RAND MNALLY

ZIP CODE FINDER

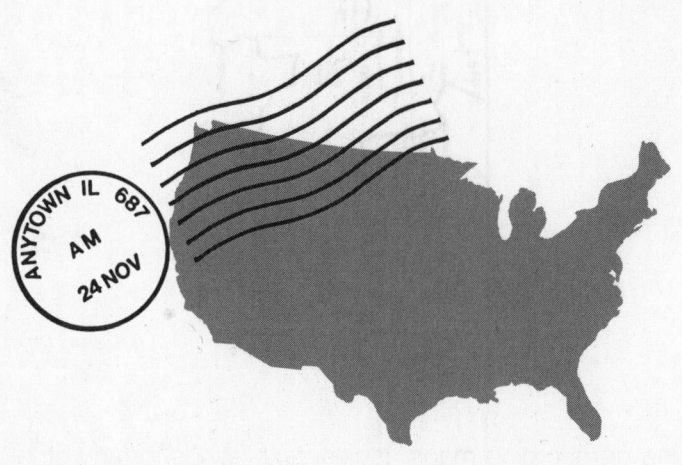

ANYTOWN IL 687
AM
24 NOV

Rand McNally Zip Code Finder
Table of Contents

INTRODUCTION

BASIC LISTINGS AND
3-DIGIT ZIP CODE MAPS

State	3-Digit Map	Listings	State	3-Digit Map	Listings
Flushing		370	South Dakota	510-511	509
Jamaica		373	Tennessee	514-515	516
Long Island City		374	Memphis		525
New York City		377	Nashville		526
Staten Island		385	Texas	534-535	536
North Carolina	390-391	389	Dallas		540
Charlotte		393	Fort Worth		543
North Dakota	406-407	408	Houston		546
Ohio	412-413	411	San Antonio		555
Cincinnati		416	Utah	562-563	561
Cleveland		417	Vermont	566-567	568
Columbus		417	Virginia	572-573	574
Oklahoma	438-439	440	Norfolk		585
Oklahoma City		443	Washington	592-593	594
Oregon	446-447	448	Seattle		599
Pennsylvania	454-455	453	West Virginia	602-603	604
Philadelphia		481	Wisconsin	616-617	615
Pittsburgh		483	Milwaukee		624
Rhode Island	496-497	498	Wyoming	632-633	631
South Carolina	500-501	502			

MAJOR CITIES WITH 5-DIGIT ZIP CODE MAPS

City	5-Digit Map	City	5-Digit Map
Atlanta, GA	125	Minneapolis, MN	296
Boston, MA	264	New York, NY	378, 379
Chicago, IL	151	Philadelphia, PA	482
Dallas, TX	541	San Francisco, CA	79
Detroit, MI	278	St. Paul, MN	299
Kansas City, KS	205	Washington, DC	102
Los Angeles, CA	72		

INTRODUCTION

The Rand McNally *Zip Code Finder* is a complete and convenient reference containing zip code listings for more than 120,000 places in the United States. Arranged alphabetically by state, these listings enable you to quickly and easily find zip codes. The *Zip Code Finder's* listings are visually enhanced by a detailed 3-digit zip code map for each state. These maps show the location of towns and cities within Zip Code Sectional Areas.

Listings for 50 major U.S. cities include zip codes for selected hospitals, military installations, hotels/motels, colleges, universities and financial institutions. The Washington, D.C. listing additionally includes zip codes for government offices.

Included in the listings is a telephone number for each multiple zip code city. By using this number, you can readily determine which of the city's zip codes you need. Five-digit zip code maps display zip code boundaries for each of thirteen multiple zip code cities.

The Rand McNally *Zip Code Finder* saves you time and money. Information provided on postal rates and regulations, plus the locations of post office division offices, helps you to mail economically and efficiently. Convenient listings of toll-free numbers for car rentals, airline reservations and hotel/motel accommodations place these services at your fingertips. In addition, telephone area code lists provide a helpful and economical reference when placing long-distance calls.

THE MEANING OF YOUR ZIP CODE

Zip codes, set up to improve mail distribution, define areas within the U.S.

The country is divided into ten geographic regions that consist of three or more states. Each of these regions is assigned a number 0-9. This number is the first digit of your zip code.

Within the ten geographic regions, states are further divided into smaller geographic units. The second and third digits of your zip code identify these units.

Together, the first three digits of your zip code identify either a particular Sectional Center or Multi-Coded City. Sectional Centers and Multi-Coded Cities have similar postal functions. A Sectional Center, usually the natural center of local transportation, is a large post office serving smaller surrounding post offices. The Multi-Coded City is a main city post office which serves its stations and branches within the city's neighborhoods.

The final two digits of your zip code identify the post offices served by the Sectional Center or branches and stations served by the city post office.

The example below further illustrates the meaning of a 5-digit zip code:

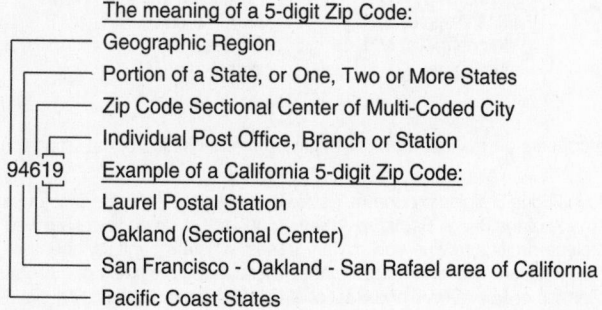

The meaning of a 5-digit Zip Code:
- Geographic Region
- Portion of a State, or One, Two or More States
- Zip Code Sectional Center of Multi-Coded City
- Individual Post Office, Branch or Station

94619   Example of a California 5-digit Zip Code:
- Laurel Postal Station
- Oakland (Sectional Center)
- San Francisco - Oakland - San Rafael area of California
- Pacific Coast States

USING THE ZIP CODE FINDER

Using the Rand McNally *Zip Code Finder* is easy. If you have the name of a city or town, but don't know its zip code, check the basic listings.

The basic listings are organized by state. Cities and towns are arranged alphabetically within each state.

Since it is not uncommon for the name of a city or town to occur more than once within a state, the *Zip Code Finder* differentiates between such cities or towns in several ways. First, if a city or town has the same name as another city or town, but is located in a different county, the *Zip Code Finder* will list the county in which the city or town is located. The county will be listed in parenthesis following the name of the city or town for all places that have a name which is identical to the name of another place within the same state. For example:

> Altamont (Effingham County)...   62411
> Altamont (Madison County)..   62035

In most cases, listing the county in which a city or town is located will differentiate between places with the same name. However, since the *Zip Code Finder* also lists townships and "towns,"* places that are "part of" other places, places that are defined by the Bureau of the Census, and several other types of localities, additional differentiation is also shown in parenthesis following the name of the place. For example:

> Ashford   06278
> Ashford (Town)..........   06250

In this case, the first listing refers to a single community that has the same name as the larger civil division which contains it and several other communities or places as well. The zip code for the larger civil division is shown in the second listing.

For places with more than one zip code, the *Zip Code Finder* provides the *range* of zip codes as shown below:

> Belleville   62220-25
> For specific Belleville Zip Codes
> call (618) 233-0391

In this example, the hyphenated numbers indicate the zip code range for Belleville. To obtain the zip code for a specific address within this multi-coded city, telephone the number shown.

In addition to the telephone number for zip code information, a 5-digit zip code map is provided for each of the following cities:

- Atlanta, GA	- Kansas City, KS	- Philadelphia, PA
- Boston, MA	- Los Angeles, CA	- San Francisco, CA
- Chicago, IL	- Minneapolis, MN	- St. Paul, MN
- Dallas, TX	- New York, NY	- Washington, DC
- Detroit, MI		

The 5-digit zip code map appears on the first full page following the beginning of the listing for each city shown above.

The *Zip Code Finder* also includes 3-digit zip code maps for the fifty states and the District of Columbia. More detailed maps of the 3-digit Sectional Areas around major urban areas are also provided. In addition to selected cities, towns and military bases, all state capitals, counties, county seats and Sectional Areas are shown on these maps. These maps provide a population key based on the 1980 Census of Population, and Sectional Centers are indicated by a circle around their respective population symbols. (Arrows show that a Sectional Area is served by a Sectional Center located in another Sectional Area.)

Zip Codes for selected hospitals, military installations, hotels, motels, banks, savings and loans, colleges, and universities are also listed for 50 of America's Largest Cities.

---

* In certain states, the civil divisions know as "townships" or "towns" have significant local importance. These civil divisions frequently include several distinct communities or places, and one of these places may bear the same name as the civil division. In the *Zip Code Finder*, "townships" are included in the listings for Illinois, Indiana, Michigan, Ohio, New Jersey and Pennsylvania, and "towns" are included for Connecticut, Maine, Massachusetts, New Hampshire, New York, Rhode Island, Vermont and Wisconsin.

STANDARD ABBREVIATIONS
FOR ADDRESSES

Listed below are two-letter state abbrevations which can be used in addressing mail.

<u>Two-Letter State Abbreviations</u>

Alabama AL	Kentucky KY	North Dakota ND
Alaska AK	Louisiana LA	Ohio OH
Arizona AZ	Maine ME	Oklahoma OK
Arkansas AR	Maryland MD	Oregon OR
California CA	Massachusetts MA	Pennsylvania PA
Colorado CO	Michigan MI	Rhode Island RI
Connecticut CT	Minnesota MN	South Carolina SC
Delaware DE	Mississippi MS	South Dakota SD
District of Columbia DC	Missouri MO	Tennessee TN
Florida FL	Montana MT	Texas TX
Georgia GA	Nebraska NE	Utah UT
Hawaii HI	Nevada NV	Vermont VT
Idaho ID	New Hampshire NH	Virginia VA
Illinois IL	New Jersey NJ	Washington WA
Indiana IN	New Mexico NM	West Virginia WV
Iowa IA	New York NY	Wisconsin WI
Kansas KS	North Carolina NC	Wyoming WY

SELECTED TOLL - FREE RESERVATION NUMBERS

To save you time and facilitate your reservations needs, the following toll-free reservation numbers are provided for selected lodging accommodations, car rental services and major airlines. (All numbers listed were effective at time of publication.)

AIRLINES

American
800-433-7300

Continental
800-525-0280

Delta
800-221-1212

Northwest
800-225-2525

TWA
800-221-2000

United
800-241-6522

U.S. Air
800-428-4322

HOTEL/MOTELS

Best Western
International, Inc.
800-528-1234

Days Inn
800-325-2525

Embassy Suites
800-EMBASSY

Fairmont Hotels
800-527-4727

Guest Quarters
800-424-2900

Harley Hotels
800-321-2323

Helmsley Hotels
800-221-4982

Holiday Inns
800-HOLIDAY

Howard Johnson's
Motor Lodges
800-654-2000

Hyatt Hotels Corp
800-228-9000

Marriott
800-228-9290

Omni/Supranational
Hotels
800-843-6664

Preferred Hotels
800-323-7500

Quality Inns
800-228-5151

Radisson Hotels Int'l
800-333-3333

Ramada Inns, Inc.
800-228-2828

Regent International
Hotels
800-545-4000

Sheraton Hotels
& Motor Inns
800-325-3535

Stouffer Hotels & Resorts
800-HOTELS-1

Westin Hotels
800-228-3000

CAR RENTAL COMPANIES

Agency Rent-A-Car
800-321-1972
800-362-1794 (Ohio only)

Alamo Rent-A-Car
800-327-9633

Allstate Rent-A-Car
800-634-6186 (except NV)

American International
Rent-A-Car
800-527-0202

Avis Reservations Center
800-331-1212 (Domestic)
800-331-1084 (International)

Budget Rent-A-Car
800-527-0700

Enterprise Rent-A-Car
800-325-8007

Hertz Corporation
800-654-3131

National Car Rental
800-328-4567

Payless Car Rental
800-PAYLESS

Sears Rent-A-Car
800-527-0770

Thrifty Rent-A-Car
800-367-2277

Value Rent-A-Car
800-327-2501

TELEPHONE AREA CODE AND TIME ZONE INFORMATION

The following tables list telephone area codes used in the United States. The first table is arranged in alphabetical order by state. The second table lists telephone area codes in numerical order.

The United States (including Alaska and Hawaii) is divided longitudinally into six time zones. If you were traveling from east to west, you would pass through the time zones in the following order: Eastern Standard Time (EST), Central Standard Time (CST), Mountain Standard Time (MST), Pacific Standard Time (PST), Alaska Time (AK), and Hawaii Time (HI).

Each time you enter a new time zone, it becomes one hour earlier. When it is 5 p.m. Eastern Standard Time (EST), it is 4 p.m. Central Standard Time (CST), 3 p.m. Mountain Standard Time (MST), etc. For your convenience, the appropriate time zone is listed in parentheses after each area code below. The map on pages 12 and 13 details the time zone boundaries.

Aphabetical List of Telephone Area Codes

Alabama	205
Montgomery (CST)	205
Alaska (AK-HI)	907
Juneau (AK)	907
Arizona (MST)	602
Phoenix (MST)	602
Arkansas	501
Little Rock (CST)	501
California	
Anaheim (PST)	714
Bakersfield (PST)	805
Eureka (PST)	707
Fresno (PST)	209
Long Beach (PST)	310
Los Angeles (PST)	213
Oakland (PST)	510
Pasadena (PST)	818
Riverside (PST)	909
Sacramento (PST)	916
San Diego (PST)	619
San Francisco (PST)	415
San Jose (PST)	408
Colorado	
Colorado Springs (MST)	719
Denver (MST)	303
Connecticut	203
Hartford (EST)	203
Delaware	302
Dover (EST)	302
District of Columbia	202
Washington (EST)	202
Florida (CST,EST)	
Jacksonville (EST)	904
Miami (EST)	305
Orlando (EST)	407
St. Petersburg (EST)	813
Tallahassee (EST)	904
Georgia	
Atlanta (EST)	404
Columbus (EST)	706
Savannah (EST)	912
Hawaii (HI)	808
Honolulu (AK-HI)	808
Idaho (MST,PST)	208
Boise (MST)	208

Illinois	
Chicago (CST)	312
Aurora (CST)	708
Peoria (CST)	309
Rockford (CST)	815
Springfield (CST)	217
West Frankfort (CST)	618
Indiana (CST,EST)	
Evansville (EST)	812
Indianapolis (EST)	317
South Bend (EST)	219
Iowa	
Council Bluffs (CST)	712
Des Moines (CST)	515
Dubuque (CST)	319
Kansas (CST,MST)	
Topeka (CST)	913
Wichita (CST)	316
Kentucky (CST,EST)	
Covington (EST)	606
Frankfort (EST)	502
Louisville (EST)	502
Louisiana	
Baton Rouge (CST)	504
New Orleans (CST)	504
Shreveport (CST)	318
Maine	207
Augusta (EST)	207
Maryland	
Annapolis (EST)	410
Rockville	301
Massachusetts	
Boston (EST)	617
Lowell (EST)	508
Springfield (EST)	413
Michigan (CST,EST)	
Detroit (EST)	313
Escanaba (EST)	906
Grand Rapids (EST)	616
Lansing (EST)	517
Minnesota	
Duluth (CST)	218
Minneapolis (CST)	612
Rochester (CST)	507
St. Paul (CST)	612

TELEPHONE AREA CODE AND TIME ZONE INFORMATION, CONT'D.

Aphabetical List of Telephone Area Codes, continued

Mississippi	601	Salem (PST)	503
Jackson (CST)	601	Pennsylvania	
Missouri		Erie (EST)	814
Jefferson City (CST)	314	Harrisburg (EST)	717
Kansas City (CST)	816	Philadelphia (EST)	215
St. Louis (CST)	314	Pittsburgh (EST)	412
Springfield (CST)	417	Rhode Island	401
Montana	406	Providence (EST)	401
Helena (MST)	406	South Carolina	803
Nebraska (CST,MST)		Columbia (EST)	803
Lincoln (CST)	402	South Dakota (CST,MST)	605
North Platte (CST)	308	Pierre (CST)	605
Omaha (CST)	402	Tennessee (CST,EST)	
Nevada	702	Memphis (CST)	901
Carson City (PST)	702	Nashville (CST)	615
New Hampshire	603	Texas (CST,MST)	
Concord (EST)	603	Abilene (CST)	915
New Jersey		Amarillo (CST)	806
Elizabeth (EST)	908	Austin (CST)	512
Newark (EST)	201	Beaumont (CST)	409
Trenton (EST)	609	Dallas (CST)	214
New Mexico	505	Fort Worth (CST)	817
Santa Fe (MST)	505	Houston (CST)	713
New York		San Antonio (CST)	210
Albany (EST)	518	Tyler (CST)	903
Binghamton (EST)	607	Utah	801
Buffalo (EST)	716	Salt Lake City (MST)	801
Hempstead (EST)	516	Vermont	802
New York (EST)	212	Montpelier (EST)	802
New York (EST)	718	Virginia	
New York (EST)	917	Richmond (EST)	804
North Carolina		Roanoke (EST)	703
Charlotte (EST)	704	Washington	
Raleigh (EST)	919	Olympia (PST)	206
North Dakota (CST,MST)	701	Seattle (PST)	206
Bismark (CST)	701	Spokane (PST)	509
Ohio		West Virginia	
Cincinnati (EST)	513	Charleston (EST)	304
Cleveland (EST)	216	Wisconsin	
Columbus (EST)	614	Eau Claire (CST)	715
Toledo (EST)	419	Madison (CST)	608
Oklahoma		Milwaukee (CST)	414
Oklahoma City (CST)	405	Wyoming	307
Tulsa (CST)	918	Cheyenne (MST)	307
Oregon (MST,PST)	503		

Numerical List of Telephone Area Codes

Area Code...	Location (Time Zone)	Area Code...	Location (Time Zone)
201......	New Jersey (EST)	210......	Texas (CST)
202......	District of Columbia (EST)	212......	New York (EST)
203......	Connecticut (EST)	213......	California (PST)
205......	Alabama (CST)	214......	Texas (CST)
206......	Washington (PST)	215......	Pennsylvania (EST)
207......	Maine (EST)	216......	Ohio (EST)
208......	Idaho (MST,PST)	217......	Illinois (CST)

TELEPHONE AREA CODE AND
TIME ZONE INFORMATION, CONT'D.

Numerical List of Telephone Area Codes, continued

Area Code...	Location (Time Zone)	Area Code...	Location (Time Zone)
218......	Minnesota (CST)	606......	Kentucky (EST)
219......	Indiana (CST,EST)	607......	New York (EST)
301......	Maryland (EST)	608......	Wisconsin (CST)
302......	Delaware (EST)	609......	New Jersey (EST)
303......	Colorado (MST)	612......	Minnesota (CST)
304......	West Virginia (EST)	614......	Ohio (EST)
305......	Florida (EST)	615......	Tennessee (CST,EST)
307......	Wyoming (MST)	616......	Michigan (EST)
308......	Nebraska (CST,MST)	617......	Massachusetts (EST)
309......	Illinois (CST)	618......	Illinois (CST)
310......	California (PST)	619......	California (PST)
312......	Illinois (CST)	701......	North Dakota (CST,MST)
313......	Michigan (EST)	702......	Nevada (PST)
314......	Missouri (CST)	703......	Virginia (EST)
315......	New York (EST)	706......	Georgia (EST)
316......	Kansas (CST,MST)	707......	California (PST)
317......	Indiana (EST)	708......	Illinois (CST)
318......	Louisiana (CST)	712......	Iowa (CST)
319......	Iowa (CST)	713......	Texas (CST)
401......	Rhode Island (EST)	714......	California (PST)
402......	Nebraska (CST,MST)	715......	Wisconsin (CST)
404......	Georgia (EST)	716......	New York (EST)
405......	Oklahoma (CST)	717......	Pennsylvania (EST)
406......	Montana (MST)	718......	New York (EST)
407......	Florida (EST)	719......	Colorado (MST)
408......	California (PST)	800......	Inward Watts
409......	Texas (CST)	801......	Utah (MST)
410......	Maryland (EST)	802......	Vermont (EST)
412......	Pennsylvania (EST)	803......	South Carolina (EST)
413......	Massachusetts (EST)	804......	Virginia (EST)
414......	Wisconsin (CST)	805......	California (PST)
415......	California (PST)	806......	Texas (CST)
417......	Missouri (CST)	808......	Hawaii (AK-HI)
419......	Ohio (EST)	812......	Indiana (CST,EST)
501......	Arkansas (CST)	813......	Florida (EST)
502......	Kentucky (CST,EST)	814......	Pennsylvania (EST)
503......	Oregon (MST,PST)	815......	Illinois (CST)
504......	Louisiana (CST)	816......	Missouri (CST)
505......	New Mexico (MST)	817......	Texas (CST)
507......	Minnesota (CST)	818......	California (PST)
508......	Massachusetts (EST)	901......	Tennessee (CST)
509......	Washington (PST)	903......	Texas (CST)
510......	California (PST)	904......	Florida (CST,EST)
512......	Texas (CST)	906......	Michigan (CST,EST)
513......	Ohio (EST)	907......	Alaska (AK-HI)
515......	Iowa (CST)	909......	California (PST)
516......	New York (EST)	912......	Georgia (EST)
517......	Michigan (EST)	913......	Kansas (CST,MST)
518......	New York (EST)	914......	New York (EST)
601......	Mississippi (CST)	915......	Texas (CST,MST)
602......	Arizona (MST)	917......	New York (EST)
603......	New Hampshire (EST)	918......	Oklahoma (CST)
605......	South Dakota (CST,MST)	919......	North Carolina (EST)

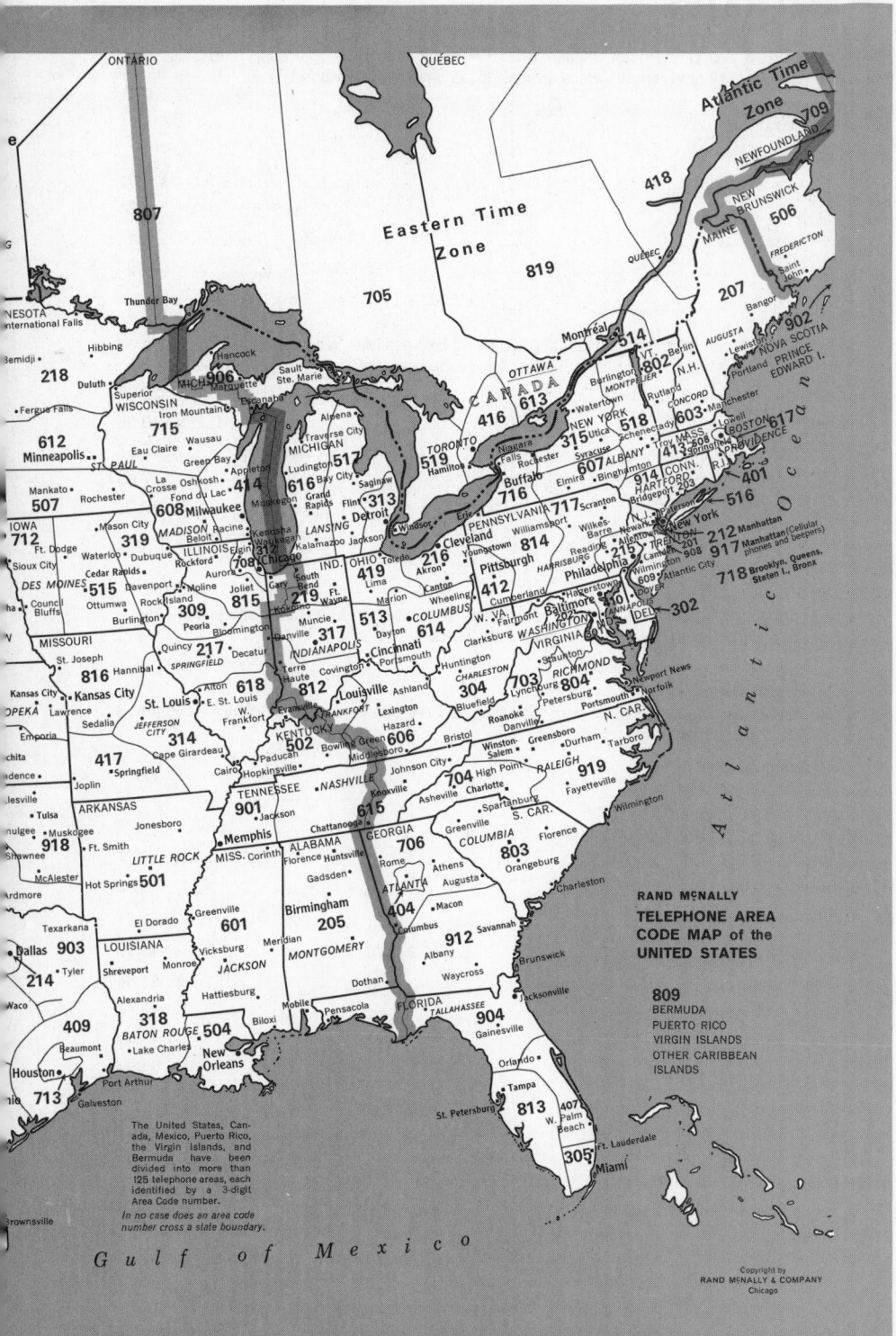

RAND M^CNALLY

**TELEPHONE AREA
CODE MAP of the
UNITED STATES**

809
BERMUDA
PUERTO RICO
VIRGIN ISLANDS
OTHER CARIBBEAN
ISLANDS

The United States, Canada, Mexico, Puerto Rico, the Virgin Islands, and Bermuda have been divided into more than 125 telephone areas, each identified by a 3-digit Area Code number.

In no case does an area code number cross a state boundary.

Copyright by
RAND M^CNALLY & COMPANY
Chicago

DOMESTIC POSTAL REGULATIONS AND RATES

Listed below are U.S. Postal Service rates for First-Class, Second-Class, Third-Class, and Express Mail. (All rates shown were current at the time of publication.)

First-Class Mail

Letters

11 oz. or less .... first oz. 29¢

each additional oz. 23¢

Over 11 oz. .... Use First Class Zone Rates (Priority Mail)

Post Cards .... 19¢

Express Mail

Packages that are taken to a postal facility offering Express Mail Service, and addressed to an area which also has Express Mail Service, will be delivered next day to the addressee.

½ lb. or less $9.95

Over 1 lb. and up to 2 lbs. $13.95

Over 2 lbs. and up to 3 lbs. $15.95

Over 3 lbs. and up to 4 lbs. $17.95

Over 4 lbs. and up to 5 lbs. $19.95

6 lbs. up to 70 lbs. .... Consult Postmaster

Second-Class Mail

Newspapers and periodicals with second-class mail privileges. Rate is applicable single piece third- or fourth-class rate for copies mailed by the general public.

Third-Class Mail

Circulars, books, catalogs, other printed matter, and merchandise, etc. weighing less than 16 oz. Over 16 oz., mail at the fourth-class rate.

Single Piece Rate

0 to 1 oz. .... 29¢

Over 1 to 2 ozs. .... 52¢

Over 2 to 3 ozs. .... 75¢

Over 3 to 4 ozs. .... 98¢

Over 4 to 6 ozs. $1.21

Over 6 to 8 ozs. $1.33

Over 8 to 10 ozs. $1.44

Over 10 to 12 ozs. $1.56

Over 12 to 14 ozs. $1.67

Over 14 but less than 16 ozs. $1.79

SMALL PARCEL RATES

Ground service rates for packages of 1 to 20 pounds are shown for the U.S. Postal Service, United Parcel Service (UPS), and Roadway Package System (RPS). Air freight rates for packages of 1 to 5 pounds and express letters, are also shown for selected air freight companies. (All rates shown were current at the time publication.)

In order to use the ground zone rate charts presented below for the U.S. Postal Service, United Parcel Service (UPS), and Roadway Package System (RPS), you will need to contact the carrier of your choice and request the zone chart that applies to your specific geographic location. This chart will enable you to determine the zone which corresponds to the destination of your parcel. Contact your local post office or UPS office; RPS may be contacted by calling the toll-free number which appears beneath the RPS Ground Zones Chart.

GROUND SERVICE RATES

United States Post Office Parcel Post Rates

First-Class Zone Rates (Priority Mail): All first-class mail weighing over 12 oz. Maximum weight is 70 lbs., size is limited to 108 inches in combined length and girth.

Weight over 12 oz. and not exceeding	Zones					
	Local 1, 2 & 3	4	5	6	7	8
1 #	$ 2.90	$ 2.90	$ 2.90	$ 2.90	$ 2.90	$ 2.90
2 #	2.90	2.90	2.90	2.90	2.90	2.90
3 #	4.10	4.10	4.10	4.10	4.10	4.10
4 #	4.65	4.65	4.65	4.65	4.65	4.65
5 #	5.45	5.45	5.45	5.45	5.45	5.45
6 #	5.55	5.75	6.10	6.85	7.65	8.60
7 #	5.70	6.10	6.70	7.55	8.50	9.65
8 #	5.90	6.50	7.30	8.30	9.40	10.70
9 #	6.10	7.00	7.95	9.05	10.25	11.75
10 #	6.35	7.55	8.55	9.80	11.15	12.80
11 #	6.75	8.05	9.20	10.55	12.05	13.80
12 #	7.15	8.55	9.80	11.30	12.90	14.85
13 #	7.50	9.10	10.40	12.05	13.80	15.90
14 #	7.90	9.60	11.05	12.80	14.65	16.95
15 #	8.30	10.10	11.65	13.55	15.55	18.00
16 #	8.70	10.65	12.30	14.30	16.45	19.05
17 #	9.10	11.15	12.90	15.05	17.30	20.10
18 #	9.50	11.65	13.55	15.80	18.20	21.10
19 #	9.90	12.20	14.15	16.50	19.05	22.15
20 #	10.30	12.70	14.75	17.25	19.95	23.20

For additional rate information, call your local Post Office.

SMALL PARCEL RATES, CONT'D.

United Parcel Service (UPS)

	Ground Zones						
Weight not to exceed	2	3	4	5	6	7	8
1 #	$ 2.08	$ 2.22	$ 2.42	$ 2.50	$ 2.58	$ 2.65	$ 2.71
2 #	2.10	2.24	2.67	2.76	2.95	3.05	3.27
3 #	2.19	2.40	2.84	2.98	3.22	3.39	3.68
4 #	2.28	2.53	2.96	3.14	3.41	3.62	4.00
5 #	2.38	2.64	3.03	3.21	3.56	3.79	4.21
6 #	2.48	2.72	3.08	3.26	3.66	3.96	4.36
7 #	2.58	2.78	3.13	3.31	3.76	4.13	4.60
8 #	2.68	2.83	3.18	3.37	3.89	4.38	4.97
9 #	2.77	2.91	3.23	3.46	4.08	4.70	5.38
10 #	2.86	2.99	3.28	3.63	4.31	5.03	5.75
11 #	2.94	3.08	3.36	3.86	4.57	5.38	6.20
12 #	3.02	3.18	3.47	4.07	4.89	5.73	6.63
13 #	3.09	3.29	3.64	4.29	5.18	6.11	7.07
14 #	3.16	3.41	3.82	4.51	5.47	6.46	7.51
15 #	3.23	3.55	4.00	4.74	5.75	6.83	7.95
16 #	3.30	3.70	4.18	4.98	6.06	7.19	8.38
17 #	3.37	3.84	4.36	5.19	6.34	7.55	8.82
18 #	3.44	3.97	4.53	5.42	6.63	7.92	9.25
19 #	3.55	4.10	4.71	5.63	6.94	8.28	9.69
20 #	3.68	4.24	4.89	5.87	7.22	8.63	10.13

For additional rate information, contact your local United Parcel Service office.

Roadway Package System (RPS)

	Ground Zones						
Weight not to exceed	2	3	4	5	6	7	8
1 #	$ 2.08	$ 2.22	$ 2.42	$ 2.50	$ 2.58	$ 2.65	$ 2.71
2 #	2.10	2.24	2.67	2.76	2.95	3.05	3.27
3 #	2.19	2.40	2.84	2.98	3.22	3.39	3.68
4 #	2.28	2.53	2.96	3.14	3.41	3.62	4.00
5 #	2.38	2.64	3.03	3.21	3.56	3.79	4.21
6 #	2.48	2.72	3.08	3.26	3.66	3.96	4.36
7 #	2.58	2.78	3.13	3.31	3.76	4.13	4.60
8 #	2.68	2.83	3.18	3.37	3.89	4.38	4.97
9 #	2.77	2.91	3.23	3.46	4.08	4.70	5.38
10 #	2.86	2.99	3.28	3.63	4.31	5.03	5.75
11 #	2.94	3.08	3.36	3.86	4.57	5.38	6.20
12 #	3.02	3.18	3.47	4.07	4.89	5.73	6.63
13 #	3.09	3.29	3.64	4.29	5.18	6.11	7.07
14 #	3.16	3.41	3.82	4.51	5.47	6.46	7.51
15 #	3.23	3.55	4.00	4.74	5.75	6.83	7.95
16 #	3.30	3.70	4.18	4.98	6.06	7.19	8.38
17 #	3.37	3.84	4.36	5.19	6.34	7.55	8.82
18 #	3.44	3.97	4.53	5.42	6.63	7.92	9.25
19 #	3.55	4.10	4.71	5.63	6.94	8.28	9.69
20 #	3.68	4.24	4.89	5.87	7.22	8.63	10.13

For additional rate information, call 1-800-ROADPAK.

SMALL PARCEL RATES, CONT'D.

AIR FREIGHT RATES FOR SELECTED PRIVATE CARRIERS

With the exception of UPS, most private carriers offer a variety of services, including overnight and second-day delivery. Most provide free envelopes and shipping containers and offer discounts for drop-off by the sender.

All of the private carriers listed provide pick-up as well as delivery. Most have drop-off boxes available in convenient locations. Next-day air and second-day air delivery times vary by carrier.

For your convenience in obtaining additional information on rates for heavier shipments, multiple shipments and frequent shipper discounts, toll-free numbers have been included in the rate tables. (All rates shown were current at the time of publication. Rates are subject to change without notice.)

United Parcel Service (UPS)

Next-Day Air Letter

$10.00 (Continental U.S.)

2nd-Day Air Letter

$5.00 (Continental U.S.)

Next-Day Air Package

Lbs.	Continental U.S.	AK & HI
1	$13.50	$17.50
2	14.00	19.00
3	15.75	20.50
4	17.50	22.00
5	19.25	23.50

2nd-Day Air Package

Lbs.	Continental U.S.	AK & HI
1	$ 5.25	$ 8.50
2	6.00	9.75
3	6.75	10.75
4	7.25	12.75
5	8.00	13.75

Federal Express (1-800-238-5355)

Overnight Letter

$15.50 (up to 8 oz.)

Priority Overnight Service (Pkg. delivery by 10:30 AM)		Standard Overnight Service (Pkg. delivery by 3:00 PM)		Economy Service (Pkg. delivery on 2nd day)	
Lbs.	Price *	Lbs.	Price *	Lbs.	Price *
1	$22.50	1	$15.50	1	$13.00
2	24.25	2	16.50	2	14.00
3	27.00	3	17.50	3	15.00
4	29.75	4	18.50	4	16.00
5	32.50	5	19.50	5	17.00

SMALL PARCEL RATES, CONT'D.

Airborne (1-800-328-4937; Washington state 1-800-562-2227)

Overnight Letter

$14.00 * (up to 8 oz.)

Non-Discounted "Express One" Service
(Next day, door-to-door pkg. delivery)

Lbs.	Price *
1	$25.00
2	25.00
3	30.00
4	36.00
5	38.00

Emery (1-800-HI-EMERY)

For specific rate information, call the toll-free number listed above.

Burlington Air Express (1-800-CALL-BAX)

Overnight Service

$23.50 (up to 11 lbs.)

2nd-Day Service

$18.50 (up to 15 lbs.)

Contact the toll-free "800" numbers for further information.

* Prices not applicable to shipments from the Continental U.S. to or between Alaska and Hawaii.

U.S. POSTAL SERVICE FIELD DIVISION OFFICES

The following is a list of Marketing and Communications Directors for each of the Postal Services 71 divisions. In the event that you have questions about mailing procedures, rates or regulations, contact the appropriate divisional office. The listings below were current at the time of publication and are subject to change.

NORTHEAST REGION

Albany, NY Division
Director, Marketing & Communications
Barry D. Brennan (518) 452-2472

Boston, MA Division
Director, Marketing & Communications
Lois A. Murphy (617) 654-5700

Brooklyn-Queens, NY Division
Director, Marketing & Communications
Betty A. Rowe (718) 321-5139

Caribbean Division
Director, Marketing & Communications
Roberto Perez de Leon (809) 767-2260

Hartford, CT Division
Director, Marketing & Communications
Bruce D. Parmiter (203) 524-6077

Manchester, NH Division
Director, Marketing & Communications
Paul F. Beaver (603) 644-4195

Newark, NJ Division
Director, Marketing & Communications
Sidney McAbee (201) 669-0770

New Brunswick, NJ Division
Director, Marketing & Communications
Joseph J. Freitas, Jr. (908) 819-3602

New York, NY Division
Director, Marketing & Communications
John L. Ghisoni (212) 330-3070

Providence, RI Division
Director, Marketing & Communications
Spiro T. Kyriakakis (401) 276-6959

Springfield, MA Division
Director, Marketing & Communications
John F. Basile (413) 731-0504

Westchester, NY Division
Director, Marketing & Communications
Teresa B. Whalen (914) 345-1238

Western New York
Director, Marketing & Communications
Nicholas A. Fabozzi (716) 846-2505

EASTERN REGION

Baltimore, MD Division
Acting Director, Marketing & Communications
Joseph H. Raia (410) 347-4516

Charleston, WV Division
Director, Marketing & Communications
Carolyn B. Drury (304) 340-4235

Cincinnati, OH Division
Director, Marketing & Communications
Kathleen Boehm (513) 684-5489

Cleveland, OH Division
Director, Marketing & Communications
Edmonia K. Page (216) 443-4076

Columbia, SC Division
Director, Marketing & Communications
Hugh Hampton (803) 731-5900

Columbus, OH Division
Director, Marketing & Communications
Edlen G. Johnson (614) 469-4412

Greensboro, NC Division
Acting Director, Marketing & Communications
Stephen F. Ashworth (919) 668-1208

Harrisburg, PA Division
Director, Marketing & Communications
Robert Chapman (717) 257-4803

Louisville, KY Division
Director, Marketing & Communications
Dennis W. Patti (502) 454-1784

Philadelphia, PA Division
Director, Marketing & Communications
Richard F. Nye (215) 895-8810

Pittsburgh, PA Division
Director, Marketing & Communications
Sarah E. Howard (412) 359-7851

Richmond, VA Division
Director, Marketing & Communications
Gail Sonnenberg (804) 775-6137

U.S. POSTAL SERVICE FIELD DIVISION OFFICES, CONT'D.

EASTERN REGION, CONT'D.

South Jersey Division
Director, Marketing & Communications
Michael E. Kurtzman (609) 933-4245

Southern MD Division
Acting Director, Marketing &
Communications
Judy Walker (301) 499-7561

SOUTHERN REGION

Atlanta, GA Division
Director, Marketing & Communications
Donald R. Warner (404) 765-7254

Birmingham, AL Division
Director, Marketing & Communications
Margie M. Cather (205) 521-0416

Dallas, TX Division
Director, Marketing & Communications
Gerald R. Carr (214) 393-6767

Houston, TX Division
Director, Marketing & Communications
Richard M. Sanchez (713) 226-3713

Jackson, MS Division
Director, Marketing & Communications
Robert Rankin (601) 968-0501

Jacksonville, FL Division
Director, Marketing & Communications
Cheryl D. Pawlowski (904) 359-2929

Little Rock, AR Division
Director, Marketing & Communications
Roxie Brown (501) 371-0301

Memphis, TN Division
Director, Marketing & Communications
John V. Rountree (901) 521-2182

Miami, FL Division
Director, Marketing & Communications
Marjorie M. Brown (305) 470-0232

Nashville, TN Division
Director, Marketing & Communications
K. M. Loggins (615) 885-9113

New Orleans, LA Division
Director, Marketing & Communications
Anthony J. Brescia (504) 589-1121

Oklahoma City, OK Division
Director, Marketing & Communications
Susan M. Plonkey (405) 278-6111

San Antonio, TX Division
Director, Marketing & Communications
Richard W. Stephens (512) 657-8500

Tampa, FL Division
Director, Marketing & Communications
Virginia Ramos (813) 877-0825

CENTRAL REGION

Chicago, IL Division
Director, Marketing & Communications
Jimmy Mason (312) 765-3034

Denver, CO Division
Director, Marketing & Communications
Marilyn Terrell (303) 297-6178

Des Moines, IA Division
Director, Marketing & Communications
Samuel C. Gonzalez (515) 283-7593

Detroit, MI Division
Acting Director, Marketing &
Communications
Richard Gentry (313) 226-8634

Grand Rapids, MI Division
Director, Marketing & Communications
Earl S. Douglas (616) 776-6156

Indianapolis, IN Division
Director, Marketing & Communications
Bernard A. Dargo (317) 464-6452

Kansas City, MO Division
Director, Marketing & Communications
Nathan W. Henderson (816) 374-9170

Milwaukee, WI Division
Director, Marketing & Communications
William Matheson (414) 287-2546

North Suburban, IL Division
Director, Marketing & Communications
Wayne J. Gardner (708) 260-5523

Omaha, NE Division
Director, Marketing & Communications
Richard S. Shaver (402) 348-2550

St. Louis, MO Division
Director, Marketing & Communications
Robert W. Roberts (314) 436-4505

South Suburban, IL Division
Director, Marketing & Communications
Betty M. Jones (708) 563-5564

U.S. POSTAL SERVICE FIELD DIVISION OFFICES, CONT'D.

CENTRAL REGION, CONT'D.

Twin Cities Division
Director, Marketing & Communications
John J. Kelliher (612) 349-4992

WESTERN REGION

Anchorage, AK Division
Director, Marketing & Communications
W. Mike Barfield (907) 261-5418

Honolulu, HI Division
Director, Marketing & Communications
Hal F. Lee (808) 423-3718

Long Beach, CA Division
Director, Marketing & Communications
Rufus F. Porter (310) 983-3002

Los Angeles, CA Division
Director, Marketing & Communications
Armando Dominguez (213) 586-1475

Oakland, CA Division
Director, Marketing & Communications
Linda A. Deaktor (510) 874-8293

Phoenix, AZ Division
Director, Marketing & Communications
Ronald C. Abalos (602) 225-3100

Portland, OR Division
Director, Marketing & Communications
Barbara Van Arsdall (503) 294-2305

Sacramento, CA Division
Director, Marketing & Communications
E. Jackson Bryant (916) 923-3141

Wichita, KS Division
Director, Marketing & Communications
Richard L. Carney (316) 946-4615

Salt Lake City, UT Division
Director, Marketing & Communications
Margaret L. Parsons (801) 974-2304

San Diego, CA Division
Director, Marketing & Communications
Gerald Vega (619) 221-3326

San Francisco, CA Division
Director, Marketing & Communications
Ruth E. Brooks (415) 550-5276

San Jose, CA Division
Acting Director, Marketing &
Communications
John DiPeri (408) 723-6100

Santa Ana, CA Division
Director, Marketing & Communications
Michael F. Flores (714) 662-6223

Seattle, WA Division
Director, Marketing & Communications
Peter A. Craft (206) 285-1335

Tucson, AZ Division
Director, Marketing & Communications
Polo J. Martinez, Jr. (602) 325-9815

Van Nuys, CA Division
Director, Marketing & Communications
Elizabeth A. Hanson (818) 908-6960

	ZIP
Abanda	36274
Abbeville	36310
Abel	36258
Abercrombie	35042
Aberfoil	36089
Abernant	35440
Abernathy	36264
Acipcoville (Part of Birmingham)	35207
Ackerville	36768
Acmar	35094
Active	36793
Ada	36069
Adamsburg	35967
Adamsville	35005
Addison	35540
Adger	35006
Adler	36779
Ai	36264
Aimwell	36782
Airport Highlands (Part of Birmingham)	35206
Akron	35441
Alabama City (Part of Gadsden)	35904
Alabama Fork	35611
Alabama Port	36523
Alabama Shores	35660
Alabaster	35007
	35144
For specific Alabaster Zip Codes call (205) 663-3971	
Alaga	36343
Alberta	36720
Alberta City (Part of Tuscaloosa)	35401
Alberton	36453
Albertville	35950
Alder Springs	35950
Aldrich	35115
Aldridge	35580
Aldridge Grove	35650
Alexander City	35010
Alexandria	36250
Alexis	35960
Aliceville	35442
Allen	36419
Allens Crossroads	35175
Allenton	36768
Allenton Station	36768
Allenville (Hale County)	36738
Allenville (Marengo County)	36738
Allgood	35013
Allsboro	35616
Allsop	36272
Alma	36501
Almeria	36089
Almond	36276
Alpine (DeKalb County)	35984
Alpine (Talladega County)	35014
Altadena Valley	35243
Alton	35015
Altoona	35952
America	35580
Andalusia	36420
Anderson (Etowah County)	35901
Anderson (Lauderdale County)	35610
Andrews Chapel	35619
Angel	36265
Annemanie	36721
Anniston	36201-06
For specific Anniston Zip Codes call (205) 236-6355	
Anniston Army Depot	36201
Ansley	36081
Antioch (Calhoun County)	36253
Antioch (Covington County)	36420
Antioch (Pike County)	36081
Appleton	36426
Aqua Vista	35645
Aquilla	36558
Arab	35016
Ararat	36921
Arbacoochee	36264
Arbor Acres (Part of Huntsville)	35810
Ardell	35053
Ardilla (Part of Dothan)	36301
Ardmore	35739
Ardmore Highway (Part of Huntsville)	35805
Argo	35173
Argo Heights	35550
Arguta	36360
Ariton	36311
Arkadelphia	35033
Arkwright (Part of Vincent)	35178
Arley	35541
Arlington	36722
Armstead	35121

	ZIP
Armstrong	36089
Arona	35957
Arrowhead	36109
Arrowwood (Part of Tuscaloosa)	35405
Asberry	36272
Asbury (Dale County)	36360
Asbury (Marshall County)	35950
Ashbank	35578
Ashby	35035
Ashford	36312
Ashland (Clay County)	36251
Ashland (Madison County)	35811
Ashridge	35565
Ashville	35953
Aspel	35768
Athens	35611
Atkinson	36784
Atmore	36502
Attalla	35954
Atwood	35571
Auburn	36830-49
For specific Auburn Zip Codes call (205) 821-3754	
Augustin	36701
Aurora	35957
Aurora Springs	35616
Austinville (Part of Decatur)	35601
Autaugaville	36003
Avalon Park (Part of Hueytown)	35020
Avant	36033
Avery (Part of Stevenson)	35772
Avoca	35653
Avon	36312
Avondale (Part of Birmingham)	35222
Avondale Mill (Part of Alexander City)	35010
Avondale Village (Part of Pell City)	35125
Avon Park (Part of Birmingham)	35234
Awin	36768
Axis	36505
Ayres	35126
Babbie	36420
Bacon Level	36274
Bagley	35062
Bailey Springs	35645
Baileyton	35019
Baileytown	35019
Baker Hill	36004
Bald Hill	36375
Baldwin Farms	36083
Balkum	36345
Ballplay	35903
Bangor	35079
Bankhead (DeKalb County)	35984
Bankhead (Walker County)	35580
Banks	36005
Bankston	35542
Barachias (Part of Montgomery)	36064
Barber	36312
Barfield	36266
Barlow	36558
Barlow Bend	36545
Barnes	36311
Barnesville	35570
Barnett Chapel	35572
Barnett Crossroads	36426
Barney	35550
Barnisdale Forest (Part of Birmingham)	35215
Barnwell	36532
Barrytown	36908
Barton	35616
Basham	35640
Bashi	36784
Basin	36323
Bass	35772
Bassetts Creek	36585
Batesville	36053
Battelle	35989
Battens Crossroads	36316
Battleground	35179
Battles Wharf	36532
Bay Minette	36507
Bayou La Batre	36509
Bay Shore Junction (Part of Prichard)	36610
Bayside (Part of Decatur)	35603
Bay Springs	35960
Bayview	35005
Bazemore	35559
Beachwood Park (Part of Birmingham)	35212
Beamon	36360
Bean Rock	35175
Bear Creek	35543

	ZIP
Bear Point	36561
Beasons Mill	36264
Beatrice	36425
Beaty Crossroads (Part of Ider)	35981
Beauregard	36801
Beaverton	35544
Beaver Town	35442
Beck	36420
Beehive	36865
Bel Air (Jefferson County)	35210
Bel Air (Mobile County)	36616
Bel Air Mall (Part of Mobile)	36616
Belforest	36526
Belgreen	35653
Belk	35545
Bellamy	36901
Bellefontaine	36567
Bellefonte	35752
Bellefountaine	36582
Bellemeade	35630
Belle Mina	35615
Belleville	36401
Bellevue (Part of Gadsden)	35901
Bell Springs	35622
Bellview	36726
Bellwood (Geneva County)	36313
Bellwood (Jefferson County)	35064
Belmont	35470
Beloit	36759
Beltline (Part of Decatur)	35601
Belview Heights (Part of Tuscumbia)	35674
Bemiston (Part of Talladega)	35160
Bendale (Part of Birmingham)	35217
Benevola	35466
Benoit	35550
Bentley Hills (Part of Mountain Brook)	35216
Benton	36785
Ben Vines Gap (Part of Maytown)	35118
Berkley	35748
Berlin	35055
Bermuda (Conecuh County)	36401
Bermuda (Monroe County)	36460
Berney Points (Part of Birmingham)	35211
Berry	35546
Bertha	36353
Bessemer	35020-23
For specific Bessemer Zip Codes call (205) 428-9163	
Bessemer Gardens (Part of Hueytown)	35020
Bessemer Homestead (Part of Bessemer)	35020
Bessie	35062
Bessie Junction	35062
Bethany	35452
Bethel (Barbour County)	36311
Bethel (Cullman County)	35055
Bethel (Limestone County)	35620
Bethlehem	36046
Beulah (Covington County)	36467
Beulah (Greene County)	35469
Beulah (Lee County)	36854
Beverly Station (Part of Birmingham)	35211
Bexar	35570
Bibbville	35188
Biddle Crossroads (Part of Henagar)	35978
Bigbee	36510
Big Creek	36301
Big Oak	35645
Big Springs	35188
Billingsley	36006
Billy Goat Hill	35960
Birdine	36740
Birdsong	35055
Birmingham	35201-61
For specific Birmingham Zip Codes call (205) 521-0451	
Birmingham Green (Part of Birmingham)	35237
Birwat (Part of Tarrant)	35217
Bishop	35616
Biven	35214
Black	36314
Blackankle	35768
Black Creek	35207
Black Diamond	35023
Black Rock	36042
Blacksher	36507
Blackwood	36345
Bladon Springs	36919
Blanche	35973
Blanton	36854
Bleecker	36874

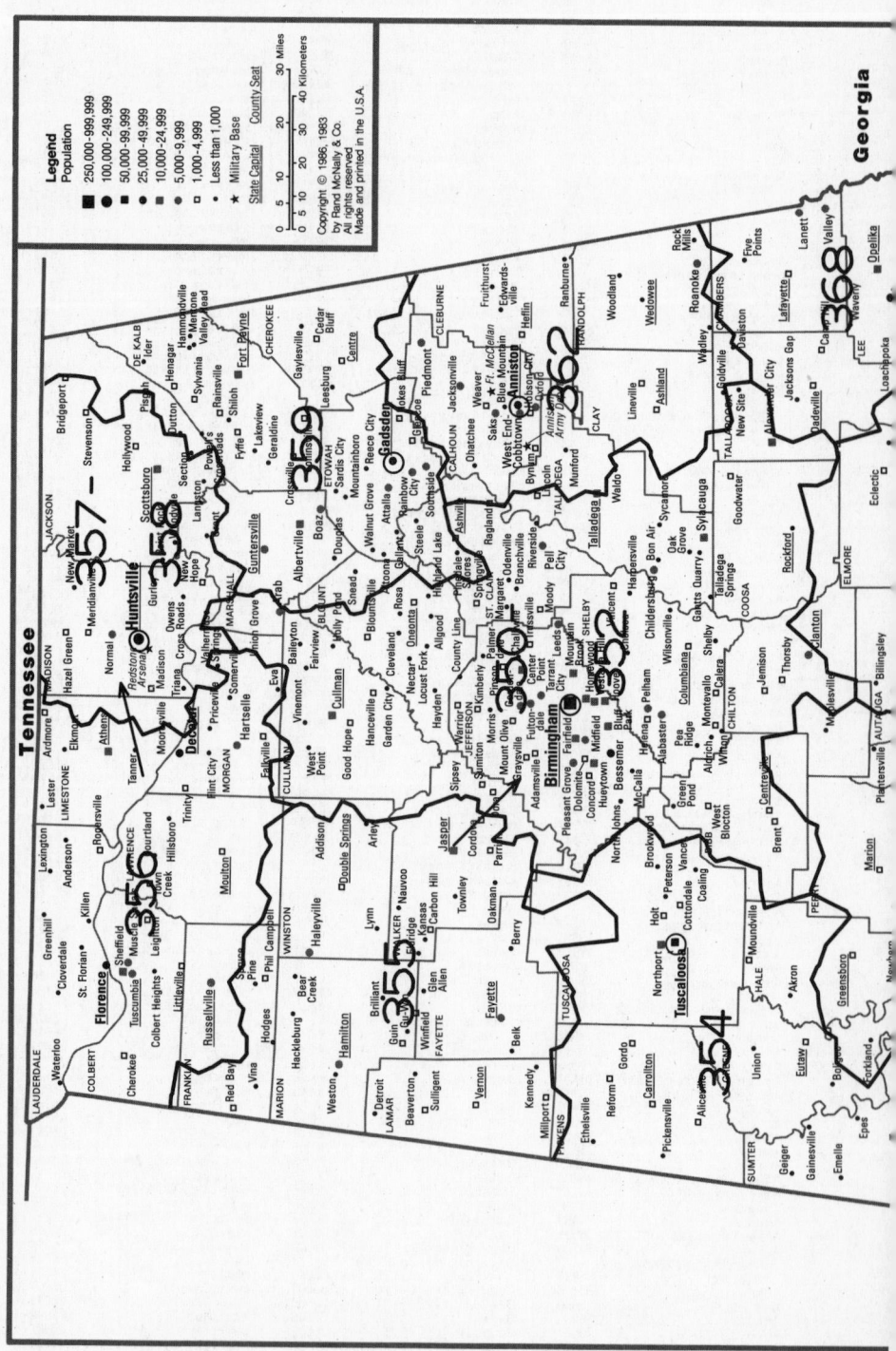

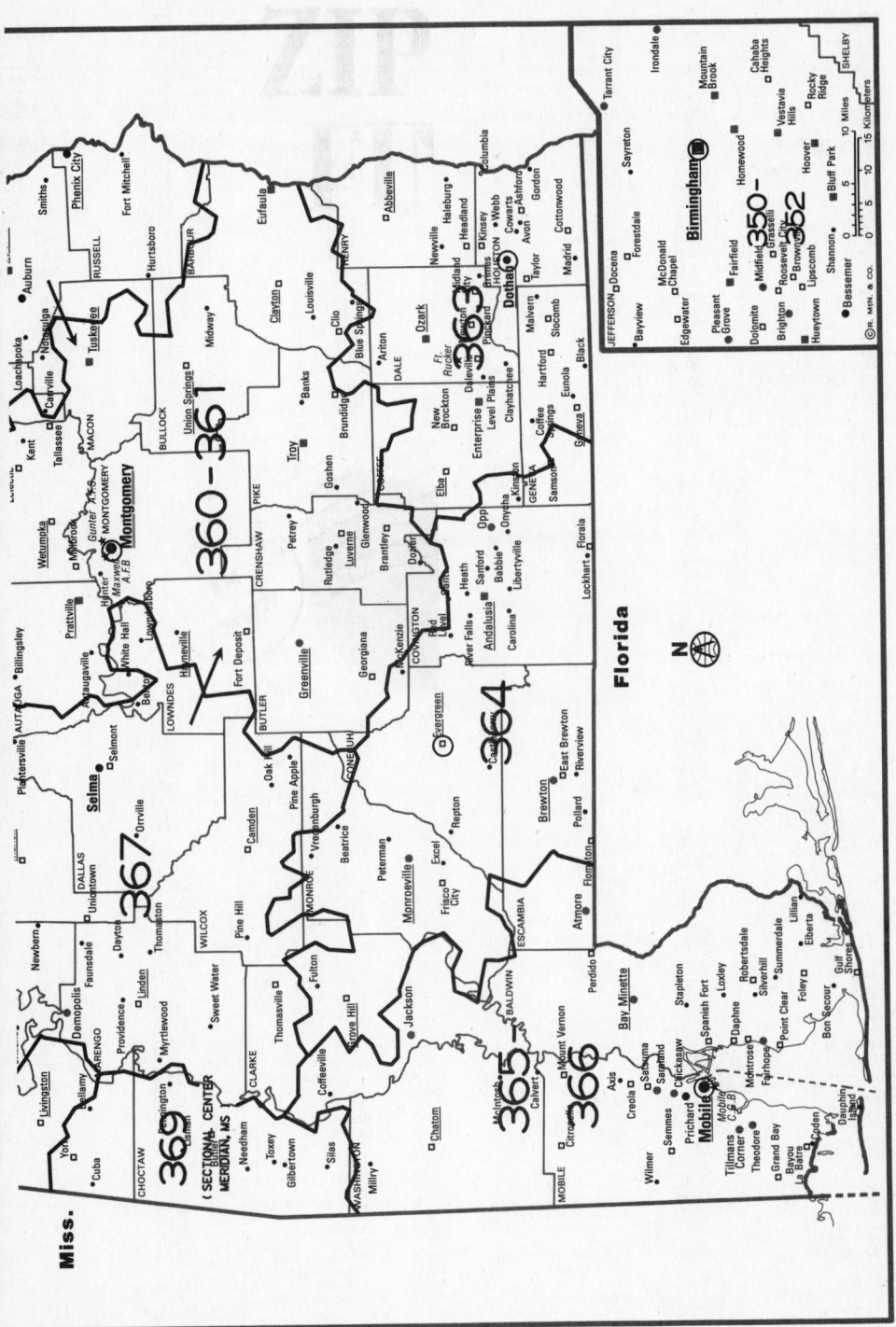

	ZIP		ZIP		ZIP
Blossburg	35073	Brooklyn (Conecuh County)	36429	Capitol Heights (Part of	
Blount Springs	35079	Brooklyn (Cullman County)	35083	Montgomery)	36107
Blountsville	35031	Brooks	36456	Capps	36353
Blow Gourd	35049	Brookside	36036	Capshaw	35742
Blue Creek	35023	Brooksville (Blount County)	35031	Carbon Hill	35549
Blue Creek Junction (Part of		Brooksville (Morgan County)	35670	Cardiff	35041
Bessemer)	35020	Brookwood	35444	Carlisle	35957
Blue Mountain	36201	Brookwood Forest (Part of		Carlowville	36761
Blue Pond	35959	Athens)	35611	Carlton	36515
Blue Ridge Estates	35226	Brookwood Village (Part of		Carns	35746
Blues Old Stand	36061	Homewood)	35209	Carolina	36420
Blue Spring (Part of		Broomtown	35973	Carolyn (Part of	
Huntsville)	35810	Broughton	36274	Montgomery)	36106
Blue Springs (Barbour		Browns	36759	Carpenter	36507
County)	36017	Brownsboro	35741	Carriger	35611
Blue Springs (Blount		Browns Corner	35773	Carr Mill	36251
County)	35031	Browns Crossroad	36310	Carrollton	35447
Blue Springs (Covington		Browns Crossroads	36360	Carrville (Part of Tallassee)	36023
County)	36467	Browntown (Jackson		Carson	36548
Blue Springs Garden	35811	County)	35978	Carter Grove	35750
Bluff	35555	Brown Town (Mobile		Cartersville	35967
Bluff Park	35226	County)	39451	Cartwright	35620
Bluff Spring	36251	Brownville (Clay County)	35072	Carver Court (Part of	
Bluff Springs	36323	Brownville (Conecuh		Tuskegee)	36088
Bluffton	30138	County)	36401	Casemore	36742
Boar Tush	35565	Brownville (Jefferson		Casey	36701
Boaz	35957	County)	35211	Castleberry	36432
Bobo (Fayette County)	35594	Brownville (Tuscaloosa		Catalpa	36081
Bobo (Madison County)	35773	County)	35476	Catherine	36728
Boiling Springs	36271	Bruceville	36089	Catoma	36108
Boldo	35501	Brundidge	36010	Cavalry Hill (Part of	
Boley Springs	35546	Brunnet Heights	35217	Huntsville)	35805
Boligee	35443	Brushy Pond	35033	Cave Spring (Etowah	
Bolinger	36903	Bryant	35958	County)	35954
Bolivar	35740	Bryant's Lower Landing	36579	Cave Spring (Madison	
Bolling	36033	Bryce Hospital (Part of		County)	35763
Bomar	35960	Tuscaloosa)	35401	Cave Springs	35674
Bon Air	35032	Buchanan Peninsula	35616	Cecil	36013
Bonita	36749	Buckhorn (Madison County)	35761	Cedar Bluff	35959
Bonneville	35611	Buckhorn (Pike County)	36081	Cedar Cove	35453
Bonnie Doone	35611	Buck Island Shores	35976	Cedar Fork	36482
Bon Secour	36511	Bucks	36512	Cedar Grove (Baldwin	
Booth	36008	Bucksnort	35747	County)	36542
Boot Hill	36048	Buena Vista	36425	Cedar Grove (Jackson	
Boothtown	36521	Buena Vista Highlands (Part		County)	35772
Boozer Heights (Part of		of Homewood)	35209	Cedar Grove (Covington	
Oxford)	36201	Buffalo	36862	County)	36420
Borden Springs	36262	Buggs Chapel	35763	Cedar Hill (Fayette County)	35555
Borden Wheeler Springs	36262	Buhl	35446	Cedar Hill (Limestone	
Borom	36860	Bull City	35468	County)	35739
Boston (Part of Brilliant)	35548	Bullock	36009	Cedar Hill Estates	35674
Boswell	36081	Bullock Correctional Facility	36089	Cedar Plains	35622
Bowles	36401	Burchfield	35444	Cedar Point	35760
Bowmans Crossroads	35744	Burgreen Corners	35758	Cedar Springs	36265
Boyd	35470	Burks Gardens (Part of		Cedrum	35549
Boyd Crossing	35490	Tuscaloosa)	35401	Center	35565
Boykin (Escambia County)	36426	Burkville	36752	Centercrest	35215
Boykin (Wilcox County)	36723	Burl	36753	Centergrove	35670
Boyles (Part of Birmingham)	35217	Burlington	36078	Center Hill (Cullman County)	35077
Boylston (Part of		Burningtree Estates (Part of		Center Hill (Lauderdale	
Montgomery)	36110	Decatur)	35603	County)	35648
Boys Ranch	36761	Burningtree Mountain	35603	Center Hill (Limestone	
Bradford	35089	Burns	36272	County)	35773
Bradley	36420	Burnsville	36703	Center Point (Clarke	
Bradleyton	36041	Burnt Corn	36431	County)	36524
Braggs	36761	Burntout	35593	Center Point (Jefferson	
Branchville	35120	Burnwell	35038	County)	35215
Brandontown (Part of		Burstall (Part of Bessemer)	35020	Center Point Gardens	35215
Huntsville)	35805	Bushy Creek	36033	Center Springs	35172
Brannon Springs	36271	Butler	36904	Center Star	35645
Brannon Stand	36301	Butler Springs	36030	Centerville	36401
Brantley (Crenshaw County)	36009	Buttston	36853	Centerwood Estates	35215
Brantley (Dallas County)	36703	Buyck	36080	Central (Cullman County)	35055
Brantleyville	35114	Bynum	36253	Central (Elmore County)	36024
Bremen	35033	Caddo	35673	Central City	36330
Brent	35034	Caffee Junction	35111	Central Crossroads	35978
Brewersville	35470	Cahaba	36767	Central Heights	35633
Brewton	36426-27	Cahaba Heights	35243	Central Highlands (Part of	
For specific Brewton Zip Codes		Cahaba Hills (Part of Leeds)	35094	Birmingham)	35206
call (205) 867-3560		Cahaba River Estates	35020	Central Mills	36773
Briar Hill	36035	Calcis	35178	Centre	35960
Brick	35660	Caldwell	35146	Centreville	35042
Bridgeport	35740	Caledonia	36753	Century Plaza (Part of	
Bridgeville	35442	Calera	35040	Birmingham)	35210
Bridlewood Forest Estates	35215	Calhoun	36047	Ceramic (Part of Phenix	
Brierfield	35035	Calumet	35580	City)	36867
Brighton	35020	Calvert	36513	Chalkville	35215
Bright Star	35980	Camden	36726	Chalybeate Springs	35643
Brilliant	35548	Camelot (Part of Huntsville)	35803	Champion	35121
Brisco Store	35772	Cameronsville	35772	Chance	36751
Broadmoor (Part of		Campbell	36727	Chancellor	36316
Bessemer)	35020	Campbells Crossroads	36266	Chandler Springs	35160
Bromley	36507	Campbellville	35063	Chapel Hill (Chambers	
Brompton	35094	Camp Hill	36850	County)	36862
Brookhurst (Jefferson		Camp Oliver	35130	Chapel Hill (Jefferson	
County)	35215	Canoe	36502	County)	35216
Brookhurst (Madison		Cantebury Heights (Part of		Chapman	36015
County)	35810	Mobile)	36609	Chapman Heights (Part of	
Brookland	36453	Cantelous Spur	36113	Huntsville)	35810
Brookley (Part of Mobile)	36605	Canton Bend	36726	Chase	35811
Brooklyn (Coffee County)	36467	Capell	36726	Chastang	36560

	ZIP
Chatom	36518
Chelsea (Madison County)	35801
Chelsea (Shelby County)	35043
Cherokee	35616
Cherokee Bluffs	36078
Cherokee Forest (Part of Mountain Brook)	35223
Cherry Grove	35611
Chesson	36029
Chesterfield	30731
Chestnut	36425
Chestnut Grove	36010
Chetopa	35139
Chickasaw	36611
Chigger Hill	35971
Childersburg	35044
Chilton	36451
China	36401
China Grove	36081
Chinneby	36268
Chisholm (Part of Montgomery)	36110
Choccolocco	36254
Choctaw Bluff	36545
Choctaw City	36904
Choctow Corner (Part of Thomasville)	36784
Chosea Springs	36201
Christiana	36258
Chrysler	36550
Chulafinnee	36264
Chunchula	36521
Circlewood (Part of Tuscaloosa)	35405
Citronelle	36522
Claiborne	36470
Clairmont Springs	35160
Clanton	35045
Clarksville	36524
Claud	36024
Clay	35048
Clay City	36532
Clayhatchee	36322
Clayhill	36784
Claysville	35976
Clayton	36016
Clear Springs	35121
Clearview (Covington County)	36028
Clearview (Crenshaw County)	36041
Cleveland (Blount County)	35049
Cleveland (Fayette County)	35542
Cleveland Crossroads	35072
Cliff Haven (Part of Sheffield)	35660
Clift Acres	35758
Clinton	35448
Clintonville	36351
Clio	36017
Clisby Park (Part of Montgomery)	36104
Clopton	36317
Cloverdale (Jefferson County)	35215
Cloverdale (Lauderdale County)	35617
Cloverdale (Mobile County)	36541
Cloverdale (Montgomery County)	36105
Cloverdale (Tuscaloosa County)	35401
Cloverdale Heights	35630
Cloverland (Part of Montgomery)	36105
Clowers Crossroads	36010
Clubview Heights (Part of Gadsden)	35901
Coal Bluff	36769
Coalburg	35068
Coal City	35131
Coal Fire	35481
Coaling	35449
Coalmont	35114
Coal Valley	35579
Coatopa	35470
Cobb City (Part of Glencoe)	35905
Cobbs Ford	36025
Cobb Town	36201
Cochrane	35442
Coden	36523
Cody	35555
Coffee Junction	35111
Coffee Springs	36318
Coffeeville	36524
Cohasset	36474
Coker	35452
Colbert Heights	35674
Cold Springs (Cullman County)	35033

	ZIP
Cold Springs (Elmore County)	36022
Coldwater (Calhoun County)	36260
Coldwater (Cleburne County)	36262
Cole Spring	35622
Collbran	35967
Collins Chapel	35045
Collinsville	35961
Collirene	36785
Coloma	35960
Colonial Gardens	35759
Colonial Heights (Part of Tuscumbia)	35674
Colony (Cullman County)	35077
Colony (Tuscaloosa County)	35476
Columbia	36319
Columbiana	35051
Columbus City	35976
Colwell	35905
Comer	36053
Concord (Blount County)	35049
Concord (Fayette County)	35555
Concord (Jefferson County)	35023
Congo	35959
Conifer	36078
Consul	36728
Cook Springs	35052
Cool Springs	35953
Coon Creek	35063
Coopers	35045
Coosa Court (Part of Childersburg)	35044
Coosada	36020
Coosa River	36022
Copeland	36558
Copeland Bridge	35961
Copper Springs	35120
Coppinville (Part of Enterprise)	36330
Corcoran (Part of Troy)	36081
Cordova	35550
Corinth (Bullock County)	36081
Corinth (Cullman County)	35179
Corinth (Randolph County)	36278
Corner	35180
Cornhouse	36274
Cornwall Furnace	35959
Corona	35579
Cortelyou	36585
Cotaco	35670
Cottage Grove	35089
Cottage Hill (Jefferson County)	35127
Cottage Hill (Mobile County)	36609
Cottondale	35453
Cottonton	36851
Cottontown	35646
Cotton Valley	36083
Cottonville	35747
Cottonwood	36320
Country Club Acres (Part of Athens)	35611
Country Club Estates (Madison County)	35201
Country Club Estates (Mobile County)	36608
Country Club Village (Part of Mobile)	36608
Country Estates (Jefferson County)	35215
Country Estates (Madison County)	36108
County Line (Blount County)	35172
County Line (Covington County)	36453
County Line (Pike County)	36034
Courtland	35618
Covin	35555
Cowarts	36321
Cox Beach (Part of Satsuma)	36572
Coxey	35611
Coy	36435
Cragford	36255
Crane Hill	35053
Crawford (Mobile County)	36608
Crawford (Russell County)	36867
Creek Stand	36089
Creeltown	35063
Creola	36525
Crescent Heights (Part of Lipscomb)	35020
Crestline (Part of Mountain Brook)	35213
Crestline Gardens (Part of Birmingham)	35210
Crestline Heights (Part of Mountain Brook)	35213
Crestline Park (Part of Birmingham)	35213

	ZIP
Crestview (Part of Mobile)	36609
Crestview Gardens (Part of Pell City)	35125
Crestwood (Part of Huntsville)	35807
Creswell	35078
Crews	35586
Crichton (Part of Mobile)	36607
	36670
For specific Crichton Zip Codes call (205) 479-2680	
Crockett Junction	35118
Cromwell	36906
Crooked Oak	35674
Cropwell (Part of Pell City)	35054
Crosby	36343
Cross Key	35620
Crossroads (Baldwin County)	36507
Cross Roads (Clarke County)	36570
Crossroads (Marshall County)	35976
Crosston	35126
Crossville (DeKalb County)	35962
Crossville (Lamar County)	35592
Crudup (Part of Reece City)	35954
Crumley Chapel	35214
Cuba	36907
Cullman	35055-56
For specific Cullman Zip Codes call (205) 734-6633	
Cullomburg	36919
Cunningham (Clarke County)	36727
Cunningham (Pickens County)	35442
Curry (Talladega County)	36268
Curry (Walker County)	35501
Currytown	36350
Curtis	36323
Curtiston (Part of Attalla)	35954
Cusseta	36852
Cypress	35474
Cyril	36912
Dadeville	36853
Daisy City	35214
Daleville	36322
Dallas (Blount County)	35172
Dallas (Madison County)	35801
Damascus (Coffee County)	36323
Damascus (Escambia County)	36426
Dancy	35442
Dancy Quarter (Part of Decatur)	35603
Danley	36323
Danville	35619
Danway	36801
Daphne	36526
Dargin	35040
Darlington	36726
Darwin Downs (Part of Huntsville)	35801
Dauphin Island	36528
Davis Hills (Part of Huntsville)	35805
Daviston	36256
Davisville	36083
Dawes	36601
Dawson	35963
Dawsons Mill	36749
Dayton	36731
De Armanville	36257
Deason Hill	35550
Deatsville	36022
Deavertown	35049
Decatur	35601-03
For specific Decatur Zip Codes call (205) 355-1211	
Deer Park	36529
DeFoor	35565
Delchamps	36523
Delmar	35551
Delta	36258
Demopolis	36732
Dempsey	35653
Deposit	35761
Detroit	35552
Devenport	36047
Dexter	36092
Diamond	35976
Dickert	36276
Dickinson	36436
Dillard	36360
Dilworth	35063
Dime	35581
Dixiana	35126
Dixie	36420
Dixieland	36867
Dixie Springs	35579

	ZIP
Forest Hills (Lauderdale County)	35630
Forest Hills (Talladega County)	35044
Forest Home	36030
Forest Park (Jefferson County)	35222
Forest Park (Mobile County)	36608
Forkland	36740
Forkville	35565
Forney	35960
Fort Benning	31905
Fort Dale	36037
Fort Davis	36031
Fort Deposit	36032
Fort McClellan	36205
Fort Mitchell	36856
Fort Morgan	36542
Fort Payne	35967
Fort Rucker	36362
Fosheeton	35010
Fosters	35463
Fostoria	36761
Fountain	36460
Fountain Heights (Part of Birmingham)	35204
Four Mile	35186
Fowlers Crossroads	35542
Fowl River	36582
Fox	35401
Frances Heights (Part of Fultondale)	35068
Francisco	37345
Francis Mill	36271
Frankfort	35653
Franklin (Macon County)	36083
Franklin (Monroe County)	36444
Frankville	36538
Fredonia	36855
Freemanville	36502
Fremont	36749
French Mill	35611
Fridays Crossing	35121
Friendship (Covington County)	36467
Friendship (Elmore County)	36078
Friendship (Montgomery County)	36036
Frisco	36010
Frisco City	36445
Frisco Quarters (Part of Jasper)	35501
Frost (Part of Centreville)	35042
Fruitdale	36539
Fruithurst	36262
Fullers Crossroads	36049
Fullerton	35973
Fulton	36446
Fulton Bridge (Part of Hamilton)	35570
Fultondale	35068
Fulton Road (Part of Mobile)	36605
Fulton Springs (Part of Fultondale)	35068
Furman	36741
Fyffe	35971
Gadsden	35901-06
	35999

For specific Gadsden Zip Codes call (205) 547-6391

	ZIP
Gadsden Mall (Part of Gadsden)	35901
Gainer	36477
Gainestown	36540
Gainesville	35464
Gallant	35972
Gallion	36742
Gamble	35501
Gandys Cove	35622
Gann Crossroad	35981
Gantt	36038
Gantts Junction (Part of Sylacauga)	35150
Gantts Quarry	35150
Garden	35442
Garden City	35070
Gardendale	35071
Garden Highlands	35211
Gardiners Gin	35550
Garland	36456
Garrards Crossroads	36375
Garth	35764
Gary Springs	35042
Garywood	35023
Gasque	36542
Gastonburg	36728
Gate City (Part of Birmingham)	35212
Gaylesville	35973
Gay Meadows (Part of Montgomery)	36111

	ZIP
Geiger	35459
Genery	35020
Geneva	36340
Gentilly Forest (Part of Vestavia Hills)	35216
Georgetown	36521
Georgia (Part of Hartselle)	35640
Georgiana	36033
Gerald (Part of Level Plains)	36322
Geraldine	35974
Germania (Part of Birmingham)	35211
Gibsonville	36251
Gilbert Crossroads	35963
Gilbertown	36908
Gilbertsboro	35647
Giles	35188
Gilliam Springs (Part of Arab)	35016
Gilmore	35020
Gipsy	35620
Girard (Part of Phenix City)	36867
G.K.Fountain Correctional Center	36502
Gladstone	35806
Glass (Part of Valley)	36854
Gleandean (Part of Auburn)	36830
Glen Allen	35559
Glen City (Part of Pell City)	35125
Glencoe (Etowah County)	35905
Glencoe (Jefferson County)	35213
Glen Hills (Part of Bessemer)	35020
Glen Mary	35577
Glenn Acres	36608
Glen Oaks (Part of Fairfield)	35064
Glenville	36871
Glenwood	36034
Gnatville	36272
Godwin Estates	35215
Goldbranch	35183
Golden Springs (Part of Anniston)	36201
Gold Mine	35548
Gold Ridge (Cullman County)	35055
Gold Ridge (Lee County)	36879
Goldville	36255
Gonce	35772
Good Hope (Cullman County)	35055
Good Hope (Elmore County)	36024
Goodman	36330
Good Springs (Limestone County)	35610
Goodsprings (Walker County)	35560
Goodwater	35072
Goodway	36449
Goodyear (Part of Gadsden)	35903
Goose Pond Crossroads (Part of Scottsboro)	35768
Gordo	35466
Gordon	36343
Gordon Heights (Part of Lipscomb)	35020
Gordonsville	36785
Gorgas	35580
Goshen	36035
Gosport	36482
Graball (Part of Abbeville)	36310
Grady	36036
Graham	36263
Grand Bay	36541
Grangeburg	36343
Grant	35747
Grantley	36272
Granttown	36268
Grasselli (Part of Birmingham)	35211
Grassy	35016
Gravel Hill (Part of Russellville)	35653
Gravelly Springs	35630
Graymont (Part of Birmingham)	35204
Grays Chapel	35745
Grayson	35572
Graystone	35013
Graysville	35073
Grayton	36271
Greeley	35111
Green Acres (Part of Birmingham)	35228
Greenbrier (Lauderdale County)	35630
Greenbrier (Limestone County)	35758
Green Chapel	35971

	ZIP
Greenhill	35630
Green Lantern (Part of Montgomery)	36111
Green Meadows	36067
Green Pond	35074
Greensboro	36744
Greens Chapel	35049
Greensport	35953
Green Valley (Etowah County)	35903
Green Valley (Jefferson County)	35216
Greenville	36037
Greenwood (Clarke County)	36451
Greenwood (Jefferson County)	35020
Greenwood (Macon County)	36088
Greenwycke Village (Part of Huntsville)	35802
Griffith Bend	35160
Grimes	36301
Grove Hill	36451
Groveoak	35975
Grove Park (Jefferson County)	35209
Grove Park (Talladega County)	35044
Grovewood Estates	36108
Guerryton	36860
Guest	35967
Guin	35563
Gulf Crest	36521
Gulf Shores	36542
	36547

For specific Gulf Shores Zip Codes call (205) 968-7000

	ZIP
Gum Pond	35621
Gum Spring	35640
Gum Springs	35031
Guntersville	35976
Gurley	35748
Guthery Crossroads	35053
Gu-Win	35563
Hackleburg	35564
Hackneyville	35010
Hacoda	36442
Hagler	35456
Haleburg	36319
Haleyville	35565
Half Acre	36763
Halls Crossroads	36445
Halltown	35582
Halsell	36912
Hamburg (Perry County)	36759
Hamburg (Wilcox County)	36768
Hamilton	35570
Hamilton Crossroads	36010
Hammondville	35989
Hamner	35460
Hampden	36722
Hanceville	35077
Hancock Crossroads	35771
Hannah (Part of Athens)	35611
Hannon	36860
Hanover	35136
Hardaway	36039
Harkins Crossroads	36251
Harlem Heights (Part of Hueytown)	35023
Harmony (Covington County)	36420
Harmony (Lawrence County)	35650
Harmony (Marshall County)	35950
Harpersville	35078
Harrell	36759
Harriman Park (Part of Birmingham)	35207
Harrisburg (Bibb County)	35034
Harrisburg (St. Clair County)	35125
Harrisville	35952
Hartford	36344
Hartselle	35640
Harvest	35749
Hatchechubbee	36858
Hatton	35672
Havana	35474
Hawk	36280
Hawthorn	36585
Hayden	35079
Haynes	36067
Haynes Crossing	35772
Hayneville	36040
Haysland (Part of Huntsville)	35802
Haysland Estates (Part of Huntsville)	35802
Hays Mill	35620
Haywood	36280
Hazel Green	35750
Hazen	36767
Headland	36345

Name	ZIP
Healing Springs	36558
Heath	36420
Hebron	35747
Hector	36029
Heflin	36264
Heiberger	36756
Helena	35080
Helicon (Crenshaw County)	36036
Helicon (Winston County)	35541
Henagar	35978
Henderson	36035
Hendrick Mill	35121
Hendrix	35121
Henryville	35976
Henson Springs	35544
Herbert	36401
Heron Bay	36523
Hester Heights (Part of Russellville)	35653
Hickory	35442
Hickory Flat	36274
Hickory Grove	35650
Hickory Hills (Lauderdale County)	35630
Hickory Hills (Morgan County)	35603
Hideaway Hills	35645
Higdon	35979
High Bluff	36344
Highland (Part of Lineville)	36266
Highland Home	36041
Highland Lake	35121
Highland Park (Part of Montgomery)	36107
Highmound	35980
High Point (DeKalb County)	35989
High Point (Marshall County)	35950
High Ridge	36089
Hightogy	35592
Hightower	36263
Hillandale (Part of Huntsville)	35805
Hillard	35587
Hillman	35020
Hillman Gardens	35020
Hillman Park	35020
Hillsboro (Lawrence County)	35643
Hillsboro (Madison County)	35761
Hillsdale (Part of Jasper)	35501
Hilltop (Part of Bessemer)	35020
Hillview	35214
Hinton	39355
Hirsch	36871
Hissop	35089
Hobbs Island	35803
Hobgood	35674
Hoboken (Barbour County)	36027
Hoboken (Marengo County)	36782
Hobson	36518
Hobson City	36201
Hodge	35744
Hodges	35571
Hodges Store	35619
Hodgesville	36301
Hodgewood	36921
Hogglesville	35474
Hog Jaw	35016
Hokes Bluff	35903
Holiday Homes (Part of Huntsville)	35807
Holiday Park Estates	35215
Holland Gin	35620
Holley Crossroads	36272
Hollins	35082
Hollis Crossroads	36264
Holly Grove	35587
Holly Pond	35083
Holly Springs	35146
Hollytree	35751
Hollywood (Jackson County)	35752
Hollywood (Jefferson County)	35209
Holman	36503
Holman Prison	36502
Holt	35404
Holt Junction (Part of Tuscaloosa)	35401
Holtville	36022
Holy Trinity	36859
Homewood	35209
Honoraville	36042
Hoods Crossroads	35121
Hoover (Jefferson County)	35216
Hoover (Madison County)	35749
Hope Hull	36043
Hopewell (Cherokee County)	35959
Hopewell (Cleburne County)	36264
Hopewell (DeKalb County)	35950
Hopewell (Jefferson County)	35020

Name	ZIP
Hoppes	36535
Hornady	36039
Horn Hill	36467
Horton	35980
Hortons Mill	35121
Houston	35572
Howard	35549
Howells Cross Roads	35960
Howelton	35952
Howton	35453
Hubbertville (Part of Glen Allen)	35555
Hudson Gardens (Part of Lipscomb)	35020
Hudson Settlement	35501
Hueytown	35023
Hueytown Crest (Part of Hueytown)	35020
Huffman (Part of Birmingham)	35215
Huffman Gardens (Part of Birmingham)	35215
Hugo	36783
Huguley	36854
Hulaco	35087
Hull (Part of Sumiton)	35063
Humpton	35776
Hunter (Part of Montgomery)	36108
Huntsville	35801-24
For specific Huntsville Zip Codes call (205) 461-6602	
Huntsville Park (Part of Huntsville)	35807
Hurricane	36507
Hurtsboro	36860
Hustleville	35950
Hustontown	35645
Huxford	36543
Hyatt	35980
Hybart	36444
Hytop	35768
Idaho	36251
Ider	35981
Independence	36067
Indian Creek	36061
Indian Hill (Part of Childersburg)	35044
Indian Hills	35244
Indian Springs (Lauderdale County)	35630
Indian Springs (Mobile County)	36613
Indian Valley	35244
Industrial City (Part of Hueytown)	35023
Industry	36033
Inglenook (Part of Birmingham)	35217
Ingram	35474
Inland	35121
Inmanfield	35540
Ino	36453
Institute	36778
Interburan Heights (Part of Fairfield)	35064
Inverness	36089
Ironaton	36268
Iron City	36201
Irondale	35210
Irvington	36544
Isabella	36750
Isbell	35653
Ishkooda (Part of Birmingham)	35211
Isney	36919
Ivalee	35954
Ivanhoe (Part of Birmingham)	35222
Jachin	36910
Jack	36346
Jackson (Choctaw County)	36921
Jackson (Clarke County)	36545
Jackson Heights (Part of Mobile)	36609
Jackson Oak	36526
Jacksons Gap	36861
Jacksonville	36265
Jack Springs	36502
Jagger	35578
Jamestown	35973
Jamesville	36879
Jarrett (Part of Valley)	36854
Jasper	35501-02
For specific Jasper Zip Codes call (205) 384-5516	
Java	36010
Jay Villa	36401
Jeddo	36480
Jeff	35806
Jefferson	36745

Name	ZIP
Jefferson Hills (Part of Birmingham)	35217
Jefferson Park	35210
Jemison	35085
Jena	35480
Jenifer	36268
Jericho	36756
Jernigan	36851
Jerusalem Heights	35405
Joe Wheeler Dam	35672
Johnsons Crossing	35077
Johnsonville	36401
Jones	36749
Jonesboro (Baldwin County)	36526
Jonesboro (Franklin County)	35653
Jonesboro (Jefferson County)	35020
Jones Chapel	35055
Jones Crossroads	35611
Jones Valley (Part of Birmingham)	35211
Jones Valley Estates (Part of Huntsville)	35802
Joppa	35087
Joquin	36035
Jordan (Elmore County)	36092
Jordan (Washington County)	36518
Jordans Mill	35593
Josephine	36530
Joseph Springs	36201
Josie	36005
Julia Tutwiler Prison for Women	36092
Kahatchie	35044
Kansas	35573
Kaolin (Part of Phenix City)	36867
Kaulton (Part of Tuscaloosa)	35401
Keego	36426
Keener	35954
Kellerman	35468
Kelly	36322
Kelly Springs (Part of Dothan)	36301
Kellyton	35089
Kendale Gardens	35630
Kennedy	35574
Kent (Elmore County)	36045
Kent (Pike County)	36035
Kenwood	35226
Ketona (Part of Tarrant)	35217
Key	35960
Keyno	35089
Keys Mill	35761
Keystone (Part of Pelham)	35007
Keyton	36330
Kilby (Part of Montgomery)	36114
Kilby Corrections Facility	36109
Kilgore	35062
Killen	35645
Killough Springs (Part of Birmingham)	35235
Kilpatrick	35950
Kimberly	35091
Kimbrel	35111
Kimbrough	36769
Kincheon	35045
Kings Landing (Baldwin County)	36567
Kings Landing (Dallas County)	36775
Kingston (Part of Birmingham)	35234
Kingsway Terrace (Part of Birmingham)	35206
Kingtown	35652
Kingville	35574
Kinsey	36301
Kinston	36453
Kinterbish	36907
Kirbytown	35755
Kirk	35466
Kirkland	36426
Kirklands Crossroads	36345
Kirks Grove	35960
Klein	35078
Klondike	35580
Knightens Crossroads	36272
Knoxville	35469
Koenton	36558
Kowaliga Beach	35010
Krafton (Part of Prichard)	36610
Kyles	35746
Kymulga	35014
Laceys Chapel	35020
Laceys Spring	35754
Lacon	35622
Ladiga	36272
Ladonia	36867
Lafayette	36862

	ZIP		ZIP		ZIP
Lagoon Park (Part of Montgomery)	36117	Linden	36748	McMullen	35442
Lake Coves	35630	Lineville	36266	Macon	36271
Lake Drive Estates (Part of Homewood)	35209	Linwood	36081	McQueen	36066
		Lipscomb	35020	McShan	35471
Lake Forest	36526	Lisman	36912	McVay	36451
Lakeside Acres	35645	Little Oak	36081	McVille	35950
		Little River (Baldwin County)	36550	McWilliams	36753
Lakeside Highlands (Part of Florence)	35630	Little River (Cherokee County)	35959	Madison	35758
				Madison Crossroads	35772
Lakeview (DeKalb County)	35971	Little Rock	36502	Madison Square Mall (Part of Huntsville)	35806
Lakeview (Marshall County)	35976	Little Shawmut	36863		
Lakeview Highlands (Part of Muscle Shoals)	35660	Little Texas	36083	Madrid	36320
		Littleton (Etowah County)	35954	Magazine (Part of Mobile)	36610
Lakewood (Jefferson County)	35234	Littleton (Jefferson County)	35073	Magnolia	36754
		Littleville (Colbert County)	35653	Magnolia Beach (Part of Fairhope)	36532
Lakewood (Limestone County)	35611	Littleville (Winston County)	35565		
		Live Oak Landing	36507	Magnolia Springs	36555
Lakewood (Madison County)	35810	Livingston	35470	Magnolia Terminal	36722
		Loachapoka	36865	Majestic	35116
Lakewood Estates (Part of Bessemer)	35020	Loango	36474	Malbis	36526
		Locke Crossroads	35620	Malcolm	36556
Lamison	36728	Lockhart	36455	Mall, The (Part of Huntsville)	35801
Land	36904	Lock Six	35645	Malone	36276
Landersville	35650	Lock Three	35652	Malta	36502
Lands Crossroads (Part of Rainsville)	35986	Locust Fork	35097	Malvern	36349
		Loflin	36851	Marnie	36052
Lane Springs	35616	Logan	35098	Manack	36752
Lanett	36863	Logton	36081	Manchester	35501
Langdale (Part of Valley)	36854	Lola City	35173	Manila	36586
Langston	35755	Lomax	35045	Manley Crossroads	35758
Langtown	35650	London (Conecuh County)	36432	Manningham	36037
Laniers (Crenshaw County)	35014	London (Montgomery County)	36064	Mansion View	35630
Lapine (Crenshaw County)	36041			Mantua	35462
Lapine (Montgomery County)	36046	Long Island	35958	Maple Hill	38449
		Longleaf Estates (Part of Decatur)	35603	Maplesville	36750
La Place	36075			Maplewood (Jefferson County)	35094
Larkinsville	35768	Longview (Cullman County)	35179		
Larkwood	35215	Longview (Shelby County)	35137	Maplewood (Madison County)	35758
Lasca	36784	Longwood (Part of Huntsville)	35801		
Latham	36579	Loop (Cherokee County)	35959	Marble City Heights (Part of Sylacauga)	35150
Lathamville	35962	Loop (Mobile County)	36606	Marble Valley	35150
Lattiwood	35950	Loree	36401	Marbury	36051
Lauderdale Beach	35630	Lott	36613	Marcoot	36862
Laurendine	36582	Lottie	36502	Margaret	35112
Lavaca	36911	Louisville	36048	Margerum	35616
Lawley	36793	Love Hill	36312	Marietta	35579
Lawrence	35959	Lovelace Crossroads	35630	Marion	36756
Lawrence Cove	35621	Loveless	35967	Marion Junction	36759
Lawrence Mill	35555	Loveless Park	35020	Markeeta	35094
Lawrenceville	36310	Lovick	35173	Marl	36477
Leatherwood	36201	Lower Peach Tree	36751	Marley Mill	36360
Lebanon (Cleburne County)	36269	Lowery	36453	Marlow	36580
Lebanon (DeKalb County)	35961	Lowerytown	35184	Mars Hill (Part of Florence)	35630
Lecta	36264	Low Gap	35120	Martins (Part of Birmingham)	35208
Leeds	35094	Lowndesboro	36752		
Leeds Mineral Well (Part of Leeds)	35094	Lowry Mill	36346	Martintown	35752
		Loxley	36551	Martinville	36502
Leesburg	35983	Loxley Heights	36551	Martling	35950
Leesdale (Part of Falkville)	35622	Lucille	35184	Marvel	35115
Leggtown	35620	Lugo	36027	Marvyn	36801
Le Grand	36105	Lumbull	35543	Marylee	35501
Leighton	35646	Luttrell	35971	Maryville	35954
Lenlock (Part of Anniston)	36201	Luverne	36049	Massey	35619
Lenox	36454	Lydia	35967	Masterson Mill	35650
Leon	36028	Lyeffion	36401	Mathews	36052
Leroy	36548	Lynn	35575	Mattawana	35121
Leslie	36790	Lynn Crossing	35073	Maud	35616
Lester	35647	Lynndale (Part of Montgomery)	36105	Maxine	35130
Letcher	35776			Maxwell	35401
Letchers	36201	Lynn Haven (Part of Tuscaloosa)	35404	Maxwellborn	36272
Letohatchee	36047			Maxwell Heights (Part of Montgomery)	36113
Level Plains	36322	Lynns Park	35550		
Levelroad	36276	Lytle	36477	Mayes Crossroads	35903
Levert	36779	Mabson	36360	Mayfair (Jefferson County)	35209
Lewis	36350	McCalla	35111	Mayfair (Madison County)	35801
Lewisburg (Part of Birmingham)	35207	McClure Town	36081	Maylene (Part of Alabaster)	35114
		McCollum	35501	Maynards Cove	35768
Lewiston	35462	McCord Crossroads	35960	Maysville	35748
Lexington	35648	McCulley Hill	35184	Maytown	35118
Liberty (Blount County)	35031	McCullough	36502	Meadow Crossroads	36874
Liberty (Butler County)	36037	McDonald Chapel	35224	Meadow Hills (Part of Huntsville)	35810
Liberty (DeKalb County)	35957	McDowell	35470		
Liberty City	36866	Macedonia (Cleburne County)	36273	Mechanicsville	36874
Liberty Highlands	35210			Media	35062
Liberty Hill (Franklin County)	35581	Macedonia (Jackson County)	35771	Meeksville	36081
Liberty Hill (Jackson County)	35966			Megargel	36457
		Macedonia (Montgomery County)	36036	Mehama	35653
Libertyville	36420			Mellow Valley	36255
Lightwood	36022	Macedonia (Walker County)	35501	Melrose (Conecuh County)	36401
Ligon Springs	35653	McElderry	36268	Melrose (Pickens County)	35471
Lillian	36549	McFarland Mall (Part of Tuscaloosa)	35405	Melton	36776
Lily Flag (Part of Huntsville)	35802			Meltonsville	35755
Lime	36274	McGhees Bend	35960	Melville	35541
Lime Kiln	35616	McGinty (Part of Valley)	36854	Melvin	36913
Limestone	36460	McIntosh	36553	Memphis	39353
Lim Rock	35776	McKenzie	36456	Mentone	35984
Lincoln (Madison County)	35810	McKestes	35963	Mercury	35811
Lincoln (Talladega County)	35096	McKinley	36728	Meridianville	35759
Lincoya Estates (Part of Vestavia Hills)	35216	McLarty	35980	Merry	36064
Lindbergh	35073	McLendon	36851	Mertz (Part of Mobile)	36606

	ZIP
Mexboro	36445
Mexia	36458
Mexia Crossing	36458
Micaville	36264
Middle Brooks Cross Roads	36879
Middleton	36271
Midfield	35228
Midland City	36350
Midtown (Part of Mobile)	36640
Midway (Bullock County)	36053
Midway (Butler County)	36042
Midway (Chilton County)	36051
Midway (Clay County)	35072
Midway (Lawrence County)	35650
Midway (Monroe County)	36768
Miflin	36530
Mignon	35150
Miles (Part of Fairfield)	35064
Millbrook	36054
Miller	36448
Millers Ferry	36760
Millertown	36613
Millerville	36267
Millport	35576
Millry	36558
Mills Quarter's	36535
Milltown	36862
Mill Village (Part of Guntersville)	35976
Milstead	36075
Milton	36749
Mineral Springs	35085
Minooka	35040
Minor	35224
Minor Terrace (Part of Childersburg)	35044
Minter	36761
Minvale (Part of Fort Payne)	35967
Mitchell	36029
Mitchell Town	35645
Mobile	36601-95
For specific Mobile Zip Codes call (205) 694-5917	
Mobile Festival Centre (Part of Mobile)	36609
Mobile Junction	35023
Moffett	36587
Mollie	36906
Molloy	35586
Mon Louis	36523
Monroeville	36460-61
For specific Monroeville Zip Codes call (205) 743-3475	
Monrovia	35806
Montague	35740
Monterey	36030
Monterey Heights	36877
Monte-Sano (Part of Birmingham)	35228
Montevallo	35115
Monte Vista (Part of Gadsden)	35901
Montgomery	36101-99
For specific Montgomery Zip Codes call (205) 244-7500	
Montgomery Mall (Part of Montgomery)	36116
Monticello	36005
Montrose	36559
Moody	35094
Moorefield	36862
Moores Bridge	35476
Moores Crossroad	35971
Moores Crossroads	36274
Moores Mill	35811
Mooresville	35649
Moreland	35572
Morgan (Part of Bessemer)	35020
Morgan City	35175
Moriah	35136
Morningside	35215
Morris	35116
Morvin	36762
Moshat	35960
Mosses	36040
Mossy Grove	36081
Mostellers	35143
Motley	36276
Moulton	35650
Moulton Heights (Part of Decatur)	35601
Moundville	35474
Mountainboro	35957
Mountain Brook (Jefferson County)	35223
Mountain Brook (Madison County)	35801
Mountain Brook Village (Part of Mountain Brook)	35223
Mountain Chest (Part of Guntersville)	35976

	ZIP
Mountain Creek	36051
Mountain Grove	35031
Mountain Home	35673
Mountain Park (Part of Birmingham)	35217
Mountain View (Part of Guntersville)	35976
Mountain Woods (Part of Vestavia Hills)	35216
Mountain Woods Park (Part of Vestavia Hills)	35216
Mount Andrew	36053
Mount Carmel (Jackson County)	35740
Mount Carmel (Marshall County)	35976
Mount Carmel (Montgomery County)	36046
Mount Hebron (Greene County)	35443
Mount Hebron (Marshall County)	35957
Mount Hester	35616
Mount Hope	35651
Mount Ida	36009
Mount Jefferson	36801
Mount Meigs	36057
Mount Nebo	36785
Mount Olive (Coosa County)	35072
Mount Olive (Jefferson County)	35117
Mount Pleasant (Coffee County)	36330
Mount Pleasant (Monroe County)	36480
Mount Rozell	35647
Mount Sinai	36113
Mount Star	35653
Mount Sterling	36904
Mount Union	36401
Mount Vernon (Cullman County)	35179
Mount Vernon (DeKalb County)	35967
Mount Vernon (Fayette County)	35555
Mount Vernon (Mobile County)	36560
Mount Willing	36032
Mount Zion	36069
Muck City	35650
Mud Creek (Jackson County)	35752
Mud Creek (Jefferson County)	35006
Mulga	35118
Mulga Mine	35118
Munford	36268
Murphy	35677
Murrays Chapel	35146
Muscadine	36269
Muscadine Junction	36269
Muscle Shoals	35661
Muscoda	35020
Mynot	35616
Myrick Chapel	36022
Myrtlewood	36763
Nadawah	36726
Naftel	36046
Nanafalia	36764
Nances Creek	36272
Napier Field	36301
Napoleon	36280
Nat	35776
Natchez	36425
Nathan (Part of Arley)	35541
Natural Bridge	35577
Nauvoo	35578
Navco (Part of Mobile)	36605
Nebo	35758
Nectar	35049
Needham	36915
Needmore (Marshall County)	35957
Needmore (Pike County)	36081
Needmore (Winston County)	35565
Neel	35640
Neenah	36726
Nellie	36726
Neshota (Part of Mobile)	36605
Nesmith (Cullman County)	35055
Ne Smith (Lawrence County)	35672
Nettleboro	36436
Newbern	36765
Newberry Crossroads	35960
New Brashier Chapel	35950
New Brockton	36351
Newburg	35653

	ZIP
New Castle	35119
New Center	35640
New Dora (Part of Dora)	35062
Newell	36270
New Georgia	35540
New Haven	35758
New Hill (Part of Lipscomb)	35020
New Home	35978
New Hope (Coffee County)	36010
New Hope (Cullman County)	35083
New Hope (Jackson County)	35768
New Hope (Madison County)	35760
New Hope (Shelby County)	35243
New Hopewell	36264
New Lexington	35546
New London	35054
New Market	35761
New Moon	35973
New Prospect (Autauga County)	36051
New Prospect (Hale County)	35441
New Sharon	35750
New Site	35010
Newsome (Part of Rainsville)	35986
Newton (Dale County)	36352
Newton (Houston County)	36301
Newtonville	35555
Newtown (Franklin County)	35653
New Town (Jackson County)	35772
Newville	36353
Nichburg	36475
Nicholsville	36784
Nitrate City	35560
Nixburg	36026
Nix Mill	35581
Nixons Chapel	35980
Noah	35960
Nokomis	36502
Nolandale (Part of Madison)	35758
Nolan Hills (Part of Madison)	35758
Normal (Part of Huntsville)	35762
Normandale Shopping Center (Part of Montgomery)	36111
North Arab (Part of Arab)	35016
North Athens (Part of Athens)	35611
North Birmingham (Part of Birmingham)	35207
North Courtland	35618
North Daye Hill	35749
North Elmore	36025
North Florence (Part of Florence)	35630
North Highlands (Part of Hueytown)	35020
North Johns	35006
North Mobile (Part of Chickasaw)	36611
Northport	35476
Northside (Part of Dothan)	36304
Northside Acres	35806
Northside Mall (Part of Dothan)	36303
North Smithfield Estates	35214
North Smithfield Manor (Part of Birmingham)	35207
North Vinemont	35179
North Walter	35055
Northwood Hills (Part of Florence)	35630
Norton	35803
Norwood (Part of Birmingham)	35234
Notasulga	36866
Nottingham	35014
Nuckols	36856
Nymph	36401
Oak	36535
Oak Bowery	36862
Oak Crossing (Part of Leeds)	35094
Oakdale	35611
Oakdale Acres	35611
Oak Grove (Autauga County)	36067
Oak Grove (Chilton County)	35085
Oak Grove (Franklin County)	35653
Oak Grove (Jefferson County)	35006
Oak Grove (Limestone County)	35739
Oak Grove (Mobile County)	36613

	ZIP
Oak Grove (Talladega County)	35150
Oak Hill (DeKalb County)	35962
Oak Hill (Wilcox County) ...	36766
Oakhurst (Part of Birmingham)	35207
Oakland	35630
Oakleigh Estates (Part of Gadsden)	35901
Oak Level	36262
Oakman	35579
Oakmulgee	36793
Oak Ridge (Morgan County)	35640
Oak Ridge (St. Clair County)	35125
Oak Ridge Park (Part of Birmingham)	35212
Oakville (Jefferson County)	35206
Oakville (Lawrence County)	35619
Oakwood (Part of Bessemer)	35020
Oakwood College	35896
Oakworth (Part of Decatur)	35601
Oaky Grove	36353
Oaky Streak	36037
Octagon	36748
Odena	35150
Oden Ridge	35621
Odenville	35120
Odom	36456
Ofelia	36266
Ohatchee	36271
Old Bethel	35646
Old Burleson	35593
Old Davistown	36201
Old Fabius	35966
Oldfield (Part of Sylacauga)	35150
Old Jonesboro	35215
Old Kingston	36067
Old Maylene (Part of Alabaster)	35114
Old Monrovia	35806
Old Nauvoo	35653
Old Samuel	36908
Old Spring Hill	36742
Old Texas	36768
Old Town (Conecuh County)	36401
Old Town (Dallas County)	36785
Oleander	35175
Oliver	35652
Ollie	36460
Olney	35442
Olustee	36081
Omaha	36274
O'Neal	35611
Oneonta	35121
Onycha	36467
Opelika	36801-03
For specific Opelika Zip Codes call (205) 745-3561	
Opine (Clarke County)	36784
Opine (Covington County)	36467
Opp	36467
Orange Beach	36561
Orchard (Part of Mobile) ...	36618
Ord (Part of Gadsden)	35901
Orion	36081
Orrville (Dallas County)	36767
Orrville (Limestone County)	35671
Osanippa	36854
Osborn	36779
Oswichee	36856
Our Town	35010
Overbrook	35150
Overlook (Part of Mobile)	36608
Overton	35210
Owassa	36401
Owens Cross Roads	35763
Owenton (Part of Birmingham)	35204
Oxford	36203
Oxford Lake (Part of Oxford)	36201
Oxmoor	35211
Oyster Bay	36535
Ozark	36360-61
For specific Ozark Zip Codes call (205) 774-5200	
Painter	35962
Paint Rock	35764
Palestine	36262
Palmerdale	35123
Palmers Crossroads	36480
Palmetto	35481
Palmetto Beach	36542
Palos	35130
Panola (Crenshaw County)	36046
Panola (Sumter County) ...	35477
Pansey	36370
Paran	36274

	ZIP
Park City	36526
Parkdale	35072
Park Hill (Part of Pell City)	35125
Parkland (Part of Jasper) ...	35501
Parkway City (Part of Huntsville)	35801
Parkway Estates (Part of Huntsville)	35802
Parkwood	35020
Parrish	35580
Partridge Crossroads	35180
Patsburg	36049
Patton	35579
Patton Chapel (Part of Hoover)	35216
Paul	36469
Pauls Hill	35020
Pawnee	35217
Peacock	36451
Pea Ridge (Escambia County)	36426
Pea Ridge (Fayette County)	35546
Pea Ridge (Madison County)	35801
Pea Ridge (Marion County)	35563
Pea Ridge (Shelby County)	35115
Pearson	35456
Pebble	35565
Peeks Corner	35961
Peeks Hill	36271
Peets Corner	35611
Pelham	35124
Pelham Heights (Part of Anniston)	36201
Pell City	35125
Penfield Heights (Part of Birmingham)	35217
Penn	35619
Pennington	36916
Pennsylvania (Part of Satsuma)	36572
Penton	36862
Pentonville	35136
Pepperell (Part of Opelika)	36801
Perdido	36562
Perdido Beach	36530
Perdue Hill	36470
Perote	36061
Perry Chapel	36586
Perry Store	36453
Perryville	36701
Peterman	36471
Peterson	35478
Petersville	35633
Petrey	36062
Petronia	36785
Pettusville	35620
Peytonia Points	35660
Phalin	35456
Phelan	35055
Phenix City	36867-69
For specific Phenix City Zip Codes call (205) 298-7871	
Phil Campbell	35581
Phillips Estates (Part of Bessemer)	35020
Phillipsville	36507
Phoenixville (Part of Birmingham)	35221
Pickensville	35447
Pickering	36758
Piedmont (Calhoun County)	36272
Piedmont (Madison County)	35801
Piedmont Springs	36272
Pierce	36587
Pigeon Creek	36037
Pike Road	36064
Pikeville	35768
Pilgrims Rest (Part of Southside)	35901
Pinckard	36371
Pinder Hill	35772
Pine Apple	36768
Pine Beach	36542
Pinebelt	36767
Pine Dale (Limestone County)	35739
Pinedale (Montgomery County)	36106
Pinedale Acres (Lauderdale County)	35645
Pinedale Acres (Limestone County)	35611
Pinedale Shores	35953
Pine Flat	36022
Pine Grove (Baldwin County)	36507
Pine Grove (Lee County)	36801
Pine Grove (Tallapoosa County)	36850
Pine Grove (Bullock County)	36053

	ZIP
Pine Grove (Cherokee County)	35960
Pine Hill (Randolph County)	36263
Pine Hill (Wilcox County) ...	36769
Pine Level (Autauga County)	36022
Pine Level (Coffee County)	36323
Pine Level (Montgomery County)	36065
Pine Mountain	35133
Pine Orchard	36471
Pine Ridge	35967
Pineview (Part of Irondale)	35210
Pinewood Terrace (Part of Childersburg)	35044
Piney	35960
Piney Bend	35593
Piney Chapel	35611
Piney Grove (Lawrence County)	35619
Piney Grove (Marion County)	35548
Piney Woods	36262
Pinkeyville	35072
Pinkney City	35214
Pinnell	36850
Pinson	35126
Pintlalla	36043
Pisgah (Jackson County)	35765
Pisgah (Limestone County)	35773
Pisgah (Montgomery County)	36036
Pittsview	36871
Plainview (Cleburne County)	36264
Plainview (DeKalb County)	35986
Plant City	36863
Plantersville (Dallas County)	36758
Plantersville (Talladega County)	35014
Plateau (Part of Prichard)	36610
Plaza De Malaga (Part of Mobile)	36685
Pleasant Acres	35811
Pleasant Gap	36272
Pleasant Grove (Chilton County)	35085
Pleasant Grove (Jackson County)	35772
Pleasant Grove (Jefferson County)	35127
Pleasant Grove (Marshall County)	35950
Pleasant Hill (Barbour County)	36027
Pleasant Hill (Franklin County)	35585
Pleasant Hill (Jefferson County)	35020
Pleasant Hill (Choctaw County)	36908
Pleasant Hill (Dallas County)	36701
Pleasant Hill (Escambia County)	36502
Pleasant Home	36420
Pleasant Plains	36312
Pleasant Ridge (Franklin County)	35653
Pleasant Ridge (Greene County)	35462
Pleasant Ridge (Pike County)	36034
Pleasant Site	35582
Pletcher	36750
Plevna	35761
Poarch	36502
Pocahontas	35549
Pogo	35582
Point Clear	36564
Polk	36785
Pollard	36441
Pollards Bend	35983
Ponderosa Estates	36575
Ponders	36853
Pondville	35034
Pool	35619
Pooles Crossroads	36274
Pools Crossroads	35045
Pope	36769
Poplarridge	35760
Poplar Springs (Marshall County)	35950
Poplar Springs (Winston County)	35578
Port Birmingham	35118
Porter	35005
Portersville	35961
Posey Mill	35565
Poseys Crossroads	36067
Postoak	36089
Potash	36274
Potter	36701

	ZIP
Powderly (Part of Birmingham)	35211
Powderly Hills (Part of Birmingham)	35211
Powell	35971
Powers	35474
Powhatan	35118
Powledge	36874
Praco	35130
Prairie	36771
Prairieville	36742
Pratt City (Part of Birmingham)	35214
Prattmont (Part of Prattville)	36067
Pratts	36016
Prattville	36066-67
For specific Prattville Zip Codes call (205) 365-6467	
Prescott	35125
Preston	35768
Prestwick	36548
Priceville	35601
Prichard	36610
Pride	35674
Primitive Ridge	35184
Princeton	35766
Pronto	36081
Prospect	35578
Providence (Butler County)	36033
Providence (Cullman County)	35179
Providence (Marengo County)	36742
Providence (Walker County)	35579
Prudence	36871
Pruitton	35630
Pulaski Pike (Part of Huntsville)	35810
Pulltight	35548
Pumpkin Center (DeKalb County)	35967
Pumpkin Center (Morgan County)	35619
Pumpkin Center (Walker County)	35130
Pushmataha	36912
Putnam	36784
Pyriton	36266
Queenstown	35173
Quintard Mall (Part of Oxford)	36201
Quinton	35130
Quintown	35130
Rabb	36401
Rabbittown (Calhoun County)	36272
Rabbit Town (Marshall County)	35950
Rabbittown (Winston County)	35565
Rabun	36507
Ragland	35131
Raimund	35020
Rainbow	35758
Rainbow City	35901
Rainbow Mountain Heights (Madison County)	35758
Rainsville	35986
Ralph	35480
Ramer	36069
Ranburne	36273
Randolph	36792
Range	36473
Rash	35772
Rayburn (Part of Guntersville)	35976
Read's Mill	36279
Red Bank	35672
Red Bay	35582
Reddock Springs	36037
Red Eagle Honor Farm	36101
Red Hill (Blount County) ...	35063
Red Hill (Elmore County)...	36078
Red Hill (Marshall County)	35976
Redland Heights (Part of Valley)	36854
Red Level	36474
Redmont Park (Part of Mountain Brook)	35213
Red Ore	35020
Red Rock	35674
Red Rock Junction	35616
Redstone Arsenal (census designated place)	35808
Redstone Arsenal	35809
Redtown	36502
Reece City	35954
Reedtown (Part of Russellville)	35653
Reeltown...................	36078
Reform.....................	35481

	ZIP
Regency (Part of Florence)	35630
Regent Forest	35226
Rehobeth	36301
Rehoboth	36720
Reid	35611
Remlap	35133
Renfroe	35160
Reno	35111
Repton	36475
Republic	35214
Rhoades	36453
Rhodesville	35630
Rice	35201
Richmond	36761
Richmond Hills (Part of Tuscumbia)	35674
Rideout Village (Part of Huntsville)	35806
Riderwood	36904
Ridgecrest	36105
Ridgeville (Butler County)	36030
Ridgeville (Etowah County)	35954
Ringgold	35973
Ripley	35611
Riverbend	35184
Riverdale (Part of Mentone)	35984
River Falls	36476
Rivermont (Colbert County)	35660
Rivermont (Lauderdale County)	35630
River Park	36532
Riverside (Blount County)	35031
Riverside (St. Clair County)	35135
Riverton	35616
River View (Chambers County)	36854
Riverview (Chambers County)	36854
Riverview (Escambia County)	36426
Riverview (Tuscaloosa County)	35401
Riverwood (Part of Tuscaloosa)	35406
Roanoke	36274
Roanoke Junction (Part of Opelika)	36801
Roba	36089
Robbins Crossroads	35062
Roberta	35040
Roberts	36420
Robertsdale	36567
Robinsons	36752
Robinson Springs	36025
Robinsonville	36502
Robinwood	35217
Rock City (Jackson County)	35771
Rock City (Marion County)	35594
Rockdale	35020
Rocket	35808
Rockford	35136
Rock Hill	36426
Rock House	35771
Rockledge	35954
Rock Mills	36274
Rock Run	36272
Rock Spring (Part of Glencoe)	35905
Rock Spring Quarry (Part of Glencoe)	35905
Rock Springs (Blount County)	35031
Rock Springs (Choctaw County)	36904
Rock Stand	36274
Rockville	36545
Rockwest	36726
Rockwood	35653
Rocky Head	36311
Rocky Hill	35672
Rocky Hollow	35550
Rocky Ridge	35243
Rodentown	35957
Roebuck (Part of Birmingham)	35206
Roebuck Crest Estates (Part of Birmingham)	35215
Roebuck Forest (Part of Birmingham)	35235
Roebuck Gardens (Part of Birmingham)	35235
Roebuck Park (Part of Birmingham)	35215
Roebuck Plaza	35235
Roebuck Springs (Part of Birmingham)	35206
Roebuck Terrace (Part of Birmingham)	35206
Roeton.....................	36010
Rogersville	35652

	ZIP
Rolling Hills (Part of Decatur)	35603
Rollins	36022
Romar Beach	36561
Rome	36420
Romulus	35446
Roper	35173
Rosa.......................	35121
Rosalie	35765
Roseboro	37328
Rosebud	36766
Rosedale (Part of Homewood)	35209
Rose Hill (Covington County)	36028
Rose Hill (Jefferson County)	35210
Rosemont (Part of Birmingham)	35221
Rose Park (Part of Florence)	35630
Rosinton	36567
Rossland City	35555
Round Hill	36784
Round Mountain	35959
Rowells Crossroad	36879
Roxana	36879
Royal	35031
Ruffner (Part of Irondale)...	35210
Russell Heights (Part of Leeds)	35094
Russell Mill (Part of Alexander City)	35010
Russell Village (Part of Decatur)	35603
Russellville	35653
Rutan	36518
Ruth	35016
Rutherford	36860
Rutledge	36071
Rutledge Heights (Jefferson County)	35064
Rutledge Heights (Madison County)	35816
Ryan	35115
Ryan Crossroads	35087
Ryland	35767
Saco	36081
Safford....................	36773
Saginaw	35137
Sahama Village (Part of Tuscaloosa)	35401
St. Bernard.................	35055
St. Clair	36752
St. Clair Correctional Facility	35120
St. Clair Springs	35146
St. Elmo	36568
St. Florian	35630
Saints Crossroads	35653
St. Stephens	36569
Saks	36201
Salem (Dallas County)	36767
Salem (Fayette County)	35546
Salem (Lee County)	36874
Salem (Limestone County)	35620
Salitpa	36570
Samantha	35482
Samford University (Part of Homewood).............	35229
Samson	36477
Samuels Chapel	35952
Sandfield	36081
Sandfort	36875
Sandhurst Park (Part of Huntsville)	35802
Sand Rock	35961
Sandtown	35546
Sandusky (Part of Birmingham)	35214
Sandy Creek	36850
Sandy Ridge	36047
Sanford	36420
Sanie	35120
San Souci Beach (Part of Bayou La Batre).........	36509
Santuck....................	36092
Sapps	35447
Saragossa	35578
Saraland	36571
Saratoga (Part of Albertville)	35950
Sardine	36441
Sardis (Bullock County)	36089
Sardis (Dallas County)	36775
Sardis (Walker County)	35550
Sardis City	35957
Sardis Springs.............	35611
Satsuma	36572
Saucer	36030
Saville	36041
Sawyerville	36776
Sayre	35139
Scant City.................	35016

	ZIP
Scarce Grease	35647
Scenic Heights (Part of Gadsden)	35901
Schenks	36279
Schmits Mill	35096
Schuster Springs	36768
Scotland	36471
Scotrock (Part of Alabaster)	35007
Scott City	35094
Scottland	36089
Scottsboro	35768
Scranage	36502
Scranton	36313
Scyrene	36436
Seaboard	36522
Seacliff (Part of Fairhope)	36532
Seale	36875
Sealy Springs (Part of Cottonwood)	36320
Searight	36028
Searles	35444
Section	35771
Segco	35580
Selbrook	36108
Selfville	35133
Sellers	36046
Sellersville	36318
Selma	36701-03
For specific Selma Zip Codes call (205) 874-4678	
Selma Mall (Part of Selma)	36703
Selmont	36703
Selmont-West Selmont	36703
Seman	36024
Seminole	36567
Semmes	36575
Service	36919
Seven Hills	36601
Seymour Bluff	36542
Shacklesville	36033
Shades Crest Estates	35226
Shady Grove (Clay County)	35072
Shady Grove (Coffee County)	36323
Shady Grove (Franklin County)	35581
Shady Grove (Pike County)	36035
Shady Lane (Part of Huntsville)	35810
Shanghai	35611
Shannon	35142
Shawmut (Part of Valley)	36854
Shawnee	36726
Sheffield	35660-62
For specific Sheffield Zip Codes call (205) 383-0252	
Shelby	35143
Shellhorn	36081
Sherman Heights (Part of Anniston)	36201
Sherwood Forest (Part of Florence)	35630
Sherwood Park (Part of Huntsville)	35206
Shiloh (DeKalb County)	35967
Shiloh (Marengo County)	36754
Shiloh (Pike County)	36005
Shinebone	36266
Shingle	35581
Shoals Acres	35645
Shopton	36029
Short Creek	35118
Shorter	36075
Shorterville	36373
Shortleaf (Part of Demopolis)	36732
Shottsville	35570
Shreve	36456
Sico	35150
Siddonsville	36738
Sigma	36319
Sikesville	36276
Silas	36919
Siloam	36907
Siluria (Part of Alabaster)	35144
Silver Cross	36919
Silverhill	36576
Silver Run	36268
Simcoe	35055
Simmons Crossroads	36879
Simmsville	35043
Sims Chapel	36553
Simsville	36089
Sipsey	35584
Six Mile	35035
Six Way	35603
Skaggs Corner (Part of Ider)	35978
Skeggs Crossroads	35072
Skinem	35750
Skinnerton	36401
Skipperville	36374

	ZIP
Skirum	35963
Skyline	35768
Skyline Acres	35758
Skyline Estates	35226
Sky Ranch	35226
Skyview (Part of Bessemer)	35020
Slackland	35901
Slocomb	36375
Smithfield (Part of Birmingham)	35204
Smith Hill	35184
Smith Institute	35957
Smiths	36877
Smiths Crossroads (Part of Glencoe)	35903
Smithson	35020
Smithsonia	35630
Smut Eye	36061
Smyer	36727
Smyrna	36301
Snead	35952
Snoddy	35462
Snowdoun	36105
Snow Hill	36778
Snowtown	35062
Socapatoy	35089
Society Hill	36801
Soleo	35072
Somerville	35670
South (Covington County)	36474
South (Montgomery County)	36116
South Calera (Part of Calera)	35040
South Gadsden (Part of Gadsden)	35901
South Gate Mall (Part of Muscle Shoals)	35660
South Guntersville (Part of Guntersville)	35976
South Haleyville (Part of Haleyville)	35565
South Highlands (Part of Birmingham)	35205
South Lowell	35501
Southmont (Part of Montgomery)	36105
South Orchard	36582
South Park Estates (Part of Huntsville)	35802
South Sheffield (Part of Tuscumbia)	35674
Southside	35901
	35903
For specific Southside Zip Codes call (205) 547-6391	
Southtown (Part of Guntersville)	35976
Southwood (Part of Homewood)	35209
Souwilpa	36919
Spanish Fort	36527
Speake	35619
Speed	36026
Speeds Water Mill	35466
Speigener	36022
Spivey's	36535
Sprague	36069
Springbrook (Part of Tuscaloosa)	35405
Springdale (Part of Tarrant)	35217
Springdale Mall (Part of Mobile)	36606
Springfield (Clarke County)	36784
Springfield (Lauderdale County)	35652
Springfield (Randolph County)	36274
Spring Garden	36275
Spring Hill (Barbour County)	36053
Spring Hill (Mobile County)	36608
Spring Hill (Pike County)	36081
Spring Hill (Walker County)	35549
Spring Valley (Colbert County)	35674
Spring Valley (Montgomery County)	36116
Springville	35146
Springville Lake Estates	35146
Sprott	36779
Spruce Pine	35585
Standard	35580
Standing Rock	36855
Stanley	36420
Stansel	35481
Stanton	36790
Stapleton	36578
Star	35576
State Line	36320
Statesville	36703
Steele	35987
Steele Crossing	37328

	ZIP
Steelwood	36551
Steenson Hollow (Part of Muscle Shoals)	35660
Steiner (Part of Montgomery)	36111
Sterrett	35147
Stevenson	35772
Stewart	35441
Stewartsville	35150
Stills Cross Road	36081
Stockdale	36268
Stockton	36579
Stokeley (Part of Andalusia)	36420
Stokes	35456
Stones	36054
Stoney Point	36022
Stotesville	35184
Stough	35555
Straight Mountain	35121
Strata	36046
Strawberry	35016
Stroud	36855
Studdards Crossroads	35549
Sturkie	36862
Suggsville	36482
Sulligent	35586
Sulphur Springs (Blount County)	35079
Sulphur Springs (DeKalb County)	30738
Sulphur Springs (Jackson County)	35966
Sulphur Springs (Madison County)	35761
Sumiton	35148
Summerdale	36580
Summerfield	36701
Summit	35031
Summit Farm	35023
Sumterville	35460
Sunflower	36581
Sunny Cove	36582
Sunny South	36769
Sunset Cove (Part of Huntsville)	35802
Sunset Mill Village (Part of Selma)	36701
Sunset Shores	36535
Sun Valley	35215
Surginer	36754
Susan Moore	35952
Suspension	36089
Suttle	36701
Swaim	35764
Swancott	35758
Swearengin	35768
Sweet Water	36782
Sycamore	35149
Sylacauga	35150
Sylvan Grove	36350
Sylvania	35988
Sylvan Springs	35118
Tabernacle (Coffee County)	36351
Tabernacle (Houston County)	36301
Tabor	35901
Taft	35973
Taits Gap	35121
Talladega	35160
Talladega Springs	35150
Tallahatta Springs	36784
Tallapoosa City (Part of Tallassee)	36023
Tallassee	36078
Tallaweka (Part of Tallassee)	36078
Talucah	35775
Tanner	35671
Tanner Crossroads	35671
Tanner Heights (Part of Hartselle)	35640
Tanner Williams	36587
Tanyard (Bullock County)	36061
Tanyard (St. Clair County)	35125
Tarentum	36010
Tarpley (Part of Birmingham)	35211
Tarrant	35217
Tarrant Heights	35217
Tasso	36767
Tattlersville	36524
Taylor	36301
Taylors Crossroads	36274
Taylorville	35405
Teals Crossroads	36311
Teasleys Mill	36052
Tecumseh	30138
Teddy	36426
Tenant	36274
Ten Broeck (Part of Lakeview)	35971

	ZIP		ZIP		ZIP
Tennala	35960	Underwood (Shelby County)	35115	Wadley	36276
Tennille	36010	Underwood Crossroads	35646	Wadsworth	36022
Tensaw	36579	Underwood-Petersville	35630	Wagar	36585
Terese (Part of Eufaula)	36027	Union (Etowah County)	35957	Wagarville	36585
Terry Heights (Part of		Union (Greene County)	35462	Wahouma (Part of	
Huntsville)	35805	Union (Henry County)	36310	Birmingham)	35206
Texasville	36016	Union (Morgan County)	35670	Walco (Part of Sylacauga)	35150
Thach	35501	Union (Tallapoosa County)	36853	Waldo	35160
Tharptown	35653	Union Academy	36330	Walker Chapel (Part of	
Thatch	35620	Union Grove (Chilton		Fultondale)	35068
The Cedars (Part of		County)	35085	Walkers Corner	35055
Florence)	35630	Union Grove (Cullman		Walker Springs	36586
The Highlands (Etowah		County)	35083	Walkerton (Part of Pell City)	35125
County)	35901	Union Grove (Jefferson		Wallace	36426
The Highlands (Madison		County)	35005	Walley	36584
County)	35810	Union Grove (Marshall		Wallsboro	36092
Theodore	36582	County)	35175	Wall Street	35758
	36590	Union Hill (Cleburne County)	36273	Walnut Grove	35990
For specific Theodore Zip Codes		Union Hill (Limestone		Walnut Hill	36853
call (205) 653-8957		County)	35610	Walnut Park (Part of	
The Ridge	36460	Union Hill (Morgan County)	35622	Gadsden)	35904
Thomas (Autauga County)	36067	Union Springs	36089	Walter	35077
Thomas (Jefferson County)	35214	Uniontown	36786	Wannville	35752
Thomas Acres (Part of		Unity (Autauga County)	36006	Ward	36922
Bessemer)	35020	Unity (Coosa County)	35183	Ware	36078
Thomas F. Station		Unity (Tuscaloosa County)	35401	Warrenton	35976
Correctional Center	36025	Universal Heights	35404	Warrior	35180
Thomas Hill (Part of		University (Part of		Warriorstand	36089
Sylacauga)	35150	Tuscaloosa)	35486	Warsaw	35477
Thomaston	36783	University Mall (Part of		Waterford (Part of Newton)	36352
Thomasville	36784	Tuscaloosa)	35401	Waterloo	35677
Thompson	36089	University of Montevallo		Water Valley	36908
Thorn Hill	35565	(Part of Montevallo)	35115	Watson (Cherokee County)	35973
Thornton	36853	University of South Alabama		Watson (Jefferson County)	35181
Thorntontown	35652	(Part of Mobile)	36608	Watsonville	36753
Thorsby	35171	Upper Coalburg	35068	Watts Mill	36266
Three Notch	36053	Upper Green Hill	35630	Wattsville	35182
Threet	35617	Upshaw	35540	Waugh	36109
Thurston	36340	Uriah	36480	Waverly	36879
Tibbie	36583	Valdosta (Part of		Wawbeek	36502
Tilden	36761	Tuscumbia)	35674	Wayne	36782
Till	36033	Valhermoso Springs	35775	Wayside	35594
Tiller Crossroads	36850	Vallegrande	36703	Weatherly Heights (Part of	
Tillery Crossroads	36854	Valley	36854	Huntsville)	35802
Tillmans Corner	36619		36872	Weaver	36277
Tinela	36481	For specific Valley Zip Codes call		Webb	36376
Titus	36080	(205) 756-3268		Webb Addition (Part of	
Toadvine	35020	Valley Creek	35020	Scottsboro)	35768
Toddtown	36451	Valley Creek Junction	36758	Webster Chapel	35903
Tompkinsville	36916	Valley Head	35989	Wedgewood	36108
Toney	35773	Valley View	35640	Wedgworth	36776
Toonersville	35652	Vance	35490	Wedowee	36278
Toulminville (Part of Mobile)	36610	Vanderbilt (Part of		Weed Crossroad	36009
Town Creek	35672	Birmingham)	35204	Weeden Heights (Part of	
Townley	35587	Vandiver	35176	Florence)	35630
Toxey	36921	Vangale	36782	Weeks	36453
Trade	35053	Vaughn	36579	Wegra	35130
Trafford	35172	Vaughn Corners	35758	Wehadkee	36274
Travis Bridge	36401	Verbena	36091	Wellington	36279
Tredegar	36265	Verlie (Part of Alabaster)	35007	Welti	35055
Trenton	35774	Vernledge	36049	Wende	36860
Triana	35758	Vernon	35592	Wenonah (Part of	
Trickem	36785	Vernontown	35184	Birmingham)	35211
Trimble	35055	Vestavia Hills	35216	Weogufka	35183
Trinity	35673	Vestavia Hills Centre (Part		Weoka	36092
Trotwood Park (Part of		of Vestavia Hills)	35216	Wessington	35040
Birmingham)	35206	Vesthaven (Part of Vestavia		West (Part of Huntsville)	35805
Troy	36081	Hills)	35216	West Alexandria	36250
Trussville	35173	Veterans Hospital (Part of		West Bend	36524
Tuckabatchie	36078	Tuscaloosa)	35401	West Blocton	35184
Tuckahoe Heights (Part of		Veto	35620	West End (Calhoun County)	36201
Gadsden)	35901	Vick (Part of Centreville)	35042	West End (Jefferson	
Tucker Crossroads	35959	Victoria	36323	County)	35211
Tumbleton	36345	Vida	36067	West End (Montgomery	
Tunnel Springs	36471	Vidette	36049	County)	36104
Tupelo	35768	Vienna	35442	West End-Cobbtown	36201
Turkestan	36753	Viewpoint	35963	West Ensley	35224
Turkey Branch	36555	Vigo	36272	Western Hills (Part of	
Turkeytown	35901	Village Creek (Part of		Mobile)	36618
Turner Crossroads	36351	Birmingham)	35207	Western Hills Estates	35749
Tuscaloosa	35401-06	Village Springs	35126	Western Hills Mall (Part of	
	35486-87	Villula	36871	Fairfield)	35064
For specific Tuscaloosa Zip Codes		Vina	35593	West Greene (Greene	
call (205) 553-6415		Vincent	35178	County)	35491
Tuscumbia	35674	Vinegar Bend	36584	West Highlands (Part of	
Tuskegee	36083	Vine Hill	36758	Hueytown)	35023
Tuskegee Institute	36087-88	Vineland	36784	West Huntsville (Part of	
For specific Tuskegee Institute Zip		Vineland Park (Part of		Huntsville)	35807
Codes call (205) 727-2880		Hueytown)	35020	West Jefferson	35130
Twilley Town	35130	Vinemont	35179	West Lake Highlands (Part	
Twin	35563	Vinesville (Part of		of Bessemer)	35020
Twin Oaks (Part of		Birmingham)	35208	Westlake Mall (Part of	
Montgomery)	36123	Virginia	35020	Bessemer)	35020
Twinsprings	36027	Virginia Shores	35660	Westlawn (Part of	
Tyler	36785	Vocation	36480	Huntsville)	35807
Tyler Crossroads	36048	Volanta (Part of Fairhope)	36532	West Monroeville (Part of	
Tyson	36043	Vredenburgh	36481	Monroeville)	36460
Tysonville	36075	Vulcan City (Part of		Weston	35570
Uchee	36858	Birmingham)	35207	Westover	35185
Underwood (Lauderdale		Waco	35653	West Point	35055
County)	35630	Wacoochee Valley	36874	West Pratt (Part of Dora)	35062

	ZIP		ZIP		ZIP
West Sayre	35062	Wiley (Montgomery County)	36105	Woodlawn Heights	
West Selmont	36703	Wiley (Tuscaloosa County)	35501	(Jefferson County)	35212
West Side (Jefferson		Wilkes (Part of Midfield)	35064	Woodley Park (Part of	
County)	35020	Wilkinstown	36081	Montgomery)	36116
West Side (Montgomery		Williamstown	35580	Woodmeadow (Part of	
County)	36108	Willowbrook (Part of		Hoover)	35226
West Wellington	36279	Huntsville)	35802	Woodmont (Part of	
Westwood	35005	Willow Springs	36092	Hueytown)	35020
Wetumpka	36092	Wills Crossroads	36310	Woodstock	35188
Whatley	36482	Wills Valley	35967	Woodstock Junction	35188
Wheat	35053	Wilmer	36587	Woodville	35776
Wheeler	35618	Wilson Lake Shores	35660	Woodward	35020
Wheelerville (Part of Mobile)	36608	Wilson Quarters	36303	Woolfolk	36268
Whistler (Part of Mobile)	36612	Wilsonville	35186	Wren	35650
White City (Autauga		Wilton	35187	Wright	35677
County)	36051	Wimberly	36921	Wright Crossroads (Lee	
White City (Cullman County)	35077	Winburn	35094	County)	36830
White Hall	36040	Windham Springs	35546	Wyatt	35130
Whitehead	35652	Windsor Highlands (Part of		Wylam (Part of Birmingham)	35224
Whitehouse	35565	Homewood)	35209	Wynnville	35952
Whitehouse Forks	36507	Winfield	35594	Yantley	36912
Whiteoak (Colbert County)	35646	Wing	36483	Yarbo	36558
White Oak (Henry County)	36310	Wingard	36035	Yelling Settlement	36526
Whiteoak (Marshall County)	35950	Winn	36545	Yellow Bluff	36769
White Plains (Calhoun		Winninger	35776	Yellow Creek Falls	35959
County)	36201	Winslow	36003	Yellowleaf	35186
White Plains (Chambers		Winterboro	35014	Yellow Pine	36539
County)	36862	Winton	35670	Yerkwood	35062
Whites Bluff	36767	Wolf Creek	35125	York	36925
Whitesboro	35957	Wolf Springs	35672	Youngblood	36081
Whitesburg Estates (Part of		Womack Hill	36908	Youngs Chapel	35903
Huntsville)	35802	Woodaire Estates	35215	Yucca	35966
Whites Chapel (Part of		Woodbluff	36727	Yupon	35555
Moody)	35173	Wooddale	35244	Zimco	36451
Whites Gap	36265	Woodford	35470	Zion (Montgomery County)	36047
Whitesville	35957	Woodland (Macon County)	36866	Zion (Pickens County)	35466
Whitfield	36925	Woodland (Randolph		Zion City (Part of	
Whitney (Part of Ashville)	35953	County)	36280	Birmingham)	35207
Whiton	35962	Woodland Forest	35405	Zion Heights (Part of	
Whorton	35960	Woodland Lake	35111	Birmingham)	35207
Wicksburg	36352	Woodlawn (Part of		Zip City	35630
Wiggins (Part of Babbie)	36420	Birmingham)	35212	Zoar	36323
Wigginsville	35611	Woodlawn Heights (Franklin			
Wiginton	35564	County)	35653		
Wilburn	35033				

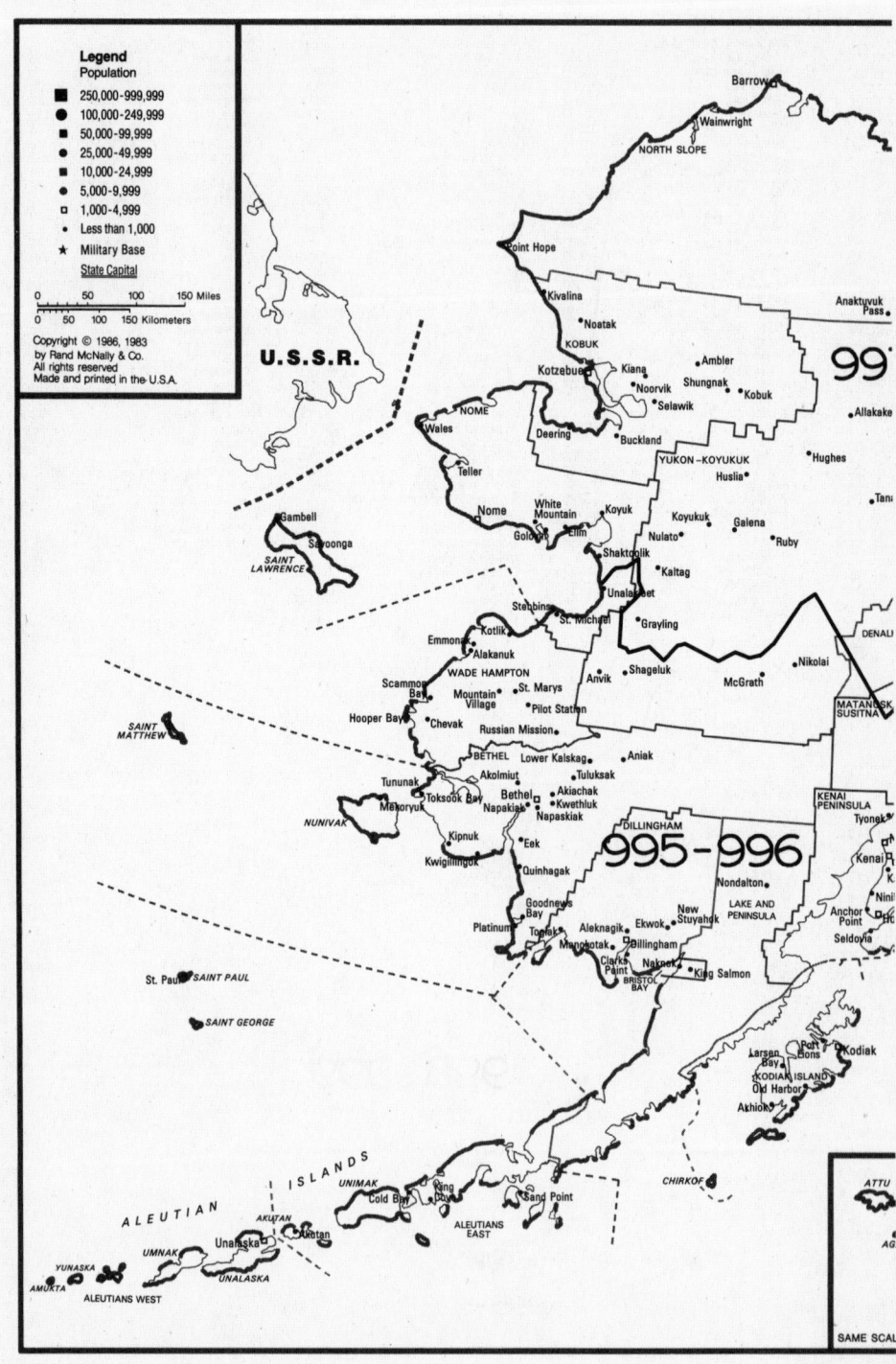

Legend
Population

- ■ 250,000-999,999
- ● 100,000-249,999
- ▪ 50,000-99,999
- • 25,000-49,999
- ▫ 10,000-24,999
- • 5,000-9,999
- ▫ 1,000-4,999
- • Less than 1,000
- ★ Military Base
- State Capital

0   50   100   150 Miles
0 50 100 150 Kilometers

U.S.S.R.

Barrow
Wainwright
NORTH SLOPE
Point Hope
Anaktuvuk Pass
Kivalina
Noatak
KOBUK
Kotzebue
Kiana
Ambler
Noorvik
Shungnak
Kobuk
Allakaket
Selawik
Hughes
NOME
Deering
Buckland
YUKON–KOYUKUK
Huslia
Tana
Wales
Teller
Nome
White Mountain
Koyuk
Koyukuk
Galena
Ruby
Golovin
Elim
Nulato
Gambell
Savoonga
SAINT LAWRENCE
Shaktoolik
Kaltag
Unalakleet
Stebbins
St. Michael
Grayling
DENALI
Kotlik
Emmonak
Alakanuk
WADE HAMPTON
Anvik
Shageluk
Nikolai
Scammon Bay
Mountain Village
St. Marys
Pilot Station
McGrath
MATANUSKA SUSITNA
SAINT MATTHEW
Hooper Bay
Chevak
Russian Mission
BETHEL
Lower Kalskag
Aniak
KENAI PENINSULA
Tununak
Akolmiut
Tuluksak
Akiachak
Tyonek
NUNIVAK
Mekoryuk
Toksook Bay
Bethel
Kwethluk
Napakiak
Napaskiak
DILLINGHAM
Kenai
Kipnuk
Eek
Nondalton
LAKE AND PENINSULA
Anchor Point
Ninil
Kwigillingok
Quinhagak
New Stuyahok
Seldovia
Goodnews Bay
Aleknagik
Ekwok
Platinum
Togiak
Manokotak
Dillingham
Clarks Point
Naknek
King Salmon
St. Paul
SAINT PAUL
BRISTOL BAY
SAINT GEORGE
Larsen Bay
Port Lions
Kodiak
KODIAK ISLAND
Old Harbor
Akhiok
ISLANDS
CHIRKOF
ATTU
ALEUTIAN
UNIMAK
Cold Bay
King Cove
Sand Point
AG
AKUTAN
Unalaska
Akutan
ALEUTIANS EAST
YUNASKA
UMNAK
AMUKTA
UNALASKA
ALEUTIANS WEST
SAME SCAL

99
995-996

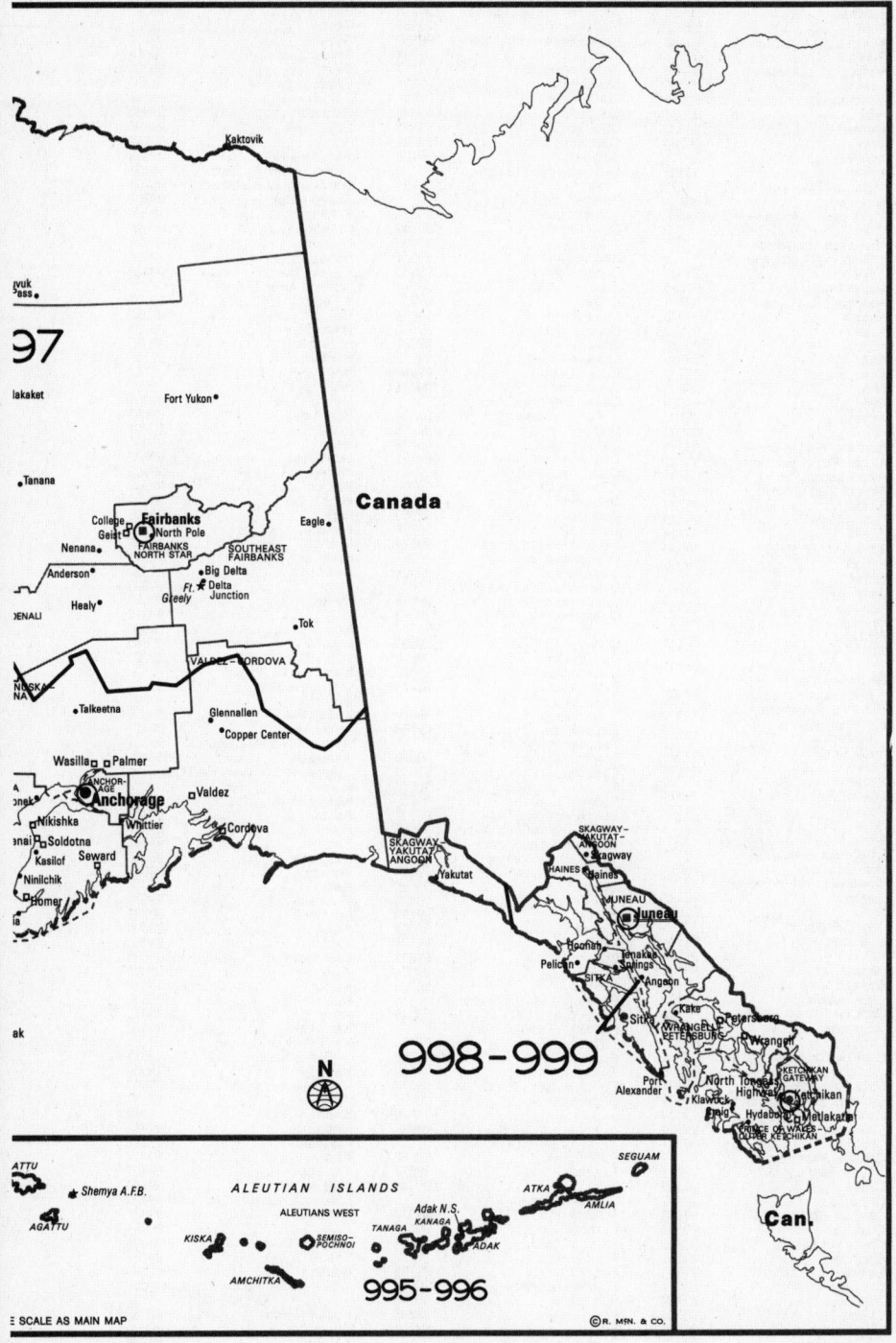

Kaktovik

vuk
ass

97

lakaket

Fort Yukon

Tanana

College
Geist
Nenana
Anderson

Fairbanks
North Pole
FAIRBANKS
NORTH STAR
SOUTHEAST
FAIRBANKS
Big Delta
Ft. Delta
Greely Junction

Eagle

Canada

DENALI
Healy

Tok

Talkeetna

VALDEZ—CORDOVA

NLSKA
NA

Glennallen
Copper Center

Wasilla Palmer
ANCHOR-
AGE
Anchorage
Whittier
Valdez

net
Nikishka
nai Soldotna
Kasilof
Ninilchik
Homer
ia

Seward
Cordova

SKAGWAY-
YAKUTAT/
ANGOON
Yakutat

SKAGWAY-
YAKUTAT-
ANGOON
Skagway
HAINES
Haines

JUNEAU
Juneau

Hoonah
Tenakee
Springs
Pelican
SITKA
Angoon

Kake
Sitka
WRANGELL-
PETERSBURG
Petersburg
Wrangell

998-999

ak

N

North Tongass
Port
Alexander
Highway
Klawock
raig
Hydaburg
PRINCE OF WALES-
OUTER KETCHIKAN

KETCHIKAN
GATEWAY
Ketchikan
Metlakatla

Can.

ATTU

AGATTU

Shemya A.F.B.

ALEUTIAN ISLANDS
ALEUTIANS WEST

KISKA

AMCHITKA

SEMISO-
POCHNOI

TANAGA
KANAGA
ADAK

Adak N.S.

ATKA
AMLIA

SEGUAM

995-996

SCALE AS MAIN MAP

©R. M9N. & CO.

	ZIP
Adak Naval Station	98791
Adak Station	98791
Akhiok	99615
Akiachak	99551
Akiak	99552
Akutan	99553
Alakanuk	99554
Alatna (Part of Allakaket)	99720
Aleknagik	99555
Alexander	99695
Alitak	99697
Allakaket	99720
Ambler	99786
Amchitka	99501
Amook	99697
Anaktuvuk Pass	99721
Anchorage	99501-24
For specific Anchorage Zip Codes call (907) 564-2842	
Anchorage 5th Avenue Shopping Center (Part of Anchorage)	99501
Anchor Point	99556
Anderson	99744
Angoon	99820
Aniak	99557
Annette	99926
Anvik	99558
Arctic Village	99722
Atka	99502
Atmautluak	99559
Atqasuk	99791
Attu	99502
Auke Bay (Part of Juneau)	99821
Aurora (Part of Fairbanks)	99701
Aurora Lodge	99701
Baranof (Part of Sitka)	99835
Barrow	99723
Bartlett Cove	99826
Beaver	99724
Bell Island Hot Springs	99950
Beluga	99695
Bethel	99559
Bettles Field	99726
Big Delta	99737
Big Horn	99701
Big Lake	99652
Birch Creek	99740
Birch Estates	99701
Birchwood (Part of Anchorage)	99567
Bird (Part of Anchorage)	99540
Bjerremark (Part of Fairbanks)	99701
Black Sand	99689
Bluff	99762
Border	99780
Boswell Bay	99574
Boundary	99780
Boyd	99701
Brevig Mission	99785
Broadmoor Acres	99701
Brooks Lodge	99613
Browerville (Part of Barrow)	99723
Buckland	99727
Butte	99645
Campbell (Part of Anchorage)	99517
Candle	99752
Cantwell	99729
Cape Lisburne	99766
Cape Newenham	99576
Cape Newenham Air Force Station	99576
Cape Pole	99950
Cape Romanzof Air Force Station	99559
Cape Yakataga	99695
Carlanna (Part of Ketchikan)	99901
Central	99730
Chalkyitsik	99788
Chandalar	99701
Charcoal Point (Part of Ketchikan)	99901
Chase	99676
Chatanika	99712
Chatham (Part of Sitka)	99803
Chefornak	99561
Chena Hot Springs	99701
Chernofski	99685
Chevak	99563
Chickaloon	99674
Chicken	99732
Chignik	99564
Chignik Lagoon	99565
Chignik Lake	99548
Chisana	99780
Chistochina	99586
Chitina	99566
Chuathbaluk	99557

	ZIP
Chugiak (Part of Anchorage)	99567
Circle	99733
Circle Hot Springs Station	99730
Clam Gulch	99568
Clark's Point	99569
Clear	99704
Clearwater Ranch	99737
Clover Pass	99901
Coffman Cove	99918
Cohoe	99610
Cold Bay	99571
Coldfoot	99701
College	99708
College (census designated place)	99701
College Village (Part of Anchorage)	99504
Collegiate Park	99701
Colorado	99695
Cooper Landing	99572
Copper Center	99573
Cordova	99574
Cosna	99756
Cottonwood	99654
Council	99762
Craig	99921
Crooked Creek	99575
Cube Cove	99850
Deadhorse	99734
Debarr Shopping Center (Part of Anchorage)	99504
Deering	99736
Delta Junction	99737
Denali National Park	99755
Derby Tract (Part of Fairbanks)	99701
Dillingham	99576
Dora Bay	99950
Dot Lake	99737
Douglas (Part of Juneau)	99824
Downtown (Part of Anchorage)	99501
Downtown (P.O. Sta.) (Part of Anchorage)	99510
Downtown (Part of Fairbanks)	99707
Driftwood Bay	99695
Duncan Canal	99833
Dutch Harbor	99692
Eagle	99738
Eagle River (Part of Anchorage)	99577
Eagle Village	99738
Eastchester (Part of Anchorage)	99520
Edna Bay	99950
Eek	99578
Egegik	99579
Eielson Air Force Base	99702
Eklutna (Part of Anchorage)	99567
Eklutna Housing Project (Part of Anchorage)	99645
Ekuk	99695
Ekwok	99580
Elfin Cove	99825
Elim	99739
Ellamar	99695
Emmonak	99581
English Bay	99603
Eska	99674
Ester	99725
Eureka (Matanuska-Susitna Borough)	99645
Eureka (Yukon-Koyukuk Census Division)	99756
Evansville	99726
Excursion Inlet	99850
Eyak	99574
Fairbanks	99701
	99706-12
For specific Fairbanks Zip Codes call (907) 474-0722	
False Pass	99583
Farewell	99627
Ferry	99743
Fire Lake (Part of Anchorage)	99577
Fishhook Junction	99645
Flat	99584
Fort Greely	99733
Fort Wainwright	99703
Fortymile Roadhouse	99737
Fort Yukon	99740
Four Corners	99645
Fox	99701
Freshwater Bay (Sitka Borough)	99803
Freshwater Bay (Skagway-Yakutat-Angoon Census Division)	99829

	ZIP
Fritz Cove (Part of Juneau)	99801
Fritz Creek	99603
Funter Bay	99850
Gakona	99586
Galena	99741
Gambell	99742
Ganes Creek	99675
Geist	99701
Girdwood (Part of Anchorage)	99587
Glennallen	99588
Gold Creek	99695
Golovin	99762
Goodnews Bay	99589
Goodnews Mining Camp	99651
Graehl (Part of Fairbanks)	99701
Granite Mountain	99762
Grayling	99590
Gulkana	99695
Gustavus	99826
Haines	99827
Halibut Cove	99603
Hamilton Acres (Part of Fairbanks)	99701
Happy Valley	99556
Harding Lake	99701
Hawk Inlet	99850
Haycock	99753
Healy	99743
Healy Lake	99737
Herring Cove	99901
Hobart Bay	99850
Hogatza	99701
Hollis	99950
Holy Cross	99602
Homer	99603
Hoonah	99829
Hooper Bay	99604
Hope	99605
Houston	99694
Hughes	99745
Huslia	99746
Hydaburg	99922
Hyder	99923
Icy Bay	99695
Igiugig	99613
Iliamna	99606
Indian (Part of Anchorage)	99540
Indian River	99720
Island Homes (Part of Fairbanks)	99701
Ivanof Bay	99695
Jakolof Bay	99695
Jennie M.	99701
Johnston (Part of Fairbanks)	99701
Juneau	99801-11
For specific Juneau Zip Codes call (907) 586-7138	
Kachemak	99603
Kake	99830
Kako	99657
Kaktovik	99747
Kalifonsky	99610
Kalskag	99607
Kaltag	99748
Kanakanak	99576
Kantishna	99755
Karluk	99608
Kasaan	99950
Kashegelok	99668
Kasigluk	99609
Kasilof	99610
Kasitsna Bay	99695
Kenai	99611
Kenai Lake	99572
Kenai Packers Cannery (Part of Kenai)	99611
Kennicott	99588
Kenny Cove	99695
Ketchikan	99901
Kiana	99749
King Cove	99612
King Salmon	99613
Kipnuk	99614
Kitoi Bay	99697
Kivalina	99750
Klawock	99925
Klukwan	99827
Knik	99654
Knudson Cove	99901
Kobuk	99751
Kodiak	99615-19
For specific Kodiak Zip Codes call (907) 486-4721	
Kodiak Station	99615
Kokhanok	99606
Kokrines	99768
Koliganek	99576
Kongiganak	99559
Kotlik	99620
Kotzebue	99752

	ZIP		ZIP		ZIP
Koyuk	99753	Nuiqsut	99789	Shemya Air Force Base	99501
Koyukuk	99754	Nulato	99765	Shemya Station	99501
Kupreanof	99833	Nunaka Valley (Part of		Shishmaref	99772
Kustatan	99682	Anchorage)	99504	Shungnak	99773
Kwethluk	99621	Nunapitchuk	99641	Sitka	99835
Kwigillingok	99622	Nyac	99557	Situk	99689
Labouchere Bay	99927	Okagamute	99607	Skagway	99840
Lake Minchumina	99757	Old Andreafski	99658	Skwentna	99667
Lake Nancy	99688	Old Harbor	99643	Slana	99586
Lakloey Hill	99701	Olnes	99701	Slaterville (Part of Fairbanks)	99701
Larsen Bay	99624	Olsonville	99576	Sleetmute	99668
Lawing	99664	Oscarville	99559	Snowball	99701
Lemeta (Part of Fairbanks)	99701	Ouzinkie	99644	Snug Harbor	99572
Lemon Creek (Part of		Palmer	99645	Soldotna	99669
Juneau)	99801	Paradise Hill	99602	Solomon	99790
Lena Cove (Part of Juneau)	99801	Parks	99697	Sourdough	99586
Levelock	99625	Paxson	99737	South (Part of Anchorage)	99511
Liberty	99738	Pederson Point	99633	South Bjerremark	99701
Lime Village	99627	Pedro Bay	99647	South Naknek	99670
Little Diomede	99762	Pelican	99832	Spenard (Part of	
Little Port Walter	99835	Peninsula Point	99901	Anchorage)	99509
Livengood	99701	Pennock Island	99901	Sprucewood	99701
Long	99768	Perryville	99648	Squaw Harbor	99661
Long Island	99654	Petersburg	99833	Stebbins	99671
Lost River (Nome Census		Peters Creek (Part of		Steele Creek	99738
Division)	99762	Anchorage)	99567	Steese	99710
Lost River (Skagway-		Pilot Point	99649	Sterling	99672
Yakutat-Angoon Census		Pilot Station	99650	Stevens Village	99774
Division)	99689	Pitkas Point	99658	Stony River	99557
Lower Kalskag	99626	Pittman	99654	Strelna	99566
Lower Mendenhall Valley		Platinum	99651	Summit	99729
(Part of Juneau)	99801	Point Baker	99927	Summit Lodge	99586
McCarthy	99695	Point Barrow DEW Station	99723	Sunnyside	99832
McGrath	99627	Point Higgins	99901	Sunshine	99695
Mack	99701	Point Hope	99766	Suntrana	99743
McKinley Acres	99701	Point Lay	99759	Sutton	99674
Main Office (Part of		Point Whiteshed	99574	Takotna	99675
Anchorage)	99502	Polk Inlet	99922	Talkeetna	99676
Manley Hot Springs	99756	Portage (Part of Anchorage)	99587	Tanacross	99776
Manokotak	99628	Portage Creek	99695	Tanana	99777
Mansfield Village	99760	Port Alexander	99836	Tatalina	99627
Marshall	99585	Port Alice	99950	Tatitlek	99677
Marvel Creek	99557	Port Alsworth	99653	Tee Harbor (Part of Juneau)	99801
Mary's Igloo	99778	Port Armstrong	99836	Telida	99695
Matanuska	99645	Port Ashton	99695	Teller	99778
May Creek	99695	Port Bailey	99697	Tenakee Springs	99841
Meade River	99791	Port Clarence	99790	Terror Bay	99697
Medfra	99627	Port Graham	99603	Tetlin	99779
Meekins Roadhouse	99645	Port Heiden	99549	Thane (Part of Juneau)	99801
Meier	99737	Port Lions	99550	Thorne Bay	99919
Mekoryuk	99630	Portlock	99663	Tiekel	99686
Mendeltna	99588	Port Moller	99571	Tin City	99783
Mendeltna Lodge	99645	Port Protection	99950	Togiak	99678
Mendenhall (Part of Juneau)	99803	Port Walter	99835	Tok	99780
Mendenhall Flats (Part of		Port Williams	99697	Tokeen	99950
Juneau)	99801	Potter (Part of Anchorage)	99501	Toksook Bay	99637
Mentasta Lake	99780	Prudhoe Bay	99734	Tonsina	99573
Metlakatla	99926	Quartz Creek	99572	Totem Bight	99901
Meyers Chuck	99903	Queen	99576	Totem Park	99701
Midtown (Part of		Quinhagak	99655	Trapper Creek	99683
Anchorage)	99503	Rainbow (Part of		Tuluksak	99679
Minto	99758	Anchorage)	99501	Tuntutuliak	99680
Montana	99688	Rampart	99767	Tununak	99681
Moose Creek	99701	Red Devil	99656	Turnagain (Part of	
Moose Pass	99631	Red Salmon	99633	Anchorage)	99517
Moser Bay	99697	Rego	99701	Turnagain by-the-Sea (Part	
Mountain Point	99901	Rodman (Part of Sitka)	99835	of Anchorage)	99517
Mountain View (Part of		Rogers Park (Part of		Turnagain Heights (Part of	
Anchorage)	99508	Anchorage)	99508	Anchorage)	99517
Mountain Village	99632	Rowan Bay	99835	Twin Hills	99576
Mount Edgecumbe (Part of		Ruby	99768	Two Rivers	99716
Sitka)	99835	Russian Jack (Part of		Tyonek	99682
Mud Bay	99901	Anchorage)	99508	Uganik	99697
Muldoon (Part of		Russian Mission	99657	Ugashik	99613
Anchorage)	99504	St. George Island	99591	Umiat	99701
Nabesna	99586	St. Marys	99658	Unalakleet	99684
Naknek	99633	St. Marys Mission (Part of		Unalaska	99685
Napakiak	99634	St. Marys)	99658	Ungalik	99684
Napaskiak	99559	St. Michael	99659	University Center (Part of	
Nelson Lagoon	99571	St. Paul Island	99660	Anchorage)	99503
Nenana	99760	Salamatof	99611	University Park	99701
Nenana Native Village (Part		Salcha	99714	Upper Mendenhall Valley	
of Nenana)	99760	Salmon Creek (Part of		(Part of Juneau)	99801
Newhalen	99606	Juneau)	99801	Upper Nickeyville (Part of	
New Stuyahok	99636	Sand Lake (Part of		Ketchikan)	99901
Newtok	99559	Anchorage)	99522	U.S. Coast Guard Station	99619
Nightmute	99690	Sand Point	99661	Usibelli	99743
Nikiski	99635	Savoonga	99769	Valdez	99686
Nikolai	99691	Saxman	99901	Vank Island	99929
Nikolski	99638	Saxman East (Part of		Venetie	99781
Ninilchik	99639	Saxman)	99901	View Cove	99950
Noatak	99761	Scammon Bay	99662	Wainwright	99782
Nome	99762	Scow Bay	99833	Wales	99783
Nondalton	99640	Seal Bay	99697	Ward Cove	99928
Noorvik	99763	Selawik	99770	Wasilla	99687
North Douglas (Part of		Seldovia	99663		99654
Juneau)	99801	Seward	99664	For specific Wasilla Zip Codes call	
North Pole	99705	Shageluk	99665	(907) 376-5327	
Northway	99764	Shaktoolik	99771		
Northway Junction	99764	Shanley (Part of Fairbanks)	99701	Waterfall	99950
Northway Village	99764	Sheldon Point	99666	West Fairwest	99701

	ZIP		ZIP		ZIP
Westgate (Part of Fairbanks)	99701	Whites Crossing	99688	Woodland Park (Part of Anchorage)	99517
West Juneau (Part of Juneau)	99801	Whitney (Part of Anchorage)	99506	Wood River	99576
West Point	99697	Whittier	99693	Wrangell	99929
Westwood	99701	Wilcox	99701	Yakutat	99689
Whale Pass	99950	Wilcox Estates	99701	Yankee Creek	99675
White Mountain	99784	Wild Lake	99726	Zachar Bay	99697
		Willow	99688		
		Wiseman	99790		

	ZIP		ZIP		ZIP
Adamana	86025	Bushman Acres	86047	Cortaro	85652
Adamsville	85232	Bylas	85530	Cottonwood	86326
Agua Caliente	85333	Cactus (Part of Phoenix)	85032	Cottonwood Station	86503
Agua Linda	85640	Cactus Flat	85546	Country Life	85201
Aguila	85320	Cactus Forest	85232	Cove	87420
Ahwatukee (Part of		Calva	85530	Covered Wells	85634
Phoenix)	85044	Camelview Plaza (Part of		Cowlic	85634
Ajo	85321	Scottsdale)	85251	Cow Springs	86044
Akchin (Pima County)	85634	Cameron	86020	Crane	85365
Ak Chin (Pinal County)	85239	Camp Creek	85331	Crestview (Part of Bisbee)	85603
Alamo Crossing	85357	Camp Verde	86322	Cross Canyon	86511
Alchesay Flat	85941	Camp Verde Indian		Crown King	86343
Ali Chuk	85634	Reservation	86322	Cuckelbur	85222
Ali Molina	85634	Cane Beds	86022	Cutter	85501
Allentown	86506	Canelo	85611	Dam View	85344
Alpine	85920	Canyon Day	85941	Date	85332
Amado	85645	Capitol (Part of Phoenix)	85009	Dateland	85333
Anegam	85634	Carefree	85377	Davis Dam	86430
Apache	88056	Carmen	85640	Davis-Monthan Air Force	
Apache Flats	85613	Carrizo	85901	Base	85707
Apache Grove	85534	Casa Blanca	85221	Deer Valley (Part of	
Apache Ho (Part of Apache		Casa Grande	85222	Phoenix)	85023
Junction)	85220		85230	Del Rio	86323
Apache Junction	85217-20	For specific Casa Grande Zip		Dennehotso	86535
	85278	Codes call (602) 836-7221		Desert (Part of Mesa)	85206
For specific Apache Junction Zip		Casas Adobes	85704	Desert Carmel	85222
Codes call (602) 982-2121		Cascabel	85602	Desert Harbor (Part of	
Apache Wells	85205	Cashion	85329	Peoria)	85381
Arcadia (Part of Phoenix)	85018	Castle Hot Springs	85342	Desert Hills (Mohave	
Arcosanti	86333	Castle Rock Shores	85344	County)	86403
Arivaca	85601	Catalina	85738	Desert Hills (Pima County)	85718
Arizola	85222	Catalina Foothills	85718	Desert Sands	85208
Arizona City	85223	Cave Creek	85331	Desert View	86023
Arizona Shores	85344	Cedar Creek	85941	Dewey	86327
Arizona State Prison		Cedar Ridge	86020	Diamond Valley	86301
Complex-Douglas	85607	Centerville (Part of		Dilkon	86047
Arizona State Prison		Clarkdale)	86324	Discovery at the Orchard	
Complex-Perryville	85338	Central	85531	(Part of Peoria)	85381
Arizona State Prison		Central Heights	85501	Dolan Springs	86441
Complex-Tucson	85706	Central Heights-Midland City	85532	Dome	85365
Arizona State Prison		Chambers	86502	Don Luis (Part of Bisbee)	85603
Complex-Florence	85232	Chandler	85224-27	Dos Cabezas	85643
Arizona State Prison-Safford	85546		85248-49	Double Adobe	85617
Arizona Sunsites	85625	For specific Chandler Zip Codes		Douglas	85607-08
Arlington	85322	call (602) 963-6643			85655
Artesa	85634	Chandler Heights	85227	For specific Douglas Zip Codes	
Artesia	85546	Cherry	86327	call (602) 364-3631	
Ash Fork	86320	Chevelon	86001	Downtown (Part of	
Avondale	85323	Chiawuli Tak	85634	Flagstaff)	86001
Avondale-Goodyear (Part of		Chilchinbito	86033	Downtown (Part of Tempe)	85281
Avondale)	85323	Childs	85321	Downtown (Part of Phoenix)	85003
	85338	Chinle	86503	Downtown (Part of	
For specific Avondale-Goodyear		Chino Valley	86323	Kingman)	86402
Zip Codes call (602) 932-2670		Chloride	86431	Downtown (Part of Tucson)	85701
Aztec	85333	Choulic	85634	Dragoon	85609
Baby Rock	86033	Christmas	85292	Drake	86334
Bacobi	86030	Chris-Town Center (Part of		Dreamland-Velda Rose	85205
Bagdad	86321	Phoenix)	85015	Dreamland Villa	85205
Bakerville (Part of Bisbee)	85603	Chuichu	85222	Drexel Heights	85706
Bapchule	85221	Chuichu	85222	Dudleyville	85292
Bayless Shopping Center		Cibecue	85911	Duncan	85534
(Part of Apache Junction)	85220	Cibola	85334	Dysart	85345
Beardsley	85373	Cienega Springs	85344	Eagar	85925
Beautys Estates	85621	Circle City	85342	Eagle Creek	85533
Beaver Dam	86432	Citrus Gardens	85201	East Flagstaff (Part of	
Bella Vista Estates (Part of		Clarkdale	86324	Flagstaff)	86001
Sierra Vista)	85635	Claypool	85532	East Fork	85943
Bellemont	86015	Clay Springs	85923	East Plantsite (Part of	
Ben Franklin (Part of		Cleator	86333	Clifton)	85540
Phoenix)	85080	Clifton	85533	Eden	85535
Benson	85602	Coal Mine Mesa	86045	Ehrenberg	85334
Beyerleville	85621	Cobblestone Village (Part of		El Con Regional Shopping	
Biltmore Fashion Park (Part		Peoria)	85381	Center (Part of Tucson)	85716
of Phoenix)	85016	Cochise	85606	Eleven Mile Corner	85222
Bisbee	85603	Cocopah Indian Reservation	85350	Elfrida	85610
Bisbee Junction	85603	College (Part of Tucson)	85722	Elgin	85611
Bitahochee	86031	Colonnade, The (Part of		El Mirage	85335
Bitter Springs	86036	Phoenix)	85016	El Mirage (mobile home	
Black Canyon City	85324	Colorado City	86021	park)	85201
Black Hills (Part of		Colorado River Indian		Eloy	85231
Clarkdale)	86324	Reservation	85344	El Pueblecito (Part of Yuma)	85364
Blackwater	85228	Commerce (Part of		Emery Park (Part of	
Blue	85922	Phoenix)	85003	Tucson)	85706
Bonita	85643	Comobabi	85634	Empire Landing	85344
Bouse	85325	Concho	85924	Fairbank	85621
Bowie	85605	Congress	85332	Falcon Estates	85203
Boys Ranch	85225	Continental	85640	Falcon Field (Part of Mesa)	85277
Braemer (Part of Peoria)	85381	Coolidge	85228	Federal Correctional	
Branding Iron	85701	Coolidge Dam	85542	Institution (Maricopa	
Brenda	85348	Co-op Village	85339	County)	85027
Bridge Canyon Country		Copper Mine	86040	Federal Correctional	
Estates	86337	Copper Queen (Part of		Institution (Pima County)	85706
Bridgeport	86326	Bisbee)	85603	Federal Prison Camp	85546
Briggs Townsite (Part of		Cordes Lakes	86333	Fiesta Mall (Part of Mesa)	85202
Bisbee)	85603	Cork	85536	Fiesta Park	85201
Buckeye	85326	Cornfields	86505	Fishers Landing	85365
Buckhorn	85205	Cornville	86325	Flagstaff	86001-16
Buena Vista	85546	Coronada Foothills Estates	85718	For specific Flagstaff Zip Codes	
Bullhead City	86430	Corona de Tucson	85726	call (602) 527-2440	
Bumble Bee	86333	Coronado (Part of Tucson)	85711	Flecha Caida Estates	85718
Burnt Water	86512	Coronado Unit	86047	Florence	85232

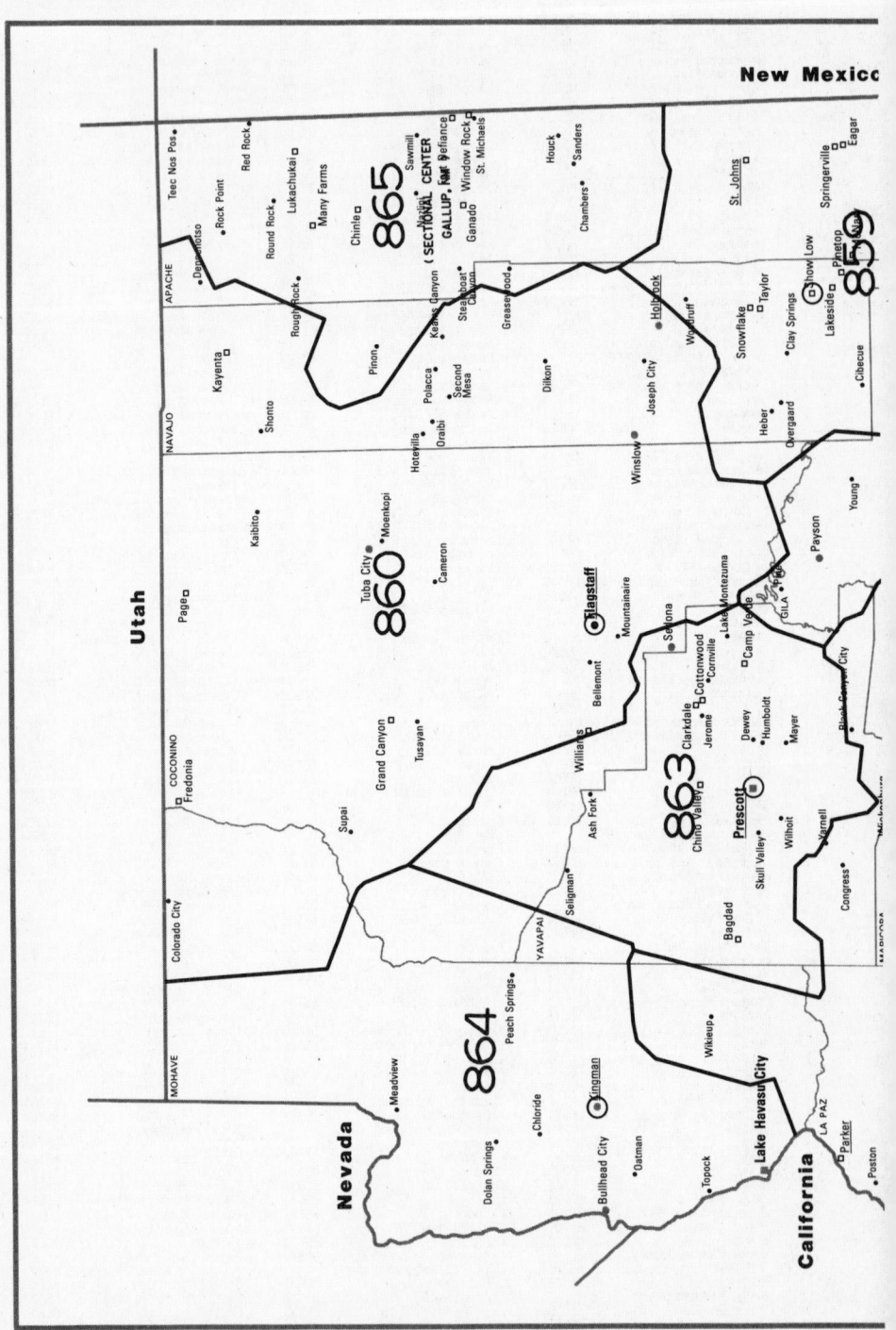

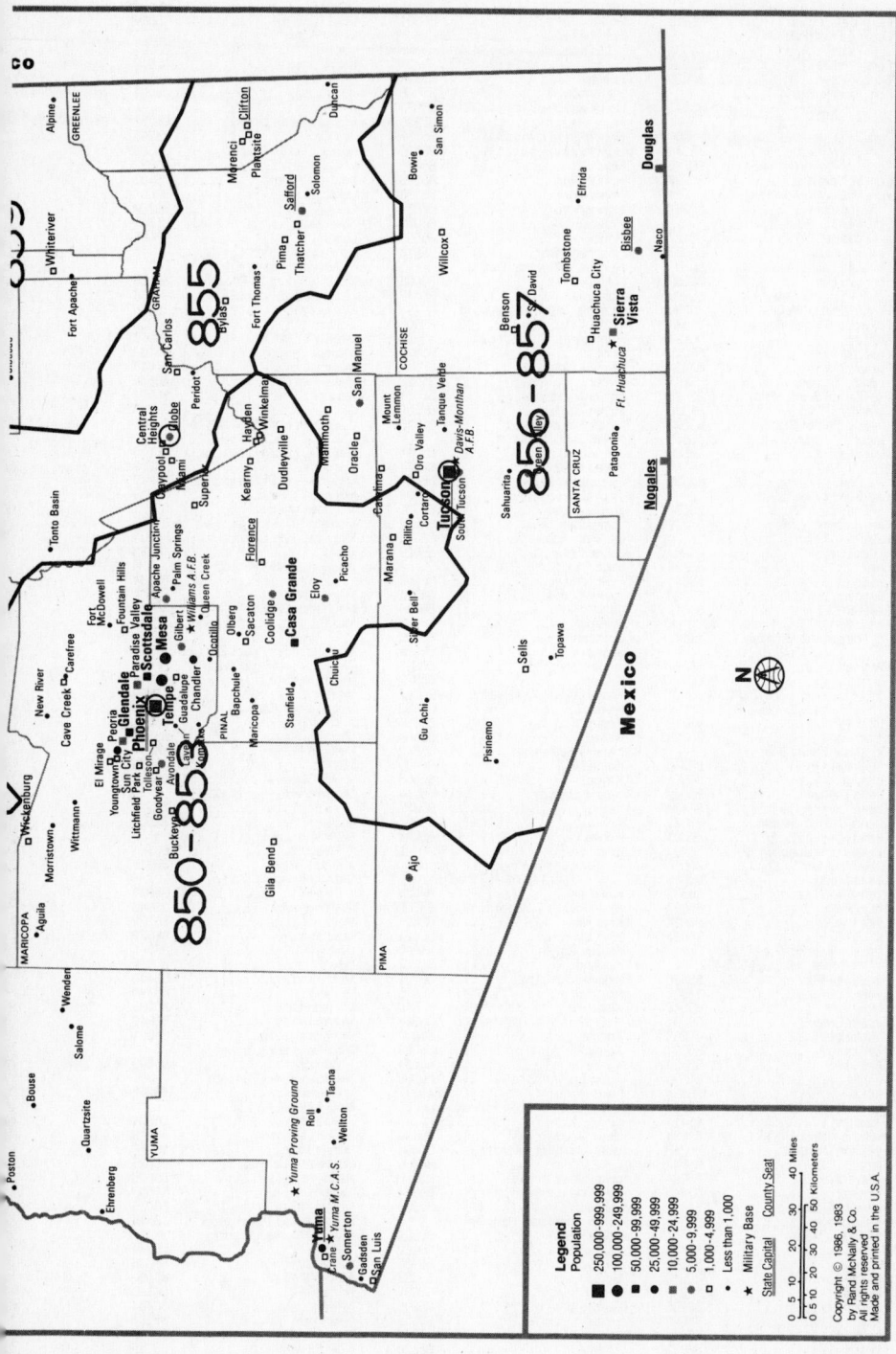

	ZIP		ZIP		ZIP
....	85279	Higley	85236	Litchfield Park	85340
For specific Florence Zip Codes call (602) 868-5651		Hillside	86301	Little Acres	85501
		Hilltop	85632	Littlefield	86432
Florence Junction	85219	Ho-Kay-Gan	86301	Little Tucson	85634
Forbing Park (Part of Prescott)	86301	Holbrook	86025-29	Lizard Acres	85373
		For specific Holbrook Zip Codes call (602) 524-3311		Lochiel	85624
Forest Lakes	85931			Loma Linda	85619
Fort Apache	85926	Holiday	85344	Lone Star	85546
Fort Apache Indian Reservation	85941	Hollywood	85546	Long Valley	86001
		Hon Dah	85935	Los Arcos Mall (Part of Scottsdale)...............	85257
Fort Apache Junction	85941	Hope	85348		
Fort Defiance..............	86504	Hopi (Part of Scottsdale)...	85258	Los Gatos	85255
Fort Grant.................	85643	Hopi Indian Reservation....	86039	Lowell (Part of Bisbee)....	85603
Fort Lowell (Part of Tucson)	85715	Horn	85333	Lower Miami	85539
Fort McDowell	85257	Horse Mesa	85290	Low Mountain	86503
Fort McDowell Indian Reservation	85264	Horse Thief	85333	Lukachukai	86507
		Hotason Vo	85634	Luke Air Force Base	85309
Fort Mohave (Part of Bullhead City)	86427	Hotevilla..................	86030	Lukeville	85341
		Houck	86506	Lupton	86508
Fort Thomas	85536	Huachuca City	85616	Lynx Estates (Part of Prescott Valley)	86301
Fountain East	85201	Huachuca Terrace (Part of Bisbee)	85603		
Fountain Hills	85269			McDowell (Part of Phoenix)	85008
Fountain of the Sun	85208	Hualapai	86412	McGees Settlement	85736
Foxfire (Part of Peoria)	85381	Hualapai Indian Reservation	86434	McGuireville	86335
Foxwood (Part of Peoria) ..	85381	Hubbell	86505	McNary	85930
Franklin	85534	Humboldt	86329	McNeal	85617
Fredonia	86022	Hunt	85924	Madera Canyon	85706
Fresnal Canyon	85634	Hunters Point..............	86511	Mammoth	85618
Friendly Corners	85231	Hyder	85333	Many Farms	86538
Fry (Part of Sierra Vista) ...	85635	Immanuel Mission	86514	Marana	85238
Gadsden	85336	Indian Gardens	86336		85653
Galena (Part of Bisbee)....	85603	Indian Ridge Estates	85715	For specific Marana Zip Codes call (602) 682-3561	
Ganado	86505	Indian School (Part of Phoenix)	85014		
Geronimo	85536			Marble Canyon	86036
Gibson	85321	Indian Wells	86031	Maricopa	85239
Gila Bend	85337	Inscription House	86044	Maricopa Indian Reservation	85247
Gila Bend Indian Reservation	85634	Inspiration	85532	Maricopa Village	85339
		Iron Springs	86330	Mariposa Manor	85621
Gila Crossing.............	85339	Jackrabbit.................	85222	Martinez Lake	85365
Gila River Indian Reservation	85247	Jackson Acres	86301	Maryvale (Part of Phoenix)	85031
		Jacob Lake	86022	Mayer	86333
Gilbert	85234	Jade Park North (Part of Phoenix)	85308	Meadow Brook (Part of Yuma)	85364
Gisela....................	85541				
Gladden	85320	Jakes Corner	85541	Meadview	86444
Gleeson...................	85610	Jeddito	86034	Mennonite Mission	86505
Glendale	85301-12	Jerome	86331	Mesa	85201-16
For specific Glendale Zip Codes call (602) 842-0099		Johnson	85609		85274-77
		Joseph City	86032	For specific Mesa Zip Codes call (602) 969-9171	
Glen Ilah	85362	Juniper Heights	86301		
Globe	85501-02	Kaibab	86022	Mesa Del Oro	85219
For specific Globe Zip Codes call (602) 425-2381		Kaibab Indian Reservation .	86022	Mescal	85602
		Kaibito	86053	Metrocenter (Part of Phoenix)	85021
Goldfield	85219	Kaihon Kug	85634		
Goodyear	85338	Kaka	85634	Mexican Town	85321
Goodyear Farms (Part of Litchfield Park)	86340	Kansas Settlement	85643	Mexican Water	86514
		Katherine	86430	Miami	85539
Graham	85552	Kayenta	86033	Miami Gardens	85539
Grand Canyon	86023	Kearns Canyon	86034	Middle Verde (Part of Camp Verde)	86322
Grand Canyon Caverns	86434	Kearny	85237		
Grand Canyon Estates.....	86023	Kelvin	85237	Midland City...............	85501
Grand View	86301	Kerwo	85634	Miller Valley (Part of Prescott)	86301
Grasshopper Junction	86401	Kingman	86401-02		
Gray Mountain	86016	For specific Kingman Zip Codes call (602) 753-2480		Miracle Valley	85615
Greasewood	86505			Miramonte Acres (Part of Bisbee)	85603
Greasewood Springs	86507	Kinlichee	86505		
Greaterville	85637	Kino (Part of Tucson)	85705	Mishongnovi	86043
Green Valley	85614	Kino Hills	85621	Mobile	85239
	85622	Kino Springs	85621	Moccasin	86022
For specific Green Valley Zip Codes call (602) 625-4221		Kinsley Ranch	85640	Moenave	86045
		Kirkland	86332	Moenkopi	86045
Greenway (Part of Glendale)	85306	Kirkland Junction	86332	Mohave Valley.............	86440
Greer	85927	Klagetoh	86505	Morenci	85540
Gripe	85546	Klondyke	85643	Mormon Lake	86038
Groom Creek	86301	Kofa (Part of Yuma)	85364	Morristown	85342
Guadalupe	85283	Kohatk	85634	Mountainaire	86001
Gunsight	85321	Komatke	85339	Mountain View (Cochise County).................	85603
Gu Oidak	85634	Ko Vaya	85634		
Guthrie...................	85533	Kykotsmovi Village	86039	Mountain View (Maricopa County)	85213
Gu Vo	85634	Lake Havasu City	86403-05		
Hacienda De Valencia	85201	For specific Lake Havasu City Zip Codes call (602) 855-2361		Mount Elden (Part of Flagstaff)	86001
Hackberry	86411				
Haivana Nakya	85634	Lake Mead City	86444	Mount Lemmon	85619
Hamilton Corner	85248	Lake Mead Rancheros	86401	Munds Park	86017
Hano	86042	Lake Mohave	86430	Na-Ah-Tee Canyon	86025
Happy Jack	86024	Lake Montezuma	86342	Naco	85620
Harcuvar	85348	Lakeside (La Paz County) ..	85344	Navajo	86509
Harmony Villa	85201	Lakeside (Navajo County) .	85929	Navajo Depot Activity	86015
Hassayampa	85343	Lampliter Village (Part of Clarkdale)................	86324	Navajo Indian Reservation .	86515
Havasupai Indian Reservation	86435			Navajo Mountain Trading Post	86044
		La Palma..................	85222		
Hawkins	85332	Las Ligas	85323	Navajo Spring	86036
Hawley Lake	85930	Laveen....................	85339	Navajo Station	86505
Hayden	85235	Lees Ferry	86036	Nazlini	86540
Hayden Junction	85235	Leisure World	85206	Nelson	86434
Heber	85928	Leupp	86035	New Hope	85201
Hereford	85615	Leupp Corner	86047	New Oraibi	86039
Hermits Rest	86023	Liberty	85326	New River	85029
Hickiwan	85634	Ligurta	85356	New Tucson (Part of Tucson)	85714
Hidden Springs............	86020	Lincon	85634		
Highland Park	85603	Litchfield Greens (Part of Litchfield Park)	85340	Nicksville	85615
Highland Pines	86301			Nogales...................	85621

	ZIP
....	85628
....	85662

For specific Nogales Zip Codes call (602) 287-9246

Nogales West	85621
Nolia	85634
Normal Junction (Part of Tempe)	85281
Northeast (Part of Phoenix)	85016
Northern Arizona University (Part of Flagstaff)	86011
Northern Hills	85704
North Komelik	85634
Northridge Park	86314
North Rim	86052
Northwest (Part of Phoenix)	85017
Nortons Corner	85225
Nutrioso	85932
Oak Creek	86341
Oak Knoll Village	86301
Oak Springs	86511
Oasis Park (Part of Apache Junction)	85220
Oatman	86433
Ocotillo	85248
Octave	85332
Olberg	85247
Old Columbine	85546
Old Oraibi	86039
Oracle	85623
Oracle Foot Hill Estates	85704
Oracle Junction	85738
Orange Grove Estates	85704
Oro Valley	85704
Osborn (Part of Phoenix)	85013
Overgaard	85933
Page	86040
Page Springs	86325
Palm Springs (Part of Apache Junction)	85219
Palominas	85615
Palomino Acres	85234
Palo Verde	85343
Pan Tak	85634
Papago (Part of Scottsdale)	85257
Papago Indian Reservation	85634
Paradise	85632
Paradise Valley	85253
Paradise Valley Mall (Part of Phoenix)	85032
Park Central Mall (Part of Phoenix)	85013
Parker	85344
Parker Creek	85501
Park Mall (Part of Tucson)	85711
Parks	86018
Patagonia	85624
Paulden	86334
Paul Spur	85607
Payson	85541
....	85547

For specific Payson Zip Codes call (602) 474-2972

Peach Springs	86434
Pearce	85625
Peeples Valley	86332
Peoria	85345
....	85380-82

For specific Peoria Zip Codes call (602) 979-1841

Peralta Estates	85219
Peridot	85542
Perkinsville	86323
Perryville	85326
Petrified Forest National Park	86028

Phoenix	85001-82

For specific Phoenix Zip Codes call (602) 225-3434

COLLEGES & UNIVERSITIES

DeVry Institute of Technology-Phoenix	85021
University of Phoenix	85040

FINANCIAL INSTITUTIONS

Bank of America, Arizona	85012
Chase Bank of Arizona	85012
Citibank (Arizona)	85012
First Interstate Bank of Arizona, N.A.	85003
Security Pacific Bank Arizona	85003
The Valley National Bank of Arizona	85004

HOSPITALS

Arizona State Hospital	85008
Carl T. Hayden Veterans Affairs Medical Center	85012

	ZIP
Good Samaritan Hospital Medical Center	85006
Humana Hospital-Phoenix	85016
John C. Lincoln Hospital and Health Center	85020
Maricopa Medical Center	85008
St. Joseph's Hospital and Medical Center	85013

HOTELS/MOTELS

Arizona Biltmore	85016
Embassy Suites Hotel	85016
Embassy Suites Camelhead	85008
Doubletree Suites Hotel at Phoenix Gateway Center	85008
Holiday Inn-Corporate Center	85029
Hyatt Regency Phoenix at Civic Plaza	85004
The Pointe Hilton Resort at Squaw Peak	85020
Ramada Inn Metrocenter	85029
Sheraton Greenway Inn	85023

MILITARY INSTALLATIONS

Arizona Air National Guard, FB6021, Sky Harbor International Airport	85034
Pia Oik	85634
Picacho	85241
Pima	85543
Pine	85544
Pinedale	85934
Pine Lake	86401
Pine Springs	86506
Pinetop (Part of Pinetop-Lakeside)	85935
Pinetop-Lakeside	85935
Pinnacle Peak Village	85255
Pinon	86510
Pioneer (Part of Mesa)	85210
Pirtleville	85626
Pisinemo	85634
Plantsite	85540
Plaza Del Rio (Part of Peoria)	85381
Polacca	86042
Poland Junction	86333
Pomerene	85627
Ponderosa Park	86301
Portal	85632
Porter Creek Estates	85929
Porter Mountain Estates	85929
Poston	85371
Prescott	86301-14

For specific Prescott Zip Codes call (602) 778-1890

Prescott Valley	86314
Presidential Estates	85616
Prinston Park	85234
Pumpkin Center	85553
Quartzsite	85346
....	85359

For specific Quartzsite Zip Codes call (602) 927-6323

Queen Creek	85242
Queen Valley	85219
Querino	86506
Rainbow Valley	85326
Ranch del Sol	85234
Rancho del Rio	85344
Randolph	85222
Reata Pass	85251
Redington	85602
Red Lake	86046
Red Mesa	86514
Red Rock (Apache County)	87420
Red Rock (Pinal County)	85245
Red Valley	85544
Rillito	85654
Rimrock	86335
Rincon (Part of Tucson)	85710
Rio Rico	85621
....	85648

For specific Rio Rico Zip Codes call (602) 281-7223

Rio Salado (Part of Phoenix)	85074
Rio Verde	85263
Riverside Stage Stop	85237
Riverside Terrace	85704
Riviera (Part of Bullhead City)	86442
Rock Point	86545
Rock Springs	85026
Roll	85347
Roosevelt	85545
Roosevelt Estates	85545
Roosevelt Resort	85545
Rough Rock	86503
Round Rock	86547

	ZIP
Royal Estates	85621
Rye	85541
Sacate	85221
Sacaton	85221
....	85221

For specific Sacaton Zip Codes call (602) 562-3681

Sacaton Flats	85247
Sacred Mountain	86001
Safford	85546
....	85548

For specific Safford Zip Codes call (602) 428-0220

Saginaw (Part of Bisbee)	85603
Sahuarita	85629
Sahuarita Heights	85629
St. David	85630
St. Johns	85936
St. Michaels	86511
Salado	85936
Salina	86503
Salome	85348
Salt River Indian Reservation	85256
Salt River Powder District Camp	85545
San Carlos	85550
San Carlos Indian Reservation	85550
Sanchez	85546
Sanders	86512
Sand Springs	86039
San Jose (Cochise County)	85603
San Jose (Graham County)	85546
San Lucy Village	85337
San Luis (Pima County)	85634
San Luis (Yuma County)	85349
San Manuel	85631
San Miguel	85634
San Pedro	85634
San Rafael Terrace (Part of Bisbee)	85603
San Simon	85632
Santa Cruz	85339
Santa Maria (Maricopa County)	85009
Santa Maria (Yavapai County)	85332
Santan	85247
Santa Rita	85640
Santa Rosa	85634
San Xavier	85746
San Xavier Indian Reservation	85634
Sasabe	85633
Sawmill	86549
Schuchk	85634
Schuchuli	85634
Scottsdale	85250-71

For specific Scottsdale Zip Codes call (602) 949-7100

Scottsdale Fashion Square (Part of Scottsdale)	85251
Second Mesa	86043
Sedona	86336
....	86340-41

For specific Sedona Zip Codes call (602) 282-3511

Seligman	86337
Sells	85634
Sentinel	85333
Shaw Butte (Part of Phoenix)	85071
Sheldon	85534
Sherwood (Part of Mesa)	85214
Shipolovi	86043
Shongopovi	86043
Shonto	86054
Shopishk	85634
Show Low	85901
Shumway	85901
Sichomovi	86042
Sierra Bonita	85643
Sierra Vista	85635-36
....	85670-71

For specific Sierra Vista Zip Codes call (602) 458-2540

Sil Nakaya	85634
Silverbell (Part of Tucson)	85745
....	85754

For specific Silverbell Zip Codes call (602) 622-5210

Site Six (Part of Lake Havasu City)	86403
Skull Valley	86338
Skyline Bel Aire Estates	85718
Skyway Village	85205
Smoke Signal	86503
Snowflake	85937
Solomon	85551
Somerton	85350

	ZIP		ZIP		ZIP
Sonoita	85637	Tierra Madre	85234	Walnut Grove	86332
Sonora Town	85234	Tintown (Part of Bisbee)	85603	Walpi	86042
South Bisbee	85603	Tolani	86047	Warren (Part of Bisbee)	85603
South Central (Part of		Tolleson	85353	Washington (Part of	
Phoenix)	85040	Toltec (Part of Eloy)	85231	Phoenix)	85021
Southgate Mall (Part of		Tombstone	85638		85051
Yuma)	85364	Tonalea	86044	For specific Washington Zip	
South Komelik	85634	Tonopah	85354	Codes call (602) 249-0028	
South Santan	85247	Tonto Basin	85553	Washington Camp	85624
South Tucson	85713	Topawa	85639	Wellton	85356
Springerville	85938	Topock	86436	Wenden	85357
Spring Valley	86333	Toreva	86043	Westbrook Village (Part of	
Stanfield	85272	Tortilla Flat	85290	Peoria)	85382
Stanton	85332	Totopitk	85634	West Chandler (Part of	
Stargo	85540	Tovrea (Part of Phoenix)	85034	Chandler)	85224
Star Valley	85541	Tower Plaza Mall (Part of		Westgate	85611
Steamboat Canyon	86505	Phoenix)	85018	Westgreen Estates (Part of	
Stoneman Lake	86024	Toyei	86505	Peoria)	85345
Strawberry	85544	Tremaine	85224	West Plaza Shopping	
Student Union (Part of		Tri-City Mall (Part of Mesa)	85201	Center (Part of Phoenix)	85017
Tucson)	85720	Truxton	86434	Westridge (Part of Phoenix)	85033
Sun (Part of Tucson)	85719	Tsaile	86556	Westridge Mall (Part of	
Sun City	85351	Tubac	85646	Phoenix)	85033
	85372-75	Tuba City	86045	West Sedona (Part of	
For specific Sun City Zip Codes		Tucson	85701-54	Sedona)	86340
call (602) 974-3623		For specific Tucson Zip Codes		Westward Quest	85201
Sun City West	85375	call (602) 620-5142		Wheatfields	86515
Sunflower	85201	Tucson Country Club		Whipple (Part of Prescott)	86313
Sunizona	85625	Estates	85715	Whippoorwill	86503
Sun Lakes	85224	Tucson Estates	85715	Whispering Hills (Part of	
Sunnyslope (Part of		Tucson National Estates	85704	Sierra Vista)	85635
Phoenix)	85020	Tumacacori	85640	White Clay	86504
Sunrise	86047	Turkey Flat	85546	White Cone	86025
Sunrise Springs	86505	Tusayan	86023	White Mountain Lake	85912
Sunset	85643	Tusconita	85706	Whiteriver (Navajo County)	85941
Sunset Acres	85603	Twin Arrows (Part of		White Tanks	85326
Sunshine Acres (Part of		Flagstaff)	86001	Why	85321
Mesa)	85201	Twin Buttes	85629	Wickenburg	85358
Sun Terra Acres	85234	Twin Knolls	85207		85390
Suntown (Part of Peoria)	85381	Two Story	86511	For specific Wickenburg Zip	
Sun Valley	86029	University of Arizona (Part		Codes call (602) 684-2138	
Supai	86435	of Tucson)	85717	Wide Ruin	86502
Superior	85273	Upper Greasewood Trading		Wikieup	86360
Superstition Estates (Part of		Post	86507	Wilhoit	86332
Apache Junction)	85220	Upper Wheatfields	86556	Willcox	85643
Supi Oidak	85634	Utting	85348	Williams	86046
Surprise	85374	Vahki	85221	Williams Air Force Base	85240
Sweetwater (Apache		Vail	85641	Willow Beach	86445
County)	87401	Vaiva Vo	85634	Willow Canyon	85619
Sweetwater (Maricopa		Valencia	85326	Willow Valley Estates	86440
County)	85326	Valentine	86437	Window Rock	86515
Sweetwater (Pinal County)	85221	Valley Farms	85291	Winkelman	85292
Swift Trail Junction	85546	Valley West Mall (Part of		Winona	86001
Tacna	85352	Glendale)	85301	Winslow	86047
Tapco	86324	Vamori	85634	Winwood	85603
Tat Momoli	85634	Vandenberg Village	85708	Wittmann	85361
Tatria Toak	85634	Vaya Chin	85634	Wood Hills	85616
Taylor	85939	Velda Rose Estates	85205	Woodruff	85942
Teec Nos Pos	86514	Velda Rose Gardens	85201	Woodsprings	86505
Tees To	86047	Ventana	85634	Yarnell	85362
Tempe	85280-85	Ventana Lakes (Part of		Yava	86301
For specific Tempe Zip Codes call		Peoria)	85382	Yavapai Indian Reservation	86301
(602) 220-0258		Venture Out	85201	York	85534
Temple Bar Marina	86443	Vernon	85940	Young	85554
Tes Nez Iah	86033	Vicksburg	85348	Youngtown	85363
Thatcher	85552	Village Meadows (Part of		Yucca	86438
Theba	85337	Sierra Vista)	85635	Yuma	85364-66
The Gap	86020	Waddell	85355	For specific Yuma Zip Codes call	
Thomas Mall (Part of		Wagoner	86332	(602) 783-2124	
Phoenix)	85018	Wahak Hotrontk	85634	Yuma Marine Corps Air	
Three Points	85714	Wahweap	86040	Station	85369
Three Way	85534	Walker	86301	Yuma Proving Ground	85364

Name	ZIP	Name	ZIP	Name	ZIP
Abbott	72944	Bates	72924	Blytheville	72315-19
Aberdeen	72134	Batesville	72501-03	For specific Blytheville Zip Codes call (501) 763-3690	
Acorn	71953	For specific Batesville Zip Codes call (501) 793-6828		Board Camp	71932
Ada	72001	Battlefield	71801	Bodcaw	71858
Adkins Lake	71601	Baucum	72117	Bogg Springs	71944
Adona	72001	Bauxite	72011	Bolding	71747
Agnos	72513	Baxter	71638	Boles	72926
Alabam	72740	Bay	72411	Bonanza	72916
Albert Pike (Part of Hot Springs National Park)	71913	Bayou Meto (Arkansas County)	72160	Bondsville	72354
Albion	72143	Bayou Meto (Lonoke County)	72086	Bonnerdale	71933
Alco	72610	Bay Village	72324	Bono (Craighead County)	72416
Alexander (Greene County)	72450	Bear Creek Springs	72601	Bono (Faulkner County)	72058
Alexander (Pulaski County)	72002	Bearden	71720	Booker	72117
Algoa	72112	Beaver	72613	Booneville	72927
Alicia	72410	Beaver Shores	72756	Booster	72645
Alix	72820	Beck	72348	Boothe	72927
Allbrook	71851	Becton	72036	Boston	72752
Alleene	71820	Beebe	72012	Boswell	72516
Allison	72560	Bee Branch	72013	Botkinburg	72031
Allport	72046	Beech Grove (Dallas County)	71742	Boughton	71857
Alma	72921	Beech Grove (Greene County)	72412	Bowen	71940
Almond	72550	Beedeville	72014	Bowman	72437
Almyra	72003	Beirne	71721	Boxley	72740
Alpena	72611	Bellaire	71638	Boyd	71837
Alpine	71920	Bella Vista	72714	Boydell	71658
Alread	72031	Bellefonte	72601	Boyd Hill	71845
Altheimer	72004	Belle Meade	72348	Boydsville	72461
Alto	72354	Belleville	72824	Boynton	72438
Altus	72821	Bells Chapel	72823	Bradford	72020
Aly	72857	Bellville	71846	Bradley	71826
Amagon	72005	Belton	71852	Brady (Part of Little Rock)	72205
Amanca	72376	Ben	72530	Bragg City	71726
Amboy (Part of North Little Rock)	72118	Ben Gay	72466	Brakebill	72478
Amity	71921	Ben Hur	72856	Branch	72928
Amy	71701	Ben Lomond	71823	Brasfield	72017
Andy	72376	Benton	72015	Bredlow Corner	72046
Annieville	72434	Bentonville	72712-14	Brentwood	72959
Antioch (Perry County)	72070	For specific Bentonville Zip Codes call (501) 273-2722		Brewer	72044
Antioch (White County)	72012	Benton Work Release and Pre Release Center	72015	Brickeys	72320
Antoine	71922	Bergman	72615	Briggsville	72828
Aplin	72126	Berryville	72616	Brighton	72450
Appleton	72822	Beryl	72032	Bright Star	71834
Apt	72401	Best	72756	Brightwater	72756
Arbor Grove	72433	Bethany	71833	Brinkley	72021
Ard	72834	Bethel	72450	Brister	71740
Arden	71822	Bethel Heights	72764	Brockett	72455
Arkadelphia	71923	Bethesda	72501	Brockwell	72517
Arkana	71826	Beulah	72017	Brookland	72417
Arkansas City	71630	Bevis Corners	72142	Brown's Crossing	71640
Arkinda	71836	Bexar	72515	Brown Springs	72104
Arkola	72940	Bidville	72959	Brownstown	71846
Arlberg	72031	Bigelow	72016	Brownsville	72067
Armorel	72310	Big Flat	72617	Bruins	72348
Armstrong	72482	Big Fork	71953	Brumley	72032
Armstrong Springs	72143	Biggers	72413	Brummitt	72160
Artesian	71744	Big Lake	72442	Bruno	72618
Artist Point	72946	Big Springs	72657	Brush Creek	72084
Ashdown	71822	Billingsley's Corner	71866	Bryant	72022
Asher (Madison County)	72727	Billstown	71958		72089
Asher (Pulaski County)	72204	Bingen	71852	For specific Bryant Zip Codes call (501) 847-2226	
Ash Flat	72513	Birdell	72455	Bryant Addition	72857
Athelstan	72370	Birdeye	72314	Buckeye	72438
Athens	71971	Birdsong	72386	Buckner	71827
Atkins	72823	Birdtown	72157	Buck Range	71851
Atlanta	71740	Birta	72853	Buckville	71956
Attica	72455	Biscoe	72017	Buena Vista	71764
Aubrey	72311	Bismarck	71929	Buffalo City	72653
Augsburg	72847	Blackburn	72959	Buie	72129
Augusta	72006	Blackfish	72346	Bullfrog Valley	72837
Aurelle	71765	Black Fork	71953	Bull Shoals	72619
Aurora	72740	Black Oak (Craighead County)	72414	Bunney	72414
Austin (Conway County)	72031	Black Oak (Poinsett County)	72386	Burdette	72321
Austin (Lonoke County)	72007	Black Rock	72415	Burg	71833
Auvergne	72112	Black Springs	71960	Burlington	72662
Avilla	72002	Blackton	72069	Burnville	72936
Avoca	72711	Blackville (Conway County)	72823	Buroak	72650
Avon	71832	Blackville (Jackson County)	72112	Burtsell	71962
Back Gate	71639	Blakely	71931	Busch	72632
Baker	72482	Blakemore	72046	Bussey	71860
Balch	72009	Blevins	71825	Butlerville	72176
Bald Knob	72010	Bloomer	72933	Butterfield	72104
Baldwin (Part of Fayetteville)	72701	Bloomfield	72734	Byron	72576
Ballard	72513	Blossom	72392	Cabanol	72616
Band Mill	72517	Blue Ball	72833	Cabot	72023
Banks	71631	Blue Eye	65601	Caddo Gap	71935
Banner	72523	Blue Hill	72118	Caddo Valley	71923
Barber	72927	Blue Mountain	72826	Cain	72946
Barcelona	72955	Blue Springs	71909	Calamine	72466
Bard	72450	Blue Springs Village	72764	Caldwell	72322
Bardstown	72350	Bluff City	71722	Cale	71828
Barfield	72315	Bluffton	72827	Caledonia	71749
Barling	72923			Calhoun	71753
Barney	72047			Calico Rock	72519
Barton	72312			Calion	71724
Bashe (Part of Fort Smith)	72901			Calmer	71665
Bass	72655			Calumet	72315
Bassett	72313			Camark	71701
Batavia	72601			Camden	71701
Batchelor	72366			Cammack Village	72207

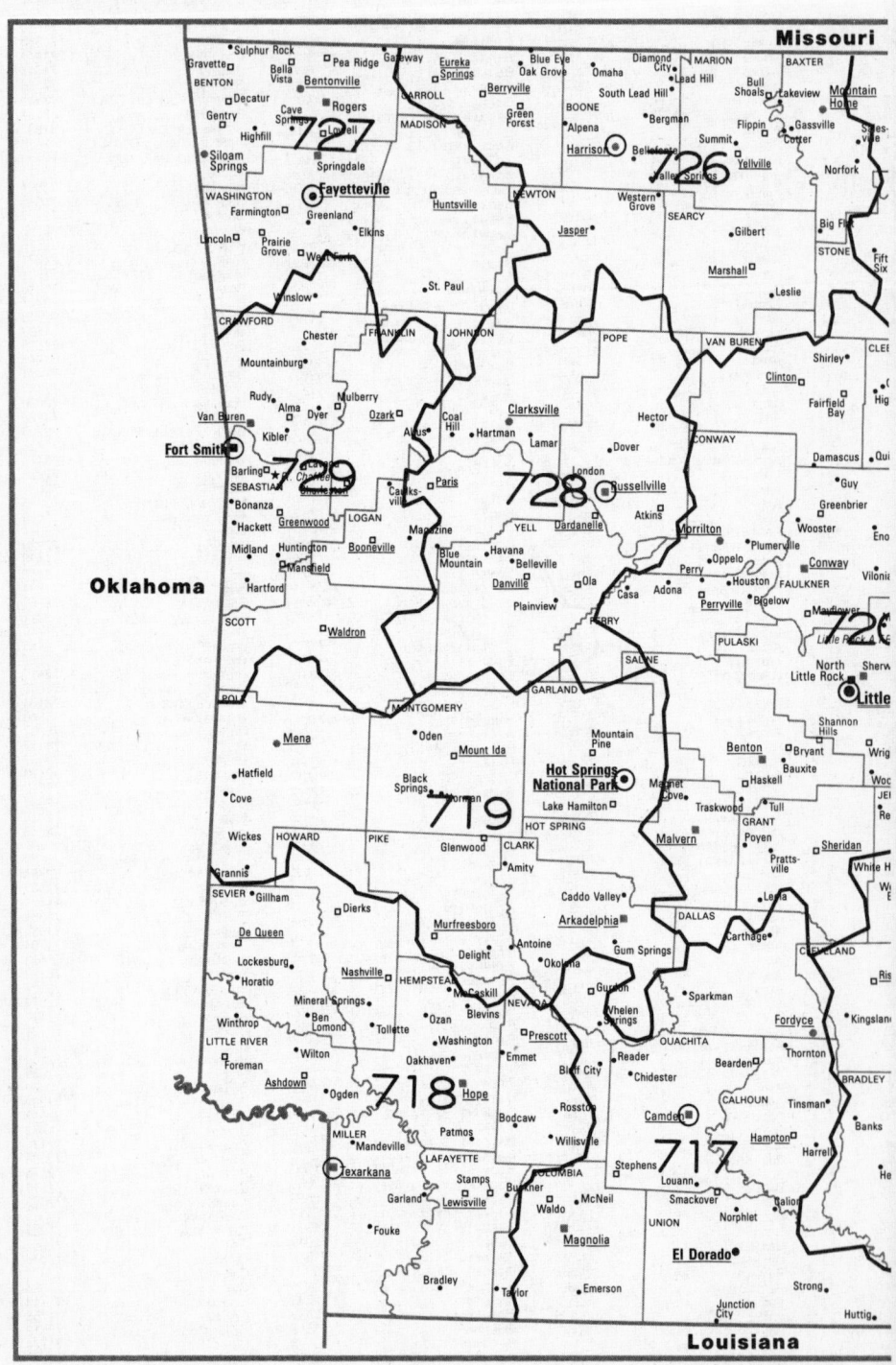

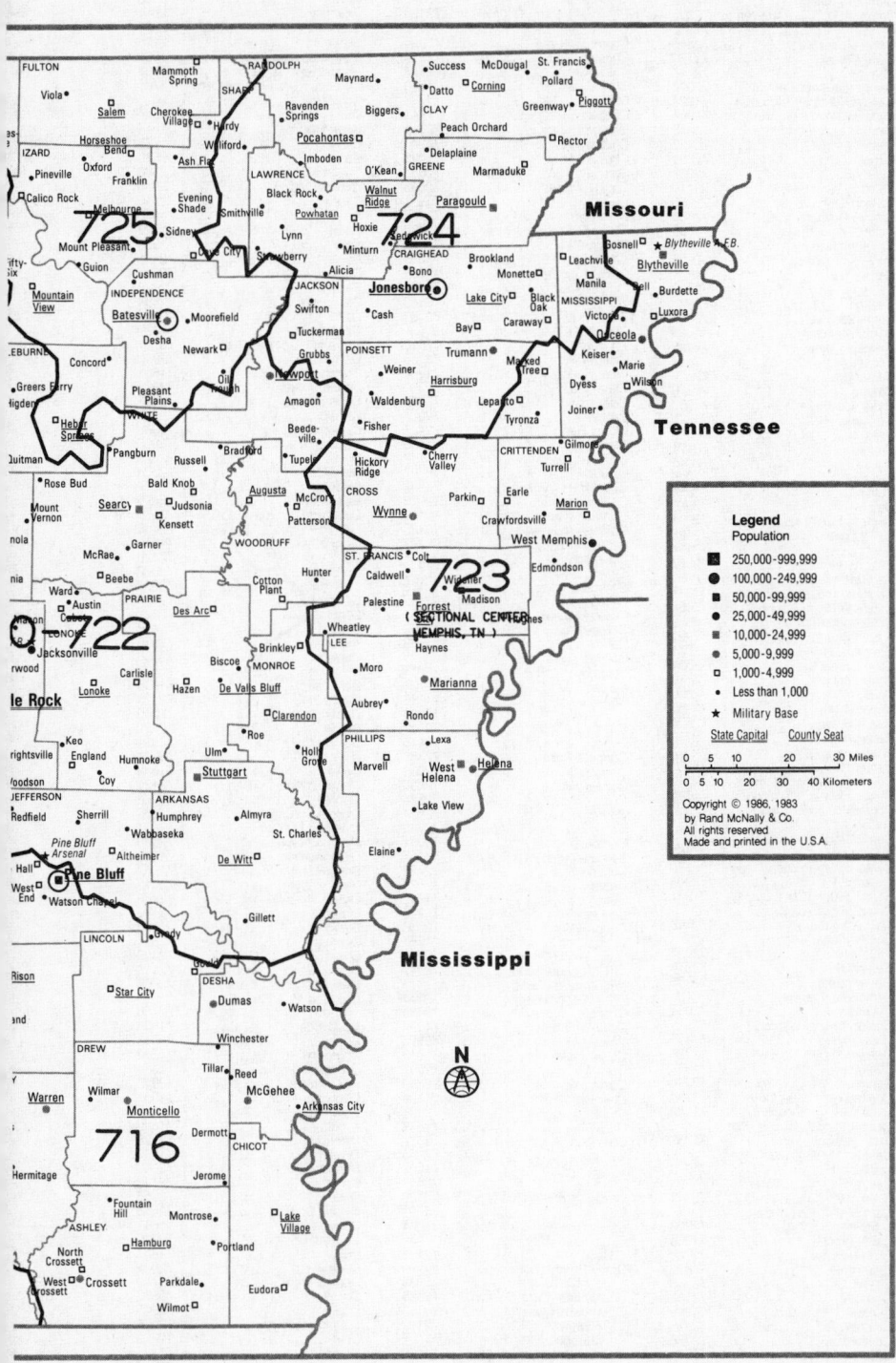

FULTON
Mammoth
Spring
Viola
Salem
Cherokee
Village
Horseshoe
Bend
IZARD
Pineville
Oxford
Franklin
Calico Rock
Melbourne
Evening
Shade
Mount Pleasant
Guion
Cushman
INDEPENDENCE
Mountain
View
Batesville
Moorefield
Desha
Newark
Concord
LEBURNE
Greers Ferry
Quitman
Pleasant
Plains
WHITE
Hebet
Springs
Pangburn
Russell
Bald Knob
Rose Bud
Mount
Vernon
Searcy
Judsonia
Kensett
McRae
Garner
Beebe
Ward
PRAIRIE
Austin
Cabot
Jacksonville
Carlisle
Lonoke
Hazen
De Valls Bluff
le Rock
Keo
England
Humnoke
Coy
Stuttgart
JEFFERSON
Redfield
Sherrill
Wabbaseka
Humphrey
Pine Bluff
Arsenal
Altheimer
De Witt
Hall
West
End
Watson Chapel
LINCOLN
Grady
rison
DESHA
Star City
Dumas
Watson
Winchester
DREW
Tillar
Reed
Warren
Wilmar
Monticello
McGehee
Dermott
716
Jerome
Hermitage
Fountain
Hill
Montrose
ASHLEY
Hamburg
Portland
North
Crossett
West
Crossett
Crossett
Parkdale
Wilmot

RANDOLPH
Maynard
Success
McDougal
St. Francis
Datto
Corning
Pollard
SHARP
Ravenden
Springs
Biggers
CLAY
Greenway
Piggott
Hardy
Williford
Pocahontas
Peach Orchard
Rector
Ash Flat
Imboden
Delaplaine
LAWRENCE
O'Kean
GREENE
Marmaduke
Black Rock
Walnut
Ridge
Paragould
Missouri
Smithville
Powhatan
Hoxie
Lynn
Minturn
Sedgwick
724
Strawberry
CRAIGHEAD
Bono
Brookland
Monette
Gosnell
Blytheville A.F.B.
JACKSON
Alicia
Jonesboro
Leachville
Blytheville
Swifton
Lake City
Manila
MISSISSIPPI
Burdette
Tuckerman
Cash
Bay
Caraway
Victoria
Osceola
Luxora
Newport
Grubbs
POINSETT
Trumann
Keiser
Oil
Trough
Weiner
Marked
Tree
Marie
Wilson
Amagon
Harrisburg
Dyess
Waldenburg
Lepanto
Joiner
Beede-
ville
Fisher
Tyronza
Tennessee
Bradford
Tupelo
Hickory
Ridge
Cherry
Valley
Gilmore
Augusta
McCrory
CROSS
Parkin
Earle
Marion
Patterson
Wynne
Crawfordsville
WOODRUFF
West Memphis
Cotton
Plant
Hunter
ST. FRANCIS
Colt
Edmondson
Des Arc
Caldwell
Widener
Madison
Palestine
Forrest
City
SECTIONAL CENTER
MEMPHIS, TN
Brinkley
Wheatley
LEE
Haynes
Biscoe
MONROE
Moro
Clarendon
Aubrey
Rondo
Roe
PHILLIPS
Lexa
Ulm
Holly
Grove
Marvell
West
Helena
Helena
Almyra
St. Charles
Lake View
ARKANSAS
Elaine

722

725

723

716

Mississippi

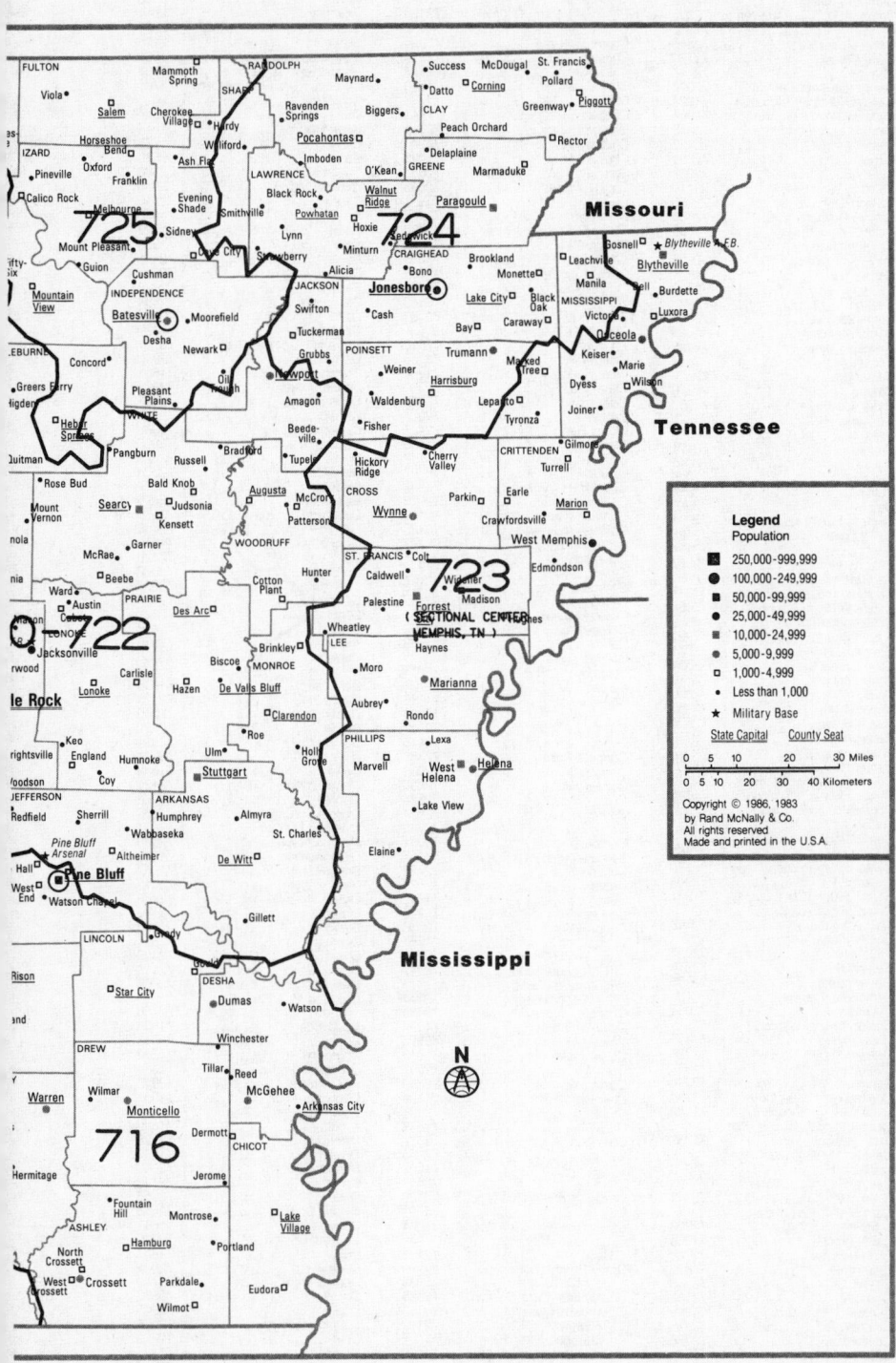

N

	ZIP
Camp	72520
Campbell Station	72473
Camp Joseph T. Robinson	72205
Canaan	72650
Canal Gardens	72348
Cane Creek	72150
Canehill	72717
Caney (Faulkner County)	72032
Caney (Hot Spring County)	71929
Caney Valley	71921
Canfield	71845
Cantwell	72422
Capps	72601
Capps City	71069
Caraway	72419
Carbon City	72855
Carden Bottoms	72834
Careyville	71765
Carlile Highland	72653
Carlisle	72024
Carmel	71671
Carmi	72438
Carolan	72927
Carpenter	71642
Carpenter Addition	71655
Carroll's Corner	72442
Carrollton	72611
Carryville	72454
Carson	72370
Carter Cove Use Area	72857
Carthage	71725
Casa	72025
Cash	72421
Cass	72949
Casscoe	72026
Catalpa	72854
Catcher	72956
Catholic Point	72027
Cathy Lake	72396
Cato	72114
Catron	72367
Caulksville	72951
Cauthron (Logan County)	72927
Cauthron (Scott County)	72958
Cavanaugh (Part of Fort Smith)	72901
Cave City	72521
Cave Creek	72501
Cave Springs	72718
Cecil	72930
Cedar Creek	72950
Cedar Grove	72534
Cedarville	72932
Center	72542
Center Hill (Greene County)	72450
Center Hill (White County)	72143
Center Point (Clark County)	71743
Center Point (Hempstead County)	71801
Center Point (Howard County)	71852
Center Point (Prairie County)	72064
Center Ridge (Clark County)	71921
Center Ridge (Cleburne County)	72543
Center Ridge (Conway County)	72027
Centerton	72719
Center Valley	72801
Centerville (Faulkner County)	72058
Centerville (Hempstead County)	71835
Centerville (Yell County)	72829
Central (Clark County)	71923
Central (Cross County)	72396
Central (Hot Spring County)	72104
Central (Sevier County)	71842
Central Baptist College (Part of Conway)	72032
Central City (Garland County)	71913
Central City (Sebastian County)	72941
Central Mall (Part of Fort Smith)	72903
Cerrogordo	71866
Chambersville	71766
Chapel Hill	71832
Charleston	72933
Charlotte	72522
Chasewood Landing	71969
Chatfield	72348
Chelford	72386
Cherokee City	72734
Cherokee Village	72525
	72529

For specific Cherokee Village Zip Codes call (50l) 257-2662

	ZIP
Cherokee Village-Hidden Valley	72525
Cherry Hill (Perry County)	72126
Cherry Hill (Polk County)	71953
Cherry Valley	72324
Chester	72934
Chickalah	72834
Chicot Junction	71640
Chidester	71726
Childress	72447
Chimes	72645
Chismville	72943
Choctaw	72028
Choctaw Acres	72031
Christy Acres	72015
Chula	72857
Cincinnati	72769
Clarendon	72029
Clarkedale	72325
Clarkridge	72623
Clarks Corner	72394
Clarksville	72830
Clay	72143
Clear Lake (Grant County)	72150
Clear Lake (Mississippi County)	72315
Clear Point	72756
Clear Spring	71962
Cleveland	72030
Clifty	72756
Clinton	72031
Clover Bend	72433
Clow	71855
Clyde	72717
Coaldale	74937
Coal Hill	72832
Coffeeville	72020
Coffman (Greene County)	72450
Coffman (Lawrence County)	72433
Coldwater	72373
Coleman	71655
Colfax	72653
College City	72476
Collegehill	71752
College Station	72053
Collegeville	72002
Collins	71638
Colt	72326
Columbus	71831
Combs	72721
Cominto	71655
Compton	72624
Concord	72523
Congo	72015
Connells Point	72366
Conway	72032
Copper Mine	72756
Cord	72524
Corinth	72824
Corley	72855
Cornerstone	72004
Cornerville	71667
Corning	72422
Cotter	72626
Cotterneck	71742
Cottonbelt	71720
Cotton Plant	72036
Cottonshed	71851
Cottonwood Corner (Craighead County)	72447
Cottonwood Corner (Mississippi County)	72370
Council	72320
Cove	71937
Cowell	72856
Cowlingsville	71846
Coy	72037
Cozahome	72639
Crabapple Point	71724
Crabtree	72031
Cravens	72949
Crawfordsville	72327
Creigh	72366
Crigler	71667
Crockett	72454
Crocketts Bluff	72038
Crosses	72701
Crossett	71635
Crossroads (Cleburne County)	72131
Cross Roads (Hot Spring County)	71933
Crossroads (Izard County)	72566
Crossroads (Jackson County)	72112
Cross Roads (Little River County)	71866
Cross Roads (Logan County)	72863
Cross Roads (Madison County)	72738

	ZIP
Crossroads (Prairie County)	72040
Crows	72015
Crumpler	72644
Crumrod	72328
Crystal Hill	72118
Crystal Springs	71968
Crystal Springs Landing	71968
Cullendale (Part of Camden)	71701
Culpeper	72031
Cumi	72544
Cummins Unit	71644
Curtis	71728
Cushman	72526
Cypert	72366
Cypress Valley	72156
Dabney	72110
Daisy	71950
Dalark	71923
Dallas	71953
Dalton	72455
Damascus	72039
Danville	72833
Dardanelle	72834
Datto	72424
Davis Creek	72129
Dawn Hill Country Club	72761
Dayton	72940
DeAnn	71801
Deans Market	72921
Dean Springs	72921
Decatur	72722
Deckerville	72386
Deep Elm	71653
Deer	72628
Deerfield	72328
Delaney	72727
Delaplaine	72425
Delaware	72835
Delfore	72438
Delight	71940
Dell	72426
De Luce	72042
Denmark	72020
Dennard	72629
Denning	72821
Denton	72458
Denver	72638
Denwood	72386
De Queen	71832
Dermott	71638
De Roche	71929
Des Arc	72040
Desha	72527
Detonti	72011
De Valls Bluff	72041
Dewey (Chicot County)	71638
Dewey (White County)	72121
De Witt	72042
Dialion	71665
Diamond Bay	72531
Diamond City	72630
Diamondhead	71913
Dian (Part of Prescott)	71857
Diaz	72043
Dickey Heights	72768
Dicus	72476
Dierks	71833
Dillen	72854
Dixie (Craighead County)	72437
Dixie (Pulaski County)	72114
Dixie (Woodruff County)	72006
Dixieland Mall (Part of Rogers)	72756
Doddridge	71834
Dogpatch	72648
Dogtown	71832
Dogwood (Part of Blytheville)	72315
Dogwood Acres	71957
Dollarway (Part of Pine Bluff)	71602
Dolph	72528
Donaldson	71941
Dongola	72650
Doniphan	72143
Dora	72956
Double Bridges	72358
Douglas	71643
Douglas Corner	72205
Dover	72837
Dowdy	72524
Drakes Creek	72740
Drasco	72530
Driggs	72943
Dripping Springs	72955
Driver	72329
Dryden	72401
Dryfork	72740
Dublin	72863
Duff	72675
Dumas	71639

	ZIP
Durham	72727
Dutch Mills	72744
Dutton	72760
Dyer	72935
Dyess	72330
Eagle Mills	71720
Eagle Point	72531
Eagleton	71953
Earle	72331
East Black Oak	72386
East Camden	71701
East End	72065
Eastview	72351
Eaton	72458
Ebenezer	71764
Ebony	72364
Echo	72927
Economy	72823
Eden Isle	72543
Edgemont	72044
Edmondson	72332
Eglantine	72153
Egypt	72427
Elaine	72333
El Dorado	71730-31
For specific El Dorado Zip Codes call (501) 863-7571	
Elevenpoint	72455
Elgin	72112
Elizabeth	72531
Elkins	72727
Elk Ranch	72632
Elliott	71701
Ellison	72152
Elm Springs	72728
Elm Store	65778
Elmwood	72601
Elnora	72455
El Paso	72045
Emerson	71740
Emmet	71835
Empire	71661
Enders	72131
Engelberg	72455
England	72046
English	72004
Enola	72047
Enterprise	72901
Eros	72633
Erwin	72112
Ethel	72048
Etna	72949
Etowah	72428
Euclid Heights (Part of Hot Springs National Park)	71901
Eudora	71640
Eula	72675
Eureka Springs	72632
Evansville	72729
Evening Shade (Hempstead County)	71801
Evening Shade (Scott County)	72958
Evening Shade (Sharp County)	72532
Evening Star	72422
Everton	72633
Excelsior	72936
Fairbanks	72131
Fairfield (Part of Little Rock)	72209
Fairfield Bay	72088
Fairmont	72160
Fair Oaks	72397
Fairview (Chicot County)	71653
Fairview (Lonoke County)	72086
Fairview (Marion County)	72650
Fairview (Ouachita County)	71701
Fairview (Sevier County)	71841
Fairwood	71913
Falcon	71827
Falls Chapel	71846
Fallsville	72854
Fancy Hill	71935
Fannie	71970
Farelly Lake	72160
Fargo	72021
Farmington	72730
Farmville	71671
Farville	72417
Fayetteville	72701-03
For specific Fayetteville Zip Codes call (501) 442-8286	
Felsenthal	71747
Felton	72360
Fender	72476
Fendley	71921
Fenter	72167
Ferguson	72328
Ferguson Crossroads	71837
Fern	72946
Ferndale	72208

	ZIP
Fifty-Six	72533
Figure Five	72956
Finch	72421
Fisher (Craighead County)	72421
Fisher (Poinsett County)	72429
Fitzgerald (Part of Diaz)	72112
Fitzgerald Crossing	72006
Fitzhugh	72006
Fivemile	72530
Flag	72645
Flat Rock	72847
Flint Springs	72583
Flippin	72634
Floodway	72442
Floral	72534
Florence	71655
Floyd	72143
Fomby	71822
Fontaine	72416
Fordyce	71742
Foreman	71836
Forest Grove (Columbia County)	71740
Forest Grove (Lafayette County)	71861
Forest Park (Part of Little Rock)	72207
Formosa	72031
Forrest City	72335
Fort Chaffee	72905
Fort Douglas	72854
Fort Lynn	71837
Fort Smith	72901-17
For specific Fort Smith Zip Codes call (501) 484-6370	
Fortune	72373
Forty Four	72585
Forum	72740
Fouke	71837
Fountain Hill	71642
Fountain Lake	71901
Fourche	72016
Fourche Junction	72857
Fourche Valley	72827
Fourmile Hill	72143
Fox	72051
Francis	72601
Franklin	72536
Free Hope	71753
Frenchmans Bayou	72338
Frenchport	71701
Fresno	71643
Friendship (Cleveland County)	71665
Friendship (Columbia County)	71860
Friendship (Hot Spring County)	71942
Friley	72752
Fritz	72461
Fryatt	72554
Frys Mill	72386
Fulton	71838
Furlow	72086
Gaines Landing	71653
Gainesville	72450
Gainsboro	72501
Gaither	72601
Galla Rock	72823
Gallatin	72761
Galloway	72117
Gamaliel	72537
Gammon	72364
Gardner	71765
Garfield	72732
Garland City	71839
Garland Springs	72111
Garner	72052
Garner's Farm	71742
Garnett	71667
Garret Grove	72368
Garrett	72476
Garrett Bridge	71639
Gassville	72635
Gateway	72733
Gaylor	72657
Geneva	71832
Genoa	71840
Gentry	72734
George Creek	72687
Georgetown (Madison County)	72773
Georgetown (Pope County)	72847
Georgetown (White County)	72143
Gepp	72538
Geridge	72046
Gethsemane	72004
Gibbs	71969
Gibson	72401
Gieseck	72373
Gifford	72104

	ZIP
Gilbert	72636
Gilchrist	72358
Giles Spur	72476
Gilkey	72853
Gillett	72055
Gillham	71841
Gilmore	72339
Gin City	71826
Gladden	72331
Gleason	72032
Glemore	72801
Glencoe	72539
Glendale	71667
Glen Rose	72104
Glenview (Part of North Little Rock)	72117
Glenwood	71943
Gobblers Point	72080
Gobell	72366
Gold Creek	72032
Golden City	72927
Golden Lake	72395
Gold Lake Estates	72032
Goobertown	72417
Good Hope	71726
Goodwin	72340
Goose Camp	72840
Goshen	72735
Gosnell	72319
Gould	71643
Gourd	71639
Gourd Neck	72101
Grady	71644
Grand Glaise	72020
Grandview	72601
Grange	72521
Grannis	71944
Grapevine	72057
Graphic	72921
Grassy Lake Bottom	72331
Gravel Hill (Van Buren County)	72030
Gravel Hill (White County)	72136
Gravelly	72838
Gravelridge (Bradley County)	71631
Gravel Ridge (Pulaski County)	72076
Graves Chapel	71846
Gravesville	72039
Gravette	72736
Gray Rock	72855
Grays	72101
Grayson	72927
Greasy Corner	72346
Green Acres	72756
Greenbrier	72058
Greene High	72450
Greenfield	72432
Green Forest	72638
Green Hill	71675
Greenland	72737
Green Tree	72031
Greenway	72430
Greenwich Village	75502
Greenwood (Franklin County)	72949
Greenwood (Sebastian County)	72936
Greers Ferry	72067
Gregory	72059
Grider	72370
Griffith Spring	71667
Griffithtown	71923
Griffithville	72060
Grubbs	72431
Guernsey	71801
Guion	72540
Gum Corner	71640
Gum Log	72801
Gum Springs (Clark County)	71923
Gum Springs (Newton County)	72641
Gurdon	71743
Guy	72061
Hackett	72937
Hagarville	72839
Half Moon	72315
Halley	71638
Halley Junction	71638
Halliday	72443
Hamburg	71646
Hamil	72460
Hamilton	72024
Hampton	71744
Hampton's Landing	72041
Hancock	72419
Hanna	71640
Hannaberry	72160
Hanover	72560
Happy	72143

	ZIP
Happy Bend	72823
Happy Corners	72438
Hardin	71602
Hardy	72542
Hargrave Corner	72461
Harlow	71766
Harmon (Boone County)	72601
Harmon (Washington County)	72701
Harmontown	72501
Harmony (Columbia County)	71753
Harmony (Johnson County)	72830
Harmony (Madison County)	72740
Harmony (White County)	72143
Harmony Grove	71701
Harness	72645
Harp	72104
Harrell	71745
Harriet	72639
Harrisburg	72432
Harrison	72601-02
For specific Harrison Zip Codes call (501) 741-3473	
Hartford	72938
Hartman	72840
Hartwell	72740
Harvey	72841
Haskell	72015
Hasty	72640
Hatchie Coon	72472
Hatfield	71945
Hattieville	72063
Hatton	71946
Havana	72842
Hayley	72040
Haynes	72341
Hazen	72064
Heafer	72331
Healing Springs	72712
Heart	72539
Heber Springs	72543
Hebron	71660
Hector	72843
Helena	72342
Helena Crossing (Part of Helena)	72342
Helena Junction	72342
Hempwallace	71964
Henderson	72544
Henderson College (Part of Arkadelphia)	71923
Hendrix College (Part of Conway)	72032
Hensley	72065
Herbine	71665
Hergett	72401
Heritage Estates	72653
Herman	72401
Hermitage (Bradley County)	71647
Hermitage (Pulaski County)	72206
Herndon	72401
Hervey	75502
Heth	72346
Hickeytown	72847
Hickman	72315
Hickoria	72422
Hickory Creek	72745
Hickory Flat	72121
Hickory Hill	72110
Hickory Plains	72066
Hickory Ridge	72347
Hickory Valley	72521
Hicks	72366
Hicks Station	72394
Hicksville	72366
Hidden Valley	72542
Higden	72067
Higgins (Part of Little Rock)	72206
Higginson	72068
Highfill	72734
Highland	72542
Highland Estates	72745
Hill Creek	72127
Hillcrest (Johnson County)	72830
Hillcrest (Pulaski County)	72205
Hilleman	72101
Hilltop	72482
Hilo	71647
Hindsville	72738
Hiram	72179
Hiwasse	72739
Hobbs Spur	72952
Holiday Hills	72531
Holiday Island	72632
Holland	72173
Hollis	72857
Holly Grove	72069
Holly Hills	72501
Holly Island	72461
Holly Ridge	71640

	ZIP
Holly Springs (Dallas County)	71763
Holly Springs (White County)	72143
Hollywood	71923
Holman	72846
Holub	72360
Homan	75502
Homewood	72025
Hon	72958
Hooker	72450
Hope	71801
Hopeville	71766
Hopewell (Cleburne County)	72137
Hopewell (Greene County)	72443
Hopewell (Lawrence County)	72433
Hopper	71935
Horatio	71842
Horseshoe	72112
Horseshoe Bend	72512
Horseshoe Lake (Crittenden County)	72348
Horseshoe Lake (Woodruff County)	72006
Horton	72326
Hot Springs Mall (Part of Hot Springs National Park)	71901
Hot Springs National Park	71901-14
For specific Hot Springs National Park Zip Codes call (501) 623-7704	
Hot Springs Village	71909
Hot Springs Village (census designated place)	71901
Houston	72070
Howell	72071
Hoxie	72433
Hudspeth	71638
Huff	72501
Huffman	72315
Hughes	72348
Hulbert (Part of West Memphis)	72301
Humnoke	72072
Humphrey	72073
Hunt	72844
Hunter	72074
Huntington	72940
Huntsville	72740
Hurricane Grove	71957
Hutchinson	72534
Huttig	71747
Hydrick	72324
Ida	72546
Imboden	72434
Immanuel	72003
Index	75502
Indian Bay	72069
Indiandale (Part of Hot Springs National Park)	71901
Indianhead Lake Estates (Part of North Little Rock)	72116
Indian Meadows	65733
Indian Springs	72002
Industrial (Part of Little Rock)	72209
Ingalls	71647
Ingleside	72112
Ingram	72478
Ink	71953
Ione	72927
Iron Springs	72206
Island Town	72112
Iuka	72519
Ivan	71748
Ivesville	72207
Ivy	71725
Jabb	72046
Jackson Heights (Part of Jacksonville)	72076
Jacksonport	72075
Jacksonville	72076
Jamestown (Independence County)	72501
Jamestown (Johnson County)	72830
Japton	72740
Jarrett	72444
Jasmine	72060
Jasper	72641
Jefferson	72079
Jefferson Square (Part of Pine Bluff)	71601
Jeffersonville	72360
Jeffrey	72118
Jennette	72327
Jennie	71649
Jenny Lind	72916

	ZIP
Jenson	72937
Jericho	72327
Jerome	71650
Jersey	71651
Jerusalem	72080
Jessieville	71949
Jesup	72466
Joan	71923
Johnson	72741
Johnson Addition	72411
Johnstown	72112
Johnsville	71647
Joiner	72350
Jolliff Store	72442
Jonesboro	72401-03
For specific Jonesboro Zip Codes call (501) 972-8400	
Jones Mill	72105
Jonesville	71837
Jonquil	72346
Joplin	71957
Jordan	72519
Joy	72143
Joyce City	71762
Joyland Park	72927
Judd Hill	72472
Judsonia	72081
Julius	72327
Jumbo	72556
Junction City	71749
Kansas	71772
Kearney	72132
Kedron	71665
Keiser	72351
Kellum	71832
Kelso	71674
Kenova	71762
Kensett	72082
Kent	71701
Kentucky	72015
Kenwood	72823
Keo	72083
Kerlin	71753
Kerr	72142
Kibler	72956
Kimberley	71958
Kindall	72374
King	71841
Kingsland	71652
Kingston (Madison County)	72742
Kingston (Yell County)	72853
Kingswood Estates	72653
Kingtown	72366
Kirby	71950
Kirkland	71751
Knob	72436
Knobel	72435
Knoxville	72845
Koch Ridge	72031
Lacey	71655
Laconia	72379
LaCrosse	72584
Ladd	71601
Ladelle	71655
Lafe	72436
Lafferty	72561
La Grange	72352
Lake Bull Shoales Estates	72687
Lake Catherine	71901
Lake City	72437
Lake Dick	72004
Lake Elmdale	72764
Lake Francis	72761
Lake Hamilton	71913
Lake Poinsett	72432
Lakeport	71653
Lakeside (Garland County)	71901
Lakeside (Ouachita County)	71701
Lakeside Country Club	72065
Lakeside Terrace	72653
Lakeview (Baxter County)	72642
Lakeview (Conway County)	72110
Lake View (Craighead County)	72437
Lake View (Phillips County)	72342
Lakeview Estates	71970
Lake Village	71653
Lakeway	72687
Lakewood (Jefferson County)	72004
Lakewood (Pulaski County)	72116
Lakewood Estates	75501
Lamar	72846
Lamartine	71770
Lambert	71929
Lambrook	72353
Landers	72472
Landis	72650
Laneburg	71844
Langford	72004
Langley	71952

	ZIP
Lanieve	72416
Lansing	72327
Lanty	72063
Lapile	71765
La Plaza Acres	72143
Larkin	72584
Larue	72756
Latour	72355
Lauratown	72433
Lavaca	72941
Lawson	71750
Lazy Acres	65733
Leachville	72438
Lead Hill	72644
Lebanon	71846
Lee Creek	72934
Lehi	72364
Leitner (Part of Pine Bluff)	71601
Leola	72084
Leonard	72461
Lepanto	72354
Leslie	72645
Lester	72437
Letona	72085
Levy (Part of North Little Rock)	72118
Lewisville	71845
Lexa	72355
Lexington	72031
Liberty	72835
Liberty Hall	72834
Liberty Valley	72010
Lick Mountain	72027
Light	72439
Limedale	72501
Limestone	72628
Lincoln	72744
Linder	72058
Lisbon	71730
Little Bay	71766
Little Flock	72756
Little Garnett	71667
Little Italy	72016
Little Red	72121
Little River	72442
Little River Country Club	71866
Little Rock	72201-31
For specific Little Rock Zip Codes call (501) 375-8148	
Little Rock Air Force Base	72099
Locke	72946
Lockesburg	71846
Locust Bayou	71701
Locust Grove	72550
Lodge Corner	72160
Lodi	71943
Logan	72761
Lollie	72106
London	72847
Lonelm	72947
Lone Pine	72650
Lono	72084
Lonoke	72086
Lonsdale	72087
Lookout (Benton County)	72756
Lookout (Monroe County)	72134
Lorado	72401
Lorine	72455
Lost Bridge Village	72732
Lost Cane	72442
Lost Corner	72080
Louann	71751
Louise	72376
Lowell	72745
Lower Boydsville	72461
Lower Poplar Ridge	72414
Lower White Oak Lake	71726
Low Gap	72641
Luber	72560
Lucas	72927
Ludwig	72830
Lumber	71770
Luna	71653
Lundell	72367
Lunenburg	72556
Lunsford	72437
Lurton	72856
Lutherville	72846
Luxora	72358
Lynch (Part of North Little Rock)	72117
Lynn	72440
Mabelvale (Part of Little Rock)	72103
McAlmont	72117
McArthur	71654
McBrides	65733
McCain Mall (Part of North Little Rock)	72116
McCaskill	71847
McClelland	72006

	ZIP
McCormick	72472
McCreanor	72024
McCrory	72101
McDonald	72373
McDougal	72441
Macedonia (Columbia County)	71753
Macedonia (Conway County)	72063
McElroy	72396
McEntre	72476
Macey	72447
McFadden	72347
McGehee	71654
McGintytown	72058
McGregor	72036
McHue	72501
McJester	72121
McKamie	71860
Macks	72112
McMilan Corner	71653
McNab	71838
McNeil	71752
McNutt	72476
Macon	72076
Macon Lake	71653
McRae	72102
Madding	72004
Madison	72359
Magazine	72943
Magic Springs	72650
Magness	72553
Magnet Cove	72104
Magnolia	71753
Main Street (Part of North Little Rock)	72119
Mallet Town	72157
Mallory Spur	72348
Malvern	72104
Mammoth Spring	72554
Mandalay	72442
Mandeville	75501
Manfred	71935
Mangrum	72414
Manila	72442
Manning	71763
Mansfield	72944
Many Island	72554
Maple	72616
Maple Corner	72374
Maple Grove	72472
Maple Springs	72571
Marble	72740
Marcella	72555
Marche	72118
Marc Lyn Estates	72687
Marianna	72360
Marie	72395
Marion	72364
Marked Tree	72365
Marmaduke	72443
Marsden	71647
Marsena	72650
Marshall	72650
Mars Hill	71860
Martindale	72204
Martinville	72204
Marvell	72366
Marvinville	72842
Marysville	71753
Mason Valley	72712
Masonville	71654
Massard (Part of Fort Smith)	72901
Maumee	72675
Maumelle	72113
Maxville	72521
Mayfield	72703
Mayflower	72106
Maynard	72444
Maysville	72747
Mazarn	71933
Meadow Cliff	72335
Meeks Settlement	71962
Melbourne	72556
Mellwood	72367
Melrose	72550
Mena	71953
Menifee	72107
Meridian	71635
Meroney	71643
Merrivale (Part of Little Rock)	72209
Mesa	72041
Metalton	72601
Middlebrook	72444
Middleton	72027
Midland	72945
Midland (Part of Ft. Smith)	72904
Midway (Baxter County)	72651
Midway (Hot Spring County)	71941
Midway (Howard County)	71852

	ZIP
Midway (Jackson County)	72479
Midway (Lafayette County)	71845
Midway (Logan County)	72865
Midway (Nevada County)	71857
Midway (White County)	72568
Midway Corner	72376
Milford	71846
Mill Creek (Pope County)	72801
Mill Creek (Sebastian County)	72901
Mill Creek Estates	72687
Milligan Ridge	72442
Milltown	72936
Milo	71646
Mimosa Circle	72513
Mineral	72841
Mineral Springs	71851
Minorca	72444
Minturn	72445
Mist	71646
Mitchell	72583
Mitchellville	71639
Mixon	72927
Moark	72422
Mohawk	71740
Moko	72557
Monarch	72687
Monette	72447
Monkey Run	72635
Monnie Springs	72135
Monroe	72108
Montana	72840
Monte Ne Shores	72756
Monterey	72373
Monticello	71655
Montongo	71655
Montreal	72940
Montrose	71658
Moore	72856
Moore Camp	71822
Moorefield	72501
Moreland	72801
Morgan	72118
Morganton	72013
Morning Star (Garland County)	71901
Morning Star (Searcy County)	72650
Morning Sun	72143
Moro	72368
Morobay	71651
Morrilton	72110
Morris	71828
Morrison Bluff	72863
Morriston	72576
Morrow	72749
Morton	72101
Mosby	72328
Moscow	71659
Mosley	72834
Mossville	72641
Mounds (Crittenden County)	72376
Mounds (Greene County)	72461
Mountainburg	72946
Mountain Crest	72727
Mountain Fork	71953
Mountain Harbor	71957
Mountain Home	72653
Mountain Pine	71956
Mountain Springs	72023
Mountain Top	72949
Mountain Valley	71901
Mountain View	72560
Mount Elba	71660
Mount Elba Edition	71665
Mount Gayler	72959
Mount George	72833
Mount Hersey	72685
Mount Holly	71758
Mount Ida	71957
Mount Judea	72655
Mount Moriah	71958
Mount Olive (Bradley County)	71647
Mount Olive (Conway County)	72127
Mount Olive (Izard County)	72556
Mount Olive (Washington County)	72727
Mount Pisgah	72143
Mount Pleasant (Izard County)	72561
Mount Pleasant (Miller County)	75502
Mount Sherman	72641
Mount Tabor	71956
Mount Vernon (Faulkner County)	72111
Mount Vernon (Johnson County)	72840
Mozart	72051

	ZIP
Muddyfork	71852
Mulberry	72947
Mull	72687
Murfreesboro	71958
Murphys Corner	72112
Mustin Lake	71701
Myron	72513
Nady	72166
Nail	72628
Nance	72087
Nashville	71852
Nathan	71852
Natural Dam	72948
Natural Steps	72135
Naylor	72173
Neal Springs	71842
Nebo	71667
Needham	72437
Needmore	72958
Nella	71953
Nelsonville	72466
Nettleton (Part of Jonesboro)	72401
Neuhardt	72376
Newark	72562
New Augusta (Part of Augusta)	72006
New Blaine	72851
Newburg	72556
New Dixie	72016
New Edinburg	71660
Newell	71730
New Gascony	72004
New Hope (Dallas County)	71763
New Hope (Drew County)	71655
New Hope (Hempstead County)	71801
New Hope (Independence County)	72501
Newhope (Pike County)	71959
New Hope (Pope County)	72801
New London	71765
Newnata	72657
Newport	72112
New Spadra	72830
New Summit (Part of Benton)	72011
New Town (Crawford County)	72921
Newtown (Jefferson County)	72004
Nimmo	72143
Nimmons	72461
Nimrod	72126
Nine Elms	72761
Noble Lake	71601
Nodena	72395
Noland	72455
Norfolk Lake Estates	72544
Norfork	72658
Norfork Village	72658
Norman	71960
Norphlet	71759
Norristown (Part of Russellville)	72801
North Bingen	71852
North Cedar (Part of Pine Bluff)	71601
North Crossett	71635
North Dardanelle	72801
Northern Ohio	72365
North Heights (Part of Texarkana)	75502
North Hughes	72348
North Little Rock	72113-20
For specific North Little Rock Zip Codes call (501) 758-1707	
Northpoint	72135
Northwest Arkansas Mall (Part of Fayetteville)	72701
Norvell (Part of Earle)	72331
Nuckles	72020
Number Nine	72315
Nunley	71953
Oak Bower	71929
Oak Forest (Lee County)	72360
Oak Forest (Pulaski County)	72201
Oak Grove (Carroll County)	72660
Oak Grove (Clark County)	71728
Oak Grove (Hot Spring County)	72104
Oak Grove (Little River County)	71822
Oak Grove (Lonoke County)	72007
Oak Grove (Nevada County)	71858
Oak Grove (Perry County)	72070
Oak Grove (Pope County)	72801
Oak Grove (Pulaski County)	72118
Oak Grove (Sevier County)	71846

	ZIP
Oak Grove (Washington County)	72764
Oak Grove Heights	72450
Oakhaven	71801
Oak Hill	71822
Oakland	72661
Oaklawn (Part of Hot Springs National Park)	71901
Oak Park (Part of Pine Bluff)	71603
Oark	72852
Oden	71961
O'Donnell Bend	72358
Ogden	71853
Ogemaw	71764
Oil Trough	72564
O'Kean	72449
Okolona	71962
Ola	72853
Old Alabam	72740
Old Austin	72007
Old Grand Glaise	72020
Old Hickory	72063
Old Jenny Lind	72901
Old Joe	72658
Old Town	72389
Old Union	71730
Old Weona	72472
Olio	72958
Oliver	72958
Olmstead	72116
Olvey	72601
Olyphant	72020
Oma	71964
Omaha	72662
Omega (Carroll County)	72616
Omega (Yell County)	72834
Onda	72774
One Horse Store	72160
Oneida	72369
Onia	72663
Onyx	72857
Opal (Polk County)	71953
Opal (White County)	72012
Oppelo	72110
Optimus	72519
Orion	72132
Orlando	71660
Osage	72638
Osage Mills	72712
Osage Village	72531
Osceola	72370
Ott	65626
Otto	72173
Otwell	72401
Ouachita	71763
Ouachita College (Part of Arkadelphia)	71923
Overcup (Conway County)	72110
Overcup (Woodruff County)	72101
Owensville	72087
Oxford	72565
Oxley	72645
Ozan	71855
Ozark	72949
Ozark Acres (Baxter County)	72635
Ozark Acres (Sharp County)	72482
Ozark Lithia	71901
Ozone	72854
Pace City	71751
Palestine	72372
Palmyra	71667
Pangburn	72121
Pankey (Part of Little Rock)	72212
Panther Forest	71653
Paradise Landing	72106
Paragould	72450-51
For specific Paragould Zip Codes call (501) 236-7636	
Paraloma	71846
Paris	72855
Parkdale	71661
Parkers	72206
Parkers Chapel	71730
Parkers-Iron Springs	72206
Park Grove	72029
Park Hill (Part of North Little Rock)	72116
Parkin	72373
Park Place	72320
Park Plaza (Part of Little Rock)	72205
Parks	72950
Parma	72044
Parmenter Addition	72315
Parnell	72023
Paron	72122
Parthenon	72666
Pastoria	72152
Patmos	71801
Patrick	72727

	ZIP
Patsville	71647
Patterson	72123
Pawheen	72438
Payneway	72472
Peach Orchard	72453
Pearcy	71964
Pea Ridge (Benton County)	72751
Pea Ridge (Desha County)	71674
Pearson	72131
Pecan Point	72350
Peel	72668
Pelsor	72856
Pencil Bluff	71965
Pendleton	71639
Penjur	72348
Pennington	72005
Pennys	71846
Penrose	72101
Peppers Landing	72041
Perla	72104
Perry	72125
Perrytown	71801
Perryville	72126
Peter Pender	72933
Peter Rock Acres	72031
Pettigrew	72752
Pettus	72086
Pettyville	72442
Pfeiffer	72501
Philadelphia	72401
Philander Smith College (Part of Little Rock)	72202
Phillips Bayou	72360
Phoenix Village (Part of Fort Smith)	72901
Pickens (Desha County)	71662
Pickens (White County)	72143
Pickering	71730
Piercetown	72641
Piggott	72454
Pike City	71958
Pilgrims Rest	72764
Pindall	72669
Pine Bluff	71601-13
For specific Pine Bluff Zip Codes call (501) 536-3535	
Pine Bluff Arsenal	71602
Pine Bluff Southeast (Part of Pine Bluff)	71601
Pine City	72069
Pine Grove	71763
Pine Grove Valley	72944
Pine Ridge	71966
Pine Tree	72326
Pineville	72566
Piney (Garland County)	71913
Piney (Johnson County)	72847
Piney Grove	71845
Pinnacle	72135
Pisgah (Pike County)	71940
Pisgah (Yell County)	72834
Pitman	72444
Pitts	72421
Plainfield	71740
Plainview (White County)	72081
Plainview (Yell County)	72857
Plant	72031
Pleasant Grove (Craighead County)	72401
Pleasant Grove (Stone County)	72567
Pleasant Grove (Van Buren County)	72030
Pleasant Hill (Crawford County)	72947
Pleasant Hill (Cross County)	72396
Pleasant Hill (Garland County)	71901
Pleasant Hill (Nevada County)	71857
Pleasant Plains	72568
Pleasant Ridge	72632
Pleasant Valley (Carroll County)	72616
Pleasant Valley (Faulkner County)	72058
Pleasant Valley (Izard County)	72519
Pleasant Valley (Lafayette County)	71826
Pleasant Valley (Perry County)	72016
Pleasant Valley (Pope County)	72837
Pleasant View (Conway County)	72110
Pleasant View (Franklin County)	72949
Pleasure Heights	72745
Plumerville	72127
Plunketts	72017

	ZIP		ZIP		ZIP
Pocahontas	72455	Rob Roy	72004	Sellers Store	72542
Point Cedar	71921	Rock Hill	71846	Selma	71670
Pollard	72456	Rockport	72104	Seyppel	72348
Ponca	72670	Rock Springs	71675	Shady	71953
Ponders	72476	Rockwell (Garland County)	71901	Shady Grove (Faulkner	
Pontoon	72025	Rockwell (Garland County)	71913	County)	72058
Poplar Grove	72374	Rocky	71953	Shady Grove (Fulton	
Portia	72457	Rocky Hill	72629	County)	72583
Portland	71663	Rocky Mound (Hempstead		Shady Grove (Johnson	
Posey	72392	County)	71801	County)	72830
Possum Grape	72020	Rocky Mound (Miller		Shady Grove (Mississippi	
Postelle	72366	County)	71837	County)	72442
Post Oak	71658	Rodney	72519	Shady Grove (Nevada	
Potter	71953	Roe	72134	County)	71857
Potter Junction	71953	Rogers	72756-57	Shady Grove (Poinsett	
Pottsville	72858	For specific Rogers Zip Codes call		County)	72472
Poughkeepsie	72569	(501) 636-3301		Shakertown	71923
Powhatan	72458	Rogers Avenue (Part of Fort		Shannon	72455
Poyen	72128	Smith)	72903	Shannondale	72348
Prairie Creek	72756	Rohwer	71666	Shannon Hills	72103
Prairie Grove	72753	Roland	72135	Shannonville	72331
Prairie View	72863	Rolla	72104	Sharman	71860
Prattsville	72129	Romance	72136	Sharum	72455
Prescott	71857	Rondo (Lee County)	72355	Shaw	72015
Preston	72032	Rondo (Miller County)	75502	Shearerville	72346
Preston Ferry	72134	Rosa	72358	Shelbyville	72521
Price Place	65729	Rosboro	71921	Shell Lake	72346
Prim	72130	Rose Bud	72137	Sheppard	71838
Princedale	72373	Rose City (Part of North		Sheridan	72150
Princeton	71725	Little Rock)	72117	Sherrill	72152
Process City	71832	Rose Hill	71655	Sherwood	72120
Proctor	72376	Roseland	72442	Sherwood Hills	72105
Promised Land (Mississippi		Rose Meadow (Part of Little		Shiloh (Howard County)	71851
County)	72315	Rock)	72206	Shiloh (Pope County)	72801
Promised Land (Poinsett		Roseville	72949	Shippen	72351
County)	72472	Rosie	72571	Shirley	72153
Providence	72081	Ross	72846	Shoffner	72112
Provo	71846	Rosston	71858	Shover Springs	71801
Pruitt	72648	Ross Van-Ness	71640	Sidney	72577
Pumpkin Bend	72101	Rotan	72370	Sidon	72137
Pyatt	72672	Round Pond	72378	Signal Hill	72560
Quarry Heights	72826	Rover	72860	Siloam Springs	72761
Quinn	71730	Rowell	71665	Silver	71957
Quitman	72131	Roy	71852	Silver Hill	72675
Raggio	72320	Royal	71968	Silver Ridge (Cleburne	
Ragtown	72069	Royal Oak	72103	County)	72530
Rainbow Island	72121	Rubicon	72015	Silver Ridge (Sevier County)	71846
Ralph	72687	Ruddell Hill	72501	Sims	71969
Rambo Riveria	72756	Rudy	72952	Simsboro	72348
Ramsey	71742	Rule	72638	Sitka	72482
Ramsey Hill	72501	Rumley	72645	Skunkhollow	72032
Ranger	72824	Runyan Acres	72120	Slaytonville	72937
Ratcliff	72951	Rupert	72031	Slonikers Mill	72372
Ratio	72333	Rushing	72051	Slovak	72160
Ravanna	75556	Russell	72139	Smackover	71762
Ravenden	72459	Russellville	72801	Smale	72021
Ravenden Springs	72460	Rutherford	72501	Smearney	71647
Rawlison	72348	Rye	71665	Smithdale	72373
Ray Lee Addition	72801	Sacred Heart	72840	Smiths Corner	72368
Reader	71726	Saddle	72554	Smithville (Lawrence	
Readland	71640	Saffell	72572	County)	72466
Rea Valley	72634	Sage	72573	Smithville (Miller County)	71834
Rector	72461	Saginaw	71941	Snow	72687
Redfield	72132	St. Charles	72140	Snowball	72650
Redland	71857	St. Francis	72464	Snow Hill	71751
Red Leaf	71653	St. Joe	72675	Snow Lake	72379
Red Onion	72447	St. Matthews	71752	Snyder	71658
Red Springs	71743	St. Paul	72760	Social Hill	72104
Red Star	72752	St. Vincent	72063	Solgohachia	72156
Red Wing	71832	Salado	72575	Sonora	72764
Reed	71670	Salem (Fulton County)	72576	South Bend	72076
Reedville	71639	Salem (Lee County)	72368	South Crossett (Part of	
Relfs Bluff	71667	Salem (Pike County)	71943	Crossett)	71635
Remmel	72112	Salem (Saline County)	72015	Southern Hills	72601
Rena	72956	Salesville	72653	Southern State College (Part	
Republican	72058	Saltillo	72032	of Magnolia)	71753
Revel	72006	Salus	72854	South Fort Smith (Part of	
Rex	72031	Sand Hill	72040	Fort Smith)	72906
Reydell	72133	Sandtown	72501	South Jacksonville (Part of	
Reyno	72462	Sandy Bend	71765	Jacksonville)	72076
Rich	72021	Sandyland	71762	Southland (Craighead	
Richardson	72004	Sandy Ridge	72315	County)	72437
Richland View	72727	Sans Souci	72370	Southland (Phillips County)	72355
Richmond	71822	Sarassa	71644	South Lead Hill	72644
Richwood	72476	Saratoga	71859	South Lewisville	71845
Richwoods	71923	Sardis	72011	South Ozark	72949
Ridgeway	72601	Savoy	72703	South Sheridan	72150
Rio Vista	72010	Schaal	71851	South Shore Park	72543
Risher	72421	Schaberg	72946	South Side (Independence	
Rison	71665	Schooley	71851	County)	72501
Rivercliff Estates	72756	Schug	72450	South Side (Pulaski County)	72206
Riverdale	72941	Scotland	72141	Southside (Van Buren	
River Mountain	72835	Scott	72142	County)	72013
Riverside	72101	Scottsville	72837	Spadra	72830
Rivervale	72377	Scott Valley	72360	Sparkman	71763
Riverview	72110	Scranton	72863	Spence Junction	72856
Riverview Addition	72501	Screeton	72064	Spirit Lake	71845
Rixey (Part of North Little		Searcy	72143	Springdale	72762-66
Rock)	72117	Seaton	72046	For specific Springdale Zip Codes	
Robertsville	72063	Seaton Dump	72046	call (501) 751-4441	
Robinson	72761	Sedgwick	72465	Springfield	72157

	ZIP		ZIP		ZIP
West Ridge	72391	Willow	72084	Woodlawn (Cleveland	
Westville	72956	Wilmar	71675	County)	71665
Westwood (Part of Little		Wilmot	71676	Woodlawn (Lonoke County)	72007
Rock)	72201	Wilson (Mississippi County)	72395	Woodrow	72130
Wharton	72740	Wilson (Pope County)	72823	Woodson	72180
Wheatley	72392	Wilton	71865	Wooster	72181
Wheeler	72775	Winchester	71677	Worden	72010
Wheeling	72576	Windamere (Part of Little		Wright	72182
Whelen Springs	71772	Rock)	72201	Wrights Corner	72010
Whispering Springs	72067	Winesburg	72401	Wrightsville	72183
Whistleville	72442	Winfield	72958	Wrightsville Unit	72183
Whitaker	72432	Winfrey	72959	Wycamp	72390
White	71635	Wing	72860	Wye	72016
White Cliffs	71846	Winslow	72959	Wyman	72701
White Hall (Drew County)	71655	Winston Terrace (Part of		Wynne	72396-97
White Hall (Jefferson		Little Rock)	72201	For specific Wynne Zip Codes call	
County)	71602	Winthrop	71866	(501) 238-2131	
Whitehall (Lee County)	72320	Wirth	72554	Wyola	72959
Whitehall (Poinsett County)	72432	Wiseman	72587	Yale	72752
Whiteoak	72949	Witcherville	72940	Yancopin	71674
White Oak Bluff	71665	Witherspoon	71923	Yancy	71855
White Rock	72701	Witter	72776	Yarbro	72315
Whitetown	71961	Wittsburg	72396	Yardelle	72685
Whiteville	72635	Witts Springs	72686	Y City	72926
Whitmore	72394	Wiville	72101	Yellow Bayou	71653
Whitton	72386	Wolf Bayou	72530	Yellville	72687
Wickes	71973	Wonderview	72063	Yocana	71953
Wideman	72585	Woodberry	71744	Yoestown	72921
Widener	72394	Woodland	72830	Yorktown	71678
Wiederkehr Village	72821	Woodland Corner	72315	Zachery	72366
Wilburn	72179	Woodland Heights (Part of		Zent	72021
Wild Cherry	72576	Little Rock)	72201	Zinc	72601
Wildwood	72346	Woodland Hills (Fulton		Zion	72556
Williamson	71842	County)	72542	Zion Hill	72110
Williford	72482	Woodland Hills (Saline			
Willisville	71864	County)	72002		

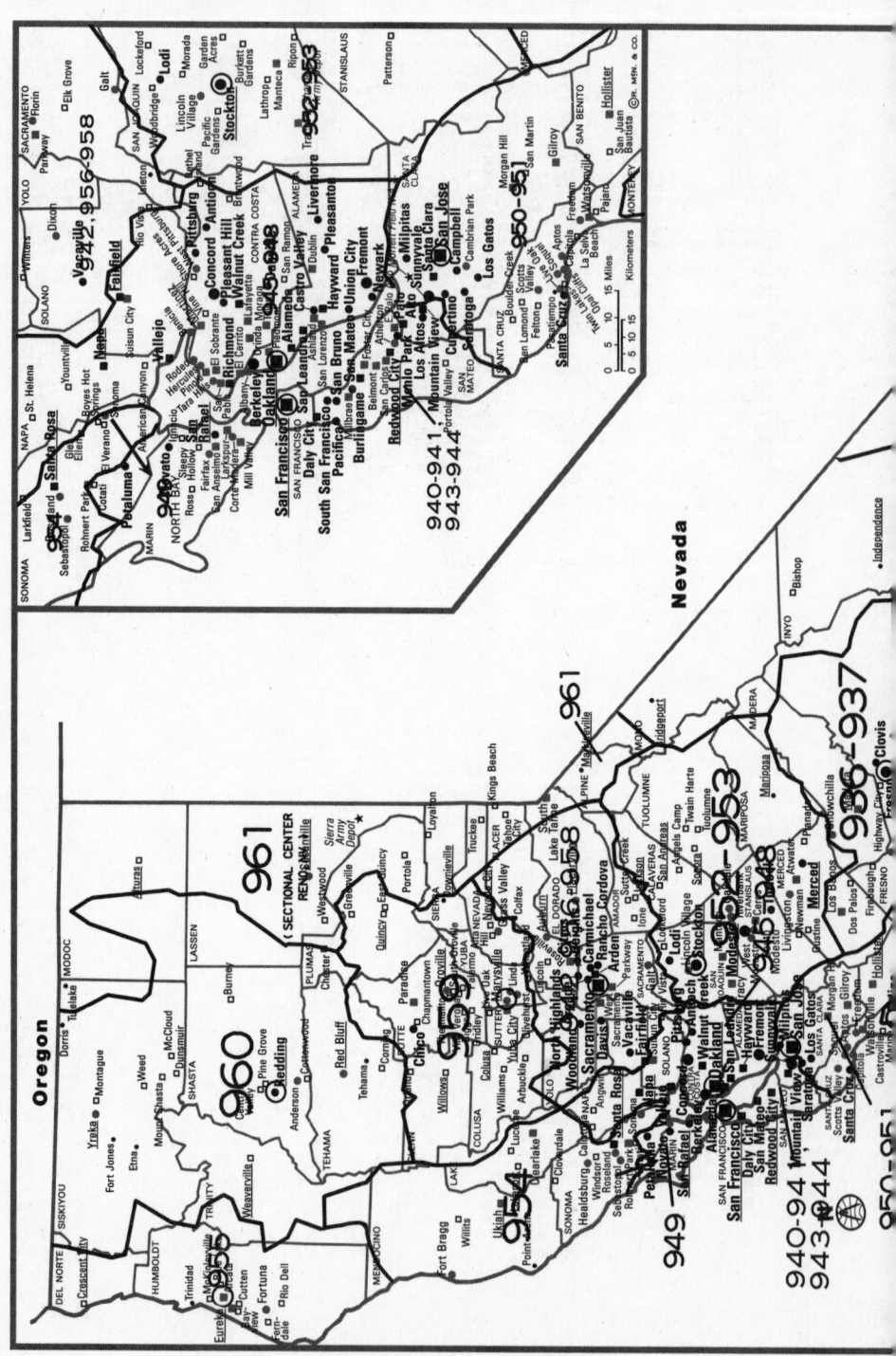

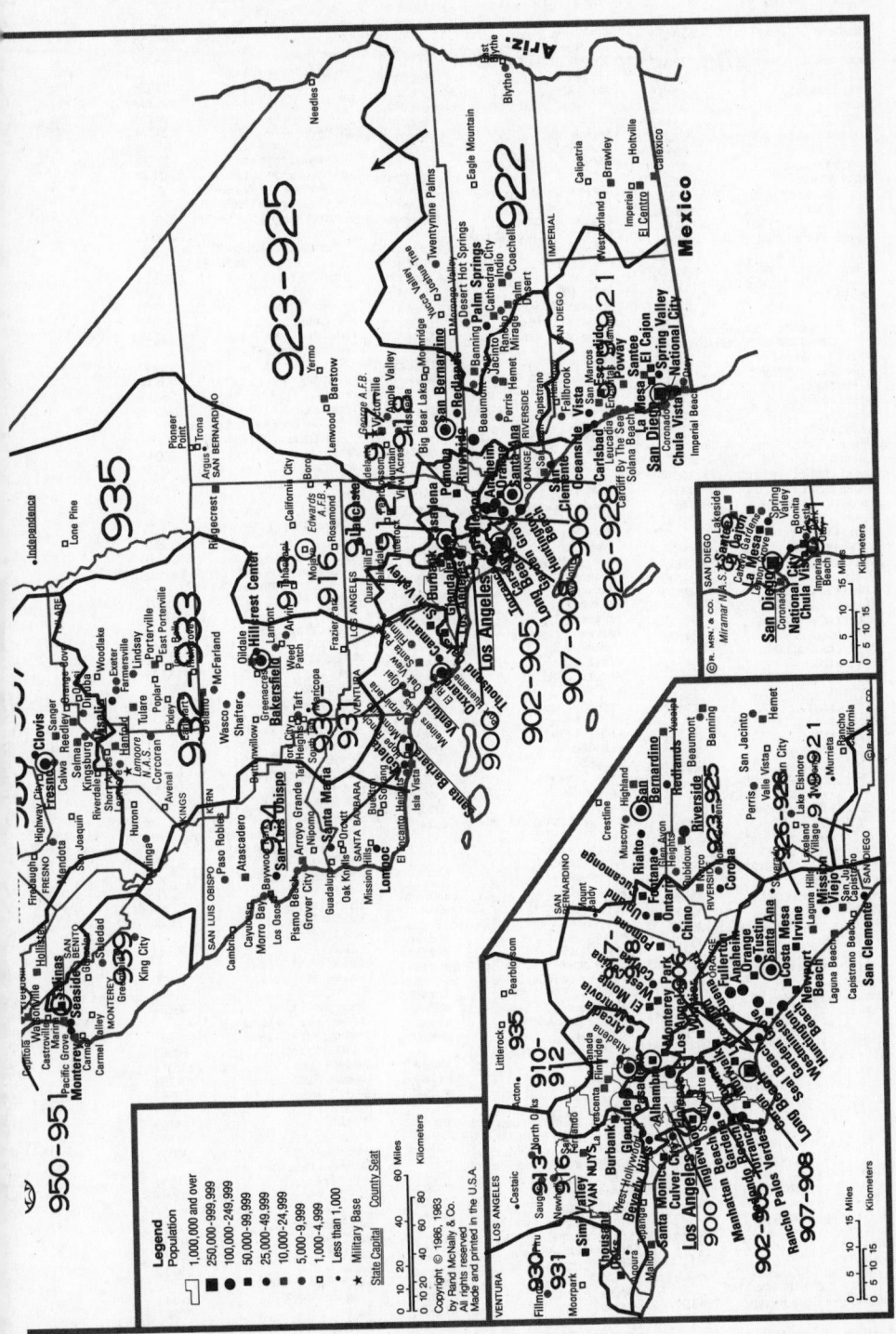

	ZIP
A	91976
Abalone Cove (Part of Rancho Palos Verdes)	90274
Aberdeen	93526
Academy	93612
Acampo	95220
Acasia Acres	93277
Actis Gardens	93501
Acton	93510
Adelaida	93446
Adelanto	92301
Adin	96006
Adobe Corners	92392
Aerial Acres	93523
Aetna Springs	94567
Afton	95920
Ager	96064
Agnew (Part of Santa Clara)	95054
	95056

For specific Agnew Zip Codes call (408) 452-4300

	ZIP
Agoura Hills	91301
	91376

For specific Agoura Hills Zip Codes call (818) 889-0266

	ZIP
Agua Caliente	95476
Agua Caliente Indian Reservation	92262
Agua Dulce	91350
Aguanga	92536
Ahwahnee	93601
Airbase (Part of Santa Maria)	93454
Airport (Part of Oakland)	94614
Alabama Hills	93545
Alameda	94501
Alamo	94507
Alamo Oaks (Part of Danville)	94526
Alamorio	92227
Albany	94706
Alberhill	92530
Albion	95410
Alcatraz (Part of San Francisco)	94123
Alderbrook Tract (Part of Cupertino)	95014
Aldercroft Heights	95030
Alderpoint	95511
Alder Springs	93602
Alessandro (Part of Riverside)	92508
Alexander Valley	95441
Alhambra	91801-99

For specific Alhambra Zip Codes call (818) 289-9101

	ZIP
Alhambra General Mail Facility	91897-98

For specific Alhambra General Mail Facility Zip Codes call (818) 289-9101

	ZIP
Alhambra Valley	94553
Alisal (Part of Salinas)	93905
Alleghany	95910
Allendale	95688
Allensworth	93219
Alliance (Part of Arcata)	95521
Almaden Plaza (Part of San Jose)	95118
Almaden Valley (Part of San Jose)	95120
Almanor (Plumas County)	95923
Almanor (Plumas County)	95947
Almondale	93553
Almonte	94941
Alondra	90249
Alpaugh	93201
Alpine	91901
	91903

For specific Alpine Zip Codes call (619) 445-6622

	ZIP
Alpine Heights	91901
Alpine Village (Riverside County)	92262
Alpine Village (Tulare County)	93265
Alta	95701
Altadena	91001-03

For specific Altadena Zip Codes call (818) 794-1147

	ZIP
Alta Heights (Part of Napa)	94558
Alta Hill	95945
Al Tahoe (Part of South Lake Tahoe)	96150
Alta Loma (Part of Cucamonga)	91701

	ZIP
	91737

For specific Alta Loma Zip Codes call (714) 987-3100

	ZIP
Alta Sierra (Kern County)	93285
Alta Sierra (Nevada County)	95949
Altaville (Part of Angels Camp)	95221
Alta Vista	95314
Alto (Part of Mill Valley)	94941
Alton	95540
Alturas	96101
Alum Rock	95127
Alvarado (Part of Union City)	94587
Alviso (Part of San Jose)	95002
Amador City	95601
Amarillo Beach	90265
Ambassador (Part of Los Angeles)	90005
Ambler Park	93901
Amboy	92304
Ambrose	94565
American Canyon	94589
American House	95981
Amphibious Base	92155

	ZIP
Anaheim	92801-25

For specific Anaheim Zip Codes call (714) 520-2600

FINANCIAL INSTITUTIONS

	ZIP
United California Savings Bank	92805

HOTELS/MOTELS

	ZIP
Anaheim Hilton & Towers	92802
Sheraton-Anaheim Hotel	92802
Anaheim Hills (Part of Anaheim)	92808
Anaheim Plaza (Part of Anaheim)	92801
Anchor Bay	95445
Anderson	96007
Anderson Springs	95461
Andrew Jackson (Part of San Diego)	92115
Angels Camp	95222
Angelus Oaks	92305
Angiola	93212
Angwin	94508
Annapolis	95412
Annex III (Part of Los Angeles)	91405
Antelope	95678
Antelope Acres	93534
Antioch	94509
	94531

For specific Antioch Zip Codes call (510) 757-4192

	ZIP
Antonio	93437
Anza	92539
Applegate	95703
Apple Valley	92307-08

For specific Apple Valley Zip Codes call (619) 247-7819

	ZIP
Aptos	95001
	95003

For specific Aptos Zip Codes call (408) 688-3192

	ZIP
Arbolada (Part of Ojai)	93023
Arbuckle	95912
Arcade (Los Angeles County)	90052
Arcade (Sacramento County)	95821
Arcadia	91006-07
	91066
	91077

For specific Arcadia Zip Codes call (818) 446-4678

	ZIP
Arcata	95521
Arch Beach Heights (Part of Laguna Beach)	92651
Arden	95825
Arden-Arcade	95821
Arden Fair Mall (Part of Sacramento)	95815
Arden Town	95825
Ardmore (Part of South Gate)	90280
Arena	95301
Argus	93562
Arleta (Part of Los Angeles)	91331
Arlington (Part of Riverside)	92503
	92513

For specific Arlington Zip Codes call (714) 788-4600

	ZIP
Arlington Heights Estate	95934
Arlynda Corners	95536
Armistead	93527
Armona	93202
Army Point	94510
Army Terminal (Part of Oakland)	94626
Arnold	95223
Arnold Heights	92508
Aromas	95004
Arrowbear Lake	92382
Arrowhead Highlands	92325
Arroyo Grande	93420-21

For specific Arroyo Grande Zip Codes call (805) 489-5923

	ZIP
Arroyo Vista (Part of Dublin)	94566
Artesia	90701-03

For specific Artesia Zip Codes call (213) 860-6694

	ZIP
Artois	95913
Arvin	93203
Arvin (labor camp)	93308
Ash Creek	96057
Ashland	94541
Asilomar (Part of Pacific Grove)	93950
Aspendell	93514
Asti	95425
Atascadero	93422-23

For specific Atascadero Zip Codes call (805) 466-1103

	ZIP
Athens	90047
Atherton	94027
Athlone	95333
Atlanta	95366
Atwater	95301
Atwood (Part of Placentia)	92601
Auberry	93602
Auburn	95603-04

For specific Auburn Zip Codes call (916) 885-7944

	ZIP
August	95201
Avalon	90704
Avalon Village (Part of Carson)	90744
Avenal	93204
Avery	95224
Avila Beach	93424
Avocado Heights	91746
Azusa	91702
Baden (Part of South San Francisco)	94080
Badger	93603
Bailey (Part of Whittier)	90601
Baker	92309
Baker Ranch	95631
Bakersfield	93301-89

For specific Bakersfield Zip Codes call (805) 861-4346

	ZIP
Bakersfield East	93305
Bakersfield Plaza (Part of Bakersfield)	93308
Bakersfield South	93304
Balance Rock	93260
Balboa (Part of Newport Beach)	92661
Balboa Island (Part of Newport Beach)	92662
Balch Camp	93649
Balderson Station	95634
Baldwin Hills Regional Shopping Mall (Part of Los Angeles)	90067
Baldwin Lake	92314
Baldwin Park	91706
Baldy Mesa	92369
Ballarat	93562
Ballard	93463
Ballico	95303
Balls Ferry	96007
Baltimore Park (Part of Larkspur)	94939
Bandini (Part of Commerce)	90022
Bangor	95914
Bankhead Springs	91934
Banner	92036
Banning	92220
Banta	95304
Barber City (Part of Westminster)	92683
Bard	92222
Bardsdale	93015
Barona	92040
Barona Ranch Indian Reservation	92040
Barrett	91917

	ZIP
Barrington (Part of Los Angeles)	90049
Barron Park (Part of Palo Alto)	94306
Barstow	92311-12
For specific Barstow Zip Codes call (619) 256-8494	
Barstow Colony	93705
Barton (Part of Fresno)	93702
Base Line (Part of San Bernardino)	92410
Bassett	91746
Bassetts	96125
Bass Lake	93604
Batavia	95620
Baxter	95701
Bay (Part of Big Bear Lake)	92315
Bay Fair Mall (Part of San Leandro)	94578
Bayliss	95943
Bayo Vista	94572
Bay Park (Part of San Diego)	92110
Bayshore (Part of Brisbane)	94005
Bayshore Mall (Part of Eureka)	95501
Bayside (Humboldt County)	95524
Bayside (Santa Clara County)	95131
	95134
	95164
For specific Bayside Zip Codes call (707) 822-1683	
Bayview (Humboldt County)	95503
Bay View (San Francisco County)	94124
Bayview Park (Contra Costa County)	94806
Bay View Park (Monterey County)	93955
Baywood-Los Osos	93402
Baywood Park	93402
Beach Center (Part of Huntington Beach)	92648
Beale Air Force Base	95903
Beale West	95903
Bear Creek	95340
Bear River	95603
Bear River Lake	95666
Bear River Pines	95945
Bear Valley (Alpine County)	95223
Bear Valley (Mariposa County)	95338
Beaumont	92223
Beckwourth	96129
Bee Rock	93426
Bel Aire Estates (Part of Tiburon)	94920
Belden	95915
Bell	90201
Bella Vista (Contra Costa County)	94565
Bella Vista (Kern County)	93240
Bella Vista (Los Angeles County)	90022
Bella Vista (Shasta County)	96008
Belle Haven (Part of Menlo Park)	94025
Belleview	95370
Bellflower	90706-07
For specific Bellflower Zip Codes call (213) 866-1775	
Bell Gardens	90201
Bell Mountain	92392
Belltown	92509
Bellview (Part of Rio Dell)	95562
Bel Marin Keys	94947
Belmont	94002
Belridge Farms	93251
Belvedere (Los Angeles County)	90022
Belvedere (Marin County)	94920
Belvedere Gardens	90022
Belvedere-Tiburon (Part of Belvedere)	94920
Belvernon Gardens (Part of Tiburon)	94920
Benbow	95542
Bend	96080
Ben Hur	93653
Benicia	94510
Ben Lomond	95005
Benton	93512
Berenda	93637
Berkeley	94701-05

	ZIP
	94707-20
For specific Berkeley Zip Codes call (415) 649-3100	
Berkeley Highlands	94707
Bernal (Part of San Francisco)	94110
Berry Creek	95916
Berryessa (Part of San Jose)	95132
Berryessa Park	94558
Berry Hill Estates (Part of Rancho Palos Verdes)	90274
Berteleda	95531
Bertsch Terrace	95531
Bethany Park (Part of Scotts Valley)	95066
Bethel Island	94511
Betteravia	93454
Beverly Center (Part of Los Angeles)	90048
Beverly Hills	90209-13
For specific Beverly Hills Zip Codes call (213) 247-3400	
Bicentennial (Part of Los Angeles)	90048
Bieber	96009
Big Bar	96010
Big Basin	95006
Big Bear City	92314
Big Bear Highlands	92386
Big Bear Lake	92315
Big Bend	96011
Big Chief	96161
Big Creek	93605
Big Flat	96091
Biggs	95917
Big Lagoon Park	95570
Big Meadows	95223
Big Oak Flat	95305
Big Pine	93513
Big Pine Indian Reservation	93513
Big River	92242
Big Springs	96064
Big Sur	93920
Big Trees	95018
Bijou (Part of South Lake Tahoe)	96156
Bijou Park (Part of South Lake Tahoe)	96150
Binghamton	95620
Biola	93606
Birch Hill	92060
Birch Meadow Acres	95945
Birdcage Walk	95610
Bird Rock (Part of San Diego)	92037
Birds Landing	94512
Bishop	93514-15
For specific Bishop Zip Codes call (619) 873-3526	
Bishop Acres	93263
Bishop Indian Reservation	93514
Bitterwater	93930
Bixby (Part of Long Beach)	90807
Black Meadow Landing	92267
Black Point	94947
Blackrock	93526
Blackstone (Part of Fresno)	93710
Blackwells Corner	93249
Blairsden	96103
Blanco	93901
Blocksburg	95514
Bloomfield	94952
Bloomfield Acres (Part of Arcata)	95521
Bloomington	92316
Blossom Hill (Part of San Jose)	95123
Blossom Valley (Part of Mountain View)	94040
Blue Canon	95715
Blue Hills (Part of Saratoga)	95070
Blue Jay	92317
Blue Lake	95525
Bluff Creek	95546
Blythe	92225-26
For specific Blythe Zip Codes call (619) 922-6157	
Bodega	94922
Bodega Bay	94923
Bodfish	93205
Bohemia	95945
Bolinas	94924
Bolsa (Part of Westminster)	92683
Bolsa Knolls	93901
Bombay Beach	92257
Bonadelle Ranchos	93637

	ZIP
Bonadelle Ranchos-Madera Ranchos	93637
Bonds Corner	92250
Bonita (Madera County)	93637
Bonita (San Diego County)	91902
	91908
For specific Bonita Zip Codes call (619) 475-4324	
Bonnie Bell	92282
Bonny Doon	95060
Bonnyview (Part of Redding)	96001
Bonsall	92003
Boonville	95415
Bootjack	95338
Boron	93516
	93596
For specific Boron Zip Codes call (619) 762-5313	
Borosolvay	93562
Borrego Springs	92004
Borrego Wells	92004
Bostonia	92021
Boston Ravine (Part of Grass Valley)	95945
Boulder Creek	95006
Boulder Oaks	91962
Boulder Park	91934
Boulevard	91905
Bouquet Canyon (Part of Santa Clarita)	91350
Bowling Green	95815
Bowman	95604
Box Springs	92507
Boyes Hot Springs	95416
Boyle (Part of Los Angeles)	90033
Boys Republic	91710
Brackney	95005
Bradbury	91010
Bradford (Part of Hayward)	94541
Bradley	93426
Brandeis	93064
Branscomb	95417
Brawley	92227
Bray	96058
Brea	92621-22
For specific Brea Zip Codes call (714) 529-3000	
Brea Mall (Part of Brea)	92621
Brentwood	94513
Briceburg	95345
Briceland	95542
Bridgehead	94509
Bridgeport (Mariposa County)	95338
Bridgeport (Mono County)	93517
Bridgeville	95526
Brisbane	94005
Bristol (Part of Santa Ana)	92703
Broadmoor	94015
Broadway (Sacramento County)	95818
Broadway (San Mateo County)	94010
Broadway Manchester (Part of Los Angeles)	90003
Broadway Plaza (Part of Walnut Creek)	94596
Brockway	96143
Broderick (Part of West Sacramento)	95605
Brookdale	95007
Brookhurst Center (Part of Anaheim)	92804
Brooks	95606
Brookside Park (Part of Portola Valley)	94028
Browns Corner (Part of Woodland)	95695
Browns Valley	95918
Brownsville	95919
Brundage (Part of Bakersfield)	93307
Bryant (Part of Long Beach)	90805
Bryn Mawr (Part of Loma Linda)	92318
Bryson	93426
Bryte (Part of West Sacramento)	95605
Buckeye (Part of Redding)	96001
Buckhorn Lodge	95666
Buckingham Park	95451
Buck Meadows	95321
Bucks Bar	95667
Bucks Lake	95971
Bucks Lake Lodge	95971
Bucktail	96052

	ZIP
Buellton	93427
Buena (Part of Vista)	92083
Buena Park	90620-24
For specific Buena Park Zip Codes call (714) 523-1960	
Buena Park Mall (Part of Buena Park)	90620
Buenaventura Plaza (Part of Ventura)	93003
Buena Vista (Amador County)	95640
Buena Vista (Sonoma County)	95476
Buffalo Hill	95634
Buhach	95340
Bummerville	95255
Burbank	91501-10
For specific Burbank Zip Codes call (818) 846-3155	
Burbank	95128
Burkett Acres (Part of Stockton)	95205
Burkett Gardens	95205
Burlingame	94010-11
For specific Burlingame Zip Codes call (415) 342-7694	
Burlingame Hills	94010
Burney	96013
Burnt Ranch	95527
Burrel	93607
Burrough	93667
Burson	95225
Butano Canyon	94060
Butte City	95920
Butte Creek	95926
Butte Meadows	95942
Buttonwillow	93206
Byron	94514
Cabazon	92230
Cabin Cove	93271
Cabrillo (Part of Long Beach)	90810
Cabrillo Estates	93402
Cache Creek	93501
Cachuma Village	93101
Cadiz	92319
Cahuilla	92539
Cahuilla Estates	92539
Cahuilla Hills	92260
Cahuilla Indian Reservation	92543
Cairns Corner	93247
Cajon Junction	92403
Calabasas	91302
	91372
For specific Calabasas Zip Codes call (818) 347-4056	
Calabasas Highlands	91302
Calabasas Park	91302
Calaveras (Part of Stockton)	95207
	95267
For specific Calaveras Zip Codes call (209) 795-1006	
Calaveras Yacht and Country Club Estates	95204
Calaveritas	95249
Calavo Gardens	91941
Calexico	92231-32
For specific Calexico Zip Codes call (619) 357-2982	
Calexico Lodge	91905
Calico	92398
Cal-Ida	95922
Caliente	93518
California City	93504-05
For specific California City Zip Codes call (619) 373-2162	
California Correctional Institution (Kern County)	93561
California Correctional Center (Lassen County)	96130
California Hot Springs	93207
California Medical Facility	95688
California Polytechnic State University-San Luis O	93407
California Rehabilitation Center (Part of Norco)	91720
California State Prison-Amador	95640
California Valley	93453
Calimesa	92320
Calipatria	92233
Calistoga	94515
Calla	95336
Callahan	96014
Calpella	95418
Calpine	96124
Calville	95521

	ZIP
Calwa	93725
Camanche Lake	95640
Camarillo	93010-12
For specific Camarillo Zip Codes call (805) 482-8894	
Camarillo Heights	93010
Cambria	93428
Cambrian Park	95124
Camden	93242
Camellia (Part of Sacramento)	95819
Cameo Acres (Part of Danville)	94526
Cameron Corners	91906
Cameron Creek Colony	93277
Cameron Park	95682
Camino	95709
Camino Heights	95709
Campbell	95008-09
	95011
For specific Campbell Zip Codes call (408) 378-2153	
Campbell Hot Springs	96126
Camp Conifer	93271
Camp Connell	95223
Camp Evers (Part of Scotts Valley)	95066
Camp Meeker	95419
Camp Nelson	93208
Campo	91906
Campo Indian Reservation	91906
Campo Seco	95226
Camp Pendleton	92055
Camp Pendleton Marine Corps Base	92055
Camp Pendleton North	92055
Camp Pendleton South	92055
Camp Richardson	96150
Camp Sierra	93664
Camp St. Michael	95585
Camp Ten	95634
Campton Heights (Part of Fortuna)	95540
Camptonville	95922
Camp Wishon	93265
Camulos	93040
Canby	96015
Canebrake	93255
Canoga Annex (Part of Los Angeles)	91304
Canoga Park	91303-09
For specific Canoga Park Zip Codes call (818) 340-7525	
Cantil	93519
Cantua Creek	93608
Canyon	94516
Canyon Country (Part of Santa Clarita)	91351
	91386
For specific Canyon Country Zip Codes call (805) 254-1684	
Canyon Crest (Part of Riverside)	92507
	92517
For specific Canyon Crest Zip Codes call (714) 788-4600	
Canyondam	95923
Canyon Lake	92587
Capay (Glenn County)	95963
Capay (Yolo County)	95607
Capetown	95536
Capistrano Beach (Part of Dana Point)	92624
Capistrano Highlands	92653
Capital Hill (Part of Paso Robles)	93446
Capitola	95010
Capitol Square (Part of San Jose)	95133
Carbona	95376
Carbon Beach	90265
Carbon Canyon	91710
Cardiff By The Sea (Part of Encinitas)	92007
Cardwell (Part of Fresno)	93704
Caribou	95965
Carlotta	95528
Carlsbad	92008-09
	92018
For specific Carlsbad Zip Codes call (619) 729-2456	
Carlton Hills (Part of Santee)	92071
Carmel	93921-23
For specific Carmel Zip Codes call (408) 625-4411	
Carmel-By-The-Sea (Part of Carmel)	93921

	ZIP
Carmel Highlands	93923
Carmel Hills	93923
Carmel Point	93923
Carmel Valley Village	93924
Carmel Woods	93923
Carmenita (Part of Santa Fe Springs)	90670
Carmet	94923
Carmichael	95608-09
For specific Carmichael Zip Codes call (916) 483-8568	
Carnelian Bay	96140
Carpinteria	93013-14
For specific Carpinteria Zip Codes call (805) 684-2219	
Carquinez Heights (Part of Vallejo)	94590
Carriage Hills	91977
Carrick Addition	96094
Carson	90745-47
	90749
For specific Carson Zip Codes call (310) 549-2800	
Carson Hill	95222
Carson Mall (Part of Carson)	90745
Cartago	93549
Caruthers	93609
Carvin Creek Homesites	96126
Casa Conejo	91359
Casa Correo (Part of Concord)	94521
Casa de Oro	91977
Casa de Oro-Mount Helix	91977
Cascadel Woods	93643
Casitas Springs	93001
Casmalia	93429
Caspar	95420
Cassel	96016
Castaic	91310
	91384
For specific Castaic Zip Codes call (805) 257-0252	
Castella	96017
Castellammare (Part of Los Angeles)	90272
Castle Air Force Base	95342
Castle Garden	95342
Castle Park	91911
Castlewood	94566
Castro Valley	94546
	94552
For specific Castro Valley Zip Codes call (510) 581-0191	
Castroville	95012
Catalina (Part of Pasadena)	91116
Cathedral City	92234-35
For specific Cathedral City Zip Codes call (619) 328-2270	
Catheys Valley	95306
Cawelo	93308
Cayucos	93430
Cazadero	95421
Cecilville	96027
Cedar (Part of Lancaster)	93534
	93584
For specific Cedar Zip Codes call (805) 948-4170	
Cedarbrook	93641
Cedar Crest	93605
Cedar Flat	96140
Cedar Glen	92321
Cedar Grove (El Dorado County)	95709
Cedar Grove (Fresno County)	93633
Cedarpines Park	92322
Cedar Ridge (Nevada County)	95924
Cedar Ridge (Tuolumne County)	95370
Cedar Slope	93265
Cedar Stock	96052
Cedarville	96104
Cedarville Indian Reservation	96104
Centerpoint Mall (Part of Oxnard)	93033
Centerville (Alameda County)	94536
Centerville (Fresno County)	93657
Central City Mall (Part of San Bernardino)	92401
Central District (Part of Pomona)	91769
Central Valley	96019
Centre	95860

ZIP

Century City (Part of Los
Angeles) 90067
Century City Shopping
Center (Part of Los
Angeles) 90067
Ceres 95307
Cerritos 90703
Cerro Villa Heights (Part of
Villa Park) 92667
Chalfant 93514
Challenge 95925
Chambless 92319
Champagne Fountain (Part
of Saratoga) 95070
Channel Islands 93030
Chapmantown 95926
Chapman Woods 91107
Chappo 92055
Charleston 93635
Charter Oak 91724
Chatsworth 91311-13
For specific Chatsworth Zip Codes
call (818) 341-9551
Chatsworth Lake Manor . . . 91311
Chawanakee 93602
Cheeseville 96037
Chemeketa Park 95030
Cherokee (Butte County) . . . 95965
Cherokee (Nevada County) . . 95959
Cherokee Strip 93263
Cherry Creek Acres 95949
Cherryland 94541
Cherry Valley 92223
Chester 96020
Chestnut (Part of South San
Francisco) 94080
Chicago Park 95712
Chico 95926-28
For specific Chico Zip Codes call
(916) 343-5531
Chilcoot 96105
Childs Meadows 96061
Chili Bar 95667
China (Part of San
Francisco) 94108
China Camp 94901
China Lake 93555
China Lake Naval Weapons
Center 93555
Chinatown (Part of San
Francisco) 94108
Chinese Camp 95309
Chino 91708-10
For specific Chino Zip Codes call
(714) 627-3631
Chinowths Corner (Part of
Visalia) 93277
Chiriaco Summit 92201
Cholame 93431
Chowchilla 93610
Christofferson 93610
Chrome 95963
Chualar 93925
Chuckwalla Valley State
Prison 92225
Chula Vista 91909-15
For specific Chula Vista Zip
Codes call (619) 422-9221
Chula Vista Shopping
Center (Part of Chula
Vista) 91910
Church of God Colony 93648
Cima 92323
Cisco 95728
Citrus 91702
Citrus Heights 95610-11
. . . . 95621
For specific Citrus Heights Zip
Codes call (916) 725-2060
City Hall (Part of San
Francisco) 94102
City Heights (Part of San
Diego) 92105
City of Industry 91715-16
For specific City of Industry Zip
Codes call (818) 855-6699
City Shopping Center, The
(Part of Orange) 92668
City Terrace 90063
Civic Center (Part of
Fresno) 93721
Civic Center (Part of Los
Angeles) 91401
Civic Center (Part of San
Rafael) 94903
Civic Center (Part of Santa
Ana) 92701

ZIP

Civic Center (Part of La
Habra) 90633
Civic Center Annex (Part of
Oakland) 94612
Clairemont (Part of San
Diego) 92117
Clam Beach 95521
Claremont 91711
Clarksburg 95612
Clarksville 95682
Clay 95638
Clayton 94517
Clear Creek (Lassen
County) 96137
Clear Creek (Siskiyou
County) 96039
Clearlake 95422
Clearlake Oaks 95423
Clearlake Park (Part of
Clearlake) 95424
Clearlake Riviera 95451
Clements 95227
Cleone 95437
Cliff Haven (Part of Newport
Beach) 92660
Clifton 90277
Clingans Junction 93646
Clinter (Part of Fresno) 93703
Clinton 95642
Clio 96106
Clipper Gap 95603
Clipper Mills 95930
Cloverdale (Shasta County) . . 96007
Cloverdale (Sonoma
County) 95425
Clovis 93612-13
For specific Clovis Zip Codes call
(209) 299-3118
Clyde 94520
Coachella 92236
Coalinga 93210
Coarsegold 93614
Cobb 95426
Cockatoo Grove (Part of
Chula Vista) 91910
Coddington Center (Part of
Santa Rosa) 95406
Coddingtown (Part of Santa
Rosa) 95406
Codora 95970
Coffee Creek 96091
Cohasset 95926
Coit 93640
Cold Fork 96080
Cole (Part of West
Hollywood) 90046
Coleville 96107
Colfax 95713
College City 95931
College Grove Center 92115
College Heights (Kern
County) 93305
College Heights (San
Bernardino County) 91786
College Heights (Santa Cruz
County) 95003
College Park (Part of
Thousand Oaks) 91360
College Plaza (Part of
Oceanside) 92056
Collegeville 95206
Collier (Part of Los Angeles) . . 91307
Collierville 95220
Collinsville 94585
Colma 94014
Coloma 95613
Colonial (Part of
Sacramento) 95820
Colonial Juarez (Part of
Fountain Valley) 92708
Colony 92363
Colorado 90404-05
. . . . 90411
For specific Colorado Zip Codes
call (310) 576-2610
Colorado River Indian
Reservation 85344
Colton 92324
Columbia 95310
Columbus (Part of
Bakersfield) 93306
Colusa 95932
Commerce 90040
Commonwealth (Part of
Fullerton) 92632
Community Center (Part of
Simi Valley) 93065

ZIP

Comptche 95427
Compton 90220-24
For specific Compton Zip Codes
call (213) 638-0394
Concepcion 93436
Concord 94518-22
. . . . 94524
. . . . 94527
. . . . 94529
For specific Concord Zip Codes
call (415) 687-1500
Concord Naval Weapons
Station 94520
Conejo 93662
Conejo Valley (Part of
Thousand Oaks) 91360
Confidence 95370
Consumne 95683
Convict Lake 93514
Cool 95614
Coopers Corner 95220
Copco 96044
Copperopolis 95228
Corbin Village (Part of Los
Angeles) 91364
Corcoran 93212
Cordelia 94585
Corning 96021
Corona 91718-20
For specific Corona Zip Codes
call (714) 737-0451
Corona Del Mar (Part of
Newport Beach) 92625
Coronado 92118
. . . . 92178
For specific Coronado Zip Codes
call (619) 435-5211
Coronado Naval
Amphibious Base 92155
Corona Mall (Part of
Corona) 91720
Coronita 91720
Corral Beach 90265
Corralitos 95076
Correctional Training Facility . 93960
Corte Madera 94925
. . . . 94976
For specific Corte Madera Zip
Codes call (415) 924-4463
Coso Junction 93542
Costa Mesa 92626-28
For specific Costa Mesa Zip
Codes call (714) 546-5330
Cotati 94931
Cotners Corners (Part of
Apple Valley) 92307
Cottage Springs 95223
Cotton Center 93257
Cottonwood 96022
Coulterville 95311
Country Club 95204
Country Club Centre 95825
Country Club Estates 93401
Country Club Plaza 95825
Country Modern 93501
County East Mall (Part of
Antioch) 94509
Court (Part of Martinez) 94553
Courtland 95615
Covelo 95428
Covina 91722-24
For specific Covina Zip Codes call
(818) 966-8391
Covington Mill 96052
Cowan Heights 92705
Cowell (Part of Concord) 94520
Coy Flat 93208
Coyote (Part of San Jose) . . . 95013
Craf 92359
Crafton 92359
Crenshaw (Part of Los
Angeles) 90008
Crenshaw-Imperial (Part of
Inglewood) 90303
Crescent City 95531
Crescent City North 95531
Crescent Mills 95934
Cressey 95312
Crest 92021
Crestline 92325
Crestmore 92316
Crestmore Heights 92509
Creston 93432
Crest Park 92326
Crestview Village 95608
Crockett 94525
Cromberg 96103

	ZIP
Crossroads (Part of Santa Rosa)	95401
Crossroads Plaza (Part of Pico Rivera)	90661
Crowley (Part of Visalia)	93277
Crowley Lake	93546
Crown Point (Part of San Diego)	92109
Crows Landing	95313
Crutcher (Part of Paramount)	90723
Crystal Court (Part of Costa Mesa)	92626
Crystal Cove	92651
Cucamonga	91729-30
	91739
For specific Cucamonga Zip Codes call (714) 987-4641	
Cudahy	90201
Cuesta-by-the-Sea	93402
Culver City	90230-33
For specific Culver City Zip Codes call (213) 391-6374	
Cummings	95454
Cunningham	95472
Cupertino	95014-16
For specific Cupertino Zip Codes call (408) 252-6798	
Curry Village	95389
Curtiss Heights (Part of Arcata)	95521
Cutler	93615
Cutten	95534
Cuyama	93214
Cypress	90630
Cypress South (Part of Cypress)	90630
Daggett	92327
Dairyville	96080
Dales	96080
Daly City	94014-17
For specific Daly City Zip Codes call (415) 756-2303	
Daphnedale Park	96101
Dardanelle	95314
Darrah	95338
Darwin	93522
Daulton	93637
Davenport	95017
Davis	95616-17
For specific Davis Zip Codes call (916) 753-3496	
Davis Creek	96108
Day	96056
Dayton	95926
Daywalt	95472
Deane Brothers	91350
Dearborn Park	94060
Death Valley	92328
Death Valley Junction	92328
Decoto (Part of Union City)	94587
Deep Springs	89010
Deer Creek	96061
Deer Lick Springs	96076
Deer Park (Napa County)	94576
Deer Park (Santa Cruz County)	95003
Del Aire	90250
Del Amo (Part of Torrance)	90503
Del Amo Fashion Center (Part of Torrance)	90503
Delano	93215-16
For specific Delano Zip Codes call (805) 725-8742	
Del Dios	92029
Delevan	95988
Delft Colony	93618
Delhi	95315
Delkern	93307
Delleker	96122
Del Loma	96010
Del Mar (San Diego County)	92014
Del Mar (Santa Cruz County)	95060
Del Mesa	94904
Del Monte Forest	93953
Del Monte Heights (Part of Seaside)	93955
Del Monte Park	93950

	ZIP
Del Monte Shopping Center (Part of Monterey)	93940
Del Paso Heights (Part of Sacramento)	95838
Del Rey	93616
Del Rey Oaks	93940
Del Rio Woods	95448
Del Rosa (Part of San Bernardino)	92404
Del Sur	93534
Delta (Part of Stockton)	95202
De Luz	92028
Del Valle (Part of Los Angeles)	90015
Delways	95695
Democrat Hot Springs	93301
Denair	95316
Denny	95527
Denverton	94585
Derby Acres	93224
Descanso	91916
Desert	92309
Desert Beach	92254
Desert Center	92239
Desert Hot Springs	92240
Desert Lake	93516
Desert Shores	92274
Desert View Highlands	93550
Des Moines (Part of La Habra)	90631
Deuel Vocational Institution	95376
Devils Den	93204
Devore	92407
Devore Heights	92407
Diablo	94528
Diamond (Part of Santa Ana)	92704
Diamond Bar	91765
Diamond Heights (Part of San Francisco)	94131
Diamond Springs	95619
Diamond Springs Heights	95619
Di Giorgio	93217
Dillon Beach	94929
Dimond (Part of Oakland)	94602
Dinkey Creek	93664
Dinsmore	95526
Dinuba	93618
Discovery Bay	94513
Dixon	95620
Dobbins	95935
Dockweiler (Part of Los Angeles)	90007
Doheny Park	92624
Dollar Ranch (Part of Walnut Creek)	94595
Dolomite	93545
Dominguez (Part of Carson)	90810
Dominguez Hills (Part of Carson)	90801
Donlon (Part of Oxnard)	93030
Donner	96162
Donner Lake	96161
Don Pedro Camp	95329
Dorrington	95223
Dorris	96023
Dos Palos	93620
Dos Rios	95429
Douglas City	96024
Douglas Flat	95229
Downey	90239-42
For specific Downey Zip Codes call (213) 923-5465	
Downieville	95936
Downtown (Part of Riverside)	92501-02
For specific Downtown Zip Codes call (714) 788-4600	
Downtown (Part of Bakersfield)	93303
Downtown (Part of Burbank)	91502
Downtown (Part of Manhattan Beach)	90266
Downtown (Part of San Bernardino)	92401
Downtown (Part of Ontario)	91761
Downtown (Part of San Diego)	92101
Downtown (Part of Sonora)	95370
Downtown Plaza (Part of Sacramento)	95814
Doyle (Lassen County)	96109
Doyle (Tulare County)	93258
Drakesbad	96020
Dryden Flight Research Center	93523

	ZIP
Drytown	95699
Duarte	91009-10
For specific Duarte Zip Codes call (818) 358-1833	
Dublin	94568
Ducor	93218
Dulzura	91917
Duncans Mills	95430
Dunlap	93621
Dunlap Acres (Part of Yucaipa)	92399
Dunmovin	93542
Dunneville Corners	95023
Dunnigan	95937
Dunsmuir	96025
Durham	95938
Dustin Acres	93268
Dutch Flat	95714
Eagle Lake Resort	96130
Eagle Mountain	92239
Eagle Rock (Part of Los Angeles)	90041
Eagle Rock Plaza (Part of Los Angeles)	90041
Eagle Tree	95690
Eagleville	96110
Earlimart	93219
Earp	92242
East (Part of Downey)	90239
East Anaheim Shopping Center (Part of Anaheim)	92806
East Applegate	95703
East Bakersfield (Part of Bakersfield)	93305
East Baldy Mesa	92369
East Blythe	92225
East Compton	90221
East Firebaugh	93622
East Fresno (Part of Fresno)	93727
Eastgate (Part of Beverly Hills)	90211
East Gridley	95948
East Guernewood	95446
East Hemet	92544
East Highlands	92346
East Irvine	92650
East La Mirada	90638
Eastland Shopping Center (Part of West Covina)	91790
East Linda	95901
East Long Beach (Part of Long Beach)	90804
East Los Angeles	90022
East Lynwood (Part of Lynwood)	90262
Eastmont (Part of Oakland)	94605
Eastmont Mall (Part of Oakland)	94605
East Nicolaus	95622
Easton	93706
East Orosi	93647
East Palo Alto (San Mateo County)	94303
East Palo Alto (Santa Clara County)	94303
East Pasadena (Part of Pasadena)	91107
	91117
For specific East Pasadena Zip Codes call (818) 304-7129	
East Porterville	93257
East Quincy	95971
East Richmond	94805
Eastridge (Part of San Jose)	95122
	95173
For specific Eastridge Zip Codes call (408) 452-4300	
East San Diego (Part of San Diego)	92105
East Santa Cruz (Part of Santa Cruz)	95060
Eastside Acres	93622
Eastside Ranch	93622
East Stockton (Part of Stockton)	95205
	95215
For specific East Stockton Zip Codes call (209) 466-9334	
East Tustin	92705
East Vallejo (Part of Vallejo)	94590
East Ventura (Part of Ventura)	93003
Eastview	90734
Echo Lake	95721
Echo Park (Part of Los Angeles)	90026

ZIP

Edendale (Part of Los
  Angeles) 90026
Edgemar (Part of Pacifica) 94044
Edgemont (Lassen County) 96114
Edgemont (Riverside
  County) 92508
Edgemont Acres 93523
Edgewater Estates 91977
Edgewood 96094
Edison 93220
Edmundson Acres.......... 93203
Edwards 93523-24
  For specific Edwards Zip Codes
    call (805) 258-5811
Edwards Air Force Base ... 93523
Edwards Estates 93523
Edwards Palisades 93523
Eel Rock 95554
Eight Mile House 95709
El Bonita 95446
El Cajon 92019-22
  For specific El Cajon Zip Codes
    call (619) 442-0727
El Camino................. 96035
El Camino North Shopping
  Center (Part of
  Oceanside) 92054
El Casco Lake 92373
El Centro................. 92243-44
  For specific El Centro Zip Codes
    call (619) 352-2494
El Cerrito (Contra Costa
  County) 94530
El Cerrito (Riverside County) 91720
El Cerrito Plaza (Part of El
  Cerrito) 94530
Elders Corner 95603
Elderwood 93286
El Dorado 95623
El Dorado Hills 95762
Eldridge.................. 95431
El Encanto Heights 93117
El Granada 94018
Elizabeth Lake 93551
Elk 95432
Elk Creek 95939
Elk Grove 95624
.... 95758-59
  For specific Elk Grove Zip Codes
    call (916) 685-5700
Elkhorn 95012
Elk River 95503
Elk River Corners 95503
Ellwood 93118
El Macero (Part of Davis) 95618
Elmhurst (Part of Oakland) 94603
Elmira................... 95625
El Mirador 93247
El Mirage................ 92301
El Modena (Part of Orange) 92667
El Monte 91731-34
  For specific El Monte Zip Codes
    call (818) 443-8995
El Monte (Part of Concord) 94521
El Monte Center (Part of El
  Monte).................. 91732
El Monte Park 92040
Elm View................. 93609
Elmwood (Part of Berkeley) 94705
El Nido 95317
El Portal (Contra Costa
  County) 94806
El Portal (Mariposa County) 95318
El Porto Beach (Part of
  Manhattan Beach)........ 90266
El Pueblo 94565
El Rio 93030
El Rio Villa 95694
El Segundo 90245
El Segundo Station (Part of
  El Segundo) 90245
El Sereno (Part of Los
  Angeles) 90026
El Sobrante 94803
.... 94820
  For specific El Sobrante Zip
    Codes call (510) 262-1960
El Sueno 93110
El Toro................... 92610
.... 92630
  For specific El Toro Zip Codes call
    (714) 837-1220
El Toro Marine Corps Air
  Station 92709
El Toro Station 92709
El Verano 95433
Elverta.................. 95626

ZIP

El Viejo 95353-54
  For specific El Viejo Zip Codes
    call (209) 523-8326
Emandal 95490
Emerald Bay 92651
Emerald Lake 94062
Emeryville 94608
.... 94662
  For specific Emeryville Zip Codes
    call (510) 251-3112
Emigrant Gap 95715
Empire................... 95319
Encanto (Part of San Diego) 92114
Encinal (Part of Sunnyvale) 94087
Encinitas 92007
.... 92023-24
  For specific Encinitas Zip Codes
    call (619) 753-6446
Encino (Part of Los
  Angeles) 91316
.... 91416
.... 91426
.... 91436
  For specific Encino Zip Codes call
    (818) 908-6919
Enterprise (Part of Redding) 96001
Escalle (Part of Larkspur) 94939
.... 95320
Escalon 95320
Escondido 92025-27
.... 92029-33
.... 92046
  For specific Escondido Zip Codes
    call (619) 745-1912
Escondido Junction (Part of
  Oceanside) 92054
Escondido Village Mall (Part
  of Escondido) 92027
Esparto 95627
Esplanade, The........... 93300
Essex 92332
Estrella 93451
Estudillo (Part of San
  Leandro) 94577
Etiwanda (Part of
  Cucamonga) 91739
Etna 96027
Ettersburg............... 95542
Eucalyptus Hills 92040
Eugene 95230
Eureka 95501-02
  For specific Eureka Zip Codes call
    (707) 442-1768
Exeter 93221
Fairfax (Kern County) 93307
Fairfax (Marin County) 94930
.... 94978
  For specific Fairfax Zip Codes call
    (415) 453-3146
Fairfield 94533
Fairhaven................ 95564
Fairmead................ 93610
Fairmont 93534
Fairmont Terrace 94577
Fairmount (Part of El
  Cerrito) 94530
Fair Oaks (Sacramento
  County).................. 95628
Fair Oaks (San Luis Obispo
  County).................. 93420
Fairview (Alameda County) 94542
Fairview (Fresno County) 93657
Fairview (Trinity County) ... 96052
Fairview (Tulare County) ... 93238
Falk..................... 95503
Fallbrook................. 92028
.... 92088
  For specific Fallbrook Zip Codes
    call (619) 728-7880
Fallbrook Junction 92055
Fallbrook Mall (Part of Los
  Angeles)................ 91307
Fallen Leaf 96151
Falling Springs 91702
Fallon 94952
Fall River Mills 96028
Fallsvale 92339
Famoso 93250
Fancher................. 93702
Farmers Market (Part of Los
  Angeles) 90036
Farmersville 93223
Farmington 95230
Fashion Valley Center (Part
  of San Diego) 92108
Fawnskin................ 92333
Fay Creek 93283
Feather Falls 95940

ZIP

Feather River............. 96020
Feather River Inn 96103
Feather River Park 96103
Federal (Part of Covina) ... 91723
Federal (Part of Los
  Angeles) 90012
Federal (Part of Anaheim) 92805
Federal Building (Part of
  San Francisco) 94102
Federal Building (Part of
  Oxnard)................. 93030
Federal Correctional
  Institution 94566
Federal Prison Camp 93516
Federal Terrace (Part of
  Vallejo) 94590
Fellows 93224
Felton (census designated
  place) 95041
Felton................... 95018
Felton Grove 95018
Fernbridge 95540
Fernbrook................ 92065
Ferndale 95536
Fern Valley 92549
Fernwood 90290
Fetters Hot Springs 95476
Fetters Hot Springs-Agua
  Caliente................ 95476
Fickle Hill 95521
Fiddletown............... 95629
Fieldbrook............... 95521
Fields Landing 95537
Fig Garden 93704
Fig Garden Village......... 93704
Figueroa (Part of Los
  Angeles) 91001
Fillmore 93015-16
  For specific Fillmore Zip Codes
    call (805) 524-1413
Finley 95435
Firebaugh 93622
Fire Mountain............ 96061
Firestone (Part of South
  Gate) 90280
Firestone Park 90001
First Street (Part of
  Oceanside) 92049
.... 92054
  For specific First Street Zip Codes
    call (619) 722-6420
Fish Camp 93623
Fish Springs 93513
Fisk (Part of San Francisco) 94122
Fitchburg (Part of Oakland) 94621
Five Brooks 94950
Five Mile Terrace 95667
Five Points (Fresno County) 93624
Five Points (San Diego
  County) 92110
Flinn Springs 92021
Flintridge (Part of La
  Canada Flintridge)....... 91011
Florence 90001
Florence-Graham 90001
Florin 95828
Florin Mall (Part of
  Sacramento) 95823
Floriston 96111
Flosden Acres (Part of
  Vallejo) 94590
Flournoy 96029
Flower Village 93305
Fly in Acres 95223
Folsom.................. 95630
Folsom Junction (Part of
  Folsom).................. 95630
Fontana.................. 92334-36
  For specific Fontana Zip Codes
    call (714) 822-8039
Foothill Farms 95841
Forbestown 95941
Ford City................ 93268
Forest................... 95910
Foresta 95389
Forest Falls 92339
Forest Glen 96041
Foresthill 95631
Forest Home (Amador
  County) 95669
Forest Home (San
  Bernardino County)...... 92339
Forest Knolls 94933
Forest Park.............. 95006
Forest Ranch 95942
Forest Springs (Nevada
  County)................. 95949

	ZIP
Forest Springs (Santa Cruz County)	95006
Forestville	95436
Forks of Salmon	96031
Forrest Park	91350
Fort Baker	94965
Fort Barry	94965
Fort Bidwell	96112
Fort Bidwell Indian Reservation	96112
Fort Bragg	95437
Fort Cronkhite	94965
Fort Dick	95538
Fort Goff	96086
Fort Hunter Liggett	93928
Fort Independence Indian Reservation	93526
Fort Irwin	92310
Fort Jones	96032
Fort Mason (Part of San Francisco)	94123
Fort McArthur (Part of Los Angeles)	90731
Fort Miley (Part of San Francisco)	94121
Fort Mohave Indian Reservation	92363
Fort Ord	93941
Fort Ord Village (Part of Seaside)	93941
Fort Seward	95511
Fort Sutter (Part of Sacramento)	95816
Fortuna	95540
Fort Yuma	85364
Fort Yuma Indian Reservation	92283
Foster City	94404
Fountainhead Springs	93257
Fountain Valley	92708
	92728
For specific Fountain Valley Zip Codes call (714) 966-0580	
Four Corners (Kramer Junction)	93516
Four Corners (Part of Twentynine Palms)	92277
Four Corners (Madera County)	93637
Fouts Springs	95979
Fowler	93625
Fox Creek	95528
Fox Hills (Part of Culver City)	90233
Fox Hills Mall (Part of Culver City)	90230
Foy (Part of Los Angeles)	90017
Franciscan Park (Part of Daly City)	94014
Franklin	95758
Frazier Park	93222
	93225
For specific Frazier Park Zip Codes call (805) 245-3801	
Fredericksburg	96120
Freedom	95019
Freestone	95472
Fremont	94536-39
	94555
For specific Fremont Zip Codes call (415) 792-8654	
Fremont Fashion Center (Part of Fremont)	94538
Fremont Hub Shopping Center (Part of Fremont)	94538
French Camp	95231
French Corral	95960
French Gulch	96033
Fresh Pond	95726
Freshwater	95503
Freshwater Corners	95503
Fresno	93650
	93701-94
For specific Fresno Zip Codes call (209) 487-7700	
Fresno Fashion Fair (Part of Fresno)	93710
Friant	93626
Friendly Hills	92252
Fruitland	95554
Fruitridge	95820
Fruitvale (Alameda County)	94601
Fruitvale (Kern County)	93308
Fruto	95988
Fullerton	92631-35
For specific Fullerton Zip Codes call (714) 525-3893	

	ZIP
Fulton	95439
Gabilan (Part of Salinas)	93906
Gabilan Acres	93901
Galleria at South Bay, The (Part of Redondo Beach)	90278
Gallinas	94903
Galt	95632
Garberville	95542
Gardena	90247-49
For specific Gardena Zip Codes call (213) 327-9114	
Garden Acres	95205
Garden Farms	93422
Garden Gate Village	95014
Garden Grove	92640-45
For specific Garden Grove Zip Codes call (714) 537-1331	
Garden Valley	95633
Garden Village (Part of Daly City)	94015
Garey	93454
Garfield	93205
Garlock	93554
Gasoline Alley	95603
Gas Point	96022
Gasquet	95543
Gateway (Los Angeles County)	90232
Gateway (Nevada County)	96161
Gaviota	93117
Gazelle	96034
Geary (Part of San Francisco)	94108
Gene	92267
Genesee	95983
Genesee Plaza (Part of San Diego)	92111
George AFB (census designated place)	92392
George Air Force Base	92394
Georgetown	95634
George Washington (Part of San Diego)	92103
Gerber	96035
Geyser Resort	95425
Geyserville	95441
Gilman Hot Springs	92583
Gilroy	95020-21
For specific Gilroy Zip Codes call (408) 842-2550	
Glamis	92227
Glassell (Part of Los Angeles)	90065
Glen Arbor	95005
Glen Avon	92509
Glenbrook Heights	95945
Glenburn	96028
Glencoe	95232
Glencove (Part of Vallejo)	94590
Glendale	91201-26
For specific Glendale Zip Codes call (818) 502-3202	
Glendale	95521
Glendale Galleria (Part of Glendale)	91210
Glendora	91740
Glen Ellen	95442
Glenhaven	95443
Glen Martin	92305
Glenn	95943
Glennville	93226
Glenoaks (Part of Burbank)	91504
Glenshire	96161
Glenview (Los Angeles County)	90290
Glenview (San Diego County)	92021
Glorietta (Part of Orinda)	94563
Goffs	92332
Golden Hill (Part of San Diego)	92102
Gold Flat	95959
Gold Gulch	95018
Gold Hill	95667
Gold River	95670
Gold Run	95717
Goleta	93117
Gonzales	93926
Goodyears Bar	95944
Gordon Valley	94585
Gorman	93243
Goshen	93227
Government Island (Part of Alameda)	94501
Graeagle	96103
Graham	90002

	ZIP
Granada Hills (Part of Los Angeles)	91344
Grand Central (Part of Glendale)	91201
	91221
For specific Grand Central Zip Codes call (818) 502-3254	
Grand Lake (Part of Oakland)	94610
Grand Terrace	92324
Grandview	92311
Grandview-Palos Verdes (Part of Rancho Palos Verdes)	90274
Grangeville	93230
Granite Bay Vista	95678
Granite Hill	95945
Graniteville	95959
Grantville (Part of San Diego)	92120
Grass Valley	95945
	95949
For specific Grass Valley Zip Codes call (916) 273-7233	
Graton	95444
Grayson	95363
Greeley	93307
Greeley Hill	95311
Green (Part of Los Angeles)	90037
Greenacres	93308
Greenbrae	94904
Greenbrook (Part of Danville)	94526
Greenfield	93927
Greenmead (Part of Los Angeles)	90059
Green Meadows	95616
Greenspot	92359
Green Valley	91350
Green Valley Estates	94585
Green Valley Lake	92341
Greenview	96037
Greenview Acres (Part of Arcata)	95521
Greenville	95947
Greenwich Village (Part of Thousand Oaks)	91360
Greenwood	95635
Grenada	96038
Gridley	95948
Griffith (Part of Los Angeles)	90039
Grimes	95950
Grizzly Flats	95636
Grossmont	91942-43
For specific Grossmont Zip Codes call (619) 466-3283	
Grossmont	91941
Grove Highlands (Part of Pacific Grove)	93950
Groveland	95321
Grover City	93433
	93483
For specific Grover City Zip Codes call (805) 489-5887	
Guadalupe	93434
Gualala	95445
Guasti	91743
Guatay	91931
Guerneville	95446
Guernewood Park	95446
Guernsey	93230
Guinda	95637
Gustine	95322
Hacienda	95436
Hacienda Heights	91745
Haiwee	93549
Halcyon	93420
Hales Grove	95585
Half Moon Bay	94019
Hall (Part of Union City)	94587
Halloran Springs	92309
Halls Corner	93245
Hallwood	95901
Hamburg	96045
Hamilton (Part of Palo Alto)	94301
Hamilton City	95951
Hammer Ranch (Part of Stockton)	95209
	95219
For specific Hammer Ranch Zip Codes call (209) 957-7972	
Hammil	93514
Hammonton	95901
Hancock (Part of Los Angeles)	90044

ZIP		ZIP		ZIP	
Hanford	93230-32	Hilltop (Contra Costa		Idyllwild-Pine Cove	92549
For specific Hanford Zip Codes		County)	94806	Idylwood Acres (Part of	
call (209) 582-2507		Hilltop (Kern County)	93307	Walnut Creek)	94596
Happy Camp	96039	Hillview (Part of San Jose)	95121	Ignacio	94947
Harbison Canyon	92020	Hilmar	95324	Igo	96047
Harbor City (Part of Los		Hilt	96044	Imola	94558
Angeles)	90710	Hilton	95436	Imperial	92251
Harbor Side	91911	Hinkley	92347	Imperial Beach	91932-33
Hardman Center (Part of		Hiouchi Valley	95531	For specific Imperial Beach Zip	
Riverside)	92504	Hirschdale	96161	Codes call (619) 423-4545	
Hardwick	93230	Hi Vista	93534	Imperial Crest (Part of	
Harlem Springs (Part of		Hoaglin	95595	Norwalk)	90650
Highland)	92346	Hobart (Part of Vernon)	90058	Incline	95318
Harmony	93435	Hobart Mills	96161	Independence	93526
Harmony Grove	92029	Hodge	92311	Indian Beach	95443
Harris	95542	Holiday (Part of Anaheim)	92802	Indian Creek	95466
Harrison Park	92036	Holiday Forest	92386	Indian Falls	95952
Hartland	93603	Holiday Lake (Part of		Indian Hill Mall (Part of	
Harvard	92398	Morgan Hill)	95037	Pomona)	91767
Haskell Creek Homesites	96126	Hollister	95023-24	Indian Lakes Estates	93614
Haskins Resort	95971	For specific Hollister Zip Codes		Indian Mission	93602
Hat Creek	96040	call (408) 637-3350		Indianola	95503
Hathaway Pines	95233	Hollydale (Los Angeles		Indian Wells	92260
Hatton Fields	93923	County)	90280	Indio	92201-02
Havasu Lake	92363	Hollydale (Sonoma County)	95436	For specific Indio Zip Codes call	
Havilah	93518	Hollywood (Part of Los		(619) 347-3442	
Hawaiian Gardens	90716	Angeles)	90028	Industrial (Part of Santa	
Hawkins Bar	95563	Hollywood Beach	93030	Ana)	92705
Hawkinsville	96097	Hollywood by the Sea	93030	Inglenook	95437
Hawthorne	90250-51	Hollywood Riviera (Part of		Ingleside (Part of San	
For specific Hawthorne Zip Codes		Torrance)	90277	Francisco)	94112
call (213) 676-2284		Holmes	95569	Inglewood	90301-12
Hawthorne Plaza (Part of		Holt	95234	For specific Inglewood Zip Codes	
Hawthorne)	90250	Holtville	92250	call (213) 301-1230	
Hayfork	96041	Holy City	95026	Ingot	96008
Hayward	94540-45	Home Garden	93239	Inland Center (Part of San	
	94557	Home Gardens	91720	Bernardino)	92408
For specific Hayward Zip Codes		Homeland	92548	Inverness	94937
call (415) 783-2400		Homestead (Kern County)	93527	Inverness Park	94956
Hayward Highlands (Part of		Homestead (Riverside		Inyokern	93527
Hayward)	94542	County)	92539	Ione	95640
Hazard	90063	Homestead (San Joaquin		Iowa Hill	95713
Healdsburg	95448	County)	95206	Irish Beach	95459
Heber	92249	Homestead Valley	94941	Iron Mountain	92242
Helena	96048	Homewood	96141	Irvine	92709-10
Helendale	92342	Honby	91350		92713-20
Helm	93627	Honcut	95965		92730
Hemet	92543-46	Honer Plaza (Part of Santa		For specific Irvine Zip Codes call	
For specific Hemet Zip Codes call		Ana)	92706	(714) 474-0407	
(714) 658-3263		Honeydew	95545	Irvington (Part of Fremont)	94538
Henderson (Part of		Hood	95639	Irwin	95324
Porterville)	93258	Hooker	96022	Irwindale	91706
Henderson Center (Part of		Hookston (Part of Pleasant		Irwin Estates	92311
Eureka)	95501	Hill)	94523	Island Mountain	95542
Henderson Village	95240	Hoopa	95546	Isla Vista	93117
Hendy Woods	95466	Hoopa Valley Indian		Isleton	95641
Henley	96044	Reservation	95546	Ivanhoe	93235
Henleyville	96021	Hope Ranch	93105	Ivanpah	92309
Herald	95638	Hopeton	95369	Jacinto Grange	95943
Hercules	94547	Hope Valley	96120	Jackie Robinson	91103-04
Herlong	96113	Hopland	95449	For specific Jackie Robinson Zip	
Hermosa Beach	90254	Hornbrook	96044	Codes call (818) 304-7134	
Hernandez	95023	Hornitos	95325	Jackson	95642
Herndon	93711	Horse Creek	96045	Jackson Gate (Part of	
Hesperia	92340	Horton Plaza (Part of San		Jackson)	95642
	92345	Diego)	92101	Jacumba	91934
For specific Hesperia Zip Codes		Hot Springs	95984	Jalama	93436
call (619) 244-2267		Howard Landing	95690	Jamesburg	93924
Heyer	94544	Howest (Part of Burlingame)	94010	Jamestown	95327
Hickman	95323	Hub City (Part of Compton)	90220	Jamul	91935
Hidden Hills	91302	Hudson	95355-57	Janesville	96114
Hidden Meadows	92025	For specific Hudson Zip Codes		Jarbo	95965
Hidden Valley	95650	call (209) 551-9444		Jarvis Landing (Part of	
Highgrove	92507	Hughes (Part of Fresno)	93705	Newark)	94560
Highland	92346	Hughson	95326	Jelly	96080
Highland Manor	93308	Humboldt Bay CGAS	95521	Jenner	95450
Highland Park (Kern		Hume	93628	Jenny Lind	95236
County)	93308	Humphreys Station	93612	Jesmond Dene	92026
Highland Park (Los Angeles		Hunters Valley	95325	Jimtown	95448
County)	90042	Huntington (Part of		Johannesburg	93528
Highway City	93706	Huntington Beach)	92646	John Adams (Part of San	
Highway Highlands (Part of		Huntington Beach	92605	Diego)	92116
Glendale)	91214		92615	Johnsondale	93238
Hilarita (Part of Tiburon)	94920		92646-49	Johnson Park	96013
Hillcrest (Los Angeles		For specific Huntington Beach Zip		Johnstonville	96130
County)	90301	Codes call (714) 847-5665		Johnstown	92020
Hillcrest (San Diego County)	92103	Huntington Center (Part of		Johnsville	96103
Hillcrest Center (Part of		Huntington Beach)	92647	Jolon	93928
Bakersfield)	93306	Huntington Lake	93629	Jonesville	95942
Hillcrest Park	94590	Huntington Park	90255	Joshua Tree	92252
Hillsborough	94010	Huron	93234	Julian	92036
Hillsdale (Part of San		Hyampom	96046	Junction City	96048
Mateo)	94403	Hydesville	95547	June Lake	93529
Hillsdale Shopping Center		Idlewild (Del Norte County)	95543	June Lake Junction	93529
(Part of San Mateo)	94403	Idlewild (Tulare County)	93260	Juniper Hills	93543
Hills Flat	95945	Idria	95023	Juniper Lake Resort	96020
		Idyllwild	92549	Juniper Springs	92548

	ZIP
Live Oak Acres (Tehama County)	96080
Live Oak Acres (Ventura County)	93022
Live Oak Canyon	91750
Live Oak Springs	91962
Livermore	94550-51
For specific Livermore Zip Codes call (510) 447-3580	
Livingston	95334
Llano	93544
Lobitos	94019
Lobo (Part of Stanton)	90680
Loch Lomond	95426
Locke	95690
Lockeford	95237
Lockhart	92347
Lockwood	93932
Lodge Pole	93262
Lodi	95240-42
For specific Lodi Zip Codes call (209) 369-9545	
Lodoga	95979
Logan Heights (Part of San Diego)	92113
Loleta	95551
Loma (Part of Long Beach)	90814
Loma Linda	92354
Loma Mar	94021
Loma Portal (Part of San Diego)	92110
Loma Rica	95901
Lomas Santa Fe (Part of Solana Beach)	92075
Loma Verda (Part of Novato)	94947
Lomita	90717
Lomita Park (Part of San Bruno)	94066
Lompico	95018
Lompoc	93436-38
For specific Lompoc Zip Codes call (805) 736-4561	
London	93618
Lone Pine	93545
Lone Pine Indian Reservation	93545
Long Barn	95335

Long Beach 90801-53
For specific Long Beach Zip
Codes call (213) 494-2371

COLLEGES & UNIVERSITIES

California State University- Long Beach	90840

FINANCIAL INSTITUTIONS

Farmers & Merchants Bank of Long Beach	90802
Guardian Savings & Loan	90803
Harbor Bank	90802
National Bank of Long Beach	90807

HOSPITALS

Long Beach Community Hospital	90804
Long Beach Memorial Medical Center	90806
St. Mary Medical Center	90801
Veterans Affairs Medical Center	90822

HOTELS/MOTELS

Golden Sails Hotel	90803
Hyatt Regency Long Beach	90802
Hotel Queen Mary	90801
Ramada Inn	90804

MILITARY INSTALLATIONS

Long Beach Naval Shipyard	90810
Naval Regional Contracting Center Detachment	90822
Supervisor of Shipbuilding, Conversion and Repair, Long Beach	90822
Long Beach Plaza (Part of Long Beach)	90802
Longvale	95490
Longview	93553
Lonoak	93930
Lonoke (Part of Gilroy)	95020
Lookout	96054
Loomis	95650
Loomis Corners	96001

	ZIP
Loraine	93518
Loree Estates	95014
Los Alamitos	90720-21
For specific Los Alamitos Zip Codes call (213) 431-6546	
Los Alamitos Naval Air Station	90720
Los Alamos	93440
Los Altos	94022-24
For specific Los Altos Zip Codes call (415) 948-6000	
Los Altos Hills	94022
Los Altos Shopping Center (Part of Long Beach)	90815
Los Amigos (Part of Downey)	90240

Los Angeles 90001-99
.... 90101
For specific Los Angeles Zip
Codes call (213) 586-1737

COLLEGES & UNIVERSITIES

California State University- Los Angeles	90032
Loyola Marymount University	90045
Mount Saint Mary's College	90049
Northrop University	90045
Occidental College	90041
University of California-Los Angeles	90024
University of Southern California	90089

FINANCIAL INSTITUTIONS

American International Bank	90017
The Bank of California, National Association	90071
Bankers Trust Company of California, N.A.	90071
California Commerce Bank	90017
California Federal Bank	90036
California Korea Bank	90010
California Overseas Bank	90010
Canadian Imperial Bank of Commerce	90071
Capital Bank of California	90067
Cathay Bank	90012
Dai-Ichi Kangyo Bank of California	90017
East-West Federal Bank, F.S.B.	90012
Family Savings Bank	90016
Far East National Bank	90012
1st Business Bank	90071
First Interstate Bank, Ltd.	90017
First Interstate Bank of California	90017
First Los Angeles Bank	90067
First Public Savings Bank	90012
Founders National Bank of Los Angeles	90008
General Bank	90012
Guardian Bank	90017
Hancock Savings Bank	90004
Hanmi Bank	90010
Highland Federal Bank	90042
Home Savings of America, F.A.	90010
Manufacturers Bank	90071
Marathon National Bank	90064
Mercantile National Bank	90067
Metrobank	90024
Security Pacific National Bank	90071
Standard Savings Bank	90012
Sterling Bank	90010
Tokai Bank of California	90014
Union Bank	90071
Western Bank	90024

HOSPITALS

California Medical Center- Los Angeles	90015
Cedars-Sinai Medical Center	90048
Childrens Hospital of Los Angeles	90027
Hospital of the Good Samaritan	90017
Kaiser Foundation Hospital	90027
LAC-King-Drew Medical Center	90059
LAC-University of Southern California Medical Center	90033
St. Vincent Medical Center	90057

	ZIP
University of California Los Angeles Medical Center	90024
Veterans Affairs Medical Center-West Los Angeles	90073

HOTELS/MOTELS

The Beverly Plaza Hotel	90048
The Biltmore Hotel	90071
Holiday Inn Crowne Plaza	90045
Holiday Inn-Downtown	90017
Hyatt Regency Los Angeles	90017
Le Parc Hotel	90069
Los Angeles Hilton & Towers	90017
The New Otani Hotel & Garden	90012
Sheraton Grande	90071
Sheraton Los Angeles Airport	90045
Sheraton Town House	90010
University Hilton-Los Angeles	90007
The Westin Bonaventure	90071

MILITARY INSTALLATIONS

Los Angeles Air Force Station	90009
Military Airlift Command	90045
United States Army Engineer District, Los Angeles	90053
Los Banos	93635
Los Berros	93420
Los Cerritos Center (Part of Cerritos)	90701
Los Coyotes Indian Reservation	92086
Los Deltos	93622
Los Feliz (Part of Los Angeles)	90027
Los Gatos	95030-32
For specific Los Gatos Zip Codes call (408) 354-6666	
Los Molinos	96055
Los Nietos	90606
Los Olivos	93441
Los Osos	93402
	93412
For specific Los Osos Zip Codes call (805) 528-0444	
Los Ranchitos	94903
Los Serranos	91709
Lost Hills	93249
Lost Lake	92225
Los Trancos Woods	94028
Los Tules	92086
Lotus	95651
Lovelock	95954
Lower Echo Lake	95721
Lower Lake	95457
Lowrey	96080
Loyalton	96118
Loyola (Part of Los Altos)	94022
Lucas Valley	94903
Lucas Valley-Marinwood	94903
Lucerne	95458
Lucerne Valley	92356
Lugo (Part of Los Angeles)	90023
Lugonia (Part of Redlands)	92375
Lunada Bay (Part of Palos Verdes Estates)	90274
Lundy	93541
Lushmeadows Mountain Estates	95338
Luther Burbank (Part of Santa Rosa)	95402
Lyman Springs	96075
Lynwood	90262
Lynwood Gardens (Part of Lynwood)	90262
Lytle Creek	92358
McArthur	96056
McCann	95569
McClellan Air Force Base	95652
McCloud	96057
Macdoel	96058
McFarland	93250
McHie	96080
McIntyre Park	92225
McKeon	95631
McKinleyville	95521
McKittrick	93251
McKnight Acres	94590
McLaren (Part of San Francisco)	94134

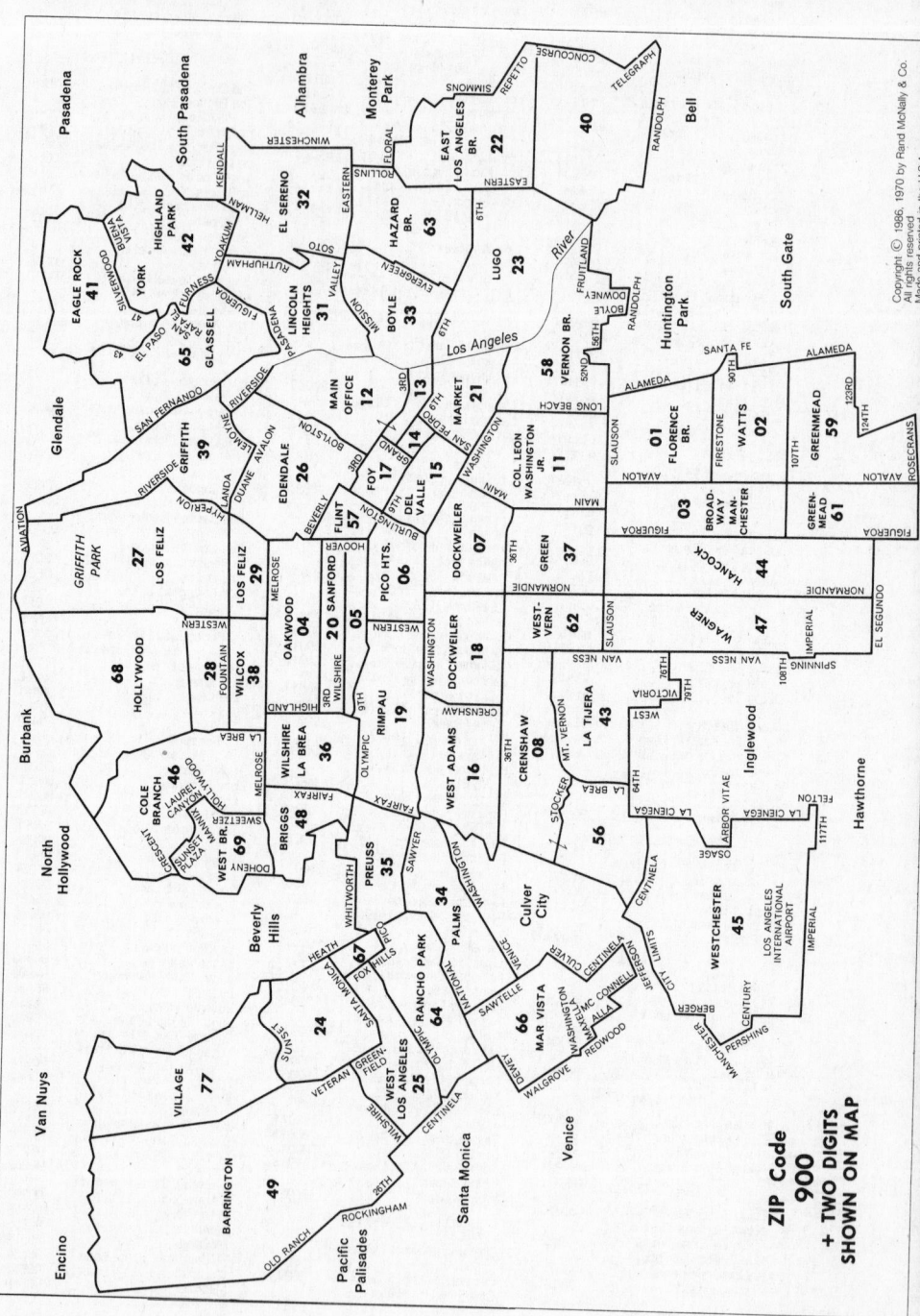

ZIP Code
900
+ TWO DIGITS
SHOWN ON MAP

ZIP	ZIP	ZIP

Maclay (Part of San
Fernando) 91340
McMillan Manor (Part of
Oxnard)................. 93030
Madeline 96119
Madera 93637-39
For specific Madera Zip Codes
call (209) 673-9288
Madera Acres 93637
Madera Country Club
Estates 93637
Madera Highlands 93637
Madera Ranchos 93637
Madison 95653
Madonna Road Plaza (Part
of San Luis Obispo) 93405
Mad River 95552
Madrone (Part of Morgan
Hill) 95037
Magalia 95954
Magnolia (Imperial County) 92227
Magnolia (Santa Barbara
County)................. 93111
Magnolia Center (Part of
Riverside) 92506
Magnolia Park (Part of
Burbank)................ 91505
MainPlace/Santa Ana (Part
of Santa Ana) 92701
Malaga.................... 93725
Malibu 90264-65
For specific Malibu Zip Codes call
(213) 456-2018
Malibu Beach 90265
Malibu Bowl 90265
Malibu Canyon Homes..... 91302
Mall at Northgate, The (Part
of San Rafael) 94903
Mall at Weberstown, The
(Part of Stockton) 95207
Mall of Orange, The (Part of
Orange) 92665
Malott (Part of El Cerrito)... 94530
Mammoth Lakes 93546
Manchester 95459
Manchester Center (Part of
Fresno) 93726
Manhattan Beach........... 90266
Manhattan Village (Part of
Manhattan Beach)....... 90266
Manila 95521
Manka's Corners 94585
Manlove................... 95826
Manor (Part of Fairfax) 94930
Manteca 95336
Manton 96059
Manzana 95444
Manzanita 95948
Manzanita Indian
Reservation............. 91905
Maple Creek 95550
Maravilla Park 90022
Marcelina (Part of Torrance) 90501
March Air Force Base 92508
Marcus Foster (Part of
Oakland)................ 94624
Maricopa.................. 93252
Marina (Monterey County) 93933
Marina (Part of San
Francisco) 94123
.... 94147
For specific Marina Zip Codes call
(408) 384-9313
Marina Del Rey............ 90292
.... 90295
For specific Marina Del Rey Zip
Codes call (310) 306-1233
Marin City 94965
Marin Country Club Estates
(Part of Novato) 94947
Marine Corps Air Station (H) 92709
Marine Corps Logistics
Support Base, Pacific ... 92311
Marine Corps Supply
Center, West Yermo Area 92398
Mariner (Part of Seal Beach) 90740
Marinwood 94903
Mariposa.................. 95338
Market (Part of Los
Angeles) 90021
Marklee Village 96120
Markleeville............... 96120
Marloma (Part of Rolling
Hills Estates)........... 90274
Marne (Part of City of
Industry) 91743
Marshall.................. 94940

Marshall Station 93612
Martell 95654
Martinez 94553
Martins Beach 94019
Mar Vista (Part of Los
Angeles)............... 90066
Marysville 95901
Massack 95971
Mather Air Force Base 95655
Mather Heights 95655
Maxwell 95955
Mayflower Village 91016
Maywood 90270
Meadowbrook 92570
Meadowbrook Woods 92326
Meadow Lake Park 96161
Meadow Lakes 93602
Meadowsweet (Part of
Corte Madera) 94925
Meadow Valley 95956
Meadow Vista 95722
Mead Valley 92570
Mecca 92254
Medicine Lake Lodge...... 96134
Meeks Bay 96142
Meiners Oaks 93023
Melbourne 95427
Melody Oaks 95642
Meloland 92243
Melsons Corner 95684
Melvin (Part of Clovis) 93612
Mendocino 95460
Mendosama 95463
Mendota 93640
Menifee 92584
Menlo Park................ 94025-28
For specific Menlo Park Zip Codes
call (415) 323-0038
Mentone 92359
Merced 95339-44
.... 95348
For specific Merced Zip Codes
call (209) 723-1063
Merced Falls 95369
Merced Mall (Part of
Merced) 95340
Meridian 95957
Mesa Camp 93514
Mesa Center (Part of Costa
Mesa) 92627
Mesa Grande 92070
Mesa Verde 92225
Metro (Part of Sacramento) 95814
Metropolitan (Humboldt
County)................. 95540
Metropolitan (Los Angeles
County)................. 90014
Mettler 93301
Mexican Colony 93263
Michigan Bluff 95631
Michillinda................ 91107
Mid City (Part of Stockton) 95202
Midco (Part of Santa Maria) 93454
Middlefield Road 94061
Middle River 95234
Middletown................ 95461
Midpines 95345
Midtown (Part of Chico).... 95926
Midway City 92655
Mikon (Part of West
Sacramento) 95605
Milford 96121
Millbrae 94030
Millbrae Meadows (Part of
Millbrae) 94030
Mill City 93546
Mill Creek 96061
Mill Creek Park 92359
Millers Corners 93637
Mills College (Part of
Oakland)............... 94613
Mills Orchard 95951
Mill Valley 94941-42
For specific Mill Valley Zip Codes
call (415) 388-8656
Millville 96062
Milo 93265
Milpas (Part of Santa
Barbara) 93103
Milpitas 95035-36
For specific Milpitas Zip Codes
call (408) 262-2322
Milton 95230
Mineral 96063
Mineral King 93271
Minkler................... 93657

Mint Canyon (Part of Santa
Clarita)................. 91350
Mirabel Heights............ 95436
Mirabel Park.............. 95436
Miracle Hot Springs........ 93301
Miracle Manor 93501
Miracle Mile (Part of Los
Angeles) 90036
Miraleste (Part of Rancho
Palos Verdes) 90274
Mira Loma 91752
Miramar (San Diego County) 92145
Miramar (San Mateo
County)................. 94018
Mira Mesa (Part of San
Diego) 92126
Miramonte (Fresno County) 93641
Mira Monte (Ventura
County)................. 93023
Miranda 95553
Mira Vista (Part of
Richmond) 94805
Mission (San Francisco
County)................. 94110
Mission (San Luis Obispo
County)................. 93406
Mission (Santa Clara
County)................. 95051
Mission Annex (Part of San
Francisco) 94103
Mission Beach (Part of San
Diego) 92109
Mission City Annex (Part of
Los Angeles)........... 91345
Mission Highlands 95476
Mission Hills (Los Angeles
County)................. 91345
Mission Hills (San Diego
County)................. 92103
Mission Hills (Santa Barbara
County)................. 93436
Mission Rafael (Part of San
Rafael)................. 94901
Mission San Jose (Part of
Fremont)............... 94539
Mission Valley Center (Part
of San Diego) 92108
Mission Viejo 92691
Mission Viejo Mall (Part of
Mission Viejo) 92691
Missouri Triangle 93251
Mitchell Mill.............. 95257
Mi-Wuk Village 95346
Moccasin 95347
Mococo (Part of Martinez) 94553
Modesto 95350-57
For specific Modesto Zip Codes
call (209) 523-8326
Modjeska 92667
Moffett Field Naval Air
Station 94035
Mohave Manor 92311
Mojave 93501-02
.... 93504-05
For specific Mojave Zip Codes call
(805) 824-4561
Mojave Heights (Part of
Victorville).............. 92392
Mojave Knolls 93501
Mokelumne Hill 95245
Monarch Bay (Part of
Laguna Niguel).......... 92677
Monmouth 93725
Mono Hot Springs 93642
Mono Lake 93541
Mono Village 93517
Mono Vista 95370
Monrovia 91016-17
For specific Monrovia Zip Codes
call (818) 359-1189
Monson 93618
Montague 96064
Montair (Part of Danville)... 94526
Montalvin Manor 94806
Montalvo (Part of Ventura) 93003
.... 93005
For specific Montalvo Zip Codes
call (805) 643-5457
Montara 94037
Monta Vista 95014
Montclair 91763
Montclair Plaza (Part of
Montclair).............. 91763
Montebello 90640
Montebello Gardens (Part of
Pico Rivera)............ 90660

	ZIP
Montebello Town Center (Part of Montebello)	90640
Montecito	93108
Monte Nido	91302
Monterey	93940
	93942-44
For specific Monterey Zip Codes call (408) 372-5803	
Monterey Park	91754
Monte Rio	95462
Monte Rosa	95446
Montesano	95446
Monte Sereno	95030
Monte Toyon	95003
Montgomery Creek	96065
Montgomery Village (Part of Santa Rosa)	95405
Montrose	91020-21
For specific Montrose Zip Codes call (818) 249-5033	
Moody (Part of Cypress)	90630
Moonridge	92315
Moonstone	95570
Moorpark	93020-21
For specific Moorpark Zip Codes call (805) 529-1477	
Moorpark Home Acres	93021
Morada	95212
Moraga	94556
Morena	92040
Moreno	92554-55
For specific Moreno Zip Codes call (714) 656-2590	
Moreno Valley	92552-57
For specific Moreno Valley Zip Codes call (714) 656-2590	
Morgan Hill	95037-38
For specific Morgan Hill Zip Codes call (408) 779-2484	
Mormon Bar	95338
Morningside Park (Part of Inglewood)	90305
Morongo Indian Reservation	92220
Morongo Valley	92256
Morro Bay	93442-43
For specific Morro Bay Zip Codes call (805) 772-2361	
Morro Palisades	93402
Moss Beach	94038
Mossdale	95330
Moss Landing	95039
Mountain Center	92561
Mountain Gate	96003
Mountain House (Alameda County)	95376
Mountain House (Butte County)	95916
Mountain Mesa	93240
Mountain Pass	92366
Mountain Ranch	95246
Mountain Spring	91934
Mountain View	94039-43
For specific Mountain View Zip Codes call (415) 967-5721	
Mountain View	93307
Mountain View Acres	92392
Mount Aukum	95656
Mount Baldy	91759
Mount Bullion	95338
Mount Eden (Part of Hayward)	94557
Mount Hamilton	95140
Mount Hannah Lodge	95451
Mount Hebron	96058
Mount Helix	91941
Mount Hermon	95041
Mount Laguna	91948
Mount Shasta	96067
Mount Shasta Mall (Part of Redding)	96003
Mount Signal	92231
Mount View	94553
Mount Whitney	93545
Mount Wilson	91023
Mugginsville	96032
Muir (Part of Willits)	95490
Muir Beach	94965
Muir Woods	94941
Murietta	93640
Murphys	95247
Murray Park (Part of Larkspur)	94939
Murrieta	92562-64
For specific Murrieta Zip Codes call (714) 677-5927	
Murrieta Hot Springs	92563
Muscoy	92405

	ZIP
Myers Flat	95554
Myrtletown	95501
Nadeau	90001
Napa	94558-59
	94581
For specific Napa Zip Codes call (707) 255-1791	
Napa Junction	94590
Nashville	95623
National City	91950-51
For specific National City Zip Codes call (619) 477-3173	
Navajo (Part of San Diego)	92119
Naval Air Facility	92243
Naval Air Station (Alameda County)	94501
Naval Air Station (Kings County)	93245
Naval Base (Part of Port Hueneme)	93043
Naval Regional Medical Center	92055
Naval Weapons Station (Contra Costa County)	94520
Naval Weapons Station (Orange County)	90740
Navarro	95463
Navelencia	93654
Nebo	92311
Nebo Center	92311
Needles	92363
Nelson	95958
Nestor (Part of San Diego)	92053
Nevada City	95959
New Almaden	95042
Newark	94560
New Auberry	93602
Newberry Springs	92365
Newburg	95540
Newbury Park	91319-20
For specific Newbury Park Zip Codes call (805) 497-8661	
Newcastle	95658
New Cuyama	93254
Newell	96134
Newhall	91321-22
	91382-83
For specific Newhall Zip Codes call (805) 259-4897	
Newhall Ranch (Part of Santa Clarita)	91350
New Helvetia (Part of Sacramento)	95815
Newman	95360
New Monterey (Part of Monterey)	93940
New Park Mall (Part of Newark)	94560
New Pine Creek	97635
Newport Beach	92657-63
For specific Newport Beach Zip Codes call (714) 640-8720	
Newport Center Fashion Island (Part of Newport Beach)	92660
Newtown (El Dorado County)	95667
Newtown (Nevada County)	95959
Newville	95963
Nicasio	94946
Nice	95464
Nichols	94565
Nicolaus	95659
Nigger Hill	95667
Nightingale	92561
Niguel Terrace (Part of Laguna Niguel)	92677
Niland	92257
Niles (Part of Fremont)	94536
Nimshew	95954
Nipinnawassee	93601
Nipomo	93444
Nipton	92364
Nob Hill (Part of San Francisco)	94108
Noe Valley (Part of San Francisco)	94114
No Mirage	92259
Norco	91760
Nord	95926
Norden	95724
Normal Heights (Part of San Diego)	92116
North (Part of Los Angeles)	91342
North Auburn	95603
North Bay View Park (Part of Seaside)	93955

	ZIP
North Beach (Part of San Francisco)	94133
North Belridge	93429
North Berkeley (Part of Berkeley)	94709
North Bloomfield	95959
North Clairemont (Part of San Diego)	92107
North Columbia	95959
North County Fair (Part of Escondido)	92025
Northcrest (Part of Crescent City)	95531
North Cucamonga (Part of Cucamonga)	91730
North Downey (Part of Downey)	90240
Northeast Modesto (Part of Modesto)	95350
North Edwards	93523
North Elsinore (Part of Lake Elsinore)	92530
Northern California Women's Facility	95213
North Fair Oaks	94025
North Fillmore (Part of Fillmore)	93015
North Fork	93643
North Gardena	90247
North Glendale (Part of Glendale)	91202
	91222
For specific North Glendale Zip Codes call (818) 502-3257	
North Highlands	95660
North Hollywood	91601-10
	91614-17
For specific North Hollywood Zip Codes call (818) 503-0695	
North Inglewood (Part of Inglewood)	90302
North Island Naval Air Station	92135
North Loma Linda (Part of Loma Linda)	92354
North Long Beach (Part of Long Beach)	90805
North Oakland (Part of Oakland)	94609
North Oaks	91350
North Palm Springs	92258
North Park (Part of San Diego)	92104
North Redondo Beach (Part of Redondo Beach)	90278
North Richmond	94804
Northridge	91324-28
For specific Northridge Zip Codes call (818) 349-4475	
Northridge Center (Part of Salinas)	93906
Northridge Fashion Center (Part of Los Angeles)	91324
North Sacramento (Part of Sacramento)	95815
North San Juan	95960
North Seal Beach (Part of Seal Beach)	90740
North Shore	92254
North Torrance (Part of Torrance)	90504
North Valley Plaza (Part of Chico)	95926
North Whittier	91746
North Whittier Heights	91745
Norwalk	90650-52
For specific Norwalk Zip Codes call (213) 868-3247	
Norwalk Manor (Part of Norwalk)	90650
Norwalk Square (Part of Norwalk)	90650
Novato	94945
	94947-49
For specific Novato Zip Codes call (415) 897-3171	
Noyo	95437
Nubieber	96068
Nuevo	92567
Nummi (Part of Fremont)	94538
Nut Tree (Part of Vacaville)	95696
Nyland Acres	93030
Oak Bottom	96095
Oakdale	95361
Oak Glen	92399
Oak Grove (Butte County)	95965

	ZIP
Oak Grove (San Diego County)	92536
Oakhills	93907
Oakhurst	93644
Oak Knoll Hills	95014
Oak Knolls	93454
Oakland	94601-07
	94609-61

For specific Oakland Zip Codes call (415) 874-8200

Oakley	94561
Oakmont (Part of Santa Rosa)	95405
Oak Park (Sacramento County)	95817
Oak Park (San Luis Obispo County)	93446
Oak Park (Ventura County)	91301
Oakridge Mall (Part of San Jose)	95122
Oak Run	96069
Oaks (Part of Arroyo Grande)	93420
Oaks, The (Part of Thousand Oaks)	91360
Oak Shores	93426
Oak View	93022
Oakville	94562
Oakwood (Part of Los Angeles)	90004
Oasis	89010
O'Brien	96070
Occidental	95465
Ocean Beach (Part of San Diego)	92107
Oceano	93445
Ocean Park (Part of Santa Monica)	90405
	90409

For specific Ocean Park Zip Codes call (310) 576-2670

Oceanside	92049-52
	92054-58

For specific Oceanside Zip Codes call (619) 433-8711

Ocean View (San Francisco County)	94112
Ocean View (Sonoma County)	94923
Ocotillo	92259
Ocotillo Wells	92004
Oildale	93308
Ojai	93023-24

For specific Ojai Zip Codes call (805) 646-4311

Olancha	93549
Old Fellows Park	95446
Old Fort Jim	95667
Old Gilroy	95020
Old Hopland	95449
Old Mammoth (Part of Mammoth Lakes)	93546
Old River	93309
Old San Diego (Part of San Diego)	92110
Old Station	96071
Old Towne (Part of Tehachapi)	93561
Old Towne Mall (Part of Torrance)	90503
Oleander	93725
Olema	94950
Oleum	94572
Olinda (Orange County)	92621
Olinda (Shasta County)	96007
Olive (Part of Orange)	92665
Olivehurst	95961
Olivenhain (Part of Encinitas)	92024
Olympia	95018
Olympic (Part of Beverly Hills)	90212
Olympic Valley	96146
Omo Ranch	95684
O'Neals	93645
One Hundred Palms	92274
Ono	96001
Ontario	91758
	91761-62
	91764

For specific Ontario Zip Codes call (714) 983-1873

Ontario Mail Facility (Part of Ontario)	91761
Onyx	93255
Opal Cliffs	95062
Ophir	95603

	ZIP
Orange	92613
	92664-69

For specific Orange Zip Codes call (714) 997-1255

Orange Cove	93646
Orangefair Mall (Part of Fullerton)	92632
Orange Glen (Part of Escondido)	92027
Orange Heights (Part of Upland)	91786
Orangehurst (Part of Fullerton)	92633
Orange Park Acres	92667
Orangevale	95662
Orangewood (Part of Pasadena)	91115
Orcutt	93455
	93457

For specific Orcutt Zip Codes call (805) 937-6664

Ordbend	95943
Oregon City	95965
Oregon House	95962
Orick	95555
Orinda	94563
Orinda Village (Part of Orinda)	94563
Orland	95963
Orleans	95556
Ormand	92509
Oro Fino	96032
Oro Grande	92368
Oro Loma	93622
Orosi	93647
Oroville	95965-66

For specific Oroville Zip Codes call (916) 533-4515

Osbourne (Part of Los Angeles)	90028
Otay	91911
Otay Mesa (Part of Chula Vista)	92154
Otterbein	91745
Outingdale	95684
Oval (Part of Visalia)	93291
Owenyo	93545
Oxnard	93030-35

For specific Oxnard Zip Codes call (805) 485-6722

Oxnard Beach	93030
Pabrico (Part of Union City)	94587
Pachappa	92506
Pacheco	94553
Pacific (Part of Long Beach)	90806
Pacifica	94044
Pacific Beach (Part of San Diego)	92109
Pacific Gardens	95204
Pacific Grove	93950
Pacific Grove Acres (Part of Pacific Grove)	93950
Pacific House	95726
Pacific Manor (Humboldt County)	95521
Pacific Manor (San Mateo County)	94044
Pacific Missile Test Center-Point Mugu	93042
Pacific Palisades (Part of Los Angeles)	90272
Pacific Villas	95204
Pacoima	91331-34

For specific Pacoima Zip Codes call (818) 896-7491

Paddison Square (Part of Norwalk)	90652
Paicines	95043
Paintersville	95615
Pajaro	95076
Pala	92059
Pala Mesa Village	92028
Palermo	95968
Pallett	93563
Palm City (Part of Palm Desert)	92260
Palmdale	93550-52
	93590-91

For specific Palmdale Zip Codes call (805) 947-4134

Palmdale East	93550
Palm Desert	92255
	92260-61

For specific Palm Desert Zip Codes call (619) 568-5803

Palm Desert Town Center (Part of Palm Desert)	92260

	ZIP
Palmer Creek	95540
Palms (Part of Los Angeles)	90034
Palm Springs	92262-64

For specific Palm Springs Zip Codes call (619) 325-9631

Palm Springs Mall (Part of Palm Springs)	92262
Palm Wells	92256
Palo Alto	94301-09

For specific Palo Alto Zip Codes call (415) 321-4310

Palo Cedro	96073
Paloma	95252
Palomares	94546
Palomar Mountain	92060
Palomar Park	94062
Palos Verdes Estates	90274
Palos Verdes Peninsula (Part of Rolling Hills Estates)	90274
Palo Verde	92266
Palo Vista (Part of Vista)	92083
Panoche	95043
Panorama Heights (Orange County)	92705
Panorama Heights (Tulare County)	93260
Panorama Mall (Part of Los Angeles)	91402
Pappas	93640
Paradise (Butte County)	95967
	95969

For specific Paradise Zip Codes call (916) 877-4445

Paradise (Stanislaus County)	95351
	95358

For specific Paradise Zip Codes call (209) 523-8326

Paradise Cay (Part of Tiburon)	94920
Paradise Hills (Part of San Diego)	92139
Paradise Park	95060
Paramount	90723
Parchers Camp	93514
Park (Part of Berkeley)	94702
Park Central (Part of Alameda)	94501
Parker Dam	92267
Parkfield	93451
Parkmoor (Part of San Jose)	95128
Parksdale	93637
Parkside (Part of San Francisco)	94116
Park Siding (Part of Petaluma)	94952
Parkway	95823
Parkway Estates	95823
Parkway Plaza (Part of El Cajon)	92020
Parkway-Sacramento South	95823
Parkwood	93637
Parlier	93648
Pasadena	91101-18

For specific Pasadena Zip Codes call (818) 304-7183

Pasatiempo	95060
Paskenta	96074
Paso Robles	93446-47

For specific Paso Robles Zip Codes call (805) 238-4904

Patata (Part of South Gate)	90280
Patrick Creek	95543
Patricks Point	95570
Patterson (Stanislaus County)	95363
Patterson (Tulare County)	93277
Patton	92369
Patton Village	96113
Pauma Valley	92061
Paxton	95952
Paynes Creek	96075
Paynesville	96120
Peanut	96041
Pearblossom	93553
Peardale	95945
Pearland	93550
Pearsonville	93527
Pebble Beach	93953
Pecwan	95546
Pedley	92509
Pedro Valley (Part of Pacifica)	94044
Pelican Bay State Prison	95531

	ZIP
Peninsula Center (Part of Rolling Hills Estates)	90274
Peninsula Village	96137
Penngrove	94951
Pennington	95953
Penn Valley	95946
Penryn	95663
Pentz	95965
Pepperwood	95565
Peralta Hills	92667
Perkins	95826
Perris	92570-72
For specific Perris Zip Codes call (714) 657-2396	
Perry (Los Angeles County)	90603
Perry (Santa Clara County)	95037
Pescadero	94060
Petaluma	94952-55
	94975
	94999
For specific Petaluma Zip Codes call (707) 762-0051	
Peters	95236
Petrolia	95558
Pheasant Hill	93065
Phelan	92329
	92371
For specific Phelan Zip Codes call (619) 868-6307	
Phelps Corner	91935
Phillipsville	95559
Philo	95466
Pico (Part of Pico Rivera)	90660
Pico Heights (Part of Los Angeles)	90006
Pico Rivera	90660-62
For specific Pico Rivera Zip Codes call (213) 942-7008	
Piedmont	94611
	94620
For specific Piedmont Zip Codes call (510) 251-3130	
Piedra	93649
Piercy	95587
Pierpoint Springs	93208
Pike	95960
Pilot Hill	95664
Pine Cove (Riverside County)	92549
Pine Cove (Trinity County)	96052
Pinecrest	95364
Pinedale (Part of Fresno)	93650
Pine Flat	93207
Pine Grove (Amador County)	95665
Pine Grove (Lake County)	95426
Pine Grove (Mendocino County)	95420
Pine Grove (Shasta County)	96079
Pine Hills (Humboldt County)	95503
Pine Hills (San Diego County)	92036
Pinehurst	93641
Pine Mountain Club	93225
Pine Mountain Lake	95321
Pine Ridge	93602
Pine Valley	91962
Pinnacles	95043
Pinole	94564
Pinon Hills	92372
Pinyon Crest	92262
Pinyon Pines	92561
Pioneer	95666
Pioneer Point	93562
Pioneertown	92268
Piru	93040
Pismo Beach	93448-49
For specific Pismo Beach Zip Codes call (805) 773-2191	
Pittsburg	94565
Pittville	96056
Pixley	93256
Placentia	92670
Placerville	95667
Plainsburg	95333
Plainview	93267
Planada	95365
Planehaven	95652
Plantation	95421
Plaster City	92243
Platina	96076
Playa (Part of Laguna Beach)	92652
Playa Del Rey (Part of Los Angeles)	90293

	ZIP
	90296
For specific Playa Del Rey Zip Codes call (310) 396-3191	
Playa Vista (Part of Los Angeles)	90094
Playmor	91911
Plaza (Los Angeles County)	91102
Plaza (Orange County)	92666
Plaza (Santa Clara County)	94086
Plaza Camino Real (Part of Carlsbad)	92008
Plaza Center (Part of Ontario)	91762
Plaza Pasadena (Part of Pasadena)	91101
Pleasant Grove	95668
Pleasant Hill	94523
Pleasanton	94566
	94588
For specific Pleasanton Zip Codes call (510) 846-5631	
Pleasant Valley	95667
Pleasant View	93260
Plymouth	95669
Poinsettia Tract	94565
Point Arena	95468
Point Dume	90265
Point Loma (Part of San Diego)	92106
Point Pleasant	95624
Point Reyes Station	94956
Point Richmond (Part of Richmond)	94807
Poker Flat	95228
Pollock Pines	95726
Pomona	91766-69
For specific Pomona Zip Codes call (714) 623-4476	
Pond	93280
Pondosa	96057
Pope Valley	94567
Poplar	93258
Port Costa	94569
Porter Ranch (Part of Los Angeles)	91326
Porterville	93257-58
For specific Porterville Zip Codes call (209) 784-4872	
Porterville Development Center	93257
Porterville West	93257
Port Hueneme	93041-44
For specific Port Hueneme Zip Codes call (805) 488-3501	
Port Kenyon	95536
Portola	96122
Portola Valley	94028
Port San Luis	93424
Portuguese Bend (Part of Rancho Palos Verdes)	90274
Posey	93260
Poso Park	93260
Postal Avenue (Part of Moreno Valley)	92556-57
For specific Postal Avenue Zip Codes call (714) 242-6459	
Post Office Annex (Part of Burlingame)	94010
Posts	93920
Potrero (San Diego County)	91963
Potrero (San Francisco County)	94110
Potter Valley	95469
Poway	92064
	92074
For specific Poway Zip Codes call (619) 748-3371	
Power Tract	93283
Pozo	93453
Prather	93651
Prattville	95923
Presidential Heights (Part of San Clemente)	92672
Preston Heights (Part of Arcata)	95521
Preuss (Part of Los Angeles)	90035
Priest Valley	93210
Princeton (Colusa County)	95970
Princeton (San Mateo County)	94019
Princeton-by-the-Sea	94019
Proberta	96078
Project City	96079
Promenade Mall (Part of Los Angeles)	91367
Prosser Lakeview Estates	96161

	ZIP
Prunedale	93907
Pruneyard, The (Part of Campbell)	95008
Pudding Creek	95437
Puente Junction (Part of City of Industry)	91744
Puerco Beach	90265
Pulga	95965
Pumpkin Center	93309
Putah Creek Park	94558
Quail Valley	92587
Quaking Aspen	93265
Quartz Hill	93536
Quincy	95971
Quincy-East Quincy	95971
Quintette	95634
Quito (Part of Saratoga)	95070
Rackerby	95972
Radec	92543
Rafael Village (Part of Novato)	94947
Rail Road Flat	95248
Rainbow	92028
Raisin	93652
Ralph	95370
Ramirez (Part of Los Angeles)	90037
Ramona	92065
Ramos Village	95336
Ranch, The (Part of Scotts Valley)	95066
Rancheria	95449
Ranch House	92055
Ranchita	92066
Rancho Bernardo (Part of San Diego)	92128
Rancho Buena	96022
Rancho California	92590
Rancho Cordova	95670
	95741-42
For specific Rancho Cordova Zip Codes call (916) 635-9876	
Rancho Del Mar	94590
Rancho Del Rey	91909
	91911
For specific Rancho Del Rey Zip Codes call (619) 422-9221	
Rancho La Costa	92008
Rancho Mirage	92270
Rancho Murieta	95683
Rancho Palos Verdes	90274
Rancho Park (Part of Los Angeles)	90064
Rancho Penasquitos (Part of San Diego)	92129
Rancho Rinconada	95014
Rancho San Diego	91941
Rancho Santa Fe	92067
Rancho Santa Margarita	92688
Randall Island	95615
Randolph	96126
Randsburg	93554
Ravendale	96123
Ravenswood (Part of East Palo Alto)	94303
Rawhide	95370
Rawson	96080
Raymond	93653
Red Bank	96080
Red Bluff	96080
Redcrest	95569
Redding	96001-03
	96049
	96099
For specific Redding Zip Codes call (916) 223-7502	
Red Hill	92705
Redlands	92373-75
For specific Redlands Zip Codes call (714) 793-2171	
Redlands Heights (Part of Redlands)	92373
Red Mountain	93558
Redondo Beach	90277-78
For specific Redondo Beach Zip Codes call (213) 376-2472	
Reds Meadow	93546
Red Top	95340
Redway	95560
Redwood City	94061-65
For specific Redwood City Zip Codes call (415) 368-4181	
Redwood Estates	95044
Redwood Grove	95006
Redwood Lodge	95437
Redwood Retreat	95020
Redwood Terrace	94020

	ZIP

MILITARY INSTALLATIONS

	ZIP
Coast Guard Air Station, San Diego	92101
Marine Corps Recruiting Depot, San Diego	92140
Naval Air Station, Miramar	92145
Naval Air Station, North Island	92135
Naval Hospital, San Diego	92134
Naval Command Control and Ocean Surveillance Center	92132
Naval Supply Center, Fuel Department, Point Lom Annex	92136
Naval Supply Center, San Diego	92136
Naval Training Center, San Diego	92133
San Diego International Airport, Military	92101
Supervisor of Shipbuilding, Conversion and Repair, San Diego	92163

San Diego Country Estates	92065
San Dimas	91773
Sandy Korner	92274
San Felipe	95023
San Fernando	91340-46
	91392-95
For specific San Fernando Zip Codes call (818) 365-0683	
Sanford (Part of Los Angeles)	90005
San Francisco	94101-88
For specific San Francisco Zip Codes call (415) 550-6500	

COLLEGES & UNIVERSITIES

Golden Gate University	94105
San Francisco State University	94132
University of California-Hastings College of Law	94102
University of California-San Francisco	94143
University of San Francisco	94117

FINANCIAL INSTITUTIONS

Bank of America National Trust & Savings Association	94104
The Bank of California, National Association	94104
Bank of Canton of California	94111
Bank of San Francisco	94111
Bank of the Orient	94104
Bank of the West	94104
California Savings & Loan, A Federal Association	94102
Continental Savings of America	94103
East-West Federal Bank	94111
Golden Coin Savings & Loan Association	94133
Hamilton Financial Corporation	94105
Home Federal Savings & Loan Association of San Francisco	94108
Homestead Savings, A Federal Savings & Loan Association	94121
Pacific Bank, National Association	94104
Redwood Bank	94111
Sanwa Bank California	94111
Security Pacific Bank	94111
The Sumitomo Bank of California	94104
Union Bank	94104
United Savings Bank, F.S.B.	94102
Wells Fargo Bank, N.A.	94163

HOSPITALS

Kaiser Foundation Hospital	94115
Laguna Honda Hospital and Rehabilitation Center	94116
Letterman Army Medical Center	94129
Mount Zion Medical Center of University of California - San Francisco	94115

	ZIP
San Francisco General Hospital Medical Center	94110
St. Francis Memorial Hospital	94109
St. Mary's Hospital and Medical Center	94117
University of California, San Francisco Medical Center	94143
Veterans Affairs Medical Center	94121

HOTELS/MOTELS

Best Western Americana	94103
Grand Hyatt San Francisco	94108
The Mark Hopkins Inter-Continental	94108
Miyako Hotel	94115
Parc 55 Hotel	94102
San Francisco Airport Hilton	94128
San Francisco Marriott Fisherman's Wharf	94133
Sir Francis Drake Hotel	94102
Stouffer Stanford Court Hotel	94108

MILITARY INSTALLATIONS

Coast Guard Air Station, San Francisco	94501
Letterman Army Medical Center	94129
Naval Station, Treasure Island	94130
Presidio of San Francisco	94129
United States Army Engineer District, San Francisco	94105

San Francisco Recreation Camp	95655
San Gabriel	91775-78
For specific San Gabriel Zip Codes call (818) 287-9661	
Sanger	93657
San Geronimo	94963
San Gregorio	94074
San Jacinto	92581-83
For specific San Jacinto Zip Codes call (714) 654-7922	
San Joaquin	93660
San Joaquin River Club	95385
San Jose	95101-96
For specific San Jose Zip Codes call (408) 452-0660	
San Jose (recreation area)	95321
San Juan Bautista	95045
San Juan Capistrano	92675
	92679
	92688-93
For specific San Juan Capistrano Zip Codes call (714) 364-5020	
San Juan Plaza (Part of San Juan Capistrano)	92675
San Lawrence Terrace	93451
San Leandro	94577-79
For specific San Leandro Zip Codes call (415) 483-0550	
San Lorenzo	94580
San Lorenzo Park	95006
San Lucas	93954
San Luis Obispo	93401-12
For specific San Luis Obispo Zip Codes call (805) 543-1882	
San Luis Rey (Part of Oceanside)	92068
San Luis Rey Heights	92028
San Marcos	92069
	92079
For specific San Marcos Zip Codes call (619) 744-1030	
San Marin (Part of Novato)	94947
San Marino	91108
	91118
For specific San Marino Zip Codes call (818) 285-6906	
San Martin	95046
San Mateo	94401-04
For specific San Mateo Zip Codes call (415) 349-2301	
San Mateo Fashion Island (Part of San Mateo)	94404
San Miguel	93451
San Onofre	92672
San Pablo	94806
San Pedro	90731-34
For specific San Pedro Zip Codes call (213) 831-3246	
San Quentin	94964

	ZIP
San Rafael	94901-15
For specific San Rafael Zip Codes call (415) 459-0944	
San Ramon	94583
San Ramon Village (Part of Dublin)	94568
San Roque (Part of Santa Barbara)	93105
San Simeon	93452
San Simeon Acres	93452
Santa Ana	92701-08
	92711-12
	92799
For specific Santa Ana Zip Codes call (714) 662-6445	
Santa Ana Heights	92701
Santa Ana Marine Corps Air Facility	92709
Santa Anita Fashion Park (Part of Arcadia)	91006
Santa Barbara	93101-90
For specific Santa Barbara Zip Codes call (805) 564-2266	
Santa Clara	95050-56
For specific Santa Clara Zip Codes call (408) 296-1881	
Santa Clarita	91310
	91321-22
	91350-51
	91354-55
	91380
	91382-86
For specific Santa Clarita Zip Codes call (805) 254-1684	
Santa Cruz	95060-65
For specific Santa Cruz Zip Codes call (408) 426-5200	
Santa Cruz Gardens	95060
Santa Fe Plaza	90605
Santa Fe Springs	90670-71
For specific Santa Fe Springs Zip Codes call (213) 868-3731	
Santa Margarita	93453
Santa Maria	93454-57
For specific Santa Maria Zip Codes call (805) 922-1911	
Santa Maria Town Center (Part of Santa Maria)	93454
Santa Monica	90401-11
For specific Santa Monica Zip Codes call (213) 576-2626	
Santa Monica Canyon (Part of Los Angeles)	90406
Santa Monica Place (Part of Santa Monica)	90401
Santa Nella	95322
Santa Paula	93060-61
For specific Santa Paula Zip Codes call (805) 525-6911	
Santa Rita (Monterey County)	93901
Santa Rita (Santa Barbara County)	93436
Santa Rita Park	93661
Santa Rosa	95401-09
For specific Santa Rosa Zip Codes call (707) 528-8763	
Santa Rosa Indian Reservation	92543
Santa Rosa Island Air Force Station	93041
Santa Rosa Plaza (Part of Santa Rosa)	95401
Santa Susana (Part of Simi Valley)	93063
Santa Venetia	94901
Santa Western (Part of Los Angeles)	90072
Santa Ynez	93460
Santa Ysabel	92070
Santa Ysabel Indian Reservation	92070
Santee	92071-72
For specific Santee Zip Codes call (619) 448-2448	
San Ysidro (Part of San Diego)	92143
	92173
For specific San Ysidro Zip Codes call (619) 428-1345	
Saranap	94596
Saratoga	95070-71
For specific Saratoga Zip Codes call (408) 867-3086	
Sather Gate (Part of Berkeley)	94704
Saticoy (Part of Ventura)	93004

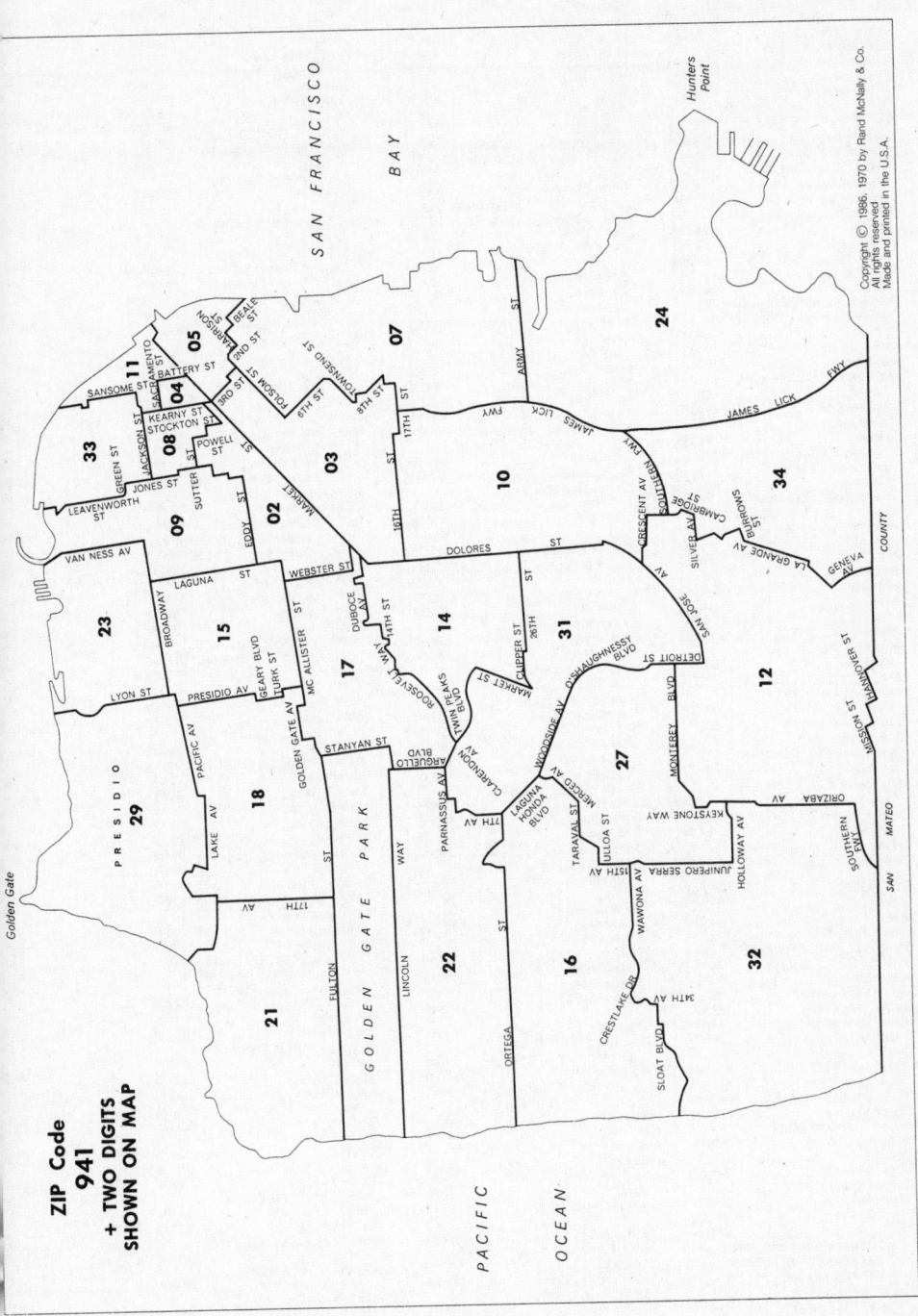

ZIP Code
941
+ TWO DIGITS
SHOWN ON MAP

	ZIP
Stewart Springs	96094
Stine Station (Part of Bakersfield)	93309
Stinson Beach	94970
Stirling City	95978
Stockdale (Part of Bakersfield)	93309
Stockton	95201-19
	95267-69
For specific Stockton Zip Codes call (209) 983-6317	
Stonegate (Part of Portola Valley)	94028
Stonehurst (Part of Oakland)	94603
Stone Lagoon	95570
Stonestown (Part of San Francisco)	94132
Stonewood Shopping Center (Part of Downey)	90241
Stonyford	95979
Storey	93637
Storrie	95980
Stovepipe Wells	92328
Stratford	93266
Strathmore	93267
Strawberry (El Dorado County)	95720
Strawberry (Tuolumne County)	95375
Strawberry Point	94941
Strawberry Valley	95981
Stuart	92055
Studebaker (Part of Norwalk)	90650
Studio City (Part of Los Angeles)	91604
	91614
For specific Studio City Zip Codes call (818) 506-0087	
Suburban Acres	96080
Success	93257
Sugarloaf	92386
Sugarloaf Mountain Park	95979
Sugar Pine (Madera County)	93644
Sugar Pine (Tuolumne County)	95346
Suisun City	94585
Sulphur Springs	93060
Sultana	93666
Summer Home	95336
Summerhome Park	95436
Summerland	93067
Summit	92345
Summit City	96089
Sun City	92584-87
For specific Sun City Zip Codes call (714) 679-1737	
Sunfair	92252
Sunkist (Part of Anaheim)	92806
Sunland	91040-41
For specific Sunland Zip Codes call (818) 353-5255	
Sunny Brae (Part of Arcata)	95521
Sunnybrook	95640
Sunny Hills (Part of Fullerton)	92632
Sunnymead	92553
Sunnyside (Fresno County)	93727
Sunnyside (San Diego County)	91902
Sunnyside (Placer County)	96145
Sunnyside-Tahoe City	96145
Sunnyslope (Butte County)	95914
Sunnyslope (Riverside County)	92509
Sunnyvale	94086-89
For specific Sunnyvale Zip Codes call (408) 732-0121	
Sunnyvale Town Center (Part of Sunnyvale)	94086
Sunny Vista (Part of Chula Vista)	91910
Sunol	94586
Sunrise Mall	95610
Sunrise Oasis (Part of Palm Springs)	92262
Sunrise Vista	95451
Sunset (Humboldt County)	95521
Sunset (San Francisco County)	94122
Sunset Beach (Orange County)	90742
Sunset Beach (Santa Cruz County)	95076
Sunset Cliffs (Part of San Diego)	92107

	ZIP
Sunset Hills	91745
Sunset Terrace	93402
Sunset Tract	93022
Sunset View	95945
Sunset Whitney Ranch (Part of Rocklin)	95677
Sunshine Homes	91350
Sunshine Summit	92536
Sun Valley	91352-53
For specific Sun Valley Zip Codes call (818) 767-0223	
Sunvalley (Part of Concord)	94520
Sun Village (Part of Palmdale)	93550
Surf	93436
Surfside (Part of Seal Beach)	90743
Susana Knolls (Part of Simi Valley)	93063
Susanville	96130
Sutter	95982
Sutter Creek	95685
Sutter Hill	95685
Sutter Island	95615
Sutter Street (Part of San Francisco)	94104
Swanton	95017
Sweet Brier	96017
Sweetwater	95451
Sycamore (Colusa County)	95957
Sycamore (Contra Costa County)	94526
Sylmar (Part of Los Angeles)	91345
Sylvia Park	90290
Table Bluff	95551
Taft	93268
Taft Heights	93268
Tahoe City	96145
Tahoe Keys (Part of South Lake Tahoe)	96150
Tahoe Paradise (Part of South Lake Tahoe)	96155
Tahoe Pines	96141
Tahoe Valley (Part of South Lake Tahoe)	96158
Tahoe Vista	96148
Tahoma	96142
Talica (Part of Oceanside)	92054
Talmage	95481
Tamalpais-Homestead Valley	94941
Tamalpais Valley	94941
Tamarack	95223
Tambs Station	95370
Tanforan (Part of South San Francisco)	94080
Tanforan Park (Part of San Bruno)	94066
Tangair	93437
Tanglewood	95018
Tara Hills	94564
Tarpey	93727
Tarzana	91356-57
For specific Tarzana Zip Codes call (818) 345-3172	
Tassajara Hot Springs	93924
Taurusa	93277
Taylorsville	95983
Tecate	91980
Tecnor	96058
Tecopa	92389
Tecopa Hot Springs	92389
Tehachapi	93561
	93581-82
For specific Tehachapi Zip Codes call (805) 822-3276	
Tehama	96090
Temecula	92589-93
For specific Temecula Zip Codes call (714) 699-1121	
Temelec	95476
Temple City	91780
Templeton	93465
Tennant	96058
Tent City (Part of Coronado)	92118
Terminal Annex (Part of Los Angeles)	90054
Terminous	95240
Termo	96132
Terra Bella	93270
Terra Linda (Part of San Rafael)	94901
Tewksbury Heights	94805
Textile (Part of Los Angeles)	90015

	ZIP
The Falls	93604
The Forks (Madera County)	93604
The Forks (Mendocino County)	95482
The Geysers	95425
The Hermitage	95585
The Oaks	95945
The Pines	93604
Thermal	92274
Thermalito	95965
The Sea Ranch	95497
Thomas Mountain	92561
Thornton	95686
Thousand Oaks	91319-20
	91359-62
For specific Thousand Oaks Zip Codes call (805) 497-8661	
Thousand Palms	92276
Three Arch Bay (Part of Dana Point)	92677
Three Point	93532
Three Rivers	93271
Three Rocks	93608
Tiburon	94920
Tierra Buena	95991
Tierra del Sol	91905
Tionesta	96134
Tipton	93272
Tivy Valley	93657
Tobin	95965
Tocaloma	94950
Todd Valley	95631
Todos Santos (Part of Concord)	94522
Tollhouse	93667
Toluca Lake (Part of Los Angeles)	91602
Tomales	94971
Toms Place	93514
Tonyville	93247
Toolville	93221
Topanga	90290
Topanga Beach	90265
Topanga Oaks	90290
Topanga Park	90290
Topanga Plaza (Part of Los Angeles)	91303
Topa Topa	93060
Topaz	96133
Top of the World (Part of Laguna Beach)	92651
Tormey	94572
Torrance	90501-10
For specific Torrance Zip Codes call (213) 328-9363	
Torres-Martinez Indian Reservation	92274
Torrey Pines Homes (Part of San Diego)	92037
Tower (Part of Fresno)	93728
Town and Country (Riverside County)	92553
Town and Country (Sacramento County)	95821
Town Center (Part of Visalia)	93291
Toyon	96019
Trabuco Canyon	92678
Tracy	95376-78
For specific Tracy Zip Codes call (209) 835-4774	
Tranquillity	93668
Traver	93673
Tres Pinos	95075
Trevarno (Part of Livermore)	94550
Trigo	93637
Trimmer	93657
Trinidad	95570
Trinity Alps	96052
Trinity Center	96091
Trinity Village	95527
Triple R Estates	93257
Trona	93562
	93592
For specific Trona Zip Codes call (619) 372-4789	
Tropico	91204-05
	91208
For specific Tropico Zip Codes call (818) 502-3250	
Tropico Village	93560
Trowbridge	95659
Truckee	96160-62
For specific Truckee Zip Codes call (916) 555-1212	

	ZIP
Tujunga	91042-43
For specific Tujunga Zip Codes call (818) 353-1197	
Tulare	93274-75
For specific Tulare Zip Codes call (209) 686-1594	
Tulelake	96134
Tule River Indian Reservation	93257
Tunitas	94109
Tuolumne	95379
Tuolumne Meadows	95389
Tupman	93276
Turlock	95380-81
For specific Turlock Zip Codes call (209) 632-3801	
Tustin	92680-81
For specific Tustin Zip Codes call (714) 544-5170	
Tustin Foothills	92680
Tuttle	95340
Tuttletown	95370
Tuxedo Country Club Estates	95204
Tuxedo Park (Part of Stockton)	95204
T.V. Bell (Part of Merced)	95340
Twain	95984
Twain Harte	95383
Tweedy (Part of South Gate)	90280
Twentynine Palms	92277-78
For specific Twentynine Palms Zip Codes call (619) 367-3501	
Twentynine Palms Base	92278
Twentynine Palms Marine Corps Base	92278
Twentytwo Mile House	93637
Twin Bridges	95735
Twin Creeks	95120
Twin Lakes	95060
Twin Oaks	92069
Twin Peaks	92391
Two Rock Coast Guard Station	94952
Tyler Mall (Part of Riverside)	92503
Ukiah	95482
Ulmar (Part of Livermore)	94550
Union (Part of Napa)	94558
Union City	94587
Union Hill	95945
Universal City	91608
University (Orange County)	92716
University (Santa Barbara County)	93107
University City (Part of San Diego)	92122
University Heights	94025
University of California-Davis	95616
University of Santa Clara (Part of Santa Clara)	95050
University Towne Centre (Part of San Diego)	92121
Upland	91785-86
For specific Upland Zip Codes call (714) 981-2824	
Upper Lake	95485
Uptown (Part of San Bernardino)	92405
Vaca (Part of Vacaville)	95687
Vacation	95446
Vacaville	95687-88
	95696
For specific Vacaville Zip Codes call (707) 448-2030	
Valencia	91354-55
	91385
For specific Valencia Zip Codes call (805) 254-1684	
Valinda	91744
Valla (Part of Santa Fe Springs)	90670
Vallco Fashion Park (Part of Cupertino)	95014
Vallecito	95251
Vallecitos Town Center (Part of San Marcos)	92069
Vallejo	94589-92
For specific Vallejo Zip Codes call (707) 642-4441	
Vallemar (Part of Pacifica)	94044
Valle Vista (Alameda County)	94541
Valle Vista (Riverside County)	92544
Valley Acres	93268
Valley Center	92082

	ZIP
Valley Estates	93283
Valley Fair (Part of San Jose)	95128
Valley Ford	94972
Valley Home	95384
Valley Lake Ranchos	93637
Valley of Enchantment	92325
Valley of the Moon	92325
Valley Plaza (Imperial County)	92243
Valley Plaza (Kern County)	93304
Valley Plaza (Los Angeles County)	91606
Valley Springs	95252
Valley View Park	92325
Valley Village (Part of Los Angeles)	91607
Valona	94525
Val Verde Park	91350
Valyermo	93563
Vandenberg Air Force Base	93437
Vandenberg Village	93436
Van Nuys	91401-02
	91404-12
For specific Van Nuys Zip Codes call (818) 908-6608	
Vanowen (Part of Los Angeles)	91405
Venice (Part of Los Angeles)	90291-96
For specific Venice Zip Codes call (213) 396-3191	
Ventucopa	93252
Ven-tu Park (Part of Thousand Oaks)	91320
Ventura	93001-09
For specific Ventura Zip Codes call (805) 643-5457	
Verdemont	92402
Verdi	89439
Verdugo City (Part of Glendale)	91046
Verdugo Viejo	91206-08
	91226
For specific Verdugo Viejo Zip Codes call (213) 586-1467	
Vernalis	95385
Vernon	90058
Verona	95659
Verona Landing	95659
Veteran Heights	94508
Veterans Administration	90073
Veterans Bureau Hospital (Part of Palo Alto)	94304
Veterans Home (Part of Yountville)	94599
Veterans Hospital (Part of Los Angeles)	91343
Victor	95253
Victoria Court (Part of Santa Barbara)	93101
Victoria Park (Part of Carson)	90247
Victorville	92392-94
For specific Victorville Zip Codes call (619) 245-7723	
Victory Center (Part of Los Angeles)	91606
Vidal	92225
View Park	90043
View Park-Windsor Hills	90043
Viking (Part of Long Beach)	90808
Village (Part of Los Angeles)	90024
Villa Grande	95486
Villa Park	92667
Villa Verona	95965
Vina	96092
Vineburg	95487
Vine Hill	94553
Vintage Faire Mall (Part of Modesto)	95356
Vinton	96135
Vinvale (Part of South Gate)	90280
Viola	96088
Virginia Colony	93021
Virner	95634
Visalia	93277-79
	93291-92
For specific Visalia Zip Codes call (209) 732-8073	
Visalia Mall (Part of Visalia)	93277
Visitacion (Part of San Francisco)	94134
Vista	92083-85
For specific Vista Zip Codes call (619) 726-0772	

	ZIP
Vista Del Mar (Part of San Clemente)	92672
Vista del Morro	93402
Vista Grande	93637
Vista La Mesa (Part of La Mesa)	91941
Vista Park	93307
Volcano	95689
Volta	93635
Vorden	95690
Waddington	95536
Wagner (Part of Los Angeles)	90047
Wagy Flats	93240
Walerga	95660
Walker (Los Angeles County)	90201
Walker (Mono County)	96107
Walker Landing	95690
Wallace	95254
Walnut	91788-89
For specific Walnut Zip Codes call (714) 594-1741	
Walnut Creek	94504
	94593-98
For specific Walnut Creek Zip Codes call (415) 935-1842	
Walnut Creek West	94598
Walnut Grove	95690
Walnut Heights	94596
Walnut Park	90255
Walteria (Part of Torrance)	90505
Warm Springs (Part of Fremont)	94539
Warner Ranch	92553
Warner Springs	92086
Wasco	93280
Washington (Part of Los Angeles)	90011
Washington (Part of Pasadena)	91114
Washington (Nevada County)	95986
Washington Flat	95543
Washington Manor (Part of San Leandro)	94579
Waterford	95386
Waterloo	95215
Watson (Part of Carson)	90744
Watsonville	95076-77
For specific Watsonville Zip Codes call (408) 724-2262	
Watts (Part of Los Angeles)	90002
Watts Valley	93667
Waukena	93282
Waverly Heights (Part of Thousand Oaks)	91360
Wawona	95389
Weaverville	96093
Webster Street (Part of Alameda)	94501
Weed	96094
Weedpatch	93241
Weimar	95736
Weitchpec	95546
Weldon	93283
Wendel	96136
Weott	95571
West Adams (Part of Los Angeles)	90016
West Arcadia (Part of Arcadia)	91006
West Athens	90247
West Butte	95953
West Carson	90502
Westchester (Part of Los Angeles)	90045
West Compton	90220
West Covina	91790-93
For specific West Covina Zip Codes call (818) 962-8611	
West Covina Fashion Plaza (Part of West Covina)	91790
Westend	93562
Western Pacific Mole (Part of Oakland)	94607
Western Village	93501
Westfield (Part of Rancho Palos Verdes)	90274
West Garden Grove (Part of Garden Grove)	92645
Westgate (Santa Clara County)	95117
Westgate (Ventura County)	91360
Westgate Mall (Part of San Jose)	95129

	ZIP
West Guernewood	95446
Westhaven (Fresno County)	93245
Westhaven (Humboldt County)	95570
West Hollywood	90046
	90048
	90069
For specific West Hollywood Zip Codes call (213) 933-8448	
Westlake (San Mateo County)	94015
Westlake (San Mateo County)	94014
Westlake Shopping Center (Part of Daly City)	94015
Westlake Village (Los Angeles County)	91361
Westlake Village (Ventura County)	91360
Westley	95387
West Los Angeles (Part of Los Angeles)	90025
West Menlo Park	94025
Westminster	92683-84
For specific Westminster Zip Codes call (714) 898-4929	
Westminster Mall (Part of Westminster)	92683
West Modesto	95351
Westmont	90044
Westmorland	92281
West Palm Springs	92282
West Parlier	93648
West Pittsburg	94565
West Point	95255
Westport	95488
West Portal (Part of San Francisco)	94127
West Puente Valley	91744
West Sacramento	95691
West Saticoy (Part of Ventura)	93001
Westside (Part of San Bernardino)	92411
Westside Pavilion (Part of Los Angeles)	90074
Westvern (Part of Los Angeles)	90062
West Whittier	90606
West Whittier-Los Nietos	90606
Westwood (Lassen County)	96137
Westwood (Los Angeles County)	90024
Westwood Manor	96001
Westwood Village (Part of Arcata)	95521
Wheatland	95692
Wheeler Ridge	93301
Wherry Housing	93523
Whiskeytown	96095
Whispering Pines (Lake County)	95461
Whispering Pines (San Diego County)	92036
White Hall	95726
White Oak (Part of Los Angeles)	91416
White Pines	95223
White River (mail Porterville)	93257
White River (mail California Hot Springs)	93207
White Rock	95630
Whitethorn	95589
White Water	92282
Whitley Gardens	93446
Whitlow	95554

	ZIP
Whitmore	96096
Whitmore Hot Springs	93546
Whitner Heights	93648
Whittier	90601-12
For specific Whittier Zip Codes call (213) 698-9921	
Whittier Quad Shopping Center (Part of Whittier)	90605
Whittwood Mall (Part of Whittier)	90603
Wiest	92227
Wilbur Springs	95987
Wilcox (Part of Los Angeles)	90038
Wildflower	93662
Wildomar	92595
Wildwood (Santa Cruz County)	95006
Wildwood (Trinity County)	96001
Wilfred	95401
Willaura Estates	95949
William H. Taft (Part of San Diego)	92117
Williams	95987
Willits	95490
Willow Brook	90222
Willow Creek (Humboldt County)	95573
Willow Creek (Plumas County)	96020
Willow Ranch	96108
Willows	95988
Willow Springs (Kern County)	93560
Willow Springs (Tuolumne County)	95372
Willow Springs (Mono County)	93517
Willow Valley	95959
Will Rogers (Part of Santa Monica)	90402
	90408
For specific Will Rogers Zip Codes call (310) 576-2616	
Wilmar (Part of Rosemead)	91770
Wilmington (Part of Los Angeles)	90744
	90748
For specific Wilmington Zip Codes call (310) 834-5204	
Wilmington Park (Part of Los Angeles)	90744
Wilseyville	95257
Wilsona	93534
Wilson Acres	96080
Wilsona Gardens	93534
Wilsonia	93633
Wilton	95693
Winchester	92596
Windsor	95492
Windsor Hills	90052
Windy Acres	93283
Winnetka (Part of Los Angeles)	91306
Winter Gardens	92040
Winterhaven	92283
Winters	95694
Winterwarm	92028
Winton	95388
Wise (Part of El Segundo)	90245
Wiseburn (Part of Hawthorne)	90250
Wishon	93669
Witch Creek	92065
Witter Springs	95493

	ZIP
Wofford Heights	93285
Wolf	95603
Wonderland	96003
Woodacre	94973
Woodbridge	95258
Woodcrest	92504
Woodfords	96120
Woodlake	93286
Woodland	95695
	95776
For specific Woodland Zip Codes call (916) 662-5976	
Woodland Hills	91302
	91364-67
For specific Woodland Hills Zip Codes call (818) 347-4056	
Woodleaf	95925
Woodruff Avenue (Part of Bellflower)	90706
Woodside	94062
Woodside Glens (Part of Woodside)	94062
Woodson Bridge Estates	96021
Woodville	93258
Woodward Park (Part of Fresno)	93710
	93720
	93729
For specific Woodward Park Zip Codes call (209) 435-2767	
Woody	93287
Workman (Part of South Gate)	90280
Worldway Postal Center (Part of Los Angeles)	90009
Wrights Lake	95720
Wrightwood	92397
Wyandotte	95965
Wynola	92070
Wyntoon	96091
Yale (Part of Hemet)	92544
Yankee Hill	95965
Yankee Jims	95631
Yerba Buena Island (Part of San Francisco)	94130
Yermo	92398
Yettem	93670
Ygnacio Valley (Part of Walnut Creek)	94598
Yolanda (Part of San Anselmo)	94960
Yolo	95697
Yorba (Part of Pomona)	91767
Yorba Linda	92686-87
For specific Yorba Linda Zip Codes call (714) 528-7601	
York (Part of Los Angeles)	90050
Yorkville	95494
Yosemite Lodge	95389
Yosemite National Park	95389
Yountville	94599
Yreka	96097
Yuba City	95991-93
For specific Yuba City Zip Codes call (916) 673-9153	
Yuba City Farm Labor Center	95991
Yucaipa	92399
Yucca Valley	92284
	92286
For specific Yucca Valley Zip Codes call (619) 365-3855	
Zamora	95698
Zayante	95018
Zenia	95595

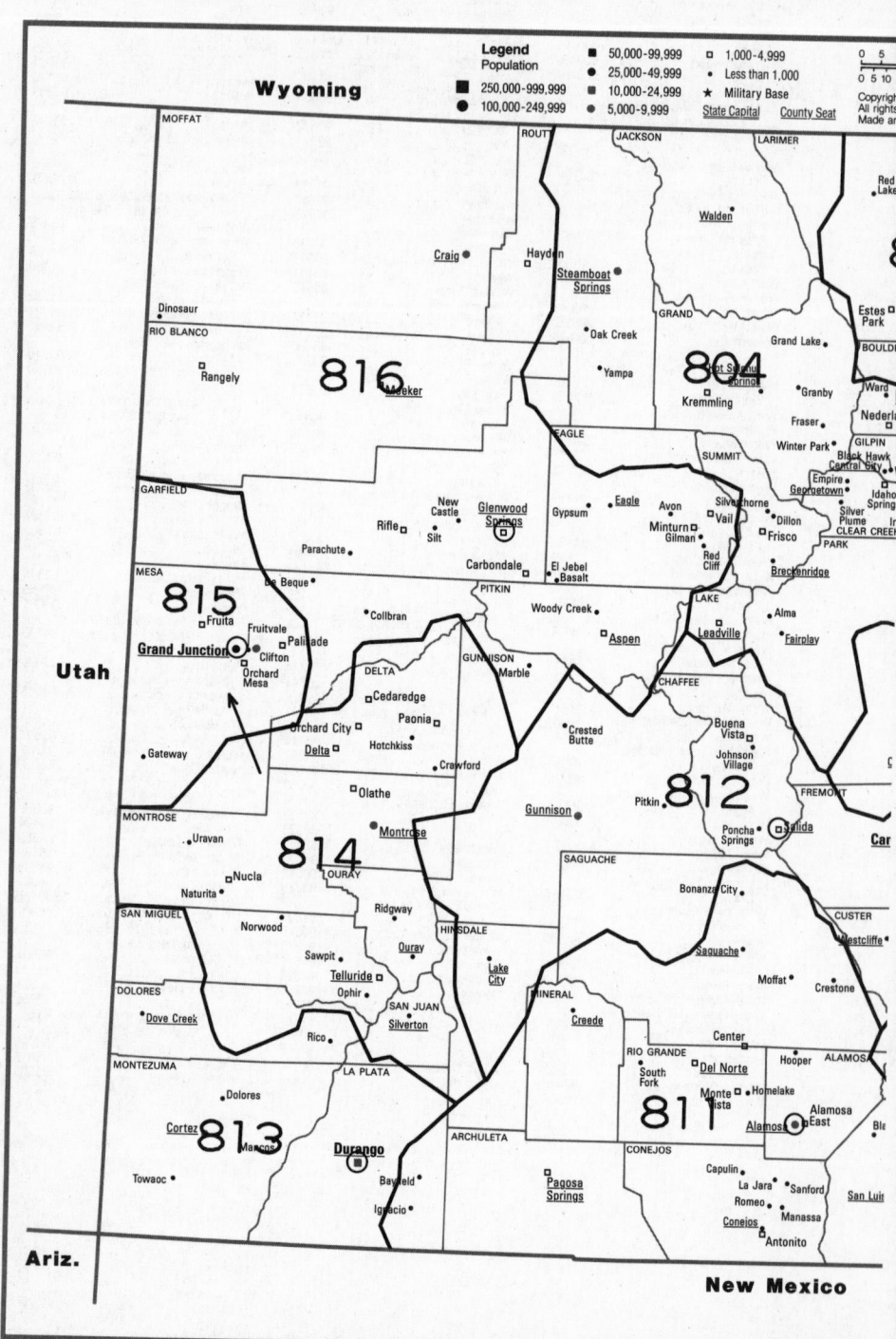

Legend
Population

■ 50,000-99,999 □ 1,000-4,999
● 25,000-49,999 • Less than 1,000
■ 250,000-999,999 ● 10,000-24,999 ★ Military Base
● 100,000-249,999 ● 5,000-9,999 State Capital County Seat

Wyoming

MOFFAT

ROUT JACKSON LARIMER

Red F
Lakes

Walden

Craig • Hayden
□ Steamboat
Springs

GRAND

Oak Creek

Grand Lake •

Estes
Park

BOULDE

Dinosaur •

RIO BLANCO

Rangely □

816

Meeker

Yampa •

804

Kremmling •

Hot Sulphur
Springs

Granby •

Fraser •

Winter Park •

Ward

Nederla

GILPIN

Black Hawk

Central City

EAGLE

SUMMIT

Empire • Georgetown •

Idaho
Spring

GARFIELD

New
Castle Glenwood
Springs

Rifle □ Silt •

Parachute •

Gypsum • Eagle •

Avon • Silverthorne
Vail □

Minturn •
Gilman •

Dillon •

Frisco •

Silver
Plume •

Ir
CLEAR CREEK

MESA

De Beque •

Carbondale •

El Jebel □
Basalt •

PITKIN

Red
Cliff •

PARK

LAKE

Breckenridge □

815

Fruita
□

Fruitvale •

Palisade □

Collbran •

Woody Creek •

Aspen □

Leadville □

Alma •

Fairplay •

Grand Junction ⊙

Clifton •

Orchard
Mesa

DELTA

GUNNISON

CHAFFEE

Cedaredge □

Marble •

Gateway •

Orchard City □

Paonia •

Hotchkiss •

Crested
Butte •

Buena
Vista •

Johnson
Village •

C

Delta □

Crawford •

Olathe □

Gunnison •

Pitkin •

812

FREMONT

MONTROSE

Uravan •

814

Montrose □

Poncha
Springs •

Salida ⊙

Car

SAGUACHE

Naturita •

Nucla □

OURAY

Bonanza City •

CUSTER

Westcliffe

SAN MIGUEL

Norwood •

Ridgway •

HINSDALE

Saguache □

Moffat •

Crestone •

Sawpit •

Ouray □

Lake
City □

Telluride □

Ophir •

SAN JUAN

MINERAL

Center •

DOLORES

Dove Creek □

Rico •

Silverton □

Creede □

RIO GRANDE

South
Fork •

Del Norte □

Hooper •

ALAMOS

MONTEZUMA

LA PLATA

Monte □ Homelake •
Vista

Alamosa
East •

Bla

Dolores •

813

ARCHULETA

CONEJOS

Alamosa ⊙

Cortez □

Mancos •

Durango ⊙

Capulin •

La Jara □ Sanford •

San Luis

Towaoc •

Bayfield •

Pagosa
Springs □

Romeo • Manassa •

Ignacio •

811

Conejos □

Antonito •

Utah

Ariz.

New Mexico

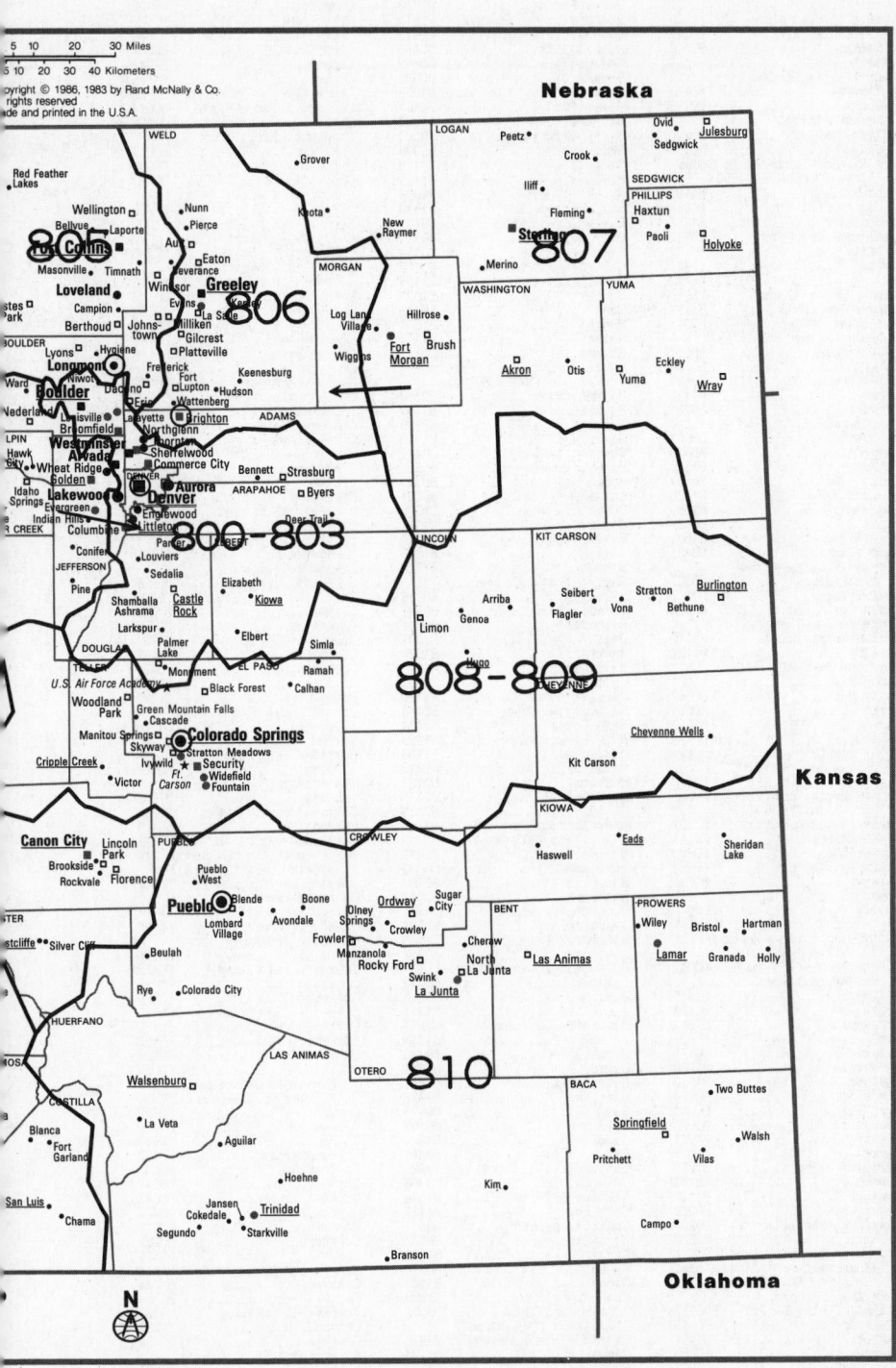

Nebraska

Kansas

Oklahoma

	ZIP		ZIP		ZIP
Acres Green	80124	Bennett	80102	Castle Rock	80104
Adams	80022	Bergen Park	80439	Castlewood	80120
Adams City (Part of		Berthoud (Larimer County)	80513	Cattle Creek	81623
Commerce City)	80022	Berthoud (Weld County)	80513	Cedar	81431
Agate	80101	Berthoud Falls	80438	Cedar Cove	80537
Aguilar	81020	Berthoud Pass	80452	Cedaredge	81413
Airport Mail Facility (Part of		Bethune	80805	Center	81125
Denver)	80207	Beulah	81023	Central City	80427
Akron	80720	Beverly Hills	80104	Chaddsford (Part of Aurora)	80014
Alameda (Part of		Big Bend	81092	Chama	81126
Lakewood)	80215	Big Elk Meadows	80540	Chambers Square (Part of	
Alamosa	81101-02	Black Forest	80908	Aurora)	80011
For specific Alamosa Zip Codes		Black Hawk	80422	Chapel Hills	80907
call (719) 589-4908		Blanca	81123	Chatfield Estates	80123
Alamosa East	81101	Blende	81006	Chautauqua (Part of	
Alcott (Part of Denver)	80212	Blue Mountain	81610	Boulder)	80302
Alder	81155	Blue Mountain Estates	80401	Cheraw	81030
Allenspark	80510	Blue Ridge	80424	Cherry Creek (Part of	
Allison	81137	Blue River	80424	Denver)	80206
Alma	80420	Blue Valley	80452	Cherry Creek Shopping	
Almont	81210	Bonanza City	81155	Center (Part of Denver)	80206
Alpine (Chaffee County)	81236	Boncarbo	81024	Cherry Hills Crest	80120
Alpine (Rio Grande County)	81154	Bond	80423	Cherry Hills Manor	80120
Altura (Part of Aurora)	80011	Bondad	81301	Cherry Hills Village	80110
Altura Annex (Part of		Boone	81025	Cherry Knolls	80120
Aurora)	80011	Boulder	80301-10	Cherry Park	80110
Alvin	80758	For specific Boulder Zip Codes		Cherry Valley	80116
American City	80427	call (303) 938-1100		Cherrywood Village	80120
Ames	81426	Boulder Heights	80302	Cheyenne Canon (Part of	
Amherst	80721	Bountiful	81140	Colorado Springs)	80907
Andersonville (Part of Fort		Bovina	80818	Cheyenne Wells	80810
Collins)	80521	Bowie	81428	Chimney Rock	81127
Angel Acres	80433	Bow Mar	80120	Chipita Park	80809
Antlers	81650	Boxelder Estates	80521	Chivington	81036
Anton	80801	Boyero	80821	Chromo	81128
Antonito	81120	Bracewell	80631	Chula Vista	80401
Apache City	81089	Brandon	81026	Cimarron	81220
Apex	80427	Branson	81027	Cimarron Hills	80906
Appleton	81501	Breckenridge	80424	Cinderella City (Part of	
Applewood	80401	Breen	81326	Englewood)	80110
Applewood Village (Part of		Brewster	81226	Citadel, The (Part of	
Wheat Ridge)	80033	Briargate (Part of Colorado		Colorado Springs)	80909
Arabian Acres	80816	Springs)	80918	Clark	80428
Arapahoe	80802	Brigadoon Glen	80501	Clifton	81520
Arapahoe East (Part of		Briggsdale	80611	Climax	80429
Greenwood Village)	80112	Brighton	80601	Coal Creek	81221
Arboles	81121	Bristol	81028	Coaldale	81222
Aristocrat Ranchettes	80621	Broadmoor (Part of		Coalmont	80430
Arlington	81021	Colorado Springs)	80906	Cokedale	81032
Aroya	80862	Broadway Estates	80120	Collbran	81624
Arriba	80804	Broken Arrow Acres	80433	College Heights (Part of	
Arriola	81323	Brook Forest	80439	Durango)	81301
Arvada	80001-06	Brook Forest Estates	80439	Colona	81401
For specific Arvada Zip Codes call		Brookridge	80120	Colorado City (El Paso	
(303) 421-2200		Brookside	81212	County)	80904
Aspen	81611-12	Brookvale	80439	Colorado City (Pueblo	
For specific Aspen Zip Codes call		Broomfield	80020-21	County)	81019
(303) 925-7523			80038	Colorado Mountain Estates	80816
Aspen (Part of Fort Collins)	80527	For specific Broomfield Zip Codes		Colorado Sierra	80401
Aspen-Gerbaz	81611	call (303) 466-1711		Colorado Springs	80901-97
Aspen Park	80433	Brownlee	80480	For specific Colorado Springs Zip	
Association Camp	80511	Brownsville	80026	Codes call (719) 570-5377	
Atwood	80722	Brush	80723	Colorado Technical College	80907
Ault	80610	Buckeye	80549	Columbine (census	
Aurora	80010-19	Buckingham (Part of Fort		designated place)	
	80040-47	Collins)	80521	(Jefferson County)	80123
For specific Aurora Zip Codes call		Buckingham Plaza (Part of		Columbine (Jefferson	
(303) 364-9215		Aurora)	80012	County)	80120
Aurora Mall (Part of Aurora)	80012	Buckingham Square (Part of		Columbine (Routt County)	80428
Austin (Part of Orchard		Aurora)	80012	Columbine Hills	80120
City)	81410	Buda	80513	Columbine Knolls	80120
Avon	81620	Buena Vista	81211	Columbine Knolls South	80123
Avondale	81022	Buena Vista Correctional		Columbine Manor	80120
Bailey	80421	Facility	81211	Columbine Valley	80123
Bakersville	80476	Buffalo Creek	80425	Commerce City	80022
Baldwin	81230	Buford	81641		80037
Balltown	81228	Burland Ranchettes	80470	For specific Commerce City Zip	
Barnesville	80624	Burlington	80807	Codes call (303) 288-2100	
Barr	80601	Burns	80426	Como	80432
Bartlett	81090	Byers	80103	Conejos	81129
Barton	81041	Caddoa	81044	Conifer	80433
Basalt	81621	Cadet	80841	Conifer Mountain	80433
Battlement Mesa	81636	Cahone	81320	Conifer Park	80433
Baxterville	81132	Calhan	80808	Cope	80812
Bayfield	81122	California Oil Camp	81648	Copper Mountain	80443
Beacon Hill	80860	Camp Bird	81427	Copper Spur	80423
Bear Valley (Part of Denver)	80227	Camp George West	80401	Cornish	80611
	80232	Campion	80537	Coronado	80229
	80236-37	Campo	81029	Cortez	81321
For specific Bear Valley Zip Codes		Canfield	80026	Cory (Part of Orchard City)	81414
call (303) 986-6808		Canon	81120	Cotopaxi	81223
Bear Valley Shopping		Canon City	81212-15	Country Acres	80534
Center (Part of Denver)	80227	For specific Canon City Zip Codes		Country Club Estates	80521
Beaver Ridge	80440	call (719) 275-6877		Country Club Park	80303
Bedrock	81411	Capitol Hill (Part of Denver)	80218	Cowdrey	80434
Beecher Island	80758	Capulin	81124	Cragmor (Part of Colorado	
Belle Plain (Part of Pueblo)	81001	Carbondale	81623	Springs)	80907
Bellvue	80512	Cardiff	81601	Craig	81625-26
Belmar (Part of Lakewood)	80226	Carr	80612	For specific Craig Zip Codes call	
Belmont (Part of Pueblo)	81001	Cascade	80809	(303) 824-5795	
Bendemeer Valley	80439	Cascade-Chipita Park	80809	Craig South Highlands	81625

	ZIP
Crawford	81415
Creede	81130
Crescent	80401
Crested Butte	81224
Crestmoor (Part of Glendale)	80222
Crestone	81131
Crestwoods	80424
Crews	80911
Cripple Creek	80813
Crisman	80302
Crook	80726
Crossroads Mall (Part of Boulder)	80301
Crowley	81033
Crystola	80863
Cuchara	81055
Cuerna Verde	81069
Dacono	80514
Dailey	80728
De Beque	81630
Deckers	80135
Deepcreek	80428
Deer Creek Valley Ranchos	80470
Deer Park	80467
Deer Trail	80105
Delhi	81059
Del Norte	81132
Delta	81416
Denver	**80201-95**

For specific Denver Zip Codes call
(303) 297-6000

COLLEGES & UNIVERSITIES

Metropolitan State College of Denver	80217
Regis University	80221
University of Colorado at Denver	80217
University of Colorado Health Sciences Center	80262
University of Denver	80208

FINANCIAL INSTITUTIONS

The Bank of Cherry Creek, N.A.	80206
Bank Western, Federal Savings Bank	80202
Central Bank, National Association	80202
Colorado National Bank	80202
Colorado State Bank of Denver	80202
Affiliated National Bank-Denver	80202
Affiliated National Bank-University Hills	80222
First Federal Savings Bank of Colorado	80226
First Interstate Bank of Denver, N.A.	80270
First National Bank of Southeast Denver	80210
Guaranty Bank & Trust Co.	80202
Affiliated National Bank-Lakeside	80212
Mountain States Bank	80218
United Bank of Bear Valley, N.A.	80227
United Bank of Denver, N.A.	80274
United Bank of Lakewood, N.A.	80226

HOSPITALS

Denver Health and Hospitals	80204
Porter Memorial Hospital	80210
Presbyterian-St. Luke's Medical Center	80203
Rose Medical Center	80220
Saint Joseph Hospital	80218
Provident Health Partners-St. Anthony Central	80204
University Hospital	80262
Veterans Affairs Medical Center	80220

HOTELS/MOTELS

The Brown Palace Hotel	80202
Denver Marriott Hotel-City Center	80202
Embassy Suites Hotel & Athletic Club	80202
Oxford Hotel	80202
Radisson Hotel Denver	80202
Warwick Hotel	80203
Westin Hotel, Tabor Center	80202

	ZIP
MILITARY INSTALLATIONS	
Defense Finance and Accounting Service	80297
Denver Merchandise Mart	80216
Derby	80022
Derby Junction	80426
Devine	81001
Dillon	80435
Dinosaur	81610
Divide	80814
Dolores	81323
Dome Rock	80441
Dorey Lakes	80401
Dory Hill	80401
Dotsero	81637
Dove Creek	81324
Downieville	80436
Downtown (Part of Englewood)	80110
Doyleville	81239
Drake	80515
Drakes (Part of Fort Collins)	80521
Dream House Acres	80120
Dry Creek Basin	81431
Dumont	80436
Dupont	80024
Durango	81301-02

For specific Durango Zip Codes
call (303) 247-3434

Eads	81036
Eagle	81631
Eagle-Vail	81620
Eastlake (Adams County)	80614
Eastlake (Pueblo County)	81004
East Portal	80474
Eastridge (Part of Aurora)	80014
Eastridge South (Part of Aurora)	80014
East Weston	81091
Eaton	80615
Echo Lake	80452
Eckert (Part of Orchard City)	81418
Eckley	80727
Edgemont (Part of Lakewood)	80401
Edgewater	80214
Edison	80864
Edith	81128
Edler	81073
Edwards	81632
Egnar	81325
Elbert	80106
Eldora	80466
Eldorado Springs	80025
Elephant Park	80439
Eleven Mile Village	80827
Elizabeth	80107
El Jebel	81628
Elk Creek Acres	80470
Elk Creek Highlands	80470
Elkdale	80478
Elkhorn Acres	80470
Elk Springs	81633
Elkton	80860
Ellicott	80808
El Moro	81082
El Rancho	80401
El Vado	80302
Elwell	80534
Emma (Eagle County)	81623
Emma (Pitkin County)	81623
Empire	80438
Englewood	80110-12
	80150-56

For specific Englewood Zip Codes
call (303) 761-0474

Erie	80516
Erie Air Park (Part of Erie)	80516
Escalante Forks	81416
Estes Park	80517
Estrella	81101
Evans	80620
Evanston	80530
Evergreen	80439
Ever Green Hills	80439
Evergreen West	80439
Fairplay	80440
Fairview	81069
Fairview Estates	80123
Fairway Estates	80521
Falcon	80908
Falcon Estates	80908
Falfa	81301
Fall Creek	81430
Farista	81040
Farmers	80631
Federal Correctional Institution	80110

	ZIP
Federal Heights	80221
Fenders	80465
Ferncliff	80510
Firestone	80520
First View	80810
Flagler	80815
Fleming	80728
Flintwood Hills	80116
Florence	81226
Florissant	80816
Florissant Heights	80816
Fondis	80816
Foothills Fashion Mall (Part of Fort Collins)	80525
Forest Hills	80401
Fort Carson	80913
Fort Collins	80521-27

For specific Fort Collins Zip Codes
call (303) 482-2837

Fort Garland	81133
Fort Logan (Part of Sheridan)	80236
Fort Lupton	80621
Fort Lyon	81038
Fort Morgan	80701
Fountain	80817
Fountain Valley School	80911
Fowler	81039
Fox Creek	81120
Foxton	80441
Franktown	80116
Fraser	80442
Frederick	80530
Friendship Ranch	80470
Friendship Ranch Estates	80470
Frisco	80443
Fruita	81521
Fruitvale	81504
Galeton	80622
Garcia	81134
Garden City	80631
Gardner	81040
Garfield	81227
Gateway (Arapahoe County)	80014
Gateway (Douglas County)	80126
Gateway (Mesa County)	81522
Gato	81147
Gem Village	81122
Genesee	80401
Genoa	80818
Georgetown	80444
Gilcrest	80623
Gill	80624
Gilman	81645
Glade Park	81523
Glen Comfort	80515
Glendale	80222
Glendevey	82063
Gleneagle	80132
Glenelk	80470
Glen Haven	80532
Glen Isle	80421
Glen Park (Part of Palmer Lake)	80133
Glentivar	80440
Glenwood Springs	81601-02

For specific Glenwood Springs Zip
Codes call (303) 945-5611

Golden	80401-03

For specific Golden Zip Codes call
(303) 278-8537

Golden Acres (Part of Longmont)	80501
Goldfield	80860
Gold Hill	80302
Goodnight	81005
Goodrich	80653
Gould	80480
Granada	81041
Granby	80446
Grand Junction	81501-06

For specific Grand Junction Zip
Codes call (303) 244-3400

Grand Lake	80447
Grand Mesa	81413
Grandview	81301
Grandview Estates	80134
Granite	81228
Grant	80448
Gray's Mary Greenwood	81069
Greeley	80631-39

For specific Greeley Zip Codes
call (303) 353-0398

Greeley Mall (Part of Greeley)	80631
Greenland	80118
Green Mountain (Part of Lakewood)	80228
Green Mountain Camp	80459
Green Mountain Estates (Part of Lakewood)	80228

	ZIP		ZIP		ZIP
Green Mountain Falls	80819	Ione	80621	Lochwood (Part of	
Green Mountain Village		Irondale	80022	Lakewood)	80215
(Part of Lakewood)	80228	Ivywild (Part of Colorado		Log Lane Village	80701
Green Towers	81069	Springs)	80906	Loma	81524
Green Valley Acres	80433	Jamestown	80455	Loma Linda	81301
Greenway Park	80020	Jansen	81082	Lombard Village	81006
Greenwood (Custer County)	81253	Jaroso	81138	Lone Pine Estates	80465
Greenwood (Pueblo		Jefferson	80456	Longmont	80501-04
County)	81069	Jefferson Heights	80456	For specific Longmont Zip Codes	
Greenwood Village	80111	Joes	80822	call (303) 776-2135	
Greystone	81640	Johnson Village	81211	Longview	80441
Grizzly	81601	Johnstown	80534	Lookout Mountain	80401
Grover	80729	Juanita	81147	Loretto Heights (Part of	
Guadalupe	81129	Julesburg	80737	Denver)	80236
Guffey	80820	Kahler	80513	Los Fuertes	81153
Gulnare	81042	Kaibab	81631	Louisville	80027
Gunbarrel	80501	Karval	80823	Louviers	80131
Gunbarrel Estates	80501	Keenesburg	80643	Loveland	80537-39
Gunbarrel Greens	80301	Kelim	80537	For specific Loveland Zip Codes	
Gunnison	81230	Kelker (Part of Colorado		call (303) 667-0344	
Gypsum	81637	Springs)	80906	Loveland Heights	80515
Hahns Peak	80428	Kellytown	80125	Lubers	81057
Hale	80735	Ken Caryl	80127	Lucerne	80646
Halfway House	81220	Ken Caryl (census		Ludlow	81082
Hallcraft Town Houses (Part		designated place)	80123	Lyons	80540
of Lakewood)	80228	Keota	80729	Lyons Park Estates	80540
Hamilton	81638	Kersey	80644	McClave	81057
Hanover	80909	Keystone	80435	McClellands (Part of Fort	
Happy Canyon	80104	Kim	81049	Collins)	80521
Hardin	80644	Kingsborough (Part of		McCoy (Chaffee County)	81201
Harmony (Part of Fort		Aurora)	80017	McCoy (Eagle County)	80463
Collins)	80521	Kingsborough South (Part		McElmo	81321
Harris Park (Adams County)	80036	of Aurora)	80012	Mack	81525
Harris Park (Park County)	80470	Kings Corner	80537	Madison Hill (Part of	
Hartman	81043	Kiowa	80117	Westminster)	80030
Hartsel	80449	Kipling Hills	80123	Madrid	81082
Hasty	81044	Kipling Villas	80123	Magnolia	80466
Haswell	81045	Kirk	80824	Maher	81421
Hawley	81067	Kit Carson	80825	Manassa	81141
Haxtun	80731	Kittredge	80457	Mancos	81328
Hayden	81639	Kline	81326	Mancos Creek	81321
Hazeltine Heights	80640	Knaus	80634	Mandalay Gardens	80021
Heather Ridge (Part of		Knob Hill (Part of Colorado		Manitou Springs	80829
Aurora)	80014	Springs)	80910	Manzanola	81058
Heatherwood	80301	Koen	81041	Marble	81623
Heeney	80459	Kornman	81052	Marshall	80302
Henderson	80640	Kremmling	80459	Marshdale Park	80439
Hereford	80732	Kuhlmann Heights	80401	Marvel	81329
Heritage Place	80110	Kutch	80832	Mary Jane	80480
Hermosa	81301	K-Z Ranchettes	80470	Maryvale	80442
Herzman Mesa	80439	Lafayette	80026	Mason Corner	80631
Hesperus	81326	La Garita	81132	Masonic Park	81154
Hiawatha Camp	82901	Laird	80758	Masonville	80541
Hidden Valley	80439	La Jara	81140	Massadona	81610
Hideaway Park (Part of		La Junta	81050	Masters	80649
Winter Park)	80482	La Junta Gardens (Part of		Matheson	80830
High Chateau Ranches	80816	La Junta)	81050	Maxeyville	81144
Highland Acres	80631	Lakeborough	80235	Maybell	81640
Highland Hills	80634	Lake City	81235	Mayday	81326
Highland Lake	80651	Lake George	80827	Maysville	81201
Highland Lakes	80814	Lakeside	80212	May Valley	81052
Highland Park	80470	Lakeside Mall (Part of		Mead	80542
Highlands (Part of Denver)	80211	Wheat Ridge)	80212	Meadow Brook Heights	80120
Highlands Ranch	80126	Lake View	80401	Meadowood (Part of	
High-Mar (Part of Boulder)	80303	Lakewood	80215	Aurora)	80013
Hi-Land Acres	80601	Lamar	81052	Medina Plaza	81091
Hill N' Park	80631	La Montana Mesa	80816	Meeker	81641
Hillrose	80733	Laporte	80535	Meeker Park	80510
Hillside	81232	La Posta	81301	Meredith	81642
Hilltop	80134	Lariat (Part of Monte Vista)	81144	Merino	80741
Hiwan Hills	80439	Larkspur	80118	Mesa	81643
Hoehne	81046	La Salle	80645	Mesa Verde National Park	81330
Hoffman Heights (Part of		Las Animas	81054	Mesita	81152
Aurora)	80012	Lasauses	81151	Messex	80741
Holiday Hills	80863	Las Mesitas	81120	Milliken	80543
Holly	81047	Last Chance	80757	Milner	80487
Holyoke	80734	La Valley	81153	Mineral Hot Springs	81143
Homelake	81135	La Veta	81055	Minnequa (Part of Pueblo)	81007
Hooper	81136	Lawson	80452	Minnequa Heights (Part of	
Hotchkiss	81419	Lay	81625	Pueblo)	81007
Hot Sulphur Springs	80451	Lazear	81420	Minturn	81645
Howard	81233	Leadville	80461	Mirage	81143
Howells (Part of Littleton)	80120	Leadville North	80461	Mission Viejo (Part of	
Hoyt	80654	Leawood	80123	Aurora)	80013
Hudson	80642	Lebanon	81323	Model	81059
Hugo	80821	Leisure Living	80516	Moffat (Moffat County)	81638
Husted	80840	Lewis	81327	Moffat (Saguache County)	81143
Hyde	80743	Leyden	80401	Mogote	81120
Hygiene	80533	Liberty Bell Village	81435	Molina	81646
Hyland Hills	80439	Limon	80828	Montbello (Part of Denver)	80239
Hyland Knolls	80634	Lincoln Park	81212	Montclair (Part of Denver)	80220
Idaho Springs	80452	Lindon	80740	Monte Vista	81144
Idalia	80735	Littleton	80120-27	Montezuma	80435
Idledale	80453		80160-62	Montrose	81401-02
Ignacio	81137	For specific Littleton Zip Codes		For specific Montrose Zip Codes	
Iliff	80736	call (303) 798-2461		call (303) 249-6654	
Ilse	81212	Livengood Hills	80134	Monument	80132
Indian Creek	80816	Livermore	80536	Monument Lake Park	81091
Indian Hills	80454	Lobatos	81120	Moore Dale	80421
Indian Springs Village	80470	Lochbuie	80601	Morgan	81140
Indian Tree (Part of Arvada)	80006			Morrison	80465

	ZIP		ZIP		ZIP
Mosca	81146	Pine	80470	Rye Ranchettes	81069
Mountain Park	80401	Pinebrook Hills	80302	Sable (Part of Aurora)	80011
Mountain View (Jefferson		Pinecliffe	80471	Saguache	81149
County)	80212	Pine Crest (Part of Palmer		Saint Charles Mesa	81006
Mountain View (Larimer		Lake)	80133	St. Elmo	81236
County)	80521	Pine Hills	80132	St. Petersburg	80728
Mountain View Acres	81101	Pine Nook	80135	Salida	81201
Mountain View Lakes	80470	Pine Park Estates	80465	Salina	80302
Mount Crested Butte	81225	Pinewood Springs	80540	Salt Creek (Part of Pueblo)	81006
Mount Massive Lakes	80461	Pinnacle Park	80631	San Acacio	81151
Mount Princeton Hot		Pinon	81008	San Antonio	81120
Springs	81236	Pinon Acres	81301	Sand Creek (Part of	
Mount Vernon Club Place	80401	Pinon Canyon	81082	Commerce City)	80022
Mutual	81089	Pitkin	81241	Sandown (Part of Denver)	80216
Nast	81642	Placerville	81430	Sanford	81151
Nathrop	81236	Plateau City	81624	Sangre De Cristo Ranches	81133
Naturita	81422	Platner	80743	San Isabel	81069
Nederland	80466	Platoro	81144	San Juan	81070
Nevadaville	80427	Platteville	80651	San Luis	81152
New Castle	81647	Plaza	81132	San Pablo	81153
New Raymer	80742	Pleasant View (Jefferson		San Pedro	81153
Nighthawk	80135	County)	80401	Santa Fe (Denver County)	80204
Nine Mile Corner	80026	Pleasant View (Montezuma		Santa Fe (Pueblo County)	81003
Niwot	80544	County)	81331	Sapinero	81247
Nob Hill	80122	Poncha Springs	81242	Sarcillo	81082
North Avondale	81022	Ponderosa	80424	Sarcillo Canon	81091
North Boulder (Part of		Ponderosa Hills	80134	Sargents	81248
Boulder)	80302	Ponderosa Park	80107	Sargents School	81144
North Cherry Creek Valley	80231	Poudre Park	80521	Sawpit	81430
North Delta	81416	Powderhorn	81243	Security	80911
North End (Part of Colorado		Powder Wash	82901	Security-Widefield	80911
Springs)	80907	Pritchett	81064	Sedalia	80135
Northglenn	80233	Proctor	80736	Sedgwick	80749
Northglenn Mall (Part of		Prospect Heights	81212	Segundo	81070
Northglenn)	80233	Prospect Valley	80643	Seibert	80834
North La Junta (Part of La		Prowers	81052	Semper	80021
Junta)	81050	Pryor	81065	Severance	80546
North Pecos	80221	Pueblo	81001-08	Shadow Mountain	80447
North Pole	80809	For specific Pueblo Zip Codes call		Shadows North	80424
North Valley Shopping		(719) 544-0132		Shaffers Crossing	80433
Center (Part of Thornton)	80229	Pueblo Army Depot	81001	Shamballa Ashrama	80135
North Washington Heights	80229	Pueblo Dam	81003	Shauano Vista	81201
North Yard (Part of Denver)	80221	Pueblo Mall (Part of Pueblo)	81008	Shaw Heights	80030
Norwood	81423	Pueblo West	81007	Shaw Heights Mesa	80030
Nucla	81424	Punkin Center	80821	Shawnee	80475
Numa	81063	Quincy (Part of Aurora)	80015	Sheridan	80110
Nunn	80648	Radium	80423	Sheridan Lake	81071
Nutria	81147	Ragged Mountain	81434	Sherrelwood	80221
Oak Creek	80467	Rainbow Valley	80814	Sherrelwood Estates	80221
Oak Grove	81401	Ramah	80832	Silt	81652
Oehlmann Park	80433	Rand	80473	Silver Cliff	81252
Ohio	81237	Rangely	81648	Silver Creek	80446
Olathe	81425	Rangeview Estates (Boulder		Silver Heights	80104
Olney Springs	81062	County)	80501	Silver Plume	80476
Olympus Heights	80515	Range View Estates (Weld		Silver Shekel	80424
Ophir	81426	County)	80631	Silver Springs	80470
Orchard	80649	Rattlesnake Buttes	81089	Silver Spruce	80301
Orchard City	81410	Raymond	80540	Silverthorne	80498
Orchard Mesa	81501	Read	81416	Silverton	81433
Ordway	81063	Red Cliff	81649	Simla	80835
Ormandale	81005	Red Feather Lakes	80545	Singleton	80475
Ortiz	81120	Redlands	81503	Skyland Village (Part of	
Otis	80743	Redmesa	81326	Westminster)	80030
Ouray	81427	Red Rock Ranch	80132	Skyline	80222
Ovid	80744	Redstone	81623	Sky Village	80465
Oxford	81137	Redvale	81431	Skyway (El Paso County)	80906
Pactolus	80401	Red Wing	81066	Skyway (Mesa County)	81643
Padroni	80745	Rembrandt Place	80121	Skyway Estates (Part of	
Pagosa	81147	Rezago	81082	Colorado Springs)	80906
Pagosa Springs	81147	Richfield	81140	Skyway Park (Part of	
Paisaje	81120	Rico	81332	Colorado Springs)	80906
Palisade	81526	Ridgeview Hills	80122	Slater	81653
Palmer Lake	80133	Ridgway	81432	Slick Rock	81333
Palos Verdes	80123	Rifle	81650	Smeltertown	81201
Palos Verdes East	80110	Rinn	80501	Smoky Hill (Part of Aurora)	80015
Pandora	81435	Rio Blanco	81650	Snowmass	81654
Paoli	80746	Riverside	80540	Snowmass Village	81615
Paonia	81428	Roberta	81050	Snow Mountain Ranch	80446
Parachute	81635	Rockvale	81244	Snyder	80750
Paradox	81429	Rocky Ford	81067	Somerset	81434
Paragon Estates	80303	Rocky Mountain Arsenal	80022	South Boulder (Part of	
Park Center	81212	Rogers Mesa	81419	Boulder)	80303
Park City	80420	Roggen	80652	South Canon (Part of	
Parker	80134	Roland Valley	80470	Canon City)	81212
Park Hill (Part of Denver)	80207	Rollinsville	80474	South Denver (Part of	
Park Vista Estates	80908	Romeo	81148	Denver)	80209
Parlin	81239	Rosedale (Part of Garden		Southern Ute Indian	
Parshall	80468	City)	80631	Reservation	81137
Peaceful Valley	80540	Rosita	81252	South Fork	81154
Peagreen	81416	Roswell (Part of Colorado		Southglenn	80122
Peak Seven West	80424	Springs)	80907	South Park City (Part of	
Peckham	80645	Rowena	80455	Fairplay)	80440
Peetz	80747	Roxborough Park	80125	South Platte	80441
Penitentiary (Part of Canon		Royal Gorge	81246	South Roggen	80652
City)	81212	Royal Ranch	80470	Southwind	80120
Penrose	81240	Ruedi	81621	Southwood	80120
Peyton	80831	Rulison	81635	Spanish Colony	80631
Pheasant Run (Part of		Rush	80833	Spanish Village	80644
Aurora)	80015	Russell Gulch	80427	Spar City	81130
Phippsburg	80469	Rustic	80512	Sparks	82901
Pierce	80650	Rye	81069	Sphinx Park	80470

	ZIP		ZIP		ZIP
Spivak (Part of Lakewood)	80214	Toponas	80479	Walsh	81090
Springfield	81073	Tordal Estates	80424	Waltonia	80515
Spring Valley	80814	Torres (Las Animas County)	81091	Wamblee Park	80433
Sprucedale	80439	Torres (Rio Grande County)	81144	Wamblee Valley	80433
Squaw Point	81324	Towaoc	81334	Wandcrest Park	80470
Stanley Park	80439	Towner	81071	Ward	80481
Starkville	81074	Tranquil Acres	80863	Waterton	80125
Steamboat 1981	80477	Trimble	81301	Watkins	80137
Steamboat Plaza (Part of		Trinchera	81081	Wattenberg	80621
Steamboat Springs)	80488	Trinidad	81082	Waverly	81101
Steamboat Springs	80477	Troutdale	80439	Welby	80229
	80487-88	Trout Haven	80814	Weldona	80653
For specific Steamboat Springs		Trout Lake	81426	Wellington	80549
Zip Codes call (303) 879-3556		Truckton	80864	Wellshire (Part of Denver)	80222
Steamboat Village (Part of		Trujillo	81147	Wellsville	81201
Steamboat Springs)	80487	Trumbull	80135	West (Part of Greeley)	80634
Sterling	80751	Twin Forks	80454	Westcliffe	81252
Stockyards (Part of Denver)	80216	Twin Lakes	81251	West End (Part of Colorado	
Stoneham	80754	Twin Rock	80816	Springs)	80904
Stoner	81323	Twin Spruce	80401	Western Hills	80221
Stonewall	81091	Two Buttes	81084	West Farm	81052
Stonington	81075	Tyrone	81059	Westland Center (Part of	
Strasburg	80136	Unaweep	81527	Lakewood)	80215
Stratmoor	80906	Uncompahgre	81401	Westminster	80030-31
Stratmoor Hills	80906	Union	80750		80035-36
Stratton	80836	Union Stockyards (Part of		For specific Westminster Zip	
Stratton Meadows (Part of		Denver)	80216	Codes call (303) 429-0340	
Colorado Springs)	80906	University (Part of Boulder)	80309	Westminster East	80221
Stratton Park (Part of		University Hills Mall (Part of		Westminster Mall (Part of	
Colorado Springs)	80907	Denver)	80222	Westminster)	80030
Stringtown	80461	University Park (Part of		Weston	81091
Sugar City	81076	Denver)	80210	Westridge	80634
Sugarloaf	80302		80250	West Vail (Part of Vail)	81657
Summit Cove	80435	For specific University Park Zip		Westwood (Part of Denver)	80219
Summitville	81132	Codes call (714) 997-1255		Westwood Lake	80863
Sunbeam	81640	Uravan	81422	Wetmore	81253
Sunnyside (Boulder County)	80466	U.S. Air Force Academy	80840-41	Wheat Ridge	80033-34
Sunnyside (La Plata County)	81301	For specific U.S. Air Force		For specific Wheat Ridge Zip	
Sunnyslopes	80020	Academy Zip Codes call (719)		Codes call (303) 421-2855	
Sunset (Part of Pueblo)	81005	472-1818		Wheeler	80401
Sunshine	80302	Ute Heights	81201	White Pine	81248
Superior	80027	Ute Mountain Indian		Whitewater	81527
Surrey Ridge	80104	Reservation	81334	Widefield	80911
Sutank	81623	Utleyville	81064	Wiggins	80654
Swallows	81003	Vail	81657-58	Wild Horse (Cheyenne	
Swede Corners	81149	For specific Vail Zip Codes call		County)	80862
Sweetwater	81637	(303) 476-5217		Wild Horse (Pueblo County)	81001
Swink	81077	Vallecito	81122	Wiley	81092
Swissvale	81201	Valley Hi Mountain Estates	80816	Willard	80741
Switzerland Village	80470	Valley of Blue	80424	Williamsburg (Fremont	
Tabernash	80478	Vancorum	81422	County)	81226
Tallahassee School	81212	Velasquez Plaza	81091	Williamsburg (Jefferson	
Tamarron	81301	Vernon	80755	County)	80127
Tanglewood Acres	81252	Victor	80860	Willowbrook	80465
Tarryall	80827	Viejo San Acacio	81151	Willow Creek	80110
Taylor Park	81210	Vigil	81091	Willow Gulch	81423
Telluride	81435	Vilas	81087	Wilson Lake Estates	80816
Templeton (Part of		Village East (Part of Aurora)	80012	Windsor	80550
Colorado Springs)	80936	Villa Grove	81155	Windsor Gardens (Part of	
Ten Mile Vista	80424	Villa Italia Center (Part of		Denver)	80231
Tennyson Heights (Part of		Lakewood)	80226	Winter Park	80482
Fort Collins)	80521	Villegreen	81049	Wolcott	81655
Terminal Annex (Part of		Vineland	81001	Wondervu	80401
Denver)	80217	Virginia Dale	80535	Woodglen (Part of	
Texas Creek	81223	Vista Grande (Part of		Thornton)	80229
Thatcher	81059	Colorado Springs)	80918	Woodland Acres	81069
The Meadows	80127	Vista Verde	80120	Woodland Park	80863
The Mesa	80904	Vollmar	80621		80866
The Pinery	80134	Vona	80861	For specific Woodland Park Zip	
The Shadows	80424	Vroman	81067	Codes call (719) 687-9184	
The Springs	80906	Waconda Hills	80132	Woodmar Village	80123
Thomasville	81642	Wagner Manor	80302	Woodmoor	80908
Thornton	80229	Wagon Wheel Gap	81154	Woodrow	80757
Thurman	80801	Wahatoya	81055	Woody Creek	81656
Tiffany	81137	Wah Keeney Park	80439	Wray	80758
Timbers (Part of Aurora)	80014	Wahketa Village	80701	Yampa	80483
Timnath	80547	Walden	80480	Yellow Jacket	81335
Timpas	81050	Wallace Village	80021	Yoder	80864
Tincup	81210	Wallstreet	80302	Yorkborough (Part of	
Tiny Town	80465	Walnut Hills	80112	Thornton)	80229
Tolland	80474	Walsenburg	81089	Yuma	80759
Toltec	81089				

	ZIP		ZIP		ZIP
Abington	06230	Branhaven Shopping Center	06405	Christy Hill Estates	06335
Addison	06033	Brendan Heights	06078	Church Hill	06794
Agua Vista (Part of Danbury)	06810	Bretton Heights (Part of Middletown)	06457	Churchwood	06357
Alien Heights	06339	Bridgeport	06601-50	Clam Island	06405
Allerton Farms (Part of Naugatuck)	06770	For specific Bridgeport Zip Codes call (203) 332-5337		Clarks Corner	06256
Allington (Part of West Haven)	06516	Bridgeport (Town)	06604	Clarks Falls	06359
Almyville	06354	Bridgewater	06752	Clarksville	02891
Alpine	06810	Bridgewater (Town)	06752	Clearview Heights	06076
Amenia Union	06069	Brighton Beach	06371	Clinton (Town)	06413
Amesville	06031	Bristol	06010-11	Clinton	06413
Amity (Part of New Haven)	06524	For specific Bristol Zip Codes call (203) 583-1371		Clinton Beach	06413
Amston	06231	Bristol Terrace (Part of Naugatuck)	06770	Clintonville	06473
Andover	06232	Broad Brook	06016	Cobalt	06414
Andover (Town)	06232	Bromica	06757	Codfish Hill	06801
Ansonia	06401	Brookfield	06804	Colburn Hill	06076
Ansonia (Town)	06401	Brookfield (Town)	06804	Colchester	06415
Ashford	06278	Brookfield Center	06804	Colchester (Town)	06415
Ashford (Town)	06250	Brooklyn	06234	Colebrook	06021
Ashford Lake	06250	Brooklyn (Town)	06234	Colebrook (Town)	06021
Aspetuck	06880	Brook Valley (Part of Naugatuck)	06770	Collinsville	06022
Attawan Beach	06357	Bruce Park	06830	Colonial Manor	06360
Attawaugan	06241	Brush Island	06820	Columbia	06237
Atwoodville	06250	Buckingham	06033	Columbia (Town)	06237
Avery Heights	06776	Buckland	06040	Compo Beach	06880
Avery Hill	06339	Bucks Corners	06073	Compo Hill	06880
Avon	06001	Bulls Bridge	06785	Conantville	06226
Avon (Town)	06001	Bunker Hill (Part of Waterbury)	06708	Congamond Lakes	06093
Baileyville	06455	Burlington	06013	Connecticut Correctional Center (New Haven County)	06410
Bakersville	06057	Burlington (Town)	06085	Connecticut Correctional Institution (Hartford County)	06082
Ballouville	06233	Burnside	06108	Connecticut Correctional Institution (Tolland County)	06071
Ball Pond	06812	Burr Hill	06419	Connecticut Post Mall (Part of Milford)	06460
Baltic	06330	Burrville (Part of Torrington)	06790	Conning Towers	06340
Banksville	06830	Burwells Beach (Part of Milford)	06460	Conning Towers-Nautilus Park	06340
Bantam	06750	Byram	06830	Copaco Shopping Center	06002
Barkhamsted (Town)	06063	Camp Bethel	06438	Cornwall	06753
Barnum (Part of Bridgeport)	06605	Camptown (Part of Derby)	06418	Cornwall (Town)	06753
Barry Square (Part of Hartford)	06134	Canaan	06018	Cornwall Bridge	06754
Bartlett Corners	06375	Canaan (Town)	06031	Cornwall Center	06796
Bayview (Part of Milford)	06460	Candleset Cove	06776	Cornwall Hollow	06031
Beacon Falls	06403	Candlewood Hill	06441	Cos Cob	06807
Beacon Falls (Town)	06403	Candlewood Hills	06810	Cottage Grove	06002
Beardsley (Part of Bridgeport)	06606	Candlewood Isle	06812	Coventry	06238
Beaverbrook (Part of Danbury)	06810	Candlewood Knolls	06810	Coventry (Town)	06238
Beckettville (Part of Danbury)	06810	Candlewood Lake Club	06804	Cranbury (Part of Norwalk)	06851
Bedlam Corner	06256	Candlewood Lake Estates	06784	Cranska Village	06354
Bel Aire Heights	06355	Candlewood Orchards	06804	Crescent Beach	06357
Belden (Part of Norwalk)	06850	Candlewood Point	06776	Cromwell (Town)	06416
Belle Haven	06830	Candlewood Shores	06804	Cromwell	06416
Bell Island (Part of Norwalk)	06853	Candlewood Springs	06776	Cromwell Hills	06416
Belltown (Part of Stamford)	06906	Candlewood Trails	06776	Crystal Lake	06029
Berkshire	06482	Cannondale	06897	Daleville	06279
Berkshire Estates	06488	Canterbury	06331	Damascus	06405
Berkshire Shopping Center (Part of Danbury)	06810	Canterbury (Town)	06331	Danbury	06810-11
Berlin	06037	Canton	06019	For specific Danbury Zip Codes call (203) 748-1230	
Berlin (Town)	06037	Canton (Town)	06019	Danbury Fair (Part of Danbury)	06810
Beseck Lake	06455	Canton Center	06020	Danbury Quarter	06098
Bethany	06524	Carl Robinson Correctional Institution	06082	Danbury Shopping Center (Part of Danbury)	06810
Bethany (Town)	06524	Carmel Hill	06751	Danielson	06239
Bethel (Town)	06801	Castle Hill	02891	Darien (Town)	06820
Bethel	06801	Cedar Beach (Part of Milford)	06460	Darien	06820
Bethlehem	06751	Cedar Heights (Part of Danbury)	06810	Dayville	06241
Bethlehem (Town)	06751	Cedarhurst	06482	Deep River	06417
Birch Groves	06776	Cedar Knolls	06776		06419
Birch Hill	06757	Cedar Lake (Part of Bristol)	06010	For specific Deep River Zip Codes call (203) 526-5970	
Birch Meadow	06479	Cedar Land	06488	Deep River (Town)	06417
Birch Mountain	06040	Center	06611	Deer Island	06758
Birchwood	06095	Centerbrook	06409	Deer Run Shores	06784
Birdland	06082	Center Groton	06340	Derby	06418
Bishop	06374	Center Hill	06057	Derby (Town)	06418
Bishops Corner	06137	Centerville	06518	Derby Junction (Part of Derby)	06418
Bissell	06074	Centerville-Mount Carmel	06518	Derby Neck (Part of Derby)	06418
Black Point	06357	Central (Part of Hartford)	06103	Devil's Backbone	06751
Black Point Beach Club	06357	Central Commons (Part of Bridgeport)	06607	Devon (Part of Milford)	06460
Bloomfield	06002	Central Village	06332	Diamond Lake	06033
Bloomfield (Town)	06002	Chaffeeville	06268	Dibble Hill	06796
Blue Hills (Bloomfield Twp.)	06002	Chalkers Beach	06475	Dickerman's Corner	06479
Blue Hills (Hartford Twp.)	06132	Chaplin	06235	Doanville	06384
Boardman Manor	06776	Chaplin (Town)	06235	Dodgingtown	06470
Boardmans Bridge	06776	Chapman Beach	06498	Dolphin Gardens	06340
Bolton	06043	Charcoal Ridge	06812	Double Beach	06405
Bolton (Town)	06043	Cherry Brook	06020	Dowd's Corner	06019
Bolton Center	06040	Cherry Hill	06796	Downersville	02891
Bonny Brook	06776	Cherrywood	06479	Drakeville (Part of Torrington)	06790
Borough (Part of Groton)	06340	Cheshire	06410	Durham	06422
Botsford	06404	Cheshire (Town)	06410	Durham (Town)	06422
Boulder Lake	06413	Chester	06412	Durham Center	06422
Bozrah	06334	Chester (Town)	06412	Eagleville	06268
Bozrah (Town)	06334	Chickahominy	06830		
Branchville	06829	Chippens Hill (Part of Bristol)	06010		
Brandy Hill	06277				
Branford	06405				
Branford (Town)	06405				
Branford Hills	06405				

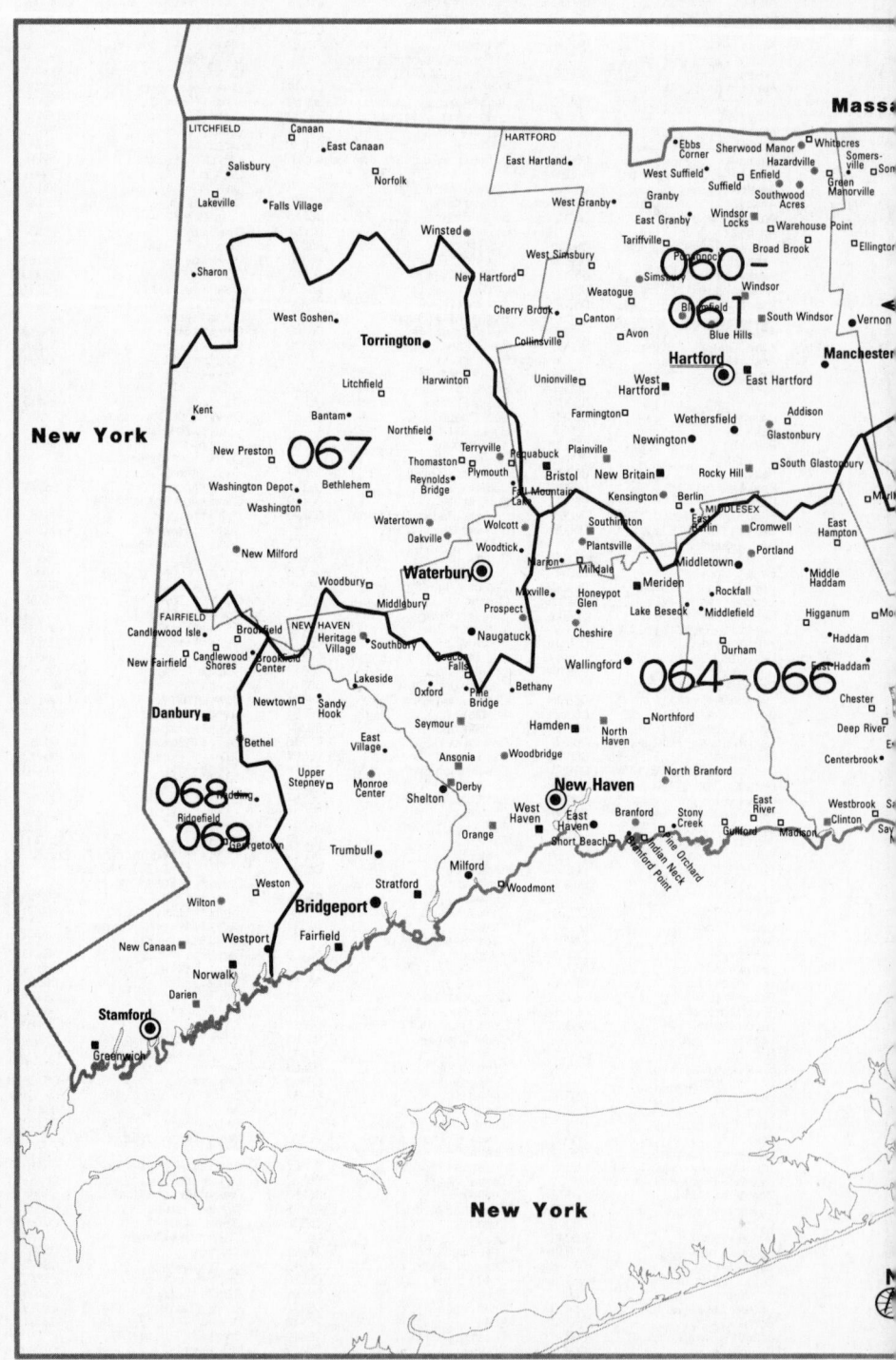

LITCHFIELD   Canaan   East Canaan
HARTFORD
Salisbury   Norfolk
East Hartland
Lakeville   Falls Village
West Granby
Sharon
Winsted
West Goshen
New Hartford
Torrington
Litchfield   Harwinton
New York
Kent
Bantam
Northfield
New Preston
Thomaston
New York

Massa...

Ebbs Corner   Sherwood Manor   Whitcres
West Suffield   Hazardville   Somers-ville   Som
Enfield
Granby   Suffield   Southwood Acres   Green Mahorville
East Granby   Windsor Locks   Warehouse Point
Tariffville   Simsbury   Windsor   Broad Brook   Ellington
West Simsbury   Weatogue   South Windsor   Vernon
Cherry Brook   Bloomfield
Canton   Avon   Blue Hills
Collinsville

060-061

Hartford   East Hartford   Manchester
Unionville   West Hartford
Farmington   Wethersfield   Addison   Glastonbury
Newington   Rocky Hill   South Glastonbury
MIDDLESEX

067

Terryville   Pequabuck   Plainville
Reynolds Bridge   Plymouth   Bristol   New Britain   Kensington   Berlin   East Berlin   Cromwell   East Hampton
Washington Depot   Bethlehem   Fall Mountain   Lake   Southington   Plantsville   Middletown   Portland   Middle Haddam
Washington   Watertown   Wolcott   Marion   Mildale   Meriden   Rockfall   Higganum   Mo
Oakville   Woodtick   Honeypot Glen   Lake Beseck   Middlefield   Haddam
New Milford   Woodbury   Waterbury   Maxville   Cheshire   Durham   East Haddam
Middlebury   Prospect   Naugatuck   Wallingford   Chester   Deep River
Heritage Village   Southbury   Beacon Falls   Bethany   North Haven   Northford   Centerbrook   E
Brookfield   NEW HAVEN   Lakeside   Oxford   Pine Bridge   Hamden   North Branford   East River   Westbrook   Sa
Candlewood Isle   Brookfield Center   Seymour   Woodbridge   New Haven   Clinton   Say
New Fairfield   Candlewood Shores   Newtown   Sandy Hook   East Village   Ansonia   Derby   West Haven   East Haven   Branford   Stony Creek   Guilford   Madison
Danbury   Bethel   Upper Stepney   Monroe Center   Shelton   Orange   Short Beach   Indian Neck
Ridding   Ridgefield   Georgetown   Trumbull   Milford   Woodmont   Pine Orchard   Branford Point

064-066

068
069

Weston   Stratford
Wilton   Bridgeport
New Canaan   Westport   Fairfield
Norwalk
Darien
Stamford
Greenwich

New York

Massa...

chusetts

TOLLAND

Staffordville
Stafford
Stafford Springs
Crystal Lake
Tolland
Storrs
Coventry
Mansfield Center
Willimantic
Windham
South Windham
Hebron
NEW LONDON
Baltic
Colchester
Fitchville
Norwich

062

WINDHAM
Quinebaug
North Grosvenor Dale
Grosvenor Dale
Thompson
South Woodstock
Putnam
Eastford
Pomfret
Abington
Ballouville
Rogers
Dayville
Danielson
Brooklyn
East Brooklyn
North Windham
Wauregan
Central Village
Moosup
Oneco
Plainfield
Jewett City

PROVIDENCE
Slatersville
Woonsocket
Diamond Hill
Harrisville
Union Village
Cumberland Hill
Arnold Mills
Glendale
Manville
Abbott Run Valley
Pascoag
Oakland
Albion
Ashton
Mapleville
Berkeley
Chepachet
Lonsdale
Valley Falls
Harmony
Esmond
Saylesville
Central Falls
Greenville
North Providence
Pawtucket

Mass.

Providence
Johnston
East Providence
Cranston

028–029

KENT
West Barrington
Barrington
Warren
Anthony
West Warwick
Warwick
BRISTOL
Coventry
Natick
Bristol
East Greenwich
Common Fence Point
Quidnessett
NEWPORT
Tiverton
Davisville
Mount View
Island Park
Portsmouth

WASHINGTON
La Fayette
North Kingstown
Allenton
Middletown
Wyoming
Jamestown
Newport East
Hope Valley
West Kingston
Kingston
Newport
Carolina
Peace Dale
Shannock
Wakefield
Montville
Uncasville
Ashaway
Gales Ferry
New London Submarine Base
Quaker Hill
U.S. Coast Guard Academy
Nautilus Park
Old Mystic
Pawcatuck
Westerly
East Lyme
Groton
West Mystic
Mystic
Wequetequock
New London
Waterford
Poquonock Bridge
Noank
Stonington
Niantic
Giants Neck
Pleasure Beach
Groton Long Point
Watch Hill
Block Point Beach Club
Fenwick

063

Montville
Quaker Hill
South Hopkinton
Bradford
Charlestown
Matunuck
Quonochontaug

Narragansett

Block Island

	ZIP		ZIP		ZIP
Kings Corner	06088	Milbrook	06830	Northford	06472
Knollcrest	06810	Milford	06460	North Franklin	06254
Knollwood	06475	Milford (Town)	06460	North Glenwood	06335
Lake Bashan	06423	Milford Lawns (Part of		North Granby	06060
Lake Beseck	06455	Milford)	06460	North Grosvenor Dale	06255
Lake Bungee	06282	Millbrook	06518	North Guilford	06437
Lake Garda	06013	Milldale	06467	North Haven (Town)	06473
Lake Hayward	06415	Millington	06423	North Haven	06473
Lake Plymouth	06782	Mill Plain (Part of Danbury)	06810	North Kent	06757
Lake Pocotopaug	06424	Millville (Part of Naugatuck)	06770	North Madison	06443
Lakeside (Litchfield County)	06758	Milton	06759	North Mianus	06807
Lakeside (New Haven		Mixville	06410	North Plain	06423
County)	06488	Mohegan	06382	North Sterling	06377
Lakeview Terrace	06076	Momauguin	06512	North Stonington	06359
Lakeville	06039	Monroe	06468	North Stonington (Town)	06359
Lakewood (Part of		Monroe (Town)	06468	North Thompsonville	06082
Waterbury)	06704	Monroe Center	06468	Northville	06776
Lattins Landing (Part of		Montowese	06473	North Westchester	06474
Danbury)	06810	Montville	06353	North Wilton	06897
Laurel (Part of Middletown)	06457	Montville (Town)	06353	North Windham	06256
Laurel Beach (Part of		Montville Manor	06370	Norwalk	06850-56
Milford)	06460	Moodus	06469	For specific Norwalk Zip Codes	
Laurel Hill (Part of Norwich)	06360	Moosup	06354	call (203) 838-4881	
Laysville	06371	Morningside (Part of Milford)	06460	Norwich	06360
Lebanon	06249	Morris	06763	Norwich (Town)	06360
Lebanon (Town)	06249	Morris (Town)	06763	Norwich Hospital	06365
Ledyard	06339	Morris Cove	06512	Norwichtown (Part of	
Ledyard (Town)	06339	Mount Carmel	06518	Norwich)	06360
Leesville	06469	Mount Hope	06250	Nut Plains	06437
Leetes Island	06437	Murphy Road Annex (Part		Oakdale	06370
Leffingwell	06360	of Hartford)	06114	Oakdale Heights	06370
Liberty Hill	06249	Murray	06430	Oakdale Manor	06488
Lime Rock	06039	Myrtle Beach (Part of		Oakland Gardens	06032
Lisbon	06351	Milford)	06460	Oakville	06779
Lisbon (Town)	06351	Mystic	06355	Oakwood Acres	06812
Litchfield	06759	Naugatuck	06770	Occum (Part of Norwich)	06360
Litchfield (Town)	06759	Naugatuck (Town)	06770	Old Greenwich	06870
Little Boston	06875	Naugatuck Gardens (Part of		Old Lyme	06371
Little City	06441	Milford)	06460	Old Lyme (Town)	06371
Long Hill (Fairfield County)	06611	Naugatuck Valley Mall (Part		Old Lyme Shores	06371
Long Hill (Middlesex		of Waterbury)	06705	Old Mystic	06372
County)	06457	Nautilus Park	06340	Old Saybrook	06475
Long Hill (New Haven		Nepaug	06057	Old Saybrook (Town)	06475
County)	06704	Newberry Corner (Part of		Old Saybrook Shopping	
Long Hill (New London		Torrington)	06790	Center	06475
County)	06340	New Britain	06050-53	Old State House (Part of	
Long Ridge (Part of		For specific New Britain Zip		Hartford)	06123
Stamford)	06901	Codes call (203) 223-3681		Oneco	06373
Lordship	06497	New Canaan (Town)	06840	Orange (Town)	06477
Lords Point	06378	New Canaan	06840	Orange	06477
Lydallville	06040	Newent	06351	Orcutts	06076
Lyme	06371	New Fairfield	06812	Oronoke (Part of Waterbury)	06708
Lyme (Town)	06371	New Fairfield (Town)	06810	Oronoque	06497
Lyons Plains	06880	Newfield	06607	Oswegatchie	06385
Macedonia	06757	Newfield Heights (Part of		Overlook (Part of	
Madison	06443	Middletown)	06457	Waterbury)	06710
Madison (Town)	06443	Newhallville (Part of New		Owenoke	06880
Manchester (Town)	06040	Haven)	06511	Oxford	06478
Manchester	06040	New Hartford	06057	Oxford (Town)	06478
	06045	New Hartford (Town)	06057	Ox Hill (Part of Norwich)	06360
For specific Manchester Zip		New Haven	06501-11	Oxoboxo Lake	06370
Codes call (203) 643-2735		For specific New Haven Zip		Pachaug	06351
Manchester Green	06040	Codes call (203) 782-7203		Palestine	06470
Mansfield (Town)	06250	Newington (Town)	06131	Palmertown	06353
Mansfield Center	06250	Newington	06111	Paradise Green	06497
Mansfield City	06268		06131	Parcel Post (Part of Milford)	06460
Mansfield Depot	06251	For specific Newington Zip Codes		Parkville (Part of Hartford)	06106
Mansfield Four Corners	06268	call (203) 666-8436		Pawcatuck	06379
Mansfield Hollow	06250	Newington Junction	06111	Pemberwick	06830
Maple Hill	06111	New London	06320	Pequabuck	06781
Maplewood (Part of Derby)	06418	New London (Town)	06320	Perkins Corner	06226
Marble Dale	06777	New London Submarine		Phoenixville	06235
Margerie Manor (Part of		Base	06349	Pine Bridge	06403
Danbury)	06810	New Milford	06776	Pine Grove (Litchfield	
Marion	06444	New Milford (Town)	06776	County)	06031
Marlborough	06447	New Preston	06777	Pine Grove (New London	
Marlborough (Town)	06447	New Preston-Marble Dale	06777	County)	06357
Maromas (Part of		Newtown	06470	Pine Meadow	06061
Middletown)	06457	Newtown (Town)	06470	Pine Orchard	06405
Mashapaug	06076	New Village	06374	Pine Rock Park (Part of	
Mason Island	06355	Niantic	06357	Shelton)	06484
Massapeag	06382	Nichols	06611	Plainfield	06374
Mayberry Village	06108	Noank	06340	Plainfield (Town)	06374
Mechanicsville	06277	Noble (Part of Bridgeport)	06608	Plainville (Town)	06062
Melrose	06049	Norfolk	06058	Plainville	06062
Melville Village	06430	Norfolk (Town)	06058	Plantsville	06479
Meriden	06450	Noroton	06820	Platts Mills (Part of	
Meriden (Town)	06450	Noroton Heights	06820	Waterbury)	06706
Meriden Square (Part of		North Ashford	06282	Plaza (Part of Waterbury)	06704
Meriden)	06450	North Bloomfield	06002	Pleasant Acres (Part of	
Merrow	06251	North Branford	06471	Danbury)	06810
Mianus	06807	North Branford (Town)	06471	Pleasant Valley	06063
Middle Beach	06443	North Bridgeport (Part of		Pleasure Beach	06385
Middlebury	06762	Bridgeport)	06601	Plymouth	06782
Middlebury (Town)	06762	North Canaan (Town)	06018	Plymouth (Town)	06782
Middlefield	06455	North Canton	06059	Point Beach (Part of Milford)	06460
Middlefield (Town)	06455	North Cornwall	06796	Point O'Woods	06376
Middle Haddam	06456	North End (Part of		Pomfret	06258
Middletown	06457	Waterbury)	06704	Pomfret (Town)	06258
Middletown (Town)	06460	North Farms	06471	Pomfret Center	06259
Midway	06340	Northfield	06778	Pomfret Landing	06259

	ZIP		ZIP		ZIP
West Hartford	06107	Westview Acres	06478	Wilton (Town)	06897
	06110	Westville (Part of New		Winchester (Town)	06094
	06117	Haven)	06515	Winchester Center	06094
	06119	West Wauregan	06387	Windham	06280
For specific West Hartford Zip		West Willington	06279	Windham (Town)	06280
Codes call (203) 231-2871		Westwood Park (Part of		Winding Lanes	06001
West Hartland	06091	Norwich)	06360	Windsor	06095
West Haven	06516	West Woods	06069	Windsor (Town)	06095
West Haven (Town)	06516	West Woodstock	06281	Windsor Locks (Town)	06096
West Lakes	06437	Wethersfield (Town)	06129	Windsor Locks	06096
West Mystic	06388	Wethersfield	06109	Windsorville	06016
West Norfolk	06058		06129	Winnipauk (Part of Norwalk)	06851
West Norwalk (Part of		For specific Wethersfield Zip		Winsted	06098
Norwalk)	06851	Codes call (203) 563-1941		Winthrop	06417
Weston	06883	Wethersfield Shopping		Wolcott	06716
Weston (Town)	06880	Center	06109	Wolcott (Town)	06716
Westport	06880-81	Wheeler Farms (Part of		Woodbridge (Town)	06525
For specific Westport Zip Codes		Milford)	06460	Woodbridge	06525
call (203) 227-9569		Whigville	06013	Woodbury	06798
West Putnam Avenue	06830	Whipstick	06877	Woodbury (Town)	06798
West Redding	06896	Whitacres	06082	Woodlake	06798
West Shore (Part of West		White Sands Beach	06371	Woodmont	06460
Haven)	06516	Whitneyville	06517	Woodstock	06281
West Side (Part of Norwich)	06360	Wildermere Beach (Part of		Woodstock (Town)	06281
West Side Hill (Part of		Milford)	06460	Woodstock Valley	06282
Waterbury)	06708	Williams Crossing	06249	Woodtick	06716
West Simsbury	06092	Willimantic	06226	Woodville	06777
West Stafford	06076	Willington (Town)	06279	Yale (Part of New Haven)	06520
West Suffield	06093	Willington Hill	06279	Yalesville	06492
West Thompson	06255	Willow Point	06388	Yantic (Part of Norwich)	06389
West Torrington (Part of		Wilsonville	06255	Zoar	06482
Torrington)	06790	Wilton	06897		

	ZIP
Adams Crossroads	19950
Adamsville	19950
Afton	19810
Alapocas	19803
Albertson Park	19808
Analine Village	19703
Andrewville	19950
Anglesey	19807
Angola	19958
Angola Beach	19951
Angola by the Bay	19958
Anne Acres	19971
Arden	19803
Ardencroft	19810
Ardentown	19810
Argos Corner	19963
Arundel	19808
Ashbourne Hills	19703
Ashland	19807
Ashley	19804
Atlanta	19933
Atlanta Estates	19973
Augustine Beach	19731
Avalon	19808
Bacon	19940
Bakers Choice	19946
Baldton (Part of New Castle)	19720
Bayard	19945
Bay Berry Dunes	19930
Bay View Beach	19709
Bay View Park	19930
Bayville	19975
Bay Vista	19971
Bear	19701
Beaver Brook Apartments	19720
Beaverdam Heights	19973
Bellefonte	19809
Bellemoor	19802
Bellevue Manor	19809
Belltown	19958
Belmont Hall	19977
Belvidere	19804
Bestfield	19804
Bethany Beach	19930
Bethany Dunes	19930
Bethany Village	19930
Bethel	19931
Big Mills Bridge	19956
Big Oak Corners	19977
Big Pine	19950
Big Stone Beach	19963
Binns Park (Part of Newark)	19711
Birchwood Park	19711
Blackbird	19734
Blackiston	19938
Blackwater Village	19939
Blades	19973
Blue Hen Mall (Part of Dover)	19901
Blue Rock Manor	19803
Bowers	19946
Bowers Beach	19946
Boxwood	19804
Brack-Ex	19805
Brandywine	19810
Brandywine Estates	19703
Brandywine Springs Manor	19808
Brandywood	19810
Breezewood (Kent County)	19943
Breezewood (New Castle County)	19713
Brenford	19977
Briar Park	19901
Bridgeville	19933
Broadacres	19973
Broad Creek	19956
Broadkill Beach	19968
Brookbend	19713
Brookdale Heights	19934
Brookhaven	19711
Brookland Terrace	19805
Brookside	19713
Brookview Apartments	19703
Brownsville	19952
Bull Pine Corners	19947
Bunting	19975
Buttonwood (Part of New Castle)	19720
Camden	19934
Camden-Wyoming (Part of Wyoming)	19934
Cannon	19933
Canterbury	19943
Capitol Green (Part of Dover)	19901
Capitol Park	19901
Cardiff	19810
Carlisle Village	19901
Carrcroft	19803

	ZIP
Carrcroft Crest	19803
Carter	19901
Castle Hills	19720
Catalina Gardens (Part of Newark)	19711
Cave Colony	19968
Cedar Beach	19963
Cedarbrook Acres	19977
Cedar Heights	19804
Centerville	19807
Chalfonte	19810
Channin	19803
Chapel Hill	19711
Chatham	19810
Chelsea Estates	19720
Cherokee Woods	19713
Chestnut Hill Estates	19713
Chestnut Knoll	19963
Cheswold	19936
Christiana	19702
Christiana Acres	19720
Clarksville	19970
Claymont	19703
Claymont (census designated place)	19702
Clayton	19938
Clearfield	19703
Clearview Manor	19720
Cleland Heights	19805
Clifton Park Manor	19802
Cocked Hat	19933
College Park (Part of Newark)	19711
Collins Park	19720
Colmar Manor	19977
Colonial Heights	19805
Colonial Park	19805
Columbia	19940
Concord	19973
Concord Mall	19803
Concord Manor	19803
Cool Spring	19968
Cooper Farm	19808
Cottonpatch Hill	19930
Country Club Estates	19963
Coventry	19720
Coverdale Crossroads	19933
Covered Bridge Farms	19711
Covey Creek	19958
Cragmere	19809
Cragmere Woods	19809
Craigs Mill	19973
Cranston Heights	19808
Crossgates (Part of Dover)	19901
Cross Keys	19966
Dagsboro	19939
Darley Woods	19810
Dartmouth Woods	19810
Deerhurst	19803
Delaplane Manor	19711
Delaware City	19706
Delaware Correctional Center	19977
Delaware Heights	19807
Del Haven Estates	19962
Delmar	19940
Del Park Manor	19808
Devon	19810
Devonshire	19810
Dewey Beach	19971
Diamond Acres	19939
Dobbinsville (Part of New Castle)	19720
Dover	19901-03
For specific Dover Zip Codes call (302) 734-5821	
Dover AFB Housing Annex	19901
Dover Base Housing	19901
Doverbrook Gardens	19901
Dover Mall (Part of Dover)	19901
Downs Chapel	19938
Drummond North	19711
Dublin Hill	19933
Dunleith	19801
Dunlinden Acres	19805
Dupont Manor	19901
Du Ross Heights	19720
Dutch Acres	19958
Eastman Heights	19963
Eastover Hills (Part of Dover)	19901
Eberton	19901
Eden Park	19901
Edge Hill (Part of Dover)	19901
Edgehill Acres (Part of Dover)	19901
Edgemoor	19809
Edgemoor (census designated place)	19802
Edgemoor Gardens	19802
Edgemoor Terrace	19802

	ZIP
Edgewater Acres	19975
Edgewood Hills	19802
Edwardsville	19943
Ellendale	19941
Elmhurst	19804
Elsmere	19805
Elsmere Junction (Part of Elsmere)	19805
English Village	19711
Evergreen Acres	19963
Fairfax	19803
Fairfield Farms	19901
Fairmount	19951
Fairwinds	19701
Farmington	19942
Faulkland	19808
Faulkland Heights	19808
Faulkwoods	19810
Federal (Part of Newark)	19711
Felton	19943
Felton Heights	19943
Felton Manor	19943
Fenwick Island	19944
Fieldsboro	19734
Fireside Park	19713
Flemings Corner	19952
Flemings Landing	19734
Forest Brook Glen	19804
Forest Hills Park	19803
Four Seasons	19702
Foxhall Courtside	19901
Fox Hollow	19958
Frankford	19945
Frederica	19946
Galewood	19803
Garfield Park	19720
Gateway Farms	19707
Georgetown	19947
Ginns Corner	19734
Glasgow	19711
Glasgow Court	19702
Glasgow Pines	19702
Glen Burne Estates	19804
Glendale	19711
Glenville	19804
Goldey Beacom College	19808
Gordon Heights	19802
Gordy Estates	19804
Granogue	19807
Gravel Hill	19947
Graylyn Crest	19810
Green Acres	19803
Green Bank	19808
Greenbriar	19720
Greenshire	19703
Greentree	19703
Greenview	19901
Greenville	19807
Greenville Place	19807
Greenwood	19950
Gulls Nest	19930
Gumboro	19945
Guyencourt	19807
Gwinhurst	19809
Hall Estates	19963
Hamilton Park	19720
Hanbys Corner	19810
Harbeson	19951
Hardscrabble	19973
Harmony Hills	19711
Harrington	19952
Hartly	19953
Hayden Park	19804
Hearns Crossroads	19956
Hearns Mill	19973
Heather Woods	19702
Henlopen Acres	19971
Henry Clay	19807
Hickman	21629
Hickory Hill	19966
Hickory Ridge	19977
Highland Acres (Kent County)	19901
Highland Acres (Sussex County)	19958
Highland West	19808
High Point Park	19946
Hillcrest	19802
Hillside Acres	19943
Hillside Heights	19711
Hilltop Manor	19809
Hitchens Crossroads	19956
Hockessin	19707
Holiday Acres	19939
Hollandsville	19943
Holletts Corners	19938
Holloway Terrace	19720
Holly Oak (New Castle County)	19809
Holly Oak (Sussex County)	19973
Holly Oak Terrace	19809

	ZIP		ZIP		ZIP
Washington Park (Part of		Williamsville (Kent County)	19954	Woodcrest (Kent County)	19901
New Castle)	19720	Williamsville (Sussex		Woodcrest (New Castle	
Webb Manor	19963	County).................	19975	County).................	19804
Webster Farms............	19803	Willow Grove	19934	Wooddale	19807
Wedgewood Acres	19720	Willow Run	19805	Woodenhawk	19950
Weisman Acres	19963	Wilmington	19801-99	Woodland (New Castle	
Wellington Woods	19702	For specific Wilmington Zip Codes		County).................	19805
Welshire	19803	call (302) 323-3783		Woodland (Sussex County)	19973
West Beach...............	19939	Wilmington College	19720	Woodland Beach	19977
Westfield.................	19804	Wilmington Manor	19720	Woodshade	19702
West Haven...............	19807	Wilmington Manor Gardens	19720	Woods Haven	19963
West Meadow..............	19711	Wilmont	19810	Woodside	19980
Westover Hills	19807	Windermer	19804	Woodside East	19980
West Park	19807	Windsor Hills	19803	Woodside Hills	19809
Westview	19804	Windy Bush	19810	Woods Manor	19901
Westwood Manor..........	19810	Windy Hills	19711	Workmans Corners	19947
Whaleys Corners	19956	Winterthur	19735	Wyoming..................	19934
Whaleys Crossroads.......	19956	Woodbine	19803	York Beach (Part of South	
Whiteleysburg	19943	Woodbrook (Kent County)	19901	Bethany)...............	19930
White Oak Farms (Part of		Woodbrook (New Castle		Yorklyn	19736
Dover)	19901	County).................	19803		
Whitesville................	19940				

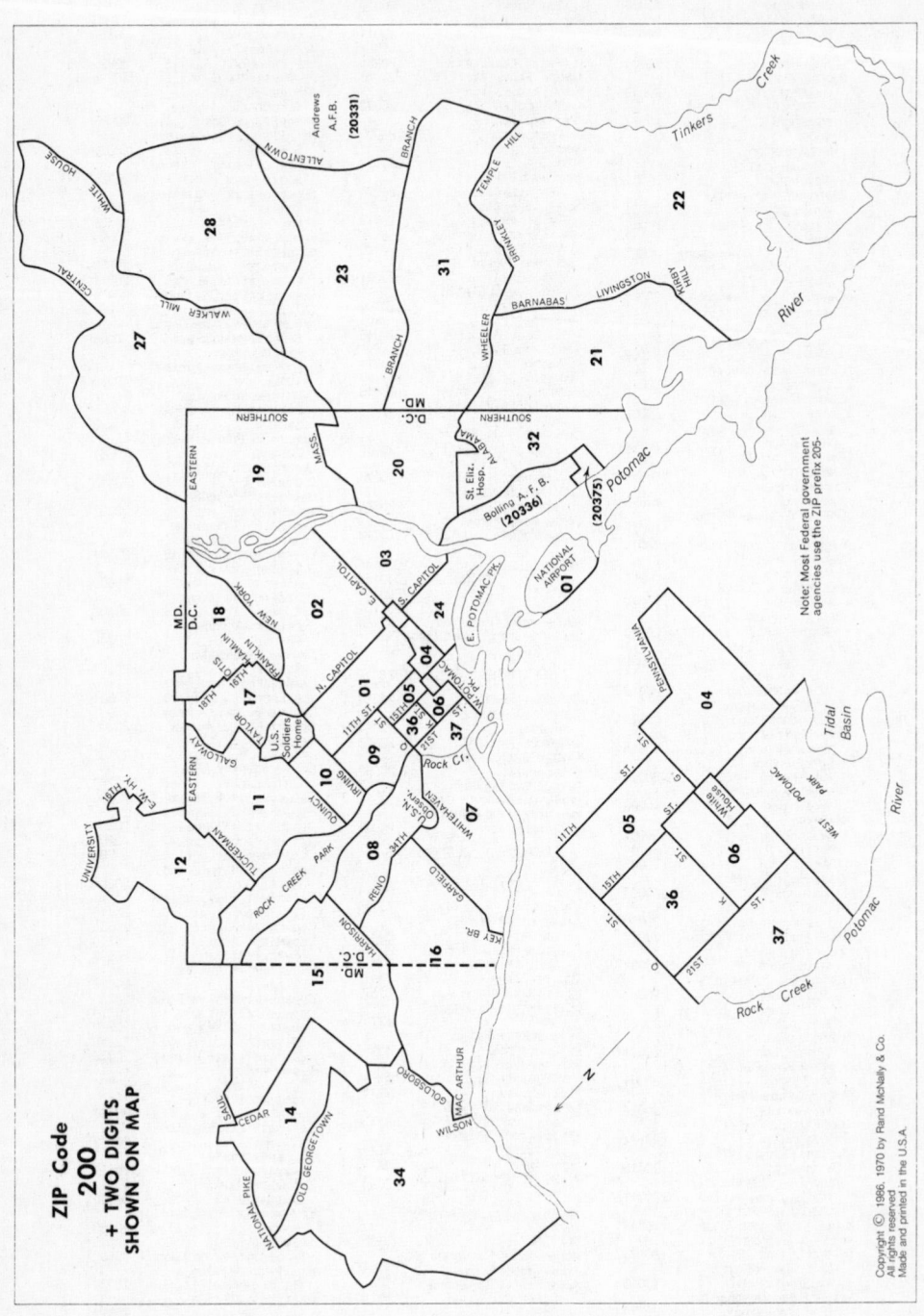

ZIP Code
200
+ TWO DIGITS
SHOWN ON MAP

Note: Most Federal government agencies use the ZIP prefix 205-

	ZIP
Comptroller and Supply Department, Naval District, Washington Navy Yard	20374
Bolling Air Force Base	20332
Coast Guard Headquarters, Washington D.C.	20593
Fort Lesley J. McNair	20319
Marine Corps Headquarters, Navy Annex	20380
Marine Barracks	20390
Military District of Washington D.C., Headquarters	20319

	ZIP
Naval Research Laboratory	20375
Naval Security Station	20390
United States Property and Fiscal Office, Washington D.C.	20315
Walter Reed Medical Center	20307
Washington Highlands (Part of Washington)	20032
Washington Square (Part of Washington)	20036
Watergate (Part of Washington)	20037

	ZIP
Wesley Heights (Part of Washington)	20016
West End (Part of Washington)	20037
Woodley Park (Part of Washington)	20008
Woodley Road (Part of Washington)	20008
Woodridge (Part of Washington)	20018

	ZIP
A (Part of Palm Beach)	33480
Aberdeen	33437
Abe Springs	32424
Acline	33950
Adams Beach	32347
Adamsville (Hillsborough County)	33534
Adamsville (Sumter County)	34785
Airport Siding (Part of Jacksonville)	32229
Alachua	32615
Aladdin City	33187
Alamana	32168
Alderman Park (Part of Jacksonville)	32211
Alford	32420
Allandale	32119
Allanton	32404
Allapattah (Part of Miami)	33142
	33242
For specific Allapattah Zip Codes call (305) 635-4461	
Allentown	32570
Alliance	32446
Alligator Point	32327
Aloma (Part of Winter Park)	32792
Alpine Heights	32433
Altamonte Mall (Part of Altamonte Springs)	32701
Altamonte Springs	32701
	32714-16
For specific Altamonte Springs Zip Codes call (407) 682-3977	
Altha	32421
Alton	32066
Altoona	32702
Alturas	33820
Alumni Village (Part of Tallahassee)	32310
Alva	33920
Amelia City	32034
Amelia Island Plantation	32034
American Beach	32034
Anclote	34691
Andalusia	32110
Andover	33169
	33179
For specific Andover Zip Codes call (305) 470-0327	
Andover Golf Estates	33169
Andover Lake Estates	33169
	33179
For specific Andover Lake Estates Zip Codes call (305) 470-0327	
Andrews	32046
Angel City	32952
Angler Park	33037
Angus Valley	33544
Anna Maria	34216
Anthony	32617
Antioch	33565
Apalachee Correctional Institution	32324
Apalachee Ridge (Part of Tallahassee)	32301
Apalachicola	32320
	32329
For specific Apalachicola Zip Codes call (904) 653-9554	
Apollo Beach	33572
Apopka	32703-04
	32712
For specific Apopka Zip Codes call (407) 886-2951	
Aquarina	32951
Araquey	32095
Arbor Hills (Part of Tallahassee)	32308
Arcadia	33821
Archer	32618
Argyle	32422
Aripeka	34679
Arlington (Part of Jacksonville)	32211
	32239
For specific Arlington Zip Codes call (904) 744-5222	
Arlington Hills (Part of Jacksonville)	32211
Arlingwood (Part of Jacksonville)	32211
Armstrong	32033
Arran	32327
Arredondo	32608
Asbury Lake	32043
Ashton	34771
Ashville	32331
Astatula	34705
Astor	32102
Astor Park	32102

	ZIP
Astronaut Trail (Part of Titusville)	32782
Athena	32347
Atlantic Beach	32233
Atlantic Boulevard (Part of Coral Springs)	33071
	33077
For specific Atlantic Boulevard Zip Codes call (305) 346-9446	
Atlantic Boulevard Estates (Part of Jacksonville)	32225
Atlantic Heights (Part of Miami Beach)	33139
Atlantis	33462
Auburn	32536
Auburndale	33823
Aucilla	32344
Audubon	32952
Aurantia	32754
Autumn Woods	34683
Avalon Beach	32583
Aventura	33160
	33180
	33280
For specific Aventura Zip Codes call (305) 567-5179	
Aventura Mall	33180
Avondale (Part of Jacksonville)	32205
Avon Park	33825
Avon Park Air Force Base	33825
Avon Park Correctional Institution	33825
Avon Park Estates	33825
Avon Park Lakes	33825
Azalea Park	32807
Babson Park	33827
Bagdad	32530
Bahia Oaks	34474
Bahia Shores (Part of St. Petersburg Beach)	33706
Baker	32531
Baker Correctional Institution	32072
Baker Settlement	32464
Bakersville	32092
Bal-Alex Estates	32561
Baldwin	32234
Bal Harbour	33154
Bal Harbour Shops (Part of Bal Harbour)	33154
Ballantine Manor	34243
Ballast Point (Part of Tampa)	33611
Balm	33503
Bamboo	34748
Barberville	32105
Bardin	32177
Bardmoor	34641
Bare Beach	33440
Barefoot Bay	32976
Barrineau Park	32533
Barry University (Part of Miami Shores)	33161
Barth	32533
Bartow	33830
Bascom	32423
Basinger	34972
Baskin	34644
	34648
For specific Baskin Zip Codes call (813) 584-2191	
Bassville Park	34788
Basswood Estates	34972
Baum	32308
Bay Acres	34229
Bayard (Part of Jacksonville)	32258
Bay Crest Park	33615
Bay Grove	32439
Bay Harbor Islands	33154
Bayhead (Bay County)....	32466
Bay Head (Pasco County)	33525
Bay Hill	32819
Bay Lake	34736
Bayonet Point	34667
Bayou George	32405
Bay Pines	33504
Bay Point (Bay County) ...	32411
Bay Point (Dade County)	33137
Bayport	34607
Bayridge	32703
Bayshore	33917
Bayshore Gardens	34207
Bayshore Manor	33917
Bay Springs	32568
Bayview	32401
Bay Vista (Dade County)..	33181
Bay Vista (Pinellas County)	33712
Bayway (Part of St. Petersburg)	33715

	ZIP
Baywood	32140
Baywood Village	34683
Beach	32963-64
For specific Beach Zip Codes call (407) 567-5206	
Beach Haven	32507
Beach Highlands	32459
Beach Park (Part of Tampa)	33609
	33629
For specific Beach Park Zip Codes call (813) 286-7599	
Beachville	32071
Beachwood (Part of Jacksonville)	32246
Beacon Beach	32403
Beacon Groves	34683
Beacon Hill	32456
Beacon Hills (Part of Jacksonville)	32225
Beacon Lakes	34691
Beacon Light (Part of Lighthouse Point)	33064
Beacon Square	34691
Bealsville	33567
Bean City	33440
Bear Creek	32401
Bear Lake	32703
Bearss Plaza	33612
Beauclere Gardens (Part of Jacksonville)	32257
Beaver Creek	32531
Becker	32097
Beckhamtown	32640
Beeghly Heights (Part of Jacksonville)	32218
Bee Ridge	34233
Bel-Air (Part of Sanford)....	32771
Belair Beach	32408
Bell	32619
Bellair	32073
Bellair-Meadowbrook Terrace	32073
Bellair Plaza (Part of Daytona Beach)	32118
Belleair	34616
Belleair Beach	34635
Belleair Bluffs	34640
Belleair Shore	34635
Belle Glade	33430
Belle Glade Camp	33430
Belle Isle	32809
Belleview	34420-21
For specific Belleview Zip Codes call (904) 245-8777	
Belleview Heights	34420
Bellview	32506
	32526
For specific Bellview Zip Codes call (904) 944-5357	
Bellwood	32780
Belvedere Homes	33409
Benbow	33440
Bennett	32466
Bent Tree Village	34241
Beresford	32720
Berkshire Estates	34241
Berry	33868
Berrydale	32565
Bertha	32792
Bethany	34251
Bethel	32327
Bethlehem	32425
Bethune Beach	32169
Betmar Acres	33541
Betton Hills (Part of Tallahassee)	32312
Beulah (Escambia County)	32526
Beulah (Orange County) ...	34787
Beverly Beach	32136
Beverly Hills	34464-65
For specific Beverly Hills Zip Codes call (904) 746-3076	
Beverly Hills (Part of Jacksonville)	32208
Beverly Terrace	34234
Bevilles Corner	33513
Big Bayou (Part of St. Petersburg)	33705
	33739
For specific Big Bayou Zip Codes call (813) 323-6516	
Big Coppitt Key	33040
Big Pine Key	33043
Big Scrub	32179
Biltmore (Part of Jacksonville)	32205
Biltmore Beach	32408
Bird Key (Part of Sarasota)	34236
Biscayne Gardens	33162

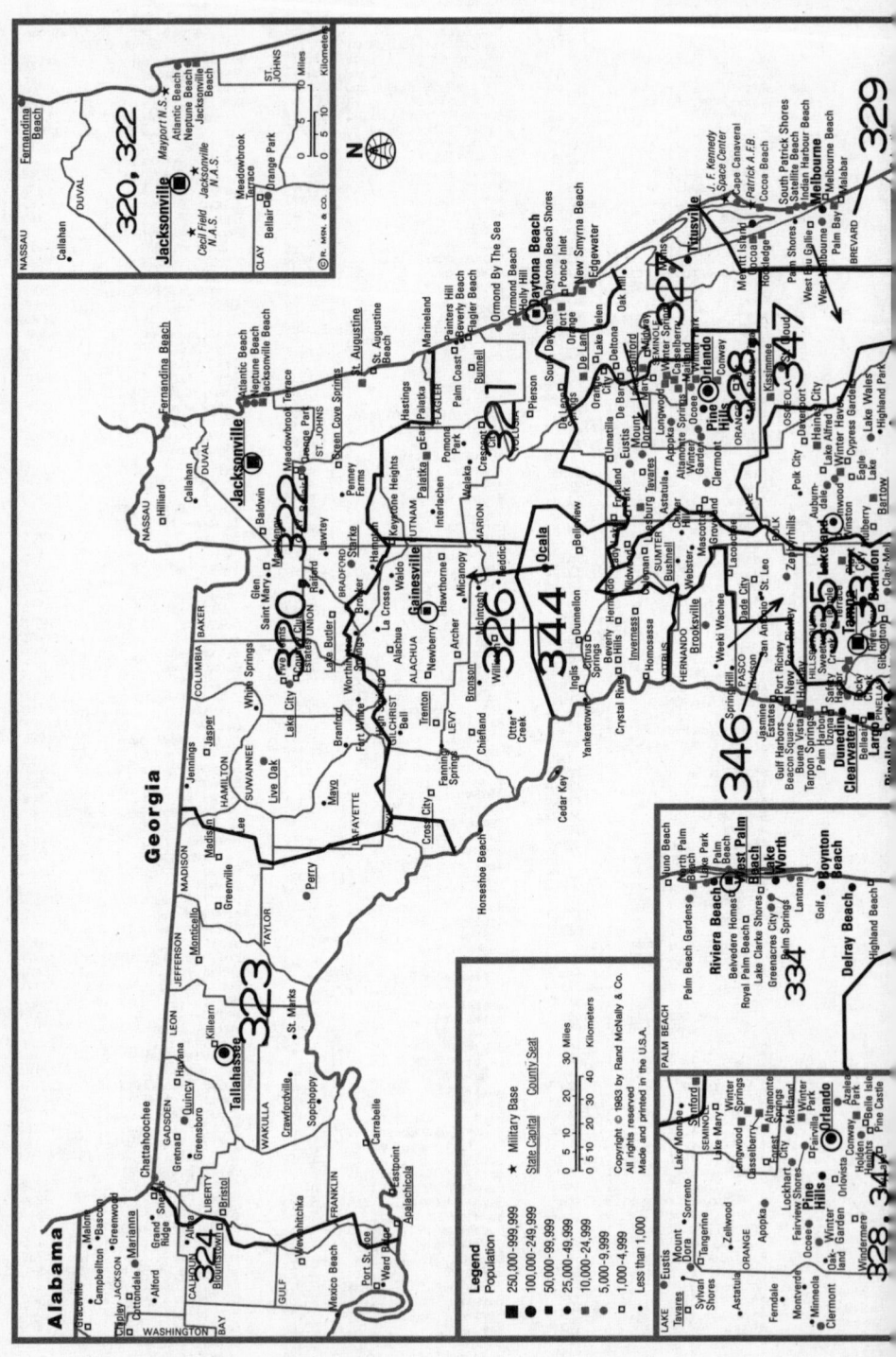

Legend

Population

- 250,000-999,999
- 100,000-249,999
- 50,000-99,999
- 25,000-49,999
- 10,000-24,999
- 5,000-9,999
- 1,000-4,999
- Less than 1,000

★ State Capital
☐ County Seat
★ Military Base

0 5 10 20 30 Miles
0 5 10 20 30 40 Kilometers

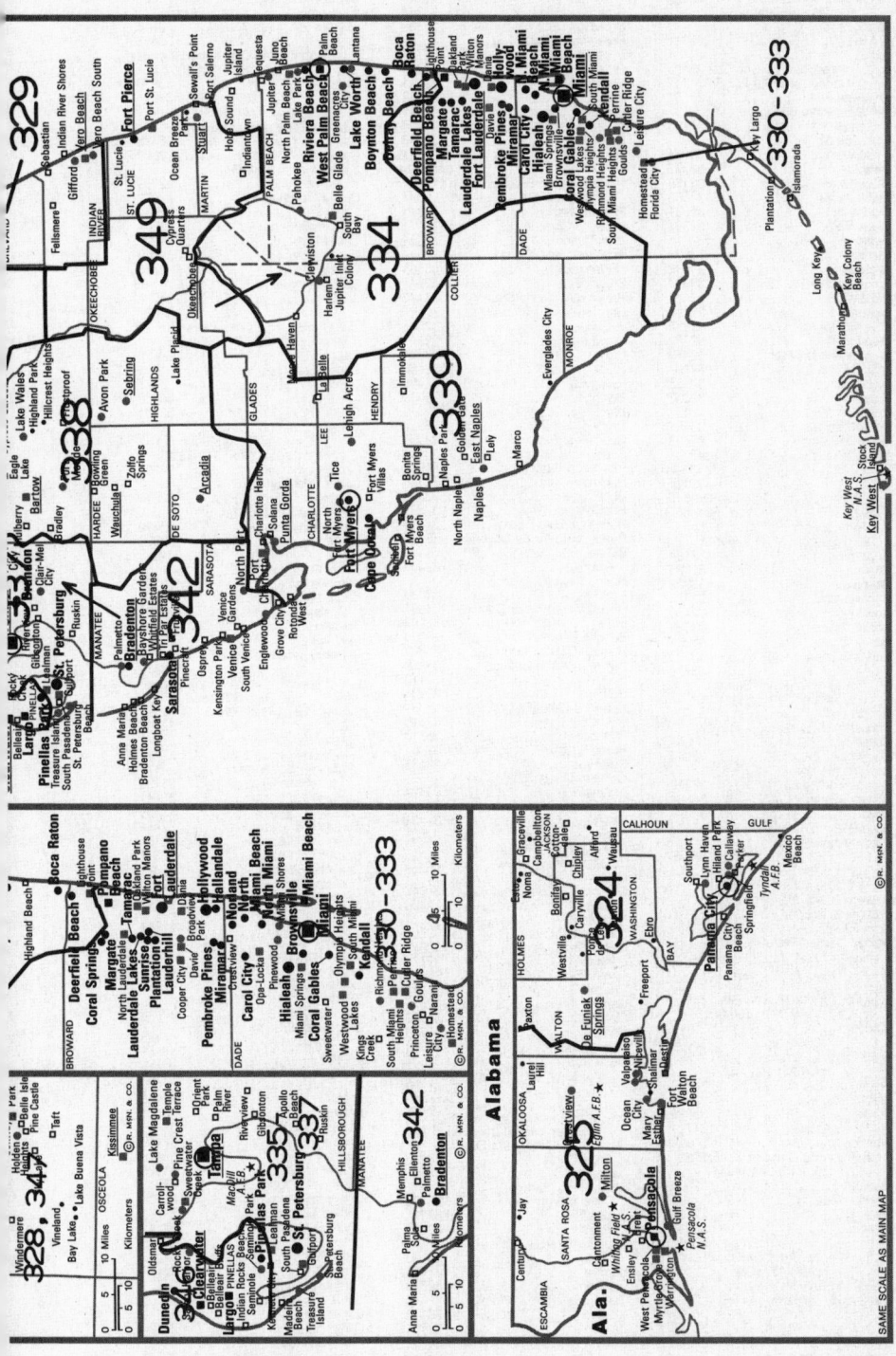

ZIP	ZIP	ZIP
.... 33351	 33146	Cudjoe.............. 33042
For specific City of Sunrise Zip	For specific Coral Gables Zip	Cudjoe Key 33044
Codes call (305) 748-8675	Codes call (305) 445-8842	Cunningham Acres 33541
Clair-Mel City........... 33619	Coral Gardens............. 34997	Curlew 34683
Clarcona 32710	Coral Ridge Shopping Plaza	Curtis Mill 32358
Clark..................... 32643	(Part of Fort Lauderdale) 33306	Cutler............. 33157-58
Clarksville 32430	 33339	For specific Cutler Zip Codes call
Clear Springs (Okaloosa	For specific Coral Ridge Shopping	(305) 233-6859
County)............... 32567	Plaza Zip Codes call (305) 563-	Cutler Ridge.............. 33157
Clear Springs (Walton	3339	 33189-90
County)............... 32567	Coral Springs............ 33065	For specific Cutler Ridge Zip
Clearwater 34615-30	 33067	Codes call (305) 233-6859
For specific Clearwater Zip Codes	 33075-76	Cutler Ridge Mall 33189
call (813) 441-4511	For specific Coral Springs Zip	Cypress (Broward County) 33060
Clearwater Beach (Part of	Codes call (305) 752-7640	Cypress (Jackson County) 32432
Clearwater).............. 34630	Coral Square (Part of Coral	Cypress Creek 33850
Clearwater Coast Guard Air	Springs) 33071	Cypress Gardens........... 33884
Station................. 34622	Coral Terrace 33144	Cypress Lake 33919
Clearwater Mall (Part of	 33156	Cypress Lake Estates 33919
Clearwater) 34624	For specific Coral Terrace Zip	Cypress Lakes 33417
Clermont.............. 34711-12	Codes call (305) 470-0327	Cypress Point 32131
For specific Clermont Zip Codes	Coral Way Village 33155	Cypress Quarters 34972
call (904) 394-2423	Coralwood Mall (Part of	Cypress Trace 33907
Cleveland 33982	Cape Coral)............ 33904	Dade City 33525-26
Cleveland Street (Part of	Cordova (Part of Pensacola) 32503	For specific Dade City Zip Codes
Clearwater)............. 34615	Cordova Lakes (Part of	call (904) 567-5179
Clewiston 33440	Bradenton)............ 34209	Dade City North 33525
Clifton (Part of Jacksonville) 32211	Cordova Mall (Part of	Dade Correctional Institution 33034
Clinton Heights 33525	Pensacola)............. 32504	Dadeland Mall 33156
Cloud Lake 33406	Corkscrew 33934	Dalkeith 32465
Cluster Springs 32433	Corley Island 34748	Dallas 34491
Coastland Center (Part of	Cornwell 33857	Dames Point (Part of
Naples) 33940	Coronet 33566	Jacksonville)............. 32226
Cobbtown................. 32565	Corry Station Naval Training	Dania 33004
Cocoa 32922-27	Center 32511	Danks Corner 34491
For specific Cocoa Zip Codes call	Cortez 34215	Darby.............. 33525
(407) 636-6565	Cortez Road (Part of	Darlington 32464
Cocoa Beach 32931-32	Bradenton)............ 34210	Davenport.............. 33837
For specific Cocoa Beach Zip	Cottage Hill 32533	Davie 33312
Codes call (407) 783-2544	Cottondale 32431	 33314
Cocoa West 32922	Cotton Plant.............. 34474	 33325-26
Coconut 33923	Country Club 33015	 33328-32
Coconut Creek 33063	Country Club Acres 33484	For specific Davie Zip Codes call
.... 33066	Country Club Estates	(305) 474-2557
.... 33073	(Columbia County) 32055	Davis Islands (Part of
For specific Coconut Creek Zip	Country Club Estates (Polk	Tampa).................. 33606
Codes call (305) 974-6080	County).............. 33805	Day 32013
Coconut Grove (Part of	Country Club Manor (Part of	Daytona Beach 32114-29
Miami) 33133	Sanford).............. 32771	 32198
.... 33233	Country Club Trail 33436-37	For specific Daytona Beach Zip
For specific Coconut Grove Zip	For specific Country Club Trail Zip	Codes call (904) 274-3500
Codes call (305) 443-0030	Codes call (407) 732-6689	Daytona Beach Shores 32116
Cody 32344	Countryside (Marion	Daytona Highbridge Estates 32114
Colee (Part of Fort	County)............... 34481	Daytona Mall (Part of
Lauderdale) 33301	Countryside (Pinellas	Daytona Beach)......... 32114
.... 33303	County)............... 34621	Daytona Park Estates...... 32720
For specific Colee Zip Codes call	Countryside Mall (Part of	De Bary 32713
(305) 764-5931	Clearwater)............. 34621	Deerfield Beach 33441-43
Coleman 33521	Countryway 33635	For specific Deerfield Beach Zip
College Park (Duval County) 32209	Courtenay................. 32952	Codes call (305) 427-3600
College Park (Marion	Cove (Part of Panama City) 32401	Deerfield Lakes............ 32011
County)............... 34474	Cox.................. 32424	Deerfield Mall (Part of
College Park (Orange	Coytown (Part of Orlando) 32803	Deerfield Beach) 33442
County)............... 32804	Crackertown (Part of Inglis) 34449	Deerland 32536
College Point............. 32444	Crandall 32097	Deer Park 32901
Collier City (Part of	Crawford 32009	Deer Point 32405
Pompano Beach)........ 33069	Crawfordville 32326-27	Deerwood (Part of
Collier Manor-Cresthaven 33064	For specific Crawfordville Zip	Jacksonville) 32256
Colonial Gables 34232	Codes call (904) 926-3256	De Funiak Springs 32433
Colonial Hills 34652	Crescent Beach (Sarasota	Dekle Beach 32347
Colonial Manor (Part of	County).............. 34242	De Land 32720-24
Jacksonville) 32207	Crescent Beach (St. Johns	For specific De Land Zip Codes
Colonial Plaza (Part of	County).............. 32086	call (904) 734-7600
Orlando) 32803	Crescent City 32112	De Land Highlands 32720
Colonialtown (Part of	Crescent Shores Heights 32157	De Land Southwest 32720
Orlando) 32803	Crestview 32536	De Leon Springs 32130
Columbia 32055	Crewsville 33890	Delespine 32927
Combee Settlement 33805	Crooked Lake Park 33853	Dellwood (Jackson County) 32442
Compass Lake 32420	Croom-A-Coochee 33597	Dellwood (Leon County) ... 32303
Compass Lake Hills 32420	Cross City 32628	Delray Beach 33444-47
Conch Key 33050	Cross City Correctional	 33483-84
Concord 32333	Institution 32628	For specific Delray Beach Zip
Concord Shopping Plaza 33165	Cross County Mall 33409	Codes call (407) 276-6047
Conner 34488	Cross Creek 32640	Delray Beach Mall (Part of
Connersville 33830	Crossroads................. 33709-10	Delray Beach)......... 33483
Conway.................. 32806	 33743	Delray Garden Estates 33484
.... 32812	For specific Crossroads Zip	Del Rio 33617
For specific Conway Zip Codes	Codes call (813) 343-1277	Deltona 32725
call (407) 240-9496	Crows Bluff 32720	 32738
Cooks Hammock 32066	Crystal Beach 34681	For specific Deltona Zip Codes
Cooper City 33328	Crystal Lake (Polk County) 33801	call (407) 574-6363
Copeland 33926	 33803	Del Tura 33903
Copeland Settlement 32609	For specific Crystal Lake Zip	Denaud 33935
Coquina Key (Part of St.	Codes call (813) 683-6245	Denver.................. 32112
Petersburg) 33705	Crystal Lake (Washington	De Soto Acres 34235
Cora 32565	County)............... 32409	De Soto City 33870
Coral Cove 34231	Crystal River 34423	DeSoto Correctional
Coral Gables 33114	 34428-29	Institution 33821
.... 33134	For specific Crystal River Zip	Desoto Lakes 34235
	Codes call (904) 795-2030	DeSoto Square 34205
	Crystal Springs 33524	

	ZIP
Floral Bluff (Part of Jacksonville)	32211
Floral City	34436
Floral Park	33462
Florence Lake	33881
Florence Villa (Part of Winter Haven)	33881
	33885

For specific Florence Villa Zip Codes call (813) 293-8423

	ZIP
Florida City	33034
Florida Correctional Institution	32663
Florida Gardens	33460
Florida International University	33199
Floridana Beach	32951
Florida Ridge	32962
Florida State Prison	32091
Florida State University (Part of Tallahassee)	32313
Florosa	32569
Flowersville	32567
Fluffy Landing	32439
Footman	32952
Forest City	32714
Forest Heights (Part of Tallahassee)	32303
Forest Hills (Hillsborough County)	33612
	33682

For specific Forest Hills Zip Codes call (813) 935-8054

	ZIP
Forest Hills (Lake County)	32720
Forest Hills (Pasco County)	34690
Forest Hills (Volusia County)	32174
Forest Island Park	33908
Forest Lakes (Pinellas County)	34677
Forest Lakes (Sarasota County)	34232
Forest Lakes Park	32179
Forest Ridge Village (Part of Fernandina Beach)	32034
Formosa (Part of Orlando)	32804
Fort Basinger	34972
Fort Caroline Club Estates (Part of Jacksonville)	32211
Fort Drum	34972
Fort George Island (Part of Jacksonville)	32226
Fort Green	33834
Fort Green Springs	33834
Fort King Acres	33541

Fort Lauderdale 33301-94

For specific Fort Lauderdale Zip Codes call (305) 527-2074

COLLEGES & UNIVERSITIES

	ZIP
Nova University	33314

FINANCIAL INSTITUTIONS

	ZIP
The Citizens and Southern National Bank of Florida	33394
Sun Bank/South Florida, N.A.	33301

HOSPITALS

	ZIP
Broward General Medical Center	33316
Florida Medical Center Hospital	33313
Holy Cross Hospital	33308
North Ridge Medical Center	33334

HOTELS/MOTELS

	ZIP
Best Western Oceanside Inn	33316
Best Western Marina Inn & Yacht Harbor	33316
Days Inn Fort Lauderdale	33312
Ft. Lauderdale Surf Hotel & Marina	33316
Crown Sterling Suites	33309
Crown Sterling Suites	33316
Holiday Inn Coral Springs	33065
Holiday Inn I-95 Airport	33312
Holiday Inn Lauderdale-by-the-Sea	33308
Holiday Inn Ft.Lauderdale North	33309
Holiday Inn Ft.Lauderdale West	33319
Howard Johnson's	33315
Howard Johnson's Hotel Resort & Villas	33308
Howard Johnson's North	33308
Howard Johnson's Oceans Edge Resort	33304

	ZIP
Oceanfront TravelLodge	33304

MILITARY INSTALLATIONS

	ZIP
Naval Surface Warfare Center, Fort Lauderdale	33315

	ZIP
Fort Lonesome	33547
Fort McCoy	32134
Fort Meade	33841
Fort Myers	33901-19
	33990-91

For specific Fort Myers Zip Codes call (813) 334-2116

	ZIP
Fort Myers Beach	33931-32

For specific Fort Myers Beach Zip Codes call (813) 463-9151

	ZIP
Fort Myers Shores (Lee County)	33905
Fort Myers Villas	33912
Fort Ogden	33842
Fort Pierce	34945-51
	34954
	34979-82

For specific Fort Pierce Zip Codes call (407) 461-2460

	ZIP
Fort Pierce Beach (Part of Fort Pierce)	34949
Fort Pierce North	34946-47

For specific Fort Pierce North Zip Codes call (407) 461-8014

	ZIP
Fort Pierce Shores	34949
Fort Pierce South	34981-82

For specific Fort Pierce South Zip Codes call (407) 461-2460

	ZIP
Fort Taylor (Part of Key West)	33040
Fort Union	32060
Fort Walton Beach	32547-49

For specific Fort Walton Beach Zip Codes call (904) 243-2311

	ZIP
Fort White	32038
Forty Ninth Street (Part of Gulfport)	33707
Fountain	32438
Four Mile Village	32459
Fowler Bluff	32626
Foxcroft (Part of Tallahassee)	32308
Fox Town	33809
Francis	32177
Franklin Park	33916
Franklintown	32034
Freeport	32439
Frink	32430
Frontenac	32927
Frostproof	33843
Fruit Cove	32259
Fruitland	32112
Fruitland Park	34731
Fruitville	34232
Fuller Heights	33860
Fussels Corner	33823
Gainesville	32601-14

For specific Gainesville Zip Codes call (904) 377-1912

	ZIP
Gainesville Mall (Part of Gainesville)	32601
Galleria at Fort Lauderdale, The (Part of Fort Lauderdale)	33304
Galliver	32564
Galloway	33809
Galt City	32583
Galt Ocean Mile (Part of Fort Lauderdale)	33308
Gandy	33702
Garden City (Duval County)	32218
Garden City (Okaloosa County)	32536
Garden Grove Estates	34609
Gardens, The (Part of Palm Beach Gardens)	33410
Gardenville	33534
Gardner	33890
Gaskin	32433
Gateway (Part of Fort Lauderdale)	33338
Gateway Center (Part of Jacksonville)	32206
Gateway Mall (Part of St. Petersburg)	33702
	33742

For specific Gateway Mall Zip Codes call (813) 577-6123

	ZIP
Gator Creek Estates	34241
Geneva	32732
Georgetown (Madison County)	32340
Georgetown (Putnam County)	32139
Georgiana	32952

	ZIP
Gibson	32333
Gibsonia	33809
Gibsonton	33534
Gifford	32960-61
	32967

For specific Gifford Zip Codes call (407) 567-5206

	ZIP
Gilberts Mill	32428
Gillett	34221
Gilmore (Part of Jacksonville)	32211
Gladeview	33147
	33150

For specific Gladeview Zip Codes call (305) 836-9710

	ZIP
Glencoe	32168
Glendale (Leon County)	32303
Glendale (Walton County)	32433
Glen Oaks (Part of Sarasota)	34232
Glen Ridge	33406
Glen Saint Mary	32040
Glenvar Heights	33143
	33155

For specific Glenvar Heights Zip Codes call (305) 661-8101

	ZIP
Glenwood (Nassau County)	32097
Glenwood (Volusia County)	32722
Glory	32351
Glynlea Park (Part of Jacksonville)	32216
Golden Beach	33160
Golden Gate (Collier County)	33999
Golden Gate (Martin County)	34997
Golden Gate Estates	33964
	33999

For specific Golden Gate Estates Zip Codes call (813) 455-5425

	ZIP
Golden Glades	33055
Golden Hills	34482
Golden Isles (Part of Hallandale)	33009
Golden Lakes	33411
Goldenrod	32733
Golden Shores	33160
Golfview	33406
Golfview Park	33853
Gomez	33455
Gonzalez	32560
Goodbys (Part of Jacksonville)	32257
Good Hope	32531
Goodland	33933
Gopher Ridge	32145
Gordon	32433
Gordon Chapel	32640
Gordonville	33830
Gotha	34734
Goulding	32501
Goulds	33170
Governor's Square Mall (Part of Tallahassee)	32301
Graceville	32440
Graham	32042
Grahamsville	34488
Grand Crossing (Part of Jacksonville)	32209
Grandin	32138
Grand Island	32735
Grand Park (Part of Jacksonville)	32209
Grand Ridge	32442
Grandview	32131
Grangers Mill	32055
Grant	32949
Grassy Key	33050
Gratigny (Part of North Miami)	33168
Grayton Beach	32459
Greater Northdale	33624
Greenacres City	33463
Greenbriar	32771
Green Cove Springs	32043
Greenhead	32428
Green Hills	32438
Greenland (Part of Jacksonville)	32256
	32258

For specific Greenland Zip Codes call (904) 642-2066

	ZIP
Greensboro	32330
Greenville	32331
Greenwood (Jackson County)	32443
Greenwood (Santa Rosa County)	32565
Grenelefe	33844
Gretna	32332
Griffin	33801

	ZIP
Gross	32097
Grove City	34224
Groveland	34736
Grove Park (Alachua County)	32640
Grove Park (Duval County)	32216
Grove Park (Polk County)	33801
Gulf Beach	32507
Gulf Beach Heights	32507
Gulf Breeze	32561-62
	32566
For specific Gulf Breeze Zip Codes call (904) 932-2662	
Gulf City	33570
Gulf Gate East	34231
	34276
For specific Gulf Gate East Zip Codes call (813) 924-8116	
Gulf Gate Estates	34231
Gulf Gate Mall	34231
Gulf Hammock	32639
Gulf Harbors	34652
Gulf Pines	32459
Gulfport	33707
	33737
For specific Gulfport Zip Codes call (813) 323-6543	
Gulf Resort Beach (Part of Panama City Beach)	32407
Gulf Stream	33483
Hague	32601
Haines City	33844-45
For specific Haines City Zip Codes call (813) 422-4477	
Hainesworth	32615
Hallandale	33008-09
For specific Hallandale Zip Codes call (305) 457-8456	
Hamilton (Part of Pompano Beach)	33072
Hammock	32137
Hammocks	33196
Hampton	32044
Hamptons at Boca Raton	33434
Hanson	32340
Harbinwood Estates	32303
Harbor Bluffs	34640
Harbor Oaks	32127
Harbor Shores	34748
Harbor View (Charlotte County)	33980
Harborview (Duval County)	32209
Harbour Heights	33983
Hardaway	32324
Hardeetown (Part of Chiefland)	32626
Hardin Heights	32324
Harlem	33440
Harmony Heights	34946
Harold	32563
Harshaw (Part of St. Petersburg)	33713
Hastings	32145
Hatchbend	32008
Havana	32333
Haverhill	33413
	33417
For specific Haverhill Zip Codes call (407) 697-2040	
Hawthorne (Alachua County)	32640
Hawthorne (Lake County)	34748
Heathrow	32746
Hedges	32097
Heilbronn	32091
Henderson Creek	33961
Hendry Correctional Institution	33934
Heritage Estates	32960
Hernando	34442
Hernando Beach	34607
Hernando City Heights	34442
Hernando Ridge	33525
Herndon (Part of Orlando)	32803
Hero	32097
Hesperides	33853
Hialeah	33010-17
For specific Hialeah Zip Codes call (305) 888-6491	
Hialeah Gardens	33016
Hialeah Lakes (Part of Hialeah)	33014
Hiawasee	32818
Hibernia	32043
Hibiscus	32757
Hickory Hill	32464
Hidden Lake Villas (Part of Sanford)	32773
Hidden Oaks	33173
Hidden River	34240
Highland	32058

	ZIP
Highland Beach	33487
Highland City	33846
Highland Lakes	34684
Highland Park (Franklin County)	33220
Highland Park (Polk County)	33853
Highland Park (Seminole County)	32771
Highlands (Part of Jacksonville)	32218
Highlands Lakes	33825
Highlands Park Estates	33852
Highland View	32456
High Point (Hernando County)	34613
High Point (Palm Beach County)	33484
Highpointe (Pinellas County)	34620
High Springs	32643
Highway Park	33852
Hiland Park	32405
Hildreth	32008
Hillcrest Heights	33827
Hilldale (Part of Tampa)	33614
	33684
For specific Hilldale Zip Codes call (813) 876-9147	
Hilliard	32046
Hill N Dale	34602
Hillsboro Beach	33062
	33072
For specific Hillsboro Beach Zip Codes call (305) 941-1844	
Hillsborough Correctional Institution	33569
Hinson	32333
Hinson Crossroads	32427
Hobe Sound	33455
	33475
For specific Hobe Sound Zip Codes call (407) 546-5630	
Hog Valley	32134
Holden Heights	32805
	32839
For specific Holden Heights Zip Codes call (407) 843-6400	
Holder	34445
Holiday	34690-91
For specific Holiday Zip Codes call (813) 942-3621	
Holiday Harbor (Part of Jacksonville)	32224
Holiday Heights	33037
Holiday Manor	33844
Holland Crossroads	32425
Holley	32561
Holliday Hill (Part of Jacksonville)	32216
Hollister	32147
Holly Ford (Part of Jacksonville)	32218
Holly Hill	32117
Holly Hills (Part of Tallahassee)	32303
Holly Point (Part of Orange Park)	32073
Hollywood	33019-29
	33081
	33083-84
For specific Hollywood Zip Codes call (305) 527-2074	
Hollywood Beach	32413
Hollywood Beach Gardens (Part of Hollywood)	33021
Hollywood Fashion Center (Part of Hollywood)	33023
Hollywood Hills (Part of Hollywood)	33021
	33081
For specific Hollywood Hills Zip Codes call (305) 981-8650	
Hollywood Mall (Part of Hollywood)	33021
Hollywood Seminole Indian Reservation	33024
Holmes Beach	34218
Holmes Correctional Institution	32425
Holmes Valley	32462
Holopaw	32901
Holt	32564
Homeland	33847
Homestead	33030-35
	33039
	33090-92
For specific Homestead Zip Codes call (305) 247-2641	
Homestead Air Force Base	33039
Homestead Ridge	32308
Homosassa	34446
	34448

	ZIP
	34487
For specific Homosassa Zip Codes call (904) 628-2396	
Homosassa Springs	34447
Honeyville	32465
Hooker Point (Hendry County)	33440
Hooker Point (Hillsborough County)	33605
Hopewell (Hillsborough County)	33566
Hopewell (Madison County)	32340
Horseshoe Beach	32648
Hosford	32334
Houston	32060
Howard	33176
Howard Creek	32465
Howey-in-the-Hills	34737
Hudson	34667
Hull	33821
Hunt Club	32703
Huntington	32112
Huntington Estates	32303
Huntington Woods (Part of Tallahassee)	32303
Hurlburt Field	32544
Hutchinson Island South	34949
Hyde Grove (Part of Jacksonville)	32210
Hyde Park (Duval County)	32210
Hyde Park (Hillsborough County)	33606
	33609
For specific Hyde Park Zip Codes call (813) 253-3140	
Hyde Park (Wakulla County)	32327
Hypoluxo	33462
Iddo	32331
Immokalee	33934
Imperial Lakes	33860
Imperial Point	34644
Indialantic	32903
Indian Bluff	32466
Indian Bluff Island	34683
Indian Creek	33154
Indian Harbour Beach	32937
Indian Head Acres (Part of Tallahassee)	32301
Indian Hills (Part of Cocoa)	32922
Indian Lake Estates	33855
Indian Mound Village	32771
Indianola	32952
Indian Pass	32456
Indian River City (Part of Titusville)	32780
Indian River Correctional Institution	32968
Indian River Estates	34982
Indian River Shores	32963
Indian Rocks Beach	34635
Indian Shores	34635
Indiantown	34956
Indian Wells	34746
Indrio	34946
Inglis	34449
Inlet Beach	32413
Innerarity Point	32507
Innisbrook	34684
Interbay (Part of Tampa)	33611
	33681
For specific Interbay Zip Codes call (813) 831-7963	
Intercession City	33848
Interlachen	32148
Inverness	32650-52
For specific Inverness Zip Codes call (904) 726-2757	
Inverrary (Part of Lauderhill)	33319
Inwood (Jackson County)	32460
Inwood (Polk County)	33881
Iona	33908
Irvine	32686
Islamorada	33036
Island Estates (Part of Clearwater)	34630
Island Grove	32654
Islandia	33131
Isleboro (Part of New Smyrna Beach)	32168
Isle of Palms (Duval County)	32250
Isle of Palms (Pinellas County)	33706
Isle Of Palms South (Part of Jacksonville)	32250
Isles of Capri	33962
Isleworth	34786
Istachatta	34636
Istokpoga Shores	33857
Ivan	32327
Ives Estates	33162
Izagora	32427

ZIP

Jacksonville 32201-98
For specific Jacksonville Zip
Codes call (904) 355-7311
Jacksonville Air Transfer
Office (Part of
Jacksonville) 32229
Jacksonville Beach 32240
.... 32250
For specific Jacksonville Beach
Zip Codes call (904) 249-9056
Jacksonville Heights (Part of
Jacksonville) 32210
Jacob City 32431
Jamaica Bay 33912
Jan Phyl Village 33880
Jarrott 32344
Jasmine Estates 34668
Jasper 32052
Jay 32565
Jena 32359
Jennings 32053
Jensen Beach 34957-58
For specific Jensen Beach Zip
Codes call (407) 334-1898
Jerome 33926
Jessamine 33525
John's Lake 34787
Johnson 32640
Johnson's Corner 32767
Jonathan's Landing 33477
Jonesville 32669
Judson 32693
Julington Forest (Part of
Jacksonville) 32258
June Park 32901
Jungle (Part of St.
Petersburg) 33710
Juniper................... 32330
Juno Beach 33408
Jupiter 33458
.... 33468-69
.... 33477-79
For specific Jupiter Zip Codes call
(407) 746-3620
Jupiter Inlet Beach Colony   33469
Jupiter Island 33455
Kathleen 33849
Keaton Beach 32347
Kenansville 34739
Kendale Lakes 33175
.... 33183
For specific Kendale Lakes Zip
Codes call (305) 235-7511
Kendale Lakes Mall 33183
Kendall 33156
.... 33173
.... 33176
.... 33256
For specific Kendall Zip Codes
call (305) 235-7511
Kendall Green 33064
Kendall Lakes West 33193
Kendall Town & Country ... 33183
Kendrick 34475
Kennedy Space Center 32815
Kenneth City 33709
Kensington Park 34235
Kerr City 32134
Keuka 32148
Key Biscayne 33149
Key Colony Beach 33051
Key Largo 33037
Key Largo Park 33037
Key Largo Village 33037
Keystone Heights 32656
Keystone Islands (Part of
North Miami) 33181
Keysville 33547
Key West 33040-41
.... 33045
For specific Key West Zip
Codes call (305) 294-2557
Key West Naval Air Station   33040
Killarney 34740
Killearn Acres 32308
Killearn Estates (Part of
Tallahassee) 32308
Killearn Lakes 32312
Kinard 32449
Kincaid Hills 32601
Kings Bay 33158
Kings Ferry............... 32046
Kingsley Lake 32091
Kingsley Village 32091
Kings Point 33484
Kings Road (Part of
Jacksonville) 32254
Kingswood Manor 32804
Kissimmee 34741-47

ZIP

.... 34758-59
For specific Kissimmee Zip Codes
call (407) 846-3121
Kissimmee Park 34772
Knights 33565
Korona 32110
Kossuthville 33823
Kynesville 32431
La Belle 33935
Lackawana Estates 32640
Lacoochee 33537
La Crosse 32658
Lady Lake 32159
La Gorce Island (Part of
Miami Beach) 33141
La Grange 32796
Laguna Beach............. 32413
Lake Alfred 33850
Lake Ashby Shores........ 32168
Lake Bird 32347
Lake Brantley 32750
Lakebreeze 32303
Lake Bryant 32179
Lake Buena Vista.......... 32830
Lake Butler............... 32054
Lake Cain Hills 32805
Lake Charm (Part of
Oviedo) 32765
Lake City 32055-56
For specific Lake City Zip Codes
call (904) 752-3373
Lake Clarke Shores........ 33406
Lake Como 32157
Lake Correctional Institution 34711
Lake Crescent Estates..... 32112
Lake Forest (Broward
County)................. 33023
Lake Forest (Duval County)   32208
Lake Forest Hills (Part of
Jacksonville) 32208
Lake Frances (Part of
Tavares) 32778
Lake Garfield 33830
Lake Geneva 32160
Lake Hamilton 33851
Lake Harbor.............. 33459
Lake Harris Shores 32778
Lake Haven Estates 33872
Lake Helen............... 32744
Lake Jem 32745
Lake Joanna 32726
Lake Josephine 33872
Lake Kathryn Heights 32720
Lakeland 33801-13
For specific Lakeland Zip Codes
call (813) 683-6245
Lakeland Highlands........ 33813
Lakeland Mall (Part of
Lakeland) 33801
Lakeland Square (Part of
Lakeland) 33809
Lake Letta 33825
Lake Lindsey............. 34601
Lake Lorraine 32579
Lake Lotela 33825
Lake Lucerne 33055-56
.... 33169
For specific Lake Lucerne Zip
Codes call (305) 470-0327
Lake Lucina (Part of
Jacksonville) 32211
Lake Mack Park 32720
Lake Magdalene........... 33612-13
For specific Lake Magdalene Zip
Codes call (813) 877-0746
Lake Marian Highlands..... 34739
Lake Mary 32746
.... 32795
For specific Lake Mary Zip Codes
call (407) 322-8420
Lake Mendelin Estates 32703
Lake Miona Heights 34785
Lake Monroe 32747
Lakemont 33825
Lake Mystic 32321
Lake of the Hills 33853
Lake Panasoffkee 33538
Lake Park 33403
Lake Pasadena Heights 33525
Lake Placid 33852
Lakeport 33471
Lake Sarasota............ 34241
Lake Saunders 32757
Lakes by the Bay 33157
.... 33190-90
For specific Lakes by the Bay Zip
Codes call (305) 233-6859
Lake Shore (Part of
Jacksonville) 32210

ZIP

.... 32238
For specific Lake Shore Zip
Codes call (904) 771-8563
Lakeside 32073
Lakeside Green 33417
Lakeside Hills 32140
Lakes Mall (Part of
Lauderdale Lakes) 33319
Lake St. George........... 34684
Lake Wales 33853
.... 33859
.... 33867
For specific Lake Wales Zip
Codes call (813) 676-2531
Lake Weir 32179
Lake Winnott 32640
Lakewood (Duval County)   32207
Lakewood (Walton County)   32433
Lakewood Heights (Part of
Tallahassee) 32311
Lakewood Park 34951
Lakewood Village 32303
Lake Worth 33460-67
For specific Lake Worth Zip
Codes call (407) 964-1102
Lamont 32336
Lamplighter (Part of
Gainesville) 32609
Lam Smith Crossroads 32425
Lanark Village 32323
Land O'Lakes 34639
Lane (Part of Jacksonville)   32254
Lantana 33462
.... 33465
For specific Lantana Zip Codes
call (407) 697-1920
Lantana Homes 33463
Largo 34640-49
For specific Largo Zip Codes call
(813) 584-2191
Largo Mall (Part of Largo)   34641
Larkin Fish Camp.......... 32321
Lauderdale-by-the-Sea 33308
Lauderdale Lakes 33309
.... 33311
.... 33313
.... 33319
For specific Lauderdale Lakes Zip
Codes call (305) 527-2077
Lauderhill 33313
.... 33319
.... 33351
For specific Lauderhill Zip Codes
call (305) 587-2450
Lauderhill Mall (Part of
Lauderhill)............. 33313
Laurel 34272
Laurel Grove (Part of
Orange Park) 32073
Laurel Hill 32567
Laurel Park (Escambia
County)................ 32505
Laurel Park (Orange
County)................ 32809
Lawtey.................. 32058
Lazy Lagoon 33982
Lazy Lake 33305
Lealman 33714
Lebanon 34431
Lecanto 34460-61
.... 34464-65
For specific Lecanto Zip Codes
call (904) 746-2424
Lee 32059
Lee Cypress 33926
Leesburg 34748-49
.... 34788-89
For specific Leesburg Zip Codes
call (904) 787-3679
Lehigh (Part of Tallahassee)   32301
Lehigh Acres 33936
.... 33970-71
For specific Lehigh Acres Zip
Codes call (813) 369-2159
Leisure City 33033
Leisure Lakes 33852
Lely..................... 33961
Lemon Bluff 32764
Lemon City (Part of Miami)   33127
.... 33137
For specific Lemon City Zip
Codes call (305) 576-0404
Lemon Grove 33873
Leon (Part of Tallahassee)   32303
.... 32315
For specific Leon Zip Codes call
(904) 877-4189
Leonards 32424
Leonia 32464
Leonton 32344
Lessie 32046

	ZIP
Liberty	32433
Liberty City (Part of Miami)	33142
Liberty Square (Part of Miami)	33147
Lido Key (Part of Sarasota)	34239
Lighthouse Point (Broward County)	33064
	33074

For specific Lighthouse Point Zip Codes call (305) 942-9555

Lighthouse Point (Martin County)	34994
Lily	33865
Limestone (Hardee County)	33865
Limestone (Jefferson County)	32344
Limona	33510
Lincoln City	32091
Lincoln Estates (Part of Gainesville)	32601
Lincoln Road Mall (Part of Miami Beach)	33139
Linden	33597
Lindgren Acres	33186
Lisbon	34788
Lithia	33547
Little Acres	34736
Little Gasparilla	33946
Little Havana (Part of Miami)	33125
Little Hollywood	32976
Little Lake City	32619
Little River (Part of Miami)	33138
	33238

For specific Little River Zip Codes call (305) 754-2524

Little River Springs	32071
Little Torch Key	33042
Live Oak (Suwannee County)	32060
Live Oak (Washington County)	32462
Live Oak Island	32327
Lloyd	32337
Lochloosa	32662
Lochmoor	33903
Lochmoor Waterway Estates	33903
Lock Arbor (Part of Sanford)	32773
Lockhart	32810
Londonderry (Part of Orlando)	32808
Longboat Key	34228
Long Key	33001
Longwood (Okaloosa County)	32579
Longwood (Seminole County)	32750
	32752
	32779
	32791

For specific Longwood Zip Codes call (407) 682-7559

Lorida	33857
Lotus	32952
Loughman	33858
Lovedale	32423
Lovett	32331
Lovewood	32431
Lowell	32663
Lower Clay Landing	32626
Lower Grand Lagoon	32401
Lower Matecumbe Key	33036
Loxahatchee	33470
Lucerne Avenue (Part of Lake Worth)	33460
Lucerne Park (Part of Winter Haven)	33881
Ludlam (Part of Miami)	33155
	33255

For specific Ludlam Zip Codes call (305) 666-0971

Lullwater Beach (Part of Panama City Beach)	32407
Lulu	32061
Lumberton	33540
Lundy	32177
Luraville	32060
Lutz	33549
Lynne	34488
Lynn Haven	32444
Mabel	33514
Mabry Manor (Part of Tallahassee)	32310
McAlpin	32062
Macclenny	32063
Macclenny II	32063
MacDill Air Force Base	33608

	ZIP
	33621

For specific MacDill Air Force Base Zip Codes call (813) 830-4438

McDavid	32568
Macedonia	32424
McGregor	33919
McIntosh	32664
McKinnon	32568
McLellen	32570
McMeekin	32640
Madeira Beach	33708
	33738

For specific Madeira Beach Zip Codes call (813) 391-8045

Madison	32340
Magnolia Beach	32408
Magnolia Gardens (Part of Jacksonville)	32209
Magnolia Springs	32043
Mainland (Part of Ormond Beach)	32174
Mainlands Center (Part of Pinellas Park)	34666
Maitland	32751
	32794

For specific Maitland Zip Codes call (407) 647-5505

Malabar	32950
Malone	32445
Manalapan	33462
Manasota	34223
Manasota Key	34223
Manatee (Part of Bradenton)	34208
Mandarin (Part of Jacksonville)	32223
	32241

For specific Mandarin Zip Codes call (904) 733-0781

Mango	33550
Mango (census designated place)	33584
Mango Hills	33584
Mangonia Park	33407
Marathon	33050
Marathon Shores	33052
Maravilla (Part of Fort Pierce)	34982
Marco	33937
	33969

For specific Marco Zip Codes call (813) 394-3621

Margate	33063
	33066
	33068

For specific Margate Zip Codes call (305) 974-6080

Marianna	32446-47

For specific Marianna Zip Codes call (904) 482-4951

Marietta (Part of Jacksonville)	32220
Marineland	32086
Mariner Mall	32505
Mariner Sands	34997
Marion Correctional Institution	32663
Marion Oaks	34473
Market Square Mall (Part of Jacksonville)	32207
Martel	34475
Martin	32617
Martin Correctional Institution and Work Camp	34956
Martin Downs	34990
Mary Esther	32569
Masaryktown	34609
Mascotte	34753
Matlacha	33909
Maxcy Quarters	33843
Maximo Moorings (Part of St. Petersburg)	33711
Maxville (Part of Jacksonville)	32234
Mayfair in the Grove (Part of Miami)	33133
Mayo	32066
Mayo Correctional Institution	32066
Mayo Junction	32066
Mayport (Part of Jacksonville)	32233
	32267

For specific Mayport Zip Codes call (904) 249-9056

Mayport Naval Station	32227-28

For specific Mayport Naval Station Zip Codes call (904) 270-5560

Meadowbrook	32808
Meadowbrook Terrace	32073

	ZIP
Meadowlawn (Part of St. Petersburg)	33702
Meadowlea on the River	32713
Meadow Wood	32824
Mecca	32771
Medart	32327
Medley	33178
Medulla	33811
Melbourne	32901-10
	32934-40
	32951

For specific Melbourne Zip Codes call (305) 723-5135

Melbourne Beach	32951
Melbourne Shores	32951
Melbourne Square (Part of Melbourne)	32901
Melbourne Village	32901
Melody Hills (Part of Tallahassee)	32308
Melrose	32666
Melrose Park (Broward County)	33312
Melrose Park (Columbia County)	32055
Memphis	34221
Memphis Heights	34221
Merritt Island	32952-54

For specific Merritt Island Zip Codes call (407) 453-1366

Merritt Square	32952
Metro Mall (Part of Fort Myers)	33916
Mexico Beach	32410
Miami	**33101-99**
	33201-99

For specific Miami Zip Codes call (305) 470-0327

COLLEGES & UNIVERSITIES

Barry University	33161

FINANCIAL INSTITUTIONS

American Savings of Florida, F.S.B.	33169
Amerifirst Federal Savings Bank	33131
Barnett Bank of South Florida, N.A.	33131
Capital Bank	33131
Chase Federal Bank	33156
Citizens Federal Bank	33131
City National Bank of Florida	33130
Coconut Grove Bank	33133
Continental National Bank of Miami	33135
Coral Gables Federal Savings & Loan Association	33134
County National Bank of South Florida	33137
Dadeland Bank	33156
Eagle National Bank of Miami	33132
Flagler Federal Savings & Loan Association	33132
Interamerican Bank	33165
Intercontinental Bank	33131
Key Biscayne Bank and Trust Company	33149
Northern Trust Bank of Florida, N.A.	33131
Ocean Bank	33126
Pacific National Bank	33131
Republic National Bank of Miami	33126
SafraBank, N.A.	33132
Sun Bank/Miami, N.A.	33131
Terrabank, N.A.	33145
TOTALBANK	33145
United National Bank	33130

HOSPITALS

AMI Kendall Regional Medical Center	33175
Baptist Hospital of Miami	33176
Cedars Medical Center	33136
Golden Glades Regional Medical Center	33169
Humana Hospital-Biscayne	33180
Jackson Memorial Hospital	33136
Mercy Hospital	33133
North Shore Medical Center	33150
South Miami Hospital	33143
Veterans Affairs Medical Center	33125

HOTELS/MOTELS

Hyatt Regency Miami	33131

ZIP ZIP ZIP

	ZIP
Ridgewood Estates	34232
Ridge Wood Heights	34231
Rio	34957
Riomar (Part of Vero Beach)	32963
Riverdale (Hernando County)	33525
Riverdale (St. Johns County)	32095
River Forest (Part of Jacksonville)	32211
Riverhaven Village	34447
River Isles (Part of Bradenton)	34208
Riverland	33312
River Park	34983
River Retreats	34431
Riverside (Dade County) ...	33135
Riverside (Duval County) ...	32204
River Trails	33917
Riverview (Duval County) ..	32208
Riverview (Hillsborough County)	33569
Riviera Beach	33404
....	33419
For specific Riviera Beach Zip Codes call (407) 844-9139	
Robin Hill	32701
Robinson Heights	32667
Robinwood	32808
....	32818
For specific Robinwood Zip Codes call (407) 293-3274	
Rochelle	32601
Rock Bluff	32321
Rockdale	33157
Rock Harbor	33037
Rock Hill (Okaloosa County)	32531
Rock Hill (Walton County)	32433
Rock Hill (Washington County)	32428
Rockledge	32955-56
For specific Rockledge Zip Codes call (407) 636-4177	
Rocksprings (Marion County)	34431
Rock Springs (Orange County)	32703
Rocky Creek	33615
Rocky Point	32608
Roeville	32583
Ro-Len Lake Gardens (Part of Hallandale)	33009
Rolling Acres	34602
Rolling Hills (Duval County)	32221
Rolling Hills (Marion County)	34474
Rolling Hills (Polk County)	33860
Rolling Ranches	34431
Romeo	34432
Roosevelt Mall (Part of Jacksonville)	32210
Rosedale	32324
Roseland	32957
Rosewood	32625
Rotonda	33946
Rotonda West	33946
Round Lake	32420
Royal	34785
Royal Gardens Estates	34209
Royal Palm Beach	33411
Royal Palm Village	33908
Royals Cross Roads	32464
Royal Terrace (Part of Jacksonville)	32209
Rubonia	34221
Runnymeade	32303
Ruskin	33570-71
....	33573
For specific Ruskin Zip Codes call (813) 645-1820	
Russell	32043
Rutland	33538
Sabal Palm Estates	33068
Saddlebunch Keys	33040
Saddle Creek	34241
Safety Harbor	34695
St. Andrews (Part of Panama City)	32401
St. Armands (Part of Sarasota)	34236
St. Augustine	32084-86
....	32092
....	32095
For specific St. Augustine Zip Codes call (904) 829-8716	
St. Augustine Beach	32086
St. Augustine Shores	32086
St. Augustine South	32086
St. Catherine	33513
St. Cloud	34769-73
For specific St. Cloud Zip Codes call (407) 892-3779	

	ZIP
St. George Island	32328
Saint James	32358
St. James City	33956
Saint Joe Beach	32456
St. Johns Park (Duval County)	32210
St. Johns Park (Flagler County)	32110
St. Johns River Estates (Putnam County)	32189
Saint Johns River Estates (Seminole County)	32771
Saint Josephs	32771
St. Leo	33574
St. Lucie	34946
St. Marks	32355
St. Nicholas (Part of Jacksonville)	32207
St. Petersburg	33701-84
For specific St. Petersburg Zip Codes call (813) 323-6516	
St. Petersburg Beach	33706
....	33715
....	33736
For specific St. Petersburg Beach Zip Codes call (813) 367-2261	
St. Teresa	32358
Saint Vincent de Paul Regional Seminary	33436
Salem	32356
Salt Springs	32134
Samoset	34208
Sample Square (Part of Pompano Beach)	33064
Sampson City	32091
Samsula	32168
Samsula-Spruce Creek	32168
San Antonio	33576
San Blas	32456
San Carlos Park	33912
Sandalfoot Cove	33428
Sandalwood (Part of Jacksonville)	32246
Sand Cut	33348
Sanderson	32087
Sandestin	32541
Sand Lake (Part of Orlando)	32819
....	32821
....	32836-37
For specific Sand Lake Zip Codes call (407) 351-9037	
Sandlefoot Cove	33428
....	33433
For specific Sandlefoot Cove Zip Codes call (407) 479-0650	
Sandy	34251
Sandy Point	32008
Sanford	32771-73
For specific Sanford Zip Codes call (407) 322-2892	
Sanibel	33957
San Jose (Part of Jacksonville)	32217
San Marco (Part of Jacksonville)	32207
San Mateo (Duval County)	32218
San Mateo (Putnam County)	32187
San Souci (Part of Jacksonville)	32216
San Souci Estates (Part of North Miami)	33181
San Souci Lakes	33917
Sans Souci	33982
Santa Fe	32616
Santa Monica	32413
Santa Rosa Beach	32459
Santa Rosa Mall (Part of Mary Esther)	32569
Santos	34474
Sarabay Acres	34229
Sarasota	34230-43
....	34276-78
For specific Sarasota Zip Codes call (813) 952-9720	
Sarasota Heights (Part of Sarasota)	34239
Sarasota Main Plaza (Part of Sarasota)	34236
Sarasota Springs	34232
Sarasota Square	34238
Saratoga	32189
Sarno Plaza (Part of Melbourne)	32935
Sasafrass Acres	32038
Satellite Beach	32937
Satsuma	32189
Saufley Field	32509
Sawdust	32351
Sawgrass	32082
Sawgrass Mills (Part of City of Sunrise)	33323

	ZIP
Scenic Heights (Part of Tallahassee)	32303
Scotland	32333
Scott Lake	33056
Scotts Ferry	32424
Scottsmoor	32775
Seaglades	32507
Seagrove Beach	32459
Sea Ranch Lakes	33062
Searstown Mall (Part of Titusville)	32780
Seascape	32541
Seaside	32459
Sebastian	32958
....	32976-78
For specific Sebastian Zip Codes call (407) 589-4397	
Sebastian Highlands (Part of Sebastian)	32958
Sebring	33870-72
For specific Sebring Zip Codes call (813) 382-1151	
Sebring Country Estates ...	33870
Sebring Hills	33872
Sebring Hills South	33870
Sebring Ridge	33870
Sebring Shores	33870
Seffner	33584
Seminole (Okaloosa County)	32578
Seminole (Pinellas County)	34642
Seminole Heights (Part of Tampa)	33603
....	33673
For specific Seminole Heights Zip Codes call (813) 232-0171	
Seminole Mall (Part of Seminole)	34642
Seminole Manor (Leon County)	32310
Seminole Manor (Palm Beach County)	33460
Seminole Park	34647
Seminole Plaza (Part of Casselberry)	32707
Seven Springs	34655
Seville	32190
Sewall's Point	34996
Shadeville	32327
Shadow Run	33569
Shady	34474
Shady Grove (Jackson County)	32442
Shady Grove (Taylor County)	32357
Shalimar	32579
Shamrock	32628
Shangri La	33584
Shannon Forest (Part of Tallahassee)	32308
Shannon Woods	32607
Sharpes	32959
Shawnee	33440
Shell Point	32327
Shenandoah (Part of Miami)	33145
....	33245
For specific Shenandoah Zip Codes call (305) 856-2206	
Sherman	34974
Sherwood Forest (Duval County)	32208
Sherwood Forest (Osceola County)	34746
Sherwood Park (Part of Delray Beach)	33445
Shockley Heights	32702
Shockley Hills	32702
Shore Acres (Part of St. Petersburg)	33705
Siesta Key	34242
Siesta Lago	34746
Silver Beach Heights	32784
Silver Lake	34788
Silver Sands (Part of Panama City Beach)	32407
Silver Springs (Marion County)	34488-89
For specific Silver Springs Zip Codes call (904) 687-4480	
Silver Springs (Okaloosa County)	32536
Silver Springs Shores	34472
Simmons Point	32346
Singer Island (Part of Riviera Beach)	33404
Sink Creek	34246
Sirmans	32331
Skycrest (Part of Clearwater)	34615
Sky Lake	32809
Skylake Mall	33162
Skyland Meadows	34442

	ZIP
Skyline Hills (Part of Lady Lake)	32159
Slavia	32765
Slones Ridge	34736
Snapper Creek	33116
	33176
	33186
	33196

For specific Snapper Creek Zip Codes call (305) 274-9050

	ZIP
Sneads	32460
Snell Isle (Part of St. Petersburg)	33705
Snow Hill	32765
Socrum	33809
Solana	33950
Sopchoppy	32358
Sorrento	32776
Sorrento Shores	34229
Sorrento Shores South	34275
South Apopka	32703
South Bay	33493
South Beach (Dade County)	33139
South Beach (Indian River County)	32963
Southboro (Part of West Palm Beach)	33405
South Bradenton	34205
South Brooksville	34601
South Clermont	34711
South Clinton Heights	33525
South Daytona	32121
Southeast Arcadia	33821
South Florida Mail Processing Center (Part of Pembroke Pines)	33082
Southgate	34239
	34277

For specific Southgate Zip Codes call (813) 955-9355

	ZIP
South Gate Plaza (Part of Sarasota)	34239
South Gate Ridge	34231
	34233

For specific South Gate Ridge Zip Codes call (813) 955-9355

	ZIP
South Jacksonville (Part of Jacksonville)	32207
	32247

For specific South Jacksonville Zip Codes call (904) 355-7311

	ZIP
South Merritt Estates	32952
South Miami	33143
	33155
	33243

For specific South Miami Zip Codes call (305) 661-1734

	ZIP
South Miami Heights	33157
South Mulberry	33860
South Palm Beach	33480
South Pasadena	33707
South Patrick Shores	32937
South Pine Lakes	32726
South Ponte Vedra Beach	32082
Southport (Bay County)	32409
South Port (Osceola County)	34746
South Punta Gorda Heights	33955
South Sarasota	34231
Southside (Part of Ft. Lauderdale)	33335
Southside (Part of Lakeland)	33807
	33811
	33813

For specific Southside Zip Codes call (305) 761-1194

	ZIP
Southside Estates (Part of Jacksonville)	32216
South Trail	34231
South Venice	34293
South Weeki Wachee	34606
Southwood	32809
Sparr	32192
Spring Creek	32327
Springfield (Bay County)	32401
Springfield (Duval County)	32206
Spring Glen (Part of Jacksonville)	32207
Springhead	33566
Spring Hill	34606-08

For specific Spring Hill Zip Codes call (904) 683-3634

	ZIP
Springhill	32071
Spring Lake (Hernando County)	34602
Spring Lake (Highlands County)	33870
Spring Oaks (Part of Altamonte Springs)	32714
Springside	32177

	ZIP
Springs Plaza (Part of Longwood)	32779
Spruce Creek	32119
Spuds	32033
Starke	32091
State Capitol (Part of Tallahassee)	32399
State Line	32426
Station A (Part of Daytona Beach)	32122
Station F (Part of Jacksonville)	32206
Steinhatchee	32359
Stetson University (Part of De Land)	32720
Stock Island	33040
Stuart	34994-97

For specific Stuart Zip Codes call (407) 287-2171

	ZIP
Stucky Still	34736
Sugar Loaf Shores	33044
Sugar Mill (Hillsborough County)	33624
Sugar Mill (Volusia County)	32168
Sugarmill Woods	34446
Sulphur Springs (Part of Tampa)	33604
	33674

For specific Sulphur Springs Zip Codes call (813) 238-5000

	ZIP
Sumatra	32335
Summerbrooke (Part of Tallahassee)	32312
Summerfield	34491-92

For specific Summerfield Zip Codes call (904) 245-2784

	ZIP
Summer Haven	32086
Summerland Key	33042
Summer Place	32960
Summerport Beach	34786
Sumner	32625
Sumter Correctional Institution	33513
Sumterville	33585
Sun City	33586
Sun City Center	33571
	33573

For specific Sun City Center Zip Codes call (813) 645-5884

	ZIP
Suncoast Estates	33917
Sun Haven	34231
Suniland	33156
Sunlake	32735
Sunland Estates	32771
Sunland Gardens	34947
Sunniland (Collier County)	33934
Sunniland (Dade County)	33156
Sun 'n Lake Acres	33852
Sun 'n Lake Estates	33852
Sun 'n Lakes	33870
Sunny Breeze Harbour	33821
Sunny Hills	32428
Sunny Isles	33160
Sunnyland	34233
Sunnyside (Bay County)	32461
Sunnyside (Lake County)	34748
Sun Ray Homes	33843
Sunrise (Part of Fort Lauderdale)	33304
Sunset	33183
	33283

For specific Sunset Zip Codes call (305) 596-9156

	ZIP
Sunset Harbor	34491
Sunset Islands (Part of Miami Beach)	33140
Sunshine Mall (Part of Clearwater)	34616
Suntree	32940
Sun Valley	33437
Surf	32346
Surfside	33154
Suwannee	32692
Suwannee Gardens	32680
Suwannee River Park Estates	32060
Suwannee Springs	32060
Suwannee Valley	32055
Svea	32567
Sweet Gum Head	32464
Sweetwater (Dade County)	33172
	33174

For specific Sweetwater Zip Codes call (305) 477-6708

	ZIP
Sweetwater (Liberty County)	32321
Sweetwater Creek	33615
Sweetwater Oaks	32750
Switzerland	32043
Sycamore	32351
Sydney	33587
Sylvania	32462

	ZIP
Sylvan Shores (Highlands County)	33852
Sylvan Shores (Lake County)	32757
Taft	32824
Talisman Estates	33525
Tallahassee	32301-04
	32306-08
	32310-17
	32399

For specific Tallahassee Zip Codes call (904) 877-4189

	ZIP
Tallahassee Mall (Part of Tallahassee)	32303
Tallevast	34270
Talleyrand (Part of Jacksonville)	32206
Tamarac	33319-21

For specific Tamarac Zip Codes call (305) 722-6080

	ZIP
Tamiami	33175
	33182
	33184

For specific Tamiami Zip Codes call (305) 261-5102

	ZIP
Tamiami (P.O. Station)	33144
Tampa	33601-97

For specific Tampa Zip Codes call (813) 877-0717

COLLEGES & UNIVERSITIES

	ZIP
Tampa College	33614
University of South Florida	33620
University of Tampa	33606

FINANCIAL INSTITUTIONS

	ZIP
Bank of Tampa	33603
Barnett Bank of Tampa, N.A.	33602
Bay Financial Savings Bank	33615
Central Bank of Tampa	33609
First Florida Bank, National Association	33602
NCNB National Bank of Florida	33602
Sun Bank of Tampa Bay	33602

HOSPITALS

	ZIP
James A. Haley Veterans Hospitals	33612
St. Joseph's Hospital	33612
Tampa General Hospital	33601
University Community Hospital	33613

HOTELS/MOTELS

	ZIP
Days Inn Conference Center	33602
Embassy Suites Tampa Airport	33609
Tampa Airport Marriott	33607
Tampa Airport Hilton at Metrocenter	33607
Tampa Marriott	33607

MILITARY INSTALLATIONS

	ZIP
MacDill Air Force Base	33608
	33621
Marine Corps Reserve Training Center, Tampa	33611
Tampa Bay Center (Part of Tampa)	33607
Tangelo Park	32819
Tangerine	32777
Tang-O-Mar Beach	32541
Tarpon Lake Village	34685
Tarpon Springs	34688-90

For specific Tarpon Springs Zip Codes call (813) 937-5741

	ZIP
Tarpon Woods	34685
Tarrytown	33597
Tavares	32778
Tavernier	33070
Taylor	32087
Taylor Creek	34974
Tee and Green Estates	33982
Telogia	32360
Temple Terrace	33617
	33687

For specific Temple Terrace Zip Codes call (813) 988-4776

	ZIP
Tenille	32356
Tequesta	33469
Terra Ceia	34250
The Forest	33908
The Fountains	33467
The Hamptons	33434
The Landings (Lee County)	33919

	ZIP
The Landings (Sarasota County)	34231
The Meadows (Clay County)	32065
The Meadows (Lake County)	32702
The Meadows (Sarasota County)	34235
Theressa	32091
The Vineyards	33999
Thomas City	32344
Thompson Estates	32778
Thonotosassa	33592
Three Rivers	32322
Three Rivers Estates	32038
Tice	33905
Tierra Verde	33715
Tiger Point	32561
Tildenville	34787
Timberline Estates	34461
Timber Pines	34606
Timberwood Estates	34785
Tisonia (Part of Jacksonville)	32218
Titusville	32780-83
	32796
For specific Titusville Zip Codes call (407) 267-4826	
Tocoi	32033
Tommytown (Part of Dade City)	33525
Tomoka Estates	32174
Torchlite	34711
Torrey	33834
Town and Country Plaza	32505
Town and River Estates	33919
Town Center At Boca Raton (Part of Boca Raton)	33431
Towne Mall (Part of Plantation)	33317
Town 'n' Country (census designated place)	33614-15
	33634
For specific Town 'n' Country (census designated place) Zip Codes call (813) 876-9147	
Town 'n' Country	33615
	33685
For specific Town 'n' Country Zip Codes call (813) 885-6296	
Town Park Estates	33165
	33174
For specific Town Park Estates Zip Codes call (305) 226-7522	
Trailer Estates	34281
Trailer Haven (Part of Melbourne)	32901
Trapnell	33567
Treasure Island (Dade County)	33141
Treasure Island (Lake County)	34788
Treasure Island (Pinellas County)	33706
Trenton	32693
Triangle Acres	32757
Trilby	33593
Tri Par Estates	34234
Tropic	32962
	32965
For specific Tropic Zip Codes call (407) 453-1366	
Tropical Acres	33569
Tropical Farms	34990
Tropical Gulf Acres	33955
Tropical Shores Manor	32778
Tropic Palms (Part of Delray Beach)	33444
Tropic Vista	33469
Truckland	33908
Turkey Creek	33567
Turner River	33943
Turquoise Beach	32459
Tuscanooga	34736
Tuskawilla (Part of Winter Springs)	32708
Twin City Mall (Part of North Palm Beach)	33408
Two Egg	32423
Tyndall Air Force Base	32403
Tyrone Square (Part of St. Petersburg)	33710
Uleta	33164
Umatilla	32784
Union Correctional Institution	32083
Union Park	32817
	32825
For specific Union Park Zip Codes call (407) 282-1421	

	ZIP
University	32603-04
For specific University Zip Codes call (904) 355-7311	
University Mall (Broward County)	33024
University Mall (Escambia County)	32504
University Of Miami (Part of Coral Gables)	33124
University of South Florida	33620
University of Tampa (Part of Tampa)	33606
University of West Florida	32514
University Park (Duval County)	32211
University Park (Orange County)	32817
University Plaza	33612
University Square	33612
University West	33612-13
For specific University West Zip Codes call (813) 935-8054	
Upper Grand Lagoon	32407
	32411
For specific Upper Grand Lagoon Zip Codes call (904) 234-9101	
USAF Hospital	32542
Useppa Island	33924
Valdez	32713
Valkaria	32905
Valparaiso	32580
Valrico	33594
Vamo	34231
Venetia (Part of Jacksonville)	32210
Venetian Islands (Part of Miami Beach)	33139
Venetian Isles (Pinellas County)	33705
Venetian Isles (Santa Rosa County)	32561
Venetia Terrace (Part of Jacksonville)	32244
Venice	34284-93
For specific Venice Zip Codes call (813) 485-9858	
Venice Acres	34292
Venice East	34293
Venice Gardens	34293
Venus	33960
Verdie	32009
Vermont Heights	32033
Verna	34251
Vernon	32462
Vero Beach	32960-68
For specific Vero Beach Zip Codes call (407) 567-5206	
Vero Beach Highlands	32962
Vero Beach South	32960
	32962
	32966
	32968
For specific Vero Beach South Zip Codes call (407) 567-5206	
Vero Lake Estates	32967
Vero Shores	32962
Vicksburg	32401
Vilano Beach	32095
Vilas	32334
Village (Part of Deerfield Beach)	33442
Village Green (Brevard County)	32955
Village Green (Manatee County)	34209
Village of Golf	33436
Village of Pine Run	32174
Villages of Oriole	33446
Villas	33912
Villa Sabine	32561
Villa Tasso	32578
Vina del Mar (Part of St. Petersburg Beach)	33706
Virginia Gardens	33166
Volusia	32102
Volusia Mall (Part of Daytona Beach)	32114
Wabasso	32970
Wacahotta	32667
Waccasassa Lake	32693
Wacissa	32361
Wadesboro	32308
Wahneta	33880
Wahoo	33513
Wakulla	32327
Wakulla Gardens	32327
Wakulla Springs	32305
Waldo	32694
Wallace	32571
Walnut Hill	32568
Walsingham	34644

	ZIP
Walton	34957
Wannee	32619
Ward Ridge	32456
Warm Mineral Springs	34287
Warrington	32507
Washington Lake Estates (Part of Jacksonville)	32218
Washington Park	33311
Washington Shores (Part of Orlando)	32805
Waters Lake	32693
Watertown	32055
Waterway Estates	33903
Wauchula	33873
Wauchula Hills	33873
Waukeenah	32344
Wausau	32463
Waverly	33877
Waverly Hills (Part of Tallahassee)	32312
Weathersfield	32714
Webster	33597
Weeki Wachee	34606
Weeki Wachee Acres	34606
Weeki Wachee Gardens	34607
Weirsdale	32195
Wekiva Springs	32750
Wekiwa Acres	32703
Welaka	32193
Welcome	33547
Wellborn	32094
Wellington	33414
Wesconnett (Part of Jacksonville)	32244
Wesley Chapel	33543-44
For specific Wesley Chapel Zip Codes call (813) 782-2013	
Wesley Manor	32223
West Atlantic (Part of Coral Springs)	33071
	33077
For specific West Atlantic Zip Codes call (305) 346-9446	
West Bay	32413
West Bradenton	34209
Westchester	33144
	33155
	33165
	33174
For specific Westchester Zip Codes call (305) 445-8841	
West Dade	33196
West De Land	32720
West End (Broward County)	33326
West End (Calhoun County)	32424
West End (Jackson County)	32446
Western Acres	33903
West Farm	32340
West Frostproof	33843
Westgate (Manatee County)	34205
Westgate (Palm Beach County)	33409
Westgate-Belvedere Homes	33409
West Holly Hill	32117
West Hollywood (Part of Pembroke Pines)	33023
	33083
For specific West Hollywood Zip Codes call (305) 983-3533	
West Jacksonville (Part of Jacksonville)	32205
West Kendall	33296
Westland Mall (Part of Hialeah)	33012
West Lantana (Part of Lantana)	33462
West Little River	33147
	33150
For specific West Little River Zip Codes call (305) 754-2524	
West Melbourne	32904
West Miami	33144
	33155
For specific West Miami Zip Codes call (305) 385-1366	
Weston	33326
West Palm Beach	33401-07
	33409-20
For specific West Palm Beach Zip Codes call (407) 697-1933	
West Palmetto Park (Part of Boca Raton)	33427
	33486
For specific West Palmetto Park Zip Codes call (407) 844-7277	
West Panama City Beach (Part of Panama City Beach)	32413
West Park	33614
West Pensacola	32505
Westridge	33433

	ZIP		ZIP		ZIP
West Samoset	34208	Wilson Neck	32097	Woodlawn Beach	32561
West Scenic Park	33853	Wilton Manors	33305-06	Wood Memorial Hospital	33821
West Shore Plaza (Part of			33311	Woodmont (Part of	
Tampa)	33609		33334	Tamarac)	33321
West Tampa (Part of		For specific Wilton Manors Zip		Woods	32321
Tampa)	33607	Codes call (305) 527-2077		Woods and Lakes	32179
	33677	Wimauma	33598	Woodville	32362
For specific West Tampa Zip		Windermere	34786	Woodward Avenue (Part of	
Codes call (813) 253-3062		Winding Lakes	33428	Tallahassee)	32304
Westview	33168	Windsor	32601		32316
Westville	32464	Winfield	32055	For specific Woodward Avenue	
Westwood (Duval County)	32244	Winston (census designated		Zip Codes call (904) 222-2861	
Westwood (Orange County)	32808	place)	33801	Worthington Springs	32697
Westwood Acres	34474		33803	Wright	32547
Westwood Lakes	33165	For specific Winston (census		Wulfert (Part of Sanibel)	33957
Wewahitchka	32465	designated place) Zip Codes call		Wynnehaven Beach	32569
Whiskey Creek	33919	(813) 688-5572		Wynwood (Dade County)	33127
Whispering Pines (Madison		Winston	33803	Wynwood (Seminole	
County)	32340	Winter Beach	32971	County)	32771
Whispering Pines		Winter Garden	34777	Yacht Club Colony	33917
(Okeechobee County)	34972		34787	Yalaha	34797
Whispering Pines (Putnam		For specific Winter Garden Zip		Yankeetown	34498
County)	32139	Codes call (407) 656-3344		Ybor City (Part of Tampa)	33605
Whisper Walk	33496	Winter Haven	33880-85		33675
White City (Gulf County)	32465	For specific Winter Haven Zip		For specific Ybor City Zip Codes	
White City (St. Lucie		Codes call (813) 294-4157		call (813) 248-2543	
	34981	Winter Haven Mall (Part of		Yeehaw Junction	C34972
Whitehouse (Part of		Winter Haven)	33880	Yellow Pine	32340
Jacksonville)	32220	Winter Park	32789-90	Yelvington	32131
White Springs (Hamilton			32792-93	York	34474
County)	32096	For specific Winter Park Zip		Youmans	33566
White Springs (Liberty		Codes call (407) 647-3621		Youngstown	32466
County)	32321	Winter Park Estates	32792	Yukon (Part of Jacksonville)	32244
Whitfield	34243	Winter Park Mall (Part of		Yulee	32097
Whitfield Estates	34243	Winter Park)	32789	Yulee Heights	32097
Whiting Field	32570	Winter Springs	32708	Yulee Woods	32097
Whitney	34748		32719	Zellwood	32798
Whitney Beach (Part of		For specific Winter Springs Zip		Zephyrhills	33539-44
Longboat Key)	34228	Codes call (407) 327-4600		For specific Zephyrhills Zip Codes	
Wilbur-By-The-Sea	32127	Wiscon	34609	call (813) 782-2013	
Wilcox	32693	Woodland (Part of Boca		Zephyrhills Correctional	
Wildwood	34785	Raton)	33431	Institution	33539
Williamsburg	32821		33481	Zephyrhills North	33540
	32823	For specific Woodland Zip Codes		Zephyrhills South	33540-41
For specific Williamsburg Zip		call (407) 997-1619		For specific Zephyrhills South Zip	
Codes call (407) 850-6200		Woodland Drives (Part of		Codes call (813) 782-2013	
Williams Point	32959	Tallahassee)	32301	Zephyrhills West	33541
Willis Landing	32465	Woodlawn (Bay County)	32407	Zolfo Springs	33890
Williston	32696	Woodlawn (Pinellas County)	33704	Zuber	34475
Williston Highlands	32696	Woodlawn (St. Johns			
Willow Oak	33860	County)	32095		
Wilson Corner	33597				

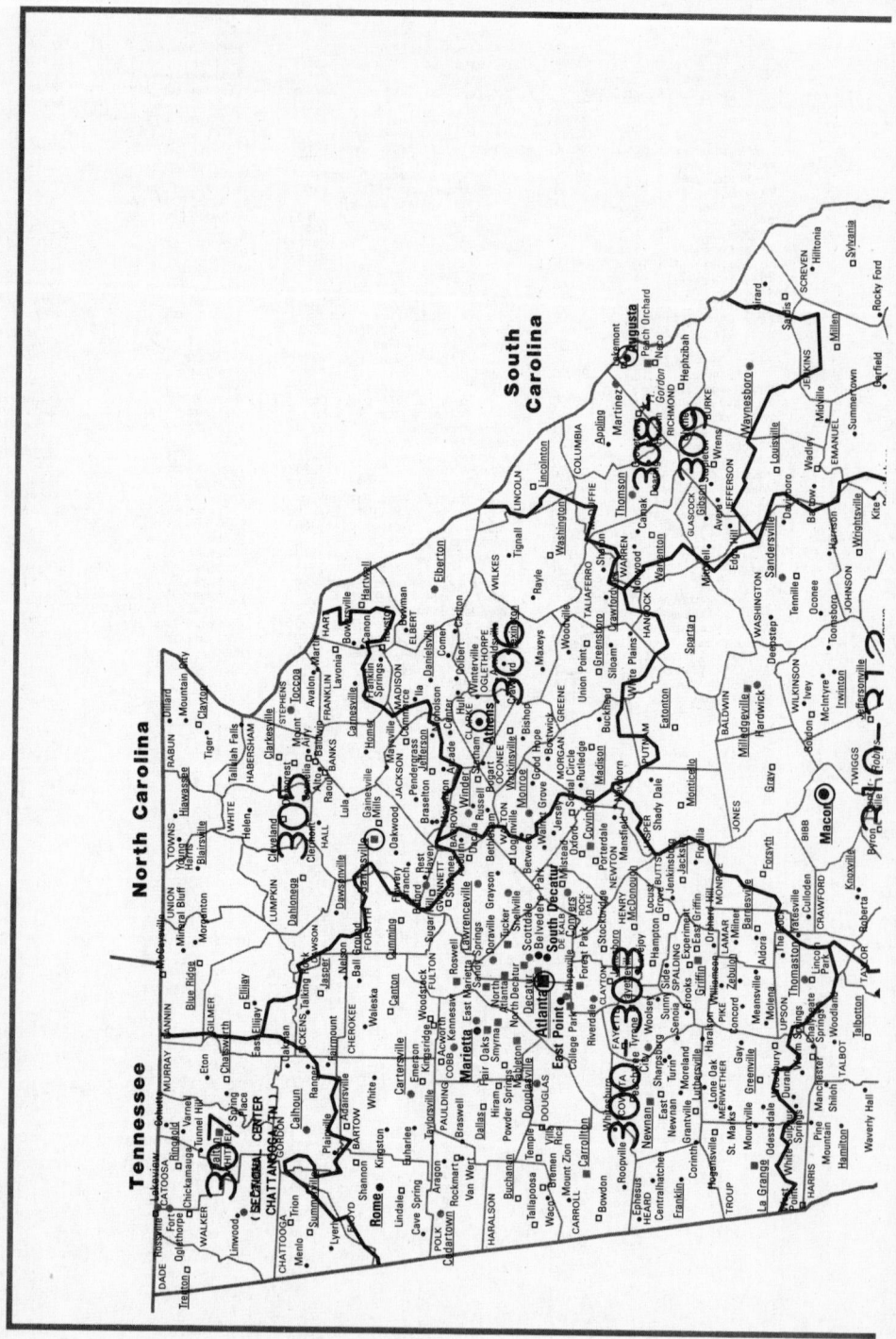

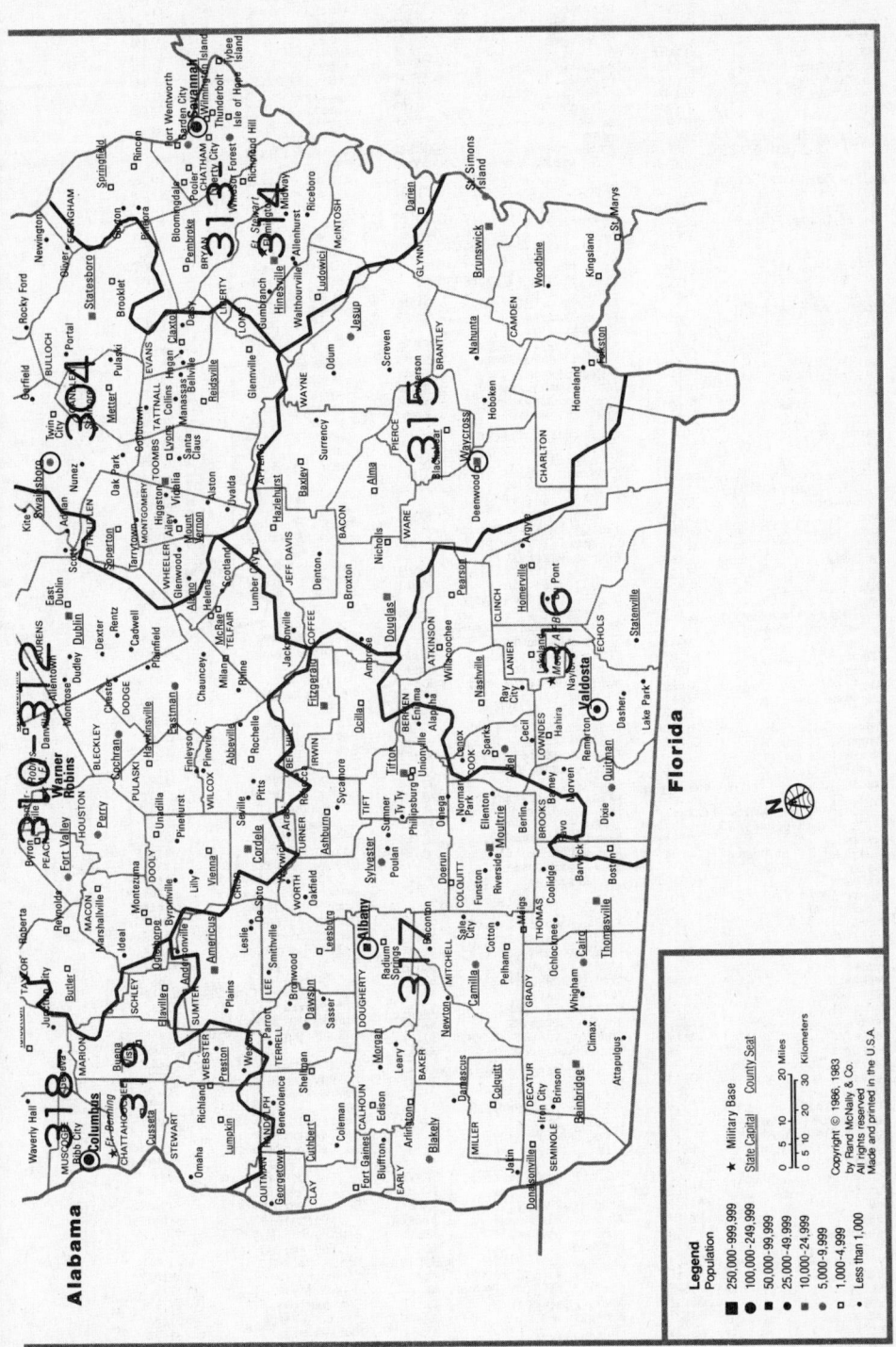

	ZIP
Aaron	30450
Abac	31794
Abba	31750
Abbeville	31001
Abbott	30207
Abbottsford	30240
Aberdeen (Part of Peachtree City)	30269
Acree	31791
Acworth	30101-02
For specific Acworth Zip Codes call (404) 974-3300	
Adairsville	30103
Adams Park (Fulton County)	30311
Adams Park (Twiggs County)	31020
Adamsville (Part of Atlanta)	30331
Adasburg	30673
Adel	31620
Adgateville	31038
Adrian	31002
Agnes	30817
Agnes Scott College (Part of Decatur)	30030
Aid	30521
Ailey	30410
Air Line	30516
Airport Mail Facility (Part of Atlanta)	30320
Airport Subdivision	31601
Akin	30415
Alamo	30411
Alapaha	31622
Albany	31701-07
For specific Albany Zip Codes call (404) 883-7600	
Albion Acres	30906
Alcovy	30209
Alcovy Shores	31064
Aldora	30204
Alexander	30456
Alfords	31791
Aline	30420
Allen City	30071
Allendale (Gwinnett County)	30245
Allendale (Muscogee County)	31904
Allenhurst	31301
Allentown	31003
Allenville	31639
Allenwood	31061
Allie	30222
Alma	31510
Almon	30209
Almond Park (Part of Atlanta)	30318
Alpharetta	30201-02
	30239
For specific Alpharetta Zip Codes call (404) 475-7235	
Alpine	30731
Alps Road (Part of Athens)	30604
Alston	30412
Altamaha	30453
Alta Vista (Part of Columbus)	31906
Altman	30467
Alto	30510
Alto Park	30161
Alvaton	30218
Amboy	31714
Ambrose	31512
Americus	31709
Amity	30817
Amos Mill	35967
Amsterdam	31734
Anderson City	31744
Andersonville	31711
Anguilla	31525
Ansley Estates	30274
Antioch (Polk County)	30125
Antioch (Troup County)	30240
Aonia	30673
Apalachee	30650
Apple Valley	30529
Appling	30802
Arabi	31712
Aragon	30104
Aragon Park	30901
Arcade	30549
Arch City	30701
Archery	31780
Arco	31520
Arcola	30415
Ardick	31331
Ardmore	31329
Ardsley Park (Part of Savannah)	31405
Argyle	31623
Arkwright	31204
Arlington	31713

	ZIP
Armstrong State College	31406
Armuchee	30105
Arnco Mills	30263
Arnoldsville	30619
Arp	31783
Arrowhead Village	30236
Ascalon	30738
Ashburn	31714
Ashford Park	30319
Ashintilly	31331
Ashland	30521
Athens	30601-13
For specific Athens Zip Codes call (404) 613-2195	
Atkinson	31543
Atlanta	30301-83
	31101-99
For specific Atlanta Zip Codes call (404) 765-7261	

COLLEGES & UNIVERSITIES

	ZIP
Clark Atlanta University	30314
Emory University	30322
Georgia Institute of Technology	30332
Georgia State University	30303
Mercer University-Atlanta	30341
Morris Brown College	30314
Oglethorpe University	30319
Spelman College	30314

FINANCIAL INSTITUTIONS

	ZIP
Bank South	30303
Citizens Trust Bank	30303
Federal Savings Bank	30305
First American Bank of Georgia, N.A.	30328
First Union National Bank of Georgia	30303
Georgia Federal Bank, F.S.B.	30303
NCNB National Bank	30319
The Prudential Bank and Trust Company	30328
Southern Federal Savings & Loan Association of Georgia	30308
Trust Company Bank	30302
Wachovia Bank of Atlanta	30383

HOSPITALS

	ZIP
Crawford Long Hospital of Emory University	30365
Emory University Hospital	30322
Georgia Baptist Medical Center	30312
Grady Memorial Hospital	30335
HCA West Paces Ferry Hospital	30327
Northside Hospital	30342
Piedmont Hospital	30309
Saint Joseph's Hospital of Atlanta	30342

HOTELS/MOTELS

	ZIP
The Atlanta Hilton & Towers	30303
Holiday Inn Buckhead	30026
Lanier Plaza Hotel & CC	30324
Marriott Perimeter Center	30346
Omni Hotel at CNN Center	30335
Ramada Hotel & Conference Center	30338
The Ritz-Carlton Atlanta	30303
Sheraton Inn Atlanta Airport	30344
Westin Peachtree Plaza	30343

MILITARY INSTALLATIONS

	ZIP
United States Army Engineer Division, South Atlantic Division	30335
United States Property and Fiscal Office for Georgia	30316
Atlanta Naval Air Station	30060
Attapulgus	31715
Attapulgus Station	31715
Attica	30606
Auburn	30203
Audubon	30735
Augusta	30901-19
For specific Augusta Zip Codes call (404) 724-7436	
Aumond Heights	30909
Aumond Place	30909
Auraria	30534
Austell	30001
Austin	30663
Autreyville	31768
Autumn Forest	30236
Avallon	30328

	ZIP
Avalon (Chatham County)	31406
Avalon (Stephens County)	30557
Avans	30752
Avera	30803
Avert Acres	31705
Avery	30114
Avondale (Bibb County)	31206
Avondale (McDuffie County)	30814
Avondale Estates	30002
Avondale Park (Part of Savannah)	31404
Avon Park (Part of Savannah)	31404
Axson	31624
Ayersville	30577
Baconton	31716
Bainbridge	31717
Bairdstown	30669
Baker Village (Part of Columbus)	31903
Baldwin	30511
Baldwinville	31812
Ball Ground (Cherokee County)	30107
Ball Ground (Murray County)	30705
Baltimore (Part of Washington)	30673
Banning	30185
Bannockburn	31639
Barksdale	31082
Barnesville	30204
Barnett	30821
Barnett Shoals	30605
Barney	31625
Barnsley	30145
Barretts	31602
Barrettsville	30534
Barrow Heights	30680
Bartletts Ferry	31808
Barton Village	30906
Bartonwoods	30307
Bartow	30413
Barwick	31720
Bascom	30467
Bass Crossroads	30230
Batesville	30523
Bath	30805
Battery Point	31404
Baughs Crossroads	31833
Baxley	31513
Bay	31756
Bayview	31316
Beach	31554
Beachton	31792
Beacon Heights	30650
Beallwood (Part of Columbus)	31904
Beaulieu	31406
Beaumount	30736
Beaverdale	30720
Beechwood Shopping Center (Part of Athens)	30606
Belair	30907
Belair Hills Estates	30909
Belfast	31324
Bellemeade	30906
Bellton (Part of Lula)	30554
Bellville	30414
Bellville Bluff	31331
Belmont (DeKalb County)	30035
Belmont (Hall County)	30507
Belmont Hills Shopping Center (Part of Smyrna)	30080
Belvedere	30032
Belvedere Park	30032
Belvedere Plaza	30032
Belvins Acres	30736
Bemiss	31602
Benedict	30125
Benevolence	31740
Ben Hill (Part of Atlanta)	30331
	31131
For specific Ben Hill Zip Codes call (912) 423-7929	
Benning Hills (Part of Columbus)	31903
Benning Park (Part of Columbus)	31903
Bentley Place	30741
Benton	30165
Bent Tree	30143
Berckman Hills	30909
Berckman Village	30909
Berkeley Lake	30136
Berkshire Woods (Part of Savannah)	31406
Berlin	31722
Berryton	30747
Berzelia	30814

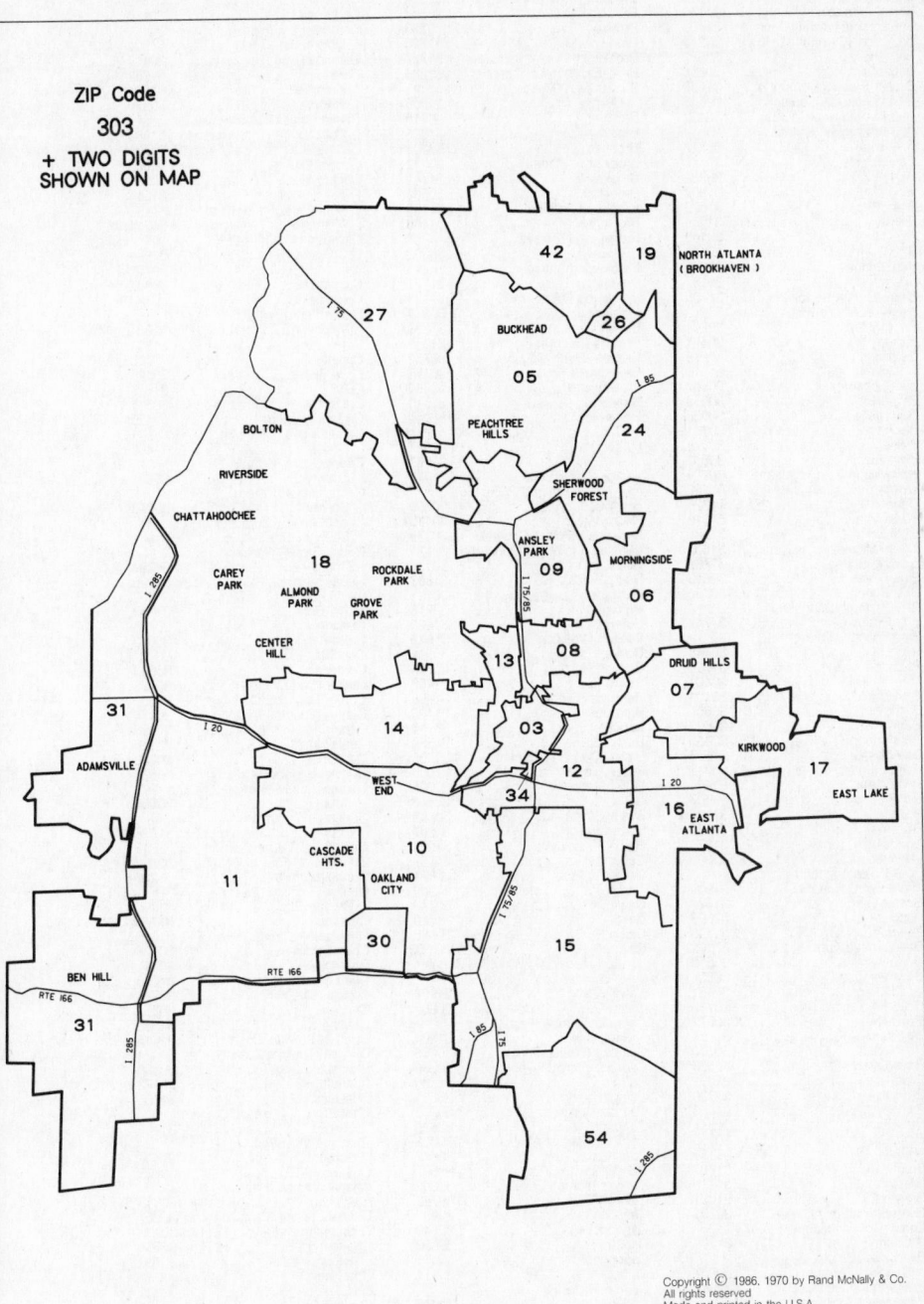

ZIP Code
303
+ TWO DIGITS
SHOWN ON MAP

42   19   NORTH ATLANTA
(BROOKHAVEN)

I 75   27

BUCKHEAD   26

05

BOLTON

PEACHTREE
HILLS

I 85   24

RIVERSIDE

CHATTAHOOCHEE

SHERWOOD
FOREST

ANSLEY
PARK

18   ROCKDALE   09   MORNINGSIDE
PARK

CAREY   ALMOND   I 75/85
PARK   PARK   GROVE   06
PARK

I 285

CENTER
HILL   13   08

31   DRUID HILLS
07

I 20   14   03

ADAMSVILLE   KIRKWOOD

WEST.   12   17
END   34   I 20

10   16   EAST   EAST LAKE
ATLANTA

CASCADE
HTS.

11   OAKLAND
CITY

I 75/85

30   15

BEN HILL   RTE 166

RTE 166

31   I 285

I 85   I 75

54   I 285

	ZIP
Bethany	31762
Bethel (Jasper County)	31064
Bethel (Randolph County)	31740
Bethesda (Chatham County)	31406
Bethesda (Gwinnett County)	30245
Bethlehem	30620
Between	30655
Beulah (Hancock County)	31087
Beulah (Lincoln County)	30668
Beulah (Paulding County)	30153
Beulah Heights (Part of Atlanta)	30312
Beverly Hills	30741
Bexton	30259
Bibb City	31904
Bibb Mills	31029
Bickley	31554
Big Canoe	30143
Big Creek	30131
Big Springs	30240
Billarp	30187
Bingville (Part of Savannah)	31405
Birdie	30223
Birmingham	30201
Bishop	30621
Blackjack	30276
Blackshear	31516
Blackshear Place	30507
Blacksville	30253
Blackwells	30066
Blackwood	30701
Blaine	30175
Blairsville	30512
Blair Village (Part of Atlanta)	30354
Blakely	31723
Blandford	31326
Bland Villa	31015
Blitchton	31308
Bloomingdale	31302
Blowing Springs	37409
Blue Ridge	30513
Blue Spring	30736
Blue Springs (Dougherty County)	31707
Blue Springs (Screven County)	30446
Bluffton	31724
Blun	30401
Blundale	30401
Blythe	30805
Bogart	30622
Bold Spring	30655
Bolingbroke	31004
Bolton (Part of Atlanta)	30318
Bona Bella	31406
Bonair	30907
Bonaire	31005
Bonanza	30236
Bonds	31020
Boneville	30806
Booker Washington Heights (Part of Columbus)	31909
Boston	31626
Bostwick	30623
Bowdon	30108
Bowdon Junction	30109
Bowersville	30516
Bowman	30624
Box Springs	31801
Boyd Highlands	30736
Boydville	30577
Boykin	31737
Boynton	30736
Boys Estate	31523
Bradley	31032
Branchville	31730
Brantley	31803
Braselton	30517
Braswell	30153
Bremen	30110
Brentwood	31707
Brest	31716
Brewton	31021
Briarcliff (Part of Atlanta)	30329
Briarwood (Chatham County)	31408
Briarwood (Columbia County)	30907
Briarwood (Fulton County)	30344
Briarwood (Rockdale County)	30207
Briar Wood Estates	30060
Brick Store	30279
Bridgeboro	31705
Bridgeman Heights	31201
Brighton	31794
Brinson	31725
Brisbon	31324
Bristol	31518
Bristol Woods	30207
Broad	30668

	ZIP
Broadhurst	31545
Broadview (Part of Atlanta)	30324
Brockton	30506
Bronco	30728
Bronwood	31726
Brookfield	31727
Brookhaven (Bibb County)	31206
Brookhaven (Muscogee County)	31906
Brooklet	30415
Brooklyn	31825
Brooks	30205
Brookstore Place	30342
Brooksville	31740
Brookton	30501
Brookvale Estates	30736
Brookview	31406
Brookwood (Forsyth County)	30202
Brookwood (Laurens County)	31021
Brookwood (Richmond County)	30904
Browndale	31036
Browns (Baldwin County)	31061
Browns (Dade County)	30752
Brownsville	30133
Brownwood	30650
Broxton	31519
Brunswick	31520-22
	31524-25
	31527
	31561
For specific Brunswick Zip Codes call (912) 265-6186	
Brynwood	30909
Buchanan	30113
Buckhead (Fulton County)	30339
Buckhead (Morgan County)	30625
Budapest	30176
Buena Vista	31803
Buffington	30114
Buford	30518
Bullard	31020
Bulloch Crossroads	31816
Bunker Hill	30512
Burning Bush	30736
Burnside	31406
Burnside Island	31406
Burroughs	31405
Burwell	30117
Bushnell	31533
Butler (Dougherty County)	31705
Butler (Taylor County)	31006
Butler Manor	30905
Butts	30442
Byers Crossroads	30185
Byromville	31007
Byron	31008
Cabaniss	31029
Cadley	30821
Cadwell	31009
Cagle	30143
Cairo	31728
Caleb	30058
Calhoun	30701-03
For specific Calhoun Zip Codes call (706) 629-3053	
Calvary	31729
Camak	30807
Camellia Terrace (Part of Savannah)	31404
Camelot (Clarke County)	30606
Camelot (Clayton County)	30236
Camilla	31730
Campania	30814
Campbellton	30213
Campton	30655
Campus (Part of Athens)	30605
Canal Lake	30512
Candler	30507
Candler-McAfee	30032
Cannon Crossing	30742
Cannon Gate	30907
Cannonville	30240
Canon	30520
Canoochee	30471
Canton	30114
Canton Plaza (Part of Marietta)	30066
Capel	31728
Capitol Hill (Part of Atlanta)	30334
Captolo	30467
Carbondale	30720
Carey Park (Part of Atlanta)	30318
Carl	30203
Carlton	30627
Carmel	30218
Carmichael Crossroads	30114
Carnegie	31740
Carnes Creek	30577

	ZIP
Carnesville	30521
Carnigan	31319
Carns Mill	30175
Caroline Park (Part of Columbus)	31904
Carrollton	30117
Carrs	31087
Carsonville	31827
Cartecay	30540
Carter Acres (Part of Columbus)	31903
Carters	30705
Carters Grove	30660
Cartersville	30120
Cary	31014
Cascade Heights (Part of Atlanta)	30311
Cascade Hills (Part of Columbus)	31904
Cash	30701
Cassandra	30707
Cassville	30123
Castle Park (Part of Valdosta)	31601
Cataula	31804
Catlett	30728
Cave Spring	30124
Cecil	31627
Cedar Creek Park	30605
Cedar Crossing	30436
Cedar Grove (Chatham County)	31406
Cedar Grove (DeKalb County)	30027
Cedar Grove (Fulton County)	30213
Cedar Grove (Laurens County)	31021
Cedar Grove (Walker County)	30707
Cedar Hammock	31406
Cedar Point	31332
Cedar Springs	31732
Cedartown	30125
Celeste	30673
Cenchat	30707
Centennial	30663
Center (Bartow County)	30120
Center (Jackson County)	30601
Center (Toombs County)	30474
Center Hill (Part of Atlanta)	30318
Center Point	30179
Centerpost	30728
Centerville (Elbert County)	30635
Centerville (Gwinnett County)	30058
Centerville (Houston County)	31028
Centerville (Talbot County)	31812
Central City (Part of Atlanta)	30303
Centralhatchee	30217
Central Junction (Part of Garden City)	31408
Century	31763
Chalybeate Springs	31816
Chamberlain	30728
Chamblee	30341
Chambliss	31709
Chapel Hill	30134
Chappel	30257
Charing	31058
Charles (Stewart County)	31815
Charles (Toombs County)	30474
Charleston South	30906
Charlotteville	30473
Chastain	31738
Chatham City (Part of Garden City)	31408
Chatham Villa (Part of Garden City)	31408
Chatsworth	30705
Chattahoochee (Part of Atlanta)	30318
Chattahoochee Plantation	30067
Chattanooga Valley	30725
Chatterton	31554
Chattoogaville	30730
Chauncey	31011
Checkero	30525
Chelsea	30731
Chennault	30668
Cherokee Forest	30188
Cherrylog	30522
Cheshire Bridge (Part of Atlanta)	30324
Chestatee	30130
Chester	31012
Chestnutflat	30728
Chestnut Mountain	30502
Chickamauga	30707
Chickasawhatchee	31742

	ZIP		ZIP		ZIP
Chicopee	30507	Council	31631	Delhi	30668
China Hill	31077	Country Club Estates	31520	Dellwood	30401
Chippewa Terrace (Part of		Country Club Hills (Part of		DeLowe (Part of East Point)	30344
Savannah)	31406	Augusta)	30904	Demorest	30535
Choestoe	30512	Country Park	30906	Denmark	30415
Chubtown	30124	Country Side (Part of		Dennis	31024
Chula	31733	Savannah)	31406	Denton	31532
Cinderella Hills	30736	County Line (Barrow		Denver	30217
Cisco	30708	County)	30680	De Soto	31743
Civic Center (Part of		County Line (DeKalb		De Soto Park	30161
Atlanta)	30308	County)	30032	Desser	31745
Clarkdale	30020	County Line (Stewart		Devereux	31087
Clarke Dale	30605	County)	31815	Dewberry	30741
Clarkesville	30523	Court Square (Part of		Dewy Rose	30634
Clarksboro	30607	Dublin)	31021	Dexter	31019
Clarkston	30021	Covena	30401	Dial	30513
Claxton	30417	Coverdale	31714	Dialtown	30267
Clayfields	31054	Covington	30209	Diamond Hill	30628
Clayton	30525	Covington Mills (Part of		Dickey	31746
Clearview (Part of		Covington)	30209	Digbey	30205
Savannah)	31401	Cox	31331	Dillard	30537
Clem	30117	Coxs Crossing	30321	Dillon	31792
Clermont	30527	Crabapple	30201	Dinglewood (Part of	
Cleveland	30528	Crandall	30711	Columbus)	31906
Cliftondale	30337	Craneeater	30701	Dixie (Brooks County)	31629
Climax	31734	Cravey	31060	Dixie (Newton County)	30209
Clinchfield	31013	Crawford	30630	Dixie Heights (Part of	
Clinton	31032	Crawfordville	30631	Albany)	31705
Cloudland	30731	Crescent	31304	Dixie Union	31503
Cloverdale	30738	Crest	30286	Dobbins Air Force Base	30060
Clubview Heights (Part of		Cresthill	31406	Dock Junction	31520
Columbus)	31906	Crest Hill Gardens (Part of		Doctortown	31545
Clyattville	31601	Savannah)	31406	Doerun	31744
Clyo	31303	Crestview	31713	Doles	31791
Coal Mountain	30130	Crestwell Heights	31204	Donald	31316
Coastal Correctional		Crosland	31771	Donalsonville	31745
Institution	31408	Cross Keys (Part of Macon)	31201	Donegal	30458
Cobb	31735	Crossroads (Hart County)	30516	Donovan	31096
Cobb Centre Mall (Part of		Crossroads (Liberty County)	31323	Doogan	30708
Smyrna)	30080	Crossroads at Stewart		Dooling	31063
Cobbtown	30420	Lakewood, The (Part of		Doraville	30340
Cochran	31014	Atlanta)	30315	Dorchester (Liberty County)	31320
Coffee	31551	Cruse	30245	Dorchester (Richmond	
Coffee Bluff Plantation (Part		Crystal Springs (Bibb		County)	30909
of Savannah)	31406	County)	31201	Dot	30108
Cogdell	31634	Crystal Springs (Floyd		Double Branches	30817
Cohutta	30710	County)	30105	Doublegate	31707
Cohutta Springs	30711	Crystal Valley (Part of		Double Run	31072
Colbert	30628	Columbus)	31907	Dougherty	30534
Cole City	30752	Culloden	31016	Douglas	31533
Coleman	31736	Culverton	31087	Douglasville	30133-35
Colemans Lake	30441	Cumberland	30339	For specific Douglasville Zip	
Colesburg	31569	Cumming	30130-31	Codes call (404) 765-7261	
Colfax	30458	For specific Cumming Zip Codes		Dove Creek	30635
College (Part of Fort Valley)	31030	call (404) 887-5777		Dover	30424
College Heights (Dougherty		Curryville	30701	Doverel	31742
County)	31705	Curtis	30513	Downtown (Part of Atlanta)	30301
College Heights (Muscogee		Cusseta	31805	Downtown (Part of	
County)	31906	Custer Terrace (Part of		Columbus)	31901
College Park	30337	Columbus)	31905	Doyle	31803
Collins	30421	Cuthbert	31740	Draketown	30179
Collinsville	30035	Cypress Mills	31520	Dranesville	31803
Colomokee	31723	Dacula	30211	Drayton	31092
Colonial Oaks (Part of		Daffin Heights (Part of		Dresden	30263
Savannah)	31406	Savannah)	31404	Drew	30130
Colonial Place	31705	Dahlonega	30533	Drexel	30663
Colonial Village (Part of		Daisy	30423	Druid Hills	30333
Savannah)	31406	Dakota	31714	Dry Branch (Jenkins	
Colony Park	30909	Dallas	30132	County)	30822
Colquitt	31737	Dallas Heights	30906	Dry Branch (Twiggs County)	31020
Columbia Heights	30907	Dallondale	30741	Dry Pond	30529
Columbus	31901-09	Dalton	30720-22	Dublin	31021
For specific Columbus Zip Codes		For specific Dalton Zip Codes call			31040
call (404) 563-0100		(404) 278-7450		For specific Dublin Zip Codes call	
Columbus Square (Part of		Damascus (Early County)	31741	(912) 272-6831	
Columbus)	31908	Damascus (Gordon County)	30701	Dubois	31026
Colwell	30541	Dames Ferry	31046	Ducktown	30130
Comer	30629	Danburg	30668	Dudley	31022
Commerce	30529	Daniel	31324	Due West	30064
Concord (Pike County)	30206	Daniel Springs	30669	Duffee	31730
Concord (Schley County)	31806	Danielsville	30633	Dugdown	30140
Coney	31015	Danville	31017	Duluth	30136
Conley	30027	Darien	31305	Dumas	31824
Constitution	30316	Dasher	31601	Dunaire	30032
Conyers	30207-08	Davisboro	31018	Duncan Park	37412
For specific Conyers Zip Codes		Davis Crossroads	30707	Dunwoody	30338
call (404) 483-8378		Dawesville	31792	Du Pont	31630
Cooksville	30230	Dawnville	30720	Durand	31830
Coolidge	31738	Dawson	31742	Dutch Island	31406
Cool Spring	31771	Dawsonville	30534	Eagle Cliff	37409
Cooper Creek Park (Part of		Days Crossroads	31751	Eagle Grove	30520
Columbus)	31907	Dearing	30808	East Albany (Part of Albany)	31701
Cooper Heights	30707	Decatur	30030-37	Eastanollee	30538
Coopers	31031		30089	East Armuchee	30728
Coosa	30129	For specific Decatur Zip Codes		East Athens	30683
Copeland	31077	call (404) 378-8857		East Atlanta (Part of	
Cordele	31015	Deenwood (Ware County)	31503	Atlanta)	30316
Corinth	30230	Deepstep	31082	East Boundary	30901
Cornelia	30531	Deer Run	30207	East Boynton	30736
Cotton	31739	Deerwood Forest	30906	East Columbus	31907
Cotton Hill	31767	Deerwood Park	30032	East Dublin	31021

	ZIP
East Edgewood (Part of Columbus)	31907
East Ellijay	30539
East Englewood (Part of Columbus)	31907
East Griffin	30223
East Highlands (Part of Columbus)	31901
East Juliette	31046
Eastman	31023
Eastman Mills	31023
East Marietta	30062
East Meadow	30605
East Newnan	30263
East Point	30344
East Side (Part of Dalton)	30721
East Town (Part of Albany)	31705
East Trion (Part of Trion)	30753
Eastview	30904
Eastville	30621
Eastwood	30316
Eastwood (Part of Atlanta)	30317
Eatonton	31024
Ebernezer	30279
Echeconnee	31008
Echota	30701
Eden	31307
Edge Hill	30810
Edgemere (Part of Savannah)	31404
Edgemoor East	30236
Edgemoor West	30236
Edgewater (Part of Savannah)	31406
Edgewater Park (Part of Savannah)	31406
Edgewood (Columbia County)	30907
Edgewood (Muscogee County)	31907
Edison	31746
Edith	31631
Egypt	31329
Elberta	31093
Elberton	30635
Elder	30677
Eldorado	31794
Eldorendo	31737
Eleanor Village	31705
Elim	31316
Elizabeth (Part of Marietta)	30060
Elko	31025
Ellabell	31308
Ellaville	31806
Ellenton	31747
Ellenwood	30049
Ellerslie	31807
Ellijay	30540
Ellwood	30805
Elmodel	31770
Elza	30453
Embry Hills	30341
Emerson	30137
Emerson Park	31503
Emit	30458
Emma	30534
Emmalane	30442
Emory University	30322
Empire	31026
Englewood (Part of Columbus)	31907
Enigma	31749
Enon Grove	30217
Enterprise	30627
Ephesus	30217
Epworth	30541
Epworth Acres	31522
Esom Hill	30138
Etna	30138
Eton	30724
Euharlee	30120
Eulonia	31331
Evans	30809
Evansville	30240
Everett	31525
Everett Springs	30105
Evergreen	31707
Excelsior	30439
Executive Park	30347
Experiment (census designated place)	30223
Experiment	30212
Faceville	31717
Fairburn	30213
Fairchild	31745
Fairfax	31552
Fairfield (Part of Savannah)	31404
Fairlawn Acres (Part of Fort Oglethorpe)	30741
Fairmount	30139
Fair Oaks	30060

	ZIP
Fairplay (Douglas County)	30187
Fairplay (Morgan County)	30663
Fairview (Habersham County)	30535
Fairview (Walker County)	30741
Fairway Oaks (Part of Savannah)	31405
Fairway Village	30906
Fantasy Hills	37409
Fargo	31631
Farmdale	30467
Farmers High	30117
Farmington	30638
Farmville	30701
Farrar	31085
Fashion	30705
Faulkner	30107
Fayetteville	30214
Federal (Part of Albany)	31702
Federal Reserve (Part of Atlanta)	30303
Felton	30140
Fence	30203
Fernwood (Part of Savannah)	31404
Ficklin	30673
Ficklings Mill	31006
Fidele	30735
Fife	30213
Fincherville	30233
Findlay	31070
Finleyson	31071
Fish Creek	30125
Fitzgerald	31750
Fitzgerald Cotton Mill	31750
Fitzpatrick	31044
Five Forks (Gwinnett County)	30245
Five Forks (Thomas County)	31626
Five Points (Fulton County)	30303
Five Points (Lowndes County)	31601
Five Points (Macon County)	31063
Five Points (Marion County)	31803
Five Points (Randolph County)	31786
Five Points (Taylor County)	31006
Five Points (Treutlen County)	30457
Five Springs	30720
Flat Rock (Muscogee County)	31907
Flat Rock (Putnam County)	31024
Flat Shoals	30516
Fleetwood (Part of Savannah)	31404
Fleming	31309
Fleming Heights	30906
Flemington	31313
Flint	31716
Flint Hill	31826
Flint River	31711
Flint River Estates	30236
Flintside	31735
Flintstone	30725
Flintwood	30274
Flippen	30253
Floral Hill	30668
Florence	31821
Flovilla	30216
Flowery Branch	30542
Floyd	30059
Floyd Springs	30105
Folkston	31537
Folsom	30103
Forest Estates	30909
Forest Lake (Part of Macon)	31204
Forest Park (Clayton County)	30050-51
For specific Forest Park Zip Codes call (404) 363-1804	
Forest Park (Dougherty County)	31701
Forest Park (Richmond County)	30904
Forest River Farms (Part of Savannah)	31406
Forrest Hills (Part of Savannah)	31404
Forsyth	31029
Fort Benning	31905
Fort Benning South	31905
Fort Gaines	31751
Fort Gillem	30050
Fort Gordon	30905
Fort Lamar	30633
Fort McAllister	31324
Fort Oglethorpe	30742
Fort Screven (Part of Tybee Island)	31328
Fortson (Part of Columbus)	31808

	ZIP
Fortsonia	30635
Fort Stewart (census designated place)	31313
Fort Stewart	31314
Fort Valley	31030
Foster Hills	30736
Fosters Mills	30161
Four Points (Part of Albany)	31705
Four Seasons	30207
Fowlstown	31752
Fox (Part of Rome)	30161
Foxboro	31601
Frances Hollow	30207
Franklin	30217
Franklin Springs	30639
Franklinton	31020
Frazier	31014
Free Home	30114
Friendship (Polk County)	30125
Friendship (Sumter County)	31709
Frolona	30217
Fruitland	31630
Fry	30555
Funston	31753
Furniture City	30001
Gabbettville	30240
Gaddistown	30572
Gaillard	31078
Gaines School	30605
Gainesville	30501-07
For specific Gainesville Zip Codes call (404) 532-3138	
Gainesville Mills	30501
Galloway	30513
Garden Acres Estates (Part of Pooler)	31322
Garden City	31408
Garden Lakes	30165
Garden Valley	31041
Gardi	31545
Gardner (Part of Oconee)	31067
Garfield	30425
Garnersville	31767
Garretta	31021
Gasco (Part of Atlanta)	30301
Gates City (Part of Atlanta)	30312
Gateway (Part of Thomasville)	31792
Gay	30218
Geneva	31810
Gentian (Part of Columbus)	31907
Georgetown (Chatham County)	31405
Georgetown (Quitman County)	31754
Georgetown Estates	30906
Georgia Diagnostic and Classification	30233
Georgia Southern (Part of Statesboro)	30458
Georgia Southwestern College (Part of Americus)	31709
Georgia State Prison	30453
Georgia Training and Development Center	30518
Georgia University (Part of Athens)	30602
Germany	30525
Gibson	30810
Gill	30668
Gillis Springs	30457
Gillsville	30543
Girard	30426
Gladesville	31064
Gladys	31622
Glasgow	31626
Glencliff	30286
Glen Haven	30032
Glenloch	30217
Glenloch Village (Part of Peachtree City)	30269
Glenmore	31503
Glenn	30217
Glenn Hills	30906
Glennville	30427
Glenwood (Floyd County)	30165
Glenwood (Wheeler County)	30428
Glenwood Hills	30032
Gloster	30245
Glynn Haven	31522
Goat Town	31082
Gobblers Hill	31805
Gober	30107
Godfrey	30650
Godwinsville	31023
Goggins	30204
Golden Isle	31410
Goldmine	30520
Goldsboro	31014
Goldson	31006

	ZIP		ZIP		ZIP
Goodes	30268	Harrington	31522	Houston Lake	31047
Good Hope	30641	Harrisburg	30747	Houston Mall (Part of	
Gorday	31791	Harris City	30222	Warner Robins)	31093
Gordon	31031	Harrison	31035	Howard	31039
Gordon Springs	30740	Harrisonville	30230	Howell	31636
Gore	30747	Harrock Hall	31406	Howell Mill (Part of Atlanta)	30325
Goss	30635	Hartford	31036	Howells Transfer (Part of	
Gough	30811	Hartsfield	31756	Atlanta)	30301
Gracewood	30812	Hartwell	30643	Howell Tower (Part of	
Grady	30125	Harvest	30523	Atlanta)	30318
Graham	31513	Haskins Crossing	31022	Huber	31201
Grange	30434	Hassier Mill	30740	Hubert	30415
Granite Hill	31087	Hatcher	31754	Hudson Mill	31804
Grantville	30220	Hatley	31015	Huffaker	30165
Gratis	30655	Hawkinsville	31036	Huffer	31533
Graves	31742	Haylow	31630	Hughland	30438
Gray	31032	Hayneville	31036	Hulett	30117
Gray Hill	31833	Hayston	30255	Hull	30646
Graymont (Part of Twin		Hazlehurst	31539	Hunter	30467
City)	30471	Head River	30731	Huntington	31709
Grays	31404	Heardville	30130	Hurst	30560
Grayson	30221	Hebardville	31503	Hutchins	30630
Graysville	30726	Helen	30545	Ideal	31041
Great Southwest Industrial		Helena	31037	Ila	30647
Park (Part of Atlanta)	30336	Hemp	30560	Imlac	30293
Green Acres (Catoosa		Henderson	31025	Imperial	31024
County)	30741	Hentown	31723	Inaha	31790
Green Acres (Chatham		Hephzibah	30815	Indian Hills	30236
County)	31404	Herndon	30441	Indianola	31601
Green Acres (Clarke		Herod	31742	Indian Springs (Butts	
County)	30605	Hiawassee	30546	County)	30216
Green Acres Estate (Part of		Hickory Bluff	31565	Indian Springs (Catoosa	
Dublin)	31021	Hickory Flat (Banks County)	30554	County)	30736
Greenbriar (Part of Atlanta)	30331	Hickory Flat (Cherokee		Industrial (Part of Atlanta)	30336
Greenbrier	30909	County)	30114	Industrial City of Gordon,	
Green Island Hills (Part of		Hickory Level	30117	Murray and Whitfield Co	30705
Columbus)	31904	Hickox	31553	Inman	30232
Greenough	31716	Hicks Circle	30207	Iron City	31759
Greensboro	30642	Hidden Acres	30207	Irondale	30236
Greens Crossing	31641	Higdon	30541	Irwins	31089
Greens Cut	30906	Higgston	30410	Irwinton	31042
Greenville (Camden County)	31548	Highfalls	30233	Irwinville	31760
Greenville (Meriwether		Highgate	30909	Isabella	31791
County)	30222	Highland Heights	31709	Islandwood	31410
Greenway (Emanuel		Highland Mills	30223	Isle of Hope	31406
County)	30441	Highland Park (Part of		Isle of Hope-Dutch Island	31406
Greenway (Fulton County)	30075	Savannah)	31406	Ivey	31031
Greenwood	31730	High Point (Newton County)	30209	Ivy Log	30512
Greenwood Forest	31649	High Point (Walker County)	30707	Jackson	30233
Gresham Park	30316	High Shoals	30645	Jacksons Crossroads	30668
Gresham Road (Part of		Hightower	30130	Jacksons Store	30668
Marietta)	30062	Hill City	30735	Jacksonville (Telfair County)	31544
Greshamville	30650	Hillcrest	30240	Jacksonville (Towns	
Gresston	31023	Hillman	30631	County)	30582
Griffin	30223-24	Hillsboro	31038	Jake	30182
For specific Griffin Zip Codes call (404) 227-2426		Hilltonia	30467	Jakin	31761
		Hilton	31723	Jamaica Estates	30907
Grimball Park	31406	Hilton Heights (Part of		James	31032
Griswoldville	31201	Columbus)	31906	Jamestown	31503
Grizzletown	30101	Hilyer	30240	Jarrell	31006
Grooverville	31626	Hinesville	31313-14	Jasper	30143
Grovania	31036	For specific Hinesville Zip Codes call (912) 876-3978		Jay Bird Springs	31011
Groveland (Bryan County)	31321			Jefferson (Jackson County)	30549
Groveland (Chatham		Hinkles	30738	Jefferson (Putnam County)	31024
County)	31405	Hinsonton	31765	Jeffersonville	31044
Grove Park	31406	Hinton	30143	Jekyll Island	31527
Grove Point	31405	Hiram	30141	Jenkinsburg	30234
Grovetown	30813	Hi Roc Shores	30207	Jersey	30235
Gumbranch	31313	Hobby	31714	Jerusalem (Camden	
Gum Log	30512	Hoboken	31542	County)	31568
Gumlong	30553	Hogansville	30230	Jerusalem (Pickens County)	30143
Guysie	31510	Holbrook	30130	Jesup	31545
Guyton	31312	Holcomb Bridge (Part of		Jewell	31045
Habersham	30544	Roswell)	30076	Jewtown	31522
Haddock	31033	Holland	30730	Jinks	31717
Hagan	30429	Hollingsworth	30510	Johnson Corner	30436
Hahira	31632	Hollis	31778	Johnson Crossroads	31822
Halcyondale	30467	Hollonville	30292	Johnstonville	30204
Halfmoon Landing	31320	Holly Hills (Part of		Jolly	30292
Halls	30145	Columbus)	31906	Jones	31323
Hallwood	31024	Holly Springs (Cherokee		Jones Acres	31201
Halycon Bluff	31401	County)	30142	Jonesboro	30236-37
Hamilton	31811	Holly Springs (Jackson		For specific Jonesboro Zip Codes call (404) 478-8286	
Hammett	31078	County)	30558		
Hampton	30228	Hollywood	30523	Jones Crossroads	31822
Handy	30263	Holt	31774	Jonesville	30108
Haney	30124	Homeland	31537	Jordan City (Part of	
Hannah	30187	Homer	30547	Columbus)	31904
Hannahs Mill	30286	Homerville	31634	Jot Em Down Store	31516
Hannatown	31717	Honey Creek	30207	Joy Lake	30260
Hapeville	30354	Honora	30817	Juliette	31046
Happy Hollow	30184	Hooker	30752	Junction City	31812
Haralson	30229	Hopeful	31730	Juniper	31801
Harbins	30620	Hopewell (Cherokee		Juno	30534
Harbor Creek	31410	County)	30114	Kansas	30182
Hardwick	31034	Hopewell (Harris County)	31822	Kathleen	31047
Harlem	30814	Horns	31078	Keith	30755
Harmony	31024	Hornsby	30901	Keithsburg	30114
Harmony Church	31905	Horseleg Estates	30165	Keller	31324
Harp	30232	Hortense	31543	Kelley Hill	31905
Harrietts Bluff	31569	Hoschton	30548	Kelleytown	30253

	ZIP
Kelly	31085
Kemp	30401
Kenilworth	30909
Kennesaw	30144
Kensington	30707
Kensington Park (Part of Savannah)	31405
Kenwood (Fayette County)	30214
Kenwood (Muscogee County)	31909
Keysville	30816
Kibbee	30474
Kiker	30540
Kildare	30446
Killarney	31761
Kimbrough	31825
Kinderlou	31601
Kings	32209
Kings Bay	31547
Kings Bay Base	31547
Kingsboro	31811
Kingsland	31548
Kingsridge	30188
Kingston (Bartow County)	30145
Kingston (Richmond County)	30909
Kings Wood (Chatham County)	31401
Kingswood (Clarke County)	30606
Kings Wood (Richmond County)	30904
Kirkland (Atkinson County)	31642
Kirkland (Jeff Davis County)	31539
Kirkwood (Part of Moultrie)	31768
Kite	31049
Klondike (DeKalb County)	30058
Klondike (Houston County)	31036
Knott	30240
Knoxville	31050
Kramer	31001
Laboon	30641
La Crosse	31806
La Fayette	30728
La Grange	30240-41
For specific La Grange Zip Codes call (404) 882-1851	
Lake	30125
Lake Arrowhead	30183
Lake Capri Estates	30058
Lake Cindy	30228
Lake City	30260
Lake Creek	30125
Lake Hills	30263
Lake Howard	30728
Lake Iodeco	30236
Lakeland	31635
Lake Lanier Islands	30518
Lake Lucerne	30247
Lakemont (Rabun County)	30552
Lakemont (Richmond County)	30901
Lake Park	31636
Lakeshore Estates (Part of Gainesville)	30501
Lakeshore Mall (Part of Gainesville)	30501
Lakeside Park	31406
Lake Talmadge	30228
Lake Tara	30236
Lakeview (Bleckley County)	31014
Lakeview (Catoosa County)	30741
Lakeview (Peach County)	31030
Lakeview Estates	30207
Lakewood (Clarke County)	30605
Lakewood (Fulton County)	30315
Lakewood Heights (Part of Atlanta)	30315
Lamara Heights (Part of Savannah)	31405
Lamarville (Part of Savannah)	31405
Landrum	30534
Laney	31784
Lanier	31321
Laroche Park (Part of Savannah)	31404
Lashley	31005
Lathamtown	30114
Laurel Hills (Part of Columbus)	31907
La Vista	30329
Lavonia	30553
Lawrenceville	30243-46
For specific Lawrenceville Zip Codes call (404) 963-7118	
Lax	31774
Leaf	30528
Leah	30802
Leary	31762
Leathersville	30817
Lebanon	30146

	ZIP
Lee Correctional Institution	31763
Leefield	30458
Lee Pope	31030
Leesburg	31763
Lees Crossing (Part of La Grange)	30240
Lees Mill	30214
Leland	30059
Leliaton	31650
Lena	30101
Lenox	31637
Lenox Square (Part of Atlanta)	30326
Leslie	31764
Lewis	30467
Lewiston	30809
Lexington	30648
Lexsy	30401
Liberty	30678
Liberty City (Part of Savannah)	31405
Liberty Hill	30257
Lifsey	30295
Lilburn	30226
	30247
For specific Lilburn Zip Codes call (404) 381-1440	
Lilly	31051
Lillypond	30701
Limestone	31014
Lincoln Hills (Part of Columbus)	31904
Lincoln Park	30286
Lincolnton	30817
Lindale	30147
Lindbergh Plaza (Part of Atlanta)	30324
Lindsey Creek (Part of Columbus)	31907
Linesville	30631
Linton	31087
Linwood	30728
Lions Gate	30327
Listonia	31015
Lithia Springs	30057
Lithonia	30038
	30058
For specific Lithonia Zip Codes call (404) 482-6554	
Little Five Points (Part of Atlanta)	30307
Little Miami	31601
Live Oak Gardens (Part of College Park)	30337
Livingston	30161
Lizella	31052
Loco	30817
Locust Grove	30248
Loftin	31816
Loganville	30249
Lollie	31021
Lone Oak	30230
Long Cane	30240
Lookout Mountain	30750
Lorane	31201
Lorenzo	31329
Lorwood (Part of Savannah)	31406
Lost Mountain	30073
Lothair	30457
Lotts	31519
Louise	30230
Louisville	30434
Louvale	31814
Lovejoy	30250
Lovett	31021
Lowell	30117
Lowndes Correctional Institution	31601
Lowry	30214
Lucile	31723
Lucius	30522
Ludowici	31316
Ludville	30175
Luella	30248
Lula	30554
Lulaton	31553
Lumber City	31549
Lumpkin	31815
Luthersville	30251
Luvdale	31701
Luxomni	30247
Lyerly	30730
Lyn Hills (Part of Columbus)	31904
Lynhurst	31406
Lynn	31717
Lynnwood	30741
Lyons	30436
Lytle	30707
Mableton	30059
McAfee	30032
McBean	30906

	ZIP
McCaysville	30555
McCollum	30263
McCutchen	30740
McDaniels	30701
McDonald Acres	30741
McDonough	30253
Macedonia (Cherokee County)	30114
Macedonia (Towns County)	30546
McElroys Mill	30249
McGregor	30410
Machen	31064
McIntosh	31320
McIntosh Mill Village	30263
McIntyre	31054
McKinnon	31545
Macland	30073
Macon	31201-95
For specific Macon Zip Codes call (912) 741-8400	
Macon Correctional Center	31201
Macon Mall (Part of Macon)	31206
McPherson	30132
McRae	31055
McWhorter	30134
Madison	30650
Madola	30541
Madras	30254
Madray Springs	31545
Magby Gap	30752
Magnet	30207
Magnolia (Chatham County)	31404
Magnolia (Fulton County)	30318
Mallorysville	30668
Manassas	30438
Manchester	31816
Manor	31550
Mansfield	30255
Manta	31805
Marblehill	30148
Maretts	30553
Marietta	30007
	30060-68
	30090
For specific Marietta Zip Codes call (404) 424-0140	
Marietta Campground	30060
Marine Corps Supply Center	31704
Marion	31020
Marketplace at North DeKalb (Part of Decatur)	30033
Marlborough	30274
Marlow	31312
Marshallville	31057
Mars Hill	30101
Martech (Part of Atlanta)	30318
Martin	30557
Martinez	30907
Massee	31620
Matt	30130
Matthews	30818
Mattox	31537
Mauk	31058
Maura Estates	30906
Maxeys	30671
Maxim	30817
Maxwell	31085
Mayday	31636
Mayfair (Part of Savannah)	31406
Mayfield	31087
Mayhaw	31723
Maysville	30558
Meadow Grove	30905
Meansville	30256
Mechanicsville	30340
Meeks	31049
Meigs	31765
Meinhard (Part of Port Wentworth)	31407
Meldrim	31318
Melrose	31636
Mendes	30427
Menlo	30731
Mercer University (Part of Macon)	31207
Meridian	31319
Merrillville	31738
Mershon	31551
Mesena	30819
Metasville	30673
Metcalf	31792
Metter	30439
Mica	30107
Middleton	30635
Midland (Part of Columbus)	31820
Midtown (Part of Atlanta)	30309
Midville	30441
Midway (Catoosa County)	30741
Midway (Liberty County)	31320
Midway (Tattnall County)	30427
Midway-Hardwick	31061

	ZIP		ZIP		ZIP
Milan	31060	Munnerlyn	30830	Oak Grove (Cherokee	
Miles Park	30906	Murphy	31738	County)	30102
Milford	31762	Murray Hills	30909	Oak Grove (DeKalb County)	30033
Mill Creek	30740	Murrays Crossroads	31806	Oak Grove (Troup County)	31822
Mill Creek Estates	30506	Murrayville	30564	Oakhaven	31707
Milledgeville	31061	Musella	31066	Oak Hill (Gilmer County)	30540
Millen	30442	Myrtle Grove	31324	Oak Hill (Newton County)	30209
Millers Mill	30281	Mystic	31769	Oakhurst (Part of Savannah)	31406
Millhaven	30467	Nahunta	31553	Oakland	30218
Millwood	31552	Nails Creek	30521	Oakland City (Part of	
Milner	30257	Nance Springs	30720	Atlanta)	30301
Milstead	30207	Nankipooh (Part of		Oakland Heights	30120
Mineola	31602	Columbus)	31909	Oakland Park (Part of	
Mineral Bluff	30559	Naomi	30728	Savannah)	31404
Minnesota	31744	Nashville	31639	Oaklawn	30263
Mission Ridge (Part of		National Hills	30904	Oakleaf Plantation	30067
Rossville)	30741	Naylor	31641	Oakman	30732
Mitchell	30820	Neal	30206	Oak Mountain	31826
Mize	30577	Nebo	30132	Oak Park	30401
Mizell	31006	Needmore	31630	Oakwood	30566
Modoc	30401	Neese	30646	Oasis	30513
Molena	30258	Nelson	30151	Oatland Island	31410
Moncrief	32301	Nevils	31321	Ocee	30202
Moniac	31646	Newark	31792	Ochillee	31905
Monroe	30655	Newborn	30262	Ochlocknee	31773
Montclair	30907	New Branch	30436	Ochwalkee	30428
Monteith (Part of Port		New Cotton Mill (Part of		Ocilla	31774
Wentworth)	31407	Canton)	30114	Oconee	31067
Montevideo	30635	New Elm	31768	Oconee Heights	30607
Montezuma	31063	New England	30752	Odessadale	30222
Montgomery (Chatham		New Era	31709	Odum	31555
County)	31406	New Georgia	30132	Offerman	31556
Montgomery Correctional		New Holland	30501	Ogeechee	30467
Institution	30445	New Home	30752	Ogeechee Farms	31405
Monticello (Jasper County)	31064	New Hope (Gwinnett		Ogeechee Road	31405
Monticello (Richmond		County)	30245	Ogeecheeton (Part of	
County)	30906	New Hope (Lincoln County)	30817	Savannah)	31401
Montreal	30033	New Hope (Paulding		Oglethorpe (Chatham	
Montrose	31065	County)	30132	County)	31406
Moody Air Force Base	31601	Newington	30446	Oglethorpe (Macon County)	31068
Moody Field	31601	Newnan	30263-65	Oglethorpe Mall (Part of	
Moons	30725	For specific Newnan Zip Codes		Savannah)	31406
Moores	31021	call (404) 253-2725		Oglethorpe Park (Part of	
Mora	31650	New Point	31780	Savannah)	31405
Moreland	30259	New Salem	30547	Oglethorpe University	30319
Morgan	31766	Newton	31770	Ogletree Woods (Part of	
Morganton	30560	Newton Factory	30209	Columbus)	31904
Morganville	30757	Newtown (Fulton County)	30202	Ohoopee	30436
Morningside (Fulton County)	30324	New Town (Gordon County)	30701	Okefenokee	31503
Morningside (Muscogee		New Town (Wilkes County)	30673	Ola	30253
County)	31904	New York (Part of Aragon)	30153	Old Damascus	31741
Morningside Hills	30501	Neyami	31763	Old National (Part of	
Morris	31767	Nicholasville	31713	Atlanta)	30349
Morris Brown (Part of		Nicholls	31554	Old South	30236
Atlanta)	30314	Nicholson	30565	Olive Branch	31827
Morris Estates	30736	Nicklesville	31042	Oliver	30449
Morris Siding (Part of		Nickleville	31797	Olney	31308
Atlanta)	30301	Nickville	30634	Omaha	31821
Morrow	30260	Noah's Station	30818	Omega	31775
Mortons	31405	Noble	30728	Oostanaula	30701
Morven	31638	Noonday	30060	Ophir	30107
Moultrie	31768	Norcross	30071	Orange	30114
	31776		30091-93	Orchard Hill	30266
For specific Moultrie Zip Codes		For specific Norcross Zip Codes		Orchard Hills	30741
call (912) 985-3535		call (404) 448-2241		Orianna	31002
Mountainbrook (Part of Pine		Norman	30668	Orland	30457
Mountain)	31822	Norman Park	31771	Ormewood (Part of Atlanta)	30312
Mountain City	30562	Normantown	30474	Oscarville	30506
Mountain Hill	31811	Norris	30828	Osierfield	31750
Mountain Park (Fulton		Norristown	30447	Other	30132
County)	30075	North Atlanta	30319	Ottawa Estates (Part of	
Mountain Park (Gwinnett		North Canton	30114	Bloomingdale)	31302
County)	30087	North Decatur	30033	Owensboro	31079
Mountain View (Clayton		North Druid Hills	30033	Owltown	30512
County)	30321	North Dublin (Part of Dublin)	31021	Oxford	30267
Mountain View (Walker		North Elberton	30635	Pace	30209
County)	30741	Northgate	31907	Pachitta	31740
Mount Airy	30563	North Highland (Part of		Palmetto (Fulton County)	30268
Mount Berry	30149	Atlanta)	30306	Palmetto (Oglethorpe	
Mount Bethel	30060	North Highlands (Part of		County)	30627
Mount Carmel	30728	Columbus)	31904	Palmyra	31763
Mount Olivet	30643	North High Shoals	30645	Pancras	31061
Mount Pleasant (Banks		Northlake	30345	Panhandle	31076
County)	30547	Northridge (Part of Conyers)	30350	Pannell	30655
Mount Pleasant (Wayne			31150	Pantertown	30559
County)	31543	For specific Northridge Zip Codes		Panthersville	30032
Mount Vernon (Montgomery		call (404) 998-3941		Paoli	30629
County)	30445	North Roswell (Part of		Paradise Park (Part of	
Mount Vernon (Walton		Roswell)	30075	Savannah)	31406
County)	30655	North Side (Part of Atlanta)	30305	Paradise Valley	30607
Mount Vernon (Whitfield		North West Point	31833	Parhams	30521
County)	30740	Norton Acres	30906	Parkchester (Part of	
Mountville	30261	Norwood	30821	Columbus)	31906
Mount Zion	30150	Note	31024	Park City (Part of Fort	
Moxley	30477	Nuberg	30634	Oglethorpe)	30741
Mulberry	30680	Nunez	30448	Parkersburg	31406
Mulberry Grove	31804	Oakdale	30080	Parkerville	31744
Mulberry Heights (Part of		Oakfield	31772	Park Hill (Part of Gainesville)	30501
Albany)	31705	Oak Forest	30236	Parkwood (Part of	
Mulberry Street (Part of		Oak Grove (Carroll County)	30117	Savannah)	31404
Macon)	31201			Parrott	31777

	ZIP		ZIP		ZIP
Tignall	30668	Villa Rica	30180	Wheat Hill (Part of Garden	
Tilton	30720	Vineland	30909	City)	31408
Timothy Estates	30606	Vinings	30339	Wheeler Heights	31201
Tippettville	31092	Vista-Grove	30033	Whigham	31797
Tison	30427	Vulcan	30738	Whistleville	30680
Titus	30546	Waco	30182	White	30184
Toccoa	30577	Wadley	30477	White Bluff (Part of	
Toccoa Falls	30598	Wahoo	30533	Savannah)	31406
Toco Hills	30329	Walden	31206	White City	30187
Toledo	31646	Waleska	30183	White Hall	30605
Tom	31049	Walker Correctional		Whitehouse	30253
Toms Creek	30557	Institution	30739	Whitemarsh Island	31404
Toomsboro	31090	Walker Park	30655	White Oak	31568
Topeka Junction	30285	Wallace	31036	White Plains	30678
Town and Country Acres	31707	Wallaceville	30707	Whitesburg	30185
Town and Country		Walls Crossing	31806	Whitestone	30175
Shopping Center (Part of		Walnut Grove (Walker		White Sulphur Springs	31822
Marietta)	30060	County)	30728	Whitesville	31833
Towns	31055	Walnut Grove (Walton		Whitworth	30553
Townsend	31331	County)	30209	Wilbanks Store	30711
Traders Hill	31537	Walnut Square (Part of		Wildwood	30757
Trans	30728	Dalton)	30720	Wiley	30581
Tremont	30907	Walthourville	31333	Willacoochee	31650
Tremont Park (Part of		Ware Correctional Institution	31503	Willard	31024
Savannah)	31401	Waresboro	31564	Williamson	30292
Trenton	30752	Wares Crossroads	30240	Williams Plaza (Part of	
Trice	30286	Waresville	30217	Warner Robins)	31093
Trickum	30755	Waring	30720	Wilmington Island	31410
Trimble	30230	Warm Springs	31830	Wilmington Park	31410
Trion	30753	Warner Robins	31088	Wilshire (Part of Savannah)	31406
Troutman	31740		31093	Wilshire Estates (Part of	
Trudie	31557		31095	Savannah)	31406
Tucker	30084-85		31098-99	Wilsons Church	30529
For specific Tucker Zip Codes call (404) 938-6920		For specific Warner Robins Zip Codes call (912) 922-3121		Wilsonville	31554
				Wimberly on the Marsh	31406
Tugalo	30577	Warner Robins	31088	Winchester	31057
Tugaloo (Part of Tallulah		Warren Terrace	30741	Winchester Hills	30207
Falls)	30573	Warrenton	30828	Winder	30680
Tunnel Hill	30755	Warsaw	30202	Windermere	30904
Turin	30289	Warthen	31094	Windsor	30249
Turner City (Part of Albany)	31705	Warwick	31796	Windsor Estates	30263
Turners Rock	31406	Washington	30673	Windsor Forest (Chatham	
Turnerville	30580	Waterloo	31733	County)	31406
Tusculum	31329	Waterport	30249	Windsor Forest (Richmond	
Tuxedo (Part of Atlanta)	30342	Watkinsville	30677	County)	30904
Twin City	30471	Waverly (Camden County)	31565	Windsor Park (Lowndes	
Twin Lakes	31636	Waverly (Richmond County)	30909	County)	31601
Tybee Island	31328	Waverly Hall	31831	Windsor Park (Muscogee	
Tyrone (Fayette County)	30290	Waverly Park	30741	County)	31904
Tyrone (Wilkes County)	30673	Wax	30104	Windward (Part of	
Ty Ty	31795	Wayback	31746	Savannah)	31405
Tyus	30108	Waycross	31501-02	Windy Ridge	30559
Unadilla	31091	For specific Waycross Zip Codes call (912) 283-2822		Winfield	30824
Union (Marion County)	31803			Winokur	31537
Union (Paulding County)	30179	Wayne Correctional		Winona Park	31503
Union (Quitman County)	31754	Institution	31555	Winston	30187
Union (Stewart County)	31821	Waynesboro	30830	Winterville	30683
Unionburg	31794	Waynesville	31566	Withers	31630
Union City	30291	Wayside	31032	Wofford Crossroads	30184
Union Hill	30201	Webb	30201	Woodbine	31569
Union Point	30669	Weber	31639	Woodbury	30293
Unionville	31794	Welcome	30263	Woodcliff	30467
Unity	30521	Welcome Hill	30753	Woodgate	30909
University Heights	30605	Wenona	31015	Woodlake	30906
Upatoi (Part of Columbus)	31829	Weracoba Heights (Part of		Woodland	31836
Upton	31533	Columbus)	31906	Woodland Hills (Laurens	
Upton Mill	31006	Wesley (Emanuel County)	30401	County)	31021
Uptonville	31537	Wesley (Taylor County)	31812	Woodland Hills (Walker	
Uvalda	30473	Wesleyan College (Part of		County)	30741
Vada	31734	Macon)	31201	Woodlawn (Part of	
Valdosta	31601-04	Wesleyan Estates	31204	Savannah)	31408
For specific Valdosta Zip Codes call (912) 242-8201		West Augusta	30901	Woodlawn Estates (Part of	
		West Bainbridge (Part of		Columbus)	31909
Valley Forge	30906	Bainbridge)	31717	Woodlawn Terrace (Part of	
Valley View	37409	West Brow	30738	Garden City)	31408
Valona	31332	West Crossing	30176	Woodridge Estates	31410
Vanceville	31794	West Dublin (Part of Dublin)	31021	Woods Grove	30582
Vandiver Heights	30060	West End (Floyd County)	30165	Wood Station	30736
Vanna	30662	West End (Fulton County)	30310	Woodstock	30188
Vans Valley	30161	Westgate (Part of Albany)	31707	Woodville (Chatham	
Van Wert	30153	Westgate Mall (Part of		County)	31401
Varnell	30756	Macon)	31206	Woodville (Greene County)	30669
Vaughn	30223	Westgate Park	30607	Woolsey	30214
Veal	30108	West Georgia College (Part		Wooster	30218
Veazey	30642	of Carrollton)	30117	Wormsloe	31406
Vega	30256	West Green	31567	Worth	31714
Veribest	30627	Westmont	30809	Worthville	30233
Vernonburg	31406	Westoak	30060	Wray	31798
Vernon View	31406	Weston	31832	Wrens	30833
Vesta	30627	West Point	31833	Wright Square (Part of	
Veterans Hospital (Part of		West Rome (Part of Rome)	30165	Savannah)	31401
Augusta)	30909	West Savannah (Part of		Wrightsville	31096
Victoria	30188	Savannah)	31401	Wymberly	31406
Victory	30108	Westside (Catoosa County)	30741	Wynngate	30907
Victory Heights (Part of		Westside (Hall County)	30501	Wynnton (Part of	
Savannah)	31404	West Valdosta	31601	Columbus)	31906
Vidalia	30474	West Vidalia (Part of Vidalia)	30434	Yahoola	30533
Vidette	30434	Westwick	30909	Yates	30263
Vienna	31092	Westwood	31750	Yates Crossroads	30217
View	30531	Wexwood	30274	Yatesville	31097
Villanow	30728			Yellow Bluff Fishing Village	31320

	ZIP		ZIP		ZIP
Yellow Dirt	30217	Young Harris	30582	Zebulon	30295
Yeomans	31742	Youngs	30125	Zenith	31078
Yonah	30510	Youngstown	30512	Zetella	30223
Yonkers	31014	Youth	30249	Zetto	31724
Yorkville	30132	Zaidee	30457	Zingara	30207
Youngcane	30512	Zebina	30833		

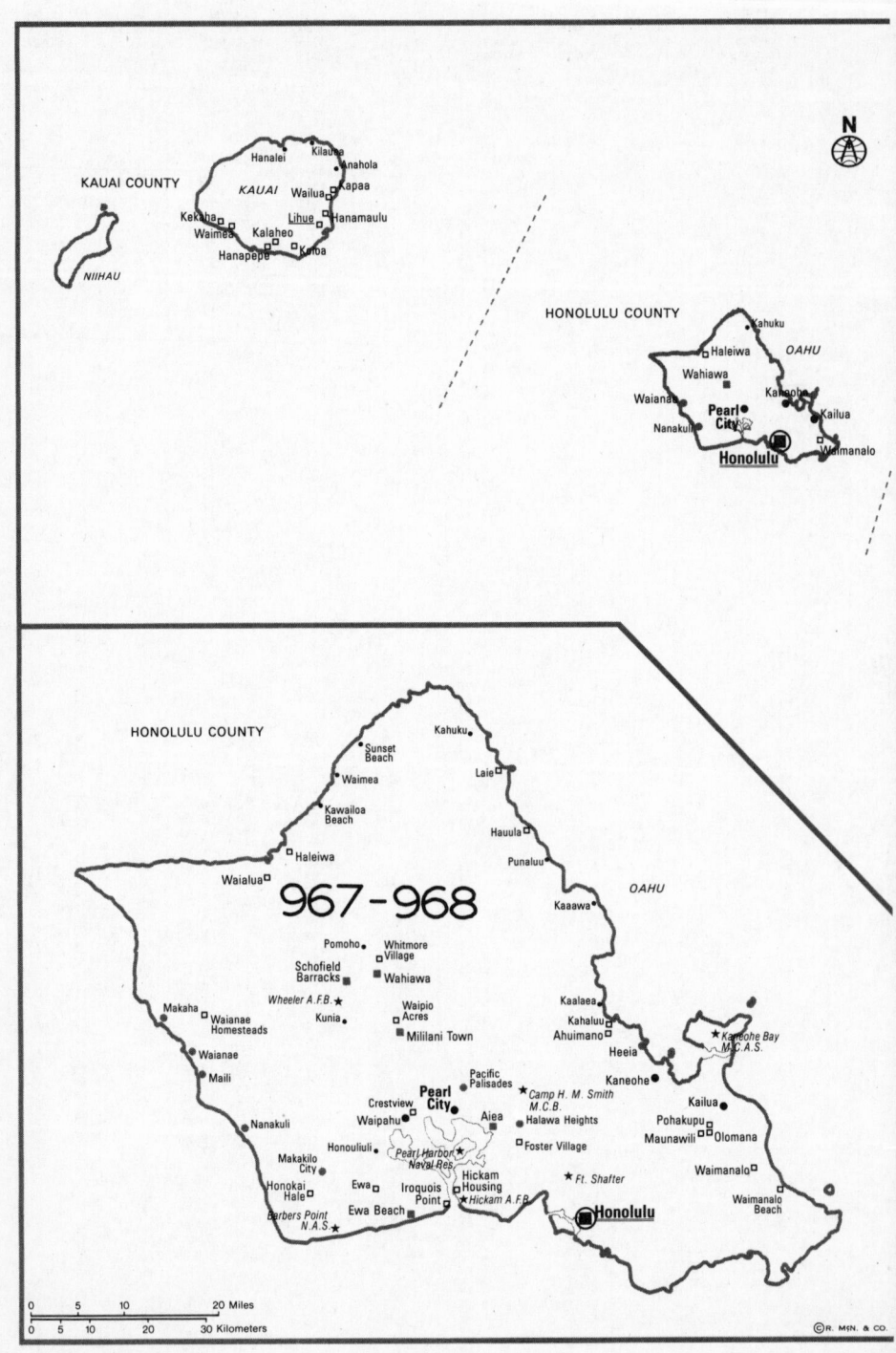

N

KAUAI COUNTY

KAUAI

Hanalei   Kilauea   Anahola
Wailua   Kapaa
Kekaha   Lihue   Hanamaulu
Waimea   Kalaheo
Hanapepe   Koloa

NIIHAU

HONOLULU COUNTY

OAHU

Kahuku
Haleiwa
Wahiawa
Waianae   Kaneohe
Pearl City   Kailua
Nanakuli
Honolulu   Waimanalo

HONOLULU COUNTY

Sunset Beach   Kahuku
Waimea   Laie
Kawailoa Beach
Hauula
Haleiwa   Punaluu
Waialua

967-968   *OAHU*

Kaaawa

Pomoho   Whitmore Village
Schofield Barracks   Wahiawa
Wheeler A.F.B. ★   Waipio Acres   Kaalaea
Makaha   Waianae Homesteads   Kunia   Kahaluu   Kaneohe Bay M.C.A.S.
Waianae   Mililani Town   Ahuimano
Maili   Heeia
Kaneohe
Nanakuli   Pacific Palisades   Kailua
Crestview   Pearl City   Camp H. M. Smith M.C.B.   Pohakupu
Waipahu   Aiea   Halawa Heights   Maunawili   Olomana
Honouliuli   Foster Village
Makakilo City   *Pearl Harbor Naval Res.*   Waimanalo
Honokai Hale   Ewa   Iroquois Point   Hickam Housing   ★ Ft. Shafter
Barbers Point N.A.S. ★   Ewa Beach   Hickam A.F.B.   Waimanalo Beach
    Honolulu

0   5   10   20 Miles
0   5   10   20   30 Kilometers

©R. M⁵N. & CO.

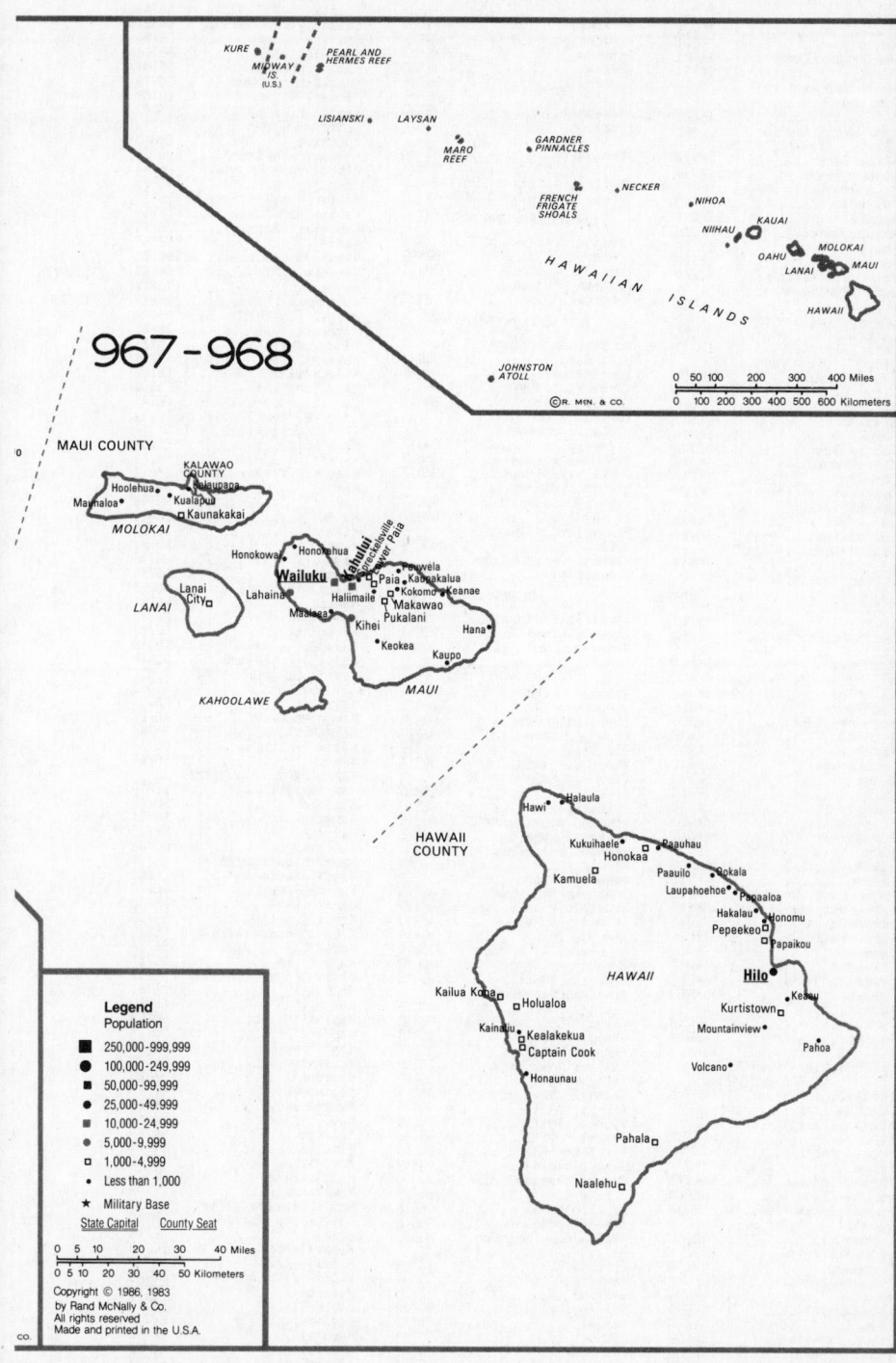

967-968

KURE
MIDWAY
IS.
(U.S.)
PEARL AND
HERMES REEF
LISIANSKI   LAYSAN
MARO
REEF
GARDNER
PINNACLES
FRENCH
FRIGATE
SHOALS
NECKER
NIHOA
NIIHAU   KAUAI
OAHU   MOLOKAI
LANAI   MAUI
HAWAII
H A W A I I A N   I S L A N D S
JOHNSTON
ATOLL
©R. M¢N. & CO.

| 0 | 50 | 100 | 200 | 300 | 400 Miles |

| 0 | 100 | 200 | 300 | 400 | 500 | 600 Kilometers |

MAUI COUNTY

KALAWAO
COUNTY
Kalaupapa
Hoolehua
Maunaloa   Kualapuu
Kaunakakai
MOLOKAI

Honokowai   Honokahua
Kaanapali
Kahului   Lower Paia
Wailuku
Honokowai
Haliimaile   Paia   Kaupakalua
Lahaina   Kokomo   Keanae
Maalaea   Makawao
Kihei   Pukalani
Lanai
City   Keokea   Hana
LANAI
Kaupo
MAUI
KAHOOLAWE

HAWAII
COUNTY

Halaula
Hawi
Kukuihaele   Paauhau
Honokaa
Kamuela   Paauilo   Ookala
Laupahoehoe   Papaaloa
Hakalau   Honomu
Pepeekeo   Papaikou
HAWAII   Hilo
Kailua Kona   Keaau
Holualoa   Kurtistown
Kainaliu   Mountainview
Kealakekua   Pahoa
Captain Cook
Honaunau   Volcano

Pahala

Naalehu

	ZIP
Ahualoa	96727
Ahuimanu	96744
Ahuimanu	96744
Aiea	96701
Aiea Heights	96701
Aiea Shopping Center	96701
Aikahi	96734
Aina Haina (Part of Honolulu)	96821
	96824

For specific Aina Haina Zip Codes call (808) 373-2555

Akasaki Camp	96774
Alabama Village	96784
Alewa Heights (Part of Honolulu)	96819
Aliamanu	96818
Amauulu Camps	96720
Anahola	96703
Andrade	96783
Barbers Point Housing	96862
Barbers Point Naval Air Station	96706
Brigham Young University-Hawaii	96762
Camp 106	96727
Camp H.M. Smith Marine Corps Base	96861
Captain Cook	96704
Chinatown (Part of Honolulu)	96817
Chin Chuck	96710
Coconut Grove	96734
Coral Gardens	96744
Crestview	96797
Downtown (Part of Hilo)	96720
Downtown (Part of Honolulu)	96813
Downtown (Maui County)	96767
Dowsett Highlands (Part of Honolulu)	96817
Eight and One-half Mile Camp	96749
Eightmile Camp	96749
Eleele	96705
Elevenmile Homestead	96760
Ewa	96706
Ewa Beach	96706-07

For specific Ewa Beach Zip Codes call (808) 689-5033

Ewa Gentry	96706
Fernandez Village	96706
Ford Island	96818
Fort Shafter	96819
Foster Village	96818
Glenwood	96771
Haaheo	96720
Haena	96714
Haiku	96708
Haiku-Pauwela	96708
Haina	96727
Hakalau	96710
Halaula	96755
Halawa (Hawaii County)	96755
Halawa (Honolulu County)	96701
Halawa (Maui County)	96748
Halawa Heights	96701
Halawa Hills	96701
Haleiwa	96712
Halepalaoa Landing	96763
Haiimaile	96768
Hamoa	96713
Hana	96713
Hanalei	96714
	96722

For specific Hanalei Zip Codes call (808) 826-6471

Hanamaulu	96715
Hanapepe	96716
Hanapepe Heights	96716
Haou	96713
Happy Valley	96793
Hauula	96717
Hawaiian Beaches	96778
Hawaiian Ocean View	96704
Hawaiian Paradise Park	96778
Hawaiian Village (Part of Honolulu)	96813
Hawaii Kai (Part of Honolulu)	96825
Hawaii National Park	96718
Hawi	96719
Hawi Camp 17	96719
Heeia	96744
Hickam Air Force Base	96818
Hickam Housing	96818
Highway Village	96728
Hilo	96720-21

For specific Hilo Zip Codes call (808) 935-2821

Hoaeae	96797

	ZIP
Hokamahoe House Lot	96764
Holualoa	96725
Honalo	96750
Honaunau	96726
Honaunau-Napoopoo	96726
Honohina	96710
Honokaa	96727
Honokahua	96761
Honokai Hale	96706
Honokohau	96725
Honokowai	96761
Honolulu	**96801-50**
	96898

For specific Honolulu Zip Codes call (808) 423-3990

COLLEGES & UNIVERSITIES

Chaminade University of Honolulu	96816
Hawaii Pacific College	96813
University of Hawaii at Manoa	96822

FINANCIAL INSTITUTIONS

American Savings Bank, F.S.B.	96813
Bank of Hawaii	96813
Central Pacific Bank	96813
City Bank	96813
First Federal Savings & Loan Association of America	96813
First Hawaiian Bank	96813
Hawaii National Bank	96817
International Savings & Loan Association, Ltd.	96813
Liberty Bank	96817
Pioneer Federal Savings Bank	96813
Territorial Savings & Loan Association	96814

HOSPITALS

Kuakini Medical Center	96817
Queen's Medical Center	96813
Tripler Army Medical Center	96859

HOTELS/MOTELS

Ambassador Hotel of Waikiki	96815
Best Western Plaza Hotel	96819
Outrigger Waikiki Tower	96815
The Breakers	96815
Colony Surf Hotel	96815
Coral Reef Aston Hotels & Resort	96815
Halekulani Hotel	96815
Hawaiian Monarch Hotel	96815
Hawaiian Regent	96815
Hawaiian Waikiki Beach Hotel	96815
Hawaiiana Hotel	96815
Hilton Hawaiian Village	96815
Holiday Inn-Honolulu Airport	96819
Hyatt Regency Waikiki	96815
Ilikai, The	96815
Ilima Hotel	96815
Kahala Hilton	96816
Miramar at Waikiki	96815
New Otani Kaimana Beach Hotel	96815
Outrigger Coral Seas Hotel	96815
Outrigger East	96815
Outrigger Malia	96815
Outrigger Prince Kuhio	96815
Outrigger Surf	96815
Outrigger Waikiki Hotel	96815
Outrigger West	96815
Pacific Beach Hotel	96815
Pagoda Hotel	96814
Park Shore Hotel	96815
Royal Hawaiian Hotel	96815
Sheraton Princess Kaiulani Hotel	96815
Sheraton-Waikiki	96815
Waikiki Beachcomber	96815
Waikikian On The Beach	96815
Honomakau	96755
Honomalino	96704
Honomu	96728
Honouliuli	96706
Honuapo	96772
Hookena	96704
Hoolehua	96729
Hoopuloa	96726
Huehue	96725
Huelo	96708
Iroquois Point	96706
Iwasaki Camp	96760

	ZIP
Kaaawa	96730
Kaahumanu Center	96732
Kaalaea	96744
Kaalawai (Part of Honolulu)	96821
Kaanapali	96761
Kaapahu	96776
Kaapoko Homesteads	96781
Kaauhuhu Homesteads	96719
Kaawanui Village	96769
Kahakuloa	96793
Kahala Mall (Part of Honolulu)	96816
Kahaluu (Hawaii County)	96725
Kahaluu (Honolulu County)	96744
Kahaluu-Keauhou	96725
Kahana (Honolulu County)	96717
Kahana (Maui County)	96761
Kahei Homesteads	96719
Kahua	96755
Kahuku (Hawaii County)	96772
Kahuku (Honolulu County)	96731
Kahului	96732-33

For specific Kahului Zip Codes call (808) 871-4710

Kaiaakea	96773
Kaieie Homesteads	96781
Kailua (Honolulu County)	96734
Kailua (Maui County)	96708
Kailua Kona	96739-40
	96745

For specific Kailua Kona Zip Codes call (808) 329-1927

Kai Malino	96704
Kaimu	96778
Kaimuki (Part of Honolulu)	96816
Kainaliu	96750
Kainalu	96748
Kaiwiki	96720
Kalae	96729
Kalaheo	96741
Kalamaula	96748
Kalaoa	96781
Kalaoa Homesteads	96725
Kalauao	96701
Kalaupapa	96742
Kalepoleopo	96753
Kalihi (Part of Honolulu)	96819
Kalihi Kai (Part of Honolulu)	96818
Kalihi Shopping Center (Part of Honolulu)	96819
Kalihiwai	96754
Kalopa Mauka	96727
Kaluaaha	96748
Kamaili	96778
Kamalo	96748
Kamehameha Heights (Part of Honolulu)	96819
Kamiloloa	96748
Kamooloa	96791
Kamuela	96743
Kaneohe	96744
Kaneohe State Hospital	96744
Kaneohe Station	96863
Kaniahiku Village	96778
Kapaa	96746
Kapaau	96755
Kapahulu (Part of Honolulu)	96815
Kapaia	96715
Kapaka	96747
Kapalama (Part of Honolulu)	96817
Kapalua	96761
Kapehu	96780
Kapoho	96778
Kapulena	96727
Kaumakani	96747
Kaumalapau	96763
Kaumana	96720
Kaunakakai	96748
Kaupakalua	96708
Kaupo	96713
Kawaihae	96743
Kawaihua	96746
Kawailoa	96712
Kawailoa Beach	96712
Kawainui	96783
Kawela (Honolulu County)	96731
Kawela (Maui County)	96748
Keaau	96749
Keaau Camp	96749
Keaau Ranch	96749
Kealakehe Homesteads	96740
Kealakekua	96750
Kealia	96751
Keanae	96708
Keauhou	96740
Keaukaha	96720
Keawakapu	96753
Keehia	96774
Keei	96726
Kehena	96778
Kekaha	96752

	ZIP		ZIP		ZIP
Kelawea	96761	Mountain View	96771	Puuiki	96713
Keokea (Hawaii County)	96704	Muolea	96713	Puukolii	96761
Keokea (Maui County)	96790	Naalehu	96772	Puunene	96784
Keolu Hills	96734	Nanakuli	96792	Puunoa	96761
Kihalani Homestead	96780	Napili	96761	Puunui (Part of Honolulu)	96819
Kihei	96753	Napili-Honokowai	96761	Puuohala	96793
Kilauea	96754	Napoopoo	96704	Puu Waawaa	96740
Kilauea Military Camp	96718	Naval Communication		Puuwai	96769
Kilauea Settlement	96785	Station	96786	Renton Village	96706
Kiolakaa Keaa Homesteads	96772	Navy Cantonment (Part of		Royal Hawaiian (Part of	
Kipahulu	96713	Honolulu)	96818	Honolulu)	96815
Kipu (Kauai County)	96766	Navy Terminal (Part of		St. Louis Heights (Part of	
Kipu (Maui County)	96757	Honolulu)	96818	Honolulu)	96822
Koali	96713	Nawiliwili	96766	Schofield Barracks	96786
Koele	96763	Newtown Estates	96782	Spanish Village B	96784
Kokee	96752	Nine Miles	96749	Spreckelsville	96779
Kokohahi	96744	Ninole	96773	Submarine Base	96818
Kokomo	96708	Niulii	96755	Sunset Beach	96712
Kolekole Beach Park	96710	Niumalu	96766	Tantalus (Part of Honolulu)	96822
Kolo	96704	Niu Valley (Part of Honolulu)	96816	Tenney	96706
Koloa	96756	Niu Valley Shopping Center		Timber Town (Part of	
Kualapuu	96757	(Part of Honolulu)	96821	Honolulu)	96826
Kualoa	96730	Niu Village	96774	Ualapue	96748
Kuhio Village	96743	Numila	96705	Ulumalu	96708
Kuhua	96761	Olinda	96768	Ulupalakua	96790
Kukaiau	96776	Olomana	96734	Umikoa	96776
Kukui	96771	Olowalu	96761	Union Mill	96719
Kukuihaele	96727	Omao	96756	University (Part of Honolulu)	96822
Kukuiula	96756	Omapio	96790	Upolu Point	96719
Kukui Village	96774	Onomea	96781	Varona Village	96706
Kula	96790	Ookala	96774	Village Park	96797
Kumukumu	96703	Opihikao	96778	Village Seven	96705
Kunia	96759	Orpheum Village	96779	Volcano	96785
Kupolo	96766	Paauhau	96775	Wahiawa (Honolulu County)	96786
Kurtistown	96760	Paauhau Mauka	96727	Wahiawa (Kauai County)	96705
Lahaina	96761	Paauilo	96776	Waiahole	96744
	96767	Pacific Heights (Part of		Waiaka	96743
For specific Lahaina Zip Codes		Honolulu)	96817	Waiakea	96720
call (808) 667-6611		Pacific Palisades	96782	Waiakea Camps	96720
Lahaina Shopping Center	96761	Pahala	96777	Waialae-Kahala (Part of	
Laie	96762	Pahoa	96778	Honolulu)	96816
Lalakoa	96763	Pahoehoe	96704	Waialua (Honolulu County)	96791
Lanai City	96763	Paia	96779	Waialua (Maui County)	96748
Lanikai	96734	Palama (Part of Honolulu)	96817	Waialua Mill	96791
Lanikai Heights	96734	Palani Junction	96725	Waianae	96792
Lau Hue Point	96720	Panaewa	96720	Waianae Homesteads	96792
Laupahoehoe	96764	Papa	96704	Waiau	96782
Laupahoehoe Point	96764	Papaaloa	96780	Waiau View Estates	96782
Lawai	96765	Papaikou	96781	Waiawa Correctional Facility	96782
Lihue	96766	Paukaa	96720	Waiehu	96793
Lihue Shopping Center	96766	Paukukalo	96793	Waiehu Village	96793
Lower Paia	96779	Paumalu	96712	Waihee	96793
Lower Village	96706	Pauwela	96708	Waihee-Waiehue	96793
Lualualei	96792	Peahi	96708	Waikane	96744
Lualualei Homesteads	96792	Pearl City	96782	Waikapu	96793
Maalaea	96793	Pearl City Heights	96782	Waikele	96797
McGerrow Village	96784	Pearl Harbor Naval		Waikiki (Part of Honolulu)	96815
McGrew Point	96701	Reservation	96818	Waikoloa	96738
Maili	96792	Pearl Harbor Naval Supply		Wailea	96710
Makaha	96792	Center	96818	Wailea-Makena	96753
Makaha Valley	96792	Pepeekeo	96783	Wailua (Kauai County)	96746
Makakilo City	96706	Pepeekeo Mill Camp	96783	Wailua (Maui County)	96708
Makapala	96755	Pihana	96793	Wailua Homesteads	96746
Makawao	96768	Piihonua	96720	Wailuku	96793
Makaweli	96769	Pohakea Homesteads	96776	Wailupe (Part of Honolulu)	96821
Makena	96753	Pohakupu	96734	Waimalu	96701
Makiki	96822-23	Pohoiki	96778	Waimanalo	96795
	96826	Poipu	96756	Waimanalo Beach	96795
For specific Makiki Zip Codes call		Pomoho	96786	Waimea (Honolulu County)	96712
(808) 536-9903		Port Allen	96705	Waimea (Kauai County)	96796
Makiki Heights (Part of		Portlock (Part of Honolulu)	96821	Wainaku	96720
Honolulu)	96822	Prince Kuhio Plaza	96720	Wainee	96761
Mana	96752	Princeville	96722	Wainiha	96714
Market (Part of Honolulu)	96816	Puako	96743	Waiohinu	96772
Mark Twain Estates	96772	Pualaea Homestead	96764	Waipahu	96797
Maulua	96780	Pua Loke	96766	Waipio (Hawaii County)	96727
Maunalani Heights (Part of		Puhi	96766	Waipio (Honolulu County)	96797
Honolulu)	96816	Pukalani	96788	Waipio Acres	96786
Maunaloa	96770	Pukoo	96748	Waipouli	96746
Maunalua (Part of Honolulu)	96816	Pulehu	96790	Waipunalei Homesteads	96764
Maunawili	96734	Punaluu (Hawaii County)	96777	Wharf	96761
Mikilua	96792	Punaluu (Honolulu County)	96717	Wheeler Air Force Base	96854
Mililani Town	96789	Puohala Village	96744	Whitmore Village	96786
Miloli	96726	Pupukea	96712	Wilhelmina Rise (Part of	
Milo Village	96774	Puuanahulu	96725	Honolulu)	96816
Moanalua (Part of Honolulu)	96819	Puueo	96720	Woodlawn (Part of	
Moiliili (Part of Honolulu)	96814	Pu'uhonua o Honaunau		Honolulu)	96816
Mokuleia	96791	National Historical Park	96726	Wood Valley Homesteads	96777
Momilani Estates	96782	Puu Hue	96719		

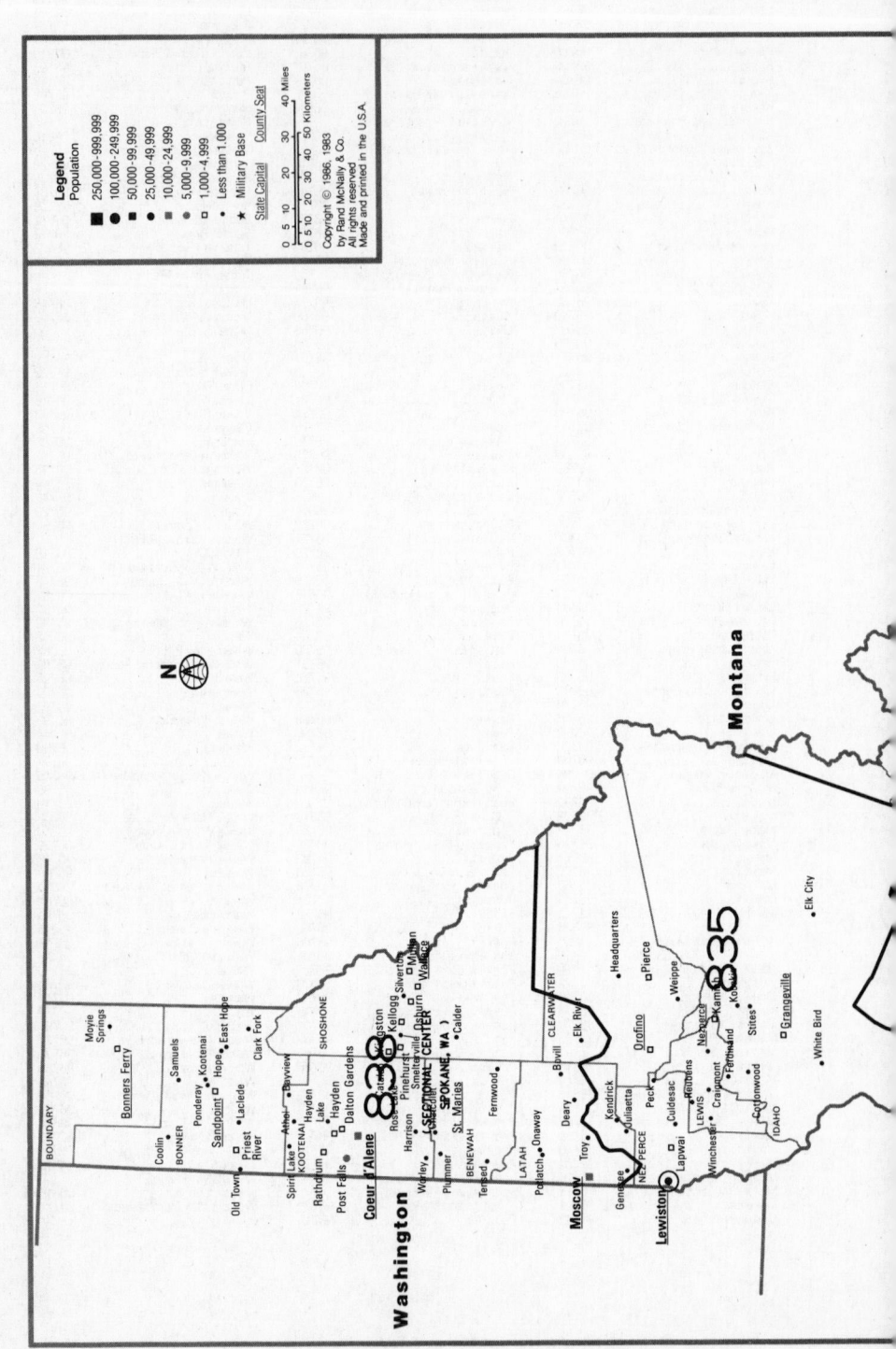

Legend
Population
250,000-999,999
100,000-249,999
50,000-99,999
25,000-49,999
10,000-24,999
5,000-9,999
1,000-4,999
Less than 1,000
Military Base
State Capital   County Seat

0 5 10   20   30   40 Miles
0 5 10 20 30 40 50 Kilometers

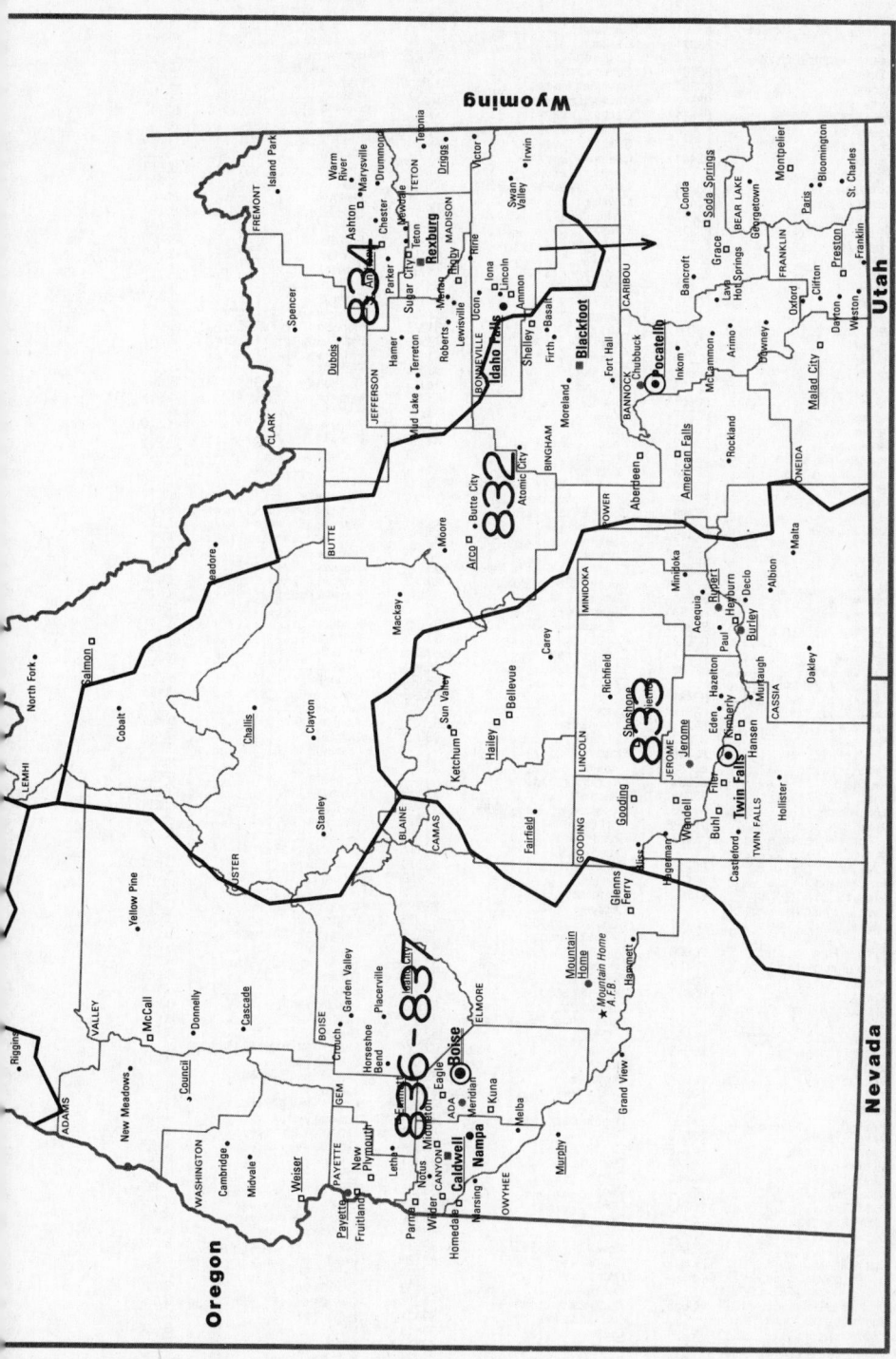

	ZIP		ZIP		ZIP
Aberdeen	83210	Carey	83320	East Hope	83836
Acequia	83350	Careywood	83809	East Kamiah	83539
Ahsahka	83520	Carlin Bay	83833	East Lewiston (Part of	
Alameda (Part of Pocatello)	83201	Carmen	83462	Lewiston)	83501
Albion	83311	Cascade	83611	Eastport	83826
Aldape Heights (Part of		Castleford	83321	Eaton	83672
Boise)	83701	Cataldo	83810	Echo Beach	83858
Algoma	83860	Cathedral Pines	83340	Eddiville	83814
Almo	83312	Cavendish	83537	Eden	83325
Alpha	83611	Central	83217	Edmonds	83440
Alpine	83610	Central Cove	83676	Egin	83445
American Falls	83211	Challis	83226	Elba	83326
Ammon	83401	Chatcolet	83851	Elk City	83525
Anderson Dam	83647	Cherry Creek	83252	Elk River	83827
Annis	83442	Cherry Lane (Part of Boise)	83705	Ellis	83235
Antelope	83443	Chester	83421	Elmira	83862
Apple Valley	83660	Chesterfield	83217	Emida	83861
Arbon	83212	Chilco	83801	Emmett	83617
Arbon Valley	83203	Chubbuck	83202	Enaville	83839
Archer	83440	Churchill	83318	Enkraft	83350
Arco	83213	Clagstone	83856	Enrose	83605
Argora	83423	Clark Fork	83811	Excelsior Beach	83858
Arimo	83214	Clarkia	83812	Fairfield	83327
Ashton	83420	Clawson	83452	Fairview (Franklin County)	83263
Athol	83801	Clayton	83227	Fairview (Twin Falls County)	83316
Atlanta	83601	Clearwater	83539	Fall Creek (Elmore County)	83647
Atomic City	83215	Clementsville	83436	Fall Creek (Idaho County)	83530
Avery	83802	Cleveland	83263	Falls City	83338
Avon	83823	Cliffs	97910	Featherville	83647
Baker	83467	Clifton	83228	Felt	83424
Bancroft	83217	Clover	83316	Fenn	83531
Banida	83263	Coats	83350	Ferdinand	83526
Banks	83602	Cobalt	83229	Fernan Lake Village	83814
Bannock (Part of Pocatello)	83204	Cocolalla	83813	Fernwood	83830
Basalt	83218	Coeur d'Alene	83814-16	Filer	83328
Basin	83346	For specific Coeur d'Alene Zip		Firth	83236
Bates	83422	Codes call (208) 773-4922		Fish Haven	83287
Bayview	83803	Coeur d'Alene Indian		Fort Hall (Bannock County)	83203
Beachs Corner	83401	Reservation	83851	Fort Hall (Bingham County)	83203
Bear	83612	Colburn	83865	Fort Hall Indian Reservation	83203
Bellevue	83313	Cold House	83636	Fox Creek	83455
Belmont	83801	Cole Village (Part of Boise)	83704	Franklin (Ada County)	83704
Bench	83241	Collister (Part of Boise)	83703	Franklin (Franklin County)	83237
Benewah	83861	Coltman	83401	Franklin Park (Part of Boise)	83704
Bennington	83254	Columbus Park (Part of		Fraser	83544
Berger	83301	Boise)	83705	Freedom	83120
Bern	83220	Conda	83230	Fruitland	83619
Big Creek	83677	Conkling Park	83876	Fruitvale	83620
Big Little Acres	83338	Conner	83342	Galena	83340
Big Springs (Part of Island		Coolin	83821	Gannett	83313
Park)	83433	Corral	83322	Gardena	83629
Black Cloud	83873	Cotterel	83323	Garden City	83704
Blackfoot	83221	Cottonwood	83522	Garden Valley	83622
Black Lake	83861	Council	83612	Garfield	83401
Blackrock	83245	Country Club Mall (Part of		Garwood	83835
Blaine	83843	Idaho Falls)	83401	Gem	83873
Blanchard	83804	Country Club Manor (Part of		Genesee	83832
Bliss	83314	Boise)	83705	Geneva	83238
Bloomington	83223	Country Club Terrace (Part		Georgetown	83239
Boise	83701-88	of Boise)	83705	Gibbonsville	83463
For specific Boise Zip Codes call		Craigmont	83523	Gibson	83221
(208) 383-4211		Crescent	83537	Gibson City (Part of	
Boise Airport (Part of Boise)	83715	Crouch	83602	Pinehurst)	83850
Boise Heights (Part of		Crystal	83672	Gifford	83541
Boise)	83702	Culdesac	83524	Glendale	83263
Boise Town Square (Part of		Cuprum	83612	Glengary	83864
Boise)	83701	Curry	83328	Glenns Ferry	83623
Bone	83401	Dalton Gardens	83814	Glenwood (Clearwater	
Bonners Ferry	83805	Daniels	83252	County)	83544
Borah (Part of Boise)	83702	Darlington	83255	Glenwood (Idaho County)	83536
Bovill	83806	David Taylor Research		Golden	83530
Bowmont	83651	Center, Acoustic		Gooding	83330
Box Canyon (Part of Island		Research Detachment	83803	Goodrich	83612
Park)	83429	Davis Acres (Part of Garden		Goshen	83274
Bradley (Part of Kellogg)	83837	City)	83704	Grace	83241
Bridge	83342	Dayton	83232	Grand Teton Mall (Part of	
Bruneau	83604	Deary	83823	Idaho Falls)	83401
Bruneau Valley	83604	Declo	83323	Grandview (Bingham	
Buhl	83316	Deep Creek	83316	County)	83210
Buist	83243	Delta	83873	Grand View (Owyhee	
Burgdorf	83638	Denton (Part of Boise)	83704	County)	83624
Burke	83873	Denver	83530	Grangemont	83544
Burley	83318	Desmet	83824	Grangeville	83530
Burmah	83349	Dietrich	83324	Granite	83801
Burton	83440	Dingle	83233	Grant	83401
Butler Bay	83861	Dixie	83525	Grasmere	83604
Butte City	83213	Doles	83605	Gray	83285
Cabinet	83811	Donnelly	83615	Greencreek	83533
Cache	83452	Dover	83825	Greenleaf	83626
Calder	83808	Downey	83234	Greenwood	83335
Caldwell	83605-06	Driggs	83422	Greer	83544
For specific Caldwell Zip Codes		Drummond	83420	Gross	83657
call (208) 459-7489		Dubois	83423	Groveland	83221
Caldwell Labor Camp	83605	Duck Valley Indian		Gwenford	83252
Cambridge (Bannock		Reservation	89832	Hagerman	83332
County)	83234	Dudley	83810	Hailey	83333
Cambridge (Washington		Eagle (Ada County)	83616	Hamer	83425
County)	83610	Eagle (Shoshone County)	83874	Hamilton Corner	83655
Cameron	83537	Eagle Rock (Part of Idaho		Hammett	83627
Cape Horn	83821	Falls)	83402	Hampton	83857
Care-Free Estates	83318	Easley Hot Springs	83340	Hansen	83334

	ZIP		ZIP		ZIP
Harpster	83539	Lenore	83541	Nezperce	83543
Harrison	83833	Leslie	83255	Nez Perce Indian	
Harvard	83834	Letha	83636	Reservation	83540
Hatwai	83501	Lewiston	83501	Niter	83241
Hauser	83854	Lewiston Orchards (Part of		Nordman	83848
Havens	83221	Lewiston)	83501	Norland	83343
Hayden	83835	Lewisville	83431	North Fork	83466
Hayden Lake	83835	Liberty	83260	North Idaho Correctional	
Hazelton	83335	Lidy Hot Springs	83423	Institution	83522
Headquarters	83534	Lincoln	83401	North Lewiston (Part of	
Heglar	83211	Linden	83537	Lewiston)	83501
Heise	83443	Linrose	83286	North Shoshone	83352
Helmer	83823	Lone Pine	83464	Northside (Ada County)	83702
Heman	83445	Lookout	83541	Northside (Gem County)	83617
Henry	83230	Lorenzo	83442	Notus	83656
Hess Point	83821	Lost River (Butte County)	83255	Nounan	83254
Heyburn	83336	Lost River (Custer County)	83255	Nuclear Power Training	
Hibbard	83440	Lowell	83539	Unit, Idaho Falls	83401
Highlands (Part of Boise)	83702	Lower Stanley	83278	Oakley	83346
Hill City	83337	Lowman	83637	Obsidian	83340
Hillview (Part of Ammon)	83401	Lucile	83542	Ola	83657
Holbrook	83243	Lund	83217	Old Town	83822
Hollister	83301	Lyman	83440	Onaway	83855
Home Acres (Part of Boise)	83704	McArthur	83847	Oreana	83650
Homedale	83628	McCall	83638	Orofino	83544
Honeysuckle Hills	83835	McCammon	83250	Orogrande	83525
Hop (Part of Greenleaf)	83626	McGuires (Part of Post		Osburn	83849
Hope	83836	Falls)	83854	Osgood	83402
Hornet	83612	Mackay	83251	Outlet Bay	83856
Horseshoe Bend	83629	Macks Inn (Part of Island		Ovid	83260
Hot Spring Landing	83313	Park)	83443	Oxford	83263
Howe	83244	Magic City	83313	Page	83868
Huetter	83854	Magic Resort	83352	Palisades	83437
Hulen Meadows	83340	Malad City	83252	Palouse Empire Mall (Part of	
Humphrey	83446	Malta	83342	Moscow)	83843
Hunt	83325	Mapleton	83263	Paradise Hot Springs	83647
Huston	83630	Marion	83346	Paris	83261
Hyland Park (Part of		Marley (Part of Richfield)	83349	Park	83823
Pocatello)	83201	Marshcenter	83214	Parker	83438
Idaho City	83631	Marsing	83639	Parma	83660
Idaho Falls	83401-06	Marysville	83420	Patterson	83253
For specific Idaho Falls Zip Codes		May	83253	Paul	83347
call (208) 523-3650		Meadow Creek	83805	Payette	83661
Idaho Maximum Security		Meadows	83654	Pearl	83616
Institution	83701	Meadowville	83276	Peck	83545
Idahome	83323	Medimont	83842	Pedee (Part of Chatcolet)	83851
Idman	83423	Melba	83641	Pegram	83254
Indian Cove	83627	Menan	83434	Pella	83318
Indian Hills (Part of		Meridian	83642	Peterson Corners	83553
Pocatello)	83204		83680	Picabo	83348
Indian Valley	83632	For specific Meridian Zip Codes		Pierce	83546
Inkóm	83245	call (208) 888-3361		Pine	83647
Iona	83427	Mesa	83643	Pinehurst (Adams County)	83654
Irwin	83428	Mica	83814	Pinehurst (Shoshone	
Island Park	83429	Midas	83864	County)	83850
Jackson	83350	Middleton	83644	Pine Ridge	83612
Jacques	83524	Midvale	83645	Pine Ridge Mall (Part of	
Jamestown	83274	Miller Creek Settlement	89832	Pocatello)	83201
Jerome	83338	Milltown	83861	Pingree	83262
Joel	83843	Milo	83401	Pinto Point	83821
Johnny Creek (Part of		Minidoka	83343	Pioneerville	83631
Pocatello)	83204	Minkcreek	83263	Placerville	83666
Jonathan	83672	Montana Junction (Part of		Plano	83440
Judge Town	83546	Pocatello)	83201	Pleasantview	83252
Juliaetta	83535	Monteview	83435	Plummer	83851
Juniper	84336	Montour	83617	Pocatello	83201-06
Kamiah	83536	Montpelier	83254	For specific Pocatello Zip Codes	
Karcher Mall (Part of		Moore	83255	call (208) 233-0800	
Nampa)	83651	Mora	83634	Polaris (Part of Osburn)	83849
Kellogg	83837	Moravia	83805	Pollock	83547
Kendrick	83537	Moreland	83256	Ponderay	83852
Ketchum	83340	Morgans Alley (Part of		Ponds Resort (Part of Island	
Keuterville	83538	Lewiston)	83501	Park)	83429
Kidder	83359	Moscow	83843	Porthill	83853
Kilgore	83423	Mountain Home	83647	Post Falls	83854
Kimball	83236	Mountain Home Air Force		Potlatch	83855
Kimberly	83341	Base	83648	Potlatch Junction	83855
King Hill	83633	Mountain View (Part of		Prairie	83647
Kingston	83839	Boise)	83704	Preston	83263
Knowlton Heights	83605	Mount Idaho	83530	Prichard	83873
Kooskia	83539	Moyie Springs	83845	Priest River	83822
Kootenai	83840	Mud Lake	83450		83856
Kuna	83634	Mullan	83846	For specific Priest River Zip Codes	
Labelle	83442	Murphy	83650	call (208) 448-1513	
Laclede	83841	Murray	83874	Princeton	83857
Lake Creek	83876	Murtaugh	83344	Raft River	83211
Lake Fork	83635	Myrtle	83535	Ramsdell (Part of Chatcolet)	83851
Lakeview	83803	Naf	83342	Rathdrum	83858
Lamont	83420	Nampa	83651-53	Raymond	83114
Lanark	83260		83686-87	Redfish Lake	83278
Lancaster Terrace (Part of		For specific Nampa Zip Codes call		Red River Hot Springs	83525
Boise)	83702	(208) 466-8938		Reno	83423
Lane	83810	Naples	83847	Reubens	83548
Lapwai	83540	Naval Administration Unit,		Rexburg	83440
Lardo (Part of McCall)	83638	Idaho Falls	83401	Reynolds	83650
Last Chance Resort (Part of		Neeley	83211	Richfield	83349
Island Park)	83429	New Centerville	83631	Riddle	83604
Lava Hot Springs	83246	Newdale	83436	Rigby	83442
Leadore	83464	New Meadows	83654	Riggins	83549
Leland	83537	New Plymouth	83655	Ririe	83443
Lemhi	83465	New Sweden	83402		

	ZIP
Riverdale	83263
Riverside (Bingham County)	83221
Riverside (Canyon County)	83605
Riverside (Clearwater County)	83544
Roberts	83444
Robin	83214
Rock Creek	83334
Rockford	83221
Rockford Bay	83814
Rockland	83271
Rocky Bar	83647
Rocky Point (Benewah County)	83851
Rocky Point (Bonner County)	83821
Rogerson	83302
Rose	83221
Roseberry	83615
Rose Lake	83810
Roseworth	83321
Roswell	83660
Roy	83271
Rupert	83350
Sagle	83860
St. Anthony	83445
St. Charles	83272
St. Joe	83861
St. John	83252
St. Leon	83401
St. Maries	83861
Salem	83440
Salmon	83467
Samaria	83252
Samuels	83862
Sanders	83870
Sandpoint	83862-65
For specific Sandpoint Zip Codes call (208) 263-2716	
Santa	83866
Selle	83864
Sharon	83260
Shelley	83274
Shelton	83401
Sherwood Beach	83821
Shoshone	83352
Shoup	83469
Silver City	83650
Silver Creek Plunge	83602
Silver Sands Beach	83858
Silverton	83867
Skyline (Part of Idaho Falls)	83401
Slate Creek	83554
Slickpoo	83524
Small	83423
Smelter Heights (Part of Kellogg)	83837
Smelterville	83868
Smiths Ferry	83602
Soda Springs	83276

	ZIP
Soldiers Home (Part of Boise)	83704
South Boise (Part of Boise)	83706
South Gate Plaza (Part of Lewiston)	83501
South Park (Part of Pocatello)	83201
Southside (Part of Boise)	83706
Southwick	83537
Spalding	83551
Spencer	83446
Spirit Lake	83869
Springdale	83318
Springfield	83277
Squirrel	83447
Standrod	83342
Stanley	83278
Star	83669
Starrhs Ferry	83318
State Line	83854
Sterling	83210
Stites	83552
Stoddard	83641
Stone	83280
Sugar City	83448
Sunbeam	83278
Sunnydell	83440
Sunnyside (Bonner County)	83864
Sunnyside (Shoshone County)	83837
Sunnyslope	83605
Sun Valley	83353-54
For specific Sun Valley Zip Codes call (208) 622-5265	
Swanlake	83281
Swan Valley	83449
Sweet	83670
Sweetwater	83540
Syringa	83539
Taber	83221
Talache	83860
Tamarack	83612
Taylor	83401
Teakean	83537
Tendoy	83468
Tenmile	83642
Tensed	83870
Terreton	83450
Teton	83451
Tetonia	83452
Thatcher	83283
Thomas	83221
Thomas Junction	83221
Thornton	83440
Three Creek	83302
Topaz	83246
Transfer (Part of Lewiston)	83501
Treasureton	83263
Trestle Creek	83836
Triumph	83333

	ZIP
Troy	83871
Turner Bay	83833
Tuttle	83314
Twin Falls	83301
	83348
For specific Twin Falls Zip Codes call (208) 733-4380	
Twin Groves	83445
Twin Lakes	83858
Twinlow	83858
Tyhee	83201
Ucon	83454
Unity	83318
University (Part of Moscow)	83843
Ustick	83702
Valley View Heights (Part of Lewiston)	83501
Victor	83455
View	83318
Viola	83872
Virginia	83234
Waha	83501
Wallace	83873
Wapello	83221
Wardboro	83254
Wardner	83837
Warm Lake	83611
Warm River	83420
Warren	83671
Washoe	83661
Wayan	83285
Webb	83540
Weippe	83553
Weiser	83672
Weitz	83605
Wendell	83355
Westgate Acres (Part of Boise)	83704
Westlake	83526
Westmond	83860
Westmoreland (Part of Boise)	83704
West Mountain	83611
Weston	83286
White Bird	83554
Whitney (Ada County)	83705
Whitney (Franklin County)	83263
Wilder	83676
Wilford	83445
Winchester	83555
Winder	83263
Wolf Lodge	83814
Wolverine	83236
Woodland	83536
Woodland Park	83873
Woodruff	83252
Woodville	83274
Worley	83876
Yellow Pine	83677

	ZIP		ZIP		ZIP
Abingdon	61410	Andover (Township)	61233	Atwater	62511
Abington (Township)	61476	Andres	60468	Atwood	61913
Acacia Acres	60525	Andrew	62707	Atwood Heights (Part of	
Acme Station (Part of		Anna	62906	Alsip)	60658
Bartonville)	61607	Anna Mental Health and		Auburn (Township)	62615
Adair	61411	Developmental Center	62906	Auburn (Clark County)	
Adams (Adams County)	62347	Annapolis	62413	(Township)	62441
Adams (La Salle County)		Annawan	61234	Auburn (Sangamon County)	62615
(Township)	60531	Annawan (Township)	61234	Auburn Park (Part of	
Adams Corner	62410	Antioch	60002	Chicago)	60620
Addieville	62214	Antioch (Township)	60002	Auburn Woods (Part of	
Addison (Township)	60101	Appanoose (Township)	62354	Palatine)	60067
Addison	60101	Apple Canyon Lake	61001	Audubon (Township)	62075
Adeline	61047	Applegate (Part of		Augsburg	62885
Aden	62895	Schaumburg)	60194	Augusta	62311
Adrian	62310	Apple River	61001	Augusta (Township)	62311
Aero Estates	60564	Apple River (Township)	61001	Aurora	60504-07
Aetna (Coles County)	61938	Appleton	61428	For specific Aurora Zip Codes call	
Aetna (Logan County)		Appletree (Part of Country		(708) 897-2221	
(Township)	61749	Club Hills)	60477	Aurora (Township)	60505
Afolkey	61018	Apple Valley (Part of		Austin (Cook County)	60644
Afton (Township)	60115	Glenview)	60025	Austin (Macon County)	
Agnew	61081	Appolaloosa West	60119	(Township)	62573
Airport	61074	Aptakisic	60069	Austin View	60463
Airport Heights	61607	Arboretum East	60137	Aux Sable (Township)	60447
Akin	62805	Arboretum Villages (Part of		Ava	62907
Akron (Township)	61559	Lisle)	60532	Avalon Park (Part of	
Alan Dale	62035	Arboretum West	60137	Chicago)	60619
Alba (Township)	61235	Arbor Trails (Part of Park		Avena	62458
Albany	61230	Forest)	60466	Avena (Township)	62458
Albany (Township)	61230	Arbury Hills	60448	Avery Hill	62223
Albers	62215	Arcadia	62650	Aviston	62216
Albion	62806	Archer	62707	Avoca (Township)	61739
Alden	60001	Archie	61876	Avon (Fulton County)	61415
Alden (Township)	60001	Arcola	61910	Avon (Lake County)	
Aldridge	62998	Arcola (Township)	61910	(Township)	60030
Aledo	61231	Arenzville	62611	Avondale (Part of Chicago)	60641
Alexander	62601	Arenzville (Township)	62611	Ayers (Township)	61816
Alexis	61412	Argenta	62501	Babcock	61244
Algonquin	60102	Argo (Part of Summit)	60501	Babson (Part of St. Charles)	60174
Algonquin (Township)	60102	Argo Fay	61053	Babylon	61415
Algonquin Shores	60102	Argyle	61011	Baden Baden (Part of	
Algonquin Trails (Part of		Arispie (Township)	61368	Pierron)	62273
Mount Prospect)	60056	Arlington	61312	Bader	62624
Alhambra	62001	Arlington Heights	60004-06	Baileyville	61007
Alhambra (Township)	62001	For specific Arlington Heights Zip		Bainbridge (Township)	62639
Allen (La Salle County)		Codes call (708) 253-7456		Baker	60531
(Township)	60470	Arlington Ridge (Part of		Baker Lake	60010
Allen (Mason County)	62682	Arlington Heights)	60004	Bakerville	62864
Allen (Whiteside County)	61071	Armington	61721	Balcom	62906
Allendale	62410	Armstrong	61812	Bald Bluff (Township)	61476
Allen Grove (Township)	62682	Arnold	62650	Bald Hill (Township)	62883
Allens Corners	60140	Aroma (Township)	60901	Baldwin	62217
Allentown	61568	Aroma Park	60910	Baldwin Beach	62644
Allenville	61951	Aroma Park Northwest	60901	Bales Lake	60948
Allerton	61810	Arrington (Township)	62886	Ball (Township)	62629
Allin (Township)	61774	Arrowhead (DuPage		Ballou	60481
Allison (Township)	62439	County)	60187	Banner (Fulton County)	
Alma	62807	Arrowhead (Kankakee		(Township)	61520
Alma (Township)	62807	County)	60914	Banner (Effingham County)	
Almora	60123	Arrowhead (McDonough		(Township)	62461
Almora Heights	60123	County)	61455	Banner	61520
Alorton	62207	Arrowhead Hills	60543	Bannister	62881
Alpha	61413	Arrowsmith (Township)	61772	Bannockburn	60015
Alsey	62610	Arrowsmith	61722	Barclay	62561
Alsip	60658	Arrow Wood	62035	Bardolph	61416
Alsip Woods (Part of Alsip)	60658	Artesia (Township)	60918	Bargerville	62960
Alta	61614	Arthur	61911	Barnett (De Witt County)	
Altamont (Effingham		Asbury (Township)	62871	(Township)	61727
County)	62411	Ashburn (Part of Chicago)	60652	Barnett (Montgomery	
Altamont (Madison County)	62035	Ash Grove (Iroquois		County)	62056
Alto (Township)	60553	County) (Township)	60953	Barnhill	62809
Alton	62002	Ash Grove (Shelby County)		Barnhill (Township)	62809
Alton (Township)	62002	(Township)	61957	Barr (Macoupin County)	
Altona	61414	Ashkum	60911	(Township)	62674
Alton Square (Part of Alton)	62002	Ashkum (Township)	60911	Barr (Sangamon County)	62613
Alto Pass	62905	Ashland	62612	Barren (Township)	62812
Altorf	60914	Ashland (Township)	62612	Barrington	60010-11
Alvin	61811	Ashley	62808	For specific Barrington Zip Codes	
Alworth	61088	Ashley (Township)	62808	call (708) 381-0514	
Amboy	61310	Ashmore	61912	Barrington Center (Part of	
Amboy (Township)	61310	Ashmore (Township)	61912	Barrington Hills)	60010
Amenia	61856	Ashton	61006	Barrington Highlands	60010
America	62996	Ashton (Township)	61006	Barrington Hills	60010
Americana Village (Part of		Assumption	62510	Barrington Square (Part of	
Glendale Heights)	60139	Assumption (Township)	62510	Hoffman Estates)	60195
Ames	62277	Astoria	61501	Barrington Woods	60074
Amity (Township)	61319	Astoria (Township)	61501	Barrow	62082
Anchor	61720	Athens	62613	Barry	62312
Anchor (Township)	61720	Athensville	62082	Barry (Township)	62312
Anchorage (Part of		Athensville (Township)	62082	Barstow	61236
Glenview)	60026	Atkinson	61235	Bartelso	62218
Ancient Tree (Part of		Atkinson (Township)	61235	Bartlett	60103
Northbrook)	60062	Atlanta	61723		60107
Ancona	61311	Atlanta (Township)	61723	For specific Bartlett Zip Codes call	
Andalusia	61232	Atlas	62370	(708) 837-1626	
Andalusia (Township)	61232	Atlas (Township)	62370	Bartonville	61607
Anderman Acres	60544	Atlee Ogles	62223	Basco	62313
Anderson (Township)	62441	Atrium (Part of Elmhurst)	60126	Base (Part of Rantoul)	61866
Anderson Lake	61501	Atterbury	62675	Batavia	60510
Andover	61233	Attila	62974	Batavia (Township)	60510

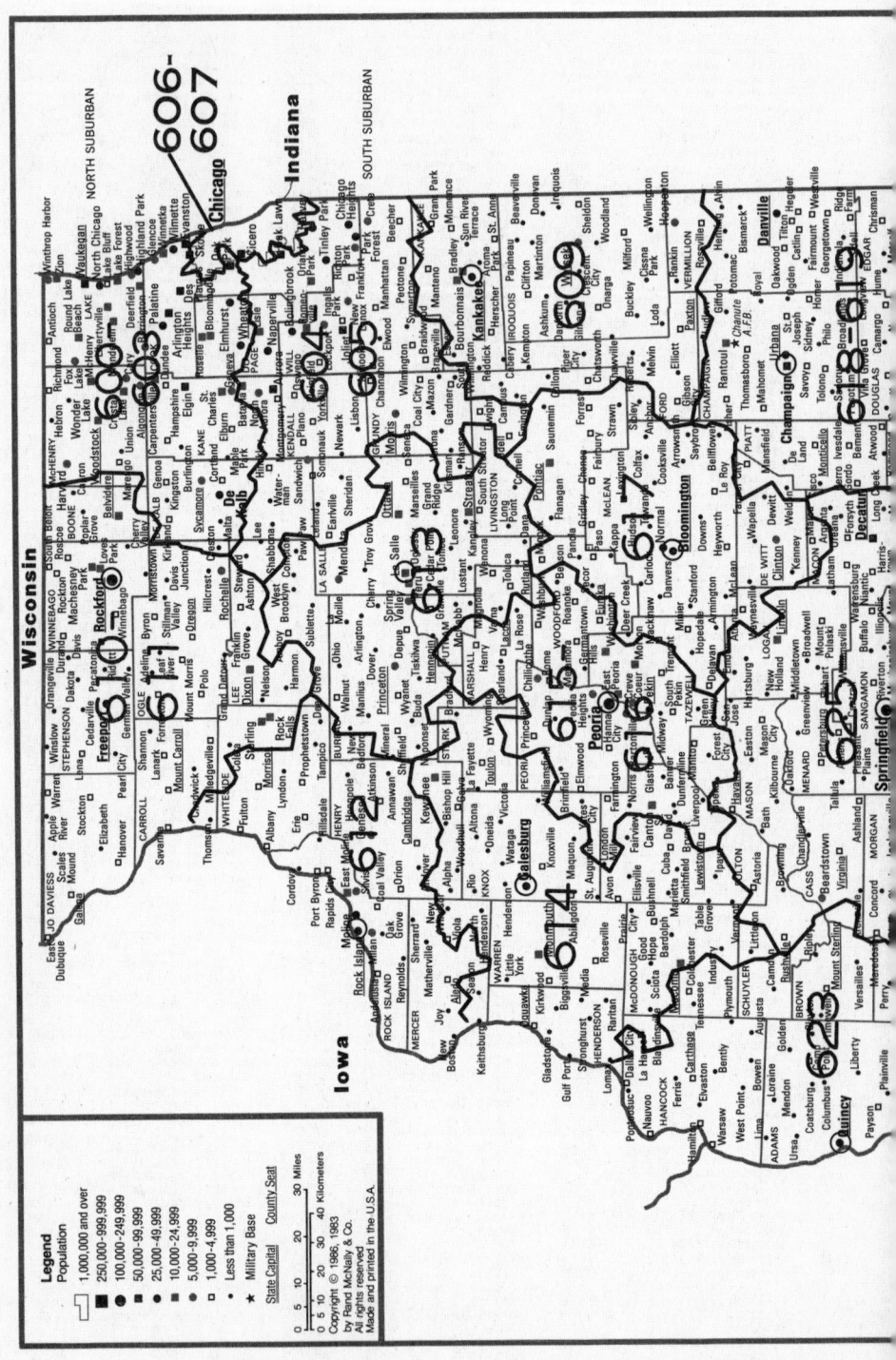

Legend

Population
- 1,000,000 and over
- 250,000-999,999
- 100,000-249,999
- 50,000-99,999
- 25,000-49,999
- 10,000-24,999
- 5,000-9,999
- 1,000-4,999
- Less than 1,000

State Capital   County Seat

★ Military Base

0 5 10   20   30 Miles
0 5 10 20 30 40 Kilometers

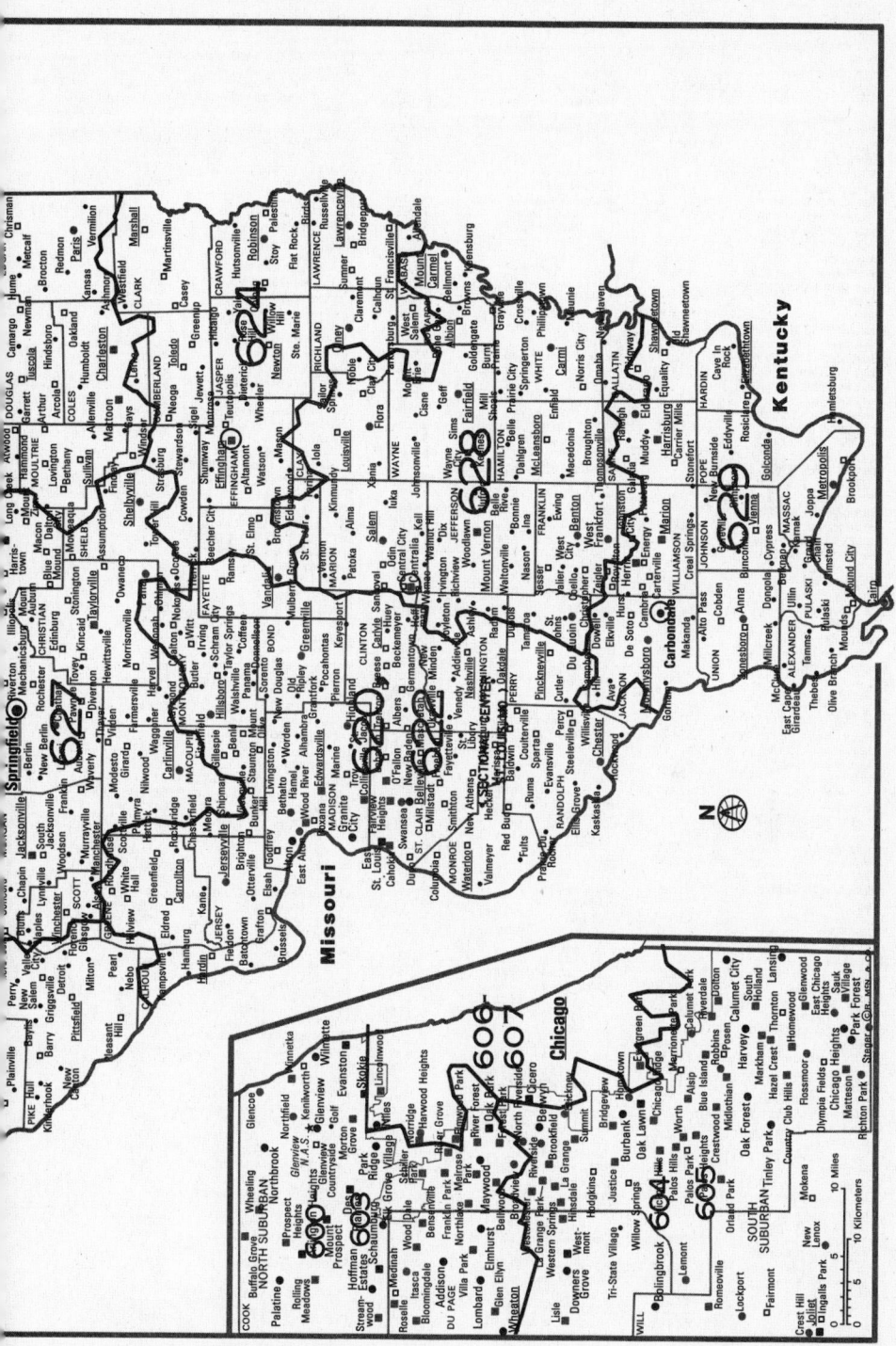

	ZIP
Braeside (Part of Highland Park)	60035
Braidwood	60408
Brainerd (Part of Chicago)	60620
Branding	62013
Brandywine	60181
Branigar Estates	60007
Breckenridge	62563
Breeds	61520
Breese	62230
Breese (Township)	62230
Bremen (Cook County) (Township)	60426
Bremen (Randolph County)	62233
Brementowne Mall (Part of Tinley Park)	60477
Brenton (Township)	60959
Brentwood (Part of Des Plaines)	60016
Brentwood Estates	60074
Brereton	61520
Brettwood (Part of Decatur)	62526
Briar Bluff	61240
Briarbrook Village (Part of Wheaton)	60187
Briarcliffe (Part of Wheaton)	60187
Briarcliffe Knolls (Part of Wheaton)	60187
Briarcliff Estates (Part of Bourbonnais)	60914
Briarwick	61938
Briarwood	61107
Briarwoods Estates (Part of Deerfield)	60015
Briarwood Trace	62901
Brickman Manor (Part of Mount Prospect)	60056
Brickyard, The (Part of Chicago)	60635
Bridgelane	61265
Bridgeport	62417
Bridgeport (Township)	62417
Bridgeview	60455
Bridgeway Addition (Part of Moline)	61265
Bridle Creek Estates	60175
Brierwood	60175
Bright Oaks (Part of Cary)	60013
Brighton	62012
Brighton (Township)	62012
Brighton Park (Part of Chicago)	60632
Brimfield	61517
Brimfield (Township)	61517
Brisbane	60451
Bristol	60512
Bristol (Township)	60512
Bristol Lake	60560
Bristol Ridge	60560
Broadlands	61816
Broadmoor	61421
Broadview	60153
Broadway (Part of Rockford)	61106
Broadwell	62634
Broadwell (Township)	62634
Brocton	61917
Brooke Estates (Part of Highland Park)	60035
Brookeridge	60515
Brookfield (Cook County)	60513
Brookfield (La Salle County) (Township)	60470
Brook Forest (Part of Oak Brook)	60521
Brookforest North	60435
Brookhaven	61277
Brookhaven Manor (Part of Darien)	60561
Brookhill	60048
Brooklyn (Schuyler County) (Township)	62367
Brooklyn (Lee County) (Township)	61318
Brooklyn	62367
Brookport	62910
Brooks	62040
Brookside (Clinton County) (Township)	62801
Brookside (Kane County)	60175
Brooks Isle	61061
Brookview	61614
Brookville	61064
Brookville (Township)	61064
Brookwood (Part of Rolling Meadows)	60008
Brookwood (Part of Prospect Heights)	60070
Brookwood (Kane County)	60174
Brookwood Estates (Part of Wood Dale)	60191

	ZIP
Brothers	61858
Broughton (Hamilton County)	62817
Broughton (Livingston County) (Township)	60934
Brouilletts Creek (Township)	61924
Brown (Township)	61845
Brownfield	62938
Browning (Schuyler County) (Township)	62624
Browning (Franklin County) (Township)	62812
Browning	62624
Browns	62818
Brownstown	62418
Brownsville	62821
Brownwood	61747
Brubaker	62807
Bruce (La Salle County) (Township)	61364
Bruce (Moultrie County)	61951
Brunning	60441
Brunswick	62534
Brushy (Township)	62935
Brushy Mound (Township)	62033
Brussels	62013
Bryant	61519
Bryce	60953
Bryn Mawr (Part of Chicago)	60649
Buck (Township)	61944
Buckeye (Township)	61013
Buckhart (Christian County) (Township)	62531
Buckhart	62545
Buckheart (Township)	61563
Buckhorn	62353
Buckhorn (Township)	62375
Buckingham	60917
Buckley	60918
Buckner	62819
Bucks	61745
Buda	61314
Budd	61313
Buena Vista (Saline County)	62946
Buena Vista (Schuyler County) (Township)	62681
Buena Vista (Stephenson County)	61032
Buffalo (Ogle County) (Township)	61064
Buffalo (Sangamon County)	62515
Buffalo Grove (Cook County)	60089
Buffalo Grove (Ogle County)	61064
Buffalo Hart	62515
Buffalo Hart (Township)	62515
Buffalo Prairie	61237
Buffalo Prairie (Township)	61237
Bull Creek	60048
Bullock Addition	61241
Bull Valley	60098
Bulpitt	62517
Buncombe	62912
Bungay	62887
Bunker Hill	62014
Bunker Hill (Township)	62014
Bunkum (Part of Fairview Heights)	62208
Bunsenville	61846
Burbank	60459
Burches	60914
Bureau	61315
Bureau (Township)	61379
Burgess (Bond County) (Township)	62275
Burgess (Mercer County)	61231
Burksville	62298
Burlington	60109
Burlington (Township)	60109
Burnham	60633
Burnham Mill (Part of Elgin)	60123
Burns (Township)	61443
Burnside (Cook County)	60617
Burnside (Hancock County)	62318
Burnside's Lakewood (Part of Richton Park)	60466
Burnt Prairie	62820
Burnt Prairie (Township)	62821
Burritt (Township)	61088
Burr Oak (Part of Blue Island)	60406
Burr Oaks (Part of Joliet)	60435
Burrowsville	61929
Burr Ridge	60521
Burt	61721
Burton	62301
Burton (Adams County) (Township)	62301

	ZIP
Burton (McHenry County) (Township)	60081
Burtons Bridge	60050
Burtonview	62656
Bush (Jackson County)	62901
Bush (Williamson County)	62924
Bushnell	61422
Bushnell (Township)	61422
Bushton	61920
Butler (Montgomery County)	62015
Butler (Vermilion County) (Township)	60960
Butler Grove (Township)	62015
Butterfield	60148
Butterfield West	60137
Button (Township)	60960
Buysse Addition	61240
Buzzville	62644
Byron	61010
Byron (Township)	61010
Byron Hills (Ogle County)	61010
Byron Hills (Rock Island County)	61275
Cabery	60919
Cable	61281
Cache	62913
Cadiz	62931
Cadwell	61911
Cahokia (Macoupin County) (Township)	62023
Cahokia (St. Clair County)	62206
Cairo	62914
Caledonia	61011
Caledonia (Township)	61011
Calhoun	62419
Calumet (Township)	60406
Calumet (Part of East Hazel Crest)	60429
Calumet City	60409
Calumet Harbor (Part of Chicago)	60633
Calumet Park	60643
Calvin	62827
Camargo	61919
Camargo (Township)	61919
Cambria	62915
Cambridge	61238
Cambridge (Township)	61238
Cambridge (Part of Libertyville)	60048
Camden	62319
Camden (Township)	62319
Camelot	62401
Cameo Terrace (Part of Wheeling)	60090
Cameron	61423
Campbell Hill	62916
Campbells Island	61244
Camp Epworth	61038
Camp Ground	62864
Camp Grove	61424
Camp Logan	60099
Camp Point	62320
Camp Point (Township)	62320
Campton (Township)	60183
Campus	60920
Campus Walk (Part of Elgin)	60120
Camridge West (Part of Mundelein)	60060
Candlewood Estates	61853
Canoe Creek (Township)	61257
Canteen (Township)	62204
Canterbury Lane (Part of Glenview)	60025
Canterbury Shopping Center (Part of Markham)	60426
Canton	61520
Canton (Township)	61520
Cantrall	62625
Capital (Township)	62707
Capitol (Part of Springfield)	62701
Capri Gardens	60074
Capri Village	60074
Capron	61012
Carbon (Part of O'Fallon)	62269
Carbon Cliff	61239
Carbondale	62901-03
For specific Carbondale Zip Codes call (618) 457-3800	
Carbon Hill	60416
Cardiff	60420
Carlinville (Township)	62626
Carlinville	62626
Carlock	61725
Carlsburg	62069
Carlyle	62231
Carlyle (Township)	62231
Carlysle (Part of Schaumburg)	60194
Carman	61425

COLLEGES & UNIVERSITIES

FINANCIAL INSTITUTIONS

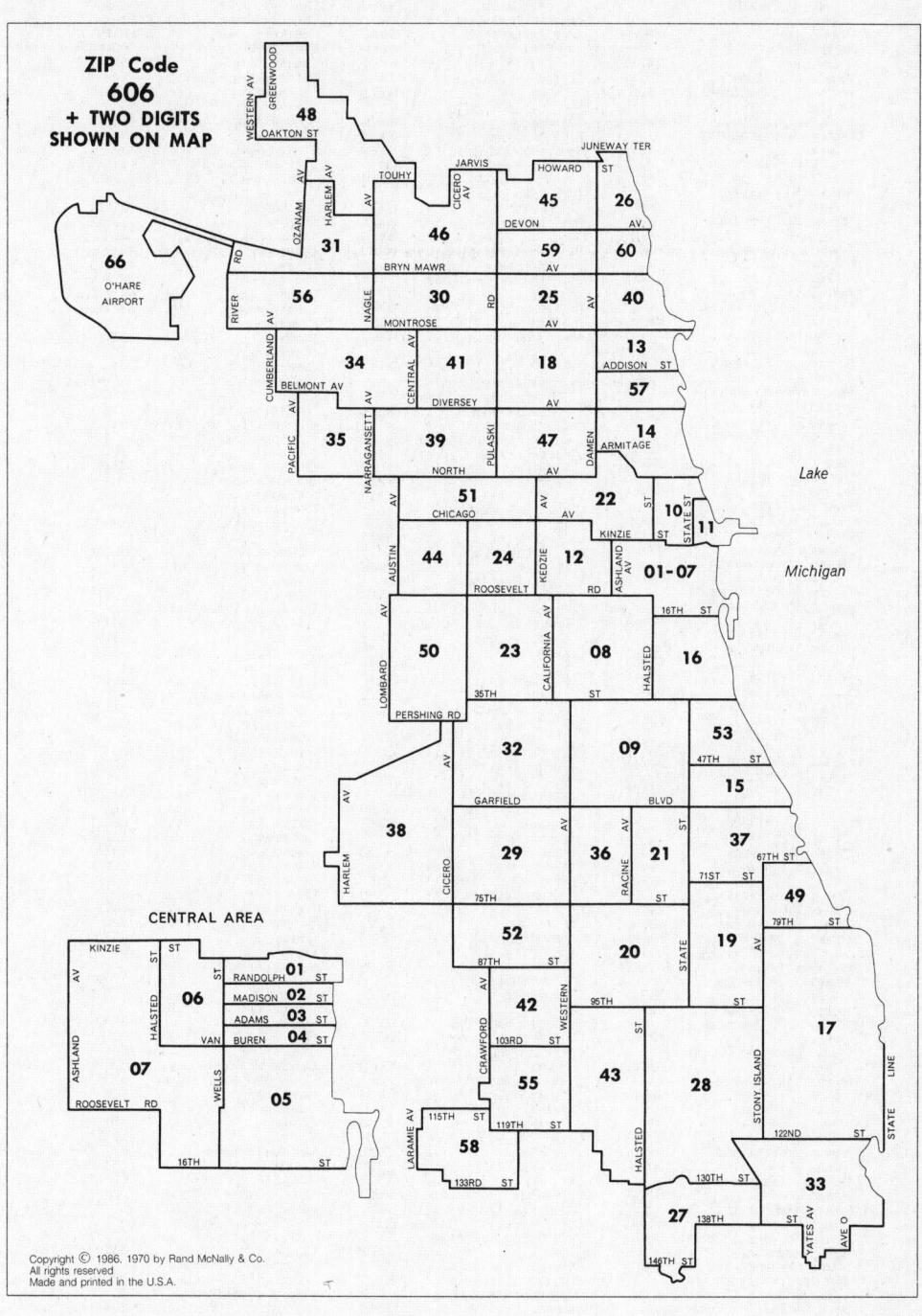

ZIP Code
606
+ TWO DIGITS
SHOWN ON MAP

	ZIP
Lincoln National Bank......	60613
Lincoln Park Federal Savings & Loan Association.............	60613
Madison Bank & Trust Company.............	60606
Manufacturer's Bank.......	60622
Marquette National Bank...	60636
Merchandise National Bank of Chicago.............	60654
Michigan Avenue National Bank.................	60602
The Mid-City National Bank of Chicago.............	60607
Midwest Bank and Trust Company.............	60635
Midwest Securities Trust Company.............	60605
Mount Greenwood Bank...	60655
National Security Bank of Chicago.............	60622
NBD Chicago Bank........	60601
Northern Trust Bank/O'Hare, N.A.	60631
The Northern Trust Company.............	60675
Northwestern Savings & Loan Association........	60647
Park National Bank and Trust Company of Chicago.............	60618
Peerless Federal Savings Bank	60630
Peterson Bank	60659
Pioneer Bank & Trust Company.............	60639
River Valley Savings Bank, F.S.B.	60606
St. Paul Federal Bank for Savings.............	60635
Seaway National Bank of Chicago.............	60619
Second Federal Savings & Loan Association of Chicago.............	60623
Security Federal Savings & Loan Association of Chicago.............	60622
South Shore Bank	60649
South Chicago Bank	60617
Standard Federal Bank for Savings.............	60632
The Steel City National Bank of Chicago	60617
LaSalle Talman Bank	60603
Uptown National Bank of Chicago	60640

HOSPITALS

	ZIP
Chicago Osteopathic Hospital and Medical Center.................	60615
Children's Memorial Hospital	60614
Columbus Hospital	60614
Cook County Hospital	60612
Edgewater Medical Center	60660
Grant Hospital of Chicago	60614
Holy Cross Hospital	60629
Illinois Masonic Medical Center.................	60657
Jackson Park Hospital	60649
Louis A. Weiss Memorial Hospital.................	60640
Mercy Hospital and Medical Center.................	60616
Humana Hospital Michael Reese	60616
Mount Sinai Hospital Medical Center of Chicago	60608
Northwestern Memorial Hospital.................	60611
Our Lady of Resurrection Medical Center..........	60634
Ravenswood Hospital Medical Center..........	60640
Resurrection Medical Center	60631
Rush-Presbyterian-St. Luke's Medical Center...	60612
Saint Mary of Nazareth Hospital Center	60622
South Chicago Community Hospital.................	60617
St. Elizabeth's Hospital	60622
St. Joseph Hospital and Health Care Center......	60657
University of Chicago Hospitals.................	60637
University of Illinois Hospital and Clinics at Chicago	60612

	ZIP
Veterans Affairs Lakeside Medical Center..........	60611
Veterans Affairs West Side Medical Center..........	60612

HOTELS/MOTELS

	ZIP
The Chicago Hilton and Towers	60605
The Congress Hotel of Chicago	60605
The Drake Hotel	60611
Holiday Inn-Mart Plaza	60654
Hyatt Regency Chicago in Illinois Center	60601
Knickerbocker-Chicago Hotel	60611
The O'Hare Hilton	60666
O'Hare Marriott Hotel	60631
The Mayfair Regent......	60611
The Palmer House Hilton...	60690
Park Hyatt on Water Tower Square	60611
The Ritz-Carlton	60611
The Tremont	60611
Westin Hotel Chicago......	60611

MILITARY INSTALLATIONS

	ZIP
Illinois Air National Guard, FB6121, Chicago O'Hare International Airport	60666
United States Army Engineer District Chicago	60606
928th Airlift Group, O'Hare Air Reserve Forces Facility	60666
Chicago Bulk Mail Center (Part of Forest Park).....	60799
Chicago Heights...........	60411
Chicago Lawn (Part of Chicago).................	60629
Chicago - Read Mental Health Center	60634
Chicago Ridge	60415
Chicago Ridge Mall (Part of Chicago Ridge)	60415
Chicken Bristle	61953
Chili.......................	62380
Chili (Township)	62380
Chillicothe.................	61523
Chillicothe (Township)	61523
Chilon Chalet (Part of Chicago Heights)........	60411
China (Township).........	61310
Chinatown (Part of Maryville)..............	62062
Chippendale (Part of Barrington)...............	60010
Chippewa	60658
Chippewa Ridge (Part of Alsip)...................	60658
Chittenden (Part of Gurnee)	60031
Chittyville (Part of Herrin)...	62948
Chouteau (Township)	62040
Chrisman	61924
Christopher.................	62822
Christy (Township).........	62466
Churchill (Part of Hoffman Estates)	60195
Churchville (Part of Bensenville).............	60126
Cicero	60650
Cicero (Township)	60650
Cimic (Part of Divernon) ...	62530
Cincinnati (Pike County) (Township)...............	62343
Cincinnati (Tazewell County) (Township)...............	61554
Cinnamon Creek (Part of Bolingbrook).............	60440
Circle Drive	61364
Circle Park	62565
Cisco	61830
Cisne	62823
Cissna Park	60924
Citation Lake Estates	60062
City Park (Part of Taylorville)	62568
Claburn (Part of Chicago)	60617
Clank	62988
Clare	60111
Claremont.................	62421
Claremont (Township)......	62421
Clarence	60960
Clarendon Hills	60514
Clarion (Township)........	61330
Clark Center	62441
Clarksburg	62565
Clarksburg (Township)	62565
Clarksdale.................	62556
Clarksville (Clark County)	62441
Clarksville (McLean County)	61753

	ZIP
Clarmin	62257
Clay City	62824
Clay City (Township)......	62824
Claypool	60450
Clays Prairie	61944
Clayton	62324
Clayton (Adams County) (Township)...............	62324
Clayton (Woodford County) (Township)...............	61516
Claytonville.................	60926
Clearing (Part of Chicago)	60638
Clear Lake (Township).....	62707
Clear Lake (Cass County)	62622
Clear Lake (Sangamon County).................	62707
Cleburne	62865
Clement (Township)	62252
Clements	62638
Cleone	62442
Cleveland	61241
Clifton	60927
Clifton Terrace	62035
Clifty Heights	62959
Clinch....................	62832
Clinton (De Witt County) ..	61727
Clinton (DeKalb County) (Township)...............	60556
Clintonia (Township)	61727
Clover (Township)	61490
Cloverdale (DuPage County)	60103
Cloverdale (Tazewell County).................	61611
Cloverleaf (Madison County)	62060
Cloverleaf (Rock Island County).................	61265
Clybourn (Part of Chicago)	60610
Clyde (Cook County)	60650
Clyde (Whiteside County) (Township)...............	61270
Coach Homes of Willow Bend (Part of Rolling Meadows)	60008
Coach Light Manor (Part of Mount Prospect)	60056
Coal City.................	60416
Coal Hollow	61356
Coalton	62075
Coal Valley	61240
Coal Valley (Township)	61240
Coatsburg	62325
Cobblestone	60025
Cobblewood (Part of Northbrook)	60062
Cobden	62920
Coe (Township)	61275
Coello....................	62825
Coffeen	62017
Colby Point	60050
Colchester	62326
Colchester (Township)	62326
Coldbrook.................	61423
Coldbrook (Township)	61401
Cold Spring (Township)	62571
Colehour (Part of Chicago)	60617
Coleman	60177
Coles	61928
Coleta	61017
Colfax (Champaign County) (Township)...............	61851
Colfax (McLean County) ...	61728
College Hills Mall (Part of Normal)...............	61761
College Park (Part of Elgin)	60123
College View	60441
Collins (Will County)	60544
Collins (Winnebago County)	61080
Collinsville	62234
Collinsville (Township)	62234
Collison	61831
Colmar	62367
Coloma (Township)	61071
Colona	61241
Colona (Township)	61241
Colonial Gardens (Part of Machesney Park)........	61111
Colonial Manor (Part of Mount Prospect)	60056
Colonial Ridge	60016
Colonial Village (Madison County).................	62035
Colonial Village (Will County).................	60440
Colonial Village (Winnebago County).................	61108
Colony Grove	61853
Colony Park (Part of Carol Stream).................	60188
Colony Point (Part of Deerfield)	60015
Colp	62921

	ZIP
Columbia	62236
Columbia Village	61801
Columbus	62328
Columbus (Township)	62320
Colusa	62329
Colvin Park	60145
Como	61081
Compromise (Township)	61862
Compton	61318
Compton Pines	60175
Conant	62274
Concord (Adams County) (Township)	62324
Concord (Bureau County) (Township)	61361
Concord (Iroquois County) (Township)	60945
Concord (Morgan County)	62631
Condit (Township)	61840
Confidence	62418
Congerville	61729
Congress Park (Part of Brookfield)	60513
Conlogue	61944
Conover	60560
Conrad	62036
Continental Village (Part of Waukegan)	60085
Cooks Mills	61931
Cooksville	61730
Cooper (Township)	62563
Cooperstown	62353
Cooperstown (Township)	62353
Copley (Township)	61485
Cora	62280
Coral	60152
Coral (Township)	60180
Coral Gable (Part of O'Fallon)	62269
Cordova	61242
Cordova (Township)	61242
Corinth	62890
Cornell	61319
Cornerville	62935
Cornland	62519
Cornwall (Township)	61235
Cortese	60901
Cortland	60112
Cortland (Township)	60112
Corwin (Township)	62666
Costin (Part of Bloomington)	61701
Cottage (Township)	62946
Cottagegrove	62930
Cottage Hills	62018
Cotton Hill (Township)	62563
Cottonwood (Cumberland County) (Township)	62468
Cottonwood (Gallatin County)	62871
Coulterville	62237
Council Hill	61075
Council Hill (Township)	61075
Council Hill Station	61075
Country Acres (La Salle County)	61360
Country Acres (St. Clair County)	62220
Country Aire (Jefferson County)	62864
Country Aire (Kane County)	60120
Country Club	61938
Country Club Acres	62626
Country Club Heights	61938
Country Club Hills	60478
Country Club Manor (Part of Country Club Hills)	60477
Country Club Place	62223
Country Club Terrace	62220
Country Courts	61265
Country Estates	61254
Country Fair (Part of Champaign)	61821
Country Gardens (Part of Prospect Heights)	60070
Country Heights (Part of Mount Vernon)	62864
Country Knolls (Kane County)	60123
Country Knolls (Knox County)	61410
Country Lake	60563
Country Lake Estates	62613
Country Manor (Coles County)	61938
Country Manor (Effingham County)	62401
Country Manor (Henry County)	61254
Country Orchard	61938
Countryside (Cook County)	60525
Countryside (Kane County)	60560

	ZIP
Countryside (Kendall County)	60560
Countryside (Lake County)	60047
Countryside Estates	60922
Countryside Lake	60060
Countryside Manor	60048
Country Squire (Part of Urbana)	61801
Country Squire Estates	61032
Countryview Estates (Kane County)	60118
Country View Estates (Will County)	60565
Covel	61701
Coventry (Part of Crystal Lake)	60014
Coventry East (Part of Crystal Lake)	60014
Coventry West (Part of Crystal Lake)	60014
Covington	62271
Covington (Township)	62271
Covington Manor	60089
Cow Bell Lane	62274
Cowden	62422
Cowling	62863
Crab Orchard	62959
Crab Orchard Estates	62901
Cragin (Part of Chicago)	60639
Cragin Junction (Part of Chicago)	60639
Craig Manor (Part of Des Plaines)	60016
Crainville	62918
Cramers	61529
Crane Creek (Township)	62633
Cravat	62801
Crawford Countryside (Part of Matteson)	60443
Creal Springs	62922
Creek (Township)	61750
Creekside (Part of Matteson)	60443
Creekside (Part of Rolling Meadows)	60008
Creekwood	60439
Crenshaw	62959
Crescent (Township)	60953
Crescent City	60928
Cress Haven (Part of Naperville)	60563
Crest Haven (Part of Fairview Heights)	62221
Crest Hill	60435
Creston	60113
Crestview	60970
Crestview Terrace (Part of Fairfield)	62837
Crestwood	60445
Crestwood Estates	62959
Crete	60417
Crete (Township)	60417
Creve Coeur	61611
Cricket Hill (Part of Matteson)	60443
Crisp	62895
Crittenden (Township)	61880
Crocketts Estates	60041
Crook (Township)	62859
Crooked Creek (Cumberland County) (Township)	62428
Crooked Creek (Jasper County) (Township)	62432
Crooked Lake	60046
Crooked Lake Oaks	60046
Cropsey	61731
Cropsey (Township)	61731
Cross County Mall (Part of Mattoon)	61938
Crossroads (Johnson County)	62995
Crossroads (St. Clair County)	62232
Crossroad Terrace (Part of Fairview Heights)	62232
Crossville	62827
Crouch (Township)	62895
Crown Estates (Part of Elmhurst)	60126
Cruger	61530
Cruger (Township)	61530
Crystal Gardens (Part of Crystal Lake)	60014
Crystal Lake (Jersey County)	62012
Crystal Lake (Madison County)	62035
Crystal Lake (McHenry County)	60012
	60014

	ZIP
	60039
For specific Crystal Lake Zip Codes call (815) 459-0140	
Crystal Lake Estates	60014
Crystal Lawns	60435
Crystal Manor (Part of Crystal Lake)	60014
Crystal Point Mall (Part of Crystal Lake)	60014
Crystal Vista (Part of Crystal Lake)	60014
Cuba (Fulton County)	61427
Cuba (Lake County) (Township)	60010
Cullom	60929
Cumberland (Part of Des Plaines)	60016
Cumberland Green (Part of St. Charles)	60174
Cumberland Heights (Part of Fairfield)	62837
Cumberland Highlands (Part of Des Plaines)	60016
Cunningham (Township)	61801
Cunningham Courts (Part of Palatine)	60067
Curran	62670
Curran (Township)	62670
Custer (Township)	60481
Custer Park	60481
Cutler	62238
Cypress	62923
Cypress Gardens	62901
D'Adrian Gardens	62035
Daggetts	61053
Dahinda	61428
Dahlgren	62828
Dahlgren (Township)	62828
Dailey	61862
Dakota	61018
Dakota (Township)	61018
Dale (Hamilton County)	62829
Dale (McLean County) (Township)	61772
Dale Valley	61853
Dallasania	62917
Dallas City	62330
Dallas City (Township)	62330
Dalton City	61925
Dalzell	61320
Damiansville	62215
Dana	61321
Danada North (Part of Wheaton)	60187
Danada West (Part of Wheaton)	60187
Danforth	60930
Danforth (Township)	60930
Danvers	61732
Danvers (Township)	61732
Danville	61832
	61834
For specific Danville Zip Codes call (217) 446-9440	
Danville (Township)	61832
Danville Junction (Part of Danville)	61832
Danway	61341
Darien	60561
Darmstadt	62255
Darrow	60966
Darwin	62477
Darwin (Township)	62477
Davis	61019
Davis Junction	61020
Dawson (McLean County) (Township)	61737
Dawson (Sangamon County)	62520
Dawson Park	60953
Daysville	61061
Dayton	61350
Dayton (Township)	61350
Dearborn Heights (Part of Oak Lawn)	60453
Decatur	62521-26
For specific Decatur Zip Codes call (217) 428-4474	
Decker (Township)	62868
Decorra	61480
Deep Lake	60046
Deep Spring Woods	60097
Deep Woods (Part of Mundelein)	60060
Deerbrook Mall (Part of Deerfield)	60015
Deer Creek	61733
Deer Creek (Township)	61733
Deerfield (Lake County) (Township)	60035

	ZIP		ZIP		ZIP
Eighty-Third Street (Part of Chicago)	60617	Emmet (Township)	61455	Fairway Estates (DuPage County)	60187
Eiker Addition	61448	Empire (Township)	61752	Fall Creek	62360
Eileen (Part of Coal City)	60416	Empire Hills	60175	Fall Creek (Township)	62360
Ela (Township)	60047	Enchanted Forest	61604	Fall River (Township)	61350
Elam Lake	61951	Energy	62933	Falmouth	62448
Elba (Gallatin County)	62871	Enfield	62835	Fancher	62444
Elba (Knox County) (Township)	61489	Enfield (Township)	62835	Fancy Creek (Township)	62684
Elba Center	61572	Engelmann (Township)	62258	Fancy Prairie	62613
Elbridge	61944	England Heights	62901	Fandon	62326
Elbridge (Township)	61944	Englewood (Part of Chicago)	60621	Fargo	62375
Elburn	60119	English (Township)	62052	Farina	62838
Elco	62929	Enion	62644	Farmer City	61842
El Dara	62312	Enos	62626	Farmers (Township)	61482
Eldena	61324	Enright	61738	Farmersville	62533
Elderville	62313	Enterprise	62823	Farmingdale (DuPage County)	60561
Eldorado (McDonough County) (Township)	61411	Eola	60519	Farmingdale (Sangamon County)	62677
Eldorado (Saline County)	62930	Eppards Point (Township)	61764	Farmingdale South (Part of Darien)	60561
Eldred	62027	Epworth	62821	Farmingdale Terrace (Part of Darien)	60561
Eleanor	61453	Equality	62934		
Eleroy	61027	Equality (Township)	62934	Farmingdale Village (Part of Darien)	60561
Elgin	60120-23	Erie	61250		
For specific Elgin Zip Codes call (708) 741-0725		Erie (Township)	61250	Farmington (Township)	61531
		Erienna (Township)	60450	Farmington (Kane County)	60174
Elgin Estates	60123	Erin (Township)	61027	Farmington (Lake County)	60047
Eliza	61272	Erontenac	60118	Farmington (Coles County)	62440
Eliza (Township)	61272	Esmen (Township)	60460	Farmington (Fulton County)	61531
Elizabeth	61028	Esmond	60129	Farm Ridge (Township)	61325
Elizabeth (Township)	61028	Essex	60935	Farmsted (Part of Naperville)	60565
Elizabethtown	62931	Essex (Kankakee County) (Township)	60935	Farnsworth (Part of Waukegan)	60088
Elk (Township)	62932				
Elk Grove (Township)	60007	Essex (Stark County) (Township)	61491	Farrington (Township)	62814
Elk Grove Village	60007			Farrow	61605
	60009	Estate Lane (Part of Glenview)	60025	Fayette (Greene County)	62044
For specific Elk Grove Village Zip Codes call (708) 439-5573		Etherton	62966	Fayette (Livingston County) (Township)	61775
		Eubanks	62301		
Elkhart	62634	Euclid Lake (Part of Mount Prospect)	60056	Fayetteville	62258
Elkhart (Township)	62634			Fayetteville (Township)	62258
Elkhorn	62353	Eureka	61530	Fayville	62990
Elkhorn Grove (Township)	61051	Evans	61377	Federal Penitentiary	62959
Elk Prairie (Township)	62816	Evans (Township)	61377	Feehanville (Part of Mount Prospect)	60056
Elk Ridge Villa (Part of Mount Prospect)	60056	Evanston	60201-04		
		For specific Evanston Zip Codes call (708) 328-6201		Felix (Township)	60416
Elkton	62268			Felker (Part of Washington)	61571
Elkville	62932	Evansville	62242	Fenton	61251
Ellery	62833	Evarts	61067	Fenton (Township)	61251
Ellington	62301	Evergreen Park	60642	Fergestown	62959
Ellington (Township)	62301	Evergreen Plaza (Part of Evergreen Park)	60642	Fernway (Part of Orland Park)	60462
Elliott	60933				
Elliottstown	62424	Ewing	62836	Ferrel	61944
Ellis	61865	Ewing (Township)	62836	Ferrin	62231
Ellis Grove	62241	Exeter	62621	Ferris	62336
Ellison (Township)	61478	Exline	60901	Fiatt	61433
Ellisville	61431	Expo Park (Part of Hoffman Estates)	60192	Ficklin	61953
Ellisville (Township)	61431			Fiday View	60435
Ellsworth	61737	Eylar	61769	Fidelity	62030
Ellwood Greens	60135	Ezra	62896	Fidelity (Township)	62030
Elm Estates (Part of Elmhurst)	60126	Factory Outlet Mall (Part of Kankakee)	60901	Field (Township)	62889
				Fieldcrest (Part of Oak Forest)	60452
Elm Grove (Township)	61554	Fairbanks	61937		
Elmhurst	60126	Fairbury	61739	Fieldon	62031
Elmira	61483	Fair City	62952	Fields West	61821
Elmira (Township)	61483	Fairdale	60146	Fifty-Fifth Street (Part of Chicago)	60615
Elmore	61451	Fairfield (Bureau County) (Township)	61283		
El Morro (Part of Oak Forest)	60452			Fifty-Ninth Street (Part of Chicago)	60637
		Fairfield (Lake County)	60047		
Elm River (Township)	62842	Fairfield (Wayne County)	62837	Fifty-Seventh Street (Part of Chicago)	60637
Elmwood	61529	Fairfield Heights	61032		
Elmwood (Township)	61529	Fair Grange	61920	Fillmore	62032
Elmwood Park	60635	Fair Haven	61014	Fillmore (Township)	62032
El Paso	61738	Fairhaven (Township)	61014	Filson	61910
El Paso (Township)	61738	Fairland	61956	Findlay	62534
El-Rancho	60901	Fairman	62882	Finley Square Mall (Part of Downers Grove)	60515
Elsah	62028	Fairmont	60441		
Elsah (Township)	62028	Fairmont City	62201	Finney Heights	62801
Elsdon (Part of Chicago)	60632	Fairmount (Madison County)	62002	First Pommier	60964
El Sierra (Part of Downers Grove)	60515	Fairmount (Pike County) (Township)	62314	Fisher	61843
				Fishhook	62314
Elva	60115	Fairmount (Vermilion County)	61841	Fithian	61844
Elvaston	62334			Five Islands Park	60177
Elvira	62912	Fairmount (Massac County)	62960	Flag Center	61068
El Vista (Cook County)	60452	Fair Oaks (Cook County)	60103	Flagg	61068
El Vista (Peoria County)	61604	Fair Oaks (DuPage County)	60185	Flagg (Township)	61068
Elwin	62532	Fair Oaks (Kane County)	60175	Flamingo Estates	62286
Elwood (Vermilion County) (Township)	61870	Fairview (Township)	61432	Flanagan	61740
		Fairview (Part of Fairview Heights)	62232	Flannigan (Township)	62890
Elwood (Will County)	60421			Flat Branch (Township)	62550
Embarrass (Township)	61949	Fairview (Christian County)	62568	Flat Rock	62427
Emden	62635	Fairview (Cook County)	60176	Flatville	61878
Emerald Green (Part of Warrenville)	60555	Fairview (Fulton County)	61432	Flat Woods	62985
		Fairview Addition	62930	Fletcher	61730
Emerald Park	60050	Fairview Avenue (Part of Downers Grove)	60515	Flickerville	60914
Emerald Terrace	62223			Flint (Township)	62340
Emerson	61081	Fairview Gardens (Part of Mount Prospect)	60056	Flora (Boone County) (Township)	61008
Emerson City	62883				
Eminence (Township)	61721	Fairview Heights	62208	Flora (Clay County)	62839
Emington	60934	Fairway	61401	Floraville	62298
Emma	62834	Fairway Estates (Cook County)	60462		
Emma (Township)	62834				

	ZIP
Florence (Stephenson County) (Township)	61032
Florence (Will County) (Township)	60481
Florence (Pike County)	62363
Florence (Stephenson County)	61032
Florid	61327
Flossmoor	60422
Flossmoor Highlands (Part of Flossmoor)	60422
Flowerfield Acres (Part of Lombard)	60148
Floyd (Township)	61423
Fondulac (Tazewell County) (Township)	61611
Fon-Du-Lac (Will County)	60544
Foosland	61845
Ford City Shopping Center (Part of Chicago)	60652
Fordham (Part of Chicago)	60619
Ford Heights	60411
Forest Acres	62201
Forest City	61532
Forest City (Township)	61532
Forest Estates	60067
Forest Gardens	60084
Forest Glen (Part of Chicago)	60630
Foresthaven	60045
Forest Heights (Part of Chicago Heights)	60411
Forest Hill (Part of Chicago)	60652
Forest Hills Estates	62471
Forest Homes	62018
Forest Lake	60047
Forest Manor	60441
Forest Park	60130
Forest River	60056
Forest View	60402
Forest View Hills (Part of Oak Forest)	60452
Forman	62908
Forrest	61741
Forrest (Township)	61741
Forrestal Village (Part of North Chicago)	60088
Forreston	61030
Forreston (Township)	61030
Forsyth	62535
Fort Dearborn (Part of Chicago)	60610
Fort Gage	62241
Fort Russell (Township)	62010
Forty-Seventh Street (Part of Chicago)	60615
Foss Acres (Part of Waukegan)	60088
Foster (Madison County) (Township)	62002
Foster (Marion County) (Township)	62807
Fosterburg	62002
Foster Pond	62298
Fountain	62295
Fountain Bluff (Township)	62950
Fountain Creek	60942
Fountain Creek (Township)	60942
Fountain Gap	62236
Fountain Green	62321
Fountain Green (Township)	62321
Four Lakes	60532
Four Mile (Township)	62895
Fowler	62338
Fox (Kendall County) (Township)	60560
Fox (Jasper County) (Township)	62448
Fox	60560
Fox Chase (Part of St. Charles)	60174
Foxcroft	60137
Foxfield	60175
Fox Lake	60020
Fox Lake Hills	60046
Fox Lake Vista	60081
Fox Lawn	60560
Fox Point (Part of Barrington)	60010
Fox Ridge (Part of South Elgin)	60177
Fox River Bluffs 2	60118
Fox River Estates	60174
Fox River Gardens	60560
Fox River Grove	60021
Fox River Heights	60174
Fox River Valley Gardens	60010
Fox Valley Center (Part of Aurora)	60505
Fox Valley East (Part of Aurora)	60505

	ZIP
Fox Valley Mail Processing Center	60598-99
For specific Fox Valley Mail Processing Center Zip Codes call (708) 897-2221	
Fox Valley Villages (Part of Aurora)	60505
Frankfort (Franklin County) (Township)	62896
Frankfort (Will County) (Township)	60423
Frankfort	60423
Frankfort Heights (Part of West Frankfort)	62840
Frankfort Square	60423
Franklin (DeKalb County) (Township)	60146
Franklin (Morgan County)	62638
Franklin Grove	61031
Franklin Park	60131
Franklin Square	60423
Franklinville	60098
Frederick	62639
Frederick (Township)	62639
Freeburg	62243
Freeburg (Township)	62243
Freedom (Carroll County) (Township)	61046
Freedom (La Salle County) (Township)	61350
Freeman Spur	62841
Freeport	61032
Freeport (Township)	61032
Fremont (Township)	60060
Fremont Center	60060
Fremont Junction (Part of Hanover Park)	60103
Frenchman's Cove (Part of Arlington Heights)	60004
French Village (Part of Fairview Heights)	62208
Frentress Lake	61025
Friends Creek (Township)	62501
Friendsville	62863
Frisco	62836
Frog City	62913
Frogtown (Clinton County)	62231
Frogtown (Washington County)	62271
Frontenac	60563
Frontenac Place	62035
Frost	62901
Fruit	62025
Fruitland	61265
Fry's Wheatland View	60565
Fulton	61252
Fulton (Township)	61252
Fults	62244
Funkhouser	62401
Funks Grove	61754
Funks Grove (Township)	61754
Future City	62914
Fyre Lake	61281
Gages Lake	60030
Galatia	62935
Galatia (Township)	62935
Gale	62990
Galena	61036
Galena Oaks	61028
Galesburg	61401-02
For specific Galesburg Zip Codes call (309) 342-6165	
Galesburg City (Township)	61401
Galesville	61854
Gallagher	62450
Galnipper Place	62047
Galt	61037
Galton	61910
Galva	61434
Galva (Township)	61434
Ganeer (Township)	60954
Ganntown	62943
Garber	60936
Gardena (Part of East Peoria)	61611
Garden Heights	62946
Garden Hill (Township)	62899
Garden Hills (Part of Champaign)	61821
Garden Homes	60655
Garden of Eden	60954
Garden Plain	61252
Garden Plain (Township)	61252
Garden Prairie	61038
Garden Quarter (Part of Elgin)	60123
Gardner (Grundy County)	60424
Gardner (Sangamon County) (Township)	62677
Gards Point	62863

	ZIP
Garfield (Grundy County) (Township)	60424
Garfield (La Salle County)	61377
Garfield Park (Part of Chicago)	60624
Garland	61917
Garrett	61913
Garrett (Township)	61913
Gary Gardens	60188
Gas Light Village	60450
Gateway Yard (Part of East St. Louis)	62207
Gays	61928
Geff	62842
Genesee (Township)	61270
Geneseo	61254
Geneseo (Township)	61254
Geneseo Hills	61254
Geneva	60134
Geneva (Township)	60134
Genoa	60135
Genoa (Township)	60135
Gent City	62959
Gentry Acres	62918
Georgetown (Township)	61846
Georgetown (Carroll County)	61046
Georgetown (McDonough County)	61455
Georgetown (Vermilion County)	61846
Gerald	61812
Gerlaw	61435
German (Township)	62421
Germantown (Clinton County)	62245
Germantown (Township)	62245
Germantown (Woodford County)	61548
Germantown Hills	61548
German Valley	61039
Germanville (Township)	60921
Gibson City	60936
Gibsonia	62954
Gifford	61847
Gila	62445
Gilberts	60136
Gilchrist	61486
Gilead	62006
Gillespie	62033
Gillespie (Township)	62033
Gillespie Lakes	62033
Gillum	61701
Gilman	60938
Gilmer (Township)	62328
Gilmore	62443
Gilmore Lake	62236
Gilson	61436
Ginger Creek (Part of Oak Brook)	60521
Ginger Hill (Part of Milan)	61264
Girard	62640
Girard (Township)	62640
Givins (Part of Chicago)	60620
Gladstone	61437
Gladstone (Township)	61437
Gladstone Commons (Part of Mount Prospect)	60056
Gladstone Park (Part of Chicago)	60630
Glasford	61533
Glasgow	62694
Glass Works (Part of Alton)	62002
Glen (Part of Glen Carbon)	62034
Glen Acres (Part of Rosemont)	60018
Glenarm	62536
Glen Arms	60041
Glenavon	61724
Glenayre (Part of Glenview)	60025
Glenayre Gardens (Part of Glenview)	60025
Glenbard South	60532
Glenbrook Countryside	60062
Glenburn	61858
Glen Carbon	62034
Glencoe	60022
Glendale (Pope County)	62985
Glendale (Rock Island County)	61282
Glendale Gardens (Part of Wood River)	62024
Glendale Heights	60139
Glen Ellyn	60137-38
For specific Glen Ellyn Zip Codes call (708) 469-1060	
Glen Ellyn Countryside	60137
Glen Ellyn Woods	60137
Glengarry (Part of Geneva)	60134
Glen Hill (Part of Glendale Heights)	60139

	ZIP
Hastings	61810
Hatcher Woods	60450
Havana	62644
Havana (Township)	62644
Haw Creek (Township)	61458
Hawthorn Center (Part of Vernon Hills)	60060
Hawthorne (Part of Chicago)	60623
Hawthorne (Part of Cicero)	60650
Hawthorne (White County) (Township)	62821
Hawthorn Woods	60047
Hawthrone Hills	62864
Hayes	61953
Hayford (Part of Chicago)	60652
Haymarket (Part of Chicago)	60606
Haypress	62027
Hazel Crest	60429
Hazelcrest Highlands (Part of Hazel Crest)	60429
Hazel Dell	62428
Hazelgreen (Part of Alsip)	60482
Hazelhurst	61064
Hazelwood	61254
Hazelwood Heights	61254
Hazelwood West	61254
Headyville	62424
Healy (Part of Chicago)	60639
Heapsville	61425
Heartville	62401
Heathercrest (Part of Northbrook)	60062
Heatherfield	60450
Heatherlea	60074
Heathsville	62427
Hebron	60034
Hebron (Township)	60034
Hecker	62248
Hegeler	61832
Hegewisch (Part of Chicago)	60633
Helena	62466
Helmar	60541
Helvetia (Township)	62249
Heman	62573
Henderson	61439
Henderson (Township)	61439
Henderson	62033
Henderson Grove	61401
Hendryx Manor	61614
Hennepin	61327
Hennepin (Township)	61327
Henning	61848
Henry	61537
Henry (Township)	61537
Hensley (Township)	61820
Henton	62565
Herald	62845
Heralds Prairie (Township)	62869
Herbert	60145
Herborn	62465
Heritage (Part of Moline)	61265
Heritage Estates (Part of Bourbonnais)	60914
Hermon	61458
Hermosa (Part of Chicago)	60639
Herod	62947
Herrick	62431
Herrick (Township)	62431
Herrin	62948
Herscher	60941
Hersman	62353
Hervey City	62549
Hettick	62649
Hewittville	62568
Heyworth	61745
Hickory (Township)	62624
Hickory Falls	60097
Hickory Grove	62301
Hickory Hill (Township)	62895
Hickory Hills (Cook County)	60457
Hickory Hills (Piatt County)	61884
Hickory Hollow	60118
Hickory Point (Macon County) (Township)	62526
Hickory Point (Shelby County)	62565
Hickoryville	63673
Hicks	62947
Hidalgo	62432
Hidden Creek	60074
Hidden Hills	61455
Higginsville	61865
High Knob	60187
High Lake	60185
Highland (Grundy County) (Township)	60437
Highland (Madison County)	62249
Highlander	62901

	ZIP
Highland Haven	60123
Highland Hills	60148
Highland Lake	60030
Highland Park (Lake County)	60035
Highland Park (Marion County)	62881
Highlands (Cook County)	60411
Highlands (DuPage County)	60521
Highlands-Clarks	60543
Highland Shores	60097
Highlawn (Part of Riverdale)	60627
High Meadows	61607
High Point (Part of Hoffman Estates)	60195
Highview Estates	60514
Highway Village (Part of East Peoria)	61611
Highwood (Lake County)	60040
Highwood (St. Clair County)	62221
Highwood Terrace (Part of Belleville)	62221
Hilcrest	62089
Hildreth	61876
Hill Correctional Center	61401
Hillcrest (Calhoun County)	62045
Hillcrest (Christian County)	62568
Hillcrest (Cook County)	60439
Hillcrest (Douglas County)	61953
Hillcrest (Henry County)	61254
Hillcrest (Ogle County)	61068
Hillcrest Shopping Center (Part of Crest Hill)	60435
Hilldale Villages (Part of Hoffman Estates)	60195
Hillerman	62941
Hillery	61832
Hillsboro	62049
Hillsboro (Township)	62049
Hillsdale	61257
Hillside (Cook County)	60162
Hillside (Kankakee County)	60901
Hillside-Berkeley (Part of Hillside)	60162
Hillside Mall (Part of Hillside)	60162
Hillside Manor	60901
Hill Top	62675
Hillview	62050
Hillyard (Township)	62676
Himrod	61883
Hinckley	60520
Hindsboro	61930
Hinsdale	60521-22
For specific Hinsdale Zip Codes call (708) 323-1490	
Hinswood (Part of Darien)	60561
Hire (Township)	62326
Hitt	61051
Hittle (Township)	61721
Hodgetown	62865
Hodgkins	60525
Hoffman	62250
Hoffman Estates	60194-95
For specific Hoffman Estates Zip Codes call (708) 885-6510	
Hoffmann Edition	60924
Holbrook	60411
Holcomb	61043
Holden	62832
Holder	61736
Holiday Hills	60050
Holiday Shores	62025
Holland	62414
Holland (Township)	62414
Hollandia	62221
Hollenback	60450
Hollendale (Part of South Holland)	60473
Holliday	62414
Hollis (Township)	61607
Hollowayville	61356
Hollydale (Part of Homewood)	60430
Hollywood (Part of Brookfield)	60513
Hollywood Heights	62232
Hollywood Ridge (Part of Wheeling)	60090
Holmes Center	61523
Homberg	62938
Home Gardens (Part of Danville)	61832
Homer (Champaign County)	61849
Homer (Will County) (Township)	60441
Homerican Villas (Part of Des Plaines)	60016
Homestead (Part of O'Fallon)	62269
Hometown	60456
Homewood (Cook County)	60430

	ZIP
Homewood (Rock Island County)	61265
Homewood Acres	60430
Homewood Shores (Part of Homewood)	60430
Homewood Terrace (Part of Homewood)	60430
Honegger	61741
Honey Bend	62056
Honey Creek (Adams County) (Township)	62325
Honey Creek (Crawford County) (Township)	62427
Honey Creek (Ogle County)	61015
Honey Point (Township)	62056
Hononegah Heights	61073
Hoodville	62859
Hookdale	62284
Hoopeston	60942
Hooppole	61258
Hoosier (Township)	62858
Hope (La Salle County) (Township)	61334
Hope (Vermilion County)	61812
Hopedale	61747
Hopedale (Township)	61747
Hopewell	61565
Hopewell (Township)	61540
Hop Hollow	62035
Hopkins (Township)	61081
Hopkins Park	60944
Hopper	61480
Horace	61924
Horatio Gardens	60069
Hord	62858
Hornsby	62056
Horseshoe	62934
Houston (Adams County) (Township)	62339
Houston (Randolph County)	62286
Howardton	62942
Howe (Part of Depue)	61322
Howe Terrace	60010
Hoyleton	62803
Hoyleton (Township)	62803
Hubbard Woods (Cook County)	60093
Hubbard Woods (Marion County)	62801
Hubly	62642
Hudgens	62959
Hudson	61748
Hudson (Township)	61748
Huegely	62803
Huey	62252
Hugh's Addition	62684
Hugo	61953
Hull	62343
Humboldt	61931
Humboldt (Township)	61931
Hume (Edgar County)	61932
Hume (Whiteside County) (Township)	61071
Humm Wye	62938
Humrick	61870
Hunt City	62480
Hunt City (Township)	62480
Hunter (Boone County)	61011
Hunter (Edgar County)	61944
Hunter (Edgar County) (Township)	61944
Hunter Trail (Part of Oak Brook)	60521
Huntington (Part of Naperville)	60540
Huntington Commons (Part of Mount Prospect)	60056
Huntington Park (Part of Elgin)	60120
Huntinton Park	62035
Huntley	60142
Huntsville	62344
Huntsville (Township)	62344
Hurlbut (Township)	62634
Hurricane (Township)	62080
Hurst	62949
Hutchins Park	61103
Hutsonville	62433
Hutsonville (Township)	62433
Hutton	61920
Hutton (Township)	61920
Hyde Park (Part of Chicago)	60653
Idaville Corner	60924
Ideal	61285
Idlewild	60030
Idlewood	62864
Iliana	47982
Illiana Heights	60954
Illini (Township)	62573
Illinois City	61259

	ZIP
La Grange Highlands	60525
La Grange Park	60525
La Grange Road (Part of La Grange)	60525
Laguna Woods	60462
La Harpe	61450
La Harpe (Township)	61450
La Hogue	60938
Lake	62283
Lake (Township)	62801
Lake Barrington	60010
Lake Bluff	60044
Lake Boulevard Addition	61832
Lake Bracken	61401
Lake Briarwood	60004
Lake Camelot	61547
Lake Carlinville	62626
Lake Catherine	60002
Lake Centralia	62801
Lake Charleston	61920
Lake Charlotte	60174
Lake City	61937
Lakecrest (Montgomery County)	62049
Lake Crest (Williamson County)	62922
Lake Estates	62959
Lake Forest	60045
Lake Forest Estates (Part of Belleville)	62221
Lake Fork	62541
Lake Fork (Township)	62548
Lake Holiday	60548
Lakehurst Shopping Center (Part of Waukegan)	60085
Lake in the Hills	60102
Lake in the Woods	60515
Lake Iroquois	60948
Lake Ka-Ho	62069
Lake Killarney	60013
Lake Lancelot	61547
Lakeland Hills (Jackson County)	62901
Lakeland Hills (St. Clair County)	62221
Lakeland Park (Part of McHenry)	60050
Lake Lawrence	47591
Lake Louise	61010
Lake Lynwood (Cook County)	60411
Lake Lynwood (Henry County)	61262
Lake Mantero	60950
Lake Marie	60002
Lake Marion	60110
Lake Mattoon	62447
Lakemoor	60050
Lake Oakland	61943
Lake of the Winds (Part of Wheeling)	60090
Lake of the Woods (Champaign County)	61820
Lake of the Woods (Peoria County)	61525
Lake Pana	62557
Lake Park (Champaign County)	61821
Lake Park (Cook County)	60615
Lake Park Estates	60067
Lake Park Forest	60067
Lake Petersburg	62675
Lake Piasa	62012
Lake Ranier	62626
Lake Sara	62401
Lakeshore Acres	62231
Lakeside Knolls	62049
Lakeside Villas (Part of Wheeling)	60090
Lake Summerset	61019
Lake Tacoma	62901
Lake Tara Estates	60118
Lake Thunderbird	61560
Lakeview (Part of Chicago)	60613
Lakeview Acres	62234
Lakeview Estate	62881
Lakeview Estates (Jefferson County)	62864
Lake View Estates (Williamson County)	62958
Lakeview Heights (Part of Fairfield)	62837
Lake Villa	60046
Lake Villa (Township)	60046
Lake Wildwood	61336
Lake Williamson	62626
Lakewood (Township)	62438
Lakewood (Cook County)	60466
Lakewood (DuPage County)	60185
Lakewood (Madison County)	62035

	ZIP
Lakewood (McHenry County)	60014
Lakewood (Shelby County)	62438
Lakewood Park	62901
Lakewood Shores	60481
Lakewood Village (Part of Carpentersville)	60110
Lake Zurich	60047
Lamard (Township)	62842
Lamb	62919
Lambert	60439
La Moille	61330
La Moille (Township)	61349
Lamoine (Township)	61415
Lamotte (Township)	62451
Lamplighter (Part of Towanda)	61776
Lanark	61046
Lancaster (Stephenson County) (Township)	61032
Lancaster (Wabash County)	62855
Landers (Part of Chicago)	60652
Landes	62466
Landings, The (Part of Lansing)	60438
Lane	61750
Lanesville	62515
Lanesville (Township)	62515
Langleyville	62568
Lansing	60438
Laona (Township)	61024
La Place	61936
La Prairie (Adams County)	62346
La Prairie (Marshall County) (Township)	61523
La Prairie Center	61565
Larchland	61462
Larkdale (Lake County)	60084
Larkdale (Macon County)	62521
Larkinsburg (Township)	62426
La Rose	61541
La Salle	61301
La Salle (Township)	61301
Latham	62543
Latona	62479
Laura	61451
La Vergne (Part of Berwyn)	60402
Lawndale (Logan County)	61751
Lawndale (McLean County) (Township)	61728
Lawn Ridge	61526
Lawrence (Lawrence County) (Township)	62439
Lawrence (McHenry County)	60033
Lawrenceville	62439
Lawrencewood Shopping Center (Part of Niles)	60714
Layton	62681
Leaf River	61047
Leaf River (Township)	61047
Leaverton Park	62451
Lebanon	62254
Lebanon (Township)	62254
Leclaire (Part of Edwardsville)	62025
Ledford	62946
Lee (Brown County) (Township)	62375
Lee (Fulton County) (Township)	61470
Lee (Lee County)	60530
Lee Center	61331
Lee Center (Township)	61331
Leech (Township)	62833
Leeds	61377
Leef (Township)	62249
Leepertown (Township)	61315
Leesburg	61501
Leesville	60964
Lehigh	60901
Leisure Lea	60543
Leisure Village (Part of Fox Lake)	60020
Leland	60531
Leland Grove	62707
Leland Lake	62650
Lemont	60439
Lemont (Township)	60439
Le Moyne (Part of Chicago)	60638
Lena	61048
Lenox (Township)	61462
Lenzburg	62255
Lenzburg (Township)	62257
Leonard	60938
Leon Corners	61277
Leonore	61332
L'Erable	60927
Lerna	62440
Le Roy (Boone County) (Township)	61012

	ZIP
Le Roy (McLean County)	61752
Levan (Township)	62966
Levee (Township)	62343
Leverett	61821
Lewistown	61542
Lewistown (Township)	61542
Lewood	60544
Lexington	61753
Lexington (Township)	61753
Leyden (Township)	60131
Liberty	62347
Liberty (Township)	62347
Liberty (Effingham County) (Township)	62414
Liberty (Saline County)	62946
Liberty Acres	60048
Liberty Lake (Part of Libertyville)	60048
Liberty Park	60559
Libertyville	60048
For specific Libertyville Zip Codes call (708) 362-2266	
Libertyville (Township)	60048
Lick	62629
Lick Creek	62912
Licking (Township)	62449
Lidice (Part of Crest Hill)	60435
Lightsville	61047
Lilac Circle Homes (Part of Lombard)	60148
Lilly	61755
Lily Cache	60544
Lily Cache Acres	60544
Lily Lake	60151
Lilymoor	60050
Lima	62348
Lima (Township)	62348
Limerick	61349
Limestone (Kankakee County) (Township)	60901
Limestone (Peoria County) (Township)	61604
Limestone (Peoria County)	61607
Lincoln (Logan County)	62656
Lincoln (Ogle County) (Township)	61064
Lincoln Addition (Part of Wood River)	62095
Lincoln Correctional Center	62656
Lincoln Developmental Center	62656
Lincoln Estates	60423
Lincoln Gardens (Part of Alton)	62002
Lincoln Highway (Part of Olympia Fields)	60461
Lincoln Hills	60137
Lincoln Mall (Part of Matteson)	60443
Lincoln Park (Part of Chicago)	60614
Lincolnshire (Lake County)	60069
Lincolnshire (Will County)	60417
Lincolnshire Fields	61821
Lincolnwood	60645
Lincolnwood Hills	60451
Lincolnwood Town Center (Part of Lincolnwood)	60645
Lindenhurst	60046
Lindenhurst Estates (Part of Lindenhurst)	60046
Lindenwood	61049
Linder (Township)	62016
Linn (Wabash County)	62410
Linn (Woodford County) (Township)	61570
Linrose Heights	62216
Lintner	61929
Lioncrest (Part of Richton Park)	60466
Lis	62448
Lisbon	60541
Lisbon (Township)	60541
Lisbon Center	60541
Lisle	60532
Lisle (Township)	60532
Litchfield (Kankakee County)	60954
Litchfield (Montgomery County)	62056
Literberry	62660
Little America	61542
Little Indian	62691
Little Mackinaw (Township)	61759
Little Rock	60545
Little Rock (Township)	60545
Little Swan Lake	61415
Littleton	61452
Littleton (Township)	61452

	ZIP		ZIP		ZIP
Little York	61453	Lynn (Henry County)		Mannon	61272
Lively Grove	62268	(Township)	61262	Mansfield	61854
Lively Grove (Township)	62268	Lynn (Knox County)		Manteno	60950
Liverpool	61543	(Township)	61414	Manteno (Township)	60950
Liverpool (Township)	61543	Lynn Center	61262	Manville	61319
Livingston (Clark County)	62441	Lynn Gardens	60901	Maplebrook (Part of	
Livingston (Madison		Lynnville (Morgan County)	62650	Naperville)	60565
County)	62058	Lynnville (Ogle County)		Maple Grove	62476
Loami	62661	(Township)	61049	Maple Lane	61081
Loami (Township)	62661	Lynnwood (Cook County)	60411	Maple Park	60151
Loch Lomond (Part of		Lynnwood (Kendall County)	60543	Maple Point	62428
Mundelein)	60060	Lynnwood (La Salle County)	61354	Maples Mill	61542
Lockhaven	62035	Lynwood	60411	Mapleton	61547
Lockport	60441	Lyons	60534	Maplewood (Cook County)	60647
Lockport (Township)	60441	Lyons (Township)	60525	Maplewood (St. Clair	
Locust (Township)	62555	Lyons (Part of Belgium)	61883	County)	62206
Loda	60948	McCall	62321	Maplewood Estates	61520
Loda (Township)	60948	McClellan (Township)	62894	Maquon	61458
Lodemia	61739	McClure	62957	Maquon (Township)	61458
Lodge	61856	McClusky	62052	Marblehead	62301
Logan (Edgar County)	61924	McConnell	61050	Marcelline	62376
Logan (Franklin County)	62856	McCook	60525	Marcoe	62864
Logan (Peoria County)		McCormick	62987	Mardell Manor	61607
(Township)	61536	McCullom Lake	60050	Marengo	60152
Logan Correctional Center	62656	McCully	61764	Marengo (Township)	60152
Logan Square (Part of		McDowell	61764	Marietta	61459
Chicago)	60647	Macedonia	62860	Marigold	62242
Log Cabin Camp	60954	McGirr	60556	Marina Terrace	60543
Lomax	61454	McHenry	60050-51	Marina Village	60543
Lomax (Township)	61454	For specific McHenry Zip Codes		Marine	62061
Lombard	60148	call (815) 385-0816		Marine (Township)	62061
Lombardville	61421	McHenry Shores (Part of		Marion (Lee County)	
London Mills	61544	McHenry)	60050	(Township)	61310
Lone Grove (Township)	62880	Machesney Park	61111	Marion (Ogle County)	
Lone Tree	61368	Machesney Park Mall (Part		(Township)	61015
Long Branch (Mason		of Machesney Park)	61111	Marion (Williamson County)	62959
County)	62644	MacIntoch	61364	Marion Circle	60554
Long Branch (Saline		McIntosh	60123	Marion Country Club	62959
County) (Township)	62935	McKee (Township)	62347	Marion Hills (Part of Darien)	60561
Long Creek	62521	McKeen	62441	Marissa	62257
Long Creek (Township)	62521	McKendree (Township)	61832	Marissa (Township)	62257
Long Grove	60047	Mackinaw (Township)	61755	Mark	61340
Long Lake	60041	Mackinaw	61755	Market Place (Part of	
Long Meadow (Part of		Mackler Heights (Part of		Champaign)	61820
Downers Grove)	60515	Chicago Heights)	60411	Markham (Cook County)	60426
Long Point	61333	McLean	61754	Markham (Morgan County)	62628
Long Point (Township)	61333	McLeansboro	62859	Markham City (Part of	
Longshadow	60175	McLeansboro (Township)	62859	Bluford)	62814
Longview	61852	McNabb	61335	Marley (Edgar County)	61944
Longwood Farms (Part of		Macomb	61455	Marley (Will County)	60448
Chicago Heights)	60411	Macomb (Township)	61438	Marlow	62872
Longwood Manor	60563	Macomb City (Township)	61455	Marnico Village	62650
Loogootee	62857	Macon (Bureau County)		Maroa	61756
Looking Glass (Township)	62265	(Township)	61314	Maroa (Township)	61756
Lookout Point	60097	Macon (Macon County)	62544	Marquette Heights	61554
Loon Lake	60002	Macoupin	62676	Marrowbone (Township)	61914
Loop (Part of Chicago)	60604	McQueen	60185	Mars (Part of Chicago)	60639
Loraine (Adams County)	62349	McVey	62640	Marseilles	61341
Loraine (Henry County)		Madison (Madison County)	62060	Marshall	62441
(Township)	61277	Madison (Richland County)		Marshall (Township)	62441
Loran	61062	(Township)	62450	Marston	61279
Loran (Township)	61062	Madonnaville	62298	Martin (Crawford County)	
Lords' Park Manor (Part of		Maeystown (Monroe		(Township)	62454
Elgin)	60120	County)	62256	Martin (McLean County)	
Lorenzo	60481	Magnet	61938	(Township)	61728
Loretto	60460	Magnolia	61336	Martinsburg	62363
Lorraine Park (Part of		Magnolia (Township)	61336	Martinsburg (Township)	62363
Wheaton)	60187	Mahomet	61853	Martinsville	62442
Lostant	61334	Mahomet (Township)	61853	Martinsville (Township)	62442
Lost Lake	61070	Maine (Cook County)		Martinton	60951
Lost Nation	61021	(Township)	60016	Martinton (Township)	60951
Lotus	61845	Maine (Grundy County)		Mary Crest (Part of Country	
Lotus Woods	60081	(Township)	60444	Club Hills)	60477
Lou Del	62298	Main Post Office (Part of		Marydale	62231
Loudon (Township)	62414	Chicago)	60607	Marydale Manor (Part of	
Louis Joliet Mall (Part of		Main Street (Part of		Dolton)	60419
Joliet)	60435	Evanston)	60202	Maryland	61064
Louisville	62858	Makanda	62958	Maryland (Township)	61007
Louisville (Township)	62858	Makanda (Township)	62958	Mary Meadows	60175
Love (Township)	61870	Malden	61337	Maryville	62062
Lovejoy (Iroquois County)		Malibu Village	62901	Mascoutah	62258
(Township)	60973	Mallard West (Part of		Mascoutah (Township)	62258
Lovejoy (St. Clair County)	62059	Schaumburg)	60194	Mason	62443
Loves Park	61111	Malone (Township)	61534	Mason (Township)	62443
Lovington	61937	Malta	60150	Mason City (Township)	62664
Lovington (Township)	61937	Malta (Township)	60150	Mason City	62664
Lowder	62662	Malvern	61270	Massbach	61028
Lowe (Township)	61911	Manchester (Boone County)		Massilon (Township)	62883
Lowell	61370	(Township)	61011	Matanzas Beach	62644
Lowpoint	61545	Manchester (Scott County)	62663	Matherville	61263
Loxa	61938	Manhattan	60442	Matteson	60443
Lucas (Township)	62424	Manhattan (Township)	60442	Mattoon	61938
Ludlow	60949	Manito	61546	Mattoon (Township)	61938
Ludlow (Township)	60949	Manito (Township)	61546	Maud	62863
Lukin (Township)	62417	Manlius	61338	Maunie	62861
Lumaghi Heights	62234	Manlius (Bureau County)		Maxwell (Township)	62661
Luther	62664	(Township)	61338	May (Christian County)	
Lyman (Township)	60962	Manlius (LaSalle County)		(Township)	62567
Lynchburg (Township)	62617	(Township)	61360	May (Lee County)	
Lyndon	61261	Mannheim (Part of Franklin		(Township)	61367
Lyndon (Township)	61261	Park)	60131		

	ZIP
Mayberry (Township)	62817
Mayfair (Cook County)	60630
Mayfair (Tazewell County)	61550
Mayfield (Township)	60178
Maynard Lake	61821
Mays	61944
Maysville	62340
Maytown	61310
Mayview	61801
Maywood	60153-54
For specific Maywood Zip Codes call (708) 344-4243	
Mazon	60444
Mazon (Township)	60444
Meacham (Township)	62854
Meadowbrook (Madison County)	62010
Meadowbrook (McDonough County)	61455
Meadowbrook East (Part of Wheeling)	60090
Meadowbrook West (Part of Wheeling)	60090
Meadowdale (Part of Carpentersville)	60110
Meadowdale Shopping Center (Part of Carpentersville)	60110
Meadow Heights (Part of Collinsville)	62234
Meadow Knolls (Part of Schaumburg)	60194
Meadowlake	61821
Meadows	61726
Meadowview (Kane County)	60175
Meadowview (Kankakee County)	60901
Mechanicsburg	62545
Mechanicsburg (Township)	62545
Medalist Park (Part of Palatine)	60067
Media	61460
Media (Township)	61460
Medina (Township)	61523
Medinah	60157
Medinah on the Lake (Part of Bloomingdale)	60108
Medora	62063
Meeks	61846
Meersman	61244
Melrose (Clark County) (Township)	62478
Melrose (Adams County) (Township)	62301
Melrose	62478
Melrose Park	60160-61
	60164
For specific Melrose Park Zip Codes call (708) 343-2150	
Melville	62035
Melvin	60952
Menard	62259
Mendon	62351
Mendon (Township)	62351
Mendota	61342
Mendota (Township)	61342
Menominee (Township)	61025
Menominee	61025
Meppen	62013
Mercer (Township)	61231
Merchandise Mart (Part of Chicago)	60654
Meredosia	62665
Meriden	61342
Meriden (Township)	61342
Meridian (Township)	62283
Meridian Heights (Part of Mounds)	62964
Mermet	62908
Merna	61758
Merriam	62837
Merrimac	62295
Merrionette Park	60655
Merritt	62650
Merry Oaks	61244
Mesa Lake	62855
Metamora	61548
Metamora (Township)	61548
Metcalf	61940
Metropolis	62960
Mettawa	60048
Meyer (Adams County)	62379
Meyer (Kankakee County)	60901
Meyerbrook	60545
Meyers Bay (Part of Fox Lake)	60050
Michael	62065
Middlebury (Part of Barrington Hills)	60010
Middle Creek (Hancock County)	62321

	ZIP
Middlecreek (Kane County)	60175
Middlefork (Township)	61865
Middle Grove	61531
Middleport (Township)	60970
Middlesworth	62565
Middletown	62666
Midland City	61727
Midland Hills	62958
Midlothian	60445
Midway (Madison County)	62067
Midway (Massac County)	62960
Midway (Tazewell County)	61554
Midway (Vermilion County)	61883
Midwest (Part of Chicago)	60612
Midwest Club (Part of Oak Brook)	60521
Milam (Township)	62544
Milan (DeKalb County) (Township)	60550
Milan (Rock Island County)	61264
Mildred	62707
Miles Station	62012
Milford	60953
Milford (Township)	60953
Milks Grove (Township)	60941
Millbrook (Kendall County)	60536
Millbrook (Peoria County) (Township)	61451
Millburn	60046
Millcreek	62961
Milledgeville	61051
Miller (Township)	61360
Miller Addition	61250
Miller City	62962
Miller Lake	62864
Millersburg	61231
Millersburg (Township)	61260
Millersville	62557
Miller Woods	60411
Millhurst	60545
Millington	60537
Mills (Township)	62246
Mill Shoals	62862
Mill Shoals (Township)	62862
Mill Spring	62035
Millstadt	62260
Millstadt (Township)	62260
Milmine	61855
Milo (Township)	61421
Milo	61421
Milton (DuPage County) (Township)	60187
Milton (Pike County)	62352
Mindale	62319
Mineral	61344
Mineral (Township)	61344
Mineral Springs	61081
Minier	61759
Minonk	61760
Minonk (Township)	61760
Minooka	60447
Missal	61364
Mission (Township)	60551
Mission Hills	60062
Mississippi (Township)	62022
Missouri (Township)	62353
Mitchell	62040
Mitchellsville	62917
Mitchie	62295
Mobet Meadows	61275
Mobile City	61401
Moccasin	62411
Moccasin (Township)	62411
Mode	62444
Modena	61491
Modesto	62667
Modoc	62261
Moecherville	60504
Mohawk (Part of Bensenville)	60106
Mokena	60448
Moline	61265
Moline (Township)	61265
Momence	60954
Momence (Township)	60954
Mona (Township)	60964
Monee	60449
Monee (Township)	60449
Money Creek (Township)	61753
Monica	61559
Monmouth	61462
Monmouth (Township)	61462
Monroe (Township)	61052
Monroe Center	61052
Monroe City	62298
Mont	62025
Montague Forest	60123
Mont Clare (Part of Chicago)	60639
Montebello (Township)	62341
Monterey	61520

	ZIP
Monterey Village (Part of University Park)	60466
Montezuma	62361
Montezuma (Township)	62361
Montgomery (Crawford County) (Township)	62427
Montgomery (Kane County)	60538
Montgomery (Woodford County) (Township)	61733
Monticello	61856
Monticello (Township)	61856
Montmorency (Township)	61071
Montrose	62445
Moon Lake Village (Part of Hoffman Estates)	60195
Moonshine	62442
Moores Prairie (Township)	62810
Mooseheart	60539
Moraine Valley Facility (Part of Bridgeview)	60455
Morea	62451
Morehaven	61073
Morgan (Township)	61943
Morgan Park (Part of Chicago)	60643
Morgan's Gate	60067
Moriah	62420
Moro	62067
Moro (Township)	62067
Morris	60450
Morris (Township)	60450
Morris Hills (Part of Collinsville)	62234
Morrison	61270
Morrisonville	62546
Morristown	61274
Morseville	61085
Morton	61550
Morton (Township)	61550
Morton Grove	60053
Morton Park (Part of Cicero)	60650
Moser Highlands (Part of Naperville)	60540
Mosquito (Township)	62547
Mossville	61552
Mound (Effingham County) (Township)	62411
Mound (McDonough County) (Township)	61455
Mound City	62963
Mounds	62964
Mountain (Township)	62946
Mountain Glen	62920
Mount Auburn	62547
Mount Auburn (Township)	62547
Mount Carbon	62966
Mount Carmel	62863
Mount Carroll	61053
Mount Carroll (Township)	61053
Mount Clair	62035
Mount Clare	62033
Mount Erie	62446
Mount Erie (Township)	62446
Mount Greenwood (Part of Chicago)	60655
Mount Hope (Township)	61754
Mount Joy	61723
Mount Morris	61054
Mount Morris (Township)	61054
Mount Olive	62069
Mount Olive (Township)	62069
Mount Palatine	61334
Mount Pleasant (Union County)	62912
Mount Pleasant (Whiteside County) (Township)	61270
Mount Prospect	60056
Mount Prospect Gardens (Part of Mount Prospect)	60056
Mount Prospect Plaza (Part of Mount Prospect)	60056
Mount Pulaski	62548
Mount Pulaski (Township)	62548
Mount Sterling	62353
Mount Sterling (Township)	62353
Mount Vernon	62864
Mount Vernon (Township)	62864
Mount Zion	62549
Mount Zion (Township)	62549
Moweaqua	62550
Moweaqua (Township)	62550
Mozier	62070
Mozier Landing	62045
Mt. Vernon	61025
Muddy	62965
Mulberry Grove	62262
Mulberry Grove (Township)	62262
Mulkeytown	62865
Muncie	61857
Mundelein	60060

	ZIP		ZIP		ZIP
Mundelein Ridge Estates		Newmansville	62612	North Henderson	
(Part of Mundelein)	60060	Newmansville (Township)	62612	(Township)	61466
Munson (Township)	61238	New Memphis	62266	North Hills	60060
Munster	61364	New Milford	61109	Northlake	60164
Murdock	61941	New Minden	62263	North Lakewood	62881
Murdock (Township)	61941	New Palatine	62297	Northland Mall (Part of	
Murphy Acres	60435	New Philadelphia	61459	Sterling)	61081
Murphysboro	62966	Newport (Lake County)		North Libertyville Estates	60048
Murphysboro (Township)	62966	(Township)	60083	North Litchfield (Township)	62056
Murrayville	62668	Newport (Madison County)	62060	Northmore	62035
Myers Lake	62568	New Salem (Township)	62357	Northmore Heights (Part of	
Mylith Park	60050	New Salem (McDonough		Effingham)	62401
Myrtle	61047	County) (Township)	61482	North Mounds	62964
Naausay (Township)	60560	New Salem (Pike County)	62357	North Muddy (Township)	62479
Nachusa	61057	Newton (Jasper County)	62448	North Okaw (Township)	61938
Nachusa (Township)	61057	Newton (Whiteside County)		North Oregon	61061
Nameoki (Township)	62040	(Township)	61250	North Otter (Township)	62690
Nameoki	62040	Newtown (Livingston		North Palmyra (Township)	62667
Nameoki Village Shopping		County) (Township)	61311	North Park (Part of	
Center (Part of Granite		Newtown (Vermilion County)	61858	Machesney Park)	61111
City)	62040	New Trier (Township)	60093	North Park Mall (Part of Villa	
Nantucket Cove (Part of		New Virginia	62951	Park)	60181
Schaumburg)	60194	New Windsor	61465	North Pekin	61554
Naperville	60540	Niantic	62551	North Plato	60140
	60563-67	Niantic (Township)	62551	Northpoint Estates (Part of	
For specific Naperville Zip Codes		North Illinois Fair		Bourbonnais)	60914
call (708) 717-2662		Association (Part of North		Northpoint Shopping Center	
Naperville (Township)	60540	Aurora)	60542	(Part of Arlington Heights)	60004
Naplate	61350	Niles	60714	North Prairie Acres	61953
Naples	62665	Niles (Township)	60076	North Riverside	60546
Nashua (Township)	61061	Nilwood	62672	North Riverside Park Mall	
Nashville	62263	Nilwood (Township)	62640	(Part of North Riverside)	60546
Nashville (Township)	62263	Nineteenth Avenue (Part of		North Shoreland	62959
Nason	62866	Melrose Park)	60160	North Suburban Facility	
Natalie Estates (Part of Oak		Niota	62358	(Part of River Grove)	60199
Forest)	60452	Nippersink Terrace	60081	Northtown (Part of Chicago)	60645
National Stock Yards	62071	Nixon (Township)	61882	North Towne Mall (Part of	
Natrona	62682	Nixon's Greenwood-Central	60025	Rockford)	61103
Nauvoo	62354	Noble	62868	North Venice (Part of	
Nauvoo (Township)	62354	Noble (Township)	62868	Venice)	62090
Navajo Hills (Part of Palos		Nokomis	62075	Northville (Township)	60551
Heights)	60463	Nokomis (Township)	62075	Northwood	61801
Neadmore	62442	Nolle Hill	62036	Northwoods (DeKalb	
Nebo	62355	Nora	61059	County)	60135
Nebraska (Township)	61740	Nora (Township)	61059	North Woods (DuPage	
Neelys	62621	Nordic Acres	61008	County)	60185
Nekoma	61490	Nordic Park	60143	Northwoods (St. Clair	
Nelson	61058	Normal	61761	County)	62269
Nelson (Township)	61058	Normal (Township)	61761	Northwoods Place (Part of	
Neoga (Township)	62447	Normal Junction (Part of		East Alton)	62024
Neoga	62447	Normal)	61761	Northwoods Shopping	
Neponset	61345	Norman (Township)	60450	Center (Part of Peoria)	61613
Neponset (Township)	61345	Normandale	61554	Norton (Township)	60917
Nerska (Part of Chicago)	60632	Normandy	61376	Nortonville	62668
Nettle Creek (Township)	60541	Normandy Heights	62864	Norway	60551
Neunert	62950	Normandy Hill (Part of		Norwood (Mercer County)	61412
Nevada (Township)	60460	Northbrook)	60062	Norwood (Peoria County)	61604
Nevins	61944	Normandy Villa (Part of		Norwood Park (Township)	60656
Newark	60541	Chicago Heights)	60411	Norwood Park (Part of	
New Athens	62264	Norpaul (Part of Franklin		Chicago)	60631
New Athens (Township)	62264	Park)	60131	Nottingham Park (Part of	
New Baden	62265	Norridge	60656	Bridgeview)	60638
New Bedford	61346	Norris	61553	Nottingham Woods	60119
New Berlin	62670	Norris City	62869	Novak Park	60174
New Berlin (Township)	62670	North (Part of Evanston)	60201	Nubbin Ridge	62835
Newbern	62022	North Alton (Part of Alton)	62002	Nunda (Township)	60012
New Blossom Hill (Part of		North Arm	61944	Nutwood	62031
Cary)	60013	North Aurora	60542	Oak	62947
New Boston	61272	North Barrington	60010	Oak Bluff Estates	61038
New Boston (Township)	61272	Northbelt Homesites (Part of		Oak Brook (DuPage	
Newburg (Macon County)	62501	Belleville)	62221	County)	60521
Newburg (Pike County)		Northbrook	60062	Oakbrook (Macoupin	
(Township)	62363		60065	County)	62626
New Burnside	62967	For specific Northbrook Zip Codes		Oakbrook Center (Part of	
Newby	61938	call (708) 272-0018		Oak Brook)	60521
New Camp	62921	Northbrook Court (Part of		Oakbrook Terrace	60181
New Canton	62356	Northbrook)	60062	Oakdale (Township)	62268
Newcastle	62987	Northbrook Knolls (Part of		Oakdale (Cook County)	60619
New Century Town (Part of		Northbrook)	60062	Oakdale (Washington	
Vernon Hills)	60060	Northbrook West	60062	County)	62268
New City	62563	North Chicago	60064	Oakdale Woods	60106
New Columbia	62943	North Chillicothe (Part of		Oakford	62673
Newcomb (Township)	61853	Chillicothe)	61523	Oak Forest	60452
New Delhi	62052	North Dixon (Part of Dixon)	61021	Oak Grove (Madison	
New Dennison	62959	Northeast (Township)	62339	County)	62035
New Douglas	62074	Northern (Township)	62860	Oak Grove (Rock Island	
New Douglas (Township)	62074	Northern Heights	61010	County)	61264
Newell (Township)	61832	Northern Hills	61032	Oak Hill	61518
New Hanover	62298	Northfield	60093	Oak Hills	62232
New Hartford	62363	Northfield (Township)	60025	Oak Hills Estates	61008
New Haven	62867	Northfield Woods	60025	Oak Knolls	60118
New Haven (Township)	62867	North Fork (Township)	62979	Oakland (Coles County)	61943
New Hebron	62454	Northgate (Part of Hanover		Oakland (Schuyler County)	
New Holland	62671	Park)	60103	(Township)	62681
New La Grange	62278	Northgate Shopping Center		Oak Lawn	60453-59
New Lebanon	60140	(Part of Aurora)	60506	For specific Oak Lawn Zip Codes	
New Lenox	60451	North Glen Ellyn	60137	call (708) 598-6305	
New Lenox (Township)	60451	North Hampton	61523	Oaklawn (Part of Danville)	61832
New Liberty	62910	North Harvey (Part of		Oakley	62552
Newman	61942	Harvey)	60426	Oakley (Township)	62552
Newman (Township)	61942	North Henderson	61466	Oak Manor	60545

	ZIP
Oak Meadows	60185
Oak Park	60301-04
For specific Oak Park Zip Codes call (708) 848-7900	
Oak Park (Township)	60302
Oak Ridge	61548
Oak Run	61428
Oak Spring Woods	60048
Oakwood (Township)	61858
Oakwood (DuPage County)	60559
Oakwood (Henderson County)	61437
Oakwood (Peoria County)	61605
Oakwood (Vermilion County)	61858
Oakwood Acres (Part of Geneseo)	61254
Oakwood Hills	60013
Oakwood Shores	60097
Obed	62510
Oblong	62449
Oblong (Township)	62449
Oconee	62553
Oconee (Township)	62553
Ocoya	61764
Odell	60460
Odell (Township)	60460
Odgen	62863
Odin	62870
Odin (Township)	62870
O'Fallon	62269
O'Fallon (Township)	62269
Ogden	61859
Ogden (Township)	61859
Ogden Park (Part of Chicago)	60636
Oglesby	61348
O'Hare Airport (Part of Chicago)	60666
Ohio	61349
Ohio (Township)	61349
Ohio Grove (Township)	61231
Ohlman	62076
Oil Center (Part of Centralia)	62801
Oilfield	62420
Okaw (Township)	62534
Okawville	62271
Okawville (Township)	62271
Oklahoma Addition	62451
Old Camp	62921
Old Du Quoin	62832
Oldenburg	62024
Olde Salem (Part of Hanover Park)	60103
Old Farm (Part of Naperville)	60563
Old Gilchrist	61231
Old Kane	62054
Old Marissa (Part of Marissa)	62257
Old Mill Creek	60083
Old Mill Grove (Part of Lake Zurich)	60047
Old Niota	62358
Old Orchard Shopping Center (Part of Skokie)	60077
Old Pearl	62361
Old Ripley	62275
Old Ripley (Township)	62275
Old Shawneetown	62984
Old Stonington	62567
Oldtown (McLean County) (Township)	61701
Oldtown (Saline County)	62987
Olena	61480
Olio (Township)	61530
Olive (Township)	62058
Olive Branch	62969
Oliver	62441
Olivet	61846
Olmsted	62970
Olney	62450
Olney (Township)	62450
Olympia Fields	60461
Olympia Gardens	60411
Olympic Terrace (Part of Naperville)	60540
Olympic Village (Part of Chicago Heights)	60411
Omaha	62871
Omaha (Township)	62871
Omega	62849
Omega (Township)	62849
Omphghent (Township)	62097
Onarga	60955
Onarga (Township)	60955
Oneco	61060
Oneco (Township)	61060
One Hundred Fourty-seventh Street (Part of Harvey)	60426

	ZIP
One Hundred Third Street (Part of Chicago)	60628
Oneida	61467
Ontario (Township)	61467
Ontario Street (Part of Chicago)	60611
Ontarioville	60103
Opdyke	62872
Opheim	61468
Ophir (Township)	61342
Oquawka	61469
Oquawka (Township)	61469
Ora (Township)	62971
Oran (Township)	62512
Orange (Clark County) (Township)	62442
Orange (Knox County) (Township)	61436
Orange Prairie	61614
Orangeville	61060
Oraville	62971
Orchard (Township)	62850
Orchard Acres	60014
Orchard Estates	60187
Orchard Heights	62450
Orchard Mines	61607
Orchard Place (Part of Des Plaines)	60018
Orchard Valley	60031
Orchardville	62899
Oreana	62554
Oregon	61061
Oregon (Township)	61061
Orel (Township)	62895
Orient	62874
Orion (Fulton County) (Township)	61520
Orion (Henry County)	61273
Orland (Township)	60462
Orland Hills	60462
Orland Hills (Westhaven)	60477
Orland Park	60462
Orland Park Place (Part of Orland Park)	60462
Orland Square (Part of Orland Park)	60462
Orleans	62601
Orleans Terrace (Part of Addison)	60101
Orvil (Township)	62635
Osage (Franklin County)	62983
Osage (La Salle County) (Township)	61377
Osbernville	62513
Osborn	61257
Osceola	61345
Osceola (Township)	61421
Osco	61274
Osco (Township)	61274
Oskaloosa	62899
Oskaloosa (Township)	62899
Osman	61843
Ospur	61727
Ossami Lake (Part of Morton)	61550
Oswego	60543
Oswego (Township)	60543
Otego (Township)	62418
Ottawa	61350
Ottawa (Township)	61350
Otter Creek (Jersey County) (Township)	62052
Otter Creek (La Salle County) (Township)	61364
Otterville	62037
Otto	60922
Otto (Township)	60922
Otto Mall (Part of Chicago Heights)	60411
Ottville	61362
Outter Creek	62031
Owaneco	62555
Owego (Township)	61764
Owen (Township)	61103
Oxford (Township)	61413
Oxville	62621
Ozark	62972
Pacesetter Park (Part of South Holland)	60473
Paderborn	62298
Padua	61737
Painesville	62948
Palatine	60067
	60074
	60078
	60094-95
For specific Palatine Zip Codes call (708) 590-8000	
Palatine (Township)	60067
Palermo	61876
Palestine (Crawford County)	62451

	ZIP
Palestine (Woodford County) (Township)	61771
Palmer	62556
Palmyra (Lee County)	61021
Palmyra (Lee County) (Township)	61021
Palmyra (Macoupin County)	62674
Paloma	62359
Palos (Township)	60464
Palos Gardens	60463
Palos Heights	60463
Palos Hills	60465
Palos Park	60464
Palos Westgate (Part of Palos Heights)	60463
Palsgrove	61053
Pam Anne Estates	60025
Pana	62557
Pana (Township)	62557
Panama	62077
Pankeyville	62946
Panola	61738
Panola (Township)	61738
Panther Creek (Township)	62627
Papineau	60956
Papineau (Township)	60956
Paradise	61938
Paradise (Township)	61938
Paradise Acres	62918
Paris	61944
Paris (Township)	61944
Park City	60085
Parker (Clark County) (Township)	62474
Parker (Johnson County)	62922
Parkersburg	62452
Parkfield Terrace	62206
Park Forest	60466
Park Hills (Part of Effingham)	62401
Parkhome (Part of Cicero)	60650
Park Lane	60964
Park Manor (Part of Chicago)	60619
Park Meadows (Part of Rolling Meadows)	60008
Park Ridge	60068
Parkville	61872
Parkway (Part of North Riverside)	60546
Parkwood (Part of Elgin)	60120
Parkwood Village (Part of Elgin)	60120
Parnell	61842
Parrish	62890
Parrish Addition	62930
Partridge (Township)	61545
Partridge Hill (Part of Hoffman Estates)	60195
Passport	62868
Patoka	62875
Patoka (Township)	62875
Patterson	62078
Patterson (Township)	62078
Patterson Heights	62035
Patterson Springs	61919
Patton (Ford County) (Township)	60957
Patton (Wabash County)	62863
Pattonsburg	61369
Paulton	62959
Pavillion	60560
Pawnee	62558
Pawnee (Township)	62558
Paw Paw (DeKalb County) (Township)	60518
Paw Paw (Lee County)	61353
Paxton	60957
Paynes Point	61015
Payson	62360
Payson (Township)	62360
Peach Orchard (Township)	60952
Pea Ridge (Township)	62375
Pearl	62361
Pearl (Township)	62361
Pearl City	61062
Pebble Beach	60450
Pecan Grove	62031
Pecatonica	61063
Pecatonica (Township)	61063
Peerless	60544
Pekin	61554-55
For specific Pekin Zip Codes call (309) 346-7878	
Pekin Heights (Part of Pekin)	61554
Pekin Mall (Part of Pekin)	61554
Pella (Township)	60959
Pembroke (Township)	60964
Pendleton (Township)	62810
Penfield	61862

	ZIP
Racine Avenue (Part of Chicago)	60628
Raddle	62950
Radford	62550
Radnor (Township)	61525
Radom	62876
Rainbow Hills	60174
Rakers Addition	62216
Raleigh	62977
Raleigh (Township)	62977
Ramona Place	62035
Ramsey	62080
Ramsey (Township)	62080
Randhurst Shopping Center (Part of Mount Prospect)	60056
Randolph	61745
Randolph (Township)	61745
Randolph Street (Part of Chicago)	60601
Range	62864
Rankin	60960
Ransom	60470
Ransom Ridge Estates (Part of Park Ridge)	60068
Rantoul	61866
Rantoul (Township)	61866
Rapatee	61544
Rapids City	61278
Rardin	61920
Raritan	61471
Raritan (Township)	61471
Rasmussen Addition	60936
Raven	61924
Ravenswood (Part of Chicago)	60625
Ravinia (Part of Highland Park)	60035
Ravinia Park (Part of Highland Park)	60035
Rawalts	61520
Rawlins (Township)	61036
Ray	62681
Raymond (Montgomery County) (Township)	62560
Raymond (Champaign County) (Township)	61852
Raymond	62560
Reader	62630
Reading	61311
Reading (Township)	61311
Rector (Township)	62930
Red Bud	62278
Reddick	60961
Redmon	61949
Red Oak	61032
Red Oak Terrace (Part of Highland Park)	60035
Reed (Township)	60408
Reed City	61547
Reeds Station	62924
Rees	62638
Reevesville	62943
Regency Grove	60515
Regency Terrace (Part of Bloomingdale)	60108
Reilly	60960
Reily Lake	62241
Rellswood Hills	61008
Renault	62279
Renchville	61523
Rend City	62812
Reno	62246
Rentchler	62221
Reseda (Part of Palatine)	60067
Resthaven	60481
Reynolds (Lee County) (Township)	61006
Reynolds (Rock Island County)	61279
Reynoldsburg	62991
Reynoldsville	62952
Rice (Jo Daviess County) (Township)	61036
Rice (Perry County)	62274
Rice Lake	61401
Rich (Township)	60471
Richards	60450
Richardson	60151
Richardson Estates	61801
Richfield	62365
Richfield (Township)	62365
Richland (La Salle County) (Township)	61334
Richland (Marshall County) (Township)	61570
Richland (Sangamon County)	62677
Richland (Shelby County) (Township)	62465
Richland Grove (Township)	61281
Richmond	60071

	ZIP
Richmond (Township)	60071
Richmond Estates (Part of Oak Forest)	60452
Richton Hills (Part of Richton Park)	60466
Richton Park	60471
Richview	62877
Richview (Township)	62877
Richwood (Township)	62031
Richwoods (Crawford County)	62451
Richwoods (Peoria County) (Township)	61614
Ricks (Township)	62546
Ridge (Township)	62565
Ridgecrest	60450
Ridge Farm	61870
Ridgefield	60012
Ridgeland (Township)	60968
Ridgemoor (Part of Willowbrook)	60521
Ridge Prairie Heights (Part of O'Fallon)	62269
Ridgeville	60955
Ridgewood (Part of Western Springs)	60558
Ridgewood East	60452
Ridgewood West (Part of Oak Forest)	60452
Ridgway	62979
Ridgway (Township)	62979
Ridott	61067
Ridott (Township)	61067
Rieuf's Meadows	61341
Riffel	62858
Riggston	62694
Riley (Township)	61038
Riley Center	60152
Rinard	62878
Ring Neck	60543
Ringwood	60072
Rio	61472
Rio (Township)	61472
Ripley	62353
Ripley (Township)	62353
Rising Sun	62821
Ritchason Addition	62896
Ritchie	60481
Riverair	62035
Riverdale (Cook County)	60627
Riverdale (Winnebago County)	61073
River Forest	60305
River Forest (Township)	60305
River Glen	60010
River Grange Lakes	60175
River Grove	60171
River Heights (Part of Danville)	61832
River Isle	60954
River Oaks Center (Part of Calumet City)	60409
River Reach	61008
River Ridge	60560
Riverside (Cook County) (Township)	60546
Riverside (Adams County) (Township)	62301
Riverside (Cook County)	60546
Riverside Island (Part of Fox Lake)	60020
Riverside Lawns	60546
Riverside Park	60050
Riverton	62561
Riverview (Carroll County)	61285
Riverview (Lee County)	61021
Riverview (Whiteside County)	61071
Riverview Heights	60543
Riverwoods	60015
Rivoli (Township)	61465
Roaches	62898
Roachtown	62260
Roanoke	61561
Roanoke (Township)	61561
Robbins	60472
Robbs	62985
Robein (Part of East Peoria)	61611
Roberts (Ford County)	60962
Roberts (Marshall County) (Township)	61375
Roberts Park (Part of Bridgeview)	60453
Robin Hill (Part of Joliet)	60435
Robinson	62454
Robinson (Township)	62454
Rob Roy Country Club (Part of Prospect Heights)	60070
Roby	62545
Rochelle	61068
Rochester	62563

	ZIP
Rochester (Township)	62563
Rochester	62863
Rock	62938
Rockbridge	62081
Rockbridge (Township)	62081
Rock City	61070
Rock Creek (Adams County)	62301
Rock Creek (Hancock County) (Township)	62321
Rock Creek (Hardin County)	62919
Rock Creek-Lima (Township)	61046
Rockdale	60436
Rock Falls	61071
Rockford	61101-32
For specific Rockford Zip Codes call (815) 229-4811	
Rockgate Estates	62035
Rock Grove	61070
Rock Grove (Township)	61070
Rock Island	61201-04
For specific Rock Island Zip Codes call (309) 793-7200	
Rock Island Arsenal	61299
Rockport	62370
Rock River Terrace	61010
Rock Run (Township)	61019
Rockton	61072
Rockton (Township)	61072
Rockvale (Township)	61061
Rock Vale Heights	61010
Rockville (Township)	60950
Rockwell (Part of La Salle)	61301
Rockwood	62280
Rocky Run (Township)	62373
Rodden	61041
Rogers (Township)	60946
Rogers Park (Part of Chicago)	60660
Rolling Acres (Champaign County)	61866
Rolling Acres (Peoria County)	61614
Rolling Green	61938
Rolling Hills (Clinton County)	62293
Rolling Hills (Piatt County)	61884
Rolling Meadows (Cook County)	60008
Rolling Meadows (McDonough County)	61455
Rollo	60518
Rome (Jefferson County) (Township)	62830
Rome (Peoria County)	61562
Rome Heights	61523
Romeoville	60441
Romine (Township)	62849
Rondout	60044
Roodhouse	62082
Roodhouse (Township)	62082
Rooks Creek (Township)	61764
Rooney Heights	60435
Roosevelt Road (Part of Chicago)	60607
Roots	62277
Root Spring	60013
Ropers Landing	62938
Rosamond	62083
Rosamond (Township)	62083
Roscoe	61073
Roscoe (Township)	61073
Rose (Township)	62565
Rosebud	62938
Rosecrans	60083
Rosedale	62031
Rosedale (Township)	62031
Rosefield (Township)	61529
Rose Hill (Cook County)	60640
Rose Hill (DuPage County)	60515
Rose Hill (Jasper County)	62432
Rose Lake (Part of Fairmont City)	62201
Roseland (Part of Chicago)	60628
Rose Lawn (Part of Chicago)	60628
Roselle	60172
Rosemont (Cook County)	60018
Rosemont (St. Clair County)	62204
Roseville	61473
Roseville (Township)	61473
Rosewood	62024
Rosewood Heights	62024
Rosiclare	62982
Roslyn	62462
Ross (Edgar County) (Township)	61924
Ross (Pike County) (Township)	62366
Ross (Vermilion County) (Township)	60963

	ZIP
Rossville	60963
Round Barn (Part of Champaign)	61821
Round Grove (Livingston County) (Township)	60420
Round Grove (Whiteside County)	61270
Round Knob	62960
Round Lake	60073
Round Lake Beach	60073
Round Lake Heights	60073
Round Lake Park	60073
Round Prairie	62823
Rountree (Township)	62094
Rowe	61764
Roxana	62084
Roxanne	62901
Roxbury	61353
Royal	61871
Royal Lake Resort (Bond County)	62262
Royal Lake Resort (Clinton County)	62231
Royal Lakes (Macoupin County)	62685
Royal Lakes (Marion County)	62870
Royal Oaks	61032
Royalton	62983
Rozetta	61469
Rozetta (Township)	61447
Rubicon (Township)	62044
Rudement	62946
Ruma	62278
Rural (Rock Island County) (Township)	61240
Rural (Shelby County) (Township)	62510
Rush (Township)	61085
Rushville	62681
Rushville (Township)	62681
Russell	60075
Russell (Township)	47591
Russellville	47591
Rutland (Kane County) (Township)	60120
Rutland (La Salle County)	61358
Rutland (La Salle County) (Township)	61341
Rutledge (Township)	61752
Ruyle (Township)	62063
Sabina	61722
Sacramento	62835
Sadorus	61872
Sadorus (Township)	61872
Sag Bridge	60439
Saidora	62627
Sailor Springs	62879
St. Albans (Township)	62380
St. Anne	60964
St. Anne (Township)	60964
St. Anne Woods	60964
St. Augustine	61474
St. Charles	60174-75
For specific St. Charles Zip Codes call (708) 584-2318	
St. Clair (Township)	62221
St. Clair Square (Part of Fairview Heights)	62208
St. David	61563
St. Elmo	62458
St. Francis (Township)	62467
St. Francisville	62460
St. George	60914
St. Jacob	62281
St. Jacob (Township)	62281
St. James	62857
St. James Estates (Part of Sauk Village)	60411
St. Joe	62298
St. Johns	62832
St. Joseph	61873
St. Joseph (Township)	61873
St. Joseph's	60557
St. Libory	62282
Ste. Marie	62459
Ste. Marie (Township)	62459
St. Mary	62367
St. Mary (Township)	62367
St. Marys	62401
Saint Morgan	62293
St. Paul	62885
St. Peter	62880
St. Regis (Part of Lombard)	60148
St. Rose	62230
St. Rose (Township)	62293
Salem (Marion County) (Township)	62881
Salem (Carroll County) (Township)	61046

	ZIP
Salem (Knox County) (Township)	61572
Salem	62881
Salina (Township)	60913
Saline (Township)	62249
Saline Landing	62919
Saline Mines	62984
Salisbury	62677
Salt Creek (Township)	62664
Samoth	62943
Samsville	62476
Sand Barrens	62460
Sandburg Mall (Part of Galesburg)	61401
Sandoval	62882
Sandoval (Township)	62882
Sandpebble Walk (Part of Wheeling)	60090
Sand Prairie (Township)	61534
Sandra Heights (Part of Chicago Heights)	60411
Sand Ridge	62940
Sand Ridge (Township)	62940
Sandusky	62988
Sandwich	60548
Sandwich (Township)	60548
Sangamon (Macon County)	62521
Sangamon (Piatt County) (Township)	61884
Sangamon Heights	61853
Sangamon Valley (Township)	62618
San Jose	62682
Santa Anna (Township)	61842
Santa Fe (Township)	62218
Santa Fe Park	60521
Saratoga (Grundy County) (Township)	60450
Saratoga (Marshall County) (Township)	61537
Saratoga (Union County)	62906
Saratoga Center	61537
Sargent (Township)	61943
Sato	62907
Sauganash (Part of Chicago)	60646
Sauget	62201
Sauk Village	60411
Saunemin	61769
Saunemin (Township)	61769
Savanna	61074
Savanna (Township)	61074
Savoy	61874
Sawyerville	62085
Say Brook (DuPage County)	60563
Saybrook (McLean County)	61770
Scales Mound	61075
Scales Mound (Township)	61075
Scarboro	60553
Schaeferville	61554
Schapville	61028
Schaumburg	60159
	60168
	60173
	60192-96
For specific Schaumburg Zip Codes call (708) 885-6500	
Schaumburg (Township)	60194
Schaumburg Green (Part of Schaumburg)	60194
Scheller	62883
Schiller Park	60176
Schram City	62049
Schrodt	62863
Schulines	62286
Schwer	60953
Sciota	61475
Sciota (Township)	61475
Scioto Mills	61076
Scotland (Edgar County)	61924
Scotland (McDonough County) (Township)	61455
Scotsboro	62959
Scott (Champaign County) (Township)	61875
Scott (Ogle County) (Township)	61020
Scott Air Force Base	62225
Scottsburg	61422
Scottswood	61801
Scottville	62683
Scottville (Township)	62683
Seagaert	61354
Seaton	61476
Seatonville	61359
Seco Park	60115
Secor	61771
Seeger (Part of Des Plaines)	60016
Seehorn	62343
Sefton (Township)	62418
Selby (Township)	61322

	ZIP
Selmaville	62881
Seminary (Fayette County) (Township)	62471
Seminary (Richland County)	62450
Senachwine (Township)	61560
Seneca (La Salle County)	61360
Seneca (McHenry County) (Township)	60098
Sepo	61542
Serena	60549
Serena (Township)	60549
Sesser	62884
Seven Hickory (Township)	61920
Seven Hills (Part of Lindenhurst)	60046
Seville	61477
Seward (Winnebago County) (Township)	61077
Seward (Kendall County) (Township)	60447
Seward	61077
Sexson Corner	61928
Seymour	61875
Shabbona	60550
Shabbona (Township)	60550
Shabbona Grove	60518
Shadetree (Part of Oak Forest)	60452
Shadow Lawn	60954
Shady Acres	62665
Shady Beach	61254
Shady Grove	62910
Shady Hill	60010
Shafter	62471
Shafter (Township)	62471
Shakerag	62951
Shale City	61231
Shanghai City	61412
Shannon	61078
Sharon (Township)	62080
Sharpsburg	62568
Shattuc	62283
Shaw	60073
Shawnee (Township)	62984
Shawnee Correctional Center	62995
Shawneetown	62984
Shaws	61310
Shaws Point (Township)	62511
Sheffield	61361
Sheffield Park (Part of Schaumburg)	60194
Shelbyville	62565
Shelbyville (Township)	62565
Sheldon	60966
Sheldon (Township)	60966
Sheldons Grove	62624
Shepherd	62343
Sherburnville	60940
Sheridan (La Salle County)	60551
Sheridan (Logan County) (Township)	62671
Sheridan Correctional Center	60551
Sheridan Village (Part of Peoria)	61614
Sherman (Mason County) (Township)	62633
Sherman (Sangamon County)	62684
Sherrard	61281
Sherwood Forest (Part of Wood Dale)	60191
Sherwood Oaks	60120
Sherwood on the Fox (Part of Carpentersville)	60110
Shields (Jefferson County)	62851
Shields (Lake County) (Township)	60045
Shiloh (Edgar County) (Township)	61917
Shiloh (Jefferson County) (Township)	62864
Shiloh (St. Clair County)	62221
Shiloh Hill	62916
Shiloh Valley (Township)	62221
Shipman	62685
Shipman (Township)	62685
Shippingsport	61348
Shires of Inverness	60067
Shirland	61079
Shirland (Township)	61079
Shirley	61772
Shoal Creek (Township)	62086
Shobonier	62885
Shokokon	61425
Shore Acres	61071
Shore Heights Manor	60543
Shore Hills	60097
Shores of Shining Waters (Part of Carol Stream)	60188

	ZIP
Shorewood (Kankakee County)	60964
Shorewood (Will County)	60435
Shull's Urban Estates (Part of Rantoul)	61866
Shumway	62461
Sibley	61773
Sicily	62558
Sidell	61876
Sidell (Township)	61876
Sidney	61877
Sidney (Township)	61877
Sigel	62462
Sigel (Township)	62462
Signal Hill	62223
Silver Creek (Township)	61032
Silver Lake	60013
Silver Ridge	61061
Silvis	61282
Silvis Heights (Part of Silvis)	61282
Simpson (Johnson County)	62985
Simpson (White County)	62827
Sims	62886
Sims Western Acres	62707
Sinclair	62650
Six Mile (Township)	62999
Sixty-seventh Street (Part of Chicago)	60649
Sixty Six Court	60452
Sixty-Third Street (Part of Chicago)	60637
Skokie	60076-77
For specific Skokie Zip Codes call (708) 676-2200	
Slap Out	62849
Sleepy Hollow	60118
Smallwood (Township)	62448
Smithboro	62284
Smithfield	61477
Smithshire	61478
Smithton	62285
Smithton (Township)	62285
Smithville	61536
Snicarte	62617
Snyder	62477
Solitt	60401
Solon Mills	60080
Somer (Township)	61820
Somerset (DuPage County)	60521
Somerset (Jackson County) (Township)	62966
Somerset (McHenry County)	60014
Somerset (Saline County)	62946
Somonauk	60552
Somonauk (Township)	60552
Songer (Township)	62899
Sonora (Township)	62354
Sorento	62086
South (Part of Evanston)	60202
South Addison (Part of Villa Park)	60181
South Barrington	60010
South Bartonville (Part of Bartonville)	61607
South Beloit	61080
South Chicago (Part of Chicago)	60617
South Chicago Heights	60411
South Crouch (Township)	62859
South Danville (Part of Danville)	61832
South Deering (Part of Chicago)	60617
South Dixon (Township)	61021
South Elgin	60177
Southern Hills	62901
Southern Illinois University	62026
Southern View	62707
South Fillmore (Township)	62032
South Flannigan (Township)	62890
South Fork (Township)	62540
South Grove (Township)	60146
South Holland	60473
South Homer (Township)	61849
South Hurricane (Township)	62011
South Jacksonville	62650
South Litchfield (Township)	62056
South Lockport (Part of Lockport)	60441
South Macon (Township)	62544
South Moline (Township)	61244
South Moline Gardens (Part of Moline)	61265
Southmore	62035
Southmore Heights	62411
South Mounds (Part of Mounds)	62964
South Muddy (Township)	62448
South Oak Park (Part of Oak Park)	60304
South Ottawa (Township)	61350

	ZIP
South Otter (Township)	62674
South Palmyra (Township)	62674
Southpark Mall (Part of Moline)	61265
South Pekin	61564
Southport	61517
South Rock Island (Township)	61201
South Rome	61523
South Ross (Township)	61848
South Roxana	62087
South Shore (Part of Chicago)	60649
South Twigg (Township)	62817
South Waukegan (Part of North Chicago)	60064
Southwest (Township)	62466
South Wheatland (Township)	62532
South Wilmington	60474
Space Valley	60521
Spanish Court (Part of Highland Park)	60035
Spankey	62031
Sparks Hill	62931
Sparland	61565
Sparta (Knox County) (Township)	61488
Sparta (Randolph County)	62286
Spaulding (Cook County)	60120
Spaulding (Sangamon County)	62561
Speer	61479
Spencer	60451
Spencer Heights	62964
Spillertown	62959
Spin Lake	61732
Sportsman Lake	62881
Spring (Township)	61008
Spring Arbor Lake	62901
Spring Bay (Township)	61611
Spring Bay	61611
Spring Creek (Township)	62355
Springerton	62887
Springfield	62701-94
For specific Springfield Zip Codes call (217) 788-7200	
Springfield (Township)	62702
Spring Garden	62846
Spring Garden (Township)	62846
Spring Grove (McHenry County)	60081
Spring Grove (Warren County) (Township)	61412
Springhaven	62035
Spring Hill	61250
Spring Hill Mall (Part of Dundee)	60118
Spring Lake (Champaign County)	61853
Spring Lake (Tazewell County)	61546
Spring Lake (Tazewell County) (Township)	61546
Spring Point (Township)	62462
Spring Valley	61362
Squaw Grove (Township)	60520
Squaw Prairie Estate	61008
Stable	62918
Stainfield	60545
Staleys	61821
Standard	61363
Standard City	62686
Stanford (Clay County) (Township)	62824
Stanford (McLean County)	61774
Stanton (Township)	61873
Stanton Point	60041
Stark	61559
Starks	60140
Starnes	62707
State Line	62423
State Park Place	62201
State Street (Part of Chicago)	60628
Staunton	62088
Staunton (Township)	62088
Stavanger	61360
Steel City	62812
Steeleville	62288
Steeple Run	60540
Steger	60475
Stelle	60919
Sterling (Township)	61081
Sterling	61081
Sterling Place (Part of Caseyville)	62232
Steuben (Township)	61565
Stevenson (Township)	62881
Steward	60553
Stewardson	62463

	ZIP
Stickney	60402
Stickney (Township)	60402
Stillman Valley	61084
Stillmeadow	60119
Stillwell	62380
Stiritz	62896
Stites (Township)	62059
Stockland (Township)	60967
Stockland	60967
Stockton	61085
Stockton (Township)	61085
Stock Yards (Part of Chicago)	60609
Stolletown	62231
Stone	62931
Stone Church	62296
Stonefort (Township)	62987
Stonefort	62987
Stonehenge	60178
Stonelake (Part of Woodstock)	60098
Stone Park	60165
Stoneyville	61350
Stonington	62567
Stonington (Township)	62567
Stony Island Avenue (Part of Chicago)	60649
Stookey (Township)	62221
Storeyland	62035
Storybrook	60512
Stoy	62464
Strasburg	62465
Stratford	61064
Stratford Hills (Part of Elmhurst)	60126
Stratford Park	61821
Stratford Square (Part of Bloomingdale)	60108
Stratton (Edgar County) (Township)	61944
Stratton (Jefferson County)	62814
Strawberry Hill	61270
Strawn	61775
Streamwood	60103
Streator	61364
Streator Junction (Part of Eureka)	61530
Stringtown	62450
Stronghurst	61480
Stronghurst (Township)	61480
Stubblefield	62246
Sublette	61367
Sublette (Township)	61367
Suburban Estates	60515
Suburban Heights	62801
Suez (Township)	61412
Sugar Brook (Part of Bolingbrook)	60440
Sugar Creek (Township)	62293
Sugar Grove	60554
Sugar Grove (Township)	60554
Sugar Grove	61231
Sugar Island	60922
Sugar Loaf (Township)	62240
Sugar Loaf	62240
Sullivan (Moultrie County) (Township)	61951
Sullivan (Livingston County) (Township)	60929
Sullivan	61951
Sullivant (Township)	61773
Summerdale (Part of Chicago)	60640
Summerfield	62289
Summerhill	60062
Summer Hill (Cook County)	60120
Summer Hill (Pike County)	62372
Summerlakes (Part of Warrenville)	60555
Summersville (Part of Mount Vernon)	62864
Summerville	62063
Summit (Cook County)	60501
Summit (Effingham County) (Township)	62461
Summit-Argo (Part of Summit)	60501
Summit Heights	62089
Summum	61501
Sumner (Kankakee County) (Township)	60940
Sumner (Lawrence County)	62466
Sumner (Warren County) (Township)	61453
Sumpter (Township)	62468
Sunbeam	61231
Sunbury	61313
Sunbury (Township)	61313
Sunfield	62832
Sunny Acres (Champaign County)	61853

	ZIP		ZIP		ZIP
Sunny Acres (Kankakee County)	60950	The Fairway of Country Lakes (Part of Naperville)	60563	Triumph	61371
Sunny Crest	60430	The Greens of Woodgate		Triumvera	60025
Sunnydale	61021	(Part of Matteson)	60443	Trivoli	61569
Sunny Hill	61273	The Grove Shopping Center		Trivoli (Township)	61569
Sunny Hill Estates	61273	(Part of Elk Grove Village)	60007	Trout Valley (Part of Cary)	60013
Sunny Hills Estates	60515	The Knolls	60175	Trowbridge	62447
Sunnyland (Tazewell County)	61571	The Laurels (Part of Justice)	60458	Troxel	60151
Sunny Land (Will County)	60435	The Ledges	61073	Troy (Madison County)	62294
Sunnyside (McHenry County)	60050	The Meadows	60532	Troy (Will County) (Township)	60435
Sunnyside (Williamson County)	62948	The Old Farm	61821	Troy Grove	61372
Sunnyside Acres	62531	Third Lake	60046	Troy Grove (Township)	61372
Sun Prairie Seed	61873	Thomas	61283	Tru Lock Acres	61455
Sun Ridge (Part of Hoffman Estates)	60195	Thomasboro	61878	Trumbull	62821
Sunrise Ridge (Part of Romeoville)	60441	Thomas Eddition	61364	Truro (Township)	61489
Sun River Terrace	60964	Thomasville	62533	Tullamore (Part of Mundelein)	60060
Sunset Acres (Lake County)	60048	Thompson (Township)	61001	Tunbridge (Township)	61749
Sunset Acres (Stephenson County)	61032	Thompson Addition	61241	Tunnel Hill	62991
Sunset Harbor	62959	Thompsonville	62890	Turnberry	60014
Sunset Hills (Part of Roselle)	60172	Thomson	61285	Tuscola	61953
Sunset Lake	62640	Thornhill (Part of Carol Stream)	60187	Tuscola (Township)	61953
Sunset Trailer Park (Part of Glenview)	60025	Thornton	60476	Twelvemile Corner	61318
Sutter	62373	Thornton (Township)	60476	Twenty-Second Street (Part of Chicago)	60616
Sutton	60010	Thornton Junction (Part of South Holland)	60473	Twenty-Seventh Street (Part of Chicago)	60616
Sutton Point (Part of Northbrook)	60062	Thornwilde (Part of Warrenville)	60555	Twenty-Third Street (Part of Chicago)	60616
Swan (Township)	61473	Thunderbird Lake	62012	Twigg (Township)	62829
Swan Creek	61473	Tice	62675	Twilight Terrace	62221
Swansea	62221	Ticona	61370	Twin City (Part of Champaign)	61801
Swanwick	62237	Tierra Grande (Part of Country Club Hills)	60477	Twin Creek Acres	61010
Swedona	61262	Tilden	62292	Twin Lakes	62294
Sweetwater	62642	Tilton	61833	Twin Oaks (Part of Joliet)	60435
Swiss Valley (Part of Crete)	60417	Timber (Township)	61533	Tyrone (Township)	62822
Swissville (Part of Dixon)	61021	Timberbrook	61254	Udina	60123
Swygert	61764	Timbercrest (Part of Schaumburg)	60194	Ulah	61238
Sycamore	60178	Timber Lake (Carroll County)	61053	Ullin	62992
Sycamore (Township)	60178	Timber Lake (Lake County)	60010	Union (Cumberland County) (Township)	62428
Sylvan Hill	60462	Timberlake Estate	62568	Union (Effingham County) (Township)	62424
Sylvan Lake	60060	Timberlake Estates	60521	Union (Fulton County) (Township)	61415
Symerton	60481	Timberlake Village (Part of Mount Prospect)	60056	Union (Livingston County) (Township)	60460
Symmes (Township)	61944	Timber Lane	61008	Union (Logan County)	62635
Table Grove	61482	Timberline	60435	Union (McHenry County)	60180
Tabor	61778	Timber Ridge (Cook County)	60457	Union Center	62428
Taggert Woods	62626	Timber Ridge (DuPage County)	60190	Union Grove	61270
Talkington (Township)	62692	Timber Terrace	60115	Union Grove (Township)	61270
Tall Trees (Part of Glenview)	60025	Timber Trails (Part of Oak Brook)	60521	Union Hill (Kankakee County)	60969
Tallula	62688	Timber View	61801	Union Hill (St. Clair County)	62232
Tamalco	62253	Timberview	61853	Union Stock Yards (Part of Chicago)	60609
Tamalco (Township)	62253	Time	62363	Uniontown	61572
Tamarac (Part of Flossmoor)	60422	Timewell	62375	Unionville (Massac County)	62910
Tamaroa	62888	Timothy	62428	Unionville (Vermilion County)	61883
Tamms	62988	Tinley Park	60477	Unionville (Whiteside County)	61270
Tampico	61283	Tinley Terrace (Part of Tinley Park)	60477	Unity (Alexander County)	62993
Tampico (Township)	61283	Tioga	62351	Unity (Piatt County) (Township)	61913
Tanbark (Part of Tinley Park)	60477	Tipton	62298	University (Part of Urbana)	61801
Tanglewood (Part of Hanover Park)	60103	Tiskilwa	61368	University Heights (Part of Charleston)	61920
Tate (Township)	62935	Todds Mill	62263	University Mall (Part of Carbondale)	62901
Tatumville	62988	Todds Point	61914	University Park	60466
Taylor (Township)	61021	Todds Point (Township)	61914	Upper Alton (Part of Alton)	62002
Taylor Ridge	61284	Toledo	62468	Uptown (Part of Chicago)	60640
Taylor Springs	62089	Tolono	61880	Urbain	62822
Taylorville	62568	Tolono (Township)	61880	Urban (Part of Taylorville)	62568
Taylorville (Township)	62568	Toluca	61369	Urbana	61801
Techny	60082	Tomahawk Bluff	61301	Urbana (Township)	61801
Teheran	62664	Tompkins (Township)	61447	Urbandale	62914
Temple Hill	62938	Toms Prairie	62837	Ursa	62376
Tenerelli	60511	Tonica	61370	Ursa (Township)	62376
Tennessee	62374	Tonti	62881	Ustick (Township)	61270
Tennessee (Township)	62374	Tonti (Township)	62881	Utica	61373
Terminal Junction (Part of Rock Island)	61201	Topeka	61567	Utica (Township)	61373
Terra Cotta	60014	Toronto	62707	Vale Vue Acres	62650
Terre Haute	61454	Toulon	61483	Valier	62891
Terre Haute (Township)	61454	Toulon (Township)	61483	Valley (Township)	61491
Teutopolis	62467	Tovey	62570	Valley City	62340
Teutopolis (Township)	62467	Towanda	61776	Valley Lo (Part of Glenview)	60025
Texas (Township)	61727	Towanda (Township)	61776	Valley View (DeKalb County)	60145
Texas City	62930	Tower Hill	62571	Valley View (DuPage County)	60137
Texico	62889	Tower Hill (Township)	62571	Valley View (Kane County)	60174
Thackeray	62859	Tower Lakes	60010	Valley View (Tazewell County)	61611
Thawville	60968	Town and Country	62901	Valmeyer	62295
Thayer	62689	Towne Oaks	61535	Van Burensburg	62032
Thebes	62990	Tradewinds	60115	Van Buren Street (Part of Chicago)	60601
Thebes Junction (Part of Thebes)	62990	Trago Lake	62839		
The Burg	61318	Tremont (Township)	61568		
The Clusters (Part of Bolingbrook)	60440	Tremont (Madison County)	62035		
The Covered Bridges (Part of Carol Stream)	60188	Tremont (Tazewell County)	61568		
		Trenton	62293		
		Trilla	62469		
		Trimble	62454		
		Triple Lance Heights	62901		
		Tri-State Village	60521		

	ZIP
Vance (Township)	61841
Vandalia	62471
Vandalia (Township)	62471
Vandalia Correctional Center	62471
Van Orin	61374
Varna	61375
Velma	62568
Venedy (Township)	62296
Venedy	62296
Venetian Village	60046
Venice	62090
Venice (Township)	62090
Venice Crossing (Part of Venice)	62090
Vera	62080
Vergennes	62994
Vergennes (Township)	62994
Vermilion (Edgar County)	61955
Vermilion (La Salle County) (Township)	61370
Vermilion Grove	61870
Vermilion Heights	61832
Vermilionville	61370
Vermilion Estates	61764
Vermont	61484
Vermont (Township)	61484
Vernon (Lake County) (Township)	60069
Vernon (Marion County)	62892
Vernon Hills	60061
Verona	60479
Versailles	62378
Versailles (Township)	62378
Versailles-on-the-Lake (Part of Schaumburg)	60194
Veterans Administration Medical Center	60064
Vets Row	61523
Vevay Park	62420
Vicic (Part of East Peoria)	61611
Victor (Township)	60556
Victoria	61485
Victoria (Township)	61485
Vienna (Grundy County) (Township)	60479
Vienna (Johnson County)	62995
Village Mall (Part of Danville)	61832
Village Square	60515
Village Square Mall (Part of Effingham)	62401
Villa Grove	61956
Villa Grove Junction (Part of Villa Grove)	61956
Villa Hills	62223
Villa Marie	62035
Villa Park	60181
Villa Ridge	62996
Villas Salceda (Part of Northbrook)	60062
Villa Verde (Part of Buffalo Grove)	60090
Villa West	60462
Villa Westbrook (Part of Macomb)	61455
Vincennes Trail	60954
Vinegar Hill (Township)	61036
Viola (Lee County) (Township)	61318
Viola (Mercer County)	61486
Virden	62690
Virden (Township)	62690
Virgil	60182
Virgil (Township)	60182
Virginia	62691
Virginia (Township)	62691
Volo	60073
Vonachen Knolls	61523
Von Glenn Acres	61010
Voorhies	61813
Vulcan (Part of East Carondelet)	62240
Wabash (Township)	62441
Wacker (Carroll County)	61053
Wacker (Kendall County)	60560
Waddams (Township)	61050
Waddams Grove	61048
Wade (Clinton County) (Township)	62231
Wade (Jasper County) (Township)	62448
Wadsworth	60083
Waggoner	62572
Wakefield	62448
Waldo (Township)	61744
Walker (Township)	62373
Walkerville	62050
Walkerville (Township)	62050
Wall (Township)	60948
Wallace (Township)	61350
Wallingford	60442

	ZIP
Walnut	61376
Walnut (Township)	61376
Walnut Grove (McDonough County) (Township)	61438
Walnut Grove (Knox County) (Township)	61414
Walnut Grove	61470
Walnut Hill	62893
Walnut Park	62231
Walnut Prairie	62477
Walpole	62817
Walsh	62297
Walshville	62091
Walshville (Township)	62091
Waltham	61373
Waltham (Township)	61373
Walton	61021
Waltonville	62894
Wamac	62801
Wanda	62025
Wanlock	61231
Wapella	61777
Wapella (Township)	61777
Wards Grove (Township)	61048
Ware	62952
Warner	61273
Warren	61087
Warren (Jo Daviess County) (Township)	61087
Warren (Lake County) (Township)	60031
Warren G. Murray Developmental Center	62801
Warrenhurst (Part of Warrenville)	60555
Warren Park (Part of Cicero)	60650
Warrensburg	62573
Warrenville	60555
Warsaw	62379
Warsaw (Township)	62379
Wartburg	62298
Wartrace	62943
Wasco	60183
Washburn	61570
Washington (Tazewell County) (Township)	61571
Washington (Will County) (Township)	60401
Washington (Carroll County) (Township)	61074
Washington	61571
Washington Heights (Part of Chicago)	60628
Washington Park	62204
Washington Square Mall (Part of Homewood)	60430
Wasson	62930
Wataga	61488
Waterford (DuPage County)	60521
Waterford (Fulton County) (Township)	61542
Waterloo	62298
Waterman	60556
Water Tower Place (Part of Chicago)	60611
Watertown (Part of East Moline)	61244
Watervalley	62920
Watseka	60970
Watson	62473
Watson (Township)	62473
Wauconda	60084
Wauconda (Township)	60084
Waukegan	60079
	60085-87
For specific Waukegan Zip Codes call (708) 662-6800	
Wauponsee (Township)	60450
Waverly	62692
Waycinden Park	60016
Wayne (Township)	60185
Wayne	60184
Wayne Center	60185
Wayne City	62895
Waynesville	61778
Waynesville (Township)	61778
Weathersfield (Part of Schaumburg)	60194
Weaver	62423
Webber (Township)	62814
Webster	62321
Webster Park (Part of Spring Valley)	61362
Wedgewood Estates	62293
Wedron	60557
Weedman	61842
Wee-Ma-Tuk Hills	61427
Weldon	61882
Welge	62288
Weller (Township)	61238
Wellington	60973

	ZIP
Wellington Heights	60435
Wells	62871
Wendelin	62448
Wenona	61377
Wenonah	62075
Wentworth Avenue (Part of Calumet City)	60409
Wesley (Tazewell County)	61611
Wesley (Will County) (Township)	60481
West (Effingham County) (Township)	62458
West (McLean County) (Township)	61722
Westaway	60504
Westbrook	61853
Westbrook Estates (Part of O'Fallon)	62269
West Brooklyn	61378
West Brook Village (Part of Macomb)	61455
Westbury (Part of Bolingbrook)	60440
Westchester	60153
West Chicago	60185-86
For specific West Chicago Zip Codes call (708) 231-2020	
West City	62812
West Clinton Estates	62265
Westdale Gardens	60126
West Deerfield (Township)	60015
West End	62890
Western (Township)	61273
Western Avenue (SOO Station) (Part of Chicago)	60612
Western Avenue (Burlington Northern Station) (Part of Chicago)	60608
Western Knolls	62707
Western Mound (Township)	62630
Western Springs	60558
Westervelt	62574
Westfield (Township)	62474
Westfield (Part of Joliet)	60435
Westfield (Bureau County) (Township)	61312
Westfield (Clark County)	62474
West Frankfort	62896
West Frankfort Lake	62896
West Galena (Township)	61036
Westgate	62959
West Glen (Part of Peoria)	61612
	61614
For specific West Glen Zip Codes call (309) 692-9816	
West Glenview	60025
West Hallock	61526
West Jersey	61483
West Jersey (Township)	61483
West Kankakee (Part of Kankakee)	60901
West Lake (Crawford County)	62454
Westlake (DuPage County)	60139
West Lake Forest (Part of Lake Forest)	60045
West Liberty	62475
West Lincoln (Township)	62656
West Meadowview (Part of Kankakee)	60901
West Miltmore	60046
Westmont	60559
Westmore (Part of Lombard)	60148
Weston	61726
West Peoria	61604
West Peoria (Township)	61604
West Point (Hancock County)	62380
West Point (Morgan County)	62650
West Point (Stephenson County) (Township)	61048
Westport (Knox County)	61401
Westport (Lawrence County)	47591
West Pullman (Part of Chicago)	60628
Westridge (Cook County)	60070
West Ridge (Douglas County)	61953
West Salem	62476
West Sandford	61944
West Twenty-Second St. (Part of Chicago)	60650
West Union	62477
Westville	61883
Westwood (Part of Addison)	60101
West York	62478
Wetaug	62926
Wethersfield (Township)	61277
Wetzel	61944

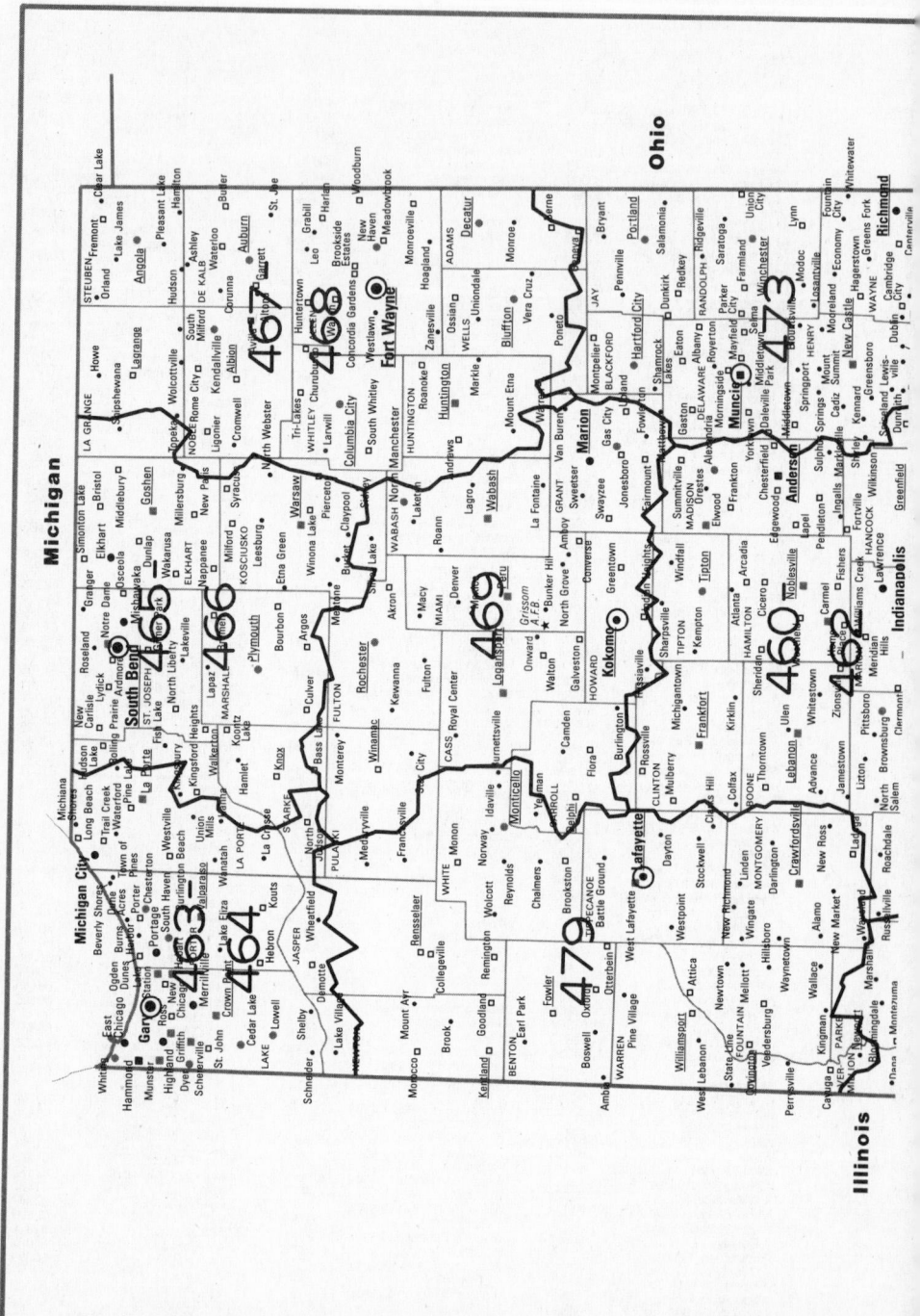

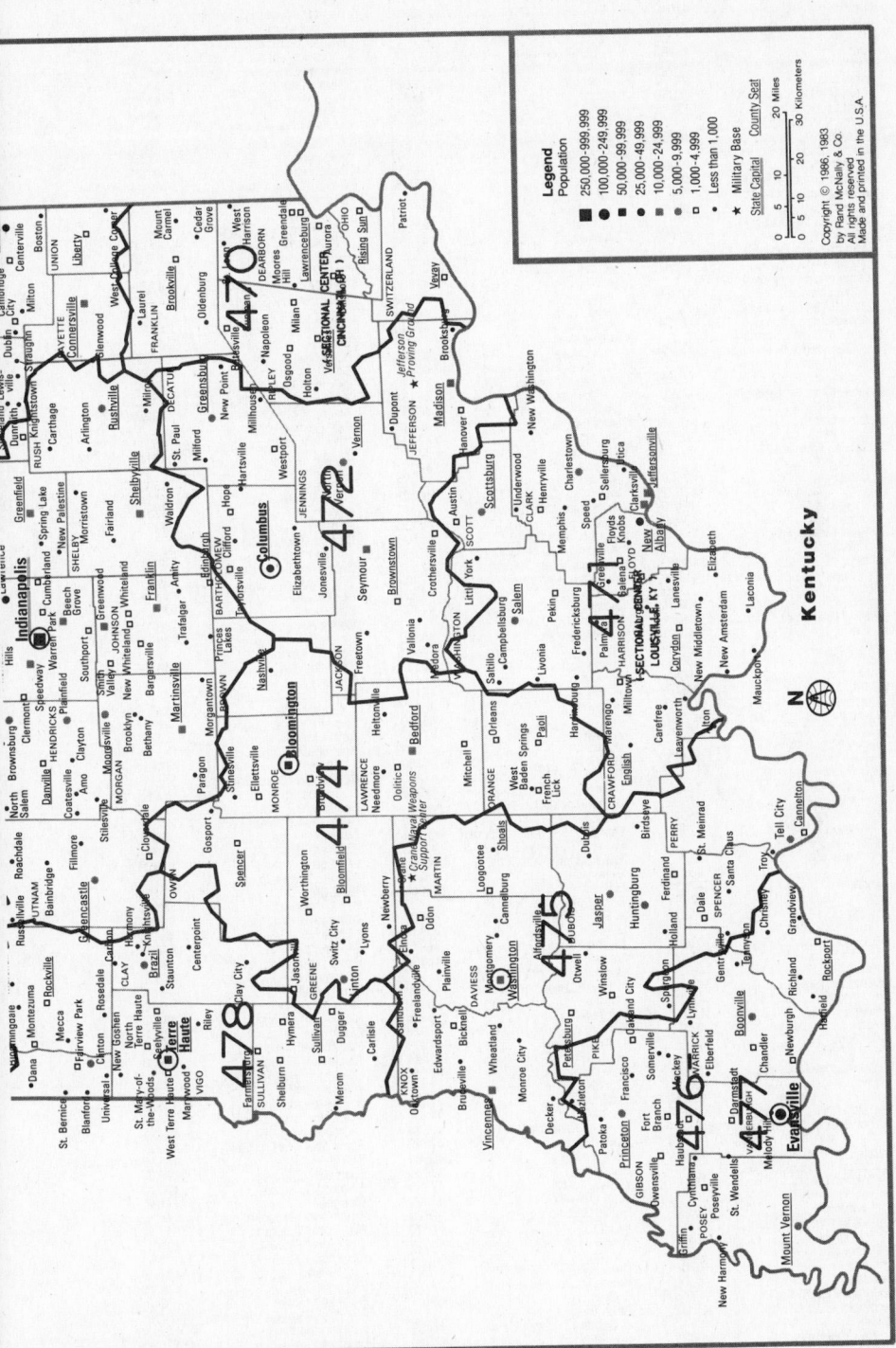

	ZIP		ZIP		ZIP
Abbey Dell	47469	Arcadia	46030	Beattys Corner	46360
Aberdeen	47040	Arcana	46952	Beaver (Newton County)	
Abington	47330	Arcola	46704	(Township)	47963
Abington (Township)	47330	Arctic Springs (Part of		Beaver (Pulaski County)	
Aboite	46783	Jeffersonville)	47130	(Township)	46996
Aboite (Township)	46804	Arda	47567	Beaver City	47922
Acme	47274	Ardmore	46628	Becks Grove	47235
Acton (Part of Indianapolis)	46259	Argos	46501	Becks Mill	47167
Adams (Township)	47272	Ari	46723	Bedford	47421
Adams (Hamilton County)		Ar'les Acres	46060	Bedford Heights (Part of	
(Township)	46069	Arlington (Monroe County)	47401	Bedford)	47421
Adams (Madison County)		Arlington (Rush County)	46104	Beecamp	47250
(Township)	46056	Arlington Park	46815	Beech Brook	46176
Adams (Morgan County)	46151	Armiesburg	47862	Beech Creek (Township)	47459
Adams (Morgan County)		Armstrong	47720	Beech Grove (Marion	
(Township)	46151	Armstrong (Township)	47720	County)	46107
Adams (Parke County)		Armuth Acres	47203	Beech Grove (Morgan	
(Township)	47872	Arney	47431	County)	46151
Adams (Ripley County)		Aroma	46031	Beechwood	47137
(Township)	47041	Arrowhead Park	46580	Bee Ridge	47834
Adams (Warren County)		Art	47834	Bell Center	47925
(Township)	47975	Arthur	47598	Bellefountain	47371
Adams (Allen County)		Artic	46721	Belle Union	46120
(Township)	46774	Ashboro	47840	Belleview	47250
Adams (Carroll County)		Asherville	47834	Belleville	46118
(Township)	47960	Ash Grove	47920	Bellmore	47830
Adams (Cass County)		Ashland (Henry County)	47362	Bell Rohr Park	46538
(Township)	46988	Ashland (Morgan County)		Belmont (Brown County)	47448
Adams (Decatur County)	47240	(Township)	46151	Belmont (Henry County)	47362
Adamsboro	46947	Ashley	46705	Belshaw	46356
Adams Lake	46795	Athens	46912	Ben Davis (Part of	
Adams Mill	46920	Atherton	47874	Indianapolis)	46241
Addison (Township)	46176	Atkinsonville	47868	Bengal	46131
Addmore (Part of		Atlanta	46031	Benham	47042
Clarksville)	47129	Attica	47918	Bennetts	46901
Ade	47922	Atwood	46502	Bennettsville	47143
Advance	46102	Aubbeenaubbee (Township)	46975	Bennington	47011
Ainsworth	46342	Auburn	46706	Benton	46526
Air Mail Field (Part of		Auburn Junction	46706	Benton (Elkhart County)	
Indianapolis)	46241	Augusta (Marion County)	46268	(Township)	46526
Akron	46910	Augusta (Pike County)	47598	Benton (Monroe County)	
Alamo	47916	Aultshire (Part of Muncie)	47302	(Township)	47401
Albany	47320	Aurora	47001	Bentonville	47322
Albion	46701	Austin	47102	Benwood	47834
Albion (Township)	46701	Avalon Hills (Part of		Berlien	46703
Aldine	46366	Indianapolis)	46250	Berne	46711
Alert	47283	Avery	46041	Berwick Manor (Part of	
Alexandria	46001	Avilla	46710	Shelbyville)	46176
Alfont	46040	Avoca	47420	Bethany	46111
Alford	47567	Avon	46168	Bethel (Posey County)	
Alfordsville	47553	Avondale	46952	(Township)	47616
Algers	47567	Ayr	46550	Bethel (Wayne County)	47341
Alida	46391	Ayrshire	47598	Bethel Village	47201
Allen (Miami County)		Azalia	47232	Bethlehem (Clark County)	
(Township)	46951	Babcock	46383	(Township)	47104
Allen (Noble County)		Bacon (Part of Indianapolis)	46220	Bethlehem (Cass County)	
(Township)	46755	Baileys Corner	47978	(Township)	46988
Allendale	47802	Bainbridge (Dubois County)		Bethlehem	47104
Allens Acres	46077	(Township)	47546	Between-the-Lakes Park	46538
Allensville	47011	Bainbridge (Putnam County)	46105	Beverly Shores	46301
Allisonville (Part of		Baker (Township)	47433	Bicknell	47512
Indianapolis)	46250	Bakers Corners	46069	Big Creek (Township)	47929
Allman	46158	Bakertown	46701	Bigger (Township)	47265
Alma Lake	47834	Balbec	47369	Big Lake	46725
Alpine	47331	Baldwin Heights (Part of		Big Springs	46069
Alquina	47331	Princeton)	47670	Billingsville	47353
Alta	47854	Bandon	47514	Billtown	47834
Alto	46902	Banquo	46940	Billville	47834
Alton	47137	Banta	46106	Bippus	46713
Altona	46738	Bar-Barry Heights (Part of		Birdseye	47513
Alvarado	46742	West Lafayette)	47906	Birmingham	46951
Amber Valley	47803	Barbee	46562	Black (Township)	47620
Ambia	47917	Bargersville	46106	Blackhawk (Allen County)	46805
Amboy	46911	Barkley (Township)	47978	Blackhawk (Vigo County)	47866
Americus	47905	Barnaby Acres	47201	Blackhawk Beach	46383
Ames (Part of		Barnard	46172	Blackhawk Forest	46805
Crawfordsville)	47933	Barr (Township)	47519	Blackiston Heights (Part of	
Amity	46131	Barrick Corner	47841	Clarksville)	47129
Amo	46103	Bartlettsville	47421	Blackiston Mill	47129
Anderson	46011-18	Bartley	47805	Blackiston Village (Part of	
For specific Anderson Zip Codes call (317) 643-3356		Barton (Township)	47613	Clarksville)	47129
Anderson (Township)	46016	Bartonia	47390	Black Oak (Part of Gary)	46406
Anderson (Perry County)		Bass Lake	46534	Blaine	47371
(Township)	47586	Batesville	47006	Blairsville	47638
Anderson (Rush County)		Bath	47010	Blanford	47831
(Township)	46156	Bath (Township)	47010	Blocher	47138
Anderson (Warrick County)		Battle Ground	47920	Bloomfield (Greene County)	47424
(Township)	47630	Baugh City	47610	Bloomfield (Lagrange	
Andersonville	47024	Baugo (Township)	46514	County) (Township)	46761
Andrews	46702	Bayfield	46562	Bloomfield (Spencer	
Angola	46703	Beal	47591	County)	47611
Annandale Estates	47448	Bean Blossom (Brown		Bloomingdale	47832
Annapolis	47832	County)	46160	Blooming Grove	47012
Anoka	46947	Bean Blossom (Monroe		Blooming Grove (Township)	47012
Ansley Acres	46804	County) (Township)	47429	Bloomingport	47355
Anthony	47302	Bear Branch	47018	Bloomington	47401-08
Antioch	46041	Bearcreek (Township)	47326	For specific Bloomington Zip Codes call (812) 334-4030	
Antiville	47371	Beard	46041	Blountsville	47354
Apache Acres	47805	Beardstown	46996	Blue Creek (Adams County)	
Arba	47355	Bear Lake	46701	(Township)	46772
		Beatrice	46341		

	ZIP		ZIP		ZIP
Blue Creek (Franklin County)	47041	Broad Ripple (Part of Indianapolis)	46220	Butler (Franklin County) (Township)	47006
Blue Lake	46723	Broadview (Grant County)	46952	Butler (Miami County) (Township)	46970
Blue Ridge	46176	Broadview (Lawrence County)	47421	Butler Center	46738
Blue River (Hancock County) (Township)	46140	Broadview (Monroe County)	47401	Butlerville	47223
Blue River (Harrison County) (Township)	47115	Bromer	47452	Byrneville	47122
		Brook	47922	Byron	46371
Blue River (Henry County) (Township)	47360	Brookfield	46126	Caborn	47620
		Brook Haven	46952	Cadiz	47362
Blue River (Johnson County) (Township)	46124	Brook Knoll (Part of Bedford)	47421	Caesar Creek (Township)	47018
Bluff Point	47371	Brooklyn	46111	Cagle Mill	47868
Bluffs	46151	Brookmoor	46158	Cain (Township)	47949
Bluffton	46714	Brooks	46060	Cairo	47906
Bobtown	47274	Brooksburg	47250	Cale	47581
Bogard (Township)	47568	Brookside Estates (Allen County)	46805	California (Township)	46534
Boggstown	46110			Calumet (Township)	46402
Bogle Corner	47438	Brookside Estates (Vigo County)	47802	Calvertville	47424
Bolivar (Township)	47970	Brookston	47923	Cambria	46041
Bonnell	47022	Brook Trails	46637	Cambridge City	47327
Bonnenburger	47130	Brookville	47012	Camby (Part of Indianapolis)	46113
Bono	47446	Brookville (Township)	47012	Camden	46917
Bono (Township)	47446	Brookville Heights	46163	Cammack	47302
Boon (Township)	47601	Brookwood (Part of Warsaw)	46580	Campbell (Jennings County) (Township)	47023
Boone (Cass County) (Township)	46978	Broom Hill	47106	Campbell (Warrick County) (Township)	47610
Boone (Crawford County) (Township)	47137	Brown (Hancock County) (Township)	47384	Campbellsburg	47108
		Brown (Hendricks County) (Township)	46112	Campbelltown	47598
Boone (Dubois County) (Township)	47546	Brown (Montgomery County) (Township)	47933	Canaan	47224
				Candleglo Village	46176
Boone (Harrison County) (Township)	47135	Brown (Morgan County) (Township)	46158	Candle Light Village (Part of Columbus)	47201
Boone (Madison County) (Township)	46036	Brown (Ripley County) (Township)	47250	Cannelburg	47519
				Cannelton	47520
Boone (Porter County) (Township)	46341	Brown (Washington County) (Township)	47108	Cannelton Heights (Part of Cannelton)	47520
Boone Grove	46302	Brownsburg	46112	Canton	47167
Boonville	47601	Browns Crossing	46151	Carbon	47837
Borden	47106	Brownstown (Township)	47220	Carbondale	47993
Boston	47324	Brownstown (Crawford County)	47118	Cardonia	47834
Boston (Township)	47324			Carefree	47137
Boswell	47921	Brownstown (Jackson County)	47220	Carey (Part of Noblesville)	46060
Boundary	47371	Browns Valley	47933	Carlisle	47838
Bourbon	46504	Brownsville	47325	Carlos City	47355
Bourbon (Township)	46504	Brownsville (Township)	47325	Carmel	46032-33
Bowers	47940	Bruce Lake	46939	For specific Carmel Zip Codes call (317) 846-1566	
Bowerstown	46750	Bruceville	47516		
Bowling Green	47833	Brummitt Acres	46304	Carp	47460
Bowman	47567	Brunswick	46303	Carpenter (Township)	47977
Bowman Acres (Part of Greenfield)	46140	Brunswick (Part of Gary)	46406	Carpentersville	46172
		Brushy Prairie	46761	Carr (Clark County) (Township)	47143
Boxley	46069	Bryant	47326		
Boyleston	46057	Bryantsburg	47250	Carr (Jackson County) (Township)	47260
Bracken	46750	Bryantsville	47446		
Bradford	47107	Buck Creek (Hancock County) (Township)	46140	Carriage Estates (Bartholomew County)	47201
Bradford Village (Part of Marion)	46952	Buck Creek (Tippecanoe County)	47924	Carriage Estates (Hancock County)	46163
Bradley	47611	Buckeye	46792	Carrollton	46913
Bramble	47553	Buckskin	47613	Carrollton (Township)	46929
Branchville	47514	Bucktown	47838	Carter (Township)	47523
Branchville Training Center	47586	Bud	46131	Cartersburg	46114
Brandywine (Hancock County) (Township)	46140	Buddha	47421	Carthage	46115
		Buena Vista	47024	Carwood	47106
Brandywine (Shelby County) (Township)	46126	Buffalo	47925	Cascade Heights (Part of Bloomington)	47401
		Buffaloville	47550		
Braytown	47043	Buffington (Part of Gary)	46406	Cass (Sullivan County) (Township)	47882
Brazil	47834	Bufkin	47620		
Brazil (Township)	47834	Bugtown	47633	Cass (White County) (Township)	47960
Breezewood	46952	Bullocktown	47601	Cass	47882
Breezewood Park	47302	Bunker Hill (Fayette County)	47331	Cass (Clay County) (Township)	47868
Breezy Point	47960	Bunker Hill (Knox County)	47591		
Bremen	46506	Bunker Hill (Miami County)	46914	Cass (Dubois County) (Township)	47541
Brems	46534	Bunker Hill (Washington County)	47167	Cass (Greene County) (Township)	47449
Brendan Wood (Part of Lebanon)	46052	Burdick	46304		
Brendonwood (Part of Indianapolis)	46226	Burglen Hills (Part of Tell City)	47586	Cass (La Porte County) (Township)	46390
		Burket	46508	Cass (Ohio County) (Township)	47040
Brent Woods (Part of Shelbyville)	46176	Burlington	46915		
Bretzville	47542	Burlington (Township)	46915	Cass (Pulaski County) (Township)	47957
Brewersville	47265	Burlington Beach	46383		
Brewington Woods	47302	Burnett	47805	Cassville	46901
Briarwood	46157	Burnettsville	47926	Castleton	46250
Brice	47371	Burney	47222	Castleton Square (Part of Castleton)	46250
Brick Chapel	46135	Burns City	47553		
Bridgeport (Part of Indianapolis)	46231	Burns Harbor	46304	Cataract	47460
		Burnsville	47201	Cates	47952
Bridgeton	47836	Burr Oak (Marshall County)	46511	Catlin	47872
Brierwood Hills	46804	Burr Oak (Noble County)	46701	Cato	47598
Bright	47025	Burrows	46916	Cavanaugh (Part of Gary)	46406
Brighton	46746	Busseron	47561	Cayuga	47928
Brightwood (Part of Indianapolis)	46218	Busseron (Township)	47561	Cedar Canyons	46825
Brimfield	46720	Butler (De Kalb County)	46721	Cedar Creek (Allen County) (Township)	46741
Brinckley	47340	Butler (De Kalb County) (Township)	46763		
Bringhurst	46913			Cedar Creek (De Kalb County)	46738
Bristol	46507			Cedar Creek (Lake County) (Township)	46356
Bristow	47515				
Broadlands	47805				

	ZIP
Cedar Grove	47016
Cedar Lake	46303
Cedar Point	47960
Cedar Shores	46741
Cedarville	46741
Celestine	47521
Cemar Estates	47805
Cementville (Part of Jeffersonville)	47129
Centenary	47842
Centennial	47952
Center (Benton County) (Township)	47944
Center (Boone County) (Township)	46052
Center (Clinton County) (Township)	46041
Center (Dearborn County) (Township)	47001
Center (Delaware County) (Township)	47302
Center (Gibson County) (Township)	47649
Center (Grant County) (Township)	46952
Center (Greene County) (Township)	47424
Center (Hancock County) (Township)	46140
Center (Hendricks County) (Township)	46122
Center (Howard County)	46902
Center (Howard County) (Township)	46902
Center (Jay County)	47371
Center (Jennings County) (Township)	47265
Center (La Porte County) (Township)	46350
Center (Lake County) (Township)	46307
Center (Marion County) (Township)	46204
Center (Marshall County) (Township)	46563
Center (Martin County) (Township)	47553
Center (Porter County) (Township)	46383
Center (Posey County) (Township)	47620
Center (Ripley County) (Township)	47037
Center (Rush County) (Township)	46148
Center (Starke County) (Township)	46534
Center (Union County) (Township)	47353
Center (Vanderburgh County) (Township)	47710
Center (Warrick County)	47601
Center (Wayne County) (Township)	47330
Centerpoint	47840
Center Square	47043
Centerton	46151
Center Valley	46158
Centerville (Spencer County)	47611
Centerville (Wayne County)	47330
Central	47110
Central Barren	47161
Centre (Township)	46614
Century Consumer Mall (Part of Merrillville)	46410
Ceylon	46740
Chain O'Lakes	46628
Chalmers	47929
Chambersburg	47454
Champlin Meadows (Part of Martinsville)	46151
Chandler	47610
Chapel Bluff (Part of Columbus)	47201
Chapel Hill (Marion County)	46224
Chapelhill (Monroe County)	47436
Chapel Manor (Part of Merrillville)	46410
Charlemac Village (Part of Indianapolis)	46259
Charlestown	47111
Charlestown (Township)	47111
Charle Sumac Estates (Part of Indianapolis)	46259
Charlottesville	46117
Chase	47921
Chelsea	47138
Cherokee Terrace	47130
Cherry Grove	47933

	ZIP
Chester (Wabash County) (Township)	46962
Chester (Wayne County)	47374
Chester (Wells County) (Township)	46781
Chesterfield	46017
Chesterton (Hamilton County)	46280
Chesterton (Porter County)	46304
Chesterville	47032
Chestnut Hill (Part of Chesterton)	46304
Chestnut Ridge	47274
Chicago Avenue (Part of East Chicago)	46312
Chili	46926
China	47250
Chippewa (Part of South Bend)	46614
Chrisney	47611
Christiansburg	47201
Christmas Lake Village (Part of Santa Claus)	47579
Churubusco	46723
Cicero (Hamilton County)	46034
Cicero (Tipton County) (Township)	46031
Cicero Heights	46072
Cincinnati	47424
Circle Park	46742
Circleville	46173
Clare	46060
Clark (Johnson County) (Township)	46142
Clark (Montgomery County) (Township)	47954
Clark (Perry County) (Township)	47515
Clarksburg	47225
Clarks Hill	47930
Clarks Landing	46742
Clarksville (Clark County)	47129
Clarksville (Hamilton County)	46060
Clay (Bartholomew County) (Township)	47201
Clay (Carroll County) (Township)	46923
Clay (Cass County) (Township)	46947
Clay (Dearborn County) (Township)	47032
Clay (Decatur County) (Township)	47240
Clay (Hamilton County) (Township)	46032-33
For specific Clay Zip Codes call (812) 939-3111	
Clay (Hendricks County) (Township)	46121
Clay (Howard County) (Township)	46901
Clay (Kosciusko County) (Township)	46580
Clay (Lagrange County) (Township)	46761
Clay (Miami County) (Township)	46914
Clay (Morgan County) (Township)	46111
Clay (Owen County) (Township)	47460
Clay (Pike County) (Township)	47640
Clay (Spencer County) (Township)	47579
Clay (St. Joseph County) (Township)	46637
Clay (Wayne County) (Township)	47345
Clay City (Clay County)	47841
Clay City (Spencer County)	47550
Claypool	46510
Claysville	47108
Clayton	46118
Clear Creek (Huntington County) (Township)	46750
Clear Creek (Monroe County)	47426
Clear Creek (Monroe County) (Township)	47401
Clear Lake (Township)	46737
Clear Lake	46737
Clear Spring (Jackson County)	47220
Clearspring (Lagrange County) (Township)	46751
Clermont	46234
Clermont Heights	46112
Cleveland (Elkhart County) (Township)	46514

	ZIP
Cleveland (Hancock County)	46140
Cleveland (Whitley County) (Township)	46787
Clifford	47226
Clifty (Township)	47246
Clifty Village	47203
Clinton (Vermillion County) (Township)	47842
Clinton (Boone County) (Township)	46052
Clinton (Cass County) (Township)	46947
Clinton (Decatur County) (Township)	47240
Clinton (Elkhart County) (Township)	46526
Clinton (La Porte County) (Township)	46382
Clinton (Putnam County) (Township)	46135
Clinton (Vermillion County)	47842
Clinton Falls	46135
Cloud Crest Hills	47448
Cloverdale	46120
Cloverdale (Township)	46120
Cloverland	47834
Clover Village	46126
Clunette	46538
Clymers	46947
Coal Bluff	47874
Coal City	47427
Coal Creek (Fountain County)	47932
Coal Creek (Montgomery County) (Township)	47994
Coalmont	47845
Coatesville	46121
Cochran (Part of Aurora)	47001
Coe	47598
Coesse	46725
Coesse Corners	46725
Coffey	47448
Cofield Corner	47040
Colburn	47931
Colburn Acres	46536
Cold Springs (Dearborn County)	47032
Cold Springs (Steuben County)	46742
Colfax (Clinton County)	46035
Colfax (Newton County) (Township)	46349
Collamer	46787
College Corner (Jay County)	47371
College Corner (Union County)	45003
College Hill (Part of Logansport)	46947
College Mall (Part of Bloomington)	47401
College Meadows	46240
Collegeville	47978
Collett	47371
Collins	46725
Coloma	47872
Colonial Hills	47630
Colonial Park	47802
Colonial Village	46040
Columbia (Fayette County) (Township)	47331
Columbia (Gibson County) (Township)	47660
Columbia (Jennings County) (Township)	47265
Columbia (Whitley County) (Township)	46725
Columbia (Dubois County) (Township)	47527
Columbia (Fayette County)	47331
Columbia City	46725
Columbus	47201-03
For specific Columbus Zip Codes call (812) 378-2089	
Commercial Place (Part of Greencastle)	46135
Commiskey	47227
Como	47371
Concord (DeKalb County) (Township)	46785
Concord (De Kalb County)	46706
Concord (Elkhart County) (Township)	46514
Concord (Tippecanoe County)	47905
Concordia Gardens (Part of Fort Wayne)	46825
Connersville	47331
Connersville (Township)	47331
Continental Camp	47616

	ZIP		ZIP		ZIP
Converse	46919	Darmstadt	47711	Dudleytown	47274
Cook (Part of Cedar Lake)	46303	Darrough Chapel	46901	Duff	47542
Cool Spring (Township)	46360	Davis (Fountain County)		Dugger	47848
Coolwood Acres	46383	(Township)	47918	Dundee	46001
Cope	46151	Davis (La Porte County)	46360	Dune Acres	46304
Coppess Corner	46772	Davis (Starke County)		Dune Acres Station (Part of	
Cordry Lake	46164	(Township)	46532	Dune Acres)	46304
Corn Brook	47203	Daylight	47711	Duneland Beach	46360
Cornettsville	47568	Dayton	47941	Dunfee	46818
Correct	47042	Dayville	47630	Dunkirk (Cass County)	46947
Correctional Industrial		Deacon	46994	Dunkirk (Jay County)	47336
Complex	46064	De Camp Gardens	46516	Dunlap	46514
Cortland	47228	Decatur (Adams County)	46733	Dunlapsville	47353
Corunna	46730	Decatur (Marion County)		Dunn	47944
Cory	47846	(Township)	46241	Dunnington	47944
Corydon	47112	Decker	47524	Dunns Bridge	46380
Cosperville	46794	Decker (Township)	47524	Dunreith	47337
Cottage Grove	47353	Deedsville	46921	Dupont	47231
Cotton (Township)	47011	Deep River	46342	Durbin	46060
Country Club Gardens	46804	Deer Creek (Carroll County)	46917	Dutch Town (Part of	
Country Club Heights	46011	Deer Creek (Carroll County)		Garrett)	46738
Country Club Meadows		(Township)	46923	Dyer	46311
(Part of Evansville)	47710	Deer Creek (Cass County)		Eagle (Township)	46077
Countryside Estates	46805	(Township)	46932	Eagle Creek (Township)	46341
Country Terrace	47302	Deer Creek (Miami County)		Eagledale Plaza Shopping	
Country Village	47303	(Township)	46959	Center (Part of	
Courter	46970	Deerfield (Bartholomew		Indianapolis)	46222
Coveyville	47421	County)	47201	Eagle Hollow	47250
Covington	47932	Deerfield (Randolph County)	47380	Eagletown	46074
Covington Dells	46804	Deerfield (Vigo County)	47802	Eagle Village	46077
Covington Plaza (Part of		Deer Park	46310	Eaglewood Estates	46077
Fort Wayne)	46804	Deers Mills	47989	Earle	47711
Cowan	47302	De Gonia	47601	Earlham (Part of Richmond)	47374
Coxville	47874	Delaware (Ripley County)		Earl Park	47942
Craig (Township)	47043	(Township)	47037	East Cedar Lake (Part of	
Craig Highlands	46060	Delaware (Delaware County)		Cedar Lake)	46303
Craigville	46731	(Township)	47320	East Chicago	46312
Crandall	47111	Delaware (Hamilton County)		East Clifford	47203
Crane	47522	(Township)	46060	East Columbus (Part of	
Crane Naval Depot	47522	Delaware	47037	Columbus)	47201
Crane Naval Weapons		Delong	46922	East Enterprise	47019
Support Center	47522	Delp	47905	Eastern Heights (Part of	
Crawfordsville	47933	Delphi	46923	Bloomington)	47401
Cree Lake	46755	Deming	46034	Eastgate (Bartholomew	
Crest Manor (Part of South		Democrat (Township)	46920	County)	47201
Bend)	46614	Demotte	46310	Eastgate (Clark County)	47130
Crestmoor (Part of		Denham	46925	East Gate (Hancock	
Shelbyville)	46176	Denmark	47427	County)	46040
Creston	46356	Denver	46926	Eastgate (Marion County)	46219
Crestview	46383	Depauw	47115	Eastgate Consumer Mall	
Crestview Heights	46158	Deputy	47230	(Part of Indianapolis)	46219
Crestwood (Part of Fort		Derby	47525	East Glenn	47803
Wayne)	46804	Desoto	47302	Eastland Gardens (Part of	
Crete	47355	Devon Park (Part of Muncie)	47304	Fort Wayne)	46816
Crisman (Part of Portage)	46368	Devonshire (Part of		Eastland Mall (Part of	
Critchfield	46142	Lawrence)	46226	Evansville)	47715
Crocker (Part of Portage)	46383	Dewey (Township)	46348	East Monticello	47960
Crompton Hill	47842	Diamond	47874	East Mount Carmel	47665
Cromwell	46732	Diamond Lake	46794	East Oolitic	47421
Crooked Lake	46703	Diamond Valley (Part of		East Park (Part of Frankfort)	46041
Cross Plains	47017	Evansville)	47710	Eastridge Manor	47203
Crothersville	47229	Dick Johnson (Township)	47834	East Shelburn (Part of	
Crown Center	46157	Dike (Part of Princeton)	47670	Shelburn)	47879
Crown Colony	46816	Dillman	46792	East Shoals (Part of Shoals)	47581
Crown Point	46307	Dillsboro	47018	East Union	46031
Crows Nest	46208	Diplomat Plaza (Part of Fort		Eastwich (Part of Lafayette)	47901
Crumley Crossing	47336	Wayne)	46806	Eaton	47338
Crump Estates (Part of		Disko	46982	Echo Heights (Part of	
Columbus)	47201	Dixon	46773	Muncie)	47302
Crumstown	46554	Doans	47424	Eckerty	47116
Crystal	47527	Dodd	47587	Economy	47339
Cuba (Allen County)	46741	Dodds Bridge	47849	Eddy	46795
Cuba (Bartholomew County)	46124	Dogwood	47135	Eden (Hancock County)	46140
Cuba (Owen County)	47460	Dolan	47401	Eden (Lagrange County)	
Culver	46511	Domestic	46714	(Township)	46571
Culver Military Academy		Donaldson	46513	Edgerton	46797
(Part of Culver)	46511	Dongola	47660	Edgewater	46383
Cumback	47501	Doolittle Mills	47118	Edgewood (Bartholomew	
Cumberland	46229	Door Village	46350	County)	47201
Cunot	46120	Dover (Boone County)	46052	Edgewood (La Porte	
Curby	47118	Dover (Dearborn County)	47022	County)	46360
Curry (Township)	47879	Dover Hill	47581	Edgewood (Lawrence	
Curryville (Adams County)	46731	Dovers View	47072	County)	47421
Curryville (Sullivan County)	47879	Dowden Acres	47802	Edgewood (Madison	
Curtisville	46036	Downtown (Part of Gary)	46402	County)	46011
Cutler	46920	Downtown (Part of		Edgewood (Marion County)	46227
Cuzco	47432	Kokomo)	46901	Edgewood Park	46818
Cyclone	46041	Downtown (Part of		Edinburgh	46124
Cynthiana	47612	Lafayette)	47902	Edison Park (Part of South	
Cypress	47712	Downtown (Part of Muncie)	47305	Bend)	46615
Dabney	47023	Dreamwold Heights	46637	Edna Mills	46065
Daggett	47427	Dresden	47453	Edwardsport	47528
Daisy Hill	47106	Dresser	47885	Edwardsville	47150
Dale	47523	Drexel Gardens (Part of		Eel (Township)	46947
Daleville	47334	Indianapolis)	46241	Eel River (Allen County)	
Dallas (Township)	46702	Driftwood (Township)	47281	(Township)	46723
Dalton	47346	Dublin	47335	Eel River (Hendricks	
Dalton (Township)	47346	Dubois	47527	County) (Township)	46165
Dana	47847	Dubois Crossroads	47527	Effner	60966
Danville	46122	Duck Creek (Township)	46036	Ege	46763
Darlington	47940	Dudley (Township)	47387	Ehrmandale	47805

	ZIP
Ekin	46031
Elberfeld	47613
El Dorado	46142
Elizabeth	47117
Elizabethtown	47232
Elizaville	46052
Elkhart	46514-17
For specific Elkhart Zip Codes call (219) 293-5502	
Elkhart (Elkhart County) (Township)	46526
Elkhart (Noble County) (Township)	46794
Elkinsville	47448
Ellettsville	47429
Ellis	47848
Elliston	47424
Elmdale	47933
Elmira	46761
Elmore (Township)	47529
Elmwood (Part of Peru)	46970
Elnora	47529
Elrod	47018
Elston	47905
Elwood	46036
Elwren	47401
Eminence	46125
Emison	47530
Emma	46571
Emporia	46056
Enchanted Hills	46732
Englewood (Part of Bedford)	47421
English	47118
English Lake	46366
Enochsburg	47240
Enos	47963
Enos Corners	47660
Epsom	47568
Epworth Forest	46555
Erie	46970
Erie (Township)	46970
Ervin (Township)	46929
Etna (Kosciusko County) (Township)	46524
Etna (Whitley County)	46725
Etna Green	46524
Etna-Troy (Township)	46764
Eugene	47928
Eugene (Township)	47928
Eureka	47635
Evanston	47531
Evansville	47701-99
For specific Evansville Zip Codes call (812) 429-3400	
Evergreen Acres (Part of Clarksville)	47129
Everroad Park East (Part of Columbus)	47203
Everroad Park West (Part of Columbus)	47203
Everton	47331
Ewing (Part of Brownstown)	47220
Fair Acres (Part of Salem)	47167
Fairbanks (Township)	47849
Fairbanks	47849
Fairfield (De Kalb County) (Township)	46730
Fairfield (Franklin County) (Township)	47012
Fairfield (Tippecanoe County) (Township)	47904
Fairfield Center	46730
Fair Grounds (Part of Indianapolis)	46205
Fairland	46126
Fairlawn (Part of Columbus)	47201
Fairmount	46928
Fairmount (Township)	46928
Fair Oaks	47943
Fairplay (Township)	47465
Fairview	47331
Fairview (Township)	47331
Fairview (Randolph County)	47373
Fairview (Switzerland County)	47011
Fairview Park	47842
Fairwood Hills (Part of Indianapolis)	46256
Fall Creek (Hamilton County) (Township)	46064
Fall Creek (Henry County) (Township)	47356
Fall Creek (Madison County) (Township)	46011
Falmouth	46127
Farlen	47562
Farmers	47431
Farmersburg	47850
Farmers Retreat	47018
Farmersville	47620

	ZIP
Farmland	47340
Farrabee	47167
Farrville	46952
Fayette (Boone County)	46052
Fayette (Vigo County) (Township)	47885
Fayetteville	47421
Federal (Part of Indianapolis)	46204
Fenn Haven	47586
Ferdinand	47532
Ferdinand (Township)	47532
Ferguson Hill	47885
Fewell Rhoades	46151
Fiat	47326
Fickle	46041
Fields	46158
Fifteenth Avenue (Part of Gary)	46407
Fillmore	46128
Fincastle	46172
Finley (Township)	47170
Finly	46129
Fishers	46038
Fishersburg	46051
Fisher's Woodland	46060
Fish Lake (La Porte County)	46574
Fish Lake (Lagrange County)	46761
Five Points (Marion County)	46239
Five Points (Morgan County)	46158
Five Points (Whitley County)	46725
Flat Rock (Bartholomew County) (Township)	47201
Flat Rock (Shelby County)	47234
Flat Rock Park	47201
Flat Rock Park North (Part of Columbus)	47201
Fleming	47274
Fletcher Lake	46939
Flint	46703
Flintwood (Part of Columbus)	47201
Flora (Carroll County)	46929
Flora (Miami County)	46970
Florence	47020
Florida (Madison County)	46011
Florida (Parke County) (Township)	47874
Floyd (Township)	46121
Floyds Knobs	47119
Folsomville	47614
Fontanet	47851
Foraker	46526
Foresman	47922
Forest	46039
Forest (Township)	46039
Forest Hill	47240
Forest Park (Part of Columbus)	47201
Forest Park Beach	46742
Forest Park Heights	47401
Forest Park North (Part of Columbus)	47201
Forest Ridge (Allen County)	46804
Forest Ridge (Grant County)	46952
Forest Ridge Estates	46804
Forrest Hills	46036
Fort Branch	47648
Fort Ritner	47430
Fortville	46040
Fort Wayne	46801-99
For specific Fort Wayne Zip Codes call (219) 427-7311	
Foster	47932
Fountain	47918
Fountain City	47341
Fountain Park (Jasper County)	47977
Fountain Park (Steuben County)	46742
Fountain Square (Part of Indianapolis)	46203
Fountaintown	46130
Fowler	47944
Fowlerton	46930
Foxglen	46060
Fox Hill	46113
Fox Lake	46703
Fox Ridge	46135
Francesville	47946
Francisco	47649
Frankfort	46041
Franklin (Johnson County) (Township)	46131
Franklin (Kosciusko County) (Township)	46910
Franklin (Marion County) (Township)	46239

	ZIP
Franklin (Montgomery County) (Township)	47940
Franklin (Owen County) (Township)	47431
Franklin (Pulaski County) (Township)	46996
Franklin (Putnam County) (Township)	46172
Franklin (Randolph County) (Township)	47380
Franklin (Ripley County) (Township)	47031
Franklin (Washington County) (Township)	47167
Franklin (Wayne County)	47346
Franklin (Wayne County) (Township)	47341
Franklin (De Kalb County) (Township)	46721
Franklin (Floyd County) (Township)	47117
Franklin (Grant County) (Township)	46952
Franklin (Harrison County) (Township)	47136
Franklin (Hendricks County) (Township)	46180
Franklin (Henry County) (Township)	47352
Franklin (Johnson County)	46131
Franklin Hills (Part of Tell City)	47586
Frankton	46044
Fredericksburg	47120
Fredonia	47137
Freedom	47431
Freeland Park	47944
Freelandville	47535
Freeman	47460
Freeport	46161
Freetown	47235
Fremont (Township)	46737
Fremont	46737
French (Adams County) (Township)	46714
French (Ohio County)	47001
French Lake	47802
French Lick	47432
French Lick (Township)	47432
Frenchtown	47115
Friendship	47021
Friendswood	46113
Fritchton	47591
Fritz Corner	47585
Fruitdale	46160
Fugit (Township)	47240
Fulda	47536
Fulton (Township)	47932
Fulton	46931
Furnace	47424
Furnessville	46304
Gadsden	46052
Galena (Floyd County)	47119
Galena (La Porte County) (Township)	46371
Galveston	46932
Gambill	47848
Gar Creek	46774
Garden Acres (Boone County)	46071
Garden Acres (Monroe County)	47401
Garden City	47201
Garfield (Part of Indianapolis)	46203
Garrett	46738
Gary	46401-11
For specific Gary Zip Codes call (219) 886-8011	
Gasburg	46158
Gas City	46933
Gaston	47342
Gatchel	47586
Gatesville	46164
Gateway Shopping Center (Part of Richmond)	47374
Gatewood (Part of Muncie)	47304
Gaynorsville	47240
Geetingsville	46041
Gem	46140
Geneva (Adams County)	46740
Geneva (Jennings County) (Township)	47273
Geneva (Shelby County)	47234
Gentryville	47537
Georgetown (Floyd County) (Township)	47122
Georgetown (Randolph County)	47340

	ZIP		ZIP		ZIP
Georgetown (St. Joseph County)	46635	Green (Noble County) (Township)	46763	Hamburg (Clark County) ...	47172
Georgetown (Allen County)	46741	Green (Randolph County) (Township)	47368	Hamburg (Franklin County)	47036
Georgetown (Cass County)	46947	Green (Wayne County)		Hamilton (Clinton County)	46058
Georgetown (Floyd County)	47122	(Township)	47393	Hamilton (Delaware County) (Township)	47302
Georgia	47446	Green (Hancock County)		Hamilton (Jackson County)	
Georgia Heights (Part of Merrillville)	46410	(Township)	46040	(Township)	47274
Gerald	47520	Green (Madison County) (Township)	46048	Hamilton (Madison County)	46011
German (Bartholomew County) (Township)	47201	Green (Marshall County) (Township)	46501	Hamilton (Steuben County)	46742
German (Marshall County) (Township)	46506	Green (Morgan County) (Township)	46151	Hamilton (Sullivan County) (Township)	47882
German (St. Joseph County) (Township)	46628	Green Acres	46410	Hamilton Park	47302
German (Vanderburgh County) (Township)	47712	Greenbriar (Marion County)	46260	Hamilton Village	47303
Germantown	47272	Greenbriar (Putnam County)	46135	Hamlet	46532
Gessie	47974	Greenbrier	47601	Hammond	46320-27
Gibson (Township)	47170	Greencastle	46135	For specific Hammond Zip Codes call (219) 932-1519	
Gifford	47978	Greencastle (Township)	46135	Hammond (Township)	47615
Gilboa (Township)	47944	Green Center	46701	Hamor Heights	47203
Gilead	46951	Greendale (Allen County)	46805	Hancock	47115
Gill (Township)	47861	Greendale (Dearborn County)	47025	Handy	47401
Gillam (Township)	46392	Greene (Jay County) (Township)	47371	Hanfield	46952
Gilman	46001	Greene (Parke County) (Township)	47989	Hanging Grove (Township)	47978
Gilmer Park	46624	Greene (St. Joseph County) (Township)	46614	Hangman Crossing	47274
Gilmour	47438	Greenfield (Hancock County)	46140	Hanna	46340
Gingrich	47960	Greenfield (Lagrange County) (Township)	46746	Hanna (Township)	46340
Gings	46173	Greenfield (Orange County) (Township)	47118	Hanover	47243
Giro	47640	Greenfield Estates	46952	Hanover (Township)	47243
Glen Aire	47803	Greenfield Mills	46746	Hanover (Lake County) (Township)	46303
Glenbrook Square (Part of Fort Wayne)	46805	Greenhill	47970	Hanover (Shelby County) (Township)	46161
Glendale	47558	Greenleaf Manor (Part of Elkhart)	46514	Hanover Beach	47243
Glendale Center (Part of Indianapolis)	46220	Green Meadows (Shelby County)	46126	Happy Hollow Heights (Part of West Lafayette)	47906
Glendale Lake	46952	Green Meadows (Tippecanoe County)	47906	Harbison (Township)	47527
Glen Eden	46703	Greenoak	46975	Harbor (Part of East Chicago)	46312
Glenhall	47992	Greensboro	47344	Hardinsburg (Dearborn County)	47025
Glenns Valley (Part of Indianapolis)	46217	Greensboro (Township)	47344	Hardinsburg (Washington County)	47125
Glen Park (Part of Gary)	46409	Greensburg	47240	Hardscrabble	46051
Glenview	47203	Greensfork (Randolph County) (Township)	47335	Harlan	46743
Glenwood	46133	Greens Fork (Wayne County)	47345	Harmony (Clay County)	47853
Glenwood Acres	47620	Greentown	46936	Harmony (Posey County) (Township)	47631
Glenwood Park (Part of Fort Wayne)	46805	Green Tree Mall (Part of Clarksville)	47129	Harmony (Union County) (Township)	47331
Glezen	47567	Greenvalley	46060	Harper	47283
Gnaw Bone	47448	Greenview	46815	Harris (Township)	46530
Goblesville	46750	Greenville	47124	Harrisburg	47331
Goff	46952	Greenville (Township)	47124	Harris City	47240
Golden Acres	46815	Greenville	46781	Harrison (Bartholomew County) (Township)	47201
Golden Hill	47960	Greenwood (Johnson County)	46142-43	Harrison (Blackford County) (Township)	47359
Golden Lake	46779	For specific Greenwood Zip Codes call (317) 881-2323		Harrison (Boone County) (Township)	46052
Goldsmith	46045	Greenwood (Lagrange County)	46795	Harrison (Cass County) (Township)	46947
Golfview Estates	47130	Greenwood Park Mall (Part of Greenwood)	46142	Harrison (Clay County) (Township)	47841
Goodland	47948	Greer (Township)	47613	Harrison (Daviess County) (Township)	47501
Goose Lake	46725	Gregg (Township)	46157	Harrison (Dearborn County) (Township)	47060
Goshen (Elkhart County)	46526	Greybrook Lake	47868	Harrison (Delaware County) (Township)	47302
Goshen (Scott County)	47170	Griffin	47616	Harrison (Elkhart County) (Township)	46526
Gospel Grove	47803	Griffith	46319	Harrison (Fayette County) (Township)	47331
Gosport	47433	Grissom Air Force Base	46971	Harrison (Harrison County) (Township)	47122
Gowdy	46173	Groomsville	46049	Harrison (Henry County) (Township)	47384
Grabill	46741	Groveland	46105	Harrison (Howard County) (Township)	46979
Graceland Heights (Part of Hagerstown)	47346	Grovertown	46531	Harrison (Knox County) (Township)	47591
Grafton	47620	Guilford (Dearborn County)	47022	Harrison (Kosciusko County) (Township)	46502
Graham (Township)	47230	Guilford (Hendricks County) (Township)	46168	Harrison (Miami County) (Township)	46911
Graham Valley	47601	Guion	47872	Harrison (Morgan County) (Township)	46151
Graham Woods	46304	Gulivoire Park	46624	Harrison (Owen County) (Township)	47433
Grammer	47236	Gurley Corner	47038	Harrison (Pulaski County) (Township)	46939
Grandview (Monroe County)	47401	Guthrie	47421	Harrison (Spencer County) (Township)	47532
Grandview (Spencer County)	47615	Guthrie (Township)	47467	Harrison (Union County) (Township)	47353
Grandview Lake	47201	Guy	46936	Harrison (Vigo County) (Township)	47807
Grandview Village	47150	Gwynneville	46144	Harrison (Wayne County) (Township)	47327
Granger	46530	Hacienda Village	46805	Harrison (Wells County) (Township)	46714
Grant (Benton County) (Township)	47944	Hackleman	46928		
Grant (De Kalb County) (Township)	46793	Haddon (Township)	47838		
Grant (Greene County) (Township)	47465	Hadley	46121		
Grant (Newton County) (Township)	47948	Hagerstown	47346		
Grant City	47384	Halbert (Township)	47581		
Grantsburg	47123	Haleysbury	47281		
Granville	47611	Hall (Dubois County) (Township)	47546		
Grass (Township)	46935	Hall (Morgan County) (Township)	46157		
Grass Creek		Halteman Village (Part of Muncie)	47304		
Grasselli (Part of East Chicago)	46312	Hamblen (Township)	46164		
Grassy Fork (Township)	47274				
Gravel Beach	46747				
Gravelton	46542				
Grayford	47265				
Graysville	47852				
Green (Grant County) (Township)	46928				

	ZIP
Harrison Hills (Part of Columbus)	47201
Harrison Lake	47201
Harristown	47167
Harrisville	47390
Harrodsburg	47434
Hart (Township)	47619
Hartford (Adams County) (Township)	46740
Hartford (Ohio County)	47001
Hartford City	47348
Hartford Place (Part of Columbus)	47201
Hartleyville	47421
Hartsdale (Part of Schererville)	46375
Hartsville	47244
Harveysburg	47952
Hashtown	47424
Haskells	46390
Hastings	46542
Hatfield	47617
Haubstadt	47639
Haw Creek (Township)	47246
Hawthorne Hills	46307
Hayden	47245
Haymond	47006
Haysville	47546
Hazelrigg	46052
Hazelwood (Allen County)	46805
Hazelwood (Hendricks County)	46118
Hazelwood (Shelby County)	46176
Hazleton	47640
Headlee	47960
Heath	47905
Heather Heights (Part of Columbus)	47201
Heather Hills (Part of Indianapolis)	46229
Heaton Lake	46514
Hebron	46341
Hedrick	47993
Heilman	47523
Helmcrest (Part of Fortville)	46040
Helmer	46744
Helmsburg	47435
Helt (Township)	47847
Heltonville	47436
Hemlock	46937
Hemlock Lakes	47952
Henderson	46173
Hendricks (Johnson County)	46142
Hendricks (Shelby County) (Township)	46176
Hendricksville	47459
Henry (Fulton County) (Township)	46910
Henry (Henry County) (Township)	47362
Henryville	47126
Hensley (Township)	46181
Herbst	46952
Heritage Lake	46128
Herr	46052
Hessen Cassel	46806
Hesston	46350
Hessville (Part of Hammond)	46323
Heth (Township)	47110
Heusler	47712
Hibbard	46511
Hibernia	47111
Hibernia Mills	47933
Hickory Grove (Township)	47984
Hickory Hills	46952
Hidden Valley	47025
Hideaway Lake	47952
Highbanks	46555
High Lake	46701
Highland (Franklin County) (Township)	47012
Highland (Greene County) (Township)	47424
Highland (Lake County)	46322
Highland (Vanderburgh County)	47710
Highland (Vermillion County)	47854
Highland (Vermillion County) (Township)	47974
Highland Meadows	46952
Highland Village (Part of Bloomington)	47401
Highwoods (Part of Indianapolis)	46222
Hiker Trace (Part of Columbus)	47201
Hildebrand Village	46176
Hill and Dale (Part of Sellersburg)	47172

	ZIP
Hillcrest (Bartholomew County)	47201
Hillcrest (Harrison County)	47112
Hillcrest (Porter County)	46383
Hillcrest Circle (Part of Bedford)	47421
Hillendale	47006
Hillham	47432
Hillisburg	46046
Hills And Dales	47383
Hillsboro (Fountain County)	47949
Hillsboro (Henry County)	47362
Hillsdale (Vanderburgh County)	47711
Hillsdale (Vermillion County)	47854
Hillview Estates	47201
Hindostan Falls	47581
Hindustan	47401
Hitchcock	47167
Hi-View (Part of South Bend)	46624
Hoagland	46745
Hobart	46342
Hobart (Township)	46342
Hobbieville	47462
Hobbs	46047
Hoffman Lake	46580
Hogan (Township)	47001
Hogtown	47140
Holaday Hills and Dales	46032
Holiday Lakes	46738
Holiday Park	46902
Holland	47541
Hollandsburg	47872
Hollybrook Lake	47433
Holly Hills	47802
Holton	47023
Home Corner	46952
Homecroft	46227
Home Place	46240
Homer	46146
Homestead (Part of Greendale)	47025
Honey Creek (Henry County)	47356
Honey Creek (Howard County) (Township)	46979
Honey Creek (Vigo County) (Township)	47802
Honey Creek (White County) (Township)	47980
Honeyville	46571
Hoosier Acres (Part of Bloomington)	47401
Hoosier Highlands	47868
Hoosierville	47834
Hoover	46947
Hope	47246
Hopewell (De Kalb County)	46706
Hopewell (Johnson County)	46131
Horace	47240
Horton	46069
Houston	47235
Hovey	47620
Howard (Howard County) (Township)	46901
Howard (Parke County)	47985
Howard (Parke County) (Township)	47859
Howard (Washington County) (Township)	47167
Howe	46746
Howell (Part of Evansville)	47712
Howesville	47438
Hubbell	47427
Hubbells Corner	47041
Hudson (La Porte County) (Township)	46552
Hudson (Steuben County)	46747
Hudson Lake	46552
Hudsonville	47558
Huff (Township)	47615
Huffman	47588
Hull Addition	46072
Hunter (Part of Indianapolis)	46239
Huntersville (Part of Batesville)	47006
Huntertown	46748
Huntingburg	47542
Huntington (Township)	46750
Huntington	46750
Huntsville (Madison County)	46064
Huntsville (Randolph County)	47358
Huron	47437
Hyde Park	47302
Hymera	47855
Hyndsdale	46151
Idaho (Part of Terre Haute)	47802
Idaville	47950
Ijamsville	46962

	ZIP
Imperial Gardens	46815
Imperial Hills (Part of Greenwood)	46227
Independence	47918
Independence Hill (Part of Merrillville)	46410
Indiana Army Ammunition Plant	47111
Indiana Beach	47960
Indiana Oaks	47172
Indianapolis	46201-90

For specific Indianapolis Zip Codes call (317) 464-6150

COLLEGES & UNIVERSITIES

	ZIP
Butler University	46208
Indiana University-Purdue University at Indianapolis	46202
Marian College	46222
University of Indianapolis	46227

FINANCIAL INSTITUTIONS

	ZIP
Bank One, Indianapolis, N.A.	46277
First of America Bank-Indianapolis	46224
INB National Bank	46266
Merchants National Bank and Trust Company of Indianapolis	46255
Peoples Bank & Trust Company	46204
Railroadmen's Federal Savings & Loan Association	46204
Union Federal Savings Bank	46204

HOSPITALS

	ZIP
Community Hospitals of Indianapolis	46219
Indiana University Medical Center	46202
Methodist Hospital of Indianapolis	46202
Richard L. Roudebush Veterans Affairs Medical Center	46202
St. Vincent Hospital and Health Care Center	46032
William N. Wishard Memorial Hospital	46202

HOTELS/MOTELS

	ZIP
Adam's Mark Indianapolis	46241
Airport Hilton Inn	46241
The Canterbury Hotel	46225
Embassy Suites-Downtown	46204
Hilton at the Circle	46204
Holiday Inn-Southeast	46203
Indianapolis Marriott	46219
Radisson Plaza Hotel Indianapolis	46240

MILITARY INSTALLATIONS

	ZIP
Naval Air Warfare Center	46219
United States Property and Fiscal Office for Indiana	46241
United States Property and Fiscal Office, Camp Atterbury	46241
Indianapolis Union Stock Yards (Part of Indianapolis)	46241
Indiana State Farm	46135
Indiana State Reformatory	46064
Indiana State University Evansville Campus	47712
Indian Creek (Lawrence County) (Township)	47421
Indian Creek (Monroe County) (Township)	47401
Indian Creek (Pulaski County) (Township)	46985
Indian Creek Settlement	47512
Indianhead Lake	46122
Indian Heights	46902
Indian Hills	47201
Indian Lake (De Kalb County)	46730
Indian Lake (Marion County)	46226
Indianola	46795
Indian Springs	47581
Indian Village (Noble County)	46732
Indian Village (St. Joseph County)	46637
Industry (Part of Muncie)	47302
Ingalls	46048

	ZIP
Kokomo	46901-04
For specific Kokomo Zip Codes call (317) 455-8300	
Koleen	47439
Koontz Lake	46574
Kossuth	47167
Kouts	46347
Kramer	47918
Kreitsburg	46311
Kriete Corners	47274
Kurtz	47249
Kyana	47575
Kyle	47001
Laconia	47135
La Crosse	46348
Ladoga	47954
Lafayette	47901-05
For specific Lafayette Zip Codes call (317) 448-9245	
Lafayette (Allen County) (Township)	46783
Lafayette (Floyd County) (Township)	47119
Lafayette (Madison County) (Township)	46011
Lafayette (Owen County) (Township)	47460
Lafayette Square (Part of Indianapolis)	46254
La Fontaine	46940
Lagrange	46761
Lagro	46941
Lagro (Township)	46941
Lake (Allen County) (Township)	46818
Lake (Kosciusko County) (Township)	46982
Lake (Newton County) (Township)	46349
Lake Bodona	46158
Lake Bruce	46939
Lake Cicott	46942
Lakecrest (Part of Noblesville)	46060
Lake Dalecarlia	46356
Lake Dilldear	47018
Lake Edgewood	46151
Lake Eliza	46383
Lake Everett	46808
Lake Front (Part of Whiting)	46394
Lake Hart	46158
Lake Hills	46375
Lake Holiday	47933
Lake James	46703
Lakeland (Part of Michigan City)	46360
Lake Latonka	46511
Lake Lincoln	47552
Lake Manitou	46975
Lake Maxine	47456
Lake McCoy	47240
Lake Mohee	47348
Lake Noji	47802
Lake of the Woods	46506
Lake Park	46552
Lakeside	46795
Lakeside Park (Part of Warsaw)	46580
Lakes of the Four Seasons	46307
Lake Station	46405
Lake Sullivan	47882
Laketon	46943
Lakeview (Franklin County)	47024
Lake View (Porter County)	46383
Lakeview (Lagrange County)	46795
Lakeview Estates	47802
Lake Village	46349
Lakeville	46536
Lake Wood (Grant County)	46952
Lakewood (Vigo County)	47802
Lakewood (White County)	47960
Lakewood Hills (Part of Evansville)	47711
Lamar	47550
Lamb	47043
Lamb Lake	46181
Lamong	46069
Lamplighter	46060
Lancaster	46750
Lancaster (Huntington County) (Township)	46750
Lancaster (Jefferson County) (Township)	47250
Lancaster (Wells County) (Township)	46714
Lancaster Park	47401
Landess	46944
Lane (Township)	47637
Lanesville	47136

	ZIP
Lantana Estate (Part of Shelbyville)	46176
Lantern Park	47302
Laotto	46763
Lapaz	46537
La Paz Junction	46563
Lapel	46051
La Porte	46350
Larimer Hill	47885
Larwill	46764
Lasalle Square (Part of South Bend)	46601
Laud	46725
Laughery (Township)	47006
Lauramie (Township)	47930
Laurel	47024
Laurel (Township)	47024
Lawndale (Part of Evansville)	47715
Lawrence	46226
Lawrence (Township)	46226
Lawrenceburg	47025
Lawrenceburg (Township)	47025
Lawrenceport	47446
Lawrenceville	47041
Lawton	46996
Laynecrest (Part of Muncie)	47304
Leases Corner	46950
Leavenworth	47137
Lebanon	46052
Lee	47978
Leesburg	46538
Leesville	47421
Leininger Acres	46072
Leipsic	47452
Leisure	46036
Leiters Ford	46945
Lena	47834
Leo	46765
Leopold	47551
Leopold (Township)	47551
Leota	47170
Leroy	46355
Letts	47240
Letts Corner	47240
Lewis (Clay County) (Township)	47438
Lewis (Vigo County)	47858
Lewisburg	46970
Lewis Creek	47234
Lewisville (Henry County)	47352
Lewisville (Morgan County)	46120
Lexington (Township)	47138
Lexington (Carroll County)	46920
Lexington (Scott County)	47138
Liber	47371
Liberty (Carroll County) (Township)	46916
Liberty (Crawford County) (Township)	47140
Liberty (Delaware County) (Township)	47383
Liberty (Fulton County) (Township)	46931
Liberty (Grant County) (Township)	46952
Liberty (Hendricks County) (Township)	46118
Liberty (Henry County) (Township)	47362
Liberty (Howard County) (Township)	46901
Liberty (Parke County) (Township)	47985
Liberty (Porter County) (Township)	46383
Liberty (Shelby County) (Township)	46182
Liberty (St. Joseph County) (Township)	46554
Liberty (Tipton County) (Township)	46068
Liberty (Union County) (Township)	47353
Liberty (Union County) (Township)	47353
Liberty (Wabash County) (Township)	46940
Liberty (Warren County) (Township)	47918
Liberty (Wells County) (Township)	46766
Liberty (White County) (Township)	47925
Liberty Center	46766
Liberty Hills	46804
Liberty Mills	46946
Liberty Park	46307
Libertyville	47885
Licking (Township)	47348
Liggett	47885
Ligonier	46767

	ZIP
Lilly Dale	47586
Lima (Township)	46746
Limberlost Hills	47803
Limedale	46135
Lincoln (Cass County)	46994
Lincoln (Hendricks County) (Township)	46112
Lincoln (La Porte County) (Township)	46365
Lincoln (Newton County) (Township)	46310
Lincoln (St. Joseph County) (Township)	46574
Lincoln (White County) (Township)	47950
Lincoln City	47552
Lincoln Heights (Clark County)	47129
Lincoln Heights (Madison County)	46001
Lincoln Hills	46383
Lincoln Park (Part of Clarksville)	47129
Lincoln Village (Part of Merrillville)	46410
Lincolnville	46992
Linden	47955
Linden Park (Part of Muncie)	47303
Lindenwood (Part of Indianapolis)	46227
Linkville	46563
Linn Grove	46769
Linnsburg	47933
Linton (Greene County)	47441
Linton (Vigo County) (Township)	47802
Linwood (Madison County)	46001
Linwood (Marion County)	46201
Lippe	47620
Lisbon	46755
Little	47567
Little Acres	47274
Little Point	46180
Little Saint Louis	47115
Little York	47139
Liverpool (Part of Lake Station)	46408
Livonia	47108
Lizton	46149
Locke	46550
Locke (Township)	46550
Lockhart (Township)	47585
Lockport	47926
Lodi	47952
Logan	47060
Logan (Township)	47060
Logan (Fountain County) (Township)	47918
Logan (Pike County) (Township)	47567
Logansport	46947
Logansport State Hospital	46947
Lomax	46374
London	46126
London Heights	46126
Long Acres	46176
Long Beach	46360
Long Lake	46962
Long Lake Island	46383
Longview Beach	47130
Loogootee	47553
Lookout	47041
Loon Lake	46725
Lorane	46725
Loree	46914
Losantville	47354
Lost Creek (Township)	47803
Lost River (Township)	47432
Lottaville (Part of Merrillville)	46410
Lotus	47353
Lovett	47265
Lovett (Township)	47265
Lowell (Bartholomew County)	47201
Lowell (Lake County)	46356
	46399
For specific Lowell Zip Codes call (219) 696-8594	
Lower Sunset Park	47960
Loyal	46975
Luce (Township)	47617
Lucerne	46950
Ludwig Park (Part of Fort Wayne)	46825
Lukens Lake	46974
Luray	47386
Luther	46787
Lutheran Lake	47274
Lydick	46628
Lyford	47874

	ZIP
Lynhurst	46241
Lynn (Posey County) (Township)	47620
Lynn (Randolph County)	47355
Lynnville	47619
Lyons	47443
Lyonsville	47331
McBride Heights	47130
McCarthy Addition (Part of Alexandria)	46001
McCarty	46142
McClellan (Township)	47963
Mc Col Place (Part of Salem)	47167
McCool (Part of Portage)	46368
McCordsville	46055
McCoysburg	47978
McCutchanville	47711
McDaniel	46151
Mace	47933
Mac-Fair-Mar	46947
McGrawsville	46911
Mackey	47654
McKinley	47108
McKinley Town and Country Shopping Center (Part of Mishawaka)	46545
McNatts	47359
Macy	46951
Madison (Allen County) (Township)	46773
Madison (Carroll County) (Township)	46923
Madison (Clinton County) (Township)	46058
Madison (Daviess County) (Township)	47562
Madison (Dubois County) (Township)	47546
Madison (Jay County) (Township)	45846
Madison (Jefferson County)	47250
Madison (Jefferson County) (Township)	47250
Madison (Montgomery County) (Township)	47933
Madison (Morgan County) (Township)	46158
Madison (Pike County) (Township)	47567
Madison (Putnam County) (Township)	46135
Madison (St. Joseph County) (Township)	46614
Madison (Tipton County) (Township)	46072
Madison (Washington County) (Township)	47108
Madison State Hospital	47250
Magley	46733
Magnet	47555
Mahalasville	46151
Mahon	46750
Majenica	46750
Malden	46383
Malott Park (Part of Indianapolis)	46205
Maltersville	47542
Manchester	47001
Manchester (Township)	47001
Manhattan	46135
Manilla	46150
Manor Woods	46804
Mansfield	47872
Manson	46041
Manville	47250
Maplecrest Shopping Center (Part of Kokomo)	46902
Maple Lane	46635
Maples	46806
Mapleton (Part of Indianapolis)	46208
Maple Valley	46117
Maplewood (Hendricks County)	46122
Maplewood (Vigo County)	47885
Maplewood Park	46805
Marco	47443
Marengo	47140
Mariah Hill	47556
Marietta	46176
Marineland Gardens	46567
Marion	46952-53
For specific Marion Zip Codes call (317) 668-8191	
Marion (Allen County) (Township)	46745
Marion (Boone County) (Township)	46069
Marion (Decatur County) (Township)	47261

	ZIP
Marion (Dubois County) (Township)	47546
Marion (Hendricks County) (Township)	46122
Marion (Jasper County) (Township)	47978
Marion (Jennings County) (Township)	47270
Marion (Lawrence County) (Township)	47446
Marion (Owen County) (Township)	47455
Marion (Pike County) (Township)	47590
Marion (Putnam County) (Township)	46128
Marion (Shelby County) (Township)	46176
Marion (Shelby County)	46176
Marion Heights	47885
Marion Manor (Part of Valparaiso)	46383
Markland	47020
Markland Mall (Part of Kokomo)	46902
Markle	46770
Markleville	46056
Marlin Hills	47401
Marquette Farm	47805
Marquette Mall (Part of Michigan City)	46360
Marrs (Township)	47620
Marrs Center	47620
Marshall (Lawrence County) (Township)	47421
Marshall (Parke County)	47859
Marshfield	47993
Mars Hill (Part of Indianapolis)	46241
Marshtown	46939
Martin Heights (Part of Salem)	47167
Martinsburg	47165
Martinsville	46151
Martz	47841
Maryland	47802
Marysville (Clark County)	47141
Marysville (Pike County)	47598
Marywood	47802
Matlock Heights (Part of Bloomington)	47401
Matthews	46957
Mattix Corner	46041
Mauckport	47142
Maumee (Township)	46797
Mauzy	46173
Max	46052
Maxinkuckee	46511
Maxville	47340
Maxwell (Hancock County)	46154
Maxwell (Morgan County)	46151
Mayfield (Part of Muncie)	47302
Maynard (Part of Munster)	46321
Mays	46155
Maysville	47501
Maywood (Part of Indianapolis)	46241
M-Dee Acres	46550
Meadowbrook (Allen County)	46774
Meadowbrook (Tippecanoe County)	47901
Meadowood (Elkhart County)	46514
Meadowood (Marion County)	46224
Meadowood Estates	46036
Meadows (Part of Terre Haute)	47803
Meadows Shopping Center (Part of Indianapolis)	46205
Meadowview	46947
Mead Village (Part of Columbus)	47201
Mecca	47860
Mechanicsburg (Boone County)	46050
Mechanicsburg (Henry County)	47356
Medaryville	47957
Medford	47302
Medina (Township)	47970
Medora	47260
Meiks	46176
Mellott	47958
Melody Acres (Part of Warsaw)	46580
Melody Hill	47711
Meltzer	46176
Memphis	47143
Mentone	46539

	ZIP
Mentor	47513
Meridian Hills	46260
Merom	47861
Merriam	46701
Merrillville	46410
Metamora (Township)	47030
Metamora	47030
Metea	46950
Metz	46703
Mexico	46958
Miami (Cass County) (Township)	46947
Miami (Miami County)	46959
Miami Bend	46947
Miami Trails Addition	46614
Michaelsville	46952
Michiana Shores	49117
Michigan (Clinton County) (Township)	46057
Michigan (La Porte County) (Township)	46360
Michigan City	46360
Michigantown	46057
Mickleyville (Part of Indianapolis)	46241
Middle (Township)	46167
Middleboro	47374
Middlebury	46540
Middlebury (Township)	46540
Middlefork (Clinton County)	46041
Middlefork (Jefferson County)	47231
Middletown (Henry County)	47356
Middletown (Shelby County)	46182
Middletown Park	47302
Midland	47445
Midway (Elkhart County)	46526
Midway (Jefferson County)	47250
Midway (Spencer County)	47601
Midwest (Part of Portage)	46368
Mier	46919
Mifflin	47118
Milan (Allen County) (Township)	46797
Milan (Ripley County)	47031
Milan Center	46774
Milford (Decatur County)	47240
Milford (Kosciusko County)	46542
Milford (Lagrange County) (Township)	46795
Milford Junction	46542
Mill (Township)	46933
Mill Creek (Fountain County) (Township)	47952
Mill Creek (Hamilton County)	46060
Mill Creek (La Porte County)	46365
Milledgeville	46052
Miller (Dearborn County) (Township)	47025
Miller (Lake County)	46403
Millersburg (Elkhart County)	46543
Millersburg (Hamilton County)	46030
Millersburg (Orange County)	47454
Millersburg (Warrick County)	47610
Millersville (Part of Lawrence)	46226
Mill Grove (Blackford County)	47348
Millgrove (Steuben County) (Township)	46776
Millhousen	47261
Milligan	47872
Milltown	47145
Millville	47362
Milners Corner	46140
Milo	46991
Milroy (Jasper County) (Township)	47978
Milroy (Rush County)	46156
Milton (Jefferson County) (Township)	47250
Milton (Ohio County)	47018
Milton (Wayne County)	47357
Mineral	47424
Mineral Springs	46538
Mishawaka	46544-46
For specific Mishawaka Zip Codes call (219) 255-9691	
Mitchell	47446
Mitchellville (Part of Indianapolis)	46201
Mitcheltree (Township)	47581
Mixerville	47010
Moberly	47115
Modesto	47401
Modoc	47358
Mohawk	46140
Mongo	46771
Monitor	47905

	ZIP		ZIP		ZIP
Pipe Creek (Miami County)		Prairie City	47834	Richland (Fulton County)	
(Township)	46914	Prairie Creek	47869	(Township)	46975
Pittsboro	46167	Prairie Creek (Township)	47869	Richland (Grant County)	
Pittsburg	46923	Prairieton	47870	(Township)	46952
Plain (Township)	46538	Prairieton (Township)	47870	Richland (Greene County)	
Plainfield	46168	Prairie Village	47802	(Township)	47424
Plainville	47568	Prather	46151	Richland (Jay County)	
Plano	46151	Preble	46782	(Township)	47373
Plato	46761	Preble (Township)	46733	Richland (Madison County)	
Plattsburg	47281	Prescott	46176	(Township)	46011
Pleasant (Allen County)		Presidential Village	46803	Richland (Miami County)	
(Township)	46798	Pretty Lake	46795	(Township)	46970
Pleasant (Grant County)		Prince Hall Plaza (Part of		Richland (Monroe County)	
(Township)	46952	Marion)	46952	(Township)	47429
Pleasant (Johnson County)		Princes Lakes	46164	Richland (Rush County)	46173
(Township)	46131	Princeton (Gibson County)	47670	Richland (Rush County)	
Pleasant (La Porte County)		Princeton (White County)		(Township)	46173
(Township)	46350	(Township)	47995	Richland (Spencer County)	47634
Pleasant (Porter County)		Progress	47302	Richland (Steuben County)	
(Township)	46347	Progress Acres	47805	(Township)	46703
Pleasant (Steuben County)		Prospect	47469	Richland (Whitley County)	
(Township)	46703	Providence	46106	(Township)	46764
Pleasant (Switzerland		Publico (Part of New		Richmond	47374-75
County)	47224	Albany)	47150	For specific Richmond Zip Codes	
Pleasant (Switzerland		Puckett	46952	call (317) 966-7631	
County) (Township)	47224	Pulaski	46996	Richmond Square (Part of	
Pleasant (Wabash County)		Pumpkin Center	47170	Richmond)	47374
(Township)	46962	Purcell	47591	Richmond State Hospital	47374
Pleasant Gardens	46171	Purdue University	47906	Richvalley	46992
Pleasant Lake	46779	Purdue University North		Riddle	47118
Pleasant Mills	46780	Central Campus	46391	Ridgemede (Part of	
Pleasant Plain	46792	Putnamville	46170	Bloomington)	47401
Pleasant Run (Township)	47436	Pyrmont	46923	Ridgeport	47424
Pleasant Valley	46544	Quail Meadows Estates		Ridgeview (Part of Peru)	46970
Pleasant View	46126	(Part of Batesville)	47006	Ridgeview Heights	46806
Pleasant View Village	46124	Queensville	47265	Ridgeville	47380
Pleasantville	47838	Quercus Grove	47040	Ridgeway	46809
Pleasure Valley	46182	Quincy	47456	Ridinger Lake	46562
Plevna	46901	Raber	46725	Rigdon	46036
Plummer	47424	Raccoon (Parke County)		Riley	47871
Plum Tree	46792	(Township)	47874	Riley (Township)	47871
Plymouth	46563	Raccoon (Putnam County)	46172	Rileysburg	47932
Poe	46819	Radioville	47957	Riley Village (Part of	
Point (Township)	47620	Radley	46938	Shelbyville)	46176
Point Commerce	47471	Radnor	46923	Ripley (Montgomery	
Point Idalawn	47468	Raglesville	47562	County) (Township)	47933
Point Isabel	46928	Ragsdale	47573	Ripley (Pulaski County)	46996
Poland	47868	Railroad (Township)	46374	Ripley (Rush County)	
Polk (Huntington County)		Rainbow (Part of		(Township)	46115
(Township)	46750	Indianapolis)	46222	Rising Sun	47040
Polk (Marshall County)		Rainsville	47918	Risse (Part of Frankfort)	46041
(Township)	46574	Raleigh	46173	Rivare	46733
Polk (Monroe County)		Ramsey	47166	River Forest	46011
(Township)	47436	Randolph (Ohio County)		Riverhaven	46802
Polk (Washington County)		(Township)	47040	River Ridge	47111
(Township)	47165	Randolph (Tippecanoe		Riverside	47129-30
Poneto	46781	County) (Township)	47981	For specific Riverside Zip Codes	
Pontiac	47837	Raub	47976	call (317) 762-3360	
Popcorn	47462	Ravenswood (Part of		Riverside	47918
Portage	46368	Indianapolis)	46240	Riverton	47861
Portage (Porter County)		Ravinamy	47906	River Vale	47446
(Township)	46368	Ray (Franklin County)		Riverview	47849
Portage (St. Joseph		(Township)	47036	Riverview Acres	47201
County) (Township)	46601	Ray (Morgan County)		Riverwood	46060
Porter	46304	(Township)	46166	Riviera Plaza (Part of Fort	
Porter (Township)	46383	Ray (Steuben County)	46737	Wayne)	46815
Portersville	47546	Raymond	47010	Roachdale	46172
Port Fulton (Part of		Rays Crossing	46176	Roann	46974
Jeffersonville)	47130	Raysville	46148	Roanoke	46783
Portland	47371	Reception Diagnostic		Robb (Township)	47633
Portland Mills	46135	Center	46168	Robertsdale (Part of	
Posey (Clay County)		Red Bridge	46911	Hammond)	46394
(Township)	47834	Red Bush	47630	Robinson (Township)	47638
Posey (Fayette County)		Redding (Township)	47274	Robinwood	47803
(Township)	47331	Reddington	47274	Roble Woods	46383
Posey (Franklin County)		Redkey	47373	Rob Roy	47918
(Township)	47024	Redmond Park	46567	Rochester	46975
Posey (Harrison County)		Reed Station	47302	Rochester (Township)	46975
(Township)	47117	Reelsville	46171	Rockcreek (Township)	46714
Posey (Rush County)		Reeve (Township)	47553	Rock Creek (Bartholomew	
(Township)	46104	Rego	47125	County) (Township)	47232
Posey (Switzerland County)		Reiffsburg	46714	Rock Creek (Carroll County)	
(Township)	47038	Remington	47977	(Township)	46923
Posey (Washington County)		Reno	46121	Rock Creek (Huntington	
(Township)	47120	Rensselaer	47978	County)	46750
Poseyville	47633	Reo	47635	Rock Creek (Huntington	
Pottawattomie Park	46360	Republican (Township)	47138	County) (Township)	46750
Pottersville	47460	Reserve (Township)	47862	Rockdale	47060
Powers	47371	Retreat	47229	Rockfield	46977
Prairie (Henry County)		Rexville	47250	Rockford (Jackson County)	47274
(Township)	47360	Reynolds	47980	Rockford (Wells County)	46714
Prairie (Kosciusko County)		Riceville	47513	Rock Island (Part of	
(Township)	46580	Richey Park	47960	Indianapolis)	46268
Prairie (La Porte County)		Rich Grove (Township)	46996	Rock Lake	46910
(Township)	46340	Richland (Benton County)		Rocklane	46142
Prairie (Tipton County)		(Township)	47942	Rockport	47635
(Township)	46049	Richland (De Kalb County)		Rockville	47872
Prairie (Warren County)		(Township)	46730	Rocky Fork Lake	47834
(Township)	47921	Richland (Fountain County)		Rocky Ripple	46208
Prairie (White County)		(Township)	47969	Roland	47469
(Township)	47923			Roll	47348

	ZIP		ZIP		ZIP
Rolling Acres	47601	Salem (Washington County)	47167	Shawville	47805
Rolling Hill Estates (Part of		Salem (Pulaski County)		Sheddfield (Part of	
Schererville)	46410	(Township)	47946	Hammond)	46320
Rolling Hills (Allen County)	46804	Salem Center	46747	Sheffield (Township)	47901
Rolling Hills (Clark County)	47111	Salem Heights	46350	Sheffield Woods (Part of	
Rolling Hills (Grant County)	46952	Saline City	47840	Indianapolis)	46229
Rolling Prairie	46371	Salt Creek (Decatur County)		Shelburn	47879
Rolling Ridge (Part of		(Township)	47240	Shelburne	46151
Shelbyville)	46176	Salt Creek (Franklin County)		Shelby (Jefferson County)	
Rollins	47581	(Township)	47024	(Township)	47250
Rome	47574	Salt Creek (Jackson		Shelby (Lake County)	46377
Rome City	46784	County) (Township)	47235	Shelby (Ripley County)	
Romney	47981	Salt Creek (Monroe County)		(Township)	47250
Romona	47460	(Township)	47401	Shelby (Shelby County)	
Root (Township)	46733	Salt Creek Commons	46383	(Township)	46176
Roseburg (Grant County)	46952	Saltillo	47108	Shelby (Tippecanoe County)	
Roseburg (Union County)	47353	Saluda	47243	(Township)	47906
Rosedale	47874	Saluda (Township)	47243	Shelbyville	46176
Rosedale Hills (Part of		Samaria	46181	Shepardsville	47880
Indianapolis)	46227	Sandborn	47578	Sheridan (Hamilton County)	46069
Rose Hill Gardens	47805	Sand Creek (Bartholomew		Sheridan (La Porte County)	46360
Rose-Hulman Institute of		County) (Township)	47232	Sherwood Forest (Part of	
Technology	47803	Sand Creek (Decatur		Indianapolis)	46240
Roseland	46635	County) (Township)	47283	Shideler	47338
Roselawn	46372	Sand Creek (Jennings		Shields	47274
Rosewood	47117	County) (Township)	47265	Shiloh Village	47201
Ross (Clinton County)		Sandcut	47805	Shipshewana	46565
(Township)	46041	Sanders	47401	Shirkieville	47885
Ross (Lake County)		Sandford	47877	Shirley	47384
(Township)	46410	Sand Ridge	47635	Shoals	47581
Ross (Lake County)	46408	Sandusky	47240	Shoe Lake	46538
Rosston	46077	Sandy Beach	47960	Shore Acres (Part of	
Rosstown	47201	Sandy Hook (Part of		Indianapolis)	46201
Rossville	46065	Columbus)	47201	Shoreland Hills	46360
Roth Park	47960	Sandytown	47842	Siberia	47515
Round Grove (Township)	47923	San Jacinto	47223	Sidney	46566
Round Lake	46755	San Pierre	46374	Silver Creek (Township)	47172
Royal Center	46978	Santa Claus	47579	Silver Hills (Part of New	
Royal Oaks	46815	Santa Fe	46970	Albany)	47150
Royalton	46077	Saratoga	47382	Silver Lake	46982
Royal View	47201	Sardinia	47283	Silver Lakes Estates	47129
Royer Lake	46761	Savah	47620	Silverville	47470
Royerton	47302	Scenic Heights	47586	Silverwood	47952
Royerton Park	47303	Scenic Hill	47553	Simonton Lake	46514
Royville	46845	Schaefer Lake	47246	Sims (Township)	46983
Rugby	47246	Schererville	46375	Sims (Bartholomew County)	47201
Rural	47394	Schneider	46376	Sims (Grant County)	46983
Rushville	46173	Schnellville	47580	Sitka	47960
Rushville (Township)	46173	Scipio (Allen County)		Skelton (Township)	47637
Russell (Township)	46172	(Township)	45813	Skinner Lake	46701
Russell Lake	46077	Scipio (Franklin County)	45053	Sleepy Hollow	46182
Russellville	46175	Scipio (Jennings County)	47273	Sleeth	46923
Russels Point	46742	Scipio (La Porte County)		Sloan	47993
Russiaville	46979	(Township)	46350	Smartsburg	47933
Rustic Hills	47630	Scircleville	46041	Smedley	47108
Rutherford (Township)	47553	Scotchtown	47848	Smith (Greene County)	
Rutland	46563	Scotland	47457	(Township)	47471
Ryan Place	47620	Scott (Kosciusko County)		Smith (Posey County)	
Rykers Ridge	47250	(Township)	46550	(Township)	47612
Saddle Lake	46733	Scott (Lagrange County)	46565	Smith (Whitley County)	
Sagers Lake	46383	Scott (Montgomery County)		(Township)	46723
Sagunay Lake	46371	(Township)	47933	Smithfield (De Kalb County)	
St. Anthony	47575	Scott (Steuben County)		(Township)	46793
St. Bernice	47875	(Township)	46703	Smithfield (Delaware	
St. Croix	47576	Scott (Vanderburgh County)		County)	47383
St. Henry	47532	(Township)	47711	Smithland	46176
St. James	47639	Scott City	47879	Smithson	47980
St. Joe	46785	Scottsburg (Pike County)	47660	Smith Valley	46142
St. John (Lake County)	46373	Scottsburg (Scott County)	47170	Smithville	47458
St. John (Township)	46373	Scottsdale Mall (Part of		Smyrna	47250
St. John (Warrick County)	47613	South Bend)	46612	Smyrna (Township)	47250
St. Johns	46738	Scottsville	47106	Snow Hill	47394
St. Joseph (Allen County)		Searcy Crossroads	47038	Solitude	47620
(Township)	46805	Sedalia	46067	Solsberry	47459
St. Joseph (Vanderburgh		Sedan	46793	Somerset	46984
County)	47720	Seelyville	47878	Somerville	47683
St. Leon	47060	Sellersburg	47172	South Bend	46601-99
St. Louis Crossing	47201	Sellers Lake	46562	For specific South Bend Zip	
St. Marks (Dubois County)	47575	Selma	47383	Codes call (219) 282-8400	
St. Marks (Perry County)	47586	Selvin	47523	South Bethany	47201
St. Mary-of-the-Woods	47876	Servia	46980	South Boston	47167
St. Marys (Adams County)		Sevastopol	46510	South Calumet Avenue (Part	
(Township)	46733	Seward (Township)	46510	of Hammond)	46324
St. Marys (Floyd County)	47119	Sexton	46173	South Center	46532
St. Marys (St. Joseph		Seymour	47274	Southeast (Township)	47140
County)	46556	Shadeland (Grant County)	46952	Southeast Grove	46341
St. Maurice	47240	Shadeland (Tippecanoe		Southeast Manor	46126
St. Meinrad	47577	County)	47905	South Edgewood (Part of	
St. Omer	47272	Shady Hills	46952	Edgewood)	46011
St. Paul	47272	Shady Hills Estates	46952	South Gate (Franklin	
St. Peters	47012	Shady Lawn	46307	County)	47060
St. Philip	47620	Shady Nook	46795	Southgate (La Porte	
St. Thomas	47591	Shady Side (Part of Burns		County)	46360
St. Wendel	47720	Harbor)	46304	South Harbor (Part of	
Salamonia	47381	Shaffer Woods	47303	Noblesville)	46060
Salamonie (Township)	46792	Shamrock Lakes	47348	South Haven	46383
Salem (Delaware County)		Shannondale	47933	South Lake	47885
(Township)	47334	Sharon	46929	Southlake Mall (Part of	
Salem (Jay County)	47390	Sharpsville	46068	Merrillville)	46410
Salem (Steuben County)		Shawnee (Township)	47987	South Marion (Part of	
(Township)	46747	Shawswick (Township)	47421	Marion)	46952

	ZIP		ZIP		ZIP
South Milford	46786	Stevenson	47610	Tanglewood (Part of New	
Southmoor (Part of		Stewart	47993	Haven)	46774
Merrillville)	46410	Stewartsville	47633	Taswell	47175
South Mud Lake	46951	Stilesville	46180	Taylor (Greene County)	
South Park	46567	Stillwell	46351	(Township)	47424
South Peru (Part of Peru)	46970	Stinesville	47464	Taylor (Harrison County)	
Southport	46227	Stockdale	46974	(Township)	47117
South Raub	47905	Stockton (Township)	47441	Taylor (Howard County)	
South Salem	47390	Stockwell	47983	(Township)	46901
Southtown Mall (Part of Fort		Stone	47394	Taylor (Owen County)	
Wayne)	46816	Stonebluff	47987	(Township)	47460
South Wanatah	46390	Stoneburner Landing	46580	Taylors	47905
South Washington	47501	Stonecrest	46952	Taylorsville	47280
Southwest	46526	Stonegate Square (Part of		Tecumseh	47885
South Whitley	46787	Newburgh)	47630	Teegarden	46574
Southwick Village	46816	Stone Head	47448	Tee Lake	46350
Southwood (La Porte		Stones Crossing	46142	Tefft	46380
County)	46360	Stoney Creek (Henry		Tell City	47586
Southwood (Vigo County)	47802	County) (Township)	47360	Temple	47118
Spades	47041	Stoney Creek (Randolph		Templeton	47986
Sparksville	47260	County) (Township)	47368	Tennyson	47637
Sparta	47032	Stonington	47446	Terhune	46069
Sparta (Dearborn County)		Stony Creek (Township)	46051	Terrace Bay	47960
(Township)	47032	Stony Lonesome	47201	Terrace Lake (Part of	
Sparta (Noble County)		Stony Ridge	46538	Columbus)	47201
(Township)	46760	Story	47448	Terre Haute	47801-08
Spartanburg	47355	Straughn	47387	For specific Terre Haute Zip	
Spearsville	46181	Strawtown	46060	Codes call (812) 231-9414	
Speed	47172	Stringtown (Boone County)	46052	Tetersburg	46072
Speedway	46224	Stringtown (Hancock		Texas (Part of Aurora)	47001
Speedway Shopping Center		County)	46140	Thayer	46381
(Part of Speedway)	46224	Stroh	46789	The Hamlet	47303
Speicher	46992	Sugar Creek (Boone		Thomas Lake	46135
Spelterville	47805	County) (Township)	46071	Thomaston	46390
Spencer (De Kalb County)		Sugar Creek (Clinton		Thorncreek (Township)	46725
(Township)	46788	County) (Township)	46050	Thornhope	46985
Spencer (Harrison County)		Sugar Creek (Hancock		Thorntown	46071
(Township)	47115	County) (Township)	46163	Thurman	46774
Spencer (Jennings County)		Sugar Creek (Montgomery		Tilden	46122
(Township)	47265	County) (Township)	46035	Tillman	46773
Spencer (Owen County)	47460	Sugar Creek (Parke County)		Timbercrest (Allen County)	46804
Spencerville	46788	(Township)	47859	Timbercrest (Cass County)	46947
Spiceland	47385	Sugar Creek (Shelby		Timberhurst	46795
Spiceland (Township)	47385	County)	46126	Tiosa	46975
Spice Valley (Township)	47437	Sugar Creek (Shelby		Tippecanoe (Carroll County)	
Spraytown	47274	County) (Township)	46110	(Township)	46923
Springersville	47325	Sugar Creek (Vigo County)		Tippecanoe (Kosciusko	
Springfield (Allen County)		(Township)	47885	County) (Township)	46555
(Township)	46743	Sugar Ridge (Township)	47840	Tippecanoe (Marshall	
Springfield (Franklin County)		Sullivan	47882	County)	46570
(Township)	45056	Sulphur	47174	Tippecanoe (Marshall	
Springfield (La Porte		Sulphur Springs	47388	County) (Township)	46570
County) (Township)	46360	Suman	46383	Tippecanoe (Pulaski	
Springfield (Lagrange		Sumava Resorts	46379	County) (Township)	46960
County) (Township)	46771	Summit Grove	47842	Tippecanoe (Tippecanoe	
Springfield (Posey County)	47620	Summit Ridge (Part of Fort		County) (Township)	47906
Spring Grove	47374	Wayne)	46805	Tippecanoe Mall (Part of	
Spring Grove Heights (Part		Summitville	46070	Lafayette)	47905
of Spring Grove)	47374	Sundown Manor	46158	Tipton (Cass County)	
Spring Hill	46208	Sunman	47041	(Township)	46994
Spring Hill Estates	47802	Sunnybrook Acres	46805	Tipton (Tipton County)	46072
Spring Lake	46140	Sunnymeadow	46815	Tipton Park (Part of	
Springport	47386	Sunnymede (Allen County)	46803	Columbus)	47201
Springtown	46122	Sunnymede (Wabash		Toad Hop	47885
Spring Valley Estates	47802	County)	46992	Tobin (Township)	47574
Springville (La Porte		Sunnymede Woods	46803	Tobinsport	47587
County)	46350	Sunny Slopes	47401	Tocsin	46790
Springville (Lawrence		Sunset Acres	46514	Toledo	46750
County)	47462	Sunset Parkway (Part of		Tolleston (Part of Gary)	46404
Springwood	47805	Seymour)	47274	Toll Gate Heights	46714
Spurgeon	47584	Sunset Village	47111	Tomahawk Village (Part of	
Spurgeons Corner	47235	Sunshine Gardens (Part of		Indianapolis)	46224
Stacer	47639	Indianapolis)	46217	Topeka	46571
Stafford (De Kalb County)		Sunview	46040	Toto	46534
(Township)	46721	Surprise	47274	Townley	46773
Stafford (Greene County)		Sussex Woods (Part of		Town of Pines	46360
(Township)	47578	Hobart)	46342	Tracy	46532
Stampers Creek (Township)	47454	Swan	46763	Traders Point (Part of	
Stanford	47463	Swan (Township)	46763	Indianapolis)	46278
Star City	46985	Swanington	47944	Trafalgar	46181
Stardust Village	46060	Swayzee	46986	Trail Creek	46360
Starlight	47106	Sweetser	46987	Travisville	46714
State Line (Vigo County)	47885	Sweetwater Lake	46164	Treaty	46992
State Line (Warren County)	47982	Switz City	47465	Tremont	46304
Staunton	47881	Sycamore	46936	Trenton	47348
Stavetown	47012	Sycamore Hills	46036	Trevlac	47448
Stearleyville	47834	Sycamore Knolls	47802	Trier Ridge Park	46806
Steele (Township)	47501	Sycamore Park	47885	Tri-Lakes	46725
Steen (Township)	47597	Sylvan Hills	46952	Trilobi Hills (Part of	
Steinbarger Lake	46784	Sylvania	47832	Lawrence)	46226
Steinmeir Estates (Part of		Sylvan Manor	46383	Trinity	47326
Indianapolis)	46250	Syndicate	47842	Trinity Springs	47581
Stendal	47585	Syracuse	46567	Troy (De Kalb County)	
Sterling (Crawford County)		Tab	47917	(Township)	46721
(Township)	47118	Tabertown (Part of		Troy (Fountain County)	
Sterling (Fountain County)	47987	Seelyville)	47878	(Township)	47932
Steuben (Steuben County)		Talbot	47984	Troy (Perry County)	
(Township)	46705	Tall Timbers	46952	(Township)	47588
Steuben (Warren County)		Talma	46975	Troy (Perry County)	47588
(Township)	47993	Tampico	47220	Tudor	47201
Steubenville	46705	Tangier	47985	Tulip	47424

	ZIP		ZIP		ZIP
Washington (Delaware County) (Township)	47342	Wayne (Huntington County) (Township)	46940	West Wabash	47712
Washington (Elkhart County) (Township)	46507	Wayne (Jay County) (Township)	47371		47719-20
Washington (Gibson County) (Township)	47640	Wayne (Kosciusko County) (Township)	46590	For specific West Wabash Zip Codes call (219) 563-3258	
Washington (Grant County) (Township)	46952	Wayne (Marion County) (Township)	46241	Westwood	47362
				Wey Lake	47834
Washington (Greene County) (Township)	47443	Wayne (Montgomery County) (Township)	47990	Wheatfield	46392
Washington (Hamilton County) (Township)	46074	Wayne (Noble County) (Township)	46755	Wheatfield (Township)	46392
Washington (Harrison County) (Township)	47110	Wayne (Owen County) (Township)	47433	Wheatland	47597
				Wheatonville	47613
Washington (Hendricks County) (Township)	46122	Wayne (Randolph County) (Township)	47390	Wheeler	46393
Washington (Jackson County) (Township)	47274	Wayne (Starke County) (Township)	46366	Wheeling (Carroll County)	46929
				Wheeling (Delaware County)	47342
Washington (Knox County) (Township)	47516	Wayne (Tippecanoe County) (Township)	47992	Whiskey Run (Township)	47145
				Whitaker	46166
Washington (Kosciusko County) (Township)	46562	Wayne (Wayne County) (Township)	47374	Whitcomb	47012
		Wayne Center	46755	Whitcomb Heights	47885
Washington (La Porte County) (Township)	46350	Waynedale (Part of Fort Wayne)	46809	White Cloud	47112
				Whitehall	47401
Washington (Marion County) (Township)	46220	Waynesburg	47244	Whiteland	46184
		Waynesville	47201	Whiteoak	47598
Washington (Miami County) (Township)	46970	Waynetown	47990	White Post (Township)	47957
		Wea (Township)	47901	White Ridge	46952
Washington (Monroe County) (Township)	47401	Webster (Wayne County) (Township)	47392	White River (Gibson County) (Township)	47666
Washington (Morgan County) (Township)	46151	Webster (Harrison County) (Township)	47112	White River (Hamilton County) (Township)	46031
Washington (Newton County) (Township)	47922	Webster (Wayne County)	47392	White River (Johnson County) (Township)	46142
		Wegan	47220	White River (Randolph County) (Township)	47394
Washington (Noble County) (Township)	46760	Wehmeir	47201	White River Bluffs (Part of Bedford)	47421
		Weisburg	47041	Whites Crossing	47441
Washington (Owen County) (Township)	47460	Wellington Heights (Part of Shelbyville)	46176	Whitestown	46075
				Whitesville	47933
Washington (Parke County) (Township)	47859	Wells	46970	Whitewater (Franklin County) (Township)	47060
		Wellsboro	46382	Whitewater (Wayne County)	47374
Washington (Pike County) (Township)	47567	Wellsburg	46714	Whitfield	47553
		West (Township)	46563	Whiting	46394
Washington (Porter County) (Township)	46383	Westacres	47302	Wickliffe	47116
		West Atherton	47874	Widner (Township)	47561
Washington (Putnam County) (Township)	46171	West Baden Springs	47469	Wilbur	46151
		West Brook Acres (Part of Batesville)	47006	Wildcat (Township)	46076
Washington (Randolph County) (Township)	47394	West Brook Downs	47401	Wilders	46348
		Westchester (Jay County)	47371	Wildwood	46952
Washington (Ripley County) (Township)	47031	Westchester (Porter County) (Township)	46304	Wildwood Lake	47454
Washington (Rush County) (Township)	46127	West College Corner	45003	Wilfred	47879
		West Creek (Township)	46356	Wilkinson	46186
Washington (Shelby County) (Township)	46176	West Elwood	46036	Williams (Adams County)	46733
		Western Acres (Part of Chesterton)	46304	Williams (Lawrence County)	47470
Washington (Starke County) (Township)	46534	Western Hills (Part of Mount Vernon)	47620	Williamsburg	47393
				Williams Creek	46240
Washington (Tippecanoe County) (Township)	47924	Westfield	46074	Williamsport	47993
		West Fork	47118	Williamstown	47240
Washington (Warren County) (Township)	47993	West Franklin	47620	Willisville	47567
		West Harrison	47060	Willow Branch	46187
Washington (Washington County) (Township)	47167	West Haven	46580	Willowbrook Estates	46151
		West Hill	46383	Willow Creek (Part of Portage)	46368
Washington (Wayne County) (Township)	47357	West Indianapolis (Part of Indianapolis)	46221	Willow Valley	47581
Washington (Whitley County) (Township)	46725	West Lafayette	47906-07	Wills (Township)	46371
			47996	Wilmington (De Kalb County) (Township)	46721
Washington Center	46725	For specific West Lafayette Zip Codes call (317) 448-9245		Wilmington (Dearborn County)	47001
Washington Place (Part of Indianapolis)	46219	Westland	46140	Wilmot	46562
Washington Square (Part of Indianapolis)	46229	Westlawn	46804	Wilshire (Part of Frankfort)	46041
		West Lebanon	47991	Wilson (Clark County)	47106
Washington Square Mall (Part of Evansville)	47715	West Liberty	46936	Wilson (Porter County)	46368
Washington Trails (Part of Indianapolis)	46229	West Middleton	46995	Wilson (Shelby County)	46176
		Westmoor (Part of Fort Wayne)	46804	Wilson Lake	46725
Waterford	46360			Winamac	46996
Waterford Mills	46526	West Muncie (Part of Yorktown)	47396	Winchester	47394
Waterloo (Township)	47331	West Newton (Part of Indianapolis)	46183	Windemere Lake	47885
Waterloo (De Kalb County)	46793	West Noblesville (Part of Noblesville)	46060	Windfall	46076
Waterloo (Fayette County)	47331	West Peru (Part of Peru)	46970	Windom	47581
Waterswolde	46825	West Petersburg (Part of Petersburg)	47567	Windsor	47368
Wathen Heights	47130			Windsor Village (Part of Indianapolis)	46219
Watson	47130	Westphalia	47596	Winfield	46307
Waugh	46075	West Point (Howard County)	46901	Winfield (Township)	46307
Wauhob Lake	46383	Westpoint (Tippecanoe County)	47992	Wingate	47994
Waveland	47989	West Point (White County) (Township)	47980	Winona	46534
Waverly	46151	Westport	47283	Winona Lake	46590
Waverly Woods	46151	Westport Addition	47302	Winslow	47598
Wawaka	46794	Westside (Part of Aurora)	47001	Winthrop	47918
Wawpecong	46901	West Terre Haute	47885	Wirt	47250
Waymansville	47201	Westville	46391	Wirt Station	47250
Wayne (Allen County) (Township)	46806	Westville Correctional Center	46391	Witmer Manor	46795
				Witts	47353
Wayne (Bartholomew County) (Township)	47201			Wolcott	47995
Wayne (Fulton County) (Township)	46939			Wolcottville	46795
				Wolff	46151
Wayne (Hamilton County) (Township)	46060			Wolflake	46796
				Wonder Lake	47802
Wayne (Henry County) (Township)	46148			Wood (Township)	47106
				Woodbridge (Part of Bloomington)	47407
				Woodburn	46797

	ZIP		ZIP		ZIP
Woodbury	46055	Worth (Township)	46075	York (Switzerland County)	
Woodcrest	46151	Worthington	47471	(Township)	47020
Woodgate	47802	Wright (Township)	47441	Yorktown	47396
Woodgate East	47802	Wrights Corners	47001	Yorkville	47022
Woodland	46619	Wyatt	46595	Young	46158
Woodland Heights	46952	Wynnedale	46208	Young America	46998
Woodland Lake	46160	Yankeetown	47630	Youngs Corner	47012
Woodland Park (Delaware		Yeddo	47952	Youngs Creek	47454
County)	47302	Yellowbanks	46555	Youngstown	47802
Woodland Park (Lagrange		Yellow Creek Lake	46510	Youngstown Acres	47802
County)	46795	Yeoman	47997	Youngstown Meadows	47802
Woodland Trace (Part of		Yockey	47446	Youngstown Shopping	
Carmel)	46032	Yoder	46798	Center (Part of	
Woodlawn Heights	46011	York (Benton County)		Jeffersonville)	47130
Woodmar Mall (Part of		(Township)	47942	Yountsville	47933
Hammond)	46320	York (Dearborn County)		Yule Estates (Part of	
Woodridge	47803	(Township)	47022	Alexandria)	46001
Woodruff	46795	York (Elkhart County)		Zanesville	46799
Woodruff Place (Part of		(Township)	46507	Zelma	47264
Indianapolis)	46201	York (Noble County)		Zenas	47223
Woodville	46304	(Township)	46701	Zionsville	46077
Woodville Hills	47401	York (Steuben County)	46737	Zoar	47585
Wooster (Kosciusko		York (Steuben County)		Zulu	46773
County)	46562	(Township)	46703		
Wooster (Scott County)	47138				

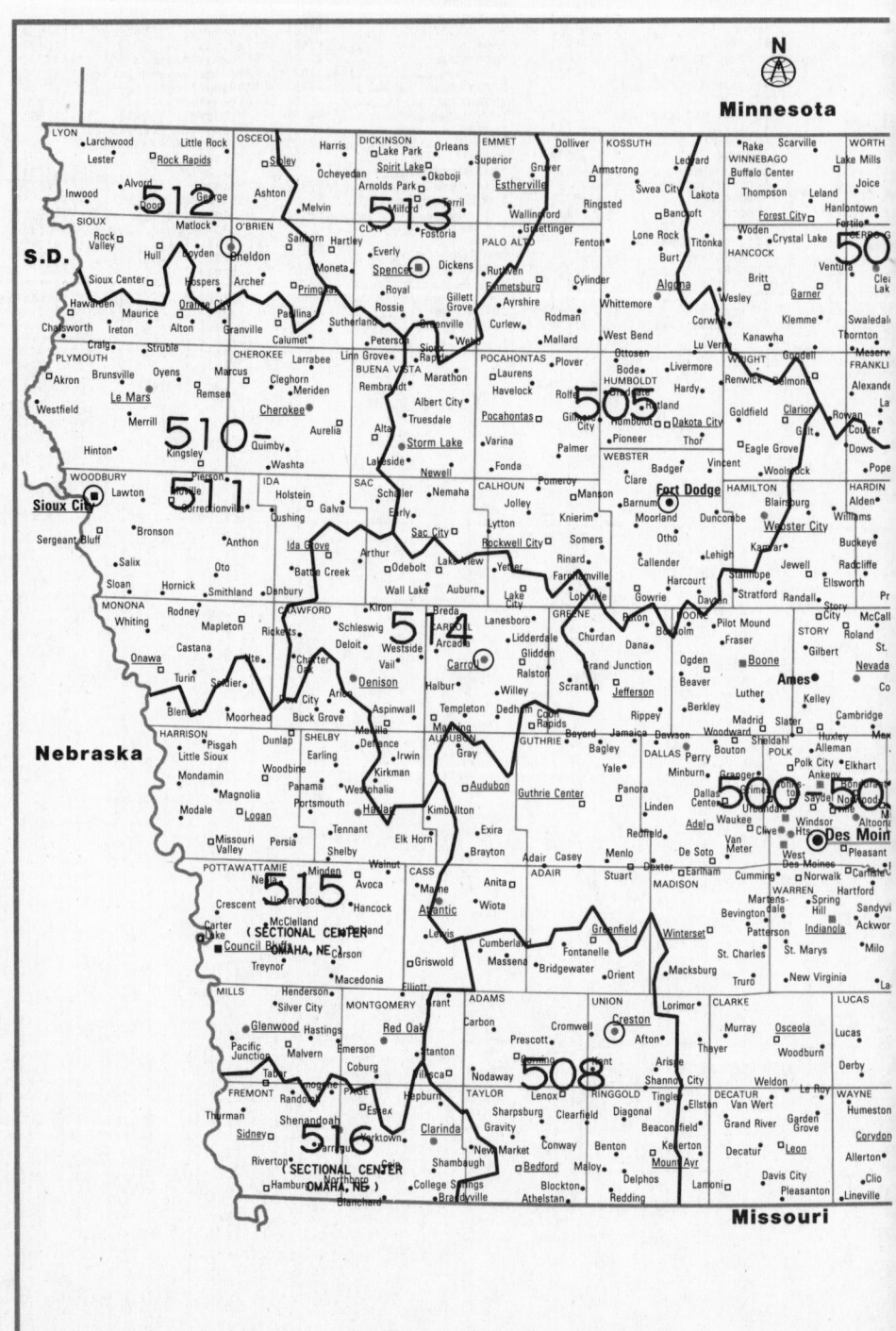

Legend
Population

- 250,000-999,999
- 100,000-249,999
- 50,000-99,999
- 25,000-49,999
- 10,000-24,999
- 5,000-9,999
- 1,000-4,999
- Less than 1,000

State Capital
County Seat

Copyright © 1986, 1983
by Rand McNally & Co.
All rights reserved
Made and printed in the U.S.A.

	ZIP		ZIP		ZIP
Abingdon	52533	Belmond	50421	Carroll	51401
Ackley	50601	Beloit	51240	Carson	51525
Ackworth	50001	Bennett	52721	Carter Lake	51510
Adair	50002	Benton	50835	Cartersville	50469
Adaza	50050	Bentonsport	52565	Cascade	52033
Adel	50003	Berkley	50220	Casey	50048
Afton	50830	Bernard	52032	Casino Beach	50588
Agency	52530	Bertram	52401	Castalia	52133
Ainsworth	52201	Berwick	50032	Castana	51010
Akron	51001	Bethlehem	50238	Cedar	52543
Albert City	50510	Bettendorf	52722	Cedar Bluff	52772
Albia	52531	Bevington	50033	Cedar Falls	50613
Albion	50005	Big Mound	52630	Cedar Rapids	52401-10
Alburnett	52202	Big Rock	52725	For specific Cedar Rapids Zip	
Alden	50006	Bingham	51601	Codes call (319) 399-2900	
Alexander	50420	Birmingham	52535	Cedar Valley	52358
Algona	50511	Bladensburg	52501	Cedar View	50616
Alleman	50007	Blairsburg	50034	Centerdale	52776
Allendorf	51330	Blairstown	52209	Center Grove (Part of	
Allerton	50008	Blakesburg	52536	Dubuque)	52003
Allison	50602	Blanchard	51630	Center Junction	52212
Alpha	52130	Blencoe	51523	Center Point	52213
Alta	51002	Blockton	50836	Centerville (Appanoose	
Alta Vista	50603	Bloomfield	52537	County)	52544
Alton	51003	Blue Grass	52726	Centerville (Boone County)	50036
Altoona	50009	Bluff Park (Part of		Central (Part of Davenport)	52801
Alvord	51230	Montrose)	52639	Central City	52214
Amana	52203	Bluffton	52101	Central College (Part of	
Amber	52205	Bode	50519	Pella)	50219
Amboy	50208	Bolan	50448	Central Heights (Part of	
Ames	50010	Bonair	52155	Mason City)	50401
Anamosa	52205	Bonaparte	52620	Centralia	52068
Anderson	51652	Bondurant	50035	Chapin	50427
Andover	52701	Boone	50036	Chariton	50049
Andrew	52030	Booneville	50038	Charles City	50616
Anita	50020	Botna	51454	Charleston	52619
Ankeny	50021	Bouton	50039	Charlotte	52731
Anthon	51004	Boxholm	50040	Charter Oak	51439
Aplington	50604	Boyd	50659	Chatsworth	51011
Arcadia	51430	Boyden	51234	Chelsea	52215
Archer	51231	Boyer	51448	Cherokee	51012
Aredale	50605	Braddyville	51631	Chester	52134
Argyle	52619	Bradford	50041	Chickasaw	50645
Arion	51520	Bradgate	50520	Chillicothe	52548
Arispe	50831	Brainard	52141	Church	52151
Arlington	50606	Brandon	52210	Churchville	50211
Armstrong	50514	Brayton	50042	Churdan	50050
Arnolds Park	51331	Brazil	52574	Cincinnati	52549
Artesian	50677	Breda	51436	Clare	50524
Arthur	51431	Bremer	50677	Clarence	52216
Asbury	52002	Bridgewater	50837	Clarinda	51632
Ashton	51232	Brighton	52540	Clarion	50525
Aspinwall	51432	Bristow	50611	Clarkdale	52544
Atalissa	52720	Britt	50423	Clarksville	50619
Athelstan	50836	Bronson	51007	Clayton	52049
Atkins	52206	Brooklyn	52211	Clayton Center	52043
Atlantic	50022	Brooks	50841	Clearfield	50840
Attica	50138	Brunsville	51008	Clear Lake	50428
Auburn	51433	Brushy	50532	Cleghorn	51014
Audubon	50025	Bryant	52727	Clemons	50051
Augusta	52658	Bryantsburg	50641	Clermont	52135
Aurelia	51005	Buchanan	52772	Cleves	50601
Aureola	50653	Buckcreek	50674	Climbing Hill	51015
Aurora	50607	Buckeye	50043	Clinton	52732-33
Austinville	50608	Buck Grove	51528	For specific Clinton Zip Codes call	
Avery	52531	Buckingham	50612	(319) 242-6214	
Avoca	51521	Buffalo	52728	Clio	50052
Avon	50047	Buffalo Center	50424	Clive	50322
Avon Lake	50047	Buffalo Heights	52728	Cloverdale	51249
Ayrshire	50515	Burchinal	50469	Cloverhills (Part of	
Badger	50516	Burlington	52601	Des Moines)	50265
Bagley	50026	Burnside	50521	Clutier	52217
Baldwin	52207	Burr Oak	52131	Coalville	50501
Balltown	52073	Burt	50522	Coburg	51566
Bancroft	50517	Bussey	50044	Coggon	52218
Bangor	50258	Cairo	52738	Coin	51636
Bankston	52045	Calamus	52729	Colesburg	52035
Barnes City	50027	Calhoun	51555	Colfax	50054
Barnum	50518	California Junction	51555	College Springs	51637
Barrett Superette	50164	Callender	50523	College Square Mall (Part of	
Bartlett	51655	Calmar	52132	Cedar Falls)	50613
Bassett	50645	Calumet	51009	Collins	50055
Batavia	52533	Camanche	52730	Colo	50056
Battle Creek	51006	Cambria	50060	Colonial Village (Part of	
Baxter	50028	Cambridge	50046	West Des Moines)	50266
Bayard	50029	Camp Dodge	50111	Columbia	50057
Beacon	52534	Canby	50048	Columbus City	52737
Beaconsfield	50030	Canton	52309	Columbus Junction	52738
Beaman	50609	Cantril	52542	Colwell	50620
Beaver	50031	Capital Square (Part of Des		Commerce (Part of West	
Beaverdale (Part of Des		Moines)	50393	Des Moines)	50265
Moines)	50310	Capitol Heights	50317	Conesville	52739
Beaverdale Heights	52655	Carbon	50839	Confidence	52569
Beckwith	52556	Carl	50841	Conger	50240
Bedford	50833	Carlisle	50047	Conover	52132
Beebeetown	51546	Carmel	51247	Conrad	50621
Beech	50025	Carnarvon	51450	Conroy	52220
Bel Air Beach	50588	Carnes	51003	Conway	50833
Belknap	52537	Carney	50021	Cool	50125
Belle Plaine	52208	Carnforth	52347	Coon Rapids	50058
Bellevue	52031	Carpenter	50426	Cooper	50059

	ZIP		ZIP		ZIP
Coppock	52654	Dows	50071	Festina	52143
Coralville	52241	Drakesville	52552	Fillmore	52033
Corley	51537	Dubuque	52001-04	Finchford	50647
Cornelia	50525	For specific Dubuque Zip Codes		First Street (Part of Cedar	
Cornell	50585	call (319) 582-3674		Rapids)	52407
Corning	50841	Duck Creek Plaza (Part of		Fiscus	50025
Correctionville	51016	Bettendorf)	52722	Five Points	52073
Corwith	50430	Dumont	50625	Flagler	50138
Corydon	50060	Dunbar	50158	Florenceville	52136
Cosgrove	52322	Duncan	50423	Floris	52560
Cotter	52738	Duncombe	50532	Floyd	50435
Cottonville	52054	Dundee	52038	Folletts	52730
Coulter	50431	Dunkerton	50626	Fonda	50540
Council Bluffs	51501-03	Dunlap	51529	Fontanelle	50846
	51593	Durango	52073	Forbush	52544
For specific Council Bluffs Zip		Durant	52747	Forest City	50436
Codes call (712) 325-0630		Durham	50119	Fort Atkinson	52144
Covington	52324	Dutchtown	52057	Fort Dodge	50501
Craig	51017	Dyersville	52040	Fort Dodge Junction (Part	
Crandalls Lodge	51360	Dysart	52224	of Fort Dodge)	50501
Cranston	52754	Eagle Center	50701	Fort Madison	52627
Crawfordsville	52621	Eagle Grove	50533	Fostoria	51340
Crescent	51526	Eagle Point (Part of		Four Corners	52635
Cresco	52136	Dubuque)	52001	Franklin	52625
Creston	50801	Earlham	50072	Frankville	52162
Crestwood (Part of Windsor		Earling	51530	Fraser	50036
Heights)	50311	Earlville	52041	Fredericksburg	50630
Crocker	50226	Early	50535	Frederika	50631
Cromwell	50842	East Amana	52203	Fredonia	52738
Crossroads Center (Part of		East Des Moines (Part of		Freeman	50401
Waterloo)	50703	Des Moines)	50309	Freeport	52101
Crossroads Mall (Part of		East Fourteenth Street (Part		Fremont	52561
Fort Dodge)	50501	of Des Moines)	50316	Froelich	52047
Croton	52626	East Pleasant Plain	52540	Fruitland	52749
Crystal Lake	50432	Eddyville	52553	Fulton	52060
Cumberland	50843	Edgewood	52042	Galesburg	50232
Cumming	50061	Edgewood Park (Part of		Galland	52639
Curlew	50527	Bettendorf)	52722	Galt	50101
Cushing	51018	Edna	51246	Galva	51020
Cylinder	50528	Egralharve	51360	Gambrill	52756
Dahlonega	52501	Elberon	52225	Garber	52048
Dakota City	50529	Eldon	52554	Garden City	50102
Dallas (Part of Melcher)	50062	Eldora	50627	Garden Grove	50103
Dallas Center	50063	Eldorado	52175	Gardiner	50039
Dana	50064	Eldridge	52748	Garnavillo	52049
Danbury	51019	Elgin	52141	Garner	50438
Danville	52623	Elkader	52043	Garrison	52229
Darbyville	52544	Elkhart	50073	Garwin	50632
Davenport	52801-09	Elk Horn	51531	Gaza	51245
For specific Davenport Zip Codes		Elkport	52044	Geneva	50633
call (319) 322-5991		Elk Run Heights	50701	George	51237
Davis City	50065	Elliott	51532	Georgetown	52531
Dawson	50066	Ellston	50074	Germantown	51046
Dayton	50530	Ellsworth	50075	German Valley	50480
Daytonville	52356	Elma	50628	Germanville	52540
Dean	52572	Elon	52170	Giard	52157
Decatur	50067	Elrick	52653	Gibson	50104
Decorah	52101	Elvira	52732	Gifford	50259
Dedham	51440	Elwood	52226	Gilbert	50105
Deep River	52222	Ely	52227	Gilbertville	50634
Defiance	51527	Emeline	52207	Gillett Grove	51341
Delaware	52036	Emerson	51533	Gilman	50106
Delhi	52223	Emery	50401	Gilmore City	50541
Delmar	52037	Emmetsburg	50536	Gladbrook	50635
Deloit	51441	Enterprise	50073	Glasgow	52556
Delphos	50844	Epworth	52045	Glendale Acres	51503
Delta	52550	Essex	51638	Glendon	50164
Denison	51442	Estherville	51334	Glenwood	51534
Denmark	52624	Evans	52577	Glidden	51443
Denver	50622	Evansdale	50707	Goddard	50054
Depew	50528	Evanston	50532	Goldfield	50542
Derby	50068	Evergreen	52804	Goodell	50439
Des Moines	50265-66	Everly	51338	Goose Lake	52750
	50301-95	Ewart	50171	Gowrie	50543
For specific Des Moines Zip		Exira	50076	Grace Hill	52353
Codes call (515) 283-7500		Exline	52555	Graettinger	51342
De Soto	50069	Fairbank	50629	Graf	52073
Dewar	50623	Fairfax	52228	Grafton	50440
Dewey	50853	Fairfield	52556	Grand (Part of Des Moines)	50309
De Witt	52742	Fair Ground (Part of		Grand Junction	50107
Dexter	50070	Dubuque)	52002	Grand Mound	52751
Diagonal	50845	Fairmount Park (Part of		Grand River	50108
Dickens	51333	Council Bluffs)	51503	Grandview	52752
Dike	50624	Fairport	52761	Granger	50109
Dillon	50158	Fairview	52205	Granger Homesteads	50109
Dinsdale	50669	Fanslers	50115	Granite	51241
Dixon	52745	Farley	52046	Grant	50847
Dodge Park (Part of Council		Farlin	50077	Grant Wood (Part of	
Bluffs)	51501	Farmersburg	52047	Bettendorf)	52722
Dodgeville	52650	Farmington	52626	Granville	51022
Dolliver	50531	Farnhamville	50538	Gravity	50848
Donahue	52746	Farragut	51639	Gray	50110
Donnan	52142	Farrar	50161	Greeley	52050
Donnellson	52625	Farson	52563	Green Castle	50054
Doon	51235	Faulkner	50601	Greene	50636
Dorchester	52140	Fayette	52142	Greenfield	50849
Douds	52551	Fenton	50539	Greenfield Plaza	50315
Dougherty	50433	Ferguson	50078	Green Island	52064
Douglas	52175	Fern	50665	Green Mountain	50637
Dow City	51528	Fernald	50201	Greenville	51343
Downey	52358	Fertile	50434	Greenwood Acres	50021

	ZIP		ZIP		ZIP
Grimes	50111	Indianola	50125	Lansing	52151
Grinnell	50112	Industry	50540	Lanyon	50544
Griswold	51535	Inwood	51240	La Porte City	50651
Grundy Center	50638	Ionia	50645	Larchwood	51241
Gruver	51344	Iowa Army Ammunition		Larrabee	51029
Guernsey	50172	Plant	52638	Latimer	50452
Gunder	52162	Iowa Center	50161	Laurel	50141
Guss	50857	Iowa City	50240	Laurens	50554
Guthrie Center	50115		52242-46	Lawler	52154
Guttenberg	52052	For specific Iowa City Zip Codes		Lawn Hill	50206
Halbur	51444	call (319) 354-1560		Lawton	51030
Hale	52230	Iowa Falls	50126	Leando	52551
Hamburg	51640	Iowa State University (Part		Lebanon (Sioux County)	51250
Hamill	52625	of Ames)	50010	Lebanon (Van Buren	
Hamilton	50116	Ira	50127	County)	52565
Hamlin	50117	Ireton	51027	Le Claire	52753
Hampton	50441	Ironhills	52060	Ledyard	50556
Hancock	51536	Irving	52208	Leeds (Part of Sioux City)	51108
Hanford	50401	Irvington	50560	Le Grand	50142
Hanley	50240	Irwin	51446	Lehigh	50557
Hanlontown	50444	Ivy	50009	Leighton	50143
Hanover	51002	Jackson Junction	52150	Leland	50453
Hansell	50640	Jacksonville	51537	Le Mars	51031
Harcourt	50544	Jamaica	50128	Lenox	50851
Hardy	50545	James	51108	Leon	50144
Harlan	51537	Jamison	50210	Le Roy	50123
Harper	52231	Janesville	50647	Lester	51242
Harpers Ferry	52146	Jefferson	50129	Letts	52754
Harris	51345	Jerico	50659	Lewis	51544
Harrisburg	52620	Jerome	52544	Liberty	50210
Hartford	50118	Jesup	50648	Liberty Center	50145
Hartley	51346	Jewell	50130	Libertyville	52567
Hartwick	52232	Joetown	52247	Lidderdale	51452
Harvard	50008	Johnston	50131	Lime City	52778
Harvey	50119	Johnston Station (Part of		Lime Springs	52155
Haskins	52201	Johnston)	50131	Linby	52580
Hastings	51540	Joice	50446	Lincoln	50652
Hauntown	52732	Jolley	50551	Lincoln Center	50841
Havelock	50546	Jordan	50036	Lindale Mall (Part of Cedar	
Haven	52339	Julien	52003	Rapids)	52402
Haverhill	50120	Juniata	50588	Linden	50146
Hawarden	51023	Kalo	50569	Lineville	50147
Hawkeye	52147	Kalona	52247	Linn Grove	51033
Hawleyville	51632	Kamrar	50132	Linwood (Part of Buffalo)	52805
Hawthorne	51566	Kanawha	50447	Lisbon	52253
Hayesville	52562	Kellerton	50133	Liscomb	50148
Hayfield	50438	Kelley	50134	Little Cedar	50454
Hazleton	50641	Kellogg	50135	Littleport	52055
Hedrick	52563	Kendallville	52136	Little Rock	51243
Henderson	51541	Kennedy Mall (Part of		Little Sioux	51545
Hepburn	51632	Dubuque)	52002	Littleton	50648
Herndon	50128	Kensett	50448	Little Turkey	52154
Herrold	50111	Kent	50850	Livermore	50558
Hesper	52101	Keokuk	52632	Livingston	52549
Hiawatha	52233	Keomah Village	52577	Lockridge	52635
Hickman Road (Part of		Keosauqua	52565	Logan	51546
Urbandale)	50322	Keota	52248	Logansport	50036
High	52203	Kesley	50649	Lohrville	51453
Highland Center	52501	Keswick	50136	Lone Rock	50559
Highland Park (Part of Des		Keystone	52249	Lone Tree	52755
Moines)	50333	Key West	52003	Long Grove	52756
Highlandville	52149	Kilbourn	52535	Lorah	50022
High Point	50103	Killduff	50137	Lorimor	50149
Highview	50595	Kimballton	51543	Lost Nation	52254
Hills	52235	Kingsley	51028	Lourdes	50628
Hillsboro	52630	Kingston	52637	Loveland	51555
Hinton	51024	Kinross	52250	Lovilia	50150
Hiteman	52531	Kirkman	51447	Lovington	50322
Hobarton	50511	Kirkville	52566	Lowden	52255
Hocking	52531	Kiron	51448	Lowell	52645
Holbrook	52325	Klemme	50449	Low Moor	52757
Holiday Lake	52211	Klinger	50668	Luana	52156
Holland	50642	Knierim	50552	Lucas	50151
Holly Springs	51026	Knittel	50668	Lundstrom Heights	50021
Holmes	50525	Knoke	50553	Luther	50152
Holstein	51025	Knoxville	50138	Luther Manor (Part of	
Holy Cross	52053	Knoxville Estates	50138	Bettendorf)	52722
Homer	50595	Konigsmark	52401	Luton	51052
Homestead	52236	Kossuth	52637	Lu Verne	50560
Honey Creek	51542	Koszta	52208	Luxemburg	52056
Hopeville	50174	Lacelle	50213	Luzerne	52257
Hopkinton	52237	Lacey	50207	Lyman	51535
Hornick	51026	Lacona	50139	Lynnville	50153
Horton	50677	Ladora	52251	Lyons (Clinton County)	52732
Hospers	51238	La Fayette	52202	Lyons (Linn County)	52302
Houghton	52631	Lake Canyada	52804	Lytton	50561
Hubbard	50122	Lake City	51449	McCallsburg	50154
Hudson	50643	Lake Mills	50450	McCausland	52758
Hull	51239	Lake Park	51347	McClelland	51548
Humboldt	50548	Lakeside	50588	Macedonia	51549
Humeston	50123	Lake View	51450	McGregor	52157
Huntington	51334	Lakewood	50211	McIntire	50455
Hurstville	52060	Lakota	50451	Macksburg	50155
Hutchins	50423	Lambs Grove	50208	McNally	51027
Huxley	50124	Lamoille	50158	Macy	50601
Iconium	52571	Lamoni	50140	Madison (Part of Council	
Ida Grove	51445	Lamont	50650	Bluffs)	51503
Imogene	51645	La Motte	52054	Madrid	50156
Independence	50644	Lanesboro	51451	Magnolia	51550
Indian Creek (Part of		Langdon	51301	Maine	52571
Marion)	52302	Langworthy	52252	Malcom	50157

	ZIP		ZIP		ZIP
Pleasanton	50065	Rowan	50470	Southern Hills Mall (Part of	
Pleasant Plain	52540	Rowley	52329	Sioux City)	51106
Pleasant Prairie	52761	Royal	51357	South Muscatine (Part of	
Pleasant Valley	52767	Rubio	52585	Muscatine)	52761
Pleasantville	50225	Rudd	50471	South Ottumwa (Part of	
Plover	50573	Runnells	50237	Ottumwa)	52501
Plymouth	50464	Russell	50238	Southridge Mall (Part of Des	
Pocahontas	50574	Ruthven	51358	Moines)	50315
Polk City	50226	Rutland	50582	Spaulding	50801
Pomeroy	50575	Ryan	50330	Spencer	51301
Popejoy	50227	Sabula	52070	Sperry	52650
Portland	50401	Sac and Fox Indian		Spillville	52168
Portsmouth	51565	Reservation	52339	Spirit Lake	51360
Postville	52162	Sac City	50583	Spragueville	52074
Powersville	50636	Sageville	52001	Springbrook	52075
Prairieburg	52219	St. Ansgar	50472	Springdale	52358
Prairie City	50228	St. Anthony	50239	Spring Grove	52601
Prairie Grove	52655	St. Benedict	50511	Spring Hill	50125
Prescott	50859	St. Catherines	52003	Springville	52336
Preston	52069	St. Charles	50240	Spruce Hills Village (Part of	
Primghar	51245	St. Donatus	52071	Bettendorf)	52722
Primrose	52625	St. Joseph	50519	Stacyville	50476
Princeton	52768	St. Lucas	52166	Stanhope	50246
Prole	50229	St. Marys	50241	Stanley	50671
Promise City	52583	St. Olaf	52072	Stanton	51573
Prospect Hill (Part of		St. Paul	52657	Stanwood	52337
Burlington)	52601	Salem	52649	Stanzel	50849
Protivin	52163	Salina	52556	State Center	50247
Pulaski	52584	Salix	51052	Steamboat Rock	50672
Quarry	50158	Sanborn	51248	Stennett	51566
Quasqueton	52326	Sand Springs	52237	Sterling	52070
Quimby	51049	Sandusky	52632	Stiles	52537
Radcliffe	50230	Sandyville	50001	Stilson	50423
Rake	50465	Santiago	50169	Stockport	52651
Ralston	51459	Saratoga	52155	Stockton	52769
Randalia	52164	Saude	52154	Stone City	52205
Randall	50231	Savannah	52537	Storm Lake	50588
Randolph	51649	Sawyer	52627	Story City	50248
Rands	50579	Saydel	50313	Stout	50673
Rathbun	52544	Saylorville	50313	Strahan	51540
Raymar	50701	Scarville	50473	Stratford	50249
Raymond	50667	Schaller	51053	Strawberry Point	52076
Readlyn	50668	Schleswig	51461	Stringtown	50851
Reasnor	50232	Schley	52136	Struble	51057
Redding	50860	Sciola	50864	Stuart	50250
Redfield	50233	Scotch Grove	52331	Suburban Heights	52556
Red Line	51447	Scotch Ridge	50047	Sully	50251
Red Oak	51566	Scranton	51462	Sulphur Springs	50588
Red Rock Lakeview	50138	Searsboro	50242	Summerset	50125
Reinbeck	50669	Sedan	52544	Summitville	52632
Rembrandt	50576	Selma	52588	Sumner	50674
Remsen	51050	Seneca	50539	Sunbury	52778
Renwick	50577	Seney	51031	Sunshine	52544
Rhodes	50234	Sergeant Bluff	51054	Superior	51363
Riceville	50466	Sewal	50060	Sutherland	51058
Richards	50579	Sexton	50483	Sutliff	52253
Richland	52585	Seymour	52590	Swaledale	50477
Richmond	52247	Shaffton	52730	Swan	50252
Rickardsville	52073	Shambaugh	51651	Swea City	50590
Ricketts	51460	Shannon City	50861	Swedesburg	52652
Ridgeport	50036	Sharon Center	52240	Sweetland Center	52761
Ridgeway	52165	Sharpsburg	50862	Swisher	52338
Rinard	50587	Shawondasse	52003	Tabor	51653
Ringsted	50578	Sheffield	50475	Taintor	50253
Rippey	50235	Shelby	51570	Talleyrand	52248
Rising Sun	50317	Sheldahl	50243	Tama	52339
Ritter	51201	Sheldon	51201	Tara	50501
Riverdale	52722	Shell Rock	50670	Teeds Grove	52771
River Heights	52240	Shellsburg	52332	Templar Park	51360
River Junction	52755	Shenandoah	51601	Templeton	51463
Riverside (Washington			51693	Ten Mile	52727
County)	52327	For specific Shenandoah Zip		Tennant	51574
Riverside (Woodbury		Codes call (712) 246-2703		Tenville	50864
County)	51109	Sheridan	50157	Tenville Junction	50864
River Sioux	51545	Sherrill	52073	Terril	51364
Riverton	51650	Sherwood	50579	Thayer	50254
Riverview Release Center	50208	Shipley	50201	Thirty	52544
Roberts	50569	Shueyville	52404	Thompson	50478
Robertson	50601	Siam	50833	Thor	50591
Robins	52328	Sibley	51249	Thornburg	50255
Robinson	52330	Sidney	51652	Thornton	50479
Rochester	52772	Sigourney	52591	Thorpe	52057
Rock Creek	50461	Silver City	51571	Thurman	51654
Rockdale (Part of Dubuque)	52003	Sinclair	50665	Ticonic	51010
Rock Falls	50467	Sioux Center	51250	Tiffin	52340
Rockford	50468	Sioux City	51101-11	Timberland Heights (Part of	
Rock Rapids	51246	For specific Sioux City Zip Codes		Ames)	50010
Rock Valley	51247	call (712) 277-6411		Tingley	50863
Rockwell	50469	Sioux Rapids	50585	Tipton	52772
Rockwell City	50579	Six Mile	52732	Titonka	50480
Rodman	50580	Slater	50244	Toddville	52341
Rodney	51051	Slifer	50543	Toeterville	50481
Roelyn	50566	Sloan	51055	Toledo	52342
Roland	50236	Smithland	51056	Toolesboro	52653
Rolfe	50581	Soldier	51572	Toronto	52343
Rome	52642	Solon	52333	Tracy	50256
Rose Hill	52586	Somers	50586	Traer	50675
Roselle	51401	South Amana	52334	Trenton	52641
Ross	50025	South Des Moines (Part of		Treynor	51575
Rossie	51357	Des Moines)	50315	Triboji Beach	51360
Rossville	52159	South English	52335	Tripoli	50676

	ZIP		ZIP		ZIP
Troy	52537	Wall Lake	51466	Westside	51467
Troy Mills	52344	Walnut	51577	West Spencer	51338
Truax	52553	Walnut City	52574	West Storm Lake (Part of	
Truesdale	50592	Wapello	52653	Storm Lake)	50588
Truro	50257	Ware	50546	West Union	52175
Turin	51059	Washburn	50706	Westwood	52641
Turkey River	52052	Washington	52353	Wever	52658
Twin View Heights	52333	Washta	51061	What Cheer	50268
Udell	52593	Waterloo	50701-07	Wheatland	52777
Ulmer	51450	For specific Waterloo Zip Codes		White Oak	50073
Underwood	51576	call (319) 291-7400		Whiting	51063
Union	50258	Waterville	52170	Whittemore	50598
Union Center	51031	Watkins	52354	Whitten	50269
Union Mills	50207	Waubeek	52214	Whittier	52336
Unionville	52594	Waucoma	52171	Wichita	50115
University Heights	52240	Waukee	50263	Wick	50240
University Park	52595	Waukon	52172	Wildwood Camp	52756
University Place (Part of		Waukon Junction	52146	Willey	51401
Des Moines)	50311	Waupeton	52073	William Penn College (Part	
Urbana	52345	Waverly	50677	of Oskaloosa)	52577
Urbandale	50322	Wayland	52654	Williams	50271
Ute	51060	Webb	51366	Williamsburg	52361
Utica	52651	Webster (Keokuk County)	52355	Williamson (Adams County)	50859
Vail	51465	Webster (Madison County)	50273	Williamson (Lucas County)	50272
Valeria	50054	Webster City	50595	Williamstown	52247
Valley West Mall (Part of		Welch Avenue (Part of		Wilton	52778
West Des Moines)	50266	Ames)	50010	Windham	52322
Van Cleve	50162	Weldon	50264	Windsor Heights	50311
Vandalia	50228	Wellman	52356	Winfield	52659
Van Horne	52346	Wellsburg	50680	Winnebago Heights	50401
Van Meter	50261	Welton	52774	Winterset	50273
Van Wert	50262	Wesley	50483	Winthrop	50682
Varina	50593	West	52357	Wiota	50274
Ventura	50482	West Ackley (Part of		Wiscotta	50233
Vernon	52565	Ackley)	50601	Woden	50484
Vernon Springs	52136	West Bend	50597	Wood	52042
Vernon View	52401	West Branch	52358	Woodbine	51579
Veterans Administration		West Broadway (Part of		Woodburn	50275
Medical Center (Part of		Council Bluffs)	51501	Woodland	50103
Knoxville)	50138	West Burlington	52655	Woodward	50276
Victor	52347	West Chester	52359	Woodward State Hospital-	
Villisca	50864	Westdale Mall (Part of		School	50276
Vincennes	52619	Cedar Rapids)	52404	Woolstock	50599
Vincent	50594	West Des Moines	50265-66	Worthington	52078
Vining	52348	For specific West Des Moines Zip		Wright	52577
Vinton	52349	Codes call (515) 255-7410		Wyman	52621
Viola	52350	Western College	52404	Wyoming	52362
Volga	52077	Westfield	51062	Yale	50277
Volney	52159	Westgate	50681	Yarmouth	52660
Voorhies	50643	West Grove	52538	Yetter	51433
Wadena	52169	West Le Mars	51031	Yorktown	51656
Wahpeton	51351	West Liberty	52776	Zaneta	50643
Walcott	52773	West Okoboji	51351	Zearing	50278
Wales	51533	Weston	51576	Zion	50858
Walford	52351	Westphalia	51578	Zook Spur	50156
Walker	52352	West Point	52656	Zwingle	52079
Wallingford	51365				

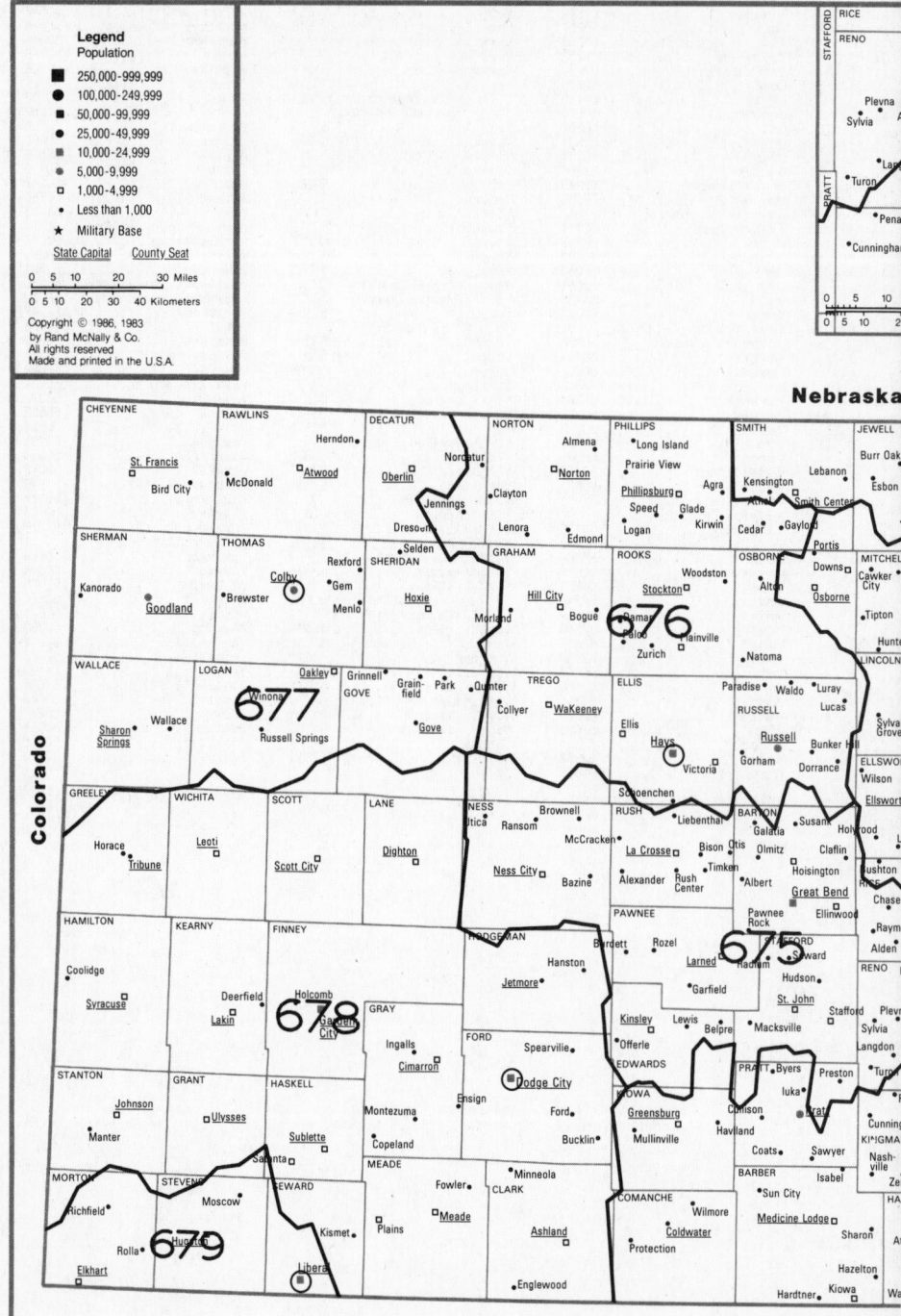

Legend

Population

- ■ 250,000-999,999
- ● 100,000-249,999
- ● 50,000-99,999
- ● 25,000-49,999
- ■ 10,000-24,999
- ▪ 5,000-9,999
- □ 1,000-4,999
- • Less than 1,000
- ★ Military Base

State Capital　County Seat

0 5 10   20   30 Miles
0 5 10 20 30 40 Kilometers

Nebraska

Colorado

Oklal

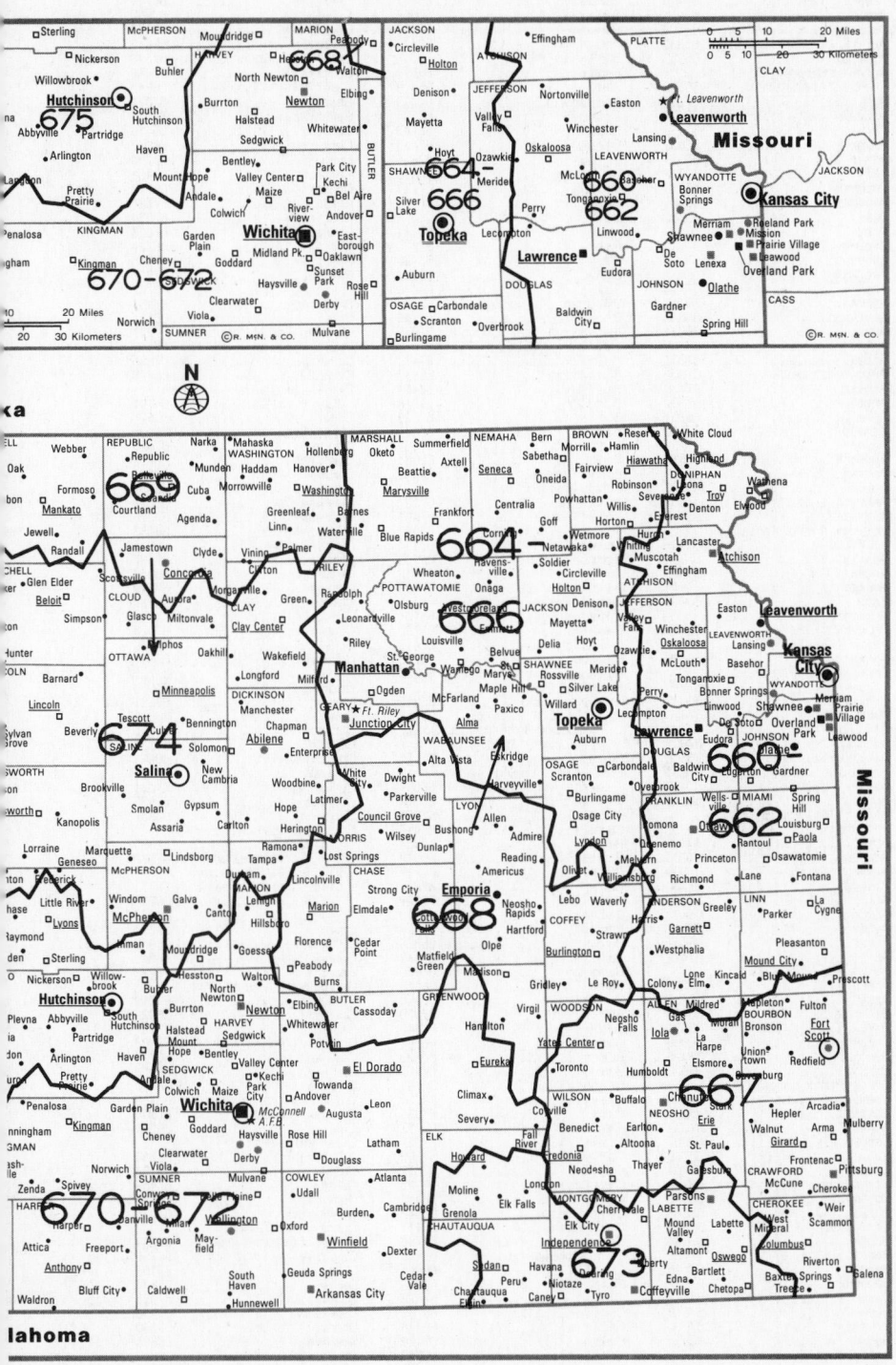

	ZIP
Abbyville	67510
Abilene	67410
Ada	67414
Adams	67128
Admire	66830
Agenda	66930
Aggieville Shopping Center (Part of Manhattan)	66502
Agra	67621
Agricola	66871
Akron	67156
Alamota	67839
Albert	67511
Alden	67512
Alexander	67513
Aliceville	66093
Allen	66833
Alma	66401
Almena	67622
Altamont	67330
Alta Vista	66834
Alton	67623
Altoona	66710
Americus	66835
Ames	66931
Amy	67850
Andale	67001
Andover	67002
Angelus	67738
Angola	67337
Anna	66701
Anness	67106
Anson	67152
Antelope	66858
Anthony	67003
Antioch	66083
Antonino	67601
Arcadia	66711
Argentine (Part of Kansas City)	66106
Argonia	67004
Arkansas City	67005
Arlington	67514
Arma	66712
Armourdale (Part of Kansas City)	66105
Arnold	67515
Arrington	66436
Arthur Heights (Part of Bel Aire)	67220
Arvonia	66523
Asherville	67420
Ash Grove	67481
Ashland (Clark County)	67831
Ashland (Riley County)	66502
Ashton	67051
Assaria	67416
Atchison	66002
Atchison Mall (Part of Atchison)	66002
Athol	66932
Atlanta	67008
Attica	67009
Atwood	67730
Aubry	66085
Auburn	66402
Augusta	67010
Aulne	66861
Aurora	67417
Aurora Park (Part of Bel Aire)	67220
Axtell	66403
Baileyville	66404
Bala	66531
Baldwin City	66006
Bancroft	66428
Barclay	66523
Barker (Part of Kansas City)	66104
Barnard	67418
Barnes	66933
Bartlett	67332
Basehor	66007
Bassett	66749
Bavaria	67401
Baxter Springs	66713
Bayard	66039
Bazaar	66845
Bazine	67516
Beagle	66064
Beardsley	67730
Beattie	66406
Beaumont	67012
Beaver	67517
Beeler	67518
Bel Aire	67220
Bellaire	66952
Belle Plaine	67013
Belleville	66935
Belmont	67068
Beloit	67420
Belpre	67519

	ZIP
Belvidere	67015
Belvue	66407
Bendena	66008
Benedict	66714
Bennington	67422
Bentley	67016
Benton	67017
Bern	66408
Berryton	66409
Berwick	66534
Beulah	66743
Beverly	67423
Big Bow	67855
Big Springs	66050
Bird City	67731
Birmingham	66436
Bismarck Grove (Part of Lawrence)	66044
Bison	67520
Black Wolf	67490
Blaine	66549
Blair	66090
Blakeman	67730
Bloom	67865
Bloomington (Butler County)	67010
Bloomington (Osborne County)	67473
Blue Mound	66010
Blue Rapids	66411
Bluff City	67018
Bogue	67625
Boicourt	66075
Bolton	67301
Bonita	66061
Bonner Springs	66012
Bonnie Brae (Part of Wichita)	67207
Bonnie Ridge	67401
Boyle	66088
Brainerd	67154
Brazilton	66743
Bremen	66412
Brenham	67059
Brenner Heights (Part of Kansas City)	66104
Brewster	67732
Bridgeport	67416
Bronson	66716
Brookhaven Estates	67230
Brookridge (Part of Overland Park)	66212
	66282
For specific Brookridge Zip Codes call (913) 831-5302	
Brookville	67425
Brookwood Shopping Center (Part of Topeka)	66614
Brownell	67521
Browns Spur	67068
Buckeye	67410
Bucklin	67834
Bucyrus	66013
Buffalo	66717
Buhler	67522
Bunker Hill	67626
Burden	67019
Burdett	67523
Burdick	66838
Burlingame	66413
Burlington	66839
Burns	66840
Burr Oak	66936
Burrton	67020
Busby	67349
Bush City	66032
Bushong	66833
Bushton	67427
Buxton	66736
Byers	67021
Cairo	67035
Caldwell	67022
Calista	67035
Callahan (Part of Wichita)	67209
Calvert	67622
Cambridge	67023
Camp Forsyth	66442
Camp Funston	66442
Camp Naish	66111
Campus	67748
Camp Whiteside	66442
Canada	66861
Caney	67333
Canton	67428
Capaldo	66762
Carbondale	66414
Carlton	67429
Carlyle	66749
Carneiro	67425
Carona	66773
Cassoday	66842
Castleton	67501

	ZIP
Catharine	67627
Cato	66711
Cave	67952
Cawker City	67430
Cedar (Johnson County)	66018
Cedar (Smith County)	67628
Cedar Bluffs	67749
Cedar Point	66843
Cedar Vale	67024
Centerville	66014
Centralia	66415
Centropolis	66067
Chanute	66720
Chapman	67431
Charleston	67853
Chase	67524
Chautauqua	67334
Cheney	67025
Cherokee	66724
Cherryvale	67335
Chetopa	67336
Chicopee	66762
Child's Acres	67101
Chiles	66071
Chisholm (Part of Wichita)	67217
Cicero	67152
Cimarron	67835
Circleville	66416
Civic Center (Part of Kansas City)	66101
Claflin	67525
Clare	66061
Claudell	67628
Clay Center	67432
Clayton	67629
Clearfield	66025
Clearview City	66019
Clearwater	67026
Clements	66843
Clifton	66937
Climax	67137
Clinton	66046
Clonmel	67149
Clyde	66938
Coalvale	66711
Coats	67028
Codell	67630
Coffeyville	67337
Colby	67701
Coldwater	67029
Collyer	67631
Colony	66015
Columbus	66725
Colwich	67030
Concordia	66901
Conway	67460
Conway Springs	67031
Coolidge	67836
Copeland	67837
Corbin (Montgomery County)	67335
Corbin (Sumner County)	67032
Corinth Square Shopping Center (Part of Prairie Village)	66208
Corning	66417
Corwin	67061
Cottonwood Falls	66845
Council Grove	66846
Countryside	66222
County Acres (Part of Wichita)	67212
Courtland	66939
Covert	67651
Cow Town (Part of Wichita)	67203
Coyville	66727
Craig	66215
Crestline	66728
Croweburg	66756
Cruppers Corner	67501
Cuba	66940
Cullen Village (Part of Topeka)	66619
Cullison	67124
Culver	67484
Cummings	66016
Cunningham	67035
Cunningham Highlands (Part of Overland Park)	66204
Curranville	66756
Dalton	67152
Damar	67632
Danville	67036
Dartmouth	67530
Dearing	67340
Deerfield	67838
De Graff	66840
Delavan	67449
Delia	66418
Delphos	67436
Denison	66419

	ZIP		ZIP		ZIP
Denmark	67455	Ford	67842	Harris	66032
Dennis	67341	Forest Hills (Part of Wichita)	67206	Hartford	66854
Densmore	67633	Forest Lake (Part of		Harveyville	66431
Denton	66017	Edwardsville)	66113	Haskell (Part of Lawrence)	66044
Denton-McWorter Addition	67101	Formoso	66942	Havana	67347
Derby	67037	Fort Dodge	67843	Haven	67543
Dermot	67954	Fort Leavenworth	66027	Havensville	66432
De Soto	66018	Fort Riley	66442	Haverhill	67010
Detroit	67410	Fort Riley-Camp Whiteside	66442	Haviland	67059
Devon	66701	Fort Riley North	66442	Hays	67601
Dexter	67038	Fort Scott	66701	Haysville	67060
Diamond Springs	66838	Fostoria (Osage County)	66413	Hazelton	67061
Dighton	67839	Fostoria (Pottawatomie		Healy	67850
Dillwyn	67557	County)	66426	Hedville	67401
Dispatch	67430	Four Corners	66537	Heizer	67530
Dodge City	67801	Fowler	67844	Hepler	66746
Doniphan	66002	Fox Town	66756	Herington	67449
Dorrance	67634	Frankfort	66427	Heritage Hills	66002
Douglass	67039	Franklin	66735	Herkimer	66433
Dover	66420	Frederick	67444	Herndon	67739
Downs	67437	Fredonia	66736	Hesper	66025
Downtown (Part of Wichita)	67202	Freeport	67049	Hessdale	66401
Dresden	67635	Friend	67871	Hesston	67062
Drury	67022	Frontenac	66762	Hewins	67024
Dubuque	67634	Fulton	66738	Hiattville	66701
Duluth	66521	Furley	67147	Hiawatha	66434
Dundee	67530	Gage Center (Part of		Hickok	67880
Dunkirk	66762	Topeka)	66604	Hickory Acres	66512
Dunlap	66846	Galatia	67565	Hicrest (Part of Topeka)	66605
Duquoin	67058	Galena	66739	Hidden Lakes (Part of	
Durham	67438	Galesburg	66740	Wichita)	67212
Dwight	66849	Galva	67443	Highland	66035
Earlton	66720	Garden City	67846	Highland Park (Part of	
East Bank (Part of Iola)	66749	Garden Plain	67050	Topeka)	66605
Eastborough	67206	Gardner	66030	Hill City	67642
East Forbes	66620	Gardner Lake	66030	Hillcrest Shopping Center	
Eastgate Shopping Center		Garfield	67529	(Part of Lawrence)	66044
(Part of Wichita)	67207	Garland	66741	Hillsboro	67063
Easton	66020	Garnett	66032	Hillsdale	66036
Eastshore	66861	Gas	66742	Hillside (Part of Wichita)	67208
Edgerton	66021	Gaylord	67638	Hitschmann	67525
Edmond	67636	Gem	67734	Hoge	66086
Edna	67342	Geneseo	67444	Hoisington	67544
Edson	67733	Geuda Springs	67051	Holcomb	67851
Edwardsville	66113	Girard	66743	Holland	67410
Effingham	66023	Glade	67639	Hollenberg	66946
Elbing	67041	Glasco	67445	Holliday (Part of Shawnee)	66218
El Dorado	67042	Glendale	67425	Holliday Square Shopping	
El Dorado Honor Camp	67042	Glen Elder	67446	Center (Part of Topeka)	66611
Elgin	67361	Glen Park (Part of Kansas		Holton	66436
Elk City	67344	City)	66102	Holyrood	67450
Elk Falls	67345	Glenville (Part of Wichita)	67217	Home	66438
Elkhart	67950	Goddard	67052	Homewood	66095
Ellinwood	67526	Goessel	67053	Hope	67451
Ellis	67637	Goff	66428	Hopewell	67557
Ellsworth	67439	Golden Belt Spur (Part of		Horace	67879
Elmdale	66850	Salina)	67401	Horton	66439
Elmhurst (Part of Overland		Goodland	67735	Howard	67349
Park)	66204	Goodrich	66072	Hoxie	67740
Elmo	67451	Gorham	67640	Hoyt	66440
Elmont	66618	Gove	67736	Hudson	67545
Elsmore	66732	Grainfield	67737	Hugoton	67951
Elwood	66024	Granada	66550	Humboldt	66748
Elyria	67460	Grand Summit	67023	Hunnewell	67140
Emmeram	67671	Grandview (Part of Bonner		Hunter	67452
Emmett	66422	Springs)	66012	Huron	66041
Empire City (Part of Galena)	66739	Grandview Plaza	66441	Huscher	66901
Empire Junction (Part of		Grantville	66429	Hutchinson	67501-04
Galena)	66739	Great Bend	67530	For specific Hutchinson Zip Codes	
Emporia	66801	Greeley	66033	call (316) 662-1295	
Englevale	66756	Green	67447	Hutchinson Mall (Part of	
Englewood	67840	Greenbush	66743	Hutchinson)	67501
Ensign	67841	Greenleaf	66943	Idana	67432
Enterprise	67441	Greensburg	67054	Imes	66079
Erie	66733	Greenwich	67055	Independence	67301
Esbon	66941	Greenwich Heights	67207	Indian Creek (Part of	
Eskridge	66423	Grenola	67346	Overland Park)	66207
Eudora	66025	Gretna	67661	Indian Ridge	66512
Eureka	67045	Gridley	66852	Indian Springs Shopping	
Eureka City Lake	67045	Grigston	67871	Center (Part of Kansas	
Everest	66424	Grinnell	67738	City)	66102
Fairfax (Part of Kansas City)	66115	Gross	66711	Indian Valley	66608
Fairmount	66048	Grove	66539	Indian Village	67337
Fairport	67665	Groveland	67546	Industry	67410
Fairview	66425	Gypsum	67448	Ingalls	67853
Fairway	66205	Hackney	67156	Inman	67546
Fall Leaf	66052	Haddam	66944	Iola	66749
Fall River	67047	Haggard	67835	Ionia	66949
Falun	67442	Half Mound	66088	Iowa Point	66035
Fanning	66087	Halford	67701	Isabel	67065
Farlington	66734	Hallowell	66725	Iuka	67066
Farlinville	66014	Halls Summit	66871	Jacobs Creek Landing	66854
Farmington	66023	Halstead	67056	Jamestown	66948
Faulkner	67336	Hamilton	66853	Jarbalo	66048
Federal Penitentiary	66048	Hamlin	66434	Jayhawk (Part of Lawrence)	66046
Fellsburg	67552	Hammond	66701	Jefferson	67301
Fleming	66762	Hanover	66945	Jennings	67643
Floral	67156	Hanston	67849	Jetmore	67854
Florence	66851	Hardtner	67057	Jewell	66949
Flush	66535	Harlan	67641	Johnson	67855
Fontana	66026	Harper	67058	Junction City	66441

	ZIP
Juniata	67423
Kackley	66948
Kalloch	67337
Kalvesta	67856
Kanona	67749
Kanopolis	67454
Kanorado	67741
Kansas City	66101-19

For specific Kansas City Zip Codes call (913) 573-2600

COLLEGES & UNIVERSITIES

University of Kansas Medical Center	66103

FINANCIAL INSTITUTIONS

Brotherhood Bank and Trust	66101
Citizens Bank & Trust of Kansas City	66103
Home State Bank Kansas	66101
Inter-State Federal Savings and Loan Association of Kansas City	66101
Security Bank of Kansas City	66101

HOSPITALS

Bethany Medical Center	66102
Providence-St. Margaret Health Center	66112
University of Kansas Hospital	66103

HOTELS/MOTELS

Best Western Flamingo Motel	66102
Best Western Inn	66103
Kansas State Penitentiary	66043
Kansas State University of Agriculture and Applied	66506
Keats	66502
Kechi	67067
Keene	66423
Kellogg	67156
Kelly	66538
Kendall	67857
Kennekuk	66439
Kenneth	66223
Kensington	66951
Kickapoo	66048
Kickapoo Indian Reservation	66439
Kimball	66733
Kimeo	66943
Kincaid	66039
Kingman	67068
Kingsdown	67858
Kinsley	67547
Kiowa	67070
Kipp	67401
Kirkwood	66762
Kiro	66539
Kirwin	67644
Kismet	67859
Labette	67356
La Crosse	67548
La Cygne	66040
Lafontaine	66736
La Harpe	66751
Lake Chaparral	66056
Lake City	67071
Lake Kahola	66846
Lake of the Forest (Part of Bonner Springs)	66012
Lake Quivira	66106
Lake Shore (Ellsworth County)	67454
Lake Shore (Jefferson County)	66070
Lakeshore (Shawnee County)	66605
Lakeside Acres Addition	67208
Lakeside Village	66070
Lakeview Heights	67230
Lake Wabaunsee	66401
Lakewood Hills	66070
Lakin	67860
Lamont	66855
Lancaster	66041
Lane	66042
Langdon	67583
Langley	67464
Lanham	68415
Lansing	66043
Larkinburg	66436
Larned	67550
Larned State Hospital	67550
Latham	67072
Latimer	67449
Lawrence	66044-47

	ZIP
	66049

For specific Lawrence Zip Codes call (913) 843-1681

Lawton	67781
Leavenworth	66048
Leawood	66206
Lebanon	66952
Lebo	66856
Lecompton	66050
Lehigh	67073
Le Loup	66091
Lenape	66052
Lenexa	66215
	66285

For specific Lenexa Zip Codes call (913) 888-5234

Lenexa Plaza (Part of Lenexa)	66215
Lenora	67645
Leon	67074
Leona	66532
Leonardville	66449
Leoti	67861
Leoville	67757
Le Roy	66857
Levant	67743
Lewis	67552
Liberal	67901-05

For specific Liberal Zip Codes call (316) 624-4031

Liberty	67351
Liebenthal	67553
Lillis	66544
Lincoln	67455
Lincolnville	66858
Lindsborg	67456
Linn	66953
Linn Valley Lakes	66040
Linwood	66052
Little River	67457
Logan	67646
Lone Elm	66039
Lone Star	66046
Longford	67458
Long Island	67647
Longton	67352
Loretta	67520
Lorraine	67459
Lost Springs	66859
Louisburg	66053
Louisville	66450
Lovewell	66942
Lowell	66713
Lowemont	66020
Lucas	67648
Ludell	67744
Luray	67649
Lydia	67861
Lyndon	66451
Lyons	67554
McConnell Air Force Base	67221
McCracken	67556
McCune	66753
McDonald	67745
McFarland	66501
Mackie	66725
Macksville	67557
McLouth	66054
McPherson	67460
Madison	66860
Mahaska	66955
Maize	67101
Manchester	67463
Manhattan	66502
Mankato	66956
Manning	67871
Manter	67862
Maple City	67102
Maple Hill	66507
Mapleton	66754
Marienthal	67863
Marietta	66518
Marion	66861
Marion County Lake	66861
Marmaton	66701
Marquette	67464
Marysville	66508
Matfield Green	66862
Mayetta	66509
Mayfield	67103
Meade	67864
Mecca Acres	67230
Medicine Lodge	67104
Medina	66073
Medora	67502
Melrose	67336
Melvern	66510
Menlo	67753
Mentor	67465
Mercier	66439
Meriden	66512

	ZIP
Merriam	66203
Metcalf South Shopping Center (Part of Overland Park)	66212
Michigan	66528
Midland (Part of Wichita)	67216
Midland Park	67216
Midway (Kingman County)	67111
Midway (Rawlins County)	67739
Milan	67105
Milberger	67665
Mildred	66039
Milford	66514
Millbrook (Part of Wichita)	67212
Miller	66868
Milton	67106
Miltonvale	67466
Mingo	67701
Minneapolis	67467
Minneola	67865
Mission	66205
Mission Hills	66205
Mission Shopping Center (Part of Mission)	66222
Mission Woods	66205
Mitchell	67554
Modoc	67863
Moline	67353
Monmouth	66753
Monrovia	66023
Montana	67356
Montara	66619
Montezuma	67867
Monticello (Part of Shawnee)	66218
Mont Ida	66091
Montrose	66956
Monument	67747
Moran	66755
Moray	66087
Morehead	66776
Morganville	67468
Morland	67650
Morrill	66515
Morrowville	66958
Morse	66061
Moscow	67952
Mound City	66056
Moundridge	67107
Mound Valley	67354
Mount Hope	67108
Mount Vernon	67025
Mulberry	66756
Mullinville	67109
Mulvane	67110
Muncie (Part of Kansas City)	66111
Munden	66959
Munger (Part of Wichita)	67208
Munjor	67601
Murdock	67111
Muscotah	66058
Narka	66960
Nashville	67112
Natoma	67651
Navarre	67469
Neal	66863
Nekoma	67559
Neodesha	66757
Neosho Falls	66758
Neosho Rapids	66864
Ness City	67560
Netawaka	66516
Neuchatel	66521
Neutral	66725
New Albany	66759
New Almelo	67652
Newbury	66526
New Cambria	67470
New Lancaster	66040
Newman	66073
New Salem	67156
Newton	67114
Nickerson	67561
Nicodemus	67625
Niles	67480
Niotaze	67355
Norcatur	67653
Normandie Shopping Center (Part of Wichita)	67206
Northbranch	66936
Northern Hills	66608
North Newton	67117
North Osage City (Part of Osage City)	66523
North Topeka (Part of Topeka)	66608
North Wichita (Part of Wichita)	67204
Norton	67654
Nortonville	66060

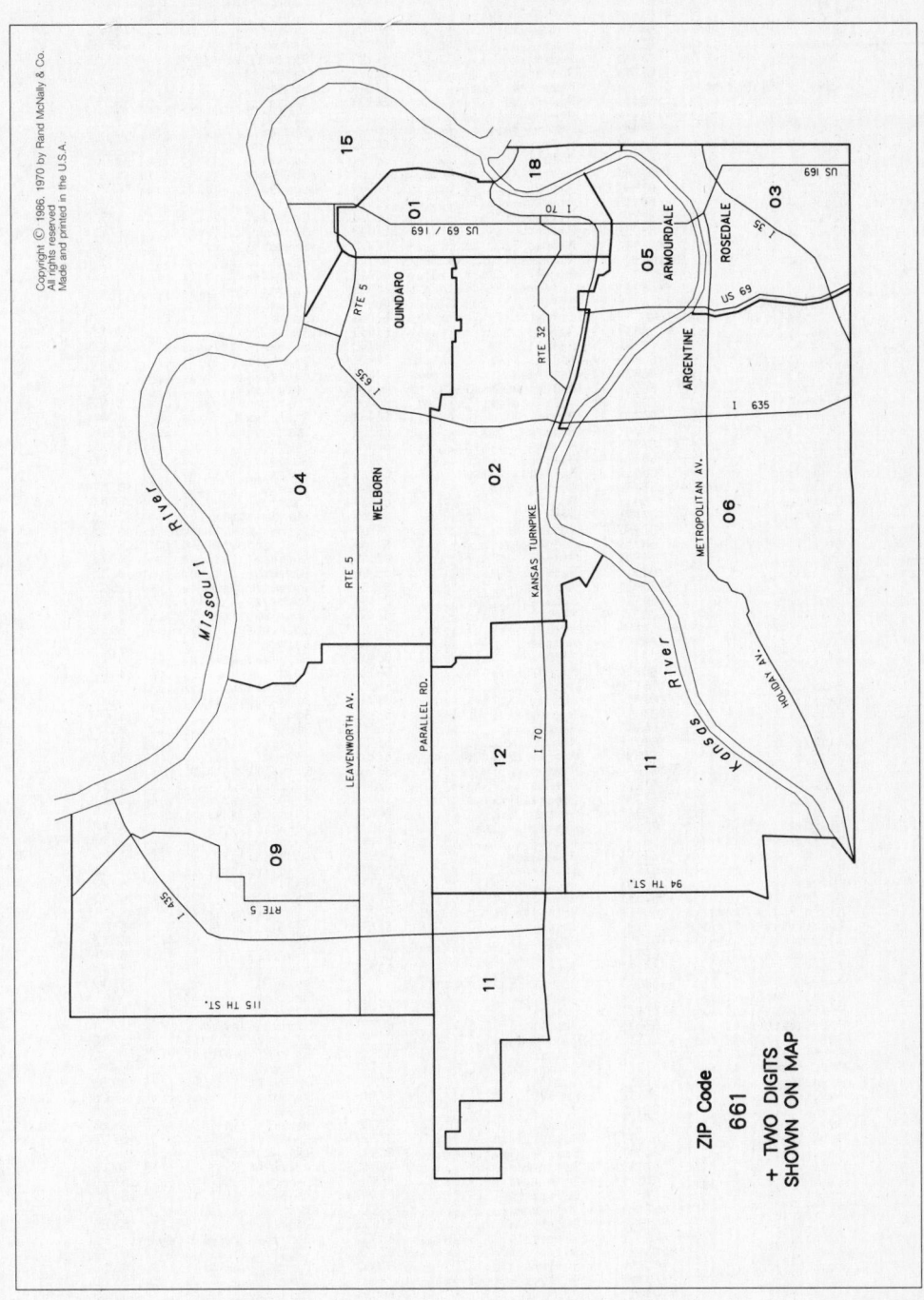

ZIP Code
661
+ TWO DIGITS
SHOWN ON MAP

	ZIP		ZIP		ZIP
Sun City	67143	Venango	67464	Westway Shopping Center	
Sunnydale	67147	Verdi	67480	(Part of Wichita)	67217
Sunset Park (Part of		Vermillion	66544	Westwood	66205
Haysville)	67060	Vernon	66783	Westwood Hills	66205
Suppesville	67106	Vesper	67455	Wetmore	66550
Susank	67544	Veterans Affairs Hospital		Wheaton	66551
Sweetbriar Shopping Center		(Part of Topeka)	66622	Wheatridge Addition (Part of	
(Part of Wichita)	67204	Victoria	67671	Wichita)	67212
Sycamore	67363	Vilas	66720	Wheeler	67756
Sylvan Grove	67481	Village Square, The (Part of		White Church (Part of	
Sylvia	67581	Dodge City)	67801	Kansas City)	66109
Syracuse	67878	Vine Creek	67458	White City	66872
Talmage	67482	Vining	66937	White Cloud	66094
Talmo	66935	Vinland	66006	White Lakes Shopping	
Tampa	67483	Viola	67149	Center (Part of Topeka)	67611
Tanglewood Lake	66040	Virgil	66870	Whitewater	67154
Tasco	67740	Vliets	66545	Whiting	66552
Tecumseh	66542	Voda	67631	Wichita	67201-78
Terra Heights (Part of		Wabaunsee	66547	For specific Wichita Zip Codes call	
Topeka)	66609	Waco	67120	(316) 946-4511	
Tescott	67484	Wagon Wheel Ranch	67010	Wichita State University	
Thayer	66776	Wagstaff	66071	(Part of Wichita)	67208
The Dell (Part of Wichita)	67209	Wakarusa	66546	Wilburton	67950
Thompsonville	66073	WaKeeney	67672	Wilder Junction	66018
Timken	67582	Wakefield	67487	Willard	66604
Tipton	67485	Waldo	67673	Williamsburg	66095
Tonganoxie	66086	Waldron	67150	Williamstown	66073
Topeka	66601-99	Walker	67674	Willis	66435
For specific Topeka Zip Codes		Wallace	67761	Willowbrook	67501
call (913) 295-9100		Walnut	66780	Willowdale	67142
Toronto	67777	Walton	67151	Wilmore	67155
Towanda	67144	Wamego	66547	Wilmot	67131
Tower Grove (Part of		Washburn University (Part		Wilroads Gardens	67801
Overland Park)	66204	of Topeka)	66621	Wilsey	66873
Towne East Square (Part of		Washington	66968	Wilson	67490
Wichita)	67207	Waterloo	67111	Winchester	66097
Towne West Square (Part		Waterville	66548	Windom	67491
of Wichita)	67209	Wathena	66090	Windsor Park	67207
Trading Post	66075	Watson	66542	Windthorst	67876
Traer	67749	Wauneta	67024	Winfield	67156
Travel Air	67206	Waverly	66871	Winfield State Hospital and	
Treece	66778	Wayne	66930	Training Center	67156
Trego Center	67672	Wayside	67301	Winifred	66427
Tribune	67879	Wea	66013	Winona	67764
Trousdale	67059	Webber	66970	Winway (Part of Parsons)	67357
Troy	66087	Webster	67669	Wolcott (Part of Kansas	
Turck	66725	Wego-Waco	67216	City)	66109
Turkville	67663	Weir	66781	Womer	66952
Turner (Part of Kansas City)	66106	Welborn (Part of Kansas		Wonsevu	66840
Turon	67583	City)	66104	Woodbine	67492
Twin Lakes Shopping		Welda	66091	Woodruff	67661
Center (Part of Wichita)	67203	Wellington	67152	Woods	67951
Tyro	67364	Wells	67488	Woodston	67675
Udall	67146	Wellsford	67059	Worden	66006
Ulysses	67880	Wellsville	66092	Wright	67882
Union Stock Yards (Part of		Weskan	67762	Wyandotte West (Part of	
Wichita)	67219	Wesleyan (Part of Salina)	67401	Kansas City)	66112
Uniontown	66779	Westboro (Part of Topeka)	66604	Xenia	66716
University (Crawford		West Coffeyville	67337	Yaggy	67501
County)	66762	Westfall	67455	Yale	66762
University (Douglas County)	66044	Westlink Shopping Center		Yates Center	66783
Urbana	66720	(Part of Wichita)	67212	Yocemento	67601
Utica	67584	Westlink Village (Part of		Yoder	67585
Valeda	67337	Wichita)	67212	Zarah (Part of Shawnee)	66218
Valencia	66604	West Mineral	66782	Zeandale	66502
Valley Center	67147	Westmoreland	66549	Zenda	67159
Valley Falls	66088	Westphalia	66093	Zenith	67578
Varner	67068	Westport (Part of Wichita)	67217	Zook	67550
Vassar	66543	West Shore	66512	Zurich	67676

India

Orchar

Louisville
Naval Ordnance Station
Shively

Pleasure Ridge Park Okolor
Valley Station JEFFEI

MEADE West
Brandenburg Point Hillvie
BULLITT

Lewisport Irvington Ekr Ft. Knox Muldraugh

Henderson Hawesville Cloverport **401-402** Lyte
HANCOCK Grove

HENDERSON Hardinsburg HARDIN Elizabethtown

Uniontown Corydon **Owensboro** BRECKINRIDGE

Morganfield Waverly DAVIESS Whitesville Fordsville Sonora Hodge

UNION OHIO Leitchfield Clarkson Upton

Caseyville Sturgis Sebree McLEAN Livermore Caneyville HART Bonniev

Wheatl SECTIONAL CENTER Calhoun **423** Hartford Beaver Dam Munfordville

Carrsville CRITTENDEN EVANSVILLE, IN Providence Sacra- McHenry Horse

Salem Nebo mento Hanson Island Rockport BUTLER Cave

Marion Madisonville S. Carrollton Central Morgantown Brownsville

LIVINGSTON Earlington Mortons Lowderly City WARREN

Dycus- Fredonia Dawson Gap Norton Greenville Rochester Smiths Grove Park City

BALLARD burg Springs St. MUHLENBERG Plum Springs

La Center Kevil **Paducah** Eddyville CALDWELL Charles **Bowling Green** Glasgow

Barlow Smithland Princeton Crofton TODD LOGAN Oakland

Wickliffe Kuttawa Lewisburg ALLEN

McCRACKEN Calvert Grand CHRISTIAN Woodburn WARREN

Bardwell City Rivers Auburn MO

CARLISLE GRAVES Benton **Hopkinsville** **422** Fulton Russellville **421** Tomp

Mo. Arlington **420** MARSHALL Pembroke Franklin Scottsville

Columbus Mayfield Hardin Trenton Allensville SIMPSON Gar

HICKMAN CALLOWAY La Fayette Oak Grove Guthrie Adairville

Clinton Wingo Ft. Campbell

FULTON **Murray**

Hickman Water Valley **Tenness**

Fulton Hazel

Illinois

Louisville

Owensboro

424

Grayson

Lewisport

HANCOCK

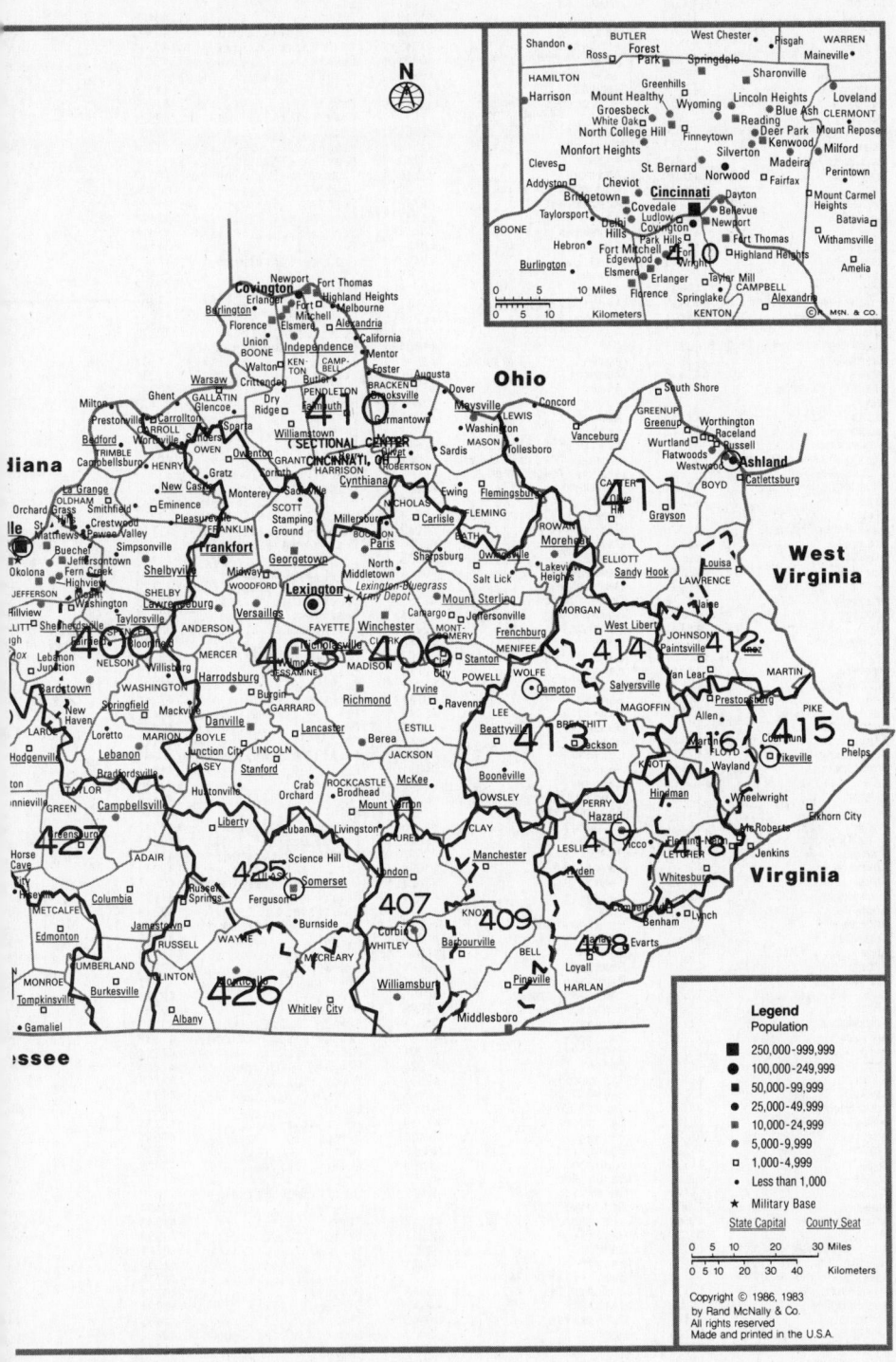

N

Legend
Population

■ 250,000-999,999
● 100,000-249,999
● 50,000-99,999
● 25,000-49,999
■ 10,000-24,999
▪ 5,000-9,999
□ 1,000-4,999
• Less than 1,000
★ Military Base

State Capital   County Seat

0 5 10   20   30 Miles

0 5 10   20   30   40
Kilometers

Copyright © 1986, 1983
by Rand McNally & Co.
All rights reserved
Made and printed in the U.S.A.

Name	ZIP	Name	ZIP	Name	ZIP
Aaron	42601	Artville	40387	Baughman	40911
Abbott	40006	Arvel	40447	Baughman Heights (Part of Danville)	40422
Abegall	41044	Ary	41712	Baxter (Harlan County)	40806
Aberdeen	42201	Ashbyburg	42456	Baxter (Jefferson County)	40204
Absher	42728	Ashcamp	41512	Bayfork	42122
Access	41164	Asher	40803	Bayou	42081
Acorn	42510	Ashers Fork	40962	Bays	41310
Acton	42718	Ashland	41101-05	Bays Branch	41222
Acup	41751	For specific Ashland Zip Codes call (606) 327-2121		Bealers Knob	42371
Adaburg	42347	Ashlock	38551	Beals	42451
Adair	42348	Askin	42343	Bear Branch	41714
Adairville	42202	Asphalt	42210	Bear Grass (Part of Louisville)	40218
Adams	41201	Atchison	42718	Beartown	41164
Adamson	41517	Athens (Part of Lexington)	40502	Bearville	41740
Add	41224	Athertonville	42748	Bear Wallow	42127
Addison	40143	Athol	41307	Beattyville	41311
Adeline	41129	Atkinstown	40434	Beaumont	42124
Aden	41142	Atlanta	40741	Beaumont Park (Part of Lexington)	40502
Adolphus	42120	Atoka	40422	Beauty	41203
Aetnaville	42368	Atwood	41063	Beaver	41604
Aflex	41529	Auburn	42206	Beaver Bottom	41522
Ages	40801	Audobon Acres	42301	Beaver Dam	42320
Ages-Brookside	40801	Audubon Park	40213	Beaver Junction (Part of Allen)	41601
Airport Gardens	41701	Augusta	41002	Beaverlick	41094
Ajax	41722	Ault	41164	Becknerville	40391
Akers (Part of Cumberland)	40823	Aurora	42048	Becks Store	42715
Akersville	42133	Austerlitz	40361	Beckton	42141
Albany	42602	Austin	42123	Beda	42347
Alberta	41031	Auxier	41602	Bedford	40006
Albia	42567	Avawam	41713	Bee	42729
Alcalde	42501	Avoca	40223	Beech (Breathitt County)	41306
Alcorn	40447	Avon (Part of Lexington)	40505	Beech (Harlan County)	40964
Alexandria	41001	Avondale (Part of Paducah)	42001	Beechburg	41093
Algonquin Manor (Part of Louisville)	40211	Avondale Heights (Part of Paducah)	42001	Beech Creek	42321
Alhambra	41055	Axtel	40103	Beech Fork	41756
Aliceton	40328	Ayers	40769	Beech Grove (Bullitt County)	40150
Alka	41562	Bachelors Rest	41040	Beech Grove (McLean County)	42322
Allais (Part of Hazard)	41701	Backusburg	42054	Beechland	42256
Allegre	42203	Bagdad	40003	Beechmont	42323
Allen	41601	Bailey Creek	40828	Beechville	42129
Allendale	42782	Bailey Mine	41168	Beechwood	40359
Allen Springs	42122	Baileys Branch	42151	Beechwood Village	40207
Allensville	42204	Baileys Switch	40906	Beechy	41175
Allock	41710	Bainbridge	42215	Beefhide	41537
Almo	42020	Baizetown	42349	Beelerton	42041
Almo Heights	42020	Baker Branch	41263	Bee Lick	40419
Alonzo	42120	Bakerton	42711	Bee Spring	42207
Alpha	42603	Bald Hill	41041	Beetle	41143
Alpine	42519	Baldrock	40741	Bel-Air (Part of Winchester)	40391
Alta	42358	Baldwin	40475	Belcher	41513
Alton	40342	Balkan	40977	Belcourt	42456
Alton Station	40342	Ballard	40342	Belcraft	41858
Altro	41306	Ballardsville	40014	Belfry	41514
Alumbaugh	40336	Balltown	40051	Belknap	41342
Alum Springs	40440	Baltimore	42066	Belknap Beach	40059
Alva	40863	Bancroft (Jefferson County)	40222	Bell City (Elliott County)	41171
Alvaton	42122	Bancroft (Muhlenberg County)	42345	Bell City (Graves County)	42040
Amandaville	42711	Bandana	42022	Bell County Forestry Camp	40977
Amba	41635	Bandy	42567	Bellefonte	41101
Amburgey	41801	Bank Lick	41094	Bellemeade	40222
Ammie	40962	Banner	41603	Bellepoint (Part of Frankfort)	40601
Ammons	40170	Banock	42261	Belleview	41005
Amos	42153	Baptist	41301	Bellevue	41073
Anchorage	40223	Barbourmeade	40222	Bellewood	40207
Anco	41759	Barbourville	40906	Bell Farm	42647
Anderson	42268	Barcreek	40972	Bells Run	42378
Andyville	40157	Bardo	40831	Belltown	40033
Anna	42270	Bardstown	40004	Belmont (Bullitt County)	40150
Anneta	42754	Bardstown Junction	40165	Belmont (Harrison County)	41031
Annville	40402	Bardwell	42023	Belton	42324
Ano	42510	Barefoot	40311	Ben Bow	41230
Ansel	42553	Bark Camp	40701	Bengal	42718
Antepast	40972	Barkley Field	42001	Benham	40807
Anthoston	42420	Barlow	42024	Benito	40849
Antioch Mills	41003	Barnesburg	42501	Bennettstown	42236
Antioch Shores	42519	Barnes Store	42445	Benson	40601
Anton	42431	Barnetts Creek	41256	Bent	42501
Apex	42464	Barnrock	41219	Benton	42025
Aqua Shores	40065	Barnsley	42431	Berea	40403
Arat	42717	Barnyard	40935	Berea College (Part of Berea)	40404
Arch	42724	Barralton	40165	Berlin	41043
Argillite	41121	Barren River	42101	Bernice	40932
Argo	41568	Barrier	42633	Bernstadt	40741
Argyle	42516	Barr Street (Part of Lexington)	40507	Berry	41003
Arista	42718	Barterville	40311	Berrys Lick	42268
Arjay	40902	Barwick	41306	Berrytown	40223
Arkansas Creek	41649	Bascom	41171	Bertha	40734
Arkle	40734	Bashford Manor Mall (Part of West Buechel)	40218	Bethanna	41465
Arlington (Carlisle County)	42021	Basil	42742	Bethany (Jefferson County)	40272
Arlington (Madison County)	40475	Basin Springs	40146	Bethany (Wolfe County)	41313
Arlington Heights (Part of Frankfort)	40601	Baskett	42402	Bethel (Bath County)	40306
Armstrong Hill	41164	Bass	42733	Bethel (Jessamine County)	40356
Arnett	41314	Bath	41836	Bethelridge	42516
Arnold	42349	Battle	40040	Bethesda	42633
Arrington Corner	42348	Battle Run	41039		
Arrowood	41316	Battletown	40104		
Artemus	40903				
Arthur	42210				
Arthurmable	41430				

	ZIP		ZIP		ZIP
Bethlehem	40007	Bolyn	41630	Brookhaven (Part of	
Betsey	42633	Bon	40769	Lexington)	40502
Betsy Layne	41605	Bon Air Hills (Part of		Brooklyn	42209
Beulah (Hickman County)	42039	Frankfort)	40601	Brooks	40109
Beulah (Hopkins County)	42408	Bonanza	41653	Brookside	40801
Beulah Heights	42607	Bonayer	42160	Brooksville	41004
Beverly	40913	Bond	40407	Broughtentown	40419
Beverly Hills (Part of		Bondurant	42050	Browder	42326
Danville)	40422	Bondville	40372	Brownies Creek	40856
Bevier	42337	Boneyville	40484	Browning	42274
Bevinsville	41606	Bon Haven (Part of		Brownings Corner	41040
Bewleyville	40146	Winchester)	40391	Browningtown	41065
Biddle	40324	Bonnie Brae	40065	Brownsboro	40014
Big Bear Creek	42025	Bonnieville	42713	Brownsboro Farm	40222
Big Bone	41091	Bonny	41332	Brownsboro Road Shopping	
Big Branch	41522	Bonnyman	41719	Center (Part of Windy	
Big Clifty	42712	Booker	40069	Hills)	40207
Big Creek	40914	Boone	40403	Brownsboro Village	40222
Big Eddy	40601	Boone Heights	40906	Browns Fork	41720
Big Fork	41777	Boonesboro (Clark County)	40475	Browns Grove	42071
Biggs	41524	Boonesboro (Madison		Brown's Valley	42376
Bighill	40405	County)	40475	Brownsville (Edmonson	
Big Laurel	40808	Booneville	41314	County)	42210
Big Ready	42275	Boons Camp	41204	Brownsville (Fulton County)	42050
Big Rock	41777	Bordley	42404	Brownwood Manor	42301
Big Sandy Junction (Part of		Boreing	40740	Bruin	41125
Catlettsburg)	41129	Borowick Farms	40031	Brush Grove	40040
Big Shoals	41501	Boston (Butler County)	42268	Brutus	40972
Big Spring	40106	Boston (Nelson County)	40107	Bryan	42629
Bigstone	41171	Boston (Pendleton County)	41006	Bryants Store	40921
Big Woods	40387	Botland	40004	Bryantsville	40410
Billows	42501	Botto	40944	Buchanan	41129
Bimble	40915	Bourbon	42501	Buck Creek	41314
Birdie	40342	Bourbon Furnace	40360	Buckettown	40475
Birdsville	42081	Bourne	40444	Buckeye	40444
Birk City	42301	Bouty	40769	Buck Grove	40117
Biscayne	41812	Bow	42714	Buckhorn	41721
Bishop (Part of Lexington)	40505	Bowen	40309	Buckingham	41636
Black Bottom	40828	Bowling Green	42101-04	Buckner	40010
Blackburn Correctional		For specific Bowling Green Zip		Buechel	40218
Complex	40504	Codes call (502) 782-4202			40261
Black Diamond (Part of		Boyce	42122	For specific Buechel Zip Codes	
Drakesboro)	42337	Boyd	41003	call (502) 454-1881	
Blackey	41804	Boyds Crossing	42782	Buel	42327
Blackford	42403	Boyds Landing	42055	Buena Vista (Garrard	
Black Gnat	42718	Boydsville	42079	County)	40444
Black Gold	42285	Boydtown	40324	Buena Vista (Harrison	
Black Jack	42134	Bracht	41030	County)	41031
Black Mountain	40847	Bracktown (Part of		Buena Vista (Lewis County)	41179
Black Rock	42754	Lexington)	40505	Buena Vista (Marshall	
Black Snake	40863	Bradford	41043	County)	42044
Blackwater	40741	Bradfordsville	40009	Buffalo (Larue County)	42716
Bladeston	41004	Bradshaw	40434	Buffalo (Trigg County)	42211
Blaine	41124	Brady (Part of Morehead)	40351	Buford	42376
Blair	40823	Brainard	41465	Bug	42602
Blairs Mills	41472	Bramlett	42743	Bugtussle	42140
Blake	41314	Brandenburg (Meade		Bulan	41722
Blanche	40902	County)	40108	Bull Creek	41653
Blanchet	41010	Brandy Keg	41653	Bullittsville	41005
Blandville	42026	Brassfield	40385	Bummer	40460
Blaze	41472	Braxton	40330	Burdick	42718
Bledsoe	40810	Brazil	40447	Burdine (Part of Jenkins)	41517
Blevins	41124	Breadens Creek	40927	Burfield	42633
Blincoe	40037	Breathitt	41340	Burgin	40310
Bloomfield	40008	Breckinridge	41031	Burke (Elliott County)	41171
Bloomingdale	40391	Breckinridge Center	42437	Burke (Henry County)	40057
Bloomington (Grayson		Breeding	42715	Burkesville	42717
County)	42754	Bremen	42325	Burkhart	41315
Bloomington (Magoffin		Brent (Part of Fort Thomas)	41075	Burk Hollow	40769
County)	41465	Brentsville	40361	Burkley	42021
Bloss	40456	Brentwood (Part of		Burkshire Terrace	40214
Blowing Spring	42743	Madisonville)	42431	Burlington (Boone County)	41005
Blowing Springs	42729	Brewers	42025	Burna	42028
Blue Bank	41041	Briartown	40069	Burnaugh	41129
Blue Diamond	41719	Briarwood	40222	Burnetta	42544
Blue Grass (Part of		Briarwood Manor (Part of		Burning Fork (Magoffin	
Lexington)	40503	Bowling Green)	42103	County)	41465
Bluegrass Estates	40422	Bridgeport	40601	Burning Fork (Pike County)	41501
Bluehole	40917	Bridge Street (Part of		Burning Springs	40962
Blue John	42519	Paducah)	42001	Burnside	42519
Blue Level	42274	Bridgeville	41004	Burnwell	41518
Blue Lick Springs	40311	Briensburg	42025	Burr	40456
Blue Moon	41655	Brighton (Part of Lexington)	40505	Burton	41612
Blue Ridge Manor	40223	Brightshade	40962	Burtonville	41189
Blue River	41607	Brinegar	41164	Bush	40724
Blue Spring	42211	Brinkley	41805	Bushong	42167
Bluestone	40351	Bristol Oakes	40299	Bushtown	40330
Blue Water Estates	42211	Bristow	42101	Buskirk (Morgan County)	41406
Bluff Boom	42743	Britmark	42220	Buskirk (Pike County)	41544
Bluff City	42420	Broad Bottom	41501	Busseyville	41230
Blythe	42151	Broad Fields	40207	Busy	41723
Board Tree	41528	Broad Ford	42726	Butler (Franklin County)	40601
Boaz	42027	Broadview Manor	40601	Butler (Pendleton County)	41006
Bobbs	41260	Broadwell	41031	Butterfly	41719
Bobs Creek	40815	Brodhead	40409	Buttimer Hill (Part of	
Bobtown	40403	Broeck Pointe	40201	Frankfort)	40601
Bohon	40330	Bromley (Kenton County)	41016	Buttonsberry	42350
Boiling Spring	42101	Bromley (Owen County)	41086	Bybee	40385
Boldman	41501	Bromo	40456	Bypro	41612
Boles	42167	Bronston	42518	Cabell	42633
Boltsfork	41168			Cabot	42343

	ZIP
Caddo	41040
Cadentown (Part of Lexington)	40505
Cadiz	42211
Cains Store	42544
Cairo	42420
Calana Shores	41097
Caldwell	41033
Caldwell Manor (Part of Danville)	40422
Caleast	40475
Caledonia	42232
Calf Creek	41224
Calhoun	42327
California	41007
Calla	40336
Callaboose	41301
Callaway	40977
Calloway	40456
Calmes	40391
Calvary	40033
Calvert City	42029
Calvin	40813
Camargo	40353
Cambridge	40220
Cambridge Shores	42044
Camelia	42086
Camelot (Part of St. Matthews)	40222
Campbellsburg	40011
Campbellsville	42718-19
For specific Campbellsville Zip Codes call (502) 465-4251	
Camp Dick Robinson	40444
Camp Dix	41127
Camp Kennedy	40444
Camp Nelson	40444
Camp Pleasant	40601
Camp Shantituck	40165
Camp Springs	41059
Campton	41301
Canada	41519
Canby	41010
Cane Creek	40741
Cane Valley	42720
Caney	41407
Caneyville	42721
Canmer	42722
Cannel City	41408
Cannon	40923
Cannonsburg	41101
Canoe	41316
Canton	42212
Canton Heights Estates	42211
Canyon Falls	41311
Capital Heights (Part of Frankfort)	40601
Capito	40965
Carbondale	42408
Carbon Glow	41832
Carcassonne	41804
Cardinal Hills (Part of Frankfort)	40601
Cardinal Valley (Part of Lexington)	40503
Cardwell	40330
Carlisle	40311
Carmen	41522
Carntown	41006
Carpenter	40906
Carr Creek	41847
Carrie	41725
Carrollton	41008
Carrs	41179
Carrsville	42081
Carter	41128
Carthage	41007
Cartwright	42602
Carver	41409
Cary	40977
Casey	42261
Casey Creek	42723
Caseyville	42459
Cash	42784
Casky	42240
Cassaday	42103
Castlewood (Part of Lexington)	40505
Castner (Part of Louisville)	40206
Catalpa	41230
Catawba	41040
Cat Creek	40380
Catlettsburg	41129
Caudell	41858
Causey	41777
Cave City	42127
Cavehill	42274
Cave Ridge	42129
Cave Spring	42276
Cawood	40815
Cayce	42041

	ZIP
Cecil	42001
Cecilia	42724
Cedar Bluff	42445
Cedar Brook	41031
Cedarcrest	42532
Cedar Flat	42129
Cedar Grove (Pulaski County)	42501
Cedar Grove (Todd County)	42220
Cedar Heights Park	40291
Cedar Hill Heights	42518
Cedar Spring	42160
Cedar Springs	42164
Cedarville (Pike County)	41522
Cedarville (Rockcastle County)	40456
Center	42214
Centerfield	40014
Center Point	42167
Center Ridge	42071
Centertown	42328
Centerview	40145
Centerview Rough River	40145
Central Avenue (Part of Paducah)	42001
Central City	42330
Centreville	40324
Ceralvo	42369
Cerulean	42215
Chad	40823
Chalybeate	42171
Chambers	42348
Chance	42728
Chandlers Chapel	42206
Chandlerville	41257
Chapel Hill	42120
Chaplin	40012
Chapman	41230
Chappell	40816
Charleston	42408
Charleswood	40229
Charley	41230
Charters	41179
Chatham	41002
Chavies	41727
Cheap (Part of Flatwoods)	41144
Chenault	40170
Chenoa	40977
Chenowee	41339
Cherokee (Jefferson County)	40205
	40255
For specific Cherokee Zip Codes call (606) 638-4840	
Cherokee (Lawrence County)	41180
Cherry	42071
Cherrywood Village	40207
Chesnutburg	40962
Chestnut Gap	41314
Chestnut Grove	40065
Chevrolet	40831
Chevy Chase (Part of Lexington)	40502
Chicken Bristle	40484
Chilesburg (Part of Lexington)	40505
Chloe	41501
Choateville	40601
Christianburg	40065
Christine	42728
Christopher	41701
Christy	40351
Church	42754
Cinda	41728
Cinderella Estates	40229
Cisco	41410
Cisselville	40069
Clabber Bottom	40324
Clare	42134
Clarence	42567
Clark Hill	41164
Clarksburg	41179
Clarkson	42726
Clark Station	40023
Clark Street (Part of Paducah)	42001
Claryville	41001
Claxton	42408
Clay	42404
Clay City	40312
Clayhole	41317
Clay Lick	40337
Claymour	42220
Claypool	42103
Claysville	41064
Clay Village	40065
Clear Creek	40977
Clear Creek Springs	40977
Clearfield	40313

	ZIP
Clear Run	42347
Cleaton	42332
Clementsville	42539
Clemons	41719
Cleopatra	42327
Clermont	40110
Cliff (Part of Prestonsburg)	41653
Clifford	41230
Clifton	40383
Clifty	42216
Climax	40456
Clinton	42031
Clintonville	40361
Clio	40769
Closplint	40927
Clover Bottom	40447
Cloverdale (Part of Frankfort)	40601
Clover-Darby	40927
Cloverleaf (Part of Louisville)	40216
Cloverport	40111
Clovertown	40831
Cloyds Landing	42752
Clutts	40823
Clyffeside (Part of Ashland)	41101
Coakley	42743
Coalgood	40818
Coal Run	41501
Coalton	41168
Cobb	42445
Cobhill	40415
Coburg	42743
Codyville (Part of Hardinsburg)	40143
Coe	42167
Cofer	42129
Cogswell	40351
Colby Hills	40391
Coldiron	40819
Cold Spring	41076
Cold Spring-Highland Heights (Part of Highland Heights)	41076
Coldstream	40202
Coldwater	42071
Coleman	41553
Colemansville	41003
Coles Bend	42171
Colesburg	40150
Coletown (Part of Lexington)	40502
Colfax	41049
College (Part of Berea)	40403
College Heights (Part of Bowling Green)	42101
College Hill	40385
College Park (Part of Frankfort)	40601
Collista	41222
Colly	41815
Colmar	40965
Colo	42501
Colonial Terrace	40222
Colson	41858
Columbia	42728
Columbus	42032
Colville	41031
Combs	41729
Comer	42327
Concord (Fleming County)	41041
Concord (Lewis County)	41131
Concord (McCracken County)	42001
Concord (Pendleton County)	41040
Concordia	40157
Conder	41514
Confederate	42038
Confederate Estates	40014
Confluence	41730
Congleton (Lee County)	41311
Congleton (McLean County)	42327
Conkling	41314
Conley	41411
Connersville	41031
Conoloway	42726
Conrad	42501
Consolation	40003
Constance	41009
Constantine	40114
Conway	40417
Cooktown	42123
Cool Springs	42320
Cooper	42633
Co Operative	42647
Cooperstown	42276
Coopersville	42611
Copebranch	41339
Coral Hill	42141
Coral Ridge	40118

ZIP

Corbin	40701-02
For specific Corbin Zip Codes call (606) 528-3912	
Cordell	41124
Cordia	41701
Cordova	41010
Corey	41142
Corinth (Grant County)	41010
Corinth (Logan County)	42276
Cork	42129
Corn Creek	40006
Corners	40146
Cornette	40729
Cornettsville	41731
Cornishville	40330
Corydon	42406
Costelow	42276
Cote	40828
Cottageville	41179
Cottle	41412
Cottonburg	40475
Country Club Heights	41056
Country Lane Estates	40601
Country Manor	40065
Countryside	40059
Country Village	40014
Counts Cross Roads	41164
Covedale	41179
Covington	41011-18
For specific Covington Zip Codes call (606) 261-4425	
Cowan	41039
Cow Creek (Estill County)	40472
Cowcreek (Owsley County)	41314
Coxs Creek	40013
Coxton	40831
Crab Orchard	40419
Cracker	41649
Crailhope	42214
Craintown	41041
Crane Nest	40906
Cranetown	40324
Craney	40351
Cranks	40820
Cranston	40351
Crawford (Laurel County)	40741
Crawford (Perry County)	41719
Crayne	42033
Craynor	41614
Creal	42764
Creekmore	42649
Creekside	42222
Creekville	40962
Creelsboro	42629
Crenshaw	40071
Crescent Hill (Part of Louisville)	40206
Crescent Park	41017
Crescent Springs	41016
Cressmont	41311
Crestmoor (Part of Bowling Green)	42101
Creston	42539
Crestview	41076
Crestview Hills	41017
Crestview Hills Mall (Part of Crestview Hills)	41017
Crestwood (Fayette County)	40503
Crestwood (Franklin County)	40601
Crestwood (Oldham County)	40014
Creswell	42411
Crider	42445
Crittenden	41030
Crix	40313
Croakes	40069
Crockett (Bell County)	40977
Crockett (Morgan County)	41413
Crocus	42741
Crofton	42217
Croley	42031
Cromona	41810
Cromwell	42333
Cropper	40057
Crossgate	40222
Cross Keys	40065
Crossland	42049
Cross Roads	42256
Crown	41811
Crowtown	42445
Crummies	40815
Crutchfield	42041
Crystal	40420
Crystal Lake	40031
Cuba	42066
Cubage	40856
Cub Run	42729
Culbertson	41129
Cullen	42437
Culver	41211

ZIP

Culvertown	40051
Cumberland	40823
Cumberland City	42602
Cumberland College (Part of Williamsburg)	40769
Cumminsville	41004
Cundiff	42730
Cunningham (Carlisle County)	42035
Cunningham (Hickman County)	42031
Cupio	40177
Curdsville (Daviess County)	42334
Curdsville (Mercer County)	40310
Curt	41339
Custer	40115
Cutshin	41732
Cutuno	41465
Cuzick	40475
Cyclone	42166
Cynthiana	41031
Dabney	42501
Dabolt	40421
Dahl	42501
Daisy	41733
Dal	40769
Dalesburg (Breathitt County)	41314
Dalesburg (Fleming County)	41041
Dalton	42445
Damron	41572
Dan (Menifee County)	40387
Dan (Ohio County)	42349
Dana	41615
Danby	42276
Daniel Boone	42442
Daniels Creek	41265
Danleytown	41144
Dants	40037
Danville	40422-23
For specific Danville Zip Codes call (606) 236-6334	
Darfork	41701
Dartmont	40828
Davella	41214
David	41616
Davis	40370
Davis Branch	41129
Davisburg	40977
Davis Cross Roads	42268
Davison Station	42361
Davisport	41262
Davistown (Garrard County)	40444
Davistown (Woodford County)	40347
Dawson Springs	42408
Day	41858
Dayhoit	40824
Daylight	42408
Daysboro	41332
Daysville	42276
Dayton	41074
Deane	41812
Deatsville	40013
Debord	41214
Decker	42721
DeCoursey (Part of Taylor Mill)	41015
Decoy	41321
Dee Acres	42366
Deep Spring (Part of Lexington)	40505
Deering Heights	40272
Deer Lick	42256
Defiance	41760
Defoe	40017
Defries	42722
Dehart	41472
De Koven	42459
Delafield (Part of Bowling Green)	42101
Delaplain	40324
Delaware	42373
Delia	41097
Dellville	40011
Delmer	42544
Delphia	41735
Delta	42613
Delvinta	41311
Dema	41859
Democrat	41858
De Mossville	41033
Demplytown	40014
Denison	42729
Denney	42633
Dennis	42574
Denniston	40316
Denton	41132
Denver	41215
Depoy	42345
Dermont	42301
Devon	41042

ZIP

Devondale (Part of Graymoor-Devondale)	40222
Dewdrop	41171
Dewitt	40930
Dewey	42036
Dexter	42261
Dexterville	42261
Diablock	41701
Diamond	42404
Diamond Springs	42256
Dice	41736
Dimple	42261
Dingus	41417
Dinwood	41619
Dione	40823
Dishman Springs	40906
Disputanta	40456
Dix Fork	41564
Dixie (Harlan County)	40849
Dixie (Henderson County)	42406
Dixie (Kenton County)	41017
Dixie Bend	42558
Dixie Manor Shopping Center	40258
Dixie Plantation (Part of Lexington)	40505
Dixon	42409
Dixville	40330
Dizney	40825
Dobbins	41180
Dock	41653
Doddy	42164
Doe Creek	40336
Doe Run	40108
Doe Valley Estates	40108
Dogcreek	42729
Dogtown	42025
Dog Walk (Lincoln County)	40419
Dogwalk (Ohio County)	42766
Dogwood	42051
Donaldson	42211
Donansburg	42743
Donerail (Part of Lexington)	40505
Dongola	41858
Dony	41647
Dortha	40701
Dorton	41520
Dorton Branch	40977
Do Stop	42721
Dot	42202
Dougan Town (Part of Burkesville)	42717
Douglas	41560
Douglass Hills	40243
Dover	41034
Downtown (Part of Louisville)	40201
Doylesville	40475
Dozier Heights (Part of Madisonville)	42431
Draffenville	42025
Draffin	41521
Drake	42128
Drakesboro	42337
Draper	40828
Drennon Springs	40011
Dressen (Part of Harlan)	40831
Dreyfus	40426
Drift	41619
Dripping Spring	42711
Drip Rock	40336
Dr. Martin Luther King Jr. (Part of Louisville)	40211
	40251
For specific Dr. Martin Luther King Jr. Zip Codes call (502) 778-7810	
Druid Hills	40207
Drum	42501
Dry Creek	41862
Dryfork (Barren County)	42131
Dry Fork (Pike County)	41561
Dryhill	41749
Dry Ridge	41035
Dublin	42039
Dubre	42731
Duckers	40347
Duckrun	40769
Duco	41465
Duff	42754
Duganville	40330
Dukedom	42085
Dukes	42348
Dulaney	42445
Duluth	40403
Dunbar	42219
Duncan (Casey County)	40442
Duncan (Mercer County)	40330
Duncannon	40475
Dundee	42338
Dunham (Part of Jenkins)	41537
Dunlap	41524
Dunleary	41522

	ZIP
Dunmor	42339
Dunnville	42528
Dunraven	41754
Durbin	41129
Durbintown	41003
Duval	40324
Dwale	41621
Dwarf	41739
Dycusburg	42037
Dyer	40115
Dykes	42501
Eadsville	42633
Eagle Creek	40363
Eagle Hill	41046
Eagle Station	41083
Earlington	42410
Earnestville	41314
East Bernstadt	40729
Easterday	41008
Eastern	41622
East Fork	42129
East Frankfort (Part of Frankfort)	40601
East Hickman	40356
East Jenkins (Part of Jenkins)	41537
Eastland (Part of Maysville)	41056
Eastland Park (Fayette County)	40505
Eastland Park (Warren County)	42103
Eastland Shopping Center (Part of Lexington)	40505
East McDowell	41647
Easton	42343
East Pineville	40977
East Point	41216
East Union	40311
Eastview	42732
Eastwood (Franklin County)	40601
Eastwood (Jefferson County)	40018
Ebenezer (Mercer County)	40372
Ebenezer (Monroe County)	42167
Ebenezer (Muhlenberg County)	42337
Eberle	40447
Echo	42154
Echols	42320
Echo Point	42518
Echo Valley	40031
Eddyville	42038
Eddyville Shores	42038
Edenton	40475
Edgewater	41534
Edgewood	41017
Edmonton	42129
Edna	41419
Edsel	41180
Edwards	42256
Eglon	40447
Egypt	40430
Eighty Eight	42130
Ekron	40117
Elamton	41472
Elba	42327
Elcomb	40831
Eldridge	41149
Elfie	42766
Elgin	42501
Eli	42642
Elihu	42501
Elizabeth	40361
Elizabethtown	42701-02
For specific Elizabethtown Zip Codes call (502) 765-7230	
Elizaville	41037
Elkatawa	41339
Elk Creek	40023
Elkfork	41421
Elk Horn	42733
Elkhorn City	41522
Elk Lake Shore	40359
Elkton	42220
Ella	42728
Ellington	42752
Elliottville	40317
Ellisburg	40437
Elliston (Grant County)	41035
Elliston (Madison County)	40475
Ellisville	40311
Ellmitch	42343
Ellwood	41538
Elmburg	40057
Elmer Davis Lake	40359
Elmrock	41640
Elmville	40379
Elna	41219
Elsie	41422
Elsinore	40601
Elsmere	41018

	ZIP
Elswick	41538
Elva	42082
Elys	40939
Emanuel	40734
Emerling	40854
Emerson	41135
Eminence	40019
Emlyn	40730
Emma	41653
Emmalena	41740
Empire	42442
Endee	41314
Endicott	41626
End of Line	41667
Engle	41727
English	41008
Ennis	42337
Enon	42411
Ensor	42301
Enterprise	41164
Eolia	40826
Epleys	42276
Epperson	42001
Epson	41465
Epworth	41189
Eriline	40962
Erlanger	41018
Ermine	41815
Erose	40970
Esco	41501
Essie	40827
Estep	41230
Estesburg	40489
Estill	41627
Esto	42642
Ethridge	41095
Etna	42567
Etoile	42131
Etterwood	40324
Etty	41572
Eubank	42567
Eunice	42728
Evanston	41340
Evarts	40828
Eveleigh	42754
Ever	41465
Everett (Logan County)	42256
Everett (Todd County)	42280
Evergreen	40601
Eversole	41314
Ewing	41039
Ewingford	40006
Ewington	40353
Exie	42743
Ezel	41425
Faber	40701
Fagan	40322
Fairbanks (Graves County)	42079
Fairbanks (Owen County)	40359
Fairdale	40118
Fairdealing	42025
Fairfield (Breckinridge County)	40144
Fairfield (Nelson County)	40020
Fair Grounds (Part of Maysville)	41056
Fairland	42602
Fairlane Acres	40065
Fairmeade	40207
Fairmont	42404
Fairplay	42735
Fairview (Anderson County)	40342
Fairview (Boyd County)	41101
Fairview (Christian County)	42221
Fairview (Fleming County)	41039
Fairview (Kenton County)	41015
Fairview (Lyon County)	42038
Fairview (Whitley County)	40769
Fairview Heights (Part of Frankfort)	40601
Fairview Hill	41146
Fairway (Part of Lexington)	40502
Falcon	41426
Fall Rock	40932
Fallsburg	41230
Falls of Rough	40119
Falmouth	41040
Fancy Farm	42039
Fannin	41171
Fariston	40741
Farler	41774
Farmers	40351
Farmers Mill	40831
Farmersville	42445
Farmington	42040
Farraday	41855
Farristown	40403
Faubush	42532
Faulconer	40422
Faxon	42071
Faye	41171

	ZIP
Fayette Mall (Part of Lexington)	40503
Faywood	40383
Fearisville	41179
Fearsville	42240
Feathersburg	42733
Federal Correctional Institution	41101
Fedscreek	41524
Fee	40863
Feliciana	42085
Felty	40962
Fencroft	40272
Fentress McMahon	40119
Fenwick	40069
Ferguson (Logan County)	42276
Ferguson (Pulaski County)	42533
Ferguson Creek (Part of Pikeville)	41501
Fern Creek	40291
Ferndale	40977
Fernleaf	41034
Fern View	40291
Ferrells Creek	41513
Fielden	41177
Fieldstone Acres	40065
Figg	40065
Fillmore	41323
Fincastle	40222
Finchville	40022
Finley	42736
Finney	42141
Firebrick	41137
Firmantown	40383
Fisher	42754
Fisherville	40023
Fishtrap	41557
Fiskburg	41033
Fisty	41743
Fitch	41164
Fitchburg	40472
Five Forks	41230
Fivemile	41339
Fixer	41397
Flag Fork	40601
Flag Spring	41007
Flaherty	40175
Flanary	41548
Flat	41301
Flat Fork	41427
Flatgap	41219
Flat Lick	40935
Flat Rock (Caldwell County)	42411
Flat Rock (McCreary County)	42653
Flat Rock (Rockcastle County)	40460
Flat Rock (Simpson County)	42134
Flatwoods	41139
Fleet	42140
Fleming (Part of Fleming-Neon)	41840
Fleming-Neon	41840
Flemingsburg	41041
Flemingsburg Junction	41041
Flener	42261
Fletcher	40741
Flingsville	41030
Flint Springs	42349
Flippin	42167
Floral	42348
Florence	41022
	41042
For specific Florence Zip Codes call (606) 371-8922	
Florress	41472
Flosie	42613
Flournoy	42437
Floyd	42567
Floydsburg	40014
Fogertown	40936
Folsom	41035
Folsomdale	42051
Fonde	40940
Fonthill	42642
Foraker	41465
Ford	40320
Fords Branch	41526
Fordsville	42343
Forest Cottage	42717
Forest Grove	40391
Forest Hill (Part of Paducah)	42001
Forest Hills (Jefferson County)	40299
Forest Hills (Kenton County)	41015
Forest Hills (Pike County)	41527
Forkton	42167
Forrest Park (Part of Winchester)	40391
Fort Campbell	42223
Fort Campbell North	42223

	ZIP
Fort Knox	40121
Fort Mitchell	41017
Fort Spring (Part of Lexington)	40504
Fort Thomas	41075
Fort Wright	41011
Foster	41043
Fount	40999
Fountain Run	42133
Four Corners	40162
Fourmile	40939
Four Oaks	41040
Fourseam	41701
Fox	40336
Foxboro	40223
Fox Chase	40165
Fox Creek	40342
Foxport	41093
Foxtown	40447
Frakes	40940
Frances	42064
Francisville	41048
Frankfort	40601-04
For specific Frankfort Zip Codes call (502) 223-3447	
Franklin	42134-35
For specific Franklin Zip Codes call (502) 586-3522	
Franklin Cross Roads	42724
Franklin Mines	42064
Franklinton	40057
Frazer	42618
Fraziertown	40014
Fredericktown	40069
Fredonia	42411
Fredville	41430
Freeburn	41528
Freedom	42157
Freetown	42140
Free Union	42409
Fremont	42001
Frenchburg	40322
Fresh Meadows	40824
Frew	41776
Friendly Hills	40219
Frisby	42633
Fritz	41465
Frogtown (Fayette County)	40383
Frogtown (Marion County)	40033
Frogue	42714
Frozen Creek	41339
Fruithill	42217
Fry	42743
Fuget	41220
Fulgham	42031
Fulton	42041
Fultz	41143
Funston	42634
Furnace	40472
Fusonia	41774
Future City	42053
Gabbard (Sebastian)	41364
Gabe	42743
Gadberry	42735
Gage	42056
Gainesville	42164
Gainesway (Part of Lexington)	40502
Gallup	41230
Galveston	41629
Gamaliel	42140
Gapcreek	42603
Gap in Knob	40165
Gapville	41433
Gardenside (Part of Lexington)	40504
Garden Springs (Part of Lexington)	40504
Garden Village	41501
Gardnersville	41033
Garfield	40140
Garlin	42728
Garner (Boyd County)	41168
Garner (Knott County)	41817
Garrard	40941
Garrett (Floyd County)	41630
Garrett (Meade County)	40117
Garrettsburg	42236
Garrison	41141
Garvin Ridge	41164
Gascon	42129
Gaskill (Part of Jenkins)	41537
Gasper	42206
Gates	40351
Gatewood	42348
Gatliff	40769
Gatun	40806
Gausdale	40906
Gaybourn	40383
Gays Creek	41745
Geddes	42134

	ZIP
Geneva (Henderson County)	42406
Geneva (Lincoln County)	40437
Gentrys Mill	42728
Georges Creek	41264
Georgetown (Harlan County)	40843
Georgetown (Scott County)	40324
Germantown	41044
Gertrude	41004
Gesling	41128
Gest	40057
Gethsemane	40051
Ghent	41045
Gibbs	40906
Gifford	41465
Gilbertsville	42044
Gillem Branch	41219
Gilley	41819
Gillmore	41327
Gilpin	42539
Gilreath	42635
Gilstrap	42349
Gimlet	41164
Girdler	40943
Girkin	42101
Gishton	42325
Glasgow	42141-42
For specific Glasgow Zip Codes call (502) 651-8859	
Gleanings	40052
Glenarm	40014
Glencoe	41046
Glendale	42740
Glen Dean	40119
Glengary	40118
Glensboro	40342
Glens Fork	42741
Glen Springs	41179
Glenview (Daviess County)	42301
Glenview (Jefferson County)	40025
Glenview (Shelby County)	40065
Glenview Heights	40222
Glenview Hills	40222
Glenview Manor	40222
Glenville	42376
Glo	41666
Globe	41164
Glomawr	41701
Goddard	41093
Goering	42348
Goffs Corner	40391
Goforth	41040
Goins	40763
Goldbug	40769
Gold City	42134
Golden Ash	40831
Golden Meadows	40272
Golden Pond	42211
Golo	42054
Goochtown	42567
Goodluck	42129
Goodnight	42127
Goodwater	42501
Goody	41529
Goose Creek	40222
Goose Rock	40944
Gordon	41819
Gordon Ford	41412
Gordonsville	42276
Goshen	40026
Gott	42101
Grab	42743
Grace	40962
Gracey	42232
Gradyville	42742
Graefenburg	40601
Graham	42344
Graham Hill	42420
Grahamville	42086
Grahn	41142
Grancer	42287
Grand Rivers	42045
Grandview (Part of Tompkinsville)	42167
Grandview Heights (Part of Frankfort)	40601
Grange City	41049
Grangertown	42459
Grants Lick	41001
Grapevine (Part of Madisonville)	42431
Grassy Creek	41332
Grassy Lick	40353
Gratz	40327
Gravel Switch	40328
Gray	40734
Gray Hawk	40434
Graymoor-Devondale	40222
Grays Branch	41144
Grays Knob	40829

	ZIP
Grayson	41143
Grayson Springs	42726
Graysville	40146
Greasy Creek	41562
Great Crossing	40324
Greear	41472
Greeley	40420
Green	41164
Green Acres (Part of Danville)	40422
Greenbriar (Daviess County)	42301
Greenbriar (Marion County)	40033
Greenbriar (Oldham County)	40031
Greenbrier	40489
Greencastle	42270
Greendale (Part of Lexington)	40505
Green Fields Estates	40391
Green Grove	42714
Green Hall	41328
Green Hill (Jackson County)	40402
Greenhill (Warren County)	42103
Green Hills	42728
Greenland Park	40065
Greenmount	40741
Greenough	41534
Green River	42374
Green Road	40946
Greensburg	42743
Green Spring	40222
Greenup	41144
Greenville	42345
Greenwood (McCreary County)	42634
Greenwood (Pendleton County)	41006
Greenwood (Warren County)	42104
Greenwood Mall (Part of Bowling Green)	42101
Grefco	41164
Gregory	42633
Gregoryville	41143
Gresham	42743
Grethel	41631
Grider	42717
Griderville	42127
Griffin	42640
Griffith	42301
Griffytown (Part of Middletown)	40243
Grove Center	42437
Grubbs	42031
Grundy	42501
Guage	41339
Gubser Mill	41007
Guerrant	41339
Guffie	42327
Gulfco (Part of Ashland)	41101
Gullett	41465
Gulnare	41501
Gulston	40830
Gum Sulphur	40419
Gum Tree	42167
Gunlock	41632
Gunns Chapel	40444
Guston	40142
Guthrie	42234
Guthrie's Ridge	42752
Guy	42101
Gwinn Island	40422
Gypsy	41438
Habit	42366
Hackley	40444
Haddix	41331
Hadensville	42234
Hadley	42235
Hager	41465
Hagerhill	41222
Hail	42501
Halcom	41171
Haldeman	40329
Halfway	42150
Halifax	42164
Hall (Jessamine County)	40356
Hall (Knott County)	41840
Hallie	41821
Halls Gap	40489
Halls Store	42263
Halo	41633
Hamlin	42046
Hammackville	42286
Hammonville	42757
Hampton	42047
Hampton Manor (Part of Winchester)	40391
Handshoe	41640
Hanly	40356
Hannah	41124
Hansford	40456
Hanson	42413

Name	ZIP	Name	ZIP	Name	ZIP
Happy	41746	Hickory Flat	42134	Horse Lick	40341
Happy Acre	42642	Hickory Grove (Cumberland		Horton	42320
Happy Landing	40403	County)	42752	Hoskinston	40844
Hardburly	41747	Hickory Grove (McCreary		Hosman	40977
Hardin	42048	County)	42638	Houston	41314
Hardinsburg	40143	Hickory Hill	40201	Houston Acres	40220
Hardin Springs	42712	Hidalgo	42633	Hovious Ridge	42723
Hard Money	42001	Hide-A-Way Hills	40359	Howard	40177
Hardshell	41348	High Bridge	40390	Howards Creek	41331
Hardwick	42618	High Falls	41301	Howardstown	40028
Hardy	41531	Highgrove	40013	Howel	42262
Hardyville	42746	High Knob	40402	Howe Valley	42724
Hare	40729	Highland (Lincoln County)	40484	Hubble	40444
Hargett	40336	Highland (Simpson County)	42134	Hubbs	40921
Harlan	40831	Highland Heights	41076	Huddy	41535
Harlan Crossroads	42167	Highplains	40106	Hudgins	42782
Harlan Gas	40831	High Point	42086	Hudson	40145
Harmony	40359	Highsplint	40828	Hueys Corners	41091
Harmony Lake Estates	40059	High Top	40741	Hueysville	41640
Harmony Village	40059	Highview (Jefferson County)	40228	Huff	42250
Harned	40144	Highview (Ohio County)	42320	Hulen	40845
Harold	41635	Highway	42602	Humble	42642
Harper	41465	Hignite	40965	Hummel	40492
Harreldsville	42256	Hi Hat	41636	Hunnewell	41121
Harrington Mill Estates	40065	Hikes Point (Part of		Hunt	40391
Harris	41179	Louisville)	40220	Hunter	41641
Harris Grove	42071		40250	Hunters	40004
Harrisonville	40076	For specific Hikes Point Zip Codes		Hunters Grove	40258
Harrodsburg	40330	call (502) 459-7616		Hunters Hollow	40165
Harrods Creek	40027	Hilda	40351	Hunters Trace	40216
Hart	40741	Hillcrest	40475	Huntertown	40383
Hartford	42347	Hillendale	41095	Huntington Woods	40601
Hartley	41572	Hill-N-Dale	40065	Huntsville	42251
Harveyton	41719	Hill Ridge	40299	Hurley	40447
Harvy	42025	Hills and Dales	40222	Hurricane Hills	40107
Haskingsville	42743	Hillsboro	41049	Hurst	41301
Hatcher	42718	Hillsdale	42134	Hurstborne Estates	40222
Hatfield	41514	Hillside	42330	Hurstbourne	40222
Hatton	40601	Hilltop (Fleming County)	41039	Hurstbourne Acres	40220
Hawesville	42348	Hilltop (Grant County)	41097	Hustonville	40437
Hayes	41040	Hilltop (Logan County)	42202	Hutch	40965
Haynesville	42368	Hill Top (McCreary County)	42647	Hutchison	40361
Hays	42171	Hillview (Bullitt County)	40229	Hyattsville	40444
Hays Crossing	40351	Hillview (Edmonson County)	42207	Hyden	41749
Hayslen	41719	Hilton	41701	Hydro	42171
Hayward	41173	Hima	40951	Iberia	42726
Haywood	42141	Himyar	40906	Ibex	41164
Hazard	41701-02	Hinda Heights (Part of		Ice	41858
For specific Hazard Zip Codes call		Lexington)	40502	Ida	42602
(606) 436-3188		Hindman	41822	Idamay	41311
Hazel	42049	Hinkle	40953	Idle Hour (Part of Lexington)	40502
Hazel Green	41332	Hinkleville	42056	Idlewild	41005
Hazel Patch	40729	Hinton	41010	Ilsley	42408
Head of Cedar	40379	Hippo	41637	Independence	41051
Head of Grassy	41135	Hiram	40823	Independence Station	41051
Headquarters	40311	Hisel	40447	Index	41472
Hearin	42404	Hiseville	42152	Indiancreek	40734
Heath	42086	Hislope	42544	Indian Fields	40391
Hebbardsville	42420	Hitchins	41146	Indian Hills (Boyle County)	40422
Hebron	41048	Hite	41649	Indian Hills (Carroll County)	41008
Hebron Estates	40165	Hitesville	42437	Indian Hills (Hardin County)	42701
Hecla	42410	Hobson	42718	Indian Hills (Jefferson	
Hector	40962	Hode	41267	County)	40207
Hedgeville	40444	Hodgenville	42748	Indian Hills (Russell County)	42642
Heekin	41097	Hogue	42553	Indian Hills (Scott County)	40324
Heenon	41545	Holbrook	41097	Indian Hills (Warren County)	42103
Heflin	42347	Holiday Hills (Part of		Indian Hills Cherokee	
Hegira	42717	Lexington)	40502	Section	40207
Heidelberg	41333	Holland	42153	Indian Lake	42348
Heidrick	40949	Holliday	41474	Indian Trail Square	40219
Heiner	41722	Hollonville	41301	Inez	41224
Helechawa	41332	Hollow Bill	42256	Ingle	42536
Helena	41055	Hollow Creek	40228	Ingleside	42053
Hellier	41534	Hollybush	41823	Ingram	40955
Helton	40840	Hollyhill	42635	Insco	42276
Hemp Ridge	40076	Hollyvilla	40118	Insko	41443
Henderson	42420	Hollywood (Part of		Inverness Estates	40601
Hendricks	41465	Lexington)	40502	Iron Hill	41143
Hendron	42001	Holmes Mill	40843	Iron Hill Camp	42055
Henry Clay (Fayette County)	40502	Holt (Breckinridge County)	40143	Ironville	41102
Henry Clay (Pike County)	41542	Holt (Lawrence County)	41230	Iroquois (Part of Louisville)	40214
Henryville	40311	Holt (Muhlenberg County)	42332	Iroquois Heights	40214
Henshaw	42437	Holy Cross	40037	Iroquois Vista (Part of	
Hensley (Breckinridge		Homer	42276	Louisville)	40214
County)	40146	Honaker	41639	Irvine	40336
Hensley (Clay County)	40962	Honeybee	42634	Irvington	40146
Herbert	42368	Honey Fork	41513	Irvins Store	42642
Herd	40435	Hooktown	41031	Island	42350
Hermitage Hills (Part of		Hootentown	40391	Island City	41338
Lexington)	40505	Hope	40334	Isom	41824
Hermon	42234	Hopeful Heights (Part of		Isonville	41149
Herndon (Christian County)	42236	Florence)	41042	Iuka	42045
Herndon (Scott County)	40324	Hopewell	41143	Ivel	41642
Herron Hill	41189	Hopkinsville	42240-41	Ivis	41822
Heselton	41179	For specific Hopkinsville Zip		Ivor	41007
Hesler	40359	Codes call (502) 886-5259		Ivy Grove	40939
Hestand	42151	Hopson	42445	Ivyton	41444
Hi Acres (Part of Lexington)	40505	Horntown	42642	Jabez	42532
Hickman	42050	Horse Branch	42349	Jackhorn	41825
Hickman Hill	40601	Horse Cave	42749	Jacks Creek	40983
Hickory	42051	Horse Creek Junction	40962	Jackson	41339

	ZIP
Lily	40740
Limaburg	41005
Limestone	41164
Limestone Springs	40165
Limeville	41175
Limp	42732
Lincoln	40962
Lincoln Ridge	40067
Lincolnshire	40220
Lindseyville	42257
Linefork	41833
Linton	42211
Linwood (Grayson County)	42726
Linwood (Hart County)	42757
Lionilli	41537
Lisletown	40391
Lisman	42404
Litsey	40069
Littcarr	41834
Little	41346
Little Barren	42743
Little Bear Creek	42044
Little Creek	40902
Little Cypress	42029
Little Dixie	41501
Little Georgetown (Part of Lexington)	40504
Little Hickman	40356
Little Mount	40071
Little Muddy	42261
Little Needmore	40422
Little Rock	40311
Little Sandy	41171
Little Tar Springs	42348
Little Texas (Part of Lexington)	40504
Littleton	40962
Little Valley	42442
Littrell	42752
Livermore	42352
Livia	42327
Livingston	40445
Lloyd	41156
Load	41144
Lockards Creek	40941
Lockport	40036
Lockwood Estates	40014
Locust	40045
Locust Grove (Clark County)	40391
Locust Grove (Pendleton County)	41040
Locust Hill	40144
Lodiburg	40146
Logana	40356
Logansport	42261
Logantown	40484
Loglick	40391
Log Mountain	40977
Logville	41465
Lola	42059
Lombard	40380
London	40741-45

For specific London Zip Codes call (606) 864-2251

	ZIP
Lone	41347
Lone Oak	42001
Lone Star	42713
Long Fork	41572
Longlick	40379
Long Ridge	40359
Long Run	40023
Long View	42701
Longview Estates	40422
Lookout	41542
Loradale (Part of Lexington)	40505
Loretto	40037
Lost Creek	41348
Lost River	42101
Lot	40769
Lothair (Part of Hazard)	41701
Lotus	40013
Louden	40769
Louellen	40828
Louisa	41230

Louisville 40201-99
For specific Louisville Zip Codes call (502) 454-1650

COLLEGES & UNIVERSITIES

	ZIP
Spalding University	40203
University of Louisville	40292

FINANCIAL INSTITUTIONS

	ZIP
Citizens Fidelity Bank and Trust Company	40202
The Cumberland Federal Savings Bank	40202
First Kentucky Trust Company	40202
First National Bank of Louisville	40202
Great Financial Federal	40202
Liberty National Bank and Trust Company of Louisville	40202
Mid-America Bank of Louisville and Trust Company	40202
Republic Bank & Trust Company	40202
Stock Yards Bank & Trust Company	40206

HOSPITALS

	ZIP
Alliant Health System	40202
Baptist Hospital East	40207
Humana Hospital-Audubon	40217
Humana Hospital-Suburban	40207
Humana Hospital-University of Louisville	40202
Jewish Hospital	40202
Methodist Evangelical Hospital	40202
Saints Mary and Elizabeth Hospital	40215
Veterans Affairs Medical Center-Louisville	40206

HOTELS/MOTELS

	ZIP
The Brown-A.Camberley Hotel	40202
The Galt House Hotel	40202
Hyatt Regency Louisville	40202
Ramada Inn Brownsboro	40207
Seelbach Hotel	40202

MILITARY INSTALLATIONS

	ZIP
Kentucky Air National Guard, FB6161 Standiford Field	40213
Naval Surface Warfare Center, Crane Division/Naval Ordinance Station, Louisville	40214
United States Army Engineer District, Louisville	40201
Lovelaceville	42060
Lovely	41231
Lowell	40461
Lower Gillmore	41327
Lower Hunters	40216
Lower Kings Addition	41175
Lower Pompey	41501
Lowes	42061
Lowmansville	41232
Loyall	40854
Lucas	42156
Lucile	41171
Lucky Fork	41364
Lucky Stop	40337
Ludlow	41016
Luner	40456
Lusby's Mill	40359
Luther Luckett Correctional Complex	40031
Luzon	42409
Lykins	41465
Lynch	40855
Lyndale	40391
Lyndon	40222
	40252

For specific Lyndon Zip Codes call (502) 425-4547

	ZIP
Lynn	41144
Lynncamp	40701
Lynn City	42372
Lynn Grove	42071
Lynnview	40213
Lynnville	42063
Lyons	40051
Lytten	41171
Mac	42718
McAfee	40330
McAndrews	41543
McBrayer	40342
McCarr	41544
McClure	41250
McCombs	41545
McCreary	40444
McCreight	40999
McDaniels	40152
McDowell	41647
Macedonia (Breathitt County)	41370
Macedonia (Christian County)	42217
Macedonia (Jackson County)	40447

	ZIP
Maceo	42355
McGowan	42445
McHenry	42354
McKee	40447
McKinney	40448
McKinneysburg	41040
Mackville	40040
Mc Neely Lake	40229
McQuady	40153
McRoberts	41835
McVeigh	41546
McVille	41005
McWhorter	40741
Madisonville	42431
Madrid	42754
Magan	42343
Maggard	41465
Maggie	42211
Magnolia	42757
Magoffin	41464
Main Street (Part of Pikeville)	41501
Majestic	41547
Major	41314
Malaga	41301
Mallie	41836
Mall in St. Matthews, The (Part of St. Matthews)	40207
Malone	41451
Maloneton	41175
Mammoth Cave	42259
Manchester	40962
Manco	41534
Manda	42333
Mangum	42516
Manila	41238
Manitou	42436
Mannington	42217
Mannsville	42758
Manor Creek	40222
Manse	40461
Manton (Floyd County)	41649
Manton (Washington County)	40037
Manuel	41701
Maple Grove (Jefferson County)	40229
Maple Grove (Trigg County)	42211
Maple Mount	42356
Maplesville	40741
Marcellus	40444
Marcum	40962
Marcus	41003
Maretburg	40456
Mariba	40345
Mariemont	40258
Marion	42064
Mark	42501
Marksbury	40444
Marlowe	41858
Marrowbone	42759
Marshall	41056
Marshallville	41452
Marshes Siding	42631
Martha	41159
Martha Mills	41041
Martin	41649
Martinsville	42159
Martwick	42330
Mary	41301
Mary Alice	40964
Marydale	41018
Marydell	40751
Maryhill Estates	40207
Maryville (Part of Hillview)	40229
Mashfork	41465
Mason (Grant County)	41054
Mason (Magoffin County)	41465
Masonic Home (Part of Louisville)	40041
Masonville (Daviess County)	42376
Massac	42001
Matanzas	42328
Matlock	42104
Matthew	41472
Mattingly	40111
Mattoon	42064
Mattoxtown	40505
Maud	40069
Maulden	40486
Mavity	41129
Maxie	40769
Maxine	42776
Maxwell	42376
Mayfield	42066
Mayflower	41501
Mayking	41837
Maynard	42164
Mayo	40330
Mayo Village	41501
Mays Lick	41055

	ZIP		ZIP		ZIP
Maysville	41056	Moct	41385	Murphyfork	41332
Maytown	41472	Modoc	42714	Murphysville	41056
Maywood	40484	Molus	40819	Murray	42071
Mazie	41160	Monford	42252	Murray Hill	40222
Meador	42164	Monica	41362	Muses Mills	41065
Meadow Branch	41301	Monitor	40006	Music	41168
Meadowbrook (Clark		Monkeys Eyebrow	42056	Myers	40311
County)	40391	Monroe	42746	Myra	41549
Meadowbrook (Shelby		Montclair (Fayette County)	40502	Mystic	40146
County)	40065	Montclair (Shelby County)	40065	Nancy	42544
Meadowbrook Farm	40223	Monterey	40359	Naomi	42544
Meadow Creek	40759	Montgomery	42211	Napfor	41754
Meadowrun	40065	Montgomerys Mill	42743	Napier	40810
Meadowthorpe (Part of		Monticello	42633	Naples	41101
Lexington)	40505	Montpelier	42763	Napoleon	41046
Meadow Vale	40222	Montrose (Part of		Narco (Part of Lexington)	40505
Meadowview	40475	Lexington)	40505	Narrows	42358
Meadowview Estates	40220	Montrose Park (Part of		Narvel	42603
Meally	41234	Frankfort)	40601	Nashtown	41189
Means	40346	Mooleyville	40143	Natlee	41010
Medora	40272	Moon	41457	Natural Bridge	40376
Meece	42501	Moon Lake Estates	40324	Nazareth	40048
Meeting Creek	42732	Moorefield	40350	Neafus	42766
Melber	42069	Moores Creek	40402	Neave	41040
Melbourne	41059	Moores Ferry	40371	Nebo (Hopkins County)	42441
Meldrum	40965	Mooresville	40069	Nebo (Muhlenberg County)	42345
Mell	42743	Moorland	40223	Ned	41339
Melody Lake	40051	Moorman	42357	Needmore (Ballard County)	42053
Melvin	41650	Moranburg	41056	Needmore (Boyle County)	40422
Memphis Junction	42101	Morcoal	41543	Needmore (Caldwell	
Mendota Village	41222	Morehead	40351	County)	42445
Mentor	41007	Moreland	40437	Needmore (Madison	
Meredith	42754	Morgan	41040	County)	40426
Meridian	41006	Morganfield	42437	Needmore (Shelby County)	40022
Merrimac	40009	Morgantown	42261	Nelse	41550
Merry Oaks	42171	Morningglory	41031	Nelson	42330
Mershons	40729	Morning View	41063	Nelsonville	40107
Meshack	42167	Morrill	40455	Neon (Part of Fleming-	
Meta	41501	Morris Fork	41314	Neon)	41840
Mexico	42064	Mortimer Station	42202	Neon Junction	41840
Midas	41640	Mortons Gap	42440	Neosheo	42134
Middleburg	42541	Mortonsville	40383	Nepton	41039
Middlefork	40447	Moscow	42031	Nerinx	40049
Middlesboro	40965	Moseleyville	42301	Nero	41265
Middleton	42134	Mossy Bottom	41501	Nevada	40330
Middleton Heights (Part of		Motley	42103	Nevelsville	42653
Shelbyville)	40065	Mount Aerial	42128	Nevin	40342
Middleton (Jefferson		Mountain Ash	40769	Nevisdale	40754
County)	40243	Mountain Top	41164	New	40359
	40253	Mountain Valley	41339	New Allen (Part of Allen)	41601
For specific Middletown Zip		Mount Auburn	41006	Newburg (Jefferson County)	40218
Codes call (502) 454-1650		Mount Carmel	41041	Newby	40475
Middletown (Madison		Mount Eden	40046	New Camp	25661
County)	40403	Mount Gilead (Green		New Castle	40050
Middletown (Russell		County)	42743	New Columbus	41010
County)	42629	Mount Gilead (Monroe		Newcombe	41149
Midland (Bath County)	40371	County)	42167	New Concord	42076
Midland (Muhlenberg		Mount Hermon	42157	New Cypress (Hickman	
County)	42325	Mount Lebanon	40356	County)	42031
Midway (Calloway County)	42049	Mount Olive (Casey County)	42566	New Cypress (Muhlenberg	
Midway (Crittenden County)	42064	Mount Olive (Lee County)	41311	County)	42345
Midway (Meade County)	40142	Mount Olivet	41064	Newfound	40972
Midway (Woodford County)	40347	Mount Pisgah	42633	Newfoundland	41171
Milburn	42070	Mount Pleasant (Ohio		Newgarden	40121
Mildred	40447	County)	42333	New Haven	40051
Milford	41061	Mount Pleasant (Trimble		New Hope	40052
Millard	41562	County)	40006	New Liberty	40355
Mill Creek	41055	Mount Salem	40437	Newman	42301
Milledgeville	40437	Mount Sherman	42764	New Market	40033
Miller (Fulton County)	42050	Mount Sterling	40353	Newport	41071-76
Miller (Nicholas County)	40311	Mount Tabor (Larue County)	42716	For specific Newport Zip Codes	
Millersburg	40348	Mount Tabor (Todd County)	42220	call (606) 291-5250	
Millers Creek	40472	Mount Union	42120	Newport Shopping Center	
Millerstown	42726	Mount Vernon (Rockcastle		(Part of Newport)	41071
Millerstown	40475	County)	40456	New Providence	42049
Million	40962	Mount Vernon (Scott		New Roe	42120
Mill Pond	42372	County)	40324	New Salem (Crittenden	
Millport	40970	Mount Victor	42104	County)	42064
Mills	41101	Mount Victory	42501	New Salem (Lincoln	
Millseat	42632	Mount Washington	40047	County)	40437
Mill Springs	41838	Mount Zion (Allen County)	42164	Newstead	42240
Millstone	42761	Mount Zion (Grant County)	41035	New Stithton	40121
Milltown (Adair County)	40350	Mount Zion (Pulaski County)	42553	Newt	42743
Milltown (Nicholas County)	40601	Mousie	41839	Newtown	40324
Millville	42762	Moutardier	42754	New Zion (Jackson County)	40447
Millwood	40383	Mouthcard	41548	New Zion (Scott County)	40505
Milner	41262	Moxley	40363	Niagara	42420
Milo	40045	Mozelle	40858	Nicholasville	40340
Milton	41456	Mud Camp	42717		40356
Mima	41062	Muddy Ford	40324	For specific Nicholasville Zip	
Minerva	41763	Mud Lick	42167	Codes call (606) 887-5666	
Miniard	41651	Muir (Part of Lexington)	40505	Nichols (Bullitt County)	40177
Minnie	40213	Mulberry	40065	Nichols (Hickman County)	42031
Minor Lane Heights	40379	Muldraugh	40155	Nicholson (Kenton County)	41051
Minorsville	42539	Mulfordtown	42459	Nicholson (Trigg County)	42215
Mintonville	40856	Mullikin Junction	42028	Nickell	41332
Miracle	41351	Mullins	40456	Nigh	41524
Mistletoe	40452	Mullins Addition	41501	Nina	40444
Mitchellsburg	41352	Mummie	40486	Nineteen	42320
Mize	40475	Munfordville	42765	Ninevah	40342
Moberly	40207	Murl	42633	Nippa	41240
Mockingbird Valley					

	ZIP
Noble	41317
Nobob	42166
Nocreek	42347
Noctor	41357
Node	42214
Noetown (Part of Middlesboro)	40965
Noland	40336
Nolansburg	40870
Nolin	42776
Nolin Lake Estates	42726
Nonesuch	40383
Nonnel	42337
Nora	42602
Norbourne Estates	40207
Norfleet	42544
Normal (Part of Ashland)	41101
Normal Heights (Part of Frankfort)	40601
Normandy	40071
North (Part of Lexington)	40505
North Corbin (Laurel County)	40701
Northfield	40222
North Irvine	40336
North Lexington (Part of Lexington)	40505
North Middletown	40357
North Pleasureville (Part of Pleasureville)	40057
Northpoint Training Center	40310
Northtown	42749
Norton Branch	41168
Nortonville	42442
Norwood (Jefferson County)	40222
Norwood (Pulaski County)	42553
Nuckols	42352
Nugent Cross Roads	40383
Nugym	40902
Number One	42633
Oakbrook	41042
Oakdale (Breathitt County)	41339
Oakdale (McCracken County)	42001
Oak Forest	42164
Oak Grove (Christian County)	42262
Oak Grove (Ohio County)	42333
Oak Hill (Hopkins County)	42442
Oak Hill (Pulaski County)	42501
Oakland	42159
Oakland Mills	40311
Oaklawn Estates	41222
Oak Level	42025
Oakley	40729
Oak Ridge (Edmonson County)	42207
Oak Ridge (Kenton County)	41015
Oaks (Bell County)	40813
Oaks (Ohio County)	42343
Oak Street (Part of Louisville)	40210
Oakton	42031
Oakville	42263
O'Bannon	40223
Octavia	41543
Oddville	41031
Odessa	40360
Offutt	41237
Ogle	40962
Oil City	42141
Oil Springs	41238
Oil Valley	42633
O. K.	42567
Okolona	40219
	40259
For specific Okolona Zip Codes call (502) 966-8049	
Olaton	42361
Old Brownsboro Place	40222
Old Christianburg	40003
Old Cypress	42031
Old Flat Lick	40935
Oldham	40077
Oldham Acres	40059
Old Landing	41358
Old Olga	42629
Old Orchard	40447
Old Pine Grove	40391
Old Taylor Place	40026
Oldtown	41163
Old Volney	42265
Olga	42629
Olin	40447
Olive	42025
Olive Branch (Fleming County)	41041
Olive Branch (Shelby County)	40065
Olive Hill	41164
Oliver	41156

	ZIP
Ollie	42264
Olmstead	42265
Olney	42408
Olympia	40358
Olympia Springs	40358
Omaha	41843
Omega	40324
Oneida	40972
Oneonta	41007
Ono	42642
Onton	42455
Open Gates (Part of Lexington)	40503
Ophir	41459
Oppy	41231
Orangeburg	41056
Orchard Grass Hills	40031
Ordinary	41171
Oregon	40372
Orinoco	41514
Orkney	41647
Orlando	40460
Orr	41180
Ortiz	42455
Orville	40057
Osborn	41635
Oscaloosa	41858
Oscar	42056
Otas (Part of Corbin)	40701
Otia	42167
Ottawa	40409
Ottenheim	40489
Otter Pond	42445
Oven Fork	40861
Overlook (Part of Eddyville)	42038
Ovesen Heights	42748
Owensboro	42301-03
For specific Owensboro Zip Codes call (502) 684-2301	
Owensboro East (Part of Owensboro)	42301
Owensboro West (Part of Owensboro)	42301
Owensby	42629
Owenton	40359
Owingsville	40360
Owsley	41501
Oxford	40324
Ozark	42728
Pactolus	41143
Paducah	42001-03
For specific Paducah Zip Codes call (502) 444-7272	
Paint Lick	40461
Paintsville	41240
Palestine	41091
Palma	42025
Palmer	40336
Panama	41472
Panco	40972
Panola	40385
Panorama Shores	42071
Panther	42276
Paris	40361-62
For specific Paris Zip Codes call (606) 987-4500	
Park City	42160
Parkers Lake	42634
Park Hills	41015
Park Lake	41093
Parksville	40464
Parkway Village	40213
Parmleysville	42640
Parnell	42633
Parrot	40465
Partridge	40862
Pascal	42746
Patesville	42348
Pathfork	40863
Patrick	41230
Patsey	40380
Pauley (Part of Pikeville)	41501
Pauline	42276
Paw Paw	41551
Paxton	41385
Payne Gap	41537
Paynes	40505
Payneville	40157
Payton	41332
Peabody	40914
Peachgrove	41006
Peach Orchard	41230
Peak	40324
Peaks Mill	40601
Pea Ridge (Scott County)	40379
Pea Ridge (Todd County)	42220
Pearl	40940
Pearman	42726
Peasticks	40360
Pebble	40360
Pebworth	41314

	ZIP
Pecksridge	41041
Peden Mill	42134
Peedee	42236
Pelfrey	40313
Pellville	42364
Pellyton	42728
Pembroke	42266
Pence	41313
Penchem	42286
Pendleton	40055
Penile	40272
Penn Run No. One	40201
Penny (Calloway County)	42071
Penny (Pike County)	41501
Pennyrile Mall (Part of Hopkinsville)	42240
Penrod	42365
Peonia	42726
Peoples	40467
Perry Park	40363
Perryville	40468
Persimmon Grove	41001
Persimon	42167
Petersburg	41080
Petersville	41179
Petra	41004
Petrie	42348
Petroleum	42120
Petros	42274
Pettit	42301
Pewee Valley	40056
Peytona	40065
Peyton Creek	41501
Peytonsburg	42768
Peytons Store	40437
Peytontown	40475
Phelps	41553
Phillipsburg	42736
Philpot	42366
Phyllis	41554
Picadome (Part of Lexington)	40503
Pickett (Adair County)	42761
Pickett (Shelby County)	40022
Pierce	42743
Pierce Acres	40272
Pigeon	41501
Pigeonroost	40962
Pike View	42757
Pikeville	41501-02
For specific Pikeville Zip Codes call (606) 432-2146	
Pilgrim	41250
Pilot Oak	42085
Pilotview	40391
Pinchem	40391
Pinckard	40383
Pinckneyville	42078
Pine Bluffs	42046
Pine Grove (Clark County)	40391
Pine Grove (Laurel County)	40740
Pine Hill	40456
Pine Knob	42721
Pine Knot	42635
Pine Meadows (Part of Lexington)	40504
Pine Mountain	40810
Piner	41063
Pine Ridge	41360
Pine Top	41843
Pineville	40977
Piney Fork	42064
Piney Grove	42501
Pink	40356
Pinnacle	41358
Pinsonfork	41555
Pioneer Village	40165
Pippa Passes	41844
Piqua	41064
Pisgah	40383
Piso	41501
Pitts	40472
Pittsburg	40755
Plainview (Part of Jeffersontown)	40224
Plank	40978
Plano	42104
Plantation	40222
Plato	42501
Pleasant Hill (Butler County)	42273
Pleasanthill (Mercer County)	40330
Pleasant Hill (Pendleton County)	41006
Pleasant Home	40359
Pleasant Ridge	42376
Pleasant Valley	41039
Pleasant View	40769
Pleasure Ridge Park	40258
	40268
For specific Pleasure Ridge Park Zip Codes call (502) 937-4154	

	ZIP
Pleasureville (Fleming County)	41093
Pleasureville (Henry County)	40057
Plummers Landing	41081
Plummers Mill	41093
Plum Springs	42101
Plumville	41056
Plymouth Village	40207
Poindexter	41031
Pointer	42544
Point Leavell	40444
Point Pleasant	42328
Polin	40040
Polksville	40371
Polkville	42159
Polly	41858
Pomeroyton	40365
Pomp	41472
Ponderosa (Fayette County)	40324
Ponderosa (Grayson County)	42726
Pondsville	42171
Pongo	40456
Poole	42444
Poortown	40356
Pope	42128
Poplar	41128
Poplar Corner	40033
Poplar Flat	41189
Poplar Grove (Fleming County)	41041
Poplar Grove (McLean County)	42372
Poplar Grove (Owen County)	41046
Poplar Highlands	41169
Poplar Hills	40218
Poplar Plains	41041
Poplarville	42501
Porter	40370
Portland (Adair County)	42761
Portland (Pendleton County)	41033
Port Royal	40058
Portsmouth	41339
Possum Trot	42029
Potters	41230
Potters Fork	41537
Pottsville (Graves County)	42051
Pottsville (Washington County)	40069
Poverty	42327
Powderly	42367
Powells Creek	41501
Powersburg	42633
Powersville	41004
Prairie Village	40272
Prater	41164
Pratt	42455
Preachersville	40419
Preece	41224
Premium	41845
Prentiss	42320
Press	41339
Preston	40366
Preston Estates	41240
Prestonsburg	41653
Prestonville	41008
Prewitt	40353
Price	41636
Prices Mill	42202
Pricetown (Casey County)	42539
Pricetown (Fayette County)	40502
Priceville	42765
Pride	42404
Primrose	41362
Princess	41102
Princeton	42445
Printer	41655
Pritchardsville	42141
Privett	40486
Proctor	41311
Prospect	40059
Prosperity	42207
Providence (Jessamine County)	40503
Providence (Knox County)	40906
Providence (Simpson County)	42134
Providence (Trimble County)	40011
Providence (Webster County)	42450
Provo	42267
Pruden	37851
Pryors	42066
Pryors Chapel	42066
Pryse	40471
Public	42501
Pueblo	42633
Pulaski	42567
Pulliam	40078
Pumpkin Center	42445

	ZIP
Puncheon	41828
Purdy	42728
Putney	40865
Pyramid	41637
Pyrus	42742
Quail	40409
Quality	42268
Queens	41179
Quicksand	41363
Quincy	41166
Quinton	42518
Rabbit Hash	41097
Rabbit Ridge	42441
Raccoon	41557
Raceland	41169
Radcliff	40159-60
For specific Radcliff Zip Codes call (502) 351-3688	
Radcliff (Part of Lexington)	40505
Ragland	42053
Railton	42160
Ralph	42378
Randolph	42129
Ransom	41531
Rapids	42134
Raven	41861
Ravenna	40472
Raymond	40176
Raywick	40060
Ready	42721
Rectorville	41056
Red Bird (Bell County)	40913
Redbird (Whitley County)	40769
Redbud	40828
Redbush	41219
Red Cross	42160
Redfox	41847
Red Hill (Allen County)	42164
Red Hill (Daviess County)	42376
Red Hill (Hardin County)	40175
Redhouse	40475
Redlick	42129
Red River	42202
Redwine	41477
Reed	42451
Reeds Crossing	40475
Reedville	41143
Reedyville	42275
Regina	41559
Region	42275
Reidland	42001
Reid Village	40353
Relief	41472
Rella	40902
Renaker	41003
Render	42320
Renfro Valley	40473
Renfrow	42349
Repton	42064
Revelo	42638
Rex	42746
Rexville	41332
Reynolds Station	42368
Reynoldsville	40374
Rhea	40806
Rheber	42528
Rhoda	42210
Rhodelia	40161
Ribolt	41189
Rice Station	40336
Ricetown	41364
Riceville (Fulton County)	42041
Riceville (Johnson County)	41258
Richardson	41253
Richardsville	42270
Richelieu	42206
Richland	42431
Richlawn	40207
Richmond	40475-76
For specific Richmond Zip Codes call (606) 369-3904	
Rich Pond	42104
Richwood	41094
Ridgeview Heights (Part of Independence)	41051
Ridgeway	40849
Riley	40328
Rineyville	40162
Ringgold	42501
Ringos Mills	41049
Risner	41649
Ritchie	41701
Ritner	42633
Rivals	40071
River	41254
River Bluff	40059
River Bluff Farms	40059
Riverfront (Part of Louisville)	40270
River Oaks	42765
River Ridge	40828
Riverside	42101

	ZIP
Riverside Gardens	40216
Riverton (Part of Greenup)	41144
Riverview	42001
Riverview Estates (Part of Harrodsburg)	40330
Riverwood	40222
Road Junction	41522
Roaring Spring	42211
Roark	40979
Robards	42452
Robinson	41031
Robinson Creek	41560
Robinsville	40475
Robinswood	40207
Rob Roy	42320
Rochester	42273
Rockbridge	42167
Rockcastle	42211
Rockdale (Boyd County)	41102
Rockdale (Owen County)	40359
Rockfield	42274
Rock Haven	40175
Rockholds	40759
Rockhouse	41561
Rockland	42101
Rockport	42369
Rock Springs	42406
Rockybranch	42640
Rocky Hill (Barren County)	42141
Rocky Hill (Edmonson County)	42163
Rodburn	40351
Rodgers Park	41570
Roederer Farm Center	40031
Roff	40178
Rogers	41365
Rogers Chapel	40380
Rogers Gap	40324
Rogersville (Part of Radcliff)	40160
Rolling Acres (Part of Frankfort)	40601
Rollingburg	42743
Rolling Fields	40207
Rolling Hills (Jefferson County)	40222
Rolling Hills (Shelby County)	40065
Rollington (Part of Pewee Valley)	40056
Rome	42301
Romine	42718
Rookwood (Part of Lexington)	40505
Roscoe	41171
Roseburg	42729
Rose Crossroads	42629
Rosefork	41301
Rose Hill (Carter County)	41164
Rose Hill (Mercer County)	40330
Rose Terrace	40121
Rosetta	40146
Roseville (Barren County)	42141
Roseville (Hancock County)	42368
Rosewood	42345
Rosine	42370
Ross	41059
Rossland	40734
Rosslyn	40380
Rosspoint	40806
Rothwell	40322
Roundhill (Edmonson County)	42275
Round Hill (Madison County)	40475
Roundstone	40456
Rouse (Part of Covington)	41014
Rousseau	41366
Routt	40299
Rowdy	41367
Rowena	42629
Rowland (Lincoln County)	40484
Rowland (McCracken County)	42001
Rowlandtown (Part of Paducah)	42001
Rowletts	42772
Roxana	41848
Royal	42726
Royalton	41464
Royrader	40402
Royville	42642
Ruckerville	40391
Ruddels Mills	41031
Ruin	41171
Rumsey	42371
Rural	25687
Rush	41168
Russell	41169
Russell Heights (Part of Russell)	41169
Russell Springs	42642
Russellville	42276

	ZIP
Ruth	42501
Rutland	41031
Ryan	41093
Ryland	41015
Ryland Heights	41015
Sacramento	42372
Sadieville	40370
Sadler	42754
St. Catharine	40061
St. Charles	42453
St. Dennis	40216
St. Elmo	42266
St. Francis	40062
St. Helens	41368
St. John	42701
St. Johns	42001
St. Joseph (Daviess County)	42373
St. Joseph (Marion County)	40060
St. Mary	40063
St. Matthews	40207
	40257
For specific St. Matthews Zip Codes call (502) 893-3478	
St. Paul (Grayson County)	42754
St. Paul (Lewis County)	41170
St. Regis Park	40220
St. Vincent	42437
Saldee	41369
Salem (Livingston County)	42078
Salem (Russell County)	42642
Salleeton	40033
Salmon	42134
Saloma	42718
Salt Gum	40935
Salt Lick	40371
Salt River (Part of Shepherdsville)	40165
Saltwell	40311
Salvisa	40372
Salyersville	41465
Sample	40143
Samuels	40013
Sandclift	42633
Sandefur Crossing	42320
Sanders	41083
Sandgap	40481
Sand Hill (Estill County)	40336
Sand Hill (Harlan County)	40823
Sand Hill (Warren County)	42101
Sand Springs (Jackson County)	40447
Sand Springs (Rockcastle County)	40456
Sandy City (Part of Catlettsburg)	41129
Sandy Hook	41171
Sano	42728
Sarah	41171
Saratoga	42445
Sardis	41056
Sargent-Sturgeon	42301
Sassafras	41759
Sassafras Ridge	42050
Saul	40981
Savage	42602
Savage Branch	41129
Savoy	40769
Savoyard	42749
Sawyer	42643
Saxton	40769
Saylor	40840
Scale	42025
Scalf	40982
Schley	42202
Schochoh	42202
Schultztown	42320
Schweizer	42134
Science Hill	42553
Scot (Part of Cumberland)	40823
Scottown	42320
Scottsburg	42445
Scotts Station	40065
Scottsville	42164
Scoville	41314
Scranton	40322
Scuddy	41760
Seaville	40030
Sebastians Branch	41370
Sebree	42455
Seco	41849
Sedalia	42079
Seitz	41466
Select	42333
Seminary	42602
Seminary Village (Part of Louisville)	40206
Semiway	42371
Seneca Gardens	40205
Senterville	41522
Se Ree	40164

	ZIP
Sergent	41858
Settle	42164
Settlers Point	40059
Seventy Six	42602
Sewell	41385
Sewellton	42629
Sextons Creek	40983
Seymour	42749
Shadeland (Part of Lexington)	40503
Shady Acres	42518
Shady Grove (Crittenden County)	42064
Shady Grove (Metcalfe County)	42214
Shadynook	41031
Shafter	42501
Shannon	41055
Sharer	42235
Sharkey	41049
Sharon	41002
Sharondale	41514
Sharon Grove	42280
Sharpe	42025
Sharpsburg	40374
Sharpsville	40330
Shawhan	41031
Shawnee Estates (Part of Bowling Green)	42104
Shawneetown (Part of Lexington)	40503
Shearer Valley	42633
Shelbiana	41562
Shelby (Part of Louisville)	40217
Shelby City (Part of Junction City)	40422
Shelby Gap	41563
Shelbyville	40065-66
For specific Shelbyville Zip Codes call (502) 633-1810	
Shepherdsville	40165
Shepola	42544
Sherburne	41041
Sheridan	41064
Sherman	41035
Sherwood Shores	42044
Shetland	40383
Shiff	40324
Shiloh	42071
Shipley	42602
Shively	40216
	40256
For specific Shively Zip Codes call (502) 449-2657	
Shoal	41730
Shop Branch	40447
Shopville	42554
Shore Acres	40601
Short Creek	42721
Short Town	40828
Shreve	42343
Shrewsbury	42721
Sibert	40962
Sidell	40962
Sideview	40353
Sideway	41164
Sidney	41564
Siler (Knox County)	40701
Siler (Whitley County)	40763
Silerville	42649
Silica	41164
Siloam	41175
Silver	42320
Silver City	42261
Silver Creek	40403
Silver Grove	41085
Silverhill	41467
Simmons	42354
Simpson	41301
Simpsonville	40067
Sims Fork	40902
Sinai	40342
Sinks	40456
Sirocco	40108
Sitka	41255
Sizerock	41762
Skibo	42345
Skillman	42348
Skinnersburg	40379
Skullbuster	40379
Skylight	40059
Skyline	41821
Slade	40376
Slat	42633
Slate Lick	40403
Slater	42087
Slate Valley	40360
Slaughters	42456
Slavans	42653
Slemp	41763
Slickford	42633

	ZIP
Slick Rock	42141
Sligo	40055
Sloan	41653
Sloans Valley	42555
Smilax	41764
Smile	40351
Smith	40867
Smithfield	40068
Smithland	42081
Smith Mills	42457
Smiths Creek	41164
Smiths Grove	42171
Smith Town	42647
Smithview	42721
Smithwood	42076
Smoky Valley	41164
Snell	42501
Snow	42602
Snow Hill	40065
Soft Shell	41831
Soldier	41173
Somerset	42501-02
	42564
For specific Somerset Zip Codes call (606) 678-5712	
Sonora	42776
Sorgho	42301
South	42754
South Buffalo	42716
South Carrollton	42374
South Columbus	42032
South Corbin (Part of Corbin)	40701
South Dixie	40272
Southdown	41815
South Elkhorn (Part of Lexington)	40503
South Fork (Breathitt County)	41339
South Fork (Lincoln County)	40437
Southfork (Owsley County)	41314
Southgate	41071
South Higginsport	41002
South Highlands	42066
South Hill	42261
South Irvine	40336
South Marshall	42048
South Park	40118
South Park View	40219
South Portsmouth	41174
South Ripley	41034
South Shore	41175
Southshores	40065
South Union	42283
Southville	40065
South Wallins	40873
South Williamson	41503
Southwire	42348
Spa	42256
Spanglin	41171
Spann	42633
Sparksville	42728
Sparta	41086
Spears	40502
Speck	42723
Speedwell	40475
Speight	41565
Spence (Part of Newport)	41071
Spencer	40353
Spencer Ridge	41311
Spider	41843
Spindletop	40324
Spiro	40456
Spottsville	42458
Spring Creek	40962
Springdale (Jefferson County)	40222
Springdale (Mason County)	41056
Springfield	40069
Spring Grove	42437
Springhill (Hickman County)	42031
Springhill (Warren County)	42101
Springlake (Kenton County)	41015
Springlake (Madison County)	40475
Spring Lake Farms	40299
Springlee	40207
Spring Lick	42779
Spring Mill	40228
Spring Station	40347
Springval	40324
Spring Valley	40216
Sprout	40350
Spruce Pine	40874
Sprule	40906
Spurlington	42718
Spurlock	40972
Squib	42501
Squiresville	40359
Stab	42557
Stacy Fork	41472

	ZIP		ZIP		ZIP
Staffordsburg	41051	Summit (Boyd County)	41102	Three Springs (Hart County)	42746
Staffordsville	41256	Summit (Hardin County)	42783	Three Springs (Warren	
Stambaugh	41257	Sumpter	42633	County)	42104
Stamping Ground	40379	Sunfish	42284	Thruston	42301
Standiford (Part of		Sunny Acres (Part of Taylor		Thurlow	42743
Louisville)	40209	Mill)	41015	Tidalwave	40701
Standing Rock	41343	Sunnybrook	42633	Tierra Linda (Part of	
Stanfill	40831	Sunny Corner	42348	Frankfort)	40601
Stanford	40484	Sunnydale	42358	Tilden	42409
Stanley	42375	Sunny Hills (Part of		Tilford	42721
Stanton	40380	Frankfort)	40601	Tiline	42083
Stanville	41659	Sunnyside	42101	Tilton	41041
Stark	41164	Sunrise	41031	Timber Lake	42518
Star Mills	42740	Sunset	41049	Timberwood Lake Shores	41010
State Line	42050	Sunshine (Greenup County)	41175	Tina	41740
Static	42602	Sunshine (Harlan County)	40831	Tinsley	40977
Station Camp	40336	Susie	42633	Tiny Town	42234
Stay	41311	Sussex Estates	40356	Tiptop	41409
Stearns	42647	Suterville	40379	Toddspoint	40065
Stedmantown	40601	Sutherland	42376	Toddville	40444
Steele	41566	Sutton (Fleming County)	41041	Toler	41569
Steff	42780	Sutton (Pike County)	41562	Toliver	41332
Stella (Calloway County)	42071	Suwanee	42055	Tollesboro	41189
Stella (Magoffin County)	41465	Swain	42635	Tolliver Town	41810
Stephens	41177	Swallowfield	40601	Tolu	42084
Stephensburg	42781	Swamp Branch	41258	Tomahawk	41262
Stephensport	40170	Swampton	41464	Tompkinsville	42167
Stepstone	40360	Swanee Shores	41097	Tonieville	42748
Steubenville	42648	Swan Lake	40906	Toonerville	41548
Stewart	42320	Swanpond	40906	Topmost	41862
Stewart Acres	42320	Sweeden	42285	Topton	40741
Stewartsville	41097	Sweeneyville	42718	Torrent	41396
Stiles	40028	Sweet Owen	40359	Totz	40870
Stillwater	41301	Switzer	40601	Toulouse	41723
Stinnett	40868	Sycamore	40222	Touristville	42633
Stinnettsville	40146	Sycamore Estates	40383	Tousey	40119
Stinson	41143	Sylvandell	41031	Tower Heights	40065
Stites	40177	Sylvania	40258	Town and Country (Daviess	
Stockholm	42257	Symbol	40729	County)	42301
Stone	41567	Symsonia	42082	Town and Country (Logan	
Stone Hedge Estates	40324	Tabernacle	42220	County)	42276
Stonestreet	40272	Tablow	40330	Tracy	42133
Stonewall (Bracken County)	41004	Tacky Town	40988	Trailwood Lakes	40003
Stonewall (Scott County)	40370	Taffy	42347	Tram	41663
Stonewall Estates (Fayette		Taft	41314	Trammel	42164
County)	40503	Talbert	41377	Trapp	40391
Stonewall Estates (Franklin		Talcum	41765	Trappist	40051
County)	40601	Tallega	41378	Travellers Rest	41314
Stoneybrook	40391	Talmage	40330	Treasure Island	40229
Stoney Fork	40988	Tanksley	40962	Tremont	40873
Stoney Point	41034	Tanner	42748	Trent	41301
Stony Fork Junction (Part of		Tannery	41179	Trenton	42286
Middlesboro)	40965	Tar Fork	40111	Tress Shop	42220
Stoops	40353	Tar Hill	42754	Tribbey	41722
Stop	42633	Tarkiln	41124	Tribune	42064
Stopover	41568	Tarryon Number One	42055	Tri City	42040
Stormking	41701	Tates Creek Estates	40356	Trigg Furnace	42211
Stovall	42160	Tateville	42558	Trimble	42544
Straight Creek	40977	Tatham Springs	40078	Trinity	41179
Strait Creek	41132	Tatumsville	42044	Trinity Station	41179
Strathmoor Gardens	40205	Taulbee	41385	Trisler	42343
Strathmoor Manor	40205	Taylor Mill	41015	Tri-State (Part of	
Strathmoor Village	40205	Taylor Mines	42320	Catlettsburg)	41129
Straw	42259	Taylorsport	41048	Trosper	40995
Strawberry	42501	Taylors Store	42049	Troublesome	41712
Stricklett	41179	Taylorsville	40071	Troy	40383
Stringtown (Anderson		Teaberry	41660	Tucker	40229
County)	40342	Tedders	40906	Tuckertown	42159
Stringtown (Boone County)	41048	Teddy	42539	Tuggleville	40863
Stringtown (Grant County)	41003	Teetersville	40831	Tunnel Hill	42701
Stringtown (Madison		Teges	40972	Turfland Mall (Part of	
County)	40475	Temperance	42134	Lexington)	40504
Stringtown (Magoffin		Temple Hill	42141	Turin	41314
County)	41465	Ten Broeck	40201	Turkey	41314
Stringtown (McLean		Teresita	40359	Turkey Creek	41570
County)	42372	Terry Manor	40258	Turkey Foot	40370
Stringtown (Mercer County)	40330	Terryville	41159	Turkeytown	40419
Stringtown (Muhlenberg		Texas	40069	Turners Station	40075
County)	42372	Texola	40471	Turnersville	40484
Strunk	42649	Thealka	41240	Turnertown (Butler County)	42268
Stubblefield	42088	The Colony (Fayette		Turnertown (Simpson	
Sturgeon	41314	County)	40504	County)	42134
Sturgis	42459	The Colony (Franklin		Tutor Key	41263
Sublett	41465	County)	40601	Tuttle	40741
Sublimity City	40741	Thelma	41260	Tway (Part of Harlan)	40831
Subtle	42129	The Meadows (Part of		Twentysix	41472
Sudith	40371	Lexington)	40505	Twila	40873
Sugar Bay	41095	The Moors Camp	42044	Twin Lakes	41091
Sugar Grove	42261	The Ridge	41171	Twin Oaks (Fayette County)	40503
Sugar Hill	42501	Thomas	41626	Twin Oaks (Jefferson	
Sugartit	41042	Thorn Hill (Franklin County)	40601	County)	40216
Sullivan	42460	Thornhill (Jefferson County)	40222	Tyewhoppety	42216
Sulphur	40070	Thornton	41855	Tygarts Valley	41144
Sulphur Lick	42166	Thorobred Acres	40222	Tyler (Part of Paducah)	42001
Sulphur Springs	42358	Thoroughbred Acres	40065	Tyner	40486
Sulphur Well (Jessamine		Thousandsticks	41766	Typo	41771
County)	40356	Threeforks (Martin County)	41261	Tyrone	40342
Sulphur Well (Metcalfe		Threeforks (Warren County)	42159	Ula	42501
County)	42129	Threelinks	40456	Ulvah	41731
Summer Shade	42166	Three Mile	41144	Ulysses	41264
Summersville	42782	Three Point	40815	Union	41091

	ZIP		ZIP		ZIP
Wolf Coal	41339	Woodsbend	41472	Yeager (Pike County)	41501
Wolf Creek	40104	Woodson Bend	42518	Yeaman	42361
Wolf Lick	42256	Woodsonville	42749	Yellow Rock	41311
Wolfpit	41522	Woodstock	42501	Yelvington	42355
Wolverine	41339	Woodville	42053	Yerkes	41778
Wonder	41626	Woolcott	41004	Yesse	42164
Wonnie	41465	Wooleyville	42718	Yocum	41472
Woodbine	40771	Woollum	40999	York	41175
Woodburn	42170	Wooton	41776	Yorktown	41501
Woodbury	42288	Worthington (Greenup		Yosemite	42566
Woodhill	40219	County)	41183	Younger Creek	42701
Woodlake	40601	Worthington (Jefferson		Youngs Creek	40701
Woodland Estates	41240	County)	40222	Youngtown	42261
Woodland Hills	40243	Worthington Hills	40201	Yuma	42733
Woodlands (Part of		Worthville	41098	Zachariah	41396
Frankfort)	40601	Wray Gap	42633	Zag	41472
Woodlawn (Campbell		Wrights	42718	Zandale (Part of Lexington)	40503
County)	41076	Wrightsburg	42327	Zebulon	41501
Woodlawn (McCracken		Wrigley	41477	Zelda	41230
County)	42001	Wurtland	41144	Zion (Grant County)	41035
Woodlawn (Nelson County)	40004	Wyett	41171	Zion (Henderson County)	42420
Woodlawn-Oakdale	42001	Wyman	42327	Zion (Todd County)	42234
Woodlawn Park	40207	Yaden	40769	Zion Hill	40347
Woodman	41574	Yancey	40831	Zoe	41397
Woodrow	40140	Yatesville	41230	Zoneton (Part of Pioneer	
Woods (Floyd County)	41653	Yeaddiss	41777	Village)	40165
Woods (Harlan County)	40828	Yeager (Knox County)	40915	Zula	42603

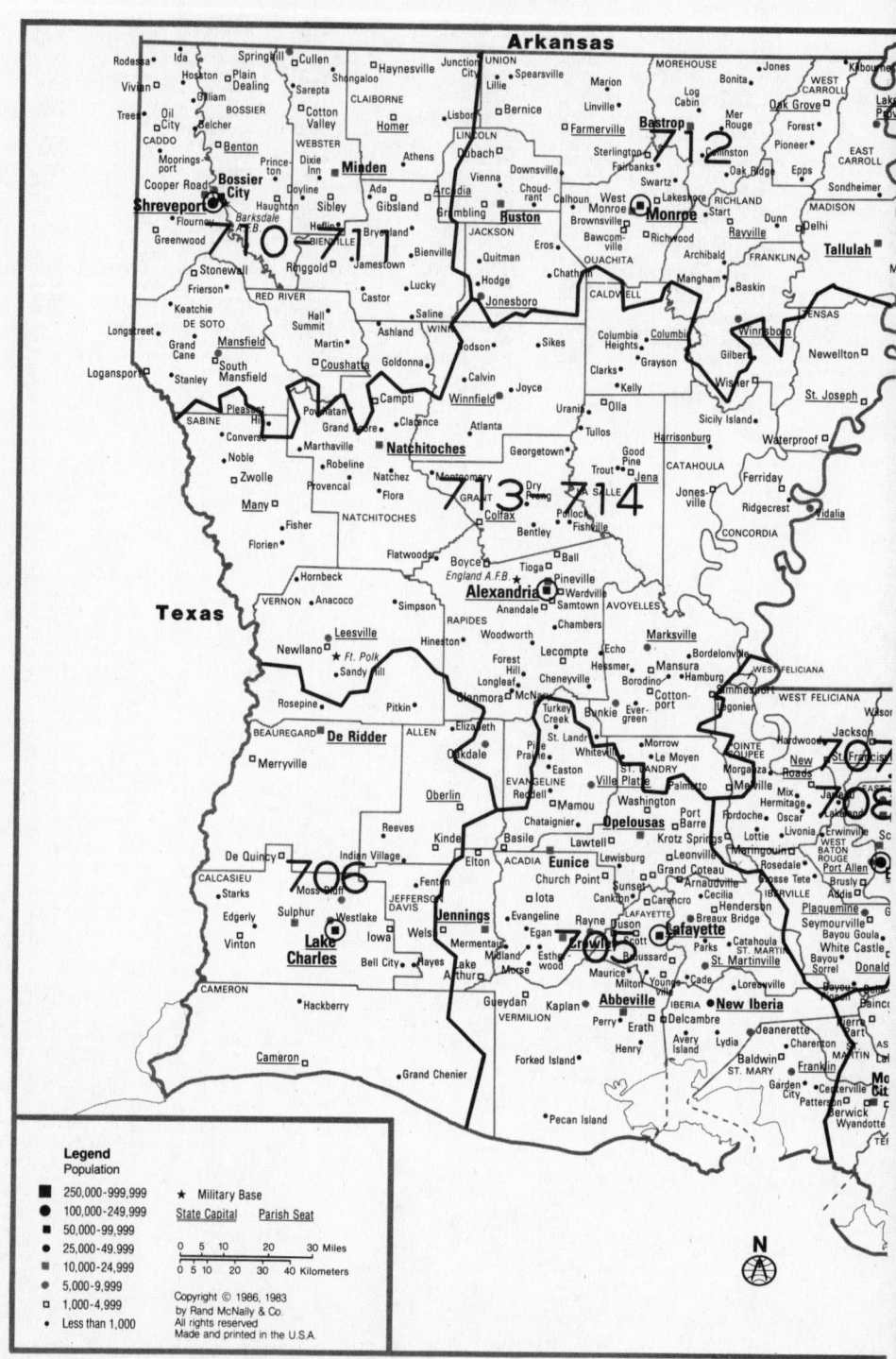

Legend
Population

■ 250,000-999,999
● 100,000-249,999
● 50,000-99,999
• 25,000-49,999
▪ 10,000-24,999
□ 5,000-9,999
□ 1,000-4,999
• Less than 1,000

★ Military Base

State Capital   Parish Seat

0 5 10   20   30 Miles
0 5 10   20   30   40 Kilometers

N

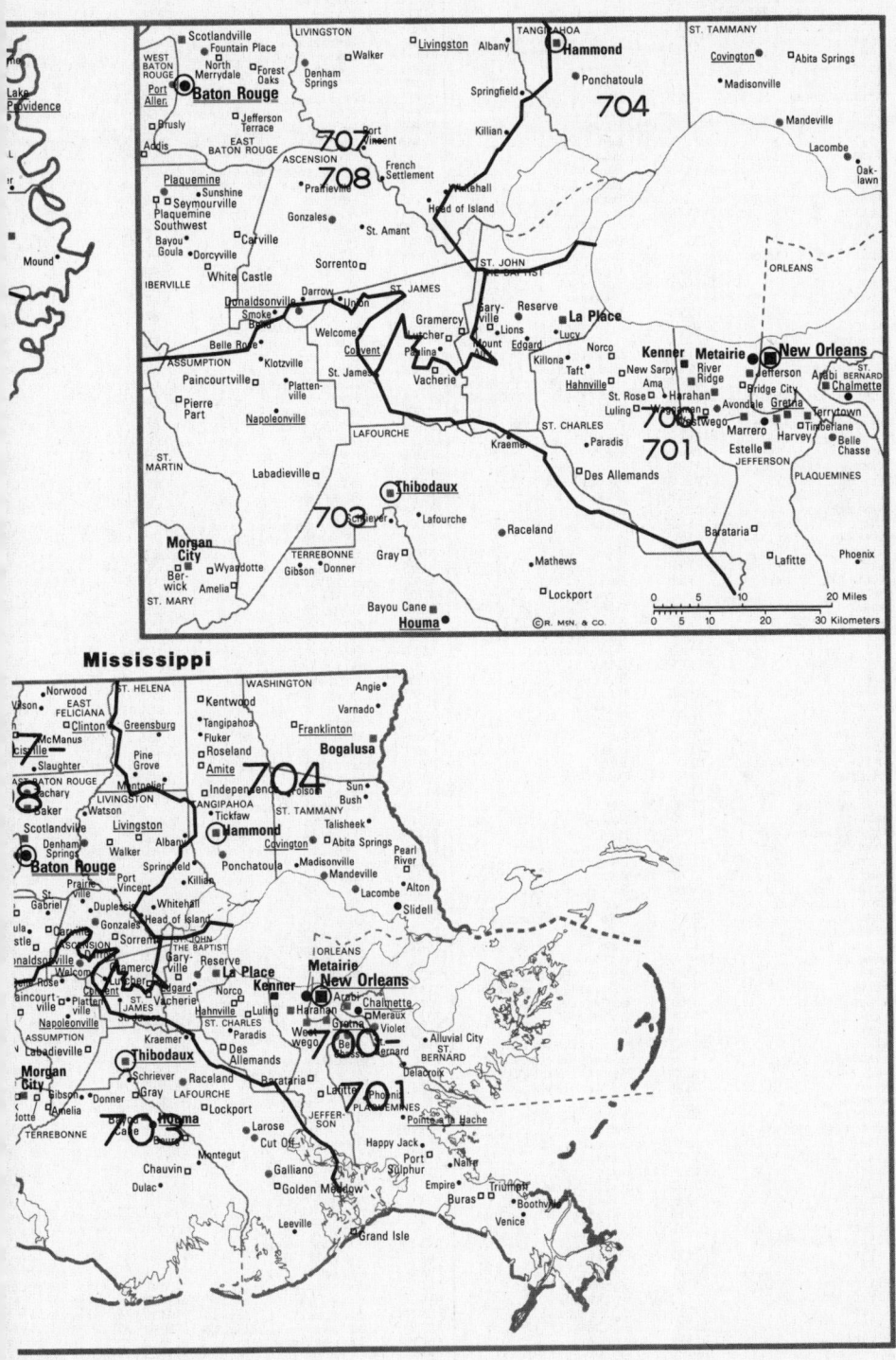

	ZIP
Abbeville	70510-11
For specific Abbeville Zip Codes call (318) 893-2972	
Abby Plantation	70301
Aben	70346
Abington	71052
Abita Springs	70420
Acadia	70301
Acadia Academy	70535
Acme	71316
Acy	70774
Ada	71080
Addis	70710
Adeline	70544
Adner	71037
Advance (Part of Hodge)	71247
Afton	71282
Aimwell	71401
Airline Park	70003
Airview Terrace (Part of Alexandria)	71301
Ajax	71450
Akers	70421
Albania	70544
Albany	70711
Alberta	71016
Alco	71446
Alden Bridge	71006
Alexandria	71301-15
For specific Alexandria Zip Codes call (318) 484-4637	
Alexandria Mall (Part of Alexandria)	71301
Alfalfa	71409
Alfords	70720
Alice B	70538
Alice C	70538
Allemand	70360
Allen	71469
Allendale	70767
Alliance	70037
Allon	70760
Alluvial City	70085
Aloha	71417
Aloysia	70788
Alsen	70807
Alto	71269
Alton	70458
Alvin Callender	70037
Ama	70031
Amelia	70340
Amite	70422
Anacoco	71403
Anandale	71301
Andrew	70548
Andrew Guillot Subdivision	70301
Angelina	70076
Angie	70426
Annadale	70788
Ansley	71270
Antioch (Claiborne Parish)	71040
Antioch (Lincoln Parish)	71275
Antonia	71467
Antonio	70767
Antrim	71064
Arabi	70032
Ararat	70601
Arbroth	70720
Arcadia	71001
Archibald	71218
Archie	71343
Arcola	70456
Ardoyne	70360
Argo	71343
Argyle	70360
Arizona	71040
Arklatex (Part of Mooringsport)	71060
Arlington	70808
Armistead	71019
Arnaudville	70512
Ashland (Natchitoches Parish)	71002
Ashland (Terrebonne Parish)	71360
Ashley	71282
Ashton	70538
Athens	71003
Atlanta	71404
Attakapas Landing	70390
Audubon (Part of Baton Rouge)	70806
Audubon Terrace	70808
Augusta (Iberville Parish)	70788
Augusta (Plaquemines Parish)	70037
Avalon	70392
Avandale	71366
Avery Island	70513
Avondale	70094
Aycock	71001
Azucena	71375

	ZIP
Bagdad	71417
Bains	70775
Baker	70704
	70714
For specific Baker Zip Codes call (504) 775-3774	
Baldwin	70514
Ball	71405
Bancroft	70653
Bankers	70582
Banks	70807
Banks Springs	71418
Baptist	70403
Barataria	70036
Barber Spur	70586
Bardel	71269
Barnet Springs (Part of Ruston)	71270
Barron	71328
Barton	70346
Basile	70515
Baskin	71219
Baskinton	71219
Bastrop	71220-21
For specific Bastrop Zip Codes call (318) 281-2672	
Batchelor	70715
Baton Rouge	70801-98
For specific Baton Rouge Zip Codes call (504) 381-0372	
Batree	70090
Bawcomville	71291
Bayou Barbary	70754
Bayou Blue	70360
Bayou Cane	70359
Bayou Chicot	70586
Bayou Crab	70390
Bayou Current	71353
Bayou Gauche	70030
Bayou Goula	70716
Bayou Pigeon	70764
Bayou Sale	70538
Bayou Sorrel	70764
Baywood	70739
Beach Grove	71277
Beachview (Part of Kenner)	70065
Bear Creek	71008
Bear Skin	71266
Beaver	71463
Bee Bayou	71269
Beech Springs	71247
Beekman	71220
Beggs	71322
Bel	70658
Belah	71371
Belair	70040
Belair Cove	70586
Belcher	71004
Bell City	70630
Belle Amie	70345
Belle Chasse	70037
Belledeau	71341
Belle Place	70552
Belle Point	70084
Belle River	70339
Belle Rose	70341
Belle Terre (Assumption Parish)	70346
Belle Terre (Iberville Parish)	70764
Belleview	70570
Bellevue (Bossier Parish)	71037
Bellevue (Caldwell Parish)	71418
Bellfontaine	70815
Bell Helene	70734
Bellwood	71468
Belmont (Sabine Parish)	71406
Belmont (St. James Parish)	70743
Belmont (West Baton Rouge Parish)	70767
Benson	71419
Bentley	71407
Benton	71006
Bermuda	71456
Bernice	71222
Bertie	70390
Bertrandville (Assumption Parish)	70390
Bertrandville (Plaquemines Parish)	70040
Berwick	70342
Bethany	71007
Bienville	71008
Big Bend	71318
Big Branch	70445
Big Cane	71356
Big Creek	71219
Big Island	71328
Big Woods	70668
Billeaud	70518
Bissonnet	70003
Bivens	70653

	ZIP
Blackburn	71038
Black Hawk	71373
Blade	71342
Blanchard	71009
Blanche	71433
Blanks	70717
Blankston	71202
Blond	70433
Bluff Creek	70722
Bob Acres	70560
Bodcau	71037
Bodoc	71329
Bogalusa	70427-29
For specific Bogalusa Zip Codes call (504) 735-5921	
Bohemia	70082
Bolden	71358
Boleyn	71450
Bolinger	71064
Bolivar	70444
Bonaire	70808
Bond	71463
Bonfouca	70458
Bonita	71223
Bon Marche Mall (Part of Baton Rouge)	70806
Bon Secour	70086
Book	71343
Boone's Corner	70605
Boothville	70038
Boothville-Venice	70038
Bordelonville	71320
Borgne Mouth	70092
Borodino	71355
Bosco	71202
Boscoville	70570
Bossier City	71111-13
	71171-72
For specific Bossier City Zip Codes call (318) 746-1481	
Boston	70533
Boudreaux Canal	70344
Bourg	70343
Boutte	70039
Boyce	71409
Braithwaite	70040
Branch	70516
Breard (Part of Monroe)	71203
Breaux Bridge	70517
Breezy Hill	71467
Brewton's Mill	71031
Bridge City	70094
Brignac	70737
Bristol	70584
Brittany	70718
Broadmoor (Lafayette Parish)	70501
Broadmoor (Orleans Parish)	70125
Broadmoor (Terrebonne Parish)	70360
Broadview (Part of Baton Rouge)	70815
Brooks	70760
Brouillette	71351
Broussard	70518
Brown	71016
Brownell	71295
Brownfields	70811
Brown Heights	70714
Brownlee	71111
Brownsville-Bawcomville	71291
Brownville (Caldwell Parish)	71418
Brownville (Ouachita Parish)	71291
Brule	70372
Brule Guillot	70301
Bruly La Croix	70788
Bruly Saint Martin	70341
Brusle Saint Vincent	70390
Brusly	70719
Bryant (Part of New Iberia)	70560
Bryceland	71014
Buckeye	71321
Buckner	71269
Bueche	70720
Buhler	70663
Bull Run	70395
Bunkie	71322
Buras	70041
Buras-Triumph	70041
Burkplace	71016
Burr Ferry	71403
Burroughs	71418
Burrwood	70091
Burton Lane	70086
Bush	70431
Bushes	71295
Bywaters (Part of New Orleans)	70117
Caddo (Part of Oil City)	71061
Caddo Station	71082
Cade	70519

	ZIP		ZIP		ZIP
Cadeville	71238	Chickama	71346	Cross Roads (Red River	
Caernarvon	70040	Chickasaw	71263	Parish)	71019
Caffery	70538	Chinchuba	70448	Crowley	70526-27
Calcasieu (Allen Parish)	71433	Chipola	70441	For specific Crowley Zip Codes	
Calcasieu (Rapides Parish)	71433	Chloe	70647	call (318) 783-2370	
Calhoun	71225	Choctaw (Iberville Parish)	70767	Crown Point	70072
Calumet	70392	Choctaw (Lafourche Parish)	70301	Crowville	71230
Calvin	71410	Chopin	71412	Crozier	70360
Camelia Gardens (Part of		Choudrant	71227	Cullen	71021
Alexandria)	71301	Choupique (Lafourche		Curry	71483
Cameron	70631	Parish)	70301	Curtis	71112
Camp Beauregard	71301	Choupique (St. Mary Parish)	70538	Cut Off	70345
Camperdown	70538	Chula	70372	Cypremort	70538
Campti	71411	Church Point	70525	Cypress (Natchitoches	
Cancienne	70390	Church Spur	70390	Parish)	71420
Canebrake	71334	Cinclare	70767	Cypress (Ouachita Parish)	71291
Caney	71446	Cindy Park	70075	Cypress Gardens (St.	
Cankton	70584	Claiborne (Ouachita Parish)	71291	Bernard Parish)	70075
Cannonburg	70788	Claiborne (St. Tammany		Cypress Gardens	
Capitan	70592	Parish)	70433	(Terrebonne Parish)	70360
Capitol (Part of Baton		Claibourne Gardens	70094	Cypress Island	70582
Rouge)	70804	Clare	71429	Daigleville (Part of Houma)	70360
Caplis	71111	Clarence	71414	Dalcour	70040
Carencro	70520	Clarks	71415	Danville	71008
Carlisle	70042	Clay	71270	D'Arbonne	71227
Carlton	71225	Clayton	71327	Darlington	70441
Carlyss	70663	Clayton Junction (Part of		Darnell	71266
Carmel	71052	Clayton)	71326	Darrow	70725
Caroline	70552	Clearview Shopping Center	70002	Daspit	70560
Carrollton (Part of New		Clearwater	71325	Davant	70046
Orleans)	70118	Clifton (Rapides Parish)	71455	Dean	71260
Carrollton Central Plaza		Clifton (Washington Parish)	70438	Dean Chapel	71291
(Part of New Orleans)	70118	Clinton	70722	De Broeck Landing	71106
Carrolwood	70068	Clio	70449	Deerford	70791
Carterville	71064	Clotilda	70394	Deer Park	71373
Carthage Bluff Landing	70462	Cloutierville	71416	Dehlco	71269
Cartwright	71227	Clovelly Farms	70345	Delacroix (St. Bernard	
Carville	70721	Cocodrie	70344	Parish)	70085
Caspiana	71115	Cocoville	71350	Delacroix (St. Martin Parish)	70582
Castle Village	71301	Coker	71052	Del Bueno Park	70075
Castor	71016	Coleman	71282	Delcambre	70528
Catahoula	70582	Colfax	71417	Delhi	71232
Catherine	70716	Colgrade	71483	Delta	71233
Cat Island	71418	College (Part of Hammond)	70401	Delta Farms	70374
Catuna	71052	Collinsburg	71064	Denham Springs	70726-27
Cavett	71004	Collinston	71229	For specific Denham Springs Zip	
Cecile	71105	Colonial Heights	71109	Codes call (504) 665-5435	
Cecilia	70521	Colquitt	71038	Dennis Mills	70726
Cedar Crest	70816	Columbia (Caldwell Parish)	71418	Denson	70449
Cedar Glen	70811	Columbia (St. John the		Dent Terrace	70808
Cedar Grove (Assumption		Baptist Parish)	70049	De Quincy	70633
Parish)	70372	Columbia Heights	71418	De Ridder	70634
Cedar Grove (Caddo		Como	71295	Derry	71421
Parish)	71106	Concession	70037	Des Allemands	70030
Cedar Grove (Plaquemines		Concord	71263	De Selle	71301
Parish)	70037	Constance Beach	70631	Dess	71429
Cedarton	71227	Consuella	71375	Destrehan	70047
Centenary (Part of		Contreras	70085	Devalls	70767
Shreveport)	71104	Convent	70723	Deville	71328
Center Point	71323	Converse	71419	Dewdrop	71220
Centerville (Evangeline		Conway	71260	Diamond	70083
Parish)	71367	Coon	70715	Dixie	71107
Centerville (St. Mary Parish)	70522	Cooper Road	71107	Dixie Acres	71280
Central (East Baton Rouge		Coopers	71446	Dixie Gardens	71105
Parish)	70811	Copenhagen	71418	Dixie Inn	71055
Central (St. James Parish)	70723	Cora	71444	Dixon Correctional Institute	70748
Central (Terrebonne Parish)	70360	Corbin (Part of Walker)	70785	Dodson	71422
Chacahoula	70395	Corey	71202	Donaldsonville	70346
Chackbay (Lafourche		Corinth	71235	Donner	70352
Parish)	70301	Cornerview	70737	Dorcyville	70788
Chalmette	70043-44	Cornor	39669	Douglas	71227
For specific Chalmette Zip Codes		Cortableau	70577	Downsville	71234
call (504) 271-4173		Cortana Mall (Part of Baton		Downtown (Part of	
Chalmette Vista	70043	Rouge)	70815	Alexandria)	71309
Chamale Cove (Part of		Coteau Holmes	70582	Downtown (Part of Monroe)	71201
Slidell)	70460	Coteau Rodaire	70512	Downtown (Part of Morgan	
Chamberlin	70767	Cotton Plant	71435	City)	70380
Chambers	71346	Cottonport	71327	Downtown (Part of	
Chandler Park (Part of		Cotton Valley	71018	Shreveport)	71101
Alexandria)	71301	Couchwood	71018	Doyle (Part of Livingston)	70754
Charenton	70523	Coulon Plantation	70301	Doyline	71023
Charles Park (Part of		Country Club Subdivision	70301	Drew (Calcasieu Parish)	70605
Alexandria)	71301	Coushatta	71019	Drew (Ouachita Parish)	71291
Charlotte	70560	Covington	70433-34	Dry Creek	70637
Chase	71324	For specific Covington Zip Codes		Dry Prong	71423
Chataignier	70524	call (504) 892-2421		Dubach	71235
Chateau Village (Part of		Covington Country Club		Dubberly	71024
Kenner)	70065	Estates	70433	Duckroost	70774
Chatham	71226	Cow Island	70510	Dufresne	70070
Chatman Town	70090	Cravens	70656	Dukedale	71006
Chauvin	70344	Creedmoor	70085	Dulac	70353
Chef Menteur (Part of New		Creole	70632	Dunbarton	71334
Orleans)	70126	Crescent (Iberville Parish)	70764	Dunn	71232
Cheneyville	71325	Crescent (Terrebonne		Duplessis	70728
Cheniere	71291	Parish)	70360	Dupont (Avoyelles Parish)	71329
Cherokee Court	70123	Creston	71020	Dupont (Pointe Coupee	
Cherokee Village (Part of		Crew Lake	71269	Parish)	70783
Alexandria)	71301	Crews	71454	Duson	70529
Cherry Grove	70655	Crichton	71019	Dutch Town	70734
Chesbrough	70444	Cross-Road	71435	Dykesville	71038
Chestnut	71070	Crossroads (Lincoln Parish)	71235	Easleyville	70441

	ZIP		ZIP		ZIP
Eastgate Plaza (Part of Shreveport)	71108	Foley (Assumption Parish)	70390	....	70737
East Hammond (Part of Hammond)	70401	Folsom	70437	For specific Gonzales Zip Codes call (504) 647-2617	
East Hodge	71247	Fondale	71201		
East Louisiana State Hospital	70748	Forbing	71106	Goodbee	70433
Easton	70586	Fordoche	70732	Good Hope	70079
East Point	71025	Foreman	70815	Good Pine	71342
East Side (Part of Lake Charles)	70601	Forest	71242	Goodwill	71263
Eastside Columbia	71418	Forest Glen	70445	Goodwood	71353
Eastwood	71037	Forest Hill	71430	Gordon	71038
Ebenezer	70526	Forest Oaks	70815	Gorum	71434
Echo	71330	Forest Park	71291	Goudeau	71333
Eden	71371	Forked Island	70510	Gouldsboro (Part of Gretna)	70053
Eden Isle	70458	Forksville	71225	Grambling	71245
Edgard	70049	Fort De Russy	71351	Gramercy	70052
Edgefield	71019	Fort Jesup	71449	Grand Bayou	71052
Edgerly	70668	Fort Necessity	71243	Grandbois	70343
Edna	70648	Fort Polk	71459	Grand Caillou	70360
Effie	71331	Fort Polk North	71459	Grand Cane	71032
Egan	70531	Fort Polk South	71459	Grand Chenier	70643
Elam	71378	Fortune Fork	71282	Grand Coteau	70541
Elba	71353	Fosters (Part of Bossier City)	71111	Grand Ecore	71457
Eliza	70764	Fosters Canal	70083	Grand Isle	70358
Elizabeth	70638	Foules	71326	Grand Lake	70605
Ellendale	70360	Fourborge	70586	Grand Point	70763
Ellis	70526	Four Corners	70538	Grand Prairie	70589
Ellsworth	70360	Four Forks (Caddo Parish)	71046	Grand River	70764
Elmer (Lafourche Parish)	70301	Four Forks (Richland Parish)	71259	Grangeville	70422
Elmer (Rapides Parish)	71424	Fowler	71240	Grant	70644
Elmfield	70390	Francis Place	70075	Gray	70359
Elm Grove	71051	Franklin	70538	Gray Point	70586
Elm Hall	70390	Franklinton	70438	Grayson	71435
Elm Hall Junction	70390	Fred	70791	Green Acres (Concordia Parish)	71373
Elm Park	70775	Freetown (Assumption Parish)	70390	Green Acres (East Baton Rouge Parish)	70811
Elton	70532	Freetown (St. Mary Parish)	70538	Green Acres (St. Charles Parish)	70030
Empire	70050	French Settlement	70733	Green Gables	71360
Encalade	70083	Frenier	70068	Greenlaw	70444
Energy (Part of Lafayette)	70598	Friendship	71008	Green Lawn (Part of Kenner)	70065
England Air Force Base	71311	Frierson	71027	Green Lawn Terrace (Part of Kenner)	70065
Englewood	71282	Frisco	70755	Greensburg	70441
English Turn	70040	Frogmore	71334	Greenwell Springs	70739
Enola	70390	Frost	70754	Greenwood (Caddo Parish)	71033
Enon	70438	Frost Town	71234	Greenwood (St. Mary Parish)	70380
Enterprise (Catahoula Parish)	71425	Fryeburg	71039	Greenwood (Terrebonne Parish)	70356
Enterprise (Iberia Parish)	70544	Fullerton	70642	Greenwood Park	71108
Eola	71322	Fulton	70657	Gretna	70053-54
Epps	71237	Funston	71049	....	70056
Erath	70533	Gaars Mill	71422	For specific Gretna Zip Codes call (504) 362-5610	
Eros	71238	Gahagan	71019		
Erwinville	70729	Galbraith	71447	Grosse Tete	70740
Essen Heights	70808	Galion	71223	Gueydan	70542
Estelle	70072	Galliano	70354	Gulf Outpost (Part of New Orleans)	70146
Esther	70510	Galva	70421	Gullett	70422
Estherwood	70534	Galvez	70769	Gum Ridge	71264
Ethel	70730	Gandy Spur	71429	Gurley	70730
Eunice	70535	Gansville	71422	Haaswood	70452
Eureka	71234	Garden City	70540	Hackberry	70645
Eva	71354	Gardere	70810	Hacketts Corner	70630
Evangeline	70537	Gardner	71431	Hackley	70438
Evans	70639	Garland	71322	Hagewood	71457
Evelyn	71052	Garyville	70051	Hahnville	70057
Evergreen (Avoyelles Parish)	71333	Gassoway	71254	Haile	71260
Evergreen (Webster Parish)	71055	Gayles	71105	Haire	70548
Evergreen Fashion Square	70808	Ged	70668	Half Way (Assumption Parish)	70346
Extension	71239	Geismar	70734	Halfway (Red River Parish)	71019
Fairbanks	71240	Gentilly (Part of New Orleans)	70122	Hall Summit	71034
Fairlane	70360	Georgetown	71432	Hamburg	71339
Fairmont	71417	Georgeville	70443	Hammet	71373
Fairview	71373	Georgia	70390	Hammond	70401-04
Farmer Spur (Part of Vienna)	71270	Getty Camp	70091	For specific Hammond Zip Codes call (504) 345-6014	
Farmerville	71241	Gheens	70355		
Faubourg	70589	Gibbstown	70630	Hanna	71019
Felixville	70722	Gibsland	71028	Hanson City (Part of Kenner)	70062
Fellowship	71371	Gibson	70356	Happy Jack	70083
Fenris	70554	Gilark	71055	Harahan	70123
Fenton	70640	Gilbert	71336	Hardwood	70775
Ferriday	71334	Gilleyville	71269	Hargis	71454
Ferry Lake	71061	Gilliam	71029	Hargrove	70633
Fields	70653	Gillis	70611	Harlem (Plaquemines Parish)	70046
Fifth Ward	71351	Girard	71269	Harlem (Vermilion Parish)	70510
Fillmore	71037	Glade	71343	Harmon	71036
Fisher	71426	Glencoe	70538	Harrisonburg	71340
Fishville	71467	Glen Dale	70049	Harvey	70058-59
Fiske	71263	Glenmora	71433	For specific Harvey Zip Codes call (504) 366-2626	
Five Forks	71483	Glenwild	70342		
Flat Creek	71479	Glenwood	70390	Hathaway	70532
Flatwoods	71427	Gloria	70037	Haughton	71037
Flora	71428	Gloster	71030	Hawthorne	71446
Florence	70538	Glynn	70736	Hayes	70646
Florien	71429	Godchaux	70394	Haynesville	71038
Florrissant	70085	Godchaux Community	70068	Hazelwood	70577
Flournoy	71109	Gold Dust	71322		
Floyd	71266	Golden Meadow	70357		
Fluker	70436	Golden Star Plantation	70090		
Foley (Allen Parish)	70655	Goldman	71375		
		Goldonna	71031		
		Goldridge	70788		
		Gonzales	70707		

	ZIP		ZIP		ZIP
Head of Island	70449	International Trade Mart		Lafourche	70301
Hearn Island	71418	(Part of New Orleans)	70130	Lagan	70086
Hebert	71418	Intracoastal City	70510	Lagonda	70380
Hecker	70647	Iota	70543	Lake	70769
Heflin	71039	Iowa	70647	Lake Arthur	70549
Helena	71366	Irish Bend	70538	Lake Bruin	71366
Henderson	70517	Irma	71457	Lake Charles	70601-16
Henfer Park	70123	Ironton	70083	For specific Lake Charles Zip	
Henry	70533	Isabel	70427	Codes call (318) 439-3631	
Hermitage	70749	Isle Labbe	70582	Lake End	71019
Hessmer	71341	Istrouma (Part of Baton		Lake Forest (Part of New	
Hester	70743	Rouge)	70805	Orleans)	70187
Hewes	70762	Ivan	71006	Lake Judge Perez	70083
Hickory (Avoyelles Parish)	71327	Jackson	70748	Lakeland	70752
Hickory (St. Tammany		Jackson Road	70748	Lake Providence	71254
Parish)	70452	Jacoby	70753	Lakeshore	71201
Hickory Grove	71328	Jamestown	71045	Lakeside (Cameron Parish)	70542
Hickory Valley	71473	Janie	71412	Lakeside (Rapides Parish)	71360
Hicks	71446	Jarreau	70749	Lakeside Shopping Center	70002
Hico	71235	Jay	70374	Lakeview (Caddo Parish)	71107
Higginbotham	70525	Jeanerette	70544	Lakeview (Natchitoches	
Highland Acres	70123	Jean Lafitte	70067	Parish)	71456
Highland Park (Part of		Jefferson (Jefferson Parish)	70121	Lakeview (Orleans Parish)	70124
Monroe)	71201	Jefferson (Lafayette Parish)	70501	Lamar	71232
Highland Park (Part of West		Jefferson Island	70560	Lamourie	71346
Monroe)	71291	Jefferson Terrace	70808	Lampman (Part of	
Highland Park (Terrebonne		Jena	71342	Abbeville)	70510
Parish)	70360	Jennings	70546	Landay Gautreaux	
Highland Park Heights	70808	Jesuit Bend	70037	Subdivision	70301
Highland Road	70808	Jewella (Part of Shreveport)	71109	Lapine	71291
Highway Park (Part of		Jigger	71249	La Place	70068-69
Kenner)	70065	Johnson (St. John the		For specific La Place Zip Codes	
Hi-Land	70092	Baptist Parish)	70049	call (504) 652-6662	
Hillaryville	70725	Johnson (St. Mary Parish)	70538	Laran	71765
Hillsdale	70422	Johnson Ridge	70301	La Reusitte	70037
Hilltop	71268	Johnson's Bayou	70631	Larose	70373
Hilly	71235	Johnson Street	70001	La Rosen (Part of	
Hineston	71438	Jones	71250	Shreveport)	71118
Hobart	70769	Jonesboro	71251	Larto	71343
Hodge	71247	Jonesburg	71269	Latanier	71346
Hohen Solms	70788	Jones Park (Part of Kenner)	70065	Laurel Grove	70301
Holden	70744	Jonesville	71343	Laurel Hill	39669
Holiday Park	70502	Jordan Hill	71483	Laurel Lea	70808
Holloway	71328	Joyce	71440	Laurel Ridge	70788
Holly	71032	Junction	70653	Laurel Valley Plantation	70301
Holly Beach	70631	Junction City	71749	Lawhon	71045
Hollybrook	71254	Kadesh	71454	Lawtell	70550
Holly Grove	71378	Kahns	70767	Lazy Acres	70360
Holly Ridge (Richland		Kaplan	70548	Leander	71445
Parish)	71269	Katy	70538	Lebeau	71345
Holly Ridge (Tensas Parish)	71375	Keatchie	71046	Le Blanc	70651
Hollywood (Calcasieu		Kedron	70422	Le Bleu	70601
Parish)	70663	Keithville	71047	Lecompte	71346
Hollywood (Terrebonne		Kelly	71441	Lee Bayou	71326
Parish)	70360	Kellys	71270	Lee Heights	71360
Hollywood (West Feliciana		Kendale	70062	Lees Creek	70427
Parish)	70775	Kendrick's Ferry	71336	Lees Landing	70454
Holmwood	70647	Kenilworth	70085	Leesville	71446
Holum	71435	Kenmore	70757		71496
Home Place	70083	Kennedy Heights	70094	For specific Leesville Zip Codes	
Homer	71040	Kenner	70062-65	call (318) 239-2841	
Hopedale	70085	For specific Kenner Zip Codes call		Leeville	70357
Hope Villa	70808	(504) 469-1506		Legonier	70753
Hornbeck	71439	Kenner Junction (Part of		Leighton	70301
Horse Bluff Landing	70462	Kenner)	70062	Leland	71368
Hosston	71043	Kentwood	70444	Leleux	70560
Hotwells	71409	Kickapoo	71030	Lemannville	70346
Houltonville	70447	Kilbourne	71253	Le Moyen	71356
Houma	70360-64	Killian	70462	Lena	71447
For specific Houma Zip Codes call		Killona	70066	Leonville	70551
(504) 868-3800		Kinder	70648	Leroy	70555
Howard	71105	King Hill	71019	Leton	71072
Hubertville (Part of		Kingston	71032	Lettsworth	70753
Jeanerette)	70544	Kingsville	71360	Levert	70582
Hudson	71422	Kiroli Woods	71291	Levins	71334
Hughes	71006	Kisatchie	71468	Lewisburg (St. Landry	
Humphreys	70356	Kleinpeter	70808	Parish)	70525
Hundley	70535	Klondyke	70343	Lewisburg (St. Tammany	
Hunter	71052	Klotzville	70341	Parish)	70448
Huron	70512	Kolin	71360	Lewiston	70444
Hurricane	71003	Kolter (Part of Keatchie)	71046	Lewistown	70394
Husser	70442	Koran	71037	Liberty	71225
Hutton	71446	Kraemer	70371	Liberty Hill	71008
Hyde (Part of Simmesport)	71369	Krotz Springs	70750	Libuse	71348
Hymel	70090	Kurthwood	71443	Liddieville	71295
Iberville	70776	Laark	71250	Lillie	71256
Ida	71044	Labadieville	70372	Linda Lee	70726
Idlewild (St. Mary Parish)	70392	Labarre	70751	Lindsay	70748
Idlewild (Terrebonne Parish)	70364	Lacamp	71444	Link	70516
Ikes	70634	Lacassine	70650	Linton	71006
Independence	70443	Lachute	71115	Linville	71260
Indian Bayou	70578	Lacombe	70445	Linwood	70514
Indian Mound	70739	Lacour	70715	Lions	70068
Indian Village (Allen Parish)	70648	Lafayette	70501-09	Lisbon	71048
Indian Village (Ouachita			70593-98	Lismore	71343
Parish)	71225	For specific Lafayette Zip Codes		Litroe	71260
Industrial (Part of		call (318) 269-4800		Little Caillou	70344
Shreveport)	71107	Lafayette Square (Part of		Little Creek	71371
Ingleside	70390	New Orleans)	70130	Little Prairie	70769
Innis	70747	Lafayette Woods	70360	Little Texas	70390
Inniswold	70809	Lafitte	70067	Live Oak	70037

	ZIP
Live Oak Hills	70433
Live Oak Manor	70094
Liverpool	70441
Livingston	70754
Livonia	70755
Lobdell	70767
Lockhart	71277
Lockport	70374
Lockport Heights	70374
Locust Ridge	71366
Logansport	71049
Log Cabin	71220
Logtown	71201
Lonepine	71367
Lone Star (Iberville Parish)	70788
Lone Star (St. Charles Parish)	70070
Longbridge (Avoyelles Parish)	71327
Long Bridge (Lafayette Parish)	70501
Longlake	71418
Longleaf	71448
Long Straw	71227
Longstreet	71049
Longview	71295
Longville	70652
Longwood (Caddo Parish)	71060
Longwood (East Baton Rouge Parish)	70780
Loranger	70446
Loreauville	70552
Lorelein	71336
Lottie	70756
Louisiana Army Ammunition Plant	71102
Louisiana Correctional and Industrial School	70633
Louisiana Correctional Institute for Women	70776
Louisiana Tech (Part of Ruston)	71272
Louisville (Part of Monroe)	71207
Lower Bonne Idee	71264
Lower Texas	70390
Loyds Bridge	71325
Lozes	70560
Lucas	71105
Lucky	71008
Lucy	70049
Ludington (Part of De Ridder)	70634
Ludvine	70374
Lukeville	70719-22
For specific Lukeville Zip Codes call (504) 749-2900	
Lula	71052
Luling	70070
Luna	71291
Lunita	70661
Lutcher	70071
Lydia	70569
Lyons Point	70526
MacArthur Village (Part of Alexandria)	71301
McBride	70360
McCall	70346
McClendon	70438
McCrea	70715
McDade	71051
McDonoghville (Part of Gretna)	70053
McGinty	71250
McIlhenny	70513
McIntyre	71055
McKneeley	70732
McLeod	70374
McManus	70748
McNary	71433
McNeely	71417
McNeese University (Part of Lake Charles)	70609
Madewood	70390
Madisonville	70447
Magda	71301
Magnolia (Assumption Parish)	70341
Magnolia (East Baton Rouge Parish)	70739
Magnolia (Livingston Parish)	70744
Magnolia (Natchitoches Parish)	71456
Magnolia (Plaquemines Parish)	70083
Magnolia (Terrebonne Parish)	70360
Magnolia Park	71417
Magnolia Woods (Part of Baton Rouge)	70808
Maitland	71326
Major (Part of New Roads)	70760

	ZIP
Mallard Junction	70647
Mamou	70554
Manchester	70647
Mandalay	70360
Mandeville	70448
	70470
For specific Mandeville Zip Codes call (504) 626-8147	
Mangham	71259
Manifest	71343
Mansfield	71052
Mansura	71350
Many	71449
Maplewood (Part of Sulphur)	70663
Marcel	70560
Marco	71447
Maringouin	70757
Marion	71260
Marksville	71351
Marrero	70072-73
For specific Marrero Zip Codes call (504) 341-1741	
Marsalis	71003
Mars Hill	71404
Marthaville	71450
Martin	71019
Martin Park (Part of Alexandria)	71301
Mason	71295
Mathews	70375
Maurepas	70449
Maurice	70555
Maxie	70526
Mayfair (Part of Baton Rouge)	70808
Mayna	71343
Meadowbrook	70056
Meadow Park Heights	71108
Meaux	70510
Mechanicsville (Part of Houma)	70360
Meeker	71346
Melder	71451
Melrose	71452
Melville	71353
Meraux	70075
Mermentau	70556
Mer Rouge	71261
Merrydale	70812
Merryville	70653
Messick	71019
Metairie	70001-11
	70033
	70055
	70060
For specific Metairie Zip Codes call (504) 831-7750	
Methvin	71019
Michoud (Part of New Orleans)	70129
Mid City (Part of New Orleans)	70119
Midland	70557
Midway (Bossier Parish)	71006
Midway (La Salle Parish)	71342
Midway (Rapides Parish)	71430
Midway (St. Mary Parish)	70538
Midway (Webster Parish)	71071
Milldale	70791
Millerton	71038
Millerville (Acadia Parish)	70543
Millerville (East Baton Rouge Parish)	70815
Millikin	71254
Milly Plantation	70764
Milton	70558
Mimosa Park	70070
Minden	71055-58
For specific Minden Zip Codes call (318) 377-1757	
Mineral Springs (Lincoln Parish)	71235
Mineral Springs (Ouachita Parish)	71225
Minerva	70360
Minorca	71334
Mira	71059
Mire	70578
Mitchell	71419
Mittie	70654
Mix	70760
Modeste	70376
Moisant Airport (Part of Kenner)	70141
Moncla	71351
Monette Ferry	71447
Monroe	71201-13
For specific Monroe Zip Codes call (318) 387-6161	
Montcalm	71275

	ZIP
Montegut	70377
Monterey	71354
Montgomery	71454
Monticello (East Baton Rouge Parish)	70815
Monticello (East Carroll Parish)	71254
Montpelier	70422
Montrose	71457
Montz	70068
Mooringsport	71060
Mora	71455
Morbihan	70560
Moreauville	71355
Moreland	71301
Morgan City	70380-81
For specific Morgan City Zip Codes call (504) 384-0277	
Morganza	70759
Morningside (Part of Shreveport)	71108
Morrisonville	70764
Morrow	71356
Morse	70559
Morvant	70301
Morville	71373
Moss Bluff	70611
Moss Lake	70663
Mossville	70663
Mot	71064
Mound	71282
Mount Airy	70076
Mount Carmel	71429
Mount Hermon	70450
Mount Lebanon	71028
Mount Moriah	71226
Mount Olive	71268
Mount Sinai	71038
Mount Union	71277
Mount Zion (Lincoln Parish)	71235
Mount Zion (Winn Parish)	71454
Mowata	70535
Mudville	71432
Mulberry	70360
Myrtle Grove (Iberville Parish)	70764
Myrtle Grove (Plaquemines Parish)	70083
Naborton	71052
Nairn	70041
Naomi	70037
Napoleonville	70390
Napoleonville Junction (Part of Thibodaux)	70301
Naquin	70301
Natalbany	70451
Natchez	71456
Natchitoches	71457-58
For specific Natchitoches Zip Codes call (318) 352-2161	
Neal Landing	70462
Nebo	71342
Negreet	71460
Nesser	70815
Newellton	71357
New Era	71354
Newhope	71266
New Iberia	70560-62
For specific New Iberia Zip Codes call (318) 364-4568	
New Light (Richland Parish)	71259
Newlight (Tensas Parish)	71357
Newllano	71461
New Orleans	70101-90
For specific New Orleans Zip Codes call (504) 589-1111	

COLLEGES & UNIVERSITIES

Dillard University	70122
Louisiana State University Medical Center	70112
Loyola University	70118
New Orleans Baptist Theological Seminary	70126
Southern University at New Orleans	70126
Tulane University	70118
University of New Orleans	70148
Xavier University of Louisiana	70125

FINANCIAL INSTITUTIONS

Alerion Bank	70130
Fidelity Homestead Association	70112
Fifth District Savings & Loan Association	70114
First National Bank of Commerce	70112
Hibernia National Bank	70130

	ZIP		ZIP		ZIP
Oak Tree Federal Savings Bank	70130	Oak Grove (Lincoln Parish)	71275	Pitreville	70525
Whitney National Bank	70130	Oak Grove (Sabine Parish)	71419	Plain Dealing	71064
		Oak Grove (West Carroll Parish)	71263	Plains	70791
HOSPITALS		Oak Hills Place	70808	Plainview	70427
Charity Hospital at New Orleans	70140	Oakland	71260	Plaisance	70570
Hotel Dieu Hospital	70112	Oaklawn (St. Mary Parish)	70538	Plantation Acres (Part of Alexandria)	71301
Ochsner Foundation Hospital	70121	Oaklawn (St. Tammany Parish)	70445	Plaquemine	70764-65
Southern Baptist Hospital	70115	Oakley	70390	For specific Plaquemine Zip Codes call (504) 687-2282	
Touro Infirmary	70115	Oak Manor	70815	Plaquemine Southwest (Part of Plaquemine)	70764
Tulane University Hospital and Clinics	70112	Oaknolia	70777	Plattenville	70393
Veterans Affairs Medical Center	70146	Oak Ridge	71264	Plaucheville	71362
		Oaks	71038	Plaza in Lake Forest, The (Part of New Orleans)	70127
HOTELS/MOTELS		Oakshire Manor	70364	Pleasant Hill (Bienville Parish)	71028
Holiday Inn Crowne Plaza	70130	Oakville	70037	Pleasant Hill (Sabine Parish)	71065
Hotel Marie Antoinette	70130	Oakwood Shopping Center (Part of Gretna)	70053	Pleasant Hills	70811
Hotel Meridien New Orleans	70130	Oberlin	70655	Pleasant Valley	71234
Hyatt Regency New Orleans at Superdome	70140	Oil Center (Part of Lafayette)	70501	Plettenberg	70775
New Orleans Hilton Riverside and Towers	70140	Oil City	71061	Point	71234
Omni Royal Orleans	70140	Okaloosa	71238	Point Au Chien	70377
Royal Sonesta Hotel	70140	Old Athens	71003	Point Blue	70586
ITT Sheraton New Orleans Hotel	70130	Oldfield	70785	Pointe a la Hache	70082
The Westin Canal Place	70130	Old Jefferson	70809-16	Pointe Coupee	70760
		For specific Old Jefferson Zip Codes call (504) 752-8994		Point Pleasant	71220
MILITARY INSTALLATIONS		Old Lafitte	70067	Poland	71301
Army National Guard, Lakefront Airfield	70126	Old Shongaloo	71072	Pollock	71467
Louisiana Air National Guard, FB6171, New Orleans Naval Air Station	70143	Olive Branch	70777	Ponchatoula	70454
MTMC Gulf Outport	70146	Oliver (Part of Hammond)	70401	Ponchatoula Beach	70454
Naval Support Activity	70142	Olivier	70560	Pontchartrain Beach (Part of New Orleans)	70122
New Orleans International Airport, Military	70141	Olla	71465	Poole	71051
Supervisor of Shipbuilding, Conversion and Repair, New Orleans	70142	Ollie	70037	Poplar Grove	70767
United States Army Engineer District, New Orleans	70160	Omega	71276	Portage	70512
United States Property and Fiscal Office for Louisiana	70146	Opelousas	70570-71	Port Allen	70767
8th Coast Guard District, New Orleans	70130	For specific Opelousas Zip Codes call (318) 942-2421		Port Barre	70577
8th Marine Corps District	70142	Orange Grove Plantation	70301	Port Barrow (Part of Donaldsonville)	70346
926th Fighter Group, New Orleans Naval Air Station (AFRES)	70143	Oretta	70633	Port Eads	70091
		Oscar	70762	Porters Curve	70450
New Roads	70760	Ossun	70583	Porterville	71071
New Rockdale	71052	Ostrica	70041	Port Fourchon	70357
New Sarpy	70078	Otis	71466	Port Gardner	70791
Newton	70601	Ouachita City	71280	Port Hickey	70791
New Verda	71404	Oubre (Part of Loreauville)	70552	Port Manchac	70421
Nibletts Bluff	70668	Oxford (De Soto Parish)	71052	Port of West Saint Mary	70538
Nicholas	70560	Oxford (St. Mary Parish)	70538	Port Sulphur	70083
Nicholls University (Part of Thibodaux)	70301	Pace	71055	Port Vincent	70726
Nickel	71465	Packton	71483	Potash	70083
Ninock	71051	Paincourtville	70391	Pot Cove	70586
Noble	71462	Palmetto	71358	Poufette	70560
Noles Landing	71073	Palo Alto	70346	Powhatan	71066
Norah	70374	Panchoville	70532	Poydras	70085
Norco	70079	Panola	71254	Prairie Ronde	70570
Normandy Park	70094	Paradis	70080	Prairieville	70769
Norris Springs	71368	Paradise	71360	Pratt	71028
Northeast Louisiana University (Part of Monroe)	71209	Paradise Manor	70123	Presque Isle	70363
Northgate Mall (Part of Lafayette)	70501	Parhams	71343	Pride	70770
North Hodge	71247	Park Manor	70003	Prien	70605
North Merrydale	70812	Parks	70582	Prien Lake Mall (Part of Lake Charles)	70601
North Monroe	71201	Parkside Manor	70123	Princeton	71067
North Plaquemine (Part of Plaquemine)	70764	Park Vista (Part of Opelousas)	70570	Promised Land	70040
North Shore	70458	Patoutville	70544	Prospect (Grant Parish)	71423
North Shore Beach	70458	Patterson	70392	Prospect (St. Charles Parish)	70078
North Slidell (Part of Slidell)	70458	Paulina	70763	Provencal	71468
Northwestern (Part of Natchitoches)	71457	Pearl River	70452	Providence	70062
Norton Shop	71072	Peason	71429	Puckett	70791
Norwood	70761	Pecan Grove	70094	Pumpkin Center	70403
Notleyville	70512	Pecaniere	70512	Punkin Center	71247
Notnac	71357	Pecan Island	70548	Quaid	71343
Numa	70560	Pecan Place	70764	Quimby	71282
Nunez	70548	Peck	71368	Quitman	71268
Oakdale	71463	Pelican	71063	Raceland	70394
Oak Forest	70356	Perkins	70633	Ragley	70657
Oak Grove (Ascension Parish)	70769	Perry	70575	Ramah	70757
Oak Grove (Cameron Parish)	70643	Perryville	71220	Rambin	71063
Oak Grove (Grant Parish)	71417	Phoenix	70042	Randolph	71256
		Pickering	71446	Rapides	71409
		Pierre Bossier Mall (Part of Bossier City)	71112	Ratliff	70390
		Pierre Part	70339	Rattan	71429
		Pierre Part Settlement	70339	Rayne	70578
		Pilottown	70081	Rayville	71269
		Pine	70438	Readhimer	71070
		Pine Coupee	71427	Red Chute	71037
		Pine Grove (Ouachita Parish)	71201	Reddell	70580
		Pine Grove (St. Helena Parish)	70453	Red Gum	71334
		Pine Island	70532	Redland (Bossier Parish)	71064
		Pine Oak Terrace (Part of Shreveport)	71108	Redland (Evangeline Parish)	70554
		Pine Prairie	70576	Red Oaks	70815
		Pineville	71360-61	Reeves	70658
		For specific Pineville Zip Codes call (318) 442-3254		Reggio	70085
		Pioneer	71266	Reids	70656
		Pitkin	70656	Remy	70763
				Reserve	70084
				Rhinehart	71363
				Rhymes	71269

	ZIP		ZIP		ZIP
Turnerville (Part of Plaquemine)	70764	Wadesboro	70454	White Hall (St. James Parish)	70723
Twin Oaks	71223	Waggaman	70094	White Hills	70714
Uncle Sam	70792	Wakefield	70784	White Sulphur Springs	71371
Union	70723	Waldheim	70433	Whiteville	71322
Union Church	71268	Walker (Jackson Parish)	71251	Whittington	71301
Union Hill (Rapides Parish)	71433	Walker (Livingston Parish)	70785	Wickland Terrace	70815
Union Hill (Winn Parish)	71483	Wallace	70049	Wickliffe	70783
Union Landing	70754	Wallace Ridge	71343	Wildsville	71377
Union Springs	71419	Walls	70720	Wildwood (Assumption Parish)	70390
Unionville	71235	Walters	71343		
University (Part of Baton Rouge)	70803	Ward	71463	Wildwood (East Baton Rouge Parish)	70808
Upland	71220	Warden	71232	Willhite	71234
Upstream	70123	Wardview	71064	Williams	71105
Urania	71480	Wardville (Morehouse Parish)	71220	Williana	71423
Utility	71343	Wardville (Rapides Parish)	71360	Willow Glen	71301
Vacherie	70090	Warnerton	70438	Wills Point	70040
Valmar	70075	Warsaw Landing	70462	Wilmer	70444
Valverda	70757	Washington	70589	Wilshire Park	71301
Vanceville	71111	Waterloo	70783	Wilson	70789
Varnado	70467	Waterproof (Tensas Parish)	71375	Wilsona	71366
Vatican	70520	Waterproof (Terrebonne Parish)	70360	Wilson Point	71301
Vaughn	71220	Watson	70786	Wilton Subdivision	71107
Velma	70422	Waverly	71232	Winnfield	71483
Venice	70091	Waxia	70589	Winnsboro	71295
Ventress	70783	Weil	71301	Wisner	71378
Verda	71481	Welcome	70086	Womack (Jackson Parish)	71226
Verdun	70754	Weldon	71222	Womack (Red River Parish)	71068
Verdunville	70538	Welsh	70591	Woodardville	71068
Vernon	71270	Wemple	71052	Woodhaven	70466
Verret	70085	Westdale	71105	Woodland	70083
Veterans Administration Hospital (Part of Shreveport)	71101	Western Kraft	71411	Woodlawn (Assumption Parish)	70390
		West Ferriday	71334		
		Westfield	70390	Woodlawn (Jefferson Davis Parish)	70647
Vick	71372	Westlake	70669		
Vidalia	71373	Westminster	70809	Woodlawn (Plaquemines Parish)	70040
Vidrine	70586	West Monroe	71291-94		
Vienna	71270	For specific West Monroe Zip Codes call (318) 387-8821		Woodlawn (Terrebonne Parish)	70360
Vieux Carre (Part of New Orleans)	70112			Woodside	71353
Village East	70360	Weston	71251	Woodville	71270
Village St. George	70808	Westover	70767	Woodworth	71485
Ville Platte	70586	West Pointe a la Hache	70083	Wyandotte	70380
Vincent Landing	70663	Westport	70656	Wyatt	71251
Vincent Park	70075	Westside	71301	Yellow Pine	71073
Vinton	70668	West Slidell (Part of Slidell)	70460	Youngsville	70592
Violet	70092	Westwego	70094-96	Zachary	70791
Vista Village Regional Shopping Center (Part of Opelousas)	70570	For specific Westwego Zip Codes call (504) 341-2411		Zebedee	71269
				Zenoria	71371
		Weyanoke	70787	Zion	71432
Vivian	71082	Whatley Landing	71371	Zion City (Part of Baton Rouge)	70811
Vixen	71418	Wheeling	71454		
Voorhies	71355	White	70301	Zwolle	71486
Vowells Mill	71469	White Castle	70788	Zylks	71069
Wade Correctional Center	71038	Whitehall (La Salle Parish)	71342		
		Whitehall (Livingston Parish)	70449		

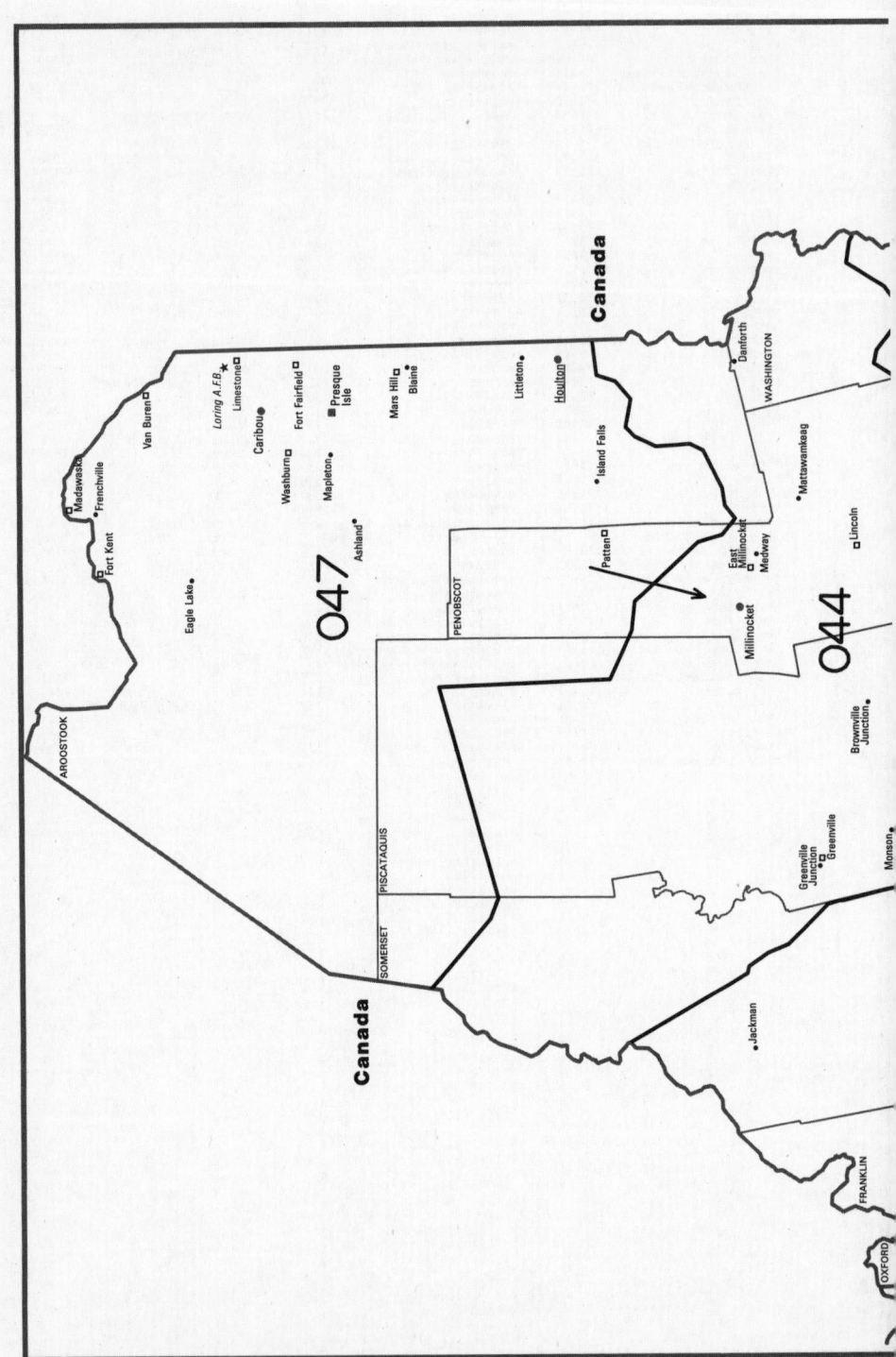

Canada

Van Buren

Madawaska
Frenchville

Fort Kent

Eagle Lake

Loring A.F.B.
Limestone

Caribou

Washburn

Fort Fairfield

Presque
Isle

Mapleton

Ashland

Mars Hill
Blaine

Littleton

Houlton

Island Falls

Patten

East
Millinocket
Medway

Millinocket

Danforth

WASHINGTON

Mattawamkeag

Lincoln

Brownville
Junction

O47

O44

PENOBSCOT

AROOSTOOK

PISCATAQUIS

SOMERSET

Greenville
Junction
Greenville

Monson

Canada

Jackman

FRANKLIN

OXFORD

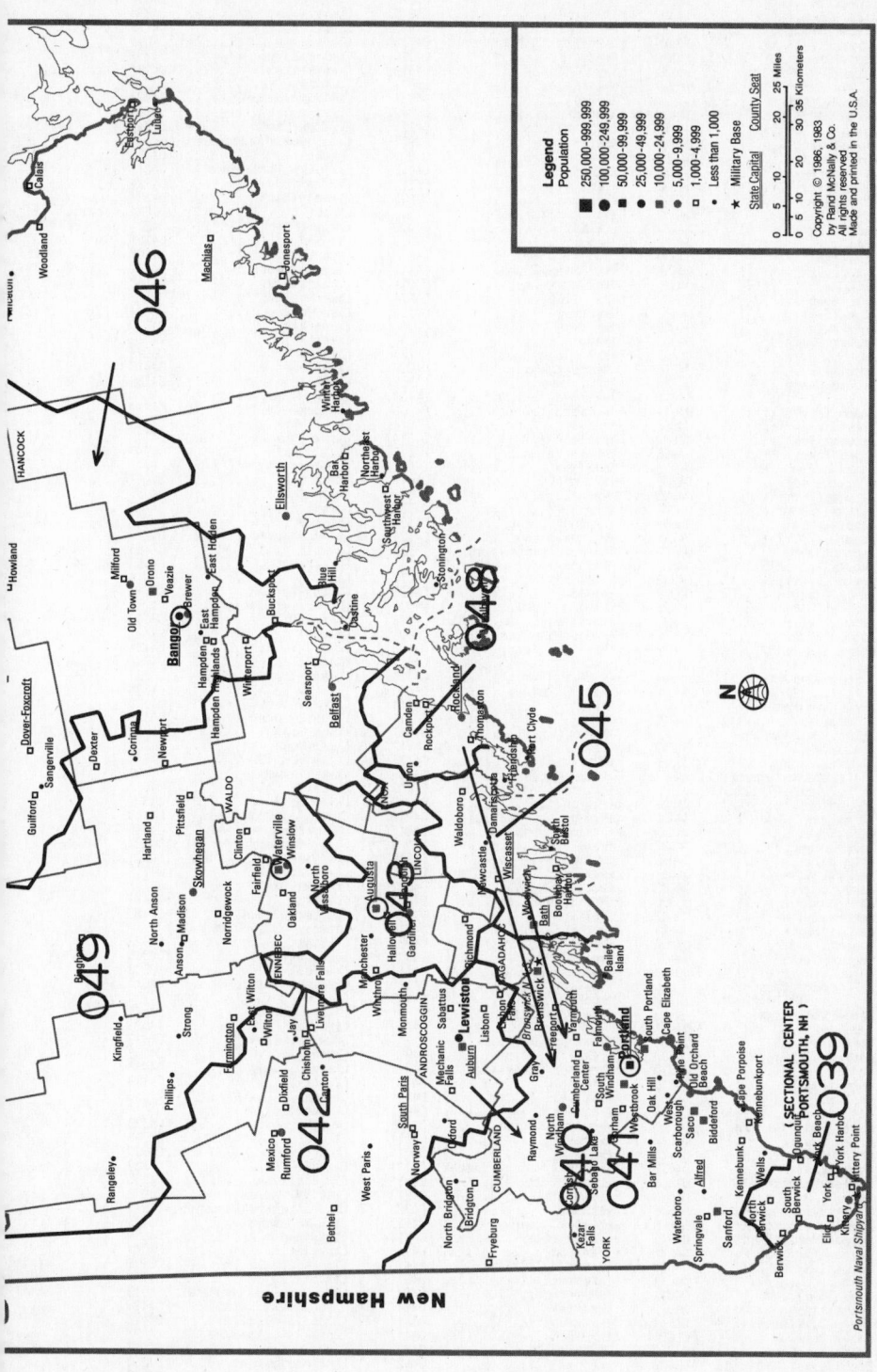

	ZIP
Abbot (Town)	04406
Abbotts Mill	04219
Abbot Village	04406
Acadia Terrace	04785
Acton	04001
Acton (Town)	04001
Addison	04606
Addison (Town)	04606
Admiralty Village	03904
Airport Mall (Part of Bangor)	04401
Albion	04910
Albion (Town)	04910
Alexander	04619
Alexander (Town)	04619
Alfred	04002
Alfred (Town)	04002
Alfred Mills	04002
Allagash (Town)	04774
Allagash	04774
Allens Mills	04938
Alna	04535
Alna (Town)	04535
Alna Center	04535
Alton (Town)	04468
Amherst	04605
Amherst (Town)	04605
Amity (Town)	04465
Andover	04216
Andover (Town)	04216
Anson	04911
Anson (Town)	04911
Appleton	04862
Appleton (Town)	04862
Argyle (Town)	04468
Aroostook Farm (Part of Presque Isle)	04769
Arrowsic (Town)	04530
Arundel (Town)	04046
Ashdale	04565
Ashland	04732
Ashland (Town)	04732
Ashville	04607
Athens	04912
Athens (Town)	04912
Atkinson (Town)	04426
Atkinson Corner	04426
Atkinson Mills	04426
Atlantic	04608
Auburn	04210-12
For specific Auburn Zip Codes call (207) 786-0604	
Auburn Mall (Part of Auburn)	04210
Auburn Plains (Part of Auburn)	04210
Augusta	04330-38
For specific Augusta Zip Codes call (207) 622-6114	
Aurora (Town)	04408
Aurora	04408
Avon (Town)	04966
Back Narrows	04537
Bailey Island	04003
Baileyville (Town)	04694
Baker Corner	04082
Balch Pond	03830
Bald Head	03907
Baldwin (Town)	04024
Bancroft	04497
Bancroft (Town)	04497
Bangor	04401-02
For specific Bangor Zip Codes call (207) 941-2016	
Bangor Mall (Part of Bangor)	04401
Bar Harbor	04609
Bar Harbor (Town)	04609
Baring	04619
Baring (Town)	04619
Bar Mills	04004
Barnard (Town)	04414
Barrett (Part of Caribou)	04736
Bartlett Mills	04043
Basin Mills	04473
Bass Harbor	04653
Batchelders Crossing	04350
Bath	04530
Bay Point	04548
Bayside (Hancock County)	04605
Bayside (Waldo County)	04915
Bayview (Part of Saco)	04072
Bayville	04536
Beals	04611
Beals (Town)	04611
Beans Corner	04225
Beaver Cove (Town)	04441
Beaver Dam	03901
Beddington (Town)	04622
Beech Ridge	03909
Belfast	04915
Belgrade	04917

	ZIP
Belgrade (Town)	04917
Belgrade Lakes	04918
Belmont (Town)	04915
Belmont Corner	04915
Benedicta	04733
Benton	04910
Benton (Town)	04910
Benton Falls	04901
Benton Station	04937
Bernard	04612
Berry Mills	04224
Berwick	03901
Berwick (Town)	03901
Bethel	04217
Bethel (Town)	04217
Biddeford	04005
Biddeford Pool (Part of Biddeford)	04006
Bingham	04920
Bingham (Town)	04920
Birch Harbor	04613
Birch Island	04011
Black Point	04074
Blackstrap	04105
Blackwell	04950
Blaine	04734
Blaine (Town)	04734
Blaisdell Corners	04027
Blake Corner	04250
Blanchard	04406
Blanchard (Town)	04406
Blue Hill	04614
Blue Hill (Town)	04614
Blue Hill Falls	04615
Blue Point	04074
Bolsters Mills	04040
Bonny Eagle	04093
Boothbay	04537
Boothbay (Town)	04537
Boothbay Harbor	04538
Boothbay Harbor (Town)	04538
Boothbay Park (Part of Saco)	04072
Bowdoin	04008
Bowdoin (Town)	04008
Bowdoinham	04008
Bowdoinham (Town)	04008
Bowerbank (Town)	04426
Bradford	04410
Bradford (Town)	04410
Bradford Center	04410
Bradley	04411
Bradley (Town)	04411
Bremen (Town)	04551
Brewer	04412
Bridgewater	04735
Bridgewater (Town)	04735
Bridgton	04009
Bridgton (Town)	04009
Brighton	04912
Brighton (Town)	04912
Bristol	04539
Bristol (Town)	04539
Brixham	03909
Broad Cove	04572
Brookhaven	04062
Brooklin	04616
Brooklin (Town)	04616
Brooks	04921
Brooks (Town)	04921
Brooksville (Town)	04617
Brooksville	04617
Brookton	04413
Brown Corner (Aroostook County)	04750
Brown Corner (Waldo County)	04915
Brownfield (Town)	04010
Brownfield	04010
Brownville	04414
Brownville (Town)	04414
Brownville Junction	04415
Brunswick	04011
Brunswick (Town)	04011
Brunswick Naval Air Station	04011
Brunswick Station	04011
Bryant Pond	04219
Buckfield	04220
Buckfield (Town)	04220
Bucks Harbor	04618
Bucksport	04416
Bucksport (Town)	04416
Bunganuc Landing	04011
Bunkers Harbor	04613
Burkettville	04574
Burlington	04417
Burlington (Town)	04417
Burnham	04922
Burnham (Town)	04922
Burnt Meadow Pond	04041
Bustins Island	04013

	ZIP
Buxton (Town)	04093
Buxton Center	04093
Byron	04275
Byron (Town)	04275
Calais	04619
Caldwel Corner	04281
Caldwell Corner	04281
Cambridge	04923
Cambridge (Town)	04923
Camden	04843
Camden (Town)	04843
Campbell (Part of Presque Isle)	04769
Camp Ellis (Part of Saco)	04072
Canaan	04924
Canaan (Town)	04924
Canton	04221
Canton (Town)	04221
Canton Point	04221
Cape Cottage	04107
Cape Elizabeth (Town)	04107
Cape Elizabeth	04107
Cape Neddick	03902
Cape Porpoise	04014
Capitol Island	04538
Caratunk	04925
Caratunk (Town)	04925
Cardville	04418
Caribou	04736
Caribou Road (Part of Presque Isle)	04769
Carmel	04419
Carmel (Town)	04419
Carrabassett	04947
Carrabassett Valley (Town)	04947
Carroll	04487
Carroll (Town)	04487
Carson	04786
Carthage	04224
Carthage (Town)	04224
Cary	04465
Cary (Town)	04465
Casco	04015
Casco (Town)	04015
Cash Corner (Part of South Portland)	04106
Castine	04421
Castine (Town)	04421
Castle Hill (Town)	04757
Caswell (Town)	04750
Cathance	04086
Cedar Grove	04342
Center Lebanon	04027
Center Lovell	04016
Center Minot	04258
Center Montville	04941
Center Vassalboro	04989
Centerville	04623
Centerville (Town)	04623
Central Aroostook (Town)	04760
Central Hancock (Town)	04640
Central Somerset (Town)	04920
Chamberlain	04541
Chapman	04757
Chapman (Town)	04757
Charleston	04422
Charleston (Town)	04422
Charleston Correctional Facility	04422
Charlotte (Town)	04666
Chases Pond	03909
Chebeague Island	04017
Chelsea	04330
Chelsea (Town)	04345
Cherryfield	04622
Cherryfield (Town)	04622
Chester	04458
Chester (Town)	04458
Chesterville	04938
Chesterville (Town)	04938
Chesuncook	04441
Chicopee	04038
China	04926
China (Town)	04926
Chisholm	04239
Christmas Cove	04568
Cider Hill	03909
City Point (Part of Belfast)	04915
Clapboard Island	04105
Clark Island	04859
Clarks Mill	04042
Clay Hill	03902
Clayton Lake	04737
Cliff Island (Part of Portland)	04019
Clifton	04428
Clifton (Town)	04428
Clinton	04927
Clinton (Town)	04927
Cobbs Bridge	04260
Coburn Gore	04936
Codyville (Town)	04490

	ZIP		ZIP		ZIP
Frye	04235	Harmony	04942	Jonesboro	04648
Fryeburg	04037	Harmony (Town)	04942	Jonesboro (Town)	04648
Fryeburg (Town)	04037	Harpswell (Town)	04079	Jones Corner	04354
Fryeburg Center	04037	Harpswell Center	04079	Jonesport	04649
Fryeburg Harbor	04037	Harrimans Point	04578	Jonesport (Town)	04649
Gardiner	04344-46	Harrington	04643	Kalers Corner	04572
For specific Gardiner Zip Codes		Harrington (Town)	04643	Keegan	04785
call (207) 582-6160		Harrison	04040	Kelleyland	04694
Garfield (Town)	04732	Harrison (Town)	04040	Kendalls Corner (Part of	
Garland	04939	Hartford	04221	Belfast)	04915
Garland (Town)	04939	Hartford (Town)	04221	Kenduskeag	04450
Georgetown	04548	Hartland	04943	Kenduskeag (Town)	04450
Georgetown (Town)	04548	Hartland (Town)	04943	Kennebago Lake	04970
Gerrishville	04693	Hartsfords Point	04442	Kennebec	04654
Gilbertville	04221	Harts Neck	04860	Kennebunk	04043
Gilead	04217	Hatch's Corner	04342	Kennebunk (Town)	04043
Gilead (Town)	04217	Haven	04616	Kennebunk Beach	04043
Glantz Corner	04062	Haynesville	04446	Kennebunk Landing	04043
Glenburn (Town)	04401	Haynesville (Town)	04446	Kennebunk Lower Village	04046
Glenburn Center	04401	Head of Tide (Part of		Kennebunkport	04046
Glen Cove	04846	Belfast)	04915	Kennebunkport (Town)	04046
Glendon	04572	Head Tide	04535	Kennedy Terrace	04785
Glenmere	04860	Hebron	04238	Kents Hill	04349
Glenwood (Town)	04497	Hebron (Town)	04238	Kezar Falls	04047
Goodings (Part of Presque		Hebron Station	04238	Kingfield	04947
Isle)	04769	Hendricks Harbor	04576	Kingfield (Town)	04947
Good Will-Hinckley School	04944	Hermon	04401	Kingman	04451
Goodwins Mills	04005	Hermon (Town)	04401	Kingman (Town)	04451
Goose Rocks Beach	04046	Hermon Center	04401	Kingsbury (Town)	04942
Gorham	04038	Heron Island	04568	Kinney Shores (Part of	
Gorham (Town)	04038	Hersey (Town)	04765	Saco)	04072
Gotts Island	04653	Hibberts (Town)	04341	Kittery	03904
Gould Landing	04401	Higgins Beach	04074	Kittery (Town)	03904
Gouldsboro	04607	Higginsville	04450	Kittery Point	03905
Gouldsboro (Town)	04607	Highland (Knox County)	04864	Knights Landing	04414
Grand Beach	04064	Highland (Somerset County)		Knightville (Part of South	
Grand Falls (Town)	04417	(Town)	04961	Portland)	04106
Grand Isle	04746	Highland Lake (Part of		Knowles Corner	04780
Grand Isle (Town)	04746	Westbrook)	04092	Knox (Town)	04986
Grand Lake Stream	04637	Highland Lake Vista	04062	Knox Center	04986
Grand Lake Stream (Town)	04637	Highpine	04090	Knox Corner	04986
Granite Hill (Part of		Hills Beach (Part of		Knox Station	04986
Hallowell)	04347	Biddeford)	04005	Kokadjo	04441
Grass Corner	04750	Hillside	04024	Lagrange	04453
Gray (Town)	04039	Hinckley	04944	Lagrange (Town)	04453
Gray (Cumberland County)	04039	Hiram	04041	Lake Arrowhead Estates	04061
Grays Corner	04676	Hiram (Town)	04041	Lake City	04843
Great Diamond Island (Part		Hodgdon	04730	Lake Moxie	04985
of Portland)	04109	Hodgdon (Town)	04730	Lake View (Town)	04463
Great Falls (Part of Auburn)	04210	Holden	04429	Lakeville (Town)	04487
Great Pond	04408	Holden (Town)	04429	Lakewood	04976
Great Pond (Town)	04408	Hollandville	04048	Lambert Lake	04454
Great Works (Part of Old		Hollis (Town)	04042	Lamoine (Town)	04605
Town)	04468	Hollis Center	04042	Lamoine	04605
Greeley Landing	04426	Holmes Mill (Part of Belfast)	04915	Lamoine Beach	04605
Greenbush	04467	Hope	04847	Lamoine Corner	04605
Greenbush (Town)	04467	Hope (Town)	04847	Larone	04937
Greene	04236	Houghton	04275	Larrabee	04655
Greene (Town)	04236	Houlton	04730	Lawry	04547
Greenfield	04423	Houlton (Town)	04730	Lebanon (Town)	04027
Greenfield (Town)	04423	Howes Corner	04282	Lee	04455
Green Lake	04429	Howland (Town)	04448	Lee (Town)	04455
Greens Corner	04988	Howland	04448	Leeds (Town)	04263
Greenville	04441	Hoyttown	04654	Leeds	04263
Greenville (Town)	04441	Hudson	04449	Leeds Junction	04263
Greenville	04441	Hudson (Town)	04449	Levant	04456
Greenville Junction	04442	Hulls Cove	04644	Levant (Town)	04456
Greenwood	04289	Hunnewell Hill	04074	Lewiston	04240-43
Greenwood (Town)	04289	Hunts Corner	04217	For specific Lewiston Zip Codes	
Grimes Mill (Part of Caribou)	04736	Hutchins Corner	04942	call (207) 783-8551	
Grindstone	04460	Indian Island	04468	Lewiston Junction (Part of	
Grindstone Neck	04693	Indian Point	04660	Auburn)	04210
Grove	04638	Indian River	04606	Lewiston Lower (Part of	
Groveville	04038	Indian Township		Lewiston)	04240
Guerette	04783	Passamaquoddy Indian		Lewiston Mall (Part of	
Guilford	04443	Reservation	04668	Lewiston)	04240
Guilford (Town)	04443	Industrial (Part of Presque		Lewiston Upper (Part of	
Guillemette	04073	Isle)	04769	Lewiston)	04240
Guinea Corner (Part of		Industry (Town)	04938	Libby Hill (Part of Gardiner)	04345
Biddeford)	04005	Ingall's Hill	04009	Liberty	04949
Hackett Mills	04258	Intervale	04260	Liberty (Town)	04949
Halldale	04986	Irish Settlement	04424	Lille	04749
Hallowell	04347	Island Falls	04747	Lily Bay	04441
Hall Quarry	04660	Island Falls (Town)	04747	Limerick	04048
Hamlin	04785	Isle au Haut	04645	Limerick (Town)	04048
Hamlin (Town)	04785	Isle Au Haut (Town)	04645	Limerick Mills	04048
Hammond (Town)	04730	Isle of Springs	04549	Limestone	04750-51
Hampden	04444	Islesboro	04848	For specific Limestone Zip Codes	
Hampden (Town)	04444	Islesboro (Town)	04848	call (207) 325-4838	
Hampden	04444	Islesford	04646	Limington	04049
Hampden Highlands	04444	Jackman	04945	Limington (Town)	04049
Hancock	04640	Jackman (Town)	04945	Lincoln (Penobscot County)	
Hancock (Town)	04640	Jackson	04921	(Town)	04457
Hancock Point	04640	Jackson (Town)	04921	Lincoln (Oxford County)	
Hanover	04237	Jackson Corners	04921	(Town)	03579
Hanover (Town)	04237	Jacksonville	04630	Lincoln	04457
Harborside	04642	Jay	04239	Lincoln Center	04458
Hardings	04011	Jay (Town)	04239	Lincoln Mills	04928
Harmon Beach	04075	Jefferson	04348	Lincolnville	04849
Harmons Corner (Part of		Jefferson (Town)	04348	Lincolnville (Town)	04849
Auburn)	04210	Jemtland	04783	Lincolnville Center	04850

	ZIP		ZIP		ZIP
Linekin	04544	Mechanic Falls	04256	New Sweden	04762
Linneus	04730	Meddybemps	04657	New Sweden (Town)	04762
Linneus (Town)	04730	Meddybemps (Town)	04657	Newtown (Part of	
Lisbon	04250	Medford	04453	Biddeford)	04005
Lisbon (Town)	04250	Medford (Town)	04453	New Vineyard	04956
Lisbon Center	04251	Medford Center	04453	New Vineyard (Town)	04956
Lisbon Falls	04252	Medomak	04551	Nicolin (Part of Ellsworth)	04605
Litchfield	04350	Medway	04460	Nobleboro	04555
Litchfield (Town)	04350	Medway (Town)	04460	Nobleboro (Town)	04555
Litchfield Corners	04350	Melvin Heights	04843	Norridgewock	04957
Litchfield Plains	04350	Mercer	04957	Norridgewock (Town)	04957
Little Deer Isle	04650	Mercer (Town)	04957	North Alfred	04002
Little Falls	04082	Merepoint	04053	North Amity	04465
Little Falls-South Windham	04082	Merrill (Town)	04780	North Anson	04958
Littlefield (Part of Auburn)	04210	Mexico	04257	North Auburn (Part of	
Littlefield Corner (Part of		Mexico (Town)	04257	Auburn)	04210
Auburn)	04210	Middledam	04216	North Augusta (Part of	
Little Machias	04626	Middle Intervale	04217	Augusta)	04330
Littleton	04730	Milbridge	04658	North Baldwin	04024
Littleton (Town)	04730	Milbridge (Town)	04658	North Bancroft	04424
Livermore	04253	Milford	04461	North Bangor (Part of	
Livermore (Town)	04253	Milford (Town)	04461	Bangor)	04401
Livermore Falls	04254	Milliken Mills	04064	North Bath (Part of Bath)	04530
Livermore Falls (Town)	04254	Millinocket (Town)	04462	North Belgrade	04963
Locke Mills	04255	Millinocket	04462	North Berwick	03906
Long Beach (Cumberland		Milltown (Part of Calais)	04619	North Berwick (Town)	03906
County)	04075	Milo	04463	North Blue Hill	04614
Long Beach (York County)	03910	Milo (Town)	04463	North Bradford	04410
Longcove	04857	Milton	04219	North Bridgton	04057
Long Island (Part of		Milton (Town)	04219	North Brooklin	04661
Portland)	04050	Minot	04258	North Brooksville	04617
Lookout	04645	Minot (Town)	04258	North Buckfield	04220
Loring Air Force Base	04751	Minturn	04659	North Castine	04472
Lovell	04051	Molunkus	04451	North Chesterville	04938
Lovell (Town)	04051	Monarda	04776	North Cutler	04630
Lowell	04433	Monhegan	04852	North Dixmont	04932
Lowell (Town)	04433	Monhegan (Town)	04852	North East Carry	04478
Lower Dennysville	04628	Monmouth	04259	Northeast Harbor	04662
Lubec	04652	Monmouth (Town)	04259	Northeast Piscataquis	
Lubec (Town)	04652	Monroe	04951	(Town)	04462
Lucerne-In-Maine	04429	Monroe (Town)	04951	Northeast Somerset (Town)	04920
Ludlow	04730	Monroe Center	04951	North Edgecomb	04556
Ludlow (Town)	04730	Monson	04464	North Ellsworth (Part of	
Lyman (Town)	04005	Monson (Town)	04464	Ellsworth)	04605
Lynchville	04231	Monticello	04760	Northern Maine Junction	04401
McFarlands Corner	04941	Monticello (Town)	04760	North Fairfield	04937
Machias	04654	Montsweag	04578	North Falmouth	04105
Machias (Town)	04654	Montville (Town)	04941	Northfield	04654
Machiasport	04655	Moody	04054	Northfield (Town)	04654
Machiasport (Town)	04655	Moody Beach	04054	North Franklin (Town)	04936
Mackworth Island	04105	Moosehead	04442	North Fryeburg	04058
Mackworth Point	04105	Moose River	04945	North Gorham	04075
MacMahan	04548	Moose River (Town)	04945	North Gray	04039
Macwahoc	04451	Moro (Town)	04780	North Guilford	04443
Macwahoc (Town)	04451	Morrill	04952	North Harpswell	04079
Madawaska	04756	Morrill (Town)	04952	North Haven	04853
Madawaska (Town)	04756	Morris Corner	04750	North Haven (Town)	04853
Madawaska Lake	04783	Morse Corners	04928	North Hermon	04401
Madison	04950	Moscow (Town)	04920	North Hill	04220
Madison (Town)	04950	Moscow	04920	North Islesboro	04848
Madrid	04966	Mount Chase (Town)	04765	North Jay	04262
Madrid (Town)	04966	Mount Desert	04660	North Lamoine	04605
Magalloway (Town)	03579	Mount Desert (Town)	04660	North Lebanon	04027
Maine Mall (Part of South		Mount Pisgah	04538	North Leeds	04263
Portland)	04106	Mount Vernon	04352	North Limington	04049
Mainstream	04942	Mount Vernon (Town)	04352	North Livermore	04254
Mallison Falls	04082	Murphy Corner	04578	North Lovell	04231
Manchester	04351	Muscongus	04551	North Lubec	04652
Manchester (Town)	04351	Muscongus Bay	04555	North Lyndon (Part of	
Manset	04656	Naples	04055	Caribou)	04736
Maple Grove	04742	Naples (Town)	04055	North Monmouth	04265
Mapleton	04757	Nashville (Town)	04732	North Monroe	04951
Mapleton (Town)	04757	Naskeag	04616	North Newcastle	04553
Maplewood	04095	Naval Air Station	04011	North New Portland	04961
Mariaville	04605	Naval Communications Unit	04630	North Norway	04268
Mariaville (Town)	04605	Naval Shipyard	03801	North Orland	04429
Marion	04628	Nequasset	04579	North Orrington	04474
Marlboro	04605	Newagen	04552	North Oxford (Town)	03579
Marrtown	04548	New Auburn (Part of		North Palermo	04354
Marshfield	04654	Auburn)	04210	North Paris	04289
Marshfield (Town)	04654	Newburgh	04444	North Parsonsfield	04047
Mars Hill	04758	Newburgh (Town)	04444	North Penobscot (Hancock	
Mars Hill (Town)	04758	New Canada (Town)	04743	County)	04476
Mars Hill-Blaine	04758	Newcastle	04553	North Penobscot	
Marshville	04643	Newcastle (Town)	04553	(Penobscot County)	
Marston Corner (Part of		Newfield	04056	(Town)	04462
Auburn)	04210	Newfield (Town)	04056	North Perry	04667
Martin	04547	New Gloucester	04260	Northport (Town)	04849
Martinsville	04860	New Gloucester (Town)	04260	Northport	04849
Masardis	04759	Newhall	04062	North Pownal	04069
Masardis (Town)	04759	New Harbor	04554	North Raymond	04274
Mason Bay	04649	New Limerick	04761	North Scarborough	04074
Mast Landing	04032	New Limerick (Town)	04761	North Searsmont	04973
Matinicus	04851	Newport	04953	North Searsport	04974
Matinicus Isle (Town)	04851	Newport (Town)	04953	North Sebago	04029
Mattawamkeag	04459	New Portland	04954	North Sedgwick	04676
Mattawamkeag (Town)	04459	New Portland (Town)	04954	North Shapleigh	04060
Maxfield (Town)	04453	Newry	04261	North Sullivan	04664
Mayberry Hill	04015	Newry (Town)	04261	North Turner	04266
Mayville	04217	New Sharon	04955	North Vassalboro	04962
Mechanic Falls (Town)	04256	New Sharon (Town)	04955	North Wade	04786

	ZIP
North Waldoboro	04572
North Warren	04864
North Washington (Town)	04686
North Waterboro	04061
North Waterford	04267
North Wayne	04284
Northwest Aroostook	04770
Northwest Aroostook (Town)	04788
Northwest Bethel	04217
Northwest Hancock (Town)	04408
Northwest Piscataquis (Town)	04441
Northwest Somerset (Town)	04945
North Whitefield	04353
North Windsor	04361
North Woodstock	04219
North Yarmouth (Town)	04021
Norumbega	04617
Norway	04268
Norway (Town)	04268
Norway Center	04268
Norway Lake	04268
Number Four	04051
Oakfield	04763
Oakfield (Town)	04763
Oak Hill (Androscoggin County)	04273
Oak Hill (Cumberland County)	04074
Oakland	04963
Oakland (Town)	04963
Oak Point	04605
Oak Ridge (Part of Biddeford)	04005
Oak Terrace	03904
Ocean Park	04063
Ocean Point	04544
Oceanview Harbor	04074
Oceanville	04681
Ogontz	04478
Ogunquit	03907
Ogunquit (Town)	03907
Olamon	04467
Olde Mill Brook	04074
Old Orchard Beach (Town)	04064
Old Orchard Beach	04064
Old Town	04468
Onawa	04443
Oquossoc	04964
Orffs Corner	04572
Orient	04471
Orient (Town)	04471
Orland	04472
Orland (Town)	04472
Orono	04473
Orono (Town)	04473
Orrington	04474
Orrington (Town)	04474
Orrington Center	04474
Orrs Island	04066
Osborn (Town)	04605
Otis	04605
Otis (Town)	04605
Otisfield	04270
Otisfield (Town)	04270
Otter Creek	04665
Owls Head	04854
Owls Head (Town)	04854
Oxbow	04764
Oxbow (Town)	04764
Oxford	04270
Oxford (Town)	04270
Paine Corner	04281
Palermo	04354
Palermo (Town)	04354
Palmyra	04965
Palmyra (Town)	04965
Paris	04271
Paris (Town)	04271
Parker Head	04562
Parkman	04443
Parkman (Town)	04443
Parsonsfield	04048
Parsonsfield (Town)	04028
Passadumkeag	04475
Passadumkeag (Town)	04475
Passamaquoddy Indian Township Indian Reservation (Town)	04668
Passamaquoddy Pleasant Point Indian Reservation (Town)	04667
Patten	04765
Patten (Town)	04765
Peabbles Cove	04107
Peaks Island (Part of Portland)	04108
Pea Ridge	04458
Pejepscot	04067
Pelton Hill (Part of Augusta)	04330

	ZIP
Pemaquid	04558
Pemaquid Beach	04554
Pemaquid Harbor	04558
Pemaquid Point	04554
Pembroke	04666
Pembroke (Town)	04666
Penley's Corner (Part of Auburn)	04210
Penobscot	04476
Penobscot (Town)	04476
Penobscot Indian Island Indian Reservation (Town)	04468
Perham	04766
Perham (Town)	04766
Perkins (Town)	04357
Perry (Town)	04667
Perry (Aroostook County)	04769
Perry (Washington County)	04667
Perrys Corner	04048
Peru	04290
Peru (Town)	04290
Peter Dana Point	04668
Phair (Part of Presque Isle)	04769
Phillips	04966
Phillips (Town)	04966
Phippsburg	04562
Phippsburg (Town)	04562
Pigeon Hill	04658
Pike Corner	04015
Pine Cliff	04576
Pine Hill	03902
Pine Park	04064
Pine Point	04074
Pittsfield	04967
Pittsfield (Town)	04967
Pittston	04345
Pittston (Town)	04345
Pittston Farm	04478
Plaisted	04767
Plantation Number Fourteen (Town)	04628
Plantation Number Twenty-one (Town)	04668
Pleasant Beach	04858
Pleasantdale (Part of South Portland)	04106
Pleasant Hill (mail Portland)	04105
Pleasant Hill (mail Freeport)	04032
Pleasant Hill (mail Scarborough)	04074
Pleasant Lake	04619
Pleasant Point	04563
Pleasant Point Indian Reservation	04667
Pleasant Pond	04925
Pleasant Ridge (Town)	04920
Pleasantville	04864
Plummer Island	04074
Plymouth	04969
Plymouth (Town)	04969
Poland	04273
Poland (Town)	04273
Poland Spring	04274
Pond Cove	04107
Poors Mills (Part of Belfast)	04915
Popham Beach	04562
Portage	04768
Portage Lake (Town)	04768
Port Clyde	04855
Porter	04068
Porter (Town)	04068
Porterfield	04047
Porter Landing	04032
Portland	04101-04
	04109
	04112
For specific Portland Zip Codes call (207) 871-8411	
Portsmouth Naval Shipyard	03801
Pownal	04069
Pownal (Town)	04069
Pownal Center	04069
Pratt Corner	04281
Prentiss	04487
Prentiss (Town)	04487
Presque Isle	04769
Prides Corner (Part of Westbrook)	04092
Princeton	04668
Princeton (Town)	04668
Promenade Mall (Part of Lewiston)	04240
Promised Land	04273
Prospect	04981
Prospect (Town)	04981
Prospect Ferry	04981
Prospect Harbor	04669
Prouts Neck	04074
Pulpit Harbor	04853
Pumpkin Valley	04009
Quimby	04770

	ZIP
Quoddy Village (Part of Eastport)	04631
Randolph (Town)	04346
Randolph	04346
Rangeley	04970
Rangeley (Town)	04970
Raymond	04071
Raymond (Town)	04071
Rayville	04270
Razorville	04574
Reach	04627
Readfield (Town)	04355
Readfield	04355
Red Beach (Part of Calais)	04619
Redding	04292
Reed (Town)	04497
Reeds	04966
Richmond	04357
Richmond (Town)	04357
Richmond Mill	04284
Richville	04075
Ridlonville	04257
Rileys	04239
Ripley	04930
Ripley (Town)	04930
Ripley	04643
Riverside	04330
Riverview (Part of Presque Isle)	04769
Robbinston	04671
Robbinston (Town)	04671
Robinhood	04530
Robinson	04758
Robinson Corner	04240
Robyville	04450
Rockland	04841
Rockport	04856
Rockport (Town)	04856
Rockville	04841
Rockwood	04478
Rogers Corners	04987
Rome	04957
Rome (Town)	04957
Roque Bluffs	04654
Roque Bluffs (Town)	04654
Ross Corner	04087
Round Pond	04564
Roxbury	04275
Roxbury (Town)	04275
Royal Corner (Part of Auburn)	04210
Rumford	04276
Rumford (Town)	04276
Rumford Center	04278
Rumford Corner	04219
Rumford Junction (Part of Auburn)	04210
Rumford Point	04279
Sabattus	04280
Sabattus (Town)	04280
Sabbathday Lake	04274
Saco	04072
St. Agatha	04772
St. Agatha (Town)	04772
St. Albans	04971
St. Albans (Town)	04971
St. David	04773
St. Francis	04774
St. Francis (Town)	04774
St. Francis College (Part of Biddeford)	04005
St. George	04857
St. George (Town)	04857
St. John	04743
St. John (Town)	04743
St. Josephs College	04062
Salem	04983
Salmon Falls	04004
Salsbury Cove	04672
Sanderson Corners	04349
Sandhill Corner	04341
Sandy Beach	04401
Sandy Creek	04009
Sandy Point	04972
Sandy River (Town)	04970
Sandy River Beach	04649
Sanford	04073
Sanford (Town)	04073
Sangerville	04479
Sangerville (Town)	04479
Sargentville	04673
Saunders (Part of Presque Isle)	04769
Scarboro Beach	04074
Scarborough	04074
Scarborough (Town)	04074
Scituate	03909
Scotland	03909
Scott (Part of Presque Isle)	04769
Scribners Mill	04040
Seabury	03909

Name	ZIP	Name	ZIP	Name	ZIP
Seal Cove	04674	South Lagrange	04453	Surry	04684
Seal Harbor	04675	South Lebanon	04027	Surry (Town)	04684
Searsmont	04973	South Levant	04456	Sutton Island	04662
Searsmont (Town)	04973	South Lewiston (Part of		Swans Island	04685
Searsport	04974	Lewiston)	04240	Swans Island (Town)	04685
Searsport (Town)	04974	South Liberty	04949	Swanville	04915
Seawall	04656	South Limington	04048	Swanville (Town)	04915
Sebago (Town)	04029	South Lincoln	04457	Sweden (Aroostook County)	04762
Sebago Lake	04075	South Livermore	04254	Sweden (Oxford County)	
Sebasco	04565	South Lubec	04652	(Town)	04040
Sebasco Estates	04565	South Monmouth	04259	Tacoma	04350
Sebec	04481	South Montville	04949	Tainter Corner	04224
Sebec (Town)	04481	South Newcastle	04556	Tallwood	04355
Sebec Corners	04426	South Orland	04472	Talmadge (Town)	04492
Sebec Lake	04482	South Orrington	04474	Tatnic	03906
Seboeis	04448	South Oxford (Town)	04267	Temple	04984
Seboeis (Town)	04448	South Paris	04281	Temple (Town)	04984
Seboomook	04478	South Parsonsfield	04048	Temple Heights	04915
Seboomook Lake (Town)	04478	South Penobscot	04476	Tenants Harbor	04860
Sedgwick	04676	Southport	04576	The Forks (Town)	04985
Sedgwick (Town)	04676	Southport (Town)	04576	The Kingdom	04941
Shady Nook	03830	South Portland	04106	The Ridge	04009
Shaker Village	04274		04116	Thomaston	04861
Shapleigh	04076	For specific South Portland Zip		Thomaston (Town)	04861
Shapleigh (Town)	04076	Codes call (207) 871-8451		Thompson's Point	04055
Shaw Mills	04075	South Princeton	04668	Thorndike	04986
Shawmut	04975	South Rangeley	04964	Thorndike (Town)	04986
Sheepscot	04578	South Rumford	04276	Thorndike Center	04986
Sheridan	04775	South Sanford	04073	Thornton Heights (Part of	
Sherman	04776	South Side	03909	South Portland)	04106
Sherman (Town)	04776	South Surry	04684	Todds Corner	04930
Sherman Mills	04776	South Thomaston	04858	Topsfield	04490
Shermans Corner	04949	South Thomaston (Town)	04858	Topsfield (Town)	04490
Sherman Station	04777	South Trescott	04652	Topsham	04086
Shin Pond	04765	South Union	04864	Topsham (Town)	04086
Shirley (Town)	04485	South Waldoboro	04572	Tory Hill	04038
Shirley Mills	04485	South Warren	04864	Town Farm Hill	04040
Sidney	04330	South Waterford	04081	Town Hill	04609
Sidney (Town)	04330	South West Bend	04252	Town House Corners	04046
Silver Ridge	04776	Southwest Harbor	04679	Tracy Corners	04606
Simonton Corners	04843	Southwest Harbor (Town)	04679	Trainor Corner	04345
Simpson Corners	04932	Southwest Harbor Coast		Trap Corner	04289
Sinclair	04779	Guard Base	04679	Tremont (Town)	04653
Skillings Corner	04210	South Windham	04082	Trenton	04605
Skowhegan	04976	South Windsor	04363	Trenton (Town)	04605
Skowhegan (Town)	04976	South Woodstock	04289	Trevett	04571
Slab City (Oxford County)	04231	South Woodville	04458	Troutdale	04985
Slab City (Waldo County)	04849	Spears Corner	04345	Troy	04987
Small Point	04567	Spragueville (Part of		Troy (Town)	04987
Smithfield	04978	Presque Isle)	04769	Troy Center	04987
Smithfield (Town)	04978	Springfield	04487	Turbats Creek	04046
Smithville	04680	Springfield (Town)	04487	Turner	04282
Smyrna (Town)	04780	Springvale	04083	Turner (Town)	04282
Smyrna Center	04780	Spruce Head	04859	Turner Center	04283
Smyrna Mills	04780	Spruce Head Island	04859	Turnpike Mall (Part of	
Soldier Pond	04781	Spruce Point	04538	Augusta)	04330
Solon	04979	Spruce Shores	04544	Twelve Corners	04254
Solon (Town)	04979	Squa Pan	04732	Twombly (Town)	04417
Somerville	04341	Square Lake (Town)	04743	Union	04862
Somerville (Town)	04341	Squirrel Island	04570	Union (Town)	04862
Sorrento	04677	Stacyville	04782	Unionville	04622
Sorrento (Town)	04677	Stacyville (Town)	04782	Unity (Town)	04988
Sound	04660	Standish	04084	Unity (Kennebec County)	
South Acton	04027	Standish (Town)	04084	(Town)	04988
South Addison	04606	Starboard	04618	Unity (Waldo County)	04988
South Andover	04216	Starks	04911	University Bookstore	04473
South Arm	04216	Starks (Town)	04911	Upper Abbot	04406
South Aroostook (Town)	04730	State Road	04769	Upper Frenchville	04784
South Bancroft	04424	Stebbins	04742	Upper Gloucester	04260
South Berwick	03908	Steep Falls	04085	Upton	04261
South Berwick (Town)	03908	Stetson	04488	Upton (Town)	04261
South Blue Hill	04615	Stetson (Town)	04488	Van Buren	04785
South Brewer (Part of		Steuben	04680	Van Buren (Town)	04785
Brewer)	04412	Steuben (Town)	04680	Vanceboro	04491
South Bridgton	04009	Stevens Corner	03830	Vanceboro (Town)	04491
South Bristol	04568	Stevensville	04742	Vassalboro	04989
South Bristol (Town)	04568	Stickney Corner	04574	Vassalborough (Town)	04989
South Buxton	04038	Stillwater (Part of Old Town)	04489	Veazie (Town)	04401
South Casco	04077	Stockholm	04783	Veazie	04401
South China	04358	Stockholm (Town)	04783	Verona	04416
South Corinth	04427	Stockton Springs	04981	Verona (Town)	04416
South Deer Isle	04681	Stockton Springs (Town)	04981	Vienna	04360
South Dover	04426	Stoneham (Town)	04231	Vienna (Town)	04360
South Durham	04032	Stonington	04681	Viking Village	04217
Southeast Piscataquis		Stonington (Town)	04681	Vinalhaven	04863
(Town)	04463	Stover Corner	04617	Vinalhaven (Town)	04863
South Eliot	03903	Stow	04058	Wade (Town)	04786
South Exeter	04928	Stow (Town)	04058	Waite	04492
South Franklin (Town)	04224	Stratton	04982	Waite (Town)	04492
South Freeport	04078	Stricklands	04263	Waites Landing	04105
South Gardiner (Part of		Strong	04983	Waldo	04915
Gardiner)	04359	Strong (Town)	04983	Waldo (Town)	04915
South Gorham	04038	Sullivan	04664	Waldoboro	04572
South Gouldsboro	04678	Sullivan (Town)	04664	Waldoboro (Town)	04572
South Gray	04039	Summerhaven (Part of		Wales (Town)	04280
South Hancock	04605	Augusta)	04330	Wales Corner	04280
South Harpswell	04079	Summit (Town)	04417	Walkers Mill	04217
South Hiram	04080	Sumner (Town)	04292	Wallagrass	04781
South Hollis	04042	Sunset	04683	Wallagrass (Town)	04781
South Hope	04862	Sunshine	04627	Walnut Hill	04021
South Jefferson	04553	Surfside	04064		

	ZIP		ZIP		ZIP
Walpole	04573	West Ellsworth (Part of		Whitneyville (Town)	04692
Waltham	04605	Ellsworth)	04605	Wildes District	04046
Waltham (Town)	04605	West End (Part of Portland)	04102	Wildwood Park	04110
Wards Cove	04075	West Enfield	04493	Wiley's Corner	04861
Wardtown	04032	West Falmouth	04105	Williamsburg	04414
Warren (Town)	04864	West Farmington	04992	Willimantic	04443
Warren	04864	Westfield	04787	Willimantic (Town)	04443
Washburn	04786	Westfield (Town)	04787	Wilson Corner (Part of	
Washburn (Town)	04786	West Forks	04985	Ellsworth)	04605
Washburn Junction (Part of		West Forks (Town)	04985	Wilsons Mills	03579
Presque Isle)	04769	West Franklin	04634	Wilton	04294
Washington	04574	West Fryeburg	04037	Wilton (Town)	04294
Washington (Town)	04574	West Gardiner (Town)	04345	Windham (Town)	04062
Waterboro	04087	West Georgetown	04548	Windham	04062
Waterboro (Town)	04087	West Gorham	04038	Windham Center	04062
Waterboro Center	04030	West Gouldsboro	04607	Windham Hill	04062
Waterford	04088	West Gray	04039	Windsor	04363
Waterford (Town)	04088	West Harpswell	04079	Windsor (Town)	04363
Waterman Beach	04858	West Harrington	04643	Winkumpaugh Corners (Part	
Water Street (Part of		West Hollis	04042	of Ellsworth)	04605
Augusta)	04330	West Jonesport	04649	Winn	04495
Waterville	04901-03	West Kennebunk	04094	Winn (Town)	04495
For specific Waterville Zip Codes		West Lebanon	04027	Winnecook	04922
call (207) 873-0714		West Leeds	04263	Winnegance	04530
Waverly	04967	West Levant	04456	Winslow	04901
Wayne	04284	West Lovell	04051	Winslow (Town)	04901
Wayne (Town)	04284	West Lubec	04652	Winslows Mills	04572
Webster	04473	Westmanland (Town)	04783	Winter Harbor	04693
Webster (Town)	04487	West Mills	04938	Winter Harbor (Town)	04693
Webster Corner	04250	West Minot	04288	Winterport	04496
Weeks Mills	04361	West Mount Vernon	04352	Winterport (Town)	04496
Welchville	04270	West Newfield	04095	Winterville	04788
Welcomes Corner (Part of		West Old Town (Part of Old		Winterville (Town)	04788
Auburn)	04210	Town)	04468	Winthrop	04364
Weld	04285	Weston	04424	Winthrop (Town)	04364
Weld (Town)	04285	Weston (Town)	04424	Winthrop Center	04364
Wellington	04942	West Paris	04289	Wiscasset	04578
Wellington (Town)	04942	West Paris (Town)	04289	Wiscasset (Town)	04578
Wells	04090	West Pembroke	04666	Wonsqueak Harbor	04613
Wells (Town)	04090	West Penobscot	04476	Woodfords (Part of	
Wells Beach	04090	West Peru	04290	Portland)	04103
Wells Branch	04090	Westpoint	04565	Woodland (Town)	04736
Wesley	04686	West Poland	04291	Woodland	04694
Wesley (Town)	04686	Westport	04578	Woodmans Mills	04973
West Appleton	04949	Westport (Town)	04578	Woodstock (Town)	04219
West Athens	04912	West Princeton	04668	Woodville (Town)	04458
West Auburn (Part of		West Rockport	04865	Woolwich	04579
Auburn)	04210	West Scarborough	04074	Woolwich (Town)	04579
West Baldwin	04091	West Seboois	04462	Worthley Pond	04290
West Bath (Town)	04530	West Southport	04576	Wyman (Franklin County)	
West Bethel	04286	West Stonington	04681	(Town)	04982
West Boothbay Harbor	04575	West Sullivan	04689	Wyman (Washington	
West Bowdoin	04287	West Sumner	04292	County)	04658
West Bridgton	04009	West Surry	04605	Wytopitlock	04497
Westbrook	04092	West Tremont	04690	Yarmouth	04096
	04098	West Trenton	04605	Yarmouth (Town)	04096
For specific Westbrook Zip Codes		West Waldoboro	04572	York	03909
call (207) 854-4651		West Washington	04341	York (Town)	03909
West Brooklin	04616	West Winterport	04496	York Beach	03910
West Brooksville	04617	Whitefield	04362	York Cliffs	03902
West Buxton	04093	Whitefield (Town)	04362	York Harbor	03911
West Central Franklin		White Rock	04038	York Harbor (census	
(Town)	04285	Whites Corner	04260	designated place)	03909
West Charleston	04422	Whiting	04691	York Heights	03909
West Corinth	04427	Whiting (Town)	04691	Youngs Corner (Part of	
West Cumberland	04021	Whitney (Town)	04487	Auburn)	04210
West Denmark	04010	Whitneyville	04692	Youngtown	04850
West Durham	04069				

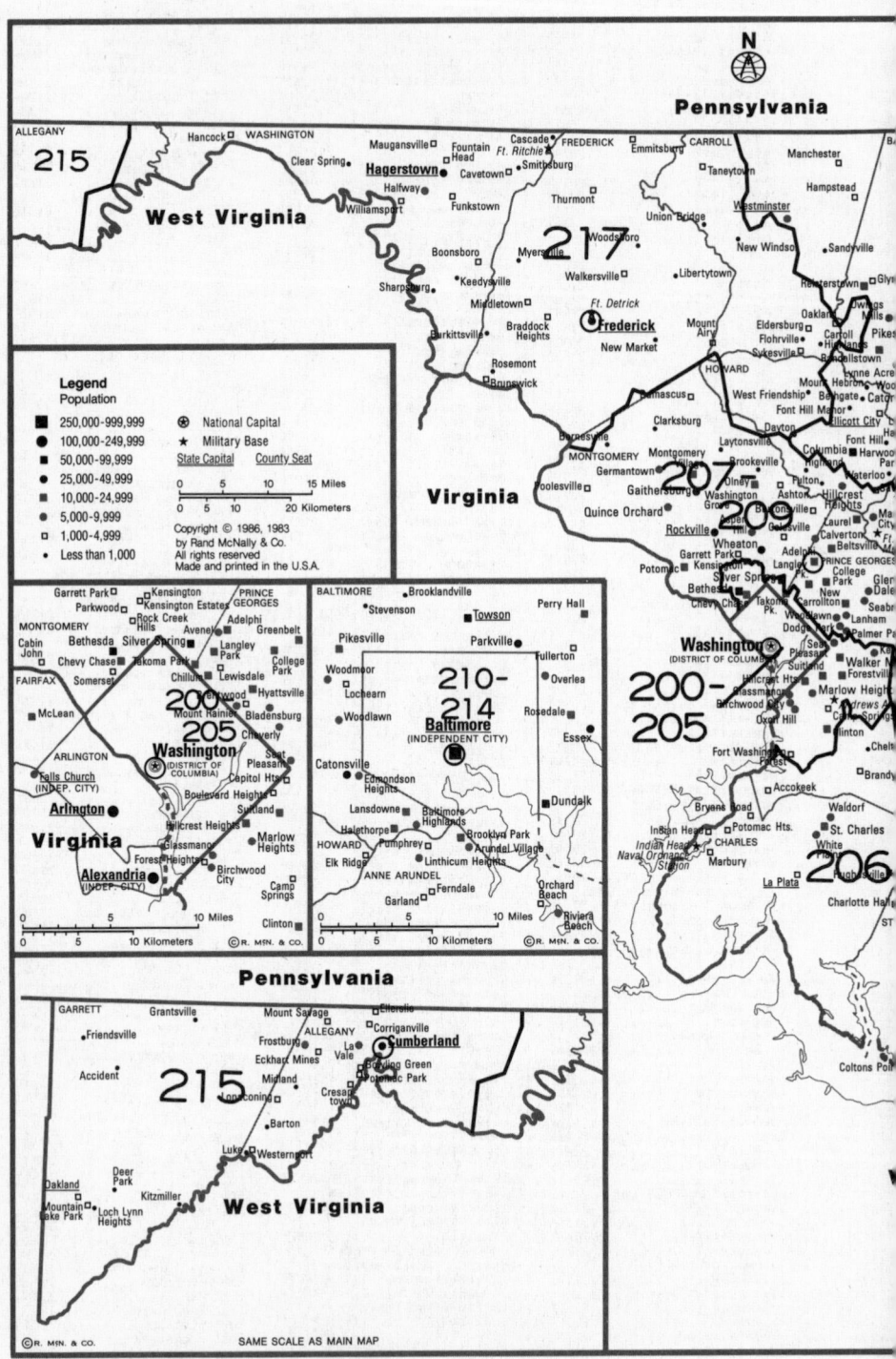

N

Pennsylvania

ALLEGANY
215
Hancock WASHINGTON
Clear Spring
Maugansville Fountain
Head Cascade FREDERICK
Ft. Ritchie Emmitsburg CARROLL
Manchester
Taneytown Hampstead

West Virginia
Halfway
Williamsport
Cavetown
Funkstown
Smithsburg
Thurmont
Union Bridge **Westminster**
New Windsor
Sandyville
Glyn

Boonsboro
Keedysville
Myersville
Walkersville
Woodsboro
217
Libertytown
Reisterstown
Oakland
Eldersburg
Flohrville
Sykesville
Carroll
Randallstown
Pikes

Sharpsburg
Middletown
Ft. Detrick
Frederick
Mount
Airy
HOWARD
Lynne Acres
Mount Hebron
West Friendship
Font Hill Manor
Dayton
Woo
Cator
Ellicott City

Burkittsville
Braddock
Heights
New Market
Damascus
Clarksburg
Laylonsville
Brookeville
Columbia
Harwood
Par
Waterloo
Font Hill

Rosemont
Brunswick
Barnesville
MONTGOMERY
Germantown
Montgomery
Gaithersburg
Olney
Ashton
207
Hillcrest
Heights

Virginia
Poolesville
Quince Orchard
Washington
Grove
Rockville
Wheaton
Gaithersburg
Fulton
Laurel
206
Calverton
Beltsville
Ft.
City

Garrett Park
Potomac
Kensington
Silver Spring
Langley
PRINCE GEORGES
College
Park
Glen
Dale

Bethesda
Chevy Chase Takoma

Washington
(DISTRICT OF COLUMBIA)
200–205
Seat
Pleasant
Walker Mill
Marlow Heights
Forestville

Garrett Park
Kensington
PRINCE
GEORGES
BALTIMORE
Brooklandville
Parkwood
Kensington Estates
Rock Creek
Hills
Adelphi
Stevenson
Perry Hall

MONTGOMERY
Bethesda
Avenel
Greenbelt
Towson
Pikesville
Parkville

Cabin
John
Chevy Chase
Silver Spring
Langley
Park
College
Park
Woodmoor
210–214
Fullerton

FAIRFAX
Somerset
Takoma Park
Chillum
Lewisdale
Hyattsville
Woodlawn
Lochearn
Baltimore
(INDEPENDENT CITY)
Overlea
Rosedale

McLean
200–205
Mount Rainier
Bladensburg
Cheverly
Catonsville
Edmondson
Heights
Essex

ARLINGTON
Washington
(DISTRICT OF
COLUMBIA)
Seat
Pleasant
Capitol Hts.
Lansdowne
Baltimore
Highlands
Dundalk

Falls Church
(INDEP. CITY)
Boulevard Heights
Suitland
Halethorpe
Brooklyn Park

Arlington
Hillcrest Heights
Marlow
Heights
HOWARD
Pumphrey
Arundel Village

Virginia
Glassmano
Birchwood
City
Elk Ridge
Linthicum Heights
Orchard
Beach

Forest Heights
Camp
Springs
ANNE ARUNDEL
Ferndale
Riviera
Beach

Alexandria
(INDEP. CITY)
Clinton
Garland
10 Miles

0   5   10 Miles
0   5   10 Kilometers
©R. MCN. & CO.
0   5   10 Miles
0   5   10 Kilometers
©R. MCN. & CO.

Bryans Road
Indian Head
Indian Head
Naval Ordnance
Station
Potomac Hts.
CHARLES
Marbury
La Plata
St. Charles
White
Plains
206
Charlotte Hall
ST.

Pennsylvania

GARRETT
Grantsville
Mount Savage
Ellerslie
Corriganville
ALLEGANY
Coltons Poin

Friendsville
Frostburg
La
Vale
Cumberland
Bowling Green
Potomac Park

Accident
Eckhart Mines
Midland
Cresaptown
215
Lonaconing
Barton

Luke
Westernport

Oakland
Deer
Park
Kitzmiller
Mountain
Lake Park
Loch Lynn
Heights

West Virginia

©R. MCN. & CO.
SAME SCALE AS MAIN MAP

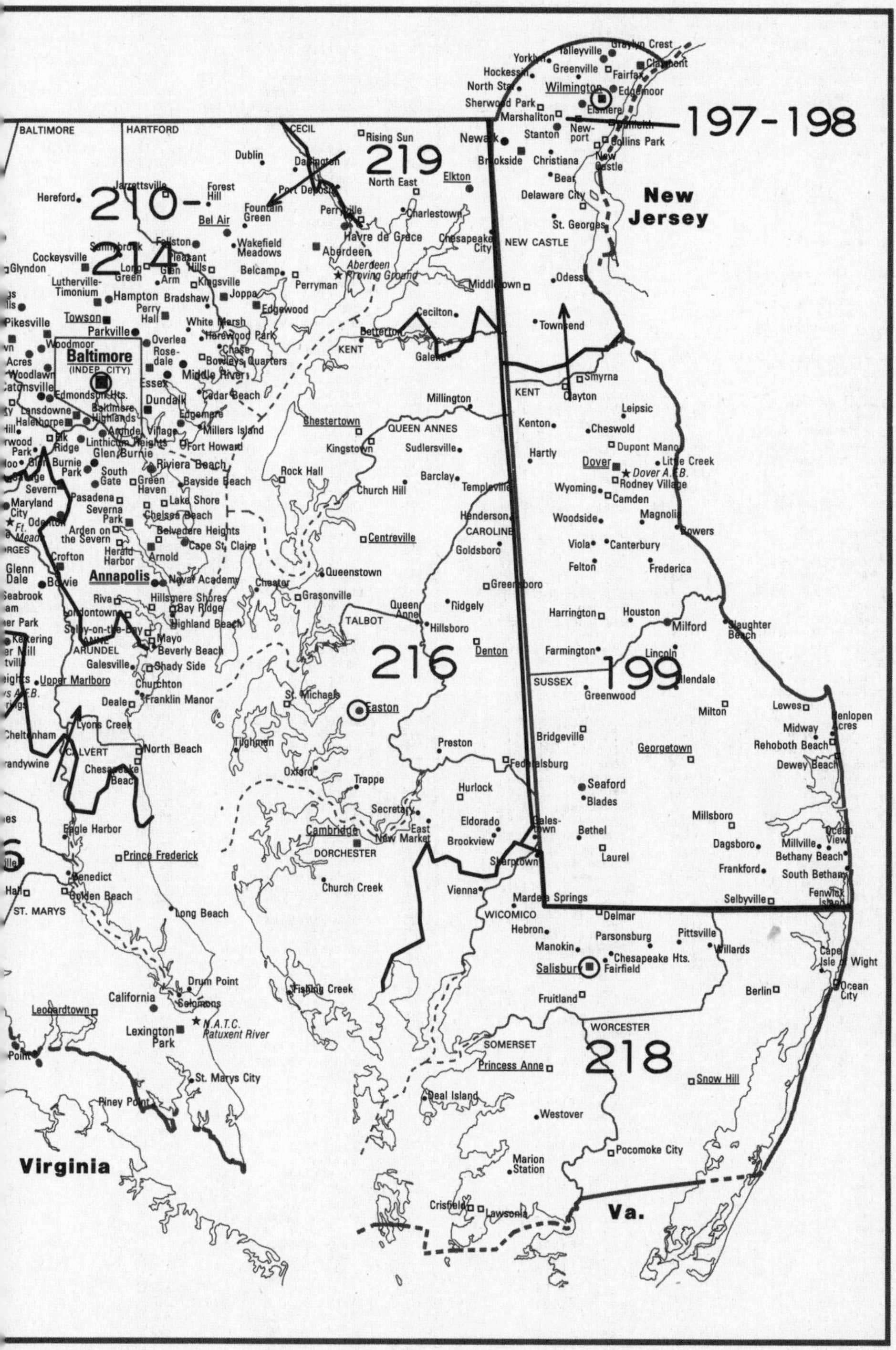

	ZIP		ZIP		ZIP
Beantown	20601		20824-27	Brandywine Country	20772
Bear Creek Junction	21222	For specific Bethesda Zip Codes		Brandywine Heights	20613
Beaufort Park	20759	call (301) 652-7401		Breathedsville	21740
Beauty Beach	21061	Bethgate	21043	Breezewood Farms	21163
Beauvue	20650	Bethlehem	21609	Breezy Point	20732
Beaver Creek	21740	Betterton	21610	Breezy Point Beach	21221
Beaver Dam	21851	Beulah	21643	Brentwood	20722
Beaverdam Estates	20785	Beverly Beach	21106	Breton Beach	20650
Beaver Heights	20743	Beverly Farms	20854	Briarcrest Heights	21755
Beckleysville	21074	Big Pines	20850	Briarwood (Charles County)	20601
Bedford	20708	Big Pool	21711	Briarwood (Prince George's	
Bedfordshire	20854	Big Spring	21722	County)	20708
Bel Air (Harford County)	21014-15	Bigwoods	21678	Briddletown	21811
For specific Bel Air Zip Codes call		Billingsley Forest	20640	Bridewell	20794
(410) 838-6262		Birchwood City	20745	Bridgeport (Frederick	
Bel Air (Allegany County)	21502	Birchwood Gardens	20708	County)	21787
Belair (Prince George's		Birdlawn	20744	Bridgeport (Washington	
County)	20715	Bird River Beach	21220	County)	21740
Bel Air Acres (Charles		Birdsville	20776	Bridgetown	21636
County)	20601	Birmingham Estates	20705	Bright Oaks	21015
Bel Air Acres (Harford		Birmingham Terrace	20705	Brighton (Baltimore County)	21244
County)	21014	Bishop	21813	Brighton (Montgomery	
Belair Buckingham (Part of		Bishops Head	21672	County)	20833
Bowie)	20715	Bishopville	21813	Brightview Woods	21108
Belair Chapel Forge (Part of		Bitter Sweet	21403	Brightwood Acres	21740
Bowie)	20715	Bittinger	21522	Brinkleigh	21042
Belair Foxhill (Part of Bowie)	20715	Bivalve	21814	Brinkleigh Manor	21042
Belair Heather Hills (Part of		Black Horse	21161	Brinkley Manor	20748
Bowie)	20715	Blackrock Estates	20874	Brinklow	20862
Belair Idlewild (Part of		Blacks Corner	21157	Bristol	20711
Bowie)	20715	Blackwater	21622	Broad Creek	21160
Belair Kenilworth (Part of		Bladensburg	20710	Broadmoor	21030
Bowie)	20715	Bladenwoods (Part of		Broad Run	21718
Belair Longridge (Part of		Bladensburg)	20710	Broadview	20748
Bowie)	20715	Blair	20910	Broadview Acres	21701
Bel Air North	21050	Blenheim	21131	Broadwater Estates	20744
Belair Overbrook (Part of		Bloomfield	21702	Broadwater Point	20733
Bowie)	20715	Blooming Rose Settlement	21531	Broadwood Manor (Part of	
Belair Rockledge (Part of		Bloomington	21523	Rockville)	20851
Bowie)	20715	Bloomsbury	21228	Brock Bridge	20708
Belair Shopping Center		Blossom Hills	21122	Brock Hall	20772
(Part of Bowie)	20715	Blueball	21921	Brock Hall Estates	20772
Belair Somerset (Part of		Blueberry Hills	20855	Brock Hall Gardens	20772
Bowie)	20715	Blue Hill (Part of Hancock)	21750	Brock Hall Manor	20772
Bel Air South	21015	Blue Mount	21111	Brookdale	20815
Belair Tulip Grove (Part of		Blue Mountain (Frederick		Brookdale Heights	21801
Bowie)	20715	County)	21788	Brooke-Jane Manor	20735
Belair White Hall (Part of		Blue Mountain (Washington		Brooke Manor	20745
Bowie)	20715	County)	21783	Brookemanor Estates	20853
Belair Yorktown (Part of		Blue Ridge Manor	20902	Brookeville	20833
Bowie)	20715	Blue Ridge View	21157	Brook Hill	21702
Bel Alton	20611	Blythedale	21903	Brooklandville	21093
Belcamp	21017	Bolivar Heights	21769	Brooklyn (Part of Baltimore)	21225
Belhaven	21122	Bolton	20601	Brooklyn-Curtis Bay	21225
Belleair Estates	20744	Bond Mill Park	20707	Brooklyn Park	21225
Belle Farm Estates	21208	Bonds	20607	Brookmead	20874
Bellefonte	20735	Bon Haven	21401	Brookmead North	20874
Belle Grove	21766	Bonnie Acres	21043	Brookmont	20816
Bellemead	20784	Bonnie Brae	21784	Brookside Forest	20901
Belleview Estates	21146	Bonnie Brook	21613	Brookside Manor	20782
Bellevue	21662	Bonnie Knob (Part of		Brookview	21659
Bellevue Estates	20607	Woodsboro)	21798	Brookville Knolls	20833
Bells Mill Village	20854	Bonnie Ridge	21209	Brookwood	20772
Bellwood Park	20601	Boonsboro	21713	Brookwood Estates	20646
Belmar	21206	Borden Shaft	21532	Broomes Island	20615
Bel Pre Estates	20906	Borden Yard	21532	Browns Corner	21617
Bel Pre Park	20906	Boring	21020	Brownsville (Queen Anne's	
Bel Pre Woods	20853	Boulevard Heights	20743	County)	21617
Beltsville	20704-05	Boulevard Park	21122	Brownsville (Washington	
For specific Beltsville Zip Codes		Bowens	20678	County)	21715
call (301) 937-3355		Bowie	20715-21	Browns Woods Villa	21401
Beltsville Heights	20705	For specific Bowie Zip Codes call		Bruceville (Carroll County)	21757
Beltway Plaza (Part of		(301) 464-0707		Bruceville (Talbot County)	21673
Greenbelt)	20770	Bowie State College	20715	Brunswick	21716
Belvedere Heights	21012	Bowleys Quarters	21220	Bryans Road	20616
Bembe Beach	21403	Bowling Green	21502	Bryantown (Charles County)	20617
Benedict	20612	Bowlings Alley	20622	Bryantown (Queen Anne's	
Benevola	21713	Boxhill North	21009	County)	21658
Bennsville	20601	Boxiron	21829	Bryant Square	21044
Ben Oaks	21146	Boxwood Village (Part of		Bryant Woods	21044
Benson	21018	Greenbelt)	20770	Buckeystown	21717
Bentley Springs	21120	Boyds	20841	Buckingham View	21157
Bentons Pleasure	21619	Boyer Mill Heights	21774	Buck Lodge	20783
Berkley	21034	Bozman	21612	Bucktown	21613
Berkshire	20747	Bradbury Heights	20743	Budds Creek	20659
Berlin	21811	Bradbury Park	20746	Buena Vista	20678
Berrett	21784	Braddock	21702	Buffalo Run	21531
Berry	20601	Braddock Estates (Part of		Burgundy Estates (Part of	
Berrywood	21122	Frostburg)	21532	Rockville)	20851
Berwyn (Part of College		Braddock Heights	21714	Burgundy Knolls (Part of	
Park)	20740	Bradley Farms	20854	Rockville)	20850
Berwyn Heights	20740	Bradley Hills	20817	Burgundy Village (Part of	
Bestgate	21401	Bradley Hills Grove	20817	Rockville)	20850
Bethany Manor	21042	Bradley Woods	20817	Burkittsville	21718
Bethel (Carroll County)	21048	Bradshaw	21021	Burning Tree Estates	20817
Bethel (Cecil County)	21915	Braebrook Village	20770	Burning Tree Manor	20817
Bethel (Frederick County)	21702	Bramble Hills	21157	Burns Corner (Part of	
Bethel (Garrett County)	21550	Branchville (Part of College		Aberdeen)	21001
Bethesda	20813-17	Park)	20740	Burnt Mills	20901
		Brandwine Farms	21047	Burnt Mills Hills	20901
		Brandywine	20613	Burnt Mills Knolls	20901

	ZIP		ZIP		ZIP
Burnt Mills Manor	20901	Carsondale	20706	Cheshaven	21919
Burnt Mills Village	20901	Carter Hill (Part of Rockville)	20850	Chester	21619
Burrisville	21617	Carvel Beach	21226	Chesterfield	21032
Burrsville	21629	Carver Heights	20653	Chesterfield Gardens	21122
Burtner	21713	Cascade	21719	Chester Harbor	21620
Burtonsville	20866	Cashell Estates	20855	Chester River Beach	21638
Bush	21009	Casselman	21536	Chestertown	21620
Bushs Corner	21132	Castle Marina	21619	Chesterville	21651
Bushwood	20618	Castleton	21034	Chesterville Forest	21651
Butler	21023	Catchpenny	21856	Chestnut Grove (Frederick	
Butlertown	21678	Catoctin	21755	County)	21701
Buttercup Estates	21794	Catoctin Furnace	21788	Chestnut Grove	
Buttonwood Beach	21919	Catoctin View	21771	(Washington County)	21756
Byford Knolls	20895	Catonsville	21228	Chestnut Hill (Baltimore	
Bynum	21050	Catonsville Heights	21228	County)	21286
Bynum Ridge	21050	Catonsville Manor	21207	Chestnut Hill (Harford	
Byrdtown	21817	Cavalier Country	20754	County)	21050
Cabin Creek	21643	Cavetown	21720	Chestnut Hill (Howard	
Cabin John	20818	Cayots	21915	County)	21043
Cabin John-Brookmont	20816	Cearfoss	21740	Chestnut Hill Estates	21043
Cabin John Park	20818	Cecilton	21913	Chestnut Hills	20705
Cactus Hill	20607	Cedar Acres	21044	Chestnut Ridge (Baltimore	
Cadillac Homes	21061	Cedar Beach	21221	County)	21117
California	20619	Cedar Grove	20876	Chestnut Ridge (Prince	
Callaway	20620	Cedar Grove Beach	21631	George's County)	20737
Caltor Manor	20744	Cedar Hall	21851	Cheverly	20785
Calvary	21028	Cedar Haven	20608	Cheverly Manor	20785
Calvert (Part of Baltimore)	21202	Cedar Heights	20743	Chevy Chase	20815
Calvert (Cecil County)	21901	Cedarhurst (Anne Arundel			20825
Calvert Beach	20685	County)	20764	For specific Chevy Chase Zip	
Calvert Beach-Long Beach	20685	Cedarhurst (Carroll County)	21048	Codes call (301) 652-8508	
Calvert Manor	20607	Cedarhurst Acres	21830	Chevy Chase Lake	20815
Calverton	20705	Cedarhurst-on-the-Bay	20764	Chevy Chase Manor	20815
Cambria	21131	Cedar Lawn	21740	Chevy Chase Section Five	20815
Cambridge	21613	Cedarmere	21117	Chevy Chase Section Three	20815
Cambridge Estates	20735	Cedar Park (Part of		Chevy Chase Terrace	20815
Camden (Part of Baltimore)	21201	Annapolis)	21401	Chevy Chase View	20895
Camden (Wicomico County)	21810	Cedar Spring	21015	Chevy Chase Village	20815
Camelback Village	20832	Cedartown	21863	Chewsville	21721
Camelot (Harford County)	21015	Cedarville	20613	Chicamuxen	20640
Camelot (Prince George's		Centennial	21042	Childs	21916
County)	20769	Centennial Estates	21042	Chillum	20783
Camotop	20854	Center Court	20879	Chillum Estates	20783
Campbell	21813	Centerville	21754	Chillum Heights	20783
Campbelltown	21813	Centreville	21617	Chillum Manor	20783
Camp Springs	20748	Ceresville	21701	Chingville	20620
Camp Springs Forest	20748	Chadwick Manor	21244	Choptank	21655
Campus Hills	21286	Chalfone Manor	21228	Christs Rock	21613
Canada Hill	21773	Chalk Point	20778	Church Creek	21622
Canal	21904	Champ	21853	Church Hill (Frederick	
Candlewood Park	20855	Chance	21816	County)	21773
Cannon Acres	21613	Chaney	20754	Church Hill (Queen Anne's	
Canton (Part of Baltimore)	21224	Chaneyville	20736	County)	21623
Cape Anne	20733	Chaneyville Farm Estates	20639	Churchill Town Sector	20874
Cape Arthur	21146	Chapel	21601	Churchton	20733
Cape Estate	21012	Chapel Gate	21113	Churchville	21028
Cape Isle of Wight	21842	Chapel Hill	20744	Cinnamon Ridge	20772
Cape Loch Haven	21037	Chapel Hill Estates	20610	Cissel Farms	20777
Cape May Beach	21221	Chapel Oaks	20743	Claggettsville	20872
Cape St. Claire	21401	Chapelview	21043	Claiborne	21624
Cape St. John	21401	Chaptico	20621	Claremont (Part of	
Capital Estates	20695	Charles Manor	21047	Baltimore)	21223
Capitol Heights	20731	Charlesmont	21222	Clarksburg	20871
	20743	Charlestown (Allegany		Clarks Landing	20636
For specific Capitol Heights Zip		County)	21539	Clarksville	21029
Codes call (301) 336-5650		Charlestown (Cecil County)	21914	Clarksville Ridge	21029
Capitol Hills	21061	Charlestown Manor Beach	21901	Clarysville	21532
Capitol Plaza (Part of		Charlesville	21702	Clayton Manor	21085
Landover Hills)	20784	Charlotte Hall	20622	Clearfield	21157
Capitol View Park	20910	Charlton	21722	Clear Spring	21722
Capri Estate	21012	Charred Oak Estates	20817	Clearview	21040
Captains Hill	21842	Chartley	21136	Clearview Manor	20745
Carderock Springs	20817	Chartridge	21146	Clearview Village	21122
Cardiff	21024	Chartwell	21146	Clearwater Beach	21226
Carea	17321	Chase	21027	Clements	20624
Carlos	21532	Chateau Valley	21042	Clifford (Part of Baltimore)	21230
Carlson Spring	20747	Chatham	20783	Cliffs City	21620
Carlton East	20706	Chattolanee	21117	Clifton	21702
Carmichael	21658	Chelsea Beach	21122	Clifton-East End (Part of	
Carmody Hills	20743	Chelsea Woods (Part of		Baltimore)	21213
Carmody Hills-Pepper Mill		Greenbelt)	20770	Clifton on the Potomac	20664
Village	20743	Cheltenham	20623	Clifton Park	20901
Carney	21234	Cheltenham Forest	20735	Clinton	20735
Carney Grove	21234	Chelten Park	20735	Clinton Acres	20613
Carney Heights	21234	Cherry Hill (Cecil County)	21921	Clinton Estates	20735
Carole Highlands	20783	Cherry Hill (Harford County)	21154	Clinton Gardens	20735
Carpenter Point	21903	Cherry Hill (mobile home		Clinton Grove	20735
Carroll (Part of Baltimore)	21229	park)	20705	Clinton Hills	20735
Carroll County Trails	21048	Cherry Hill (Prince George's		Clinton Park	20735
Carroll Heights (Part of		County)	20740	Clinton Vista	20735
Hagerstown)	21740	Cherrywalk	21830	Clinton Woods	20735
Carroll Highlands	21784	Chesaco Park	21237	Clopper	20878
Carroll Island	21220	Chesapeake Beach	20732	Cloverfields	21666
Carroll Knolls	20910	Chesapeake City	21915	Clover Hill	21702
Carroll Manor (Part of		Chesapeake Estates	21666	Cloverlea	21106
Takoma Park)	20912	Chesapeake Heights	21801	Cloverly	20904
Carrollton	21784	Chesapeake Isle	21901	Club of Stedwick	20879
Carrollton Manor	21146	Chesapeake Landing	21620	Clubside	20879
Carrollwood	21220	Chesapeake Ranch Estates	20657	Clydesdale Acres	21048
Carrollwood Estate	21157	Chesapeake Terrace	21222	Cobb Island	20625
Carsins Run	21001				

	ZIP		ZIP		ZIP
Cockeysville	21030-31	Crellin	21550	Devonshire Forest	21093
For specific Cockeysville Zip Codes call (410) 771-0780		Cremona	20659	Diamond Farms (Part of Gaithersburg)	20878
Cohasset	20814	Cresaptown	21502	Dickerson	20842
Cohill Estates	21750	Crescendo	21676	Discovery-Spring Garden	21793
Cokesburg	21851	Cresthaven	20903	District Heights-Forestville	20747
Cokesbury	21904	Crestleigh	21042		20753
Cold Spring Estates	20854	Crestview	20814	For specific District Heights-Forestville Zip Codes call (301) 735-5464	
Coleman	21678	Crestview Manor	20735		
Colesville	20904-05	Crestwood (Anne Arundel County)	21090		
For specific Colesville Zip Codes call (301) 384-0656		Crestwood (Wicomico County)	21801	Dodge Park	20785
				Dogwood Flats	21521
Colesville Farm Estates	20904	Crestwood Acres	21040	Dogwood Hills	21286
Colesville Gardens	20904	Creswell	21015	Dominion	21619
Colesville Manor	20904	Crisfield	21817	Doncaster	20640
Colesville Park	20904	Crisp (Part of Baltimore)	21225	Doncaster Village	21234
College (Part of Westminster)	21157	Criswood Manor	21029	Donleigh	21046
		Crocheron	21627	Donnybrook	21204
College Estates (Part of Frederick)	21701	Crofton	21114	Dorceytown	21771
		Cromwood	21234	Dorchester Estates	20735
College Gardens (Part of Rockville)	20850	Croom	20772	Dorsey	21227
		Crosby	21661	Dorseys Regard	20879
College Heights Estates	20783	Crowder	21043	Doubs	21710
College Park	20740-41	Crownsville	21032	Dowell	20629
For specific College Park Zip Codes call (301) 345-1714		Crownsville Hospital Center	21032	Downsville	21795
		Croydon Park (Part of Rockville)	20850	Drayden	20630
College Park Woods (Part of College Park)	20740			Dresden Green	20706
		Crumpton	21628	Drexel Woods	21228
College View	20902	Crystal Beach	21919	Druid (Part of Baltimore)	21217
Colmar Manor	20722	Cub Hills	21234	Drumcliff	20636
Colonial Acres (Cecil County)	21921	Cuckhold Creek	20664	Drumeldra Hills	20904
		Cumberland	21501-05	Drum Point	20657
Colonial Acres (Harford County)	21014	For specific Cumberland Zip Codes call (301) 722-8190		Drury	20711
				Drybranch	21161
Colonial Gardens	21228	Curtis Bay (Part of Baltimore)	21225	Dry Run	21722
Colonial Heights	21502			Dublin	21034
Colonial Park (Baltimore County)	21207	Cypress Creek	21146	Dufief	20878
		Dailsville	21613	Dulaney Village	21204
Colonial Park (Washington County)	21740	Daisy	21797	Dulls Corner	21401
		Dalton	21045	Dumbarton	21208
Colonial Village	21208	Damascus	20872	Dumbarton Heights	21208
Colony Ridge	21113	Dameron	20628	Dunbrook	21122
Colora	21917	Dames Quarter	21820	Dundalk	21222
Coltons Point	20677	Dam No. 4	21782	Dundalk Shopping Center	21222
Columbia	21044-46	Daniel	21797	Dundalk-Sparrows Point	21222
For specific Columbia Zip Codes call (301) 381-0121		Daniels Park (Part of College Park)	20740	Dundee Village	21220
				Dunkirk	20754
Columbia Beach	20764	Danville	21557	Dunlaney Village	21093
Columbia Hills	21043	Danwood	21801	Dunloggin	21042
Columbia Park	20785	Darcy Manor	20746	Dunwood	21085
Colvilla	21157	Dares Beach	20678	Dupont Heights	20746
Compton	20627	Dargan	25425	Dynard	20621
Comus	20842	Darleigh Manor	21236	Eagle Harbor	20608
Concord	21632	Darlington	21034	Eakles Mill	21756
Congressional Forest Estates	20817	Darnestown	20874	Earleigh Heights	21146
		Darryl Gardens	21162	Earleville	21919
Connecticut Avenue Estates	20902	Daugherty Town	21817	Earlton	21078
Connecticut Avenue Hills	20902	Davidsonville	21035	East Columbia Park	20785
Connecticut Avenue Park	20906	Dawson	26726	Eastfield	21222
Connecticut Gardens	20902	Dawsonville	20841	East Fort Foote Village	20744
Conowingo	21918	Day	21797	East Meadow	20745
Conowingo Village	21918	Daysville	21793	East New Market	21631
Contee	20708	Dayton	21036	Easton	21601
Cooksville	21723	Deale	20751	Easton Point	21601
Coopersville	21023	Deale Beach	20751	Eastover Knolls	20745
Coopstown	21050	Deal Island	21821	East Park Village	21061
Copenhaver	20854	Deanwood Park	20743	Eastpines	20737
Copperville (Carroll County)	21787	Decatur Heights (Part of Bladensburg)	20710	Eastpoint	21222
Copperville (Talbot County)	21601			Eastpoint Mall	21224
Coral Hills	20743	Deep Creek	21012	Eastport (Part of Annapolis)	21403
Corbett (Baltimore County)	21111	Deep Creek Lake	21541	East Riverdale	20737
Corbett (Washington County)	21740	Deep Landing Estates	20639	East Springbrook	20904
		Deerfield (Harford County)	21034	Eastview (Carroll County)	21048
Cordova	21625	Deerfield (Montgomery County)	20817	Eastview (Frederick County)	21702
Cornersville	21613			Eastview Estates	21048
Cornfield Harbor	20687	Deerfield Run	20708	Eckhart Mines	21528
Corriganville	21524	Deer Harbour	21801	Eden	21822
Costen	21851	Deer Park (Garrett County)	21550	Eder	21921
Cottage City	20722	Deer Park (Montgomery County)	20877	Edesville	21661
Country Club Acres	21550			Edgemere	21221
Country Club Estate	21061	Deer Park (Prince George's County)	20748	Edgemont (Frederick County)	21702
Country Club Manor	21061			
Country Club Park	21093	Deer Park Estates	21048	Edgemont (Washington County)	21783
Country Club Village	20814	Deer Park Heights	20748	
Country Place	20866	Deers Head	21801	Edgemoor	20814
Country Road Estates	20754	Defense Heights (Baltimore County)	21222	Edgewater	21037
Courthouse (Part of Rockville)	20850			Edgewater Beach	21037
		Defense Heights (Prince George's County)	20784	Edgewater Village	21040
Courtleigh	21133			Edgewood (Frederick County)	21702
Cove	21520	Delight	21117	
Coventry	21234	Dellmont	21048	Edgewood (Harford County)	21040
Cove Point	20657	Delmar	21875	Edgewood (Montgomery County)	20814
Covers Corner	21776	Delmont	21144	
Cowentown	21921	Den Lee Acres	20735	Edgewood Arsenal	21040
Coxby Estates	21037	Dennings	21776	Edgewood Meadows	21040
Cox Creek Acres	21619	Dennis Grove Apartments	20745	Edmondson Ridge	21228
Crabtree	21561	Denton	21629	Edmonson Heights	21207
Craigtown	21904	Dentsville	20646	Edmonston	20781
Cranberry	21157	Derwood	20855	Ednor	20905
Crapo	21626	Detmold	21539	Ednor Acres	20904
Creagerstown	21788	Detour	21725	Elberon	20854

	ZIP		ZIP		ZIP
Elder Hill	21531	Farmington (Montgomery		Franklinville (Baltimore	
Eldersburg	21784	County)	20815	County)	21087
Eldorado	21659	Farmsbrook	21702	Franklinville (Frederick	
Elioak	21044	Faulkner	20632	County)	21788
Elk Mills	21920	Faulkner Ridge	21044	Frederick	21701-02
Elkmore	21921	Fawsett Farms	20854	For specific Frederick Zip Codes	
Elk Neck	21901	Feagaville	21702	call (301) 662-2131	
Elk Ranch Park	21921	Federal Hill	21084	Frederick Junction	21701
Elkridge	21227	Federalsburg	21632	Frederick Shopping Center	
Elkton	21921-22	Felicity Cove	20764	(Part of Frederick)	21701
For specific Elkton Zip Codes call		Fellowship Forest	21204	Frederick Towne Mall (Part	
(410) 398-4040		Ferdinand Heights	21061	of Frederick)	21702
Elkton Heights (Part of		Ferndale	21061	Frederick Village	21228
Elkton)	21921	Fernglen Manor	21061	Freedom Forest	21784
Elktonia	21401	Fernwood (Montgomery		Freeland	21053
Elkton Landing (Part of		County)	20817	Free State Mall (Part of	
Elkton)	21921	Fernwood (Prince George's		Bowie)	20715
Elkwood Estates	21921	County)	20737	Frenchtown	21903
Ellerslie	21529	Fernwood (mobile home		Friendly	20744
Ellerton	21773	park)	20743	Friendly Farms	20744
Ellicott City	21041-43	Fiddlersburg	21740	Friends Creek	21727
For specific Ellicott City Zip Codes		Figgs Landing	21863	Friendship (Anne Arundel	
call (410) 465-0440		Finksburg	21048	County)	20758
Ellicott City (census		Finzel	21532	Friendship (Frederick	
designated place)	21043	Fishing Creek	21634	County)	21791
Ellicott Mills (Baltimore		Fleishman Village	20746	Friendship (Worcester	
County)	21228	Flickersville	21756	County)	21811
Ellicott Mills (Howard		Flintstone	21530	Friendship Heights	20813
County)	21043	Flohrville	21784	Friendship Park	21740
Elliott	21869	Florence	21797	Friendsville	21531
Elmwood	21206	Flower Valley	20853	Frizzelburg	21158
Elvaton Acres	21108	Flower Valley Estates	20853	Frostburg	21532
Elvatone Town	21061	Fontana Village	21237	Frostown	21769
Elwood	21643	Font Hill	21042	Fruitland	21826
Emmitsburg	21727	Font Hill Manor	21042	Fullerton	21206
Emmorton	21009	Forest Estates	20910	Fulton	20759
Emory Church	21155	Forest Glen	20910	Fulton Junction (Part of	
Emory Grove (Baltimore		Forest Greens	21001	Baltimore)	21217
County)	21071	Forest Heights	20745	Funkstown	21734
Emory Grove (Montgomery		Forest Hill	21050	Furnace Branch	21061
County)	20877	Forest Knolls (Montgomery		Gaither	21735
Emory Hills	21048	County)	20901	Gaithersburg	20877-79
Engles Mill	21520	Forest Knolls (Prince			20882-86
Englewood	20785	George's County)	20744		20898
English Manor	20853	Forest Lake	21050	For specific Gaithersburg Zip	
English Village	20814	Forest Lawn	21014	Codes call (301) 948-1894	
Enterprise Estates	20721	Forest Manor	20747	Galena	21635
Enterprise Shopping Center	20706	Forest Oaks	21784	Galestown	19973
Epping Forest	21401	Forest Park	20705	Galesville	20765
Ernstville	21711	Forestville	20747	Gallant Green	20601
Essex	21221	Forestville Estates	20747	Gamber	21048
Estonian Estates	20772	Forge Acres	21128	Gambrills	21054
Etchison	20877	Forge Heights	21128	Gannon	21562
Eudowood	21204	Fork	21051	Gapland	21736
	21286	Forrest Hall	20659	Garfield	21783
For specific Eudowood Zip Codes		Fort Foote Estates	20747	Garland	21061
call (410) 825-4888		Fort Foote Village	20744	Garrett Forest	20906
Eutaw Forest	20601	Fort George G. Meade	20755	Garrett Park	20896
Evanston	20747	Fort Howard	21052	Garrett Park Estates	20895
Evergreen Estates	21146	Fort Meade	20755	Garretts Mill	21758
Evergreen Hills	21048	Fort Ritchie	21719	Garrison	21055
Evergreen Overlook	20745	Fort Sumner	20816	Gatts Corner	21106
Evergreen Park	21221	Fort Washington	20744	Gayfields	20906
Evergreen Valley Estates	21042		20749	George Island Landing	21864
Evitts Creek	21502	For specific Fort Washington Zip		Georgetown (Anne Arundel	
Ewell	21824	Codes call (301) 292-4200		County)	20794
Ewingville	21620	Fort Washington Estates	20744	Georgetown (Cecil County)	21930
Fahrney Keedy Memorial		Fort Washington Forest	20744	Georgetown (mail	
Home	21713	Foundry Siding (Part of		Chestertown)	21620
Fairbank	21671	Westernport)	21562	Georgetown (mail	
Fairfield (Part of Baltimore)	21226	Fountaindale	21769	Georgetown)	21930
Fairfield (Carroll County)	21157	Fountain Green	21015	Georgetown Estates	20852
Fairfield Knolls	20747	Fountain Green Heights	21015	Georgetown Village	20812
Fairgreen	20772	Fountain Head	21740	Georgian Forest	20902
Fairgreen Acres	21740	Fountain Mills	21754	Germantown (Montgomery	
Fair Haven	20754	Fountain Rock (Part of		County)	20874-76
Fairhaven on the Bay	20754	Walkersville)	21793	For specific Germantown Zip	
Fair Hill	21921	Fountain Valley	21157	Codes call (301) 428-3839	
Fairidge	20877	Four Locks	21722	Germantown (census	
Fairknoll	20905	Four Seasons Estates	21113	designated place)	20874
Fairland	20904	Four Winds	21204	Germantown (Worcester	
Fairland Acres	20866	Fowblesburg	21155	County)	21811
Fairland Heights	20904	Fowlers Concord	20747	Germantown Estates	20874
Fairlee	21620	Fox Chapel	20876	Germantown Park	20874
Fairmont	21014	Fox Chapel North	20876	Germantown View	20874
Fairmount	21871	Fox Chase	21061	Gibson Island	21056
Fairmount Heights	20743	Foxhall	20906	Gibson Manor	21015
Fair Play	21733	Foxhall Estates	21035	Gilmore	21532
Fairview (mobile home park)	20707	Fox Hills	20854	Gingerville Manor Estates	21037
Fairview (Anne Arundel		Fox Hills West	20854	Girdletree	21829
County)	21122	Foxley Manor	21620	Gist	21784
Fairview (Washington		Fox Rest	20708	Glade Towne (Part of	
County)	21722	Fox Rest South	20708	Walkersville)	21793
Fairview Estates	20904	Foxridge	21078	Gladstone Acres	21034
Fairway	21015	Fox Run Estates	20735	Glassmanor	20745
Fairway Hills	20812	Foxville	21780	Glazewood Manor (Part of	
Fairway Island	20879	Franklin (Part of Baltimore)	21223	Takoma Park)	20912
Fallsmont	21047	Franklin Manor Beach	20733	Glebe Heights	21037
Fallston	21047	Franklin Manor on-the-Bay	20733	Glenallen	20902
Family Estates	20743	Franklin Park	20852	Glenarden	20706
Farmington (Cecil County)	21911	Franklin Square	20744	Glen Arm	21057

	ZIP		ZIP		ZIP
Glen Brook	21042		20770	Harborview (Queen Anne's	
Glenbrook Knolls	20814	For specific Greenbelt Zip Codes		County)	21619
Glenbrook Village	20814	call (301) 345-1721		Hardesty Estates	21035
Glen Burnie	21060-61	Greenberry Hills	21740	Harewood	21220
For specific Glen Burnie Zip		Greenbriar	21713	Harewood Park	21220
Codes call (410) 766-8880		Greenbrier (Part of		Harford Estates	21050
Glen Burnie (census		Greenbelt)	20770	Harford Farms	21234
designated place)	21061	Greendale Estates	21047	Harford Furnace	21015
Glen Burnie Mall	21061	Greenfield	20735	Harford Hills	21234
Glen Burnie Park	21061	Greenfield Mills	21710	Harford Mall (Part of Bel Air)	21014
Glencoe (Baltimore County)	21152	Green Glade	21561	Harford Park	21234
Glencoe (Kent County)	21645	Green Haven	21122	Harford Square	21040
Glen Cove	20816	Green Hill	21856	Harmans	21077
Glendale (Baltimore County)	21204	Green Hill Acres	21740	Harmony (Caroline County)	21655
Glendale (Wicomico		Green Meadows (Charles		Harmony (Frederick County)	21769
County)	21801	County)	20616	Harmony Grove	21701
Glendale Heights	20769	Green Meadows (Prince		Harmony Hall	20744
Glen Echo	20812	George's County)	20782	Harmony Hills	20906
Glen Echo Heights	20816	Greenmount	21074	Harness Woods	21403
Glenelg	21737	Green Ridge (Allegany		Harney	21787
Glen Ellen	21286	County)	21766	Harpers Choice	21044
Glen Elyn	21047	Green Ridge (Baltimore		Harpers Corner	20659
Glen Farms	19711	County)	21093	Harpers Mill	21108
Glen Gardens	21060	Greenridge (Harford		Harris Heights	21061
Glen Hills	20850	County)	21015	Harrison Ferry	21643
Glen Isle	21401	Greensboro	21639	Harrisonville	21133
Glen Kyle	19711	Greensburg	21783	Harrisville (Carroll County)	21771
Glenmar (Baltimore County)	21220	Green Spring Hills	21085	Harrisville (Cecil County)	21917
Glenmar (Howard County)	21043	Greentop Manor	21030	Harundale	21060
Glen Mar Park	20814	Greentree (Anne Arundel		Harundale Mall	21061
Glen Mary Heights (Part of		County)	21061	Harvest Hills	21047
Elkton)	21921	Greentree (Montgomery		Harwood (Anne Arundel	
Glenmont (Baltimore		County)	20879	County)	20776
County)	21239	Green Tree Manor	20817	Har-Wood (Howard County)	21227
Glenmont (Montgomery		Greenvale Village	21783	Harwood Estates	20748
County)	20902	Green Valley	21771	Harwood Park	21227
Glenmont Park	20906	Greenview Knolls	20653	Havenwood Hills	21783
Glenmore	21061	Greenwich Forest	20814	Haverhill	21234
Glen Morris	21136	Greenwood Acres	21401	Havre de Grace	21078
Glenn Dale	20769	Greenwood Farms	20777	Havre de Grace Heights	21078
Glenn Heights	21078	Greenwood Forest	20706	Hawbottom	21769
Glen Oaks	20854	Gregg Neck	21635	Hawkeye	21631
Glenora Hills (Part of		Greystone Manor (Part of		Hayes Landing	21811
Rockville)	20850	Hagerstown)	21740	Hazelhurst	21561
Glen Park	20854	Grimesville	21053	Hazelmoor	21919
Glen Ridge	20784	Grosstown	20637	Head of the Creek	21856
Glenside Park	21234	Grove	21655	Hearn Bailey Farm	21801
Glenville	21034	Grove Hill	21702	Heather Heights	21784
Glen Westover	19711	Guilford	20794	Heather Hill Apartments	20748
Glen Willows	20743	Guilford Manor	21225	Hebbville	21244
Glenwood (Harford County)	21014	Gum Springs	20868	Hebron	21830
Glenwood (Howard County)	21738	Gum Springs Farm	20868	Helen	20635
Glenwood Estates	21738	Gunners Lake Village	20874	Helen Estates	20635
Glenwood Park	20706	Gunpowder (Baltimore		Henderson	21640
Glover Acres	21157	County)	21021	Henryton	21080
Glymont	20640	Gunpowder (Harford		Herald Harbor	21032
Glyndon	21071	County)	21010	Herald Square	21244
Goddard	20770	Gunpowder Estates	21128	Hereford	21111
Goddard Space Flight		Gwenlee Estates	21738	Heritage Farm	20854
Center	20770	Gwynn	21042	Heritage Harbor	21401
Golden Beach	20659	Gwynn Acres	21042	Heritage Hills	21061
Golden Hill	21622	Gwynnbrook	21117	Heritage Walk	20852
Golden Ring	21237	Gwynn Oak (Part of		Hermanville	20653
Golden Ring Mall	21237	Baltimore)	21207	Hermitage Park	20906
Goldsboro	21636		21244	Hernwood Heights	21133
Golf Club Shores	21811	For specific Gwynn Oak Zip		Herrington Manor	21550
Golts	21637	Codes call (410) 944-9300		Hickman	21629
Good Acres (Part of		Hack Point	21919	Hickory	21014
Hagerstown)	21740	Hacks Point Acre	21919	Hickory Hills (Part of Bel Air)	21014
Good Hope	20905	Hagerstown	21740-42	Hickory Ridge	21044
Goodwill	21851	For specific Hagerstown Zip		Hicksburg	21631
Gorman	26720	Codes call (301) 797-8100		Hidden Point	21401
Gortner	21550	Halethorpe	21227	High Bridge	20720
Goshen	20879	Halfway	21740	High Bridge Estates	20720
Goshen Estates	20879	Halfway Manor	21740	Highfield (Montgomery	
Gotts	21032	Hallett Heights	21863	County)	20879
Govans (Part of Baltimore)	21212	Halley Estates	20695	Highfield (Washington	
Governors Run	20676	Halpine Village	20852	County)	21719
Graceham	21788	Hambleton Estates	21140	Highland (Frederick County)	21773
Graceton	21160	Hamilton (Part of Baltimore)	21214	Highland (Howard County)	20777
Grahamtown	21532	Hamilton Park (Part of		Highland Beach	21403
Granby Woods	20855	Hagerstown)	21740	Highland Park (Prince	
Grand Bel Manor	20906	Hamlet North	20855	George's County)	20743
Grandview	21784	Hammondell Heights	21108	Highland Park (Worcester	
Granite	21163	Hammond Park	20723	County)	21811
Grantsville	21536	Hampden (Part of		Highlands	20854
Grasonville	21638	Baltimore)	21211	Highlands of Olney	20832
Gratitude	21661	Hampshire Knolls	20783	Highland Stone	20854
Gray Haven	21222	Hampstead	21074	Highlandtown (Part of	
Gray Manor	21222	Hampton	21286	Baltimore)	21224
Gray Rock	21042	Hampton Gardens	21286	High Meadows	21770
Grayton	20662	Hance Point	21901	High Point (Anne Arundel	
Greater Capitol Heights	20743	Hancock	21750	County)	21122
Greater Upper Marlboro	20772	Hanesville	21678	High Point (Montgomery	
Great Mills	20634	Hanover (Anne Arundel		County)	20814
Green Acres (Harford		County)	21076	Highpoint Heights	20705
County)	21085	Hanover (Howard County)	21076	High Point Manor	21050
Green Acres (Montgomery		Hanson Valley View	20744	High Ridge	20723
County)	20817	Hansonville	21701	High Ridge Park	20723
Greenbelt	20768	Harbor View (Anne Arundel		High View	21771
		County)	21037		

	ZIP		ZIP		ZIP
High-View Estates (Carroll County)	21102	Huntsville	20785	Kemptown	21770
Highview Estates (Howard County)	21042	Hunt Valley	21031	Ken Gar	20895
		Hunt Valley Mall	21030	Kennedyville	21645
Highview on the Bay	20779	Hurlock	21643	Kensington	20895
Hillandale	20903	Hurry	20621	Kensington Estates	20895
Hillandale Forest	20907	Hutton	21550	Kensington Heights	20902
Hillandale Heights	20903	Huyett	21740	Kensington View	20895
Hillcrest (Anne Arundel County)	21225	Hyattstown	20871	Kent Island Estates	21666
		Hyattsville	20780-89	Kentland	20785
Hill Crest (Montgomery County)	20912	For specific Hyattsville Zip Codes call (301) 699-8905		Kentmore Park	21645
				Kentmorr	21666
Hillcrest (Prince George's County)	20748	Hyde Park (Baltimore County)	21221	Kent Village	20785
Hillcrest Estates	20748	Hyde Park (Wicomico County)	21801	Kenwood (Baltimore County)	21206
Hillcrest Heights (Howard County)	20723	Hydes	21082	Kenwood (Montgomery County)	20815
Hillcrest Heights (Prince George's County)	20748	Hynesboro	20706	Kenwood Beach	20676
		Hynson	21632	Kerby Hills	20744
Hillcrest Terrace	20748	Idlewild	20764	Kettering	20772
Hillendale Shopping Center	21204	Idlewylde	21204	Kettering Estate Park	20772
Hillmead	20817	Ijamsville	21754	Keymar	21757
Hillmeade	20769	Ilchester	21043	Keysers Ridge	21536
Hillmeade Manor	20769	Imperial Gardens	21133	Keystone Manor	20747
Hillsboro	21641	Indian Creek Estates	20622	Keysville	21787
Hillsborough	20707	Indian Head	20640	Kilbirnie Estates	21801
Hillside	21157	Indian Head Manor	20616	Kilbourn Estates	20748
Hillsmere Estates	21403	Indian Head Naval Ordnance Station	20640	Kilmarock	20912
Hillsmere Shores	21403	Indian Queen East	20744	Kimberly Gardens	20708
Hills Point	21613	Indian Queen Estates	20744	Kings Contrivance	21045
Hill Top	20693	Indian River Estates	20659	Kings County	21087
Hillwood Manor	20783	Indian Springs (Frederick County)	21702	Kings Creek Estate	20772
Hobbs	21629			Kingsford	20721
Hoffman	21532	Indian Springs (Washington County)	21711	Kings Grove	21529
Holabird (Part of Baltimore)	21224	Indiantown	21863	Kings Manor	20695
Holbrook	21133	Ingleside	21644	Kings Park	21208
Holiday Acres	21783	Inverness	21222	Kings Ransom	21113
Holiday Beach	20732	Inverness Forest	20854	Kings Ridge	21234
Holiday Hills	21044	Inverness Woods	20854	Kingston	21871
Holiday Park	20906	Iron Hill	21920	Kingston Manor	20772
Holland Cliff Shores	20639	Ironshire	21811	Kingstown	21620
Holland Heights	21801	Ironsides	20643	Kingsville	21087
Hollaway Estates	20772	Isabella Park	20783	Kingwood Common	21244
Hollinsworth Manor (Part of Elkton)	21921	Island Creek	20685	Kirkham	21601
		Island View Beach	21221	Kirkwood	20782
Holly Beach	21221	Issue	20645	Kitzmiller	21538
Holly Gaf. Acres	20636	Iverson Mall	20748	Klej Grange	21851
Holly Hall Terrace	21921	Ivy Hills	21043	Knapps Meadow	21539
Holly Hill Harbor	21037	Ivytown	21601	Knettishall	21204
Holly Lake Estates	21801	Jackson	21903	Knollview	21043
Holly Spring	20747	Jacksonville (Baltimore County)	21131	Knollwood (Baltimore County)	21204
Holly Tree	20601			Knollwood (Prince George's County)	20783
Hollywood (Prince George's County)	20740	Jacksonville (Somerset County)	21817	Knoxville	21758
Hollywood (St. Mary's County)	20636	Jacktown	21613	Kump Station	21787
		Jacobsville	21122	Ladiesburg	21759
Hollywood Beach	21915	James	21613	Lakeland (Anne Arundel County)	21146
Hollywood Estates (Part of College Park)	20740	Jarrettsville	21084		
		Jefferson	21755	Lakeland (Prince George's County)	20740
Hollywood Park	20904	Jefferson Heights (Prince George's County)	20743	Lake Linganore	21701
Hollywood Shores	20636			Lake Normandy Estates	20854
Holmehurst	20720	Jefferson Heights (Washington County)	21740	Lake Roland	21209
Home Acres	20705			Lake Shore	21122
Homecrest	20906	Jennings	21536	Lakeside Manor	21801
Homestead Estates	20904	Jersey Heights	21801	Lakeside Park	21740
Homewood (Allegany County)	21502	Jerusalem (Baltimore County)	21087	Lakeside Terrace	20854
				Lakeside Vista	21085
Homewood (Montgomery County)	20895	Jerusalem (Frederick County)	21773	Lakesville	21622
Honga	21622	Jerusalem (Montgomery County)	20837	Lakeview (Howard County)	20723
Hood College (Part of Frederick)	21701	Jessup	20794	Lakeview (Montgomery County)	20817
		Jesterville	21814	Lakewood	21801
Hoods Mill	21723	Jewell	20754	Lakewood Estates (Calvert County)	20754
Hoopersville	21634	Johnsontown	21620		
Hope Hill	21701	Johnstown	20688	Lakewood Estates (Montgomery County)	20850
Hopewell	21817	Johnsville (Carroll County)	21784	Lancaster	20601
Hopkins Mead	21029	Johnsville (Frederick County)	21791	Land-O-Lakes	20636
Horizon Run	20877			Landon Woods	20817
Houcksville	21074	Jones	21146	Landover (census designated place)	20784
Howard Heights	21042	Jonestown	21655		
Howardville	21208	Joppa	21085	Landover	20785
Hoyes Run	21531	Joppa Heights	21234	Landover Estates	20784
Hudson	21613	Joppatowne	21085	Landover Hills	20789
Hughesville	20637	Joppa View	21128	Landover Knolls	20785
Hungerford Towne (Part of Rockville)	20852	Josenhans Corner	21221	Landover Park (Part of Cheverly)	20785
		Joyce Acres	21012		
Hunt Club Estates (Charles County)	20601	Kalma Ridge	21032	Lane Beach	20650
		Kalmia	21015	Langley Park	20783
Hunt Club Estates (Howard County)	21227	Kalmia Farms	21036	Lanham	20706
		Kalten Acres	21158	Lanham Heights	20706
Hunt Crest Estates	21286	Kastle Estates	20735	Lanham-Seabrook	20703
Hunters Harbor	21122	Kaywood Gardens (Part of Mount Rainier)	20712		20706
Hunters Hill	21093			For specific Lanham-Seabrook Zip Codes call (301) 577-1842	
Hunters Ridge	20610	Keedysville	21756		
Huntersville	20659	Keeler Glade	21531	Lanham Woods	20706
Hunting Hills	20639	Keifer	25434	Lansdowne	21227
Hunting Lodge	21234	Kemp Mill Estates	20902	Lansdowne-Baltimore Highlands	21227
Hunting Park	21801	Kemp Mill Farms	20902		
Huntington Terrace	20814	Kempton	26292	Lantz	21780
Huntingtown	20639				
Huntsmoor	21227				

	ZIP
Lapidum	21078
La Plata	20646
Lappans	21733
Larchmont Knolls	20895
Largo	20772
Largo/Kettering	20775
Largo Knolls	20772
Laurel	20707-09
	20723-26
For specific Laurel Zip Codes call	
(301) 498-1400	
Laurel Acres	21122
Laurel Brook	21047
Laureldale	21234
Laurel Grove	20659
Laurel Mall (Part of Laurel)	20707
	20726
For specific Laurel Mall Zip Codes	
call (301) 498-1567	
Laurel Pines	20708
Laurel Wood	20708
La Vale	21502
Lawndale Acres	21048
Lawsonia	21817
Lawyer Heights	21788
Layhill	20906
Layhill Gardens	20906
Layhill Village	20906
Laytonia	20877
Laytonsville	20879
Lees Woods	21014
Legion Avenue (Part of Annapolis)	21401
Le Gore	21757
Leisure World	20906
Leitersburg	21740
Leon	20711
Leonardtown	20650
Leslie	21901
Level	21078
Lewis Corner	21811
Lewisdale	20783
Lewis Heights	20783
Lewis Spring Manor	20735
Lewistown (Frederick County)	21701
Lewistown (Talbot County)	21625
Lexington Park	20653
Liberty Grove	21918
Liberty Manor	21244
Libertytown (Frederick County)	21762
Libertytown (Worcester County)	21811
Lime Kiln	21701
Linchester	21655
Lincoln Avenue	21740
Lincoln Heights (Part of Salisbury)	21801
Lincoln Manor	21102
Lincoln Park (Part of Rockville)	20850
Lindamoor on the Severn	21401
Linden	20907
Linden Chapel Hills	21036
Lineboro	21088
Linganore-Bartonsville	21701
Linhigh	21206
Linkwood	21835
Linsey Acres	20748
Linsted on the Severn	21146
Linthicum	21090
Linthicum Heights	21090
Linthicum Hills	21090
Linthicum Oaks	21090
Linwood (Carroll County)	21764
Linwood (Howard County)	21043
Linwood Village	21122
Lipins Corner	21122
Lisbon	21765
Little Orleans	21766
Little Washington	20747
Livingston Grove	20607
Llandaff	21601
Lloyds	21613
Loartown	21532
Lochearn	21207
Loch Haven	21234
Loch Hill	21212
Loch Lynn Heights	21550
Loch Raven	21234
Loch Raven Heights	21234
Loch Raven Village	21234
Locust Grove (Allegany County)	21502
Locust Grove (Kent County)	21645
Locust Grove (Washington County)	21779
Locust Grove Beach	20732
Locust Grove Station	21788
Locust Hill Estates	20814

	ZIP
Locust Valley	21769
Lodgecliffe	21613
Lodge Forest	21222
Lonaconing	21539
Londontown	21037
Londontowne	21037
London Woods	20743
Lone Oak	20814
Long	21502
Long Bar Harbor	21009
Long Beach	20685
Long Corner	21771
Longfellow	21043
Longfield Estates	20747
Long Green	21092
Long Meadow (Carroll County)	21784
Long Meadow (Washington County)	21740
Long Meadow Estates	20814
Long Meadow Shopping Center (Part of Hagerstown)	21740
Long Meadow West	21208
Long Point	21122
Long Reach	21045
Longview Beach	20618
Longwood	20817
Longwoods	21601
Lord	21532
Lord Calvert Estates	20639
Loreley	21162
Loretta Heights	21401
Lothian	20711
Louisville	21048
Lou Mar Estates	21009
Love Point	21666
Loveville	20656
Lower Magothy Beach	21146
Lower Marlboro	20736
Loyola (Part of Baltimore)	21210
Lucas Heights	21502
Luke	21540
Lusby	20657
Lusby Crossroads	21401
Lute	20906
Lutherville	21093
Lutherville-Timonium	21093-94
For specific Lutherville-Timonium	
Zip Codes call (410) 252-3056	
Lutz Hill	21237
Luxmanor	20852
Lynch	21646
Lynch Point	21222
Lynnbrook (Anne Arundel County)	21225
Lynnbrook (Charles County)	20601
Lynne Acres	21244
Lyons Creek (Anne Arundel County)	20711
Lyons Creek (Calvert County)	20754
Lyons Homes	21222
Mac Alpine	21042
McCahill Estates	20707
McCanns Corner	21154
McComas Beach	21550
McCoole	26726
McDaniel	21647
Mc Daniel City	20601
Mac Donald Farms	20639
McDonogh	21208
Mc Donogh Park	21133
Maceys Corner	21146
McHenry	21541
McKaig	21771
McKay Beach	20650
Mc Kendree	20879
McKenney Hills	20910
McKinleyville	21661
McKinstrys Mill	21791
Maddox	20621
Madison	21677
Madonna	21084
Madonna Manor	21084
Magnolia	21101
Magnolia Springs	20784
Magothy Beach	21122
Magothy Park Beach	21122
Mago Vista Beach	21012
Magruder Landing	20613
Main Street (Part of Salisbury)	21801
Malcolm	20601
Mall in Columbia, The	21044
Malvern	21204
Manchester	21102
Manchester Estates	20746
Manhattan Woods	21146
Manokin (Somerset County)	21836
Manokin (Wicomico County)	21801

	ZIP
Manor	21111
Manor Lake	20853
Manor Park	20853
Manor View	21057
Manor Woods	20853
Maple Crest (Baltimore County)	21220
Maplecrest (Carroll County)	21157
Maple Park	21801
Maple Plains	21801
Mapleside (Part of Cumberland)	21502
Maple View	21157
Mapleville (Frederick County)	21771
Mapleville (Washington County)	21713
Maplewood (Howard County)	21042
Maplewood (Montgomery County)	20814
Maplewood (Prince George's County)	20744
Marbury	20658
Mardela Springs	21837
Margate	21060
Mariners	21817
Marion Station	21838
Marley	21060
Marley Heights	21061
Marley Station	21060
Marling Farms	21619
Marlow Heights	20748
Marlton	20772
Marlywood	21286
Marriottsville	21104
Mars Estates	21221
Marshall Hall	20616
Marshalls Corner	20646
Marston	21776
Martin's Additions	20815
Martinsburg	20842
Martins Woods	20706
Marwood	21061
Marydel	21649
Maryland City	20724
Maryland Correctional Institution for Women	20794
Maryland Correctional Pre-Release System	20794
Maryland Line	21105
Maryland Park	20743
Maryland Point	20662
Marymount	20814
Maryvale (Part of Rockville)	20850
Marywood	21050
Masons Beach	20751
Mason Springs	20640
Massey	21650
Mattapex	21666
Mattapony (Part of Bladensburg)	20710
Matthews	21601
Maugansville	21767
Mayberry	21158
Maydale	20868
Mayfield (Anne Arundel County)	21113
Mayfield (Howard County)	21043
Mayo	21106
Mays Chapel	21093
Mays Chapel Village	21093
Meadowbrook (Part of Bowie)	20715
Meadowbrook Estates	20876
Meadowcliff	21057
Meadowland	21093
Meadowood	20904
Meadowood of Davidsonville	21035
Meadowvale Manor (Part of Havre de Grace)	21078
Meadowview Park	21921
Mechanicsville	20659
Medford	21776
Melitota	21620
Mellwood Hills	20772
Melody Acres	20622
Melrose	21102
Melson	21875
Merchants (Part of Baltimore)	21201
Merrimack Park	20817
Merritt Heights	21801
Merrymount	21244
Michigan Park Hills	20782
Middleborough	21221
Middlebrook	20876
Middleburg	21768
Middlepoint	21773
Middle River	21220

Name	ZIP
Middlesex	21221
Middlesex Shopping Center	21221
Middleton Valley	20748
Middletown (Baltimore County)	21053
Middletown (Frederick County)	21769
Middletown Heights	21769
Midland	21542
Midlothian	21543
Milford	21207
Milford Mill	21244
Milford Park	21117
Milford Ridge	21244
Millbrook (Part of Laurel)	20707
Mill Creek South	20855
Mill Creek Towne	20707
Mill Creek Towne East	20855
Miller	21532
Millers	21107
Millers Island	21219
Millersville	21108
Mill Green	21154
Millington	21651
Millison Plaza	20653
Mill Point	20621
Mill Point Shores	20621
Millrace	21108
Mill Run	21562
Mills Choice	20879
Millwood	20743
Millwood Towne	20743
Mimosa Cove	20751
Minefield	21154
Mitchell Manor	21550
Mitchellville (Prince George's County)	20717
Mondawmin/Metro Plaza (Part of Baltimore)	21215
Monie	21853
Monkton	21111
Monrovia	21770
Montego (Part of Ocean City)	21842
Montevideo (Anne Arundel County)	21076
Montevideo (Howard County)	20794
Montgomery Knolls	21043
Montgomery Square	20854
Montgomery Village	20879
Montgomery White Oak	20904
Montpelier	20708-09
For specific Montpelier Zip Codes call (301) 490-1818	
Montpelier Woods	20708
Montrose	20852
Monumental	21227
Mooresfield	20759
Morgan	21797
Morgantown (Allegany County)	21532
Morgantown (Charles County)	20664
Morganza	20660
Morningside	20746
Moscow	21521
Mount Aetna	21740
Mountain	21085
Mountaindale	21788
Mountain Lake Park	21550
Mountain View	21157
Mountain View Estates	20878
Mountain Wood	21122
Mount Airy	21771
Mount Briar	21756
Mount Carmel	21122
Mount Clare (Part of Baltimore)	21223
Mount De Sales	21228
Mount Harmony	20736
Mount Hebron	21042
Mount Hermon	21801
Mount Hope (Part of Baltimore)	21215
Mount Lena	21713
Mount Olive	21771
Mount Pleasant (Frederick County)	21701
Mount Pleasant (Washington County)	21713
Mount Pleasant (Wicomico County)	21874
Mount Pleasant Beach	21122
Mount Rainier	20712
Mount Saint Mary's College	21727
Mount Savage	21545
Mount Vernon	21853
Mount Victoria	20661
Mountview	21104
Mountville	21701

Name	ZIP
Mount Washington (Part of Baltimore)	21209
Mount Westley	21863
Mount Zion (Caroline County)	21649
Mount Zion (Frederick County)	21702
Mount Zoar	21918
Mousetown	21713
Muirkirk	20705
Mulberry Hills	21401
Murray Hills	20745
Myersdale (Part of Hancock)	21750
Myersville	21773
Nanjemoy	20662
Nanticoke	21840
Narrows	21638
Narrows Park	21502
National Naval Medical Center	20814
Naval Academy	21402
Naval Air Facility	20390
Naval Ordnance Station	20640
Naval Surface Weapons Center	20903
Naylor	20772
Neavitt	21652
Needwood Estates	20855
Neeld Estates	20639
Neelsville	20876
Neilwood	20852
New Addition	21758
Newark	21841
New Birmingham Manor	20866
Newburg	20664
New Carrollton	20784
Newcomb	21653
New Germany	21536
New Hampshire Estates	20903
New Hampshire Gardens (Part of Takoma Park)	20912
Newhope	21874
New London	21771
New Mark Commons (Part of Rockville)	20850
New Market (Frederick County)	21774
New Market (St. Mary's County)	20622
New Market View	21771
New Midway	21775
New Orchard Estates	20772
Newport	20622
Newport Hills	20895
Newton	21655
Newton Village	20781
Newtown (Charles County)	20646
Newtown (Kent County)	21678
Newtown (Talbot County)	21625
New Valley	21918
New Windsor	21776
Nikep	21546
Nob Hill (Howard County)	21042
Nob Hill (Montgomery County)	20903
Nomira Heights (Part of Elkton)	21921
Norbeck	20906
Normandy Heights	21043
Normans	21666
Norris Corner	21009
Norrisville	21161
Northampton (Baltimore County)	21093
Northampton (Prince George's County)	20772
Northamton	20772
North Barnaby	20745
North Beach	20714
North Beach Park	20714
North Bethesda	20814
North Branch	21502
North Brentwood	20722
North Chevy Chase	20815
North College Park (Part of College Park)	20740
North Deale	20751
North East	21901
Northeast Heights	21901
North Englewood	20785
Northern (Part of Hagerstown)	21740
North Forestville	20747
North Fort Foote Village	20744
North Glade	21561
North Indian Head Estates	20616
North Junction (Part of Hagerstown)	21740
North Kensington	20902

Name	ZIP
North Laurel (census designated place)	21784
North Laurel	20723
North Laurel Park	20723
North Linthicum	21090
North Ocean City (Part of Ocean City)	21842
North Point	21222
North Point Village	21222
North Potomac	20878
North Potomac Vista	20745
Northridge Manor	21740
North Roblee Acres	20772
North Sherwood Forest	20904
Northshire	21222
North Shore	21122
North Springbrook	20904
North Wellham	21061
Northwest Park (mail Bethesda)	20814
Northwest Park (mail Silver Spring)	20903
Northwood (Part of Baltimore)	21239
Northwood Park	20901
Northwood Village	20901
Norwood Corner	20906
Norwood Estates	20905
Notch Cliff	21057
Nottingham	21237
Nottingham Woods	21236
Oak Acres	21701
Oak Court	21401
Oakcrest	20707
Oakcrest Towers	20743
Oakdale	20853
Oak Estates	20622
Oak Forest	21228
Oak Hollow	21122
Oakhurst	20866
Oakington	21078
Oakland (Baltimore County)	21053
Oakland (Carroll County)	21784
Oakland (Garrett County)	21550
Oakland (Prince George's County)	20747
Oakland Acres	20622
Oakland Mills	21045
Oakland Park	21133
Oakland Terrace	20895
Oaklawn	20744
Oakleigh	21234
Oakleigh Forest	21146
Oakleigh Manor	21234
Oakley	20609
Oaklyn Manor	21085
Oakmont	20814
Oak Orchard	20735
Oak Park (Baltimore County)	21227
Oak Park (Garrett County)	21550
Oak Ridge	21740
Oak Springs	20868
Oak Summit	21234
Oak View	20903
Oakville (Somerset County)	21853
Oakville (St. Mary's County)	20659
Oakwood	21918
Oakwood Knolls	20817
Ocean City	21842
Ocean City Harbor	21842
Ocean Pines	21811
Odenton	21113
Odenton Gardens	21113
Odenton Heights	21113
Odenton Park	21113
Odyssey	20754
Oella	21228
Old Bay Trail	20772
Old Country Estates	21146
Olde Colonial Woods	20832
Olde Fort Village	20744
Olde Towne Village (Part of District Heights-Forestville)	20747
Old Farm	20852
Old Field (Dorchester County)	21622
Oldfield (Frederick County)	21791
Old Field (Montgomery County)	20854
Old Fort Hills	20744
Old Glory Beach	21060
Old Salem Village	20904
Old Severna Park	21146
Oldtown	21555
Olive	21758
Oliver Beach	21220
Olivet	20657
Olivet Hill	21637

	ZIP		ZIP		ZIP
Olney	20830-32	Perryman	21130	Port Deposit	21904
For specific Olney Zip Codes call		Perry Point	21902	Porters Park	21221
(301) 774-4660		Perrys Corner	21638	Porterstown	21756
Olney (census designated		Perry View	21128	Port Herman	21915
place)	20832	Perryville	21903	Port Republic	20676
Olney Mills	20832	Perrywood Estates	20866	Port Tobacco	20677
Olney Square	20832	Perry Wright	20640	Port Tobacco Riviera	20677
Orangeville (Part of		Petersburg	21643	Potomac (census	
Baltimore)	21224	Petersville	21758	designated place)	20851
Oraville	20659	Pfeiffer Corners	21045	Potomac	20854
Orchard Beach	21226	Pheasant Run	20708	Potomac Commons	20854
Orchard Hills (Baltimore		Phoenix	21131	Potomac Falls Estates	20854
County)	21093	Picketts Corner	21797	Potomac Green	20854
Orchard Hills (Washington		Pike (Part of Rockville)	20852	Potomac Heights (Charles	
County)	21740	Pikesville	21208	County)	20640
Oregon	21030	Pilot Town	21918	Potomac Heights	
Oriole	21853	Pindell	20711	(Washington County)	21740
Otter Point	21009	Pine Cliff	21701	Potomac Hills	20854
Overlea	21206	Pinecrest (Part of Takoma		Potomac Park	21502
Owen Brown	21045	Park)	20912	Potomac Ranch	20854
Owings	20736	Pinedale	21128	Potomac Shores (Charles	
Owings Beach	20751	Pinefield	20601	County)	20677
Owings Mills	21117	Pine Grove	21801	Potomac Shores (St. Mary's	
Owings Wood	20714	Pine Grove Village	21122	County)	20650
Oxford	21654	Pine Hill Estates	20601	Potomac View	20664
Oxon Hill	20745	Pinehurst Estates	20744	Potomac View Estates	20854
	20750	Pinehurst on the Bay	21122	Potomac Village	20854
For specific Oxon Hill Zip Codes		Pine Knoll	21157	Potomac Vista	20745
call (301) 839-5616		Pine Knoll Terrace	21801	Potomac Woods (Part of	
Oxon Hill-Glassmanor	20745	Pineleigh	21286	Rockville)	20854
Oxon Hill Village	20745	Pine Orchard Meadows	21042	Pot Spring	21093
Oxon Run Hills	20748	Pine Ridge	21234	Powder Mill Estates	20783
Oyster Harbor	21401	Pinesburg	21795	Powder Mill Village	20705
Padonia	21030	Pines on the Severn	21012	Powellville	21852
Pagetts Corner	20748	Pinewiff Beach	21037	Powhatan Beach	21122
Paint Branch Estates	20904	Pinewood Hill	20744	Powhattan Mill	21207
Paint Branch Farm	20904	Piney Glen Farms	20854	Prathertown	20879
Palmer Park	20785	Piney Grove	21766	Presidential Park	20783
Palmers Corner	20744	Piney Point	20674	Presidential Towers	20783
Palmetto	21853	Pinto	21556	Presley Manor	20784
Paradise	21228	Pioneer City	21144	Preston	21655
Paradise Beach	21122	Piscataway	20607	Preston Manor	21009
Paramount	21740	Piscataway Bay	20744	Price	21656
Paramount Manor	21740	Piscataway Estates	20744	Priceville	21152
Paris	20736	Piscataway Hills	20744	Prince Frederick	20678
Parkertown	21811	Pisgah	20640	Princess Anne	21853
Parker Wharf	20685	Pittsville	21850	Princeton	20746
Park Hall (St. Mary's		Plainfield	21801	Principio Furnace	21903
County)	20667	Plane Number Four	21771	Prophecy	20744
Park Hall (Washington		Pleasant Fields	20874	Prospect Knolls	20720
County)	21713	Pleasant Grove (Baltimore		Prospect Walk	21044
Parkhead	21711	County)	21136	Providence (Baltimore	
Parkhurst Manor	21801	Pleasant Grove (Frederick		County)	21286
Parkland	20747	County)	21771	Providence (Cecil County)	21921
Parkland Apartments	20747	Pleasant Hill (Baltimore		Public Landing	21863
Parkland Terrace	20746	County)	21117	Pumphrey	21227
Park Mills	21710	Pleasant Hill (Cecil County)	21921	Puncheon Landing	21851
Park Overlook	20855	Pleasant Hills	21087	Putnam	21050
Parkridge	20877	Pleasant Point	21060	Putty Hill	21236
Parkside	20814	Pleasant Ridge	21157	Pylesville	21132
Parkside Estates	20855	Pleasant Springs	20613	Quail Ridge	21227
Parkton	21120	Pleasant Valley (Allegany		Quail Run	20878
Parktowne	21234	County)	21502	Quaint Acres	20904
Parkview	20735	Pleasant Valley (Carroll		Quaker Neck Landing	21620
Parkville	21234	County)	21158	Quaker Ridge	20772
Park West	21061	Pleasant Valley (Washington		Quantico	21856
Parkwood	20814	County)	21783	Queen Anne	21657
Parole	21401	Pleasant View (Frederick		Queen Anne Colony	21666
Parrsville	21771	County)	21710	Queens Chapel Manor (Part	
Parsonsburg	21849	Pleasant View (Howard		of Hyattsville)	20782
Partridge Place	20879	County)	21043	Queenstown (Prince	
Pasadena	21122	Pleasantville (Anne Arundel		George's County)	20712
Patapsco	21048	County)	21061	Queenstown (Queen Anne's	
Patterson (Part of Baltimore)	21231	Pleasantville (Washington		County)	21658
Patuxent	21113	County)	25425	Queenswood	20772
Patuxent Beach	20619	Pleasant Walk	21773	Quince Orchard	20878
Patuxent Institution	20794	Plumgar	20876	Quincy Manor	20784
Patuxent Manor	21035	Plum Point	20639	Rabbit Town	21869
Patuxent Naval Air Test		Pocomoke City	21851	Radiant Valley	20784
Center	20670	Pointer Ridge (Part of		Ramblewood Village	20735
Patuxent Palisades	20754	Bowie)	20716	Ramgate	20744
Patuxent Park	20653	Point Lookout	20687	Rancleigh (Part of	
Patuxent River	20670	Point of Rocks	21777	Baltimore)	21209
Peach Orchard Heights	20866	Point of Rocks Estates	21777	Rancleigh	21209
Peachwood	20905	Poland	21562	Randalia	21915
Peacock Corners	21651	Pomfret	20675	Randallstown	21133
Pearl	21701	Pomona	21620	Randle Cliff Beach	20732
Pectonville	21711	Pomonkey	20640	Randolph Farms	20852
Pendennis Mount	21401	Ponder Cove	21037	Randolph Hills	20852
Peninsula General Hospital		Pondsville	21783	Random Heights	21157
(Part of Salisbury)	21801	Pooks Hill	20814	Raspeburg (Part of	
Pen Mar	21719	Poole	21034	Baltimore)	21206
Pen-Mar Shopping Center	20747	Poolesville	20837	Rawlings	21557
Penn Mary Junction (Part of		Popes Creek	20664	Rawlings Heights	21557
Baltimore)	21224	Poplar Grove	21154	Raynor Heights	21090
Pepper Mill Village	20743	Poplar Hill	20608	Rayville	21120
Perry Hall	21128	Poplar Hill Estates	20735	Red Coat Woods	20854
Perry Hall Estates	21236	Poplar Knob	21788	Reddings Corner	21678
Perry Hall Manor	21128	Poplar Springs	21771	Redford Estates	20744
Perry Hall Shopping Center	21128	Port Covington (Part of		Red Hill	20658
Perry Hall Village	21128	Baltimore)	21230	Redhouse	21550

	ZIP
Sherwood (Talbot County)	21665
Sherwood Forest (Anne Arundel County)	21405
Sherwood Forest (Montgomery County)	20904
Sherwood Forest (Prince George's County)	20772
Sherwood Manor (Prince George's County)	20715
Sherwood Manor (Wicomico County)	21801
Shetland Hills	21093
Shiloh (Charles County)	20664
Shiloh (Dorchester County)	21643
Shipley	21090
Shookstown	21702
Shore Acres	21012
Shoreham Beach	21037
Shoreland	21061
Shorwood Estates	21637
Showell	21862
Sierra Manor	21801
Silesia	20744
Sillery Bay	21122
Siloam	21822
Silver Gate Village	21236
Silver Grove	21740
Silver Hill	20746
Silver Hill Park	20746
Silver Meadow	21128
Silver Rock (Part of Rockville)	20850
Silver Run	21158
Silver Sands	21060
Silver Spring	20901-18
For specific Silver Spring Zip Codes call (301) 588-9068	
Silver Valley	20746
Simpsonville	21150
Sinepuxent	21811
Singerly	21916
Skidmore	21401
Skipton	21625
Skyline	20746
Skyline Additions	20746
Sky Valley	21561
Slabtown	21545
Sligo Park Knolls	20901
Smallwood	21157
Smithsburg	21783
Smithville (Caroline County)	21632
Smithville (Dorchester County)	21669
Smoketown	21713
Smugglers Cove	21146
Snowden Manor	21157
Snowden Oaks	20708
Snow Hill	21863
Snow Hill Manor	20708
Snug Harbor (Anne Arundel County)	20764
Snug Harbor (Worcester County)	21811
Snydersburg	21074
Social Security Administration	21207
Society Hill	20650
Sollers Homes	21222
Sollers Point	21222
Solley Heights	21060
Solomons	20688
Somerset	20815
Sonoma	20814
South (Part of Baltimore)	21230
Southampton	20653
South Cheverly Forest	20784
South Cumberland (Part of Cumberland)	21502
Southdown Shores	21037
Southeast (Part of Baltimore)	21224
Southerland	20601
Southern Garden Apartments	20032
Southern Maryland Facility	20743-50
	20752-53
	20790-91
For specific Southern Maryland Facility Zip Codes call (202) 682-9595	
South Fort Foote Village	20744
South Gate	21061
South Haven	21401
South Kensington	20895
Southland Hills	21204
South Laurel	20708
South Lawn	20745
South Layhill	20906
South Piscataway	20607
South River Park	21037

	ZIP
South Salisbury (Part of Salisbury)	21801
South Tantallon	20748
Southview	20745
South Woodside Park	20910
Sparks	21152
Sparks Glencoe	21152
Sparrows Point	21219
Spaulding Heights	20747
Spence	21863
Spencerville	20868
Spielman	21733
Spoolsville	21769
Springbrook (Baltimore County)	21133
Springbrook (Montgomery County)	20904
Springbrook Forest	20902
Springbrook Manor	20904
Springbrook Village	20904
Springdale (Baltimore County)	21030
Springdale (Prince George's County)	20706
Springdale Gardens	20706
Springfield	20814
Spring Gap	21560
Spring Garden Estates	21793
Spring Grove	21837
Spring Hill	21830
Springhill Acres	21801
Springhill Lake (Part of Greenbelt)	20770
Springlake	20817
Spring Meadow	21084
Spring Mills	21157
Spring Valley	21740
Squires Woods	20744
Stablersville	21161
Stafford	21034
Stanbrook	21222
Stansbury Estates	21220
Stansbury Manor	21220
Starkeys Corner	21623
Starr	21617
Stemmer's Run	21220
Stepney	21001
Steuart Level	21037
Stevenson	21153
Stevensville	21666
Stevensville South	21666
Stewartown	20879
Stillmeadows	21144
Still Pond	21667
Stockton	21864
Stonecrest	21043
Stonegate	20905
Stone Haven	21060
Stoneleigh	21212
Stoneybrook Estates	20906
Stony Beach	21226
Stony Run	21076
Stratford	21093
Strathmore At Bel Pre	20906
Strathmore Estates	20906
Stratton Woods	20817
Strawberry Hills Estates	20616
Strawbridge Estates	21784
Strawleigh	21702
Street	21154
Stronghold	20842
Suburban Acres	21801
Suburbia	21061
Sudbrook Park	21208
Sudlersville	21668
Sugarland	20837
Sugarloaf Estates	21710
Suitland	20746
	20752
For specific Suitland Zip Codes call (301) 735-1938	
Suitland-Silver Hill	20746
Sullivan Heights	21157
Summerhill (Anne Arundel County)	21032
Summerhill (Montgomery County)	20837
Summit Farms	21237
Summit Park	21209
Sumner	20816
Sunair (Part of Salisbury)	21801
Sunderland	20689
Sunny Acres	20747
Sunnybrook	21131
Sunnybrook Hills	21131
Sunny Isle of Kent	21666
Sunrise	20744
Sunrise Beach	21032
Sunset Acres	21740
Sunset Beach	21122
Sunset Heights	21801

	ZIP
Sunset Hills	21702
Sunset Knoll	21122
Sunshine	20833
Sunshine Acres	20639
Sun Valley	21061
Surratt Gardens	20735
Susquehanna Hills	21078
Sussex Square	21108
Sutton Acres	20677
Swallow Falls	21550
Swan Creek	21001
Swanton	21561
Sweet Air Manor	21013
Sweetser Heights	21090
Sycamore Acres	20853
Sycamore Heights	21740
Sykesville	21784
Sylmar	21911
Sylvan View	21122
Table Rock	26720
Takoma Park	20912
Tall Timbers	20690
Tammany Manor	21795
Tanager Forest	21108
Taneytown	21787
Tanglewood	21401
Tantallon	20744
Tantallon North	20744
Tantallon on the Potomac	20748
Tantallon Square	20744
Tanterra	20833
Tanyard	21655
Tarquin Village	20735
Taylor Mill Village	21801
Taylors Island	21669
Taylorsville	21771
Taylorville	21811
Temple Heights	20748
Temple Hills	20748
	20757
For specific Temple Hills Zip Codes call (301) 723-6181	
Temple Hills Park	20748
Templeton Estates	20737
Templeton Manor	20737
Templeville	21670
Temple Woods	20744
Terrace Gardens	21012
Terrace View Estates	21225
Texas	21030
Thayerville	21550
The Colony	20874
The Crest of Wickford	20852
The Downs	21401
The Glen	20854
The Hamlet	20815
The Highlands	21061
The Lakes	21093
The Meadows	20639
The Oaks (Calvert County)	20639
The Oaks (Howard County)	21043
Theodore	21911
The Orchards	21043
The Pines	20772
The Points	20879
Thomas	21613
Thomas Choice	20879
Thomas Run	21015
Thomas Town	21629
Thompson Corner	20659
Thompsontown	21631
Thomson Estates	21921
Thornleigh	21139
Thornwood Knoll	20744
Thorwood Park	21234
Thunder Hill	21045
Thurmont	21788
Thurston	20842
Tilden Woods	20852
Tilghman	21671
Tilghmanton	21713
Timber Grove	21117
Timber Ridge (Anne Arundel County)	21076
Timber Ridge (Carroll County)	21157
Timberview	21227
Timonium	21093
Tintop Hill	20650
Tobytown	20854
Todd Village	21048
Toddville	21672
Tolchester Beach	21620
Tollgate	21117
Tompkinsville	20664
Tonytank	21801
Tower Acres	20723
Tower Garden on the Bay	21666
Town Creek	25434
Town Creek Estates	20619
Town Creek Manor	20653

	ZIP
Town Crest	20855
Towne and Country North	21030
Towne Center	20708
Town Point	21915
Townsend	20735
Townsontown Centre	21286
Towson	21204
	21286

For specific Towson Zip Codes
call (410) 825-4888

	ZIP
Towson Estates	21204
Towson Marketplace	21204
Towson Park	21286
Towson Plaza Shopping Center	21286
Tracys Landing	20779
Trappe (St. Mary's County)	20628
Trappe (Talbot County)	21673
Trappe (Worcester County)	21811
Trappe Station	21654
Travilah	20854
Treetops	21122
Trengall Acres	21740
Trent Hall	20659
Trenton	21155
Trescher Heights	21502
Triple Lakes	21502
Troutville	21798
Truman Heights	20748
Tulip Hill (Frederick County)	21702
Tulip Hill (Montgomery County)	20816
Tunis Mills	21601
Turkey Neck	21561
Turkey Point (Anne Arundel County)	21037
Turkey Point (Baltimore County)	21221
Turnbull Estates	21037
Turners Station	21222
Tuscarora	21790
Tuxedo (Part of Cheverly)	20785
Tuxedo Colony	20785
Twinbrook (Part of Rockville)	20851
Twinbrook Estates	20601
Twin Brook Forest (Part of Rockville)	20851
Twinbrook Park (Part of Rockville)	20851
Twin Harbors	21012
Tyaskin	21865
Tydings on the Bay	21401
Tylerton	21866
Tyrone	21158
Ulmsted Acres	21012
Ulmsted Estate	21012
Ulmsted Gardens	21012
Ulmsted Point	21012
Union Bridge	21791
Union Corner	21636
Union Mills	21158
Uniontown	21158
Unionville (Baltimore County)	21092
Unionville (Frederick County)	21791
Unionville (Talbot County)	21601
Unionville (Worcester County)	21851
Unity	20833
University City	20783
University Gardens	20783
University Hills	20783
University Park	20784
Upperco	21155
Upper Crossroads	21047
Upper Fairmount	21867
Upper Falls	21156
Upper Ferry Estates	21801
Upper Hill	21867
Upper Homewood	21502
Upper Marlboro	20772-75

For specific Upper Marlboro Zip
Codes call (301) 627-4330

	ZIP
Urbana	21701
Utica	21788
Vale	21015
Vale Summit	21532
Valley Crest	21093
Valley Lee	20692
Valley Mede	21042
Valley Stream Estates	20866
Valley View (Howard County)	21043
Valley View (Prince George's County)	20744
Valleywood (Baltimore County)	21093
Valleywood (Wicomico County)	21801

	ZIP
Van Bibber	21040
Van Bibber Manor	21040
Van Lear Manor	21795
Vansville	20705
Venice on the Bay	21122
Venton	21853
Vernon	21161
Veterans Administration Medical Center	21902
Victory Villa	21220
Vienna	21869
Viers Mill Village	20906
View More Acres	21701
Villa Cresta	21234
Village of Vanderway	21234
Villages of Montpelier	20708
Villa Heights	20784
Villa Monticello	21723
Villa Nova	21207
Villa Toscano	21122
Villa Verdi	21054
Waggaman Heights	20748
Wakefield (Baltimore County)	21093
Wakefield (Carroll County)	21776
Wakefield Meadows	21014
Walbrook (Part of Baltimore)	21216
Waldon Woods	20735
Waldorf	20601-04

For specific Waldorf Zip Codes
call (301) 645-5231

	ZIP
Walker Hill	20707
Walker Mill	20743
Walker Mill Estates	20743
Walkersville	21793
Wallington Estates	20747
Wallville	20685
Walnut Hill	20877
Walnut Ridge	21157
Walnut Woods	20852
Walston	21849
Walter Heights	20748
Wango	21801
Warburton Oaks	20744
Wards Chapel	21133
Warfield Estates	21738
Warfieldsburg	21157
Warington Hills (Part of Indian Head)	20640
Warlinda	20646
Warren	21030
Warwick	21912
Washington Grove	20880
Waterbury	21032
Waterloo	21227
Wateroak Point	21122
Watersville	21771
Waterview	21840
Watkins Glen	20854
Waverly (Part of Baltimore)	21218
Wayside	20664
Webster Village	21078
Weems Creek	21401
Weisburg	21161
Welcome	20693
Welhams	21061
Wellington Estates	20707
Wenona	21870
Wesley	21626
Wesmond (Part of Poolesville)	20837
West Baltimore (Part of Baltimore)	21227
West Beach (Part of Chesapeake Beach)	20732
West Bethesda	20817
	20827

For specific West Bethesda Zip
Codes call (301) 365-0045

	ZIP
Westboro	20814
West Bowie (Part of Bowie)	20719
Westchester (Baltimore County)	21228
Westchester (Montgomery County)	20902
Westchester Estates	20748
Westchester Park (Part of College Park)	20740
West Denton	21629
West Edmondale	21229
West Elkridge	21227
West End (Part of Annapolis)	21401
West End Park (Part of Rockville)	20850
Westerlea	21228
Westernport	21562
Western Shores Estates	20676
West Friendship	21794
Westgate	20816
West Gate Woods	20706

	ZIP
West Hills (Baltimore County)	21207
West Hills (Frederick County)	21702
West Hyattsville (Part of Hyattsville)	20782
Westlake	21801
West Lanham Estates	20784
West Lanham Hills	20784
West Laurel	20707
West Laurel Acres	20707
West Liberty	21161
West Magothy Manor	21012
Westminster (Carroll County)	21157-58

For specific Westminster Zip
Codes call (301) 848-4780

	ZIP
Westminster (Montgomery County)	20852
Westminster South	21157
Westmore (Part of Rockville)	20850
Westmoreland Hills	20816
West Nottingham	21917
West Ocean City	21842
Westover	21871
Westowne	21229
Westphalia Estates	20772
Westphalia Woods	20772
West River	20778
West Severna Park	21146
West Shady Side	20764
West Shore	21106
West Twin River Beach	21220
Westview	21801
Westview Mall	21228
Westview Park	21228
West View Shores	21919
West Vindex	21538
Westwood	20613
Westwood Estates (Charles County)	20601
Westwood Estates (Prince George's County)	20623
Wetipquin	21856
Weverton	21758
Wexford	21012
Whaleysville	21872
Wheaton	20902
Wheaton Crest	20902
Wheaton Forest	20902
Wheaton-Glenmont	20902
Wheaton Hills	20902
Wheaton Plaza Regional Center	20902
Wheaton Woods	20853
Whetstone	20879
Whipporwill Estates	21122
Whiskey Bottom	20723
Whiteburg	21863
White Crystal Beach	21919
Whitefield Knolls	20706
Whitefield Woods	20706
White Flint Mall	20895
White Flint Park	20895
Whiteford	21160
White Hall (Baltimore County)	21161
Whitehall (Prince George's County)	20607
Whitehall Beach	21401
Whitehall Manor	20814
Whitehaven	21856
Whitehouse Heights	20785
White Landing	20613
Whiteleysburg	21639
White Marsh	21162
White Oak	20904
White Oak (census designated place)	20901
White Oak Manor	20904
White Oak Park	20904
White Oak Shopping Center	20904
White Oak Tower	20904
White Plains	20695
White Point Beach	20650
White Rock	21702
White Sands	20657
Whiton	21863
Wicomico	20622
Wicomico Beach	20664
Wilburn Estates	20743
Wilde Lake	21044
Wildercroft	20737
Wild Rose Shores	21403
Wild Wood Beach	21221
Wildwood Estates	20735
Wildwood Hills	20817
Wildwood Manor	20817
Wildwoods	21133
Wilelinor Estates	21037

	ZIP
Aberdeen (Part of Boston)	02135
Abington	02351
Abington (Town)	02351
Acapesket	02536
Accord	02018
Acoaxet	02801
Acton	01720
Acton (Town)	01720
Acton Center	01720
Acushnet	02743
Acushnet (Town)	02743
Adams (Town)	01220
Adams	01220
Adamsdale	02760
Adams Shore (Part of Quincy)	02169
Adamsville	01340
Agawam	01001
Agawam (Town)	01001
Agawam Beach	02571
Agawam Shopping Center	01001
Airport Mail Facility (Part of Boston)	02109
Aldenville (Part of Chicopee)	01013
Alford	01230
Alford (Town)	01230
Allendale (Part of Pittsfield)	01201
Allendale Shopping Center (Part of Pittsfield)	01201
Allerton	02045
Allston (Part of Boston)	02134
Amesbury	01913
Amesbury (Town)	01913
Amesbury (census designated place)	01913
Amesbury Center	01913
Amherst	01002-04
For specific Amherst Zip Codes call (413) 549-0523	
Amrita	02534
Andover	01810
Andover (Town)	01810
Annisquam (Part of Gloucester)	01930
Antassawamock Beach	02739
Apponagansett Village	02748
Arlington (Town)	02174
Arlington	02174
Arlington Heights	02175
Armory (Part of Springfield)	01101
Army Materials and Mechanics Research Center	02172
Arsenal Mall	02172
Ashburnham	01430
Ashburnham (Town)	01430
Ashby	01431
Ashby (Town)	01431
Ashdod	02332
Ashfield	01330
Ashfield (Town)	01330
Ashland (Town)	01721
Ashland	01721
Ashley Falls	01222
Ashley Heights	02717
Ashmont (Part of Boston)	02124
Assinippi	02339
Assonet	02702
Assonet Bay Shores	02702
Assumption College (Part of Worcester)	01609
Astor (Part of Boston)	02123
Athol (Town)	01331
Athol	01331
Athol Junction (Part of Springfield)	01101
Atlantic (Part of Quincy)	02169
Attleboro	02703
Attleboro Falls	02763
Auburn (Town)	01501
Auburn	01501
Auburndale (Part of Newton)	02166
Auburn Shopping Mall	01501
Avon (Town)	02322
Avon	02322
Ayer	01432-33
For specific Ayer Zip Codes call (508) 772-2083	
Ayer (Town)	01432
Ayer (census designated place)	01432
Ayers Village (Part of Haverhill)	01830
Babson Park	02157
Back Bay Annex (Part of Boston)	02115
Bakers Grove	01473
Bakers Island (Part of Salem)	01970
Baldwinville	01436

	ZIP
Ballardvale	01810
Bancroft	01243
Baptist Corner	01370
Barkerville (Part of Pittsfield)	01201
Barnstable	02630
Barnstable (Town)	02630
Barre	01005
Barre (Town)	01005
Barre Plains	01606
Barrowsville	02766
Bass Point	01908
Bass River	02664
Bass Rocks (Part of Gloucester)	01930
Bay State (Part of Northampton)	01060
Bay State Correctional Center	02056
Baystate West Shopping Center (Part of Springfield)	01103
Bayview (Bristol County)	02748
Bayview (Essex County)	01930
Beach (Part of Revere)	02151
Beachmont (Part of Revere)	02151
Beach Point	02652
Beachwood	01262
Beacon Hill (Part of Boston)	02108
Beaver Brook (Middlesex County)	02154
Beaver Brook (Worcester County)	01602
Becket	01223
Becket (Town)	01223
Becket Center	01011
Bedford (Town)	01730
Bedford	01730
Bedford Springs	01730
Beechwood	02025
Belcher Square	01230
Belchertown	01007
Belchertown (Town)	01007
Belchertown State School	01007
Bellingham (Town)	02019
Bellingham	02019
Bell Rock (Part of Malden)	02148
Belmont (Town)	02178
Belmont	02178
Belvidere (Part of Lowell)	01852
Bennetts Corner	02379
Berkley	02780
Berkley (Town)	02780
Berkshire	01224
Berkshire Heights	01230
Berlin	01503
Berlin (Town)	01503
Bernardston	01337
Bernardston (Town)	01337
Beverly	01915
Beverly Cove (Part of Beverly)	01915
Beverly Farms (Part of Beverly)	01915
Beverly Junction (Part of Beverly)	01915
Big Pond	01029
Billerica	01821-22
For specific Billerica Zip Codes call (508) 663-8301	
Birch Island	01570
Blackinton (Part of North Adams)	01247
Black Rock	02025
Blackstone	01504
Blackstone (Town)	01504
Blandford	01008
Blandford (Town)	01008
Bleachery (Part of Lowell)	01852
Bleachery (Part of Waltham)	02154
Bliss Corner	02748
Blissville	01364
Bloomingdale (Part of Worcester)	01604
Blue Hills	02186
Blush Hollow	01243
Bolton	01740
Bolton (Town)	01740
Bondsville	01009
Boston	02101-37
	02163
	02201-22
For specific Boston Zip Codes call (617) 654-5768	

COLLEGES & UNIVERSITIES

	ZIP
Berklee College of Music	02215
Boston University	02215
Emerson College	02116
Massachusetts College of Art	02215

	ZIP
Massachusetts College of Pharmacy and Allied Health Sciences	02115
Northeastern University	02115
School of the Museum of Fine Arts	02115
Suffolk University	02108
University of Massachusetts at Boston	02125
Wentworth Institute of Technology	02115

FINANCIAL INSTITUTIONS

	ZIP
Advantage Bank for Savings	02152
BayBank Boston, N.A.	02110
Boston Safe Deposit and Trust Company	02108
Brookline Savings Bank	02147
Brown Brothers Harriman & Co	02109
CambridgePort Savings Bank	02139
East Boston Savings Bank	02128
The First National Bank of Boston	02110
Fleet Bank of Massachusetts, N.A.	02109
Greater Boston Bank	02135
Grove Bank	02146
Guaranty-First Trust Company	02154
Hibernia Savings Bank	02170
Hyde Park Savings Bank	02136
Malden Trust Company	02148
The Massachusetts Company	02110
Medford Savings Bank	02155
Neworld Bank	02110
Olympic International Bank and Trust Company	02210
Pioneer Financial	02148
The Provident Institution for Savings	02111
Shawmut Bank, N.A.	02211
South Boston Savings Bank	02127
South Weymouth Savings Bank	02190
State Street Bank and Trust Company	02110
Sterling Bank	02154
Stoneham Savings Bank	02180
U.S. Trust Company	02108
Watertown Savings Bank	02172
Weymouth Savings Bank	02188
Workingmens Co-Operative Bank	02110

HOSPITALS

	ZIP
Beth Israel Hospital	02215
Boston City Hospital	02118
Brigham and Women's Hospital	02115
Carney Hospital	02124
Children's Hospital	02115
Faulkner Hospital	02130
Hebrew Rehabilitation Center for Aged	02131
Lemuel Shattuck Hospital	02130
Massachusetts General Hospital	02114
New England Deaconess Hospital	02215
New England Medical Center	02111
Spaulding Rehabilitation Hospital	02114
St. Elizabeth's Hospital of Boston	02135
University Hospital	02118
Veterans Administration Medical Center	02130

HOTELS/MOTELS

	ZIP
Boston Park Plaza Hotel & Towers	02117
Le Hotel Meridien Boston	02110
The Ritz-Carlton, Boston	02117
Sheraton-Boston Hotel	02199
The Westin Hotel, Copley Place	02116

MILITARY INSTALLATIONS

	ZIP
Army Materials Technology Laboratory	02172
Coast Guard Support Center, Boston	02109
Naval Air Station, South Weymouth	02190
Naval Recruiting District, Boston	02210

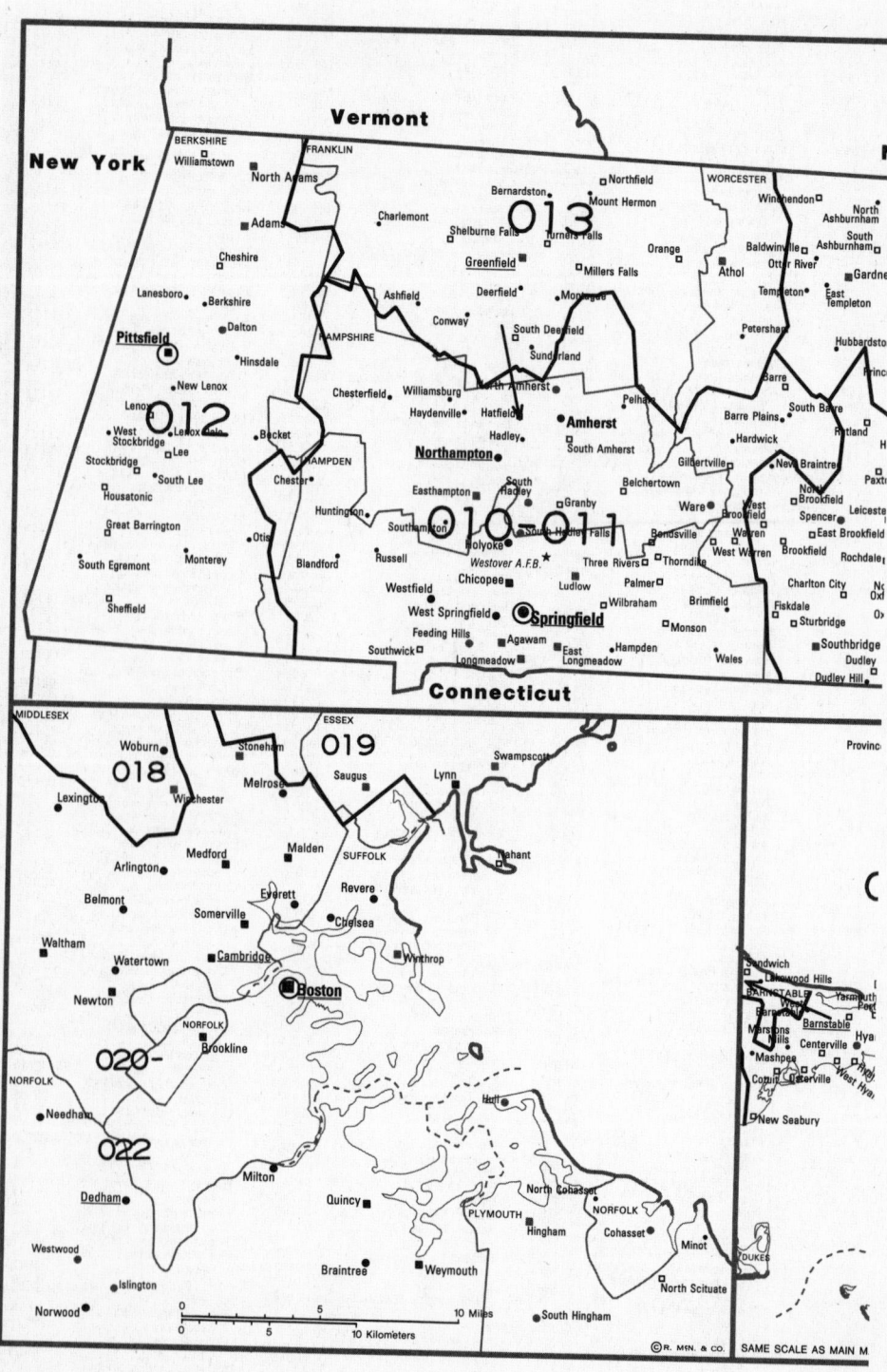

Vermont

New York

BERKSHIRE
Williamstown

FRANKLIN

Northfield

WORCESTER

North Adams

Charlemont

Bernardston

Mount Hermon

Winchendon

North Ashburnham

Adams

Shelburne Falls

Turners Falls

013

South Ashburnham

Cheshire

Greenfield

Orange

Baldwinville

Otter River

Gardner

Lanesboro

Berkshire

Deerfield

Millers Falls

Athol

Templeton

East Templeton

Dalton

Ashfield

Montague

Pittsfield

Hinsdale

HAMPSHIRE

Conway

South Deerfield

Petersham

Hubbardston

New Lenox

Chesterfield

Williamsburg

North Amherst

Sunderland

Prince

Lenox

012

Haydenville

Hatfield

Pelham

Barre

South Barre

West Stockbridge

Lenox Dale

Becket

Hadley

Amherst

Barre Plains

Hardwick

New Braintree

Rutland

H

Stockbridge

Lee

HAMPDEN

Northampton

South Amherst

Gilbertville

Paxt

Housatonic

South Lee

Chester

Easthampton

South Hadley

Belchertown

West Brookfield

North Brookfield

Leiceste

Great Barrington

Monterey

Otis

Huntington

Southampton

010-011

Granby

South Hadley Falls

Ware

Spencer

East Brookfield

Rochdale

South Egremont

Blandford

Russell

Holyoke

Three Rivers

Bondsville

West Warren

Warren

Brookfield

Rochdale

Sheffield

Westover A.F.B.

Chicopee

Ludlow

Thorndike

Charlton City

No
Oxt

Westfield

Palmer

Fiskdale

Sturbridge

O

West Springfield

Springfield

Wilbraham

Brimfield

Monson

Southbridge

Dudley

Feeding Hills

Agawam

East Longmeadow

Hampden

Wales

Dudley Hill

Southwick

Longmeadow

Connecticut

MIDDLESEX

ESSEX

Woburn

Stoneham

019

Swampscott

Provinc

018

Melrose

Saugus

Lynn

Lexington

Winchester

Medford

Malden

SUFFOLK

Nahant

Arlington

Everett

Revere

C

Belmont

Somerville

Chelsea

Waltham

Watertown

Cambridge

Winthrop

Sandwich

Lakewood Hills

Yarmouth

Newton

Boston

BARNSTABLE

Pool

NORFOLK

Barnstable

Barnstable

Hyal

Brookline

Marstons Mills

Centerville

020-

Mashpee

West Hyan

NORFOLK

Hull

Cotuit

Osterville

Needham

New Seabury

022

Milton

North Cohasset

Dedham

Quincy

PLYMOUTH

Hingham

NORFOLK

Cohasset

Minot

Westwood

Braintree

Weymouth

DUKES

Islington

North Scituate

Norwood

South Hingham

0   5   10 Miles

0   5   10 Kilometers

©R. MᴺN. & CO.   SAME SCALE AS MAIN M.

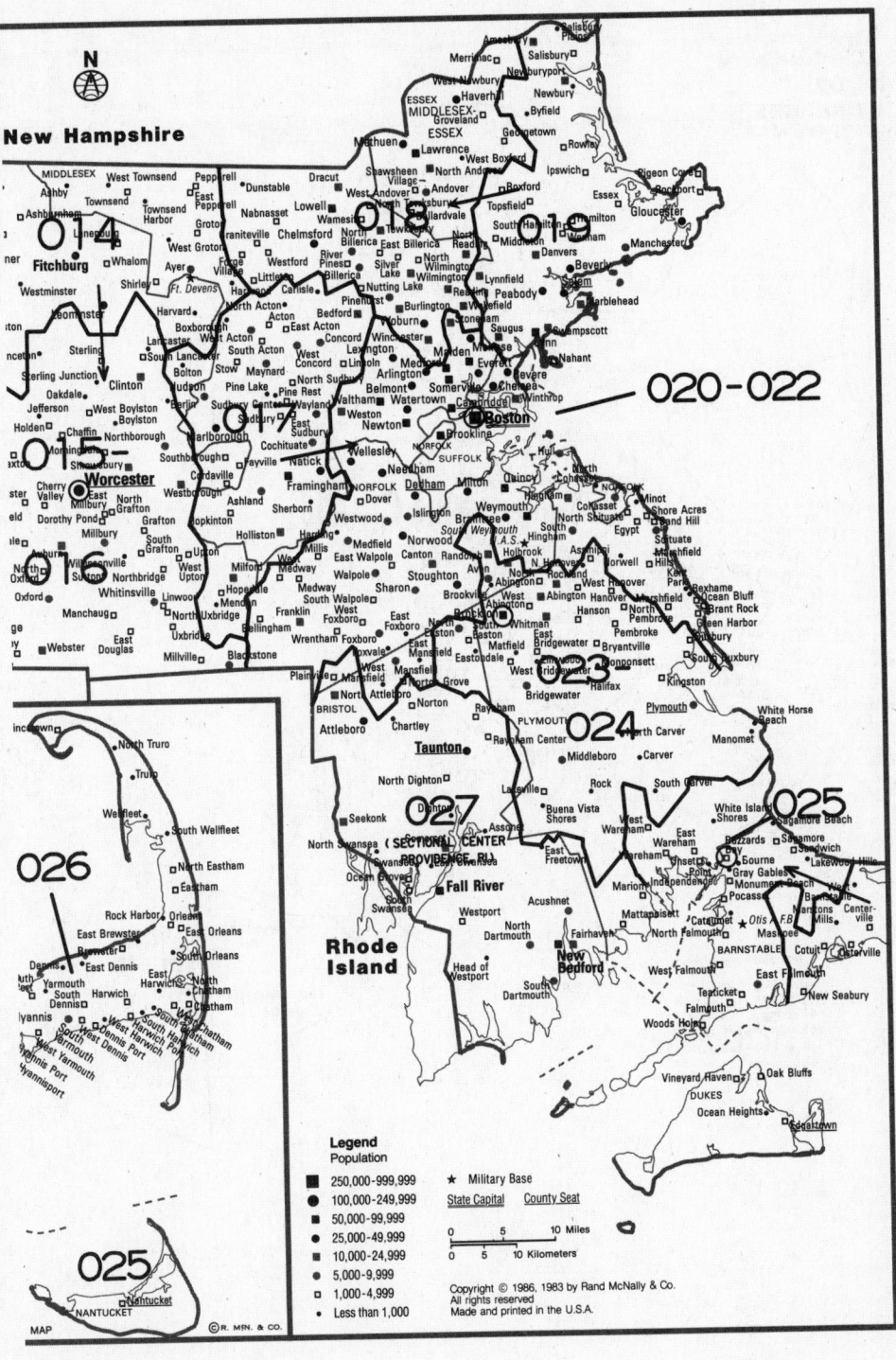

New Hampshire

020-022

026

025
NANTUCKET

MAP   ©R. McN. & CO.

Rhode
Island

Legend
Population
■ 250,000-999,999
● 100,000-249,999
■ 50,000-99,999
▪ 25,000-49,999
▫ 10,000-24,999
▫ 5,000-9,999
▫ 1,000-4,999
▫ Less than 1,000

★ Military Base
State Capital   County Seat

0   5   10 Miles
0 5   10 Kilometers

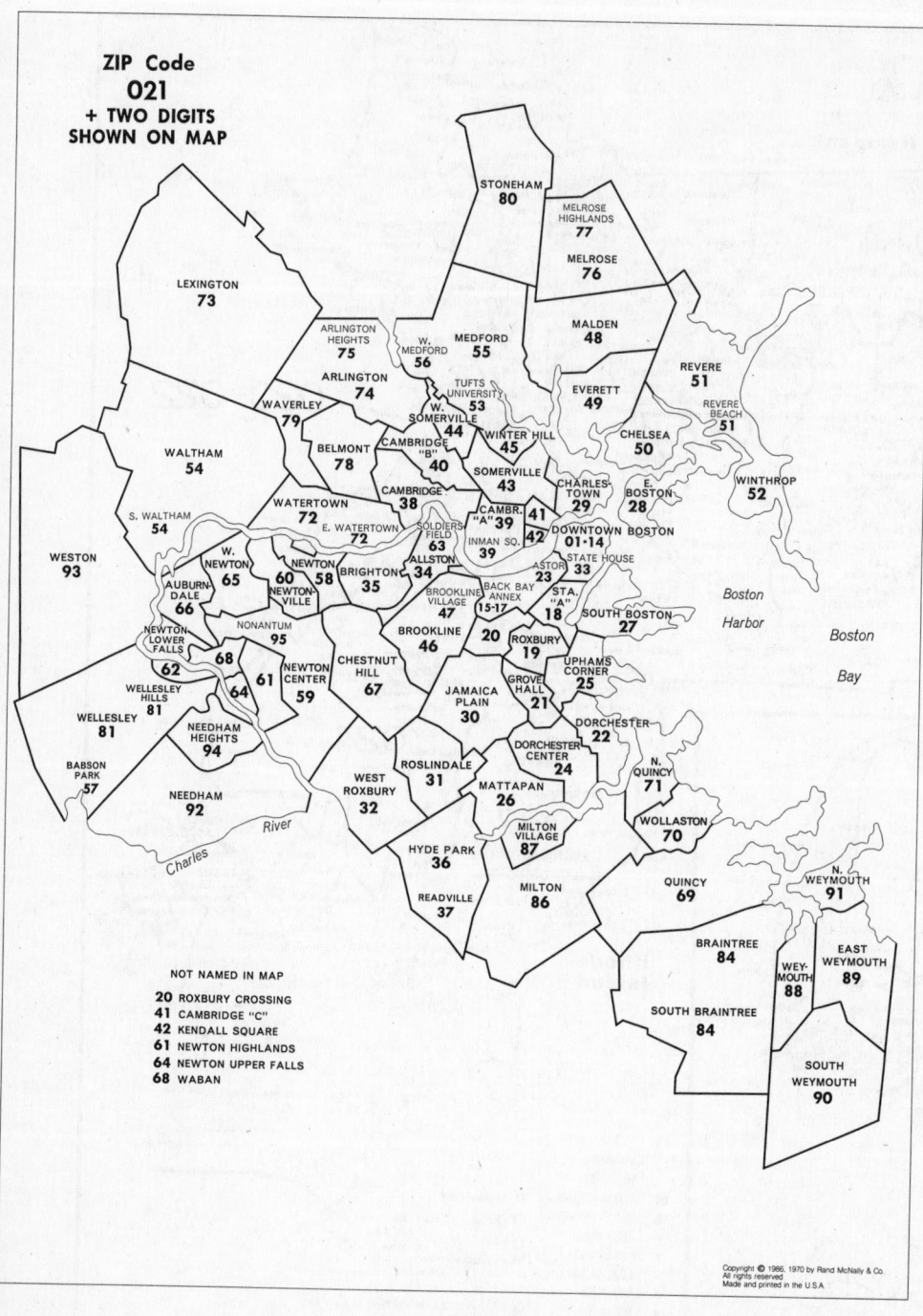

ZIP Code
021
+ TWO DIGITS
SHOWN ON MAP

STONEHAM 80

MELROSE HIGHLANDS 77

MELROSE 76

LEXINGTON 73

ARLINGTON HEIGHTS 75

W. MEDFORD 56

MEDFORD 55

MALDEN 48

REVERE 51

WAVERLEY 79

ARLINGTON 74

TUFTS UNIVERSITY 53

W. SOMERVILLE 44

WINTER HILL 45

EVERETT 49

REVERE BEACH 51

WALTHAM 54

BELMONT 78

CAMBRIDGE "B" 40

SOMERVILLE 43

CHELSEA 50

WINTHROP 52

S. WALTHAM 54

WATERTOWN 72

CAMBRIDGE 38

CAMBR. "A" 39

CAMBR. "C" 41

CHARLES-TOWN 29

E. BOSTON 28

WESTON 93

W. NEWTON 65

NEWTON 60

E. WATERTOWN 72

SOLDIERS FIELD 63

INMAN SQ. 39

KENDALL SQ. 42

DOWNTOWN BOSTON 01-14

STATE HOUSE 33

Boston Harbor

AUBURN DALE 66

NEWTON-VILLE 58

BRIGHTON 35

ALLSTON 34

BROOKLINE VILLAGE 47

BACK BAY ANNEX 15-17

ASTOR 23

STA. "A" 18

SOUTH BOSTON 27

Boston Bay

NONANTUM 95

NEWTON LOWER FALLS 62

68

61

NEWTON CENTER 59

CHESTNUT HILL 67

BROOKLINE 46

20

ROXBURY 19

UPHAMS CORNER 25

WELLESLEY HILLS 81

64

NEEDHAM HEIGHTS 94

JAMAICA PLAIN 30

GROVE HALL 21

DORCHESTER 22

N. QUINCY 71

WELLESLEY 81

BABSON PARK 57

NEEDHAM 92

Charles River

WEST ROXBURY 32

ROSLINDALE 31

DORCHESTER CENTER 24

MATTAPAN 26

WOLLASTON 70

HYDE PARK 36

MILTON VILLAGE 87

QUINCY 69

N. WEYMOUTH 91

READVILLE 37

MILTON 86

BRAINTREE 84

WEY-MOUTH 88

EAST WEYMOUTH 89

SOUTH BRAINTREE 84

SOUTH WEYMOUTH 90

NOT NAMED IN MAP

20 ROXBURY CROSSING
41 CAMBRIDGE "C"
42 KENDALL SQUARE
61 NEWTON HIGHLANDS
64 NEWTON UPPER FALLS
68 WABAN

	ZIP
Supervisor of Shipbuilding, Conversion and Repair, Boston	02210
United States Army Engineer Division, New England	02254
Boston College (Part of Newton)	02167
Boston University (Part of Boston)	02215
Bourne	02532
Bourne (Town)	02532
Bourne	02532
Bournedale	02532
Boxborough	01719
Boxborough (Town)	01719
Boxford	01921
Boxford (Town)	01921
Boylston	01505
Boylston (Town)	01505
Bradford (Part of Haverhill)	01830
Bradstreet	01038
Braintree (Town)	02184
Braintree	02184
Braintree Highlands	02184
Braleys	02717
Bramanville	01527
Brant Rock	02020
Brayton Point	02725
Brewster	02631
Brewster (Town)	02631
Briarwood Beach	02571
Bridgewater	02324
Bridgewater (Town)	02324
Brier Neck (Part of Gloucester)	01930
Brigadoon Village	01949
Briggsville	01247
Brighton (Part of Boston)	02135
Brightside (Part of Holyoke)	01040
Brightwood (Part of Springfield)	01107
Brimfield	01010
Brimfield (Town)	01010
Brittan Square (Part of Worcester)	01605
Broadway (Part of Malden)	02148
Brockton	02401-05
For specific Brockton Zip Codes call (508) 559-1800	
Brookfield	01506
Brookfield (Town)	01506
Brookline (Town)	02146
Brookline	02146
Brookline Hill	02146
Brookline Village	02147
Brooks Place	02379
Brookville	02343
Brownell Corner	02790
Browns Point	01950
Brushwood	02038
Bryantville	02327
Buckland	01338
Buckland (Town)	01338
Buena Vista Shores	02346
Buffington Corner	02725
Buffumville	01540
Bullardville	01475
Burlington (Town)	01803
Burlington	01803
Burlington Mall	01803
Burncoat (Part of Worcester)	01606
Buzzards Bay	02532
Byfield	01922
Cabot (Part of Newton)	02158
Cambridge	02138-42
	02238
For specific Cambridge Zip Codes call (617) 876-0620	
Campello	02403-04
For specific Campello Zip Codes call (508) 559-1824	
Campground Landing	02651
Camp Grounds	01564
Canterbury Estates	02563
Canton (Town)	02021
Canton	02021
Canton Junction	02021
Cape Cod Mall	02601
Carletonville (Part of Salem)	01970
Carlisle	01741
Carlisle (Town)	01741
Carver	02330
Carver (Town)	02330
Castle Hill (Part of Salem)	01970
Cataumet	02534
Cathedral (Part of Boston)	02118
Cedar Bushes	02345
Cedarville	02532

	ZIP
Center (Middlesex County)	01801
Center (Plymouth County)	02360
Centerville (Barnstable County)	02632
Centerville (Essex County)	01915
Central Massachusetts Mail Processing Center	01546
Central Village	02790
Centralville (Part of Lowell)	01850
Chadwick Square (Part of Worcester)	01605
Chaffin	01520
Chandler Hill (Part of Worcester)	01609
Chapel Hill Estates	02359
Chappaquiddick Island	02539
Chappaquoit	02574
Charlemont	01339
Charlemont (Town)	01339
Charles River Grove	02019
Charles Street (Part of Boston)	02114
Charlestown (Part of Boston)	02129
Charlton	01507
Charlton (Town)	01507
Charlton City	01508
Charlton Depot	01509
Chartley	02712
Chaseville	01571
Chatham	02633
Chatham (Town)	02633
Chelmsford	01824
Chelmsford (Town)	01824
Chelsea	02150
Cherry Brook	02193
Cherry Valley	01611
Cheshire	01225
Cheshire (Town)	01225
Cheshire Harbor	01220
Chester	01011
Chester (Town)	01011
Chester Center	01011
Chesterfield	01012
Chesterfield (Town)	01012
Chestnut Hill (Part of Newton)	02167
Chicopee	01013-22
For specific Chicopee Zip Codes call (413) 592-9451	
Chicopee Center (Part of Chicopee)	01020
Chilmark	02535
Chilmark (Town)	02535
Chiltonville	02360
Churchill Shores	02346
City Mills	02056
City Point (Part of Boston)	02127
Clarendon Hills (Part of Boston)	02131
Clarksburg (Town)	01247
Clayton	06018
Clematis Brook (Part of Waltham)	02154
Clevelandtown	02539
Clicquot	02054
Cliftondale	01906
Clinton (Town)	01510
Clinton	01510
Cochesett	02379
Cochituate	01778
Cohasset	02025
Cohasset (Town)	02025
Cohasset Army Ammunition Activity	02043
Cold Spring	01253
Cole Corner	02043
College Hill (Part of Worcester)	01610
Collinsville	01826
Colonial Park	01570
Colrain	01340
Colrain (Town)	01340
Coltsville (Part of Pittsfield)	01201
Columbus Park (Part of Worcester)	01603
Cominsville	01542
Concord	01742
Concord (Town)	01742
Congamond	01077
Conomo	01929
Conway	01341
Conway (Town)	01341
Cooks Brook Beach	02651
Cooleyville	01355
Copley Place (Part of Boston)	02116
Cordaville	01772
Cotley (Part of Taunton)	02780
Cottage Hill	02152
Cottage Park	02152

	ZIP
Cotuit	02635
Country View Estates	02038
Court Park	02152
Coury Heights	02743
Cow Yard	02748
Craigville	02636
Craigville Beach	02636
Crescent Beach (Plymouth County)	02739
Crescent Beach (Suffolk County)	02151
Crescent Mills	01050
Crooks Corner	02019
Cummaquid	02637
Cummington	01026
Cummington (Town)	01026
Cushman	01002
Cuttyhunk	02713
Dalton	01226-27
For specific Dalton Zip Codes call (413) 684-0364	
Danvers (Town)	01923
Danvers	01923
Danversport	01923
Dartmouth	02714
Dartmouth (Town)	02714
Davisville	02536
Dawson	01520
Dedham (Town)	02026
Dedham	02026
Dedham Mall	02026
Deerfield	01342
Deerfield (Town)	01342
Deer Island (Part of Boston)	02152
Dennis	02638
Dennis (Town)	02638
Dennis Port	02639
Devenscrest	01432
Devereux	01945
Dighton	02715
Dighton (Town)	02715
Division Street (Part of New Bedford)	02744
Dodge	01507
Dorchester (Part of Boston)	02122
Dorchester Center (Part of Boston)	02124
Dorchester Lower Mills (Part of Boston)	02124
Dorothy Manor	01527
Dorothy Pond	01527
Douglas	01516
Douglas (Town)	01516
Dover	02030
Dover (Town)	02030
Dracut (Town)	01826
Dracut	01826
Drury	01343
Drury Square	01501
Dry Pond	02072
Dudley	01570-71
For specific Dudley Zip Codes call (508) 943-8090	
Dudley (Town)	01571
Dudley Hill	01571
Dunstable	01827
Dunstable (Town)	01827
Duxbury	02331-32
For specific Duxbury Zip Codes call (617) 934-5551	
Duxbury (Town)	02332
Dwight	01007
Eagleville	01364
East Acton	01720
East Arlington	02174
East Billerica	01821
East Blackstone	01504
East Boston (Part of Boston)	02128
East Boxford	01921
East Braintree	02184
East Brewster	02631
East Bridgewater	02333
East Bridgewater (Town)	02333
East Brimfield	01010
East Brookfield	01515
East Brookfield (Town)	01515
East Cambridge (Part of Cambridge)	02141
East Carver	02355
East Charlemont	01370
East Chelmsford	01824
East Dedham	02026
East Deerfield	01342
East Dennis	02641
East Douglas	01516
East Fairhaven	02719
East Falmouth	02536
Eastfield Mall (Part of Springfield)	01109
East Foxboro	02035

	ZIP
East Freetown	02717
East Gloucester (Part of Gloucester)	01930
East Greenfield	01301
Eastham	02642
Eastham (Town)	02642
Easthampton (Town)	01027
Easthampton	01027
East Harwich	02645
East Holliston	01746
East Junction (Part of Attleboro)	02703
East Lee	01238
East Leverett	01054
East Longmeadow (Town)	01106
East Longmeadow	01106
	01116
For specific East Longmeadow Zip Codes call (413) 525-3309	
East Lynn (Part of Lynn)	01904
East Mansfield	02031
East Marion	02738
East Middleboro	02346
East Millbury	01527
East Milton	02186
East Northfield	01360
Easton	02334
Easton (Town)	02334
Eastondale	02375
East Orleans	02643
East Otis	01029
East Pembroke	02359
East Pepperell	01463
East Princeton	01541
East Sandwich	02537
East Saugus	01906
East Springfield (Part of Springfield)	01101
East Sudbury	01776
East Swansea	02777
East Taunton (Part of Taunton)	02718
East Templeton	01438
Eastview Park (Part of Waltham)	02154
East Village	01570
Eastville	02557
East Walpole	02032
East Wareham	02538
East Watertown	02172
East Weymouth	02189
East Windsor	01270
East Woburn (Part of Woburn)	01801
Eddyville	02346
Edgartown	02539
Edgartown (Town)	02539
Edgemere	01545
Edgewater Estates	02359
Edgeworth (Part of Malden)	02148
Egleston Square (Part of Boston)	02116
Egremont (Town)	01252
Egypt	02066
Ellisville	02532
Elmdale	01569
Elm Grove	01340
Elm Square	02379
Elmwood (Hampden County)	01040
Elmwood (Plymouth County)	02337
Endicott	02026
Erving	01344
Erving (Town)	01344
Essex	01929
Essex (Town)	01929
Essex (Part of Boston)	02112
Everett	02149
Factory Hollow	01002
Fairfield Mall (Part of Chicopee)	01020
Fairhaven (Town)	02719
Fairhaven	02719
Fairlawn	01545
Fairmount (Part of Boston)	02136
Fairview (Part of Chicopee)	01020
Fall River	02720-26
For specific Fall River Zip Codes call (508) 675-7438	
Falls	01075
Falmouth	02540-41
For specific Falmouth Zip Codes call (508) 548-1071	
Falmouth (Town)	02540
Falmouth Heights	02540
Farley	01344
Farm Hill	02180
Farnams	01225
Farnumsville	01560
Faulkner (Part of Malden)	02148
Fayville	01745

	ZIP
Federal (Part of Worcester)	01601
Feeding Hills	01030
Felchville	01760
Fellsway (Part of Medford)	02155
Fentonville	01069
Fields Corner (Part of Boston)	02122
Fieldston	02065
Findlen	02026
First Cliff	02066
Fiskdale	01518
Fitchburg	01420
Five Corners	02356
Flint (Part of Fall River)	02723
Florence (Part of Northampton)	01060
Florida	01343
Florida (Town)	01343
Forbes Park	02019
Fore River (Part of Quincy)	02169
Forestdale	02644
Forestdale Estates	02359
Forest Hills (Part of Boston)	02130
Forest Lake	01069
Forest Park (Part of Springfield)	01108
Forest River (Part of Salem)	01970
Forge Village	01886
Fort Banks (U.S. Army) (inactive)	02152
Fort Bellingham	02019
Fort Devens (Middlesex County)	01433
Fort Devens (Worcester County)	01433
Fort Heath	02152
Foundry Village	01340
Foxboro	02035
Foxborough (Town)	02035
Foxvale	02035
Framingham (Town)	01701
Framingham	01701
Framingham Center	01701
Franklin (Town)	02038
Franklin	02038
Franklin Park (Part of Revere)	02151
Freetown (Town)	02702
Fresh Pond (Part of Cambridge)	02138
Freshwater Cove (Part of Gloucester)	01930
Fuller Shores	02346
Furnace Pond Colony	02359
Furnace Village	02334
Galleria at Worcester Center (Part of Worcester)	01608
Gardner	01440
Gay Head	02535
Gay Head (Town)	02535
Georgetown	01833
Georgetown (Town)	01833
Germantown (Part of Quincy)	02169
Gilbertville	01031
Gill (Town)	01376
Gillett Corner	01077
Gleasondale	01775
Glendale	01229
Glen Echo	02072
Glen Grove	01508
Glen Grove Annex	01508
Glenridge	02030
Gloucester	01930-31
For specific Gloucester Zip Codes call (508) 283-0474	
Goodrichville	01462
Goshen	01032
Goshen (Town)	01032
Gosnold (Town)	02713
Goss Heights	01050
Goulding Village	01331
Grafton	01519
Grafton (Town)	01519
Granby	01033
Granby (Town)	01033
Graniteville	01886
Granville	01034
Granville (Town)	01034
Granville Center	01034
Gray Gables	02532
Great Barrington	01230
Great Barrington (Town)	01230
Great Brook Valley (Part of Worcester)	01605
Greenbush	02040
Greendale (Part of Worcester)	01606
Greenfield	01301-02
For specific Greenfield Zip Codes call (413) 773-3654	

	ZIP
Greenfield Center	01301
Green Harbor	02041
Green Harbor-Cedar Crest	02041
Greenlodge	02026
Green Ridge Park	01226
Greenview Estates	02035
Greenville	01542
Greenwood	01880
Greenwood Manor Estates	02359
Greylock (Part of North Adams)	01247
Griswoldville	01340
Grosvenor Corner	01844
Groton	01450
Groton (Town)	01450
Grove Hall (Part of Boston)	02121
Groveland	01834
Groveland (Town)	01834
Hadley	01035
Hadley (Town)	01035
Halfway Pond	02532
Halifax	02338
Halifax (Town)	02338
Halifax Beach	02338
Hamilton	01936
Hamilton (Town)	01936
Hamilton (Part of Worcester)	01604
Hamilton Beach	02571
Hampden	01036
Hampden (Town)	01036
Hampshire Mall	01035
Hampton Mills	01027
Hancock	01237
Hancock (Town)	01237
Hancock Village	02146
Hanover	02339
Hanover (Town)	02339
Hanover Center	02339
Hanover Street (Part of Boston)	02113
Hanson	02341
Hanson (Town)	02341
Happy Hills	02019
Harbor Beach	02739
Harbour Mall (Part of Fall River)	02721
Harding	02052
Hardwick	01037
Hardwick (Town)	01037
Harrubs Corner	02367
Harthaven	02557
Hartsville	01230
Harvard	01451
Harvard (Town)	01451
Harvard Square (Part of Cambridge)	02138
Harwich	02645
Harwich (Town)	02645
Harwich Port	02646
Harwood	01460
Hastings	02193
Hatchville	02536
Hatfield	01038
Hatfield (Town)	01038
Hathorne	01937
Haverhill	01830-32
For specific Haverhill Zip Codes call (508) 373-5643	
Hawley	01339
Hawley (Town)	01339
Haydenville	01039
Head of Westport	02790
Heath	01346
Heath (Town)	01346
Heaven Heights	02717
Hebronville (Part of Attleboro)	02703
Hemlocks	02346
Hickory Hills Lake	01462
Hicksville	02747
Highland (Part of Springfield)	01109
Highland Lake	02056
Highland Park (Part of Holyoke)	01040
Highlands (Hampden County)	01040
Highlands (Middlesex County)	01851
Hillcrest Acres	02790
Hilltop Acres	02346
Hingham (Town)	02043
Hingham	02043
Hingham Center	02043
Hinsdale	01235
Hinsdale (Town)	01235
Hinsdale Estates	02019
Hodges Village	01540
Holbrook	02343
Holbrook (Town)	02343
Holden	01520

	ZIP
Holden (Town)	01520
Holland	01521
Holland (Town)	01521
Holliston (Town)	01746
Holliston	01746
Holly Woods	02739
Holyoke	01040-41
For specific Holyoke Zip Codes call (413) 534-4577	
Holyoke Mall at Ingleside (Part of Holyoke)	01040
Hoosac Tunnel	01367
Hopedale (Town)	01747
Hopedale	01747
Hopkinton	01748
Hopkinton (Town)	01748
Horseneck Beach	02790
Hortonville	02777
Houghs Neck (Part of Quincy)	02169
Houghtonville	01247
Housatonic	01236
Hovey's Corner	01463
Howe	01949
Hubbardston	01452
Hubbardston (Town)	01452
Huckleberry Corner	02576
Huckleberry Shores	02346
Hudson (Town)	01749
Hudson	01749
Hull (Town)	02045
Hull	02045
Humarock	02047
Huntington	01050
Huntington (Town)	01050
Hyannis	02601
Hyannis Port	02647
Hyde Park (Part of Boston)	02136
Idlewell	02188
Idlewood	02747
Indian Mound Beach	02532
Indian Orchard (Part of Springfield)	01151
Indian Shore	02346
Ingleside (Part of Holyoke)	01040
Inman Square (Part of Cambridge)	02139
Interlaken	01266
Ipswich	01938
Ipswich (Town)	01938
Island Creek	02332
Islington	02090
Jamaica Plain (Part of Boston)	02130
Jefferson	01522
Jefferson Shores	02532
Jeffries Point (Part of Boston)	02128
John Fitzgerald Kennedy (Part of Boston)	02114
John W. Mc Cormack (Part of Boston)	02109
Katama	02539
Kearney Square (Part of Lowell)	01852
Kempton Croft	02747
Kendal Green	02193
Kendall Square (Part of Cambridge)	02142
Kenmore (Part of Boston)	02215
Kent Park	02050
Kenwood	01826
Killdeer Island	01570
Kingsbury Beach	02642
Kings Forest	01921
Kingston	02364
Kingston (Town)	02364
Knightville	01050
Knollmere	02719
Konkapot	01244
Lafayette Place (Part of Boston)	02111
Lagoon Heights	02557
Lake Attitash	01913
Lake Forest Park	01760
Lake Hiawatha	02019
Lake Mattawa	01364
Lake Pleasant	01347
Lakeside (Bristol County)	02790
Lakeside (Plymouth County)	02346
Lake Street	02174
Lakeview (Middlesex County)	02154
Lake View (Worcester County)	01604
Lakeview Heights	02717
Lakeview Terrace (Part of Pittsfield)	01201
Lakeville (Town)	02346
Lakewood (Part of Pittsfield)	01201
Lakewood Hills	02537

	ZIP
Lakewood Park	01473
Lambs Grove	01562
Lancaster	01523
Lancaster (Town)	01523
Lanesboro	01237
Lanesborough (Town)	01237
Lanesville (Part of Gloucester)	01930
Lane Village	01430
Larrywaug	01262
Laurel Park (Part of Northampton)	01060
Laurence G. Hanscom Air Force Base	01731
Lawrence	01840-43
For specific Lawrence Zip Codes call (508) 691-4500	
Le Count Hollow	02663
Lee	01238
Lee (Town)	01238
Leeds (Part of Northampton)	01053
Leicester	01524
Leicester (Town)	01524
Leino Park	01473
Lenox	01240
Lenox (Town)	01240
Lenox Dale	01242
Leominster	01453
Leverett (Town)	01054
Leverett	01054
Lexington (Town)	02173
Lexington	02173
Leyden (Town)	01301
Liberty Tree Mall	01923
Lincoln	01773
Lincoln (Town)	01773
Lincoln Center	01773
Lincoln Square (Part of Worcester)	01601
Linden (Part of Malden)	02148
Lindenwood	02180
Linwood	01525
Lithia	01032
Little Acres	02327
Little Harbor Beach	02571
Little Nahant	01908
Little Neck (Bristol County)	02777
Little Neck (Essex County)	01938
Little River (Part of Westfield)	01085
Littleton	01460
Littleton (Town)	01460
Lobsterville	02535
Lockerville	01760
Locks Village	01072
Long Beach	01930
Long Hill Acres	02359
Long Island Hospital (Part of Boston)	02169
Longmeadow (Town)	01106
Longmeadow	01106
	01116
For specific Longmeadow Zip Codes call (413) 731-0567	
Long Plain	02743
Long Pond Village	02532
Longwood	02146
Loudville	01027
Lovell Corners	02188
Lowell	01850-54
For specific Lowell Zip Codes call (508) 934-0500	
Lower Mills (Part of Boston)	02126
Lower Village	01775
Ludlow (Hampden County) (Town)	01056
Ludlow (Hampden County)	01056
Ludlow (Worcester County)	01603
Lunds Corner (Part of New Bedford)	02745
Lunenburg	01462
Lunenburg (Town)	01462
Lynn	01901-05
For specific Lynn Zip Codes call (617) 595-5700	
Lynnfield (Town)	01940
Lynnfield	01940
Lynnhurst	01906
Lyonsville	01340
Madaket	02554
Magnolia (Part of Gloucester)	01930
Mahkeenac Heights	01240
Main Street	02532
Malden	02148
Manchaug	01526
Manchester (Town)	01944
Manchester	01944
Manleys Corner	02379
Manomet	02345

	ZIP
Manomet Beach	02345
Manomet Bluffs	02345
Mansfield	02048
Mansfield (Town)	02048
Maple Park	01844
Maplewood (Middlesex County)	02148
Maplewood (Worcester County)	01536
Mara Vista	02536
Marblehead (Town)	01945
Marblehead	01945
Marblehead Neck	01945
Marion	02738
Marion (Town)	02738
Marlboro	01833
Marlborough	01752
Marshfield	02050
Marshfield (Town)	02050
Marshfield Hills	02051
Marstons Mills	02648
Mashnee Island	02532
Mashpee	02649
Mashpee (Town)	02649
Masons Corner	02717
Massachusette Correctional Institution (mail South Carver)	02366
Massachusetts Correctional Institution (Middlesex County)	01701
Massachusetts Correctional Institution (Norfolk County)	02071
Massachusetts Correctional Institution (mail Bridgewater)	02324
Matfield	02379
Mattapan (Part of Boston)	02126
Mattapoisett (Town)	02739
Mattapoisett Center	02739
Maynard (Town)	01754
Maynard	01754
Mayo Beach	02667
Medfield	02052
Medfield (Town)	02052
Medford	02155
Medway (Town)	02053
Medway	02053
Meeting House Hill (Part of Boston)	02122
Megansett	02556
Melrose	02176
Melrose Highlands (Part of Melrose)	02177
Menauhant	02536
Mendon	01756
Mendon (Town)	01756
Menemsha	02552
Merrick	01089
Merrimac	01860
Merrimac (Town)	01860
Merrimack College	01845
Merrimacport	01860
Merrymount (Part of Quincy)	02169
Methuen (Town)	01844
Methuen	01844
Methuen Mall	01844
Middleboro	02346
Middleborough (Town)	02346
Middlefield (Town)	01243
Middlefield	01243
Middleton (Town)	01949
Middleton	01949
Midland	02019
Mile Oak Center	01095
Milford (Town)	01757
Milford	01757
Millbury	01527
Millbury (Town)	01527
Millers Falls	01349
Millerville	01504
Millis	02054
Millis (Town)	02054
Millis-Clicquot	02054
Mill River	01244
Millville (Town)	01529
Millville	01529
Millville Center	01529
Milton (Town)	02186
Milton	02186
Milton Center	02186
Milton Village	02187
Minot	02055
Mirror Lake	02093
Mishaum Point	02748
M.I.T. (Massachusetts Institute of Technology) (Part of Cambridge)	02139
Monomoy	02554
Monponsett	02350

	ZIP
Monroe (Town)	01350
Monroe Bridge	01350
Monson	01057
Monson (Town)	01057
Montague	01351
Montague (Town)	01351
Montague City	01376
Montello (Part of Brockton)	02403
	02405
For specific Montello Zip Codes call (508) 559-1823	
Monterey	01245
Monterey (Town)	01245
Montgomery	01085
Montgomery (Town)	01085
Montserrat (Part of Beverly)	01915
Montville	01255
Monument Beach	02553
Moores Corner	01054
Morningdale	01505
Morrills	02062
Morseville	01760
Mount Auburn	02172
Mount Bowdoin (Part of Boston)	02121
Mount Hermon	01354
Mount Saint James (Part of Worcester)	01610
Mount Tom	01027
Mount Washington	12517
Mount Washington (Town)	12517
Myricks	02718
Mystic Grove	01507
Mystic Wharf (Part of Boston)	02109
Nabnasset	01886
Nahant (Town)	01908
Nahant	01908
Nantucket	02554
	02584
For specific Nantucket Zip Codes call (508) 228-1067	
Nantucket (Town)	02554
Nashaquitsa	02535
Natick (Town)	01760
Natick	01760
Natick Development Center	01760
Natick Laboratories	01760
Natick Mall	01760
Needham (Town)	02192
Needham	02192
Needham Heights	02194
Nelsons Grove	02346
Nelsons Shores	02346
Neponset (Part of Boston)	02122
New Ashford	01237
New Ashford (Town)	01237
New Bedford	02740-48
For specific New Bedford Zip Codes call (508) 996-8523	
New Boston	01255
New Braintree	01531
New Braintree (Town)	01531
Newbury	01951
Newbury (Town)	01950
Newburyport	01950-51
For specific Newburyport Zip Codes call (508) 462-4403	
New England Shopping Center	01906
New Lenox	01240
New Marlboro	01230
New Marlborough (Town)	01230
New Salem	01355
New Salem (Town)	01355
New Seabury	02649
Newton	02158
Newton Center (Part of Newton)	02159
Newton Highlands (Part of Newton)	02161
Newton Lower Falls (Part of Newton)	02162
Newton Upper Falls (Part of Newton)	02164
Newtonville (Part of Newton)	02160
New Town	02258
New Village	01588
Nobska Beach	02571
Nonantum (Part of Newton)	02195
Nonquitt	02748
Noquochoke	02790
Norfolk	02056
Norfolk (Town)	02056
North (Part of New Bedford)	02746
North Abington	02351
North Acton	01720
North Adams	01247
North Adams Junction (Part of Pittsfield)	01201

	ZIP
North Amherst	01059
Northampton	01060-61
For specific Northampton Zip Codes call (413) 584-0960	
North Andover (Town)	01845
North Andover	01845
North Andover Center	01845
North Ashburnham	01430
North Attleboro	02760-63
For specific North Attleboro Zip Codes call (508) 699-7556	
North Attleborough (Town)	02760
North Bellingham	02019
North Beverly (Part of Beverly)	01915
North Billerica	01862
North Blandford	01008
Northborough	01532
Northborough (Town)	01532
Northbridge	01534
Northbridge (Town)	01534
Northbridge Center	01588
North Brighton (Part of Boston)	02135
North Brookfield	01535
North Brookfield (Town)	01535
North Cambridge (Part of Cambridge)	02138
North Carver	02355
North Chatham	02650
North Chelmsford	01863
North Chester	01050
North Cohasset	02025
North Dartmouth	02747
North Dartmouth Mall	02747
North Dighton	02764
North Duxbury	02332
North Eastham	02651
North Easton	02356
North Egremont	01252
Northey Point (Part of Salem)	01970
North Falmouth	02556
Northfield	01360
Northfield (Town)	01360
Northgate Shopping Center (Part of Revere)	02151
North Grafton	01536
North Hadley	01035
North Hancock	01267
North Hanover	02339
North Harwich	02645
North Hatfield	01066
North Lakeville	02346
North Lancaster	01523
North Leominster (Part of Leominster)	01453
North Leverett	01054
North Littleton	01460
North Marshfield	02059
North Middleboro	02346
North Milford	01757
North Natick	01760
North New Salem	01364
North Orange	01364
North Otis	01253
North Oxford	01537
North Pembroke	02358
North Pepperell	01463
North Plymouth	02360
North Plympton	02364
North Quincy (Part of Quincy)	02171
North Randolph	02368
North Reading (Town)	01864
North Reading	01864
North Rehoboth	02769
North Rutland	01543
North Salem (Part of Salem)	01970
North Saugus	01906
North Scituate	02060
North Seekonk	02771
Northshore Shopping Center (Part of Peabody)	01960
North Sommerville (Part of Somerville)	02143
North Stoughton	02072
North Sudbury	01776
North Swansea	02777
North Tewksbury	01876
North Tisbury	02568
North Truro	02652
North Uxbridge	01538
North Waltham (Part of Waltham)	02154
Northwest Harwich	02645
North Weymouth	02191
North Wilmington	01887
North Woburn (Part of Woburn)	01801

	ZIP
North Worcester (Part of Worcester)	01606
Norton	02766
Norton (Town)	02766
Norton Grove	02766
Norwell	02061
Norwell (Town)	02161
Norwood (Town)	02062
Norwood	02062
Norwood Central	02062
Nutting Lake	01865
Oak Bluffs (Town)	02557
Oak Bluffs	02557
Oakdale (Hampden County)	01040
Oakdale (Norfolk County)	02026
Oakdale (Worcester County)	01583
Oak Grove (Part of Malden)	02148
Oakham	01068
Oakham (Town)	01068
Oak Island (Part of Revere)	02151
Oakland Vale	01906
Ocean Bluff	02065
Ocean Bluff-Brant Rock	02020
Ocean Grove	02777
Ocean Heights	02539
Ocean Spray	02152
Old City	01474
Old Common	01527
Old Furnace	01031
Oldham Pines	02359
Oldham Village	02359
Old Silver Beach	02556
Old Sturbridge Village	01566
Onset	02558
Orange	01364
Orange (Town)	01364
Orient Heights (Part of Boston)	02128
Orleans	02653
Orleans (Town)	02653
Osceola	01254
Osterville	02655
Otis	01253
Otis (Town)	01253
Otis Air Force Base	02542
Otter River	01436
Overbrook	02181
Oxford	01540
Oxford (Town)	01540
Oyster Harbors	02655
Packard Heights	01331
Padanaram Village	02748
Pages Beach	01430
Painting Island	02738
Pakachoag	01501
Palmer	01069
Palmer (Town)	01069
Park Street (Part of Medford)	02155
Parkwood Beach	02571
Patuisset	02559
Pawtucketville (Part of Lowell)	01854
Paxton	01612
Paxton (Town)	01612
Payson Park	02172
Peabody	01960-61
For specific Peabody Zip Codes call (508) 531-5400	
Pelham	01002
Pelham (Town)	01002
Pembroke	02359
Pembroke (Town)	02359
Pembroke Heights	02358
Pepperell	01463
Pepperell (Town)	01463
Perryville	02769
Peru	01235
Peru (Town)	01235
Petersham	01366
Petersham (Town)	01366
Phelps Mills (Part of Peabody)	01960
Phillipston	01331
Phillipston (Town)	01331
Phillipston Four Corners	01331
Pierceville	02576
Piety Corner (Part of Waltham)	02154
Pigeon Cove	01966
Pilgrim Heights	02652
Pilgrim Pines Estates	02327
Pilgrim Village	02019
Pine Bluffs	02346
Pinefield	01938
Pine Grove (Part of Northampton)	01060
Pinehurst	01866
Pinehurst Beach	02571
Pine Island	01951
Pine Island Lake	01060

	ZIP
Pine Lake	01776
Pine Point (Part of Springfield)	01101
Pine Rest	01776
Piney Point Beach	02738
Pingryville	01460
Pittsfield	01201-03
For specific Pittsfield Zip Codes call (413) 442-6961	
Plainfield	01070
Plainfield (Town)	01070
Plainville (Hampshire County)	01002
Plainville (Norfolk County)	02762
Plainville (Norfolk County) (Town)	02762
Pleasant Lake	02645
Plimptonville	02081
Plumbush	01951
Plum Island (Part of Newburyport)	01950
Plummer Corner	01588
Plymouth	02360-62
For specific Plymouth Zip Codes call (508) 746-0058	
Plympton	02367
Plympton (Town)	02367
Pocasset	02559
Pocomo	02554
Podunk	01515
Point Independence	02532
Point of Pines (Part of Revere)	02151
Point Pleasant	01570
Point Shirley	02152
Polpis	02554
Pomponotto Pines	02333
Ponakin Mill	01523
Pond Village (mail North Truro)	02652
Pond Village (mail Barnstable)	02630
Pondville (Norfolk County)	02093
Pondville (Worcester County)	01501
Pondville (Plymouth County)	02532
Pontoosuc Gardens (Part of Pittsfield)	01201
Pope Beach	02719
Popponesset Beach	02649
Porter Square (Part of Cambridge)	02140
Potoosuc Lake	01237
Pratt Corner	01072
Precinct	02346
Prentice Gardens	01588
Prides Crossing (Part of Beverly)	01965
Princeton	01541
Princeton (Town)	01541
Priscilla Beach	02360
Provincetown	02657
Provincetown (Town)	02657
Provincetown (census designated place)	02657
Provincetown Wharf	02657
Prudential Center (Part of Boston)	02199
Quaise	02554
Queen Lake	01331
Quidnet	02554
Quincy	02169
Quincy Adams (Part of Quincy)	02169
Quincy Center (Part of Quincy)	02169
Quincy Point (Part of Quincy)	02169
Quinsigamond Village (Part of Worcester)	01607
Quissett	02540
Rakeville	02019
Randolph (Town)	02368
Randolph	02368
Raynham	02767
Raynham (Town)	02767
Raynham Center	02768
Reading (Town)	01867
Reading	01867
Readville (Part of Boston)	02137
Redstone Shopping Center	02180
Rehoboth	02769
Rehoboth (Town)	02769
Renfrew	01220
Reservoir	02146
Revere	02151
Revere Beach (Part of Revere)	02151
Rexhame	02050
Rice Square (Part of Worcester)	01604

	ZIP
Richmond	01254
Richmond (Town)	01254
Richmond Furnace	01254
Rings Island	01950
Rio Vista	01862
Risingdale	01230
Riverdale (Essex County)	01930
Riverdale (Norfolk County)	02026
Riverdale (Worcester County)	01534
Rivermoor	02066
River Pines	01821
Riverside (Essex County)	01830
Riverside (Franklin County)	01376
Riverside (Hampden County)	01040
Riverside (Plymouth County)	02558
Riverview (Essex County)	01930
Riverview (Middlesex County)	02154
Roberts (Part of Waltham)	02154
Rochdale	01542
Rochester	02770
Rochester (Town)	02770
Rock	02346
Rockdale	01236
Rock Harbor	02653
Rockland (Town)	02370
Rockland	02370
Rockport	01966
Rockport (Town)	01966
Rocks Village (Part of Haverhill)	01830
Rock Valley (Part of Holyoke)	01040
Rockville	02054
Rocky Hill	01757
Rolling Acres Estates	01886
Roosterville	01255
Roslindale (Part of Boston)	02131
Rowe	01367
Rowe (Town)	01367
Rowley	01969
Rowley (Town)	01969
Roxbury (Part of Boston)	02119
Roxbury Crossing (Part of Boston)	02120
Royalston	01368
Royalston (Town)	01368
Russell	01071
Russell (Town)	01071
Russellville	01085
Rutland	01543
Rutland (Town)	01543
Saconesset Hills	02540
Sagamore	02561
Sagamore Beach	02562
Sagamore Highlands	02562
Salem	01970-71
For specific Salem Zip Codes call (508) 744-8600	
Salem Neck (Part of Salem)	01970
Salem State College (Part of Salem)	01970
Salisbury	01952
Salisbury (Town)	01950
Salisbury Beach	01950
Salisbury Heights (Part of Worcester)	01609
Salisbury Plains	01950
Salters Point	02748
Sandersdale	01550
Sand Hill	02066
Sandisfield	01255
Sandisfield (Town)	01255
Sandwich	02563
Sandwich (Town)	02563
Sandy Beach (Norfolk County)	02025
Sandy Beach (Worcester County)	01543
Santuit	02635
Sassaquin (Part of New Bedford)	02745
Saugus (Town)	01906
Saugus	01906
Saugus Center	01906
Saundersville	01560
Savin Hill (Part of Boston)	02125
Savoy	01256
Savoy (Town)	01256
Saxonville	01701
Scituate	02040
	02066
For specific Scituate Zip Codes call (617) 545-9122	
Scituate (Town)	02066
Scorton Shores	02537
Scott Hill Acres	02019
Searstown Mall (Part of Leominster)	01453

	ZIP
Searsville	01096
Sea View	02050
Second Cliff	02066
Seekonk (Town)	02771
Seekonk	02771
Segreganset	02715
Shaker Village	01451
Sharon (Town)	02067
Sharon	02067
Sharon Heights	02067
Shattuckville	01369
Shawkemo	02554
Shawsheen Heights	01810
Shawsheen Village	01810
Sheffield	01257
Sheffield (Town)	01257
Shelburne	01370
Shelburne (Town)	01370
Shelburne Falls	01370
Sheldonville	02070
Shell Beach	02739
Shepardville	02762
Sherborn	01770
Sherborn (Town)	01770
Sherwood Forest (Berkshire County)	01223
Sherwood Forest (Bristol County)	02743
Shimmo	02554
Shirley	01464
Shirley (Town)	01464
Shirley Center	01464
Shoppers' World	01701
Shore Acres (Bristol County)	02748
Shore Acres (Plymouth County)	02066
Shrewsbury (Town)	01545
Shrewsbury	01545
Shutesbury	01072
Shutesbury (Town)	01072
Siasconset	02564
Silver Beach	02565
Silver Hill	02193
Silver Lake (Middlesex County)	01887
Silver Lake (Plymouth County)	02360
Silver Shell Beach	02719
Silver Spring Beach	02651
Simon's Rock of Bard College	01230
Sippewisset	02540
Sixteen Acres (Part of Springfield)	01101
Smith Highlands (Part of Chicopee)	01020
Smith Mills	02747
Smiths Ferry (Part of Holyoke)	01040
Smoke Rise Heights	02777
Snug Harbor	02332
Soldiers Field (Part of Boston)	02163
Somerset (Town)	02725
Somerset	02725
Somerset Centre	02725
Somerville	02143
South (Part of Fall River)	02724
South Acton	01720
South Amherst	01002
Southampton	01073
Southampton (Town)	01073
South Ashburnham	01466
South Ashfield	01330
South Athol	01331
South Attleboro (Part of Attleboro)	02703
South Barre	01074
South Bellingham	02019
South Berlin	01503
South Billerica	01730
South Bolton	01740
Southborough	01772
Southborough (Town)	01772
South Boston (Part of Boston)	02127
South Braintree	02184
Southbridge (Town)	01550
Southbridge	01550
South Byfield	01922
South Carver	02366
South Charlton	01507
South Chatham	02659
South Chelmsford	01824
South Dartmouth	02748
South Deerfield	01373
South Dennis	02660
South Duxbury	02332
Southeastern Correctional Center	02324
South Easton	02375

	ZIP
South Egremont	01258
Southfield	01259
South Foxboro	02035
South Framingham	01701
South Georgetown	01833
South Grafton	01560
South Groveland	01834
South Hadley	01075
South Hadley (Town)	01075
South Hadley Falls	01075
South Hamilton	01982
South Hanover	02339
South Harwich	02661
South Hingham	02043
South Lakeville	02346
South Lancaster	01561
South Lawrence (Part of Lawrence)	01842
South Lee	01260
South Lowell	01876
South Lynnfield	01940
South Mashpee	02649
South Middleboro	02346
South Milford	01747
South Natick	01760
South Orleans	02662
South Peabody (Part of Peabody)	01960
South Postal Annex (Part of Boston)	02109
South Quincy (Part of Quincy)	02169
South Rehoboth	02769
South Royalston	01331
South Salem (Part of Salem)	01970
South Sandisfield	01255
South Sandwich	02563
South Shore Plaza	02184
South Springfield (Part of Springfield)	01101
South Stoughton	02072
South Sutton	01516
South Swansea	02777
South Truro	02666
South Uxbridge	01569
Southville	01772
South Walpole	02071
South Waltham (Part of Waltham)	02154
South Wareham	02571
South Wellfleet	02663
South Westport	02790
South Weymouth	02190
South Weymouth Naval Air Station	02190
Southwick	01077
Southwick (Town)	01077
South Williamstown	01267
South Wilmington (Part of Woburn)	01801
South Worthington	01050
South Yarmouth	02664
Spencer	01562
Spencer (Town)	01562
Spindleville	01747
Springdale (Part of Holyoke)	01040
Springdale Mall (Part of Springfield)	01101
Springfield	01101-05
	01107-52
For specific Springfield Zip Codes call (413) 785-6300	
Springfield Plaza (Part of Springfield)	01104
Squantum (Part of Quincy)	02171
Standish (Part of Taunton)	02780
Staples Shore	02346
State House (Part of Boston)	02133
State Line	01266
Sterling	01564
Sterling (Town)	01564
Sterling Junction	01564
Stetson Road	02359
Stevens Corner	01201
Still River	01467
Stockbridge	01262
Stockbridge (Town)	01262
Stoneham (Town)	02180
Stoneham	02180
Stoneville (Franklin County)	01344
Stoneville (Worcester County)	01501
Stony Brook	02193
Stoughton (Town)	02072
Stoughton	02072
Stow	01775
Stow (Town)	01775
Sturbridge	01566
Sturbridge (Town)	01566
Sudbury	01776

	ZIP
Sudbury (Town)	01776
Sudbury Center	01776
Summit (Part of Worcester)	01606
Sunderland	01375
Sunderland (Town)	01375
Sunderland (Part of Worcester)	01604
Sunken Meadow Beach	02651
Sunnyside	01571
Surfside	02554
Sutton	01527
Sutton (Town)	01527
Swampscott (Town)	01907
Swampscott	01907
Swansea	02777
Swansea (Town)	02777
Swansea Center	02777
Sweets Corner	01267
Swift River	01026
Swifts Beach	02571
Symmes Corner	01890
Tafts Corner	01562
Tahanto Beach	02559
Tapleyville	01923
Tatnuck (Part of Worcester)	01602
Taunton	02718
	02780
For specific Taunton Zip Codes call (508) 823-0709	
Teaticket	02536
Templeton	01468
Templeton (Town)	01468
Tewksbury	01876
Tewksbury (Town)	01876
Tewksbury Hospital	01876
Texas	01537
The Green	02346
The Pines	01866
Thomastown	02346
Thorndike	01079
Three Rivers	01080
Thumpertown Beach	02651
Tihonet	02571
Tinkertown	02332
Tinkhamtown	02739
Tisbury (Town)	02568
Tobeys Island	02553
Tolland	01034
Tolland (Town)	01034
Tonset	02653
Topsfield	01983
Topsfield (Town)	01983
Touisset	02777
Town Crest Village	01225
Town Hall	02341
Townsend	01469
Townsend (Town)	01469
Townsend Harbor	01469
Tozier Corner	01844
Tri-Town Shopping Center	02021
Truro	02666
Truro (Town)	02666
Tufts University (Part of Medford)	02153
Tully	01331
Turkey Hill Shores	01543
Turners Falls	01376
Turnpike	01545
Twin City Plaza (Part of Fitchburg)	01420
Tyngsboro	01879
Tyngsborough (Town)	01879
Tyringham	01264
Tyringham (Town)	01264
Union Market	02172
Union Point	01570
Unionville (Norfolk County)	02038
Unionville (Worcester County)	01520
University Park (Part of Worcester)	01605
Uphams Corner (Part of Boston)	02125
Upton	01568
Upton (Town)	01568
Upton-West Upton	01568
Uxbridge	01569
Uxbridge (Town)	01569
Vallersville	02532
Valley View	02019
Van Deusenville	01236
Varnumtown	01826
Veterans Administration Hospital (Part of Boston)	02130
Victory Hill (Part of Pittsfield)	01201
Village	02053
Village Mall, The	02021
Village of Nagog Woods	01718
Vineyard Haven	02568
Vineyard Highlands	02557
Waban (Part of Newton)	02168

	ZIP
Wachusett (Part of Fitchburg)	01420
Wakeby	02563
Wakefield (Town)	01880
Wakefield	01880
Wakefield Center	01880
Wakefield Junction	01880
Wales	01081
Wales (Town)	01081
Wallis Street (Part of Peabody)	01960
Walnut Hill (Part of Woburn)	01801
Walpole	02081
Walpole (Town)	02081
Walpole Mall, The	02032
Waltham	02154
Waltham Highlands (Part of Waltham)	02154
Wamesit	01876
Wampun Corner	02093
Wapping	01342
Waquoit	02536
Ward Hill (Part of Haverhill)	01830
Ware	01082
Ware (Town)	01082
Wareham	02571
Wareham (Town)	02571
Warren	01083
Warren (Town)	01083
Warren Terrace	02359
Warrentown	02346
Warwick	01378
Warwick (Town)	01378
Washington	01223
Washington (Town)	01223
Watertown	02172
Watertown	02172
Waterville (Plymouth County)	02346
Waterville (Worcester County)	01475
Watuppa (Part of Fall River)	02721
Wauwinet	02554
Waverley	02179
Wawela Park	01570
Wayland	01778
Wayland (Town)	01778
Wayside Inn	01776
Webster	01570-71
For specific Webster Zip Codes call (508) 943-0809	
Webster Square (Part of Worcester)	01603
Wedgemere	01890
Weir Village (Part of Taunton)	02780
Wellesley (Town)	02181
Wellesley	02181
Wellesley Farms	02181
Wellesley Fells	02181
Wellesley Hills	02181
Wellfleet	02667
Wellfleet (Town)	02667
Wellington (Part of Medford)	02155
Wellville	01430
Wendell	01379
Wendell (Town)	01379
Wendell Depot	01380
Wenham (Town)	01984
Wenham	01984
West Abington	02351
West Acton	01720
West Andover	01810
West Auburn	01501
West Barnstable	02668
West Becket	01238
West Bedford	01730
West Berlin	01503
West Billerica	01862
Westborough (Town)	01581
Westborough	01581
West Boxford	01885
West Boylston	01583
West Boylston (Town)	01583
West Bridgewater	02379
West Bridgewater (Town)	02379
West Brimfield	01069
West Brookfield	01585
West Brookfield (Town)	01585
West Cambridge (Part of Cambridge)	02138
West Chatham	02669
West Chelmsford	01863
Westchester (Part of Worcester)	01605
West Chesterfield	01084
West Chop	02573
West Concord	01742
West Cummington	01026
Westdale	02333
West Deerfield	01342

	ZIP
West Dennis	02670
West Dudley	01550
West Duxbury	02332
West Falmouth	02574
West Farms (Part of Northampton)	01060
Westfield	01085-86
For specific Westfield Zip Codes call (413) 562-2221	
West Fitchburg (Part of Fitchburg)	01420
Westford	01886
Westford (Town)	01886
West Foxboro	02035
Westgate Mall (Part of Brockton)	02401
West Gloucester (Part of Gloucester)	01930
West Granville	01034
West Groton	01472
Westhampton	01027
Westhampton (Town)	01027
West Hanover	02339
West Harwich	02671
West Hatfield	01088
West Hawley	01339
West Hingham	02043
West Hyannisport	02672
Westlands	01824
West Leominster (Part of Leominster)	01453
West Leyden	01337
West Lynn (Part of Lynn)	01905
West Manchester	01944
West Mansfield	02048
West Medford (Part of Medford)	02156
West Medway	02053
West Millbury	01586
Westminster	01473
Westminster (Town)	01473
West Natick	01760
West New Boston	01255
West Newbury	01985
West Newbury (Town)	01985
West Newton (Part of Newton)	02165
Weston (Town)	02193
Weston	02193
West Otis	01245
Westover Air Force Base	01022
West Peabody (Part of Peabody)	01960
West Pelham	01002
Westport (Town)	02790
Westport	02790
Westport Factory	02790
Westport Point	02791

	ZIP
West Quincy (Part of Quincy)	02169
West Roxbury (Part of Boston)	02132
West Royalston	01331
West Side (Part of Worcester)	01602
West Somerville (Part of Somerville)	02144
West Springfield	01089-90
For specific West Springfield Zip Codes call (413) 734-6911	
West Sterling	01564
West Stockbridge	01266
West Stockbridge (Town)	01266
West Stockbridge Center	01266
West Stoughton	02072
West Sutton	01527
West Tatnuck (Part of Worcester)	01602
West Tisbury	02575
West Tisbury (Town)	02575
West Townsend	01474
West Upton	01587
Westview	02038
Westville (Part of Taunton)	02780
West Walpole	02081
West Wareham	02576
West Warren	01092
West Watertown	02172
West Whately	01039
West Wind Shores	02532
Westwood	02090
Westwood (Town)	02090
West Worthington	01098
West Wrentham	02070
West Yarmouth	02673
Wethersfield	02019
Weweantic	02571
Weymouth (Town)	02188
Weymouth	02188
Weymouth Heights	02188
Weymouth Landing	02188
Whalom	01420
Whately (Town)	01093
Whately (station)	01373
Whately	01093
Wheelockville	01569
Wheelwright	01094
White City	01747
White City Shopping Center	01545
White Horse Beach	02381
White Island Shores	02538
White Oaks	01267
Whitinsville	01588
Whitman (Town)	02382
Whitman	02382
Whittenton (Part of Taunton)	02780

	ZIP
Wigginsville (Part of Lowell)	01850
Wilbraham	01095
Wilbraham (Town)	01095
Wilkinsonville	01527
Williamsburg	01096
Williamsburg (Town)	01096
Williamstown	01267
Williamstown (Town)	01267
Williamsville (Berkshire County)	01236
Williamsville (Worcester County)	01452
Wilmington	01887
Wilmington (Town)	01887
Wilson (Part of Gloucester)	01930
Winchendon	01475
Winchendon (Town)	01475
Winchendon Springs	01477
Winchester (Town)	01890
Winchester	01890
Winchester Highlands	01890
Windsor	01270
Windsor (Town)	01270
Winmere	01803
Winnecunnet	02766
Winslows	02062
Winter Hill (Part of Somerville)	02145
Winthrop (Town)	02152
Winthrop	02152
Winthrop Highlands	02152
Woburn	01801
Wollaston (Part of Quincy)	02170
Woodland Park	01501
Woods Hole	02543
Woods Hole Coast Guard Base	02543
Woodville	01784
Worcester	01601-15
For specific Worcester Zip Codes call (508) 795-3666	
Woronoco	01097
Woronoco Heights	01097
Worthington	01098
Worthington (Town)	01098
Worthington Center	01098
Wrentham	02093
Wrentham (Town)	02093
Wyben	01085
Wyoming (Part of Melrose)	02176
Yankee Orchards (Part of Pittsfield)	01201
Yarmouth	02675
Yarmouth (Town)	02675
Yarmouth Port	02675
Zoar	01367
Zylonite	01220

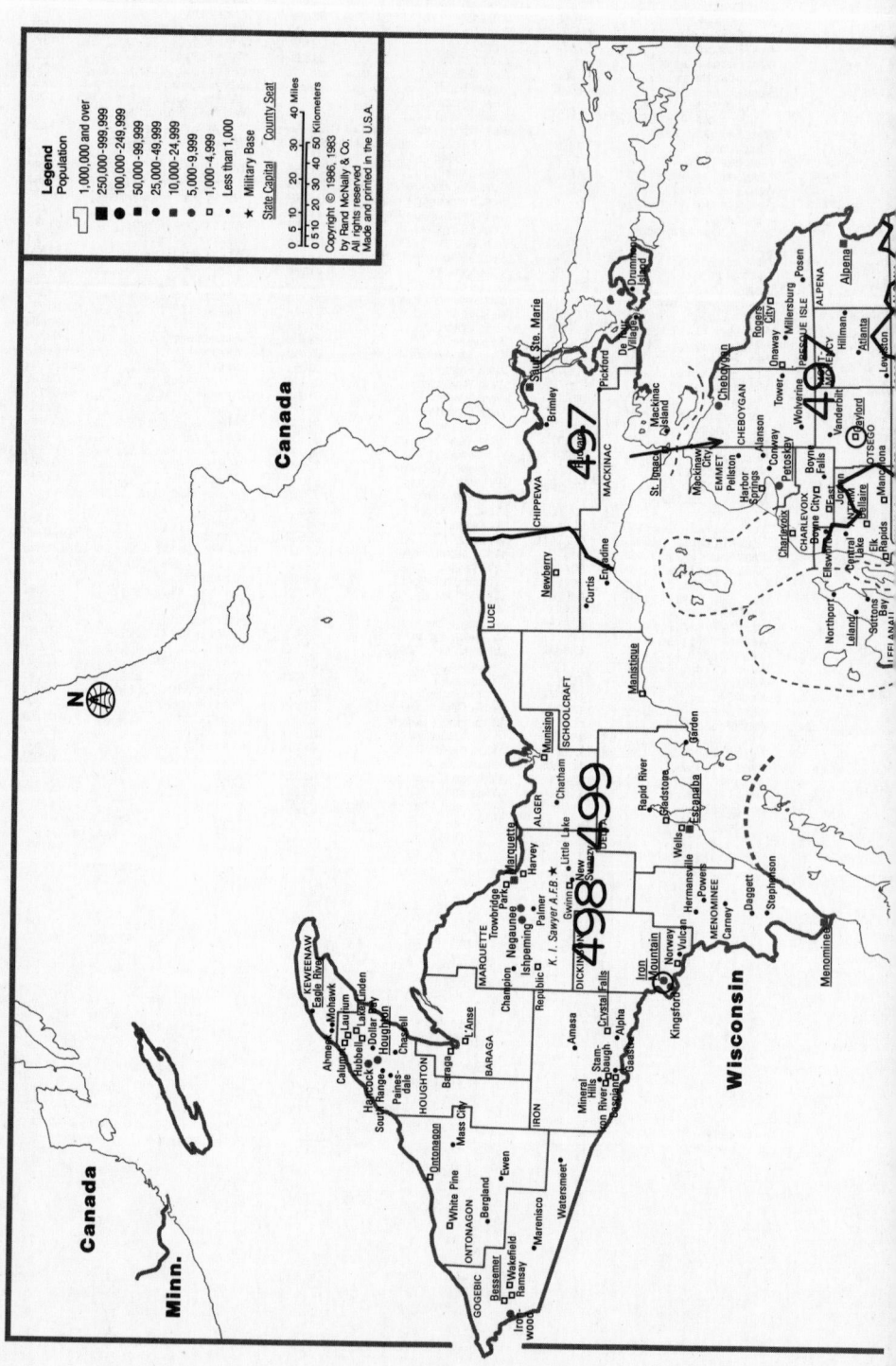

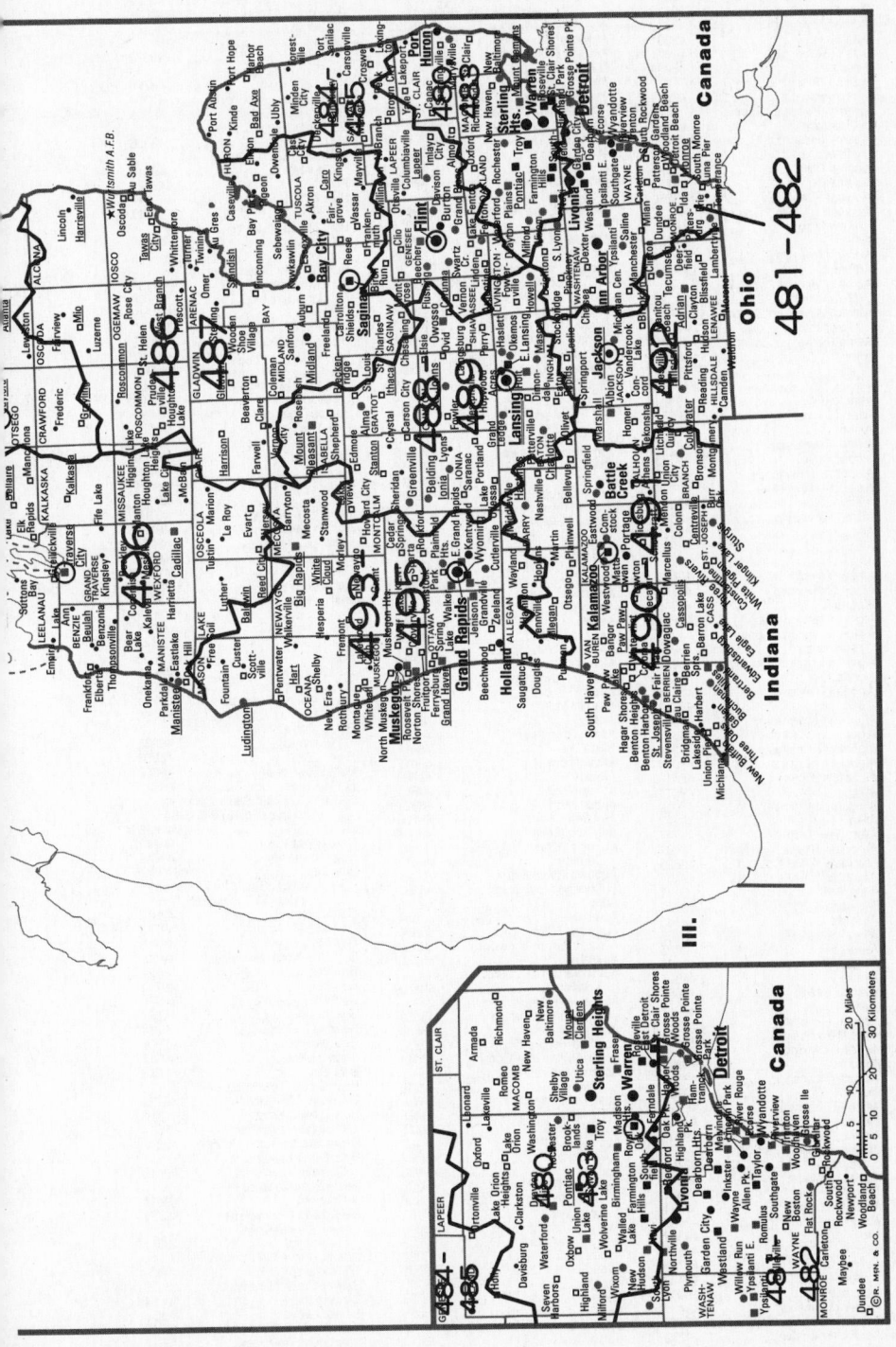

	ZIP
Abscota	49029
Ackerson Lake	49201
Acme	49610
Acme (Township)	49610
Ada	49301
Ada (Township)	49301
Adair	48064
Adams (Arenac County) (Township)	48659
Adams (Hillsdale County) (Township)	49262
Adams (Houghton County) (Township)	49963
Adams Park	49097
Adamsville	49112
Addison (Lenawee County)	49220
Addison (Oakland County) (Township)	48367
Adrian	49221
Adrian (Township)	49221
Advance	49712
Aetna (Mecosta County) (Township)	49336
Aetna (Missaukee County) (Township)	48632
Aetna (Newaygo County)	49412
Afton	49705
Agate	49967
Agnew	49460
Ahmeek	49901
Airport Forest	48625
Akron	48701
Akron (Township)	48701
Alabaster	48763
Alabaster (Township)	48763
Alaiedon (Township)	48854
Alamo	49009
Alamo (Township)	49009
Alanson	49706
Alaska	49302
Alba	49611
Albee (Township)	48655
Albert (Township)	49756
Alberta	49946
Albion (Calhoun County)	49224
Albion (Calhoun County) (Township)	49224
Albion (Houghton County)	49913
Alcona	48740
Alcona (Township)	48721
Alden	49612
Algansee (Township)	49082
Alger	48610
Algoma (Township)	49341
Algonac	48001
All Bright Shores	48612
Allegan	49010
Allegan (Township)	49010
Allen	49227
Allen (Township)	49227
Allendale (Township)	49401
Allendale (Clare County)	48625
Allendale (Ottawa County)	49401
Allen Park	48101
Allenton	48002
Allenville	49760
Allis (Township)	49765
Allouez	49805
Allouez (Township)	49805
Alma	48801
Almeda Beach	48653
Almena	49079
Almena (Township)	49079
Almer (Township)	48723
Almira (Township)	49630
Almont	48003
Almont (Township)	48003
Aloha	49721
Aloha (Township)	49721
Alpena	49707
Alpena (Township)	49707
Alpena Junction (Part of Alpena)	49707
Alpha	49902
Alpine	49321
Alpine (Township)	49321
Alston	49958
Alto	49302
Altona	49336
Alverno	49721
Amador	48422
Amasa	49903
Amber (Township)	49431
Amble	49329
Amboy (Township)	49232
Anchorville	48004
Andersonville	48350
Andrews	49104
Ann Arbor	48103-08

	ZIP
	48113
For specific Ann Arbor Zip Codes call (313) 665-1100	
Ann Arbor (Township)	48105
Antioch (Township)	49688
Antoine (Part of Iron Mountain)	49801
Antrim (Antrim County)	49659
Antrim (Shiawassee County) (Township)	48418
Antwerp (Township)	49065
Anvil Location	49911
Aplin Beach	48706
Applegate	48401
Arbela (Township)	48746
Arborland Consumer Mall (Part of Ann Arbor)	48104
Arbutus Beach	49735
Arcada (Township)	48801
Arcade (Part of Ann Arbor)	48104
Arcadia (Manistee County) (Township)	49613
Arcadia (Lapeer County) (Township)	48412
Arcadia	49613
Arenac (Township)	48749
Argentine	48451
Argentine (Township)	48451
Argyle	48410
Argyle (Township)	48410
Arlington (Township)	49013
Armada	48005
Armada (Township)	48005
Armstrong Corners	49079
Arnheim	49958
Arnold	49819
Artesia Beach	48656
Arthur (Township)	48617
Arvon (Township)	49962
Ash (Township)	48117
Ashland (Township)	49327
Ashland Center	49327
Ashley	48806
Ashmore	48767
Ashton	49655
Askel	49958
Assyria	49021
Assyria (Township)	49021
Athens	49011
Athens (Township)	49011
Atlanta	49709
Atlantic Mine	49905
Atlas	48411
Atlas (Township)	48438
Attica	48412
Attica (Township)	48412
Atwood	49729
Auburn	48611
Auburn Hills	48321
Au Gres	48703
Au Gres (Township)	48703
Augusta (Kalamazoo County)	49012
Augusta (Washtenaw County) (Township)	48191
Aura	49946
Aurelius	48854
Aurelius (Township)	48854
Aurora (Part of Ironwood)	49938
Au Sable	48750
Au Sable (Iosco County) (Township)	48750
Au Sable (Roscommon County) (Township)	48653
Au Sable River Park	48656
Austin (Hillsdale County)	49232
Austin (Marquette County)	49841
Austin (Mecosta County) (Township)	49346
Austin (Sanilac County) (Township)	48475
Austin Center	48475
Austin Lake (Part of Portage)	49081
Au Train	49806
Au Train (Township)	49806
Auvinen Corner	49938
Avalon Beach	48161
Averill	48640
Avery (Township)	49709
Avoca	48006
Avondale	49631
Azalia	48110
Bach	48759
Backus (Township)	48656
Backus Beach	48762
Bad Axe	48413
Bagley (Menominee County)	49821
Bagley (Otsego County) (Township)	49735
Baie de Wasai	49783

	ZIP
Bailey	49303
Bainbridge (Township)	49022
Bainbridge Center	49022
Bakertown	49107
Baldwin (Delta County) (Township)	49872
Baldwin (Iosco County) (Township)	48770
Baldwin (Lake County)	49304
Baltic	49905
Baltimore (Barry County) (Township)	49058
Baltimore (Ontonagon County)	49912
Banat	49821
Bancroft	48414
Banfield	49017
Bangor (Bay County) (Township)	48706
Bangor	49013
Bangor (Van Buren County) (Township)	49103
Bangor Township	48706
Bankers	49242
Banks (Township)	49729
Banksons Lake	49065
Bannister	48807
Baraga	49908
Baraga (Township)	49908
Barbeau	49710
Barker Creek	49690
Bark River	49807
Bark River (Township)	49807
Bar Lake	49660
Barnard	49720
Barnes Lake-Millers Lake	48421
Baroda	49101
Baroda (Township)	49101
Barron Lake	49120
Barry (Township)	49060
Barryton	49305
Barton (Township)	49338
Barton City	48705
Barton Hills	48105
Barton Lake	49097
Base Line Lake	49055
Bass Lake	49449
Batavia	49036
Batavia (Township)	49036
Batavia Center	49036
Bates (Grand Traverse County)	49690
Bates (Iron County) (Township)	49935
Bath	48808
Bath (Township)	48808
Battle Creek	49015-17
For specific Battle Creek Zip Codes call (616) 965-3284	
Bauer	49426
Baw Beese Lake	49242
Bay (Township)	49712
Bay City	48706-08
For specific Bay City Zip Codes call (517) 895-5555	
Bay de Noc (Township)	49878
Bay Mills (Township)	49715
Bay Mills	49715
Bay Mills Indian Reservation	49715
Bay Port	48720
Bayshore	49711
Bay View	49770
Beachwood	48654
Beacon	49814
Beacon Hill	49905
Beadle Lake	49017
Beal City	48858
Bear Creek (Township)	49770
Bearinger (Township)	49759
Bear Lake (Manistee County) (Township)	49614
Bear Lake (Hillsdale County)	49242
Bear Lake (Kalkaska County) (Township)	49646
Bear Lake (Manistee County)	49614
Beaugrand (Township)	49721
Beaver (Bay County) (Township)	48611
Beaver (Newaygo County) (Township)	49309
Beaver Creek (Township)	48653
Beaverdam	49464
Beaver Grove	49855
Beaverton	48612
Beaverton (Township)	48612
Bedford	49020
Bedford (Township)	49017
Bedford (Township)	48182
Beebe	48847

	ZIP
Beecher	48458
Beechwood (Iron County)	49909
Beechwood (Ottawa County)	49423
Belding	48809
Belknap (Township)	49743
Bell	49707
Bellaire	49615
Belleville	48111-12

For specific Belleville Zip Codes call (313) 697-8003

Bellevue	49021
Bellevue (Township)	49021
Bell Oak	48892
Belmont	49306
Belsay (Part of Burton)	48503
Belvedere	49720
Belvidere (Township)	48886
Bendon	49643
Bengal (Township)	48879
Bennington	48867
Bennington (Township)	48867
Benona (Township)	49455
Bentheim	49419
Bentley (Bay County)	48613
Bentley (Gladwin County) (Township)	48652
Bentleys Corners	49245
Benton (Cheboygan County) (Township)	49721
Benton (Eaton County) (Township)	48876
Benton Charter (Township)	49022
Benton Harbor	49022-23

For specific Benton Harbor Zip Codes call (616) 926-8227

Benton Heights	49022
Benzonia	49616
Benzonia (Township)	49616
Bergland	49910
Bergland (Township)	49910
Berkley	48072
Berlamont	49026
Berlin (Ionia County) (Township)	48846
Berlin (Monroe County) (Township)	48166
Berlin (St. Clair County) (Township)	48002
Berne	48755
Berrien (Township)	49102
Berrien Center	49102
Berrien Springs	49103
Bertrand	49120
Bertrand (Township)	49120
Berville	48002
Bessemer	49911
Bessemer (Township)	49959
Bete Grise	49950
Bethany (Township)	48880
Bethany Beach	49125
Bethel (Township)	49028
Betzer	49271
Beulah	49617
Beverly Hills (Marquette County)	49866
Beverly Hills (Oakland County)	48009
Big Bay	49808
Big Creek (Township)	48647
Biggs Settlement	48647
Big Prairie (Township)	49349
Big Rapids	49307
Big Rapids (Township)	49307
Big Rock	49709
Billings (Township)	48612
Bingham (Clinton County) (Township)	48879
Bingham (Huron County) (Township)	48475
Bingham (Leelanau County) (Township)	49684
Bingham Farms	48025
Birch Beach	48450
Birch Creek	49858
Birch Run	48415
Birch Run (Township)	48415
Birchwood (Berrien County)	49115
Birchwood (Cheboygan County)	49721
Birmingham	48009-12

For specific Birmingham Zip Codes call (313) 646-4431

Birmingham Farms	48010
Bismarck (Township)	49779
Bitely	49309
Black Lake Bluffs	49765
Blackman (Township)	49202
Black River	48721
Black River Harbor	49938

	ZIP
Blaine (Benzie County) (Township)	49635
Blaine (St. Clair County)	48032
Blair (Township)	49684
Blanchard	49310
Blaney Park	49836
Blendon (Township)	49426
Bliss	49755
Bliss (Township)	49755
Blissfield	49228
Blissfield (Township)	49228
Bloomer (Township)	48811
Bloomfield (Huron County) (Township)	48468
Bloomfield (Missaukee County) (Township)	49651
Bloomfield (Oakland County) (Township)	48302
Bloomfield Glens	48322
Bloomfield Hills	48301-04

For specific Bloomfield Hills Zip Codes call (313) 642-7030

Bloomfield Hills North	48302
Bloomfield Township	48301-02

For specific Bloomfield Township Zip Codes call (313) 626-9873

Bloomfield Town Square	48302
Bloomfield Village	48301
Bloomingdale	49026
Bloomingdale (Township)	49026
Blue Jacket	49913
Blue Lake (Kalkaska County) (Township)	49646
Blue Lake (Muskegon County) (Township)	49461
Blue Water Beach	48450
Bluff Beach	49099
Blumfield (Township)	48757
Blumfield Corners	48757
Boardman (Township)	49680
Bohemia (Township)	49965
Boichott Acres	48906
Bois Blanc (Township)	49775
Bolles Harbor	48161
Bombay	48642
Boon	49618
Boon (Township)	49618
Bootjack	49945
Borculo	49464
Boston (Houghton County)	49930
Boston (Ionia County) (Township)	48881
Bostwick Lake	49341
Bourret (Township)	48610
Bowens Mills	49333
Bowne (Township)	49302
Boyne City	49712
Boyne Falls	49713
Boyne Valley (Township)	49713
Bradley	49311
Brady (Kalamazoo County) (Township)	49097
Brady (Saginaw County) (Township)	48649
Brampton	49837
Brampton (Township)	49837
Branch	49402
Branch (Township)	49458
Brandon (Township)	48462
Brandywine Lake	49055
Brant	48614
Brant (Township)	48614
Brassar	49783
Bravo	49408
Breckenridge	48615
Breedsville	49027
Breen (Township)	49834
Breezy Beach	49099
Breitung (Township)	49876
Brent Creek	48433
Brethren	49619
Bretton Woods	48917
Brevort	49760
Brevort (Township)	49760
Briarwood (Part of Ann Arbor)	48108
Bridgehampton (Township)	48419
Bridgeport	48722
Bridgeport Charter (Township)	48722
Bridgeton	49327
Bridgeton (Township)	49327
Bridgeville	48879
Bridgewater	48115
Bridgewater (Township)	48158
Bridgman	49106
Brightmoor (Part of Detroit)	48223
Brighton	48116
Brighton (Township)	48116
Briley (Township)	49709
Brimley	49715

	ZIP
Brinton	48632
Bristol	49688
Britton	49229
Broad Acres	48035
Brockway	48097
Brockway (Township)	48097
Brohman	49312
Bronson	49028
Bronson (Township)	49028
Brookfield	48813
Brookfield (Eaton County) (Township)	48813
Brookfield (Huron County) (Township)	48754
Brooklyn	49230
Brooks (Township)	49337
Brookside	49412
Brookville	48170
Broomfield (Township)	49340
Brown (Township)	49660
Brown City	48416
Brownlee Park	49017
Brownstown (Township)	48134
Brownsville	49031
Brownwood Lake	49079
Bruce (Chippewa County) (Township)	49783
Bruce (Macomb County) (Township)	48065
Bruce Crossing	49912
Bruningville	49779
Brunswick	49313
Brutus	49716
Buchanan	49107
Buchanan (Township)	49107
Buckeye (Township)	48624
Buckley	49620
Bucks Corners	49449
Buel (Township)	48422
Buena Vista	48601
Buena Vista Charter (Township)	48601
Bullock Creek	48642
Bumbletown	49805
Bunker Hill	49251
Bunker Hill (Township)	49251
Bunny Run	48362
Burdell (Township)	49688
Burdickville	49664
Burgess	49720
Burleigh (Township)	48770
Burley Corner	49017
Burlington	49029
Burlington (Township)	49029
Burlington (Township)	48727
Burnips	49314
Burns (Township)	48418
Burnside (Township)	48416
Burr Oak	49030
Burr Oak (Township)	49030
Burt (Alger County) (Township)	49839
Burt (Cheboygan County) (Township)	49721
Burt (Saginaw County)	48417
Burtchville (Township)	48059
Burt Lake	49717
Burton (Genesee County)	48509
Burton (Shiawassee County)	48867
Burton-Northeast (Part of Burton)	48509
Burton-Southeast (Part of Burton)	48529
Bushnell (Township)	48884
Butler (Township)	49082
Butman (Township)	48624
Butterfield (Township)	48632
Butternut	48811
Byron (Kent County) (Township)	49315
Byron (Shiawassee County)	48418
Byron Center	49315
Cadillac	49601
Cadmus	49231
Cady	48035
Calcite (Part of Rogers City)	49779
Calderwood	49967
Caldwell (Township)	49651
Caledonia (Alcona County) (Township)	48762
Caledonia (Kent County)	49316
Caledonia (Kent County) (Township)	49316
Caledonia (Shiawassee County) (Township)	48817
California	49255
California (Township)	49255
Calumet	49913
Calumet (Township)	49913
Calvin (Township)	49031

	ZIP
Calvin Center	49031
Cambria	49242
Cambria (Township)	49242
Cambridge (Township)	49265
Cambridge Junction	49230
Camden	49232
Camden (Township)	49232
Campbell (Township)	48815
Campbells Corner	48367
Campbells Corners	48661
Camp Grayling	49739
Canada Corners	49318
Canada Creek Ranch	49709
Canada Shores	49036
Canal (Part of Sault Ste. Marie)	49783
Canandaigua	49235
Canfield Beach	49765
Cannon (Township)	49341
Cannonsburg	49317
Canton (Township)	48184
Canton	48187
Capac	48014
Caribou Lake	49725
Carland	48810
Carleton	48117
Carlisle	49508
Carlshend	49885
Carlton (Township)	49058
Carlton Center	49325
Carmel (Township)	48813
Carney	49812
Caro	48723
Carp Lake	49718
Carp Lake (Emmett County) (Township)	49718
Carp Lake (Ontonagon County) (Township)	49953
Carrollton (Township)	48724
Carrollton	48724
Carr Settlement	49402
Carson City	48811
Carsonville	48419
Cascade	49506
Cascade (Township)	49506
Casco (Allegan County) (Township)	49090
Casco (St. Clair County) (Township)	48064
Case (Township)	49759
Caseville	48725
Caseville (Township)	48725
Cash	48471
Casnovia	49318
Casnovia (Township)	49318
Caspian	49915
Cass City	48726
Cassidy Lake Technical School	48118
Cassopolis	49031
Castle Park	49423
Castleton (Township)	49073
Cathro	49707
Cato (Township)	48850
Cedar (Leelanau County)	49621
Cedar (Osceola County) (Township)	49631
Cedar Bluff	49090
Cedar Creek (Barry County)	49046
Cedar Creek (Muskegon County) (Township)	49457
Cedar Creek (Wexford County) (Township)	49663
Cedar Lake (Montcalm County)	48812
Cedar Lake (Van Buren County)	49067
Cedar River	49813
Cedar Springs	49319
Cedarville (Mackinac County)	49719
Cedarville (Menominee County) (Township)	49813
Cement City	49233
Centennial Heights	49913
Center (Township)	49769
Center Line	48015
Centerville (Township)	49621
Central	49950
Central Lake	49622
Central Lake (Township)	49622
Centreville	49032
Ceresco	49033
Chamberlains	49067
Champion	49814
Champion (Township)	49814
Chandler (Charlevoix County) (Township)	49712
Chandler (Huron County) (Township)	48731
Channing	49815

	ZIP
Chapin	48841
Chapin (Township)	48841
Charleston (Kalamazoo County) (Township)	49053
Charleston (Sanilac County)	48456
Charlevoix	49720
Charlevoix (Township)	49720
Charlotte	48813
Charlton (Township)	49751
Chase	49623
Chase (Township)	49623
Chassell	49916
Chassell (Township)	49916
Chatham	49816
Chatham Corners (Part of Chatham)	49816
Chauncey	49306
Cheboygan	49721
Chelsea	48118
Cherry Beach	48039
Cherry Bend	49684
Cherry Grove (Township)	49601
Cherry Hill	48187
Cherry Island (Part of Rockwood)	48173
Cherryland Mall (Part of Traverse City)	49684
Cherry Valley (Township)	49623
Chesaning	48616
Chesaning (Township)	48616
Cheshire (Township)	49010
Cheshire Center	49010
Chester	48813
Chester (Eaton County) (Township)	48813
Chester (Otsego County) (Township)	49735
Chester (Ottawa County) (Township)	49403
Chesterfield	48051
Chesterfield (Township)	48051
Chestonia (Township)	49611
Chicagon Lake	49920
Chicora	49010
Chief Lake	49645
Chikaming (Township)	49116
China (Township)	48054
Chippewa (Chippewa County) (Township)	49790
Chippewa (Isabella County) (Township)	48858
Chippewa (Mecosta County) (Township)	49320
Chippewa Lake	49320
Chippewa Vista	49305
Chocolay (Township)	49855
Christie Lake	49064
Christmas	49862
Churchill (Muskegon County)	49441
Churchill (Ogemaw County) (Township)	48661
Circle Pine Center	49046
Cisco Lake	49969
Clam Lake (Township)	49601
Clam River	49615
Clam Union (Township)	48632
Clare	48617
Clarence (Township)	49224
Clarendon	49245
Clarendon (Township)	49245
Clarion	49713
Clark (Township)	49719
Clarklake	49234
Clarkston	48346-48
For specific Clarkston Zip Codes call (313) 625-0032	
Clarksville	48815
Clawson	48017
Clay (Township)	48001
Claybanks (Township)	49452
Clayton (Arenac County) (Township)	48659
Clayton (Genesee County) (Township)	48473
Clayton (Lenawee County)	49235
Clear Lake	48661
Clearwater (Township)	49676
Clement (Township)	48610
Cleon (Township)	49625
Cleveland (Township)	49664
Clifford	48727
Climax	49034
Climax (Township)	49034
Clinton (Lenawee County)	49236
Clinton (Lenawee County) (Township)	49236
Clinton (Macomb County) (Township)	48035-36

	ZIP
	48038
For specific Clinton Zip Codes call (313) 465-1936	
Clinton (Oscoda County) (Township)	48619
Clinton Village	48906
Clio	48420
Cloverdale	49035
Cloverville	49444
Clyde (Allegan County) (Township)	49408
Clyde (Oakland County)	48356
Clyde (St. Clair County) (Township)	48049
Coats Grove	49058
Coddes Beach	49765
Cody (Part of Flint)	48507
Coe	48880
Coe (Township)	48880
Cohoctah	48816
Cohoctah (Township)	48816
Cohoctah Center	48816
Cold Springs (Township)	49646
Coldwater (Branch County)	49036
Coldwater (Branch County) (Township)	49036
Coldwater (Isabella County) (Township)	48632
Coleman	48618
Colfax (Benzie County) (Township)	49683
Colfax (Huron County) (Township)	48413
Colfax (Mecosta County) (Township)	49307
Colfax (Oceana County) (Township)	49459
Colfax (Wexford County) (Township)	49663
College Park (Part of Detroit)	48221
College Town	48706
Colling	48767
Collins	48851
Coloma	49038
Coloma (Township)	49038
Colon (Township)	49040
Colon	49040
Columbia (Jackson County) (Township)	49230
Columbia (Tuscola County) (Township)	48767
Columbia (Van Buren County) (Township)	49056
Columbiaville	48421
Columbus (Luce County) (Township)	49853
Columbus (St. Clair County) (Township)	48063
Colwood	48767
Comins	48619
Comins (Township)	48621
Commerce	48387
Commerce (Township)	48382
Comstock	49041
Comstock (Township)	49041
Comstock Northwest	49041
Comstock Park	49321
Concord	49237
Concord (Township)	49237
Condit	49245
Cone	48160
Conklin	49403
Connorville	49968
Constantine	49042
Constantine (Township)	49042
Convis (Township)	49017
Conway (Emmet County)	49722
Conway (Livingston County) (Township)	48836
Cooks	49817
Cooks Corners	48809
Cooper (Township)	49004
Cooper Center	49004
Coopersville	49404
Copemish	49625
Copenhagen	49854
Copper City	49917
Copper Harbor	49918
Coral	49322
Corey	49093
Corinne	49838
Cornell	49818
Cornell (Township)	49818
Corrections Camp Program	49240
Corunna	48817
Corwith (Township)	49795
Coryell Islands	49719
Cottage Grove	48653
Cottage Park	49724
Cottrellville (Township)	48039

	ZIP
Court (Part of Kalamazoo)	49007
Courtland (Township)	49341
Courtland Center (Part of Burton)	48509
Covert	49043
Covert (Township)	49043
Covington	49919
Covington (Township)	49919
Cranbrook (Part of Bloomfield Hills)	48303
Crescent Lake Estates	48327
Crisp	49423
Crockery (Township)	49448
Crofton	49680
Crooked Lake (Barry County)	49046
Crooked Lake (Livingston County)	48116
Crossroads, The (Part of Portage)	49081
Cross Village	49723
Cross Village (Township)	49723
Croswell	48422
Croton	49337
Croton (Township)	49337
Croton Heights	49337
Crump	48634
Crystal	48818
Crystal (Oceana County) (Township)	49420
Crystal (Montcalm County) (Township)	48818
Crystal Beach	49036
Crystal Falls (Township)	49920
Crystal Falls	49920
Crystal Lake (Township)	49635
Crystal Valley	49420
Cumber	48475
Cumming (Township)	48635
Cunard	49847
Curran	48728
Curtis (Alcona County) (Township)	48737
Curtis (Mackinac County)	49820
Curtisville	48761
Custer (Mason County) (Township)	49405
Custer (Sanilac County) (Township)	48471
Custer (Antrim County) (Township)	49659
Custer	49405
Cutlerville	49508
Dafter	49724
Dafter (Township)	49724
Daggett	49821
Daggett (Township)	49821
Dailey	49031
Dallas (Township)	48835
Dalton	49445
Dalton (Township)	49445
Damon	48654
Danby (Township)	48890
Danish Landing	49738
Dansville	48819
Darragh	49646
Davis	48094
Davisburg	48350
Davison	48423
Davison (Township)	48423
Day (Township)	48852
Dayton (Berrien County)	49113
Dayton (Newaygo County) (Township)	49412
Dayton (Tuscola County) (Township)	48744
Dayton Center	49412
Dearborn	48120-21
	48128
For specific Dearborn Zip Codes call (313) 337-4711	
Dearborn Heights	48127
Decatur (Township)	49045
Decatur	49045
Decker	48426
Deckerville	48427
Deep River (Township)	48659
Deerfield (Lenawee County) (Township)	49238
Deerfield (Livingston County) (Township)	48451
Deerfield (Mecosta County) (Township)	49336
Deerfield (Isabella County) (Township)	48858
Deerfield (Lapeer County) (Township)	48421
Deerfield	49238
Deerfield Center (Isabella County)	48858

	ZIP
Deerfield Center (Livingston County)	48451
Deer Park	49868
Deerton	49822
Deford	48729
Dehoco	48175
Delano	48703
Delaware (Township)	48456
Delhi Charter (Township)	48842
Delray (Part of Detroit)	48217
Delta (Township)	48917
Delta Mills	48917
Delton	49046
Delwin	48858
Denmark (Township)	48758
Denton (Roscommon County) (Township)	48651
Denton (Wayne County)	48111
Denver (Isabella County) (Township)	48858
Denver (Newaygo County) (Township)	49421
Derby	49127
Detour (Township)	49725
De Tour Village	49725
Detroit	48201-44
For specific Detroit Zip Codes call (313) 271-6544	
COLLEGES & UNIVERSITIES	
Marygrove College	48221
University of Detroit Mercy	48221
FINANCIAL INSTITUTIONS	
Comerica Bank	48275
Detroit Savings Bank	48226
First Federal of Michigan	48226
First of America Bank-Southeast Michigan, N.A.	48226
Manufacturers Bank,N.A.	48243
NBD Bank	48226
HOSPITALS	
Children's Hospital of Michigan	48201
Detroit Receiving Hospital and University Health Center	48201
Detroit-Macomb Hospital Corporation	48214
Grace Hospital	48235
Harper Hospital	48201
Henry Ford Hospital	48202
Holy Cross Hospital	48234
Hutzel Hospital	48201
North Detroit General Hospital	48212
Samaritan Health Center	48213
Sinai Hospital	48235
St. John Hospital and Medical Center	48236
HOTELS/MOTELS	
Mariott Detroit Airport	48242
Radisson Hotel Pontchartrain	48226
The Westin Hotel	48243
MILITARY INSTALLATIONS	
Coast Guard Base, Detroit	48207
Detroit Marine Terminal, Inc.	48218
United States Army Engineer District, Detroit	48231
United States Army Engineer District, Detroit Area Office	48209
Detroit Beach	48161
Detroit River (Part of Detroit)	48222
Devereaux	49224
Devils Lake	49253
De Witt	48820
De Witt (Township)	48820
Dexter	48130
Dexter (Township)	48169
Diamond Lake	49349
Diamond Shores	49031
Diamond Springs	49419
Dice Corners	48640
Dickson (Township)	49619
Diffin	49891
Dighton	49688
Dimondale	48821
Diorite	49814
Disco	48315
Dixboro	48105
Dodgeville	49921
Dollar Bay	49922
Dollar Settlement	49715
Dollarville	49868

	ZIP
Dolph	49632
Donaldson	49783
Donken	49965
Donoghue Beach	49707
Doriva Beach	49721
Dorr	49323
Dorr (Township)	49323
Doster	49080
Doughertys Corners	49009
Douglas	49406
Douglass (Township)	48888
Dover (Lake County) (Township)	49656
Dover (Lenawee County) (Township)	49235
Dover (Otsego County) (Township)	49738
Dowagiac	49047
Dowling	49050
Downington	48427
Downtown (Part of Flint)	48502
Downtown (Part of Lansing)	48924
Downtown (Part of Midland)	48640
Doyle (Township)	49840
Drayton Plains	48330
Drenthe	49464
Drummond (Township)	49726
Drummond Island	49726
Dryburg	49780
Dryden	48428
Dryden (Township)	48428
Dublin	49689
Duck Lake (Allegan County)	49055
Duck Lake (Calhoun County)	49224
Duel	48640
Duffield	48473
Dukes	49885
Duncan (Township)	48131
Dundee	48131
Dundee (Township)	48131
Dunham Lake	48092
Dunningville	49010
Duplain	48879
Duplain (Township)	48831
Durand	48429
Dutton	49316
Dwight (Township)	48445
Eagle	48822
Eagle (Township)	48822
Eagle Harbor	49950
Eagle Harbor (Township)	49950
Eagle Lake (Cass County)	49112
Eagle Lake (Van Buren County)	49079
Eagle Point	49031
Eagle River	49924
East Bay (Township)	49684
Eastbrook Mall (Part of Grand Rapids)	49508
East China (Township)	48054
East Cooper	49004
East Dayton	48723
Eastgate Shopping Center (Part of Roseville)	48066
East Gilead	49028
East Grand Rapids	49506
East Houghton (Part of Houghton)	49931
East Jordan	49727
East Kingsford	49801
Eastlake	49626
Eastland Center (Part of Harper Woods)	48225
East Lansing	48823-26
For specific East Lansing Zip Codes call (517) 351-3205	
East Leroy	49051
Eastmanville	49404
Easton (Ionia County) (Township)	48846
Easton (Shiawassee County)	48867
East Paris (Part of Kentwood)	49508
Eastpointe	48021
Eastport	49627
East Rockwood	48173
East Saugatuck	49419
East Sebewa	48890
East Side (Part of Saginaw)	48601
East Tawas	48730
Eastview	48065
Eastwood	49001
Eaton (Township)	48813
Eaton Rapids	48827
Eaton Rapids (Township)	48827
Eau Claire	49111
Eben Junction	49825
Echo (Township)	49622

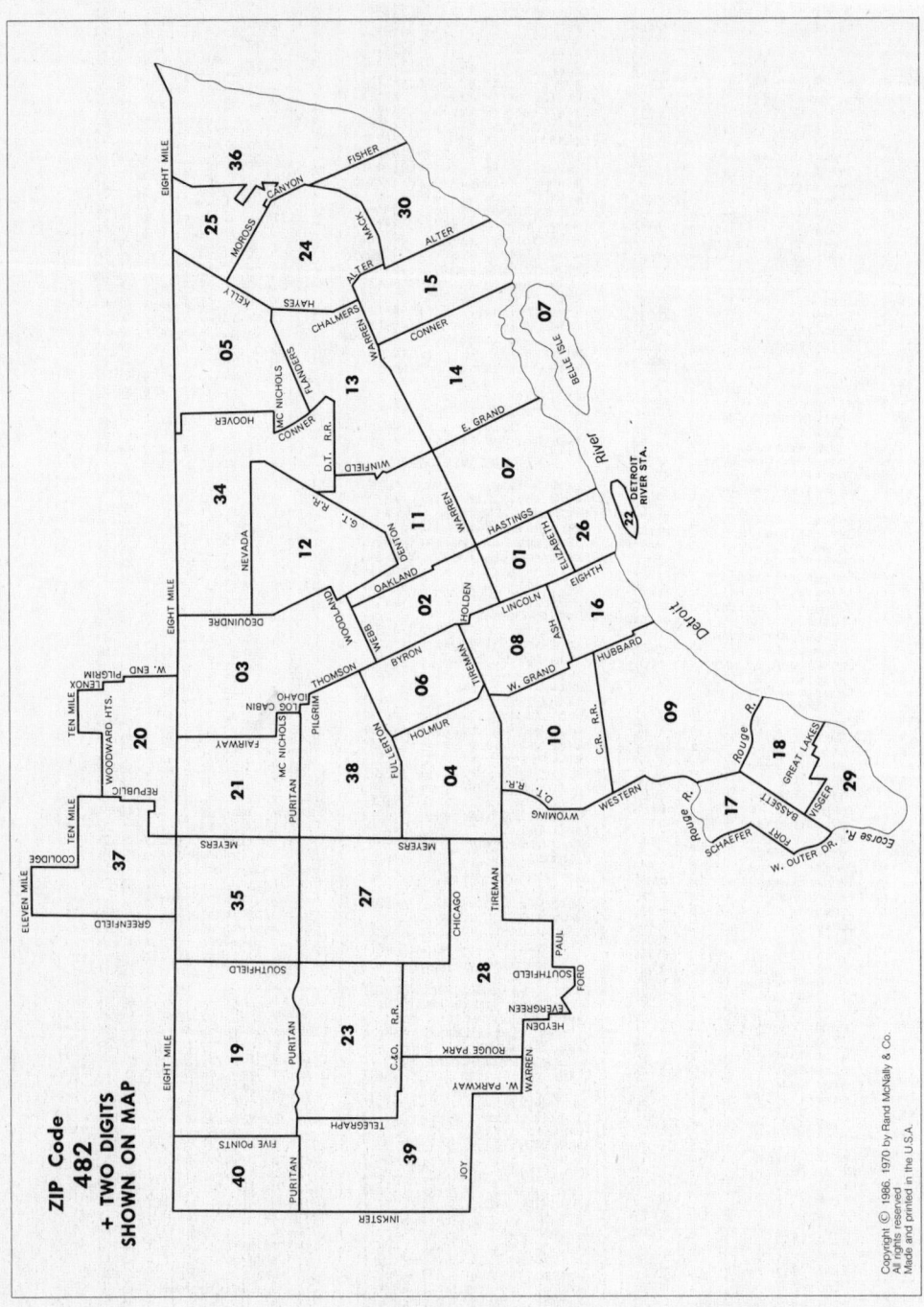

ZIP Code
482
+ TWO DIGITS
SHOWN ON MAP

	ZIP		ZIP		ZIP
Eckerman	49728	Ewing (Township)	49880	Forest (Missaukee County)	
Eckford	49245	Excelsior (Township)	49646	(Township)	49651
Eckford (Township)	49245	Exeter (Township)	48159	Forester	48419
Ecorse	48229	Eyedywild Beach	49735	Forester (Township)	48419
Eden (Ingham County)	48854	Fabius (Township)	49093	Forest Grove	49426
Eden (Lake County)		Factoryville	49066	Forest Grove Station	49426
(Township)	49644	Fairbanks (Township)	49817	Forest Hill	48801
Eden (Mason County)		Fairfax	49040	Forest Hills	49506
(Township)	49454	Fairfield	49221	Forest Home (Township)	49615
Edenville (Township)	48620	Fairfield (Lenawee County)		Forest Lake	49862
Edenville	48620	(Township)	49221	Forestville	48434
Edgemont Park	48917	Fairfield (Shiawassee		Fork (Township)	49305
Edgerton	49341	County) (Township)	48831	Forsyth (Township)	49833
Edmore	48829	Fairgrove	48733	Fort Dearborn (Part of	
Edwards (Township)	48661	Fairgrove (Township)	48733	Dearborn)	48124
Edwardsburg	49112	Fairhaven (Huron County)		Fort Gratiot (Township)	48059
Edwards Corners	49067	(Township)	48720	Fortune Lake	49920
Egelston (Township)	49442	Fair Haven (St. Clair		Foster (Township)	48661
Eight Point Lake	48632	County)	48023	Foster City	49834
Elba (Lapeer County)		Fairlane Town Center (Part		Fosters	48415
(Township)	48446	of Dearborn)	48126	Fostoria	48435
Elba (Gratiot County)		Fair Plain (Berrien County)	49022	Fountain	49410
(Township)	48807	Fairplain (Montcalm County)		Fountain Park	49266
Elba	48446	(Township)	48838	Four Mile Corner	49868
Elberta	49628	Fairplain Plaza	49022	Fowler	48835
Elbridge (Township)	49459	Fairport	49817	Fowlerville	48836
Elizabeth Lake Estates	48327	Fairview	48621	Fox	49813
Elk (Lake County)		Fairview Heights	48197	Fox Creek (Part of Detroit)	48215
(Township)	49644	Faithorn	49892	Francisco	49240
Elk (Sanilac County)		Faithorn (Township)	49892	Frandor Shopping Center	
(Township)	48466	Falmouth	49632	(Part of Lansing)	48917
Elkland (Township)	48726	Fargo	48006	Frankenlust (Township)	48706
Elk Rapids	49629	Farmers Creek	48455	Frankenmuth	48734
Elk Rapids (Township)	49629	Farmington	48331-36	Frankenmuth (Township)	48734
Elkton	48731	For specific Farmington Zip Codes		Frankentrost	48601
Ellington (Township)	48723	call (313) 474-9409		Frankfort	49635
Ellis (Township)	49705	Farmington Hills	48331-34	Franklin (Clare County)	
Ellsworth (Antrim County)	49729	For specific Farmington Hills Zip		(Township)	48625
Ellsworth (Lake County)		Codes call (313) 553-3910		Franklin (Houghton County)	
(Township)	49656	Farrandville	48420	(Township)	49930
Elmdale	48815	Farwell	48622	Franklin (Lenawee County)	
Elmer (Oscoda County)		Fawn River	49091	(Township)	49287
(Township)	48647	Fawn River (Township)	49091	Franklin (Oakland County)	48025
Elmer (Sanilac County)		Fayette (Delta County)	49817	Franklin Mine	49930
(Township)	48471	Fayette (Hillsdale County)		Fraser (Bay County)	
Elm Hall	48830	(Township)	49250	(Township)	48634
Elmira	49730	Federal (Part of Saginaw)	48606	Fraser (Macomb County)	48026
Elmira (Township)	49730	Federal Correctional		Freda	49905
Elm River (Township)	49965	Institution	48160	Frederic	49733
Elmwood (Leelanau County)		Felch	49831	Frederic (Township)	49733
(Township)	49684	Felch (Township)	49831	Fredonia (Township)	49068
Elmwood (Tuscola County)		Felch Mountain	49801	Freedom (Township)	48158
(Township)	48726	Fenkell (Part of Detroit)	48238	Freeland	48623
Elo	49958	Fennville	49408	Freeman (Township)	48632
Eloise (Part of Westland)	48185	Fenton	48430	Freeport	49325
Elsie	48831	Fenton (Township)	48430	Free Soil	49411
Elwell	48832	Fenwick	48834	Free Soil (Township)	49411
Ely (Township)	49814	Ferndale	48220	Freiburger	48475
Emerson (Township)	48615	Ferris (Township)	48891	Fremont (Isabella County)	
Emmett (St. Clair County)		Ferry	49455	(Township)	49310
(Township)	48022	Ferry (Township)	49455	Fremont (Newaygo County)	49412
Emmett (Calhoun County)		Ferrysburg	49409	Fremont (Saginaw County)	
(Township)	49017	Fibre	49780	(Township)	48655
Emmett	48022	Fife Lake	49633	Fremont (Sanilac County)	
Empire	49630	Fife Lake (Township)	49633	(Township)	48097
Empire (Township)	49630	Filer (Township)	49660	Fremont (Tuscola County)	
Engadine	49827	Filer City	49634	(Township)	48744
Ensign	49878	Filion	48432	French Landing (Part of	
Ensign (Township)	49878	Fillmore (Township)	49423	Romulus)	48174
Ensley (Township)	49329	Filmore	49423	Frenchtown (Marquette	
Ensley Center	49343	Findley	49030	County)	49849
Enterprise (Township)	49667	Fisher (Part of Wyoming)	49509	Frenchtown (Monroe	
Entrican	48888	Fisher Building (Part of		County) (Township)	48161
Epoufette	49762	Detroit)	48211	French Town (Oceana	
Epsilon	49770	Fisherville	48611	County)	49449
Erie	48133	Fitchburg	49285	Friendship (Township)	49740
Erie (Township)	48133	Five Lakes	48446	Frontier	49239
Erwin (Township)	49938	Five Points	48867	Frost (Township)	48625
Escanaba	49829	Flat Rock (Delta County)	49837	Frost Corners	48875
Escanaba (Township)	49829	Flat Rock (Wayne County)	48134	Fruitland (Township)	49461
Essex (Township)	48879	Flint	48501-32	Fruitport	49415
Essexville	48732	For specific Flint Zip Codes call		Fruitport Charter (Township)	49415
Estey	48652	(313) 257-1574		Fruitport Siding (Part of	
Estral Beach	48166	Flint (Township)	48532	Norton Shores)	49444
Eureka (Clinton County)	48833	Florence (Township)	49042	Fulton (Gratiot County)	
Eureka (Montcalm County)		Florida	49913	(Township)	48871
(Township)	48838	Flowerfield	49093	Fulton (Kalamazoo County)	49052
Evangeline (Township)	49712	Flowerfield (Township)	49093	Fulton (Keweenaw County)	49950
Evans	49319	Floyd	48640	Fulton Center	48871
Evans Lake	49287	Flushing	48433	Gaastra	49927
Evart	49631	Flushing (Township)	48433	Gagetown	48735
Evart (Township)	49631	Flynn (Township)	48453	Gaines	48436
Eveline (Township)	49727	Foote Site Village	48750	Gaines (Genesee County)	
Everett (Township)	49349	Ford Lake	49410	(Township)	48436
Evergreen (Montcalm		Ford River (Township)	49829	Gaines (Kent County)	
County) (Township)	48884	Ford River (station)	49807	(Township)	49508
Evergreen (Sanilac County)		Ford River	49829	Galesburg	49053
(Township)	48426	Forest (Cheboygan County)		Galien	49113
Evergreen Acres	48161	(Township)	49792	Galien (Township)	49113
Evergreen Shores	49781	Forest (Genesee County)		Ganges	49408
Ewen	49925	(Township)	48463		

	ZIP		ZIP		ZIP
Ganges (Township)	49408	Grand Junction	49056	Greenwood (Wexford	
Garden	49835	Grand Ledge	48837	County) (Township)	49663
Garden (Township)	49835	Grand Marais	49839	Gregory	48137
Garden City	48135-36	Grand Rapids	49501-88	Greilickville	49684
For specific Garden City Zip		For specific Grand Rapids Zip		Gresham	48813
Codes call (313) 421-8160		Codes call (616) 776-1415		Grim (Township)	48652
Garden Corners	49817	Grand Rapids Charter		Grind Stone City	48467
Gardendale	48059	(Township)	49505	Groos	49837
Gardenville	49783	Grand River (Part of Detroit)	48208	Groscap	49781
Gardner	49821	Grand View Acres	48167	Grosse Ile (Township)	48138
Garfield (Bay County)		Grand View Beach		Grosse Ile	48138
(Township)	48634	(Cheboygan County)	49749	Grosse Pointe	48230
Garfield (Clare County)		Grandview Beach (Monroe		Grosse Pointe (Township)	48236
(Township)	49684	County)	48145	Grosse Pointe Farms	48236
Garfield (Grand Traverse		Grandville	49418	Grosse Pointe Park	48230
County) (Township)	49684		49468	Grosse Pointe Shores	48236
Garfield (Kalkaska County)		For specific Grandville Zip Codes		Grosse Pointe Woods	48225
(Township)	49633	call (616) 534-8239		Grosvenor	49228
Garfield (Mackinac County)		Grant (Cheboygan County)		Grout (Township)	48624
(Township)	49827	(Township)	49721	Groveland (Township)	48462
Garfield (Newaygo County)		Grant (Clare County)		Gulliver	49840
(Township)	49337	(Township)	48617	Gull Lake	49083
Garnet	49762	Grant (Grand Traverse		Gunplain (Township)	49080
Garth	49878	County) (Township)	49647	Gustin (Township)	48740
Gay	49945	Grant (Huron County)		Gwinn	49841
Gaylord	49735	(Township)	48726	Hadley	48440
General Post Office (Part of		Grant (Iosco County)		Hadley (Township)	48455
Detroit)	48233	(Township)	48763	Hagar (Township)	49038
Genesee	48437	Grant (Keweenaw County)		Hagar Shores	49039
Genesee (Township)	48437	(Township)	49918	Hagensville	49779
Geneva (Midland County)		Grant (Mason County)		Hagerman Lake	49935
(Township)	48618	(Township)	49411	Haight (Township)	49912
Geneva (Van Buren County)		Grant (Mecosta County)		Hale	48739
(Township)	49056	(Township)	49307	Halfway Corners	48441
Genoa (Township)	48116	Grant (Newaygo County)	49327	Hamburg	48139
Georgetown (Township)	49426	Grant (Newaygo County)		Hamburg (Township)	48169
Gera	48734	(Township)	49327	Hamilton (Allegan County)	49419
Germfask	49836	Grant (Oceana County)		Hamilton (Clare County)	
Germfask (Township)	49836	(Township)	49452	(Township)	48625
Gerrish (Township)	48653	Grant (St. Clair County)		Hamilton (Gratiot County)	
Gibraltar	48173	(Township)	48032	(Township)	48847
Gibson (Allegan County)	49423	Grant Center	49307	Hamilton (Van Buren	
Gibson (Bay County)		Grape	48161	County) (Township)	49045
(Township)	48613	Grass Lake (Township)	49240	Hamlin (Eaton County)	
Gilbo Corners	49679	Grass Lake (Gladwin		(Township)	48827
Gilchrist	49762	County)	48624	Hamlin (Mason County)	
Gilead	49028	Grass Lake (Jackson		(Township)	49431
Gilead (Township)	49028	County)	49240	Hammond Bay	49759
Gilford	48736	Grassmere	48731	Hampton (Township)	48732
Gilford (Township)	48736	Gratiot (Part of Detroit)	48207	Hamtramck	48212
Gilmore (Benzie County)		Grattan	48809	Hancock	49930
(Township)	49628	Grattan (Township)	48809	Hancock (Township)	49930
Gilmore (Isabella County)		Gravel Lake	49065	Handy (Township)	48836
(Township)	48622	Grawn	49637	Hannah	49649
Gingellville	48359	Grayling	49738	Hanover	49241
Girard	49036	Grayling (Township)	49738	Hanover (Jackson County)	
Girard (Township)	49036	Greater Galesburg	49053	(Township)	49241
Gladstone	49837	Great Lake Beach	48450	Hanover (Wexford County)	
Gladwin	48624	Great Lakes Bible College	48917	(Township)	49620
Gladwin (Township)	48624	Great Western (Part of		Harbert	49115
Glen Arbor	49636	Crystal Falls)	49920	Harbor Beach	48441
Glen Arbor (Township)	49636	Greeley	49753	Harbor Point	49740
Glencoe Hills Apartments		Green (Alpena County)		Harbor Springs	49740
(Part of Ann Arbor)	48108	(Township)	49753	Harbor View	49777
Glendale	49079	Green (Mecosta County)		Hardwood	49807
Glendora	49107	(Township)	49338	Haring (Township)	49601
Glen Haven	49621	Green (Ontonagon County)	49953	Harlan	49625
Glenn	49416	Greenbush	48738	Harlem	49423
Glenn Haven Shores	49090	Greenbush (Alcona County)		Harper (Part of Detroit)	48213
Glennie	48737	(Township)	48738	Harper Woods	48225
Glenn Shores	49090	Greenbush (Clinton County)		Harrietta	49638
Glenside (Part of Norton		(Township)	48833	Harris	49845
Shores)	49441	Greendale (Township)	48883	Harris (Township)	49845
Glenwood	49047	Greenfield Village (Part of		Harrisburg	49451
Gobles	49055	Dearborn)	48124	Harrison (Clare County)	48625
Goetzville	49736	Green Lake (Allegan		Harrison (Macomb County)	48045
Golden (Township)	49436	County)	49316	Harrison (Township)	48045
Golfcrest	48161	Green Lake (Grand		Harrison Beach	49854
Goodar (Township)	48761	Traverse County)		Harrisville	48740
Goodells	48027	(Township)	49684	Harrisville (Township)	48740
Good Hart	49737	Greenland	49929	Harsens Island	48028
Goodison	48306	Greenland (Township)	49929	Hart	49420
Goodland (Township)	48444	Greenleaf (Township)	48726	Hart (Township)	49420
Goodrich	48438	Greenmead (Part of Livonia)	48153	Hartford	49057
Goodwell (Township)	49349	Green Oak (Township)	48116	Hartford (Township)	49057
Gordon Beach	49129	Green River	49659	Hartland	48353
Gordonville	48640	Green Road (Part of Ann		Hartland (Township)	48353
Gore (Township)	48468	Arbor)	48113	Hartwick (Township)	49631
Gotts Corners	48725	Greenville	48838	Harvard	49319
Gould City	49838	Greenwood (Clare County)		Harvey	49855
Gourley (Township)	49812	(Township)	48625	Haslett	48840
Gowen	49326	Greenwood (Marquette		Hastings	49058
Graafschap	49423	County)	49849	Hastings (Township)	49058
Grace	49759	Greenwood (Oceana		Hatton (Township)	48625
Graham Lake	49017	County) (Township)	49412	Hautala Corner	49938
Grand Beach	49117	Greenwood (Ogemaw		Hawes (Township)	48742
Grand Blanc	48439	County)	48610	Hawkhead	49416
Grand Blanc (Township)	48439	Greenwood (Oscoda		Hawkins	49677
Grand Haven	49417	County) (Township)	49756	Hawks	49743
Grand Haven (Township)	49417	Greenwood (St. Clair		Hay (Township)	48624
Grand Island (Township)	49862	County) (Township)	48006		

	ZIP
Hayes (Charlevoix County) (Township)	49720
Hayes (Clare County) (Township)	48625
Hayes (Otsego County) (Township)	49735
Haynes (Township)	48742
Hazelhurst Camp	49115
Hazel Park	48030
Hazelton (Township)	48433
Heath (Township)	49419
Hebron (Township)	49755
Helena (Township)	49612
Hell	48169
Helmer	49853
Helps	49873
Hemans	48426
Hematite (Township)	49903
Hemlock	48626
Henderson (Shiawassee County)	48841
Henderson (Wexford County) (Township)	49601
Hendricks (Township)	49762
Henrietta (Township)	49259
Henry Street (Part of Norton Shores)	49441
Herman	49946
Hermansville	49847
Herron	49744
Hersey	49639
Hersey (Township)	49639
Hesperia	49421
Hessel	49745
Hetherton	49751
Hiawatha (Township)	49854
Hickory Corners	49060
Higgins (Township)	48653
Higgins Lake	48627
Highland	48356-57
For specific Highland Zip Codes call (313) 887-2211	
Highland (Township)	49665
Highland Lakes	48167
Highland Park (Kalamazoo County)	49083
Highland Park (Wayne County)	48203
Highway	49913
Hi Hill Villa	48360
Hill (Township)	48739
Hillcrest	49938
Hillcrest Orchard	48145
Hilliards	49328
Hillman	49746
Hillman (Township)	49746
Hillsdale	49242
Hillsdale (Township)	49242
Hinchman	49103
Hinton (Township)	48850
Hockaday	48624
Hodunk	49094
Holland	49422-24
For specific Holland Zip Codes call (616) 396-5201	
Holland (Missaukee County) (Township)	48632
Holland (Ottawa County) (Township)	49423
Holloway	49229
Holly	48442
Holly (Township)	48442
Holmes (Township)	49821
Holt	48842
Holton	49425
Holton (Township)	49425
Home (Montcalm County) (Township)	48829
Home (Newaygo County) (Township)	49309
Home Acres (Part of Wyoming)	49508
Homer	49245
Homer (Calhoun County) (Township)	49245
Homer (Midland County) (Township)	48640
Homestead (Benzie County) (Township)	48640
Homestead (Chippewa County)	49783
Hongore Bay	49765
Honor	49640
Hooper	49080
Hope (Midland County) (Township)	48628
Hope (Barry County) (Township)	49058
Hope	48628
Hopkins	49328
Hopkins (Township)	49328

	ZIP
Hopkinsburg	49328
Hopwood Acres	48912
Horr	48893
Horton (Jackson County)	49246
Horton (Ogemaw County) (Township)	48661
Houghton (Houghton County)	49931
Houghton (Keweenaw County) (Township)	49924
Houghton Lake	48629
Houghton Lake Heights	48630
Houghton Point	48629
Howard (Township)	49120
Howard City	49329
Howardsville	49067
Howell	48843-44
For specific Howell Zip Codes call (517) 546-2560	
Hoxeyville	49601
Hubbard Lake	49747
Hubbardston	48845
Hubbell	49934
Hudson (Charlevoix County) (Township)	49730
Hudson	49247
Hudson (Lenawee County) (Township)	49247
Hudson (Mackinac County) (Township)	49762
Hudsonville	49426
Hulbert	49748
Hulbert (Township)	49748
Humboldt (Township)	49814
Hume (Township)	48467
Hunters Creek	48446
Huntington Woods	48070
Huron (Huron County) (Township)	48467
Huron (Wayne County) (Township)	48164
Huron Gardens	48341
Huronia Heights	48450
Huron Mountain	49808
Hurontown	49931
Huron Valley Men's Facility	48197
Huron Valley Women's Facility	48197
Hylas	49807
Ida	48140
Ida (Township)	48140
Idlewild	49642
Imlay (Township)	48444
Imlay City	48444
Imperial Heights	49861
Ina	49688
Independence (Township)	48346
Indianfield (Part of Portage)	49081
Indianfields (Township)	48723
Indian Lake	49047
Indian River	49749
Indiantown	48601
Ingalls	49848
Ingallston (Township)	49893
Ingersoll (Township)	48623
Ingham (Township)	48819
Ingleside	49755
Inkster	48141
Inland (Township)	49643
Inland Corners	49643
Interior (Township)	49967
Interlochen	49643
Inverness (Township)	49721
Inwood (Township)	49817
Ionia	48846
Ionia (Township)	48846
Ionia Maximum Correctional Facility	48846
Ionia Temporary Facility	48846
Iosco (Township)	48836
Ira (Township)	48023
Iron Mountain	49801-02
For specific Iron Mountain Zip Codes call (906) 774-6804	
Iron River	49935
Iron River (Township)	49935
Irons	49644
Ironton	49720
Ironwood	49938
Ironwood (Township)	49938
Irving	49058
Irving (Township)	49058
Isabella (Delta County)	49878
Isabella (Isabella County) (Township)	48878
Isabella Indian Reservation	48858
Isadore	49621
Ishpeming	49849
Ishpeming (Township)	49849
Ithaca	48847
Iva	48626

	ZIP
Ivanrest (Part of Grandville)	49418
Jackson	49201-04
For specific Jackson Zip Codes call (517) 789-2400	
Jacobsville	49945
Jam	48637
James (Township)	48609
Jamestown	49427
Jamestown (Township)	49426
Jasper (Lenawee County)	49248
Jasper (Midland County) (Township)	48880
Jeddo	48032
Jefferson (Cass County) (Township)	49112
Jefferson (Hillsdale County) (Township)	49266
Jefferson (Jackson County)	49230
Jefferson (Wayne County)	48214
Jenison	49428-29
For specific Jenison Zip Codes call (616) 457-2600	
Jennings	49651
Jericho Corners	49090
Jerome (Hillsdale County)	49249
Jerome (Midland County) (Township)	48657
Jessieville (Part of Ironwood)	49938
Johannesburg	49751
Johnstown (Township)	49050
Jones	49061
Jonesfield (Township)	48637
Jonesville	49250
Joppa	49051
Jordan (Township)	49729
Joyfield (Benzie County) (Township)	49616
Joyfield (Wayne County)	48228
Juddville	48817
Jugville	49349
Juhl	48453
Juniata	48744
Juniata (Township)	48768
Kaiserville	48137
Kalamazoo	49001-09
For specific Kalamazoo Zip Codes call (616) 388-7211	
Kalamazoo (Township)	49004
Kalamo	49096
Kalamo (Township)	49096
Kaleva	49645
Kalkaska	49646
Kalkaska (Township)	49646
Karlin	49647
Kasson (Township)	49664
Kawkawlin	48631
Kawkawlin (Township)	48631
Kearney (Township)	49615
Kearsarge	49942
Keego Harbor	48320
Keeler	49057
Keeler (Township)	49057
Keene (Township)	48881
Kegomic	49770
Kellogg	49010
Kelloggsville (Part of Kentwood)	49508
Kellys Corners	49451
Kelsey Lake	49031
Kendall	49062
Kenockee (Township)	48006
Kensington (Part of Detroit)	48224
Kent City	49330
Kenton	49943
Kentwood	49508
Kerby	48817
Kessington	49112
Kewadin	49648
Keweenaw Bay	49908
Keystone	49684
Kibbie Corners	49090
Killarney Beach	48706
Killmaster	48740
Kilmanagh	48759
Kimball (Township)	48074
Kincheloe	49788
Kinde	48445
Kinderhook	49036
Kinderhook (Township)	49036
King Arthur's Court	48906
Kingsford	49801
Kingsley	49649
Kings Mill	48461
Kingston	48741
Kingston (Township)	48729
Kinneville	48827
Kinross	49752
Kinross (Township)	49752
Kinross Correctional Facility	49788
Kipling	49837

	ZIP
K. I. Sawyer Air Force Base	49843
Kissipee	49751
Kiva	49881
Klacking (Township)	48654
Klinger Lake	49091
Klingville	49916
Klondike	49421
Kneeland	48647
Knollwood Park	49203
Kochville (Township)	48604
Koehler (Township)	49705
Koss	49887
Koylton (Township)	48741
Krakow (Township)	49776
La Branch	49873
Lacey	49021
Lachine	49753
Lac La Belle	49950
Lacota	49063
Lafayette (Township)	48662
Lagoon Beach	48706
La Grange	49031
La Grange (Township)	49031
Laing	48472
Laingsburg	48848
Laird (Township)	49952
Lake (Benzie County) (Township)	49640
Lake (Clare County)	48632
Lake (Huron County) (Township)	48725
Lake (Lake County) (Township)	49304
Lake (Macomb County) (Township)	48236
Lake (Menominee County) (Township)	49821
Lake (Missaukee County) (Township)	49651
Lake (Roscommon County) (Township)	48629
Lake Angeline (Part of Ishpeming)	49849
Lake Angelus	48326
Lake Ann	49650
Lake Charter (Township)	49106
Lake City	49651
Lake Fenton	48430
Lakefield (Luce County) (Township)	49853
Lakefield (Saginaw County) (Township)	48637
Lake George	48633
Lakeland	48143
Lake Lansing	48840
Lake Leelanau	49653
Lake Linden	49945
Lake Margrethe	49738
Lake Mine	49948
Lake Nepessing	48446
Lake Odessa	48849
Lake Orion	48360-62
For specific Lake Orion Zip Codes call (313) 693-8368	
Lake Orion Heights (Part of Lake Orion)	48362
Lake Pleasant	48412
Lakeport	48059
Lake Roland	49968
Lakeside (Berrien County)	49116
Lakeside (Huron County)	48467
Lakeside (Macomb County)	48078
Lakeside Landing	48430
Laketon (Township)	49445
Laketown (Township)	49423
Lakeview (Berrien County)	49129
Lakeview (Calhoun County)	49015
Lakeview (Montcalm County)	48850
Lakeview Square (Part of Battle Creek)	49017
Lakeville	48366
Lakewood (Kalamazoo County)	49002
Lakewood (Monroe County)	48157
Lakewood Club	49457
Lamar (Part of Wyoming)	49509
Lambertville	48144
Lambs	48027
Lamont	49430
Lamotte (Township)	48426
Lanewood (Part of Chelsea)	48118
Langston	48888
L'Anse	49946
L'Anse (Township)	49946
L'Anse Indian Reservation	55401
Lansing	48901-33
For specific Lansing Zip Codes call (517) 337-8711	
Lansing (Township)	48912
Lapeer	48446

	ZIP
Lapeer (Township)	48446
Laporte	48623
Larkin (Township)	48642
Larson Beach	48762
La Salle	48145
La Salle (Township)	48145
La Salle Gardens	48341
Lathrup Village	48076
Laurium	49913
Lawrence	49064
Lawrence (Township)	49064
Lawson	49885
Lawton	49065
Layton Corners	48118
Leaton	48858
Leavitt (Township)	49459
Lebanon (Township)	48845
Ledyard (Part of Grand Rapids)	49523
Lee (Allegan County) (Township)	49450
Lee (Calhoun County) (Township)	49068
Lee (Midland County) (Township)	48640
Lee Center	49076
Leelanau (Township)	49670
Leighton (Township)	49316
Leisure	49090
Leland	49654
Leland (Township)	49654
Lemon Park	49097
Lennon	48449
Lennon Green Estates	48449
Lenox (Township)	48050
Leonard	48367
Leoni	49201
Leoni (Township)	49201
Leonidas	49066
Leonidas (Township)	49066
Le Roy (Township)	49655
Leroy (Calhoun County) (Township)	49051
Leroy (Ingham County) (Township)	48892
Le Roy (Osceola County)	49655
Les Cheneaux Club	49719
Leslie	49251
Leslie (Township)	49251
Level Park	49017
Level Park-Oak Park	49017
Levering	49755
Lewiston	49756
Lewisville	48468
Lexington	48450
Lexington (Township)	48450
Lexington Heights	48450
Liberty	49233
Liberty (Jackson County) (Township)	49234
Liberty (Washtenaw County)	48107
Liberty (Wexford County) (Township)	49663
Liberty Corners	48144
Lilley (Township)	49309
Lima (Township)	48118
Lima Center	48130
Lime Island	49736
Limestone	49816
Limestone (Township)	49816
Lincoln (Alcona County)	48742
Lincoln (Arenac County) (Township)	48658
Lincoln (Berrien County) (Township)	49127
Lincoln (Clare County) (Township)	48633
Lincoln (Huron County) (Township)	48432
Lincoln (Isabella County) (Township)	48883
Lincoln (Midland County) (Township)	48640
Lincoln (Newaygo County) (Township)	49349
Lincoln (Osceola County) (Township)	49677
Lincoln Park (Muskegon County)	49441
Lincoln Park (Wayne County)	48146
Linden	48451
Linden Hills	49042
Linkville	48755
Linwood (Bay County)	48634
Linwood (Wayne County)	48206
Linwood Beach	48634
Lisbon	49403
Liske	49743
Litchfield	49252
Litchfield (Township)	49252

	ZIP
Littlefield (Township)	49706
Little Lake	49833
Little Point Sable	49455
Little Traverse (Township)	49740
Livernois (Part of Detroit)	48210
Livingston (Township)	49735
Livonia	48150-54
For specific Livonia Zip Codes call (313) 425-8050	
Livonia Mall (Part of Livonia)	48152
Loch Alpine	48103
Locke (Township)	48895
Lockport (Township)	49032
Lodi (Kalkaska County)	49646
Lodi (Washtenaw County) (Township)	48103
Logan (Mason County) (Township)	49402
Logan (Ogemaw County) (Township)	48756
London (Township)	48159
Long Lake (Clare County)	48625
Long Lake (Grand Traverse County) (Township)	49684
Long Lake (Ionia County)	48865
Long Lake (Iosco County)	48743
Long Lake Shores	48323
Long Point	49721
Long Rapids (Township)	49753
Longrie	49887
Loomis	48617
Loretto	49852
Lost Lake Woods	48762
Loud (Township)	48619
Lovells	49738
Lovells (Township)	49738
Lowell	49331
Lowell (Township)	49331
Lucas	49657
Ludington	49431
Lulu	48140
Lum	48452
Luna Pier	48157
Lupton	48635
Luther	49656
Luzerne	48636
Lyndon (Township)	48118
Lynn (Township)	48097
Lyon (Oakland County) (Township)	48167
Lyon (Roscommon County) (Township)	48653
Lyon Lake	49068
Lyons	48851
Lyons (Township)	48851
Mable	49690
Macatawa	49434
McBain	49657
McBrides	48852
McCords	49302
McDonald	49013
McFarlands	49880
McGregor	48427
McIntyre Landing	49738
McIvor	48748
Mackinac Island	49757
Mackinaw (Township)	49701
Mackinaw City	49701
McKinley (Emmet County) (Township)	49769
McKinley (Huron County) (Township)	48755
McKinley (Oscoda County)	48647
McLean	49412
McLeods Corner	49868
McMillan	49853
McMillan (Luce County) (Township)	49868
McMillan (Ontonagon County) (Township)	49925
McMillan Corner	49853
Macomb	48042
	48044
For specific Macomb Zip Codes call (313) 465-1936	
Macomb (Township)	48042
Macomb Mall (Part of Roseville)	48066
Macon	49236
Macon (Township)	49236
Madison Center (Part of Madison Heights)	48071
Madison Charter (Township)	49221
Madison Heights	48071
Mancelona	49659
Mancelona (Township)	49659
Manchester	48158
Manchester (Township)	48158
Manistee	49660
Manistee (Township)	49660
Manistique	49854

Name	ZIP
Manistique (Township)	49854
Manitou Beach (Lenawee County)	49253
Manitou Beach (Presque Isle County)	49779
Manitou Beach-Devils Lake	49253
Manlius (Township)	49408
Manning	49721
Mansfield (Township)	49920
Mansfield	49881
Manton	49663
Maple (Part of Dearborn)	48126
Maple City	49664
Maple Forest (Township)	49738
Maple Grove	49073
Maple Grove (Barry County) (Township)	49073
Maple Grove (Manistee County) (Township)	49645
Maple Grove (Saginaw County) (Township)	48460
Maple Grove Corners	49090
Maple Hill	49339
Maple Lake (Part of Paw Paw)	49079
Maple Rapids	48853
Maple Ridge (Alpena County) (Township)	49707
Maple Ridge (Arenac County)	48766
Maple Ridge (Delta County) (Township)	49880
Maple River (Township)	49716
Mapleton (Grand Traverse County)	49684
Mapleton (Midland County)	48640
Maple Valley (Montcalm County) (Township)	49347
Maple Valley (Roscommon County)	48656
Maple Valley (Sanilac County) (Township)	48416
Marathon (Township)	48421
Marcellus	49067
Marcellus (Township)	49067
Marengo	49224
Marengo (Township)	49224
Marenisco	49947
Marenisco (Township)	49947
Marilla (Township)	49625
Marine City	48039
Marion (Township)	49665
Marion (Charlevoix County) (Township)	49720
Marion (Livingston County) (Township)	48843
Marion (Osceola County)	49665
Marion (Saginaw County) (Township)	48614
Marion (Sanilac County) (Township)	48426
Marion Springs	48614
Markey (Township)	48629
Marlette	48453
Marlette (Township)	48453
Marne	49435
Marquette (Mackinac County) (Township)	49774
Marquette	49855
Marquette (Marquette County) (Township)	49855
Marshall	49068
Marshall (Township)	49068
Martin	49070
Martin (Township)	49070
Martiny (Township)	49342
Marysville	48040
Mason (Arenac County) (Township)	48766
Mason (Cass County) (Township)	49112
Mason (Houghton County)	49930
Mason (Ingham County)	48854
Masonville (Township)	49878
Mass City	49948
Mastodon (Township)	49902
Matchwood (Township)	49925
Matherton	48845
Mathias (Township)	49891
Mattawan	49071
Matteson (Township)	49028
Matteson Lake	49028
Max Myers Addition	49120
Maybee	48159
Mayfield	49666
Mayfield (Grand Traverse County) (Township)	49649
Mayfield (Lapeer County) (Township)	48446
Mayflower	49913
Mayville	48744
Maywood	49878
Meade (Huron County) (Township)	48432
Meade (Macomb County)	48048
Meade (Mason County) (Township)	49411
Meads Landing	48629
Mears	49436
Meauwataka	49601
Mecosta	49332
Mecosta (Township)	49346
Medina	49247
Medina (Township)	49247
Melita	48659
Mellen (Township)	49848
Melrose (Township)	49796
Melstrand	49884
Melvin	48454
Melvindale	48122
Memphis	48041
Mendon	49072
Mendon (Township)	49072
Menominee	49858
Menominee (Township)	49858
Menonaqua Beach	49740
Mentha	49055
Mentor (Cheboygan County) (Township)	49799
Mentor (Oscoda County) (Township)	48647
Meredith	48624
Meridian (Township)	48823
Meridian Mall	48864
Merrill (Newaygo County) (Township)	49309
Merrill (Saginaw County)	48637
Merriman	49801
Merritt (Bay County) (Township)	48747
Merritt (Missaukee County)	49667
Merriweather	49947
Merson	49010
Mesick	49668
Metamora	48455
Metamora (Township)	48455
Metropolitan	49801
Metropolitan Airport (Part of Romulus)	48242
Metropolitan Airport South Terminal (Part of Romulus)	48242
Metz	49776
Metz (Township)	49776
Meyer (Township)	49847
Miami Park	49090
Michiana	49117
Michigamme	49861
Michigamme (Township)	49861
Michigan Center	49254
Michigan Reformatory	48846
Michigan State University Residence Halls	48825
Michigan State University	48824
Michigan Training Unit	48824
Middlebelt (Part of Romulus)	48174
Middle Branch (Township)	49665
Middlebury (Township)	48866
Middleton	48856
Middletown	48817
Middle Village	49737
Middleville	49333
Midland	48640-42
For specific Midland Zip Codes call (517) 631-6580	
Midland (Township)	48642
Midland Park	49060
Mikado	48745
Mikado (Township)	48745
Milan (Monroe County) (Township)	48160
Milan (Washtenaw County)	48160
Milford	48380-81
For specific Milford Zip Codes call (313) 684-0775	
Milford (Township)	48381
Millbrook	49334
Millbrook (Township)	49334
Millburg	49022
Millecoquins	49827
Millen (Township)	48705
Millersburg	49759
Millett	48917
Milleville Beach	48173
Mill Grove	49010
Millington	48746
Millington (Township)	48746
Mill Lake	49055
Mills (Houghton County)	49934
Mills (Midland County) (Township)	48652
Mills (Ogemaw County) (Township)	48756
Mills (Sanilac County)	48427
Millville	49285
Milnes	49250
Milton (Antrim County) (Township)	49648
Milton (Cass County) (Township)	49120
Minards Mill	49269
Minden (Township)	48456
Minden City	48456
Mineral Hills	49935
Minor Beach	49854
Mio	48647
Missaukee Park	49651
Mitchell (Township)	48728
M & M Plaza (Part of Menominee)	49858
Moddersville	48632
Moffatt (Township)	48610
Mohawk	49950
Moline	49335
Moltke (Township)	49779
Monitor (Township)	48706
Monongahela Location	49920
Monroe	48161
Monroe (Monroe County) (Township)	48161
Monroe (Newaygo County) (Township)	49349
Monroe Center	49637
Montague	49437
Montague (Township)	49437
Montcalm (Township)	48838
Monterey (Township)	49010
Monterey Center	49010
Montgomery	49255
Montmorency (Township)	49746
Montrose	48457
Montrose (Township)	48457
Moore (Township)	48471
Moore Park	49093
Moorestown	49651
Mooreville	48160
Moorland	49451
Moorland (Township)	49451
Moran	49760
Moran (Township)	49781
Morenci	49256
Morgan	49073
Morgan Corners	49017
Morley	49336
Morrice	48857
Morseville	48415
Morton (Township)	49332
Moscow	49257
Moscow (Township)	49257
Mosherville	49258
Mosherville Station	49250
Motley	49952
Mott Park (Part of Flint)	48504
Mottville	49099
Mottville (Township)	49099
Mound Spring	49091
Mountain Beach	49460
Mount Clemens	48043-46
For specific Mount Clemens Zip Codes call (313) 465-1936	
Mount Clemens Southeast	48043
Mount Elliott (Part of Detroit)	48234
Mount Forest	48650
Mount Forest (Township)	48650
Mount Haley (Township)	48637
Mount Morris	48458
Mount Morris (Township)	48458
Mount Pleasant	48804
	48858-59
For specific Mount Pleasant Zip Codes call (517) 773-3653	
Mount Pleasant	49090
Mount Vernon	48306
Mueller (Township)	49840
Muir	48860
Mullet Lake	49761
Mullett (Township)	49791
Mulliken	48861
Mundy (Township)	48507
Munger	48747
Munising	49862
Munising (Township)	49895
Munith	49259
Munro (Township)	49755
Munson	49256
Muskegon	49440-45
For specific Muskegon Zip Codes call (616) 722-7292	
Muskegon (Township)	49445
Muskegon Heights	49444
Muskegon Mall (Part of Muskegon)	49440

	ZIP		ZIP		ZIP
Mussey (Township)	48014	North Shade (Township)	48856	Onsted	49265
Muttonville	48062	North Shores	48145	Ontonagon	49953
Nadeau	49863	North Side (Part of Flint)	48505	Ontonagon (Township)	49953
Nadeau (Township)	49863	North Star	48862	Ontwa (Township)	49112
Nagel Corner	49743	North Star (Township)	48862	Orange (Ionia County)	
Nahma	49864	North Street	48049	(Township)	48846
Nahma (Township)	49864	Northview	49505	Orange (Kalkaska County)	
Napoleon	49261	Northville (Kent County)	49505	(Township)	49646
Napoleon (Township)	49261	Northville (Wayne County)	48167	Orangeville	49080
Nashville	49073	Northville (Township)	48167	Orangeville (Township)	49080
Nathan	49821	Northville Commons	48167	Orchard Beach	49721
National (Part of Crystal		Northville Regional		Orchard Lake	48323-24
Falls)	49920	Psychiatric Hospital	48167	For specific Orchard Lake Zip	
National City	48748	Northwest (Part of Grand		Codes call (313) 626-9873	
National Mine	49865	Rapids)	49504	Orchard Park (Part of Battle	
Naubinway	49762	Northwestern (Part of		Creek)	49017
Nazareth (Part of		Detroit)	48204	Oregon (Township)	48446
Kalamazoo)	49074	North Wheeler	48662	Orient (Township)	49679
Needmore	48813	Northwood	49004	Orion	48360-62
Neeley	49080	Norton Shores	49441	For specific Orion Zip Codes call	
Negaunee	49866	Norvell	49263	(313) 693-8368	
Negaunee (Township)	49866	Norvell (Township)	49263	Orleans	48865
Nelson (Kent County)		Norwalk	49660	Orleans (Township)	48865
(Township)	49343	Norway	49870	Oronoko (Township)	49103
Nelson (Saginaw County)	48626	Norway (Township)	49892	Ortonville	48462
Nessen City	49683	Norwich (Missaukee		Osceola	49913
Nester (Township)	48624	County) (Township)	49651	Osceola (Houghton County)	
Nestoria	49861	Norwich (Newaygo County)		(Township)	49913
New Allouez	49901	(Township)	49307	Osceola (Osceola County)	
Newark (Gratiot County)		Norwood	49720	(Township)	49631
(Township)	48847	Norwood (Township)	49720	Oscoda	48750
Newark (Oakland County)	48442	Nottawa (Township)	49075	Oscoda (Township)	48750
Newaygo	49337	Nottawa (Isabella County)		Oscoda Indian Mission	48745
New Baltimore	48047	(Township)	48858	Oshtemo	49077
Newberg (Township)	49061	Nottawa (St. Joseph		Oshtemo (Township)	49077
Newberry	49868	County)	49075	Osier	49878
New Boston	48164	Novesta (Township)	48729	Oskar	49931
New Bristol Location	49920	Novi	48374-70	Osseo	49266
New Buffalo	49117	For specific Novi Zip Codes call		Ossineke	49766
New Buffalo (Township)	49117	(313) 349-2100		Ossineke (Township)	49747
New Era	49446	Novi (Township)	48375	Otisco (Township)	48809
Newfield (Township)	49421	Nunda (Township)	49799	Otisville	48463
New Greenleaf	48726	Nunica	49448	Otsego	49078
New Haven (Gratiot County)		Oakfield (Township)	48838	Otsego (Township)	49078
(Township)	48889	Oak Grove (Livingston		Otsego Lake	49735
New Haven (Macomb		County)	48863	Otsego Lake (Township)	49735
County)	48048	Oak Grove (Otsego County)	49735	Ottawa Beach	49423
New Haven (Shiawassee		Oak Grove (Roscommon		Ottawa Center	49404
County) (Township)	48867	County)	48653	Ottawa Lake	49267
New Holland	49423	Oak Hill	49660	Otterburn (Part of Swartz	
New Hudson	48165	Oakhurst	48701	Creek)	48473
Newkirk (Township)	49656	Oakland	49419	Otter Lake	48464
Newland	49660	Oakland Charter (Township)	48363	Otto (Township)	49421
New Lothrop	48460	Oakley	48649	Overisel	49423
Newport	48166	Oak Manor	49120	Overisel (Township)	49423
New, Richmond	49447	Oak Park (Calhoun County)	49017	Ovid (Clinton County)	
New Salem	49315	Oak Park (Oakland County)	48237	(Township)	48866
New Swanzy	49841	Oak Shade Park	49230	Ovid (Branch County)	
Newton (Calhoun County)		Oakville	48160	(Township)	49036
(Township)	49017	Oakwood (Oakland County)	48371	Ovid	48866
Newton (Mackinac County)		Oakwood (St. Joseph		Owasippe	49457
(Township)	49838	County)	49099	Owendale	48754
New Troy	49119	Oakwood (Wayne County)	48122	Owosso	48867
Nicholsville	49067	Oceola (Township)	48843	Owosso (Township)	48867
Niles	49120	Ocqueoc	49759	Owosso Junction (Part of	
Niles (Township)	49120	Ocqueoc (Township)	49759	Owosso)	48867
Nirvana	49623	Oden	49764	Oxford	48370-71
Nisula	49952	Odessa (Township)	48849	For specific Oxford Zip Codes call	
Noble (Township)	49028	Odgers Location	49920	(313) 628-2557	
Noordeloos	49423	Ogden (Township)	49228	Oxford (Township)	48371
Norman (Township)	49689	Ogden Center	49228	Ozark	49760
North Adams	49262	Ogemaw (Township)	48661	Paavola	49930
North Allis (Township)	49765	Ogemaw Springs	48661	Painesdale	49955
North Bell	48815	Oil City	48883	Paka Plaza (Part of	
North Blendon	49426	Okemos	48805	Jackson)	49202
North Bradley	48618	For specific Okemos Zip Codes		Palestine	49887
North Branch (Township)	48461	call (517) 349-2461		Palisades Park	49043
North Branch	48461	Old Mission	49673	Palmer	49871
North Dorr	49323	Old Redford (Part of Detroit)	48219	Palms	48465
Northeast (Part of Livonia)	48152	Olive (Clinton County)		Palmyra	49268
North End (Part of Detroit)	48202	(Township)	48879	Palmyra (Township)	49268
North Epworth	49431	Olive (Ottawa County)		Palo	48870
Northfield (Township)	48189	(Township)	49460	Paradise (Chippewa	
Northgate	49505	Olive Center	49423	County)	49768
North Kent Mall	49505	Olive Hills	49460	Paradise (Grand Traverse	
North Lake (Lapeer County)	48464	Oliver (Huron County)		County) (Township)	49649
North Lake (Marquette		(Township)	48731	Parchment	49004
County)	49849	Oliver (Kalkaska County)		Paris (Huron County)	
North Lake (Van Buren		(Township)	49646	(Township)	48470
County)	49055	Olivet	49076	Paris (Mecosta County)	49338
North Lakeport	48059	Olson	48640	Parisville	48470
Northland	49869	Omena	49674	Park (Ottawa County)	
Northland Shopping Center		Omer	48749	(Township)	49423
(Part of Southfield)	48075	Onaway	49765	Park (St. Joseph County)	
North Manitou	49654	Oneida Charter (Township)	48837	(Township)	49093
North Morenci	49256	Onekama	49675	Parkdale	49660
North Muskegon	49445	Onekama (Township)	49675	Parkers Corners	48836
North Paynesville	49912	Onondaga	49264	Park Grove (Part of Detroit)	48205
North Plains (Township)	48845	Onondaga (Township)	49264	Park Lake	48808
Northport	49670	Onota (Township)	49822	Park Plaza (Part of Lincoln	
Northport Point	49670			Park)	48146

	ZIP
Rives Junction	49277
Roberts Corners	49868
Roberts Landing	48001
Robin Glen-Indiantown	48601
Robinson (Township)	49460
Rochester	48306-09
For specific Rochester Zip Codes call (313) 651-8551	
Rochester Hills	48306-07
	48309
For specific Rochester Hills Zip Codes call (313) 651-8551	
Rock	49880
Rockford	49341
Rockland	49960
Rockland (Township)	49960
Rock River (Township)	49825
Rockwood	48173
Rodney	49342
Rogers (Township)	49779
Rogers City	49779
Roger's Plaza (Part of Wyoming)	49509
Rolland (Township)	49310
Rollin	49278
Rollin (Township)	49278
Rome (Township)	49221
Rome Center	49221
Romeo	48065
Romulus	48174
Ronald (Township)	48846
Rondo	49799
Roosevelt Park	49441
Roscommon	48653
Roscommon (Township)	48653
Rose (Oakland County) (Township)	48442
Rose (Ogemaw County) (Township)	48654
Roseburg	48097
Rosebush	48878
Rose Center	48442
Rose City	48654
Rosedale	49783
Rose Island	48759
Rose Lake (Township)	49655
Roseville	48066
Roseville Plaza (Part of Roseville)	48066
Ross (Township)	49012
Rothbury	49452
Round Lake (Lenawee County)	49253
Round Lake (Mason County)	49410
Rousseau	49948
Rowes Corner	48158
Roxand (Township)	48837
Royal Oak	48067-68
	48073
For specific Royal Oak Zip Codes call (313) 546-7108	
Royal Oak (Township)	48220
Royal Oak Beach	48721
Royalton (Township)	49085
Rubicon (Township)	48468
Ruby	48027
Rudyard	49780
Rudyard (Township)	49780
Rumely	49826
Rush (Township)	48841
Rush Lake	48169
Rusk	49464
Russell Island	48001
Russellville	48423
Rust	49746
Rust (Township)	49746
Ruth	48470
Rutland (Township)	49058
Ryan	48637
Sac Bay	49817
Saddle Lake	49056
Sage (Township)	48624
Saginaw	48601-09
For specific Saginaw Zip Codes call (517) 771-5725	
Saginaw (Township)	48603
Saginaw Township North	48603
Saginaw Township South	48603
Saginaw Valley State College	48604
Sagola	49881
Sagola (Township)	49881
St. Anthony	48182
St. Charles	48655
St. Charles (Township)	48655
St. Clair	48079
St. Clair (Township)	48079
St. Clair Shores	48080-82
For specific St. Clair Shores Zip Codes call (313) 775-5050	

	ZIP
St. Helen	48656
St. Ignace	49781
St. Ignace (Township)	49781
St. Jacques	49878
St. James	49782
St. James (Township)	49782
St. Johns	48879
Saint John's Provincial Seminary	48170
St. Joseph	49085
St. Joseph Charter (Township)	49022
St. Louis	48880
St. Marys Lake	48017
St. Nicholas	49880
Salem (Allegan County) (Township)	49314
Salem (Washtenaw County) (Township)	48178
Salem	48175
Saline	48176
Saline (Township)	49236
Salisbury (Part of Ishpeming)	49849
Samaria	48177
Sanborn (Township)	49766
Sand Beach (Township)	48441
Sand Creek	49279
Sand Lake (Iosco County)	48748
Sand Lake (Kent County)	49343
Sand Lake Corners	49265
Sand River	49822
Sands	49841
Sands (Township)	49841
Sandstone (Township)	49201
Sandusky	48471
Sandy Beach	49091
Sanford	48657
Sanilac (Township)	48469
San Souci Beach	49036
Santiago	48765
Saranac	48881
Sauble (Township)	49402
Saugatuck	49453
Saugatuck (Township)	49453
Sault Ste. Marie	49783
Sault Ste. Marie Air Force Station	49783
Sawyer	49125
Sawyer Lake	49815
Schaffer	49807
Schoolcraft	49087
Schoolcraft (Houghton County) (Township)	49945
Schoolcraft (Kalamazoo County)	49087
Schuck Island	48759
Schultz	49058
Scio (Township)	48130
Sciota (Township)	48848
Scipio (Township)	49250
Scott Correctional Facility	48170
Scottdale	49085
Scott Lake	49927
Scotts	49088
Scottville	49454
Sears	49679
Sears Lincoln Park Shopping Center (Part of Lincoln Park)	48146
Sebewa (Township)	48875
Sebewa Center	48875
Sebewaing	48759
Sebewaing (Township)	48759
Secord (Township)	48624
Seidler Corners	48611
Selfridge Air Force Base	48045
Selkirk	48661
Selma (Township)	49601
Seneca	49280
Seneca (Township)	49280
Seneca Location	49950
Seney	49883
Seney (Township)	49883
Senter	49922
Seven Harbors	48356
Seven-Mile & Mack Shopping Center (Part of Detroit)	48236
Seven Oaks (Part of Detroit)	48235
Seville (Township)	48832
Seymour Square (Part of Grand Rapids)	49510
Shabbona	48426
Shady Shores	48635
Shadyside	49266
Shafer Location	49920
Shaftsburg	48882
Shanghai Corners	49111
Sharon (Township)	48158
Sharon Hollow	48158

	ZIP
Sharps Corners	48653
Shawnee Shores	49036
Shelby Charter (Township)	48315-16
For specific Shelby Charter Zip Codes call (616) 861-2356	
Shelby	49455
Shelby (Township)	49455
Shelbyville	49344
Sheldon	48111
Shepardsville	48866
Shepherd	48883
Sheridan (Calhoun County) (Township)	49224
Sheridan (Clare County) (Township)	48617
Sheridan (Huron County) (Township)	48413
Sheridan (Mason County) (Township)	49410
Sheridan (Mecosta County) (Township)	49305
Sheridan (Montcalm County)	48884
Sheridan Charter (Township)	49412
Sherman (Gladwin County) (Township)	48624
Sherman (Huron County) (Township)	48456
Sherman (Iosco County) (Township)	48748
Sherman (Isabella County) (Township)	48632
Sherman (Keweenaw County) (Township)	49945
Sherman (Mason County) (Township)	49410
Sherman (Newaygo County) (Township)	49412
Sherman (Osceola County) (Township)	49688
Sherman (St. Joseph County) (Township)	49091
Sherman (Wexford County)	49668
Sherman City	48632
Sherwood	49089
Sherwood (Township)	49089
Sherwood Corners	48647
Shiawassee (Township)	48429
Shiawasseetown	48429
Shields	48609
Shiloh	48865
Shingleton	49884
Shoreham	49085
Shore Line Junction (Part of Hancock)	49930
Shorewood Hills	49125
Shorewood-Tower Hills-Harbert	49115
Sibley (Part of Trenton)	48183
Sidnaw	49961
Sidney	48885
Sidney (Township)	48885
Sid Town	48750
Sigel (Township)	48441
Silver City	49953
Silver Creek (Township)	49047
Silverwood	48760
Simar	49948
Sims (Township)	48703
Sister Lakes	49047
Sitka	49412
Six Lakes	48886
Skandia (Township)	49885
Skandia	49885
Skanee	49962
Skeels	48624
Skidway Lake	48756
Slagle (Township)	49638
Slapneck	49816
Sleepy Hollow	49912
Slocum	49451
Smith Corners	49420
Smiths Creek	48074
Smyrna	48887
Snover	48472
Snyderville	48063
Sodus	49126
Sodus (Township)	49126
Sokol Camp	49117
Solon (Leelanau County) (Township)	49621
Solon (Kent County) (Township)	49319
Solon	49621
Somerset	49281
Somerset (Township)	49281
Somerset Center	49282
Somerset Mall (Part of Troy)	48084
Sonoma	49017
Soo (Township)	49783
South Arm (Township)	49727
South Blendon	49426

	ZIP		ZIP		ZIP
Utica	48310-14	Waterford	48327-29		49019
	48317-18	For specific Waterford Zip Codes		For specific Westwood Zip Codes	
For specific Utica Zip Codes call		call (313) 623-0020		call (616) 343-2560	
(313) 731-9412		Waterloo	49240	Westwood Heights	48504
Valley (Township)	49010	Waterloo (Township)	49240	Wetmore	49895
Valley Center	48416	Watermill Lake	49642	Wetzel	49659
Valley Farms	48906	Waters	49797	Wexford (Township)	49668
Van	49755	Watersmeet	49969	Wheatfield (Township)	48895
Van Buren (Township)	48111	Watersmeet (Township)	49969	Wheatland (Hillsdale	
Vandalia	49095	Watertown (Sanilac County)		County) (Township)	49220
Vanderbilt	49795	(Township)	48471	Wheatland (Mecosta	
Vandercook Lake	49203	Watertown (Tuscola County)		County) (Township)	49340
Van Meer	49884	(Township)	48435	Wheatland (Sanilac County)	
Vantown	48892	Watertown (Clinton County)		(Township)	48427
Vassar	48768	(Township)	48820	Wheeler	48662
Vassar (Township)	48768	Watertown	48471	Wheeler (Township)	48662
Venice (Township)	48817	Watervale	49613	White	49952
Vergennes (Township)	49331	Watervliet	49098	White Cloud	49349
Vermontville	49096	Watervliet (Township)	49098	Whitefish (Township)	49728
Vermontville (Township)	49096	Watrousville	48768	Whitefish Point	49768
Vernon (Township)	48429	Watson	49078	Whiteford (Township)	49267
Vernon (Isabella County)		Watson (Township)	49078	Whiteford Center	49267
(Township)	48617	Watson Corners	49078	Whitehall	49461
Vernon (Shiawassee		Wattles Park	49017	Whitehall (Township)	49461
County)		Watton	49970	White Lake	48383
Vernon City	48617	Waucedah	49892	White Lake (Township)	48383
Verona (Township)	48413	Waucedah (Township)	49892	White Oak (Township)	49285
Verona (Calhoun County)	49017	Waverly (Cheboygan		White Pigeon	49099
Verona (Gogebic County)	49968	County) (Township)	49765	White Pigeon (Township)	49099
Verona (Huron County)	48413	Waverly (Eaton County)	48917	White Pine	49971
Verona Park	49017	Waverly (Van Buren County)		White River (Township)	49437
Vestaburg	48891	(Township)	49079	Whites Beach	48658
Veterans Administration		Wawatam (Township)	49701	Whitewater (Township)	49690
Hospital (Part of Iron		Wawatam Beach (Part of		Whitmore Lake	48189
Mountain)	49801	Mackinaw City)	49701	Whitney (Township)	48765
Vevay (Township)	48854	Wayland	49348	Whittaker	48190
Vickery Landing	49050	Wayland (Township)	49348	Whittemore	48770
Vickeryville	48884	Wayne	48184-88	Wickware	48726
Vicksburg	49097	For specific Wayne Zip Codes call		Wilber (Township)	48730
Victor (Township)	48848	(313) 728-4100		Wilcox (Township)	49349
Victoria	49960	Wayne (Township)	49047	Wildwood (Cheboygan	
Victory (Township)	49454	Weadlock	49755	County)	49706
Vienna (Genesee County)		Weale	48720	Wildwood (Manistee	
(Township)	48420	Weare (Township)	49420	County)	49614
Vienna (Montmorency		Webber (Township)	49304	Willard	48611
County) (Township)	49751	Webberville	48892	Williams (Township)	48611
Virginia Park	49423	Webster (Township)	48130	Williamsburg	49690
Vogel Center	49657	Weesaw (Township)	49128	Williamston	48895
Volinia	49045	Weidman	48893	Williamston (Township)	48895
Volinia (Township)	49045	Welcome Corners	49058	Williamsville (Cass County)	49095
Volney	49309	Weldon (Township)	49683	Williamsville (Livingston	
Vriesland	49464	Wellington (Township)	49753	County)	48137
Vulcan	49892	Wells	49894	Willis	48191
Wabaningo	49463	Wells (Delta County)		Willow	48164
Wacousta	48837	(Township)	49894	Willow Run	48198
Wadhams	48074	Wells (Marquette County)		Willwalk	49783
Wagarville	48624	(Township)	49818	Wilmot (Cheboygan County)	
Wahjamega	48723	Wells (Tuscola County)		(Township)	49799
Wainola	49948	(Township)	48723	Wilmot (Tuscola County)	48729
Wakefield	49968	Wellston	49689	Wilson (Alpena County)	
Wakefield (Township)	49968	Wellsville	49228	(Township)	49707
Wakelee	49067	Wenona Beach	49707	Wilson (Charlevoix County)	
Wakeshma (Township)	49052	Wequetonsing	49740	(Township)	49729
Waldenburg	48044	West Bloomfield	48322-25	Wilson (Menominee County)	49896
Waldron	49288	For specific West Bloomfield Zip		Windemere	48917
Wales (Township)	48027	Codes call (313) 626-9873		Windsor (Township)	48821
Walhalla	49458	West Bloomfield Township	48323-24	Winegars	48624
Walker (Cheboygan County)		For specific West Bloomfield		Winfield (Township)	48850
(Township)	49705	Township Zip Codes call (313)		Winn	48896
Walker (Kent County)	49504	626-9873		Winona	49965
Walkers Point	49721	West Branch (Ogemaw		Winsor (Township)	48755
Walkerville	49459	County) (Township)	48661	Winterfield (Township)	49665
Wallace	49893	West Branch (Dickinson		Winters	49878
Walled Lake	48390	County) (Township)	49877	Winthrop Junction (Part of	
Wallin	49683	West Branch (Marquette		Ishpeming)	49849
Wall Lake	49046	County) (Township)	49885	Wise (Township)	48618
Walloon Lake	49796	West Branch (Missaukee		Wisner	48701
Walnut Lake	48010	County) (Township)	49667	Wisner (Township)	48733
Walnut Point	49068	West Branch	48661	Witch Lake	49879
Walters	48346	Westchester Village	48010	Wixom	48393
Walton (Township)	49076	Western Wayne		Wolf Lake (Jackson County)	49201
Waltz	48164	Correctional Facility	48170	Wolf Lake (Muskegon	
Wardcliff	48823	West Ishpeming	49849	County)	49442
Warner (Township)	49730	Westland	48185	Wolverine	49799
Warren	48089-93	Westland Shopping Center		Wolverine Lake	48390
For specific Warren Zip Codes call		(Part of Westland)	48185	Wonderland Mall (Part of	
(313) 751-4900		West Leroy	49051	Livonia)	48150
Warren (Township)	48618	West Millbrook	49310	Woodard Lake	48834
Wasepi	49032	West Monroe	48161	Woodbridge (Township)	49242
Washington (Macomb		West Olive	49460	Woodbury	48849
County) (Township)	48094-95	Weston	49289	Wooden Shoe Village	48624
For specific Washington Zip		Westphalia	48894	Woodhaven	48183
Codes call (313) 781-4251		Westphalia (Township)	48894	Woodhull (Township)	48872
Washington (Gratiot County)		West Sebewa	48875	Woodland	48897
(Township)	48806	West Side (Part of Saginaw)	48603	Woodland (Township)	48897
Washington (Sanilac		West Traverse (Township)	49740	Woodland (Part of	
County) (Township)	48401	Westville	48888	Kentwood)	49508
Washington Harbor	55605	West Willow	48198	Woodland Beach	48161
Washington Heights (Part of		West Windsor	48813	Woodland Lake	48116
Battle Creek)	49017	Westwood	49006	Woodland Park	49309
			49009	Woods Corner	48622

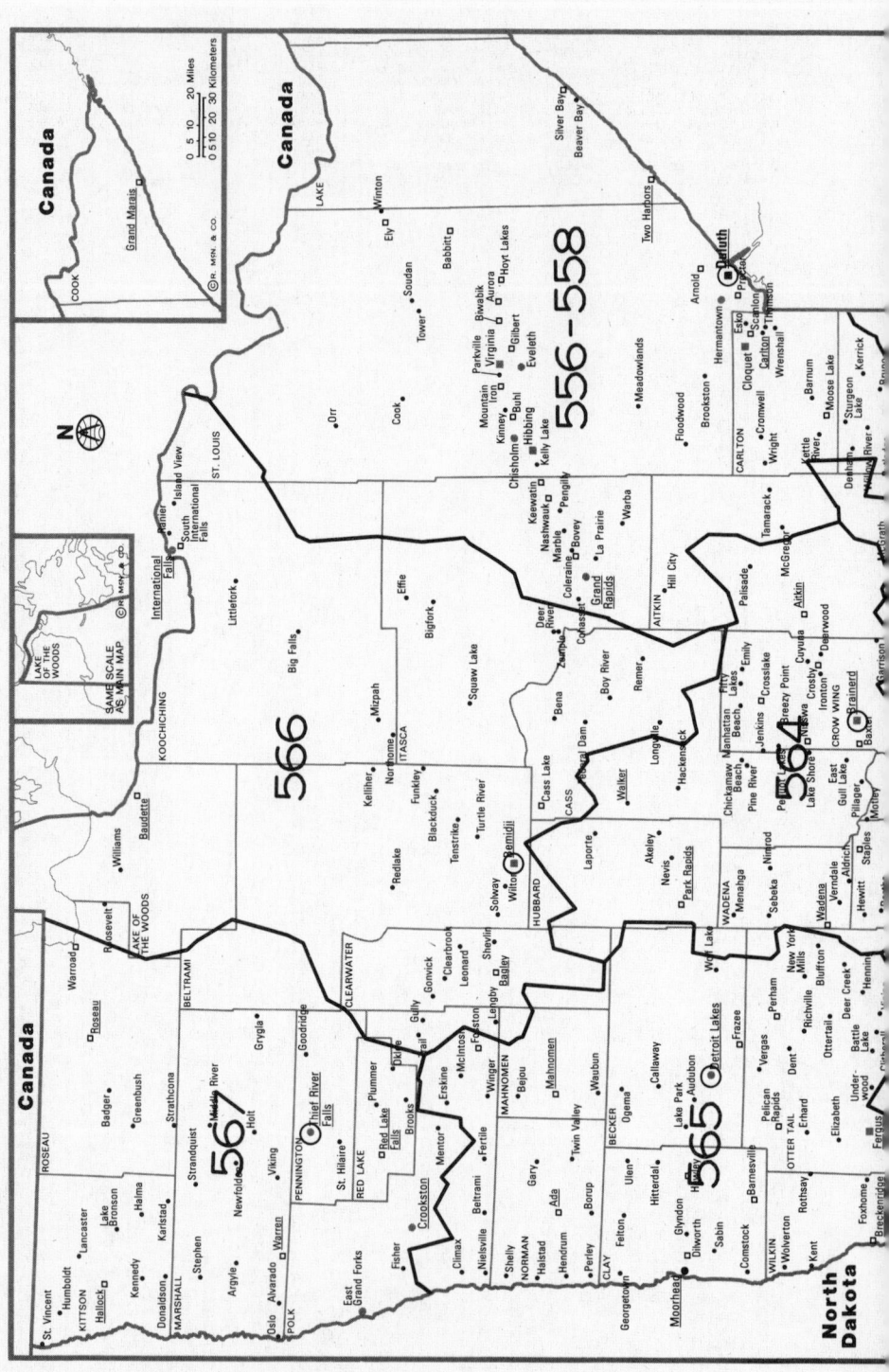

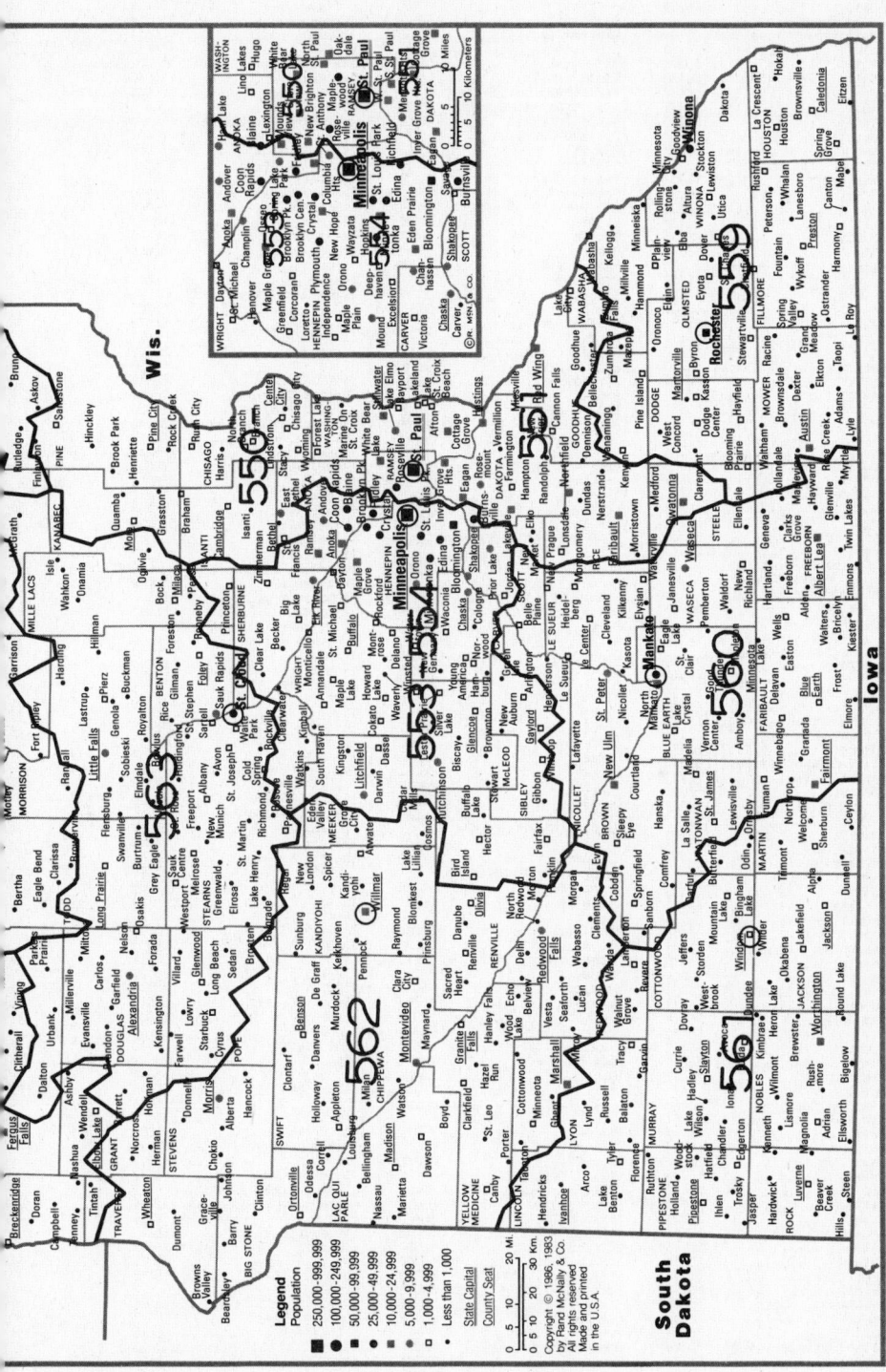

	ZIP		ZIP		ZIP
Ada	56510	Barry	56210	Bovey-Coleraine (Part of	
Adams	55909	Bassett	56602	Bovey)	55709
Adolph (Part of		Basswood	56576	Bowlus	56314
Hermantown)	55701	Basswood Grove	55033	Bowstring	56631
Adrian	56110	Battle Lake	56515	Boyd	56218
Afton	55001	Battle River	56630	Boy River	56632
Ah-Gwah-Ching	56430	Baudette	56623	Bradford	55040
Aitkin	56431	Baudette Air Force Station,		Braham	55006
Akeley	56433	692nd Air Force Defenc	56623	Brainerd	56401
Albany	56307	Baxter	56425	Brainerd Regional Human	
Alberta	56207	Bay Lake	56444	Services Center	56401
Albert Lea	56007	Bayport	55003	Branch	55056
Albertville	55301	Bayview	56359	Brandon	56315
Albion Center	55302	Beardsley	56211	Bratsberg	55971
Alborn	55702	Bear River	55723	Breckenridge	56520
Alden	56009	Bear Valley	55041	Breezy Point	56472
Aldrich	56434	Beauford	56065	Bremen	55957
Alexandria	56308	Beaulieu	56557	Brennyville	56329
Alida	56676	Beaver	55910	Brevik	56655
Allen Junction (Part of Hoyt		Beaver Bay	55601	Brewster	56119
Lakes)	55750	Beaver Creek	56116	Bricelyn	56014
Alma City	56048	Beaver Falls	56270	Bridge Court (Part of	
Almelund	55002	Bechyn	56283	Anoka)	55303
Almora	56551	Becida	56625	Bridgeman	56473
Alpha	56111	Becker	55308	Bridgewater	55021
Altura	55910	Beckville	55355	Brimson	55602
Alvarado	56710	Bejou	56516	Bristol	55939
Alvwood	56630	Belgrade	56312	Britt	55710
Amboy	56010	Bellaire	55110	Brookdale Shopping Center	
Amherst	55922	Bellechester	55027	(Part of Brooklyn Center)	55430
Amiret	56175	Belle Creek	55009	Brooklyn (Part of Hibbing)	55746
Amor	56515	Belle Plaine	56011	Brooklyn Center	55429
Andover	55304	Belle Prairie	56345	Brooklyn Park	55443
Andree	55006	Belleriver	56319	Brook Park	55007
Andyville	55912	Bellingham	56212	Brooks	56715
Angle Inlet	56711	Beltrami	56517	Brookston	55711
Angora	55703	Belview	56214	Brooten	56316
Angus	56712	Bemidji	56601-19	Browerville	56438
Annandale	55302	For specific Bemidji Zip Codes call		Brownsdale	55918
Anoka	55303-04	(218) 751-5600		Browns Valley	56219
For specific Anoka Zip Codes call		Bena	56626	Brownsville	55919
(612) 421-1114		Benedict	56436	Brownton	55312
Antlers Park (Part of		Bennettville	56431	Bruno	55712
Lakeville)	55044	Benson	56215	Brunswick	55051
Apache Mall (Part of		Bergen	56101	Brush Creek	56014
Rochester)	55902	Bergville	56661	Brushvale	56520
Apache Plaza (Part of St.		Bernadotte	56054	Buckman	56317
Anthony)	55421	Berne	55985	Buffalo	55313
Appleton	56208	Berner	56644	Buffalo Lake	55314
Apple Valley	55124	Berning Mill	55376	Buhl	55713
Arco	56113	Beroun	55004	Bunde	56222
Arcturus (Part of Taconite)	55786	Bertha	56437	Burchard	56115
Arden Hills	55112	Bethany	55910	Burnett	55727
Arendahl	55962	Bethel	55005	Burnsville	55337
Argonne (Part of Lakeville)	55044	Big Bend City	56262	Burnsville Center (Part of	
Argyle	56713	Bigelow	56117	Burnsville)	55337
Arlington	55307	Big Falls	56627	Burr	56220
Armstrong	56009	Bigfork	56628	Burschville (Part of	
Arnesen	56673	Big Island (Part of Orono)	55331	Corcoran)	55357
Arnold	55803	Big Lake	55309	Burtrum	56318
Arthyde	56350	Big Spring	55939	Butler	56567
Artichoke Lake	56227	Big Stone City (Part of		Butterfield	56120
Ashby	56309	Ortonville)	56278	Butternut	56055
Ashcreek	56173	Big Woods	56744	Buyck	55771
Ash Lake	55771	Bingham Lake	56118	Bygland	56721
Askov	55704	Birch Beach	56686	Byron	55920
Aspelund	55946	Birchdale	56629	Cable	56301
Assumption	55338	Birchwood Village	55110	Caledonia	55921
Atkinson	55718	Bird Island	55310	Callaway	56521
Atwater	56209	Biscay	55336	Calumet	55716
Atwood (Part of Edina)	55424	Biwabik	55708	Cambria	56073
Audubon	56511	Bixby	55917	Cambridge	55008
Augusta	55318	Blackberry	55744	Camden Place (Part of	
Aure	56676	Blackduck	56630	Minneapolis)	55412
Aurora	55705	Black Hammer	55974	Campbell	56522
Austin	55912	Blaine	55434	Camp Lacupolis	55041
Austin Acres	55912		55449	Camp Ripley	56345
Auto Club (Part of		For specific Blaine Zip Codes call		Canby	56220
Bloomington)	55420	(612) 784-1029		Cannon City	55021
Automba	55757	Blakeley	56011	Cannon Falls	55009
Averill	56547	Blomford	55040	Cannon Lake	55021
Avoca	56114	Blomkest	56216	Canton	55922
Avon	56310	Bloom Dale (Part of		Canyon	55717
Babbitt	55706	Bloomington)	55431	Cardigan Junction (Part of	
Backus	56435	Blooming Prairie	55917	Shoreview)	55112
Badger	56714	Bloomington	55420	Caribou	56735
Bagley	56621	Blue Earth	56013	Carimona	55965
Baker	56513	Blue Grass	56477	Carlisle	56537
Balaton	56115	Bluffton	56518	Carlos	56319
Bald Eagle	55110	Bock	56313	Carlton	55718
Balkan	55719	Bodum	55040	Carp	56623
Ball Bluff	55752	Boisberg	56296	Carver	55315
Ball Club	56636	Bois Fort	55772	Cashtown (Part of	
Balmoral	55515	Bombay	55946	Ortonville)	56278
Bancroft	56007	Bonanza Grove	56211	Casino	56473
Barden (Part of Shakopee)	55379	Bongards	55368	Cass Lake	56633
Barnesville	56514	Bonnie Glen	55013	Castle Danger	55616
Barnum	55707	Border	56629	Castle Rock	55010
Barr	55992	Borup	56519	Cedar	55011
Barrett	56311	Bovey	55709	Cedar Beach	55960
Barrows	56401				

	ZIP		ZIP		ZIP
Cedar Grove (Part of Eagan)	55111	Credit River	55372	East Gull Lake	56401
Cedar Mills	55350	Croftville	55604	East Hastings (Part of Hastings)	55033
Cedar Riverside (Part of Minneapolis)	55440	Cromwell	55726	East Lake	55760
Celina	55723	Crookston	56716	East Lake Francis Shores	55040
Center City	55012	Crosby	56441	Easton	56025
Centerville (Anoka County)	55038	Crosby Beach	56444	East Prairieville	55021
Centerville (Winona County)	55987	Crosslake	56442	Eastside (Part of Minneapolis)	55418
Central	56401	Crown	55070	East Union	55315
Central Lakes	55734	Crow River	56243	Ebro	56621
Ceylon	56121	Crow Wing	56401	Echo	56237
Champlin	55316	Crystal	55428	Echols	56081
Chandler	56122	Crystal Bay (Part of Orono)	55323	Eddsville	55310
Chanhassen	55317	Crystal Shopping Center (Part of Crystal)	55428	Eden	55927
Charlesville	56583	Culver	55727	Eden Prairie	55344
Chaska	55318	Cummingsville	55923	Eden Prairie Center (Part of Eden Prairie)	55344
Chatfield	55923	Currie	56123	Eden Valley	55329
Cherry	55751	Cushing	56443	Edgerton	56128
Cherry Grove	55975	Cusson	55771	Edgewood	55008
Chester	55904	Cutler	56431	Edina	55410
Chicago Bay	55606	Cuyuna	56444		55424
Chickamaw Beach	56474	Cyrus	56323		55435-36
Chisago City	55013	Dakota	55925	For specific Edina Zip Codes call (612) 920-5226	
Chisholm	55719	Dalbo	55017		
Choice	55954	Dale	56549	Effie	56639
Chokio	56221	Dalton	56324	Eidswold	55020
Chowens Corner (Part of Deephaven)	55391	Danube	56230	Eitzen	55931
Circle Pines	55014	Danvers	56231	Elba	55910
City (Part of Rochester)	55904	Darfur	56022	Elbow Lake	56531
City Center (Part of Minneapolis)	55402	Darling	56345	Eldes Corner	55810
Civic Center (Part of Duluth)	55802	Darwin	55324	Eldred	56523
Clara City	56222	Dassel	55325	Elgin	55932
Claremont	55924	Dawson	56232	Elizabeth	56533
Clarissa	56440	Day	55006	Elkland	55021
Clarkfield	56223	Dayton (Anoka County)	55303	Elko	55020
Clarks Grove	56016	Dayton (Hennepin County)	55327	Elk River	55330
Clearbrook	56634	Daytons Bluff (Part of St. Paul)	55106	Elkton	55933
Clear Lake	55319	Debs	56676	Ellendale	56026
Clearwater	55320	Deephaven	55391	Ellsworth	56129
Clements	56224	Deer Creek	56527	Elmdale	56314
Clementson	56623	Deerfield	55049	Elmer	55765
Cleveland	56017	Deer River	56636	Elmore	56027
Cliff (Part of Lilydale)	55118	Deerwood	56444	Elmwood (Part of St. Louis Park)	55416
Climax	56523	De Graff	56233	Elrosa	56325
Clinton	56225	Delano	55328	Elway (Part of St. Paul)	55116
Clinton Falls	56060	Delavan	56023	Ely	55731
Clitherall	56524	Delft	56124	Ely Lake	55734
Clontarf	56226	Delhi	56283	Elysian	56028
Cloquet	55720	Dell	56013	Embarrass	55732
Clotho	56347	Dellwood	55110	Emco (Part of Hoyt Lakes)	55750
Cloverdale	55037	Denham	55728	Emily	56447
Cloverton	55072	Dennison	55018	Emmons	56029
Clyde	55979	Dent	56528	Empire	55024
Coates	55068	Detroit Lakes	56501-02	Enfield	55362
Cobden	56085	For specific Detroit Lakes Zip Codes call (218) 847-8379		Englund	56758
Cohasset	55721			Erdahl	56531
Coin	56358	Dexter	55926	Erhard	56534
Cokato	55321	Diamond Lake (Part of Minneapolis)	55419	Ericksonville	56359
Colby (Part of Hoyt Lakes)	55750	Dilworth	56529	Ericsburg	56649
Cold Spring	56320	Dinkytown (Part of Minneapolis)	55414	Erie	56725
Coleraine	55722	Dodge Center	55927	Erskine	56535
Collegeville	56321	Donaldson	56720	Esden	56444
Collis	56236	Donnelly	56235	Esko	55733
Cologne	55322	Dora Lake	56661	Essig	56030
Columbia Heights	55421	Doran	56522	Estes Brook	56357
Comfrey	56019	Dorothy	56750	Etna	55975
Commerce (Part of Minneapolis)	55415	Dorset	56470	Etter	55089
Como (Part of St. Paul)	55108	Douglas	55960	Euclid	56722
Comstock	56525	Douglas Lodge	56460	Evan	56238
Conception	55945	Dover	55929	Evansville	56326
Concord	55985	Dovray	56125	Eveleth	55734
Conger	56020	Downer	56514	Everdell	56520
Constance (Part of Andover)	55303	Dresbach	55947	Evergreen	56544
Cook	55723	Duelm	56329	Excelsior	55331
Cooley	55769	Duluth	55801-16	Eyota	55934
Coon Lake Beach (Part of East Bethel)	55092	For specific Duluth Zip Codes call (218) 723-2500		Fairbanks	55602
Coon Rapids	55433	Duluth International Airport, 4787th Air Base Group	55814	Fairfax	55332
	55448	Dumfries	55981	Fairhaven	55382
For specific Coon Rapids Zip Codes call (612) 755-1150		Dumont	56236	Fairmont	56031
		Dundas	55019	Faith	56584
Copas	55073	Dundee	56126	Falcon Heights	55113
Corcoran	55340	Dunnell	56127	Faribault	55021
Cordova	56057	Dunvilla	56572	Farming	56368
Cormorant	56572	Duquette	55729	Farmington	55024
Corning	55912	Duxbury	55072	Farris	56633
Correll	56227	Eagan	55121	Farwell	56327
Corvuso	56228	Eagle Bend	56446	Federal Correctional Institution	55072
Cosmos	56228	Eagle Lake	56024	Federal Dam	56641
Cottage Grove	55016	East Beaver Bay	55601	Felton	56536
Cotton	55724	East Bethel	55005	Fergus Falls	56537-38
Cottonwood	56229	East Chain	56031	For specific Fergus Falls Zip Codes call (218) 736-7840	
Courtland	56021	East Cottage Grove (Part of Cottage Grove)	55016		
Cove	56359	Eastern Heights (Part of St. Paul)	55119	Fernando	55385
Craigville	56639			Fertile	56540
Crane Lake	55725	East Grand Forks	56721	Fifty Lakes	56448
				Fillmore	55990
				Finland	55603

	ZIP
Finland Air Force Station, 756th Radar Squadron	55603
Finlayson	55735
Fisher	56723
Flensburg	56328
Fletcher	55369
Flintwood Hills (Part of Ramsey)	55303
Flom	56541
Floodwood	55736
Florence	56170
Florenton	55792
Florian	56758
Foley	56329
Fond du Lac Indian Reservation	55720
Forada	56308
Forbes	55738
Fordson (Part of Eagan)	55121
Forest City	55355
Forest Grove	56660
Forest Lake	55025
Forest Mills	55992
Foreston	56330
Fork	56744
Fort Ripley	56449
Fort Snelling	55111
Fosston	56542
Fossum	56584
Fountain	55935
Four Corners	55811
Fourtown	56727
Foxhome	56543
Fox Lake	56181
Franconia	55074
Franklin (Renville County)	55333
Franklin (St. Louis County)	55792
Franklin Avenue (Part of Minneapolis)	55404
Frazee	56544
Freeborn	56032
Freeburg	55921
Freedhem	56345
Freeport	56331
Fremont	55979
French Lake	55302
French River	55804
Fridley	55432
Friesland	55037
Frontenac	55026
Frost	56033
Fulda	56131
Funkley	56630
Garden City	56034
Garfield	56332
Garrison	56450
Garvin	56132
Gary	56545
Gatzke	56724
Gaylord	55334
Gem Lake	55110
Gemmell	56660
Geneva	56035
Genoa (Olmsted County)	55920
Genoa (St. Louis County)	55734
Genola	56364
Gentilly	56716
Georgetown	56546
Georgeville	56312
Gheen	55740
Gheen Corner	55740
Ghent	56239
Gibbon	55335
Giese	55735
Gilbert	55741
Gilfillan	56283
Gilman	56333
Gladstone (Part of Maplewood)	55109
Glen	56431
Glencoe	55336
Glendale	55771
Glendorado	55371
Glen Lake (Part of Minnetonka)	55345
Glenville	56036
Glenwood	56334
Glenwood Junction (Part of Golden Valley)	55427
Glory	56431
Gloster (Part of Maplewood)	55109
Gluek	56260
Glyndon	56547
Godahl	56081
Golden Hill	55901
Golden Hills (Part of St. Louis Park)	55416
Golden Valley	55427
Gonvick	56644
Goodhue	55027
Goodland	55742

	ZIP
Goodridge	56725
Good Thunder	56037
Goodview	55987
Gordon	56036
Gotha	55322
Graceton	56686
Graceville	56240
Granada	56039
Grand Falls	56627
Grand Marais	55604
Grand Meadow	55936
Grand Portage	55605
Grand Portage Indian Reservation	55605
Grand Rapids	55730
	55744
For specific Grand Rapids Zip Codes call (218) 326-3956	
Grand View Heights	56573
Grandy	55029
Granger	55937
Granite Falls	56241
Grass Lake	55006
Grasston	55030
Grattan	56661
Greaney	55740
Greater Leech Lake Indian Reservation	56633
Greenbush	56726
Greenfield	55357
Green Isle	55338
Greenland	56028
Greenleaf	55355
Greenleafton	55965
Green Valley	56258
Greenwald	56335
Greenwood	55331
Grey Eagle	56336
Grogan	56081
Groningen	55072
Grove City	56243
Grove Lake	56316
Grygla	56727
Guckeen	56013
Gully	56646
Gutches Grove	56347
Guthrie	56461
Hackensack	56452
Hackett	56623
Hader	55992
Hadley	56133
Hagan	56262
Hallock	56728
Halma	56729
Halstad	56548
Hamburg	55339
Hamel	55340
Hamilton	55975
Ham Lake	55304
Hammond	55938
Hampton	55031
Hancock	56244
Hanley Falls	56245
Hanover	55341
Hanska	56041
Happyland	56653
Harding	56364
Hardwick	56134
Har-Mar Mall (Part of Roseville)	55113
Harmony	55939
Harnell Park	55779
Harris	55032
Hart	55971
Hartland	56042
Hassan	55374
Hassman	56431
Hastings	55033
Hasty	55320
Hatfield	56135
Havana	55060
Hawick	56246
Hawley	56549
Hay Creek	55066
Haydenville	56256
Hayfield	55940
Haypoint	55748
Hayward	56043
Hazel Run	56247
Hazelwood	55057
Heatwole	55350
Hector	55342
Heiberg	56584
Heidelberg	56071
Heinola	56567
Henderson	56044
Hendricks	56136
Hendrum	56550
Henning	56551
Henriette	55036
Henrytown	55939

	ZIP
Herman	56248
Hermantown	55811
Heron Lake	56137
Hewitt	56453
Hiawatha Spur (Part of Eagan)	55111
Hibbing	55746-47
For specific Hibbing Zip Codes call (218) 263-4086	
Hidden Creek (Part of Andover)	55303
High Forest	55976
Highland (Fillmore County)	55986
Highland (Hennepin County)	55411
Highland (Lake County)	55616
Highland (Wright County)	55349
High Landing	56725
Highland Park (Part of St. Paul)	55116
Hill City	55748
Hillman	56338
Hills	56138
Hilltop	55421
Hillview	56477
Hinckley	55037
Hines	56647
Hitterdal	56552
Hoffman	56339
Hoffmans Corners (Part of Gem Lake)	55110
Hokah	55941
Holdingford	56340
Holland	56139
Hollandale	56045
Holloway	56249
Hollywood	55388
Holmes City	56341
Holt	56738
Holyoke	55749
Homer	55942
Hoot Lake (Part of Fergus Falls)	56537
Hope	56046
Hopkins	55305
	55343
	55345
For specific Hopkins Zip Codes call (612) 935-8606	
Hopper (Part of Mountain Iron)	55792
Houston	55943
Hovland	55606
Howard Lake	55349
Hoyt Lakes	55750
Hubbard	56470
Hugo	55038
Humboldt	56731
Huntersville	56464
Huntley	56047
Husby Spur (Part of Arden Hills)	55112
Hutchinson	55350
Hydes Lake	55322
Ideal Corners	56472
Idington	55703
Ihlen	56140
Illgen City	55614
Imogene	56039
Independence (Hennepin County)	55359
Independence (St. Louis County)	55727
Indus	56629
Industrial (Part of St. Paul)	55104
Inger	56636
Inguadona	56655
International Falls	56649
Inver Grove Heights	55076-77
For specific Inver Grove Heights Zip Codes call (612) 451-1243	
Iona	56141
Iron	55751
Ironhub	56431
Ironton	56455
Isabella	55607
Isanti	55040
Island Lake	56667
Island Park (Part of Mound)	55364
Island View	56649
Isle	56342
Ivanhoe	56142
Iverson	55718
Jackson	56143
Jacobson	55752
Jacobs Prairie	56320
Jakeville	56329
Jameson	56649
Janesville	56048
Jarretts	55957
Jasper	56144
Jeffers	56145

	ZIP
Jenkins	56456
Jennie	55325
Jessenland	56044
Jessie Lake	56637
Johnsburg	55909
Johnson	56250
Johnsville (Part of Blaine)	55434
Jonathan (Part of Chaska)	55318
Jordan	55352
Judson	56055
Kabekona	56461
Kabetogama	56669
Kanaranzi	56110
Kandi Mall Shopping Center (Part of Willmar)	56201
Kandiyohi	56251
Karlstad	56732
Kasota	56050
Kasson	55944
Katrine	56444
Keewatin	55753
Kelliher	56650
Kellogg	55945
Kelly Lake (Part of Hibbing)	55754
Kelsey	55755
Kennedy	56733
Kenneth	56147
Kensington	56343
Kent	56553
Kenwood (Hennepin County)	55403
Kenwood (St. Louis County)	55811
Kenyon	55946
Kerkhoven	56252
Kerr (Part of Hibbing)	55746
Kerrick	55756
Kettle River	55757
Kiester	56051
Kilkenny	56052
Kimball	55353
Kimberly	56431
Kinbrae	56126
Kingsdale	55072
Kings Park	55960
Kingston	55325
Kinmount	55771
Kinney	55758
Kitzville (Part of Hibbing)	55746
Kjellberg Park	56362
Klossner	56053
Knapp	55321
Knife River	55609
Knollwood Mall (Part of St. Louis Park)	55426
Komensky	55350
Kragnes	56560
Kroschel	55037
Lac qui Parle	56265
La Crescent	55947
Lafayette	56054
Lagoona Beach	56278
Lake Benton	56149
Lake Bronson	56734
Lake Center	56511
Lake City	55041
Lake Crystal	56055
Lake Elmo	55042
Lake Eunice	56501
Lakefield	56150
Lake George	56458
Lake Henry	56362
Lake Hubert	56459
Lake Itasca	56460
Lakeland	55043
Lakeland Shores	55043
Lake Lillian	56253
Lake Netta (Part of Ham Lake)	55303
Lake Nichols	55717
Lake Park	56554
Lake Sarah (Part of Greenfield)	55357
Lake Shore	56401
Lake Shore Park (Part of White Bear Lake)	55110
Lakeside (Renville County)	55314
Lakeside (St. Louis County)	55804
Lake St. Croix Beach	55043
Lake Street (Part of Minneapolis)	55408
Lakeville	55044
Lake Wilson	56151
Lamberton	56152
Lamoille	55987
Lamson	55325
Lancaster	56735
Landfall	55128
Lanesboro	55949
Langdon (Part of Cottage Grove)	55016
Lansing	55950

	ZIP
Laporte	56461
La Prairie	55744
Larsmont	55616
La Salle	56056
Lastrup	56344
Lauderdale	55113
Lavinia	55746
Lawler	55760
Lawndale	56579
Lax Lake	55614
Leader	56466
Leaf Lake	56551
Leaf Valley	56332
Leavenworth	56085
Le Center	56057
Leetonia (Part of Hibbing)	55746
Le Hillier	56001
Lengby	56651
Lenora	55922
Leonard	56652
Leonidas	55734
Leota	56153
Lerdal	56007
Le Roy	55951
Lester Prairie	55354
Le Sueur	56058
Lewis Lake	55006
Lewiston	55952
Lewisville	56060
Lexington (Anoka County)	55112
Lexington (Le Sueur County)	56057
Libby	55760
Lilydale	55118
Lime Creek	56131
Lincoln	56443
Linden Grove	55723
Lindford	56653
Lindstrom	55045
Lino Lakes	55014
Linwood	55005
Lismore	56155
Litchfield	55355
Litomysl	56060
Little Canada	55110
Little Chicago	55057
Little Falls	56345
Littlefork	56653
Little Marais	55614
Little Pine	56431
Little Rock (Beltrami County)	56671
Little Rock (Morrison County)	56373
Little Sauk	56347
Little Swan (Part of Hibbing)	55746
Local	56501
Lockhart	56510
Loman	56654
London	56061
Long Beach	56334
Long Lake	55356
Long Point	56686
Long Prairie	56347
Long Siding	55371
Longville	56655
Lonsdale	55046
Loop (Part of Minneapolis)	55402
Loretto	55306
	55357
For specific Loretto Zip Codes call (612) 479-2656	
Loring (Part of Minneapolis)	55403
Louisburg	56254
Louriston	56260
Lower Sioux Indian Reservation	56270
Lowry	56349
Lucan	56255
Lude	56686
Lutsen	55612
Luverne	56156
Luxemburg	56301
Lydia	55352
Lyle	55953
Lynd	56157
Lyndale (Part of Independence)	55359
Lynwood (Part of Hibbing)	55746
Mabel	55954
McCauleyville	56553
McGrath	56350
McGregor	55760
McHugh	56501
McIntosh	56556
McKee (Part of Eagan)	55121
McKinley	55761
Madelia	56062
Madison	56256
Madison East (Part of Mankato)	56001

	ZIP
Madison Lake	56063
Magnolia	56158
Mahkonce	56557
Mahnomen	56557
Mahtomedi	55115
Mahtowa	55762
Maine	56586
Maine Prairie	55353
Makinen	55763
Mall (Part of Fairmont)	56031
Malmo	56431
Manannah	56243
Manchester	56064
Manhattan Beach	56463
Manitou	56629
Mankato	56001-03
For specific Mankato Zip Codes call (507) 625-1781	
Mansfield	56009
Mantorville	55955
Maple	55387
Maple Bay	56736
Maple Grove	55369
Maple Hill	55604
Maple Island	56045
Maple Lake	55358
Maple Plain	55359
Mapleton	56065
Mapleview	55912
Maplewood	55109
Maplewood Mall (Part of Maplewood)	55109
Marble	55764
Marcell	56657
Margie	56658
Marietta	56257
Marine On St. Croix	55047
Marion	55901
Markham	55763
Markville	55072
Marshall	56258
Martin Lake	55079
Marysburg	56063
Marystown	55379
Matawan	56072
Mattson	56728
Max	56659
Mayer	55360
Mayhew	56379
Mayhew Lake	56379
Maynard	56260
Mayville	55912
Mazeppa	55956
M&D Junction (Part of White Bear Lake)	55110
Meadowlands	55765
Medford	55049
Medicine Lake	55441
Meire Grove	56352
Melby	56326
Melrose	56352
Melrude	55766
Menahga	56464
Mendota	55150
Mendota Heights	55118
Mentor	56736
Meriden	56067
Merrifield	56465
Merton	56060
Mesaba (Part of Hoyt Lakes)	55750
Middle River	56737
Midway (Becker County)	56464
Midway (Ramsey County)	55104
Midway (St. Louis County)	55792
Midway Center (Part of St. Paul)	55104
Miesville	55009
Milaca	56353
Milan	56262
Mille Lacs Indian Reservation	56359
Miller Hill (Part of Duluth)	55811
Miller Hill Mall (Part of Duluth)	55811
Millersburg	55021
Millerville	56315
Millville	55957
Milroy	56263
Miltona	56354
Mineral Center	55605
Minneapolis	**55401-84**
For specific Minneapolis Zip Codes call (612) 452-3800	
COLLEGES & UNIVERSITIES	
Augsburg College	55454
North Central Bible College	55404
University of Minnesota-Twin Cities	55455

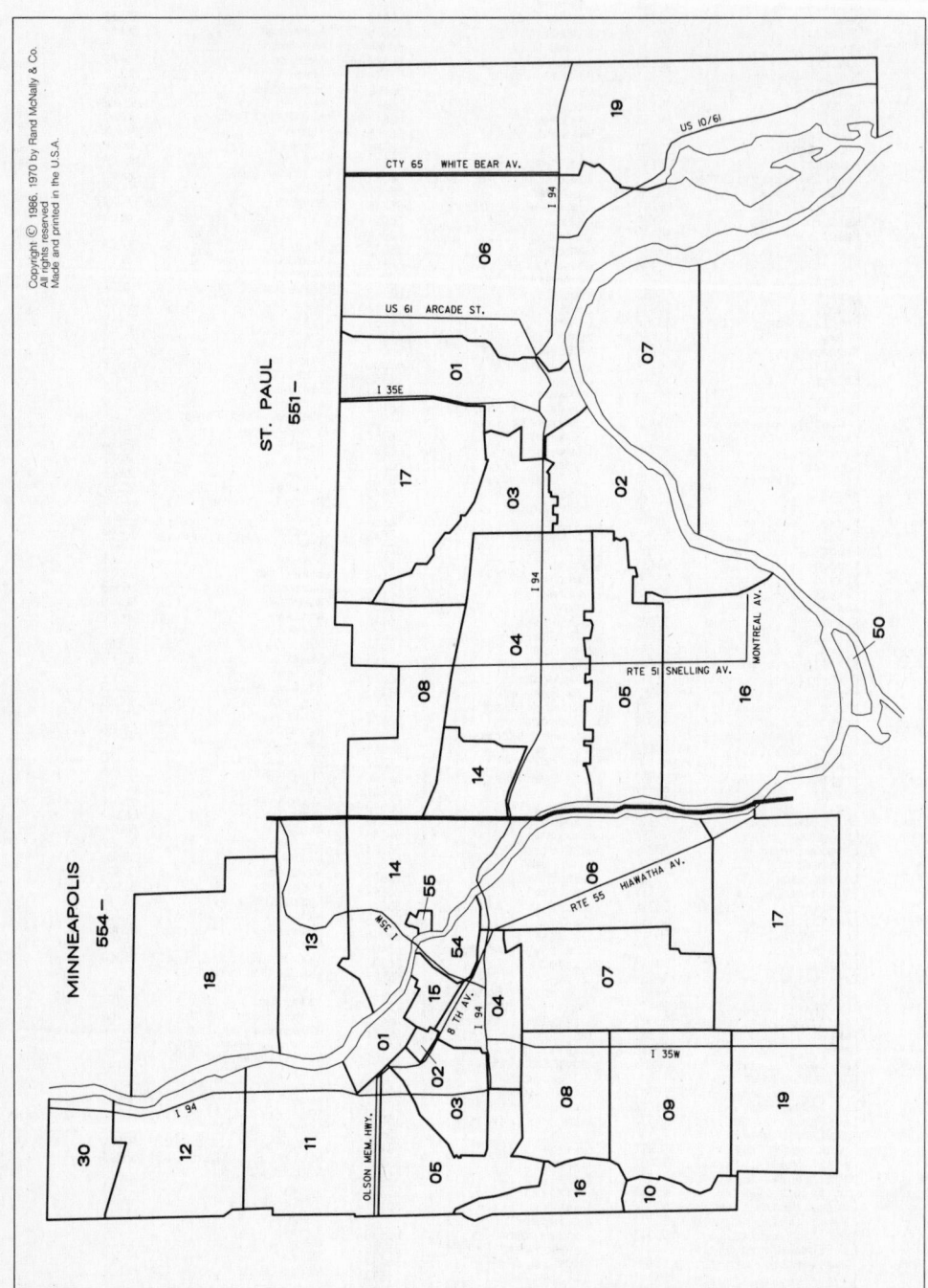

	ZIP		ZIP		ZIP
FINANCIAL INSTITUTIONS		Nelson	56355	Ortonville	56278
		Nerstrand	55053	Osage	56570
First Bank N.A.	55480	Nett Lake	55772	Osakis	56360
IDS Bank and Trust	55402	Nett Lake Indian		Oshawa	56082
Investors Savings Bank,		Reservation	55772	Oslo (Dodge County)	55940
F.S.B.	55402	Nevis	56467	Oslo (Marshall County)	56744
Marquette Bank		New Auburn	55366	Oslund	56680
Minneapolis, N.A.	55480	New Brighton	55112	Osseo	55311
Firstar Bank of Minnesota	55425	Newburg	55954		55369
National City Bank of		Newfolden	56738	For specific Osseo Zip Codes call	
Minneapolis	55402	New Germany	55367	(612) 425-2843	
Norwest Bank Minnesota,		New Hartford	55925	Ostrander	55961
National Association	55479	New Hope	55428	Otisco	56077
Park National Bank of St.		Newhouse	55954	Otisville	55073
Louis Park	55416	New London	56273	Ottawa	56058
Richfield Bank & Trust Co	55423	New Market	55054	Otter Creek	55718
TCF Bank Savings, F.S.B.	55402	New Munich	56356	Ottertail	56571
		Newport	55055	Outing	56662
HOSPITALS		New Prague	56071	Owatonna	55060
Abbott-Northwestern		New Richland	56072	Oxlip	55040
Hospital	55407	New Rome	55307	Oylen	56481
Fairview Riverside Medical		Newry	56045	Padua	56378
Center	55454	New Trier	55031	Palisade	56469
Fairview Southdale Hospital	55435	New Ulm	56073	Palmdale	55084
Health One Corporation		New York Mills	56567	Palmers	55804
Metropolitan Hospitals	55433	Nickerson	55797	Palo	55705
Hennepin County Medical		Nicollet	56074	Parent	56329
Center	55415	Nicols (Part of Eagan)	55121	Parkers Prairie	56361
University of Minnesota		Nicolville	55912	Park Rapids	56470
Hospital and Clinic	55455	Nielsville	56568	Park View (Part of	
Veterans Affairs Medical		Nimrod	56478	Crookston)	56716
Center	55417	Nininger	55033	Parkville (Part of Mountain	
		Nisswa	56468	Iron)	55773
HOTELS/MOTELS		Nodine	55925	Payne	55765
Hyatt Regency Minneapolis-		Nokomis (Part of		Paynesville	56362
Nicollet Mall	55403	Minneapolis)	55417	Pearl Lake	55353
Sheraton Park Place Hotel	55416	Nopeming	55810	Pease	56363
The Marquette	55402	Norcross	56274	Pelican Rapids	56572
		Normandale (Part of Edina)	55439	Pelland	56649
MILITARY INSTALLATIONS		Norseland	56082	Pemberton	56078
934th Mission Support		North Benton	56329	Pencer	56751
Squadron, Minneapolis-St.		North Branch	55056	Pengilly	55775
Paul Air Reserve Base	55450	Northcote	56728	Pennington	56663
		Northdale (Part of Coon		Pennock	56279
Minnehaha (Part of		Rapids)	55433	Pequaywan Lake	55801
Minneapolis)	55406	North Douglas (Part of		Pequot Lakes	56472
Minneiska	55910	Crystal)	55422	Perham	56573
Minneota	56264	Northfield	55057	Perkins	55943
Minnesota City	55959	North Mankato	56003	Perley	56574
Minnesota Lake	56068	North Oaks	55110	Petersburg	56143
Minnesota Transfer (Part of		Northome	56661	Peterson	55962
St. Paul)	55114	North Prairie	56314	Petran	56043
Minnetonka	55345	North Redwood	56283	Phelps	56586
Minnetonka Beach	55361	Northrop	56075	Philbrook	56466
Minnetonka Mills (Part of		Northside (Part of Albert		Pickwick	55987
Minnetonka)	55305	Lea)	56007	Pierz	56364
Minnetrista	55364	North St. Paul	55109	Pigeon River	55605
Minnewawa	55760	Northtown Shopping Center		Pike Lake	55811
Mizpah	56660	(Part of Blaine)	55434	Pillager	56473
Moland	55946	Northwest Terminal (Part of		Pillsbury	56382
Money Creek	55943	Minneapolis)	55418	Pilot Grove	56027
Montevideo	56265	Norway Lake	56289	Pilot Mound	55923
Montgomery	56069	Norwood	55368	Pine Bend (Dakota County)	55068
Monticello	56362		55383	Pine Bend (Mahnomen	
	55365	For specific Norwood Zip Codes		County)	56651
For specific Monticello Zip Codes		call (612) 467-2242		Pine Brook	55008
call (612) 295-2213		Nowthen	55303	Pine Center	56401
Montrose	55363	Noyes	56740	Pine City	55063
Moorhead	56560-61	Oak Center	55041	Pinecreek	56751
For specific Moorhead Zip Codes		Oakdale	55128	Pine Island	55963
call (218) 236-6001		Oakhill	56347	Pine River	56474
Moose Lake	55767	Oak Island	56741	Pine Springs	55115
Moose Lake State Hospital	55767	Oak Knoll (Part of		Pineville	55705
Mora	55051	Minnetonka)	55305	Pinewood	56676
Morgan	56266	Oakland	56076	Pioneer (Part of St. Paul)	55101
Morgan Park (Part of		Oak Park (Anoka County)	55434	Pipestone	56164
Duluth)	55808	Oak Park (Benton County)	56357	Pitt	56665
Morningside (Part of Edina)	55424	Oak Park Heights	55082	Plainview	55964
Morrill	56329	Oakport	56560	Plato	55370
Morris	56267	Oak Ridge	55910	Pleasant Grove	55976
Morristown	55052	Odessa	56276	Pleasant Lake	56301
Morton	56270	Odin	56160	Plummer	56748
Moscow	55912	Ogema	56569	Plymouth	55441
Motley	56466	Ogilvie	56358	Point Douglas	55033
Mound	55364	Okabena	56161	Ponemah	56666
Mounds View	55432	Oklee	56742	Ponsford	56575
Mountain Iron	55768	Old Frontenac	55041	Poplar	56479
Mountain Lake	56159	Olga	56646	Popple Creek	56379
Mount Royal (Part of		Olivia	56277	Port Cargill (Part of Savage)	55378
Duluth)	55803	Onamia	56359	Porter	56280
Munger	55806	Onigum	56484	Post Town	55920
Murdock	56271	Opole	56340	Potsdam	55932
Murphy City	55603	Orchard Lake (Part of		Powderhorn (Part of	
Muskoda	56549	Lakeville)	55044	Minneapolis)	55407
Myrtle	56070	Org	56187	Prairie Island Indian	
Nashua	56565	Orleans	56735	Reservation	55089
Nashwauk	55769	Ormsby	56162	Prairieville	55021
Nassau	56272	Orono	55323	Pratt	55060
Navarre (Part of Orono)	55392	Oronoco	55960	Predmore	55934
Naytahwaush	56566	Orr	55771	Preston	55965
Nebish	56667	Orrock	55309	Priam	56282

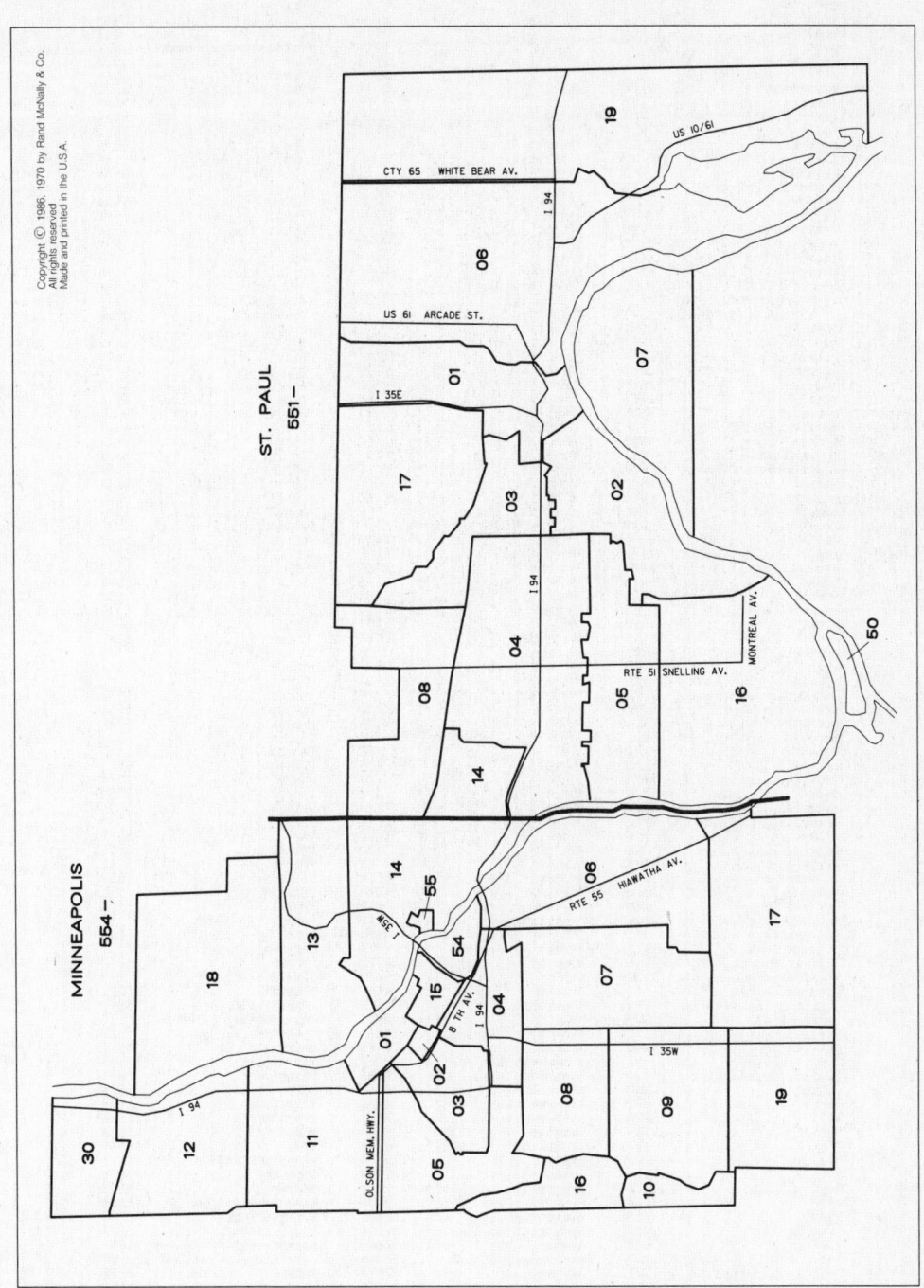

	ZIP
Abbeville	38601
Abbott	39773
Aberdeen	39730
Ackerman	39735
Acona	39095
Adams	39175
Adaton	39759
Addie	38744
Agricola	39452
Airey	39574
Airport Mail Facility (Part of Jackson)	39208
Albin	38966
Alcorn State University	39096
Algoma	38820
Allen	39083
Alligator	38720
Alpine	38849
Altitude	38829
Alva	38925
Amory	38821
Anchor	39776
Anchorage	39194
Anding	39040
Anguilla	38721
Anse	39073
Ansley	39558
Antioch	39440
Apple Ridge (Part of Jackson)	39204
Arcola	38722
Ariel	39638
Arkabutla	38602
Arlington (Lincoln County)	39629
Arlington (Neshoba County)	39350
Arm	39663
Arnold Line	39402
Artesia	39736
Ashland	38603
Askew	38621
Athens	39730
Atlanta	39776
Atway	38635
Auburn (Lee County)	38801
Auburn (Lincoln County)	39666
Austin	38676
Avalon	38912
Avera	39451
Avon	38723
Bailey	39320
Baird	38751
Baker	38652
Bald Hill	38652
Baldwyn	38824
Ballard	39046
Ballardsville	38801
Ballentine	38621
Ball Ground	39156
Baltzer	38732
Banks	38664
Banner	38913
Barlow	39083
Barnes	39051
Barnesville	38109
Barnett	39347
Barr	38668
Barrontown	39465
Bartahatchie	39740
Barth	39470
Barto	39648
Barton (George County)	39452
Barton (Marshall County)	38017
Basic	39330
Basin	39452
Bassfield	39421
Batesville	38606
Batson	39401
Battlefield (Hinds County)	39204
Battle Field (Newton County)	39325
Battles	39362
Baugh	38669
Baxter	39338
Baxterville	39455
Bayland	39194
Bay Saint Louis	39520-29
For specific Bay Saint Louis Zip Codes call (601) 467-5788	
Bayside Park	39520
Bay Springs	39422
Beacon Hill	38652
Beans Ferry	38843
Bear Town	39648
Beasley	39755
Beatline	39350
Beatrice	39330
Beatty	39176
Beaumont	39423
Beauregard	39191
Becker	38825
Beech Springs	38866

	ZIP
Beechwood	39645
Beelake	39172
Belden	38826
Belen	38609
Bellefontaine	39737
Belle Isle	39572
Belleville	39462
Bellewood	38754
Bells School	39759
Belmont	38827
Belzoni	39038
Benjoe	39456
Benndale	39456
Benoit	38725
Benson	39437
Bentley	39751
Bent Oak	39701
Benton	39039
Bentonia	39040
Benwood	38922
Berclair	38941
Berwick	39645
Bethany	38849
Betheden	39339
Bethel	39345
Bethlehem (Marshall County)	38659
Bethlehem (Pontotoc County)	38863
Bethsaida	39350
Bett	38618
Beulah (Bolivar County)	38726
Beulah (Newton County)	39337
Beulah Hubbard	39337
Bewelcome	39638
Bexley	39452
Bigbee	38821
Bigbee Valley	39738
Big Creek	38914
Biggersville	38834
Big Level	39573
Bigpoint	39581
Billups	39701
Biloxi	39530-35
For specific Biloxi Zip Codes call (601) 432-0311	
Binford	39730
Binnsville	39358
Birmingham Ridge	38828
Bissell	38801
Black Bayou Junction	38928
Black Hawk	38923
Blackjack	39759
Blackland	38829
Blackwater (Kemper County)	39326
Blackwater (Lafayette County)	38685
Blaine	38778
Blair	38849
Blakely	39180
Blanton	39159
Bloody Springs	38827
Bloomfield (Kemper County)	39328
Bloomfield (Neshoba County)	39350
Blue Hills	39144
Blue Lake	38737
Blue Mountain	38610
Blue Springs	38828
Bluff Springs (Kemper County)	39328
Bluff Springs (Panola County)	38666
Bobo (Coahoma County)	38614
Bobo (Quitman County)	38646
Boggan Bend	38849
Bogue Chitto (Kemper County)	39350
Bogue Chitto (Lincoln County)	39629
Boice	39367
Bolatusha	39160
Bolivar	38725
Bolton	39041
Bond (Neshoba County)	39350
Bond (Stone County)	39577
Bon Homme	39401
Bonita (Part of Meridian)	39301
Boon	39339
Boone	38614
Booneville	38829
Bothwell	39476
Bounds Crossroads	35582
Bourbon	38756
Bovina	39180
Bowdre	38664
Bowling Green	39063
Bowman	38618
Boyer	38751
Boyette	39160

	ZIP
Boyle	38730
Bradley	39759
Branch	39117
Brandon	39042-43
	39047
For specific Brandon Zip Codes call (601) 825-2552	
Branyan	38828
Brasfield	39096
Braxton	39044
Brazil	38963
Brewer (Clarke County)	39355
Brewer (Lee County)	38868
Brewer (Perry County)	39476
Bright	38632
Bristers Store	39641
Brockton (Part of Meridian)	39301
Brody	38603
Brookhaven	39601
Brook Hollow	39212
Brooklyn	39425
Brooks	38737
Brooksville	39739
Brownfield	38683
Browning	38930
Brownsville	39041
Brown Town	39452
Brozville	39095
Bruce	38915
Brunswick	39180
Bryant	38922
Buchannan	38863
Buckatunna	39322
Buckhorn	38864
Bude	39630
Buena Vista (Chickasaw County)	38851
Buena Vista (Tippah County)	38663
Buena Vista Lakes	38632
Bunker Hill	39429
Bunkley	39653
Burgess	38655
Burns	39153
Burnside	39350
Burnsville	38833
Burrell	38628
Burtons	38829
Bush	39149
Busy Corner	39638
Butler	39169
Byhalia	38611
Byram	39212
	39272
For specific Byram Zip Codes call (601) 968-0520	
Cadamy	38876
Cadaretta	38929
Caesar	39466
Caile	38754
Cairo	38873
Caledonia	39740
Calhoun (Jones County)	39440
Calhoun (Newton County)	39345
Calhoun City	38916
Calyx	39361
Cambridge	38601
Camden	39045
Cameron	39146
Cameta	39159
Campbell (Part of Ripley)	38663
Canaan	38603
Candlestick (Part of Jackson)	39212
Candlestick Park (Part of Jackson)	39212
Cannonsburg	39120
Canton	39046
Cardsville	38858
Carlisle	39049
Carlos	39191
Carmack	39176
Carmichael (Clarke County)	39360
Carmichael (Perry County)	39423
Carnes	39455
Carolina	38858
Carpenter	39086
Carriere	39426
Carrollton	38917
Carson	39427
Carter	39194
Carterville (Part of Petal)	39465
Carthage	39051
Cary	39054
Cascilla	38920
Caseyville	39191
Cato	39042
Cayce	38017
Cayuga	39159
Cedarbluff	39741
Cedar Hill (Madison County)	39071

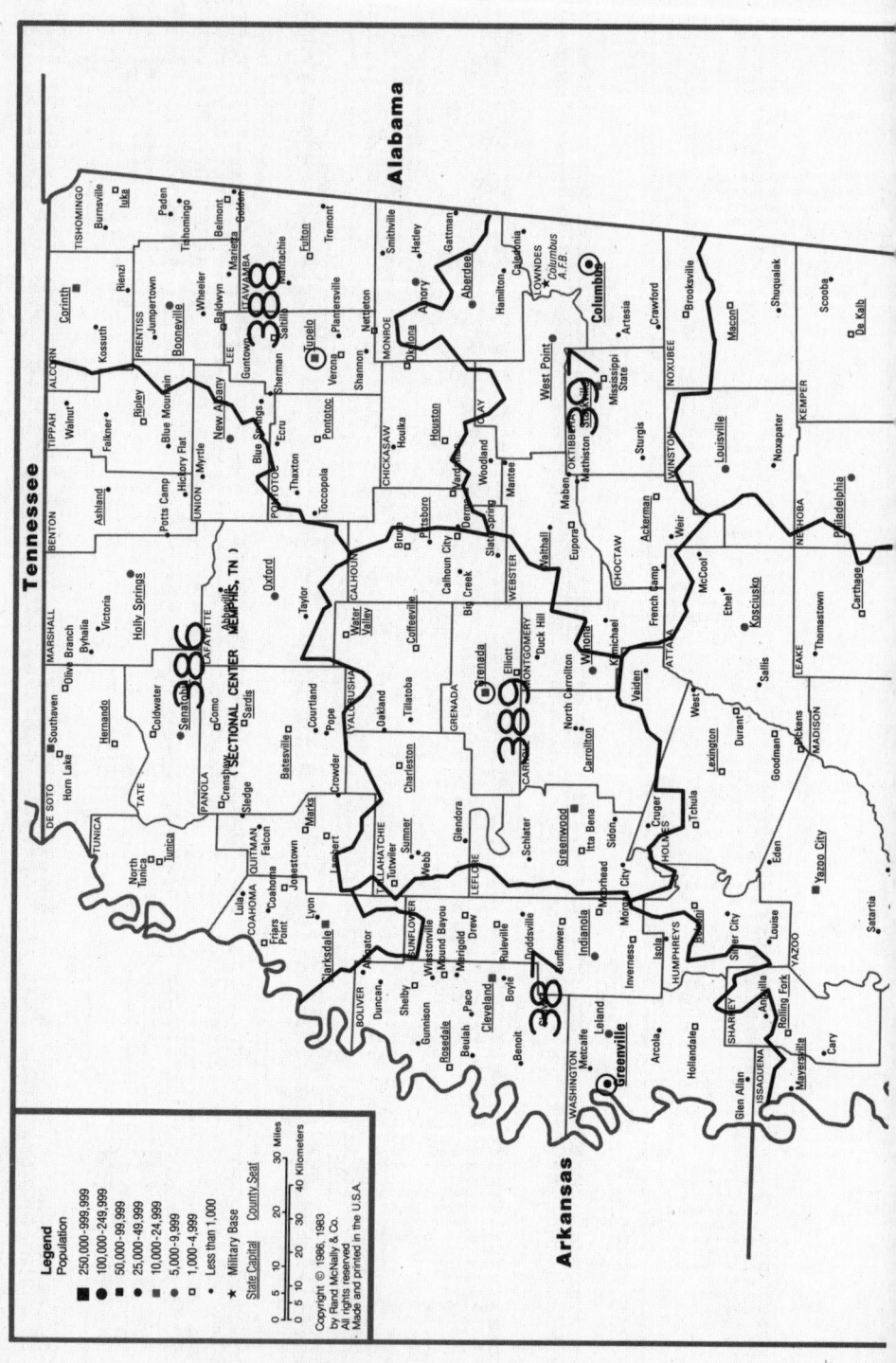

Legend
Population
■ 250,000-999,999
● 100,000-249,999
■ 50,000-99,999
● 25,000-49,999
■ 10,000-24,999
□ 5,000-9,999
□ 1,000-4,999
• Less than 1,000
★ Military Base
<u>State Capital</u> <u>County Seat</u>

0   5 10   20   30 Miles
0 5 10 20   30   40 Kilometers

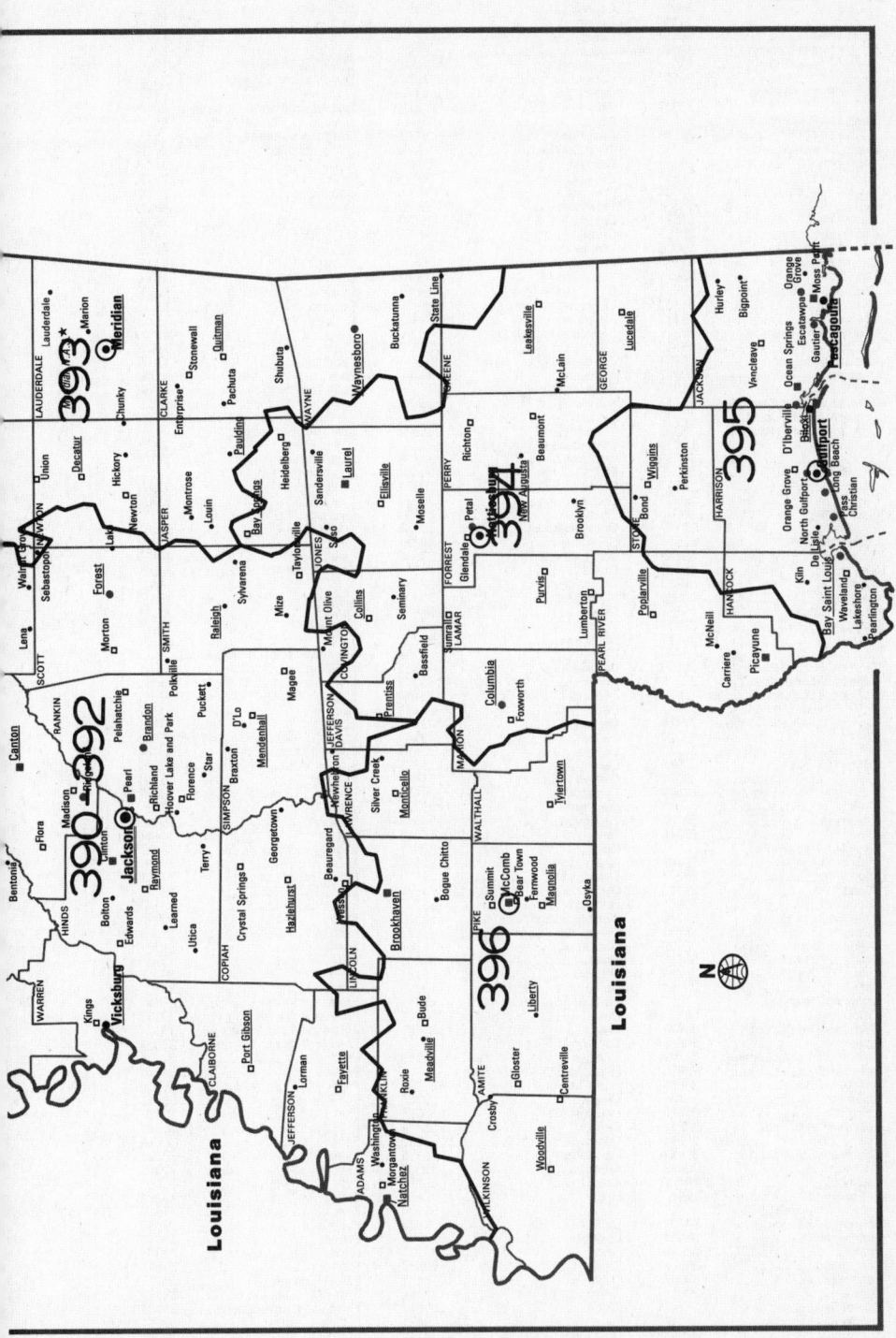

	ZIP		ZIP		ZIP
Johnson	39437	Little Rock	39337	Marion	39342
Johnston	39666	Little Texas	38676	Maris Town (Part of Canton)	39046
Jonathan	39451	Little Yazoo	39040	Markette	38655
Jonestown (Coahoma		Litton	38773	Markham	38761
County)	38639	Lizana	39503	Marks	38646
Jonestown (Yazoo County)	39194	Lobdell	38726	Mars Hill	39666
Jug Fork	38828	Lobutcha	39108	Martin	39325
Jumpertown	38829	Loch Leven	39669	Martin Bluff	39553
Junction City	39355	Locke Station	38606	Martinsville	39083
Kalem	39117	Lockhart	39335	Martintown	38652
Keirn	38924	Lodi (Humphreys County)	39166	Martinville	39114
Kellis Store	39354	Lodi (Montgomery County)	39767	Marydell	39051
Kelona	39366	Lombardy	38774	Mashulaville	39341
Kendrick	38834	Long	38756	Matherville	39360
Keownville	38652	Long Beach	39560	Mathiston	39752
Kewanee	39364	Longino	39350	Mattson	38758
Key Field (Part of Meridian)	39301	Long Lake (Coahoma		Maxie	39425
Kilmichael	39747	County)	38617	Maybank	39401
Kiln	39556	Long Lake (Warren County)	39180	Maybell	39437
King and Anderson	38614	Longshot	38773	Mayersville	39113
Kings	39180	Longtown	38665	Mayhew	39753
Kingston	39120	Longview (Oktibbeha		Mayton	39042
Kinlock	38751	County)	39759	Maywood	38654
Kipling	39328	Longview (Pontotoc		Meadville	39653
Kirby	39661	County)	38863	Mechanicsburg	39040
Kirkville	38843	Looxahoma	38668	Meehan	39301
Kittrell	39423	Lorena	39074	Meeks	38924
Klem	39074	Lorenzen	39159	Melba	39482
Klondike	39320	Lorman	39096	Meltonville	39046
Knobtown	39362	Louin	39338	Memphis	38680
Knoxo	39667	Louise	39097	Mendenhall	39114
Knoxville	39661	Louisville	39339	Meridian	39301-07
Kokomo	39643	Love	38632	For specific Meridian Zip Codes	
Kola	39428	Loyd	38878	call (601) 693-2581	
Kolola Springs	39740	Loyd Star	39601	Meridian Naval Air Station	39309
Kosciusko	39090	Lucas	39474	Meridian Station	39309
Kossuth	38834	Lucedale	39452	Merigold	38759
Kreole (Part of Moss Point)	39563	Lucern	39365	Merit	39114
Lackey	39730	Lucien	39601	Merrill	39452
Lafayette Springs	38655	Luckney	39208	Mesa	39667
Lake	39092	Ludlow	39098	Metcalfe	38760
Lake Center	38659	Lula	38644	Metrocenter (Part of	
Lake City (Prentiss County)	38829	Lumberton	39455	Jackson)	39204
Lake City (Yazoo County)	39194	Lurand	38614	Meyers	39401
Lake Como	39422	Lux	39401	Michigan City	38647
Lake Cormorant	38641	Lyman	39503	Midnight	39115
Lakeland (Part of Richland)	39218	Lynchburg (DeSoto County)	38109	Midway (Copiah County)	39191
Lake of Hills	38632	Lynn Creek	39739	Midway (Hinds County)	39170
Lakeshore	39558	Lynville	39354	Midway (Leake County)	39051
Lake View	38680	Lyon	38645	Midway (Scott County)	39074
Lamar	38642	Maben	39750	Midway (Tishomingo	
Lamar Park	39401	McAdams	39107	County)	38852
Lambert	38643	McBride	39144	Midway (Yazoo County)	39039
Lamkin	39166	McCall Creek	39647	Mileston	39169
Lamont	38755	McCallum	39401	Millard	39470
Lampton	39429	McCarley	38943	Mill Creek (Jones County)	39440
Landon	39503	McComb	39648	Mill Creek (Pearl River	
Langford	39042	McCondy	38854	County)	39426
Langsdale	39360	McCool	39108	Mill Creek (Rankin County)	39042
Larue	39564	McCrary	39701	Millcreek (Winston County)	39339
Latimer	39564	McCutcheon	38722	Mill Creek Cabin Area	38852
Latonia	39452	Mc Donald (Leake County)	39094	Miller	38654
Lauderdale	39335	McDonald (Neshoba		Millington	39358
Laurel	39440-42	County)	39365	Mill Town (Part of Canton)	39046
For specific Laurel Zip Codes call		Macedonia (Forrest County)	39401	Mimms	38606
(601) 425-1408		Macedonia (Lee County)	38801	Mineral Wells	38648
Laurelhill	39350	Macedonia (Union County)	38650	Mingo	38873
Lawrence	39336	Macel	38950	Minter City	38944
Laws Hill	38685	McElveen	39666	Missionary	39356
Leaf	39456	McHenry	39561	Mississippi City (Part of	
Leakesville	39451	McLain	39456	Gulfport)	39501
Learned	39154	McLaurin	39401	Mississippi College (Part of	
Lebanon (Hinds County)	39154	McLaurin Heights (Part of		Clinton)	39058
Lebanon (Marshall County)	38659	Pearl)	39208	Mississippi State	39762
Lee Donald	39366	McLeod	39341	Mississippi Valley State	
Leedy	38833	McMillan	39339	University	38941
Leesburg	39117	McNair	39069	Mitchell	38663
Leesdale	39661	McNeal	39338	Mize	39116
Leeville	39401	McNeill	39457	Money	38945
Lefleur (Part of Jackson)	39211	Macon	39341	Monroe	39653
Leflore	38940	McSwain	39476	Monterey	39073
Leigh Mall (Part of		McVille	39090	Monte Vista	39744
Columbus)	39701	Madden	39109	Montgomery	39191
Leland	38756	Madison	39110	Monticello	39654
Lemon	39074		39130	Montpelier	39754
Lena	39094	For specific Madison Zip Codes		Montrose	39338
Lessley	39669	call (601) 856-4641		Moon	38662
Le Tourneau	39180	Madisonville	39046	Moores Mill	38838
Leverett	38920	Magee	39111	Mooreville	38857
Lewisburg	38654	Magnolia	39652	Moorhead	38761
Lexie	39667	Mahned	39462	Morgan City	38946
Lexington	39095	Main (Part of Meridian)	39302	Morgans	39170
Liberty (Amite County)	39645	Malone	38685	Morgantown (Adams	
Liberty (Kemper County)	39328	Malvina	38769	County)	39120
Lightsey	39440	Mannassa	39355	Morgantown (Marion	
Lillian	39074	Mantachie	38855	County)	39484
Linn	38736	Mantee	39751	Morgantown (Oktibbeha	
Linwood (Neshoba County)	39365	Marcella	39169	County)	39769
Linwood (Yazoo County)	39179	Marianna	38635	Morning Star	39066
Little Creek	39423	Marie	38751	Morriston	39401
Little Italy	39092	Marietta	38856	Morton	39117

	ZIP
Moscow	39328
Moselle	39459
Moss	39460
Moss Point	39562-63
For specific Moss Point Zip Codes call (601) 475-3951	
Mossy Lake	38959
Mound Bayou	38762
Mound City (Bolivar County)	38726
Mound City (Union County)	38828
Mount Carmel	39474
Mount Nebo	39328
Mount Olive (Covington County)	39119
Mount Olive (Franklin County)	39653
Mount Olive (Jones County)	39440
Mount Pleasant (Itawamba County)	38876
Mount Pleasant (Marshall County)	38649
Mount Vernon	38801
Mount Zion	39111
Movella	39452
Muldon	39730
Mullins Store	38655
Murphy	38748
Murry	38663
Muskegon	39092
Myrick	39440
Myrleville	39039
Myrtle	38650
Nancy	39366
Nason	38940
Natchez	39120-22
For specific Natchez Zip Codes call (601) 442-4361	
National Cemetery (Part of Vicksburg)	39180
Necaise	39573
Neely	39461
Nelieburg	39307
Nesbit	38651
Neshoba	39365
Nettleton	38858
Nevada	39041
New Albany	38652
New Augusta	39462
New Byram	39212
New Canaan	38603
New Fitler	39070
New Garden	38618
New Harmony	38828
New Hebron	39140
New Hope	39702
Newman	39066
Newmans	39180
Newmans Grove	39154
Newport (Attala County)	39160
Newport (DeSoto County)	38641
New Salem	38843
New Sight	39601
New Site	38859
Newton	39345
New Town	38668
New Wren	39730
Nichols	38959
Nicholson	39463
Nida	39172
Nitta Yuma	38763
Nixon (Humphreys County)	39115
Nixon (Pontotoc County)	38863
Nod	39039
Nola	39665
Norfield	39629
Norfolk	38641
Norris	39074
North (Hinds County)	39206
North (Lauderdale County)	39305
North Bay (Part of D'Iberville)	39532
North Bend	39350
North Carrollton	38947
North Crossroads	38852
North Greenville (Part of Greenville)	38701
North Gulfport	39503
North Gulfport (census designated place)	39501
North Haven	38652
North Long Beach (Part of Long Beach)	39560
Northpark Mall (Part of Ridgeland)	39157
North Tunica	38676
Northwest Junior College (Part of Senatobia)	38668
Norton	38663
Noxapater	39346
Oak Bowery	39437
Oak Grove (Holmes County)	39169

	ZIP
Oak Grove (Jones County)	39437
Oak Grove (Lamar County)	39401
Oak Grove (Perry County)	39423
Oakland (Itawamba County)	38843
Oakland (Pike County)	39666
Oakland (Yalobusha County)	38948
Oakley	39154
Oak Ridge	39180
Oak Vale	39656
Obadiah	39320
Ocean Springs	39564-65
For specific Ocean Springs Zip Codes call (601) 875-4431	
Ocobla	39350
Ofahoma	39051
Oil City	39040
Okahola	39475
Oklahoma	38917
Okolona	38860
Oktoc	39759
Old Cairo	38829
Old Dominion	38946
Oldenburg	39661
Oldham	38852
Old Hamilton	39746
Old Houlka	38850
Old Red Star	39601
Old Union	38868
Olive Branch	38654
Oloh	39482
Oma	39654
Omega	39169
Onward	39159
Ora	39428
Orange	39347
Orange Grove (Harrison County)	39503
Orange Grove (Jackson County)	39581
Orange Hill	39041
O'Reilly	38730
Orwood	38655
Osborn	39759
Osborne Creek	38829
Osyka	39657
Ovett	39464
Owens Wells	39095
Oxberry	38940
Oxford (Amite County)	39638
Oxford (Lafayette County)	38655
Ozona	39426
Pace	38764
Pachuta	39347
Paden	38873
Palmer	39401
Palmetto	38801
Panther Burn	38765
Parchman	38738
Parham	38848
Paris	38949
Parks	38652
Parksplace	38619
Pascagoula	39562-63
	39567-69
	39581
For specific Pascagoula Zip Codes call (601) 762-5722	
Pascagoula River Estates	39466
Pass Christian	39571
Patosi	39194
Pattison	39144
Paul	38920
Paulding	39348
Paulette	39341
Paynes	38920
Pearl (Rankin County)	39208
Pearl (Simpson County)	39073
Pearl City (Part of Pearl)	39208
Pearlington	39572
Pearl River	39350
Pearson	39208
Pecan	39581
Pecan Grove	39437
Pelahatchie	39145
Penantly	39356
Pendorff	39440
Penns Station	39743
Penton	38664
Peoples	38663
Peoria	39645
Percy	38748
Perdue	39337
Perkinston	39573
Perrytown	39633
Perth	39069
Perthshire	38746
Petal	39465
Peteet	38946
Peyton	39144
Pheba	39755

	ZIP
Philadelphia	39350
Philipp	38950
Phillipstown	38954
Phoenix	39040
Piave	39476
Picayune	39466
Pickens	39146
Pickwick	39483
Pierce Crossroads	39194
Piggtown	39094
Piketown	39074
Pinckneyville	39669
Pinebluff	39751
Pinebur	39429
Pinedale	38627
Pine Flat (Lafayette County)	38965
Pine Flat (Tishomingo County)	38852
Pine Grove (Benton County)	38633
Pine Grove (Lamar County)	39475
Pine Grove (Lee County)	38868
Pine Grove (Tippah County)	38829
Pine Ridge (Adams County)	39120
Pine Ridge (Lamar County)	39475
Pine Springs	39301
Pine Valley	38965
Pineview	39440
Pineville	39074
Piney Woods	39148
Pinola	39149
Pisgah (Greene County)	39452
Pisgah (Prentiss County)	38865
Pisgah (Rankin County)	39042
Pistol Ridge	39455
Pittman	39483
Pittsboro	38951
Plainview (Part of Richland)	39218
Plantersville	38862
Plattsburg	39350
Pleasant Grove	38657
Pleasant Hill (Copiah County)	39668
Pleasant Hill (DeSoto County)	38651
Pleasant Hill (Union County)	38652
Pleasant Ridge (Jones County)	39440
Pleasant Ridge (Union County)	38625
Plum Point	38671
Pluto	39169
Poagville	38618
Pocahontas	39072
Pokal	39140
Polfrey	39564
Polkville	39117
Pollock	38751
Pond	39669
Ponta	39301
Pontotoc	38863
Poolville	38650
Pope	38658
Poplar Corners	38680
Poplar Creek	39747
Poplar Springs (Holmes County)	39063
Poplar Springs (Montgomery County)	39747
Poplar Springs (Newton County)	39345
Poplarville	39470
Porterville	39352
Port Gibson	39150
Posey Mound	38623
Post	39325
Potts Camp	38659
Powell	38626
Powers	39440
Prairie	39756
Prairie Point	39353
Prentiss	39474
Presidential Hills (Part of Jackson)	39213
Preston	39354
Pricedale	39666
Prichard	38676
Prince Chapel	39354
Priscilla	38701
Prismatic	39320
Progress (Jefferson Davis County)	39474
Progress (Perry County)	39423
Progress (Pike County)	39648
Prospect	39057
Puckett	39151
Pulaski	39152
Pumpkin Center	38652
Purvis	39475
Pyland	38851
Quentin	39647
Quincy	38848

	ZIP		ZIP		ZIP
Tippo	38962	Vernon (Madison County)	39339	West Poplarville	39470
Tishomingo	38873	Vernon (Winston County)	39339	Westside	39150
Toccopola	38874	Verona	38879	West Union	38650
Tocowa	38620	Vickland	39159	Westville	39114
Tomnolen	39744	Vicksburg	39180-82	Wheeler	38880
Toomsuba	39364	For specific Vicksburg Zip Codes		Whistler	39367
Topeka	39641	call (601) 636-1071		White Apple	39661
Topisaw	39662	Victoria	38679	Whitebluff	39483
Topton	39301	Vidalia	39571	White Cap	39638
Touchstone	39044	Village Fair Mall (Part of		Whitehead	38928
Tougaloo (Part of Jackson)	39174	Meridian)	39301	Whiteoak	39111
Townsend	39352	Vimville	39301	Whites (Clay County)	39773
Tralake	38756	Virlilia	39046	Whites (Rankin County)	39073
Trapp	39350	Vossburg	39366	Whitesand (Jefferson Davis	
Traxler	39111	Waco	38753	County)	39140
Trebloc	38875	Waddell	39741	White Sand (Pearl River	
Tremont	38876	Wade (Jackson County)	39581	County)	39470
Triangle (Part of Biloxi)	39534	Wade (Sunflower County)	38737	Whites Crossing	39577
Tribbett	38779	Wahalak	39358	Whitfield (Jones County)	39464
Trinity (DeSoto County)	38632	Wakefield	38618	Whitfield (Rankin County)	39193
Trinity (Lowndes County)	39743	Wakeland	38930	Whitney	38737
Troy	38863	Waldrup	39422	Whitten Town	38663
Truitt	39146	Wallerville	38652	Whynot	39301
Tucker	39350	Wallhill	38618	Wickware	39345
Tuckers Crossing	39440	Walls	38680	Wiggins (Leake County)	39051
Tula	38675	Walnut (Quitman County)	38964	Wiggins (Stone County)	39577
Tunica	38676	Walnut (Tippah County)	38683	Wilco Estates	38632
Tupelo	38801-03	Walnut Grove (Coahoma		Wildwood	38930
For specific Tupelo Zip Codes call		County)	38767	Wilkinson	39669
(601) 842-4482		Walnut Grove (Leake		Willet	38748
Turnbull	39669	County)	39189	Williamsburg	39428
Turnerville	39338	Walters	39437	Williamsville (Attala County)	39090
Turon	38870	Waltersville	39180	Williamsville (Neshoba	
Tuscola	39094	Walthall	39771	County)	39350
Tutwiler	38963	Wanilla	39654	Willowood	39212
Twin	39478	Wardwell	38878	Willows	39150
Twin Lakes	38680	Warrenton	39180	Winborn	38633
Tylertown	39667	Warsaw	38611	Winchester	39367
Tyro	38668	Washington	39190	Windsor Park	39564
Union (Jones County)	39437	Waterford	38685	Wingate (Part of New	
Union (Lee County)	38862	Water Oak	39367	Augusta)	39462
Union (Newton County)	39365	Water Valley	38965	Winona	38967
Union (Simpson County)	39149	Watson (Forrest County)	39401	Winstonville	38781
Union Church	39668	Watson (Marshall County)	38611	Winterville	38782
Union Hall	39601	Wautubbee	39330	Wolf Springs	39301
Unity	38849	Waveland	39576	Woodburn	38751
University (Part of Oxford)	38677	Waxhaw	38746	Woodland (Chickasaw	
University Medical Center		Way	39046	County)	39776
(Part of Jackson)	39216	Waynesboro	39367	Woodland (Pontotoc	
University of Mississippi	38677	Wayside	38780	County)	38863
Usrytown	39074	Weathersby	39114	Woodland Lake	38632
Utica	39175	Webb	38966	Woodville	39669
Utica Junior College	39175	Weir	39772	Woodwards	39367
Vaiden	39176	Wells (Part of Caledonia)	39740	Woolmarket	39532
Valewood	38744	Wells Town	39455	Wortham	39574
Valley	39194	Wenasoga	38834	Wren	39730
Valley Hill	38917	Wesson	39191	Wright	38746
Valley Park	39177	West (Holmes County)	39192	Wyatte	38668
Value (Part of Brandon)	39042	West (Lauderdale County)	39305	Yazoo City	39194
Van Buren	38858	West Biloxi (Part of Biloxi)	39531	Yocona	38655
Vance	38964	West Days	38641	Yokena	39180
Vancleave (census		West Gulfport	39501	Youngs	38922
designated place)	39564	West Hattiesburg	39401	Zama	39090
Van Cleave	39564	West Hill	39063	Zemuly	39160
Van Vleet	38877	West Jackson (Part of		Zero	39301
Vardaman	38878	Jackson)	39207	Zetus	39601
Vaughan	39179	Westland (Part of Jackson)	39209	Zieglerville	39039
Vaughn	39601	West Lincoln	39601	Zion	38863
Velma	38965	West Marks	38646	Zumbro	38732
Vernal	39452	West Point	39773		

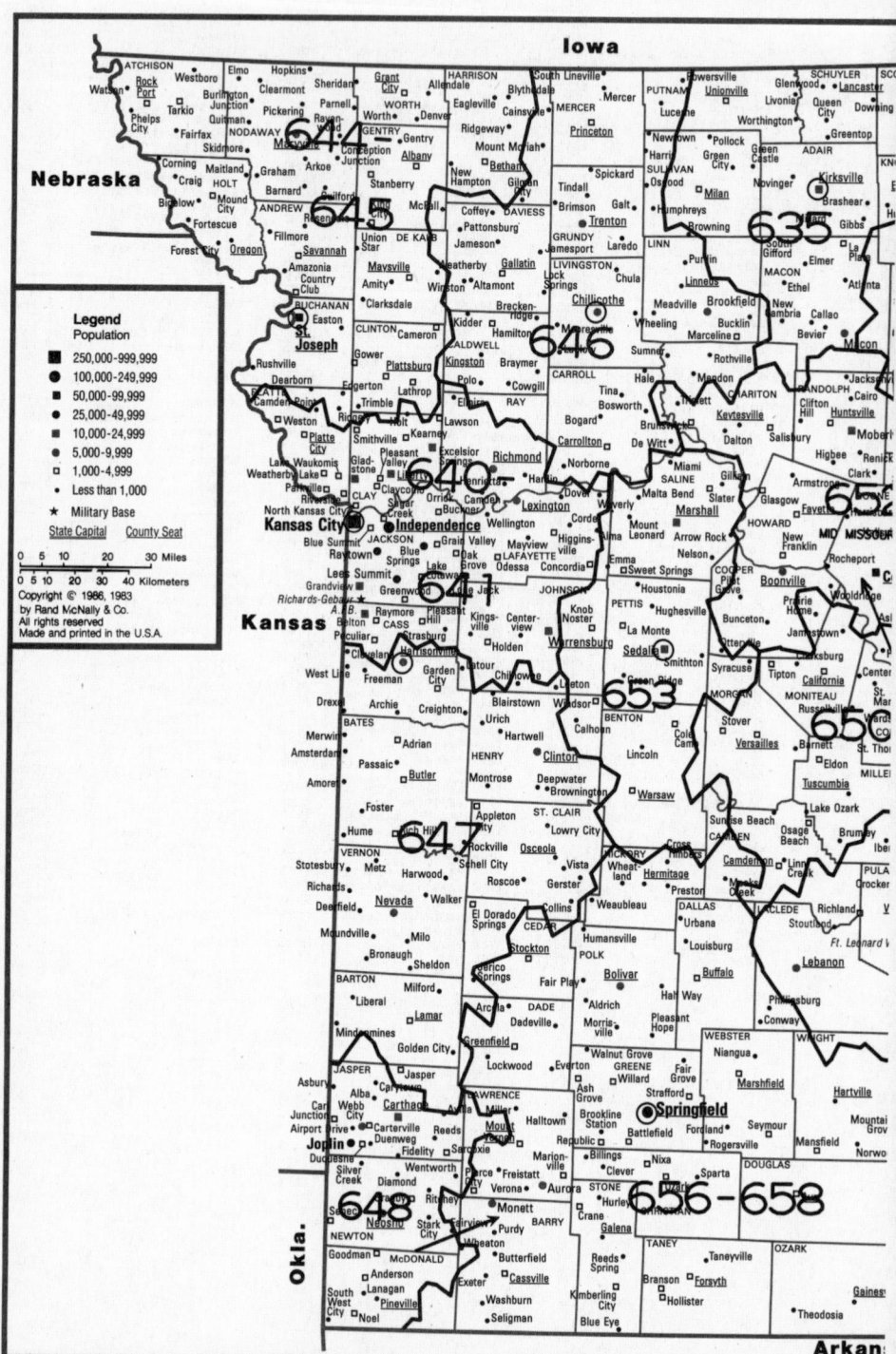

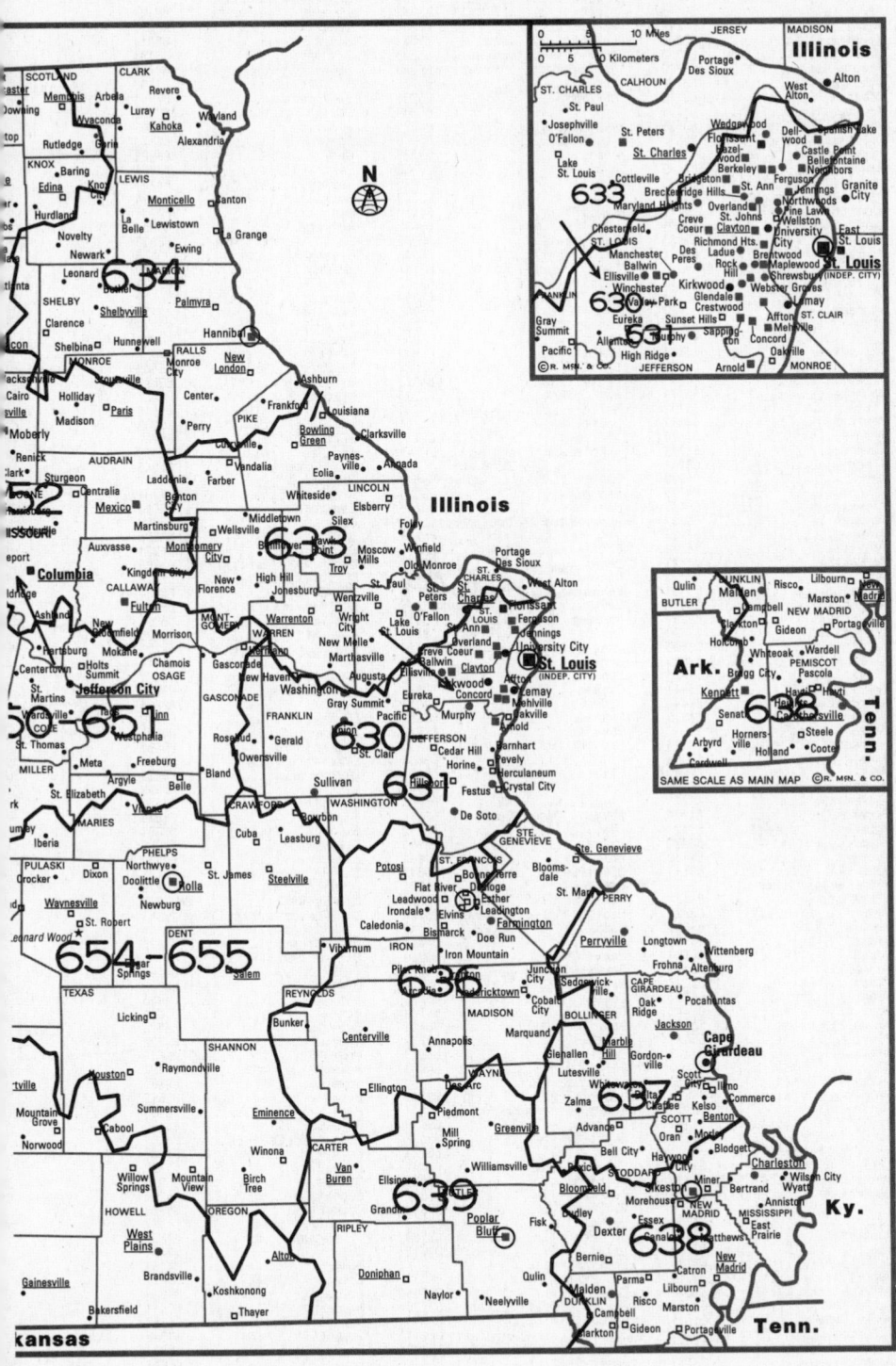

	ZIP		ZIP		ZIP
Boys Town	65559	California	65018	Chambersburg	63445
Bracken	65706	Callao	63534	Chamois	65024
Bradfield	65705	Calm	63942	Champ	63042
Bradleyville	65614	Calton Mill	65769	Champion	65717
Braggadocio	63826	Calumet	63336	Champion City	63056
Bragg City	63827	Calverton Park	63136	Chandler	64060
Braley	64477	Calwood	65251	Channel	63877
Branch	65786	Cambridge	65330	Chapel Hill	64011
Brandon	65360	Camden	64017	Chapel Hills	65785
Brandsville	65688	Camden Point	64018	Chariton	63565
Branson	65616	Camdenton	65020	Charity	65644
Brashear	63533	Cameron	64429	Charlack	63114
Braymer	64624	Campbell	63933	Charles Nagel (Part of St.	
Brays	65486	Campbellton	63068	Louis)	63115
Brazeau	63737	Camp Clark	64772	Charleston	63834
Brazil	63664	Canaan	65014	Charteroak	63833
Brazito	65101	Canalou	63828	Cherokee Pass	63645
Breckenridge	64625	Cane Hill	65635	Cherry Box	63451
Breckenridge Hills	63114	Caney Creek	63771	Cherry Valley Estates	65804
Breen Acres (Part of		Cannon Mines	63630	Cherryville	65446
Kansas City)	64152	Canton	63435	Chesapeake	65712
Brentwood	63144	Cantwell (Part of Desloge)	63601	Chesterfield	63005-06
Brewer	63775	Cape Fair	65624		63017
Briar	63931	Cape Girardeau	63701-02	For specific Chesterfield Zip	
Brickeys	63627	For specific Cape Girardeau Zip		Codes call (314) 532-3482	
Bridgeton	63044	Codes call (314) 335-5501		Chestnutridge	65630
Bridgeton Terrace (Part of		Capital Mall (Part of		Chicopee	63965
Bridgeton)	63044	Jefferson City)	65101	Chilhowee	64733
Bridlecroft	64083	Capitol Hill	63136	Chillicothe	64601
Brighton	65617	Caplinger Mills	65607	Chilton	63965
Brimson	64642	Cappeln	63348	Chitwood (Part of Joplin)	64801
Brinktown	65443	Capps	65082	Chloride	63646
Briscoe	63379	Cardwell	63829	Chouteau (Part of St. Louis)	63110
Bristow	64772	Carl Junction	64834	Chula	64635
Brixey	65618	Carlow	64648	Circle City	63846
Broadway (Part of St. Louis)	63147	Carmack	64402	Civic Center (Part of	
Brock	63555	Carola	63961	Kansas City)	64106
Bronaugh	64728	Carondelet (Part of St.		Civil Bend	64670
Brookdale	63141	Louis)	63111	Clapper	63456
Brookfield	64628	Carr (Part of Florissant)	63031	Clara	65483
Brooking Park	65301	Carrington	65251	Clarence	63437
Brookline Station	65619	Carr Lane	72616	Clark	65243
Brooklyn	64481	Carrollton	64633	Clark City	63445
Brooklyn Heights	64836	Carsonville	63121	Clarksburg	65025
Broseley	63932	Carterville	64835	Clarksdale	64430
Brownbranch	65608	Carthage	64836	Clarkson Valley	63017
Brownfield	65556	Caruth	63857	Clarksville	63336
Browning	64630	Caruthersville	63830	Clarkton	63837
Brownington	64740	Carytown	64836	Claryville	63775
Browns	65202	Cascade	63632	Claycomo	64119
Browns Spring	65610	Case	65041	Claysvill	65039
Brownwood	63738	Cash	63534	Clayton	63105
Brumley	65017	Cassel Addition	65785	Clear Creek	65276
Bruner	65620	Cassidy	65714	Clearmont	64431
Brunot	63636	Cassville	65625	Clear Spring	63965
Brunswick	65236	Castle Point	63136	Clear Springs	65793
Brushcreek	65536	Castle Rock (Part of Joplin)	64801	Clearview	65202
Brushyknob	65608	Castlewood	63011	Clearwater	63670
Buck Donic	63829	Catawba	64624	Cleavesville	65014
Buckhart	65638	Catawissa	63015	Cleveland	64734
Buckhorn (Madison County)	63655	Catherine Place	63645	Clever	65631
Buckhorn (Pulaski County)	65583	Cato	65605	Cliff Village	64801
Bucklin	64631	Catron	63833	Clifton City	65348
Buckner	64016	Caulfield	65626	Clifton Hill	65244
Bucoda	63876	Cave	63379	Climax Springs	65324
Bucyrus	65444	Cave Hill	65041	Clines Island	63846
Buell	63361	Caverna	72739	Clinton	64735
Buffalo	65622	Cave Spring	65770	Cliquot	65640
Buffington	63846	Cawood	64427	Clover Bottom	63090
Bullion	63501	Cedar City (Part of		Cloverdale	65590
Bunceton	65237	Jefferson City)	65022	Clubb	63934
Bunker	63629	Cedarcreek	65627	Clyde	64432
Bunker Hill	65257	Cedar Gap	65746	Coal	64735
Burbank	63944	Cedar Hill	63016	Coal Hill	64744
Burdett	64720	Cedar Hill Lakes	63016	Coatsville	63535
Burfordville	63739	Cedar Lake (Boone County)	65201	Cobalt City	63645
Burgess	64769	Cedar Lake (Jefferson		Cody	65742
Burke City	63135	County)	63070	Coffey	64636
Burksville	63434	Cedar Ridge	65590	Coffeyton	65441
Burlington Junction	64428	Cedar Springs	64744	Coffman	63670
Burnham	65793	Cedar Valley	63901	Coldspring	65717
Burns	65613	Cedarville	64756	Cold Springs	65355
Burr	72478	Celt	65764	Coldwater	63964
Burton	65248	Center	63436	Cole Camp	65325
Burtville	65336	Center Square (Part of		Cole Camp Junction	65325
Butcher	65774	Kansas City)	64196	College Mound	65247
Butler	64730	Centertown	65023	Collins	64738
Butler Hill Estates	63128	Centerview	64019	Coloma	64622
Butterfield	65623	Centerville	63633	Colony	63563
Butts	65441	Central (Jackson County)	64142	Columbia	65201-05
Bynumville	65281	Central (Madison County)	63645		65299
Byrnes Mill	63051	Central City	64801	For specific Columbia Zip Codes	
Byron	65013	Centralia	65240	call (314) 876-7829	
Cabanne (Part of St. Louis)	63112	Central Missouri		Columbia Mall (Part of	
Cabool	65689	Correctional Center	65101	Columbia)	65201
Caddo	65706	Centropolis (Part of Kansas		Columbus	64019
Cadet	63630	City)	64126	Commerce	63742
Cainsville	64632	Chadwick	65629	Commerce Tower (Part of	
Cairo	65239	Chaffee	63740	Kansas City)	64199
Caledonia	63631	Chain of Rocks	63369	Commercial (Part of	
Calhoun	65323	Chain-O-Lakes	65625	Springfield)	65803

Name	ZIP
Competition	65470
Conception	64433
Conception Junction	64434
Conclay (Part of Ladue)	63124
Concord (Callaway County)	65231
Concord (St. Louis County)	63128
Concord Hill	63357
Concordia	64020
Connelsville	63559
Conran	63838
Converse	64465
Conway	65632
Cook Station	65449
Cool Valley	63135
Cooper Hill	65014
Cooter	63839
Cora	63556
Corder	64021
Cornelia	64093
Corning	64435
Cornwall	63645
Corridon	63633
Corry	65635
Corsicana	65734
Corso	63377
Corticelli	65074
Cosby	64436
Cossville	64849
Cottage Farm	63050
Cottleville	63338
Cotton Plant	63855
Cottonwood Point	63830
Couch	65690
Coulstone	65542
Country Club (Andrew County)	64505
Country Club (Jackson County)	64113
Country Club Hills	63136
Country Club Plaza (Part of Kansas City)	64113
Country Lake Woods (St. Louis County)	63011
Country Life Acres	63131
Countryside (Part of Kansas City)	64152
Courtney (Part of Sugar Creek)	64050
Courtois	65565
Cowgill	64637
Coy	64831
Crabbs	65746
Craig	64437
Crane	65633
Creighton	64739
Crescent	63025
Crescent Hill	64720
Crescent Lake (Part of Excelsior Springs)	64024
Crestwood	63126
Crestwood Plaza (Part of Crestwood)	63126
Cretcher	65351
Creve Coeur	63141
Crider	65790
Crites Corner	63937
Crocker	65452
Cross Keys	63031
Cross Keys Shopping Center (Part of Florissant)	63033
Cross Roads (Douglas County)	65608
Cross Roads (Ozark County)	65637
Cross Timbers	65634
Crosstown	63775
Cross Way	65706
Crowder	63801
Crown	65706
Cruise Mill	63626
Crump	63785
Crystal City	63019
Crystal Lake Park	63131
Crystal Lakes	64024
Cuba	65453
Cunningham	64681
Curdton	63960
Cureall	65790
Currentview	63935
Curryville	63339
Custer	65501
Cyclone	64856
Cyrene	63334
Dadeville	65635
Daisy	63743
Daleview	64446
Dalton	65246
Damascus	64776
Dameron	63343
Damsel (Part of Osage Beach)	65065

Name	ZIP
Danby	63627
Danforth	63559
Danville	63361
Dardenne	63366
Dardenne Prairie	63366
Darien	65560
Daris Crossing	63601
Darksville	65259
Darlington	64438
Daugherty	64701
Davis (Lincoln County)	63379
Davis (St. Francois County)	63601
Davis Store	63932
Davisville	65456
Dawn	64638
Dawson	65711
Dawsonville	64428
Dawt	65760
Dayton	64747
Daytown (St. Francois County)	63653
Daytown (rural) (St. Francois County)	63601
Dearborn	64439
Decaturville	65536
Deckard-Y	65690
Dederick	64744
Deepwater	64740
Deerfield	64741
Deering	63840
Deer Land	63857
Deer Park	65201
Deer Ridge	63447
Deer Run	63965
Defiance	63341
Deicke	63025
De Kalb	64440
De Lassus	63640
Delaware	65438
Delbridge	63664
Dell Junction	65355
Dellwood	63136
Delmar	64735
Delmo	63801
Delta	63744
Dennis Acres	64801
Denton	63877
Denver	64441
Derby	63601
Des Arc	63636
Desloge	63601
De Soto	63020
Des Peres	63131
Dessa	64850
Detmold	63068
Devils Elbow	65457
De Witt	64639
Dexter	63841
Diamond	64840
Dickens	65759
Diehlstadt	63834
Diggins	65636
Dikeland	64083
Dillard	65456
Dillon	65401
Dissen	63068
Dittmer	63023
Dixie	65063
Dixon	65459
Dockery	64085
Doc Long Estates	65355
Doe Run	63637
Dogwood (Douglas County)	65746
Dogwood (Mississippi County)	63845
Dolly Siding (Part of Bonne Terre)	63628
Dongola	63730
Doniphan	63935
Doolittle	65401
Dora	65637
Dorena	63845
Doss	65560
Dotham	64446
Dove	65536
Dover (Lafayette County)	64022
Dover (Lewis County)	63448
Downing	63536
Drake	65066
Dresden	65301
Drexel	64742
Dripping Spring	65202
Drury	65638
Dudenville	64748
Dudley	63936
Duenweg	64841
Dugginsville	65761
Duke	65461
Duncans Bridge	63437
Duncans Point	65324
Dundee	63090

Name	ZIP
Dunksburg	65351
Dunlap	64683
Dunn	65711
Dunnegan	65640
Duquesne	64801
Durham	63438
Dutchtown	63745
Dutzow	63342
Dye	64098
Dykes	65444
Eagle Rock	65641
Eagleville	64442
Easley	65203
East Bonne Terre	63628
East End	63623
East Hills Mall (Part of St. Joseph)	64506
East Independence (Part of Independence)	64056
East Kirkwood (Part of Kirkwood)	63122
East Leavenworth	64079
East Lynne	64743
East Mexico (Part of Mexico)	65265
Easton	64443
East Prairie	63845
East Purdy	65734
Eastwood	63965
Ebenezer	65803
Ebo (Washington County)	63664
Eccles	65261
Echo Valley	65065
Economy	63530
Ectonville	64089
Edgar Springs	65462
Edge Acres	65785
Edgehill	63625
Edgerton	64444
Edgerton Junction	64439
Edgewater Beach	65653
Edgewood	63334
Edina	63537
Edinburg	64683
Edmonson	65338
Edmundson	63134
Edwards	65326
Egypt Grove	65626
Egypt Mills	63701
El Chaparral	65201
Eldon	65026
El Dorado Springs	64744
Eldridge	65463
Elgin	63434
Elijah	65626
Elk Creek	65464
Elkhead	65753
Elkhorn	64077
Elkhurst	65201
Elkland	65644
Elk Springs	64854
Elkton	65650
Ellington	63638
Ellis	64772
Ellis Prairie	65444
Ellisville	63011
Ellsinore	63937
Elm	64061
Elmdale Village (Part of St. Johns)	63114
Elmer	63538
Elmira	64062
Elmo	64445
Elmont	63080
Elmwood	65321
Elsberry	63343
Elsey	65633
Elston	65101
Elvins	63601
Elwood	65802
Ely	63461
Emden	63439
Emerald Beach	65658
Emerson	63454
Eminence	65466
Emma	65327
Empire Prairie	64463
Englewood (Boone County)	65010
Englewood (Jackson County)	64052
Enon (Moniteau County)	65074
Enon (St. Charles County)	63385
Enyart	64453
Eolia	63344
Epworth	63469
Erie	64843
Ernestville	64020
Essex	63846
Estes	63359
Esther	63601
Estill	65274

	ZIP		ZIP		ZIP
Ethel	63539	Fordland	65652	Glenallen	63751
Ethlyn	63369	Forest City	64451	Glencoe	63038
Etlah	63014	Forest Green	65281	Glendale (Putnam County)	63551
Etterville	65031	Forest Hills	65355	Glendale (St. Louis County)	63122
Eudora	65645	Foristell	63348	Glen Echo Park	63121
Eugene	65032	Forker	64651	Glennon	63764
Eunice	65468	Forkners Hill	65632	Glennonville	63933
Eureka	63025	Forrest Mill	64859	Glen Park	63070
Evans	65608	Forsyth	65653	Glensted	65084
Evansville (Buchanan		Fortescue	64452	Glenstone (Part of	
County)	64507	Fort Henry	65259	Springfield)	65804
Evansville (Monroe County)	65270	Fort Leonard Wood	65473	Glenwood	63541
Eve	64741	Fortuna	65034	Glenwood Junction (Part of	
Eveningshade	65552	Fort Zumwalt	63366	Glenwood)	63541
Everett	64725	Foster	64745	Glidewell	65803
Eversonville	64688	Fountain Grove	64659	Glover	63646
Everton	65646	Fox Creek	63069	Gobler	63849
Ewing	63440	Fox Haven	64083	Golden	65658
Excello	65247	Foxwood Springs	64083	Golden City	64748
Excelsior	65084	Frailie	63848	Golden Oak (Part of Kansas	
Excelsior Estates	64062	Frankclay	63644	City)	64117
Excelsior Springs	64024	Frankenstein	65016	Goldman	63050
Excelsior Springs Junction	64077	Frankford	63441	Goldsberry	63539
Exeter	65647	Franklin	65250	Gooch Mill	65068
Fagus	63938	Franks	65459	Goodhope	65608
Fairdealing	63939	Frazier	64401	Goodland	63623
Fairfax	64446	Fredericksburg	65061	Goodman	64843
Fairgrounds (Part of St.		Fredericktown	63645	Goodson	65659
Louis)	63107	Fredville	64850	Gordonville	63752
Fair Grove	65648	Freeburg	65035	Gorin	63543
Fair Haven	64750	Freedom (Camden County)	65052	Goshen	64673
Fairleigh (Part of St.		Freedom (Osage County)	65024	Gospel Ridge (Part of St.	
Joseph)	64506	Freeman	64746	Robert)	65583
Fairmont	63474	Freistatt	65654	Gower	64454
Fairmount (Part of		Fremont	63941	Graff	65660
Independence)	64053	Fremont Hills	65721	Graham	64455
Fair Play	65649	French Village	63036	Grain Valley	64029
Fairport	64447	Friedheim	63747	Granby	64844
Fairview (Newton County)	64842	Friendly Valley	63775	Grand Center	63534
Fairview (Taney County)	65744	Frisbee	63852	Grand Falls	64801
Fairview (Texas County)	65689	Frisco	63846	Grandin	63943
Fairview Acres (Part of Flat		Fristoe	65355	Grand Pass	65339
River)	63601	Frohna	63748	Grandview (Benton County)	65355
Falcon	65470	Frontenac	63131	Grandview (Jackson	
Fanchon	65788	Fruitland (Cape Girardeau		County)	64030
Fanning	65453	County)	63755	Granger	63442
Farber	63345	Fruitland (Greene County)	65648	Graniteville	63650
Farewell	64478	Fulton	65251	Grant (Part of Grantwood	
Farley	64028	Gaines	64735	Village)	63123
Farmer	63339	Gainesville	65655	Grant City	64456
Farmersville	64683	Galena	65656	Grantwood Village	63123
Farmington	63640	Galesburg	64855	Granville	65275
Farmington Correctional		Gallatin	64640	Grassy	63753
Center	63640	Galloway (Part of		Gravelhill	63739
Farrar	63746	Springfield)	65804	Gravelton	63655
Farrenberg	63869	Galmey	65779	Gravois (Part of St. Louis)	63116
Faucett	64448	Galt	64641	Gravois Mills	65037
Fayette	65248	Gamburg	63955	Grayridge	63850
Fayetteville	64093	Game	63830	Grayson	64492
Federal	63601	Gamma	63333	Grays Point	65707
Fee Fee	63141	Garden City	64747	Gray Summit	63039
Femme Osage	63332	Gardenview	63033	Graysville	63551
Fenton	63026	Garfield	65690	Green Acres	64801
Ferguson	63135	Garland	64735	Green Bay Terrace	65079
Fern Ridge	63141	Garrison	65657	Greenbrier	63730
Fernview Estates	63141	Garwood	63957	Green Castle	63544
Ferrelview	64163	Gasconade	65036	Green City	63545
Fertile	63630	Gascondy	65013	Greendale	63133
Festus	63028	Gashland (Part of Kansas		Greenfield	65661
Fidelity	64836	City)	64155	Green Forest	63901
Field (Part of St. Louis)	63108	Gateway Drive (Part of		Green Grove	63559
Filley	64744	Joplin)	64801	Green Lawn	63462
Fillmore	64449	Gateway South	65201	Green-Mar	63026
Fisk	63940	Gatewood	63942	Green Mound Ridge	65669
Flag Springs (Andrew		Gaynor	64475	Green Mountain	65711
County)	64494	Gazette	63359	Green Oaks	63936
Flag Springs (Phelps		Geneva	72438	Green Ridge	65332
County)	65559	Gentry	64453	Greensburg	63531
Flat	65550	Gentryville (Douglas County)	65608	Greenstreet	63013
Flat River	63601	Gentryville (Gentry County)	64402	Greentop	63546
Flatwood	65466	Georgetown (Boone		Green Trail	63026
Fleming	64077	County)	65203	Greenville (Clay County)	64060
Flemington	65650	Georgetown (Pettis County)	65301	Greenville (Wayne County)	63944
Fletcher	63030	Gerald	63037	Greenwood	64034
Flinthill	63346	Germantown	64770	Greer	65606
Flordell Hills	63136	Gerster	64776	Gregory	63435
Florence (Buchanan		Gibbs	63540	Gregory Heights	65202
County)	64504	Gibson	63847	Gretna	65616
Florence (Morgan County)	65329	Gideon	63848	Grimmet	65775
Florida	65283	Gilbert	63855	Grisham	63764
Florissant	63031-34	Gilliam	65330	Grogan	65464
For specific Florissant Zip Codes		Gilman City	64642	Grover	63040
call (314) 837-1810		Gilmore	63385	Grovespring	65662
Floyd	64077	Ginger Blue	64854	Grubville	63041
Flucom	63020	Gipsy	63750	Guilford	64457
Foil	65755	Girdner	65608	Gumbo	63601
Foley	63347	Gladden	65560	Gunn City	64760
Folk	65085	Gladstone	64118	Guthrie	65063
Foose	65622	Glasgow	65254	Hagers Grove	63437
Forbes	64473	Glasgow Village	63137	Hahatonka	65020
Ford City	64463	Glenaire	64068	Hahn	63764

	ZIP
Hailey	65605
Hale	64643
Half Rock	64679
Half Way	65663
Halls	64504
Hallsville	65255
Halltown	65664
Hamilton	64644
Hammond	65762
Hams Prairie	65251
Hancock	65452
Handy	63941
Hanley Hills	63133
Hannibal	63401
Hannon	64762
Happy Hollow	63630
Hardeman	65340
Hardenville	65666
Hardin	64035
Harg	65201
Harper	64776
Harris	64645
Harrisburg	65256
Harrisonville	64701
Harry S. Truman (Part of Independence)	64055
Hart	64865
Hartford	63565
Hartsburg	65039
Hartshorn	65479
Hartville	65667
Hartwell	64788
Hartzell	63848
Harvester	63302
Harviell	63945
Harwood	64750
Haseltine	65802
Hassard	63456
Hastain	65326
Hatfield	64458
Hatton	65231
Havenhurst	64856
Hawkeye	65452
Hawk Point	63349
Hayden	65459
Hayes Park (Part of Sibley)	64088
Hayti	63851
Hayti Heights	63851
Hayward	63873
Hay-Wood City	63736
Hazelgreen	65556
Hazel Run	63628
Hazelwood	63042-45
For specific Hazelwood Zip Codes call (314) 731-1116	
Heatonville	65707
Hebron	65775
Hecla	64653
Hedge City	63460
Helena	64459
Helm	65459
Heman Park (Part of University City)	63130
Hematite	63047
Hemple	64490
Henderson	65742
Hendrickson	63967
Henley	65040
Henrietta	64036
Henry's Acres	65338
Henry Winfield Wheeler (Part of St. Louis)	63101
Herbs	65338
Herculaneum	63048
Hercules	65614
Heritage Hills	64083
Hermann	65041
Hermitage	65668
Hermondale	63877
Hickman Mills (Part of Kansas City)	64134
Hickory Creek	64683
Hickory Hill	65040
Higbee	65257
Higdon	63645
Higginsville	64037
High Gate	65559
High Hill	63350
Highland	63775
Highlandville	65669
Highley Heights (Part of Desloge)	63601
High Point	65042
High Ridge	63049
Hilda	65680
Hill City	65625
Hillhouse Addition (Part of Richland)	65556
Hilliard	63901
Hillsboro	63050
Hillsdale	63133

	ZIP
Hill Top	63935
Hinch	65441
Hinton	65202
Hiram	63947
Hoberg	65712
Hobson	65560
Hocomo	65626
Hodge	64096
Hoene Spring	63025
Hoffman Junction	63628
Holcomb	63852
Holden	64040
Holiday Shores	65326
Holland	63853
Holliday	65258
Holliday Landing	63944
Hollister	65672
Hollow	63069
Hollywood	63821
Holman	65757
Holmes Park (Part of Kansas City)	64131
Holstein	63357
Holt	64048
Holts Summit	65043
Homestead	64024
Homestown	63879
Honey Creek	65101
Hooker	65550
Hoover	64079
Hopewell (Warren County)	63357
Hopewell (Washington County)	63660
Hopkins	64461
Horine	63070
Hornersville	63855
Hornet	64865
Hortense	64735
Horton	64751
House Creek	63965
House Springs	63051
Houston	65483
Houstonia	65333
Houston Lake	64152
Howards Ridge	65655
Howardville	63869
Howell	63303
Howes Mill	65560
H. S. Jewell (Part of Springfield)	65802
Hudson	64724
Huggins	65484
Hughesville	65334
Hugo	65052
Humansville	65674
Hume	64752
Humphreys	64646
Hunnewell	63443
Hunter	63943
Hunters Mill	63664
Hunterville	63846
Huntingdale	64735
Huntington	63456
Huntleigh	63131
Huntsdale	65203
Huntsville	65259
Hurdland	63547
Hurley	65675
Hurlingen	64443
Huron	65613
Hurricane	63764
Hurricane Deck	65079
Hurryville	63640
Hutton Valley	65793
Iantha	64759
Iatan	64098
Iberia	65486
Iconium	64776
Idalia	63825
Idlewild	63960
Ike	65737
Ilasco	63401
Illmo (Part of Scott City)	63780
Imperial	63052
Independence	64050-58
For specific Independence Zip Codes call (816) 836-1440	
Independence Center (Part of Independence)	64057
Indian Creek	63456
Indian Ford	65582
Indian Grove	65236
Indian Hills (Part of Kansas City)	64114
Indian Lake	65453
Indian Point	65616
Indian Springs	64783
Ink	65466
Ionia	65335
Irena	64456
Irondale	63648

	ZIP
Iron Gates	64801
Iron Mountain	63650
Iron Mountain Lake	63624
Ironton	63650
Irwin	64759
Isabella	65676
Isadora	64456
Ishmael	63664
Ives	63936
Jack	65560
Jacket	65745
Jackson (Benton County)	65355
Jackson (Cape Girardeau County)	63755
Jacksonville	65260
Jadwin	65501
James Crews (Part of Kansas City)	64127
Jameson	64647
Jamesport	64648
Jamestown	65046
Jamesville	65631
Jane	64856
Japan	63080
Jarvis	63050
Jasper	64755
Jaudon	64012
Jawdea	64083
Jaywye	63873
Jedburg	63011
Jefferson City	65101-10
For specific Jefferson City Zip Codes call (314) 636-4186	
Jefferson Memorial (Part of St. Louis)	63102
Je-Ke-Ki	65326
Jenkins	65605
Jennings	63136
Jerico	65746
Jerico Springs	64756
Jerk Tail	65667
Jerome	65529
Jesse M. Donaldson (Part of Kansas City)	64195
Jewett	63620
J&G Junction (Part of Joplin)	64801
Johnson City	64724
Johnstown (Bates County)	64770
Johnstown (Jasper County)	64835
Jonesburg	63351
Joplin	64801-04
For specific Joplin Zip Codes call (417) 623-6176	
Jordan	65634
Jordan W Chambers (Part of St. Louis)	63106
Josephville	63385
Judge	65051
Junction City	63645
Junland	63901
Kahoka	63445
Kaiser	65047
Kampville	63301
Kampville Beach	63301
Kampville Court	63301
Kansas City	64101-99
For specific Kansas City Zip Codes call (816) 842-2800	
Karr's	65355
Kaseyville	63534
Kearney	64060
Keener Cave	63967
Keenland	64083
Keethtown	65486
Keightley's Beach	65355
Kellerville	63469
Kelso	63758
Keltner	65720
Kendricktown	64836
Kennett	63857
Kenoma	64759
Keota	63532
Kerr	64429
Kersey Coates (Part of Kansas City)	64105
Ketterman	64790
Kewanee	63860
Keys Summit	63122
Keysville	65565
Keytesville	65261
Kidder	64649
Kiel	63068
Killarney Shores	63650
Kilwinning	63555
Kimberling City (Part of Kimberling City)	65686
Kimberling Hills (Part of Kimberling City)	65686
Kimble	65542
Kime	63944
Kimmswick	63053

	ZIP
Maryville College-Saint Louis	63141
Maryville Gardens (Part of St. Louis)	63118
Masters	65649
Matson	63341
Mattese	63129
Matthews	63867
Maud	63437
Maupin	63061
Mayesburg	64788
Mayfield	63662
Maysville	64469
Mayview	64071
Maywood	63454
Meacham Park (Part of Kirkwood)	63122
Meadowbrook Acres	64083
Meadowbrook Downs (Part of Overland)	63114
Meadowbrook West	65203
Meadville	64659
Mecca	64492
Medford	64040
Medill	63445
Medoc	64855
Mehlville	63129
Meinert	65682
Melbourne	64642
Melrose	63069
Memphis	63555
Mendon	64660
Menfro	63765
Mentor	65742
Mercer	64661
Mercyville	63538
Merriam Woods	65653
Merritt	65720
Merwin	64723
Mesler	63772
Meta	65058
Metro North Mall (Part of Kansas City)	64155
Metz	64765
Mexico	65265
Miami	65344
Michelles Corner	65444
Micola	63877
Middle Brook	63656
Middle Grove	65263
Middletown	63359
Mid Rivers Mall (Part of St. Peters)	63376
Midvale	65571
Midway	65202
Mike	64658
Milan	63556
Mildred	65679
Milford	64766
Millard	63501
Millcreek	63645
Miller	65707
Millersburg	65251
Millersville	63766
Mill Grove	64673
Millheim	63775
Mill Spring	63952
Millville	64085
Millwood	63377
Milo	64767
Milton (Atchison County)	64446
Milton (Randolph County)	65270
Mincy	65679
Mindenmines	64769
Mine La Motte	63645
Mineola	63361
Miner	63801
Mineral Point	63660
Mineral Spring	65625
Mineville (Part of Kansas City)	64161
Mingo	63960
Minimum	63620
Mint Hill	65024
Mirabile	64671
Missionary Acres	63944
Missouri City	64072
Missouri Eastern Correctional Center	63069
Missouri Training Center for Men	65270
Mitchell	63601
Moberly	65270
Modena	64673
Mokane	65059
Moline Acres	63136
Molino	65265
Monark Springs	64850
Monegaw Springs	64776
Monett	65708
Monkey Run	63401
Monroe City	63456

	ZIP
Montague	65669
Montague Hill	65340
Montevallo	64767
Montgomery City	63361
Monticello	63457
Montier	65546
Montreal	65591
Montrose	64770
Montserrat	65336
Moody	65777
Mooresville	64664
Mora	65345
Morehouse	63868
Morgan	65632
Morgan Heights	64836
Morley	63767
Morrison	65061
Morrisville	65710
Morse Mill	63066
Morton	64085
Mosby	64073
Moscow Mills	63362
Moselle	63084
Mosher	63670
Mound City	64470
Moundville	64771
Mountain	65772
Mountain Grove	65711
Mountain View	65548
Mount Airy	65259
Mount Freedom	65050
Mount Hope	63077
Mount Hulda	63525
Mount Leonard	65339
Mount Moriah	64665
Mount Pleasant	65026
Mount Shira	64854
Mount Sterling	65062
Mount Vernon	65712
Mount Zion (Douglas County)	65608
Mount Zion (Henry County)	64740
Mulberry (Barton County)	66756
Mulberry (Bates County)	64722
Mullendike	64083
Munsell	65588
Murphy	63026
Murry	65255
Musicks Ferry	63034
Musselfork	65261
Myrtle	65778
Mystic	63545
Napier	64451
Napoleon	64074
Napton	65340
Nashua (Part of Kansas City)	64155
Nashville	64855
Naylor	63953
Nebo	65470
Neck City	64849
Neelys	63755
Neelyville	63954
Neeper	63445
Neier	63084
Nelson	65347
Nelsonville	63440
Nemo	65724
Neola	65661
Neosho	64850
Netherlands	63851
Nettleton	64644
Nevada	64772
Newark	63458
New Bloomfield	65063
New Boston	63557
Newburg	65550
New Cambria	63558
New Florence	63363
New Frankfort	65349
New Franklin	65274
New Hamburg	63736
New Hampton	64471
New Harmony	63339
New Hartford	63364
New Haven	63068
New Hope	63343
New Lebanon	65237
New Liberty	65588
New London	63459
New Madrid	63869
New Market	64439
New Melle	63365
New Offenburg	63661
New Piper	64788
New Point	64473
Newport	64759
New Santa Fe (Part of Kansas City)	64145
New Survey	63877
Newtonia	64853

	ZIP
Newtown	64667
New Truxton	63381
New Wells	63732
New Woolam	65066
New York	64644
Niangua	65713
Niangua Junction	65713
Nichols (Part of Springfield)	65802
Nind	63501
Ninnescah Park	64740
Nishnabotna	64482
Nixa	65714
Noble	65715
Nodaway	64421
Noel	64854
Norborne	64668
Normandy	63121
Normandy Shopping Center (Part of Northwoods)	63121
Norris	64726
North Boonville	65274
North County	63138
Northeast (Part of Kansas City)	64123
Northern Heights (Part of Kansas City)	64152
North Kansas City	64116
Northland Shopping Center (Part of Jennings)	63136
North Lilbourn	63862
Northmoor	64152
North Noel (Part of Noel)	64854
North Park Mall (Part of Joplin)	64801
North Patton	63662
North Salem	63566
North Shores	65355
Northview	65706
North Wardell	63879
Northwest Plaza (Part of St. Ann)	63074
Northwood Acres	64152
Northwoods	63121
Northwye	65401
Norwood	65717
Norwood Court	63121
Nottinghill	65762
Novelty	63460
Novinger	63559
Number Eight	63532
Nyhart	64730
Nyssa	63932
Oak	64422
Oak Grove (Franklin County)	63080
Oak Grove (Jackson County)	64075
Oak Grove Heights	65801
Oak Hill	65453
Oakland (Laclede County)	65536
Oakland (St. Louis County)	63122
Oakland Park	64870
Oak Leaf	65065
Oak Ridge	63769
Oaks	64118
Oakside	65548
Oakton	64759
Oakview	64118
Oakville	63129
Oakwood (Clay County)	64116
Oakwood (Marion County)	63401
Oakwood Park	64116
Oasis	63347
Oates	63625
Ocie	65761
Octa	63876
Odessa	64076
Odin	65667
O'Fallon	63366
Ogborn	63640
Oglesville	63961
Ohio	64763
Okete	63379
Olathia	65704
Old Appleton	63770
Old Bland	65014
Old Chilhowee	64733
Olden	65789
Oldfield	65720
Old Fredonia	65355
Oldham	65010
Old Linn Creek	65052
Old Merritt	65720
Old Mines	63630
Old Monroe	63369
Old Orchard (Part of Webster Groves)	63119
Old Post Office (Part of St. Louis)	63169
Old Success	65570
Old Woollam	65066

	ZIP		ZIP		ZIP
Olean	65064	Peoria	63622	Princeton	64673
Olive (Dallas County)	65648	Pepsin	64844	Principia	63131
Olive (Part of St. Louis)	63101	Perkins	63774	Prospect	65713
Olivette	63132	Perrin	64477	Prospect Hill (Part of	
Olivewood	64083	Perry	63462	Riverview)	63137
Olney	63370	Perryville	63775	Prosperity	64801
Olympia	64744	Pershing	65061	Protem	65733
Olympian Village	63020	Peru	64730	Pulaski	63935
Omaha	63565	Peruque	63301	Pulaskifield	65708
Ongo	65753	Petersburg	65250	Pumpkin Center	64423
Opolis	66760	Petersville	63055	Purcell	64857
Oran	63771	Pevely	63070	Purdin	64674
Orange	65605	Phelps	64848	Purdy	65734
Orchard Farm	63301	Phelps City	64482	Pure Air	63559
Orchard Lakes	63141	Philadelphia	63463	Purina Farm	63039
Orearville	65349	Phillipsburg	65722	Purman	63935
Oregon	64473	Pickering	64476	Purvis	65079
Oriole	63701	Piedmont	63957	Puxico	63960
Orla	65536	Pierce City	65723	Pyletown	63841
Oronogo	64855	Pierpont	65201	Pyrmont	65078
Orrick	64077	Pierre Laclede (Part of St.		Quarles	64735
Orrsburg	64475	Louis)	63108	Queen City	63561
Osage	65101	Pilot Grove	65276	Quincy	65735
Osage Beach	65065	Pilot Knob	63663	Quitman	64478
Osage Bend	65101	Pinckney	63357	Qulin	63961
Osage Bluff	65101	Pine	63935	Racine	64858
Osage Hill (Part of		Pine Cove	65324	Racket	64735
Kirkwood)	63122	Pine Crest	65571	Racola	63630
Osborn	64474	Pine Lawn	63120	Rader (Maries County)	65582
Oscar	65542	Pineville	64856	Rader (Webster County)	65713
Osceola	64776	Piney Park	63077	Ralls	63401
Osgood	64641	Pinhook	63845	Randles	63740
Osiris	64756	Pioneer	65734	Randolph	64116
Oskaloosa	64762	Piper	64770	Ravanna	64673
Otterville	65348	Pisgah	65237	Ravena (Part of Pleasant	
Otto	63052	Pittsburg	65724	Valley)	64068
Overland	63114	Pittsville	64040	Ravena Gardens (Part of	
Overton	65233	Plad	65764	Pleasant Valley)	64068
Owens	65717	Plato	65552	Ravenwood	64479
Owensville	65066	Platte City	64079	Raymondville	65555
Owsley	65332	Platte Woods	64152	Raymore	64083
Oxford	64475	Plattin	63028	Raytown	64133
Oxly	63955	Plattsburg	64477	Rayville	64084
Oyer	64744	Plaza (Part of Kansas City)	64112	Rea	64480
Ozark	65721	Plaza Shopping Center (Part		Readsville	65067
Ozark Beach	65653	of Springfield)	65804	Rector	65560
Ozark Correctional Center	65652	Pleasant Gap	64730	Redbird	65014
Ozark Springs	65583	Pleasant Green	65276	Red Bridge (Part of Kansas	
Ozark View	63122	Pleasant Grove	65068	City)	64131
Pacific	63069	Pleasant Hill	64080	Redford	63665
Pack	64854	Pleasant Hope	65725	Redings Mill	64801
Pagedale	63133	Pleasant Ridge (Barry		Redman	63431
Painton	63772	County)	65769	Red Oak	64848
Palisades	63011	Pleasant Ridge (Bates		Red Top	65757
Palmer	63664	County)	64780	Reeds	64859
Palmyra	63461	Pleasant Valley (Clay		Reeds Spring	65737
Palopinto	65338	County)	64068	Regal	64624
Papin	63020	Pleasant Valley (Jasper		Reger	63556
Papinsville	64780	County)	64836	Renick	65278
Paradise	64089	Plevna	63464	Rensselaer	63401
Paradise Point	65355	Plew	64848	Renz Correctional Center	65022
Paris	65275	Plymouth	64624	Republic	65738
Paris Springs	65646	Pocahontas	63779	Rescue	64848
Parkcrest Village (Part of		Point Lookout	65726	Revere	63465
Springfield)	65807	Point Pleasant	63873	Reynolds	63666
Parkdale (Jefferson County)	63049	Polk	65727	Rhineland	65069
Parkdale (Platte County)	64152	Pollock	63560	Rhyse	65560
Parker Lake	63775	Polo	64671	Richards	64778
Parkers Park	63347	Pomona	65789	Richards-Gebaur Air Force	
Park Forest (Part of Kansas		Pom-o-sa Heights	65355	Base	64030
City)	64152	Ponce de Leon	65728	Rich Fountain	65035
Parkville	64152	Pond	63038	Rich Hill	64779
Parkway (Franklin County)	63077	Pondfork	65762	Richland	65556
Parkway (Jackson County)	64130	Pontiac	65729	Richmond	64085
Parma	63870	Pony Express (Part of St.		Richmond Heights	63117
Parnell	64475	Joseph)	64503	Richville (Douglas County)	65637
Pasadena Hills	63121	Poplar	65355	Richville (Holt County)	64473
Pasadena Park	63121	Poplar Bluff	63901	Richwoods	63071
Pascola	63871	Portage Des Sioux	63373	Ridgedale	65739
Passaic	64777	Portageville	63873	Ridgely	64444
Passo	65355	Port Hudson	63068	Ridgeway	64481
Patterson	63956	Portland	65067	Ridgley	65647
Patton	63662	Possumwalk	64428	Riggs	65284
Patton Junction	63662	Post Oak	64761	Rimby	65659
Pattonsburg	64670	Potosi	63664	Ripley (Part of	
Paulding	63821	Pottersville	65790	Independence)	64056
Paulina Hills	63010	Powe	63822	Risco	63874
Paydown	65582	Powell	65730	Rise Branch	65324
Paynesville	63371	Powersite	65731	Ritchey	64844
Peace Valley	65788	Powersville	64672	River Aux Vases	63670
Peach Orchard	63848	Poynor	63935	River Bend Estates	63017
Peaksville	63465	Prairie City	64780	Rivermines	63601
Pea Ridge	63080	Prairie Hill	65281	River Roads (Part of	
Pebble Acres	63141	Prairie Home	65068	Jennings)	63136
Peculiar	64078	Prairie Meadows Estate	65201	Riverside (Dunklin County)	63829
Peerless Park	63088	Prathersville (Boone County)	65202	Riverside (Platte County)	64150
Peers	63357	Prathersville (Clay County)	64024	Riverside Inn	64854
Pendleton	63383	Pratt	63935	Riverton	65606
Penermon	63846	Prescott	65483	Riverview	63137
Pennsboro	65752	Preston (Hickory County)	65732	Rives	63875
Pennville	63545	Preston (Jasper County)	64836	Roach	65787

	ZIP
Roads	64668
Roanoke	65230
Roanridge (Part of Kansas City)	64152
Robertson	63042
Robertsville	63072
Robinwood East	63141
Robinwood West	63141
Roby	65557
Rocheport	65279
Rochester	64459
Rockaway Beach	65740
Rockbridge	65741
Rockbridge Estate	65201
Rock Hill	63124
Rockingham	64035
Rock Port	64482
Rock Springs	63601
Rockview	63740
Rockville	64780
Rocky Comfort	64861
Rocky Mount	65072
Rocky Ridge	63670
Rogersville	65742
Rolla	65401
Rolling Hills	64083
Rombauer	63962
Rome	65608
Rondo	65650
Roosterville (Part of Liberty)	64068
Rosati	65559
Roscoe	64781
Rosebud	63091
Rosedale (Part of St. Louis)	63112
Roseland	65323
Roselle	63650
Rosendale	64483
Rothville	64676
Roubidoux	65444
Round Grove	65707
Round Spring	65466
Rover	65775
Rowena	65240
Royal	65559
Royal Heights (Part of Joplin)	64801
Royal Oak	65606
Ruble	63638
Rucker	65243
Rueter	65744
Running Deer	65065
Rush Hill	65280
Rush Tower	63028
Rushville	64484
Russ	65536
Russellville (Cole County)	65074
Russellville (Ray County)	64035
Rutledge	63563
Sabula	63620
Saco	63645
Sac Valley Estates	65785
Safe	65559
Sage Hill	65605
Saginaw	64864
St. Albans	63073
St. Ann	63074
St. Ann Shopping Center	63074
St. Anthony	65486
St. Catharine	64677
St. Charles	63301-04
For specific St. Charles Zip Codes call (314) 724-4810	
St. Clair	63077
St. Clement	63334
St. Cloud	65441
St. Elizabeth	65075
St. Francisville	63430
St. Francois (Part of Flat River)	63601
Ste. Genevieve	63670
St. George (St. Louis County)	63125
St. George (Wright County)	65667
St. James	65559
St. Johns	63114
St. Johns Station (Part of St. Johns)	63114
St. Joseph	64501-08
For specific St. Joseph Zip Codes call (816) 364-3503	
St. Joseph Stock Yards (Part of St. Joseph)	64501
St. Louis	63101-88
For specific St. Louis Zip Codes call (314) 436-4454	

COLLEGES & UNIVERSITIES

	ZIP
Harris-Stowe State College	63103
Maryville University-St. Louis	63141
St. Louis University	63103

	ZIP
University of Missouri-St. Louis	63121
Washington University	63130
Webster University	63119

FINANCIAL INSTITUTIONS

	ZIP
The Boatmen's National Bank of St. Louis	63101
Cass Bank & Trust Company	63127
Citizens National Bank of Greater St. Louis	63143
Commerce Bank of St. Louis, National Association	63105
The First National Bank of St. Louis	63105
Heartland Savings Bank, F.S.B.	63101
Home Federal Savings Bank of Missouri	63141
Jefferson Bank & Trust Co.	63103
Magna Bank of St. Louis	63144
Lemay Bank and Trust Company	63125
Mark Twain Bank	63124
Mercantile Bank of St. Louis, National Association	63101
Pulaski Bank, a Savings Bank	63141
St. Johns Bank and Trust Company	63114
Southern Commercial Bank	63111
South Side National Bank In St. Louis	63116
Southwest Bank of St. Louis	63110
United Missouri Bank of St. Louis, National Association	63102
United Postal Savings Association	63122

HOSPITALS

	ZIP
Barnes Hospital	63110
Christian Hospital Northeast	63136
Deaconess Hospital	63139
Jewish Hospital of St. Louis	63110
Lutheran Medical Center	63118
Metropolitan Medical Center	63121
St. Anthony's Medical Center	63128
St. John's Mercy Medical Center	63141
St. Mary's Health Center	63117
St. Louis University Hospital	63110
Veterans Affairs Medical Center	63125

HOTELS/MOTELS

	ZIP
Frontenac Grand Hotel	63131
Harley of St. Louis	63144
Holiday Inn Southwest	63127
Marriott Pavilion Hotel	63102
Radisson Hotel Clayton	63105
Sheraton at Westport	63146
Stouffer Concourse Hotel	63134

MILITARY INSTALLATIONS

	ZIP
Aviation Systems Command	63120
Coast Guard Base, St. Louis	63111
Defense Mapping Agency, Aerospace Center, Installation One	63118
Defense Mapping Agency, Aerospace Center, Installation Two	63125
United States Army Aviation Troop Command	63120
United States Army Engineer District, St. Louis	63103
United States Army Publications Distribution Center	63114
United States Army Reserve Personnel Center	63132
St. Louis Centre (Part of St. Louis)	63102
St. Louis Galleria (Part of Richmond Heights)	63117
St. Luke	63632
St. Martins	65101
St. Mary	63673
St. Patrick	63466
St. Paul	63366
St. Peters	63376
St. Robert	65583

	ZIP
St. Thomas	65076
Salcedo	63801
Salem	65560
Saline	64632
Saline City	65349
Salisbury	65281
Salt Springs	65340
Samford	63877
Sampsel	64601
Sampson	65713
San Antonio	64443
Sandhills	63563
Sandstone	64767
Sandy Hook	65046
Santa Fe	65282
Santa Rosa	64670
Sapp	65203
Sappington	63126
Saratoga	64854
Sarcoxie	64862
Sarvis Point	65746
Savannah	64485
Saverton	63467
Saxton	64507
Schell City	64783
Schlatitz	63730
Schluersburg	63332
Schofield	65663
Scholten	65605
Schubert	65101
Schuermann Heights (Part of Woodson Terrace)	63114
Scobeville	63857
Scopus	63764
Scotland	64836
Scotsdale	63051
Scott City	63780
Scotts Corner	63352
Scrivner	65074
Scrub Ridge	63873
Seaton	65560
Sedalia	65301-02
For specific Sedalia Zip Codes call (816) 826-8887	
Sedgewickville	63781
Seligman	65745
Sellers	63457
Selma	63028
Selmore	65721
Selsa (Part of Independence)	64057
Senate Grove	63068
Senath	63876
Seneca	64865
Sequoita (Part of Springfield)	65804
Sereno	63775
Seymour	65746
Shackelford	65340
Shade	63851
Shady Dell	63901
Shady Grove (Christian County)	65753
Shady Grove (Pulaski County)	65583
Shady Slope	65065
Shamrock	63361
Shannondale	65560
Sharon	65349
Shaw	65202
Shawnee Mound	64733
Shawneetown	63755
Shearwood	64648
Sheffield (Part of Kansas City)	64125
Shelbina	63468
Shelbyville	63469
Sheldon	64784
Shell Knob	65747
Sheridan	64486
Sherrill	65542
Shibboleth	63630
Shibleys Point	63559
Shirley	63664
Shoal Creek Drive	64801
Shoal Creek Estates	64801
Shook	63963
Short Bend	65560
Shoveltown	63031
Shrewsbury	63119
Sibley	64088
Sigsbee	63434
Sikeston	63801
Silex	63377
Silica	63028
Siloam Springs	65775
Silva	63964
Silver Creek	64801
Silver Dollar City	65616
Silver Lake (Cass County)	64083
Silver Lake (Perry County)	63775

	ZIP		ZIP		ZIP
Silver Mine	63645	Steele	63877	Tempo	63141
Simcoe	64861	Steeles	63935	Ten Brook (Part of Arnold)	63010
Simmons	65689	Steelville	65565	Tenmile	63552
Sinsabaugh	63953	Steffenville	63470	Ten Mile Corner	64784
Sitze Store	63753	Steinmetz	65254	Teresita	65573
Skidmore	64487	Stella	64867	Terre DuLac	63628
Slabtown	65542	Stephens (Boone County)	65202	Thayer	65791
Slagle	65613	Stephens (Callaway County)	65201	The Landing	63456
Slater	65349	Stet	64680	Theodosia	65761
Sleeper	65536	Stewartsville	64490	Thomas Hill	65244
Sligo	65560	Stillings	64079	Thomasville	65438
Smallett	65608	Stinson	65707	Thompson	65285
Smelter Hill (Part of Joplin)	64801	Stockton	65785	Thornfield	65762
Smithfield	64834	Stockton Hills	65785	Thorpe	65644
Smithton	65350	Stockyards (Buchanan		Thox Rock	65550
Smithville	64089	County)	64504	Thrush	64735
Smoky Hollow	65560	Stockyards (Jackson		Tiff	63674
Sni Mills	64075	County)	64102	Tiffany Springs (Part of	
Snow Hollow Lake	63656	Stone Hill	65560	Kansas City)	64152
Snyder	65286	Stoneridge	65737	Tiff City	64868
Solo	65564	Stony Hill	63068	Tiffin	64744
Souder	65773	Stotesbury	64752	Tightwad	64735
Soulard (Part of St. Louis)	63157	Stotts City	65756	Tillman	63730
South Carrollton (Part of		Stoutland	65567	Tilsit	63755
Carrollton)	64633	Stoutsville	65283	Timber	65560
South Cedar City (Part of)	65022	Stover	65078	Times Beach	63025
South County	63129	Strafford	65757	Tina	64682
	63151	Strain	63080	Tindall	64683
For specific South County Zip		Strasburg	64090	Tinkerville	63857
Codes call (314) 846-2728		Stringtown (Butler County)	63901	Tin Town	65622
Southeast (Part of Kansas		Stringtown (Cole County)	65053	Tipperary	63559
City)	64132	Stringtown (Jasper County)	64834	Tipton	65081
Southeast Missouri Mental		Stults	65737	Tipton Ford	64801
Health Center	63640	Stultz	65464	Tip Top (Benton County)	65355
Southern Hills	65301	Sturdivant	63782	Tip Top (Iron County)	63621
South Fork	65776	Sturgeon	65284	Toga	63730
Southgate Shopping Center		Sturges	64601	Toledo	65755
(Part of Springfield)	65804	Sublette	63546	Tolona	63452
South Gifford	63549	Success	65570	Torch	63953
South Greenfield	65752	Sugar Creek	64054	Tower Grove (Part of St.	
South Lee (Part of Lees		Sugar Lake	64484	Louis)	63163
Summit)	64063	Sugartree	64668	Town and Country	63131
South Liberty (Part of		Sullivan	63080	Tracy	64079
Liberty)	64068	Sulphur Springs	63083	Trask	65548
South Lineville	50147	Sumach	63852	Treloar	63378
South Mall (Part of		Summerfield	65013	Trenton	64683
Warrensburg)	64093	Summerset Lake	63020	Trimble	64492
South Point (Part of		Summersville	65571	Triplett	65286
Washington)	63090	Summit	63660	Troutt	63664
South Saint Joseph (Part of		Summit Shopping Center		Troy	63379
St. Joseph)	64504	(Part of Lees Summit)	64063	Truesdail	63383
South Shore	63301	Sumner	64681	Truman Corners (Part of	
South Side (Part of		Sundown	65761	Grandview)	64030
Springfield)	65806	Sunland Hills	63031	Truxton	63381
South Troost (Part of		Sunlight	63622	Tuckahoe	64801
Kansas City)	64131	Sunny Slope (Part of		Tucker	63942
South Troy	63379	Kansas City)	64110	Tuckers Corner	64849
South Van Buren	63965	Sunnyvale (Part of Joplin)	64801	Tunas	65764
Southwest (Part of St.		Sunrise	63855	Turners	65765
Louis)	63139	Sunrise Beach	65079	Turnerville	65548
South West City	64863	Sunrise Lake	63020	Turney	64493
Spalding	63401	Sunset Hills	63127	Turtle	65560
Spanish Lake	63138	Sutherland	65360	Tuscumbia	65082
Sparta	65753	Swan	65759	Tuxedo Park (Part of	
Speed	65233	Swedeborg	65572	Webster Groves)	63119
Spencerburg	63339	Sweden	65608	Twelve Mile	63645
Sperry	63501	Sweet Springs	65351	Twin	65355
Spickard	64679	Sweetwater (Newton		Twin Bridges	65536
Splitlog	64843	County)	64850	Twin Oaks	63011
Spokane	65754	Sweetwater (Reynolds		Twin Springs	63079
Sprague	64779	County)	63638	Tyler	63877
Spring Bluff	63080	Swift	63851	Tyrone	65483
Spring City	64801	Swinton	63730	Udall	65766
Spring Creek	65461	Swiss	65041	Ulman	65083
Springfield	65801-10	Sycamore	65758	Umber	65785
For specific Springfield Zip Codes		Sycamore Hills	63114	Umberland	65785
call (417) 864-0101		Sycamore Valley	65355	Umber View	65785
Spring Garden	65032	Syenite	63651	Umber View Heights	65785
Springhill	64601	Sylvania	65682	Union (Franklin County)	63084
Spring Lake	63501	Syracuse	65354	Union (Ray County)	64062
Springtown	63660	Taberville	64780	Union City	65610
Spring Valley (Camden		Table Rock	65616	Union Star	64494
County)	65065	Taitsville	64671	Uniontown	63783
Spring Valley (McDonald		Tallapoosa	63878	Unionville	63565
County)	64854	Taneyville	65759	Unity Village	64063
Sprott	63670	Tanner	63801	University City	63130
Spruce	64730	Tan Tar Estates	65065	Uplands Park	63121
Spurgeon	64850	Tanyard	64801	Upton	65552
Squires	65755	Taos (Buchanan County)	64448	Urbana	65767
Stahl	63559	Taos (Cole County)	65101	Urbandale (Part of Moberly)	65270
Stanberry	64489	Tara	63123	Urich	64788
Stanhope	65339	Tarkio	64491	Useful	65051
Stanley	63851	Tarrants	63334	Utica	64686
Stanton	63079	Tarsney Lakes	64075	Vale (Part of Kansas City)	64138
Star City	65734	Taskee	63967	Valles Mines	63087
Stark	63353	Tauria	65737	Valley City	65336
Stark City	64866	Taylor	63471	Valley Park	63088
Starkenburg	65069	Tea	63091	Valley View (Benton	
State Correctional Pre-		Teal Bend	65355	County)	65355
release Center	65081	Tebbetts	65080	Valley View (Ste. Genevieve	
Steedman	65077	Tecumseh	65760	County)	63627

	ZIP		ZIP		ZIP
Valley Water Mills	65803	Weaubleau	65774	Williamsburg	63388
Van	65613	Webb City	64870	Williamstown	63473
Van Buren	63965	Weber Hill	63051	Williamsville	63967
Vance	65713	Webster Groves	63119	Willmathsville	63546
Vancleve	65058	Webster Park (Part of		Willow Brook	64448
Vandalia	63382	Webster Groves)	63119	Willow Springs	65793
Vandiver	65265	Wedgewood	63031	Wilson City	63882
Vanduser	63784	Wedgewood Green	63031	Wilton	65039
Vanzant	65768	Weingarten	63670	Winchester (Clark County)	63435
Vastus	63954	Wela	64865	Winchester (St. Louis	
Velda Village	63133	Weldon Spring	63301	County)	63011
Velda Village Hills	63121	Weldon Spring Heights	63301	Winchester Gap	65536
Vera	63334	Wellington	64097	Windsor	65360
Verdella	64762	Wellston (St. Louis County)	63112	Windsor Springs (Part of	
Verona	65769	Wellston (Part of St. Louis)	63112	Kirkwood)	63122
Verona Hills (Part of Kansas		Wellsville	63384	Windyville	65783
City)	64145	Wentworth	64873	Winfield	63389
Versailles	65084	Wentzville	63385	Winigan	63566
Veterans Hospital (Part of		Wesco	65586	Winnwood (Part of Kansas	
Kansas City)	64128	West Alton	63386	City)	64117
Vibbard	64062	West Aurora	65026	Winnwood Gardens (Part of	
Viburnum	65566	Westboro	64498	Kansas City)	64117
Vichy	65580	Westbrooke	65201	Winnwood Lake (Part of	
Victoria	63020	West County Center (Part		Kansas City)	64117
Vida	65401	of Des Peres)	63131	Winona	65588
Vienna	65582	West Ely	63401	Winston	64689
Vigus	63042	West Eminence	65466	Winthrop	64484
Village of Charlack	63114	Western Missouri		Wisdom	65355
Village of Four Seasons	65049	Correctional Center	64429	Wishart	65710
Villa Heights (Part of Joplin)	64801	West Hermondale	63877	Withers Mill	63401
Villa Ridge	63089	West Line	64734	Wittenberg	63786
Vineland	63020	Weston	64098	Wolf Island	63881
Vinita Park	63114	West Park Mall (Part of		Womack	63645
Vinita Terrace	63114	Cape Girardeau)	63701	Woodbine Heights (Part of	
Vinson	63841	Westphalia	65085	Kirkwood)	63122
Viola	65747	West Plains	65775	Woodcliffe	65804
Virgil City	64744	Westport (Part of Kansas		Woodland	63461
Virginia	64730	City)	64111	Woodland Park	65026
Vista	64789	West Quincy	63471	Woodland Shores	65355
Vulcan	63675	Westview	64850	Woodlandville	65279
Waco	64869	Westville	64658	Woodridge	63033
Wagoner	65785	Westwood	63131	Woodruff	64098
Wainwright	65043	Wet Glaize	65567	Woods Heights	64024
Wakenda	64687	Wheatland	65779	Woodson Terrace	63134
Waldo (Part of Kansas City)	64114	Wheaton	64874	Woodville	65247
Waldron	64092	Wheelerville	65605	Woolam	65014
Walker	64790	Wheeling	64688	Wooldridge	65287
Wallace	64439	Whispering Hills	63141	Worland	64752
Wall Street	65590	Whispering Pines	65401	Worlds of Fun (Part of	
Walnut Grove	65770	Whitakerville	65355	Kansas City)	64161
Walnut Shade	65771	White Branch	65355	Wornall (Part of Kansas	
Wanamaker	65340	White Church	65789	City)	64114
Wanda	64866	White City	65020	Worth	64499
Wappapello	63966	White Cloud	65779	Wortham	63601
Wardell	63879	White Hall Fields (Part of		Worthington	63567
Ward Parkway Center (Part		Liberty)	64068	Wright City	63390
of Kansas City)	64114	Whiteman Air Force Base	65305	Wyaconda	63474
Wardsville	65101	Whiteoak	63880	Wyatt	63882
Ware	63050	Whiteside	63387	Wyatt Park (Part of St.	
Warren	63456	Whitesville	64480	Joseph)	64507
Warrensburg	64093	Whitewater	63785	Wyeth	64483
Warrenton	63383	Whiting	63845	Yacht Club Harbor	65065
Warsaw	65355	Whitman	65286	Yarrow	63501
Warson Woods	63122	Wien	63558	Yates	65257
Washburn	65772	Wilbur Park	63123	Yonkerville	65723
Washington	63090	Wilcox	64468	Youngstown	63559
Washington Center	64467	Wilderness	63941	Yount	63775
Wasola	65773	Wildwood	64424	Yukon	65589
Waterloo	64097	Wildwood Estates	65804	Zalma	63787
Watson	64496	Wildwood Lake (Part of		Zanoni	65784
Waverly	64096	Raytown)	64133	Zell	63670
Wayland	63472	Wilhelmina	63933	Zion	63645
Wayne	65772	Willard	65781	Zion Hill	65559
Waynesville	65583	William M Chick (Part of		Zora	65078
Weatherby	64497	Kansas City)	64124		
Weatherby Lake	64152				

	ZIP		ZIP		ZIP
Absarokee	59001	Cameron	59720	Dutton	59433
Acton	59002	Canyon Creek	59633	Eagleton	59520
Adel	59421	Canyon Ferry	59601	East Butte (Part of Butte)	59701
Agawam	59422	Capitol	57724	East Glacier Park	59434
Agency	59831	Cardwell	59721	East Helena	59635
Alberton	59820	Carlyle	59353	East Missoula (Part of	
Albion	59311	Carter	59420	Missoula)	59801
Alder	59710	Cartersville	59347	Ekalaka	59324
Alhambra	59634	Cascade	59421	Elkhorn Hot Springs	59746
Alloy (Part of Butte)	59701	Castle Rock	59327	Elliston	59728
Alpine	59071	Castner Falls	59421	Elmdale	59213
Alzada	59311	Cat Creek	59017	Elmo	59915
Amazon	59632	Centennial (Part of Billings)	59108	Emigrant	59027
Amsterdam	59741	Centerville (Cascade		Enid	59243
Anaconda	59711	County)	59472	Ennis	59729
Anceney	59741	Centerville (Silver Bow		Epsie	59317
Andes	59218	County)	59701	Essex	59916
Angela	59312	Central Park	59714	Ethridge	59435
Antelope	59211	Champion (Part of		Eureka	59917
Apgar	59936	Anaconda)	59722	Evaro	59801
Argenta	59725	Chapman	59537	Evergreen	59901
Arlee	59821	Charles M. Russell (Part of		Everson	59430
Armington	59412	Great Falls)	59405	Fairfield	59436
Ashland	59003	Charlo	59824	Fairview	59221
Ashuelot	59443	Charlos Heights	59840	Fallon	59326
Augusta	59410	Checkerboard	59053	Farmington	59422
Avon	59713	Chester	59522	Feely (Part of Butte)	59727
Babb	59411	Chico Hot Springs	59065	Ferdig	59466
Bainville	59212	Chinook	59523	Fergus	59451
Baker	59313	Choteau	59422	Findon	59053
Ballantine	59006	Christina	59541	Finley Point	59860
Bannack	59725	Church Hill	59741	First Creek	59538
Basin	59631	Circle	59215	First Electronic Combat	
Bearcreek	59007	Clancy	59634	Range Group -	
Bearmouth	59832	Clinton	59825	Detachment 1	59501
Bear Spring	59430	Clyde Park	59018	Fishtail	59028
Beaverton	59261	Coalridge	59219	Flathead Indian Reservation	59831
Beehive	59061	Coalwood	59351	Flatwillow	59087
Belfry	59008	Cobden	59872	Flaxville	59222
Belgrade	59714	Coffee Creek	59424	Floral Park (Part of Butte)	59701
Belknap	59874	Cohagen	59322	Florence	59833
Belle Creek	59317	Colorado Gulch	59601	Floweree	59440
Belmont	59046	Colstrip	59323	Forestgrove	59441
Belt	59412	Columbia Falls	59912	Forest Park	59330
Beltower	59324	Columbia Gardens (Part of		Forsyth	59327
Benchland	59462	Butte)	59701	Fort Belknap	59526
Benteen	59031	Columbia Heights	59912	Fort Belknap Indian	
Biddle	59314	Columbus	59019	Reservation	59526
Big Arm	59910	Comanche	59015	Fort Benton	59442
Bigfork	59911	Condon	59826	Fortine	59918
Bighorn	59010	Conner	59827	Fort Keogh	59301
Big Sandy	59520	Conrad	59425	Fort Kipp	59213
Big Sky	59716	Cooke City	59020	Fort Peck	59223
Big Timber	59011	Coram	59913	Fort Peck Indian	
Billings	59101-08	Corbin	59638	Reservation	59255
For specific Billings Zip Codes call		Corvallis	59828	Fort Shaw	59443
(406) 657-5709		Corwin Springs	59021	Four Buttes	59224
Billings Heights	59105	Crackerville (Part of		Fourchette	59538
Birch Creek Colony	59486	Anaconda)	59711	Four Corners	59466
Birney	59012	Craig	59648	Frazer	59225
Black Eagle	59414	Crane	59217	Frenchtown	59834
Blackfeet Indian Reservation	59417	Creston	59902	Froid	59226
Blackfoot	59417	Crow Agency	59022	Fromberg	59029
Bloomfield	59315	Crow Indian Reservation	59022	Galata	59444
Blossburg	59728	Crow Rock	59301	Galen (Part of Anaconda)	59722
Bonner	59823	Culbertson	59218	Gallatin Gateway	59730
Bonner-West Riverside	59801	Cushman	59046	Gardiner	59030
Boulder	59632	Custer	59024	Garland	59301
Box Elder	59521	Cut Bank	59427	Garneill	59445
Boyd	59013	Dagmar	59219	Garrison	59731
Boyes	59316	Danvers	59457	Garryowen	59031
Bozeman	59715	Darby	59829	Georgetown (Part of	
	59771-72	Dawson (Part of Butte)	59748	Anaconda)	59711
For specific Bozeman Zip Codes		Dayton	59914	Geraldine	59446
call (406) 586-1508		Dearborn	59648	Geyser	59447
Bozeman Hot Springs	59715	De Borgia	59830	Gibson Flats	59401
Brady	59416	Decker	59025	Gildford	59525
Brandenberg	59301	Deerfield Colony	59457	Gilt Edge	59457
Brandon	59749	Deer Lodge	59722	Glacier Colony	59427
Bridger (Carbon County)	59014	Del Bonita	59427	Glasgow	59230
Bridger (Gallatin County)	59722	Dell	59724	Glasgow Air Base	59231
Broadus	59317	Delphia	59073	Glen	59732
Broadview	59015	Dempsey	59722	Glendive	59330
Brock Creek	59731	Denton	59430	Glentana	59240
Brockton	59213	Dentons Point (Part of		Goldcreek	59733
Brockway	59214	Anaconda)	59711	Golden Ridge	59436
Brooks	59457	Devon	59474	Goldstone	59540
Brown (Part of Anaconda)	59711	Dewey	59727	Grace (Part of Butte)	59759
Brown Addition	59472	Dillon	59725	Grant	59725
Browning	59417	Divide (Part of Butte)	59727	Grantsdale	59835
Brusett	59318	Dixon	59831	Grass Range	59032
Buffalo	59418	Dodson	59524	Great Falls	59401-06
Busby	59016	Donald (Part of Butte)	59759	For specific Great Falls Zip Codes	
Butte	59701-03	Dover	59479	call (406) 761-4894	
		Dovetail	59087	Greenfield	59436
For specific Butte Zip Codes call		Downtown (Part of Billings)	59101	Greenough	59836
(406) 494-2107		Drummond	59832	Gregson (Part of Butte)	59748
Buxton (Part of Butte)	59750	Dublin Gulch (Part of Butte)	59701	Greycliff	59033
Bynum	59419	Dunkirk	59474	Hackney (Part of Butte)	59748
Camas	59845	Dupuyer	59432	Half Moon	59912
Camas Prairie	59859	Durant (Part of Butte)	59748	Hall	59837

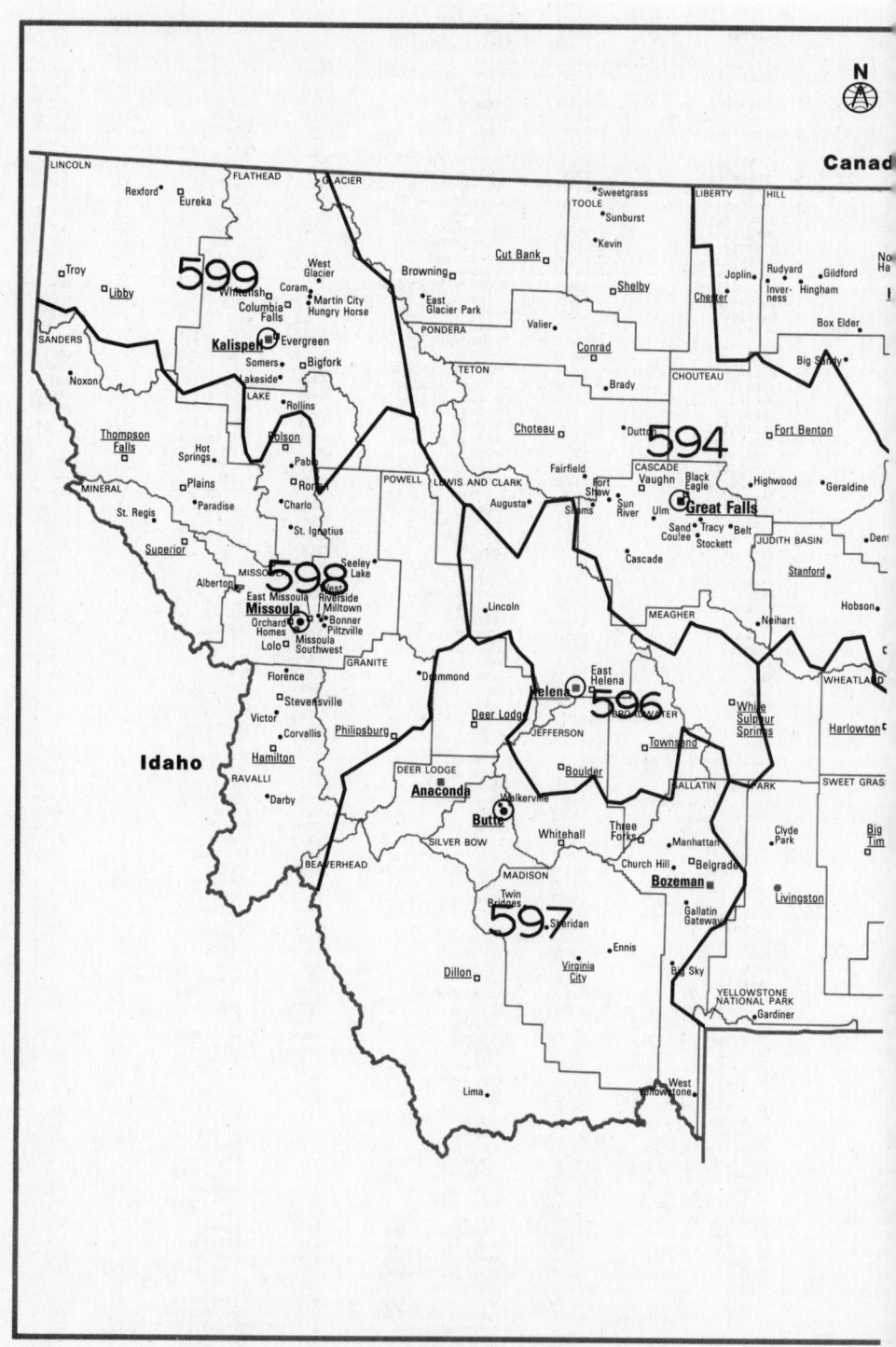

N

Canad

LINCOLN

Rexford • FLATHEAD • Eureka GLACIER

Troy • 599

Libby • West Glacier

SANDERS • Whitefish • Coram • Martin City

Columbia Falls • Hungry Horse

Kalispell • Evergreen

Noxon • Somers • Bigfork

Lakeside

LAKE • Rollins

Thompson Falls • Hot Springs • Polson

Plains • Pablo

Paradise • Ronan

St. Regis • Charlo

MINERAL • St. Ignatius

Superior

MISSOULA • Seeley Lake

Alberton • 598

East Missoula • West Riverside Milltown

Missoula • Bonner Piltzville

Orchard Homes • Missoula Southwest

Lolo

GRANITE • Drummond

Florence • Deer Lodge

Stevensville • Philipsburg

Idaho • Victor • Corvallis

Hamilton • DEER LODGE

RAVALLI • Anaconda • Walkerville

Darby • Butte

BEAVERHEAD • SILVER BOW • Whitehall

MADISON • Twin Bridges

Dillon • 597 • Sheridan

Virginia City • Ennis

Lima

Sweetgrass

TOOLE • Sunburst

Kevin

Cut Bank • LIBERTY • HILL

Browning • Shelby • Chester • Joplin • Rudyard • Gildford

East Glacier Park • Inverness • Hingham

PONDERA • Valier • Box Elder

Conrad • CHOUTEAU • Big Sandy

TETON • Brady

Choteau • Dutton • 594 • Fort Benton

Fairfield • CASCADE • Black Eagle • Highwood • Geraldine

Vaughn

Fort Shaw • Great Falls

LEWIS AND CLARK • Sun River • Sand • Tracy • Belt

Augusta • Ulm • Coulee • Stockett • JUDITH BASIN

Cascade • Stanford

Hobson

Lincoln • MEAGHER • Neihart

WHEATLAND

Helena • East Helena • White Sulphur Springs

596 • BROADWATER • Harlowton

JEFFERSON • Townsend

Boulder • GALLATIN • PARK • SWEET GRAS

Three Forks • Manhattan • Clyde Park • Big Tim

Church Hill • Belgrade

Bozeman • Livingston

Gallatin Gateway

Big Sky • YELLOWSTONE NATIONAL PARK

Gardiner

West Yellowstone

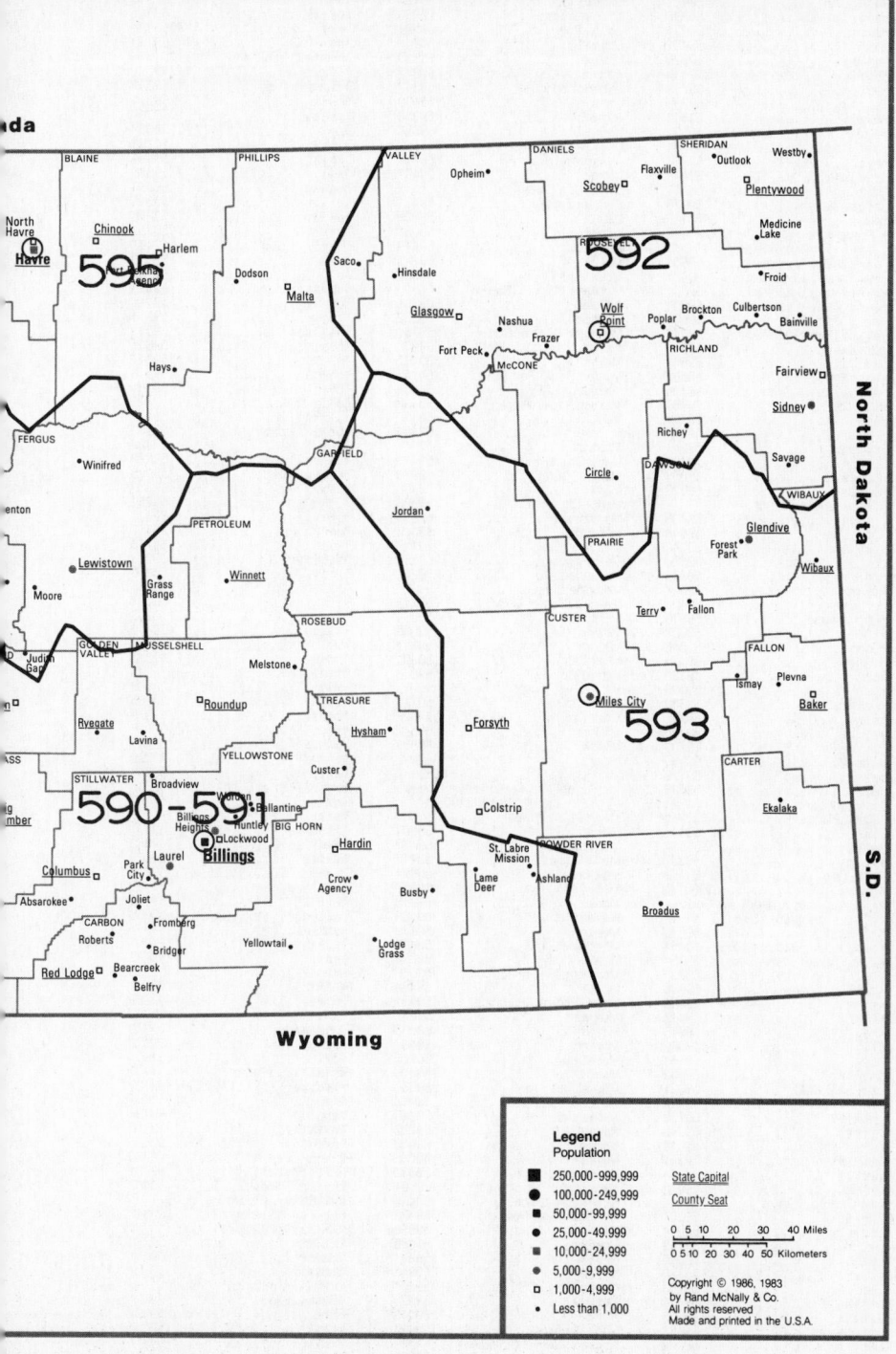

da

| BLAINE | PHILLIPS | VALLEY | DANIELS | SHERIDAN | Westby |

North
Havre
Havre
Chinook
Harlem
595
Ft. Belknap
Agency

Dodson
Malta
Saco
Hinsdale

Glasgow
Nashua
Frazer

Fort Peck
McCONE

Hays

Opheim
Scobey
Flaxville
Outlook
Plentywood

Medicine
Lake

ROOSEVELT
592
Froid

Wolf
Point
Poplar
Brockton
Culbertson
Bainville

RICHLAND
Fairview

Richey
Sidney

FERGUS
Winifred

GARFIELD

Circle
DAWSON
Savage

WIBAUX

PETROLEUM

Lewistown
Jordan

Moore

Winnett

Grass
Range

PRAIRIE
Glendive

Forest
Park
Wibaux

ROSEBUD

CUSTER
Terry
Fallon

Judith
Gap

GOLDEN
VALLEY
MUSSELSHELL

Melstone

FALLON
Ismay
Plevna
Baker

Ryegate
Lavina

Roundup

TREASURE

Hysham
Forsyth

Miles City
593

YELLOWSTONE

Custer

CARTER

STILLWATER
Broadview
Worden
Ballantine
BIG HORN

590-591

Billings
Heights
Huntley
Lockwood
Billings

Columbus
Park
City
Laurel

Absarokee
Joliet

CARBON
Roberts
Fromberg

Red Lodge
Bearcreek
Belfry

Bridger

Hardin

Crow
Agency
Busby

Yellowtail

Lodge
Grass

Colstrip

St. Labre
Mission
POWDER RIVER

Lame
Deer
Ashland

Broadus

Ekalaka

North Dakota

S.D.

Wyoming

	ZIP
Hamilton	59840
Hammond	59332
Hammond Valley	59327
Happys Inn	59923
Happy Valley	59937
Hardin	59034
Hardy	59421
Harlem	59526
Harlowton	59036
Harrison	59735
Hathaway	59333
Haugan	59842
Havre	59501
Havre North	59501
Hays	59527
Heart Butte	59448
Heath	59457
Hedgesville	59078
Helena	59601-26
For specific Helena Zip Codes call (406) 443-3304	
Helena Valley Northeast	59601
Helena Valley Northwest	59601
Helena Valley Southeast	59601
Helena Valley West Central	59601
Helena West Side	59601
Hellgate (Part of Missoula)	59802
Helmville	59843
Heron	59844
Herron Park	59501
Hesper	59106
Highwood	59450
Hilger	59451
Hingham	59528
Hinsdale	59241
Hobson	59452
Hodges	59353
Hogeland	59529
Holiday Village (Part of Great Falls)	59405
Holter Dam	59648
Homestead	59242
Hopp	59520
Hot Springs	59845
Howard	59327
Hughesville	59463
Hungry Horse	59919
Huntley	59037
Huson	59846
Hysham	59038
Iliad	59520
Ingomar	59039
Inverness	59530
Ismay	59336
Jackson	59736
Janney (Part of Butte)	59701
Jardine	59030
Jeffers	59729
Jefferson City	59638
Jefferson Island	59721
Jellison Place	59085
Joliet	59041
Joplin	59531
Jordan	59337
Judith Gap	59453
Kalispell	59901-04
For specific Kalispell Zip Codes call (406) 755-6450	
Kenilworth	59520
Kevin	59454
Kicking Horse	59864
Kila	59920
Kingsbury Colony	59486
Kinsey	59338
Kiowa	59417
Kirby	59016
Klein	59072
Kolin	59451
Kremlin	59532
Lake McDonald	59921
Lakeside	59922
Lakeview	59739
Lambert	59243
Lame Deer	59043
Landusky	59524
Larslan	59244
LaSalle	59912
Last Chance (Part of Helena)	59601
Laurel	59044
Laurin	59749
Lavina	59046
Lavon	59732
Lebo	59053
Ledger	59456
Lennep	59053
Lewistown	59457
Libby	59923
Lima	59739
Limestone	59061
Lincoln	59639

	ZIP
Lindsay	59339
Livingston	59047
Lloyd	59535
Lockwood	59101
Lodge Grass	59050
Lodge Pole	59524
Logan	59741
Lohman	59523
Lolo	59847
Lolo Hot Springs	59847
Loma	59460
Lonepine	59848
Loring	59537
Lost Creek (Part of Anaconda)	59711
Lothair	59461
Lower Sun River (Part of Great Falls)	59401
Lustre	59225
Luther	59051
McAllister	59740
McCabe	59245
McClellans Creek	59635
McGlone Heights (Part of Butte)	59701
McLeod	59052
McQueen (Part of Butte)	59701
Madoc	59222
Maiden	59457
Maiden Rock (Part of Butte)	59743
Malmstrom AFB	59402
Malmstrom Air Force Base	59402
Malta	59538
Manchester	59404
Manhattan	59741
Many Glacier Hotel	59411
Marion	59925
Marsh	59326
Martin City	59926
Martinsdale	59053
Marysville	59640
Maudlow	59714
Maxville	59858
Medicine Lake	59247
Medicine Springs	59827
Melrose (Part of Butte)	59743
Melstone	59054
Melville	59055
Mildred	59341
Miles City	59301
Milford Colony	59648
Mill Creek (Part of Anaconda)	59711
Miller Colony	59422
Mill Iron	59342
Milltown	59851
Miner	59027
Missoula	59801-07
For specific Missoula Zip Codes call (406) 329-2200	
Missoula Southwest	59801
Mizpah	59301
Moccasin	59462
Moffit Canyon	59715
Moiese	59824
Molt	59057
Mona	59213
Monarch	59463
Monida	59739
Montague	59442
Montana City	59634
Montanapolis Springs	59065
Moore	59464
Morel (Part of Anaconda)	59711
Morgan	59537
Mosby	59058
Moulton	59451
Mount Ellis	59715
Muddy	59016
Musselshell	59059
Myers	59038
Nashua	59248
Navajo	59222
Neihart	59465
Nevada City	59755
New Chicago	59832
Newcomb (Part of Butte)	59701
New Miami Colony	59425
New Rockport Colony	59422
Niarada	59852
Nibbe	59088
Nickwall	59201
Nine Mile	59846
Nissler (Part of Butte)	59701
Nohle	59221
Norris	59745
North Browning	59417
Northern Cheyenne Indian Reservation	59043
Northridge Heights (Part of Kalispell)	59901

	ZIP
Noxon	59853
Nye	59061
Oilmont	59466
Olive	59343
Ollie	59313
Olney	59927
Opheim	59250
Opportunity (Part of Anaconda)	59711
Orchard Homes	59801
Ossette	59244
Oswego	59201
Otter	59062
Outlook	59252
Ovando	59854
Pablo	59855
Paradise	59856
Park City	59063
Park Grove	59248
Peerless	59253
Pendroy	59467
Perma	59859
Petrolia	59087
Philipsburg	59858
Piegan	59411
Piltzville	59801
Pine Creek	59047
Pinegrove	59801
Pinesdale	59841
Pinnacle	59916
Pioneer (Silver Bow County)	59701
Pioneer (Yellowstone County)	59102
Pioneer Junction	59923
Plains	59859
Pleasant Prairie	59222
Pleasant Valley	59925
Pleasant View	59330
Plentywood	59254
Plevna	59344
Plum Creek	59457
Polaris	59746
Polebridge	59928
Polson	59860
Pompeys Pillar	59064
Pony	59747
Poplar	59255
Portage	59440
Post Creek	59865
Potomac	59823
Powderville	59345
Power	59468
Pray	59065
Proctor	59929
Pryor	59066
Quinn (Part of Butte)	59743
Racetrack	59722
Radersburg	59641
Ramsay (Part of Butte)	59748
Rapelje	59067
Rattlesnake (Part of Missoula)	59801
Ravalli	59863
Ravenna	59825
Raymond	59256
Raynesford	59469
Red Bluff	59745
Red Lodge	59068
Redstone	59257
Reedpoint	59069
Regina	59538
Reserve	59258
Rexford	59930
Richey	59259
Richland	59260
Ridgelawn	59270
Ridgway	59332
Rimini	59601
Rimrock Mall (Part of Billings)	59102
Ringling	59642
Rising Sun	59434
Riverside	59840
Rivulet	59820
Roberts	59070
Rocker (Part of Butte)	59701
Rockport Colony	59467
Rock Springs (Rosebud County)	59312
Rock Springs (Sheridan County)	59258
Rockvale	59041
Rocky Boy	59521
Rocky Boys Indian Reservation	59521
Rollins	59931
Ronan	59864
Roosville	59917
Roscoe	59071
Rosebud	59347
Rossfork	59457

	ZIP		ZIP		ZIP
Roundup	59072	State Capitol (Part of		Volborg	59351
Roy	59471	Helena)	59601	Volt	59201
Ruby	59710	Staton (Part of Anaconda)	59711	Wagner	59538
Rudyard	59540	Stemple	59633	Walkerville	59701
Ryegate	59074	Stevensville	59870	Wan-i-gan	59065
Saco	59261	Stockett	59480	Ware	59457
Sage Creek	59522	Stone	59837	Warmsprings (Part of	
St. Ignatius	59865	Straw	59418	Anaconda)	59756
St. Labre Mission	59004	Stryker	59933	Warren	82423
St. Marie	59230	Stuart (Part of Anaconda)	59711	Warrick	59520
St. Mary	59417	Suffolk	59451	Washoe	59007
St. Peter	59421	Sula	59871	Waterloo	59759
St. Regis	59866	Sumatra	59083	Wayne	59412
St. Xavier	59075	Summit	59434	Webster	59313
Salmon Prairie	59911	Summit Valley	59721	Weldon	59215
Saltese	59867	Sunburst	59482	Westby	59275
Sand Coulee	59472	Sunnyside (Part of		West Glacier	59936
Sand Creek	59201	Anaconda)	59711	West Lewistown	59457
Sanders	59076	Sun Prairie (Cascade		West Park Plaza (Part of	
Sand Springs	59077	County)	59487	Billings)	59102
Santa Rita	59473	Sun Prairie (Phillips County)	59538	West Riverside	59801
Sapphire Village	59452	Sun River	59483	West Valley (Part of	
Savage	59262	Sunset	59836	Anaconda)	59711
Savoy	59526	Superior	59872	West Yellowstone	59758
Scobey	59263	Swan Lake	59911	Whately	59248
Seaver Park	59601	Sweetgrass	59484	Wheeler	59230
Sedan	59086	Swiftcurrent	59411	Whitefish	59937
Seeley Lake	59868	Tampico	59230	Whitehall	59759
Shawmut	59078	Tarkio	59872	White Haven	59923
Shelby	59474	Teigen	59084	Whitepine	59874
Shepherd	59079	Terry	59349	White Sulphur Springs	59645
Sheridan	59749	The Pines	59859	Whitetail	59276
Shonkin	59450	Thompson Falls	59873	Whitewater	59544
Sidney	59270	Three Forks	59752	Whitlash	59545
Silesia	59041	Toston	59643	Wibaux	59353
Silver Bow (Part of Butte)	59750	Townsend	59644	Wickes	59638
Silver Bow Park (Part of		Tracy	59472	Willard	59354
Butte)	59701	Trego	59934	Williamsburg (Part of Butte)	59701
Silver Gate	59081	Trident	59752	Willow Creek	59760
Silver Star	59751	Trout Creek	59874	Wilsall	59086
Simms	59477	Troy	59935	Windham	59479
Simpson	59501	Truly	59485	Winifred	59489
Sipple	59464	Turah	59825	Winnett	59087
Sleeping Buffalo	59261	Turner	59542	Winston	59647
Smelter Hill	59414	Turner Colony	59542	Wisdom	59761
Somers	59932	Twin Bridges	59754	Wise River	59762
Sonnette	59348	Twin Creeks	59823	Wolf Creek	59648
South Browning	59417	Twodot	59085	Wolf Point	59201
Southern Cross (Part of		Ulm	59485	Woods Bay	59911
Anaconda)	59711	Unionville	59601	Woodside	59875
Southgate Mall (Part of		Utica	59452	Woodworth	59836
Missoula)	59801	Valier	59486	Worden	59088
Spring Creek Colony	59457	Vandalia	59273	Wyola	59089
Springdale	59082	Varney	59729	Yaak Valley	59935
Springdale Colony	59645	Vaughn	59487	Yellowtail	59035
Square Butte	59442	Victor	59875	York	59601
Stanford	59479	Vida	59274	Zortman	59546
Stark	59846	Virgelle	59520	Zurich	59547
Starr School	59417	Virginia City	59755		

Legend
Population

■ 250,000-999,999
● 100,000-249,999
■ 50,000-99,999
● 25,000-49,999
■ 10,000-24,999
● 5,000-9,999
□ 1,000-4,999
• Less than 1,000

★ Military Base

State Capital   County Seat

0 5 10   20   30   40 Miles
0 5 10 20   30 40 50 Kilometers

Copyright © 1986, 1983
by Rand McNally & Co.
All rights reserved
Made and printed in the U.S.A.

N

South Dakota

Wyoming

Colorado

SIOUX

DAWES

SHERIDAN

CHERRY

KEYA PAHA

Whitney   Chadron   Clinton   Gordon   Merriman   Cody Nenzel   Crookston   Springview
Harrison   Crawford   Rushville   Kilgore   Valentine   **692**   BROWN
Hay Springs   Wood Lake   Ainsworth
Marsland   Johnstown   Long Pine

BOX BUTTE   **693**
Hemingford
Alliance

Henry   GRANT   HOOKER   BLAINE
Morrill   Mullen   Seneca   Thedford   Brewster
Lyman Mitchell   MORRILL   GARDEN   Hyannis   THOMAS   Halsey   Dunning
Scottsbluff Terrytown
Gering Minatare
SCOTTS Melbeta   McGrew   Bayard   ARTHUR   McPHERSON   LOGAN   CUSTER
BLUFF   Bridgeport   Anselmo
BANNER   Broadwater   Arthur   Tryon   Stapleton   M
Harrisburg   Gandy   Arnold   Broken Bow
KIMBALL   CHEYENNE   Dalton   Oshkosh   KEITH   **691**   Callaway
Bushnell   Gurley   Lewellen   LINCOLN   Oconto
Dix   Ogallala   Sutherland   North Platte   DAWSON   Eddyvill
Kimball   Potter   Lodgepole   DEUEL   Paxton   Hershey   Gothenburg   Cozad   Le
Sidney   Chappell   Brule   Maxwell   Brady
Big Springs   Farnam
PERKINS   Grant   Elsie   Wallace   Dickens   Wellfleet
Venango   Madrid   Grainton   Maywood   Eustis   Elwood
CHASE   HAYES   Curtis   Moorefield   Smithfield
Lamar   Imperial   Hayes   FRONTIER   Stockville   GOSPER
Center   Holbrook
Wauneta   Hamlet   Arapah
DUNDY   HITCHCOCK   **690**   RED WILLOW   Cambridge   Edison
Indianola   Bartley   FURNAS
Stratton   Trenton   McCook   Hendley   Beave
Haigler   Benkelman   Wilsonville   City
Danbury   Lebanon

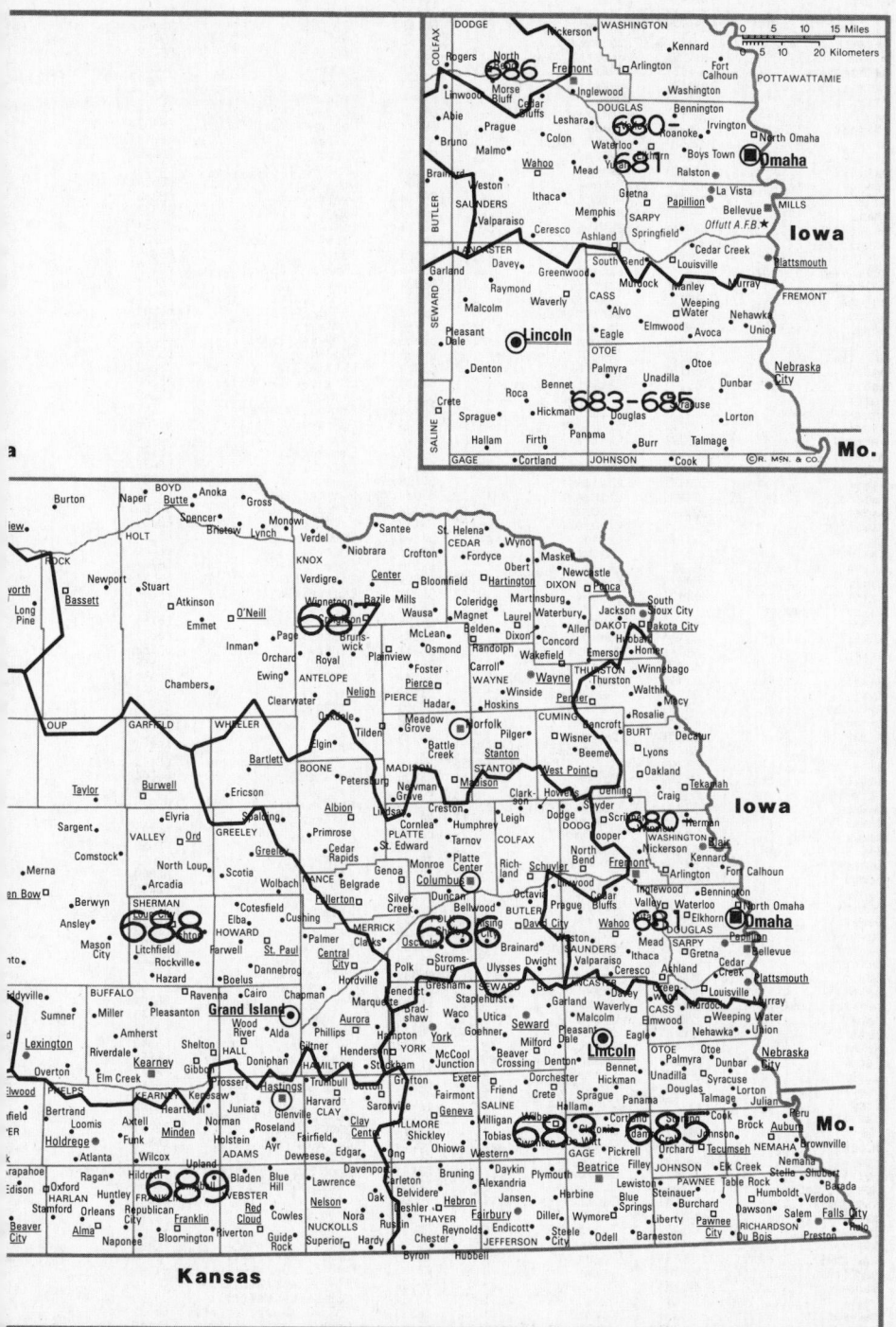

	ZIP		ZIP		ZIP
Abie	68001	Broadwater	69125	Deweese	68934
Adams	68301	Brock	68320	De Witt	68341
Agnew	68428	Broken Bow	68822	Dickens	69132
Ainsworth	69210	Brownlee	69166	Diller	68342
Air Mail Facility (Part of		Brownson	69162	Dix	69133
Omaha)	68119	Brownville	68321	Dixon	68732
Air Park West	68524	Brule	69127	Dodge	68633
Akron	68620	Bruning	68322	Doniphan	68832
Albion	68620	Bruno	68014	Dorchester	68343
Alda	68810	Brunswick	68720	Douglas	68344
Alexandria	68303	Burchard	68323	Downtown (Part of Omaha)	68102
Allen	68710	Burkett (Part of Grand		Du Bois	68345
Alliance	69301	Island)	68801	Dunbar	68346
Alma	68920	Burr	68324	Duncan	68634
Almeria	68879	Burress	68354	Dunning	68833
Aloys	68788	Burton	68778	Dwight	68635
Altona	68787	Burwell	68823	Eagle	68347
Alvo	68304	Bushnell	69128	Eddyville	68834
Amelia	68711	Butte	68722	Edgar	68935
Ames	68621	Byron	68325	Edison	68936
Ames Avenue (Part of		Cadams	68978	Elba	68835
Omaha)	68111	Cairo	68824	Elgin	68636
Amherst	68812	Callaway	68825	Eli	69201
Angora	69331	Cambridge	69022	Elk City	68064
Angus	68961	Campbell	68932	Elk Creek	68348
Anoka	68722	Carleton	68326	Elkhorn	68022
Anselmo	68813	Carroll	68723	Ellis	68310
Ansley	68814	Cedar Bluffs	68015	Ellsworth	69340
Antioch	69340	Cedar Creek	68016	Elm Creek	68836
Arapahoe	68922	Cedar Rapids	68627	Elmwood	68349
Arcadia	68815	Center	68724	Elmwood Park (Part of	
Archer	68816	Central City	68826	Omaha)	68106
Arlington	68002	Ceresco	68017	Elsie	69134
Arnold	69120	Chadron	69337	Elsmere	69135
Arthur	69121	Chalco	68046	Elwood	68937
Ashby	69333	Chambers	68725	Elyria	68837
Ashland	68003	Champion	69023	Emerald	68502
Ashton	68817	Chapman	68827	Emerson	68733
Assumption	68955	Chappell	69129	Emmet	68734
Aten	68730	Cheneys	68506	Enders	69027
Atkinson	68713	Chester	68327	Endicott	68350
Atlanta	68923	Clarks	68628	Enola	68701
Auburn	68305	Clarkson	68629	Ericson	68637
Aurora	68818	Clatonia	68328	Ericson Lake	68637
Autumn Hills (Part of		Clay Center	68933	Eustis	69028
Omaha)	68134	Clearwater	68726	Ewing	68735
Avoca	68307	Clinton	69343	Exeter	68351
Axtell	68924	Cody	69211	Fairbury	68352
Ayr	68925	Coleridge	68727	Fairfield	68938
Bancroft	68004	College View (Part of		Fairmont	68354
Barada	68355	Lincoln)	68506	Falls City	68355
Barneston	68309	Colon	68018	Farnam	69029
Bartlett	68622	Colton	69162	Farwell	68838
Bartley	69020	Columbus	68601-02	Filley	68357
Bassett	68714	For specific Columbus Zip Codes		Firth	68358
Battle Creek	68715	call (402) 564-3208		Florence (Part of Omaha)	68112
Bayard	69334	Comstock	68828	Fontanelle	68044
Bazile Mills	68729	Concord	68728	Fordyce	68736
Beatrice	68310	Conestoga Mall (Part of		Fort Calhoun	68023
Beaver City	68926	Grand Island)	68801	Fort Robinson	69339
Beaver Crossing	68313	Constance	68730	Foster	68737
Bee	68314	Cook	68329	Franklin	68939
Beemer	68716	Cordova	68330	Fremont	68025
Belden	68717	Cornlea	68642	Friend	68359
Belgrade	68623	Cortland	68331	Fullerton	68638
Bellevue	68005	Cotesfield	68829	Funk	68940
Bellwood	68624	Cowles	68930	Gandy	69163
Belvidere	68315	Cozad	69130	Garland	68360
Benedict	68316	Crab Orchard	68332	Garrison	68632
Benkelman	69021	Craig	68019	Gates	68822
Bennet	68317	Crawford	69339	Gateway Shopping Center	
Bennington	68007	Creighton	68729	(Part of Lincoln)	68505
Benson (Part of Omaha)	68104	Creston	68631	Geneva	68361
Berea	69301	Crete	68333	Genoa	68640
Bertrand	68927	Crofton	68730	Gering	69341
Berwyn	68819	Crookston	69212	Gibbon	68840
Bignell	69151	Crossroads Mall (Part of		Gilead	68362
Big Springs	69122	Omaha)	68114	Giltner	68841
Bingham	69335	Crowell	68057	Gladstone	68352
Bixby	68979	Crown Point (Part of		Glen	69339
Bladen	68928	Omaha)	68122	Glenover (Part of Beatrice)	68310
Blair	68008	Culbertson	69024	Glenvil	68941
Bloomfield	68718	Curtis	69025	Glenwood Park	68847
Bloomington	68929	Cushing	68873	Goehner	68364
Blue Hill	68930	Dakota City	68731	Good Samaritan Village	
Blue River Lodge	68333	Dalton	69131	(Part of Hastings)	68901
Blue Springs	68318	Dana College	68008	Gordon	69343
Boelus	68820	Danbury	69026	Gothenburg	69138
Boone	68625	Dannebrog	68831	Grafton	68365
Bostwick	68978	Darr	69130	Grainton	69169
Bow Valley	68739	Davenport	68335	Grand Island	68801-03
Boys Town	68010	Davey	68336	For specific Grand Island Zip	
Bradshaw	68319	David City	68632	Codes call (308) 381-5581	
Brady	69123	Dawson	68337	Grand Island Mall (Part of	
Brainard	68626	Daykin	68338	Grand Island)	68801
Brandon	69140	Debolt (Part of Omaha)	68152	Grant	69140
Breslau	68765	Decatur	68020	Greeley	68842
Brewster	68821	Denman	68956	Green Meadows	68164
Bridgeport	69336	Denton	68339	Greenwood	68366
Briggs	68122	Deshler	68340	Gresham	68367
Bristow	68719	De Soto	68023	Gretna	68028

	ZIP		ZIP		ZIP
Ringgold	69167	Sparks	69220	Valparaiso	68065
Rising City	68658	Sparta	68783	Venango	69168
Riverdale	68870	Spencer	68777	Venice	68069
Riverside Lakes	68069	Spencer Park (Part of		Verdel	68760
Riverton	68972	Hastings)	68901	Verdigre	68783
Roanoke (Part of Omaha)	68134	Sprague	68438	Verdon	68457
Roca	68430	Springfield	68059	Vesta	68450
Rockford	68310	Springview	68778	Veterans' Administration	
Rockville	68871	Stamford	68977	Hospital (Part of Omaha)	68105
Rogers	68659	Stanton	68779	Virginia	68458
Rosalie	68055	Staplehurst	68439	Wabash	68407
Roscoe	69153	Stapleton	69163	Waco	68460
Rose	68772	State House (Part of		Wagners Lake	68601
Roseland	68973	Lincoln)	68509	Wahoo	68066
Rosemont	68930	Steele City	68440	Wakefield	68784
Rosenburg	68644	Steinauer	68441	Walkers Valley View	68730
Royal	68773	Stella	68442	Wallace	69169
Rulo	68431	Sterling	68443	Walthill	68067
Rushville	69360	Still Meadow (Part of		Walton	68461
Ruskin	68974	Omaha)	68122	Wann	68003
Saddle Creek (Part of		Stockham	68818	Washington	68068
Omaha)	68132	Stockville	69042	Waterbury	68785
St. Bernard	68644	Stock Yards (Part of		Waterloo	68069
St. Columbans	68056	Omaha)	68107	Wauneta	69045
St. Edward	68660	Strang	68444	Wausa	68786
St. Helena	68774	Stratton	69043	Waverly	68462
St. James	68792	Stromsburg	68666	Wayne	68787
St. Libory	68872	Stuart	68780	Wayside	69337
St. Mary	68432	Sumner	68878	Weeping Water	68463
St. Paul	68873	Sunnyslope (Part of Omaha)	68134	Weissert	68880
St. Stephens	68957	Sunol	69149	Wellfleet	69170
Salem	68433	Superior	68978	Western	68464
Santee	68760	Surprise	68667	Westerville	68881
Santee Indian Reservation	68760	Sutherland	69165	West Omaha (Part of	
Sarben	69155	Sutton	68979	Omaha)	68114
Sargent	68874	Swanton	68445	Weston	68070
Saronville	68975	Swedeburg	68066	West Point	68788
Schaupps	68817	Syracuse	68446	Westroads Shopping Center	
Schuyler	68661	Table Rock	68447	(Part of Omaha)	68114
Scotia	68875	Talmage	68448	Westwood Plaza (Part of	
Scottsbluff	69361-63	Tamora	68434	Omaha)	68144
For specific Scottsbluff Zip Codes		Tarnov	68642	Whiteclay	69365
call (308) 635-1121		Taylor	68879	Whitman	69366
Scribner	68057	Tecumseh	68450	Whitney	69367
Seneca	69161	Tekamah	68061	Wilber	68465
Seward	68434	Telbasta	68002	Wilcox	68982
Seymour Park (Part of		Terrytown	69341	Willis	68743
Ralston)	68127	Thayer	68460	Willow Island	69171
Shelby	68662	Thedford	69166	Wilsonville	69046
Shelton	68876	Thompson	68352	Winnebago	68071
Shickley	68436	Thurston	68062	Winnebago Indian	
Sholes	68771	Tilden	68781	Reservation	68071
Shubert	68437	Tobias	68453	Winnetoon	68789
Sidney	69162	Touhy	68065	Winside	68790
Silver Creek	68663	Trenton	69044	Winslow	68072
Skyline	68022	Trumbull	68980	Wisner	68791
Smithfield	68976	Tryon	69167	Wolbach	68882
Snyder	68664	Uehling	68063	Wood Lake	69221
South Bend	68058	Ulysses	68669	Woodland Park	68701
South Minden (Part of		Unadilla	68454	Wood River	68883
Minden)	68959	Union	68455	Worms	68872
South Omaha (Part of		University Place (Part of		Wymore	68466
Omaha)	68107	Lincoln)	68504	Wynot	68792
Southroads Shopping		Upland	68981	York	68467
Center (Part of Bellevue)	68005	Utica	68456	Yossem's Paradise Valley	
South Sioux City	68776	Valentine	69201	(Part of Omaha)	68134
South Yankton	57078	Valley	68064	Yutan	68073
Spalding	68665				

	ZIP		ZIP		ZIP
Alamo	89001	Fallon Indian Reservation	89406	Meadowood Mall (Part of	
Amargosa Valley	89020	Fallon Naval Air Station	89406	Reno)	89502
Arthur	89833	Fallon Station	89406	Meadows, The (Part of Las	
Ash Springs	89017	Federal (Part of Las Vegas)	89101	Vegas)	89107
Atlanta	89043	Fernley	89408	Mercury	89023
Austin	89310	Fish Spring	89410	Mesquite	89024
Baker	89311	Flanigan	89501	Metropolis	89835
Basalt	93512	Fort McDermitt Indian		Midas	89414
Battle Mountain	89820	Reservation (NV part)	89421	Mill City	89418
Beatty	89003	Fort Mojave Indian		Mina	89422
Belmont	89022	Reservation (NV part)	92363	Minden	89423
Beowawe	89821	Gabbs	89409	Moapa	89025
Black Springs	89506	Galena (Part of Reno)	89502	Moapa River Indian	
Blue Diamond	89004	Galena Forest Estates	89511	Reservation	89025
Bluffs (Part of Elko)	89801	Gardnerville	89410	Moapa Valley	89040
Bonanza (Part of Las		Gardnerville Ranchos	89410	Mogul	89523
Vegas)	89106	Garside (Part of Las Vegas)	89412	Montello	89830
Boulder City	89005-06	Genoa	89411	Mottsville	89410
For specific Boulder City Zip		Gerlach	89412	Mountain City	89831
Codes call (702) 293-2618		Glenbrook	89413	Mountain Springs	89101
Boulevard Mall	89109	Glendale (Clark County)	89025	Mountain View Estates (Part	
Buckeye	89410	Glendale (Washoe County)	89431	of Elko)	89801
Bunkerville	89007	Golconda	89414	Mount Montgomery	93512
Cactus Springs	89101	Golden Valley	89501	Mustang	89431
Caliente	89008	Goldfield	89013	Naval Ammunition Depot	89415
Cal-Nev-Ari	89039	Gold Hill	89440	Nellis Air Force Base	89191
Carlin	89822	Gold Point	89013	Nelson	89046
Carlton Square (Part of		Goodsprings	89019	New Empire (Part of Carson	
North Las Vegas)	89030	Goshute Indian Reservation		City)	89701
Carp	89008	(NV part)	84034	New Washoe City	89701
Carson City	89701-21	Greenbrae (Part of Sparks)	89431	Nixon	89424
For specific Carson City Zip		Halleck	89824	North Battle Mountain	89820
Codes call (702) 887-7000		Hawthorne	89415-16	North 7 Estates (Part of	
Carson Meadows (Part of		For specific Hawthorne Zip Codes		Elko)	89801
Carson City)	89701	call (702) 945-2850		North Fork	89801
Carvers	89045	Hazen	89408	North Las Vegas	89030-36
Caselton	89043	Henderson	89009	For specific North Las Vegas Zip	
Centerville	89410		89011-12	Codes call (702) 642-6384	
Chambers Field	89410		89014-16	Northridge (Part of Elko)	89801
Chaparral Ridge (Part of		For specific Henderson Zip Codes		North Valley (Part of Reno)	89501
Elko)	89801	call (702) 565-8388		Oasis	89835
Charleston	89801	Hidden Valley	89502	Oreana	89419
Charleston Park	89108	Highland Estates	89705	Orovada	89425
Charleston Plaza (Part of		Hiko	89017	Overton	89040
Las Vegas)	89104	Horizon Hills	89501	Owyhee	89832
Cherry Creek	89301	Huffakers (Part of Reno)	89501	Pahrump	89041
Circus Circus	89114	Humboldt	89418	Palomino Valley	89433
Clover Hills (Part of Elko)	89801	Humboldt Conservation		Panaca	89042
Coaldale	89049	Camp	89445	Panther Valley (Part of	
Cobre	89835	Huntridge (Part of Las		Reno)	89501
Cold Springs	89406	Vegas)	89104	Paradise	89109
Contact	89825	Imlay	89418	Paradise Hill	89445
Cottonwood Cove	89046	Incline Village	89450-52	Paradise Valley (Clark	
Country Lane Estates	89410	For specific Incline Village Zip		County)	89119
Crescent Valley	89821	Codes call (702) 831-0382		Paradise Valley (Humboldt	
Crystal Bay	89450-52	Incline Village-Crystal Bay	89450	County)	89426
For specific Crystal Bay Zip		Indian Hills	89705	Park Lane Center (Part of	
Codes call (702) 831-0654		Indian Springs	89018	Reno)	89502
Crystal Bay	89402	Indian Springs Air Force		Park Terrace (Part of	
Currant	89301	Auxiliary Field	89018	Carson City)	89701
Currie	89301	Ione	89310	Patrick	89431
Dayton (Lyon County)	89403	Jackpot	89825	Pinenut	89410
Deep Creek	89801	Jacks Valley	89705	Pioche	89043
Deeth	89823	Jarbidge	89826	Pittman (Part of Henderson)	89015
Denio	89404	Jean	89019	Pleasant Valley	89511
Dixie Valley	89406	Jiggs	89801	Preston	89301
Downtown (Part of Las		Johnson Lane	89423	Pyramid Lake Indian	
Vegas)	89101	Kingsbury	89449	Reservation	89424
Downtown (Part of Reno)	89501	Kingston	89310	Quail Ridge	89403
Dresslerville	89410	Lake Mead Base	89191	Rachel	89001
Duck Valley Indian		Lakeridge	89448	Raleigh Heights (Part of	
Reservation (NV part)	89832	Lake Village	89449	Reno)	89506
Duckwater	89314	Lamoille	89828	Rancho Estates	89410
Duckwater Indian		Lane	89301	Rancho Haven	89501
Reservation	89314	Las Vegas	89101-85	Rancho Vista	89403
Dunphy	89820		89193-99	Red Rock Estates	89501
Dyer	89010	For specific Las Vegas Zip Codes		Red Rock Vista (Part of Las	
East Elko (Part of Elko)	89802	call (702) 361-9450		Vegas)	89128
East Ely (Part of Ely)	89315	Las Vegas Highlands (Part			89133
Eastland Hills (Part of Elko)	89801	of North Las Vegas)	89030	For specific Red Rock Vista Zip	
East Las Vegas	89112	Laughlin	89028-29	Codes call (702) 256-7580	
Echo Bay	89040	For specific Laughlin Zip Codes		Reno	89501-70
Edgewood	89449	call (702) 298-6161		For specific Reno Zip Codes call	
Elburz	89824	Lawton	89503	(702) 788-0600	
Eldorado Lakes	89403	Lee	89801	Rhyolite	89003
Elgin	89008	Lemmon Valley	89501	Ridgeview Estates	89705
Elko	89801-03	Lida	89013	Riverside	89007
For specific Elko Zip Codes call		Lincoln Park	89413	River Village	89403
(702) 738-6444		Lockwood	89431	Rixie's	89820
Elk Point	89448	Logandale	89021	Round Hill Village	89448
Ely	89301	Lovelock	89419	Round Mountain	89045
	89314-15	Lower Kingsbury	89449	Rowland	83604
For specific Ely Zip Codes call		Lund	89317	Ruby Valley	89833
(702) 289-4537		Luning	89420	Ruby Valley Indian	
Empire	89405	McDermitt	89421	Reservation	89701
Enterprise	89118	McGill	89318	Ruhenstroth	89410
Etna	89008	Majors Place	89301	Ruth	89319
Eureka	89316	Manhattan	89022	Sagecrest Complex (Part of	
Fallon	89406-07	Mason	89447	Elko)	89801
For specific Fallon Zip Codes call		Mayberry-Highland Park		Sage Hills 2 (Part of Elko)	89801
(702) 423-4442		(Part of Reno)	89501	Sandy	89019

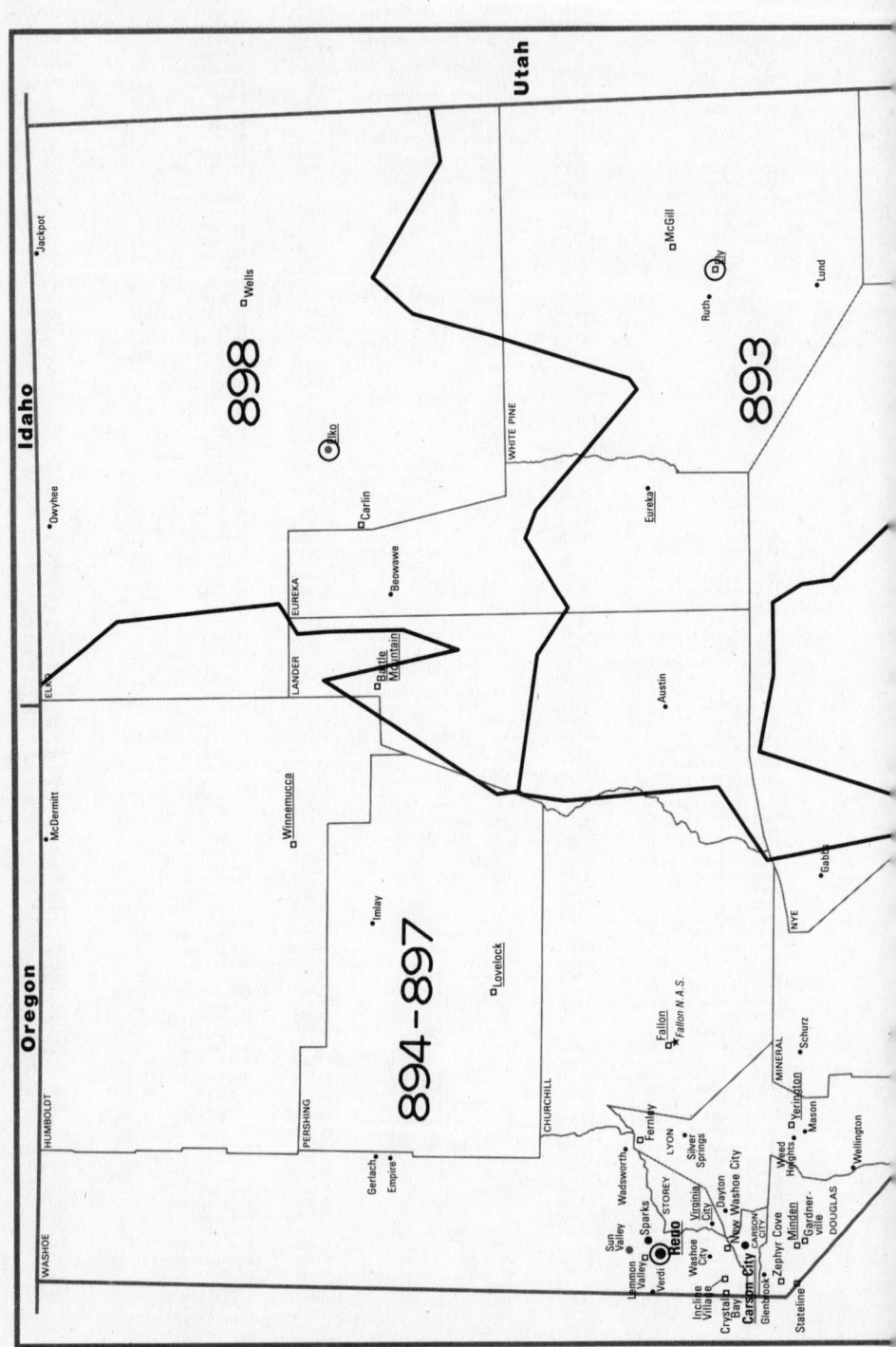

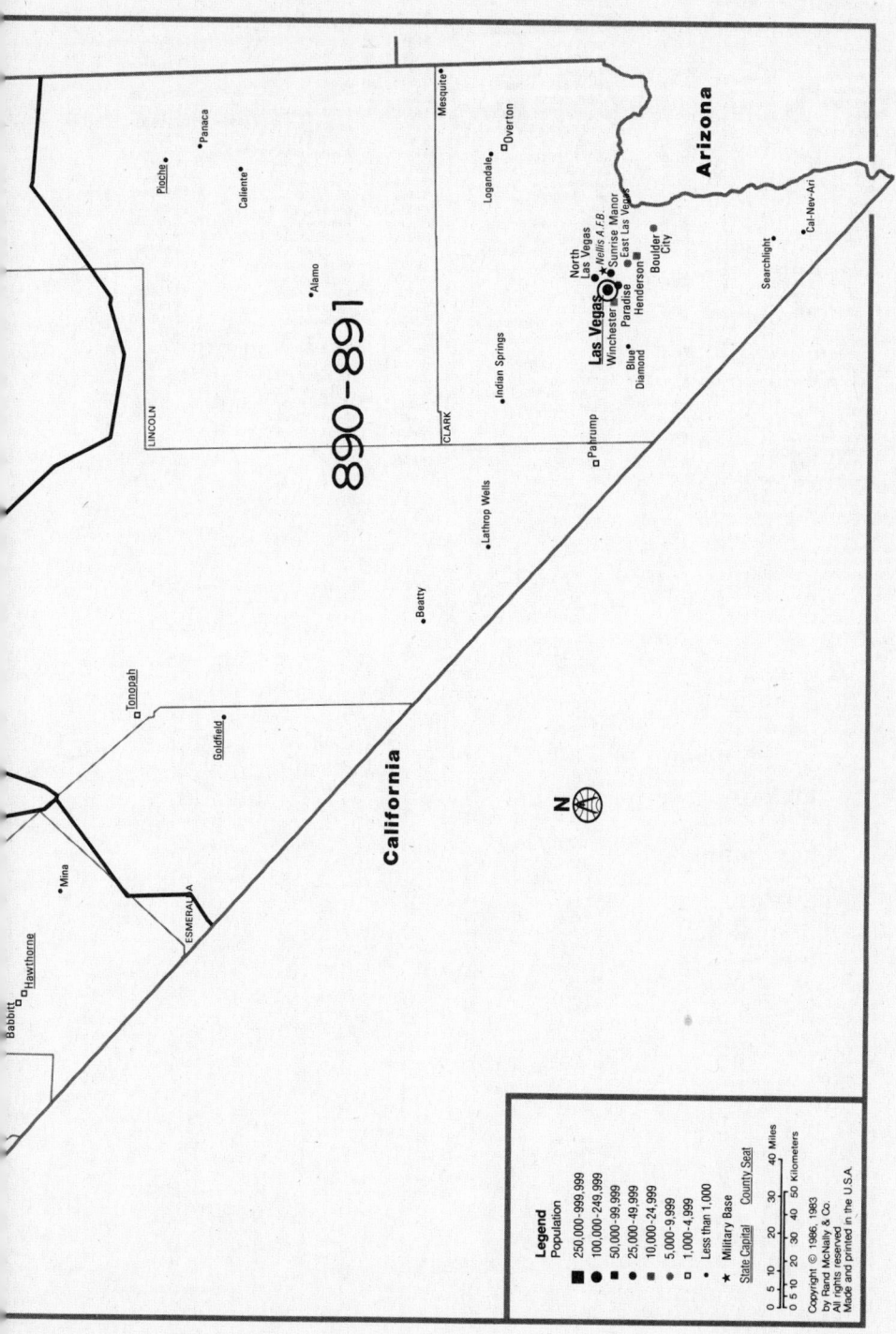

Arizona

Mesquite•

Panaca•

Overton•
Logandale•

Cal-Nev-Ari•

North
Las Vegas• Nellis A.F.B
Winchester Sunrise Manor
Las Vegas Paradise East Las Vegas
Blue Henderson• Boulder•
Diamond City

Searchlight•

Ploche
□

Caliente•

Alamo•

Indian Springs•

890-891

LINCOLN

CLARK

Pahrump
□

Lathrop Wells•

Beatty•

California

Tonopah
□

Goldfield

Mina•

ESMERALDA

Baabitt
□ Hawthorne

N

Legend
Population
■ 250,000-999,999
● 100,000-249,999
■ 50,000-99,999
■ 25,000-49,999
● 10,000-24,999
● 5,000-9,999
● 1,000-4,999
□ Less than 1,000
★ Military Base
State Capital County Seat

0 5 10 20 30 40 Miles
0 5 10 20 30 40 50 Kilometers

	ZIP		ZIP		ZIP
San Jacinto	89825	Stateline (Douglas County)	89449	Verdi	89439
Satalite Hills (Part of Sparks)	89431	Steamboat	89511	Virginia City	89440
Schurz	89427	Steptoe	89318	Vista (Part of Sparks)	89434
Scotty's Junction	89013	Stewart (Part of Carson		Vya	96104
Searchlight	89046	City)	89701	Wabuska	89447
Shafter	89835	Stewarts Point	89040	Wadsworth	89442
Sheridan	89410	Stillwater	89406	Walker Lake	89415
Sheridan Acres	89410	Summit Lake Indian		Walker River Indian	
Shoshone	89301	Reservation	89701	Reservation	89427
Sierra (Part of Reno)	89506	Suncrest (Part of Elko)	89801	Warm Springs	89049
Silverada Mall (Part of		Sundance Estates (Part of		Washington (Part of Reno)	89503
Reno)	89431	Elko)	89801	Washoe City	89701
Silverado Heights	89705	Sunrise Manor	89110	Washoe-Dresslerville Indian	
Silver City	89428	Sun Valley	89433	Reservation	89410
Silverpeak	89047	Sutcliffe	89501	Weed Heights	89447
Silver Springs	89429	Tahoe Village	89449	Wellington	89444
Skyland	89448	Tempiute	89001	Wells	89835
Sloan	89103	Thomas Creek Estates	89501	Wendover	89883
Smith	89430	Thousand Springs	89835	Westland Mall (Part of Las	
Smith Valley	89430	Timberline Estates (Part of		Vegas)	89102
Southern Nevada		Carson City)	89703	West Wendover	89883
Correctional Center	89019	Tonopah	89049	Westwood Village	89423
South Fork Indian		Topaz Junction	89410	Willow Beach	89005
Reservation	89801	Topaz Lake	89410	Winchester	89101
Southgate	89801	Topaz Ranch Estates	89444	Winnemucca	89445-46
South Hills	89501	Tracy-Clark	89431	For specific Winnemucca Zip	
Spanish Springs Valley	89433	Tuscarora	89834	Codes call (702) 623-2456	
Sparks	89431-36	Tyrolean Village	89450	Yerington	89447
For specific Sparks Zip Codes call		Unionville	89418	Yerington Indian	
(702) 359-1161		University (Part of Reno)	89507	Reservation	89447
Spring Creek	89801	Upper Kingsbury	89449	Yomba Indian Reservation	89310
Spring Valley	89103	Ursine	89043	Zephyr Cove	89448
Stagecoach	89429	Valmy	89438	Zephyr Cove-Round Hill	
Stanton Park (Part of		Vegas View (Part of North		Village	89448
Carson City)	89701	Las Vegas)	89030		
Stateline (Clark County)	89019				

Name	ZIP	Name	ZIP	Name	ZIP
Ackerman's Trailer Park	03079	Cambridge (Town)	03588	Danville (Town)	03819
Acworth	03601	Camp Hedding	03042	Davisville	03229
Acworth (Town)	03601	Campton	03223	Deerfield	03037
Albany	03818	Campton (Town)	03223	Deerfield (Town)	03037
Albany (Town)	03818	Campton Hollow	03264	Deerfield Parade	03037
Alexandria	03222	Campton Lower Village	03223	Deering	03244
Alexandria (Town)	03222	Campton Upper Village	03223	Deering (Town)	03244
Allenstown	03275	Canaan	03741	Derry	03038
Allenstown (Town)	03275	Canaan (Town)	03741	Derry (Town)	03038
Alstead	03602	Canaan Center	03741	Derry Village	03038
Alstead (Town)	03602	Canaan Street	03741	Dixs Grant (Town)	03576
Alstead Center	03602	Candia	03034	Dixville (Town)	03576
Alton	03809	Candia (Town)	03034	Dixville Notch	03576
Alton (Town)	03809	Candia Four Corners	03034	Dorchester	03266
Alton Bay	03810	Candia Village	03034	Dorchester (Town)	03266
Amherst	03031	Canobie Lake	03079	Dover	03820
Amherst (Town)	03031	Canterbury (Town)	03224	Dover Point (Part of Dover)	03820
Andover	03216	Canterbury	03224	Drewsville	03604
Andover (Town)	03216	Carroll (Town)	03595	Dublin	03444
Antrim	03440	Cascade	03581	Dublin (Town)	03444
Antrim (Town)	03440	Cedar Pond	03570	Dummer (Town)	03588
Arlington Park	03073	Center Barnstead	03225	Dunbarton	03301
Ashland	03217	Center Conway	03813	Dunbarton (Town)	03301
Ashland (Town)	03217	Center Effingham	03882	Durham	03824
Ashuelot	03441	Center Harbor	03226	Durham (Town)	03824
Atkinson	03811	Center Harbor (Town)	03226	East Alstead	03602
Atkinson (Town)	03811	Center Haverhill	03774	East Alton	03809
Atkinson and Gilmanton		Center Ossipee	03814	East Andover	03231
Academy (Town)	03579	Center Sandwich	03227	East Candia	03040
Atkinson Heights	03811	Center Strafford	03815	East Concord (Part of	
Auburn	03032	Center Tuftonboro	03816	Concord)	03301
Auburn (Town)	03032	Central Park (Part of		East Conway	04037
Baboosic Lake	03031	Somersworth)	03878	East Deering	03244
Bagley	03278	Chandlers Purchase (Town)	03595	East Derry	03041
Bank Village	03048	Charlestown	03603	East Dummer	03588
Barnstead	03218	Charlestown (Town)	03603	East Grafton	03240
Barnstead (Town)	03218	Chase Village	03281	East Grantham	03753
Barrington	03825	Chateau Richelieu (Part of		East Hampstead	03826
Barrington (Town)	03825	Nashua)	03060	East Haverhill	03780
Barry Villa (Part of		Chatham	04058	East Hebron	03232
Rochester)	03867	Chatham (Town)	04058	East Holderness	03217
Bartlett	03812	Cheever	03266	East Kingston	03827
Bartlett (Town)	03812	Chesham	03455	East Kingston (Town)	03827
Base	03595	Chester	03036	East Lempster	03605
Bath	03740	Chester (Town)	03036	East Merrimack	03054
Bath (Town)	03740	Chesterfield	03443	East Milford	03055
Bayside	03840	Chesterfield (Town)	03443	Easton	03580
Beans Grant (Town)	03595	Chichester	03263	Easton (Town)	03580
Beans Island	03077	Chichester (Town)	03263	East Plainfield	03766
Beans Purchase (Town)	03581	Chicks Corner	03259	East Rindge	03461
Beaver Lake	03041	Chocorua	03817	East Rochester (Part of	
Bedford	03102	Christian Hollow	03608	Rochester)	03868
	03110	Cilleyville	03265	East Sandwich	03226
For specific Bedford Zip Codes		Claremont	03743	East Sullivan	03445
call (603) 625-2728		Claremont Center (Part of		East Sutton	03278
Bedford (Town)	03110	Claremont)	03743	East Swanzey	03446
Beebe River	03223	Claremont Junction (Part of		East Tilton	03252
Belmont	03220	Claremont)	03743	East Unity	03773
Belmont (Town)	03220	Clarks Landing	03226	Eastview	03450
Bennington	03442	Clarksville (Town)	03576	East Wakefield	03830
Bennington (Town)	03442	Clinton Grove	03281	East Washington	03244
Benton	03785	Clinton Village	03440	East Westmoreland	03467
Benton (Town)	03785	Clovelly (Part of Nashua)	03060	East Wilder (Part of	
Berlin	03570	Coburn Woods (Part of		Lebanon)	03784
Berlin Mills (Part of Berlin)	03570	Nashua)	03060	East Wolfeboro	03894
Bethlehem	03574	Cold Regions Research and		Eaton (Town)	03832
Bethlehem (Town)	03574	Engineering Laboratory	03755	Eaton Center	03832
Bethlehem Junction	03598	Cold River	03608	Effingham	03814
Birch Hill	03855	Colebrook	03576	Effingham (Town)	03814
Blair	03264	Colebrook (Town)	03576	Effingham Falls	03814
Blais Park (Part of Berlin)	03570	Collettes Grove	03841	Elkins	03233
Blodgett Landing	03255	Columbia (Town)	03576	Ellsworth (Town)	03264
Bonds Corner	03458	Columbia Valley	03576	Elmwood (Hillsborough	
Boscawen	03301	Concord	03301-06	County)	03449
Boscawen (Town)	03301	**For specific Concord Zip Codes**		Elmwood (Merrimack	
Bow	03301	**call (603) 225-5536**		County)	03230
Bow (Town)	03301	Contoocook	03229	Enfield	03748
Bow Center	03301	Contoocook Lake	03452	Enfield (Town)	03748
Bowkerville	03465	Converseville	03461	Enfield Center	03749
Box Corner	03220	Conway	03818	Epping	03042
Bradford	03221	Conway (Town)	03818	Epping (Town)	03042
Bradford (Town)	03221	Cornish (Town)	03746	Epsom	03234
Bradford Center	03221	Cornish Center	05089	Epsom (Town)	03234
Brentwood	03042	Cornish City	05089	Errol	03579
Brentwood (Town)	03042	Cornish Flat	03746	Errol (Town)	03579
Brentwood Corner	03848	Cornish Mills	05089	Ervings Location (Town)	03576
Bretton Woods	03575	Cotton Mountain	03894	Etna	03750
Bridgewater	03222	Crawford Notch	03595	Exeter	03833
Bridgewater (Town)	03222	Crawfords Purchase (Town)	03595	Exeter (Town)	03833
Bristol	03222	Cricket Corner	03031	Exeter Hampton Mobile	
Bristol (Town)	03222	Croydon	03773	Village	03833
Broad Acres (Part of		Croydon (Town)	03773	Exeter Villa	03833
Nashua)	03060	Croydon Flat	03773	Exeter West	03833
Brookfield	03872	Crystal	03570	Fabyan	03595
Brookfield (Town)	03872	Cushman	03598	Farmington	03835
Brookline	03033	Cutts Grant (Town)	03595	Farmington (Town)	03835
Brookline (Town)	03033	Dalton	03598	Fitzwilliam	03447
Brook Village North (Part of		Dalton (Town)	03598	Fitzwilliam (Town)	03447
Nashua)	03060	Danbury	03230	Fitzwilliam Depot	03447
Bungy	03576	Danbury (Town)	03230	Forest Lake	03470
Burkehaven	03782	Danville	03819		

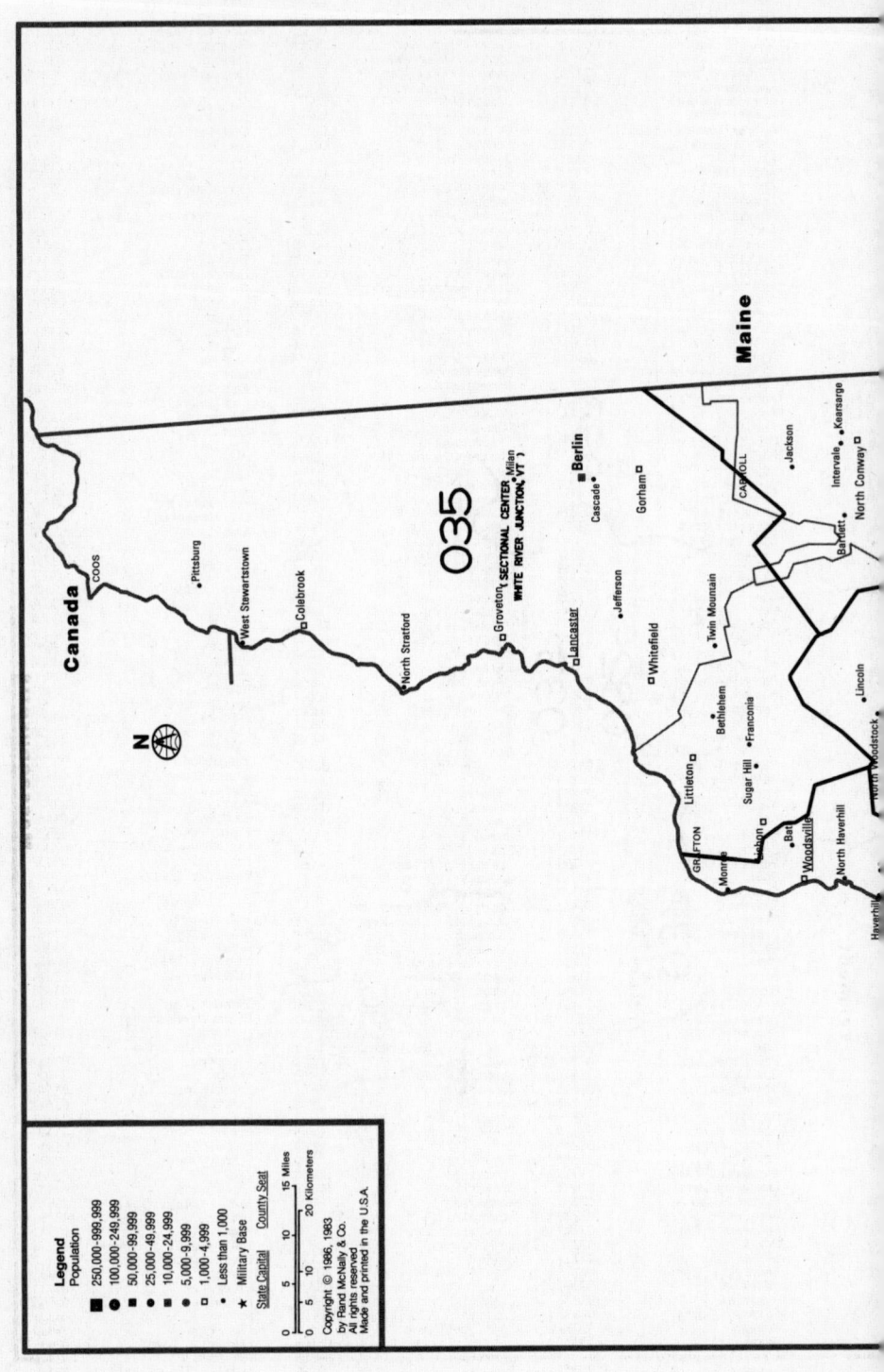

Legend
Population
■ 250,000-999,999
● 100,000-249,999
■ 50,000-99,999
● 25,000-49,999
■ 10,000-24,999
● 5,000-9,999
□ 1,000-4,999
• Less than 1,000
★ Military Base
State Capital   County Seat

0   5   10   15 Miles
0   5   10   20 Kilometers

Canada

Maine

COOS

035

•Pittsburg

•West Stewartstown

□Colebrook

•North Stratford

□Groveton SECTIONAL CENTER
WHITE RIVER JUNCTION, VT)
Milan

■Berlin

Cascade•

Gorham□

□Lancaster

•Jefferson

Whitefield•

•Twin Mountain

CARROLL

•Jackson

Intervale • •Kearsarge
North Conway

Bartlett•

•Lincoln

North Woodstock

GRAFTON

Littleton□

Bethlehem•

•Franconia

Sugar Hill•

•Monroe

Bath•

□Woodsville

North Haverhill

Haverhill

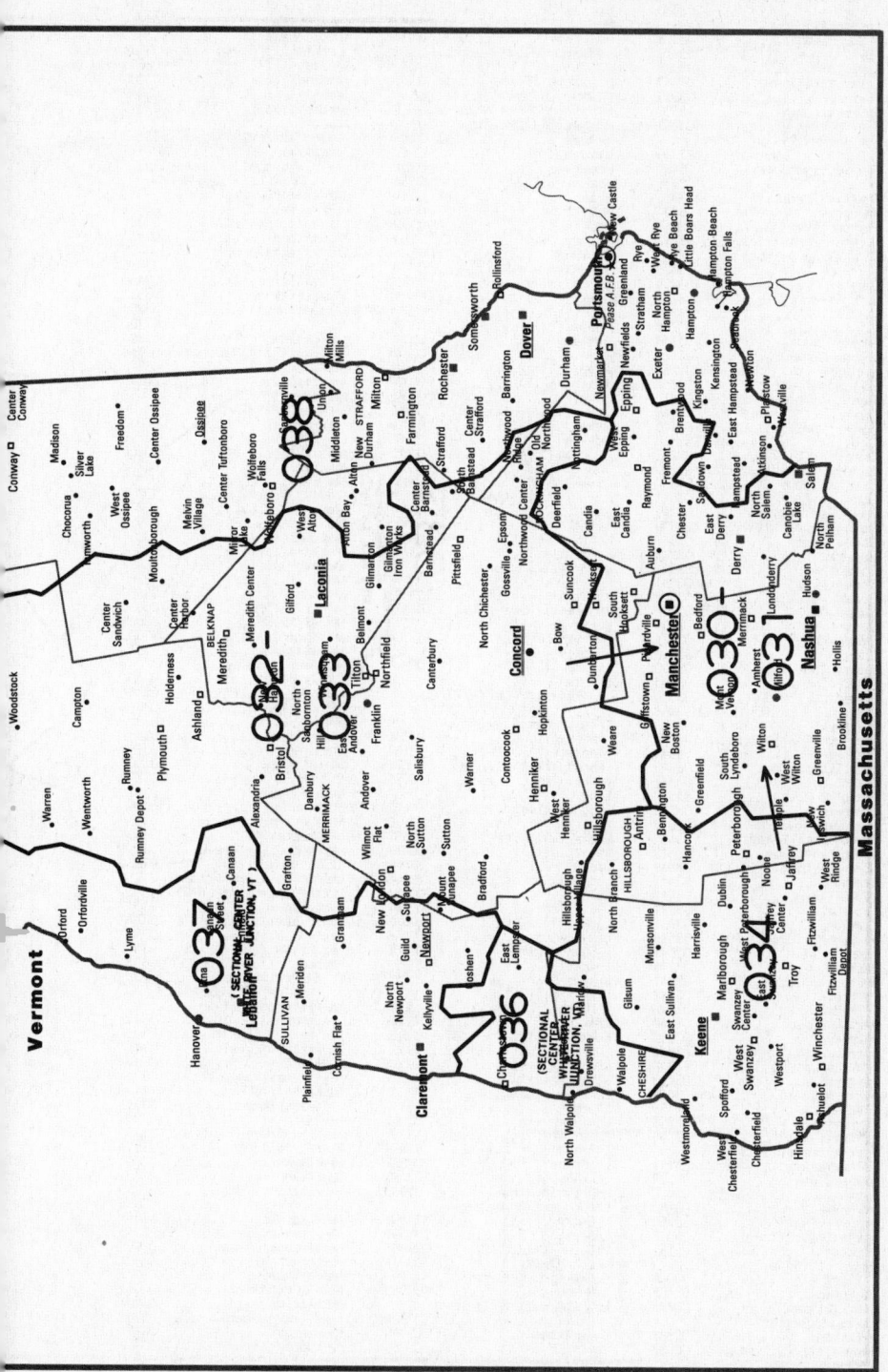

Name	ZIP
Forest Ridge (Part of Nashua)	03060
Foundry (Part of Somersworth)	03878
Foyes Corner	03870
Francestown	03043
Francestown (Town)	03043
Franconia	03580
Franconia (Town)	03580
Franklin	03235
Franklin Falls (Part of Franklin)	03235
Franklin Pierce College	03461
Freedom	03836
Freedom (Town)	03836
Fremont	03044
Fremont (Town)	03044
Gardners Grove	03252
Gates Corner (Part of Dover)	03820
Gaza	03269
Georges Mills	03751
Gerrish	03301
Gilford	03246
Gilford (Town)	03246
Gilmans Corner	03777
Gilmanton	03237
Gilmanton (Town)	03237
Gilmanton Iron Works	03837
Gilsum	03448
Gilsum (Town)	03448
Glen	03838
Glencliff	03238
Glendale	03246
Glenmere Village	03857
Goffstown	03045
Goffstown (Town)	03045
Gonic (Part of Rochester)	03839
Goodrich Falls	03846
Goose Hollow	03223
Gorham	03581
Gorham (Town)	03581
Goshen	03752
Goshen (Town)	03752
Gosport	03801
Gossville	03234
Grafton	03240
Grafton (Town)	03240
Grafton Center	03240
Grange	03584
Granite	03864
Grantham	03753
Grantham (Town)	03753
Grasmere	03045
Great Boars Head	03842
Greenfield	03047
Greenfield (Town)	03047
Greenland	03840
Greenland (Town)	03840
Greens Grant (Town)	03581
Greenville	03048
Greenville (Town)	03048
Groton	03241
Groton (Town)	03241
Groveton	03582
Guild	03754
Hadleys Purchase (Town)	03595
Hale's Location (Town)	03845
Hampstead	03841
Hampstead (Town)	03841
Hampton	03842
Hampton (Town)	03842
Hampton Beach	03842
Hampton Falls	03844
Hampton Falls (Town)	03844
Hampton Landing	03842
Hancock	03449
Hancock (Town)	03449
Hanover	03755
Hanover (Town)	03755
Hanover Center	03750
Hanover Street (Part of Manchester)	03101
Happy Corner	03592
Happy Valley	03458
Harrisville	03450
Harrisville (Town)	03450
Hart's Location (Town)	03812
Hastings	03257
Haven Hill (Part of Rochester)	03868
Haverhill	03765
Haverhill (Town)	03765
Hayes (Rockingham County)	03833
Hayes (Strafford County)	03867
Hebron	03241
Hebron (Town)	03241
Hedding	03042
Hell Hollow	03746
Henniker	03242
Henniker (Town)	03242
High Bridge	03048
Hill	03243
Hill (Town)	03243
Hill Center	03243
Hillsboro	03244
Hillsborough (Town)	03244
Hillsborough Center	03244
Hillsborough Lower Village	03244
Hillsborough Upper Village	03244
Hinsdale	03451
Hinsdale (Town)	03451
Holderness	03245
Holderness (Town)	03245
Hollis	03049
Hollis (Town)	03049
Hooksett	03106
Hooksett (Town)	03106
Hopkinton	03229
Hopkinton (Town)	03229
Horses Corner	03263
Hudson	03051
Hudson (Town)	03051
Hudson Center	03051
Intervale	03845
Jackson	03846
Jackson (Town)	03846
Jady Hill	03833
Jaffrey	03452
Jaffrey (Town)	03452
Jaffrey Center	03452
Jefferson	03583
Jefferson (Town)	03583
Jenness Beach	03871
Jones Corner	03461
Joslin (Part of Keene)	03431
Kearsarge	03847
Keene	03431
Kelleys Corner	03263
Kellyville	03743
Kelwyn Park (Part of Somersworth)	03878
Kensington	03827
Kensington (Town)	03827
Kidderville	03576
Kilkenny (Town)	03584
Kingston	03848
Kingston (Town)	03848
Laconia	03246-47
For specific Laconia Zip Codes call (603) 524-6271	
Lakeport (Part of Laconia)	03246
Lancaster (Town)	03584
Lancaster	03584
Landaff (Town)	03585
Landaff Center	03585
Langdon	03602
Langdon (Town)	03602
Langs Corner	03870
Laskey Corner	03887
Laurel Lake	03447
Leavitts Hill	03034
Lebanon	03766
Lee	03824
Lee (Town)	03857
Lee's	03833
Lempster	03606
Lempster (Town)	03606
Lincoln	03251
Lincoln (Town)	03251
Lincoln Park (Part of Nashua)	03060
Lisbon	03585
Lisbon (Town)	03585
Litchfield	03051
Litchfield (Town)	03051
Little Boars Head	03862
Little Island Pond	03076
Littleton	03561
Littleton (Town)	03561
Livermore (Town)	03251
Livermore Falls	03264
Lochmere	03252
Lockehaven	03748
Londonderry (Town)	03053
Londonderry (Rockingham County)	03053
Loudon	03301
Loudon (Town)	03301
Loudon Center	03301
Louisburg Square (Part of Nashua)	03060
Low And Burbanks Grant (Town)	03581
Lower Bartlett	03845
Lower Gilmanton	03263
Lower Village (Cheshire County)	03448
Lower Village (Merrimack County)	03278
Lyman (Town)	03585
Lyme	03768
Lyme (Town)	03768
Lyme Center	03769
Lyndeborough	03082
Lyndeborough (Town)	03082
Madbury	03820
Madbury (Town)	03820
Madison	03849
Madison (Town)	03849
Mall of New Hampshire, The (Part of Manchester)	03103
Manchester	03101-10
For specific Manchester Zip Codes call (603) 644-4111	
Maple Haven (Part of Portsmouth)	03801
Maplewood	03281
Marlborough	03455
Marlborough (Town)	03455
Marlow	03456
Marlow (Town)	03456
Marshall Corner	03833
Marshall Farms	03833
Martin	03106
Martins Location (Town)	03581
Mascoma (Part of Lebanon)	03748
Mason	03048
Mason (Town)	03048
Meadows	03587
Melrose Corner (Part of Rochester)	03867
Melvin Mills	03278
Melvin Village	03850
Meredith	03253
Meredith (Town)	03253
Meredith Center	03246
Meriden	03770
Merrimack	03054
Merrimack (Town)	03054
Middleton (Town)	03887
Middleton Corners	03887
Milan	03588
Milan (Town)	03588
Milford	03055
Milford (Town)	03055
Mill Hollow	03602
Millsfield (Town)	03579
Mill Village (Cheshire County)	03464
Mill Village (Sullivan County)	03781
Millville Lake	03079
Milton	03851
Milton (Town)	03851
Milton Mills	03852
Mirror Lake	03853
Monroe	03771
Monroe (Town)	03771
Mont Vernon	03057
Mont Vernon (Town)	03057
Moultonboro	03254
Moultonborough (Town)	03254
Moultonborough Falls	03254
Moultonville	03814
Mountain View Estates (Part of Nashua)	03060
Mount Sunapee	03772
Mount Washington	03589
Munsonville	03457
Nashua	03060-63
For specific Nashua Zip Codes call (603) 882-2646	
Nashua Mall (Part of Nashua)	03060
Nelson	03457
Nelson (Town)	03457
New Boston	03070
New Boston (Town)	03070
New Boston Air Force Tracking Station	03031
Newbury	03255
Newbury (Town)	03255
New Castle	03854
New Castle (Town)	03854
New Durham	03855
New Durham (Town)	03855
Newfields	03856
Newfields (Town)	03856
New Hampton	03256
New Hampton (Town)	03256
Newington (Town)	03801
New Ipswich	03071
New Ipswich (Town)	03071
New London	03257
New London (Town)	03257
Newmarket	03857
Newmarket (Town)	03857
Newport	03773
Newport (Town)	03773
New Rye	03275
Newton	03858
Newton (Town)	03858

	ZIP		ZIP		ZIP
Newton Junction	03859	Portsmouth	03801-04	South Effingham	03882
Noone	03458	For specific Portsmouth Zip Codes		South Hampton	03827
North Barnstead	03225	call (603) 431-1300		South Hampton (Town)	03827
North Beach	03842	Post Office Annex (Part of		South Hooksett	03106
North Branch	03440	Portsmouth)	03801	South Keene (Part of	
North Brookline	03055	Potter Place	03265	Keene)	03431
North Charlestown	03603	Puckershire (Part of		South Kingston	03848
North Chatham	04058	Claremont)	03743	South Lee	03857
North Chichester	03263	Quaker City	03603	South Lyndeboro	03082
North Conway	03860	Quincy	03266	South Merrimack	03060
North Danville	03044	Quintown	03777	South Milford	03055
Northfield	03276	Rand	03461	South Newbury	03272
Northfield (Town)	03276	Randolph	03570	South Pittsfield	03263
North Grantham	03766	Randolph (Town)	03570	South Stoddard	03464
North Groton	03266	Raymond	03077	South Sutton	03273
North Hampton	03862	Raymond (Town)	03077	South Tamworth	03883
North Hampton (Town)	03862	Redstone	03813	South Weare	03281
North Hampton Center	03862	Reeds Ferry	03054	South Wolfeboro	03894
North Haverhill	03774	Richardson	03055	Spofford	03462
North Holderness	03264	Richmond	03470	Spofford Lake	03462
North Londonderry	03053	Richmond (Town)	03470	Springfield	03284
North Newport	03773	Rindge	03461	Springfield (Town)	03284
North Pelham	03076	Rindge (Town)	03461	Squantum	03452
North Pembroke	03301	Rivercrest	03755	Stark	03582
North Richmond	03470	Riverdale	03045	Stark (Town)	03582
North Salem	03073	Riverhill (Part of Concord)	03301	State Line	03447
North Sanbornton	03269	Riverside	03874	Stewartstown	03576
North Sandwich	03259	Riverside Plaza (Part of		Stewartstown (Town)	03576
North Stratford	03590	Keene)	03431	Stewartstown Hollow	03576
North Sutton	03260	Robinson Corner	03240	Stinson Lake	03274
North Swanzey	03431	Roby	03278	Stoddard	03464
Northumberland	05905	Rochester	03839	Stoddard (Town)	03464
Northumberland (Town)	05905		03867-68	Strafford	03884
North Village	03458	For specific Rochester Zip Codes		Strafford (Town)	03884
North Walpole	03609	call (603) 332-1433		Stratford	03590
North Wilmot	03230	Rockwold	03245	Stratford (Town)	03590
North Wolfeboro	03894	Rollinsford	03869	Stratham	03885
Northwood	03261	Rollinsford (Town)	03869	Stratham (Town)	03885
Northwood (Town)	03261	Roxbury (Town)	03431	Strawberry Banke (Part of	
Northwood Center	03261	Royal Crest Estates (Part of		Portsmouth)	03801
Northwood Ridge	03261	Nashua)	03060	Success (Town)	03570
North Woodstock	03262	Rumney	03266	Sugar Hill	03585
Nottingham	03290	Rumney (Town)	03266	Sugar Hill (Town)	03585
Nottingham (Town)	03290	Rumney Depot	03266	Sullivan	03431
Noyes Terrace	03079	Ryder Corner	03773	Sullivan (Town)	03431
Nuttings Beach	03222	Rye	03870	Sunapee	03782
Odell	03582	Rye (Town)	03870	Sunapee (Town)	03782
Old Millstream Estates	03833	Rye Beach	03871	Suncook	03275
Old Northwood	03261	Rye North Beach	03870	Surry	03431
Onway Lake	03077	Sachem Village (Part of		Surry (Town)	03431
Orange	03741	Lebanon)	03784	Sutton	03221
Orange (Town)	03741	Salem	03079	Sutton (Town)	03221
Orford	03777	Salem (Town)	03079	Swanzey (Town)	03431
Orford (Town)	03777	Salem Center	03079	Swanzey Center	03431
Orfordville	03777	Salem Depot	03079	Swiftwater	03785
Ossipee	03864	Salisbury	03268	Tamworth	03886
Ossipee (Town)	03864	Salisbury (Town)	03268	Tamworth (Town)	03886
Pages Corner	03301	Salisbury Heights	03268	Temple	03084
Pannaway Manor (Part of		Sanbornton	03269	Temple (Town)	03084
Portsmouth)	03801	Sanbornton (Town)	03269	The Glen	03592
Parker Hill	03585	Sanbornville	03872	Thomas	03461
Park Hill	03467	Sandown	03873	Thompson And Meserves	
Partridge Lake	03561	Sandown (Town)	03873	Purchase (Town)	03595
Passaconaway	03818	Sandwich	03227	Thornton	03285
Pearls Corner	03301	Sandwich (Town)	03227	Thornton (Town)	03285
Pelham	03076	Sargents Purchase (Town)	03589	Tilton	03276
Pelham (Town)	03076	Sawyers (Part of Dover)	03820	Tilton (Town)	03276
Pembroke (Town)	03275	Scotland	03470	Tilton-Northfield	03276
Penacook (Part of Concord)	03303	Seabrook	03874	Tinkerville	03585
Pendleton Beach (Part of		Seabrook (Town)	03874	Trapshire	03603
Laconia)	03246	Seabrook Beach	03874	Troy	03465
Pequawket	03875	Seacrest Village (Part of		Troy (Town)	03465
Percy	03582	Portsmouth)	03801	Tuftonboro	03864
Peterborough	03458	Second College Grant		Tuftonboro (Town)	03864
Peterborough (Town)	03458	(Town)	03576	Twin Mountain	03595
Peterborough	03458	Severance	03105	Union	03887
Pheasant Lane Mall (Part of		Sharon	03458	Unity	03603
Nashua)	03063	Sharon (Town)	03458	Unity (Town)	03603
Pickering (Part of		Shelburne (Town)	03581	Upper Kidderville	03576
Rochester)	03867	Sherwood Forest	03833	Wadley Falls	03857
Pickpocket Woods	03833	Shirley Hill	03045	Wakefield	03872
Piermont	03779	Short Falls	03234	Wakefield (Town)	03872
Piermont (Town)	03779	Silver Lake	03875	Wallis Sands	03870
Pike	03780	Simoneau Plaza (Part of		Walpole	03608
Pinardville	03045	Nashua)	03060	Walpole (Town)	03608
Pine Brook Estates	03833	Smiths Point	03246	Warner	03278
Pinecrest	03833	Smithtown	03874	Warner (Town)	03278
Pine Valley	03086	Smithville	03071	Warren	03279
Pinkhams Grant (Town)	03581	Snowville	03849	Warren (Town)	03279
Pittsburg	03592	Snumshire	03603	Washington	03280
Pittsburg (Town)	03592	Somersworth	03878	Washington (Town)	03280
Pittsfield	03263	Soo Nipi	03257	Waterloo	03278
Pittsfield (Town)	03263	South Acworth	03607	Water Village	03864
Plaice Cove	03842	South Barnstead	03225	Waterville Estates	03223
Plainfield	03781	South Brookline	03033	Waterville Valley	03223
Plainfield (Town)	03781	South Charlestown	03603	Waterville Valley (Town)	03223
Plaistow	03865	South Chatham	04037	Wawbeek	03853
Plaistow (Town)	03865	South Conway	03813	Weare	03281
Plymouth	03264	South Cornish	05089	Weare (Town)	03281
Plymouth (Town)	03264	South Danville	03819	Webster	03301
Ponemah	03055	South Deerfield	03037	Webster (Town)	03301

	ZIP		ZIP		ZIP
Webster Lake (Part of Franklin)	03235	West Hampstead	03841	Whittier	03890
Webster Place (Part of Franklin)	03235	West Henniker	03242	Willey House	03812
		West Hopkinton	03229	Wilmot	03287
Weirs Beach (Part of Laconia)	03246	West Lebanon (Part of Lebanon)	03784	Wilmot (Town)	03287
Wendell	03782	West Milan	03570	Wilmot Flat	03287
Wentworth (Grafton County)	03282	Westmoreland	03467	Wilton	03086
Wentworth (Coos County)	03579	Westmoreland (Town)	03467	Wilton (Town)	03086
Wentworth (Grafton County) (Town)	03282	West Nottingham	03291	Wilton Center	03086
		West Ossipee	03890	Winchester	03470
Wentworth By The Sea	03854	West Peterborough	03468	Winchester (Town)	03470
West Alton	03246	West Plymouth	03264	Windham (Town)	03087
West Andover	03265	Westport	03469	Windham (Rockingham County)	03087
West Brentwood	03848	West Rindge	03461	Windsor (Town)	03244
West Campton	03223	West Rumney	03266	Winnisquam	03289
West Canaan	03741	West Rye	03870	Winona	03217
West Center Harbor	03217	West Salisbury	03216	Wolfeboro	03894
West Chesterfield	03466	West Springfield	03284	Wolfeboro (Town)	03894
West Claremont (Part of Claremont)	03743	West Stewartstown	03597	Wolfeboro	03894
		West Swanzey	03469	Wolfeboro Center	03894
West Deering	03440	West Thornton	03285	Wolfeboro Falls	03896
West Dummer	03570	West Unity	03743	Wonalancet	03897
West Epping	03042	Westville	03865	Woodman	03830
West Franklin (Part of Franklin)	03235	West Wilton	03086	Woodmere	03452
		West Windham	03087	Woodstock	03293
West Gonic (Part of Rochester)	03839	Whiteface	03259	Woodstock (Town)	03293
		Whitefield	03598	Woodsville	03785
		Whitefield (Town)	03598		

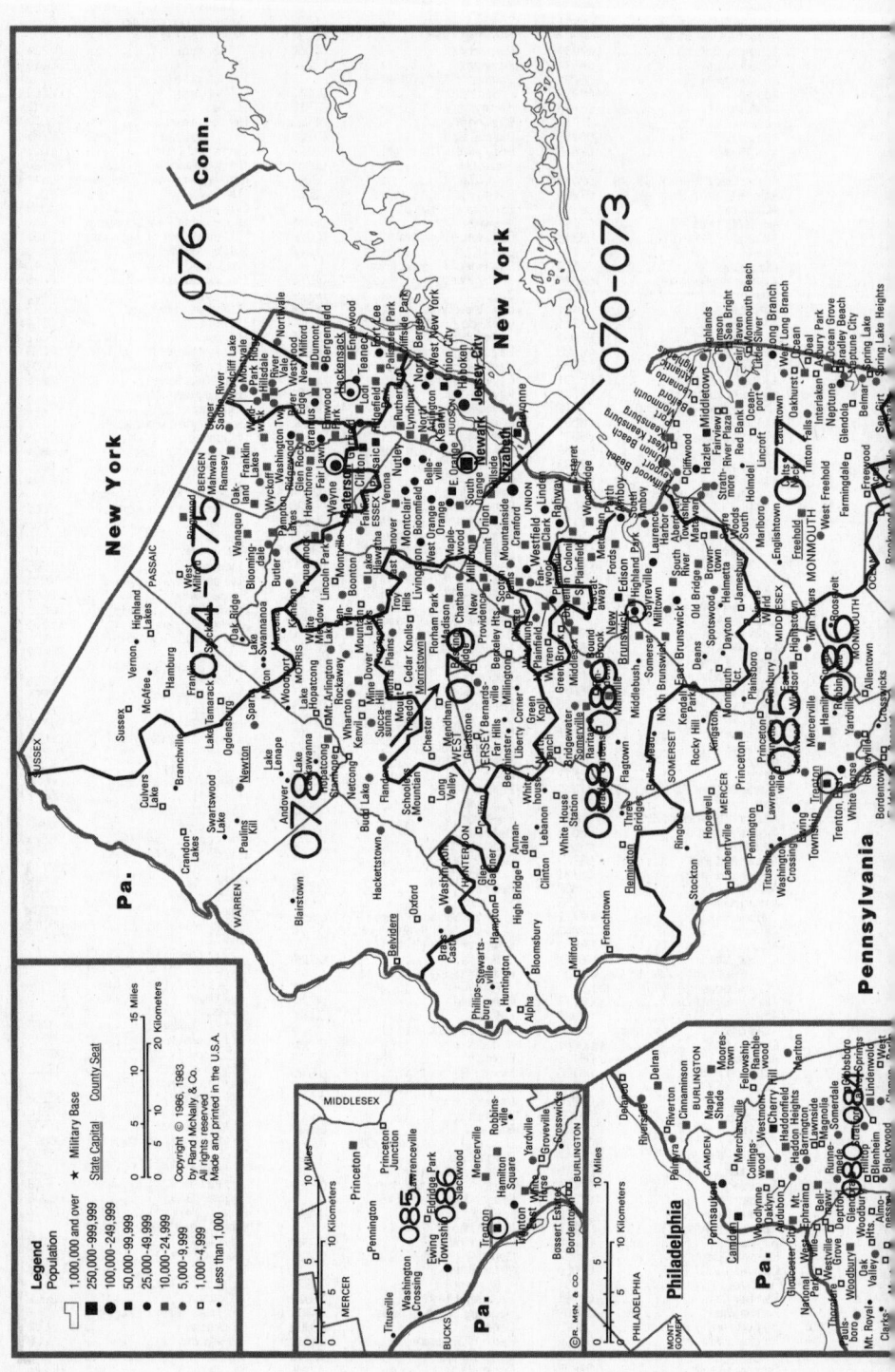

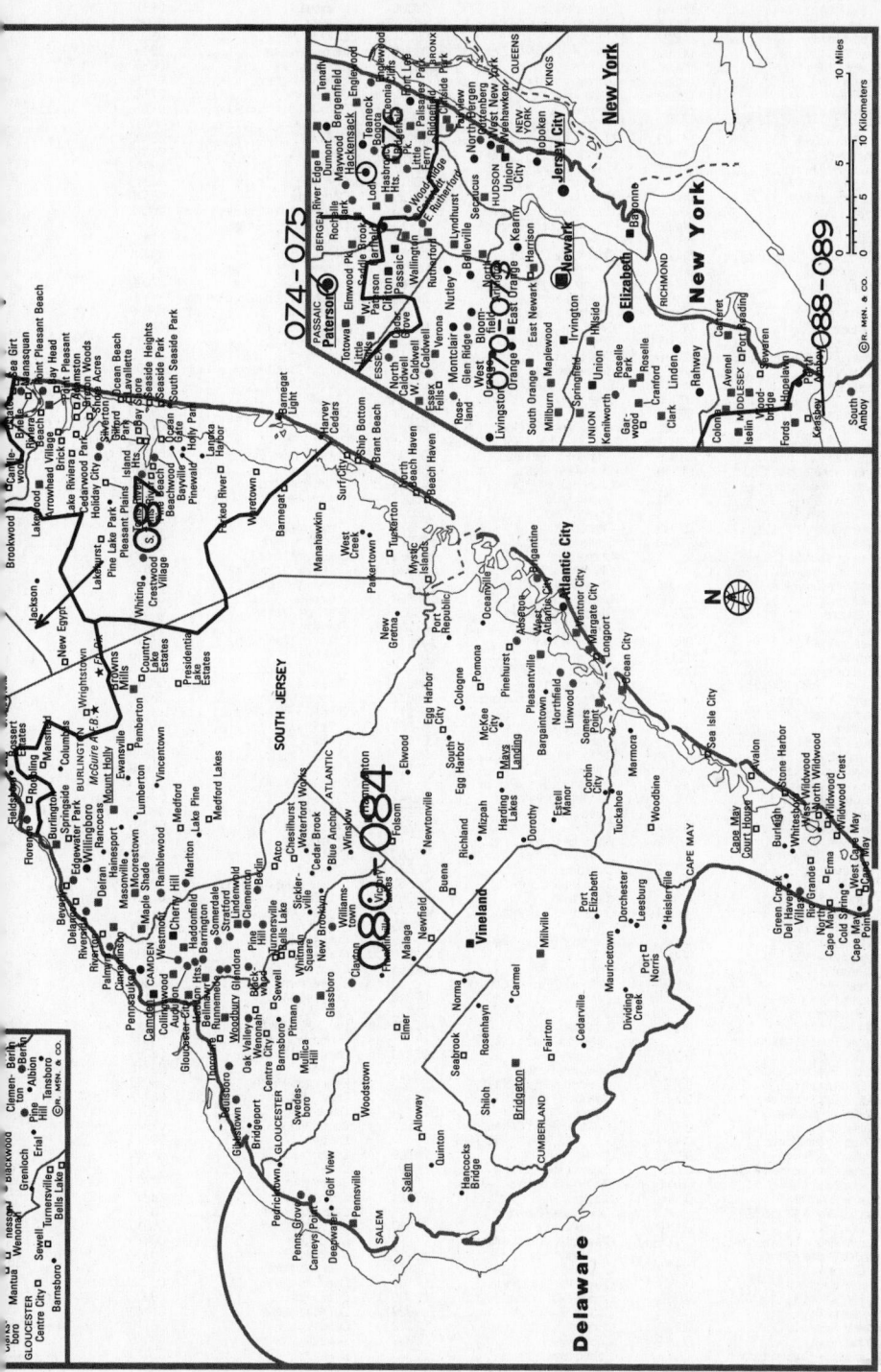

	ZIP
Brookville (Hunterdon County)	08559
Brookville (Ocean County)	08005
Brookwood	08527
Brotmanville	08302
Browns Mills	08015
Browntown	08857
Brunswick Acres	08852
Brunswick Gardens	08857
Brunswick Shopping Center (Part of New Brunswick)	08902
Brunswick Square	08816
Brush Hollow	08053
Buckingham Village	08080
Buckshutem	08332
Budd Lake	07828
Buddtown	08088
Buena	08310
Buena Vista (Township)	08360
Bulltown	08215
Bunker Hill	08080
Bunnvale	07830
Burcliff Farms	08638
Burleigh	08210
Burlington	08016
Burlington (Township)	08016
Burnt Mills	07921
Bustleton	08016
Butler	07405
Butler Park	07882
Butlers Park	07882
Butterworth Farms	07801
Buttzville	07829
Byram (Hunterdon County)	08559
Byram (Sussex County) (Township)	07821
Byram Cove (Part of Hopatcong)	07843
Caldwell	07006-07
For specific Caldwell Zip Codes call (201) 288-1700	
Caldwell (Township)	07004
Califon	07830
Callahans	07849
Cambridge	08075
Cambridge Park	08053
Camden	08101-05
For specific Camden Zip Codes call (609) 757-0330	
Camp Tecumseh	08867
Candlewood	08701
Canton	08079
Cape Breton	08723
Cape May	08204
Cape May Court House	08210
Cape May Point	08212
Capitol Hill	08010
Cardiff	08232
Carls Corner	08302
Carlstadt	07072
Carlton Hill (Part of Rutherford)	07073
Carmel	08332
Carmerville	07719
Carneys Point (Township)	08069
Carneys Point (Salem County)	08069
Carpenterville	08865
Carteret	07008
Cassville	08527
Castle Point (Part of Hoboken)	07030
Cecil	08094
Cedar Beach (Monmouth County)	07758
Cedar Beach (Ocean County)	08721
Cedar Bonnet Island	08050
Cedar Bridge Manor	08723
Cedar Brook	08018
Cedar Crest Manor	08069
Cedar Croft	08723
Cedar Glen Homes East	08757
Cedar Glen Lakes	08759
Cedar Glen West	08733
Cedar Grove (Cape May County)	08210
Cedar Grove (Township)	07009
Cedar Grove (Essex County)	07009
Cedar Heights	08801
Cedar Knolls	07927
Cedar Lake	07834
Cedar Ridge	08857
Cedar Run	08092
Cedarville (Cumberland County)	08311
Cedarville (Salem County)	08098
Cedarwood Park	08723
Centennial Lake	08053
Center (Part of Trenton)	08608

	ZIP
Center Grove	07869
Center Square	08085
Centerton (Burlington County)	08054
Centerton (Salem County)	08318
Centerville (Mercer County)	08534
Centerville (Somerset County)	08853
Central (Part of East Orange)	07018
Central Park	08070
Centre City	08051
Centre Grove	08332
Ceramics	08817
Chadwick Beach	08739
Chairville	08055
Chambersburg (Part of Trenton)	08611
Chambers Corner	08060
Changewater	07831
Chapel Heights	08080
Charlotteburg	07435
Charlton Village	07747
Chatham	07928
Chatham (Township)	07928
Chatsworth	08019
Cheesequake	08857
Cheesequake Estates	07747
Cherry Hill	08002-03
	08034
For specific Cherry Hill Zip Codes call (609) 424-4324	
Cherry Hill Estates	08002
Cherry Hill Mall	08002
Cherry Quay	08723
Cherry Ridge	08002
Cherry Valley	08002
Cherryville	08822
Cherrywood	08012
Chesilhurst	08089
Chester	07930
Chester (Township)	07930
Chesterfield	08650
Chesterfield (Township)	08650
Chestnut	07083
Chewalla Park	08619
Chews Landing	08012
Chrome (Part of Carteret)	07008
Churchtown	08070
Cinnaminson (Township)	08077
Cinnaminson	08077
Clark (Township)	07066
Clark	07066
Clarksboro	08020
Clarksburg	08510
Clarks Landing (Part of Point Pleasant)	08742
Clarktown	08330
Clayton	08312
Claytons Corner	07746
Clayville (Part of Vineland)	08360
Clearbrook Park	08831
Clear View Lake	07860
Clementon	08021
Clermont (Burlington County)	08060
Clermont (Cape May County)	08210
Cliffdale Park	07865
Cliff Park (Part of Cliffside Park)	07010
Cliffside Park	07010
Cliffwood	07721
Cliffwood Beach (Middlesex County)	08879
Cliffwood Beach (Monmouth County)	07735
Cliffwood Lake	07460
Clifton	07011-15
For specific Clifton Zip Codes call (201) 472-7900	
Clinton	08809
Clinton (Township)	08801
Clinton Hill (Part of Newark)	07108
Closter	07624
Cloverdale (Camden County)	08300
Cloverdale (Cumberland County)	08332
Cloverhill	08822
Clover Hill at Holmdel	07733
Clover Leaf Lakes	08330
Coffins Corner	08026
Cohansey	08302
Cokesbury	08833
Cold Indian Springs	07712
Cold Spring	08204
Colesville	07461
Collings Lakes	08094
Collingswood	08108
Collingwood Park	07727

	ZIP
Collinsville	07960
Cologne	08213
Colonia	07067
Colonial Arms	08527
Colonial Manor	08096
Colonial Park	08520
Colonial Terrace	07712
Colts Neck	07722
Colts Neck (Township)	07722
Columbia	07832
Columbia Lakes	08002
Columbus	08022
Colwick	08002
Commercial (Township)	08349
Concordia	08512
Congressional Estates	08002
Conklintown (Part of Ringwood)	07465
Conovertown	08201
Constable Hook (Part of Bayonne)	07002
Constable Junction (Part of Bayonne)	07002
Convent Station	07961
Cookstown	08511
Coontown	07060
Cooper Park Village	08002
Cooper Village	08096
Copper Hill	08551
Corbin City	08270
Cornish	07823
Country Farms	07733
Country Lake Estates	08015
Country Manor	08857
Country Woods	07733
Coytesville (Part of Fort Lee)	07024
Cozy Lake	07438
Cragmere Park	07430
Cranberry Lake	07821
Cranbury (Township)	08512
Cranbury (Middlesex County)	08512
Cranbury Manor	08512
Crandon Lakes	07860
Cranford (Township)	07016
Cranford	07016
Cranford Junction	07016
Creamridge	08514
Crescent Heights	08068
Crescent Park (Part of Bellmawr)	08030
Cresskill	07626
Crestmoor	07853
Creston	08619
Crestwood Village	08759
Cropwell	08053
Cross Keys	08080
Crossroads	08055
Crosswicks	08515
Croton	08822
Crowfoot	08004
Crystal Lake (Bergen County)	07436
Crystal Lake (Ocean County)	08721
Culvers Lake	07826
Cumberland	08332
Cumberland Mall (Part of Vineland)	08360
Cuthbert Manor	08108
Cyn-Wyd	08016
Da Costa (Part of Hammonton)	08037
Danceys Corner	08069
Daretown	08318
Darlington Heights	08088
Darts Mills	08822
Davis	08514
Davis Bridge	07946
Dayton	08810
Deacons	08060
Deal	07723
Deal Park	07723
Deans	08852
Deauville Beach	08739
De Cou Village	08610
Deepwater	08023
Deerfield (Township)	08352
Deerfield Park	08087
Deerfield Street	08313
Deer Park	08002
Deer Trail Lake	07460
Delair	08110
Delanco (Township)	08075
Delanco	08075
Delawanna (Part of Clifton)	07014
Delaware (Hunterdon County) (Township)	08822
Delaware (Warren County)	07833
Delaware Gardens	08110

	ZIP		ZIP		ZIP
Delaware Park	08865	Edgewater Park Estates	08016	Fenwick	08098
Delcrest	08075	Edgewood	08210	Fernwood Terrace	08618
Del Haven	08251	Edgewood Park	08527	Ferrell	08343
Delmont	08314	Edinburg	08691	Ferry Road Manor	08628
Delran (Township)	08075	Edison	08817-20	Fieldsboro	08505
Delran	08075		08837	Fieldstone	07920
Delwood	08002		08899	Finderne	08807
Demarest	07627	For specific Edison Zip Codes call		Finesville	08865
Dennis (Township)	08214	(908) 287-4311		Firthtown (Part of	
Dennisville	08214	Egg Harbor (Township)	08221	Phillipsburg)	08865
Denville	07834	Egg Harbor City	08215	Fish House	08110
Denville (Township)	07834	Eilers Corner	08520	Fish House Junction	08110
Deptford	08096	Elberon (Part of Long		Fishing Creek	08204
Deptford (Township)	08096	Branch)	07740	Five Corners (Part of Jersey	
Deptford Mall	08096	Elberon Park	07755	City)	07308
Deptford Terrace	08097	Eldora	08270	Five Points (Salem County)	08067
Devonshire	08215	Eldridge Park	08638	Five Points (Sussex County)	07860
Dias Creek	08210	Eldridges Hill	08098	Flagtown	08821
Dicktown	08081	Elizabeth	07201-08	Flanders	07836
Dividing Creek	08315	For specific Elizabeth Zip Codes		Flatbrookville	07832
Doddtown (Part of East		call (908) 352-8400		Flemington	08822
Orange)	07017	Elizabethport (Part of		Flemington Junction	08822
Dolphin (Part of Northfield)	08225	Elizabeth)	07206	Floral Hill	07928
Dorchester	08316	Elk (Township)	08028	Florence (Township)	08518
Dorothy	08317	Elks Terrace	08079	Florence (Camden County)	08009
Dover	07801-02	Ellisburg	08002	Florence (station)	
For specific Dover Zip Codes call		Ellisdale	08501	(Burlington County)	08554
(210) 366-6750		Elm	08037	Florence (Burlington	
Dover (Township)	08753	Elmer	08318	County)	08518
Dover Hills	07801	Elmora (Part of Elizabeth)	07202	Florence-Roebling	08518
Dover Shores	08753	Elmwood Park	07407	Florham Park	07932
Dover Walk	08753	Elsinboro (Township)	08079	Folsom	08037
Downe (Township)	08315	Elsmere (Part of Glassboro)	08028	Ford Estates	08096
Downer	08094	Elwood	08217	Ford Landing	08065
Downs Farms	08002	Elwood-Magnolia	08217	Fords	08863
Downtown (Part of Trenton)	08608	Emerson	07630	Forest Grove	08360
Drakestown	07840	Emmelville	08330	Forest Hill (Camden County)	08002
Drew University (Part of		Englewood	07631-32	Forest Hill (Ocean County)	08721
Madison)	07940	For specific Englewood Zip Codes		Forked River	08731
Dumont	07628	call (201) 568-0086		Forked River Beach	08731
Dunbarton	08004	Englewood Cliffs	07632	Forrest Lake Estates	08328
Dundee (Part of Passaic)	07055	English Creek	08330	Fort Dix	08640
Dunellen	08812	Englishtown	07726	Fort Elfsborg	08079
Dunham's Corner	08816	Erial	08081	Fortescue	08321
Dunham Siding	07047	Erlton	08002	Fort Hancock	07732
Dunns Mills	08505	Erma	08204	Fort Lee	07024
Durham	08817	Erma Park	08204	Fort Mercer (Part of	
Durham Park	08854	Ernston (Part of Sayreville)	08859	National Park)	08063
Dutch Neck	08550	Erskine (Part of Ringwood)	07456	Fort Mott	08079
Dutchtown	08802	Erskine Lakes (Part of		Fort Plains	07728
Eagleswood (Township)	08092	Ringwood)	07456	Forty-third Street (Part of	
Earle	07722	Essex Fells	07021	Union City)	07087
East (Part of Paterson)	07514	Essex Fells (Township)	07021	Fostertown	08060
Eastampton (Township)	08060	Essex Green Mall	07052	Foster Village (Part of	
East Amwell (Township)	08551	Estell Manor	08319	Bergenfield)	07621
East Berlin	08009	Estelville (Part of Estell		Foul Rift	07823
East Bound Brook (Part of		Manor)	08319	Four Bridges	07853
Middlesex)	08846	Estling Lake	07834	Foxborough Village	08857
East Bridgeton (Part of		Etra	08520	Fox Chase	08088
Bridgeton)	08302	Everett	07735	Fox Hills (Part of Mountain	
East Brunswick	08816	Everittstown	08867	Lakes)	07046
East Brunswick (Township)	08816	Evesboro	08053	Fox Hollow Woods	08002
East Burlington (Part of		Evesham (Township)	08053	Francis Mills	08527
Burlington)	08016	Ewan	08025	Frankford (Township)	07826
East Camden (Part of		Ewansville	08060	Franklin (Gloucester County)	
Camden)	08105	Ewing (Township)	08618	(Township)	08322
East Freehold	07728	Ewing	08618	Franklin (Hunterdon County)	
East Greenwich (Township)	08020	Ewing Park	08638	(Township)	08822
East Hanover (Township)	07936	Ewingville	08638	Franklin (Somerset County)	
East Hanover	07936	Extonville	08501	(Township)	08873
East Keansburg	07734	Fairfield (Cumberland		Franklin (Sussex County)	07416
East Long Branch (Part of		County) (Township)	08320	Franklin (Warren County)	
Long Branch)	07740	Fairfield (Essex County)		(Township)	08808
East Millstone	08873	(Township)	07101	Franklin Lakes	07417
East Newark	07029	Fairfield (Essex County)	07004	Franklin Park	08823
East Orange	07017-19	Fairfield (Monmouth County)	07728	Franklinville	08322
For specific East Orange Zip		Fair Haven	07704	Frazier Park	08008
Codes call (201) 673-5555		Fair Lawn	07410	Fredon (Township)	07860
East Pennsauken	08110	Fairmount	07830	Free Acres	07922
East Riverton	08077	Fairton	08320	Freehold	07728
East Rutherford	07073	Fairview (Bergen County)	07022	Freehold (Township)	07728
East Side (Part of		Fairview (Medford twp.)	08075	Freewood Acres	07727
Bridgeton)	08302	Fairview (Delran twp.)	08055	Frelinghuysen (Township)	07825
East Spotswood (station)	08884	Fairview (Gloucester		Frenchtown	08825
East Spotswood	08857	County)	08080	Freneau (Part of Matawan)	07747
East Trenton Heights	08638	Fairview (Hudson County)	07047	Friendship (Upper Pittsgrove	
East Vineland (Part of		Fairview (Monmouth		twp.)	08343
Vineland)	08360	County)	07701	Friendship (Carneys Point	
East Wenonah	08090	Falcon Courts North	08562	twp.)	08069
East Windsor	08520	Fanwood	07023	Fries Mill	08322
East Windsor (Township)	08520	Far Hills	07931	Galilee (Part of Monmouth	
East Woodbury	08096	Farmersville	07830	Beach)	07750
Eatontown	07724	Farmingdale	07727	Galloping Hill	07920
Echelon	08043	Farmington	08232	Galloway (Township)	08213
Echo Lake	07435	Farrington Lake Heights	08816	Gandys Beach	08345
Edgar	07095	Fashion Center, The (Part		Garden City	08096
Edgebrook (Part of New		of Paramus)	07652	Gardendale	08079
Brunswick)	08901	Fawn Lakes	08050	Garden Lake (Part of	
Edgewater	07020	Fayson Lakes (Part of		Lindenwold)	08021
Edgewater Park (Township)	08010	Kinnelon)	07405	Gardens (Part of Ocean	
Edgewater Park	08010	Fellowship	08057	City)	08226

	ZIP		ZIP		ZIP
Gardens of Pleasant Plains	08753	Grove	07003	Heyden	07095
Garden State (Part of		Grove Chapel (Part of		Hibernia	07842
Paramus)	07652	Vineland)	08344	Hibernia Junction (Part of	
Garden State Plaza (Part of		Grovers Mill	08550	Rockaway)	07866
Paramus)	07652	Groveville	08620	Hickory Acres	08520
Gardenville	08096	Gum Tree Corner	08302	Hickory Tree	07928
Gardenville Center	08096	Guttenberg	07093	Hickstown	08012
Garfield	07026	Hackensack	07601-02	Higbee Town	08201
Garwood	07027	For specific Hackensack Zip		High Bridge	08829
Genasco	08861	Codes call (201) 440-7820		High Crest Lake	07480
General Lafayette (Part of		Hackettstown	07840	Highland Beach (Part of	
Jersey City)	07304	Haddon (Township)	08108	Sea Bright)	07760
Georgetown	08022	Haddonfield	08033	Highland Lakes	07422
Georgetowne	08053	Haddon Heights	08035	Highland Park (Part of	
Georgia	07728	Haddon Hills	08033	Gloucester City)	08012
Germania	08215	Haddon Leigh	08033	Highland Park (Camden	
Germania Gardens	08213	Haddontowne	08002	County)	08030
Gibbsboro	08026	Hainesburg	07832	Highland Park (Middlesex	
Gibbstown	08027	Haines Corner	08620	County)	08904
Giffordtown	08057	Hainesport	08036	Highlands	07732
Gilford Park	08753	Hainesport (Township)	08036	High Point (Part of Harvey	
Gillespie (Part of Sayreville)	08872	Hainesville	07826	Cedars)	08008
Gillette	07933	Haledon	07508	High Point Manor	08857
Gilman Lake	08343		07538	Highs Beach	08210
Glacier Hills	07950	For specific Haledon Zip Codes		Hightstown	08520
Gladstone	07934	call (210) 977-4581		Hightstown Heights	08520
Glassboro	08028	Haleyville	08349	Highview Park	08736
Glasser (Part of Hopatcong)	07837	Halsey	07860	Hillcrest (Camden County)	08109
Glen Cove	08721	Hamburg	07419	Hillcrest (Passaic County)	07502
Glendale (Camden County)	08043	Hamden	08801	Hillcrest (Warren County)	08865
Glendale (Mercer County)	08618	Hamilton (Atlantic County)		Hilliard	08050
Glendola	07719	(Township)	08330	Hillsborough (Township)	08853
Glendora	08029	Hamilton (Mercer County)		Hillsdale	07642
Glen Gardner	08826	(Township)	08619	Hillsdale Manor (Part of	
Glen Oaks	08021	Hamilton (Monmouth		Hillsdale)	07642
Glen Ridge	07028	County)	07753	Hillside (Township)	07205
Glen Ridge (Township)	07028	Hamilton Square	08690	Hillside	07205
Glen Rock	07452	Hammond Heights	08090	Hilltop	08012
Glenside	08070	Hammonton	08037	Hilltop Terrace	08816
Glenview	08002	Hampton (Hunterdon		Hilltown	07885
Glenwood	07418	County)	08827	Hillwood Lakes	08638
Gloucester (Township)	08012	Hampton (Sussex County)		Hilton (Part of Atlantic	
Gloucester City	08030	(Township)	07860	Highlands)	07716
Godfrey Manor	08723	Hancocks Bridge	08038	Hinchman	08002
Golf Hill	07876	Hanover (Township)	07981	Hi-Nella	08083
Golf Manor	08069	Hanover Neck	07936	Hoboken	07030
Golf View	08069	Hanover Township	07981	Hoffmans	07830
Gordon Lakes	07405	Harbourton	08530	Hoffner	08518
Goshen	08218	Harding (Township)	07940	Ho Ho Kus	07423
Gouldtown	08302	Harding Lakes	08330	Holgate	08008
Grandin	08801	Hardingville	08343	Holiday City	08753
Granton Junction	07047	Hardistonville (Part of		Holiday City at Berkeley	08757
Grasselli (Part of Linden)	07036	Hamburg)	07419	Holiday City-Berkeley	08753
Grassy Sound	08260	Hardwick (Township)	07825	Holiday City-Dover	08753
Gravel Hill	07726	Hardyston (Township)	07460	Holiday City South	08757
Great Meadows	07838	Harfield	08527	Holiday City West	08757
Great Meadows-Vienna	07838	Harker Village	08096	Holiday Heights	08757
Great Notch	07424	Harlingen	08502	Holiday on the Bay	08753
Green (Township)	07821	Harmersville	08079	Holland	08848
Green Acres	08618	Harmony (Township)	08865	Holland (Township)	08848
Green Bank	08215	Harmony (Monmouth		Holly Brook	08060
Green Brook (Township)	08812	County)	07748	Holly Crest	08723
Green Brook	08812	Harmony (Ocean County)	08527	Holly Hills	08060
Green Creek	08219	Harmony (Warren County)	08865	Holly Park	08721
Green Curve Heights	08638	Harrington Park	07640	Holmansville	08527
Greendell	07839	Harrison (Gloucester		Holmdel	07733
Greenfield	08230	County) (Township)	08062	Holmdel (Township)	07733
Greenfield Heights	08096	Harrison (Hudson County)	07029	Holmdel Village	07733
Greenfields Village	08096	Harrison Mountain Lake		Holmeson	08526
Green Grove	07712	(Part of Ringwood)	07456	Homes Mills	08514
Green Haven	08002	Harrisonville (Gloucester		Homestead	07047
Green Hills	08876	County)	08039	Homestead Park	07933
Green Hut Park	07801	Harrisonville (Salem County)	08079	Homestead Run	08753
Green Island	08753	Hartford	08057	Homestead Village	07920
Green Knoll	08876	Harvey Cedars	08008	Hootens Hollow	08002
Greenland (Part of		Hasbrouck Heights	07604	Hoot Owl Estates	08055
Magnolia)	08049	Haskell (Part of Wanaque)	07420	Hoover Village	08302
Green Pond	07435	Haven Beach	08008	Hopatcong	07843
Green Pond Junction (Part		Haworth	07641	Hopatcong Heights (Part of	
of Kinnelon)	07405	Hawthorne	07506-07	Hopatcong)	07843
Greensand	08817	For specific Hawthorne Zip Codes		Hopatcong Hills (Part of	
Greens Bridge (Part of		call (201) 977-4579		Hopatcong)	07843
Phillipsburg)	08865	Hazen	07823	Hope (Township)	07844
Green Village	07935	Hazlet	07730	Hope	07844
Greenville (Hudson County)	07305	Hazlet (Township)	07730	Hopelawn	08861
Greenville (Ocean County)	08701	Head Of River (Part of Estell		Hopewell (Cumberland	
Greenville (Salem County)	08318	Manor)	08270	County) (Township)	08302
Greenwich (Cumberland		Headquarters	08557	Hopewell (Mercer County)	08525
County)	08323	Heathcote	08528	Hopewell (Mercer County)	
Greenwich (Cumberland		Heather Hills	07439	(Township)	08560
County) (Township)	08323	Hedding	08505	Hornerstown	08514
Greenwich (Gloucester		Heislerville	08324	Howell (Township)	07727
County)	08027	Helmetta	08828	Howell (P.O.)	07731
Greenwich (Warren County)		Helmetta Park	08828	Howell (rural)	07728
(Township)	08886	Hensfoot	08827	Hudson City (Part of Jersey	
Greenwich Pier	08323	Herbertsville	08723	City)	07307
Greenwood Park	08071	Heritage Village	08053	Hudson Heights	07047
Grenloch	08032	Herman	08215	Hudson Shopping Plaza	
Grenloch Terrace	08032	Herwood	08002	(Part of Jersey City)	07304
Greystone Park	07950	Hesstown	08332	Hughesville	08848
Griggstown	08540	Hewitt	07421	Huntington	08865

	ZIP		ZIP		ZIP
Mahwah	07430	Meriden	07005	Morris Plains	07950
	07495	Metedeconk	08723	Morris Street (Part of	
For specific Mahwah Zip Codes		Metedeconk Park	08723	Morristown)	07960
call (201) 529-3366		Metedeconk Pines	08723	Morristown (Morris County)	07960-63
Mahwah (Township)	07430	Metropark	07095	For specific Morristown Zip Codes	
Main Avenue (Cumberland		Mettler	08873	call (201) 539-5890	
County)	08360	Metuchen	08840	Morristown (Middlesex	
Main Avenue (Passaic		Meyersville	07933	County)	07747
County)	07011	Miami Beach	08251	Morrisville	08110
Malaga	08328	Mickleton	08056	Morsemere (Part of	
Malapardis	07981	Middle (Township)	08210	Ridgefield)	07657
Mall at Short Hills, The	07078	Middlebush	08873	Morses Creek (Part of	
Manahawkin	08050	Middlesex	08846	Linden)	07036
Manalapan	07728	Middletown	07748	Mountain Lake	07823
Manalapan (Township)	07728	Middletown (Township)	07748	Mountain Lakes	07046
Manasquan	08736	Middletown	07866	Mountainside	07092
Manasquan Park	08736	Middle Valley	07853	Mountain Spring Lakes	07405
Manasquan Shores	08736	Middleville	07855	Mountain Station	07079
Manchester (Township)	08759	Midland Park	07432	Mountain View	07470
Mandalay	08723	Midstreams	08723	Mountainville	08833
Mannington (Township)	08079	Midstreams Park	08723	Mount Airy	08530
Manor Park	08723	Midtown (Part of Newark)	07102	Mount Arlington	07856
Mansfield	08022	Midvale (Part of Wanaque)	07465	Mount Bethel	07865
Mansfield (Burlington		Mile Hollow	08505	Mount Ephraim	08059
County) (Township)	08022	Milford	08848	Mount Fern	07801
Mansfield (Warren County)		Military Ocean Terminal		Mount Freedom	07970
(Township)	07863	(Part of Bayonne)	07002	Mount Hermon	07825
Mansfield Square	08022	Millbridge	08021	Mount Holly	08060
Mantoloking	08738	Millbrook (Morris County)	07869	Mount Holly (Township)	08060
Mantua	08051	Millbrook (Warren County)	07832	Mount Hope	07885
Mantua (Township)	08051	Millburn (Township)	07041	Mount Hope Mineral	
Mantua Grove	08061	Millburn	07041	Junction (Part of	
Mantua Heights	08051	Millhurst	07728	Wharton)	07885
Mantua Terrace	08051	Millington	07946	Mount Kemble Lake	07960
Manunka Chunk	07832	Millside Heights	08075	Mount Laurel	08054
Manville	08835	Millside Manor	08075	Mount Laurel (Township)	08054
Maplecrest	07040	Millstone (Monmouth		Mount Olive (Township)	07828
Maple Glen	08527	County) (Township)	08510	Mount Pleasant (Cape May	
Maple Shade (Township)	08052	Millstone (Somerset County)	08876	County)	08270
Maple Shade	08052	Milltown (Middlesex County)	08850	Mount Pleasant (Hunterdon	
Maple Tree	08753	Milltown (Union County)	07081	County)	08848
Maple View	08857	Millville	08332	Mount Pleasant (Warren	
Maplewood (Township)	07040	Milmay	08340	County)	07832
Maplewood	07040	Milton	07438	Mount Rose	08525
Marcella	07866	Mimosa Lake	08053	Mount Royal	08061
Margate City	08402	Mine Brook (Part of		Mount Salem	07461
Marksboro	07825	Bernardsville)	07931	Mounts Mills	08831
Marlboro (Township)	07746	Mine Hill (Township)	07801	Mount Tabor (Denville twp.)	07834
Marlboro (Burlington		Mine Hill	07801	Mount Tabor (Parsippany-	
County)	08053	Minotola (Part of Buena)	08341	Troy Hills twp.)	07878
Marlboro (Cumberland		Miramar	08223	Mount Vernon	07832
County)	08302	Mizpah	08342	Muhlenberg (Part of	
Marlboro (Monmouth		Money Island	08753	Plainfield)	07060
County)	07746	Monitor (Part of West New		Mullica (Township)	08217
Marlboro Heights	07726	York)	07093	Mullica Hill	08062
Marlton	08053	Monksville (Part of		Murray Hill (Part of New	
Marlton Heights	08098	Ringwood)	07465	Providence)	07974
Marlton Hills	08053	Monmouth (Part of		Myrtle Grove	07860
Marlton Lakes	08004	Eatontown)	07724	Mystic Islands	08087
Marlyn Manor	08242	Monmouth Beach	07750	Mystic Shores	08087
Marmora	08223	Monmouth Heights	07746	Natco (Part of Union Beach)	07735
Marshalls Corner	08525	Monmouth Hills	07732	National Park	08063
Marshalltown	08079	Monmouth Junction	08852	Naughright	07853
Martins Beach	08046	Monmouth Park (Part of		Naval Air Propulsion Test	
Martinsville	08836	Oceanport)	07757	Center	08628
Maryland	08527	Monroe (Gloucester County)		Navesink	07752
Maskell Mill	08079	(Township)	08094	Navesink Beach (Part of	
Masonville	08054	Monroe (Middlesex County)		Sea Bright)	07760
Matawan	07747	(Township)	08520	Nejecho Beach	08723
Maurice River (Township)	08327	Monroe (Morris County)	07981	Neptune	07753-54
Mauricetown	08329	Monroe (Sussex County)	07871	For specific Neptune Zip Codes	
Maxim	08701	Monroeville	08343	call (908) 776-8811	
Mayetta	08092	Montague (Township)	12771	Neptune City	07753
Mayfair at Marlton	08053	Montague	07827	Nesco	08037
Mayfair Gardens	08080	Montana	08865	Neshanic	08853
Mays Landing	08330	Montclair	07042-43	Neshanic Station	08853
Mayville	08210	For specific Montclair Zip Codes		Netcong	07857
Maywood	07607	call (201) 744-2660		Netherwood (Part of	
Meadowbrook	08109	Montgomery (Township)	08558	Plainfield)	07062
Meadowbrook Village	08527	Montrose	07722	New Albany	08077
Meadowview	07047	Montvale	07645	New Amsterdam Village	08879
Meadow Village	07009	Montville	07045		
Mechanicsville (Middlesex		Montville (Township)	07045	**Newark**	07101-08
County)	08879	Moonachie	07074		07112-75
Mechanicsville (Monmouth		Moores Corner	08079	For specific Newark Zip Codes	
County)	07730	Moores Meadows	08088	call (201) 596-5146	
Medford	08055	Moorestown	08057		
Medford (Township)	08055	Moorestown (Township)	08057	*COLLEGES & UNIVERSITIES*	
Medford Farms	08088	Moorestown-Lenola	08057		
Medford Lakes	08055	Moorestown Mall	08057	Rutgers-The State University	07102
Melrose (Burlington County)	08055	Moosepack Lake	07439	University of Medicine and	
Melrose (Middlesex County)	08879	Morehousetown	07039	Dentistry of New Jersey	07103
Menantico (Part of Millville)	08332	Morgan (Part of Sayreville)	08879		
Mendham	07945	Morgan Beach	08879	*FINANCIAL INSTITUTIONS*	
Mendham (Township)	07926	Morganville	07751		
Menlo Park	08837	Morris (Camden County)	08110	Broad National Bank,	
Menlo Park Mall	08817	Morris (Morris County)		Newark	07102
Menlo Park Terrace	08840	(Township)	07961	First Fidelity Bank, National	
Mercerville	08619	Morris Beach	08330	Association	07102
Mercerville-Hamilton Square	08619	Morris Park	08865	The Howard	07101
Merchantville	08109			Midlantic National Bank	07102
				Penn Federal Savings Bank	07105

	ZIP
HOSPITALS	
Newark Beth Israel Medical Center	07112
Saint Michael's Medical Center	07102
United Hospitals Medical Center	07107
University of Medicine and Dentistry of New Jersey-University Hospital	07103
Newark Heights	07040
Newbakers Corners	07825
New Bedford	07719
Newbolds Corner	08060
New Bridge (Part of New Milford)	07646
New Brooklyn	08081
New Brunswick	08901-06
For specific New Brunswick Zip Codes call (908) 819-3200	
New Canton	08501
New Durham	07047
New Egypt	08533
Newfield	08344
Newfoundland	07435
New Freedom	08009
New Gretna	08224
New Hampton	08827
New Hanover (Township)	08511
New Italy (Part of Vineland)	08360
New Jersey & New York Junction (Part of East Rutherford)	07073
New Jersey State Prison	08327
New Lisbon	08064
New Milford	07646
New Milford (Part of Oradell)	07649
New Monmouth	07748
Newport (Cumberland County)	08345
Newport (Hunterdon County)	08826
New Providence	07974
New Sharon (Gloucester County)	08080
New Sharon (Mercer County)	08691
Newton	07860
Newton Heights	08816
Newtonville	08346
New Vernon	07976
New Village	08886
New York & Greenwood Lake Junction (Part of Kearny)	07032
Nixon	08817
Norma	08347
Normandie (Part of Sea Bright)	07760
Normandy Beach	08739
Normandy Harbor	08739
North (Part of Newark)	07104
North Arlington	07031
North Asbury Park (Part of Asbury Park)	07712
North Beach	08008
North Beach Haven	08008
North Bergen	07047
North Bergen (Township)	07047
North Branch	08876
North Brunswick (Township)	08902
North Brunswick	08902
North Caldwell	07006
North Caldwell (Township)	07006
North Cape May	08204
North Cedarville	08311
North Center	07003
North Church	07416
North Church Estates	07416
North Crosswicks	08515
North Dennis	08214
North Edison	08817
North Elizabeth (Part of Elizabeth)	07208
Northfield (Atlantic County)	08225
Northfield (Essex County)	07039
North Hackensack (Part of River Edge)	07661
North Haledon	07508
North Hanover (Township)	08562
North Hawthorne (Part of Hawthorne)	07507
North Highlands Beach	08251
North Long Branch (Part of Long Branch)	07740
North Merchantville (Part of Merchantville)	08109
North Middletown	07758

	ZIP
Northmont (Part of Mount Ephraim)	08059
North Plainfield	07060
North Port Norris	08349
North Stelton	08854
Northvale	07647
North Vineland (Part of Vineland)	08360
North Wildwood	08260
North Woodbury (Part of Woodbury)	08096
Norton	08827
Nortonville	08085
Norwood	07648
Nottingham	08619
Nugentown	08087
Nutley	07110
Nutley (Township)	07110
Oak Dale	08060
Oak Glen	07731
Oak Hill	07748
Oakhurst	07755
Oakland	07436
Oaklyn	08107
Oak Ridge (Ocean County)	08753
Oak Ridge (Passaic County)	07438
Oak Ridge Lake	07438
Oak Shades	07747
Oak Tree (Middlesex County)	08817
Oak Tree (Ocean County)	08527
Oak Valley	08090
Oakview	08096
Oakwood	08055
Oakwood Beach	08079
Oakwood Park (Part of New Providence)	07974
Ocean (Monmouth County) (Township)	07755
Ocean (Ocean County) (Township)	08758
Ocean Acres	08050
Ocean Beach	08735
Ocean City	08226
Ocean City Gardens	08226
Ocean County Mall	08753
Ocean Gate	08740
Ocean Grove	07756
Ocean Heights (Part of Linwood)	08221
Oceanport	07757
Ocean View	08230
Oceanville	08231
Ogdensburg	07439
Old Bridge	08857
Old Bridge (Township)	08857
Old Bridge	08857
Old Charleston Woods	08002
Old Forge Village	07960
Old Manor	07730
Oldmans (Township)	08067
Old Orchard	08002
Old Tappan	07675
Oldwick	08858
Olivet	08318
Oradell	07649
Orange	07050-51
For specific Orange Zip Codes call (201) 673-2372	
Orchard Center	08302
Orchard View	08016
Orston (Part of Audubon)	08106
Ortley Beach	08751
Osage	08043
Osbornsville	08723
Othello	08302
Outcalt	08831
Outwater (Part of Garfield)	07026
Overbrook (Camden County)	08021
Overbrook (Essex County)	07009
Owens	07461
Oxford	07863
Oxford (Township)	07863
Oyster Creek	08220
Packanack Lake	07470
Pahaquarry (Township)	07832
Palatine	08318
Palermo	08223
Palisade (Part of Fort Lee)	07024
Palisades Park	07650
Palmer Square (Part of Princeton)	08540
Palmyra (Burlington County)	08065
Palmyra (Hunterdon County)	08867
Pamrapo (Part of Bayonne)	07002
Pancoast	08310
Panther Lake	07821
Paradise Lakes	08001

	ZIP
Paramus	07652-53
For specific Paramus Zip Codes call (201) 262-6886	
Paramus Park Shopping Center (Part of Paramus)	07652
Park (Part of Paterson)	07513
Park Avenue	07087
Parker	07853
Parkertown	08087
Park Ridge	07656
Park Ridge Farms	08505
Parkside	08865
Park Village	07016
Parkway Pines	08701
Parkway Village	08628
Parlin (Part of Sayreville)	08859
Parry	08077
Parsippany (Morris County)	07054
Parsippany (Part of Mountain Lakes)	07046
Parsippany-Troy Hills (Township)	07054
Parsippany-Troy Hills Township (census designated place)	07005
Pasadena	08759
Passaic (Morris County) (Township)	07946
Passaic (Passaic County)	07055
Passaic Junction	07662
Passaic Park (Part of Passaic)	07055
Paterson	07501-05
For specific Paterson Zip Codes call (201) 977-4738	
Patricks Corner	08816
Pattenburg	08802
Paulina	07825
Paulins Kill	07860
Paulsboro	08066
Peahala Park	08008
Peapack (Part of Gladstone)	07977
Pedricktown	08067
Peermont (Part of Avalon)	08202
Pelican Island	08751
Pellet Pond	07480
Pellettown	07822
Pemberton	08068
Pemberton (Township)	08015
Pemberton Heights	08068
Penbryn	08009
Penekum	08021
Pennington	08534
Pennsauken	08110
Pennsauken (Township)	08110
Pennsauken (Shopping Center)	08110
Penns Beach	08070
Penns Grove	08069
Penns Neck	08540
Pennsville	08070
Pennsville (Township)	08070
Penny Pot (Part of Folsom)	08037
Penton	08079
Penwell	07865
Peppermill Farms	08002
Pequannock	07440
Pequannock (Township)	07440
Pequest	07863
Perrineville	08535
Perth Amboy	08861-62
For specific Perth Amboy Zip Codes call (908) 826-2090	
Petersburg	08270
Philips Mills	07734
Phillipsburg	08865
Phoenix	08817
Picatinny Arsenal	07806
Pierces Point	08210
Piersonville	08620
Pilesgrove (Township)	08093
Pine Acres (Part of Woodbury Heights)	08090
Pine Beach	08741
Pine Brook (Monmouth County)	07724
Pine Brook (Morris County)	07058
Pine Brook (Somerset County)	08502
Pine Cliff Lake	07480
Pine Grove	08053
Pine Hill	08021
Pinehurst	08201
Pine Lake Park	08753
Pine Ridge	08857
Pine Ridge at Crestwood	08759
Pines Lake	07470
Pine Terrace	08753
Pinetree Village	08857
Pine Valley	08021
Pinewald	08721

	ZIP		ZIP		ZIP
Shore Crest	07067	Southwood	08857	Taylortown	07005
Short Hills	07078	South Woodstown (Part of		Teabo	07885
Shrewsbury	07702	Woodstown)	08098	Teaneck (Township)	07666
Shrewsbury (Township)	07724	Sparta	07871	Teaneck	07666
Shrewsbury Road	08501	Sparta (Township)	07871	Tenafly	07670
Sicklerville	08081	Sparta Junction	07871	Tennent	07763
Sidney	08867	Sparta Lake	07871	Teterboro	07608
Siloam	07728	Sperry Springs (Part of		Tewksbury (Township)	08833
Silver Bay	08753	Hopatcong)	07843	The Acres (Part of	
Silver Lake (Essex County)	07109	Spotswood	08884	Glassboro)	08028
Silver Lake (Warren County)	07825	Spray Beach	08008	The Dunes	08008
Silver Ridge	08753	Springdale (Camden		The Orchards	08619
Silver Ridge Park	08757	County)	08002	Thompson Beach	08324
Silver Ridge Park West	08757	Springdale (Sussex County)	07860	Thorofare	08086
Silver Springs	07850	Springfield (Burlington		Three Bridges	08887
Silverton	08753	County) (Township)	08041	Timber Lakes	08094
Sim Place	08005	Springfield (Union County)		Timbuctoo	08060
Singac	07424	(Township)	07081	Tinton Falls	07724
Sinnickson Landing	08079	Springfield	07081	Titusville	08560
Six Points	08302	Spring Gardens	08618	Toms River	08753-57
Skillman	08558	Spring Lake	07762	For specific Toms River Zip	
Skylands (Part of		Spring Lake Heights	07762	Codes call (908) 349-0710	
Ringwood)	07456	Spring Mills	08848	Totowa	07512
Sky Line Lake (Part of		Springside	08016	Towaco	07082
Ringwood)	07465	Springtown (Cumberland		Town Bank	08204
Slackwoods	08638	County)	08302	Town Brook	07748
Sloop Creek Estates	08721	Springtown (Warren County)	08865	Town Center	07052
Sloping Hills	07920	Springville	08057	Town Estates	08016
Smithburg	07728	Squire Village	08753	Townley	07083
Smiths Mills	07405	Stafford (Township)	08050	Townsbury	07863
Smith Tract	08008	Staffordville	08092	Townsends Inlet (Part of	
Smithville (Atlantic County)	08201	Stanhope	07874	Sea Isle City)	08243
Smithville (Burlington		Stanton	08885	Tranquility	07879
County)	08060	Stanton Station	08822	Tremley (Part of Linden)	07036
Smoke Rise (Part of		Stanwick	08057	Tremley Point (Part of	
Kinnelon)	07405	Stanwick Glen	08057	Linden)	07036
Snow Hill (Part of Lawnside)	08045	Star Cross	08322	Trenton	08601-91
Society Hill	08857	State Hospital	08625	For specific Trenton Zip Codes	
Soho	07109	Staten Island Junction	07016	call (609) 581-3030	
Somerdale	08083	Steelmantown	08270	Trenton Gardens	08610
Somerset (Somerset		Steelmanville	08221	Trenton Highlands	08619
County)	08873-75	Stephensburg	07865	Troy Hills	07054
For specific Somerset Zip Codes		Stevens	08016	Tuckahoe	08250
call (908) 873-8600		Stewartsville	08886	Tuckerton	08087
Somerset (Mercer County)	08628	Still Valley	08865	Tuckerton Shores (Part of	
Somers Point	08244	Stillwater	07875	Tuckerton)	08087
Somerville	08876-77	Stillwater (Township)	07875	Turkey Point Corner	08349
For specific Somerville Zip Codes		Stirling	07980	Turnersville	08012
call (908) 725-0570		Stockholm	07460	Tuttles Corner	07826
South (Part of Newark)	07114	Stockton	08559	Twin Rivers	08520
South Amboy	08879	Stockton State College	08240	Tyler Park	07047
Southampton (Township)	08088	Stone Harbor	08247	Undercliff (Part of	
Southard	08701	Stone House	07946	Edgewater)	07020
South Belmar	07719	Stone Tavern	08514	Union (Hunterdon County)	
South Bound Brook		Stonetown (Part of		(Township)	08802
(Middlesex County)	08846	Ringwood)	07465	Union (Union County)	
South Bound Brook		Stoney Brook Estates	08096	(Township)	07083
(Somerset County)	08880	Stony Hill	07922	Union	07083
South Branch	08876	Stoutsburg	08525	Union Beach	07735
South Brunswick	08540	Stow Creek (Township)	08302	Union Center	07083
South Brunswick (Township)	08852	Stow Creek Landing	08302	Union City	07087
South Camden (Part of		Stratford	08084	Union Hill	07801
Camden)	08104	Strathmere	08248	Union Mills	08060
South Dennis	08245	Strathmore	07747	Union Square (Part of	
South Egg Harbor	08215	Styertowne Shopping		Elizabeth)	07201
Southern State 1 & 2	08314	Center (Part of Clifton)	07012	Uniontown	08865
South Glassboro (Part of		Suburban	07701	Union Valley	08512
Glassboro)	08028	Succasunna	07876	Unionville	08060
South Hackensack		Succasunna-Kenvil	07876	Upper (Township)	08250
(Township)	07606	Summerfield	07823	Upper Berkshire Valley	07885
South Hackensack	07606	Summit	07901-02	Upper Deerfield (Township)	08313
South Harrison (Township)	08039	For specific Summit Zip Codes		Upper Freehold (Township)	08501
South Kearny (Part of		call (908) 277-1737		Upper Greenwood Lake	07421
Kearny)	07032	Summit Avenue (Part of		Upper Harmony	08865
South Lakewood	08701	Union City)	07087	Upper Mohawk	07871
South Livingston	07039	Sunbury	08068	Upper Montclair	07043
South Mantoloking	08738	Sunnyside	08801	Upper Montvale (Part of	
South Merchantville (Part of		Sunrise Beach	08731	Montvale)	07645
Merchantville)	08109	Sunrise Park	07876	Upper Pittsgrove (Township)	08318
South Ogdensburg (Part of		Sunset Hills	08540	Upper Saddle River	07458
Ogdensburg)	07439	Surf City	08008	Uptown (Part of Hoboken)	07030
South Orange	07079	Sussex	07461	V.A. Hospital (Part of East	
South Orange Village		Sutton Park	07836	Orange)	07018
(Township)	07079	Swainton	08210	Vail Homes	07724
South Paterson (Part of		Swartswood	07877	Vails	07832
Paterson)	07503	Swartswood Lake	07860	Vailsburg (Part of Newark)	07106
South Pemberton (Part of		Swedesboro	08085	Valley (Middlesex County)	08817
Pemberton)	08068	Sweet Briar	07733	Valley (Passaic County)	07470
South Penns Grove	08069	Sweetwater	08037	Vanada Woods	08723
South Plainfield	07080	Sykesville	08562	Vanhiseville	08527
South River	08882	Sylvan Glen	08505	Van Marters Corner	07730
South Seaside Park	08752	Sylvan Lake	08016	Vasa Home	07840
South Seaville	08246	Tabernacle	08088	Vauxhall	07088
South Toms River	08757	Tabernacle (Township)	08088	Ventnor City	08406
South Vineland (Part of		Tanglewood Farms	07733	Ventnor Heights (Part of	
Vineland)	08360	Tanners Corner	08816	Ventnor City)	08406
South Westville (Part of		Tansboro	08004	Verga	08093
Westville)	08093	Taunton Lakes	08053	Vernon	07462
Southwest Vinland (Part of		Taurus (Part of West New		Vernon (Township)	07462
Vineland)	08360	York)	07093	Vernon Valley	07418
Southwind	08527	Tavistock	08033		

	ZIP
Abbott	87747
Abeytas	87006
Abiquiu	87510
Abo	87036
Abuelo	87732
Acoma	87049
Acoma Indian Reservation	87031
Acomita	87034
Acomita Lake	87034
Adelino	87031
Adobe Acres	87105
Agua Fria	87501
Air Mail Facility (Part of Albuquerque)	87119
Alameda	87114
Alamillo	87831
Alamo	87825
Alamogordo	88310-11
For specific Alamogordo Zip Codes call (505) 437-9390	
Alamo Indian Reservation	87825
Albert	87733
Albuquerque	87101-99
For specific Albuquerque Zip Codes call (505) 848-3872	
Alcalde	87511
Algodones	87001
Alire	87518
Allison	87301
Alma	88039
Alpine Village	88345
Alto	88312
Alto Crest (Part of Ruidoso)	88345
Amalia	87512
Ambrosia Lake	87020
Amistad	88410
Anaconda	87020
Ancho	88301
Angel Fire	87710
Angostura (Dona Ana County)	87940
Angostura (Taos County)	87579
Angus	88316
Animas	88020
Animas Valley Mall (Part of Farmington)	87402
Anthony	88021
Anton Chico	87711
Apache Creek	87830
Apache Park	88345
Apodaca	87527
Arabela	88351
Aragon	87820
Arch	88130
Arenas Valley	88022
Arkansas Junction	88240
Armijo	87105
Arrey	87930
Arroyo del Agua	87012
Arroyo Hondo	87513
Arroyo Seco	87514
Artesia	88210-11
For specific Artesia Zip Codes call (505) 746-4412	
Artesia Camp	88347
Atoka	88210
Atrisco (Part of Albuquerque)	87105
Aurora (Mora County)	87734
Aurora (San Miguel County)	87583
Aztec	87410
Bacaville (Part of Belen)	87002
Bard	88411
Barelas (Part of Albuquerque)	87102
Barranca	87510
Bayard	88023
Becenti	87313
Beclabito	87420
Belen	87002
Bell Ranch	88441
Bellview	88111
Bennett	88252
Bent	88314
Berino	88024
Bernal	87569
Bernalillo	87004
Bernardo	87006
Beulah	87745
Bibo	87055
Bingham	87815
Bisti	87401
Black Forest (Part of Ruidoso)	88345
Black Lake	87734
Black River Village	88220
Black Rock	87327
Blanchard	87569
Blanco	87412
Blanco Trading Post	87037
Bloomfield	87413

	ZIP
Bluewater (Cibola County)	87005
Bluewater (Lincoln County)	88351
Boles	88311
Boles Acres	88311
Bonito	88341
Bosque	87006
Bosque Farms	87068
Boys Ranch	87002
Brazos	87551
Bread Springs	87301
Brimhall	87310
Broadmoor (Part of Roswell)	88201
Broadview	88112
Broadview Acres	87020
Buckeye	88260
Buckhorn	88025
Buena Vista	87712
Bueyeros	88412
Burnham	87401
Butterfield Park	88001
Caballo	87931
Cameron	88120
Campus (Part of Socorro)	87801
Canada de los Alamos	87501
Canjilon	87515
Cannon AFB (census designated place)	88101
Cannon Air Force Base	88103
Canon	87571
Canoncito (rural) (Bernalillo County)	87008
Canoncito (Bernalillo County)	87026
Canoncito (Rio Arriba County)	87527
Canoncito (San Miguel County)	87745
Canoncito (Santa Fe County)	87505
Canoncito Indian Reservation	87026
Canones	87516
Canon Plaza	87581
Canova	87582
Canyon	87024
Canyoncito	87535
Capitan	88316
Caprock	87213
Capulin	88414
Carlsbad	88220-21
For specific Carlsbad Zip Codes call (505) 885-5717	
Carlsbad North	88220
Carnuel	87112
Carrizo	88345
Carrizozo	88301
Carson	87517
Casa Blanca	87007
Causey	88113
Cebolla	87518
Cedar Creek	88345
Cedar Crest	87008
Cedar Grove	87056
Cedar Hill	87410
Cedarvale	87009
Cedro Village	87059
Central	88026
Central New Mexico Correctional Facility	87031
Cerrillos	87010
Cerro	87519
Chacon	87713
Chama	87520
Chamberino	87027
Chamisal	87521
Chamita	87566
Chaparral	88021
Chapelle	87569
Chaperito	87701
Chelwood Park (Part of Albuquerque)	87112
Chical	87031
Chi Chil Tah	87326
Chili	87537
Chilili	87059
Chimayo	87522
Chippeway Park	88317
Chloride	87943
Chupadero	87501
Church Rock	87311
Cimarron	87714
Claunch	87011
Clayton	88415
Cleveland	87715
Cliff	88028
Clines Corners	87070
Cloud Country Estates	88317
Cloudcroft	88317
Cloverdale	88020

	ZIP
Clovis	88101-03
For specific Clovis Zip Codes call (505) 763-5556	
Cochiti	87072
Cochiti Indian Reservation	87041
Cochiti Lake	87083
Colonias	88435
Columbine	87556
Columbus	88029
Conchas Dam	88416
Continental Divide	87312
Contreras	87028
Coolidge	87312
Corazon	87701
Cordova	87523
Corona	88318
Coronado (Part of Santa Fe)	87501
Coronado Center (Part of Albuquerque)	87110
Corrales	87048
Coruco	87560
Costilla	87524
Cotton City	88020
Counselor	87018
Country Club Estates (Bernalillo County)	87114
Country Club Estates (Lincoln County)	88345
Country Club Heights (Part of Ruidoso)	88345
Cowles	87573
Coyote	87012
Cree Meadows Heights (Part of Ruidoso)	88345
Crossroads	88114
Crownpoint	87313
Cruzville	87830
Crystal	87328
Cuba	87013
Cubero	87014
Cuchillo	87932
Cuervo	88417
Cundiyo	87522
Cuyamungue	87501
Dahlia	87711
Dalies	87031
Dalton Pass	87313
Datil	87821
Del Norte (Part of Ruidoso)	88345
Deming	88030-31
For specific Deming Zip Codes call (505) 546-9461	
Derry	87933
Des Moines	88418
De Vargas Shopping Center (Part of Santa Fe)	87501
Dexter	88230
Dilia	87724
Dixon	87527
Dog Canyon Estates	88310
Domingo	87052
Dona Ana	88032
Dora	88115
Downtown (Part of Albuquerque)	87103
Dulce	87528
Dunken	88344
Duran	88319
Dusty	87943
Eagle Nest	87718
East Grand Plains	88201
East Pecos	87552
Edgewood (Santa Fe County)	87015
El Ancon	87560
El Cerrito	87583
El Cerro	87031
Eldorado (Part of Albuquerque)	87111
Eldorado at Santa Fe	87505
El Duende	87537
Elephant Butte	87935
Elephant Butte Estates	87935
El Gauche	87566
El Guique	87566
Elida	88116
Elk	88339
Elkins	88201
El Llanito	87004
El Llano (Rio Arriba County)	87532
El Llano (San Miguel County)	87701
El Morro	87034
El Portero	87522
El Porvenir	87731
El Prado	87529
El Pueblo	87560
El Rancho	87532
El Rancho Loma Linda	87579
El Renz-O-Ranch	87718
El Rincon de los Trujillos	87522

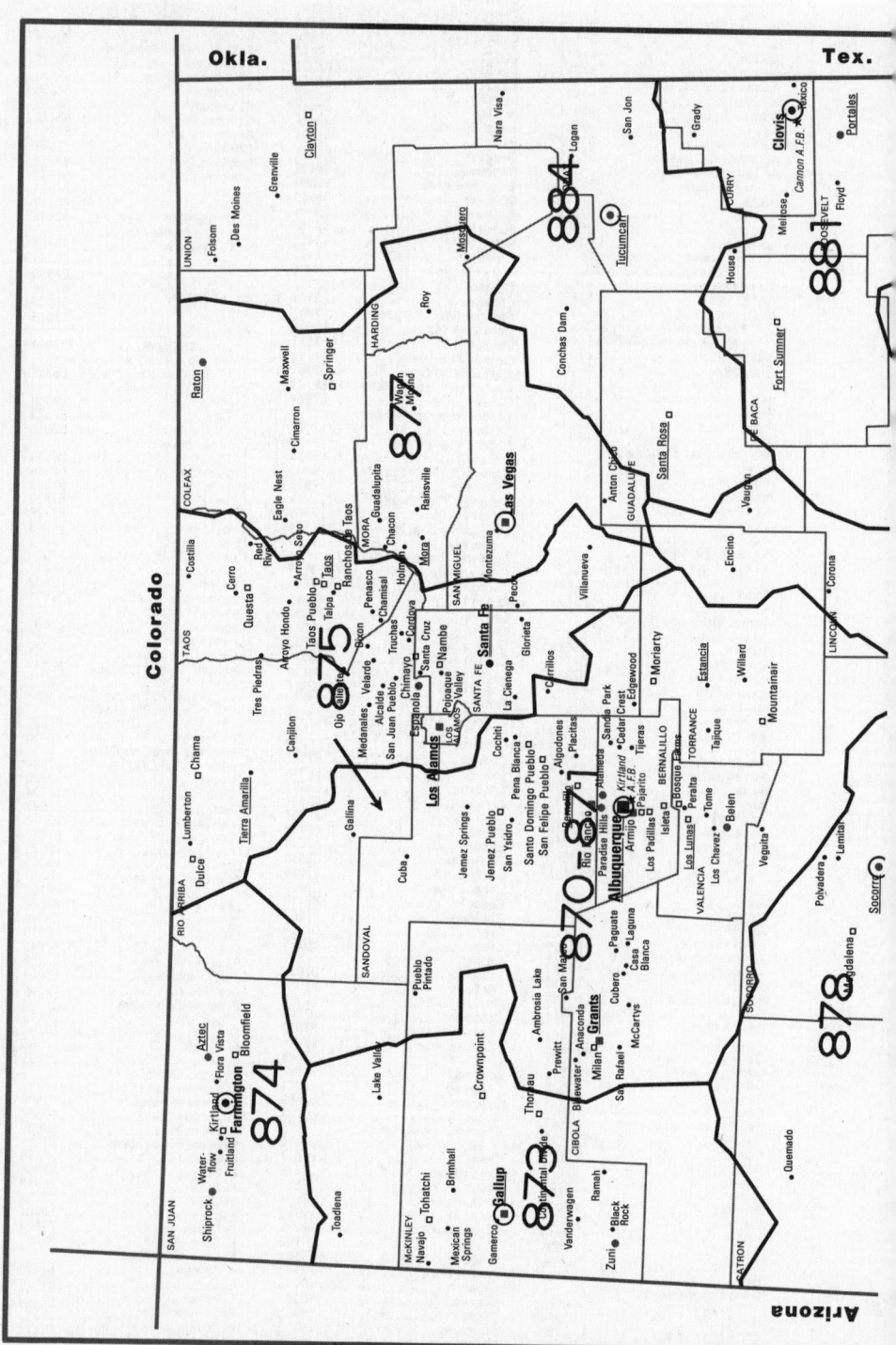

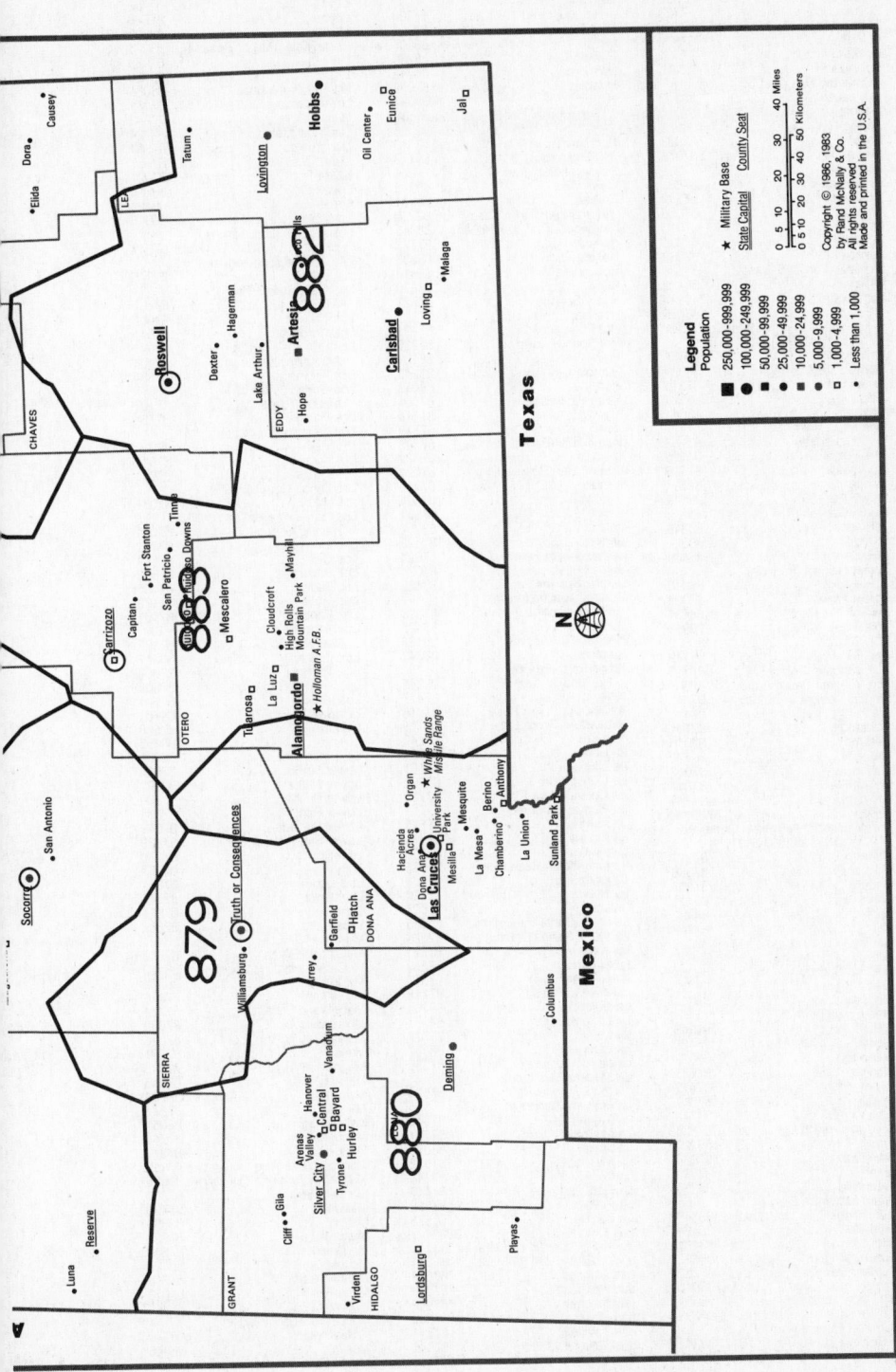

	ZIP		ZIP		ZIP
Mesquite	88048	Pilar	87571	Sabinal	87006
Mexican Springs	87320	Pine	87552	Sabinoso	87746
Miami	87729	Pinedale	87301	Sacramento	88347
Midway	88201	Pine Hill	87321	St. Vrain	88133
Milagro	88321	Pine View	87579	Salem	87941
Milan	87021	Pineywoods Estates	88317	San Acacia	87831
Mills	87730	Pinon	88344	San Antonio (Bernalillo	
Milnesand	88125	Pinos Altos	88053	County)	87008
Mimbres	88049	Pinoswells	87009	San Antonio (San Miguel	
Mimbres Hot Springs	88041	Pintada	88435	County)	87701
Mineral Hill	87701	Placita	87579	San Antonio (Socorro	
Mission Park	87031	Placitas (Dona Ana County)	87937	County)	87832
Mogollon	88039	Placitas (Rio Arriba County)	87515	San Antonio de Padua del	
Monero	87547	Placitas (Sandoval County)	87043	Rancho	87501
Monte Aplanado	87732	Placitas (Sierra County)	87939	San Antonito (Bernalillo	
Monte Verde (Part of Angel		Playas	88009	County)	87047
Fire)	87718	Plaza Blanca	87563	San Antonito (Socorro	
Montezuma	87731	Pleasant Hill	88135	County)	87832
Montgomery Plaza Mall		Pleasanton	88039	Sanchez	87746
(Part of Albuquerque)	87110	Pojoaque Indian Reservation	87501	San Cristobal	87564
Monticello	87939	Pojoaque Valley	87501	Sanctuario	87522
Montoya	88401	Polvadera	87828	Sandia	87047
Monument	88265	Ponderosa	87044	Sandia Base	87115
Moqino	87040	Ponderosa Heights (Part of		Sandia Heights	87004
Mora	87732	Ruidoso)	88345	Sandia Indian Reservation	87004
Moriarty	87035	Ponderosa Pines	87059	Sandia Knolls	87047
Mosquero	87733	Portales	88130	Sandia Park	87047
Mountainair	87036	Pot Creek	87571	Sandia Pueblo	87004
Mountain Park	88325	Prairie Dog Trading Post	87013	San Felipe Indian	
Mountain View (Bernalillo		Prairieview	88260	Reservation	87004
County)	87105	Prewitt	87045	San Felipe Pueblo	87001
Mountain View (Chaves		Progresso	87063	San Fidel	87049
County)	88201	Pueblito	87566	San Francisco	87006
Mount Dora	88429	Pueblitos	87002	San Francisco Plaza	87830
Mule Creek	88051	Pueblo of Acoma	87034	San Geronimo	87701
Nadine	88240	Pueblo Pintado	87013	San Ignacio	87745
Nageezi	87037	Puerto de Luna	88432	San Ildefonso Indian	
Nambe	87501	Punta de Agua	87036	Reservation	87502
Nambe Indian Reservation	87501	Quarris Acres	88317	San Ildefonso Pueblo	87501
Nambe Pueblo	87501	Quarteles	87532	San Jon	88434
Nara Visa	88430	Quay	88433	San Jose (Bernalillo County)	87102
Naschitti	87325	Queen	88220	San Jose (Rio Arriba	
Navajo	87328	Quemado	87829	County)	87537
Navajo Dam	87419	Questa	87556	San Jose (San Miguel	
Navajo Estates	87375	Radium Springs	88054	County)	87565
Navajo Indian Reservation	86515	Rainsville	87736	San Juan (Grant County)	88041
Navajo Wingate Village	87311	Ramah	87321	San Juan (Rio Arriba	
Newcomb	87455	Ramah Navajo Indian		County)	87566
Newkirk	88431	Reservation	87327	San Juan (San Miguel	
New Laguna	87038	Ramon	88136	County)	87565
New York	87014	Ranchito	87571	San Juan Indian	
Nogal	88341	Ranchitos	87532	Reservation	87566
North Acomita Village	87034	Rancho Grande Estates	87830	San Juan Pueblo	87566
North Carmen	87732	Ranchos de Taos	87557	San Lorenzo	88041
North Hurley	88043	Ranchos Lake Conchas	88416	San Mateo	87050
North San Ysidro	87538	Ranchvale	88101	San Miguel (Dona Ana	
North Valley	87107	Raton	87740	County)	88058
Nutrias	87575	Red Hill	87829	San Miguel (Rio Arriba	
Ocate	87734	Red River	87558	County)	81120
Oil Center	88266	Redrock (Grant County)	88055	San Miguel (San Miguel	
Ojito (Rio Arriba County)	87029	Red Rock (McKinley		County)	87560
Ojito (Taos County)	87521	County)	87420	Sanostee	87461
Ojitos Frios	87701	Regina	87046	San Pablo	87701
Ojo Amarillo	87417	Rehoboth	87322	San Patricio	88348
Ojo Caliente (Cibola		Rencona	87562	San Pedro	87532
County)	87327	Reserve	87830	San Rafael (Cibola County)	87051
Ojo Caliente (Taos County)	87549	Ribera	87560	San Rafael (San Miguel	
Ojo Feliz	87735	Rincon	87940	County)	88439
Ojo Sarco	87550	Rinconada	87531	San Sebastian	87501
Old Albuquerque (Part of		Rincon Montoso	87745	Santa Ana Indian	
Albuquerque)	87104	Rio Chiquito	87522	Reservation	87004
Old Picacho	88033	Rio Communities	87002	Santa Ana Pueblo	87004
Omega	87829	Rio Grande Estates	87002	Santa Clara Indian	
Organ	88052	Rio Lucio	87553	Reservation	87532
Orogrande	88342	Rio Puerco	87064	Santa Clara Pueblo	87532
Oscura	88301	Rio Rancho	87124	Santa Cruz	87567
Otis	88220	Rio West Mall (Part of		Santa Fe	87501-06
Paguate	87040	Gallup)	87301		87538
Pajarito (Bernalillo County)	87105	Rito de las Sillas	87064		87540
Pajarito (Santa Fe County)	87532	Riverside (Eddy County)	88210	For specific Santa Fe Zip Codes	
Paradise Hills	87114	Riverside (Lincoln County)	88201	call (505) 988-6351	
Park Springs	87701	Robin Hood Park	88317	Santa Rosa	88435
Pastura	88435	Rociada	87742	Santa Teresa	88008
Paxton Springs	87020	Rock Canyon	87935	Santo Domingo Indian	
Pecos	87552	Rock Springs	87301	Reservation	87052
Pena Blanca	87041	Rodarte	87561	Santo Domingo Pueblo	87052
Penasco	87553	Rodeo	88056	Santo Nino	87567
Penasco Blanco	87742	Rodey	87937	Santo Tomas	88044
Pendaries	87742	Rogers	88132	San Ysidro	87053
Penitentiary of New Mexico	87501	Romeroville	87701	Sapello	87745
Pep	88126	Rosebud	88410	Seama	87014
Peralta	87042	Roswell	88201-02	Seboyeta	87055
Perea	87316	For specific Roswell Zip Codes		Sedan	88436
Pescado	87327	call (505) 622-3741		Sedillo Hill	87059
Petaca	87554	Roswell Mall (Part of		Sena	87568
Philadelphia	87014	Roswell)	88201	Seneca	88437
Philmont	87714	Rowe	87562	Separ	88045
Picacho	88343	Roy	87743	Serafina	87569
Picuris	87553	Ruidoso	88345	Servilleta Plaza	87539
Picuris Indian Reservation	87553	Ruidoso Downs	88346	Seton Village	87501
Pie Town	87827	Rutheron	87563	Seven Lakes	87313

	ZIP		ZIP		ZIP
Seven Rivers	88254	Tierra Amarilla	87575	Valmora	87750
Seven Springs	87025	Tierra Monte	87742	Val Verde	87718
Shady Brook	87571	Tijeras	87059	Vanadium	88023
Sheep Springs	87364	Timberon	88350	Vanderwagen	87326
Shiprock	87420	Tinian	87401	Vaughn	88353
Sierra Vista	88312	Tinnie	88351	Veguita	87062
Sierra Vista Estates	87008	Tiptonville	87753	Velarde	87582
Sile	87041	Toadlena	87324	Ventero	87512
Silver Acres	88061	Tocito	87461	Vermejo Park	87740
Silver City	88061-62	Tohatchi	87325	Villa Linda Mall (Part of	
For specific Silver City Zip Codes		Tohlakai	87301	Santa Fe)	87505
call (505) 538-2831		Tolar	88134	Villa Madonna	88312
Sipapu	87579	Tome	87060	Villanueva	87583
Sixteen Springs	88317	Tome-Adelino	87060	Virden	85534
Skyline-Ganipa	87034	T-O Ranch	87740	Volcano Cliffs (Part of	
Smith Lake	87323	Torreon (Sandoval County)	87013	Albuquerque)	87120
Socorro	87801	Torreon (Torrance County)	87061	Wagon Mound	87752
Sofia	88424	Tortugas	88047	Walker (Part of Roswell)	88201
Soham	87565	Totavi	87544	Waterfall	88317
Solano	87746	Trampas	87576	Waterflow	87421
Sombrillo	87532	Trechado	87315	Watrous	87753
South Carmen	87725	Trementina	88439	Weed	88354
Southern New Mexico		Tres Piedras	87577	Western New Mexico	
Correctional Facility	88004	Tres Ritos	87579	Correctional Facility	87020
South San Ysidro	87565	Truchas	87578	Westgate Heights (Part of	
South Springs Acres	88201	Trujillo	87701	Albuquerque)	87105
South Valley	87102	Truth or Consequences	87901	West Las Vegas (Part of	
Spencerville	87410	Tse Bonito	86515	Las Vegas)	87701
Springer	87747	Tucumcari	88401	White Horse	87013
Springstead	87311	Tularosa	88352	White Lakes	87056
Squirrel Springs	87325	Turley	87412	White Oaks	88301
Standing Rock	87313	Turn	87002	White Rock (Los Alamos	
Stanley	87056	Twin Forks Estates	88317	County)	87544
Star Lake	87013	Twin Lakes	87301	White Rock (San Juan	
Stead	88438	Two Gray Hills	87325	County)	87313
Sumner Lake State Park	88119	Two Wells	87326	White Sands	88002
Sunland Park	88063	Tyrone	88065	White Sands Missile Range	88002
Sunshine	88030	University (Bernalillo County)	87106	Whites City	88268
Sunspot	88349	University (Roosevelt		White Signal	88061
Sun Valley	88312	County)	88130	Willard	87063
Taiban	88134	University Park	88003	Williams Acres	87301
Tajique	87057	Upper Anton Chico	87711	Williamsburg	87942
Talpa	87557	Upper Dilia	87724	Willow Creek	88039
Taos	87571	Upper Pueblo	87560	Winrock Center (Part of	
Taos Indian Reservation	87571	Upper Rociada	87742	Albuquerque)	87110
Taos Pueblo	87571	Uptown (Part of		Winston	87943
Taos Ski Valley	87525	Albuquerque)	87110	Wyoming Mall, The (Part of	
Tatum	88267	Ute Mountain Indian		Albuquerque)	87112
Tecolote	87701	Reservation	81334	Yah-Ta-Hey	87375
Tecolotito	87711	Ute Park	87749	Yeso	88136
Tererro	87573	Vadito	87579	Youngsville	87064
Tesuque	87574	Vado	88072	Zamora	87059
Tesuque Indian Reservation	87574	Valdez	87580	Zia Indian Reservation	87053
Tesuque Pueblo	87501	Valencia	87031	Zia Pueblo	87053
Texico	88135	Vallecitos	87581	Zuni	87327
Thoreau	87323	Vallecitos de los Indios	87025	Zuni Indian Reservation	87327
Three Rivers	88352	Valle Escondido	87571		

ZIP

Abbotts	14727
Academy (Albany County)	12208
Academy (Ontario County)	14424
Accord	12404
Acidalia	12760
Acra	12405
Adams	13605
Adams (Town)	13605
Adams Basin	14410
Adams Center	13606
Adams Corners	10579
Adams Cove	13634
Adamsville	12827
Addison	14801
Addison (Town)	14801
Addison Hill	16920
Adelphi (Part of New York)	11238
Adirondack	12808
Adrian	14823
Afton	13730
Afton (Town)	13730
Afton Lake	13730
Airmont	10901
Airmont Heights	10901
Akins Corners	12563
Akron	14001
Alabama	14003
Alabama (Town)	14003
Albany	12201-60
For specific Albany Zip Codes call (518) 452-2499	
Albany Medical Center (Part of Albany)	12208
Albertson	11507
Albia (Part of Troy)	12180
Albion	14411
Albion (Orleans County) (Town)	14411
Albion (Oswego County) (Town)	13302
Albion Correctional Facility	14411
Alcove	12007
Alden	14004
Alden (Town)	14004
Alden Bend	12910
Alden Center	14004
Alden Manor	11003
Alder Creek	13301
Alexander	14005
Alexander (Town)	14005
Alexander Corners	13650
Alexander Shopping Center (Part of Yonkers)	10710
Alexandria (Town)	13607
Alexandria Bay	13607
Alfred	14802
Alfred (Town)	14802
Alfred Station	14803
Allaben	12480
Allard Corners	12586
Allegany	14706
Allegany (Town)	14706
Allegany Indian Reservation (Town)	14081
Allegany Indian Reservation	14081
Allen (Town)	14709
Allen Center	14735
Allens Hill	14469
Allentown	14707
Allenwood	11021
Allerton (Part of New York)	10467
Alligerville	12440
Alloway	14489
Alma	14708
Alma (Town)	14708
Almond	14804
Almond (Town)	14804
Aloquin	14561
Alpine	14805
Alplaus	12008
Alps	12018
Alsen	12415
Altamont (Albany County)	12009
Altamont (Franklin County) (Town)	12986
Altay	14837
Altmar	13302
Alton	14413
Altona	12910
Altona (Town)	12910
Amagansett	11930
Amawalk	10501
Amber	13110
Amberville	13843
Amboy (Onondaga County)	13031
Amboy (Oswego County) (Town)	13493
Amboy Center	13493
Amchir (Part of Middletown)	10940
Amenia	12501
Amenia (Town)	12501

ZIP

Amenia Union	12501
Ames	13317
Amherst	14226
Amherst (Town)	14226
Amity (Allegany County) (Town)	14813
Amity (Orange County)	10990
Amity Harbor	11701
Amityville	11701
Amsdell Heights	14075
Amsterdam	12010
Amsterdam (Town)	12010
Ancram	12502
Ancram (Town)	12502
Ancramdale	12503
Andes	13731
Andes (Town)	13731
Andover	14806
Andover (Town)	14806
Andrea Park Estates	10598
Angelica	14709
Angelica (Town)	14709
Angola	14006
Angola on the Lake	14006
Annandale-on-Hudson	12504
Annsville (Oneida County) (Town)	13471
Annsville (Westchester County)	10566
Ansonia (Part of New York)	10023
Antwerp	13608
Antwerp (Town)	13608
Apalachin	13732
Apex	13783
Appleton	14008
Apulia	13159
Apulia Station	13020
Aquebogue	11931
Aqueduct	12308
Aquetuck	12143
Arcade	14009
Arcade (Town)	14009
Arcade Junction (Part of Arcade)	14009
Arcadia (Town)	14513
Archdale	12834
Archville	10510
Arden	10910
Ardonia	12515
Ardsley	10502
Ardsley-on-Hudson (Part of Irvington)	10503
Argusville	13459
Argyle	12809
Argyle (Town)	12809
Arietta (Town)	12139
Arkport	14807
Arkville	12406
Arkwright (Town)	14718
Arlington	12603
Arlyn Oaks	11758
Armonk	10504
Armor	14075
Arnolds Mill	12037
Arrochar (Part of New York)	10305
Arthur Manor (Part of Scarsdale)	10583
Arthursburg	12533
Arverne (Part of New York)	11692
Asharoken	11768
Ashford	14731
Ashford (Town)	14171
Ashford Hollow	14171
Ashland (Town)	12407
Ashland (Chemung County) (Town)	14894
Ashland (Greene County)	12407
Ashokan	12481
Ashville	14710
Ashville Bay	14710
Ashwood	14098
Aspenwood	12065
Aspinwall Corners	13650
Assembly Point	12845
Association Island	13651
Astoria (Part of New York)	11102
Athens	12015
Athens (Town)	12015
Athol	12810
Athol Springs	14010
Atlanta	14808
Atlantic (Part of New York)	10307
Atlantic Beach	11509
Atlantique	11706
Attica	14011
Attica (Town)	14011
Attica Center	14011
Attica Correctional Facility	14011
Attlebury	12581
Atwater	13081
Atwell	13338

ZIP

Atwood	12484
Auburn	13021-22
For specific Auburn Zip Codes call (315) 252-9554	
Audubon (Part of New York)	10032
Augusta	13425
Augusta (Town)	13425
Aurelius (Town)	13034
Auriesville	12016
Aurora (Cayuga County)	13026
Aurora (Erie County) (Town)	14052
Aurora Tract	13088
Au Sable (Town)	12944
Au Sable Chasm	12944
Au Sable Forks	12912
Austerlitz	12017
Austerlitz (Town)	12017
Ava	13303
Ava (Town)	13303
Averill Park	12018
Avoca	14809
Avoca (Town)	14809
Avon	14414
Avon (Town)	14414
Axeville	14726
Babcock Hill	13318
Babcock Lake	12138
Babylon	11702-04
For specific Babylon Zip Codes call (516) 669-1318	
Bacon Hill	12871
Baggs Corner	13601
Bainbridge	13733
Bainbridge (Town)	13733
Baiting Hollow	11933
Bakers Mills	12811
Bakerstand	14101
Balcom	14138
Balcom Beach	14777
Bald Mountain	12834
Baldwin (Chemung County) (Town)	14861
Baldwin (Nassau County)	11510
Baldwin Harbor	11510
Baldwin Heights (Part of Olean)	14760
Baldwin Place	10505
Baldwin Place Shopping Center	10505
Baldwinsville	13027
Ballina	13035
Ballston (Town)	12019
Ballston Center	12020
Ballston Lake	12019
Ballston Spa	12020
Balltown	14062
Balmat	13609
Balmville	12550
Baltimore	13141
Bangall (Dutchess County)	12506
Bangall (Onondaga County)	13112
Bangor	12966
Bangor (Town)	12966
Bangor Station	12966
Bank Plaza	11566
Barberville	12018
Barcelona	14787
Barclay Heights (Part of Saugerties)	12477
Bardonia	10954
Bare Hill Correctional Facility	12953
Barker (Broome County) (Town)	13746
Barker (Niagara County)	14012
Barkers Grove	12154
Barkersville	12850
Barkertown	14836
Barnegat	12603
Barnerville	12092
Barnes Corners	13610
Barnes Hole	11930
Barneveld	13304
Barnum Island	11558
Barre (Town)	14411
Barre Center	14411
Barrington (Town)	14837
Barrytown	12507
Barryville	12719
Bartlett	13440
Bartlett Corners	14468
Bartlett Hollow	13775
Barton	13734
Barton (Town)	13734
Basket	12760
Basom	14013
Batavia	14020-21
For specific Batavia Zip Codes call (716) 343-0491	
Batchellerville	12134

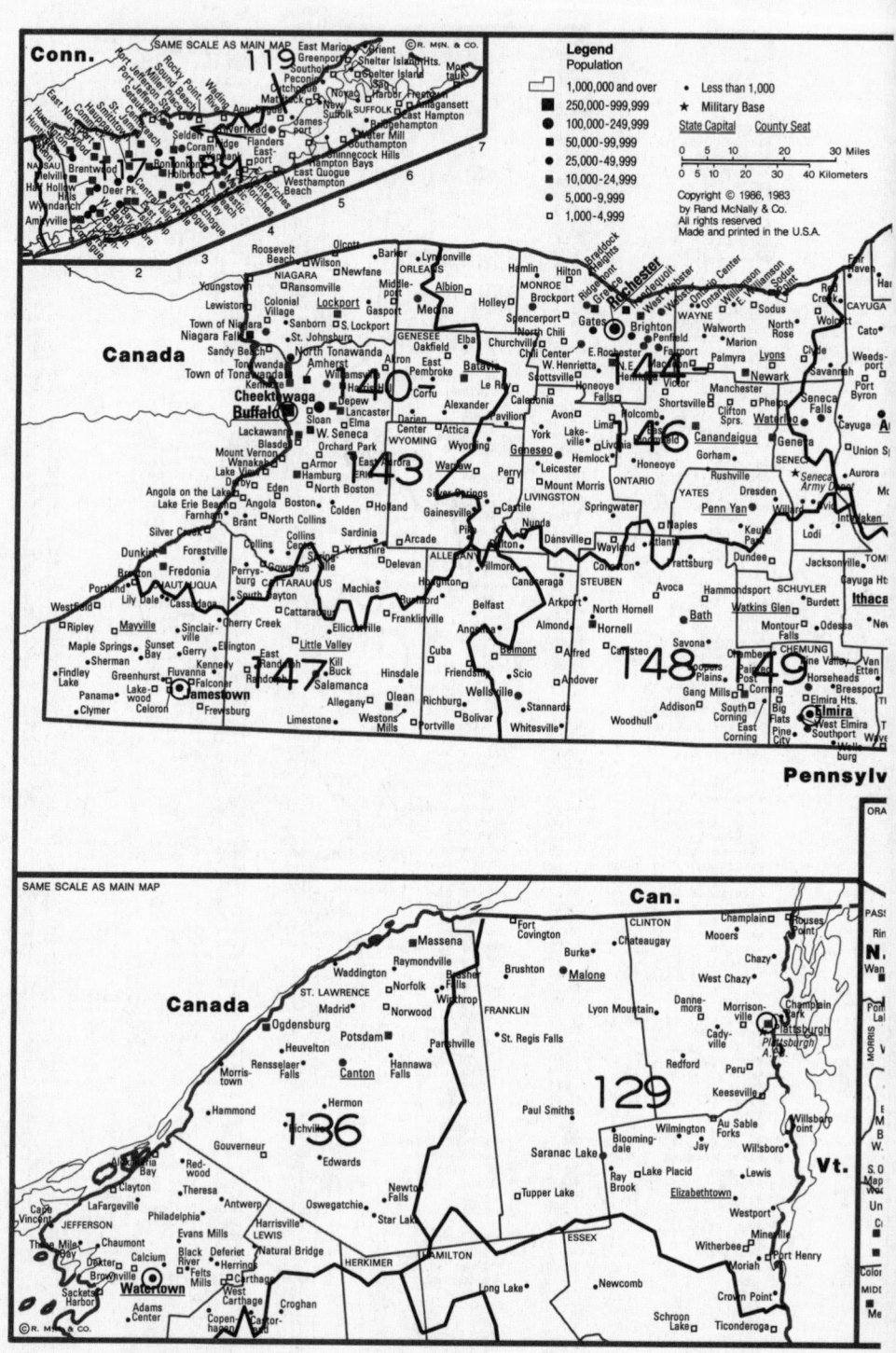

Legend
Population

▢	1,000,000 and over
■	250,000-999,999
●	100,000-249,999
●	50,000-99,999
●	25,000-49,999
■	10,000-24,999
▪	5,000-9,999
▫	1,000-4,999

• Less than 1,000
★ Military Base
<u>State Capital</u>   <u>County Seat</u>

0 5 10   20   30 Miles
0 5 10 20 30   40 Kilometers

Conn.

Canada

Pennsylv

Can.

N.

Vt.

	ZIP		ZIP		ZIP
Bates	12469	Bellmont Center	12920	Bliss	14024
Bath	14810	Bellmore	11710	Blockville	14710
Bath (Town)	14810	Bellona (station)	14527	Blodgett Mills	13738
Bath Beach (Part of New		Bellona	14415	Bloomfield (Part of New	
York)	11214	Bellow Corners	14171	York)	10314
Battenville	12834	Bellport	11713	Bloomingburg	12721
Battery Park City (Part of		Bellvale	10912	Bloomingdale	12913
New York)	10007	Bellville	14717	Blooming Grove	10914
Baxter Estates	11050	Belmont	14813	Blooming Grove (Town)	10914
Bay (Part of New York)	11235	Belvidere	14813	Bloomington	12411
Bayberry	13088	Bemis Heights	12170	Bloomville	13739
Bayberry Dunes	11772	Bemus Point	14712	Blossvale	13308
Bayberry Park (Part of New		Benedict Beach	14464	Blue Mountain	12477
Rochelle)	10804	Bennett Bridge	13302	Blue Mountain Lake	12812
Bayberry Shopping Center	13088	Bennettsburg	14818	Blue Point	11715
Baychester (Part of New		Bennettsville	13733	Blue Ridge	12534
York)	10469	Bennington	14011	Blue Stores	12526
Bay Park	11518	Bennington (Town)	14011	Bluff Point	14478
Bay Point	11963	Benson	12134	Blythebourne (Part of New	
Bayport	11705	Benson (Town)	12134	York)	11219
Bay Ridge (Part of New		Benson Mines	13690	Boardmanville (Part of	
York)	11220	Benton (Town)	14527	Olean)	14760
Bay Shore	11706	Benton Center	14527	Boerum Hill (Part of New	
Bay Shores	13110	Berea	12549	York)	11201
Bayside (Part of New York)	11360	Bergen	14416	Boght Corners	12047
Bay Terrace (Queens		Bergen (Town)	14416	Bohemia	11716
County)	11360	Bergen Beach	14847	Boiceville	12412
Bay Terrace (Richmond		Bergen Park	11746	Bolivar	14715
County)	10306	Bergholtz	14304	Bolivar (Town)	14715
Bay View (Erie County)	14075	Berkshire (Town)	13736	Bolton	12824
Bayview (Suffolk County)	11971	Berkshire (Fulton County)	12078	Bolton (Town)	12824
Bayville	11709	Berkshire (Onondaga		Bolton Landing	12814
Baywood	11706	County)	13066	Bolts Corners	13147
Beach Hampton	11930	Berkshire (Tioga County)	13736	Bombay	12914
Beach Ridge	14120	Berkshire Terrace	10512	Bombay (Town)	12914
Beach Shopping Center		Berlin	12022	Bon Air Heights (Part of	
(Part of Peekskill)	10566	Berlin (Town)	12022	Suffern)	10901
Beachville	14807	Berne	12023	Bonney	13464
Beacon	12508	Berne (Town)	12023	Bonni Castle	14590
Beacon Hill	12508	Bernhards Bay	13028	Bonnie Crest (Part of New	
Beantown	14859	Berryville	12068	Rochelle)	10804
Bear Mountain	10911	Berwyn	13084	Bonny Lee Estates	12184
Bearsville	12409	Best	12018	Boonville	13309
Beaver Brook	12764	Bethany	14054	Boonville (Town)	13309
Beaverdam Lake-Salisbury		Bethany (Town)	14054	Borden	14801
Mills	12553	Bethel (Town)	12720	Border City (Ontario	
Beaver Dams	14812	Bethel (Dutchess County)	12567	County)	14456
Beaver Falls	13305	Bethel (Sullivan County)	12720	Border City (Seneca	
Beaverkill	12758	Bethel Corners	13111	County)	14456
Beaver Meadow	13832	Bethel Grove	14850	Borodino	13152
Beaver River	13367	Bethford	14219	Borough Hall (Part of New	
Beckers Corners	12158	Bethlehem (Town)	12054	York)	11424
Becks Grove (Part of		Bethlehem Center	12077	Boston	14025
Rome)	13308	Bethlehem Heights	12161	Boston (Town)	14025
Bedell	12430	Bethpage	11714	Boston Corners	12546
Bedford (Town)	10506	Beukendaal	12302	Botanical (Part of New	
Bedford (Kings County)	11210	Beverly Inn Corners	13315	York)	10458
Bedford (Westchester		Bible School Park (Part of		Bouckville	13310
County)	10506	Johnson City)	13737	Boughton Hill	14564
Bedford Hills	10507	Bidwell (Part of Buffalo)	14222	Boulevard (Part of New	
Bedford Hills Correctional		Big Brook	13486	York)	10459
Facility	10507	Big Flats	14814	Boulevard Mall	14226
Bedford-Stuyvesant (Part of		Big Flats (Town)	14814	Boultons Beach (Part of	
New York)	11233	Big Flats Airport	14814	Sackets Harbor)	13685
Beecher Corners	12442	Big Fresh Pond	11968	Bouquet	12936
Beechertown	13697	Big H Shopping Center	11743	Bournes Beach	14787
Beech Hill (Part of Yonkers)	10710	Big Indian	12410	Bovina (Town)	13740
Beechmont (Part of New		Big Island	10924	Bovina Center	13740
Rochelle)	10804	Big Moose	13331	Bowen	14772
Beechmont Woods (Part of		Big Tree	14219	Bowens Corners	13069
New Rochelle)	10804	Big Wolf Lake	12986	Bowerstown	13326
Beechurst (Part of New		Billings	12510	Bowling Green (Part of New	
York)	11357	Billington Bay	13030	York)	10004
Beechwood (Part of		Billington Heights	14052	Bowmansville	14026
Rochester)	14609	Biltmore Shores	11758	Boylston (Town)	13083
Beehive Crossing	12090	Bingham Mills	12526	Boyntonville	12090
Beekman	12533	Binghamton	13901-05	Boysen Bay	13039
Beekman (Town)	12570	For specific Binghamton Zip		Braddock Heights	14612
Beekman Corners	13459	Codes call (607) 773-2142		Bradford	14815
Beekmantown	12901	Binghamton (Town)	13902	Bradford (Town)	14815
Beekmantown (Town)	12901	Binghamton Plaza (Part of		Bradley	12754
Beixedon Estates	11971	Binghamton)	13901	Braeside	12123
Belair Road (Part of New		Bingley	13035	Brainard	12024
York)	10305	Binnewater	12401	Brainards Corners	13315
Belcher	12865	Birchwood Estates	12184	Brainardsville	12915
Belcoda	14546	Birdsall	14709	Braman Corners	12053
Belden	13787	Birdsall (Town)	14709	Bramans Corners	12186
Belfast	14711	Bishopville	14807	Bramanville	12092
Belfast (Town)	14711	Black Brook	12912	Brambler Ridge	14450
Belfort	13327	Black Brook (Town)	12912	Branchport	14418
Belgium	13027	Black Creek	14714	Brandon (Town)	12966
Belle Isle	13209	Blackmans Corners	12959	Brandon Center	12966
Bellerose (Nassau County)	11426	Black River	13612	Brandreth	12847
Bellerose (Queens County)	11426	Black Rock (Part of Buffalo)	14207	Brant	14027
Bellerose Terrace	11426	Blackwatch Hills	14450	Brant (Town)	14027
Belle Terre	11777	Blakeley	14052	Brantingham	13312
Belleview	14712	Blasdell	14219	Brant Lake	12815
Belleville	13611	Blauvelt	10913	Brasher (Town)	13613
Bellevue	14225	Bleecker	12078	Brasher Center	13613
Bellevue Gardens	12151	Bleecker (Town)	12078	Brasher Falls	13613
Bellmont (Town)	12917	Blenheim (Town)	12131	Brasher Falls-Winthrop	13613

	ZIP
Brasie Corners	13642
Breakabeen	12122
Breesport	14816
Breezy Point (Part of New York)	11697
Brentwood	11717
Brevoort (Part of New York)	11216
Brewerton	13029
Brewster	10509
Brewster Heights	10509
Brewster Hill	10509
Briarcliff Manor	10510
Briar Park	11793
Bridge (Part of Niagara Falls)	14305
Bridgehampton	11932
Bridgeport..................	13030
Bridgeville	12701
Bridgewater	13313
Bridgewater (Town)........	13313
Brier Hill	13614
Brighton (Franklin County) (Town)	12970
Brighton (Kings County) ...	11235
Brighton (Monroe County) (Town)	14610
Brighton (Monroe County)	14610
Brighton (Otsego County)	13439
Brighton Beach (Part of New York)	11235
Brightside	13436
Brightwaters	12524
Brinckerhoff	12524
Brisben	13830
Briscoe	12783
Bristol	14469
Bristol (Town)	14469
Bristol Center..............	14424
Bristol Springs	14512
Broadacres.................	13905
Broadalbin	12025
Broadalbin (Town).........	12025
Broad Channel (Part of New York)	11693
Broadway (Part of New York)	11106
Brockport	14420
Brockville	14411
Brocton	14716
Brodhead	12494
Bronx	10401-75

For specific Bronx Zip Codes call
(212) 960-5009

COLLEGES & UNIVERSITIES

City University of New York-Lehman College	10468
Fordham University	10458
Manhattan College	10471
State University of New York Maritime College ...	10465

FINANCIAL INSTITUTIONS

North Side Savings Bank	10463
City and Suburban Federal Savings Bank	10467

HOSPITALS

Bronx Municipal Hospital Center	10461
Bronx-Lebanon Hospital Center	10457
Bronx Psychiatric Center...	10461
Lincoln Medical and Mental Health Center	10451
Montefiore Medical Center	10467
North Central Bronx Hospital	10467
Our Lady of Mercy Medical Center	10466
St. Barnabas Hospital......	10457
Veterans Affairs Medical Center	10468
Bronxville	10708
Bronxville Heights (Part of Yonkers)................	10708
Brookdale	13668
Brookfield	13314
Brookfield (Town).........	13314
Brookhaven	11719
Brookhaven (Town).......	11719
Brooklyn	11201-56

For specific Brooklyn Zip Codes
call (718) 834-3000

COLLEGES & UNIVERSITIES

Brooklyn Law School	11201

	ZIP
City University of New York-Brooklyn College	11210
City University of New York-Medgar Evers College ...	11225
City University of New York-New York City Technical College	11201
Long Island University-Brooklyn Campus	11201
Polytechnic University......	11201
Pratt Institute	11205
St. Francis College	11201
State University of New York Health Science Center at Brooklyn	11203

FINANCIAL INSTITUTIONS

Bay Ridge Federal Savings & Loan Association	11209
Brooklyn Federal Savings Bank	11201
Crossland Savings Bank ...	11201
Dime Savings Bank of Williamsburgh	11211
East New York Savings Bank	11207
Flatbush Federal Savings & Loan Association........	11210
The Green Point Savings Bank	11222
Hamilton Federal Savings & Loan Association........	11209
The Home Savings Bank	11237
Independence Savings Bank	11201

HOSPITALS

Brookdale Hospital Medical Center	11212
Brooklyn Hospital Center...	11201
Catholic Medical Center of Brooklyn and Queens ...	11214
Coney Island Hospital.....	11235
Interfaith Medical Center ...	11238
Kings County Hospital Center	11203
Kingsbrook Jewish Medical Center	11203
Long Island College Hospital	11201
Lutheran Medical Center ...	11220
Maimonides Medical Center	11219
Methodist Hospital	11215
University Hospital of Brooklyn-State University of N.Y. Health Sciences Center at Brooklyn	11203
Veterans Affairs Medical Center	11209
Victory Memorial Hospital	11228
Woodhull Medical and Mental Health Center	11206
Wyckoff Heights Medical Center	11237

MILITARY INSTALLATIONS

Coast Guard Supply Center, Brooklyn	11232
Fort Hamilton and New York Area Command	11252
Supervisor of Shipbuilding, Conversion and Repair, Brooklyn	11251
Brooks Avenue Station (Part of Rochester)	14624
Brooksburg	12496
Brooks Grove	14510
Brooktondale	14817
Brookview	12026
Brookville	11545
Brookville Park	11751
Broome (Town)...........	12122
Broome Center	12076
Broughton Park...........	13760
Browns Bridge	13625
Browns Hollow	13317
Brownsville (Kings County)	11212
Brownsville (Ontario County)	14564
Brownville	13615
Brownville (Town)........	13615
Bruceville	12440
Brunswick (Town)	12180
Brushton	12916
Brutus (Town)	13166
Bruynswick...............	12589
Bryant (Part of New York)	10036
Bryn Mawr Park (Part of Yonkers)................	10701
Buchanan	10511
Buckingham Estates	10989

	ZIP
Buckleyville................	12037
Bucks Bridge..............	13660
Buckton...................	13697
Buel	13317
Buellville	13104
Buena Vista	14823
Buffalo	14201-40

For specific Buffalo Zip Codes call
(716) 846-2538

Buffalo Creek (Part of Buffalo)	14224
Buffalo Junction (Part of Buffalo)	14201
Buffalo Lake (Part of Buffalo)	14222
Bull Hill	13324
Bulls Head (Monroe County)	14611
Bulls Head (Richmond County)................	10314
Bullville	10915
Bundys	13126
Burden Lake	12018
Burdett...................	14818
Burgoyne	12871
Burke	12917
Burke (Town)..............	12917
Burke Center	12917
Burlingham	12722
Burlington	13315
Burlington (Town)..........	13315
Burlington Flats............	13315
Burnhams (Part of Cassadaga)..............	14718
Burns	14807
Burns (Town)..............	14807
Burnside	12543
Burns-Whitney Estates	12110
Burnt Hills	12027
Burnwood	13756
Burrs Mills	13601
Burt	14028
Burtonsville	12066
Bushes Landing	13367
Bushnell Basin	14534
Bushnellsville	12480
Bush Terminal (Part of New York)	11232
Bushville (Genesee County)	14020
Bushville (Sullivan County)	12701
Bushwick (Part of New York)	11221
Buskirk	12028
Busti	14701
Busti (Town)	14701
Butler (Town).............	14590
Butler Center	14590
Butlerville	10519
Butterfield (Part of Utica) ...	13503
Butternut Grove	12776
Butternuts (Town)	13776
Byersville.................	14517
Byrden	12526
Byron	14422
Byron (Town)..............	14422
Cabinhill	13752
Cadiz	14737
Cadosia...................	13783
Cadyville	12918
Cahoonzie.................	12780
Cairo	12413
Cairo (Town)	12413
Calcium	13616
Calcutta	12064
Caldor Shopping Center (Part of Port Chester)....	10573
Caledonia	14423
Caledonia (Town)..........	14423
Calico Colony	12065
Callicoon	12723
Callicoon (Town)	12791
Callicoon Center...........	12724
Calverton	11933
Cambria (Town)	14094
Cambria Heights (Part of New York)	11411
Cambridge	12816
Cambridge (Town).........	12816
Camden	13316
Camden (Town)...........	13316
Cameron	14819
Cameron (Town)	14819
Cameron Mills	14820
Camillus	13031
Camillus (Town)	13031
Camillus Plaza............	13031
Campbell	14821
Campbell (Town)..........	14821
Campbell Hall	10916
Camp Hemlock............	12721
Camp Hill (Part of Pomona)	10970
Camps Mills	13601

	ZIP		ZIP		ZIP
Campville	13760	Cattaraugus Indian Reservation (Cattaraugus County)	14081	Chautauqua (Town)	14722
Camroden	13440			Chautauqua Mall (Part of Lakewood)	14750
Canaan	12029	Cattaraugus Indian Reservation (Chautauqua County) (Town)	14081	Chazy	12921
Canaan (Town)	12029			Chazy (Town)	12921
Canaan Center	12029			Chazy Lake	12935
Canada Lake	12032	Cattaraugus Indian Reservation (Erie County) (Town)	14081	Chazy Landing	12921
Canadice	14560			Chedwel	14712
Canadice (Town)	14560	Cattown	13337	Cheektowaga (Town)	14225
Canajoharie	13317	Caughdenoy	13036	Cheektowaga	14225
Canajoharie (Town)	13317	Cayuga	13034	Cheektowaga Northwest	14225
Canal Street (Part of New York)	10013	Cayuga Correctional Facility	13118	Cheektowaga Southwest	14227
Canandaigua	14424-25	Cayuga Heights	14850	Chelsea (Dutchess County)	12512
For specific Canandaigua Zip Codes call (716) 394-1500		Cayuta	14824	Chelsea (Richmond County)	10314
Canarsie (Part of New York)	11236	Cayuta (Town)	14824	Chemung	14825
Canaseraga	14822	Cayutaville	14805	Chemung (Town)	14825
Canastota	13032	Caywood	14860	Chemung Center	14825
Canawaugus	14423	Cazenovia	13035	Chenango (Town)	13745
Candor	13743	Cazenovia (Town)	13035	Chenango Bridge	13745
Candor (Town)	13743	Cecil Park (Part of Yonkers)	10707	Chenango Forks	13746
Caneadea	14717	Cedar Cliff	12542	Chenango Lake	13815
Caneadea (Town)	14717	Cedarcrest	14487	Cheneys Point	14710
Canisteo	14823	Cedar Flats	10980	Cheningo	13158
Canisteo (Town)	14823	Cedar Hill	12158	Cherokee (Part of New York)	10028
Cannon Corners	12959	Cedarhurst	11516	Cherry Creek	14723
Canoe Place	11946	Cedar Knolls (Part of Yonkers)	10708	Cherry Creek (Town)	14723
Canoga	13148	Cedarvale	13215	Cherry Grove	11782
Canterbury Hill (Part of Rome)	13440	Cedarville	13357	Cherry Lane (Part of Fredonia)	14063
Canterbury Woods	13116	Celoron	14720	Cherry Plain	12040
Canton	13617	Cementon	12415	Cherrytown	12446
Canton (Town)	13617	Centenary	10956	Cherry Valley	13320
Cape Vincent	13618	Center Avenue (Part of East Rockaway)	11518	Cherry Valley (Town)	13320
Cape Vincent (Town)	13618			Cherry Valley Junction	12043
Capitol (Part of Albany)	12224	Center Brunswick	12180	Cheshire	14424
Capitol Annex (Part of Albany)	12225	Centereach	11720	Chester	10918
		Center Falls	12834	Chester (Orange County) (Town)	10918
Capitol Hills	10950	Centerfield	14424		
Cardiff	13084	Centerlisle	13797	Chester (Warren County) (Town)	12860
Carle Place	11514	Center Moriches	11934		
Carle Terrace	12449	Centerport (Cayuga County)	13166	Chesterfield (Town)	12944
Carlisle	12031	Centerport (Suffolk County)	11721	Chester Heights (Part of Yonkers)	10701
Carlisle (Town)	12031	Centerville	14029		
Carlisle Center	12035	Centerville (Town)	14029	Chester Hill Park (Part of Mount Vernon)	10550
Carlisle Gardens	14094	Centerville	13756		
Carlton	14411	Center White Creek	12057	Chestertown	12817
Carlton (Town)	14411	Central (Part of New York)	11435	Chestnut Hill	13088
Carman	12303	Central Bridge	12035	Chestnut Ridge (Niagara County)	14094
Carmel	10512	Centralia	14782		
Carmel (Town)	10512	Central Islip	11722	Chestnut Ridge (Rockland County)	10952
Carmel Park Estates	10512	Central Nyack	10960		
Carnegie	14075	Central Park (Part of Buffalo)	14215	Cheviot	12526
Caroga (Town)	12032			Chichester	12416
Caroga Lake	12032	Central Park Shopping Center (Part of Buffalo)	14214	Childs	14411
Caroline	14817			Childwold	12922
Caroline (Town)	14817	Central Square	13036	Chili (Town)	14428
Caroline Center	14817	Central Valley	10917	Chili Center	14624
Carousel Center (Part of Syracuse)	13290	Centre Island	11771	Chilson	12883
		Centre Village	13787	Chinatown (Part of New York)	10013
Carroll (Town)	14738	Centuck (Part of Yonkers)	10710		
Carroll Gardens (Part of New York)	11231	Ceres	14721	Chipmonk	14706
		Chadwicks	13319	Chippewa Bay	13623
Carrollton	14748	Chaffee	14030	Chittenango	13037
Carrollton (Town)	14753	Chamberlain Corners	13660	Chittenango Falls	13035
Carson	14823	Chambers	14812	Choconut Center	13905
Carthage	13619	Champion	13619	Church Street (Part of New York)	10007
Cascade	13118	Champion (Town)	13619		
Case	13084	Champion Huddle	13619	Churchtown	12521
Casowasco	13118	Champlain	12919	Churchville (Monroe County)	14428
Cassadaga	14718	Champlain (Town)	12919	Churchville (Oneida County)	13478
Cassville	13318	Champlain Park	12901	Churubusco	12923
Castile	14427	Chapel Hill Estates	10598	Cicero	13039
Castile (Town)	14427	Chapin	14424	Cicero (Town)	13039
Castile Center	14427	Chappaqua	10514	Cicero Center	13041
Castle (Part of New Rochelle)	10801	Charleston (Montgomery County) (Town)	12066	Cincinnatus	13040
				Cincinnatus (Town)	13040
Castle Creek	13744	Charleston (Richmond County)	10301	Circleville	10919
Castle Hill (Part of New York)	10462			City Island (Part of New York)	10464
		Charleston Four Corners	12166		
Castle Point	12511	Charlotte (Chautauqua County) (Town)	14782	Clairemont Farms	13088
Castleton Corners (Part of New York)	10314			Clare (Town)	13684
		Charlotte (Monroe County)	14612	Claremont Park (Part of New York)	10457
Castleton on Hudson	12033	Charlotte Center	14782		
Castorland	13620	Charlotteville	12036	Clarence	14031
Catatonk	13827	Charlton	12019	Clarence (Town)	14031
Catharine	14869	Charlton (Town)	12019	Clarence Center	14032
Catharine (Town)	14869	Charwood Manor	12065	Clarendon	14429
Cathedral (Part of New York)	10025	Chase Lake	13343	Clarendon (Town)	14429
		Chase Mills	13621	Clark Heights	12569
Catlin (Town)	14812	Chaseville	12116	Clark Mills	13321
Cato	13033	Chasm Falls	12953	Clarksburg	14057
Cato (Town)	13033	Chateaugay	12920	Clarks Corners	14747
Caton	14830	Chateaugay (Town)	12920	Clarks Mills	12834
Caton (Town)	14830	Chatham	12037	Clarkson	14430
Catskill	12414	Chatham (Town)	12037	Clarkson (Town)	14430
Catskill (Town)	12414	Chatham Center	12184	Clarkstown (Town)	10956
Cattaraugus	14719	Chaumont	13622	Clarksville (Albany County)	12041
Cattaraugus Indian Reservation (Cattaraugus County) (Town)	14081	Chauncey (Part of Dobbs Ferry)	10502	Clarksville (Allegany County) (Town)	14786
		Chautauqua	14722	Claryville	12725

	ZIP		ZIP		ZIP
Clason Point (Part of New York)	10473	Collingwood Estates	14174	Corinth	12822
Classon (Part of New York)	11238	Collins	14034	Corinth (Town)	12822
Claverack	12513	Collins (Town)	14034	Cornell (Part of New York)	10473
Claverack (Town)	12513	Collins Center	14035	Corners (Part of Cayuga Heights)	14850
Claverack-Red Mills	12513	Collins Correctional Facility	14079	Corning	14830
Clay	13041	Collins Landing	13607	Corning (Town)	14830
Clay (Town)	13041	Collinsville	13433	Corning Manor	14830
Clayburg	12981	Colonial Acres	12077	Cornwall	12518
Clayton	13624	Colonial Green	12188	Cornwall (Town)	12518
Clayton (Town)	13624	Colonial Heights (Dutchess County)	12603	Cornwall on Hudson	12520
Clayville	13322	Colonial Heights (Westchester County)	10708	Cornwallville	12418
Clear Creek	14726	Colonial Park (Part of New York)	10039	Corona-A (Part of New York)	11368
Clearfield	14221	Colonial Springs	11798	Corona-Elmhurst (Part of New York)	11373
Clemons	12819	Colonial Village (Part of Lewiston)	14092	Cortland	13045
Clermont	12526	Colonie	12212	Cortlandt (Town)	10520
Clermont (Town)	12526	Colonie (Town)	12212	Cortlandville (Town)	13045
Cleveland	13042	Colonie Center	12205	Cortland West	13045
Cleveland Hill	14225	Colosse	13131	Cosmos Heights	13045
Cleverdale	12820	Colton	13625	Cossayuna	12823
Cliff Haven	12901	Colton (Town)	13625	Coss Corners	14810
Clifford	13069	Columbia (Town)	13357	Cottage	14138
Cliffside	12116	Columbia Center	13357	Cottage City	14424
Clifton (Monroe County)	14428	Columbia University (Part of New York)	10025	Cottage Park	14750
Clifton (Richmond County)	10304	Columbia University Extension	10926	Cottam Hill	12590
Clifton (St. Lawrence County) (Town)	13666	Columbiaville	12050	Cottekill	12419
Clifton Gardens	12065	Columbus	13411	Cottonwood Point	14435
Clifton Heights	14085	Columbus (Town)	13411	Council Meadows	12027
Clifton Knolls	12065	Columbus Circle (Part of New York)	10023	Country Knolls	12151
Clifton Park	12065	Colvin Elmwood (Part of Syracuse)	13205	Country Knolls (census designated place)	12019
Clifton Park (Town)	12065	Commack	11725	Country Knolls South	12065
Clifton Park Center	12065	Commack Corners Shopping Center	11725	Country Life Press (Part of Garden City)	11530
Clifton Springs	14432	Comstock	12821	Country Ridge Estates	10573
Climax	12042	Comstock Tract	13027	County Line	14098
Clinton (Clinton County) (Town)	12923	Concord (Erie County) (Town)	14141	Cove Neck	11771
Clinton (Dutchess County) (Town)		Concord (Richmond County)	10304	Coventry	13778
Clinton (Oneida County)	13323	Conesus	14435	Coventry (Town)	13778
Clinton Corners	12514	Conesus (Town)	14435	Coventryville	13733
Clintondale	12515	Conesville	12076	Covert	14847
Clinton Heights	12144	Conesville (Town)	12076	Covert (Town)	14847
Clinton Hollow	12578	Conewango	14726	Coveytown Corners	12917
Clinton Park	12144	Conewango (Town)	14726	Covington	14525
Clintonville	12924	Conewango Valley	14726	Covington (Town)	14525
Clockville	13043	Coney Island (Part of New York)	11224	Cowlesville	14037
Clough Corners	13862	Conger Corners	13480	Coxsackie	12051
Clove	12043	Congers	10920	Coxsackie (Town)	12051
Clover Bank	14075	Conifer	12986	Coxsackie Correctional Facility	12192
Cloverville	12430	Conklin	13748	Crafts	10512
Clyde	14433	Conklin (Town)	13748	Cragsmoor	12420
Clymer	14724	Conklin Forks	13903	Craigville	10918
Clymer (Town)	14724	Conklingville	12835	Crains Mills	13158
Cobb	11976	Connelly	12417	Cranberry Creek	12117
Cobble Hill (Part of New York)	11201	Connelly Park	14710	Cranberry Lake	12927
Cobleskill	12043	Conquest	13140	Crandall Corners	12154
Cobleskill (Town)	12043	Conquest (Town)	13140	Cranes Corners	13340
Cochecton	12726	Constable	12926	Cranesville	12010
Cochecton (Town)	12726	Constable (Town)	12926	Cranford (Part of New York)	10470
Cochecton Center	12727	Constableville	13325	Crary Mills	13617
Coeymans	12045	Constantia	13044	Craryville	12521
Coeymans (Town)	12045	Constantia (Town)	13044	Craterclub	12936
Coeymans Hollow	12046	Constantia Center	13028	Crawford (Town)	12566
Coffins Mills	13670	Continental Village	10566	Creek Locks	12411
Cohocton	14826	Cook Corners	13625	Crescent	12188
Cohocton (Town)	14826	Cooksburg	12469	Crescent Beach (Monroe County)	14612
Cohoes	12047	Cooks Falls	12776	Crescent Beach (Richmond County)	10301
Cokertown	12571	Cookville	14036	Crescent Estates	12065
Colchester	13856	Coolidge Beach	14172	Crescent Estates North	12065
Colchester (Town)	13755	Coonrod (Part of Rome)	13440	Crestview Heights	13760
Cold Brook (Herkimer County)	13324	Co-op City (Part of New York)	10475	Crestwood (Part of Yonkers)	10710
Coldbrook (Schenectady County)	12303	Cooper (Part of New York)	10003	Crestwood (Part of Tuckahoe)	10707
Colden	14033	Coopers Plains	14827	Crestwood Gardens (Part of Yonkers)	10710
Colden (Town)	14033	Cooperstown	13326	Crittenden	14038
Coldenham	12549	Cooperstown Junction	12116	Crocketts	13156
Coldspring (Cattaraugus County) (Town)	14783	Coopersville (Clinton County)	12919	Crofts Corners	10579
Cold Spring (Putnam County)	10516	Coopersville (Livingston County)	14517	Croghan	13327
Cold Spring Harbor	11724	Copake	12516	Croghan (Town)	13327
Cold Springs (Onondaga County)	13027	Copake (Town)	12516	Crompond	10517
Cold Springs (Steuben County)	14810	Copake Falls	12517	Cropseyville	12052
Cold Spring Terrace	11743	Copake Lake	12521	Cross Country Center (Part of Yonkers)	10704
Coldwater	14624	Copenhagen	13626	Crossgates Mall	12203
Colemans Mills	13492	Copiague	11726	Cross River	10518
Colesville (Town)	13787	Coram	11727	Cross Roads Estates	10598
Colgate (Part of Hamilton)	13346	Coram Hill	11763	Croton	14864
Collabar	12549	Corbett	13755	Crotona Park (Part of New York)	10460
Collamer	13057	Corbettsville	13749	Croton Falls	10519
College (Part of New York)	10030	Coreys	12986	Croton Heights	10598
College Park	12571	Corfu	14036	Croton-on-Hudson	10520
College Point (Part of New York)	11356			Crotonville	10562
Colliersville	13747				
Collingwood	13084				

	ZIP
East Moriches	11940
East Nassau	12062
East Neck	11743
East New York (Part of New York)	11207
East Nichols	13812
East Northport	11731
East Norwich	11732
East Olean (Part of Olean)	14760
Easton (Town)	12834
East Otto	14729
East Otto (Town)	14729
East Palermo	13036
East Palmyra	14444
East Part	12538
East Part	13697
East Patchogue	11772
East Pembroke	14056
East Penfield	14450
East Pharsalia	13758
East Pitcairn	13648
East Pittstown	12028
East Poestenkill	12018
Eastport	11941
East Quogue	11942
East Quogue	11942
East Randolph	14730
East Ripley	14775
East River	13056
East Rochester	14445
East Rockaway	11518
East Rodman	13601
East Salamanca (Part of Salamanca)	14779
East Schodack	12063
East Schuyler	13340
East Seneca	14224
East Setauket	11733
East Shelby	14103
East Shoreham	11786
East Side (Broome County)	13904
Eastside (Suffolk County)	11937
East Sidney	13775
East Springfield	13333
East Steamburg	14886
East Stone Arabia	13428
East Syracuse	13057
East Taghkanic	12502
East Varick	14541
East Vestal	13902
East Victor	14564
East View	10595
East Watertown	13601
East Wawarsing	12489
East White Plains (Part of Harrison)	10604
East Williamson	14449
East Williston	11596
East Windham	12439
East Windsor	13865
East Winfield	13491
Eastwood (Part of Syracuse)	13206
East Worcester	12064
Eaton	13334
Eaton (Town)	13334
Eatons Neck	11768
Eavesport	12490
Ebenezer	14224
Ebenezer Junction	14224
Echota (Part of Niagara Falls)	14302
Eddy	13617
Eddyville (Cattaraugus County)	14755
Eddyville (Ulster County)	12401
Eden	14057
Eden (Town)	14057
Edenville	10990
Edgemere (Part of New York)	11691
Edgemont	10583
Edgewater Beach	13308
Edgewater Park	13669
Edgewood (Greene County)	12450
Edgewood (Suffolk County)	11717
Edgewood Garden	13164
Edinburg	12134
Edinburg (Town)	12134
Edmeston	13335
Edmeston (Town)	13335
Edson	13865
Edwards	13635
Edwards (Town)	13635
Edwards Hill	12811
Edwards Park	12029
Edwardsville	13646
Egbertville (Part of New York)	10306
Eggertsville	14226
Egypt	14450

	ZIP
Einstein (Part of New York)	10475
Elayne Meadows	12188
Elba	14058
Elba (Town)	14058
Elbridge	13060
Elbridge (Town)	13060
Eldred	12732
Elizabethtown	12932
Elizabethtown (Town)	12932
Elizaville	12523
Elka Park	12427
Elk Brook	12776
Elk Creek	12155
Elkdale	14779
Ellenburg	12933
Ellenburg (Town)	12933
Ellenburg Center	12934
Ellenburg Depot	12935
Ellenville	12428
Ellery (Town)	14756
Ellery Center	14712
Ellicott (Chautauqua County) (Town)	14733
Ellicott (Erie County)	14127
Ellicott (Part of Buffalo)	14203
Ellicottville	14731
Ellicottville (Town)	14731
Ellington	14732
Ellington (Town)	14732
Ellisburg	13636
Ellisburg (Town)	13636
Ellis Hollow	14850
Ellistown	14892
Elma	14059
Elma (Town)	14059
Elmdale	13642
Elm Grove	13808
Elmhurst	14701
Elmhurst-A (Part of New York)	11373
Elmira	14901-25
For specific Elmira Zip Codes call (607) 737-5100	
Elmira (Town)	14902
Elmira Heights	14903
Elmira Heights North	14903
Elmont	11003
Elm Park (Part of New York)	10303
Elmsford	10523
Elm Valley	14895
Elnora	12065
Elsmere	12054
Eltingville (Part of New York)	10312
Elton	14042
Elton Station	14042
Elwood	11731
Elwood Farms	11731
Embogcht	12414
Emerson	13140
Emerson Hill (Richmond County)	10304
Emerson Hill (Richmond County)	10301
Emeryville	13642
Eminence	12175
Emmons	13820
Empeyville	13316
Empire State (Part of New York)	10001
Empire State Plaza (Part of Albany)	12220
Endicott	13760-61
	13763
For specific Endicott Zip Codes call (607) 748-8207	
Endwell	13760
Enfield	14850
Enfield (Town)	14850
Ensenore	13118
Ephratah	13339
Ephratah (Town)	13339
Erieville	13061
Erin	14838
Erin (Town)	14838
Erwin (Town)	14870
Erwins	14870
Escarpment	14092
Esopus	12429
Esopus (Town)	12429
Esperance	12066
Esperance (Town)	12066
Esplanade (Part of New York)	10469
Essex	12936
Essex (Town)	12936
Etna	13062
Euclid	13041
Evans (Town)	14006
Evans Center	14006
Evans Mills	13637

	ZIP
Exeter (Town)	13315
Exeter Center	13315
Fabius	13063
Fabius (Town)	13063
Factory Village	12020
Factoryville	12928
Fairdale	13074
Fairfield	13336
Fairfield (Town)	13336
Fairfield Farms	13066
Fairfield Gardens	12205
Fair Harbor	11706
Fair Haven	13064
Fairlawn Estates	12110
Fairmount	13219
Fairmount (census designated place)	13031
Fairmount Fair Mall	13219
Fair Oaks	10940
Fairport	14450
Fairview (Allegany County)	14060
Fairview (Dutchess County)	12601
Fairview (Westchester County)	10603
Fairview (Wyoming County)	14427
Falconer	14733
Falcon Manor	14304
Falconwood	14072
Falls (Part of Niagara Falls)	14303
Fallsburg	12733
Fallsburg (Town)	12733
Fancher	14452
Fargo	14036
Farleys Point	13160
Farmers Mills	10512
Farmersville (Town)	14060
Farmersville Center	14737
Farmersville Station	14060
Farmingdale	11735
Farmington	14425
Farmington (Town)	14425
Farmingville	11738
Farnham	14061
Farragut (Part of New York)	11203
Far Rockaway	11601-97
For specific Far Rockaway Zip Codes call (718) 327-7700	
HOSPITALS	
Peninsula Hospital Center	11691
St. John's Episcopal Hospital-South Shore	11691
MILITARY INSTALLATIONS	
Fort Tilden	11695
Fawn Ridge	13027
Fayette	13065
Fayette (Town)	13065
Fayetteville	13066
Federal (Part of Rochester)	14614
Federal Correctional Institution	10963
Federal Reserve (Part of New York)	10045
Felts Mills	13638
Fenimore	12801
Fenner (Town)	13035
Fenton (Town)	13833
Ferenbaugh	14830
Fergusons Corners	14456
Fergusonville	12155
Ferndale	12734
Fernwood (Oswego County)	13142
Fernwood (Sullivan County)	12760
Ferry Village	14072
Feura Bush	12067
Fieldston (Part of New York)	10463
Filer Corners	13808
Fillmore	14735
Finchville	10940
Findley Lake	14736
Fine	13639
Fine (Town)	13639
Fineview	13640
Finger Lakes Manor (Part of Canandaigua)	14424
Fink Basin	13365
Finnegans Corners	10924
Fire Island Pines	11782
Firthcliffe Heights	12584
Fish Creek (Lewis County)	13325
Fish Creek (Ulster County)	12477
Fish Creek Landing	13308
Fishers	14453
Fishers Island	06390
Fishers Landing	13641
Fisherville	14903
Fish House	12025
Fishkill	12524

	ZIP		ZIP		ZIP
Fishkill (Town)	12524	Forest Park (Dutchess		Fulmer Valley	14806
Fishkill Plains	12590	County)	12572	Fulton (Oswego County)	13069
Fishs Eddy	13774	Forestport	13338	Fulton (Schoharie County)	
Five Corners (Madison		Forestport (Town)	13338	(Town)	12122
County)	13421	Forestport Station	13338	Fultonham	12071
Five Corners (Oneida		Forestville	14062	Fultonville	12072
County)	13480	Forge Hollow	13328	Furnace Brook	10925
Fivemile Point	13795	Forks	14225	Furnaceville	14519
Five Points	14456	Forsonville	10524	Furnace Woods	10566
Five Town Plaza	11598	Forsyth	14775	Furniss	13126
Flackville	13669	Fort Ann	12827	Fyler Settlement	13082
Flanders	11901	Fort Ann (Town)	12827	Gabriels	12939
Flatbrook	12029	Fort Covington	12937	Gaines	14411
Flatbush (Kings County)	11226	Fort Covington (Town)	12937	Gaines (Town)	14411
Flatbush (Ulster County)	12477	Fort Covington Center	12937	Gainesville	14066
Flat Creek (Montgomery		Fort Drum	13612	Gainesville (Town)	14066
County)	13317	Fort Edward	12828	Galatia	13803
Flat Creek (Schoharie		Fort Edward (Town)	12828	Gale	12973
County)	12076	Fort George (Part of New		Galen (Town)	14433
Fleetwood (Part of Mount		York)	10040	Galeville (Onondaga	
Vernon)	10552	Fort Herkimer	13407	County)	13088
Fleischmanns	12430	Fort Hunter (Albany County)	12303	Galeville (Ulster County)	12589
Fleming	13021	Fort Hunter (Montgomery		Gallatin	12567
Fleming (Town)	13021	County)	12069	Gallatin (Town)	12567
Flemingville	13827	Fort Jackson	12938	Galleria of White Plains (Part	
Flint	14561	Fort Johnson	12070	of White Plains)	10601
Floral Park	11001-05	Fort Miller	12828	Gallupville	12073
For specific Floral Park Zip Codes		Fort Montgomery	10922	Galway	12074
call (516) 354-3297		Fort Niagara Beach	14174	Galway (Town)	12074
Florence	13316	Fort Plain	13339	Galway Lake	12025
Florence (Town)	13316	Fort Salonga	11768	Ganahgote	12525
Florida (Montgomery		Fortsville	12831	Gang Mills	14870
County) (Town)	12010	Fort Washington (Part of		Gansevoort	12831
Florida (Orange County)	10921	New York)	10032	Garbutt	14546
Floridaville	13033	Foster	13827	Garden City	11530
Flowerfield Estates (Part of		Fosterdale	12726	Garden City Park	11040
Lake Grove)	11755	Fosterville	13021	Garden City South	11530
Flower Hill	11050	Foster-Wheeler Junction		Garden Park Estates	12203
Flowers	13865	(Part of Dansville)	14437	Gardenville	14224
Floyd	13440	Fourth Lake	12846	Gardiner	12525
Floyd (Town)	13440	Fowler	13642	Gardiner (Town)	12525
		Fowler (Town)	13642	Gardiner Manor Mall	11706
Flushing	11301-86	Fowlersville	13433	Gardiners Bay Estates	11939
For specific Flushing Zip Codes		Fowlerville	14423	Gardnersville	12043
call (718) 670-4743		Fox Hill	12134	Gardnertown	12550
		Fox Meadows (Part of		Gardnertown (census	
COLLEGES & UNIVERSITIES		Scarsdale)	10583	designated place)	12250
City University of New York-		Frankfort	13340	Garfield	12168
Queens College	11367	Frankfort (Town)	13340	Garland	14420
		Frankfort Center	13340	Garnerville (Part of West	
FINANCIAL INSTITUTIONS		Franklin	13775	Haverstraw)	10923
Asia Bank, N.A.	11354	Franklin (Delaware County)		Garnet Lake	12843
Bayside Federal Savings		(Town)	13775	Garoga	12095
Bank	11361	Franklin (Franklin County)		Garrattsville	13342
Cross County Federal		(Town)	12913	Garrison	10524
Savings Bank	11379	Franklin Correctional Facility	12953	Garrison Four Corners	10524
Flushing Savings Bank	11354	Franklin D. Roosevelt (Part		Garwoods	14822
Maspeth Federal Savings &		of New York)	10022	Gaskill	13827
Loan Association	11378	Franklin Park	13057	Gasport	14067
Pioneer Savings & Loan		Franklin Springs	13341	Gates (Town)	14624
Association	11357	Franklin Square	11010	Gates	14624
Queens County Savings		Franklinton	12122	Gates Center	14611
Bank	11354	Franklinville	14737	Gates-North Gates	14626
		Franklinville (Town)	14737	Gayhead	12533
HOSPITALS		Franks Corner	13045	Gay Ridge Estates	10598
Booth Memorial Medical		Fraser	13753	Gayville	13044
Center	11355	Fredonia	14063	Geddes (Town)	13209
Elmhurst Hospital Center	11373	Freedom	14065	Gedney (Part of White	
Flushing Hospital Medical		Freedom (Town)	14065	Plains)	10605
Center	11355	Freedom Plains	12569	Geers Corners	13648
LaGuardia Hospital	11375	Freehold	12431	Genegantslet	13778
		Freeman	14801	Genesee (Town)	14754
HOTELS/MOTELS		Freeport	11520	Genesee Falls (Town)	14536
Best Western Midway Hotel	11368	Freetown (Cortland County)		Geneseo	14454
Metropole Hotel	11368	(Town)	13803	Geneseo (Town)	14454
Pan American Motor Inn	11373	Freetown (Suffolk County)	11937	Geneva	14456
		Freetown Corners	13803	Geneva (Town)	14456
MILITARY INSTALLATIONS		Freeville	13068	Genoa	13071
Fort Totten	11359	Fremont (Steuben County)		Genoa (Town)	13071
		(Town)	14807	Georgetown	13072
Fluvanna	14701	Fremont (Sullivan County)		Georgetown (Town)	13072
Fly Creek	13337	(Town)	12736	Georgetown	14450
Flying Point	11976	Fremont Center	12736	Georgetown Square (Part of	
Fly Summit	12834	Fremont Heights	13057	Williamsville)	14221
Fonda	12068	Fremont Hills	13057	Georgetown Station	13334
Foots Corners	14435	French Creek (Town)	14724	German	13040
Fordham (Part of New York)	10458	Frenchville	13486	German (Town)	13040
Forest	12935	French Woods	13783	German Flatts (Town)	13407
Forestburgh	12777	Fresh Meadows (Part of		Germantown	12526
Forestburgh (Town)	12701	New York)	11365	Germantown (Town)	12526
Forest Glen (Part of		Fresh Pond (Part of New		Germantown (Part of Port	
Hamburg)	14075	York)	11385	Jervis)	12771
Forest Hills (Part of New		Frewsburg	14738	German Village	14617
York)	11375	Friend	14527	Germonds	10956
Forest Home	14850	Friendship	14739	Gerry	14740
Forest Knolls (Part of New		Friendship (Town)	14739	Gerry (Town)	14740
Rochelle)	10804	Friends Point	12836	Getzville	14068
Forest Lawn	14580	Frontenac	13624	Geyser Crest	12866
Forest Park (Chautauqua		Fruitland	14519	Ghent	12075
County)	14787	Fruit Valley	13126	Ghent (Town)	12075
		Fullerville	13642	Gibson (Nassau County)	11580

	ZIP
Hardys	14066
Harford	13784
Harford (Town)	13784
Harford Mills	13835
Harkness	12972
Harlem (Part of New York)	10030
Harlemville	12075
Harmon Park	12302
Harmony (Town)	14767
Harmony Corners	12020
Harpersfield	13786
Harpersfield (Town)	13786
Harpursville	13787
Harriet	14223
Harrietstown (Town)	12983
Harriman	10926
Harris	12742
Harrisburg (Cattaraugus County)	14753
Harrisburg (Lewis County) (Town)	13367
Harrisburg (Warren County)	12878
Harris Corners	14145
Harris Hill	14221
Harrison	10528
Harrison (Town)	10528
Harrisville	13648
Harrower	12010
Hartfield	14728
Hartford	12838
Hartford (Town)	12838
Hartland	14067
Hartland (Town)	14067
Hartmans Corners	12009
Hartsdale	10530
Harts Hill	13492
Hartson Point	14487
Hartsville	14843
Hartsville (Town)	14843
Hartwick	13348
Hartwick (Town)	13348
Hartwick Seminary	13349
Hartwood	12729
Harvard	13756
Hasbrouck	12788
Haskell Flats	14727
Haskinville	14826
Hastings	13076
Hastings (Town)	13076
Hastings Center	13036
Hastings-on-Hudson	10706
Hatch's Corner	13684
Hauppauge	11788
Haven	12790
Haverstraw	10927
Haverstraw (Town)	10927
Haviland	12538
Hawkeye	12912
Hawkins Corner	13440
Hawkinsville	13309
Hawleys	13856
Hawleyton	13903
Hawthorne	10532
Hawthorne Hill	12309
Hawthorne Park	14787
Hawversville	12122
Hay Beach Point	11964
Haydenville	14760
Hayt Corners	14521
Hazel	12758
Head of the Harbor	11780
Heathcote (Part of New Rochelle)	10801
Heathcote (Part of Scarsdale)	10583
Heatherwood North	11733
Heatherwood South	11720
Heath Grove	13110
Heavenly Valley	12466
Hebron (Town)	12832
Hecla	13490
Hector	14841
Hector (Town)	14841
Hedgesville	14801
Helena	13649
Hell Gate (Part of New York)	10029
Helmuth	14079
Hemlock	14466
Hempstead	11550-51
For specific Hempstead Zip Codes call (516) 560-1700	
Hempstead Gardens	11552
Hemstreet Park	12118
Henderson	13650
Henderson (Town)	13650
Henderson Harbor	13651
Hendy Creek	14871
Henrietta	14467
Henrietta (Town)	14467
Hensonville	12439

	ZIP
Heritage (Part of Schenectady)	12303
Heritage Hills	12020
Heritage Knolls	12020
Herkimer	13350
Herkimer (Town)	13350
Hermitage (Steuben County)	14810
Hermitage (Wyoming County)	14066
Hermon	13652
Hermon (Town)	13652
Herrick Grove	13622
Herricks	11040
Herrings	13619
Hertel (Part of Buffalo)	14216
Herthum Heights	13492
Hervey Street	12418
Hessville	13339
Heuvelton	13654
Hewittville	13668
Hewlett	11557
Hewlett Bay Park	11557
Hewlett Harbor	11557
Hewlett Neck	11598
Hickeys Corners (Part of Saratoga Springs)	12866
Hickorybush	12401
Hickory Grove	13126
Hicks	14859
Hicksville	11801-02
	11805
For specific Hicksville Zip Codes call (516) 933-2476	
Higgins	14065
Higgins Bay	12108
Higginsville	13054
High Bank	12981
High Bridge (Bronx County)	10452
High Bridge (Onondaga County)	13066
High Falls	12440
High Flats	13625
Highland (Sullivan County) (Town)	12732
Highland (Ulster County)	12528
Highland Falls	10928
Highland Lake	12743
Highland Mills	10930
Highland-on-the-Lake	14047
Highlands (Town)	10928
Highlawn (Part of New York)	11223
High Mills	12027
Highmount	12441
High View	12721
High Woods	12477
Hiler	14223
Hillburn	10931
Hillcrest (Broome County)	13901
Hillcrest (Rockland County)	10977
Hiller Heights	13041
Hillis	12603
Hillsboro	13316
Hillsdale	12529
Hillsdale (Town)	12529
Hillside (Part of New York)	10469
Hillside Heights	11040
Hillside Lake	12590
Hillside Manor	11040
Hillside Park (Part of Johnstown)	12095
Hillview	12144
Hilton	14468
Himrod	14842
Hinckley	13352
Hinckleyville	14559
Hindsburg	14411
Hinmans Corners	13905
Hinmanville	13135
Hinsdale	14743
Hinsdale (Town)	14743
Hoag Corners	12062
Hobart	13788
Hoboken	13411
Hoffmans	12302
Hoffmeister	13353
Hogansburg	13655
Hogtown	12827
Holbrook	11741
Holcomb	14469
Holcombville	12853
Holiday Manor (Part of Geneva)	14456
Holland	14080
Holland (Town)	14080
Holland Cove	14589
Holland Patent	13354
Holley	14470
Hollis (Part of New York)	11423
Hollis Court (Part of New York)	11429

	ZIP
Holliswood (Part of New York)	11352
Hollowville	12530
Hollywood	12922
Holmes	12531
Holmesville	13843
Holton Beach	14847
Holtsville	11742
Homecrest (Part of New York)	11229
Homer	13077
Homer (Town)	13077
Homer Hill (Part of Olean)	14760
Homestead Park (Part of New Rochelle)	10801
Homestead Village	11727
Homewood	13066
Homewood Park	14225
Honeoye	14471
Honeoye Falls	14472
Honest Hill	14470
Honeywell Corners	12025
Honk Hill	12458
Honnedaga Lake	13338
Hoosick	12089
Hoosick (Town)	12089
Hoosick Falls	12090
Hoosick Junction	12133
Hope (Town)	12134
Hope Falls	12134
Hope Farm	12545
Hope Valley	12134
Hopewell (Town)	14424
Hopewell Center	14424
Hopewell Junction	12533
Hopkinton	12940
Hopkinton (Town)	12940
Horace Harding (Part of New York)	11362
Horicon (Town)	12815
Hornby	14812
Hornby (Town)	14812
Hornell	14843
Hornellsville (Town)	14807
Horseheads	14844-45
For specific Horseheads Zip Codes call (607) 739-0371	
Horseheads (Town)	14845
Horseheads North	14845
Horton	12776
Horton Estates	10587
Hortonville	12745
Hospital (Part of Binghamton)	13904
Houghton	14744
Hounsfield (Town)	13685
Houseville	13473
Housons Corners	12122
Howard (Town)	14809
Howard (New York County)	10013
Howard (Steuben County)	14809
Howard Beach (Part of New York)	11414
Howardville	13302
Howells	10932
Howes Cave	12092
Howlett Hill	13031
Hub (Part of New York)	10455
Hubbardsville	13355
Hubbardtown	13743
Hudson	12534
Hudson Falls	12839
Hudson Upper (Part of Hudson)	12534
Hughsonville	12537
Huguenot (Orange County)	12746
Huguenot (Richmond County)	10301
Huguenot Park (Part of New Rochelle)	10801
Hulberton	14470
Huletts Landing	12841
Hullsville	13827
Hume	14745
Hume (Town)	14745
Humphrey (Town)	14741
Humphrey Center	14741
Hungerford Corners	13650
Hunt	14846
Hunter	12442
Hunter (Town)	12442
Hunter Lake	12768
Huntersland	12122
Huntington (Town)	11743
Huntington	11743
Huntington Bay	11743
Huntington Beach	11721
Huntington Square	11731
Huntington Station	11746
Huntingtonville	13601

	ZIP
Hunts Corners (Cortland County)	13803
Hunts Corners (Erie County)	14031
Hunts Corners (Sullivan County)	12764
Hurd Corners	12564
Hurley	12443
Hurley (Town)	12443
Hurleyville	12747
Huron (Town)	14590
Hyde Park	12538
Hyde Park (Town)	12538
Hyde Park	13326
Hylan Shopping Plaza (Part of New York)	10306
Hyndsville	12043
Idle Hour	11769
Idlewood	14085
Ilion	13357
Imperial Plaza (Part of Wappingers Falls)	12590
Inavale	14739
Independence	14806
Independence (Town)	14806
Index	13326
Indian Castle	13365
Indian Cove	13118
Indian Falls	14036
Indian Kettles	12836
Indian Lake	12842
Indian Lake (Town)	12842
Indian Park	10925
Indian River	13327
Indian Springs	13027
Indian Village	13120
Industry	14474
Ingham Mills	13365
Ingleside	14512
Ingraham	12992
Inlet	13360
Inlet (Town)	13360
Inman	12968
Inter County Shopping Center	11758
Interlaken	14847
Interlaken Beach	14847
International Junction	14223
Inwood (Nassau County)	11696
Inwood (New York County)	10034
Ionia (Onondaga County)	13112
Ionia (Ontario County)	14475
Ira	13033
Ira (Town)	13033
Ira Station	13033
Ireland Corners	12525
Irelandville	14891
Irish Settlement	13625
Irona	12910
Irondequoit (Town)	14617
Irondequoit	14617
Irondequoit Manor	14617
Irongate	13088
Ironville	12928
Irving	14081
Irvington	10533
Ischua	14743
Ischua (Town)	14743
Island (Part of New York)	10044
Island Cottage Beach	14612
Islandia	11722
Island Park	11558
Isle of San Souci (Part of New Rochelle)	10805
Islip	11751
Islip (Town)	11751
Islip Manor	11751
Islip Terrace	11752
Italy	14512
Italy (Town)	14512
Itaska	13862
Ithaca	14850-53
For specific Ithaca Zip Codes call (607) 272-5454	
Ithaca College	14850
Ivanhoe	13839
Ives Corner	12018
Jackson (Town)	12816
Jacksonburg	13407
Jackson Corners	12571
Jackson Heights (Part of New York)	11372
Jackson Summit	12117
Jacksonville (Onondaga County)	13135
Jacksonville (Tompkins County)	14854
Jacks Reef	13112
Jamaica	11401-36
For specific Jamaica Zip Codes call (718) 990-1111	

	ZIP
COLLEGES & UNIVERSITIES	
City University of New York-York College	11451
FINANCIAL INSTITUTIONS	
Chase Manhattan Bank, N.A.	11432
HOSPITALS	
Jamaica Hospital	11418
Queens Hospital Center	11432
HOTELS/MOTELS	
JFK Airport Hilton	11436
Kennedy Inn	11434
MILITARY INSTALLATIONS	
John F. Kennedy International Airport, Military	11430
Jamesport	11947
Jamestown	14701-02
For specific Jamestown Zip Codes call (716) 488-0785	
Jamestown West	14701
Jamesville	13078
Janesville	12043
Jasper	14855
Jasper (Town)	14855
Java (Town)	14082
Java Center	14082
Java Lake	14009
Java Village	14083
Jay	12941
Jay (Town)	12941
Jeddo	14103
Jefferson	12093
Jefferson (Town)	12093
Jefferson Heights	12414
Jefferson Park	13650
Jefferson Valley	10535
Jefferson Valley Mall	10598
Jefferson Valley-Yorktown	10535
Jeffersonville	12748
Jenksville	13736
Jericho (Clinton County)	12910
Jericho (Nassau County)	11753
Jericho (Suffolk County)	11937
Jerome Avenue (Part of New York)	10468
Jersey Colony	11971
Jerusalem (Town)	14418
Jerusalem Corners	14047
Jewell	13042
Jewel Manor	13088
Jewett	12444
Jewett (Town)	12444
Jewett Center	12442
Jewettville	13634
John F. Kennedy Airport (Part of New York)	11430
Johnsburg	12843
Johnsburg (Town)	12843
Johnson	10933
Johnsonburg	14167
Johnson City	13790
Johnson Creek	14067
Johnsonville	12094
Johnstown	12095
Johnstown (Town)	12078
Jones Point	10986
Jonesville	12065
Jordan	13080
Jordanville	13361
Junction Boulevard (Part of New York)	11372
Junius (Town)	13165
Kabob	14782
Kaisertown	12549
Kanona	14856
Kasoag	13302
Katonah	10536
Katsbaan	12477
Kattelville	13901
Kattskill Bay	12844
Kauneonga Lake	12749
Kaydeross Park (Part of Saratoga Springs)	12866
Kayuta Lake	13338
Kecks Center	12095
Keefers Corners	12067
Keene	12942
Keene (Town)	12942
Keene Valley	12943
Keeseville	12944
Kelleys	12056
Kelloggsville	13118
Kelly Corners	12455
Kelsey	13783

	ZIP
Kendaia	14541
Kendall	14476
Kendall (Town)	14476
Kendall Mills	14470
Kenilworth (Part of Kings Point)	11024
Kenmore	14217
Kennedy	14747
Kenoza Lake	12750
Kensington (Erie County)	14215
Kensington (Kings County)	11218
Kensington (Nassau County)	11021
Kent (Orleans County)	14477
Kent (Putnam County) (Town)	10512
Kent Cliffs	10512
Kents Corners	13630
Kenwood (Part of Oneida)	13421
Kenwood Estates	10512
Kenyonville	14571
Kerhonkson	12446
Kerleys Corners	12571
Kernan (Part of Utica)	13502
Ketchums Corner	12170
Ketchumville	13736
Keuka	14837
Keuka Park	14478
Kew Gardens (Part of New York)	11415
Kew Gardens Hills (Part of New York)	11366
Kiamesha Lake	12751
Kiantone	14701
Kiantone (Town)	14701
Kidders	14847
Killawog	13794
Kill Buck	14748
Kimball Stand	14701
Kinderhook	12106
Kinderhook (Town)	12106
King Ferry	13081
Kings Bridge (Part of New York)	10463
Kingsbury	12839
Kingsbury (Town)	12839
Kings Ferry	13081
Kings Park	11754
Kings Park Psychiatric Center	11754
Kings Plaza Shopping Center and Marina (Part of New York)	11234
Kings Point	11024
Kings Settlement	13815
Kings Station	12831
Kingston	12401
Kingston (Town)	12401
Kingston Plaza (Part of Kingston)	12401
Kingsway (Part of New York)	11229
Kipps	10924
Kirk	13844
Kirkland	13323
Kirkland (Town)	13323
Kirkville	13082
Kirkwood	13795
Kirkwood (Town)	13795
Kirschnerville	13327
Kiryas Joel	10950
Kisco Park	10549
Kiskatom	12414
Kismet	11706
Kitchawan	10562
Knapp Creek	14749
Knapps Corner	12603
Knickerbocker (Part of New York)	10002
Knights Creek	14880
Knights Eddy	12780
Knowelhurst	12878
Knowlesville	14479
Knox	12107
Knox (Town)	12107
Knoxboro	13362
Koenig's Point	13021
Komar Park	12019
Kortright	13739
Kortright (Town)	13739
Kossuth	14715
Kringsbush	13452
Kripplebush	12484
Krumville	12461
Kyserike	12440
Lackawanna	14218
Lacona	13083
Ladentown (Part of Pomona)	10970
LaFargeville	13656
La Fayette	13084

	ZIP
LaFayette (Town)	13084
Lafayetteville	12571
La Grange (Dutchess County) (Town)	12540
Lagrange (Wyoming County)	14525
Lagrangeville	12540
La Guardia Airport (Part of New York)	11371
Lairdsville	13323
Lake	10990
Lake Bluff	14590
Lake Bonaparte	13648
Lake Carmel	10512
Lake Charles	12563
Lake Clear	12945
Lake Como	13045
Lake Delta	13440
Lake Erie Beach	14006
Lake Gardens	10541
Lake George	12845
Lake George (Town)	12845
Lake Grove	11755
Lake Hill	12448
Lake Huntington	12752
Lake Katonah	10536
Lake Katrine	12449
Lake Kitchawan	10590
Lakeland (Onondaga County)	13209
Lakeland (Suffolk County)	11779
Lake Lincolndale	10541
Lake Lucille	10956
Lake Luzerne	12846
Lake Luzerne (Town)	12846
Lake Luzerne-Hadley	12835
Lake Mahopac	10541
Lakemont	14857
Lake Moraine	13346
Lake Muskoday	12776
Lake Osceola	10535
Lake Osiris Colony	12586
Lake Panamoka	11961
Lake Peekskill	10537
Lake Placid	12946
Lake Placid Club Resort (Part of Lake Placid)	12946
Lake Pleasant	12108
Lake Pleasant (Town)	12108
Lakeport	13037
Lake Purdy	10578
Lake Ronkonkoma	11779
Lake Ronkonkoma Heights	11779
Lake Secor	10541
Lakeside (Orange County)	10930
Lakeside (Wayne County)	14519
Lakeside Park (Albany County)	12205
Lakeside Park (Orleans County)	14571
Lake Station	10990
Lake Success	11040
Lake Success Shopping Center	11040
Lake Sunnyside	12845
Lake Vanare	12846
Lake View (Erie County)	14085
Lakeview (Nassau County)	11552
Lakeview (Oswego County)	13126
Lakeview Correctional Facility	14716
Lakeville (Livingston County)	14480
Lakeville (Nassau County)	11040
Lakeville Estates	11040
Lakewood	14750
Lamberton	14063
Lambs Corner	12083
Lamont	14427
Lamson	13135
Lancaster	14086
Lancaster (Town)	14086
Lane (Part of Batavia)	14020
Lanesville	12450
Langdon	13795
Langdon Corners	13617
Langford	14057
Lansing (Town)	14882
Lansing (Oswego County)	13126
Lansing (Tompkins County)	14882
Lansingburg (Part of Troy)	12182
Laona	14063
Lapala	12401
Lapeer (Town)	13803
Laphams Mills	12972
Larchmont	10538
Larchmont North	10538
La Salle	14304
Lassellsville	13452
Latham	12110
Latham Circle Mall	12110

	ZIP
Lathams Corners	13843
Lattingtown	11560
Laughing Waters	11971
Laurel	11948
Laurel Hollow	11791
Laurelton (Monroe County)	14617
Laurelton (Queens County)	11431
Laurens	13796
Laurens (Town)	13796
Lava	12764
Lawrence (Nassau County)	11559
Lawrence (St. Lawrence County) (Town)	12965
Lawrence Farms	10514
Lawrence Park (Part of Yonkers)	10708
Lawrenceville	12949
Lawtons	14091
Lawyersville	12113
Lebanon	13085
Lebanon (Town)	13085
Lebanon Center	13332
Lebanon Springs	12114
Ledyard	13081
Ledyard (Town)	13026
Lee	13440
Lee (Town)	13440
Lee Center	13363
Leeds	12451
Leedsville	12501
Leeside	10512
Leesville	13459
Lefever Falls	12472
Lefferts (Part of New York)	11225
Leibhardt	12404
Leicester	14481
Leicester (Town)	14481
LeMarr Estates	12184
Lenox (Town)	13032
Lenox Furnace	13032
Lenox Hill (Part of New York)	10021
Lenox Park	14456
Leon	14751
Leon (Town)	14751
Leonardsville	13364
Leonta	13775
Le Ray (Town)	13637
Le Roy	14482
Le Roy (Town)	14482
Le Roy Island	14590
Levanna	13026
Levant	14733
Levittown	11756
Lewbeach	12753
Lewis	12950
Lewis (Town)	12950
Lewisboro (Town)	10590
Lewiston	14092
Lewiston (Town)	14092
Lewiston Heights (Part of Lewiston)	14092
Lewiston Manor	13224
Lexington	12452
Lexington (Town)	12452
Leyden (Town)	13433
Liberty	12754
Liberty (Town)	12754
Liberty Gardens (Part of Rome)	13440
Libertypole	14437
Lido Beach	11561
Lily Dale	14752
Lima	14485
Lima (Town)	14485
Lime Lake	14042
Lime Lake-Machias	14042
Limerick	13657
Lime Rock	14482
Limestone	14753
Limestreet	12414
Lincklaen	13052
Lincklaen (Town)	13052
Lincoln (Madison County) (Town)	13043
Lincoln (Wayne County)	14502
Lincolndale	10540
Lincoln Park (Erie County)	14223
Lincoln Park (Monroe County)	14611
Lincoln Park (Ulster County)	12401
Lincolnshire	13760
Lincolnton (Part of New York)	10037
Lindbergh Court (Part of Colonie)	12205
Linden	14054
Linden Acres	12571
Linden Hill (Part of New York)	11354

	ZIP
Lindenhurst	11757
Lindley	14858
Lindley (Town)	14858
Linlithgo	12526
Linwood	14486
Lisbon	13658
Lisbon (Town)	13658
Lisle	13797
Lisle (Town)	13797
Litchfield (Town)	13456
Lithgow	12545
Little America	13144
Little Bow	13642
Little Britain	12575
Little Canada	14054
Little Falls	13365
Little Falls (Town)	13407
Little Falls Park (Part of Wappingers Falls)	12590
Little France	13036
Little Genesee	14754
Little Neck (Part of New York)	11363
Little Plains	11731
Little Ram Island	11964
Little Utica	13135
Little Valley	14755
Little Valley (Town)	14755
Littleville	14424
Little York (Cortland County)	13087
Little York (Orange County)	10969
Liverpool	13088-90
For specific Liverpool Zip Codes call (315) 451-3060	
Livingston	12541
Livingston (Town)	12541
Livingston (Part of New York)	11201
Livingston Manor	12758
Livingstonville	12122
Livonia	14487
Livonia (Town)	14487
Livonia Center	14488
Lloyd (Town)	12528
Lloyd Harbor	11743
Lochada Lake	12719
Loch Muller	12857
Loch Sheldrake	12759
Lock Berlin	14489
Locke	13092
Locke (Town)	13092
Lockport	14094-95
For specific Lockport Zip Codes call (716) 434-1440	
Locksley Park	14075
Lockwood	14859
Locust Grove (Lewis County)	13309
Locust Grove (Nassau County)	11791
Locust Manor (Part of New York)	11431
Locust Point (Part of New York)	10465
Locust Valley	11560
Lodi	14860
Lodi (Town)	14860
Lodi Center	14860
Lodi Point	14860
Logan	14818
Logtown	12771
Lomala	12533
Lombard	14775
Lomond Shore	14476
Lomontville	12401
London Terrace (Part of New York)	10011
Lonelyville	11706
Long Beach	11561
Long Branch	13088
Long Branch Manor	13088
Long Bridge	13153
Long Eddy	12760
Long Island City	**11101-06**
For specific Long Island City Zip Codes call (718) 349-4626	
FINANCIAL INSTITUTIONS	
Astoria Federal Savings & Loan Association	11103
Financial Federal Savings & Loan Association	11104
The Long Island City Savings & Loan Association	11103
Long Island University Southampton Center	11968
Long Lake	12847
Long Lake (Town)	12847

	ZIP		ZIP		ZIP
Long Ridge Mall	14626	Malden Bridge	12115	Markhams	14070
Long View	14710	Malden on Hudson	12453	Marlboro	12542
Longwood (Part of New		Mall	11706	Marlborough (Town)	12542
York)	10459	Mall at New Rochelle, The		Marshall (Allegany County)	14711
Loomis	12754	(Part of New Rochelle)	10801	Marshall (Oneida County)	
Loomises	14710	Mallory	13103	(Town)	13328
Loon Lake	12968	Malone	12953	Marshfield	14091
Loon Lake Junction	12968	Malone (Town)	12953	Marshland Heights	13760
Lordville	13783	Malta	12020	Marshville (Montgomery	
Lorenz Park	12534	Malta (Town)	12020	County)	13317
Lorings	13045	Malta Ridge	12020	Marshville (St. Lawrence	
Lorraine	13659	Maltaville	12020	County)	13652
Lorraine (Town)	13659	Maltbie Heights	14070	Martindale Depot	12521
Lost Valley	12010	Malverne	11565	Martinsburg	13404
Loudonville	12211	Malvic Manor	13088	Martinsburg (Town)	13404
Louisville	13662	Mamakating (Town)	12790	Martisco	13108
Louisville (Town)	13662	Mamakating Park	12790	Martville	13111
Lounsberry	13812	Mamaroneck	10543	Maryknoll	10545
Lower Chateaugay Lake	12920	Mamaroneck (Town)	10543	Maryland	12116
Lower Cincinnatus	13040	Manchester	14504	Maryland (Town)	12116
Lower Genegantslet Corner	13778	Manchester (Town)	14504	Marymount (Part of	
Lower Melville	11747	Manchester Bridge	12603	Tarrytown)	10591
Lower Oswegatchie	13670	Mandana	13152	Masonville	13804
Lower Rotterdam	12306	Manhasset	11030	Masonville (Town)	13804
Lower South Bay	13041	Manhasset Hills	11040	Maspeth (Part of New York)	11378
Low Hampton	05743	Manhattan	10001-99	Massapequa	11758
Lowman	14861		10101	Massapequa Park	11762
Lowville	13367		10201-82	Massawepie	12986
Lowville (Town)	13367	For specific Manhattan Zip Codes		Massena	13662
Ludingtonville	12531	call (212) 330-3601		Massena (Town)	13662
Ludlow (Part of Yonkers)	10705	Manhattan Park (Part of		Massena Center	13662
Ludlowville	14882	White Plains)	10601	Massena Springs (Part of	
Lumberland (Town)	12770	Manhattanville (Part of New		Massena)	13662
Luther	12061	York)	10027	Masten Lake	12790
Lutheranville	12064	Manhattanville College (Part		Mastic	11950
Lycoming	13093	of Harrison)	10577	Mastic Beach	11951
Lyell (Part of Rochester)	14606	Manheim (Town)	13329	Matinecock	11560
Lykers	12166	Manheim Center	13365	Matteawan (Part of Beacon)	12508
Lyme (Town)	13693	Manitou	10524	Mattituck	11952
Lynbrook	11563	Manitou Beach	14468	Mattydale	13211
Lyncourt	13208	Manlius	13104	Maybrook	12543
Lyndon (Cattaraugus		Manlius (Town)	13104	Mayfair	12302
County) (Town)	14737	Manlius Center	13066	Mayfair Shopping Center	11725
Lyndon (Onondaga County)	13066	Mannetto Hills	11747	Mayfield	12117
Lyndonville	14098	Manning	14470	Mayfield (Town)	12117
Lynelle Meadows	13088	Mannsville	13661	Mayville	14757
Lyon Mountain	12952	Mannville	12189	Maywood (Albany County)	12205
Lyons	14489	Manny Corners	12010	Maywood (Suffolk County)	11701
Lyons (Town)	14489	Manor	13413	Meacham	11003
Lyonsdale	13368	Manorhaven	11050	Meadowbrook	12550
Lyonsdale (Town)	13368	Manorkill	12076	Meadowdale	12009
Lyons Falls	13368	Manors	11507	Meadow Hill	12550
Lyonsville	12404	Manorville (Suffolk County)	11949	Meadow Lane Estates	12184
Lysander	13094	Manorville (Ulster County)	12477	Meadowmere Park	11598
Lysander (Town)	13094	Mansfield (Town)	14755	Meadow Run (Part of	
Mabbettsville	12545	Maple Bay	14710	Hamburg)	14075
McClure	13754	Maplecrest	12454	Meadows	14420
McConnellsville	13401	Mapledale	12406	Meads	12498
MacDonnell Heights	12603	Maple Grove (Hamilton		Meads Creek	14870
McDonough	13801	County)	12134	Mechanicville	12118
McDonough (Town)	13801	Maple Grove (Otsego		Mecklenburg	14863
MacDougall	14541	County)	13808	Meco	12078
Macedon	14502	Maple Hill	12401	Medford	11763
Macedon (Town)	14502	Maplehurst	14743	Medina	14103
Macedon Center	14502	Maples	14755	Medusa	12120
McGraw	13101	Maple Springs	14756	Medway	12042
McGrawville	14777	Mapleton	13021	Melcourt (Part of New York)	10451
Machias (Town)	14101	Mapletown	13317	Mellenville	12544
Machias	14101	Maple Transit	14221	Melrose	12121
McKeever	13338	Maple Valley	13488	Melrose Park	13021
Mackey	12076	Maple View	13107	Melville	11747
McKinley	13428	Maplewood (Albany County)	12189	Memphis	13112
McKinstry Hollow	14042	Maplewood (Sullivan		Menands	12204
McKown Park	12203	County)	12701	Mendon	14506
McKownville	12203	Marathon	13803	Mendon (Town)	14506
McKownville Estates	12203	Marathon (Town)	13803	Mendon Center	14472
McLaughlin Acres	10541	Marble Hill (Part of New		Mendon Farms	14506
McLean	13102	York)	10463	Menteth Point	14424
McMasters Corners	13201	Marbletown	12401	Mentz (Town)	13140
McNalls	14067	Marbletown (Town)	12401	Meredith	13753
Macomb (Town)	13642	Marbletown	14513	Meredith (Town)	13753
McPherson Point	14487	Marcellus	13108	Meridale	13806
Madison	13402	Marcellus (Town)	13108	Meridian	13113
Madison (Town)	13402	Marcellus Falls	13108	Merillon Avenue (Part of	
Madison Park	11731	Marcy (Kings County)	11206	Garden City)	11530
Madison Square (Part of		Marcy (Oneida County)		Merrick	11566
New York)	10010	(Town)	13503	Merrickville	13839
Madrid	13660	Marcy Correctional Facility	13403	Merriewold	12701
Madrid (Town)	13660	Marengo	14433	Merriewold Lake	10950
Magnolia	14757	Margaretville	12455	Merrifield	13147
Mahopac	10541	Mariaville	12137	Merrill	12955
Mahopac Falls	10542	Marietta	13110	Merrillsville	13421
Mahopac Hills	10541	Marilla	14102	Merriville	12986
Mahopac Point	10541	Marilla (Town)	14102	Merriweather Campus (Part	
Mahopac Ridge	10541	Marine Hospital (Part of		of Brookville)	11548
Maidstone Park	11937	New York)	10301	Mertensia	14564
Maine	13802	Mariners Harbor (Part of		Messengerville	13803
Maine (Town)	13802	New York)	10303	Metropolitan (Part of New	
Main Settlement	14770	Marion	14505	York)	11206
Main Village (Part of		Marion (Town)	14505	Mettacahonts	12404
Williamsville)	14221	Mariposa	13155		

	ZIP
Newburgh	12550-52

For specific Newburgh Zip Codes
call (914) 561-1818

	ZIP
New Cassel	11590
New Castle (Town)	10514
New City	10956
New City Park	10956
Newcomb	12852
Newcomb (Town)	12852
New Concord	12060
New Dorp (Part of New York)	10306
New Dorp Beach (Part of New York)	10306
New Ebenezer	14224
New Falconwood	14072
Newfane	14108
Newfane (Town)	14108
Newfield	14867
Newfield (Town)	14867
New Hackensack	12590
New Hamburg	12590
New Hampton	10958
New Hartford	13413
New Hartford (Town)	13413
New Hartford Shopping Center (Part of New Hartford)	13413
New Haven	13121
New Haven (Town)	13121
New Hempstead	10977
New Hope	13118
New Hudson (Town)	14714
New Hurley	12525
New Hyde Park	11040-42

For specific New Hyde Park Zip
Codes call (516) 775-3980

	ZIP
New Ireland	13905
New Kingston	12459
Newkirk (Part of New York)	11226
New Lebanon	12125
New Lebanon (Town)	12125
New Lebanon Center	12125
New Lisbon	13415
New Lisbon (Town)	13415
New Lots (Part of New York)	11208
New Market (Part of Niagara Falls)	14301
New Milford	10959
New Oregon	14057
New Paltz	12561
New Paltz (Town)	12561
Newport	13416
Newport (Town)	13416
Newport (Monroe County)	14617
Newport (Onondaga County)	13164
New Rochelle	10801-02
	10804-05

For specific New Rochelle Zip
Codes call (914) 632-5906

	ZIP
New Russia	12964
New Salem (Albany County)	12186
New Salem (Ulster County)	12401
New Scotland	12159
New Scotland (Town)	12159
Newsday	11747
New Springville (Part of New York)	10314
New Square	10977
Newstead (Town)	14001
New Suffolk	11956
Newton Falls	13666
Newton Hook	12173
Newtonville	12128
Newtown	11946
New Vernon	10940
Newville	13365
New Windsor	12553
New Windsor (Town)	12553
New Woodstock	13122
New York	10001-99
	10101-99
	10201-92

For specific New York Zip Codes
call (212) 967-8585

COLLEGES & UNIVERSITIES

	ZIP
Barnard College	10027
City University of New York-Baruch College	10010
City University of New York-City College	10031
City University of New York-Hunter College	10021
City University of New York-John Jay College of Criminal Justice	10019
College of Insurance	10007

	ZIP
Columbia University-Columbia College	10027
Cooper Union	10003
Fashion Institute of Technology	10001
The Juilliard School	10023
Marymount Manhattan College	10021
New York Law School	10013
New York University	10011
School of Visual Arts	10010
Touro College	10036
Yeshiva University	10033

FINANCIAL INSTITUTIONS

	ZIP
Amalgamated Bank of New York	10003
Apple Bank for Savings	10017
Atlantic Bank of New York	10001
Banco Central of New York	10004
Banco de Bogota Trust Company	10152
Bank Audi	10020
Bankers Federal Savings, B.F.S.	10038
Bankers Trust Company	10017
Bank Leumi Trust Company of New York	10017
The Bank of New York Company, Inc.	10286
The Bank of Tokyo Trust Company	10005
Barclays Bank, PLC	10265
Bowery Savings Bank	10017
Brown Brothers Harriman & Co	10005
Canadian Imperial Bank of Commerce	10017
Carver Federal Savings Bank	10027
The Chase Manhattan Bank, N.A.	10081
Chemical Bank	10017
The Chinese American Bank	10038
Citibank, N.A.	10043
Daiwa Bank Trust Company	10019
The Depository Trust Company	10041
East River Savings Bank	10007
Emigrant Savings Bank	10017
E.A.B.	10005
Fiduciary Trust Company International	10048
First American Bank of New York	10022
The First New York Bank for Business	10010
Fourth Federal Savings Bank	10021
French American Banking Corporation	10022
The Fuji Bank and Trust Company	10048
The Greater New York Savings Bank	10119
IBJ Schroder Bank & Trust Company	10004
The Industrial Bank of Japan Trust Company	10167
Israel Discount Bank of New York	10017
The Manhattan Savings Bank	10017
Manufacturers Hanover	10017
The Merchants Bank of New York	10013
Mitsubishi Trust & Banking Corporation (USA)	10022
Morgan Guaranty Trust Company of New York	10260
National Westminster Bank USA	10038
Republic National Bank of New York	10018
Safra National Bank of New York	10036
Security Pacific National Trust Company	10006
State Street Bank and Trust Company, N.A.	10006
Sterling National Bank & Trust Company of New York	10022
Sumitomo Trust & Banking Co. (U.S.A.)	10022
UBAF Arab American Bank	10022
UMB Bank and Trust Company	10020
Union Chelsea National Bank	10017

	ZIP
United States Trust Company of New York	10036

HOSPITALS

	ZIP
Bellevue Hospital Center	10016
Beth Isreal Medical Center	10003
Cabrini Medical Center	10003
Coler Memorial Hospital	10044
Goldwater Memorial Hospital	10044
Harlem Hospital Center	10037
Lenox Hill Hospital	10021
Memorial Hospital for Cancer and Allied Diseases	10021
Metropolitan Hospital Center	10029
Mount Sinai Medical Center	10029
New York Infirmary-Beekman Downtown Hospital	10038
New York University Medical Center	10016
Presbyterian Hospital in the City of New York	10032
Society of the New York Hospital	10021
St. Clare's Hospital and Health Center	10019
St. Luke's-Roosevelt Hospital Center	10019
St. Vincent's Hospital and Medical Center of New York	10011
Veterans Affairs Medical Center	10010

HOTELS/MOTELS

	ZIP
Algonquin	10036
Doral Park Avenue	10016
Essex House	10019
Grand Hyatt New York	10017
The Helmsley Middletowne Hotel	10017
The Helmsley Palace Hotel	10022
Hotel Inter-Continental New York	10017
Hotel Parker Meridien	10019
The Swissotel N.Y.-The Drake Hotel	10022
The New York Hilton at Rockefeller Center	10019
The Pierre	10021
The Ritz Carlton New York	10019
United Nations Plaza Park Hyatt	10017
The Waldorf-Astoria	10022
The Plaza Hotel	10019
The Wyndham Hotel	10019

MILITARY INSTALLATIONS

	ZIP
United States Engineer District, New York	10278

	ZIP
New York Mills	13417
New York Mills Gardens	13492
Niagara (Town)	14302
Niagara Falls	14301-05

For specific Niagara Falls Zip
Codes call (716) 285-7561

	ZIP
Niagara Falls International Airport (AFB 6670) 914	14304
Niagara Square (Part of Buffalo)	14202
Niagara University	14109
Nichols (Town)	13812
Nichols (Steuben County)	16920
Nichols (Tioga County)	13812
Nichols Plaza (Part of Watertown)	13601
Nichols Run	14749
Nicholville	12965
Niets Crest	14710
Nile	14739
Niles	13152
Niles (Town)	13152
Nimmonsburg	13901
Nineveh	13813
Nineveh Junction	13730
Niobe	14758
Niskayuna (Town)	12309
Niskayuna	12309
Nissequogue	11780
Niverville (Columbia County)	12130
Noblesboro	13324
Norfolk	13667
Norfolk (Town)	13667
Normansville	12054
North (Part of Yonkers)	10703
North Afton	13730
North Amityville	11701

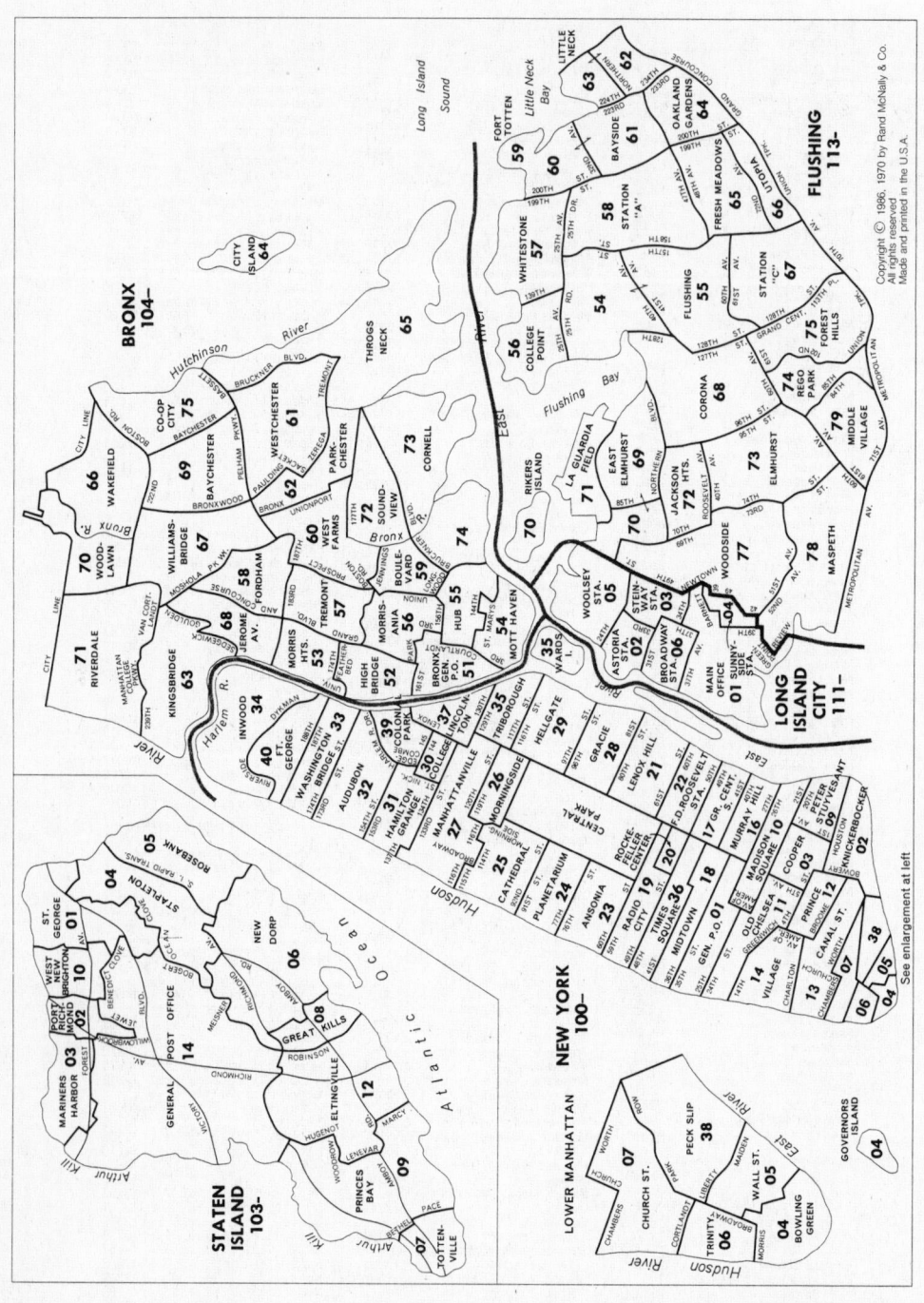

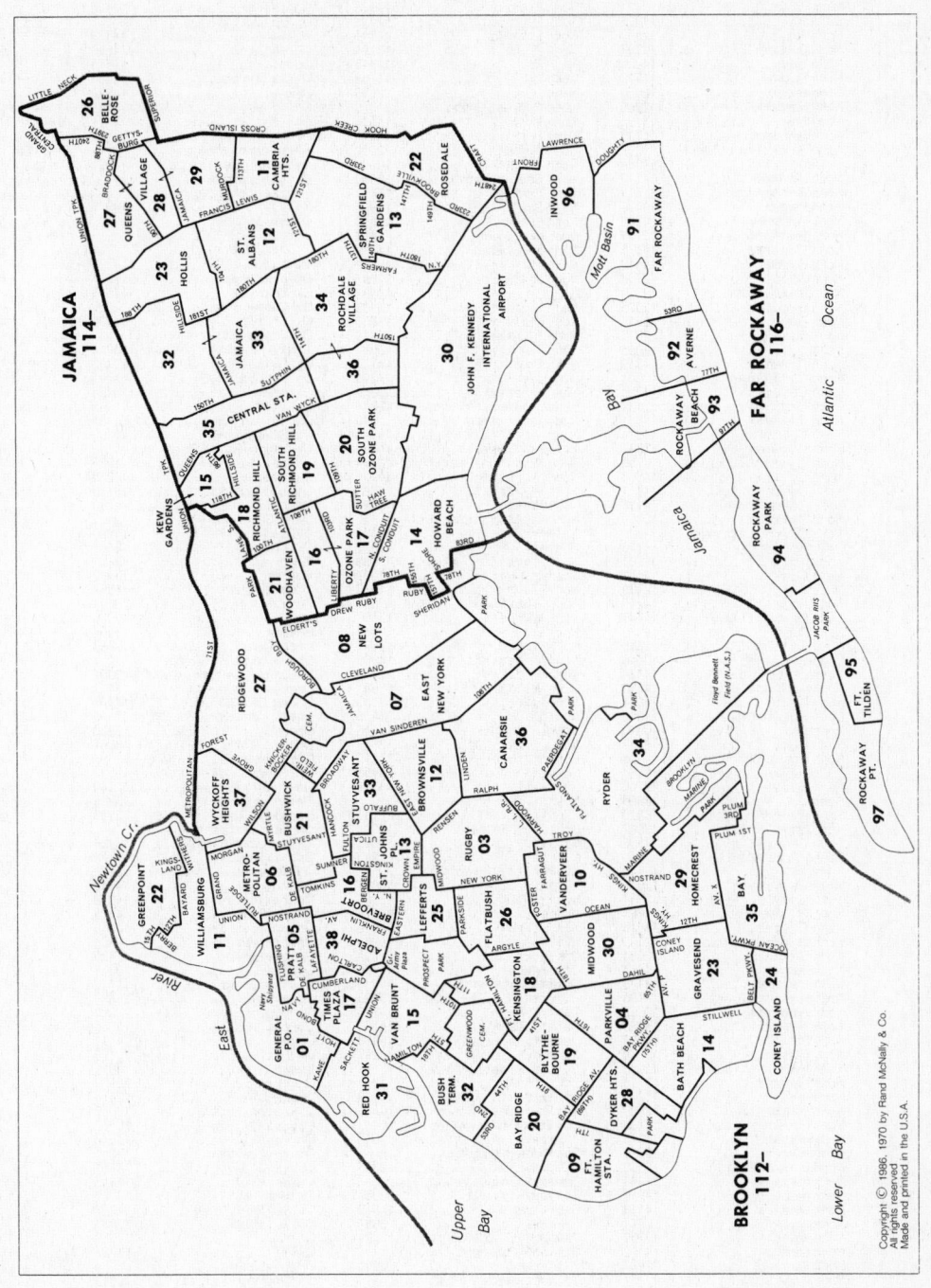

	ZIP		ZIP		ZIP
Northampton (Fulton		North Olean (Part of Olean)	14760	Oceanside	11572
County) (Town)	12134	North Patchogue	11772	Odessa	14869
Northampton (Suffolk		North Pembroke	14020	Ogden (Bronx County)	10452
County)	11901	North Petersburg	12138	Ogden (Monroe County)	
North Argyle	12809	North Pharsalia	13844	(Town)	14559
North Babylon	11703	North Pitcher	13124	Ogden Center	14559
North Bailey	14226	North Pole	12946	Ogdensburg	13669
North Baldwin	11510	Northport	11768	O'Hara Corners	12083
North Ballston Spa	12020	North River	12856	Ohio	13324
North Bangor	12966	North Rockville Centre	11570	Ohio (Town)	13324
North Bay	13123	North Rose	14516	Ohioville	12561
North Bay Shore	11706	North Rush	14543	Oil Springs Indian	
North Beach (Part of New		North Russell	13617	Reservation (Allegany	
York)	11369	North Salem	10560	County) (Town)	14081
North Bellmore	11710	North Salem (Town)	10560	Oil Springs Indian	
North Bellport	11713	North Sanford	13754	Reservation (Allegany	
North Bergen	14416	North Sea	11968	County)	14081
North Bethlehem	12203	North Selden	11784	Oil Springs Indian	
North Blenheim	12131	North Settlement	12496	Reservation (Cattaraugus	
North Bloomfield	14472	North Shore Beach	11778	County) (Town)	14081
North Boston	14110	Northside (Part of Corning)	14830	Olcott	14126
North Branch	12766	North Smithtown	11787	Old Bethpage	11804
North Bridgewater	13318	North Spencer	14883	Old Brookville	11545
North Broadalbin	12025	North Stephentown	12168	Old Central Bridge	12035
North Brookfield	13418	North Stockholm	13668	Old Chatham	12136
North Burke	12917	North Syracuse	13212	Old Chelsa (Part of New	
Northbush	12095	North Tarrytown	10591	York)	10011
North Cameron	14819	North Tonawanda	14120	Old Field	11733
North Castle (Town)	10504	Northtown Plaza	14226	Old Field South	11790
North Centereach	11720	Northumberland	12871	Old Forge	13420
North Chatham	12132	Northumberland (Town)	12871	Old Mastic	11951
North Chemung	14861	North Valley Stream	11580	Old Orchard Point	14487
North Chili	14514	North Victory	13111	Old Stony Brook	11790
North Chittenango	13037	Northview Gardens	14094	Old Village (Part of Great	
North Clymer	14759	Northville (Fulton County)	12134	Neck)	11023
North Cohocton	14868	Northville (Suffolk County)	11901	Old Westbury	11568
North Collins	14111	North Wantagh	11793	Olean (Town)	14760
North Collins (Town)	14111	North Waverly	14892	Olean	14760
North Corners	13658	Northway Mall/Off-Price		Olean Center Mall (Part of	
North Country Shopping		Center, The	12205	Olean)	14760
Center (Part of		Northway Plaza	12801	Olive (Town)	12461
Plattsburgh)	12901	North Western	13486	Olivebridge	12461
North Creek	12853	Northwest Harbor	11937	Oliverea	12462
Northcrest	12065	Northwest Ithaca	14850	Olmstedville	12857
North Cuba	14727	North White Plains	10603	Omar	13607
North Dansville (Town)	14437	North Wilmurt	13438	Omi	12075
North Darien	14036	North Wilna	13608	Onativia	13084
North East (Town)	12546	North Winfield	13491	Onchiota	12968
Northeast Center	12546	North Wolcott	14590	One Hundred Thirty Eight	
Northeast Henrietta	14534	Northwood	12188	(Part of New York)	10001
Northeast Ithaca	14850	North Woodmere	11581	Oneida	13421
North Easton	12834	Norton Hill	12135	Oneida Castle	13421
North Elba (Town)	12946	Norway	13416	Oneida Correctional Facility	13440
North End	10940	Norway (Town)	13416	Oneonta	13820
North Evans	14112	Norwich	13815	Oneonta (Town)	13861
North Fair Haven (Part of		Norwich (Town)	13815	Onesquethaw	12067
Fair Haven)	13064	Norwich Corners	13456	Oniontown	12522
North Fenton	13746	Norwood	13668	Onleys Station	10940
Northfield	13856	Nostrand (Part of New		Onondaga	13215
North Franklin	13820	York)	11235	Onondaga (Town)	13215
North Gage	13502	Nottingham Estates	14094	Onondaga Indian	
North Gainesville	14550	Noxon	12603	Reservation (Town)	13120
Northgate Estates (Part of		Noyack	11963	Onondaga Indian	
Rome)	13440	Number Forty (Part of New		Reservation	13120
North Germantown	12526	York)	10001	Ontario	14519
North Granville	12854	Number Four	13367	Ontario (Town)	14519
North Great River	11722	Nunda	14517	Ontario Center	14520
North Greece	14515	Nunda (Town)	14517	Ontario on the Lake	14519
North Greenbush (Town)	12198	Nyack	10960	Onteo Beach	14464
North Greenwich	12834	Oak Beach	11702	Onteora Park	12485
North Hamlin	14464	Oakdale	11769	Oot Park	13057
North Hannibal	13126	Oakdale Mall (Part of		Open Meadows	14710
North Harmony (Town)	14785	Johnson City)	13790	Oppenheim	13329
North Harpersfield	12093	Oakfield	14125	Oppenheim (Town)	13329
North Hartland	14008	Oakfield (Town)	14125	Oquaga Lake	13754
North Haven	11963	Oak Hill	12460	Oramel	14711
North Hebron	12832	Oakland	14517	Oran	13125
North Hempstead (Town)	11040	Oakland Gardens (Part of		Orange (Town)	14812
North Highland	10516	New York)	11364	Orangeburg	10962
North Hills	11040	Oak Orchard	14103	Orange Lake	12550
North Hillsdale	12529	Oak Point (Bronx County)	10455	Orangeport	14067
North Hoosick	12133	Oak Point (St. Lawrence		Orangetown (Town)	10960
North Hornell	14843	County)	13646	Orangeville (Town)	14569
North Hudson	12855	Oak Ridge (Montgomery		Orangeville Center	14011
North Hudson (Town)	12855	County)	12066	Orangeville Corners	14167
North Ilion	13340	Oakridge (Onondaga		Orchard Knoll	14845
North Jasper	14819	County)	13088	Orchard Park	14127
North Java	14113	Oaks Corners	14518	Orchard Park (Town)	14127
North Jay	12941	Oaksville	13337	Orchard Village	13031
North Kortright	13739	Oakwood (Cayuga County)	13021	Oregon	11952
North Lansing	14852	Oakwood (Richmond		Orient	11957
North Lawrence	12967	County)	10301	Orienta (Part of	
North Lindenhurst	11757	Oakwood Beach (Part of		Mamaroneck)	10543
North Litchfield	13340	New York)	10301	Oriental Park	14712
North Lynbrook	11563	Oakwood Heights (Part of		Orient Point	11957
North Manlius	13082	New York)	10301	Oriskany	13424
North Massapequa	11758	Obernburg	12767	Oriskany Falls	13425
North Merrick	11566	Obi	14715	Orlando	14755
North New Hyde Park	11040	Occanum	13865	Orleans (Jefferson County)	
North Norwich	13814	Ocean Bay Park	11706	(Town)	13656
North Norwich (Town)	13814	Ocean Beach	11770	Orleans (Ontario County)	14432

	ZIP		ZIP		ZIP
Orleans Four Corners	13656	Parkway (Part of New York)	10462	Pierceville	13334
Orwell	13426	Parma (Town)	14468	Piermont	10968
Orwell (Town)	13426	Parma Center	14468	Pierrepont	13617
Oscawana Corners	10579	Parma Corners	14559	Pierrepont (Town)	13617
Oscawana Lake	10579	Parson Farms	13031	Pierrepont Manor	13674
Osceola	13316	Pastime Park	14456	Pierstown	13326
Osceola (Town)	13316	Pataukunk	12446	Piffard	14533
Ossian (Town)	14437	Patchin (Part of New York)	10011	Pike	14130
Ossian Center	14437	Patchinville	14572	Pike (Town)	14130
Ossining	10562	Patchogue	11772	Pike Five Corners	14024
Ossining (Town)	10562	Patchogue Highlands	11772	Pilgrim (Part of New York)	10461
Oswegatchie	13670	Patria	12187	Pilgrim Corners (Part of	
Oswegatchie (Town)	13654	Patroon (Part of Albany)	12204	Middletown)	10940
Oswego	13126	Patterson	12563	Pilgrimport	14489
Oswego (Town)	13126	Patterson (Town)	12563	Pillar Point	13634
Oswego Bitter	13031	Pattersonville	12137	Pilot Knob	12844
Oswego Center	13126	Paul Smiths	12970	Pinckney (Town)	13610
Otego	13825	Pavilion	14525	Pine (Part of Albany)	12203
Otego (Town)	13825	Pavilion (Town)	14525	Pine Aire	11706
Otisco	13159	Pavilion Center	14525	Pinebrook (Part of New	
Otisco (Town)	13159	Pawling	12564	Rochelle)	10804
Otisco Valley	13110	Pawling (Town)	12564	Pinebrook Heights (Part of	
Otisville	10963	Payne Beach	14468	New Rochelle)	10804
Otisville Correctional Facility	10963	Peabrook	12760	Pine Bush	12566
Otsego (Town)	13337	Peach Lake	10509	Pine City	14871
Otselic	13072	Peakville	13756	Pine Grove (Lewis County)	13343
Otselic (Town)	13072	Pearl Creek	14591	Pine Grove (Schoharie	
Otselic Center	13072	Pearl River	10965	County)	12122
Otter Creek	13343	Peas Eddy	13783	Pinegrove Park	12205
Otter Lake	13338	Peasleeville	12985	Pine Hill (Erie County)	14225
Ott Meadows	13088	Peat Corners	13036	Pine Hill (Oneida County)	13471
Otto	14766	Pebble Beach	14480	Pine Hill (Ulster County)	12465
Otto (Town)	14766	Peck Slip (Part of New		Pinehill Estates	12303
Ouaquaga	13826	York)	10038	Pinehurst	14085
Overlook	12822	Peconic	11958	Pine Island	10969
Ovid	14521	Peekskill	10566	Pine Knolls	13760
Ovid (Town)	14521	Pekin	14132	Pine Lake	12032
Ovid Center	14847	Pelham	10803	Pine Meadows	13302
Ovington (Part of New York)	11220	Pelham (Town)	10803	Pine Neck	11963
Owasco	13021	Pelham Manor	10803	Pine Plains	12567
Owasco (Town)	13021	Pelham Parkway (Part of		Pine Plains (Town)	12567
Owego	13827	New York)	10462	Pine Ridge	12203
Owego (Town)	13827	Pellets Island	10958	Pine Ridge Estates	10573
Owens Mills	14825	Pembroke	14036	Pine Valley (Chemung	
Owls Head	12969	Pembroke (Town)	14036	County)	14872
Oxbow	13671	Penataquit	11706	Pine Valley (Suffolk County)	11901
Oxford	13830	Pendleton	14094	Pineville (Delaware County)	13856
Oxford (Town)	13830	Pendleton (Town)	14094	Pineville (Oswego County)	13302
Oxford	10918	Pendleton Center	14094	Pinewood Estates	12303
Oyster Bay	11771	Penfield	14526	Pine Woods	13310
Oyster Bay (Town)	11771	Penfield (Town)	14526	Pioneer	12020
Oyster Bay Cove	11771	Pennellville	13132	Piseco	12139
Ozone Park (Part of New		Penn Yan	14527	Pitcairn	13648
York)	11416	Peoria	14525	Pitcairn (Town)	13648
Pacama	12401	Perch River	13601	Pitcher	13136
Pace University		Perinton (Town)	14450	Pitcher (Town)	13136
Pleasantville-Briarcliff		Perkinsville	14529	Pitcher Hill	13212
Campus	10570	Perry	14530	Pitt (Part of New York)	10002
Paddlefords	14424	Perry (Town)	14530	Pittsfield	13411
Paddy Hill	13615	Perry Center	14530	Pittsfield (Town)	13411
Paines Hollow	13407	Perry City	14886	Pittsford	14534
Painted Post	14870	Perrysburg	14129	Pittsford (Town)	14534
Palatine Bridge	13428	Perrysburg (Town)	14129	Pittstown	12094
Palatine Bridge	13428	Perrys Mills	12919	Pittstown (Town)	12094
Palentown	12446	Perryville	13133	Place Corners	12431
Palenville	12463	Persia (Town)	14070	Plainedge	11714
Palermo	13069	Perth (Town)	12010	Plainfield (Town)	13491
Palermo (Town)	13069	Perth (Cattaraugus County)	14741	Plainfield Center	13491
Palisades	10964	Perth (Fulton County)	12010	Plainview	11803
Palmyra	14522	Peru	12972	Plainview Shopping Center	11803
Palmyra (Town)	14522	Peru (Town)	12972	Plainville	13137
Pamelia (Town)	13637	Peru	13112	Plandome	11030
Pamelia	13637	Peruville	13073	Plandome Heights	11030
Panama	14767	Peterboro	13134	Plandome Manor	11030
Panorama	14625	Petersburg	12138	Planetarium (Part of New	
Panther Lake	13028	Petersburg (Town)	12138	York)	10024
Pantigo	11937	Peter Stuyvesant (Part of		Plato	14171
Paradise Hill	12051	New York)	10009	Platte Clove	12427
Paradox	12858	Petries Corners	13367	Plattekill	12568
Parcells Corner	14062	Petrolia	14895	Plattekill (Town)	12568
Paris	13429	Pharsalia (Town)	13758	Platten	14098
Paris (Town)	13429	Phelps	14532	Plattsburgh	12901
Parish	13131	Phelps (Town)	14532	Plattsburgh (Town)	12918
Parish (Town)	13131	Philadelphia	13673	Plattsburgh Air Force Base	12903
Parishville	13672	Philadelphia (Town)	13673	Plattsburgh West	12962
Parishville (Town)	13672	Philipse Manor (Part of		Plaza (Part of New York)	11101
Parishville Center	13676	North Tarrytown)	10591	Pleasantbrook	13320
Paris Station	13456	Philipstown (Town)	10516	Pleasantdale	12182
Parkchester (Part of New		Phillipsburg	10940	Pleasant Plains (Dutchess	
York)	10462	Phillips Creek	14813	County)	12580
Park Hill (Onondaga		Phillips Mills	14712	Pleasant Plains (Richmond	
County)	13057	Phillipsport	12769	County)	10309
Park Hill (Westchester		Philmont	12565	Pleasant Point	13126
County)	10705	Phoenicia	12464	Pleasantside	10566
Parkside (Part of New York)	11375	Phoenix	13135	Pleasant Valley	12569
Park Slope (Part of New		Phoenix Mills	13326	Pleasant Valley (Town)	12569
York)	11215	Picketts Corners	12981	Pleasant Valley (Oneida	
Parkston	12758	Pickettsville	13672	County)	13480
Parksville	12768	Piercefield	12973	Pleasant Valley (Steuben	
Park Terrace	13903	Piercefield (Town)	12973	County)	14810
Parkville (Part of New York)	11204	Pierces Corner	13642		

	ZIP
Pleasantville	10570-72
For specific Pleasantville Zip	
Codes call (914) 769-1517	
Plessis	13675
Plymouth	13832
Plymouth (Town)	13832
Pocantico Hills	10591
Poestenkill	12140
Poestenkill (Town)	12140
Point Au Rouche	12901
Point Breeze	14477
Point Chautauqua	14728
Point Lookout	11569
Point O'Woods	11706
Point Peninsula	13693
Point Pleasant	14622
Point Rochester	14512
Point Rock	13471
Point Stockholm	14742
Point Vivian	13607
Poland (Chautauqua	
County) (Town)	14747
Poland (Herkimer County)	13431
Poland Center	14747
Polkville	13101
Pomfret (Town)	14063
Pomona	10970
Pomona Heights (Part of	
Pomona)	10901
Pomonok (Part of New	
York)	11365
Pompey	13138
Pompey (Town)	13138
Pompey Center	13104
Ponck Hockie (Part of	
Kingston)	12401
Pond Eddy	12770
Ponquogue	11946
Poolville	13432
Poospatuck Indian	
Reservation (Town)	11950
Poospatuck Indian	
Reservation	11950
Pope Mills	13654
Poplar Beach	14541
Poplar Ridge	13139
Poquott	11733
Portage	14846
Portage (Town)	14846
Portageville	14536
Port Authority (Part of New	
York)	10011
Port Byron	13140
Port Chester	10573
Port Crane	13833
Port Dickinson	13901
Porter (Town)	14131
Porter Center	14131
Porter Corners	12859
Porterville	14052
Port Ewen	12466
Port Gibson	14537
Port Henry	12974
Port Jefferson	11777
Port Jefferson Station	11776
Port Jervis	12771
Port Kent	12975
Portland	14769
Portland (Town)	14769
Portlandville	13834
Port Leyden	13433
Port Richmond (Part of New	
York)	10302
Portville	14770
Portville (Town)	14770
Port Washington	11050
Port Washington North	11050
Post Corners	12057
Post Creek	14812
Potsdam	13676
Potsdam (Town)	13676
Potter	14527
Potter (Town)	14527
Potter Hollow	12469
Pottersville	12860
Poughkeepsie	12601-03
For specific Poughkeepsie Zip	
Codes call (914) 452-3421	
Poughkeepsie (Town)	12602
Poughquag	12570
Pound Ridge	10576
Pound Ridge (Town)	10576
Pratt (Part of New York)	11205
Pratt Corners	13087
Prattsburg	14873
Prattsburg (Town)	14873
Pratts Hollow	13434
Prattsville	12468
Prattsville (Town)	12468
Preble	13141
Preble (Town)	13141

	ZIP
Prendergast Point	14757
Presho	14858
Preston	13830
Preston (Town)	13830
Preston Hollow	12469
Prince (Part of New York)	10012
Princes Bay (Part of New	
York)	10309
Princetown	12056
Princetown (Town)	12056
Progress	12078
Prospect	13435
Prospect Heights	12144
Prospect Hill	12188
Prospect Park West (Part of	
New York)	11215
Providence (Town)	12850
Pulaski	13142
Pulteney	14874
Pulteney (Town)	14874
Pultneyville	14538
Pulvers	12075
Pulvers Corners	12567
Pumpkin Hill	14422
Pumpkin Hollow	12529
Purchase (Part of Harrison)	10577
Purdys	10578
Purdys Mills	12910
Purling	12470
Putnam (Town)	12861
Putnam Lake	10509
Putnam Station	12861
Putnam Valley	10579
Putnam Valley (Town)	10579
Pyramid Mall Ithaca (Part of	
Lansing)	14850
Pyrites	13677
Quackenbush Hill	14830
Quackenkill	12052
Quail (Part of Albany)	12206
Quaker Basin	13052
Quaker Hill	12564
Quaker Ridge (Part of New	
Rochelle)	10801
Quaker Springs	12871
Quaker Street	12141
Quarry Heights	10603
Quarryville	12477
Queechy	12029
Queens	11001-06
	11101-06
	11301-86
	11401-36
For specific Queens Zip Codes	
call (718) 321-5000	
Queensbridge (Part of New	
York)	11101
Queensbury	12801
Queensbury (Town)	12801
Queens Center (Part of	
New York)	11373
Queens Village (Part of New	
York)	11428
Quigley Park	14710
Quinneville	13746
Quioque	11978
Quogue	11959
Raceville	05764
Radio City (Part of New	
York)	10019
Radison	13027
Rainbow Lake	12976
Ralmar Park	12302
Ramapo	10931
Ramapo (Town)	10931
Ram Island	11964
Rampasture	11946
Randall	12072
Randallsville	13346
Randolph	14772
Randolph (Town)	14772
Ransomville	14131
Rapids	14094
Raquette Lake	13436
Rathbone	14801
Rathbone (Town)	14801
Ravena	12143
Ravenwood (Part of	
Colonie)	12205
Rawson	14727
Ray Brook	12977
Raymertown	12180
Raymondville	13678
Rayville	12136
Reading (Town)	14876
Reading Center	14876
Reber	12996
Red Creek (Suffolk County)	11946
Red Creek (Wayne County)	13143
Redfalls	12468
Redfield	13437

	ZIP
Redfield (Town)	13437
Redford	12978
Red Hook	12571
Red Hook (Town)	12571
Red Hook (Part of New	
York)	11231
Red House (Town)	14779
Red Mills (Columbia	
County)	12513
Red Mills (St. Lawrence	
County)	13669
Red Oaks Mill	12603
Red Rock (Columbia	
County)	12060
Red Rock (Onondaga	
County)	13027
Redwood (Jefferson	
County)	13679
Redwood (Suffolk County)	11963
Reeds Corner	14437
Reeds Corners	14437
Reeves Park	11901
Rego Park (Part of New	
York)	11374
Reidsville	12186
Remsen	13438
Remsen (Town)	13438
Remsenburg	11960
Remsenburg-Speonk	11960
Rensselaer	12144
Rensselaer Falls	13680
Rensselaerville	12147
Rensselaerville (Town)	12147
Residence Park (Part of	
New Rochelle)	10805
Retsof	14539
Rexford	12148
Rexville	14877
Reydon Shores	11971
Reynoldsville	14818
Rheims	14840
Rhinebeck	12572
Rhinebeck (Town)	12572
Rhinecliff	12574
Ricard	13302
Rice Grove	13110
Riceville (Cattaraugus	
County)	14171
Riceville (Fulton County)	12078
Riceville Station	14171
Richburg	14774
Richfield	13439
Richfield (Town)	13439
Richfield Springs	13439
Richford	13835
Richford (Town)	13835
Richland	13144
Richland (Town)	13144
Richmond	10301-14
For specific Richmond Zip Codes	
call (718) 442-0647	
Richmond (Town)	14471
Richmond Hill (Part of New	
York)	11418
Richmond Valley (Part of	
New York)	10307
Richmondville	12149
Richmondville (Town)	12149
Richs Corners	14411
Richville	13681
Riders Mills	12024
Ridge (Livingston County)	14510
Ridge (Suffolk County)	11961
Ridgebury	10973
Ridgelea Heights	14094
Ridge Mills (Part of Rome)	13440
Ridgemont Plaza	14626
Ridgeway	14103
Ridgeway (Town)	14103
Ridgeway (Part of White	
Plains)	10601
Ridgewood (Niagara	
County)	14094
Ridgewood (Oneida	
County)	13501
Ridgewood (Queens	
County)	11385
Rifton	12471
Riga (Town)	14428
Rigney Bluff	14612
Riley Cove	12020
Ringdahl Court (Part of	
Rome)	13440
Rio	12780
Riparius	12862
Ripley	14775
Ripley (Town)	14775
Rippleton	13035
Risingville	14820
River (Part of Rochester)	14627

	ZIP		ZIP		ZIP
Riverdale (Part of New		Rose	14542	St. Regis Indian Reservation	
York)	10471	Rose (Town)	14542	(Town)	13655
Riverhead	11901	Rosebank (Part of New		St. Remy	12401
Riverhead (Town)	11901	York)	10305	Saintsville	13116
Riverside (Broome County)	13795	Roseboom	13450	Salamanca	14779
Riverside (Erie County)	14207	Roseboom (Town)	13450	Salamanca (Town)	14779
Riverside (Otsego County)	13838	Rosecrans Park	12123	Salem	12865
Riverside (Saratoga County)	12118	Rosedale (Part of New		Salem (Town)	12865
Riverside (Steuben County)	14830	York)	11422	Salem Center	10578
Riverside (Suffolk County)	11901	Rose Grove	11968	Salina (Town)	13088
Riverside Estates	11901	Rose Hill	13110	Salina	13208
Riverside Mall (Part of Utica)	13502	Rosemont Park (Part of		Salisbury	13365
Riverside Manors	14172	Rensselaer)	12144	Salisbury (Town)	13365
Riverside Park	12401	Rosendale	12472	Salisbury	11801
Riverview	12981	Rosendale (Town)	12472	Salisbury Center	13454
Riverview Correctional		Roseton	12550	Salisbury Mills	12577
Facility	13669	Rosiere	13618	Salmon River	12901
Roanoke	14143	Roslyn	11576	Saltaire	11706
Robbins Rest	11770	Roslyn Estates	11576	Salt Point	12578
Roberts Corner	13650	Roslyn Harbor	11576	Salt Springville	13320
Rochdale	12603	Roslyn Heights	11577	Sammonsville	12095
Rochdale Village (Part of		Rossburg	14776	Samsondale (Part of West	
New York)	11434	Ross Corners	13850	Haverstraw)	10993
Rochelle Heights (Part of		Rossie	13646	Samsonville	12481
New Rochelle)	10801	Rossie (Town)	13646	Sanborn	14132
Rochelle Park (Part of New		Rossman	12173	Sandford Boulevard (Part of	
Rochelle)	10801	Ross Mill	14733	Mount Vernon)	10550
Rochester	14601-92	Rosstown	14871	Sandfordville	13676
For specific Rochester Zip Codes		Rossville (Part of New York)	10309	Sand Hill (Erie County)	14001
call (716) 272-8090		Rotterdam	12303	Sand Hill (Montgomery	
Rochester (Town)	12404	Rotterdam (Town)	12303	County)	13339
Rockaway Beach (Part of		Rotterdam Junction	12150	Sand Lake	12153
New York)	11693	Round Lake	12151	Sand Lake (Town)	12153
Rockaway Park (Part of		Roundout Harbor	12466	Sand Ridge	13132
New York)	11694	Round Top	12473	Sands Point	11050
Rockaway Point (Part of		Rouses Point	12979	Sandusky	14133
New York)	11697	Roxbury	12474	Sandy Beach	14072
Rock City (Cattaraugus		Roxbury (Town)	12474	Sandy Creek	13145
County)	14760	Roxbury (Part of New York)	11697	Sandy Creek (Town)	13145
Rock City (Dutchess		Royalton	14067	Sandy Harbour Beach	14464
County)	12571	Royalton (Town)	14067	Sanford (Town)	13754
Rock City Falls	12863	Ruby	12475	Sangerfield	13455
Rock Cut	13078	Ruby Corner	13646	Sangerfield (Town)	13455
Rockdale	13809	Rugby (Part of New York)	11203	Sanitaria Springs	13833
Rockefeller Center (Part of		Rumsey Ridge	14092	San Remo	11754
New York)	10020	Rural Grove	12166	Santa Clara	12980
Rock Glen	14550	Rural Hill	13650	Santa Clara (Town)	12980
Rock Hill	12775	Rush	14543	Santapoque	11707
Rockhurst	12801	Rush (Town)	14543	Saranac	12981
Rockland (Town)	12776	Rushford	14777	Saranac (Town)	12981
Rockland (Rockland		Rushford (Town)	14777	Saranac Inn	12983
County)	10962	Rushford Lake	14717	Saranac Lake	12983
Rockland (Sullivan County)	12776	Rushville	14544	Saratoga (Town)	12871
Rockland Lake	10989	Russell	13684	Saratoga Springs	12866
Rockland Psychiatric Center	10962	Russell (Town)	13684	Sardinia	14134
Rock Stream	14878	Russell Gardens	11021	Sardinia (Town)	14134
Rock Tavern	12575	Russia	13431	Saugerties	12477
Rockton	12010	Russia (Town)	13431	Saugerties (Town)	12477
Rock Valley	12760	Rutland (Town)	13638	Saugerties South	12477
Rockville (Allegany County)	14711	Rutland Center	13601	Sauquoit	13456
Rockville (Orange County)	10940	Ryder (Part of New York)	11234	Savannah	13146
Rockville Centre	11570-71	Rye	10580	Savannah (Town)	13146
For specific Rockville Centre Zip		Rye (Town)	10573	Savona	14879
Codes call (516) 766-0479		Rye Brook	10573	Sawkill	12401
Rockville Lake	14711	Rye Hills	10573	Sawyers Corners	13021
Rockwells Mills	13843	Sabael	12864	Saxon Park	11706
Rockwood	12095	Sabattis	12847	Sayville	11782
Rocky Point (Clinton		Sabbath Day Point	12874	Scarborough (Part of	
County)	12901	Sacandaga	12134	Briarcliff Manor)	10510
Rocky Point (Suffolk		Sackets Harbor	13685	Scarsdale	10583
County)	11778	Sacketts Lake	12701	Scarsdale (Town)	10583
Rodman	13682	Saddle Rock	11023	Schaghticoke	12154
Rodman (Town)	13682	Saddle Rock Estates	11021	Schaghticoke (Town)	12154
Roe Park	10566	Sagaponack	11962	Schaghticoke Hill	12154
Roessleville	12205	Sages Cottages	11944	Schenectady	12301-08
Rolling Acres	14559	Sagetown	14871	For specific Schenectady Zip	
Rolling Hills (Monroe		Sag Harbor	11963	Codes call (518) 395-5400	
County)	14450	Sailors Snug Harbor (Part of		Schenevus	12155
Rolling Hills (Nassau		New York)	10301	Schermerhorn Corners	14747
County)	11507	St. Albans (Part of New		Schodack (Town)	12033
Rolling Meadows	12401	York)	11412	Schodack Center	12033
Romanoff	10512	St. Andrew	12586	Schodack Landing	12156
Rombout Ridge	12603	St. Armand (Town)	12913	Schoharie	12157
Rome	13440	St. Bonaventure	14778	Schoharie (Town)	12157
	13442	St. George (Part of New		Schonowe	12306
For specific Rome Zip Codes call		York)	10301	Schroeppel (Town)	13135
(315) 336-1500		St. Huberts	12943	Schroon (Town)	12870
Romulus	14541	St. James	11780	Schroon Lake	12870
Romulus (Town)	14541	St. James Heights	11780	Schultzville	12572
Rondaxe	13420	St. John Fisher College	14618	Schuluski Estates	12188
Rondout (Part of Kingston)	12401	St. Johnsburg	14302	Schuyler (Town)	13340
Ronkonkoma	11779	St. Johns Place (Part of		Schuyler Falls	12985
Ronkonkoma West	11779	New York)	11213	Schuyler Falls (Town)	12985
Roosa Gap	12721	St. Johnsville	13452	Schuyler Lake	13457
Roosevelt	11575	St. Johnsville (Town)	13452	Schuylerville	12871
Roosevelt Beach	14172	St. Josephs	12701	Scio	14880
Roosevelt Field (Part of		St. Lawrence Park	13607	Scio (Town)	14880
Garden City)	11530	St. Mary's Park (Part of		Sciota	12992
Rooseveltown	13683	New York)	10455	Scipio (Town)	13147
Root (Town)	12166	St. Regis Falls	12980	Scipio Center	13147
Roscoe	12776	St. Regis Indian Reservation	13655	Scipioville	13147

	ZIP		ZIP		ZIP
Sconondoa	13421	Sholam	12458	Solsville	13465
Scotchbush (Fulton County)	13452	Shongo	16923	Solvay	13209
Scotch Bush (Montgomery		Shooktown (Part of		Somers	10589
County)	12010	Lockport)	14094	Somers (Town)	10589
Scotchtown	10940	Shoppingtown Mall	13214	Somerset	14012
Scotia	12302	Shore Acres (Chautauqua		Somerset (Town)	14012
Scott	13077	County)	14712	Somerset Lake	13783
Scott (Town)	13077	Shore Acres (Monroe		Somerville	13642
Scottsburg	14545	County)	14468	Sonora	14879
Scottsville	14546	Shore Acres (Suffolk		Sonyea	14556
Scranton	14075	County)	11952	Sound Beach	11789
Scriba (Town)	13126	Shore Acres (Westchester		Soundview (Part of New	
Scriba Center	13126	County)	10543	York)	10472
Sea Breeze	14617	Shoreham	11786	South (Part of Yonkers)	10705
Sea Cliff	11579	Shore Haven	14787	South Addison	14801
Seaford	11783	Shorelands	14728	South Alabama	14013
Seager	12406	Shore Oaks	13126	South Albion	13302
Searingtown	11507	Shorewood	11721	South Amenia	12592
Searsburg	14886	Shortsville	14548	Southampton	11968-69
Sears Corners	10509	Short Tract	14735	For specific Southampton Zip	
Searsville	12549	Shrub Oak	10588	Codes call (516) 283-0268	
Seaview	11770	Shumla	14063	Southampton (Town)	11968
Second Milo	14527	Shushan	12873	Southampton College	11946
Seeley Creek	14871	Shutter Corners	12157	South Amsterdam (Part of	
Selden	11784	Shutts Corners	12043	Amsterdam)	12010
Selkirk	12158	Sibleyville	14472	South Apalachin	13732
Selkirk Beach	13142	Sidney	13838	South Argyle	12809
Sellecks Corners	13625	Sidney (Town)	13838	South Bay	13032
Sempronius	13118	Sidney Center	13839	South Bay Shopping Center	11702
Sempronius (Town)	13118	Siena	12211	South Bay Village	12827
Seneca (Town)	14561	Sillimans Corners	14030	South Bethlehem	12161
Seneca Army Depot	14541	Silver Bay	12874	South Bloomfield	14469
Seneca Castle	14547	Silver Creek	14136	South Bolivar	14715
Seneca Falls	13148	Silver Lake (Orange County)	10940	South Bombay	12957
Seneca Falls (Town)	13148	Silver Lake (Wyoming		South Bradford	14879
Seneca Hill	13126	County)	14549	South Bristol	14512
Seneca Knolls	13209	Silver Lake Village	10940	South Bristol (Town)	14512
Seneca Mall (Erie County)	14224	Silver Springs	14550	South Brookfield	13485
Seneca Mall (Onondaga		Simmons Island (Part of		South Buffalo (Part of	
County)	13088	Cohoes)	12047	Buffalo)	14210
Seneca Point	14512	Simpsonville	12155	South Butler	13154
Sennett	13150	Sinclairville	14782	South Byron	14557
Sennett (Town)	13150	Sissonville	13676	South Cairo	12482
Sentinel Heights	13078	Skaneateles	13152	South Cambridge	12028
Setauket	11733	Skaneateles (Town)	13152	South Canisteo	14823
Setauket-East Setauket	11733	Skaneateles Falls	13153	South Centereach	11720
Settlers Hill	10509	Skaneateles Junction	13060	South Chili	14546
Seven Hills	10512	Skerry	12966	South Colton	13687
Seventh Day Hollow	13072	Skinnerville	13697	South Columbia	13439
Severance	12872	Sky Meadow Farms	10573	South Corinth	12822
Seward	12043	Slab City (Cortland County)	13141	South Corning	14830
Seward (Town)	12043	Slab City (St. Lawrence		South Cortland	13045
Shackport	13757	County)	13676	South Danby	13864
Shadigee	14098	Slate Hill	10973	South Dansville	14807
Shady	12409	Slaterville Springs	14881	South Dayton	14138
Shandaken	12480	Sleightsburg	12401	South Dover	12522
Shandaken (Town)	12480	Slingerlands	12159	South Durham	12405
Shandelee	12758	Sloan	14225	Southeast (Town)	10509
Sharon	13459	Sloansville	12160	Southeast Owasco	13118
Sharon (Town)	13459	Sloatsburg	10974	South Edmeston	13466
Sharon Springs	13459	Slyboro	12832	South Edwards	13635
Shawangunk (Town)	12589	Smallwood	12778	South Fallsburg	12779
Shawnee	14132	Smartville	13083	South Farmingdale	11735
Sheds	13151	Smithboro	13840	Southfields	10975
Shekomeko	12546	Smith Corners	13407	South Floral Park	11001
Shelby	14103	Smithfield (Dutchess		South Flushing (Part of New	
Shelby (Town)	14103	County)	12501	York)	11365
Shelby Basin	14103	Smithfield (Madison County)		Southgate Plaza	14224
Shelby Center	14103	(Town)	13134	Southgate Shopping Center	
Sheldon	14145	Smith Haven Mall (Part of		(Part of Massapequa	
Sheldon (Town)	14145	Lake Grove)	11755	Park)	11762
Sheldrake	14521	Smiths Basin	12827	South Gilboa	12167
Sheldrake Springs	14847	Smiths Corner	12120	South Glens Falls	12801
Shelter Island	11964	Smiths Mills	14062	South Granville	12832
Shelter Island (Town)	11964	Smithtown (Town)	11787	South Greece	14626
Shelter Island Heights	11965	Smithtown	11787	South Hamilton	13332
Shenandoah	12533	Smithtown Branch	11787	South Hannibal	13074
Shenorock	10587	Smithtown Pines	11787	South Hartford (Otsego	
Sherburne	13460	Smithtown Shopping Center	11787	County)	13810
Sherburne (Town)	13460	Smith Valley	14805	South Hartford (Washington	
Sheridan	14135	Smithville (Chenango		County)	12838
Sheridan (Town)	14135	County) (Town)	13778	South Haven	11719
Sheridan Park (Part of		Smithville (Jefferson County)	13605	South Hempstead	11550
Geneva)	14456	Smithville Center	13778	South Highland	10524
Sherman	14781	Smithville Flats	13841	South Hill	14850
Sherman (Town)	14781	Smyrna	13464	South Holbrook	11741
Sherman Park	10594	Smyrna (Town)	13464	South Horicon	12815
Shermerhorn Landing	13646	Snooks Corners	12010	South Hornell	14843
Sherrill	13461	Snufftown	10924	South Huntington	11746
Sherwood Forest	12065	Snyder	14226	South Ilion	13357
Sherwood Knolls	13031	Snyder Crossing	13116	South Jamesport	11970
Sherwood Park	12144	Snyders Corners	12180	South Jefferson	12167
Shinhopple	13837	Snyders Lake	12180	South Jewett	12442
Shinnecock Hills	11946	Sodom (Putnam County)	10509	South Kortright	13842
Shinnecock Indian		Sodom (Warren County)	12853	South Lake	10512
Reservation (Town)	11968	Sodus	14551	South Lebanon	13332
Shinnecock Indian		Sodus (Town)	14551	South Lima	14558
Reservation	11968	Sodus Center	14554	South Livonia	14487
Shirewood	12065	Sodus Point	14555	South Lockport	14094
Shirley	11967	Solon	13055	South Millbrook	12545
Shokan	12481	Solon (Town)	13055	South New Berlin	13843

	ZIP
South Newstead	14001
South Nineveh	13787
South Nyack	10960
Southold	11971
Southold (Town)	11971
South Olean (Part of Olean)	14760
South Onondaga	13120
South Otselic	13155
South Owego	13827
South Oxford	13830
South Ozone Park (Part of New York)	11420
South Park (Part of Buffalo)	14220
South Plainedge	11758
South Plymouth	13844
South Pole (Part of New York)	10090
Southport	14904
Southport (Town)	14904
South Richmond Hill (Part of New York)	11419
South Ripley	14775
South Russell	13684
South Rutland	13688
South Salem	10590
South Schodack	12162
South Schroon	12870
South Setauket	11733
South Shore Mall	11706
South Side (Part of Elmira)	14904
South Sodus	14489
South St. Johnsville	13339
South Stockton	14782
South Stony Brook	11790
South Trenton	13304
South Utica (Part of Utica)	13501
South Valley (Cattaraugus County) (Town)	14779
South Valley (Otsego County)	13320
South Valley Stream	11581
South Vandalia	14706
South Vestal	13850
Southview (Part of Binghamton)	13903
South Wales	14139
South Warsaw	14569
South Westbury	11590
South Westerlo	12163
Southwest Oswego	13126
Southwood	13078
South Worcester	12197
Spackenkill	12603
Spafford	13077
Spafford (Town)	13077
Sparkill	10976
Sparkle Lake	10598
Sparrow Bush	12780
Sparta (Livingston County) (Town)	14437
Sparta (Westchester County)	10562
Spawn Hollow	12161
Speculator	12164
Speedsville	13736
Speigletown	12182
Spencer	14883
Spencer (Town)	14883
Spencerport	14559
Spencer Settlement	13440
Spencertown	12165
Speonk	11972
Split Rock	13031
Spragueville	13642
Sprakers	12166
Spring Brook	14140
Spring Creek (Part of New York)	11239
Springfield (Town)	13468
Springfield Center	13468
Springfield Gardens (Part of New York)	11413
Spring Glen	12483
Spring Lake	13140
Spring Mills	14897
Springport (Town)	13160
Springs	11937
Springtown	12561
Springvale	13815
Spring Valley (Rockland County)	10977
Spring Valley (Westchester County)	10562
Springville (Erie County)	14141
Springville (Suffolk County)	11946
Springwater	14560
Springwater (Town)	14560
Springwood Village	12538
Sprout Brook	13317
Spruceton	12492

	ZIP
Spuyten Duyvil (Part of New York)	10463
Squiretown	11946
Staatsburg	12580
Stacy Basin	13054
Stadium (Part of New York)	10452
Stafford	14143
Stafford (Town)	14143
Stamford	12167
Stamford (Town)	12167
Standish	12952
Stanford (Town)	12581
Stanford Heights	12301
Stanfordville	12581
Stanley	14561
Stanley Manor	13031
Stannards	14895
Stanwix (Part of Rome)	13440
Stanwix Heights (Part of Rome)	13440
Stanwood	10549
Stapleton (Part of New York)	10304
Starbuckville	12817
Stark (Town)	13339
Starkey	14837
Starkey (Town)	14837
Starks Knob	12871
Starkville	13339
Star Lake	13690
State Bridge	13054
State Line	14775

Staten Island 10301-14
For specific Staten Island Zip
Codes call (718) 816-2790

COLLEGES & UNIVERSITIES

	ZIP
City University of New York-College of Staten Island	10301
Wagner College	10301

FINANCIAL INSTITUTIONS

	ZIP
Gateway State Bank	10304
Northfield Savings Bank, F.S.B.	10314
Richmond County Savings Bank	10310
Staten Island Savings Bank	10304

HOSPITALS

	ZIP
St. Vincent's Medical Center of Richmond	10310
Staten Island University Hospital	10305
Staten Island Mall (Part of New York)	10314
State School	10990
State University (Part of Old Westbury)	11568
State University of New York at Binghamton	13901
State University of New York at Stony Brook	11794
Steamburg	14783
Steam Valley	14760
Stears Corners	13659
Steelton	14219
Steinway (Part of New York)	11103
Stella	13905
Stella Niagara	14144
Stephens Mills	14843
Stephentown	12168
Stephentown (Town)	12168
Stephentown Center	12168
Sterling	13156
Sterling (Town)	13156
Sterling Forest	10979
Sterling Valley	13156
Stetsonville	13415
Steuben (Town)	13354
Steuben Valley	13354
Stever Mill	12025
Stewart Air Force Base	12550
	12553

For specific Stewart Air Force
Base Zip Codes call (914) 564-
2100

	ZIP
Stewart Manor	11530
Stilesville	13754
Stillman Village	12138
Stillwater (Town)	12170
Stillwater (Chautauqua County)	14701
Stillwater (Putnam County)	10541
Stillwater (Saratoga County)	12170
Stillwater Hill	10562
Stirling	11944
Stissing	12581
Stittville	13469

	ZIP
Stockbridge	13409
Stockbridge (Town)	13409
Stockholm (Town)	13697
Stockholm Center	13697
Stockport	12534
Stockport (Town)	12534
Stockport	13783
Stockport Station	12534
Stockton	14784
Stockton (Town)	14784
Stockwell	13480
Stokes	13363
Stone Arabia	13339
Stone Church	14416
Stonedam	16923
Stone Gate	10950
Stone Mills	13656
Stone Ridge (Montgomery County)	12072
Stone Ridge (Ulster County)	12484
Stony Brook	11790
Stony Creek	12878
Stony Creek (Town)	12878
Stony Creek Estates	12065
Stony Hollow	12401
Stony Point	10980
Stony Point (Town)	10980
Stormville	12582
Stottville	12172
Stow	14785
Straits Corners	13827
Stratford	13470
Stratford (Town)	13470
Strathmore	11030
Streeters Corners	14094
Streetroad	12883
Strykersville	14145
Stuyvesant	12173
Stuyvesant (Town)	12173
Stuyvesant (Part of New York)	11233
Stuyvesant Falls	12174
Suffern	10901
Suffern Park	10901
Sugarbush	12968
Sugar Loaf	10981
Sugartown	14741
Sullivan	13037
Sullivan (Town)	13037
Sullivanville	14845
Summerhill	13092
Summerhill (Town)	13092
Summit	12175
Summit (Town)	12175
Summit Park	10977
Summit Park Mall (Part of Niagara Falls)	14304
Summitville	12781
Sun	12917
Sundown	12782
Sun Haven (Part of New Rochelle)	10801
Sunmount (Part of Tupper Lake)	12986
Sunny Side (Chautauqua County)	14701
Sunnyside (Columbia County)	12106
Sunnyside (Queens County)	11104
Sunrise Mall	11758
Sunrise Terrace	13902
Sunset (Part of New York)	11220
Sunset Bay (Hanover twp.)	14081
Sunset Bay (Ellery twp.)	14712
Sunset Beach	14172
Sunset City Shopping Center	11703
Sunset Manor	13492
State University of New York (Part of Albany)	12203
Surprise	12176
Svahn Manor	10989
Swain	14884
Swan Lake	12783
Swartwood	14889
Swastika	12985
Swazy Acres	12188
Sweden (Town)	14420
Sweden Center	14420
Sweet Meadows	12401
Swenson Drive (Part of Wappingers Falls)	12590
Swifts Mills	14001
Swormville	14051
Sycaway	12180
Sylvan Beach	13157
Sylvan Lake	12533
Syosset	11791
Syracuse	13201-90

For specific Syracuse Zip Codes
call (315) 470-3486

	ZIP		ZIP		ZIP
Taberg	13471	Tonawanda (Town)	14150	Underwood Club	12964
Tabor Corners	14572	Tonawanda (census		Union (Town)	13760
Taborton	12153	designated place)	14223	Union	13760
Taconic Correctional Facility	10507	Tonawanda Indian			13763
Taconic Lake	12138	Reservation (Erie County)	14150	For specific Union Zip Codes call
Taghkanic	12502	Tonawanda Indian		(607) 785-1181
Taghkanic (Town)	12502	Reservation (Erie County)		Union Center	13760
Talcottville	13309	(Town)	14150	Uniondale	11553
Talcville	13635	Tonawanda Indian		Union Falls	12912
Tallman	10982	Reservation (Genesee		Union Hill	14563
Tanglewood Hills	11727	County) (Town)	14150	Union Mills	12025
Tannersville	12485	Tonawanda Junction	14223	Union Shopping Center
Tappan	10983	Torrey (Town)	14441	(Part of Endicott)	13760
Tarrytown	10591	Tottenville (Part of New		Union Springs	13160
Tarrytown Heights (Part of		York)	10307	Union Vale (Town)	12585
Tarrytown)	10591	Towerville Corners	14701	Union Valley	13052
Taunton	13219	Towlesville	14810	Unionville (Albany County)	12054
Taylor	13040	Town (Part of Newburgh)	12550	Unionville (Ontario County)	14532
Taylor (Town)	13040	Towners	12531	Unionville (Orange County)	10988
Taylor Center	13040	Town Line	14086	Unionville (St. Lawrence
Teall (Part of Syracuse)	13217	Town Pump	14559	County)	13676
Teboville	12953	Townsend	14891	United Nations New York
Ten Mile River	12764	Townsendville	14847	(Part of New York)	10017
Tennanah	12776	Tracy Creek	13850	University (Part of Syracuse)	13210
Tennanah Lake	12776	Trainsmeadow (Part of New		University Gardens	11020
Terminal (Part of New York)	10301	York)	11370	University Heights (Part of
Terrace Park	13669	Transitown	14221	New York)	10452
Terry's Corners	14067	Travis (Part of New York)	10301	Upper Benson	12134
Terryville	11776	Travis Corners	10524	Upper Brookville	11545
Texas	13114	Treadwell	13846	Upper Grand View	10960
Texas Valley	13803	Tremont (Part of New York)	10457	Upper Hollowville	12530
Thayer Corners	12917	Trenton (Town)	13304	Upper Jay	12987
The Bridges	14477	Trenton Assembly Park	13304	Upper Lisle	13862
The Forge	12920	Trenton Falls	13304	Upper Little York	13087
The Forks	14030	Triangle	13778	Upper Little York Lake	13141
The Glen	12885	Triangle (Town)	13778	Upper Mongaup	12737
The Hook	12809	Triangle Lake	12122	Upper Nyack	10960
The Narrows	14737	Tribes Hill	12177	Upper Red Hook	12571
Thendara	13472	Triborough (Part of New		Upper St. Regis	12945
Theresa	13691	York)	10035	Upper Union	12309
Theresa (Town)	13691	Triphammer Mall (Part of		Upperville	13464
The Terrace	11050	Lansing)	14852	Upton Lake	12514
The Vly	12484	Tripoli	12827	Uptonville (Part of
Thiells	10984	Troupsburg	14885	Rochester)	14617
Thomaston	11021	Troupsburg (Town)	14885	Uptown (Part of Kingston)	12401
Thompson (Ontario County)	14489	Troutburg	14464	Urbana (Town)	14840
Thompson (Sullivan County)		Trout Creek	13847	United States Cadet Corps	10997
(Town)	12701	Trout River	12926	Ushers	12151
Thompson Ridge	10985	Troy	12180-83	U.S. Military Academy	10996
Thompsons Lake	12009	For specific Troy Zip Codes call		Utica	13501-05
Thompsonville	12784	(518) 272-7300		For specific Utica Zip Codes call
Thomson	12834	Truesdale Lake	10590	(315) 738-5354
Thornton	14723	Trumansburg	14886	Utopia (Part of New York)	11366
Thornton Grove	13152	Trumbulls Corners	14867	Vail Mills	12025
Thornton Heights	13152	Truthville	12854	Vails Gate	12584
Thornwood	10594	Truxton	13158	Vail's Grove	10509
Thousand Island Park	13692	Truxton (Town)	13158	Valatie	12184
Three Mile Bay	13693	Tuckahoe (Suffolk County)	11968	Valcour	12972
Three Rivers	13041	Tuckahoe (Westchester		Valhalla	10595
Throg's Neck (Part of New		County)	10707	Valley Cottage	10989
York)	10465	Tucker Heights	12019	Valley Falls	12185
Throop (Town)	13021	Tucker Terrace	13662	Valley Mills	13409
Throopsville	13021	Tudor (Part of New York)	10017	Valley Pond Estates	10536
Thruway Mall	14225	Tully	13159	Valley Stream	11580-82
Thurman (Town)	12885	Tully (Town)	13159	For specific Valley Stream Zip
Thurston	14821	Tunnel	13848	Codes call (516) 825-2220
Thurston (Town)	14821	Tupper Lake	12986	Valley View Manor (Part of
Thurston Road (Part of		Turin	13473	Rome)	13440
Rochester)	14619	Turin (Town)	13473	Vallonia Springs	13813
Tiana	11946	Turnwood	12758	Valois	14888
Tiana Shores	11942	Tuscan	12197	Van Brunt (Part of New
Ticonderoga	12883	Tuscarora (Livingston		York)	11215
Ticonderoga (Town)	12883	County)	14510	Van Buren (Town)	13027
Tillson	12486	Tuscarora (Steuben County)		Van Buren Bay	14048
Times Plaza (Part of New		(Town)	14801	Van Buren Point	14166
York)	11217	Tuscarora Indian		Van Burenville	10940
Times Square (Part of New		Reservation (Town)	14094	Van Cortlandtville	10566
York)	10036	Tuscarora Indian		Van Cott (Part of New York)	10467
Timothy Heights	12569	Reservation	14094	Vandalia	14706
Tinkertown	14803	Tusten (Town)	12764	Van Del (Part of Kenmore)	14217
Tioga (Town)	13845	Tuthill	12525	Van Deusenville	13317
Tioga Center	13845	Tuxedo (Town)	10987	Vandever (Part of New
Tioga Terrace	13732	Tuxedo Park	10987	York)	11210
Tiona	13811	Twelve Corners	14618	Van Etten	14889
Titusville	12603	Twilight Park	12436	Van Etten (Town)	14889
Tivoli	12583	Twin Lakes Village	10590	Van Fleet	16920
Toddsville	13326	Twin Orchards	13850	Van Hornesville	13475
Toddville	10566	Tyner	13830	Van Nest (Part of New
Todt Hill (Part of New York)	10301	Tyre	13148	York)	10462
Toll Gate Corner	14770	Tyre (Town)	13148	Van Schaick Island (Part of
Tomhannock	12185	Tyrone	14887	Cohoes)	12047
Tomkins Cove	10986	Tyrone (Town)	14887	Varick (Town)	14541
Tompkins (Town)	13754	Ulster (Town)	12401	Varna	14850
Tompkins Corners	14845	Ulster Heights	12428	Varysburg	14167
Tompkins Square (Part of		Ulster Landing	12477	Vaughs Corners	12839
New York)	10009	Ulster Park	12487	Vega	12455
Tompkinsville (Part of New		Ulsterville	12566	Venice	13147
York)	10301	Ulysses (Town)	14886	Venice (Town)	13147
Tonawanda	14150-51	Unadilla	13849	Venice Center	13147
For specific Tonawanda Zip		Unadilla (Town)	13849	Verbank	12585
Codes call (716) 693-4560		Unadilla Forks	13491	Verbank Village	12585

	ZIP
Westminster Park	13607
West Monroe	13167
West Monroe (Town)	13167
Westmore Estates	12203
Westmoreland	13490
Westmoreland (Town)	13490
Westmoreland	11965
West Newark	13811
West New Brighton (Part of New York)	10310
West Newburgh (Part of Newburgh)	12550
West Nyack (census designated place)	10960
West Nyack	10994
Weston	14837
West Oneonta	13861
Westons Mills	14788
Westover	13790
West Park	12493
West Pawling	12564
West Perrysburg	14129
West Perth	12010
West Phoenix	13135
West Pierrepont	13617
West Point	10996-97
For specific West Point Zip Codes call (914) 446-2004	
Westport	12993
Westport (Town)	12993
West Portland	14787
West Potsdam	13676
West Ridge (Part of Rochester)	14615
West Ronkonkoma	11779
West Rush	14543
West Salamanca (Part of Salamanca)	14779
West Sand Lake	12196
West Saugerties	12477
West Sayville	11796
West Schuyler	13502
West Seneca	14224
West Seneca (Town)	14224
West Shelby	14103
West Shokan	12494
West Side (Part of Elmira)	14905
West Slaterville	14881
West Smithtown	11787
West Somerset	14008
West Sparta (Town)	14437
West Stephentown	12168
West St. James	11787
West Stockholm	13696
West Taghkanic	12502
West Tiana	11946
Westtown	10998
West Turin (Town)	13325
West Union (Town)	14877
West Utica (Part of Utica)	13501
Westvale	13219
West Valley	14171
West Valley Falls (Part of Valley Falls)	12185
Westview (Broome County)	13905
Westview (Livingston County)	14437
West Village (Part of New York)	10014
Westville	12926
Westville (Town)	12926
Westville	12155
Westville Center	12926
West Walworth	14502
West Waterford (Part of Waterford)	12188
West Webster	14580
West Windsor	13865
West Winfield	13491
West Yaphank	11980
Wethersfield (Town)	14569
Wethersfield Springs	14569
Wevertown	12886
Whaley Lake	12531
Whallonsburg	12994
Wheatfield (Town)	14150
Wheatland (Town)	14546
Wheatley (Part of Old Westbury)	11568
Wheatley Heights	11798
Wheatville	14013
Wheeler	14810
Wheeler (Town)	14810
Wheeler Estates	12019
Wheelers	14469
Wheelerville	12032
Whig Corners	13326
Whippleville	12995
Whippoorwill	10504
White Bay	13650

	ZIP
White Creek	12057
White Creek (Town)	12057
White Fathers	12968
Whitehall	12887
Whitehall (Town)	12887
White Lake (Oneida County)	13494
White Lake (Sullivan County)	12786
Whitelaw	13032
White Plains	10601-07
For specific White Plains Zip Codes call (914) 287-2500	
Whiteport	12401
Whitesboro	13492
Whites Store	13843
Whitestone (Part of New York)	11357
Whitestone Shopping Center (Part of New York)	11357
Whitestown (Town)	13492
White Sulphur Springs	12787
Whitesville	14897
Whitfield	12404
Whitman	13804
Whitney Country	14450
Whitney Farms	14450
Whitney Highlands	14450
Whitney Point	13862
Wiccopee	12533
Wickham Knolls	10990
Wickham Village	10990
Wilbur (Part of Kingston)	12401
Wildwood	11792
Wileyville	14877
Willard	14588
Willet	13863
Willet (Town)	13863
Williams Bridge (Part of New York)	10467
Williamsburg (Part of New York)	11211
Williams Grove	13110
Williams Lake	12472
Williamson	14589
Williamson (Town)	14589
Williamstown	13493
Williamstown (Town)	13493
Williamsville	14221
Willing (Town)	14895
Williston Park	11596
Willoughby	14741
Willow	12495
Willow Brook (Chautauqua County)	14712
Willowbrook (Richmond County)	10301
Willow Brook Estates	12303
Willow Brook Park	12302
Willowemac	12758
Willow Glen (Saratoga County)	12118
Willow Glen (Tompkins County)	13053
Willow Grove	13140
Willow Point	13850
Willow Ridge Estates	14150
Willsboro	12996
Willsboro (Town)	12996
Willsboro Point	12996
Willseyville	13864
Wilmington	12997
Wilmington (Town)	12997
Wilna (Town)	13619
Wilson	14172
Wilson (Town)	14172
Wilton	12866
Wilton (Town)	12866
Winchester	14224
Winderest Park	13031
Windham	12496
Windham (Town)	12496
Windham Ridge	12496
Winding Ways	13152
Windmill Farms	10504
Windom	14219
Windsor	13865
Windsor (Town)	13865
Windsor Beach	14617
Winebrook Hills	12852
Winfield (Town)	13491
Wingdale	12594
Winona Lake	12550
Winthrop	13697
Wirt (Town)	14774
Wiscoy	14536
Wisner	10990
Witherbee	12998
Wittenberg	12409
Wolcott	14590

	ZIP
Wolcott (Town)	14590
Wolcottsburg	14032
Wolcottsville	14001
Woodberry Hills	13413
Woodbourne	12788
Woodbury (Nassau County)	11797
Woodbury (Orange County) (Town)	10930
Woodbury Falls	10930
Woodcliff Park	11933
Woodgate	13494
Wood Haven (Part of New York)	11421
Woodhull	14898
Woodhull (Town)	14898
Woodinville	12564
Woodland	12464
Woodland Hills	12065
Woodlands	10607
Woodlawn (Bronx County)	10470
Woodlawn (Chautauqua County)	14710
Woodlawn Beach	14219
Woodmere	11598
Woodridge	12789
Woodrow (Part of New York)	10309
Woodruff Heights	12302
Woodsburgh	11598
Woods Corners	13815
Woods Falls	12910
Woodside (Part of New York)	11377
Woods Mill	13608
Woods Mills	12918
Woodstock	12498
Woodstock (Town)	12498
Woodsville	14437
Woodville (Jefferson County)	13650
Woodville (Ontario County)	14512
Wooglin	14728
Woolsey (Part of New York)	11105
Worcester	12197
Worcester (Town)	12197
Worley Heights	10950
Worth	13659
Worth (Town)	13659
Worthington (Part of White Plains)	10607
Wright (Town)	12073
Wright Park Manor (Part of Rome)	13440
Wrights Corners (Niagara County)	14094
Wrights Corners (Onondaga County)	13135
Wurtemburg	12572
Wurtsboro	12790
Wurtsboro Hills	12790
Wyandanch	11798
Wyatts	12302
Wycoff Heights (Part of New York)	11237
Wykagyl (Part of New Rochelle)	10804
Wykagyl Park (Part of New Rochelle)	10804
Wynantskill	12198
Wyomanock	12168
Wyoming	14591
Yaddo	12866
Yagerville	12458
Yaleville	13668
Yankee Lake	12790
Yaphank	11980
Yates (Town)	14098
Yates Center	14098
Yatesville	14527
Yonkers	10701-10
For specific Yonkers Zip Codes call (914) 378-3600	
York	14592
York (Town)	14592
York Corners	14895
Yorkshire	14173
Yorkshire (Town)	14173
Yorktown	10598
Yorktown (Town)	10598
Yorktown Heights	10598
Yorkville	13495
Yosts	12068
Young Hickory	14885
Youngstown	14174
Youngstown Estates	14174
Youngsville	12791
Yulan	12792
Zena	12498
Zoar	13682

ZIP

Name	ZIP
Aarons Corner	27053
Abbottsburg	28320
Aberdeen	28315
Abner	27356
Abshers	28635
Acme	28456
Acorn Hill	27979
Acorn Woods	28079
Acre	27865
Addie	28779
Addor	28315
Adoniram	24598
Advance	27006
Advent Crossroads	28601
Afton	27589
Aho	28607
Ahoskie	27910
Ai	27583
Airboro (Part of Goldsboro)	27530
Airlie	27850
Airport (Part of Charlotte)	28219
Alamance	27201
Alamance Correctional Center	27253
Alarka	28713
Albemarle	28001-02
For specific Albemarle Zip Codes call (704) 982-4114	
Albemarle Beach	27970
Albertson	28508
Albrittons	28501
Alert	27589
Alexander	28701
Alexander Correctional Center	28681
Alexander Mills	28043
Alexis	28006
Alfordsville	28383
Allen	28212
Allen Grove	27839
Allen Jay (Part of High Point)	27263
Allens Crossroads	28174
Allensville	27573
All Healing Springs	28681
Alliance	28509
Alligator	27925
Allison	27326
Allreds	27356
Alma	28364
Almond	28702
Altamahaw	27202
Altamahaw-Ossipee	27202
Altamont	28657
Altan	28112
Altapass	28777
Amantha	28679
Amerotron Mill (Part of Red Springs)	28377
Airport Mail Facility (Part of Greensboro)	27425
Amity	27013
Amity Gardens (Part of Charlotte)	28205
Ammon	28337
Anderson (Caswell County)	27215
Anderson (Dare County)	27949
Anderson Creek	28323
Anderson Crossroads	27850
Andrews	28901
Angier	27501
Anson Correctional Center	28135
Ansonville	28007
Antioch (Brunswick County)	28422
Antioch (Hoke County)	28377
Antioch (Madison County)	28753
Apex	27502
Appie	27888
Apple Grove	28643
Aquadale	28128
Aquone	28703
Arabia	28376
Arapahoe	28510
Ararat	27007
Arba	28580
Arcadia	27292
Archdale	27263
Archer	27520
Arcola	27589
Arden	28704
Ardmore (Part of Winston-Salem)	27113
Ardulusa	28301
Argura	28783
Arlington	28642
Armour	28456
Arnold	27292
Arran Hills	28304
Arrowhead Beach	27932
Arrowhead Place	28025
Arrowood (Part of Charlotte)	28273

ZIP

Name	ZIP
Artesia	28442
Asbury	27330
Ash	28420
Asheboro	27203-04
For specific Asheboro Zip Codes call (919) 629-9118	
Asheville	28801-16
For specific Asheville Zip Codes call (704) 257-4112	
Asheville Mall, The (Part of Asheville)	28805
Ashford	28752
Ash Hill	27007
Ashland (Ashe County)	28615
Ashland (Bertie County)	27957
Ashland (Caswell County)	27320
Ashland (Rockingham County)	27320
Ashley Heights	28315
Ashton	28425
Ashton Forrest	28304
Ashwood	28571
Askewville	27983
Askin	28527
Aspen	27850
Atkinson	28421
Atlantic	28511
Atlantic Beach	28512
Atlantic Christian College (Part of Wilson)	27893
Auburn	27610
Audubon (Part of Wilmington)	28403
Aulander	27805
Aurelian Springs	27850
Aurora	27806
Austin	28621
Autryville	28318
Avalon Valley	27253
Avent Ferry Road (Part of Raleigh)	27606
Aventon	27891
Averasboro	28334
Avery Correctional Center	28657
Avery Creek	28704
Avery Shores	27974
Avon	27915
Axtell	27563
Ayden	28513
Aydlett	27916
Ayersville	27027
Azalea (Buncombe County)	28805
Azalea (New Hanover County)	28403
Bachelor	28532
Badin	28009
Bagley	27542
Bahama	27503
Bailey	27807
Bailey Town	27052
Baker Rhyne Apartments	28152
Bakers	28110
Bakersville	28705
Bald Creek	28714
Bald Head Island	28461
Bald Mountain	28714
Baldwin (Ashe County)	28694
Baldwin (Moore County)	27341
Baldwin Woods (Part of Whiteville)	28472
Balfour	28792
Ballantree	28803
Ballard	27840
Ballards Crossroad	27834
Ballew Store	28714
Balm	28604
Balsam	28707
Balsam Grove	28708
Baltic	28398
Baltimore	28434
Bamboo	28605
Bandana	28705
Bandy	28609
Banks Creek	28714
Banner Elk	28604
Bannertown	27030
Banoak	28168
Barber	27008
Barclaysville	27501
Barco	27917
Barham	27587
Barium Springs	28010
Barker Heights	28792
Barkers Creek	28789
Barker Ten Mile	28358
Barnard	28753
Barnardsville	28709
Barnesfield	28570
Barnesville	28319
Barrett	28623
Barriers Mill	28124

ZIP

Name	ZIP
Bass Crossroads	27882
Basstown	28328
Bat Cave	28710
Batchelor Crossroads	27882
Bath	27808
Baton	28630
Battleboro	27809
Bay	27925
Bayboro	28515
Bayleaf	27609
Baynes	27302
Bayshore	28405
Baytree	27609
Bayview	27808
Beach Spring	27944
Bear Creek (Chatham County)	27207
Bear Creek (Onslow County)	28539
Beard	28301
Bear Grass	27892
Bearpond	27536
Bear Poplar	28125
Bearskin	28328
Bearwallow	28735
Beatties Ford	28216
Beaufort	28516
Beaufort Heights	27889
Beaver Creek	28694
Beaverdam (Buncombe County)	28715
Beaver Dam (Cleveland County)	28152
Beaver Dam (Columbus County)	28431
Beaverdam (Cumberland County)	28318
Beaverdam (Halifax County)	27823
Beaverdam (Haywood County)	28716
Beckwith	27865
Beech	27787
Beech Bottom	28657
Beechbrook (Part of Belmont)	28012
Beech Creek	28604
Beechertown	28781
Beech Mountain	28604
Beechwood Shores	27958
Bee Log	28714
Beesons Crossroads	27284
Belair	28306
Belcross	27921
Belews Creek	27009
Belfast	27530
Belgrade	28555
Belhaven	27810
Bellarthur	27811
Belle Mead	28601
Bellemont	27216
Bell Island	27929
Bells Cross Roads	28166
Bells Fork (Onslow County)	28546
Bells Fork (Pitt County)	27858
Belltown	27565
Bell View	28906
Belmont (Gaston County)	28012
Belmont (Halifax County)	27870
Belmont Abbey College	28012
Belva	28753
Belvedere	27834
Belvidere	27919
Belville	28451
Belvoir	27834
Belwood	28090
Benham	28621
Bennett	27208
Benson	27504
Bent Creek	28806
Benton Heights (Part of Monroe)	28110
Bentons Crossroad	28110
Berea	27565
Berkeley (Part of Goldsboro)	27534
Bertha	27965
Bertie (Part of Windsor)	27983
Bessemer (Part of Greensboro)	27405
Bessemer City	28016
Bests	28551
Beta	28779
Bethabara (Part of Winston-Salem)	27116
Bethania	27010
Bethany	27320
Bethel (Caswell County)	27311
Bethel (Columbus County)	28432
Bethel (Haywood County)	28716
Bethel (Hoke County)	28376
Bethel (Perquimans County)	27944

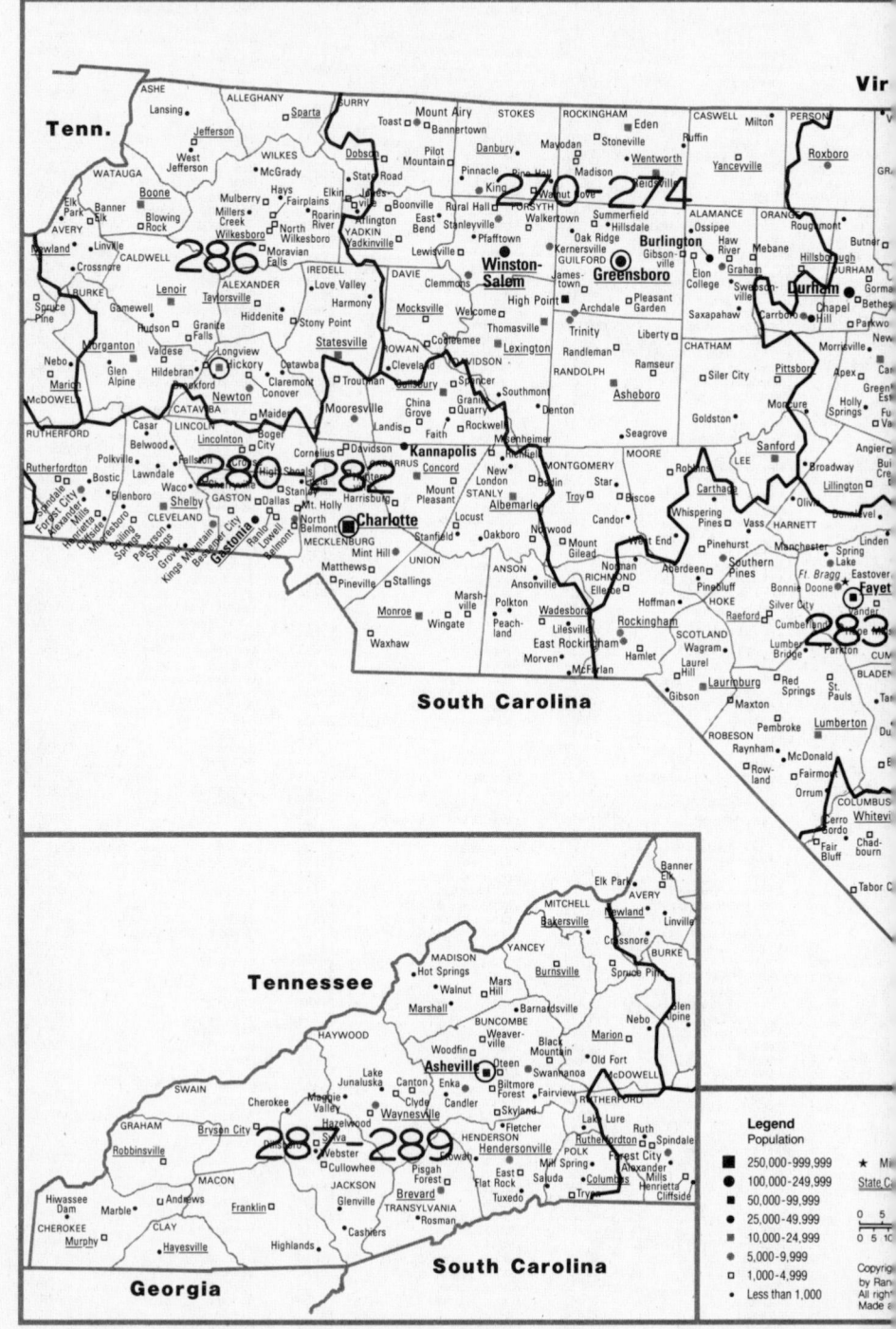

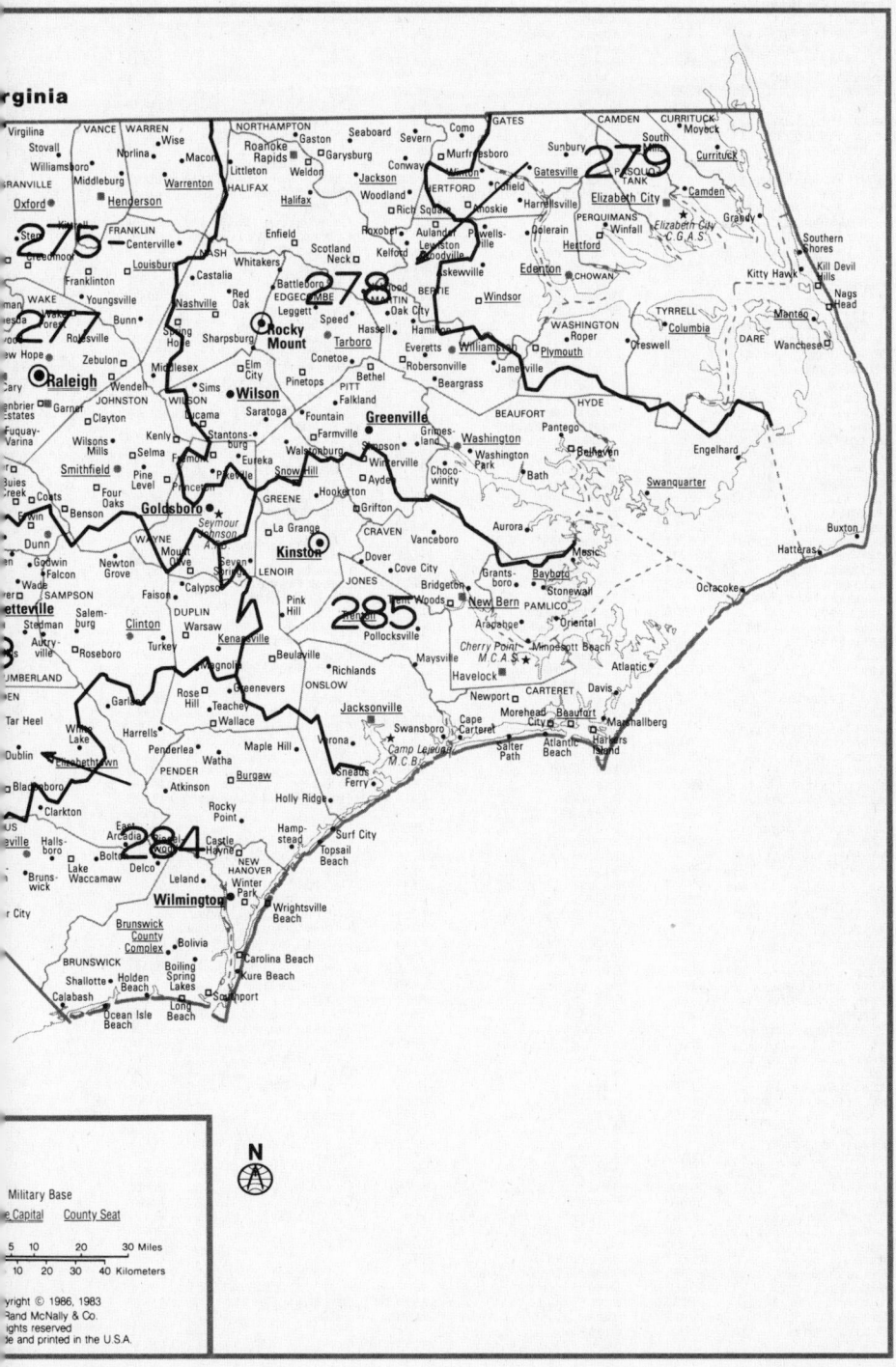

	ZIP
Bethel (Pitt County)	27812
Bethel Hill	27573
Bethesda (Davidson County)	27292
Bethesda (Durham County)	27703
Bethlehem (Alexander County)	28601
Bethlehem (Hertford County)	27922
Bettie	28516
Beulah (Hyde County)	27875
Beulah (Polk County)	28756
Beulahtown	27542
Beulaville	28518
Beverly Woods (Part of Charlotte)	28210
Bexley (Part of Wilmington)	28403
Biddleville (Part of Charlotte)	28216
Big Cove	28719
Biggs Park (Part of Lumberton)	28358
Big Laurel	28753
Big Lick	28129
Big Pine	28753
Big Ridge (Carteret County)	28570
Big Ridge (Jackson County)	28736
Biltmore (Part of Asheville)	28803
Biltmore Forest	28803
Birchwood	27215
Bird Cage	28431
Birdtown	28719
Biscoe	27209
Bishops Cross	27860
Bixby	27006
Blackburn	28658
Black Creek	27813
Black Jack	27858
Blackman	27524
Black Mountain	28711
Black Mountain Sanatorium	28711
Blackwell	27311
Blackwood	27514
Bladenboro	28320
Bladenboro North (Part of Bladenboro)	28320
Bladen Correctional Center	28337
Bladen Springs	28434
Blaine	27239
Blanch	27212
Blantyre	28768
Blevins Crossroads	28675
Blevins Store	27017
Blizzards Crossroads	28365
Bloomingdale	28369
Blossomtown	28734
Blounts Creek	27814
Blowing Rock	28605
Blue Ridge (Buncombe County)	28711
Blue Ridge (Henderson County)	28792
Blue Ridge Mall (Part of Hendersonville)	28792
Bluff	28743
Boardman	28438
Boat Club Road	28012
Bobbitt	27544
Boddies Pond	27856
Boger City	28092
Bogue	28570
Boiling Spring Lakes	28461
Boiling Springs (Cherokee County)	28906
Boiling Springs (Cleveland County)	28017
Bolivia	28422
Bolton	28423
Bolyston Creek	28768
Bon Air (Part of Winston-Salem)	27105
Bonaparte Landing	28459
Bonham Heights (Part of Morehead City)	28557
Bonlee	27213
Bonnerton	27806
Bonnetsville	28328
Bonnie Doone	28303
Bonsal	27562
Boomer	28606
Boone	28607
Boones Crossroads	27845
Boone Trail	27552
Boonford	28705
Boonville	27011
Bordeaux (Part of Fayetteville)	28304
Bostian Heights	28023
Bostic	28018
Bostwood Estates	28025
Botany Woods	28805
Bottom	27030

	ZIP
Boulevard (Part of Eden)	27288
Bowdens	28398
Bowditch	28714
Bowmore	28376
Boyles Chapel	27021
Bracey	28383
Bradfords Cross Roads	28677
Braggtown (Part of Durham)	27704
Branon	27055
Brantleys Grove	27910
Brasstown	28902
Braswell	28431
Brendletown	28734
Brentwood (Cumberland County)	28304
Brentwood (Wake County)	27604
Brettonwood	28311
Brevard	28712
Briarwood Terrace	28144
Brices Crossroads	28458
Brickhaven	27559
Bricks	27891
Brickton	28732
Bridgersville	27852
Bridgeton	28519
Brief	28107
Briertown	28781
Brigand Bay	27920
Brightwood (Part of Greensboro)	27214
Brindle Town	28655
Brinkleyville (Hertford County)	27910
Brinkleyville (Lee County)	27823
British Acres	27215
Broad Acres	27253
Broad Creek	28570
Broadway	27505
Brocks	28574
Brogden	27530
Brook Cove	27052
Brookdale	28792
Brookford	28601
Brookhaven	27609
Brookland Manor	28792
Brooks Cross Roads	27020
Brooksdale	27573
Brookside (Part of Goldsboro)	27530
Brookston	27536
Brook Valley	27858
Broughton Hospital	28655
Browns Summit	27214
Brown Town (Part of Belmont)	28012
Brownwood	28684
Bruce	27834
Brunswick	28424
Brutonville	27229
Bryantown	27869
Bryantville Park	27818
Bryson City	28713
Buckhorn	27243
Buckhorn Cross Roads	27542
Buckland	27937
Bucklesberry	28551
Buckner	28754
Buck Shoals	27020
Buena Vista	27983
Buffalo Cove	28645
Bug Hill	28455
Buie	28377
Buies Creek	27506
Buladean	28705
Bullhead	27863
Bullock	27507
Bunn	27508
Bunnlevel	28323
Bunyan	27889
Burbage Crossroads	27808
Burden	27805
Burgaw	28425
Burgess	27944
Burke Chapel	28601
Burkemont	28655
Burlington	27215-17
For specific Burlington Zip Codes call (919) 227-4293	
Burney	28399
Burningtown	28734
Burnsville (Anson County)	28135
Burnsville (Yancey County)	28714
Burnt Mills	27976
Busbee (Part of Asheville)	28803
Bushy Fork	27541
Busick (Guilford County)	27214
Busick (Yancey County)	28714
Butlers Crossroads	28328
Butner	27509
Butters	28324
Buxton	27920

	ZIP
Buzzards Crossroads	27924
Bynum	27228
Byrum Crossroads	27980
Cabarrus	28107
Cabarrus Correctional Center	28124
Cabin	28572
Cairo	28119
Cajah's Mountain	28645
Calabash	28459
Calahaln	27028
Caldwell (Mecklenburg County)	28078
Caldwell (Orange County)	27572
Caldwell Correctional Center	28638
Caledonia Correctional Center	27887
California (Dare County)	27954
California (Hertford County)	27986
California (Pitt County)	27828
Callisons	28571
Cal-Vel	27573
Calvert	28712
Calvin Heights	28570
Calypso	28325
Camden	27921
Camelot	27529
Cameron	28326
Cameron Village (Part of Raleigh)	27605
Campbell Creek	27806
Camp Glenn (Part of Morehead City)	28557
Camp Leach	27889
Camp Lejeune	28542
Camp Lejeune Central	28542
Camp MacKall	28347
Camp Springs	27320
Camp Sutton (Part of Monroe)	28110
Cana	27028
Candler	28715
Candler Heights	28715
Candlewick Estates	27834
Candor	27229
Cane Creek	28167
Cane Mountain	27349
Cane River	28714
Cannon Ferry	27980
Canto	28748
Canton	28716
Cape Carteret	28584
Cape Colony	27932
Cape Fear	27562
Capella	27021
Capelsie	27229
Carbonton	27330
Carmel (Part of Charlotte)	28226
	28270
	28276
For specific Carmel Zip Codes call (704) 541-7851	
Caroleen	28019
Carolina	22217
Carolina Beach	28428
Carolina Circle Mall (Part of Greensboro)	27405
Carolina East Mall (Part of Greenville)	27834
Carolina Forest	27371
Carolina Mall (Part of Concord)	28025
Carolina Pines	28303
Carolina Trace	27330
Carolina Village	28792
Carova Beach	27927
Carpenter	27560
Carpenter Bottom	28657
Carr	27302
Carrboro	27510
Carr Creek	27330
Carroll	28398
Carter	27938
Carteret Correctional Center	28570
Cartersville	28466
Carthage	28327
Cartoogechaye	28734
Carvers	28434
Cary	27511-13
	27518-19
For specific Cary Zip Codes call (919) 831-3661	
Cary Village Mall (Part of Cary)	27511
Casar	28020
Cashiers	28717
Cason Old Field	28170
Castalia	27816
Castle Hayne	28429
Castoria	27888
Casville	27326

	ZIP
Caswell Beach	28461
Caswell Correctional Center	27379
Catawba	28609
Catawba Correctional Center	28658
Catawba Heights	28012
Catawba Mall (Part of Hickory)	28601
Catherine Lake	28574
Catherine Square	28518
Cat Square	28168
Ca-Vel (Part of Roxboro)	27573
Cayton	28527
Cedar Creek	28301
Cedar Croft	28081
Cedar Falls	27230
Cedar Fork	28518
Cedar Grove (Orange County)	27231
Cedar Grove (Randolph County)	27203
Cedar Hill (Anson County)	28170
Cedar Hill (Brunswick County)	28451
Cedar Island	28520
Cedar Lodge	27360
Cedar Mountain	28718
Cedar Point	28584
Cedarrock	27816
Ceffo	27573
Celeste Hinkle	28677
Celo	28714
Celotex	28333
Center (Davie County)	27028
Center (Yadkin County)	27055
Center City (Part of Winston-Salem)	27120
Center Pigeon	28716
Centerview (Part of Kannapolis)	28083
Centerville	27549
Central	28677
Central Falls (Part of Asheboro)	27203
Central Heights	28025
Century (Part of Raleigh)	27601
Cerro Gordo	28430
Chadbourn	28431
Chadwick Acres	28460
Chalybeate Springs	27526
Champion	28624
Chantilly (Camden County)	27921
Chantilly (Mecklenburg County)	28205
Chapanoke	27944
Chapel Hill	27514-16
For specific Chapel Hill Zip Codes call (919) 942-4179	
Charity	28458
Charles	28677
Charlotte	28201-99
For specific Charlotte Zip Codes call (704) 393-4555	

COLLEGES & UNIVERSITIES

Johnson C. Smith University	28216
Queens College	28274
University of North Carolina at Charlotte	28223

FINANCIAL INSTITUTIONS

First Federal Savings & Loan Association of Charlotte	28233
First Union National Bank of North Carolina	28288
Home Federal Savings & Loan Association	28202
NationsBank of North Carolina	28255
Republic Bank & Trust Company	28204

HOSPITALS

Carolinas Medical Center	28203
Mercy Hospital	28207
Presbyterian Hospital	28204

HOTELS/MOTELS

Adam's Mark Charlotte	28204
Guest Quarters Suite Hotel	28211
Holiday Inn-Woodlawn	28217
The Park Hotel	28211
Ramada Inn-Central	28217

MILITARY INSTALLATIONS

Naval and Marine Corps Reserve Center, Charlotte	28256

	ZIP
North Carolina Air National Guard, FB6331, Morris Field	28208
Charlotte Correctional Center	28208
Chatham	27514
Cheeks	27316
Cherokee	28719
Cherokee Indian Reservation	28719
Cherry	27928
Cherryfield	28712
Cherry Grove	28430
Cherry Lane	28627
Cherry Oaks	27858
Cherry Point	28533
Cherry Springs	28762
Cherryville	28021
Chesterfield	28655
Chestnut Dale	28657
Chestnut Grove	27021
Chestnut Hill (Ashe County)	28617
Chestnut Hill (Henderson County)	28735
Chimney Rock	28720
China Grove	28023
China Grove Cotton Mill Village	28023
Chinquapin	28521
Chip (Craven County)	28586
Chip (Montgomery County)	27306
Choco Village	27817
Chocowinity	27817
Chowan Beach (Chowan County)	27932
Chowan Beach (Hertford County)	27855
Chublake	27573
Church Crossroads	27871
Churchill	27551
Churchland	27292
Cid	27292
Cisco	27980
City View (Part of Winston-Salem)	27101
Claremont	28610
Clarendon	28432
Clark	28562
Clarkton	28433
Clarrissa	28705
Clay	27565
Clayroot	28513
Clayton	27520
Clear Creek	28212
Clear Run	28441
Clegg	27560
Clemmons	27012
Clemont	28318
Cleveland	27013
Cleveland Correctional Center	28152
Cleveland Springs	28150
Clifdale	28304
Cliffside	28024
Clifton	28693
Climax	27233
Clinchfield	28752
Clingman	28670
Clinton	28328
Cloverdale (Part of Garner)	27529
Clover Garden	27217
Cloverleaf	28304
Club Pines	27834
Clyde	28721
Coakley	27886
Coalville	28901
Coats	27521
Coats Cross Roads	27504
Cobb Town	27829
Cofield	27922
Cognac	28363
Coinjock	27923
Cokesbury (Harnett County)	27526
Cokesbury (Vance County)	27536
Cold Springs	28025
Cold Water	28025
Cole Park	27514
Colerain	27924
Coleridge	27316
Colewood Acres	27604
Colfax	27235
Colington	27948
College (Part of Durham)	27708
College Downs	28213
College Lakes	28301
College Park (Cabarrus County)	28075
College Park (Guilford County)	27403

	ZIP
College Park (Richmond County)	28345
Collettsville	28611
Collinstown	24171
Colly	28448
Colon	27330
Colonial Heights (Beaufort County)	27889
Colonial Heights (Wake County)	27603
Colony Park (Part of Durham)	27705
Columbia	27925
Columbia Heights (Part of Winston-Salem)	27107
Columbus	28722
Columbus Correctional Center	28424
Comfort	28522
Commodore Peninsula	28115
Como	27818
Concord	28025-27
For specific Concord Zip Codes call (704) 786-3161	
Concord (Duplin County)	28453
Concord (Person County)	27573
Concord (Rutherford County)	28018
Concord (Sampson County)	28382
Conetoe	27819
Congleton	27871
Connarista	27805
Connelly Springs	28612
Conover	28613
Conway	27820
Cooksville	28168
Cooktown	28705
Cooleemee	27014
Cool Spring	27013
Cool Springs	27330
Cooper Estates	27253
Copeland	27017
Coral Bay	28557
Corapeake	27926
Corbett	27302
Cordova	28330
Core Creek	28516
Core Point	27814
Corinth (Chatham County)	27559
Corinth (Nash County)	27856
Corinth (Rutherford County)	28040
Cornatzer	27028
Cornelius	28031
Cornwall	27565
Corolla	27927
Correll Park	28146
Corriher Heights	28023
Costin	28421
Cotswold Mall (Part of Charlotte)	28211
Cottonade	28303
Cotton Grove	27292
Cottonville	28128
Council	28434
Country Club Estates	28472
Country Hills	27529
Country Homes Estates	27258
Countyline	28634
Courtney	27055
Cove City	28523
Cove Creek	28786
Covington	27306
Cowee	28734
Cox Crossing	27858
Coxville	28513
Cozart	27522
Crab Point	28557
Crabtree	28721
Crabtree Valley Mall (Part of Raleigh)	27612
Craggy	28804
Craggy Correctional Center	28802
Cramerton	28032
Cranberry	28614
Cranberry Gap	28657
Crater Park	28213
Creedmoor	27522
Creeksville	27820
Cremo	27924
Crescent	28138
Crestmont	28601
Creston	28615
Crestview	27344
Creswell	27928
Cricket	28659
Crisp	27852
Croatan	28562
Cross Landing	27925
Cross Mill	28752
Crossnore	28616
Cross Road	27030

	ZIP		ZIP		ZIP
Enterprise (Davidson County)	27292	Five Forks (Rowan County)	28023	Friendship (Cherokee County)	28906
Enterprise (Warren County)	27850	Five Forks (Warren County)	27551	Friendship (Duplin County)	28398
Ephesus	27028	Five Point (Part of Raleigh)	27608	Friendship (Guilford County)	27410
Epsom	27536	Five Points (Beaufort County)	27889	Friendship (Wake County)	27502
Erastus	28723	Five Points (Columbus County)	28431	Friendship (Yadkin County)	27018
Erect	27341			Frisco	27936
Ernul	28527	Five Points (Hoke County)	28376	Frog Level	27834
Ervintown	28574	Five Points (Richmond County)	28379	Frog Pond	28129
Erwin	28339	Flat Branch (Gates County)	27938	Frogsboro	27314
Erwin Heights (Part of Thomasville)	27360	Flat Branch (Harnett County)	27546	Fruitland	28792
Essex	27844	Flat Creek	28787	Frying Pan Landing	27925
Estatoe	28777	Flat Rock (Henderson County)	28731	Fulchers Landing	28460
Estelle	27305			Fullers	27360
Ether	27247	Flat Rock (Stokes County)	27043	Fulp	27052
Etowah	28729	Flat Rock (Surry County)	27030	Funston	28479
Eufola	28677	Flats	28781	Fuquay Springs (Part of Fuquay-Varina)	27526
Eure	27935	Flat Shoals	27019	Fuquay-Varina	27526
Eureka	27830	Flat Springs	28622	Furches	28644
Eureka Springs	28301	Flay	28021	Furnitureland (Part of High Point)	27264
Eutaw (Part of Fayetteville)	28303	Fleetwood	28626	Galatia	27876
Evansdale	27893	Fleetwood Acres	28052	Gales Creek	28570
Everetts	27825	Fletcher	28732	Galloway Crossroads	27858
Everetts Crossroads	27865	Flint Hill (Montgomery County)	27371	Gallup Acres	28304
Evergreen (Beaufort County)	27817	Flint Hill (Randolph County)	27350	Gamble Hill	28016
Evergreen (Columbus County)	28438	Flint Hill (Yadkin County)	27018	Gamewell	28645
Evergreen Estates	28304	Florence	28556	Garden Homes (Part of Greensboro)	27408
Exum	28420	Florence Town	27302	Gardnerville	28513
Exway	27306	Flowes Store	28025	Gardner Webb College (Part of Boiling Springs)	28017
Fair Bluff	28439	Floytan Crossroads	27536	Garland	28441
Fairfield (Hyde County)	27826	Folkstone	28445	Garner	27529
Fairfield (Union County)	28103	Folly	27979	Garysburg	27831
Fair Field Estate	28150	Fontana Dam	28733	Gaston	27832
Fairfield Harbour	28560	Footsville	27055	Gaston Correctional Center	28034
Fairfield Sapphire Valley	28774	Forbes	28740	Gastonia	28051-56
Fair Grove	27360	Forestburg	27944	For specific Gastonia Zip Codes call (704) 867-6311	
Fairlane	28303	Forest City	28043		
Fairmont	28340	Forest Hills (Cumberland County)	28303	Gaston Mall (Part of Gastonia)	28054
Fairmont Junction	28383	Forest Hills (Forsyth County)	27105	Gates	27937
Fairplains	28659	Forest Hills (Gaston County)	28120	Gates Correctional Center	27938
Fairport	27544	Forest Hills (New Hanover County)	28403	Gates Four	28306
Fairview (Buncombe County)	28730			Gatesville	27938
Fairview (Orange County)	27278	Forest Hills (Rockingham County)	27320	Gateway	28789
Fairview (Rockingham County)	27288	Forest Oaks	27406	Gause Landing	28459
Fairview (Union County)	28110	Forest Ridge	28152	Gay	28779
Fairview Cross Roads	27017	Forestville (Anson County)	28091	Gaylord	27808
Fairview Park	28636	Forestville (Wake County)	27587	Gela	27582
Fairway Hills	28786	Fork Church	27028	Gentry Store	27573
Faison	28341	Fort Barnwell	28526	George	27897
Faisons	27876	Fort Bragg	28307	Georgetown (Buncombe County)	28748
Faith	28041	Fort Caswell	28461		
Falcon	28342	Fort Junction	28307	Georgetown (Davidson County)	27284
Falkland	27827	Fort Landing	27925	Georgetown (Lenoir County)	28501
Fall Creek	27018	Fort Macon Coast Guard Base	28512	Georgeville	28025
Falling Creek	28501			Germanton	27019
Falling Creek Estates	28601	Fort Point	27817	Germantown	27875
Falls	27609	Foscoe	28604	Gerton	28735
Fallston	28042	Foster Creek	28753	Gethsemane	27891
Far Away Place	28025	Fountain (Duplin County)	28521	Gibson	28343
Farmer	27203	Fountain (Pitt County)	27829	Gibsontown	28716
Farmington	27028	Fountain Hill	28133	Gibsonville	27249
Farmville (Chatham County)	27330	Four Oaks	27524	Giddensville	28341
Farmville (Pitt County)	27828	Four Seasons (Part of Hendersonville)	28739	Gilkey	28139
Faro	27883			Gill	27536
Farrington	27514	Four Seasons Towncenter (Part of Greensboro)	27407	Gillburg	27536
Faust	28754	Fourway	28538	Glade Valley	28627
Fayblock (Part of Fayetteville)	28301	Fox Fire (Cumberland County)	28303	Glady	28715
Fayetteville	28301-06	Foxfire (Moore County)	27281	Glass (Part of Kannapolis)	28081
	28309-14	Foxwood Acres	28025	Glen Alpine	28628
For specific Fayetteville Zip Codes call (919) 486-2311		Francisco	27053	Glen Ayre	28705
		Francis Mill	27805	Glenbrook	28304
Fayetteville North (Part of Fayetteville)	28311	Francktown	28574	Glencoe	27217
Fearrington	27312	Frank	28657	Glendale Acres (Part of Fayetteville)	28304
Fearrington Post	27312	Franklin (Macon County)	28734	Glendale Springs	28629
Federal Building (Part of Elizabeth City)	27909	Franklin (Rowan County)	28144	Glendon	27251
		Franklin Correctional Center	27508	Glenhaven	28304
Federal Correctional Institution	27509	Franklin Grove	28713	Glen Lennox (Part of Chapel Hill)	27514
Feezor	27292	Franklin Street (Part of Chapel Hill)	27514	Glenn	27705
Feltonville	27502	Franklinton	27525	Glenola	27263
Ferguson	28624	Franklinville	27248	Glen Raven	27215
Ferncliff Estates	28025	Frazier Crossroads	27557	Glenview	27823
Fibreville (Part of Canton)	28716	Fraziers Crossroads	27910	Glenville	28736
Fields	28551	Frederick	27817	Glenwood (Guilford County)	27403
Fines Creek	28721	Freedom (Part of Charlotte)	28208	Glenwood (McDowell County)	28737
Finger	28124	Freedom Mall (Part of Charlotte)	28208	Glenwood (Richmond County)	28379
Fires Creek	28904			Globe	28645
First Union (Part of Charlotte)	28202	Freeland	28420	Gloucester	28528
		Freeman	28423	Gneiss	28734
Fisher Park (Part of Greensboro)	27401	Fremont	27830	Goat Neck	27925
Fisher Town	28081	Friendly Acres	28027	Godwin	28344
Fitch	27379	Friendly Center-Forum VI (Part of Greensboro)	27404	Golden Forest	27604
Five Forks (Person County)	27573				

	ZIP		ZIP		ZIP
Golden Gate (Part of		Guilford (Part of		Hayti (Part of Durham)	27701
Greensboro)	27405	Greensboro)	27409	Haywood	27559
Gold Hill (Rockingham		Guilford College (Part of		Haywood Road (Part of	
County)	27025	Greensboro)	27410	Asheville)	28806
Gold Hill (Rowan County)	28071	Guilford Correctional Center	27301	Hazelwood	28738
Gold Mine	28741	Guilford Hills (Part of		Hazelwood Park	27864
Gold Point	27871	Greensboro)	27408	Healing Springs	27239
Goldrock	27891	Gulf	27256	Heathsville	27823
Goldsboro	27530-34	Gull Rock	27824	Heaton	28622
For specific Goldsboro Zip Codes		Gumberry	27838	Hedrick Grove	27292
call (919) 734-3521		Gumbranch	28540	Helens Crossroads	28513
Goldston	27252	Gum Neck	27925	Helton	28631
Gold Valley Crossroads	27557	Gum Springs	27312	Hemby Acres	28079
Goodsonville	28092	Guntertown	28753	Hemby Bridge	28079
Goose Creek	27974	Gupton	27549	Henderson	27536
Gooseneck	28456	Guthrie	27284	Henderson Correctional	
Goose Pond	27924	Guyton	28320	Center	27839
Gordonton	27541	Haddocks Crossroads	28590	Hendersonville	28739
Gordontown	27292	Hairtown	28302		28792-93
Gorman	27704	Half Hell	28422	For specific Hendersonville Zip	
Goshen	28697	Half Moon	28540	Codes call (704) 692-2547	
Governors Island	28713	Halifax	27839	Hendrix Estates	28144
Grace (Part of Asheville)	28814	Halifax Correctional		Henrico	27842
Grace Chapel	28630	Institution	27839	Henrietta	28076
Gradys	28365	Hallsboro	28442	Henry	28168
Graham	27253	Halls Ferry Junction	28127	Henry River	28602
Graingers	28501	Halls Mills	28649	Hepco	28721
Grandfather	28646	Halls Store	28385	Heritage Hill	27516
Grandview	28906	Hallsville	28518	Heritage Woods	28025
Grandview Heights (Part of		Hamer	27212	Herrings Crossroads (Duplin	
Boone)	28607	Hamilton	27840	County)	28508
Grandy	27939	Hamilton Lakes (Part of		Herrings Crossroads	
Granite Falls	28630	Greensboro)	27408	(Greene County)	27888
Granite Quarry	28072	Hamlet	28345	Hertford	27944
Grantham	27530	Hampstead	28443	Hester	27581
Granthams	28560	Hamptonville	27020	Hesters Store	27541
Grantsboro	28529	Hamrick	28714	Hestertown	28358
Grape Creek	28906	Hancheys Store	28466	Hewitt	28781
Grapevine	28753	Hancock	27932	Hexlena	27805
Graphite	28762	Handy	27239	Hibbs Acres	28570
Grassy Creek (Ashe		Hanes Mall (Part of		Hickmans Crossroads	28459
County)	28631	Winston-Salem)	27103	Hickory	28601-03
Grassy Creek (Mitchell			27130	For specific Hickory Zip Codes	
County)	28777	For specific Hanes Mall Zip Codes		call (704) 328-5503	
Grays Chapel	27248	call (919) 760-9818		Hickory Crossroads	27919
Grayson	28632	Hanrahans	28530	Hickory Grove (Cumberland	
Great Neck Landing	28539	Happy Valley (Buncombe		County)	28304
Green Acres (Alamance		County)	28805	Hickory Grove (Gaston	
County)	27217	Happy Valley (Caldwell		County)	28056
Green Acres (Gaston		County)	28645	Hickory Grove	
County)	28012	Harbinger	27941	(Mecklenburg County)	28215
Green Acres (Wake County)	27603	Harbor Island (Part of		Hickory Knoll	28734
Green Acres Park	28025	Wrightsville Beach)	28480	Hickory Point	27806
Greenbrier Estates	27603	Hardees Cross Road	27504	Hickory Rock	27549
Greene Correctional Center	28554	Hardins	28034	Hicks Crossroads	
Greene Cove	28705	Hare	28627	(Mecklenburg County)	28078
Greenevers	28458	Hargetts Cross Roads	28574	Hicks Crossroads (Vance	
Green Farm	27834	Harkers Island	28531	County)	27565
Greenfield	27932	Harlem Heights	28170	Hiddenite	28636
Greenhill (Haywood County)	28716	Harlowe	28570	Higdonville	28734
Green Hill (Rutherford		Harmony	28634	Higgins	28714
County)	28139	Harper's Crossroads	27207	High Crossroads	27807
Greenlee	28762	Harrells	28444	Highfalls	27259
Greenlevel (Alamance		Harrellsville	27942	High Hampton	28717
County)	27217	Harrelsonville	28472	Highland Park	28345
Green Level (Wake County)	27502	Harris (Moore County)	28327	Highland Park West (Part of	
Greenmountain	28740	Harris (Rutherford County)	28074	Greensboro)	27407
Greenriver	28722	Harrisburg	28075	Highlands	28741
Greensboro	27401-55	Harrisburg Estates	28075	High Point	27260-65
For specific Greensboro Zip		Harris Crossroads (Franklin		For specific High Point Zip Codes	
Codes call (919) 271-5481		County)	27596	call (919) 884-8344	
Greens Creek	28779	Harris Crossroads (Vance		High Rock	27239
Green Valley	28615	County)	27536	High Shoals	28077
Greenville	27834-36	Harris Landing	27932	Highsmiths	28382
	27858	Harrison Cross Roads	27320	Hightowers	27379
For specific Greenville Zip Codes		Hartland	28645	Hildebran	28637
call (919) 752-2153		Hartman	27016	Hillcrest (Hoke County)	28376
Greenwood Homes (Part of		Hartsease	27886	Hill Crest (Moore County)	28327
Fayetteville)	28303	Harveytown	28501	Hilliardston	27856
Gregory	27973	Hassell	27841	Hillsborough	27278
Gregory Crossroads (Bertie		Hastings Corner	27921	Hills Crossroads	27839
County)	27957	Hasty	28352	Hillsdale (Davie County)	27006
Gregory Crossroads		Hatteras	27943	Hillsdale (Guilford County)	27405
(Onslow County)	28574	Havelock	28532	Hillsville	27350
Greystone	27536	Havelock Station (Part of		Hilltop (Guilford County)	27417
Griffins Crossroads	27312	Havelock)	28532	Hilltop (Lincoln County)	28092
Grifton	28530	Haw Branch (Moore		Hilltop Acres	28570
Grimesdale	28792	County)	27330	Hill View	28580
Grimesland	27837	Haw Branch (Onslow		Hines Crossroad	27834
Grissettown	28459	County)	28574	Hinsons Crossroads	28439
Grissom	27522	Haw Creek (Part of		Hiwassee Dam	28906
Grist	28431	Asheville)	28805	Hobbsville	27946
Grove Hill	27551	Hawfields	27302	Hobbton	28366
Grovemont	28778	Hawk	28705	Hobgood	27843
Grove Park (Part of		Haw River	27258	Hobucken	28537
Charlotte)	28215	Haws Run	28454	Hodges Gap	28607
Grover	28073	Hayesville	28904	Hodman	27028
Grovestone	28778	Haymount (Part of		Hoffman	28347
Growers Crossroads	27924	Fayetteville)	28305	Hog Island	28394
Guide	28463	Hayne	28318	Ho-Ho Village	28570
Guideway	28463	Hays	28635	Holden Beach	28462

	ZIP
Langley Store	27801
Lansdowne (Part of Charlotte)	28226
Lansing	28643
Lanvale	28451
Lasker	27848
Last Chance	27824
Latham Town (Part of Greensboro)	27407
Lattimore	28089
Lauada	28713
Laurel	28753
Laurel Hill (Buncombe County)	28715
Laurel Hill (Scotland County)	28351
Laurel Hills	27609
Laurel Park	28739
Laurel Springs	28644
Laurinburg	28352-53
For specific Laurinburg Zip Codes call (919) 276-0911	
Lawndale (Cleveland County)	28090
Lawndale (Guilford County)	27408
Lawrence	27886
Lawsonville (Rockingham County)	27320
Lawsonville (Stokes County)	27022
Laytown	28645
Leaksville (Part of Eden)	27288
Leaman	27325
Leasburg	27291
Leatherman	28734
Ledbetter	28379
Ledger	28705
Leechville	27810
Lee's Ridge	28806
Leewood Acres	28092
Leggett	27886
Leicester	28748
Leland	28451
Lemon Springs	28355
Lennon Crossroads	28422
Lennons Crossroads	28438
Lennoxville	28516
Lenoir	28645
Lenoir Mall (Part of Lenoir)	28645
Lenoir Rhyne (Part of Hickory)	28601
Letitia	28906
Level Cross (Randolph County)	27317
Level Cross (Surry County)	27017
Levels	27925
Lewis	27565
Lewisburg	28714
Lewiston Woodville	27849
Lewisville	27023
Lexington	27292-93
For specific Lexington Zip Codes call (704) 249-8196	
Liberia	27589
Liberty (Cherokee County)	37391
Liberty (Randolph County)	27298
Liberty (Rowan County)	28071
Liberty Hill	27306
Liddell	28578
Light Oak	28150
Liledown	28681
Lilesville	28091
Lillington	27546
Lilly	27976
Lincoln Correctional Center	28092
Lincolnton	28092-93
For specific Lincolnton Zip Codes call (704) 735-7321	
Lindell	27883
Linden	28356
Lindley Park (Part of Greensboro)	27403
Lineberry	27233
Linville	28646
Linville Falls	28647
Linwood	27299
Lisbon	28434
Little Creek	28754
Littlefield	28513
Little Horse Creek	28643
Little Mountain	28761
Little Pinecreek	28753
Little Richmond	28621
Little River (Alexander County)	28681
Little River (Transylvania County)	28766
Little Switzerland	28749
Littleton	27850
Livingstons Quarters	28351
Lizard Lick	27591
Lizzie	28580
Lloyd Crossroads	27942

	ZIP
Loafers Glory	28705
Lobelia	28394
Lochlommond	28304
Locust	28097
Locust Grove	28740
Locust Hill	27320
Loftins Crossroads	28501
Logan	28139
Lola	28520
Lomax	28669
Lone Hickory	27055
Long Acres (Part of Jacksonville)	28546
Long Beach	28461
Longcreek	28457
Longisland	28648
Long John Mountain Estates	28739
Longleaf	28570
Long Leaf Park (Part of Wilmington)	28403
Long Pine	28170
Long Ridge	28754
Long Shoals	28092
Longs Store	27573
Longtown (Burke County)	28761
Longtown (Yadkin County)	27011
Long View (Bladen County)	28448
Longview (Catawba County)	28601
Longview (Cumberland County)	28301
Longwood	28452
Longwood Park	28345
Loray	28677
Louisburg	27549
Love Field	28779
Lovejoy	27371
Love Valley	28677
Lowell	28098
Lowes Grove	27713
Lowesville	28164
Lowgap	27024
Lowland	28552
Luart	27546
Lucama	27851
Lucia	28120
Luck	28743
Lumber Bridge	28357
Lumberton	28358-59
For specific Lumberton Zip Codes call (919) 738-2451	
Luther	28715
Lyman	28521
Lynchs Corner	27909
Lynn	28750
Lynndale	27858
Lynnwood Jr. Estate	28025
Lynwood Lakes	27406
Mabel	28698
McAdenville	28101
McAdoo Heights (Part of Greensboro)	27405
McArthers Crossroads	28352
Macclesfield	27852
McConnell (Beaufort County)	27814
McConnell (Moore County)	27325
McCray	27215
McCullen	28328
McCullers	27603
Mc Cutcheon Field	28545
McDade	27231
McDaniel	28382
McDonald	28340
McDowell Correctional Center	28752
Macedonia (Wake County)	27606
Macedonia (Washington County)	27962
McFarlan	28102
MacGee Crossroads	27501
McGehees Mill	27343
McGinnis Crossroads	28722
McGowans Crossroads	27858
McGrady	28649
Machpelah	28080
Mackeys	27970
Macks Village	27526
McLamb Crossroads	28366
McLeansville	27301
Maco	28451
Macon	27551
Madison	27025
Maggie Valley	28751
Magnolia	28453
Maiden	28650
Maine	27028
Main Street (Part of Garner)	27529
Makatoka	28420
Makleyville	27875
Malmo	28451

	ZIP
Malpass Corner	28425
Maltby	28905
Malvern Hills (Part of Asheville)	28806
Mamers	27552
Mamie	27966
Manchester (Part of Spring Lake)	28390
Mangum	27306
Manly	28387
Manns Harbor	27953
Manor Station (Part of Winston-Salem)	27114
Mansfield	28557
Mansfield Park	28557
Manson	27553
Manteo	27954
Maple	27956
Maple Cypress	28530
Maple Hill	28454
Maple Springs	28665
Mapleton	27855
Mapleville	27549
Maplewood (Part of Rockingham)	28379
Marble	28905
Marcus	27281
Maready	28521
Margaretsville	27853
Maribel	28515
Marietta	28362
Marion	28752
Mariposa	28164
Marlboro	27828
Marler	27020
Marlwood Acres (Part of Charlotte)	28212
Mar-Mac	27530
Mar-Man	28532
Marshall	28753
Marshallberg	28553
Mars Hill	28754
Marshville	28103
Marston	28363
Martel Village (Part of Woodfin)	28804
Martin Correctional Center	27892
Martins Creek	28906
Marvin	28173
Marys Grove	28086
Mashoes	27953
Masonboro	28403
Masons Crossroads	28343
Mason Store	27546
Masontown	28581
Massapoag (Part of Lincolnton)	28092
Mast	28692
Mathews Crossroads	27816
Matkins	27249
Matney	28604
Matthews	28105-06
For specific Matthews Zip Codes call (704) 847-9185	
Maury	28554
Mavaton	27932
Maxton	28364
Mayfair	28304
Mayfield	27326
Mayhew	28115
Mayodan	27027
Maysville	28555
Mazeppa	28115
Meadow (Johnston County)	27504
Meadow (Stokes County)	27052
Meadowood	28379
Meadowood Lakes	27302
Meadow Summit (Part of Eden)	27288
Meadow Wood	28304
Meat Camp	28607
Mebane	27302
Mecklenburg Correctional Center	28078
Medfield	27607
Melanchton	27298
Melrose	28773
Melville	27302
Melvin Hill	28722
Menola	27910
Meredith College (Part of Raleigh)	27601
Merrimon	28516
Merritt	28556
Merry Hill	27957
Merry Oaks	27559
Mesic	28515
Metcalf	28150
Method (Part of Raleigh)	27606
Methodist College	28301
Mewborns Crossroads	28501

	ZIP		ZIP		ZIP
Micaville	28755	Morrisville	27560	Needmore (Swain County)	28713
Micro	27555	Mortimer	28645	Neel Estates	28144
Middleburg	27556	Morven	28119	Nelson	27560
Middle Fork	28712	Moss	28127	Neuse	27661
Middlesex	27557	Moss Hill	28501	Neuse Crossroads	27661
Middletown	27824	Mother Vineyard	27954	Neuse Forest	28560
Midland	28107	Motleta	27203	Neverson	27880
Midpine	28086	Mountain Home	28758	New Bern	28560-64
Midway (Alexander County)	28636	Mountain Island	28120	For specific New Bern Zip Codes	
Midway (Beaufort County)	27808	Mountain Park	28676	call (919) 638-6111	
Midway (Bertie County)	27957	Mountain Valley	28790	New Bern Junction (Part of	
Midway (Brunswick County)	28422	Mountain View (Catawba		Wilmington)	28405
Midway (Cabarrus County)	28081	County)	28601	New Bethel	27572
Midway (Richmond County)	28379	Mountain View (Gaston		Newbold (Part of	
Midway (Rockingham		County)	28086	Fayetteville)	28301
County)	27320	Mountain View (Orange		New Bridge (Part of	
Midway Park	28544	County)	27278	Woodfin)	28804
Midwood (Part of Charlotte)	28205	Mountain View (Stokes		Newdale	28714
Milburnie	27604	County)	27021	Newell	28126
Mildred	27886	Mount Airy	27030	Newfound	28748
Miles	27302	Mount Carmel	27306	New Hanover Correctional	
Millboro	27248	Mount Carmel Acres	28806	Center	28401
Mill Branch	28420	Mount Energy	27522	New Haven	28675
Millbridge	28144	Mount Gilead (Avery		New Hill	27562
Millbrook (Part of Raleigh)	27658	County)	28622	New Holland	27885
Mill Creek (Ashe County)	28684	Mount Gilead (Cabarrus		New Hope (Chatham	
Mill Creek (Brunswick		County)	28025	County)	27559
County)	28479	Mount Gilead (Montgomery		New Hope (Franklin County)	27549
Mill Creek (Carteret County)	28570	County)	27306	New Hope (Iredell County)	28689
Mill Crossroads	27932	Mount Gould	27957	New Hope (Orange County)	27514
Millennium Church	27805	Mount Herman	28638	New Hope (Randolph	
Millers Creek	28651	Mount Holly	28120	County)	27239
Millersville	28681	Mount Mourne	28123	New Hope (Wake County)	27604
Millingport	28001	Mount Olive (Bladen		New Hope (Wayne County)	27534
Mill Spring	28756	County)	28337	New Hope (Wilson County)	27893
Mills River	28742	Mount Olive (Columbus		New House	28150
Milltown	28771	County)	28472	Newland	28657
Milton	27305	Mount Olive (Hyde County)	27810	New Lands	27925
Milwaukee	27854	Mount Olive (Stokes		New Leaksville	27288
Mimosa Shores	27889	County)	27021	Newlife	28635
Mineral Springs (Anson		Mount Olive (Wayne		New London	28127
County)	28135	County)	28365	New Market	27350
Mineral Springs (Union		Mount Pleasant (Avery		Newport	28570
County)	28108	County)	28657	New River Marine Corps Air	
Mingo	28334	Mount Pleasant (Cabarrus		Station	28540
Minneapolis	28652	County)	28124	New River Plaza (Part of	
Minnesott Beach	28510	Mount Pleasant (Cherokee		Jacksonville)	28540
Minpro	28777	County)	28906	New River Station	28542
Mint Hill	28212	Mount Pleasant (Moore		New Salem (Randolph	
Mintons Store	27897	County)	28326	County)	27317
Mintonsville	27946	Mount Pleasant (Nash		New Salem (Union County)	28103
Mintz	28382	County)	27807	Newsom	27239
Mirror Lake	28741	Mount Pleasant (Richmond		Newton	28658
Misenheimer	28109	County)	28338	Newton Grove	28366
Mitchells Fork	27946	Mount Pleasant (Yadkin		Newton Park	27893
Mitchell Village	28557	County)	27011	Newtons Crossroads	28478
Mitcheners Crossroads	27525	Mount Sterling	37821	Newtowne Plaza (Part of	
Mocksville	27028	Mount Tabor (Forsyth		Statesville)	28677
Moffitt Hill	28762	County)	27106	Niagara	28387
Mollie	28432	Mount Tabor (Washington		Nixons Beach	27932
Moltonville	28328	County)	27928	Nixonton	27909
Momeyer	27856	Mount Tirzah	27583	Nobles Cross Roads	28525
Moncure	27559	Mount Ulla	28125	Nocarva	27551
Monks Crossroads	28366	Mount Vernon (Rowan		Nocho Park (Part of	
Monroe	28110-12	County)	27013	Greensboro)	27406
For specific Monroe Zip Codes		Mount Vernon (Rutherford		Norfleet	27874
call (704) 289-4507		County)	28139	Norlina	27563
Monroe Mall (Part of		Mount Vernon Springs	27344	Norman	28367
Monroe)	28110	Mount Zion (Part of		Norrington Crossroads	27546
Monroetown (Moore		Greensboro)	27406	North (Part of Winston-	
County)	28374	Moxley	28635	Salem)	27115
Monroetown (Rockingham		Moyock	27958	North Albemarle (Part of	
County)	27320	Mt. Pleasant	27592	Albemarle)	28001
Montague	28435	Muddy Cross	27946	North Asheboro (Part of	
Montclair	28304	Mulberry	28659	Asheboro)	27203
Montezuma	28653	Murdocksville	28374	North Belmont (Part of	
Montgomery Correctional		Murfreesboro	27855	Belmont)	28012
Center	27371	Murphey	28458	North Brevard	28712
Monticello	27214	Murphy	28906	North Burlington (Part of	
Montreat	28757	Murray Hills	28081	Burlington)	27215
Montrose	28376	Murrays Mills	28609	North Charlotte (Part of	
Moores Beach	27810	Murraysville	28405	Charlotte)	28225
Mooresboro	28114	Murray Town	28425	North Chase (Part of	
Moores School House	27542	Musgraves Crossroads	27863	Wilmington)	28405
Moores Springs	27053	Myers Park (Part of		North Concord (Part of	
Mooresville	28115	Charlotte)	28207	Concord)	28025
Mooresville Junction (Part of		Myrick Estates	27850	North Cooleemee (Part of	
Mooresville)	28115	Myrtle Grove	28403	Cooleemee)	27014
Moravian Falls	28654	Nags Head	27959	North Cove	28752
Mordecai (Part of Raleigh)	27604	Nahunta	27863	North Durham (Part of	
Morehead City	28557	Nakina	28455	Durham)	27704
Morgans Corner	27909	Nantahala	28781	North Elkin	28621
Morganton	28655	Naples	28760	Northgate (Part of Durham)	27701
	28680	Nashville	27856	Northgate Mall (Part of	
For specific Morganton Zip Codes		Nathans Creek	28617	Durham)	27701
call (704) 437-3484		Naval Hospital	28542	North Harbor	28516
Morgantown	27215	Navassa	28404	North Harlowe	28532
Moriah	27572	Nebo (McDowell County)	28761	North Henderson (Part of	
Morlan Park	28146	Nebo (Yadkin County)	27011	Henderson)	27536
Morning Star	28716	Nebraska	27824	North Hickory	28601
Morris Landing	28445	Needmore (Rowan County)	27054	North Hills (Part of Raleigh)	27619

ZIP

Pleasant Grove (Washington County)	27970
Pleasant Hill (Jones County)	28572
Pleasant Hill (Northampton County)	27866
Pleasant Hill (Wilkes County)	28621
Pleasant Plains	27910
Pleasant View	27925
Pleasantville	27025
Plott Farm Addition	28716
Plumtree	28664
Plyler	28001
Plymouth	27962
Pocomoke	27525
Point Caswell	28421
Point Harbor	27964
Pole Creek	28715
Polks Landing	27514
Polkton	28135
Polkville	28136
Pollocksville	28573
Pomona (Part of Greensboro)	27407
Ponderosa (Cumberland County)	28303
Ponderosa (Harnett County)	28334
Ponzer	27810
Pooletown	28137
Poor Town	27910
Pope Air Force Base	28308
Poplar	28740
Poplar Branch	27965
Poplar Grove	28341
Poplar Springs	27021
Poplar Tent	28027
Porter	28128
Portsmouth	27960
Postell	28906
Potecasi	27867
Pot Neck	28551
Potters Curve	28431
Potters Hill	28572
Pottertown	28684
Powell Crossroads	27946
Powells Point	27966
Powells Store	27326
Powellsville	27967
Powhatan	27520
Prentiss	28734
Prestonville	27025
Price	27048
Price Creek	28714
Princeton	27569
Princeville	27886
Proctors Corner	27910
Proctorville	28375
Propst Crossroads	28601
Prospect	28462
Prospect Hill	27314
Prosper	28436
Providence (Caswell County)	27315
Providence (Granville County)	27565
Providence (McDowell County)	28752
Providence (Mecklenburg County)	28105
Providence Square (Part of Charlotte)	28211
Proximity (Part of Greensboro)	27405
Pumpkin Center (Lincoln County)	28092
Pumpkin Center (Onslow County)	28540
Pumpkintown	28779
Pungo	27860
Pungo Stores	27810
Purlear	28665
Purley	27379
Purnell	27587
Purvis	28383
Putnam	28327
Pyatte	28657
Quail Corners (Part of Charlotte)	28210
Quail Ridge (Craven County)	28532
Quail Ridge (Cumberland County)	28306
Quail Ridge (Lee County)	27330
Quaker Gap	27019
Qualla	28789
Quebec	28747
Queen	27371
Quick	27326
Quinerly	28530
Quinns Store	28518
Quitsna	27983

ZIP

Rabbit Corner	27909
Radical	28649
Radio Island	28516
Raeford	28376
Raemon	28364
Rainbow Springs	28734
Raleigh	27601-76
For specific Raleigh Zip Codes call (919) 831-3661	
Rama Woods	28025
Ramseur	27316
Ramseytown	28714
Randleman	27317
Randolph (Mecklenburg County)	28211
Randolph (Pitt County)	27834
Randolph Correctional Center	27203
Randolph Mall (Part of Asheboro)	27203
Ranger	28906
Rangewood	27603
Rankin (Guilford County)	27405
Rankin (Pender County)	28421
Ranlo	28054
Ransomville	27810
Rawls	27526
Rayconda	28304
Raynham	28383
Rebel Acres	27604
Red Banks	28364
Redbug	28442
Red Cross (Randolph County)	27233
Red Cross (Stanly County)	28129
Reddies River	28696
Red Hill (Bladen County)	28433
Red Hill (Edgecombe County)	27891
Red Hill (Mitchell County)	28705
Redland	27006
Red Oak (Nash County)	27868
Red Oak (Pitt County)	27834
Red Springs	28377
Reeds Cross Roads	27292
Reedy Creek	27292
Reelsboro	28560
Reepsville	28168
Reese	28692
Reeves Ferry	28455
Regal	28906
Regan	28420
Register	28458
Rehoboth	27845
Reidsville	27320-23
For specific Reidsville Zip Codes call (919) 342-0391	
Relief	28740
Rena	27020
Rennert	28386
Renston	28513
Republican	27983
Rest Haven	27808
Revolution (Part of Greensboro)	27405
Rex (Gaston County)	28054
Rex (Robeson County)	28378
Reynolda (Part of Winston-Salem)	27109
Reynolda Park (Part of Winston-Salem)	27107
Rheasville	27870
Rhems	28562
Rhems Landing	28562
Rhodes	27805
Rhodes-Rhyne	28092
Rhodhiss	28667
Rhodo	28901
Rhyne Crossroads	28425
Riceville	28805
Richardson	28320
Richfield	28137
Richlands	28574
Richmond Hill (Alamance County)	27215
Richmond Hill (Yadkin County)	27011
Richmond Mills	28351
Rich Square	27869
Rico	28472
Riddle	27973
Ridgecrest	28770
Ridge Haven	27591
Ridge Run	28025
Ridgeville	27314
Ridgeway	27570
Ridgewood	28379
Riegelwood	28456
Riley	27596
Rimer	28025
Ringwood	27823

ZIP

River Acres	27889
River Bend	28562
Riverdale	28560
River Hills	27858
Rivermont	28501
River Neck	27925
River Road	27889
Riverside (Craven County)	28530
Riverside (Part of New Bern)	28560
Riverside (Yancey County)	28714
Riverton	27932
Roanoke Rapids	27870
Roaring Creek	28657
Roaring Gap	28668
Roaring River	28669
Robbins	27325
Robbinsville	28771
Roberdel	28379
Roberdo	27306
Roberson Store	27892
Robersonville	27871
Roberta Mill	28027
Robeson Correctional Center	28358
Robin Hood Forest	27545
Robinson's	28570
Rock Creek	27349
Rockdale (Part of Belwood)	28090
Rockefeller Estates	28326
Rockfish	28376
Rockford	27011
Rock Hill	28025
Rockingham	28379
Rockingham Correctional Center	27320
Rockingham Lake	27320
Rock Ridge	27893
Rockwell	28138
Rockwell Park (Part of Charlotte)	28213
Rocky Cross	27557
Rocky Ford	27544
Rockyhock	27932
Rocky Mount	27801-04
For specific Rocky Mount Zip Codes call (919) 977-3123	
Rocky Pass	28761
Rocky Point	28457
Rocky River	28025
Rocky Springs	28636
Rodanthe	27968
Roduco	27969
Rolesville	27571
Rollingwood	28301
Rominger	28604
Ronda	28670
Rooks	28421
Roper	27970
Rose Bay	27885
Roseboro	28382
Roseborough	28646
Rosebud (Stokes County)	27052
Rosebud (Wilson County)	27822
Rose Hill (Duplin County)	28458
Rose Hill (Warren County)	27553
Roseland (Columbus County)	28432
Roseland (Lincoln County)	28092
Roseland (Moore County)	28315
Rosemary Park	28079
Rosemead	27924
Rosemont (Part of Winston-Salem)	27107
Roseneath	27874
Roseville	27573
Rosewood	27530
Rosindale	28434
Rosman	28772
Ross Store	27052
Rougemont	27572
Roughedge	28112
Round Peak	27030
Roundtree	28513
Rowan Correctional Center	28145
Rowan Mill	28144
Rowes Corner	28560
Rowland	28383
Roxboro	27573
Roxobel	27872
Royal	27806
Royal Oaks (Part of Kannapolis)	28083
Royal Pines	28704
Royster	28451
Rudd	27214
Ruffin	27326
Rural Hall	27045
Ruskin	28399
Russtown	28420
Ruth	28139

	ZIP
Rutherford College	28671
Rutherford Correctional Center	28043
Rutherfordton	28139
Rutherwood	28607
Ryland	27980
Saddle Mountain	28623
Saddletree	28358
Sadler	27320
St. Helena	28425
St. John	27910
St. Johns	27932
St. Lewis	27852
St. Martin	28001
St. Pauls	28384
St. Stephens	28601
Salem (Burke County)	28655
Salem (Forsyth County)	27108
Salem (Lincoln County)	28092
Salem (Nash County)	27891
Salem (Randolph County)	27317
Salem (Surry County)	27030
Salemburg	28385
Salisbury	28144-46
For specific Salisbury Zip Codes call (704) 636-0231	
Salter Path	28575
Salty Shores	28570
Saluda	28773
Salvo	27972
Samarcand	27242
Samaria	27557
Sampson Correctional Center	28328
Sanderling	27948
Sand Hill (Buncombe County)	28806
Sandhill (Pamlico County)	28560
Sandhill Acres	27229
Sands	28607
Sandy Bottom	28501
Sandy Bottoms	28352
Sandy Creek	28451
Sandy Cross (Gates County)	27946
Sandy Cross (Nash County)	27856
Sandy Cross (Rockingham County)	27320
Sandy Grove (Davidson County)	27292
Sandy Grove (Hoke County)	28376
Sandymush (Buncombe County)	28753
Sandy Mush (Rutherford County)	28043
Sandy Plain (Columbus County)	28463
Sandy Plain (Duplin County)	28572
Sandy Plains	28782
Sandy Ridge (Guilford County)	27235
Sandy Ridge (Stokes County)	27046
Sandy Ridge Correctional Center	27265
Sanford	27330-31
For specific Sanford Zip Codes call (919) 774-7044	
Santeetlah	28771
Sapona	28301
Sapphire	28774
Saratoga	27873
Sarecta	28349
Sarecta Junction	28349
Sarvis Heights	28052
Sassers Mill	28526
Satterwhite	27565
Saulston	27534
Saunook	28786
Savannah	28779
Saw	28023
Sawmills	28630
Saxapahaw	27340
Sayles Village (Part of Asheville)	28803
Scalesville	27358
Scaly Mountain	28775
Schley	27278
Scholl	28345
Schrams Beach	27810
Scotch Grove	28352
Scotland Correctional Center	28396
Scotland Neck	27874
Scotsdale (Cumberland County)	28304
Scotsdale (Scotland County)	28352
Scott Acres	27302
Scott Park (Part of Greensboro)	27401

	ZIP
Scotts (Iredell County)	28699
Scotts (Wilson County)	27851
Scotts Hill	28405
Scotts Store (Duplin County)	28365
Scotts Store (Pamlico County)	28560
Scottville	28672
Scranton	27875
Scuffleton	28513
Scuppernong	27928
Seaboard	27876
Seabreeze	28403
Seagate	28403
Seagate IV	28516
Seagrove	27341
Sealevel	28577
Seaside	28459
Sedalia	27342
Sedgefield (Guilford County)	27407
Sedgefield (Mecklenburg County)	28203
Sedgefield Lakes	27407
Sedgefield Park	27407
Sedges Garden	27105
Selica	28712
Selma	27576
Selwin	27946
Selwyn Park (Part of Charlotte)	28209
Seminole	27505
Semora	27343
Senia	28657
Seven Devils	28604
Seven Lakes	27376
Seven Paths	27549
Seven Springs	28578
Severn	27877
Seversville (Part of Charlotte)	28208
Sevier	28752
Seward	27040
Seymour Johnson Air Force Base	27531
Shacktown	27055
Shadey Oaks Acres	28150
Shady Banks	27889
Shady Brook (Part of Kannapolis)	28081
Shady Forest	28459
Shady Grove	28501
Shale Brick	27360
Shallotte	28459
Shallotte Point	28459
Shallowell	27330
Shanghai (Cleveland County)	28150
Shanghai (Sampson County)	28458
Shankletown	28027
Shannon	28386
Shannon Plaza (Part of Durham)	27717
Sharon (Camden County)	27976
Sharon (Iredell County)	28677
Sharonbrook (Part of Charlotte)	28210
Sharp Point	27829
Sharpsburg	27878
Shatley Springs	28617
Shawboro	27973
Shaw Heights	28303
Sheffield	27028
Shelby	28150-52
For specific Shelby Zip Codes call (704) 487-4324	
Shell Rock Landing	28539
Shelmerdine	28513
Shelter Neck	28425
Shelton	27311
Shelton Town	27030
Shepard (Part of Durham)	27707
Shepherds	28115
Sherrills Ford	28673
Sherron Acres (Part of Durham)	27703
Sherwood	28692
Sherwood Forest (Buncombe County)	28778
Sherwood Forest (Part of Asheville)	28805
Sherwood Forest (Forsyth County)	27104
Sherwood Forest (Transylvania County)	28712
Sherwood Forrest	27893
Sherwood Park	28306
Sherwood Terrace	28712
Sherwood Village (Part of High Point)	27260
Shields Commissary	27874

	ZIP
Shiloh (Buncombe County)	28803
Shiloh (Camden County)	27974
Shiloh (Rutherford County)	28043
Shines Crossroads	28580
Shingle Hollow	28139
Shinnville	28115
Shoal	27043
Shoofly	27581
Shooting Creek	28904
Shopton	28210
Short Off	28741
Shotwell	27545
Shuffletown	28214
Shulls Mills	28607
Shupings Mill	28138
Sidestown	28027
Sidney (Beaufort County)	27810
Sidney (Columbus County)	28472
Signal Hill Mall (Part of Statesville)	28677
Sign Pine	27980
Siler City	27344
Silk Hope	27344
Siloam	27047
Silver City	28376
Silverdale	28539
Silver Hill (Davidson County)	27292
Silver Hill (Pamlico County)	28560
Silver Lake	28403
Silverstone	28698
Silver Valley	27292
Simpson	27879
Sims	27880
Sioux	28740
Sivey Town	28462
Six Forks	27609
Six Forks (Part of Raleigh)	27615
Skibo	28304
Skinnersville	27970
Skyco	27954
Skycrest Village	27604
Skyland	28776
Skyline	28394
Skyway Terrace	28364
Sladesville	27875
Slatestone Hills	27889
Sligo	27958
Sloan	28466
Slocomb	28356
Slocum	27824
Small	27806
Small Cross Roads	27932
Smallwood (Part of Washington)	27889
Smethport	28694
Smith Creek	28480
Smith Crossing	28442
Smithfield	27577
Smith Grove	27028
Smithtown (Beaufort County)	27810
Smithtown (Perquimans County)	27944
Smithtown (Yadkin County)	27018
Smyre	28054
Smyrna	28579
Sneads Ferry	28460
Sneads Grove	28352
Snow Camp	27349
Snowden	27958
Snow Hill (Chowan County)	27980
Snow Hill (Greene County)	28580
Snow Hill (Sampson County)	28382
Snug Harbor	27944
Soapstone Mountain	27355
Sodom	28753
Somerset (Chowan County)	27932
Somerset (Person County)	27573
Somerset Hills	27604
Sophia	27350
Soul City	27553
Sound Side (Dare County)	27959
Sound Side (Tyrrell County)	27925
South Albemarle (Part of Albemarle)	28001
South Aulander	27805
South Belmont (Part of Belmont)	28012
South Creek	27806
Southern Correctional Center	27371
Southern Hills	28025
Southern Pines	28387-88
For specific Southern Pines Zip Codes call (919) 692-2431	
Southern Shores (Dare County)	27949
Southern Shores (Perquimans County)	27944

	ZIP
Williston	28589
Willits	28779
Wil-Lotta Acres	28025
Willow	27946
Willow Green	28513
Willow Spring	27592
Wilmar	28586
Wil-Mar Park (Part of Concord)	28025
Wilmington	28401-12
For specific Wilmington Zip Codes call (919) 762-3700	
Wilmington Beach	28428
Wilmore (Part of Charlotte)	28203
Wilmot	28789
Wilshire Park (Part of Asheville)	28806
Wilson	27893-96
For specific Wilson Zip Codes call (919) 237-4161	
Wilsons Mills	27593
Wilsonville	27502
Wilton	27525
Wind Blow	27281
Windemere	28405
Winders Cross Roads	27020
Windom	28714
Windsor	27983
Windy Gap	28659
Winfall	27985
Wing	28705
Wingate	28174
Winnabow	28479
Winstead Crossroads	27822
Winsteadville	27810
Winston-Salem	27101-27
For specific Winston-Salem Zip Codes call (919) 721-6058	

	ZIP
Wintergreen	28523
Winterville	28590
Winton	27986
Wise	27594
Wise Forks	28526
Witherspoon Crossroads	28610
Wittys Crossroads	27320
Wolf Creek	37317
Wolf Laurel	28754
Wolf Mountain	28783
Wood	27549
Woodard (Bertie County)	27983
Woodard (Wilson County)	27893
Woodburn	28451
Wood Crest	28570
Wood Dale	28401
Woodfin	28804
Woodford	28684
Woodington	28501
Woodland	27897
Woodland Acres	27892
Woodland Hills	28804
Woodlawn (Alamance County)	27302
Woodlawn (McDowell County)	28752
Woodlea	28304
Woodleaf	27054
Woodrow (Craven County)	28560
Woodrow (Haywood County)	28716
Woodrun	27306
Woodsdale	27573
Woodside	28081
Woodside Hills	28715
Woodville (Bertie County)	27849

	ZIP
Woodville (Perquimans County)	27944
Woodville (Surry County)	27030
Woodworth	27536
Wootens Crossroads (Columbus County)	28433
Wootens Crossroads (Greene County)	27888
Wootens Crossroads (Lenoir County)	28501
Worley	28753
Worthingtons Crossroads	27858
Worthville	27317
Wrightsboro	28401
Wrightsville	28480
Wrightsville Beach	28480
Yadkin	28144
Yadkin Correctional Center	27055
Yadkin Valley	28645
Yadkinville	27055
Yamacraw	28435
Yanceyville	27379
Yancy Correctional Center	28714
Yaupon Beach	28461
Yeatsville	27808
Yellow Creek	28771
Yeopim	27932
Yorick	28399
Yorkmont Park (Part of Charlotte)	28217
Yorkwood	28052
Youngsville	27596
Zebulon	27597
Zephyr	28621
Zionville	28698
Zirconia	28790

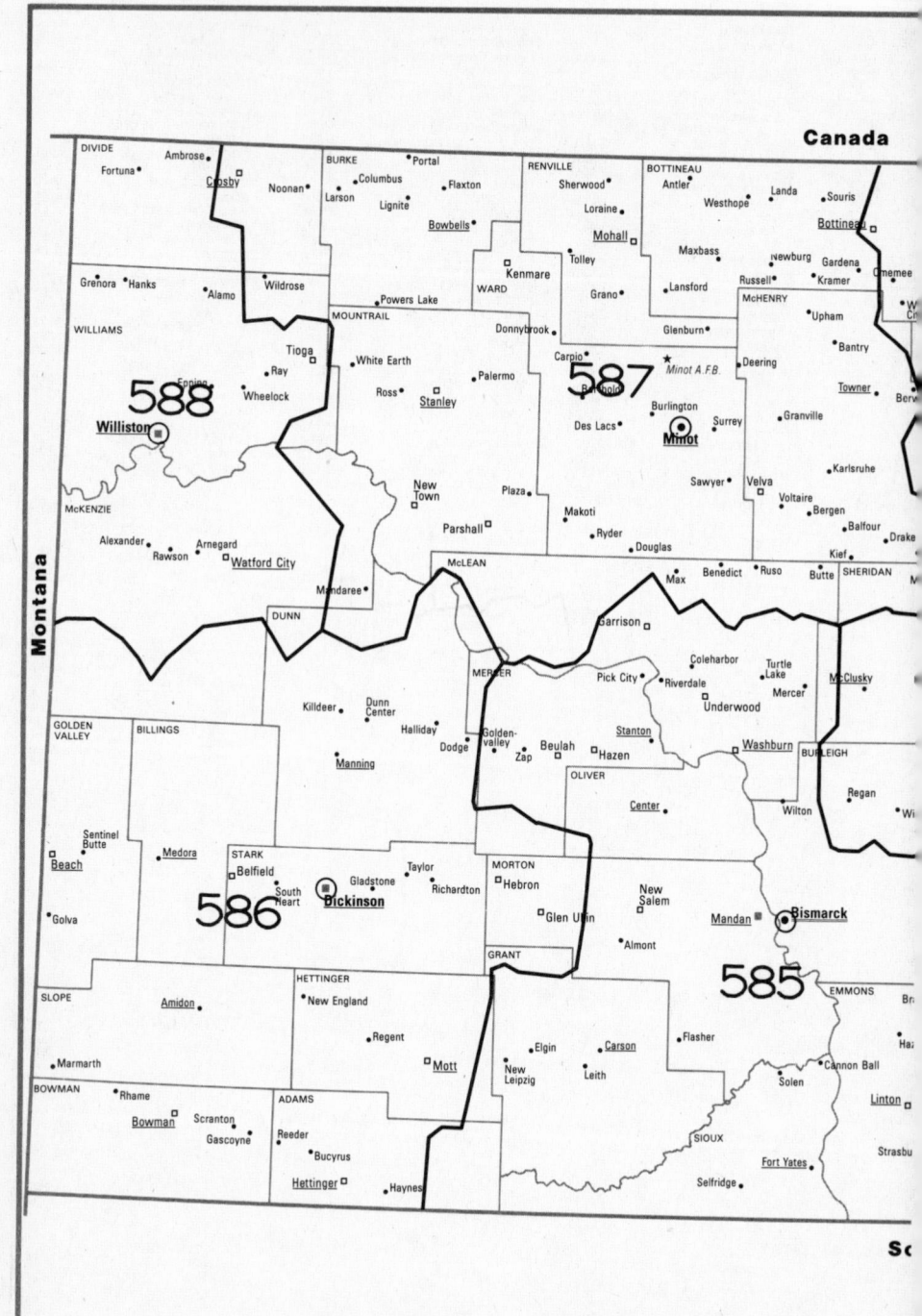

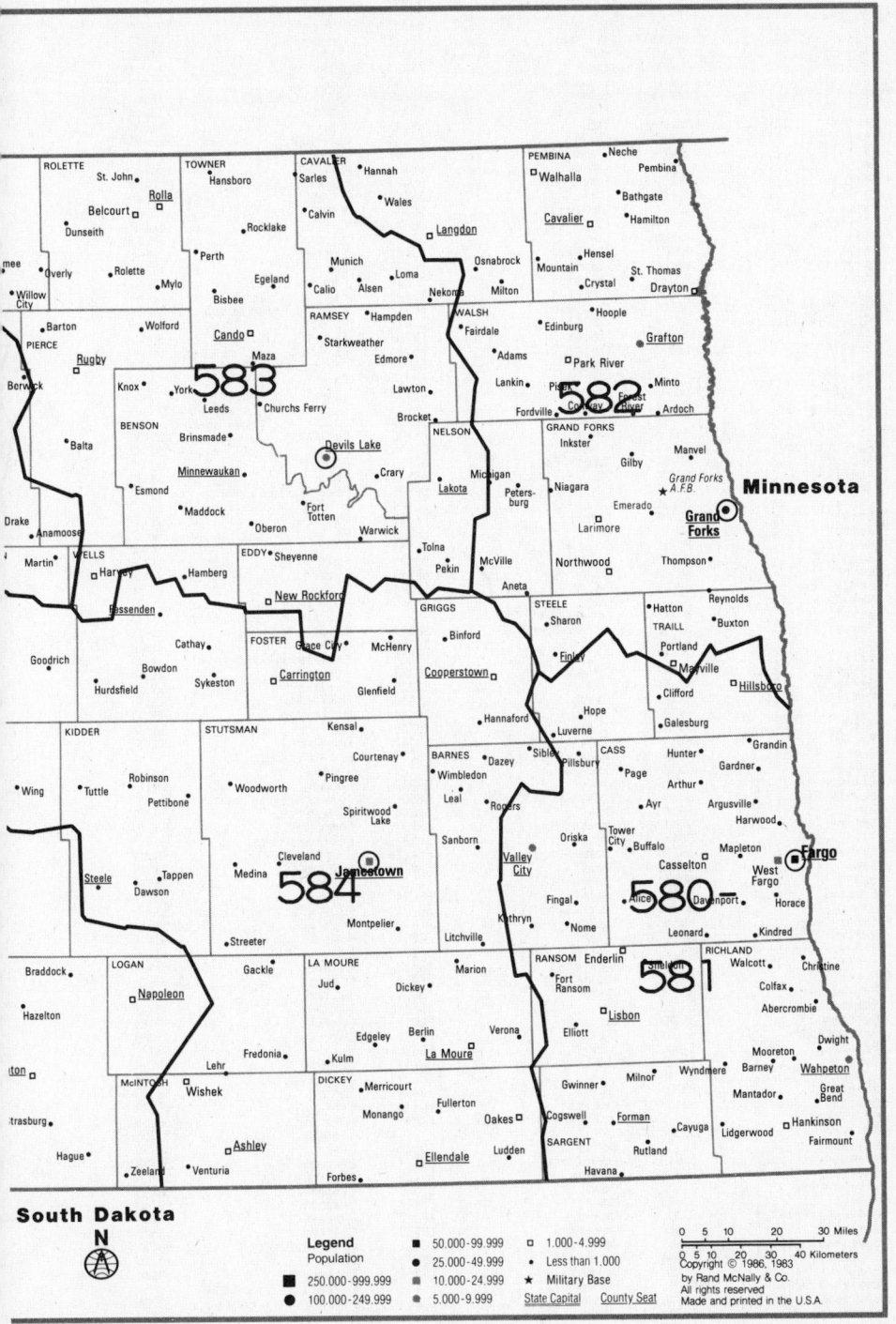

ROLETTE
St. John
Rolla
Belcourt
Dunseith
Overly
Willow City

TOWNER
Hansboro
Rocklake
Perth
Egeland
Bisbee

CAVALIER
Sarles
Hannah
Wales
Calvin
Langdon
Munich
Loma
Calio
Alsen
Nekoma
Milton

PEMBINA
Neche
Walhalla
Pembina
Bathgate
Cavalier
Hamilton
Hensel
Mountain
Crystal
St. Thomas
Drayton

Osnabrock

Barton
Wolford
Cando
Maza

RAMSEY
Hampden
Starkweather
Edmore

WALSH
Fairdale
Adams
Lankin
Fordville

Hoople
Edinburg
Grafton
Park River
Pisek
Conway
Forest River
Minto
Ardoch

583

582

Knox
Leeds
Churchs Ferry
York
Brinsmade
Devils Lake

NELSON
Michigan
Lakota
Petersburg

GRAND FORKS
Inkster
Gilby
Niagara
Manvel
Grand Forks A.F.B.
Emerado
Larimore
Grand Forks

Balta
Esmond
Minnewaukan
Maddock
Oberon
Fort Totten
Warwick
Crary

Minnesota

Drake
Anamoose
Martin
WELLS
Harvey
Hamberg
EDDY
Sheyenne
Pekin
Tolna
McVille
Aneta
Northwood
Thompson

Fessenden
New Rockford

GRIGGS
STEELE
Hatton
Sharon
Reynolds
Buxton
TRAILL
Portland
Mayville
Hillsboro

Goodrich
Cathay
FOSTER
Grace City
McHenry
Binford
Finley
Clifford

Bowdon
Hurdsfield
Sykeston
Carrington
Glenfield
Cooperstown
Hope
Luverne
Galesburg

KIDDER
STUTSMAN
Kensal
Hannaford
BARNES
Dazey
Sibley
Pillsbury
CASS
Hunter
Grandin

Wing
Tuttle
Robinson
Pettibone
Woodworth
Courtenay
Pingree
Wimbledon
Leal
Rogers
Page
Arthur
Gardner
Ayr
Argusville
Harwood

Spiritwood Lake
Sanborn
Oriska
Tower City
Buffalo
Casselton
Mapleton
West Fargo
Fargo

Steele
Dawson
Tappen
Medina
Cleveland
Jamestown
584
Montpelier
Litchville
Valley City
Fingal
Kathryn
Nome
Leonard
Davenport
Alice
580
Horace
Kindred

Streeter

Braddock
LOGAN
Napoleon
Hazelton
Gackle
Jud
LA MOURE
Dickey
Marion
Fort Ransom
RANSOM
Enderlin
Sheldon
581
RICHLAND
Walcott
Colfax
Christine
Abercrombie

Edgeley
Berlin
Verona
Elliott
Lisbon
Dwight
Moreton
Wahpeton

ton
McINTOSH
Lehr
Fredonia
Kulm
La Moure
Gwinner
Milnor
Wyndmere
Barney
Mantador
Great Bend

strasburg
Wishek
DICKEY
Merricourt
Fullerton
Monango
Oakes
Cogswell
Forman
Cayuga
Lidgerwood
Hankinson
Fairmount

Hague
Zeeland
Ashley
Venturia
Ellendale
Ludden
SARGENT
Rutland
Havana
Forbes

South Dakota

N

	ZIP		ZIP		ZIP
Abercrombie	58001	Bucyrus	58639	Eastside Estates	58701
Absaraka	58002	Buffalo	58011	East Valley City	58072
Acres A-Plenty	58504	Buffalo Springs	58623	Eckelson	58432
Adams	58210	Burke Addition	58201	Eckman	58760
Adrian	58472	Burlington	58722	Edgeley	58433
Agate	58310	Burnstad	58495	Edinburg	58227
Akra	58220	Burt	58646	Edmore	58330
Alamo	58830	Butte	58723	Edmunds	58476
Alexander	58831	Buttzville	58054	Egeland	58331
Alfred	58411	Buxton	58218	El Dorado Acres	58601
Alice	58003	Caledonia	58219	Eldridge	58401
Alkabo	58845	Calio	58322	Elgin	58533
Almont	58520	Calvin	58323	Ellendale	58436
Alpha	58654	C and L Estates	58504	Elliott	58033
Alsen	58311	Cando	58324	Embden	58079
Ambrose	58833	Cannon Ball	58528	Emerado	58228
Amenia	58004	Carbury	58783	Emmet	58540
Amidon	58620	Carlsbad	58504	Emrick	58422
Anamoose	58710	Carolville	58801	Enderlin	58027
Anderson Acres	58504	Carpio	58725	Englevale	58033
Aneta	58212	Carrington	58421	Epping	58843
Anselm	58068	Carson	58529	Erie	58029
Antler	58711	Cartwright	58838	Esmond	58332
Appam	58830	Cashel	58225	Evergreen	58051
Apple Creek Country Club	58501	Casselton	58012	Faiman's Sunrise Addition	58504
Apple Creek Estates	58558	Cathay	58422	Fairdale	58229
Apple Valley	58558	Cavalier	58220	Fairfield	58627
Ardoch	58213	Cayuga	58013	Fairmount	58030
Arena	58412	Center	58530	Falconer Estates	58504
Argusville	58005	Chaffee	58014	Falkirk	58577
Arnegard	58835	Charbonneau	58831	Fargo	58102-09
Arthur	58006	Charlson	58763	For specific Fargo Zip Codes call	
Arvilla	58214	Chaseley	58423	(701) 241-6100	
Ashley	58413	Chrisan	58102	Fessenden	58438
Ashlund Estates	58504	Christine	58015	Fillmore	58332
Auburn	58237	Churchs Ferry	58325	Fingal	58031
Aurelia	58734	Circle K Estates	58501	Finley	58230
Ayr	58007	City View Heights	58504	Finley Air Force Station,	
Backoo	58282	Cleveland	58424	785th Radar Squadron	58230
Baker	58386	Clifford	58016	Flasher	58535
Baldwin	58521	Clyde	58352	Flaxton	58737
Balfour	58712	Cogswell	58017	Flora	58348
Balta	58813	Coleharbor	58531	Fonda	58366
Bantry	58713	Colfax	58018	Forbes	58439
Bar-D Estates	58504	Colgan	58844	Fordville	58231
Barks Spur	58331	Colgate	58046	Forest River (Cass County)	58102
Barlow	58421	Columbia Mall (Part of		Forest River (Walsh County)	58233
Barney	58008	Grand Forks)	58201	Forest River Colony	58231
Bartlett	58344	Columbus	58727	Forman	58032
Barton	58315	Concrete	58220	Fort Berthold Indian	
Bathgate	58216	Conway	58233	Reservation	58763
Battleground Addition	58701	Cooperstown	58425	Fort Buford	58853
Battleview	58714	Corinth	58830	Fort Clark	58530
Bayshore	58072	Coteau	58728	Fort Ransom	58033
Beach	58621	Coulee	58746	Fort Rice	58537
Belcourt	58316	Country Acres	58047	Fort Totten	58335
Belden	58784	Country-Side Addition	58201	Fort Totten Indian	
Belfield	58622	Courtenay	58426	Reservation	58335
Benedict	58716	Crary	58327	Fortuna	58844
Bentley	58562	Crested Butte Addition	58501	Fortuna Air Force Station,	
Berea	58072	Crete	58040	780th Radar Squadron	59275
Bergen	58792	Crosby	58730	Fort Yates	58538
Berlin	58415	Crystal	58222	Four Bears Village	58763
Berthold	58718	Crystal Springs	58427	Four K's Estates	58501
Berwick	58788	Cuba	58072	Foxholm	58738
Beulah	58523	Cummings	58223	Fox Island	58504
Big Bend	58531	Dahlen	58224	Fradet	58047
Binford	58416	Dakota Boys Ranch	58701	Frazier (Part of Wimbledon)	58492
Bisbee	58317	Dakota Square (Part of		Fredonia	58440
Bismarck	58501-07	Minot)	58701	Fried	58401
For specific Bismarck Zip Codes		Davenport	58021	Frison	58301
call (701) 221-6517		Dawson	58428	Frontier	58104
Blabon	58046	Dazey	58429	Fryburg	58622
Blacktail Lake	58801	Decker	58601	Fullerton	58441
Blaisdell	58720	Deering	58731	Gackle	58442
Blanchard	58009	De Lamere	58060	Galchutt	58075
Bluffview Estates	58504	Denbigh	58788	Galesburg	58035
Bonetraill	58801	Denhoff	58430	Gardar	58227
Bordulac	58421	Des Lacs	58733	Gardena	58739
Bottineau	58318	Devils Lake	58301	Gardner	58036
Bowbells	58721	Dickey	58431	Garrison	58540
Bowdon	58418	Dickinson	58601-02	Garske	58382
Bowesmont	58225	For specific Dickinson Zip Codes		Gascoyne	58653
Bowman	58623	call (701) 225-6701		Geneseo	58053
Braddock	58524	Dodge	58625	Gilby	58235
Brampton	58017	Donnybrook	58734	Gladstone	58630
Brantford	58356	Douglas	58735	Glasser	58504
Breen's Addition	58501	Doyon	58328	Glasston	58236
Breien	58570	Drake	58736	Glenburn	58740
Brekke Addition	58701	Drayton	58225	Glenfield	58443
Bremen	58319	Dresden	58249	Glen Ullin	58631
Brentwood Estates	58501	Driscoll	58532	Glenwood Estates	58501
Briardale	58504	Dunn Center	58626	Glover	58474
Briarwood	58104	Dunning	58760	Golden Valley	58541
Bridgeview Addition	58701	Dunseith	58329	Goldfines Shopping Center	
Brinsmade	58320	Durbin	58059	(Part of Grand Forks)	58201
Brocket	58321	Dwight	58075	Golva	58632
Brookfield Estates	58501	Eagle Bend Estates	58301	Goodrich	58444
Brooks Addition	58701	Eastdale	58601	Gorham	58627
Brooktree Park	58042	East Dunseith	58329	Grace City	58445
Buchanan	58420	East Fairview	59221	Grafton	58237

	ZIP		ZIP		ZIP
Grandberg	58102	Kensal	58455	Menoken	58558
Grand Forks	58201-06	Kief	58747	Mercer	58559
For specific Grand Forks Zip		Killdeer	58640	Merricourt	58469
Codes call (701) 775-5329		Kindred	58051	Michigan	58259
Grand Forks AFB (census		Kings Court	58701	Millarton	58472
designated place)	58205	Kintyre	58549	Mills	58504
Grand Forks Air Force Base	58201	Kirkwood Plaza (Part of		Milnor	58060
Grandin	58038	Bismarck)	58504	Milton	58260
Grand Prairie Estates	58501	Kloten	58254	Minnewaukan	58351
Grand Rapids	58458	KMK Estates	58501	Minot	58701-02
Grandview	58801	Knox	58343	For specific Minot Zip Codes call	
Grano	58750	Kongsberg	58792	(701) 852-3296	
Granville	58741	Kralicek	58601	Minot AFB (census	
Grassy Butte	58634	Kramer	58748	designated place)	58701
Great Bend	58039	Kubishta	58601	Minot Air Force Base	58704
Green Acres Estates	58501	Kulm	58456	Minot Air Force Station,	
Greene	58787	Lake Jessie	58801	786th Radar Squadron	58759
Greenvale	58601	Lake Metigoshe	58318	Minto	58261
Grenora	58845	Lake Park	58801	Mirror Lake	58639
Guelph	58447	Lake Side Estate	58401	Missouri River Estates	58504
Guthrie	58736	Lake Tschida	58533	Moffit	58560
Gwinner	58040	Lake Williams	58478	Mohall	58761
Hague	58542	Lakewood Park	58301	Monango	58471
Halliday	58636	Lakota	58344	Montpelier	58472
Hallson	58220	Lamoine Addition	58201	Mooreton	58061
Hamar	58380	La Moure	58458	Mott	58646
Hamberg	58337	Landa	58783	Mountain	58262
Hamilton	58238	Langdon	58249	Mount Carmel	58249
Hamlet	58795	Lankin	58250	Mouse River Park	58787
Hampden	58338	Lansford	58750	Mr. B's	58501
Hankinson	58041	Larimore	58251	Munich	58352
Hanks	58856	Lark	58535	Mylo	58353
Hanks Corner	58220	Larson	58727	Nanson	58366
Hannaford	58448	Lawton	58345	Napoleon	58561
Hannah	58239	Leal	58479	Nash	58237
Hannover	58563	Leeds	58346	Neche	58265
Hansboro	58339	Lefor	58641	Nekoma	58355
Happy Valley	58701	Lehigh	58601	Newburg	58762
Harlow	58346	Lehr	58460	New England	58647
Hartland	58725	Leisure World Estates	58504	New Hradec	58601
Harvey	58341	Leith	58551	New Leipzig	58562
Harwood	58042	Leonard	58052	New Rockford	58356
Hastings	58049	Leroy	58282	New Salem	58563
Hatton	58240	Lewis and Clark Estates	58504	New Town	58763
Havana	58043	Leyden	58282	Niagara	58266
Havelock	58647	Lidgerwood	58053	Niobe	58746
Hay Creek	58501	Lignite	58752	Nome	58062
Hay Creek Pines	58501	Lincoln	58501	Noonan	58765
Haynes	58639	Lincoln Valley	58430	Norma	58746
Hazelton	58544	Linka Addition	58701	North Dakota Penitentiary	58501
Hazen	58545	Linton	58552	North Dakota State	
Heaton	58450	Lisbon	58054	University (Part of Fargo)	58105
Hebron	58638	Litchville	58461	North Forty Estates	58501
Heil	58533	Little Ponderosa	58701	Northgate	58737
Heimdal	58342	Logan	58701	North Grand Forks	58201
Hensel	58241	Loma	58311	North Lemmon	57638
Hensler	58547	Lone Tree	58718	North River	58102
Heritage Hills Estates	58102	Loraine	58761	North Star Acres	58501
Hesper	58348	Lostwood	58784	North Valley City	58072
Hettinger	58639	Lucca	58027	Northwood (Cass County)	58102
Hickson	58047	Ludden	58447	Northwood (Grand Forks	
Hi-Land Heights	58801	Lunds Valley	58784	County)	58267
Hillcrest Acres	58501	Luverne	58056	Northwood Estates	58501
Hillsboro	58045	Lynchburg	58059	Nortonville	58454
Holiday Colony	58701	McCanna	58253	Norwich	58768
Holmes	58275	McClusky	58463	Oakes	58474
Home on the Range for		McGregor	58755	Oak Ridge	58270
Boys	58654	McHenry	58464	Oakwood	58237
Honeyford	58235	McKenzie	58553	Oberon	58357
Hoople	58243	McLeod	58057	Olga	58249
Hope	58046	McVille	58254	Omemee	58384
Horace	58047	Maddock	58348	Oriska	58063
Horseshoe Bend	58102	Maida	58255	Orr	58244
Huff	58537	Makoti	58756	Orrin	58359
Hull	58542	Mandan	58554	Osnabrock	58269
Hunter	58048	Mandaree	58757	Overly	58360
Hurdsfield	58451	Manfred	58465	Oxbow	58047
Hutterite Colony	58458	Manitou	58776	Page	58064
Imperial Manor	58701	Manning	58642	Palermo	58769
Imperial Valley	58504	Mantador	58058	Palm Beach	58601
Inkster	58244	Manvel	58256	Park Manor (Part of Grand	
Jamestown	58401-02	Mapes	58344	Forks)	58201
For specific Jamestown Zip		Mapleton	58059	Park River	58270
Codes call (701) 252-2970		Marion	58466	Parshall	58770
Jessie	58452	Marmarth	58643	Patterson Lake	58601
Jewett Landing	58072	Marshall	58644	Pekin	58361
Jiran	58504	Martin	58758	Pembina	58271
Johnsons Corner	58847	Mary College	58501	Penn	58362
Johnstown	58235	Max	58759	Perth	58363
Joliette	58271	Maxbass	58760	Petersburg	58272
Juanita	58443	Mayville	58257	Pettibone	58475
Jud	58454	Maza	58324	Pheasant Lake	58436
Judson	58563	Meadowbrook	58701	Picardville	58463
Karlsruhe	58744	Meadow View (Part of		Pick City	58545
Kathryn	58049	Bismarck)	58504	Pillsbury	58065
Keene	58847	Medina	58467	Pingree	58476
Kelso	58045	Medora	58645	Pisek	58273
Kelvin	58329	Mee's Country Home		Pitcher Park	58301
Kempton	58267	Estates	58558	Plaza	58771
Kenaston	58746	Mekinock	58258	Pleasant Lake	58368
Kenmare	58746	Melville	58421	Ponderosa Riverside Village	58501

	ZIP		ZIP		ZIP
Porcupine	58568	Sheyenne Valley Addition	58072	Tuttle	58488
Portal	58772	Shields	58569	Twin Butte	58504
Portland	58274	Shryock	58801	Twin Buttes	58636
Powell	58201	Sibley	58429	Underwood	58576
Powers Lake	58773	Sibley Island Estates	58504	Union	58279
Prairie Rose	58104	Silva	58368	University of North Dakota	
Prairie View Acres	58501	Simcoe	58741	(Part of Grand Forks)	58202
Price	58547	Sims	58520	Upham	58789
Prosper	58042	Sioux Village	58538	Urbana	58481
Raleigh	58564	Sisseton Indian Reservation	57262	Valley City	58072
Raub	58779	Skyline Estates	58501	Velva	58790
Raulston	58801	Sleepy Hollow	58047	Venturia	58489
Rawson	58831	Solen	58570	Verona	58490
Ray	58849	Sorenson Addition	58701	Veseleyville	58237
Raymond Lee	58801	Souris	58783	Vista South	58504
Red Willow Lake	58416	Southam	58327	Vohs Dapplegrey	58801
Reeder	58649	South Forks Plaza (Part of		Voltaire	58792
Regan	58477	Grand Forks)	58201	Voss	58261
Regent	58650	South Heart	58655	Wabek	58771
Reile's Acres	58102	Southview	58801	Wahpeton	58074-75
Reynolds	58275	Southview Estates	58601	For specific Wahpeton Zip Codes	
Rhame	58651	Spiritwood	58481	call (701) 642-6174	
Richards West (Part of		Spiritwood Lake	58401	Walcott	58077
Grand Forks)	58201	Spring Brook	58843	Wales	58281
Richardton	58652	Standing Rock Indian		Walhalla	58282
Ridgeview Acres	58504	Reservation (ND part)	58538	Walum	58448
Rio Vista Heights	58801	Stanley	58784	Warren	58021
River Bend	58047	Stanton	58571	Warsaw	58261
Riverdale	58565	Starkweather	58377	Warwick	58381
Riverside (Part of West		State Hospital (Part of		Washburn	58577
Fargo)	58078	Jamestown)	58401	Watford City	58854
River View Acres	58504	Steele	58482	Webster	58382
Robinson	58478	Sterling	58572	Welle	58501
Rocklake	58365	Stirum	58069	Wellsburg	58341
Rogers	58479	Strasburg	58573	West Acres Estates	58801
Rolette	58366	Straubville	58017	Westbrook	58047
Rolla	58367	Streeter	58483	West Fargo	58078
Rolling Meadows	58501	Stromquist (Part of Devils		Westfield	58542
Roseglen	58775	Lake)	58301	West Heart Estates	58504
Roshau	58601	Strong	58301	Westhope	58793
Ross	58776	Sunnyside Addition	58102	West Industrial Park	58601
Roth	58783	Sunny Slope	58701	West Jamestown	58401
Round Hill Estates	58102	Surrey	58785	West Oakwood	58237
Rugby	58368	Sutton	58484	West Town	58401
Ruso	58778	Swansonville	58504	Westwood on the River	58501
Russell	58762	Sykeston	58486	Wheatland	58079
Ruthville	58701	Taft	58045	Wheelock	58849
Rutland	58067	Tagus	58718	White Earth	58794
Ryder	58779	Talbotts	58701	White Shield	58540
Sabot's First	58501	Tappen	58487	Whitman	58259
St. Anthony	58566	Tatley Meadows	58504	Wild Rice	58047
St. Benedict	58047	Taylor	58656	Wildrose	58795
St. Gertrude	58564	Temvik	58552	Williston	58801-02
St. John	58369	Thompson	58278	For specific Williston Zip Codes	
St. Michael	58370	Thorne	58366	call (701) 572-3121	
St. Thomas	58276	Tilden	58351	Williston Park	58801
Sanborn	58480	Timber Lake Place	58504	Willow City	58384
San Haven	58329	Tioga	58852	Wilton	58579
Sanish	58763	TJ Ranch Estates	58501	Wimbledon	58492
Sarles	58372	Tokio	58379	Windsor	58424
Sawdwood	58270	Tolley	58787	Wing	58494
Sawyer	58781	Tolna	58380	Wishek	58495
Scenic East	58801	Tower City	58071	Wolford	58385
Schefield	58647	Town and Country	58801	Wolseth	58740
Scranton	58653	Town and Country Estates	58504	Woodland	58051
Secluded Acres	58504	Town And Country		Woods	58052
Selfridge	58568	Shopping Center (Part of		Woodworth	58496
Selz	58373	Minot)	58701	Wutzke	58501
Sentinel Butte	58654	Towner	58788	Wyndmere	58081
Shamrock Acres	58501	Trenton	58853	York	58386
Sharon	58277	Trestle Valley	58701	Ypsilanti	58497
Sheldon	58068	Trotters	58657	Zahl	58856
Shell Valley	58316	Turtle Lake	58575	Zap	58580
Shepard	58425	Turtle Mountain Indian		Zeeland	58581
Sherwood	58782	Reservation	58316		
Sheyenne	58374				

	ZIP		ZIP		ZIP
Abanaka	45874	Amanda	43102	Auburn Center (Crawford	
Abbottsville	45304	Amanda (Hancock County)		County)	44875
Aberdeen	45101	(Township)	45867	Auburn Center (Geauga	
Academia	43050	Amberley	45213	County)	44022
Acme	44281	Amberly	43227	Auburn Corners	44021
Ada	45810	Amboy (Ashtabula County)	44030	Augersburg	44266
Adams (Champaign		Amboy (Fulton County)		Auglaize (Allen County)	
County) (Township)	43070	(Township)	43540	(Township)	45850
Adams (Clinton County)		Amelia	45102	Auglaize (Paulding County)	
(Township)	45177	American (Township)	45807	(Township)	43512
Adams (Coshocton County)		Ames (Township)	45711	Augusta	44607
(Township)	43832	Amesville	45711	Augusta (Township)	44607
Adams (Darke County)		Amherst	44001	Ault	43947
(Township)	45308	Amherst (Township)	44001	Aultman	44630
Adams (Defiance County)		Amity (Hamilton County)	45236	Aurelius (Township)	45746
(Township)	43512	Amity (Knox County)	43050	Aurora	44202
Adams (Guernsey County)		Amity (Madison County)	43064	Aurora East	44240
(Township)	43725	Amity (Montgomery County)	45309	Aurora Meadows	44202
Adams (Monroe County)		Amlin	43002	Ausdale Ave. (Part of	
(Township)	43914	Amlin Heights	45385	Mansfield)	44906
Adams (Muskingum		Amsden	44803	Austin	45628
County) (Township)	43821	Amsterdam (Jefferson		Austinburg	44010
Adams (Seneca County)		County)	43903	Austinburg (Township)	44010
(Township)	44867	Amsterdam (Licking		Austintown (Township)	44515
Adams (Washington		County)	43076	Austintown	44512
County) (Township)	45744	Anderson (Township)	45230	Austintown Plaza	44515
Adams Mills	43821	Anderson (Hamilton County)	45255	Austin Village (Part of	
Adamsville (Gallia County)	45614	Anderson (Ross County)	45601	Warren)	44481
Adamsville (Muskingum		Anderson Ferry (Part of		Autumn Acres	45239
County)	43802	Cincinnati)	45238	Ava	43711
Adario	44837	Andersonville	45601	Avalon (Butler County)	45042
Addison	45631	Andis	45645	Avalon (Perry County)	43107
Addison (Township)	45631	Andover	44003	Avalon Heights (Part of	
Addyston	45001	Andover (Township)	44003	Lebanon)	45036
Adelphi	43101	Angle	45631	Avon	44011
Adena	43901	Ankenytown	43019	Avondale (Belmont County)	43947
Adrian	44801	Anlo	45344	Avondale (Hamilton County)	45229
Africa	43021	Anna	45302	Avondale (Licking County)	43076
Afton	45103	Annapolis	43910	Avondale (Logan County)	43331
Aid	45645	Ansonia	45303	Avondale (Montgomery	
Aid (Township)	45645	Antioch	43793	County)	45404
Ainger	43543	Antiquity	45771	Avondale (Muskingum	
Air Mail Facility (Part of		Antrim (Guernsey County)	43773	County)	43777
Dayton)	45490	Antrim (Wyandot County)		Avondale (Stark County)	44708
Air Material Command	45433	(Township)	43323	Avon Lake	44012
Airport (Cuyahoga County)	44181	Antwerp	45813	Avon Park (Part of Girard)	44420
Airport (Franklin County)	43219	Apple Creek	44606	Axtel	44089
Airway	45431	Apple Grove	45771	Ayersville	43512
Akron	44301-72	Appleton	43031	Bachman	45309
For specific Akron Zip Codes call		Aquilla	44024	Badgertown	43719
(216) 379-0600		Arabia	45659	Bailey Lakes	44805
Albany	45710	Arcadia	44804	Baileys Mills	43713
Al Bar Meadows (Part of		Arcanum	45304	Bainbridge	44023
The Village of Indian Hill)	45243	Archbold	43502	Bainbridge (Township)	44023
Albion	44287	Archer (Township)	43986	Bainbridge	45612
Alcony	45373	Archers Fork	45767	Bainbridge Center	44022
Alexander (Township)	45701	Arion	45652	Bairdstown	45872
Alexanders (Part of		Arkoe	45661	Bakersville	43803
Independence)	44131	Arlington (Hancock County)	45814	Ballville	43420
Alexandersville (Part of		Arlington (Montgomery		Ballville (Township)	43420
West Carrollton City)	45449	County)	45309	Baltic	43804
Alexandria	43001	Arlington Heights	45215	Baltimore	43105
Alexis Place (Part of		Armstrongs Mills	43933	Bangs	43050
Toledo)	43612	Arnheim	45121	Bannock	43972
Alfred	45723	Arnold (Miami County)	45383	Bantam	45103
Alger	45812	Arnold (Union County)	43064	Barberton	44203
Alikanna	43952	Arrow Head (Part of Xenia)	45385	Bardwell	45154
Alledonia	43902	Artanna	43022	Barlow	45712
Allen (Darke County)		Arthur	43512	Barlow (Township)	45712
(Township)	45362	Ashland	44805	Barnesburg	45239
Allen (Hancock County)		Ashley	43003	Barnesville	43713
(Township)	45889	Ashley Corner	45694	Barnhill	44663
Allen (Ottawa County)		Ash Ridge	45121	Barretts Mills	45612
(Township)	43412	Ashtabula	44004	Barrs Mills	44681
Allen (Union County)		Ashtabula (Township)	44004	Bartles	45659
(Township)	43070	Ashville	43103	Bartlett	45713
Allen Center	43040	Assumption	43558	Bartley Estates	45414
Allensburg	45133	Athalia	45669	Bartlow (Township)	43516
Allensville	45651	Athens	45701	Barton	43905
Allentown (Allen County)	45807	Athens (Athens County)		Bartramville	45669
Allentown (Scioto County)	45694	(Township)	45701	Bascom	44809
Alliance	44601	Athens (Harrison County)		Bashan	45743
Alma	45690	(Township)	43981	Bass Lake	44024
Alpha	45301	Atlanta	43145	Batavia (Township)	45103
Alpine Village (Part of Valley		Atlas	43713	Batavia	45103
Hi)	43360	Attica	44807	Batemantown	43019
Alta	44903	Attica Junction	44807	Batesville	43773
Altamont Hills	43938	Atwater	44201	Bath (Summit County)	
Altamont Park (Part of		Atwater (Township)	44201	(Township)	44210
Mingo Junction)	43938	Atwater Center	44201	Bath (Allen County)	
Alton	43119	Auburn (Butler County)	45013	(Township)	45801
Alvada	44802	Auburn (Crawford County)		Bath (Greene County)	
Alvordton	43501	(Township)	44887	(Township)	45324
Amanda (Allen County)		Auburn (Geauga County)		Bath	44210
(Township)	45807	(Township)	44255	Battlesburg	44626
Amanda (Fairfield County)		Auburn (Tuscarawas		Baughman (Township)	44667
(Township)	43102	County) (Township)	44681	Bay (Township)	43452

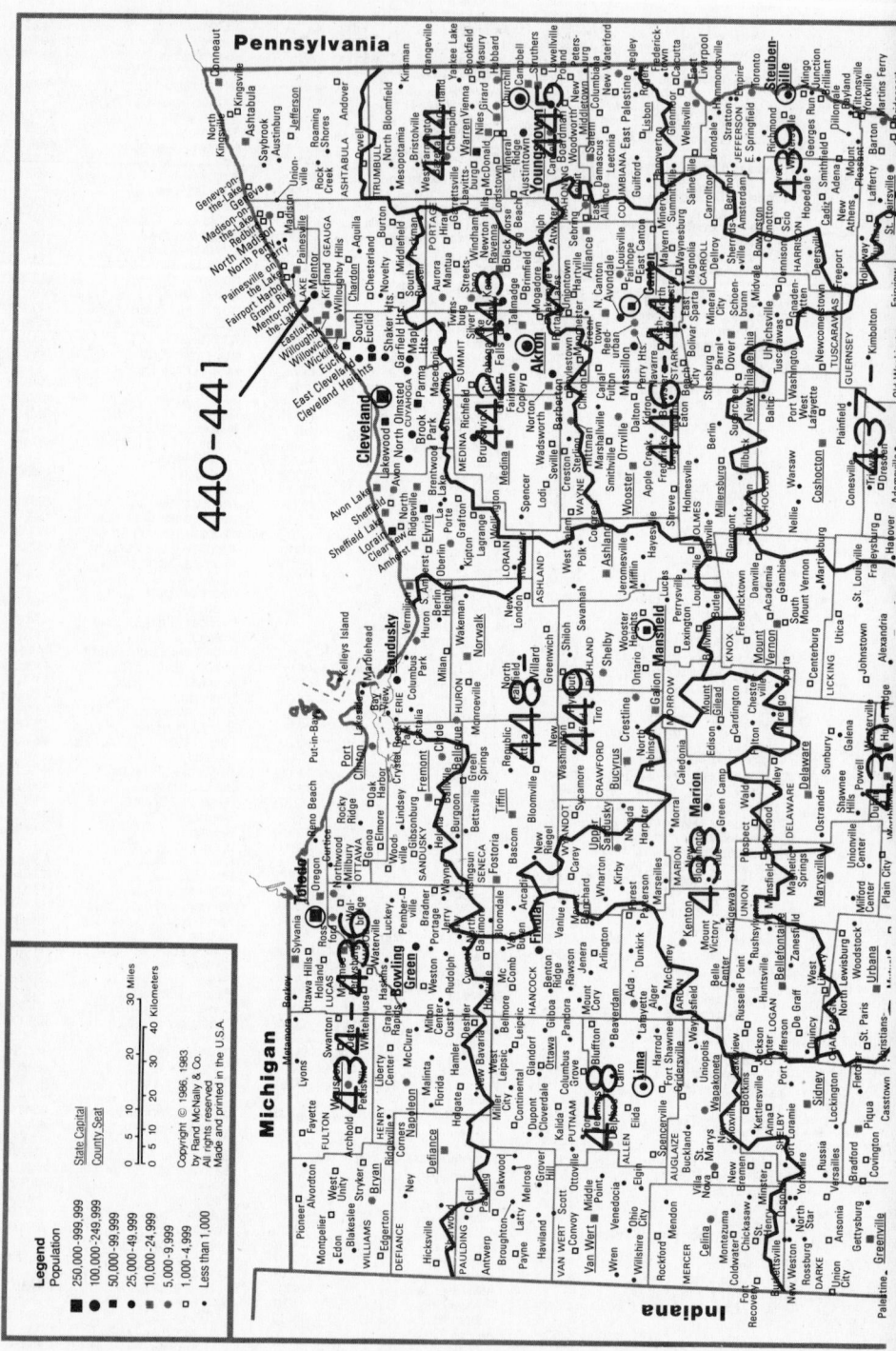

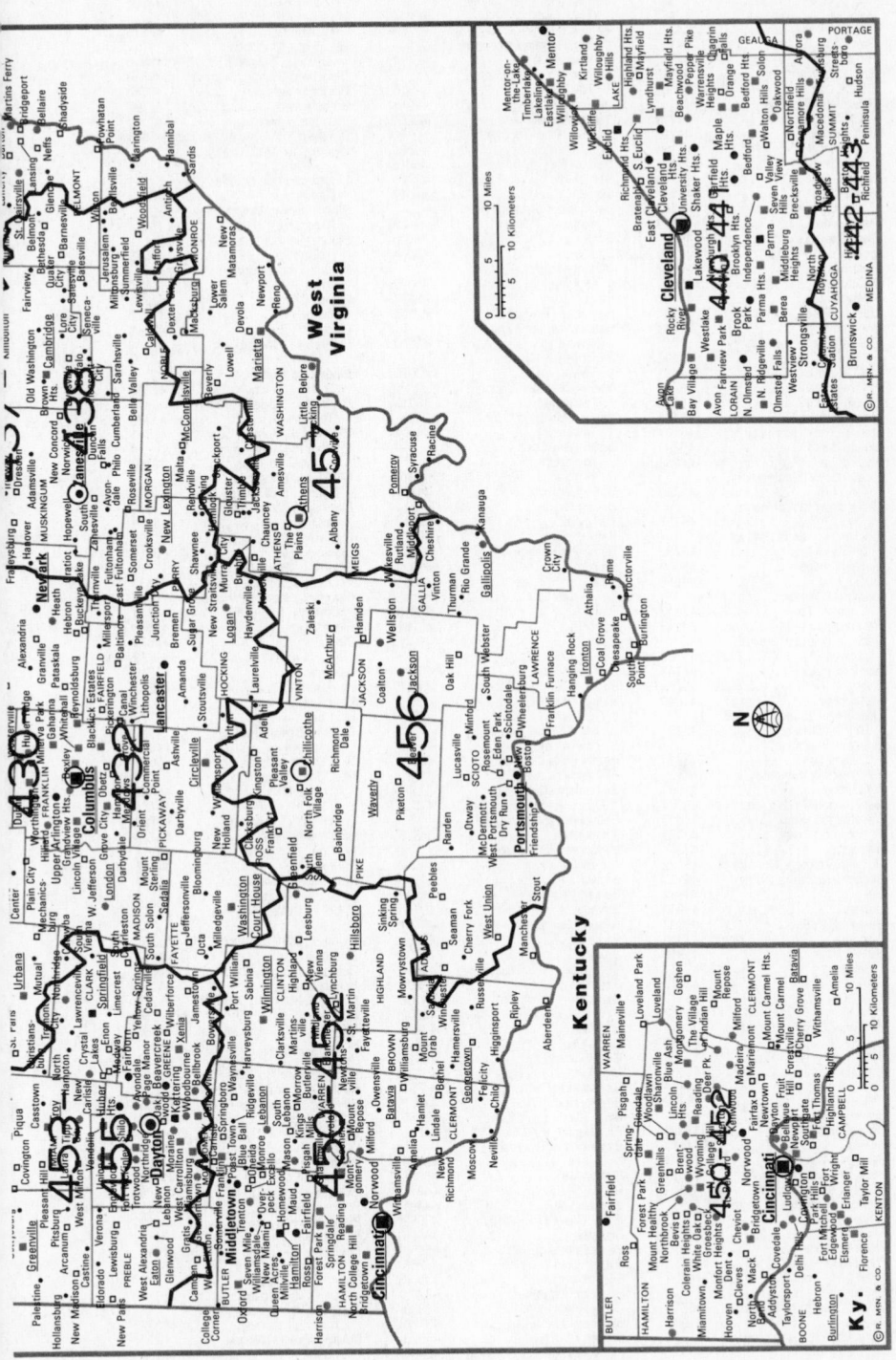

	ZIP
Bayard	44657
Bay Bridge	44870
Bays	43462
Bay View	44870
Bay Village	44140
Bazetta	44410
Bazetta (Township)	44410
Beach City	44608
Beachland (Part of Cleveland)	44119
Beachwood	44122
Beachwood Place (Part of Beachwood)	44122
Beacon Hill	45241
Beallsville	43716
Beals (Part of Pickerington)	43147
Beamsville	45303
Bear Creek	45657
Bearfield (Township)	43730
Beartown	44622
Beatty	45506
Beaumont	45701
Beaver (Pike County) (Township)	45690
Beaver (Mahoning County) (Township)	44408
Beaver (Noble County) (Township)	43773
Beaver (Pike County)	45613
Beavercreek	45434
Beavercreek (Township)	45401
Beaverdam	45808
Beaver Park (Part of Lorain)	44053
Beavertown (Montgomery County)	45429
Beavertown (Washington County)	45767
Becker Highlands (Part of Steubenville)	43952
Beckett Ridge	45069
Becks Mills	44654
Bedford (Coshocton County) (Township)	43812
Bedford (Cuyahoga County)	44146
Bedford (Meigs County) (Township)	45769
Bedford Heights	44146
Beebe	45778
Beechcrest	44240
Beechview Estates (Part of Cincinnati)	45201
Beechwood (Part of Columbus)	43214
Beechwood (Jefferson County)	43952
Beechwood (Preble County)	45064
Beechwood (Stark County)	44601
Beechwood Trails	43062
Belden	44044
Belfast (Clermont County)	45122
Belfast (Highland County)	45133
Belfort	44641
Bellaire	43906
Bellaire Gardens	43302
Bellbrook	45305
Belle Center	43310
Bellefontaine	43311
Bellepoint	43015
Belle Valley	43717
Belle Vernon	44882
Belleview Heights (Preble County)	45347
Belleview Heights (Ross County)	45601
Bellevue	44811
Bellview	45305
Bellview Estates	45305
Bellview Heights	43906
Bellville	44813
Belmont (Allen County)	45801
Belmont (Belmont County)	43718
Belmont (Butler County)	45015
Belmont Meadows (Part of Springfield)	45505
Belmont Park	44420
Belmont Ridge	43983
Belmore	45815
Beloit	44609
Belpre	45714
Belpre (Township)	45714
Belvedere	43952
Bennington (Licking County) (Township)	43011
Bennington (Morrow County) (Township)	43334
Bentley (Part of Lowellville)	44436
Bentleyville	44022

	ZIP
Benton (Crawford County)	44882
Benton (Hocking County) (Township)	43152
Benton (Holmes County)	44654
Benton (Monroe County) (Township)	45767
Benton (Ottawa County) (Township)	43432
Benton (Paulding County) (Township)	45880
Benton (Pike County) (Township)	45690
Benton Ridge	45816
Bentonville	45105
Berea	44017
Berea (Part of Middleburg Heights)	44130
Bergholz	43908
Berkey	43504
Berkley Heights (Part of Kettering)	45429
Berkshire	43074
Berkshire (Township)	43074
Berlin (Holmes County) (Township)	44610
Berlin (Knox County) (Township)	43019
Berlin (Delaware County) (Township)	43015
Berlin (Mahoning County) (Township)	44401
Berlin (Erie County) (Township)	44814
Berlin	44610
Berlin Center	44401
Berlin Heights	44814
Berlinville	44814
Bern (Township)	45770
Berne (Township)	43155
Bernice	43832
Berryman	45805
Berrysville	45133
Berwick	44853
Bessemer	45764
Bethany	45042
Bethel (Clark County) (Township)	45344
Bethel (Clermont County)	45106
Bethel (Miami County) (Township)	45371
Bethel (Monroe County) (Township)	45745
Bethel (Pike County)	45661
Bethesda	43719
Bethlehem (Coshocton County) (Township)	43812
Bethlehem (Richland County)	44875
Bethlehem (Stark County) (Township)	44662
Bettsville	44815
Beulah Beach	44089
Beverly	45715
Beverly Gardens	45431
Bevis	45239
Bexley	43209
Bidwell	45614
Big Island	43302
Big Island (Township)	43302
Biglick (Township)	44802
Big Plain	43140
Big Prairie	44611
Big Rock	45613
Big Run	45724
Big Spring (Township)	44853
Big Springs	43347
Birds Run	43749
Birmingham (Erie County)	44816
Birmingham (Guernsey County)	43749
Bishopville	45732
Bismarck	44811
Blachleyville	44691
Black Creek (Township)	45882
Blackfork	45656
Black Fork Junction	45656
Black Horse	44266
Blacklick	43004
Blacklick Estates	43227
Black Run	43830
Blacktop	43780
Bladen	45623
Bladensburg	43005
Blaine	43909
Blainesville	43950
Blairmont	43901
Blakeslee	43505

	ZIP
Blanchard (Hardin County) (Township)	45836
Blanchard (Putnam County) (Township)	45875
Blanchard (Hancock County) (Township)	45816
Blanchard (Hardin County)	45836
Blanches Addition	43062
Blanchester	45107
Blendon (Township)	43081
Blissfield	43805
Bloom (Fairfield County) (Township)	43136
Bloom (Morgan County) (Township)	43756
Bloom (Scioto County) (Township)	45682
Bloom (Seneca County) (Township)	44818
Bloom (Wood County) (Township)	44817
Bloom Center	43318
Bloomdale	44817
Bloomer	45318
Bloomfield (Columbiana County)	43920
Bloomfield (Jackson County) (Township)	45640
Bloomfield (Logan County) (Township)	43333
Bloomfield (Morrow County)	43011
Bloomfield (Muskingum County)	43762
Bloomfield (Trumbull County) (Township)	44450
Bloomfield (Washington County)	45734
Bloomingburg	43106
Bloomingdale	43910
Blooming Grove (Morrow County)	44833
Blooming Grove (Richland County) (Township)	44878
Bloomington	45169
Bloomingville	44870
Bloom Junction	45682
Bloomville	44818
Blue Ash	45242
Blue Ball	45005
Blue Bell	43772
Bluebird Beach (Part of Vermilion)	44089
Blue Creek (Adams County)	45616
Blue Creek (Paulding County) (Township)	45886
Blue Rock	43720
Blue Rock (Township)	43720
Blue Valley Acres	43130
Bluffton	45817
Boardman	44512
Boardman (Township)	44512
Boardman Plaza	44512
Bobo	45613
Boden	43762
Bokes Creek (Township)	43358
Bolindale	44484
Bolivar	44612
Bolton	44601
Bond Hill (Part of Cincinnati)	45237
Boneta	44256
Bonn	45788
Bono	43445
Bookwalter	43128
Booth (Lucas County)	43618
Booth (Tuscarawas County)	43832
Borromeo College of Ohio	44092
Boston (Highland County)	45133
Boston (Summit County) (Township)	44264
Boston Heights	44236
Boston Mill	44264
Botkins	45306
Boudes Ferry	45121
Boughtonville	44890
Bourneville	45617
Bowerston	44695
Bowersville	45307
Bowling Green (Licking County) (Township)	43076
Bowling Green (Marion County) (Township)	43332
Bowling Green (Wood County)	43402
Bowlusville	43078
Boydsville	43912
Braceville	44444
Braceville (Township)	44444

	ZIP
Carrollton	44615
Carrothers	44807
Carryall (Township)	45813
Carthage (Township)	45735
Carthagena	45822
Carysville	45317
Cass (Hancock County) (Township)	44804
Cass (Muskingum County) (Township)	43821
Cass (Richland County) (Township)	44878
Cassell	43725
Cassella	45883
Cassinelli Square (Part of Springdale)	45246
Casstown	45312
Castalia	44824
Castine	45304
Catawba (Champaign County)	43044
Catawba (Clark County)	43010
Catawba Island	43452
Catawba Island (Township)	43452
Causeway Manor	44003
Cavallo	43843
Cavett	45891
Caywood	45750
Cecil	45821
Cedar Center Plaza (Part of University Heights)	44125
Cedarhill	43102
Cedar Mills	45616
Cedar Point (Part of Sandusky)	44870
Cedar Valley	44214
Cedarville	45314
Cedarville (Township)	45314
Cedron	45121
Celeryville	44890
Celina	45822
Centenary	45631
Center	43725
Center (Carroll County) (Township)	44615
Center (Columbiana County) (Township)	44432
Center (Guernsey County) (Township)	43725
Center (Mercer County) (Township)	45822
Center (Monroe County) (Township)	43793
Center (Morgan County) (Township)	45715
Center (Noble County) (Township)	43724
Center (Williams County) (Township)	43506
Center (Wood County) (Township)	43402
Centerburg	43011
Centerfield	45123
Centerpoint	45656
Center Station	45659
Centerton	44890
Center Village	43021
Centerville (Belmont County)	43718
Centerville (Brown County)	45154
Centerville (Marion County)	43342
Centerville (Montgomery County)	45459
Centerville (Wayne County)	44676
Central (Part of Toledo)	43604
Central College (Part of Westerville)	43081
Cessna (Township)	43326
Ceylon	44839
Chagrin Falls	44022
Chagrin Falls (Township)	44022
Chagrin Falls Annex	44023
Chagrin Falls Park	44022
Chagrin Harbor (Part of Eastlake)	44094
Chalfants	43739
Chambersburg (Columbiana County)	44657
Chambersburg (Gallia County)	45631
Champion (Township)	44481
Champion Heights	44481
Chandler	43910
Chandlersville	43727
Chapel Hill Shopping Center (Part of Akron)	44310
Chapmans	45692

	ZIP
Chardon	44024
Chardon (Township)	44024
Charity Rotch (Part of Massillon)	44646
Charlestown	44266
Charlestown (Township)	44266
Charloe	45873
Charm	44617
Chase	45710
Chasetown	45118
Chaseville	43772
Chaska Beach (Part of Huron)	44839
Chateau Estates	45502
Chateau Ridge (Part of Marion)	43302
Chatfield	44825
Chatfield (Township)	44825
Chatham (Township)	44275
Chatham (Licking County)	43055
Chatham (Medina County)	44256
Chattanooga	45882
Chauncey	45719
Chautauqua	45342
Cherokee	43324
Cherry Fork	45618
Cherry Grove (Clermont County)	45230
Cherry Grove (Hamilton County)	45230
Cherry Grove Plaza	45230
Cherry Valley	44003
Cherry Valley (Township)	44003
Chesapeake	45619
Cheshire (Township)	45620
Cheshire (Delaware County)	43021
Cheshire (Gallia County)	45620
Chesswood Acres	45239
Chester	45720
Chester (Clinton County) (Township)	45177
Chester (Geauga County) (Township)	44026
Chester (Meigs County) (Township)	45720
Chester (Morrow County) (Township)	43338
Chester (Wayne County) (Township)	44691
Chester Center	44026
Chesterfield (Township)	43567
Chesterhill	43728
Chesterland	44026
Chesterville	43317
Cheviot	45211
Cheviot Hills	45502
Chevy Chase	44833
Chickasaw	45826
Chickwan	43901
Chili	43824
Chillicothe	45601
Chillicothe Correctional Institute	45601
Chillicothe Manor	45601
Chilo	45112
Chipman	45805
Chippewa (Township)	44230
Chippewa Lake	44215
Chippewa Lake Park	44215
Chocktou Lake	43140
Christiansburg	45389
Chuckery	43029
Churchill	44505
Churchills (Part of Sylvania)	43560
Churchtown	45750

	ZIP
Cincinnati	**45201-75**

For specific Cincinnati Zip Codes call (513) 684-5571

COLLEGES & UNIVERSITIES

God's Bible School and College	45210
University of Cincinnati	45221
Xavier University	45207

FINANCIAL INSTITUTIONS

Centennial Savings Bank, F.S.B.	45211
The Central Trust Company, N.A.	45202
Century Bank	45209
Charter Oak Federal Savings Bank	45242
The Cheviot Building & Loan Company	45211

	ZIP
Cottage Savings Association, F.A.	45243
Fidelity Federal Savings & Loan Association	45212
The Fifth Third Bank	45243
First Financial Savings F.A.	45209
Franklin Savings & Loan Company	45202
Gateway Federal Savings Bank	45202
Hunter Savings Association	45236
Merit Savings Association	45213
North Side Bank & Trust Co.	45223
Oak Hills Savings & Loan Company, F.A.	45248
The Provident Bank	45202
Star Bank, N.A., Cincinnati	45202
Suburban Federal Savings Bank	45242
Winton Savings & Loan Company	45247

HOSPITALS

Bethesda North Hospital	45242
Bethesda Oak Hospital	45206
Children's Hospital Medical Center	45229
Christ Hospital	45219
Drake Center	45216
Deaconess Hospital	45219
Good Samaritan Hospital	45220
Jewish Hospital of Cincinnati	45229
Providence Hospital	45239
St. Francis-St. George Hospital	45238
University of Cincinnati Hospital	45267
Veterans Affairs Medical Center	45220

HOTELS/MOTELS

Clarion Hotel	45202
The Hampshire House Hotel	45246
Harley of Cincinnati	45236
Holiday Inn-Kings Gate Area	45241
Hyatt Regency Cincinnati-Saks Fifth Avenue Center	45202
Omni Netherland Plaza	45202
Ramada Hotel-Blue Ash	45202
The Vernon Manor Hotel	45219

MILITARY INSTALLATIONS

United States Army Engineer District, Ohio River Division, Laboratory	45240

Circle Green	43908
Circle Hill (Athens County)	45764
Circle Hill (Miami County)	45308
Circleville	43113
Circleville (Township)	43113
Circleville Bible College	43113
City View Heights	45013
Claiborne	43344
Claibourne (Township)	43344
Claridon	44024
Claridon (Township)	44024
Claridon	43314
Claridon (Township)	43314
Clarington	43915
Clark (Coshocton County) (Township)	43844
Clark (Holmes County) (Township)	43804
Clark (Brown County) (Township)	45130
Clark (Clinton County) (Township)	45146
Clark (Coshocton County)	43812
Clark Corners (Ashtabula County)	44030
Clark Corners (Medina County)	44281
Clarksburg (Belmont County)	43960
Clarksburg (Ross County)	43115
Clarksfield	44889
Clarksfield (Township)	44889
Clarks Lake	43143
Clarkson	44455
Clarksville (Clinton County)	45113
Clarksville (Perry County)	43748
Clarktown	45648

ZIP

Clay (Auglaize County)
(Township) 45895
Clay (Gallia County)
(Township) 45631
Clay (Highland County)
(Township) 45171
Clay (Jackson County)..... 45656
Clay (Knox County)
(Township) 43080
Clay (Montgomery County)
(Township) 45354
Clay (Muskingum County)
(Township) 43777
Clay (Ottawa County)
(Township) 43430
Clay (Scioto County)
(Township) 45662
Clay (Tuscarawas County)
(Township) 44629
Clay Center 43408
Clay Lick 43055
Claysville 43725
Clayton (Adams County) .. 45144
Clayton (Miami County) 45318
Clayton (Montgomery
County) 45315
Clayton (Township) 43764
Clear Creek (Ashland
County) (Township) 44874
Clear Creek (Fairfield
County) (Township) 43102
Clear Creek (Warren
County) (Township) 45066
Clearport 43130
Clearview (Athens County) . 45701
Clearview (Lorain County) .. 44055
Clearview (Stark County)... 44646
Clermontville 45157
Clertoma (Part of Milford) .. 45150

Cleveland 44101-99
For specific Cleveland Zip Codes
call (216) 443-4444

COLLEGES & UNIVERSITIES

Case Western Reserve
University 44106
Cleveland State University . 44114
Dyke College 44115
John Carroll University 44118
Ursuline College 44124

FINANCIAL INSTITUTIONS

AmeriTrust Company
National Association 44115
Bank One, Cleveland, N.A. . 44114
The First Federal Savings
Bank 44114
First Federal Savings &
Loan Association of
Lakewood 44107
Home Federal Savings
Bank, Northern Ohio 44107
National City Bank 44114
Ohio Savings Bank 44114
Security Federal Savings &
Loan Association 44124
Society National Bank 44114
The Strongsville Savings
Bank 44136
Third Federal Savings &
Loan Association of
Cleveland 44105
Transohio Savings Bank ... 44114
Women's Federal Savings
Bank 44113

HOSPITALS

Cleveland Clinic Hospital ... 44195
Deaconess Hospital of
Cleveland 44109
Fairview General Hospital .. 44111
Meridia Huron Hospital 44112
Mt. Sinai Medical Center ... 44106
Saint Luke's Hospital 44104
St. Vincent Charity Hospital
and Health Center 44115
University Hospitals of
Cleveland 44106
Veterans Affairs Medical
Center 44106

HOTELS/MOTELS

Cleveland South Hilton Inn . 44131
Sheraton Airport Hotel 44135

Cleveland Heights 44118
Cleves 45002

ZIP

Clifton (Greene County).... 45316
Clifton (Hamilton County) .. 45220
Clifton Farms (Part of
Middletown).............. 45044
Climax 43320
Clinton (Franklin County)
(Township) 43224
Clinton (Fulton County)
(Township) 43567
Clinton (Knox County)
(Township) 43050
Clinton (Seneca County)
(Township) 44883
Clinton (Shelby County)
(Township) 45365
Clinton (Summit County) ... 44216
Clinton (Vinton County)
(Township) 45634
Clinton (Wayne County)
(Township) 44676
Clintonville (Part of
Columbus) 43202
Clipper Mills 45631
Cloverdale 45827
Cloverhill 43764
Cluff 45244
Clyde 43410
Coach Lite Village 43528
Coal (Jackson County)
(Township) 45621
Coal (Perry County)
(Township) 43766
Coalburg 44425
Coal Grove 45638
Coalport (Part of
Newcomerstown) 43832
Coal Ridge 43711
Coal Run 45721
Coalton 45621
Coddingville 44256
Coffee Corners 44062
Coitsville (Township) 44436
Coitsville Center 44505
Colby 43410
Cold Springs 45502
Coldwater 45828
Colebrook 44076
Colebrook (Township) 44076
Colerain 43916
Colerain (Belmont County)
(Township) 43916
Colerain (Hamilton County)
(Township) 45251
Colerain (Ross County)
(Township) 45644
Colerain Heights 45239
Coles Park 45663
Coletown 45331
College (Township) 43022
College Corner 45003
College Hill (Guernsey
County) 43725
College Hill (Hamilton
County) 45224
College Hill Junction (Part
of Cincinnati) 45224
College Hills 45324
Collins 44826
Collinsville 45004
Collinwood (Part of
Cleveland) 44110
Colonial Hills (Part of
Worthington) 43085
Colony Square (Part of
Zanesville) 43701
Colton 43510
Columbia (Hamilton County)
(Township) 45243
Columbia (Stark County) ... 44646
Columbia (Tuscarawas
County) 44622
Columbia (Williams County) 43518
Columbia (Lorain County)
(Township) 44028
Columbia (Meigs County)
(Township) 45710
Columbia Center (Licking
County) 43062
Columbia Center (Lorain
County) 44028
Columbia Hills Corners..... 44028
Columbiana 44408
Columbia Station 44028

Columbus 43201-40

ZIP

COLLEGES & UNIVERSITIES

Capital University 43209
Columbus College of Art
and Design 43215
DeVry Institute of
Technology-Columbus ... 43209
Ohio Dominican College ... 43219
Ohio State University 43210

FINANCIAL INSTITUTIONS

BancOhio National Bank ... 43251
Bank One, Columbus, N.A. . 43271
City Loan Bank 43220
The Fifth Third Bank 43215
Household Bank, F.S.B..... 43231
The Huntington National
Bank 43215
Society Bank, N.A. 43215
Star Bank Central Ohio 43215
State Savings Bank 43215

HOSPITALS

Children's Hospital 43205
Columbus Community
Hospital 43207
Doctors Hospital 43201
Grant Medical Center 43215
Mount Carmel Health
Center 43222
Ohio State University
Hospitals 43210
Riverside Methodist Hospital 43214

HOTELS/MOTELS

The Christopher Inn 43215
Columbus Marriott/North ... 43229
Harley of Columbus 43229
Holiday Inn Crowne Plaza-
Columbus 43215
Hyatt Regency Columbus .. 43215
Parke Hotel 43229
Ramada Inn-North 43229

MILITARY INSTALLATIONS

Defense Construction
Supply Center.......... 43215
Rickenbacker Air National
Guard Base 43217
For specific Columbus Zip Codes
call (614) 469-4332

Columbus Circle (Part of
Ashland) 44805
Columbus City Center (Part
of Columbus) 43215
Columbus Grove 45830
Columbus Park 44870
Comet 44216
Commercial Point......... 43116
Compton Park............ 45231
Compton Woods (Part of
Wyoming)............... 45215
Conant................... 45887
Concept 45807
Concord (Champaign
County) (Township) 43072
Concord (Delaware County)
(Township) 43015
Concord (Fayette County)
(Township) 43160
Concord (Highland County)
(Township) 45697
Concord (Lake County) 44060
Concord (Lake County)
(Township) 44077
Concord (Licking County) .. 43031
Concord (Miami County)
(Township) 45373
Concord (Ross County)
(Township) 45628
Condit 43074
Conesville 43811
Congo 43730
Congress (Wayne County)
(Township) 44287
Congress (Morrow County)
(Township) 43338
Congress 44287
Congress Lake 44632
Conneaut 44030
Conneaut Harbor (Part of
Conneaut) 44030
Connett 45764
Connor 43943
Conotton 44695
Conover 45317
Constitution 45750

	ZIP
Continental	45831
Converse	45887
Convoy	45832
Conway Addition	43731
Cook	43143
Cool Ridge Heights (Part of Mansfield)	44905
Coolville	45723
Coonville	45654
Cooperdale	43821
Coopersville	45657
Copley	44321
Copley (Township)	44321
Copley Center	44321
Corinth	44417
Cork	44041
Corner	45714
Cornersburg (Part of Youngstown)	44511
Cornerville	45773
Corning	43730
Correctional Reception Center	43146
Corryville (Hamilton County)	45219
Corryville (Lawrence County)	45619
Cortland	44410
Cortsville	45368
Corwin	45068
Coryville	45638
Coshocton	43812
Cottage Grove	44319
Country Acres	45324
Country Acres (Part of Beavercreek)	45430
Country Club Estates (Part of Steubenville)	43952
Country Club Hills	45801
Country Estates	45371
Country Fair Station (Part of Canton)	44708
Cove	45640
Covedale	45238
Coventry (Township)	44319
Covington	45318
Cozaddale	45122
Crabapple	43950
Craig Beach	44429
Craigton	44676
Cranberry (Township)	44854
Cranberry Prairie	45883
Crandenbrook	43551
Crane (Paulding County) (Township)	45821
Crane (Wyandot County) (Township)	43351
Cranwood (Part of Cleveland)	44128
Crawford (Wyandot County) (Township)	43316
Crawford (Coshocton County) (Township)	43804
Crawford	43316
Crawford Corners	44254
Cream City (Part of Irondale)	43932
Creola	45622
Crescent	43950
Crescent Gardens	44646
Crescentville (Part of Sharonville)	45241
Crestline	44827
Creston	44217
Crestwood Hills (Part of Vandalia)	45377
Cridersville	45806
Crissey	43528
Cromers	44883
Crooked Tree	45727
Crooksville	43731
Crosby (Township)	45030
Cross Creek (Township)	43952
Crossenville	43107
Crosstown	45176
Crosswick	45068
Croton	43013
Crown City	45623
Crystal Lake	44003
Crystal Lakes	45341
Crystal Rock Park	44870
Crystal Springs	44614
Cuba	45114
Cumberland	43732
Cumminsville (Part of Cincinnati)	45223
Curtice	43412
Custar	43511

	ZIP
Cutler	45724
Cuyahoga Falls	44221-24
For specific Cuyahoga Falls Zip Codes call (216) 945-5807	
Cuyahoga Heights	44125
Cygnet	43413
Cynthian (Township)	45845
Cynthiana	45624
Dabel (Part of Dayton)	45420
Dadsville	45381
Dailyville	45690
Dale	43787
Dallas (Township)	44849
Dallasburg	45140
Dalton	44618
Dalzell	45745
Daman Park	45044
Damascus (Henry County) (Township)	43534
Damascus (Mahoning County)	44619
Danbury (Township)	43452
Danville (Highland County)	45133
Danville (Knox County)	43014
Danville (Meigs County)	45741
Darby (Madison County) (Township)	43064
Darby (Pickaway County) (Township)	43146
Darby (Union County) (Township)	43064
Darbydale	43123
Darbyville	43136
Darlington (Muskingum County)	43701
Darlington (Richland County)	44813
Darrowville (Part of Stow)	44224
Darrtown	45056
Dart	45773
Darwin	45769
Davisville	45692
Dawn	45303
Dawson	45333
Day Heights	45150
Dayton	45401-90
For specific Dayton Zip Codes call (513) 227-1100	
Dayton View (Part of Dayton)	45406
Dean Dale (Part of Mingo Junction)	43938
Deavertown	43731
Decatur (Brown County)	45115
Decatur (Lawrence County) (Township)	45659
Decatur (Washington County) (Township)	45742
Decaturville	45712
Decrow Corners	43031
Dee	44824
Deep Run	43935
Deer Creek (Madison County) (Township)	43140
Deer Creek (Pickaway County) (Township)	43164
Deerfield (Portage County) (Township)	44411
Deerfield (Ross County) (Township)	43115
Deerfield (Warren County) (Township)	45040
Deerfield (Morgan County) (Township)	43758
Deerfield (Portage County) (Township)	44411
Deering	45638
Deer Park	45236
Deersville	44693
Defiance	43512
Defiance (Township)	43512
Defiance Junction (Part of Defiance)	43512
DeForest	44484
De Graff	43318
Dekalb	44887
Delaware (Delaware County) (Township)	43015
Delaware (Hancock County) (Township)	45897
Delaware (Defiance County) (Township)	43556
Delaware	43015
Delhi (Township)	45238
Delhi	45238
Delhi Hills	45238
Delightful	44470
Delisle	45304

	ZIP
Dellroy	44620
Delmont	43130
Delphi	44890
Delphos	45833
Delta	43515
Denmark (Ashtabula County) (Township)	44047
Denmark (Morrow County)	43320
Denmark Center	44047
Dennison	44621
Densons	43533
Dent	45211
Denver	45690
Derby	43117
Derwent	43733
Deshler	43516
Deunquat	44882
Devil Town	44691
Devola	45750
Deweyville	45858
Dexter	45741
Dexter City	45727
Deyarmonville	43917
Dialton	45502
Diamond	44412
Dicken	43138
Dilles Bottom	43947
Dillon Falls	43701
Dillonvale (Hamilton County)	45236
Dillonvale (Jefferson County)	43917
Dilworth	44417
Dinsmore (Township)	45306
Dixie	43782
Dixie Heights (Butler County)	45042
Dixie Heights (Montgomery County)	45414
Dixon (Preble County) (Township)	45320
Dixon (Van Wert County)	45832
Dixonville	43920
Doanville	45764
Dobbston	45678
Dodds	45036
Dodgeville	44085
Dodson (Highland County) (Township)	45142
Dodson (Montgomery County)	45309
Dodsonville	45142
Dola	45835
Dolly Varden	45368
Donald L Marrs (Part of Cincinnati)	45258
Doneys (Part of Whitehall)	43213
Donnelsville	45319
Donnersville	43950
Dorcas	45771
Dornbusch	45239
Dorset	44032
Dorset (Township)	44032
Dover (Tuscarawas County) (Township)	44622
Dover (Union County) (Township)	43040
Dover (Athens County) (Township)	45761
Dover (Fulton County) (Township)	43567
Dover	44622
Dowling	43551
Downtown (Part of Columbus)	43215
Downtown (Part of Akron)	44308
Doylestown	44230
Drakes	43730
Drakesburg	44288
Dresden	43821
Drexel	45427
Driftwood (Ashtabula County)	44041
Driftwood (Lake County)	44041
Drinkle	43102
Dry Run (Hamilton County)	45244
Dry Run (Scioto County)	45663
Dublin	43016-17
For specific Dublin Zip Codes call (614) 889-0763	
Dublin (Township)	45882
Dublin Village Center (Part of Dublin)	43017
Duchouquet (Township)	45895
Dudley (Hardin County) (Township)	43326
Dudley (Noble County)	43724
Dueber (Part of Canton)	44706

	ZIP		ZIP		ZIP
Fairway View Estates	45805	Forest Park (Hamilton County)	45240	Fredericktown (Knox County)	43019
Fairwind Acres (Part of Montgomery)	45242	Forest Park (Montgomery County)	45405	Fredonia	43023
Falls (Hocking County) (Township)	43138	Forest Park Plaza	45405	Freeburg	44669
Falls (Muskingum County) (Township)	43701	Forest View	43952	Freedom (Portage County) (Township)	44288
Fallsburg	43822	Forestville	45230	Freedom (Wood County) (Township)	43450
Fallsbury (Township)	43822	Fort Jefferson	45331	Freedom (Henry County) (Township)	43545
Fargo	43074	Fort Jennings	45844	Freedom (Portage County)	44288
Farmdale	44417	Fort Loramie	45845	Freeport	43973
Farmer	43520	Fort McKinley	45426	Freeport (Township)	43973
Farmer (Township)	43520	Fort Meigs Place	43551	Fremont	43420
Farmers	45146	Fort Miami Addition (Part of Maumee)	43537	Frenchtown (Darke County)	45380
Farmerstown	43804	Fort Recovery	45846	Frenchtown (Seneca County)	43316
Farmersville	45325	Fort Scott Camps	45030	Fresno	43824
Farmington (Belmont County)	43912	Fort Seneca	44829	Friendship	45630
Farmington (Trumbull County) (Township)	44491	Fort Shawnee	45806	Frischkorn Heights	43968
Farnham (Part of Conneaut)	44030	Fort Steuben Mall (Part of Steubenville)	43952	Frontier Park	45239
Farrington	45373	Foster	45039	Frontier Town	44514
Fashion Heights	45238	Fosterville (Part of Youngstown)	44511	Frost	45723
Fawcett	45616	Fostoria	44830	Fruitdale	45123
Fayette (Fulton County)	43521	Fountain Park	43084	Fruit Hill	45230
Fayette (Lawrence County) (Township)	45680	Fountain Square (Part of Cincinnati)	45202	Fryburg (Auglaize County)	45895
Fayetteville	45118	Fowler	44418	Fryburg (Holmes County)	44654
Fay Gardens	45140	Fowler (Township)	44418	Frys Corners	45331
Fearing (Township)	45788	Fowlers Mill	44024	Frytown	45418
Federal Reserve (Part of Cleveland)	44101	Fox (Carroll County) (Township)	43945	Fulda	43724
Feed Springs	44683	Fox (Pickaway County)	43113	Fulton (Fulton County) (Township)	43558
Feesburg	45119	Foxboro Manor (Part of Vandalia)	45377	Fulton (Morrow County)	43321
Felicity	45120	Foxborough Commons	44870	Fultonham	43738
Fernald	45030	Fox Chase	43502	Funk	44691
Fernbank (Part of Cincinnati)	45233	Fox Hollow	43542	Fursville	43062
Fernell Heights	45244	Frank	44811	Gabels Corner	43420
Fernwood	43952	Frankfort	45628	Gage	45658
Ferry (Erie County)	44870	Franklin (Adams County) (Township)	45660	Gageville	44048
Ferry (Greene County)	45068	Franklin (Brown County) (Township)	45121	Gahanna	43230
Fields Terrace	45619	Franklin (Clermont County) (Township)	45120	Galatea	45872
Filburns Island	45865	Franklin (Columbiana County) (Township)	43962	Galaxy Acres	45239
Fincastle	45171	Franklin (Coshocton County) (Township)	43811	Galena	43021
Findlater Garden (Part of Cincinnati)	45232	Franklin (Darke County) (Township)	45304	Galion	44833
Findlay	45839-40	Franklin (Franklin County) (Township)	43204	Gallia	45658
For specific Findlay Zip Codes call (419) 423-1264		Franklin (Fulton County) (Township)	43502	Gallipolis	45631
Findlay Mall (Part of Findlay)	45840	Franklin (Harrison County) (Township)	44699	Gallipolis (Township)	45631
Findley Gardens	43964	Franklin (Jackson County) (Township)	45640	Galloway	43119
Finneytown	45224	Franklin (Licking County) (Township)	43055	Gambier	43022
Fire Brick	45656	Franklin (Mercer County) (Township)	45866	Ganges	44875
Fireside	44811	Franklin (Monroe County) (Township)	43754	Gano	45241
Firestone Park (Part of Akron)	44301	Franklin (Morrow County) (Township)	43338	Garden	45735
Fishack	43452	Franklin (Portage County) (Township)	44240	Garden Acres (Clark County)	45503
Fitchville	44851	Franklin (Richland County) (Township)	44875	Garden Acres (Jefferson County)	43952
Fitchville (Township)	44851	Franklin (Ross County) (Township)	45601	Garden City	45694
Five Forks	43945	Franklin (Shelby County) (Township)	45363	Garden Hill Top (Part of Cincinnati)	45232
Five Mile	45154	Franklin (Summit County) (Township)	44216	Garden Isle	44254
Five Points (Greene County)	45324	Franklin (Tuscarawas County) (Township)	44680	Garden Terrace (Part of Steubenville)	43952
Five Points (Mahoning County)	44452	Franklin (Warren County)	45005	Garfield	44460
Five Points (Pickaway County)	43143	Franklin (Warren County) (Township)	45005	Garfield Heights	44125
Five Points (Trumbull County)	44404	Franklin (Wayne County) (Township)	44627	Garrettsville	44231
Five Points (Warren County)	45066	Franklin Furnace	45629	Gaslight Village	45122
Flatiron (Perry County)	43731	Franklin Park Mall (Part of Toledo)	43623	Gasper (Township)	45320
Flat Iron (Warren County)	45005	Franklin Square	44431	Gates Mills	44040
Flatrock (Henry County) (Township)	43545	Frazeysburg	43822	Gath	45171
Flat Rock (Seneca County)	44828	Frederick (Miami County)	45371	Gavers	44432
Fleatown	43055	Frederick (Scioto County)	45694	Geauga Lake (Part of Aurora)	44202
Fleetwood Addition	43040	Fredericksburg	44627	Geeburg	44406
Fleming	45712	Fredericksdale	43779	Geneva	44041
Fletcher	45326	Fredericktown (Columbiana County)	43920	Geneva (Township)	44041
Flint	43085			Geneva	43107
Florence (Belmont County)	43935			Geneva-on-the-Lake	44041
Florence (Erie County)	44814			Genntown	45036
Florence (Erie County) (Township)	44814			Genoa (Delaware County) (Township)	43081
Florence (Noble County)	43724			Genoa (Ottawa County)	43430
Florence (Williams County) (Township)	43518			Genung Corners	44057
Florida	43545			Georges Run	43938
Flushing	43977			Georgesville	43123
Flushing (Township)	43977			Georgetown	45121
Fly	45730			Gepharts	45694
Footville	44084			Gerald	43545
Foraker	45812			German (Auglaize County) (Township)	45869
Forest	45843			German (Clark County) (Township)	45504
Forestdale	45638			German (Fulton County) (Township)	43502
Forest Hills	45502			German (Harrison County) (Township)	43976
Forest Hills Estates	45230			German (Montgomery County) (Township)	45327

	ZIP		ZIP		ZIP
Germano	43986	Graceland Shopping Center		Greenfield (Fairfield County)	
Germantown (Montgomery		(Part of Columbus)	43214	(Township)	43130
County)	45327	Grafton	44044	Greenfield (Gallia County)	
Germantown (Washington		Grafton (Township)	44044	(Township)	45658
County)	45745	Grand (Township)	45843	Greenfield (Highland	
Getaway	45619	Grand Prairie (Township)	43302	County)	45123
Gettysburg (Darke County)	45328	Grand Rapids	43522	Greenfield (Huron County)	
Gettysburg (Preble County)	45347	Grand Rapids (Township)	43522	(Township)	44855
Geyer	45895	Grand River	44045	Greenfield Village	45224
Ghent	44333	Grandview (Township)	45767	Greenford	44422
Gibisonville	43149	Grandview (Hamilton		Green Hills (Greene County)	45324
Gibson (Guernsey County)	43778	County)	45002	Greenhills (Hamilton County)	45218
Gibson (Mercer County)		Grandview (Washington		Greenland	43115
(Township)	45846	County)	45767	Greenlex	43302
Gibsonburg	43431	Grandview Estates		Green Meadows	45323
Gilbert	43701	(Delaware County)	43015	Greensburg (Putnam	
Gilboa	45875	Grandview Estates (Marion		County) (Township)	45875
Gilead (Township)	43338	County)	43302	Greensburg (Summit	
Gillivan	43140	Grandview Heights		County)	44232
Gilmore	43837	(Champaign County)	43072	Green Springs	44836
Ginghamsburg	45371	Grandview Heights (Franklin		Greens Run	45732
Girard	44420	County)	43212	Greens Store	45640
Girton	43457	Grandview Homes (Part of		Greentown	44630
Gist Settlement	45159	Lima)	45804	Greenview	45415
Givens	45690	Grange Hall	43143	Greenville	45331
Glade	45613	Granger	44256	Greenville (Township)	45331
Gladstone	45314	Granger (Township)	44256	Greenwich	44837
Glandorf	45848	Grants	45843	Greenwich (Township)	44837
Glasgow (Columbiana		Granville	43023	Greer	44628
County)	43968	Granville (Licking County)		Grelton	43523
Glasgow (Tuscarawas		(Township)	43023	Griffith (Part of North Bend)	45052
County)	43837	Granville (Mercer County)		Griggs	44047
Glass Rock	43739	(Township)	45883	Grimms Bridge	43920
Glenbrook Acres	45305	Granville South	43023	Groesbeck	45239
Glencoe (Belmont County)	43928	Grape Grove	45335	Groton (Township)	44839
Glencoe (Hamilton County)	45231	Gratiot	43740	Grove City	43123
Glendale	45246	Gratis	45330	Groveport	43125
Glendwell (Part of		Gratis (Township)	45330	Grover Hill	45849
Steubenville)	43952	Graysville	45734	Guerne	44691
Glen Este	45103	Graytown	43432	Guernsey	43749
Glenford	43739	Greasy Ridge	45678	Guilford (Columbiana	
Glengary Heights	43081	Greater State Road		County)	44432
Glen Karn	45332	Shopping Center (Part of		Guilford (Medina County)	
Glenmary (Part of Fairfield)	45246	Cuyahoga Falls)	44223	(Township)	44273
Glenmont	44628	Great Lakes Mall (Part of		Gunnerville	45335
Glenmoor	43920	Mentor)	44060	Gurneyville	45177
Glenmore	45874	Great Northern Mall (Part of		Gustavus	44417
Glenns Run	43935	North Olmsted)	44070	Gustavus (Township)	44417
Glen Robbins	43943	Great Southern Shoppers		Gutman	45895
Glen Roy	45692	City (Part of Columbus)	43207	Guyan (Township)	45623
Glenwillow	44139	Great Western Shoppers		Guysville	45735
Glenwood	45381	Mart (Part of Columbus)	43213	Gypsum	43433
Glenwood Acres	44087	Green (Adams County)		Hackney	45715
Gloria Glens Park	44215	(Township)	45684	Hagan Addition	43901
Glouster	45732	Green (Ashland County)		Hageman Junction	45036
Glynwood	45885	(Township)	44842	Hale (Township)	43340
Gnadenhutten	44629	Green (Brown County)		Hallock	43506
Goes	45387	(Township)	45154	Hallsville	45633
Golden Corners	44214	Green (Clark County)		Hambden	44024
Golden Gate Shopping		(Township)	45502	Hambden (Township)	44024
Center (Part of Mayfield		Green (Clinton County)		Hamburg (Fairfield County)	43130
Heights)	44124	(Township)	45159	Hamburg (Preble County)	45321
Goldsboro	45692	Green (Fayette County)		Hamden	45634
Golf Manor	45237	(Township)	45135	Hamer (Township)	45133
Golfway Acres	45239	Green (Gallia County)		Hamersville	45130
Gomer	45809	(Township)	45658	Hametown (Part of Norton)	44203
Good Hope (Fayette		Green (Hamilton County)		Hamilton	45011-13
County)	43160	(Township)	45211		45015-18
Good Hope (Hocking		Green (Harrison County)		For specific Hamilton Zip Codes	
County) (Township)	43149	(Township)	43976	call (513) 867-8877	
Goodland Acres	44688	Green (Hocking County)		Hamilton (Franklin County)	
Goodyear Heights (Part of		(Township)	43138	(Township)	43137
Akron)	45305	Green (Mahoning County)		Hamilton (Jackson County)	
Goose Run	45732	(Township)	44406	(Township)	45656
Gordon	45329	Green (Monroe County)		Hamilton (Lawrence County)	
Gore	43138	(Township)	43793	(Township)	45638
Gorham (Township)	43521	Green (Ross County)		Hamilton (Warren County)	
Goshen (Auglaize County)		(Township)	45644	(Township)	45039
(Township)	43331	Green (Scioto County)		Hamilton Meadows	43207
Goshen (Belmont County)		(Township)	45629	Hamler	43524
(Township)	43719	Green (Shelby County)		Hamlet	45102
Goshen (Champaign		(Township)	45365	Hamley Run	45701
County) (Township)	43044	Green (Summit County)		Hammansburg	43413
Goshen (Clermont County)	45122	(Township)	44720	Hammondsville	43930
Goshen (Clermont County)		Green (Summit County)	44720	Hampton Woods	45502
(Township)	45122	Green (Wayne County)		Hanersville	45631
Goshen (Hardin County)		(Township)	44667	Hanging Rock	45638
(Township)	43326	Green Acres	45042	Hanley Village	44904
Goshen (Mahoning County)		Greenbush (Brown County)	45154	Hanna Hills	44266
(Township)	44460	Greenbush (Preble County)	45064	Hannibal	43931
Goshen (Tuscarawas		Green Camp	43322	Hanover (Township)	43055
County) (Township)	44663	Green Camp (Township)	43322	Hanover	43055
Goshen (Tuscarawas		Greencastle	43112	Hanover (Ashland County)	
County)	44663	Green Creek (Township)	43410	(Township)	44842
Gould Park	43230	Greendale	43138	Hanover (Butler County)	
Goulds	43938	Greene (Township)	44450	(Township)	45013

	ZIP		ZIP		ZIP
Hanover (Columbiana County) (Township)	44625	Hartsgrove	44085	Hilltop (Franklin County)	43204
Hanover (Harrison County)	43988	Hartsgrove (Township)	44085	Hilltop (Trumbull County)	44437
Hanoverton	44423	Hartshorn	45734	Hilltop Acres (Part of Wyoming)	45215
Hanville Corners	44855	Hartville	44632	Hinckley	44233
Happy Hollow	44626	Hartwell (Part of Cincinnati)	45216	Hinckley (Township)	44233
Harbor (Part of Ashtabula)	44004	Harveysburg	45032	Hiram	44234
Harbor Hills	43025	Haskins	43525	Hiram (Township)	44234
Harbor Point	45822	Hasting Hill	45662	Hiram Rapids	44234
Harbor View	43434	Hatch	45661	Hiramsburg	43732
Hardin (Shelby County)	45365	Hatton	43457	Hitchcock	45656
Harding (Township)	43558	Havana	44890	Hoadley	45658
Hardy (Township)	44654	Havens Corners	43004	Hoagland	45133
Harewood Acres	45236	Havensport	43112	Hoaglin (Township)	45891
Harlan (Township)	45162	Haven View	45373	Hobson	45760
Harlan Park (Part of Middletown)	45042	Haverhill	45636	Hocking (Township)	43130
Harlem	43021	Haviland	45851	Hocking Correctional Facility	45764
Harlem (Township)	43021	Hayden	43002	Hockingport	45739
Harlem Springs	44631	Haydenville	43127	Hoke	45383
Harmar (Part of Marietta)	45750	Hayes Colony (Part of Delaware)	43015	Holden	45896
Harmon	44662	Hayes Corners	44062	Holgate	43527
Harmons Landing	45885	Hayesville	44838	Holiday Acres	45236
Harmony	45502	Haynes	43135	Holiday Hills	45502
Harmony (Clark County) (Township)	45502	Hazelwood (Part of Blue Ash)	45242	Holiday Lakes	44890
Harmony (Morrow County) (Township)	43315	Heath	43056	Holiday Valley	45324
Harper	43311	Heatherdowns (Part of Toledo)	43614	Holland	43528
Harpersfield	44041	Hebbardsville	45701	Hollansburg	45332
Harpersfield (Township)	44041	Hebron	43025	Hollister	45732
Harpster	43323	Hecla	45638	Holloway	43985
Harriett (Guernsey County)	43725	Hegemans Landing	45865	Hollowtown	45171
Harriett (Highland County)	45133	Heidelburg Beach	44089	Holman-Stonybrook Shopping Center (Part of Loveland)	45140
Harriettsville	45745	Helena	43435	Holmes (Township)	44820
Harris (Ottawa County) (Township)	43416	Helmick	43844	Holmesville	44633
Harris (Ross County)	45612	Hemlock	43730	Home Acres (Butler County)	45044
Harrisburg (Franklin County)	43126	Hemlock Grove	45769	Home Acres (Miami County)	45373
Harrisburg (Gallia County)	45614	Hempstead (Part of Kettering)	45429	Homedale (Part of Columbus)	43085
Harrisburg (Stark County)	44641	Hendrysburg	43713	Home Orchards (Part of Springfield)	45503
Harrison (Carroll County) (Township)	44615	Henley	45652	Homer (Licking County)	43027
Harrison (Champaign County) (Township)	43357	Henrietta (Township)	44889	Homer (Medina County) (Township)	44235
Harrison (Darke County) (Township)	45346	Henry (Township)	45872	Homer (Morgan County) (Township)	45732
Harrison (Gallia County) (Township)	45631	Hepburn	43326	Homerville	44235
Harrison (Hamilton County)	45030	Heritage	45805	Homeside	43950
Harrison (Hamilton County) (Township)	45030	Heritage Hills	44087	Homeville	44870
Harrison (Henry County) (Township)	43545	Heritage Park	44212	Homewood (Part of Hamilton)	45015
Harrison (Knox County) (Township)	43022	Hessville	43431	Homeworth	44634
Harrison (Licking County) (Township)	43033	Hickman	43055	Honeytown	44691
Harrison (Logan County) (Township)	43311	Hicksville	43526	Hooker	43130
Harrison (Montgomery County) (Township)	45415	Hicksville (Township)	43526	Hooksburg	43787
Harrison (Muskingum County) (Township)	43771	Hide-A-Way Hills	43107	Hooring	45766
Harrison (Paulding County) (Township)	45880	Higginsport	45131	Hooven	45033
Harrison (Perry County) (Township)	43731	Highland (Defiance County) (Township)	43512	Hopedale	43976
Harrison (Pickaway County) (Township)	43103	Highland (Highland County)	45132	Hopetown	45601
Harrison (Preble County) (Township)	45338	Highland (Muskingum County) (Township)	43762	Hopewell (Jefferson County)	43943
Harrison (Ross County) (Township)	45601	Highland Heights	44124	Hopewell (Licking County) (Township)	43740
Harrison (Scioto County) (Township)	45653	Highland Hills	44122	Hopewell (Mercer County) (Township)	45822
Harrison (Van Wert County) (Township)	45891		44128	Hopewell (Muskingum County) (Township)	43746
		For specific Highland Hills Zip Codes call (216) 443-4444			
Harrison (Vinton County) (Township)	45647	Highland Holliday	45133	Hopewell (Perry County) (Township)	43739
Harrison Furnace	45662	Highland Park (Hamilton County)	45238	Hopewell (Seneca County) (Township)	44809
Harrison Mills	45682	Highland Park (Mercer County)	45822	Hopewell	43746
Harrisonville	45769	Highland Park (Scioto County)	45629	Hopkinsville	45039
Harrisville (Harrison County)	43974	Highland Park (Stark County)	44646	Horatio	45331
Harrisville (Medina County) (Township)	44214	Highlands (Part of Springfield)	45503	Horns Mill	43130
Harrod	45850	Highland Terrace	43950	Hoskinsville	43724
Harshasvile	45660	Highlandtown	43945	Houck Meadows (Part of Enon)	45502
Hartford (Trumbull County) (Township)	44424	Highland Trails	45133	Houcktown	45814
Hartford (Licking County) (Township)	43013	Highpoint	45242	Houston	45333
Hartford	44424	High Water	43055	Howard	43028
Hartland	44826	Hill Addition (Part of East Liverpool)	43920	Howard (Township)	43028
Hartland (Township)	44857	Hill And Hollow (Part of Oxford)	45056	Howenstein	44626
Hartland Center	44826	Hillcrest (Columbiana County)	43968	Howland (Township)	44484
Hartleyville	45732	Hillcrest (Warren County)	45036	Howland Center	44484
		Hill Crest (Wayne County)	44691	Hoytville	43529
		Hillcrest (Williams County)	43543	Hubbard	44425
		Hill Grove	45390	Hubbard (Township)	44425
		Hilliar (Township)	43011	Huber Heights	45424
		Hilliard	43026	Huber Ridge	43081
		Hills and Dales (Montgomery County)	45429	Huber South	45439
		Hills and Dales (Stark County)	44708	Hudson	44236
		Hillsboro (Highland County)	45133	Hudson (Township)	44236
		Hillsboro (Jefferson County)	43938	Hue	45622
				Hughes	45042
				Hulington	45106
				Humboldt	45612
				Hume	45806

	ZIP		ZIP		ZIP
Hunt	43050	Jackson (Highland County)		Jefferson (Guernsey	
Hunter	43719	(Township)	45133	County) (Township)	43755
Hunterdon	45732	Jackson (Jackson County)	45640	Jefferson (Jackson County)	
Huntington (Lorain County)		Jackson (Jackson County)		(Township)	45656
(Township)	44090	(Township)	45640	Jefferson (Knox County)	
Huntington (Ross County)		Jackson (Knox County)		(Township)	44628
(Township)	45601	(Township)	43005	Jefferson (Logan County)	
Huntington (Brown County)		Jackson (Mahoning County)		(Township)	43311
(Township)	45101	(Township)	44451	Jefferson (Madison County)	
Huntington (Gallia County)		Jackson (Monroe County)		(Township)	43162
(Township)	45686	(Township)	45730	Jefferson (Mercer County)	
Huntington	44090	Jackson (Montgomery		(Township)	45822
Huntington Hills	43147	County) (Township)	45325	Jefferson (Montgomery	
Huntington Park (Part of		Jackson (Muskingum		County) (Township)	45345
Aberdeen)	45101	County) (Township)	43822	Jefferson (Muskingum	
Hunting Valley	44022	Jackson (Noble County)		County) (Township)	43821
Huntsburg	44046	(Township)	45727	Jefferson (Noble County)	
Huntsburg (Township)	44046	Jackson (Paulding County)		(Township)	43724
Hunts Corners	44811	(Township)	45855	Jefferson (Preble County)	
Huntsville (Butler County)	45042	Jackson (Perry County)		(Township)	45347
Huntsville (Logan County)	43324	(Township)	43748	Jefferson (Richland County)	
Hurford	43901	Jackson (Pickaway County)		(Township)	44813
Huron	44839	(Township)	43113	Jefferson (Ross County)	
Huron (Township)	44839	Jackson (Pike County)		(Township)	45601
Hustead	45502	(Township)	45690	Jefferson (Scioto County)	
Hyatts	43065	Jackson (Preble County)		(Township)	45648
Hyde Park (Hamilton		(Township)	45320	Jefferson (Tuscarawas	
County)	45208	Jackson (Putnam County)		County) (Township)	43840
Hyde Park (Montgomery		(Township)	45844	Jefferson (Wayne County)	44691
County)	45429	Jackson (Richland County)		Jefferson (Williams County)	
Hyde Park Plaza (Part of		(Township)	44875	(Township)	43543
Cincinnati)	45209	Jackson (Sandusky County)		Jefferson Estates	43113
Iberia	43325	(Township)	43407	Jefferson Heights	43938
Idaho	45661	Jackson (Seneca County)		Jeffersonville	43128
Idlewild (Part of Cincinnati)	45201	(Township)	44830	Jelloway	43014
Iler	44830	Jackson (Shelby County)		Jenera	45841
Ilesboro	43138	(Township)	45334	Jenkins Addition	43701
Immergrun (Part of Oregon)	43618	Jackson (Stark County)		Jennings (Putnam County)	
Independence (Cuyahoga		(Township)	44646	(Township)	45844
County)	44131	Jackson (Union County)		Jennings (Van Wert County)	
Independence (Defiance		(Township)	43344	(Township)	45894
County)	43512	Jackson (Van Wert County)		Jep	45659
Independence (Township)	45767	(Township)	45863	Jericho	45042
Indian Camp	43725	Jackson (Vinton County)		Jerome	43064
Indian Knolls (Part of		(Township)	45651	Jerome (Township)	43064
Milford)	45150	Jackson (Wood County)		Jeromesville	44840
Indian Ridge	45231	(Township)	43529	Jerry City	43437
Indianview	45147	Jackson (Wyandot County)		Jersey	43062
Ingle Mann (Part of New		(Township)	45843	Jersey (Township)	43062
Paris)	45347	Jackson Belden (Part of		Jerusalem (Lucas County)	
Ingomar	45381	Canton)	44718	(Township)	43412
Ink	44883	Jacksonburg	45067	Jerusalem (Monroe County)	43747
Ira	44333	Jackson Center (Mahoning		Jesse C Owens (Part of	
Iradale	44313	County)	44451	Cleveland)	44104
Irondale (Jefferson County)	43932	Jackson Center (Shelby		Jewell	43530
Irondale (Muskingum		County)	45334	Jewett	43986
County)	43821	Jackson Heights (Jackson		Jobs	45732
Ironspot	43777	County)	45640	Joetown	43758
Ironton	45638	Jackson Heights (Jefferson		Johnson (Township)	43072
Irvington	45414	County)	43943	Johnsons Corners (Part of	
Irwin	43029	Jackson Lake	44656	Barberton)	44203
Island Creek (Township)	43964	Jacksontown	43030	Johnston	44417
Island View	43331	Jacksonville (Adams		Johnston (Township)	44417
Isle Saint George	43436	County)	45660	Johnston	44622
Isleta	43845	Jacksonville (Athens		Johnstown	43031
Israel (Township)	45003	County)	45740	Johnsville (Part of New	
Ithaca	45304	Jacksonville (Clark County)	45502	Lebanon)	45345
Ivorydale (Part of St.		Jacktown	45042	Jonesboro (Clinton County)	45146
Bernard)	45217	Jacobsburg	43933	Jonesboro (Fayette County)	43160
Ivorydale Junction (Part of		Jaite (Part of Brecksville)	44141	Jonestown	45894
St. Bernard)	45217	Jamestown	45335	Jordanville	44432
Jackson (Allen County)		Jasper (Fayette County)		Joy	43728
(Township)	45854	(Township)	43128	Jug Run	43917
Jackson (Ashland County)		Jasper (Pike County)	45642	Jumbo	43326
(Township)	44287	Jasper Mills	43160	Jump	43326
Jackson (Auglaize County)		Jays	45331	Junction	43512
(Township)	45865	Jefferson (Adams County)		Junction City	43748
Jackson (Brown County)		(Township)	45684	Junior Furnace	45629
(Township)	45697	Jefferson (Ashtabula		Justus	44662
Jackson (Champaign		County)	44047	Kalida	45853
County) (Township)	45389	Jefferson (Ashtabula		Kamms (Part of Cleveland)	44111
Jackson (Clermont County)		County) (Township)	44047	Kanauga	45631
(Township)	45145	Jefferson (Brown County)		Kansas	44841
Jackson (Coshocton		(Township)	45168	Karen Woods	45502
County) (Township)	43812	Jefferson (Clinton County)		Kay	45005
Jackson (Crawford County)		(Township)	45148	Keays (Part of Middletown)	45044
(Township)	44827	Jefferson (Coshocton		Keene	43828
Jackson (Darke County)		County) (Township)	43844	Keene (Township)	43828
(Township)	45390	Jefferson (Crawford County)		Keist Manor	43130
Jackson (Franklin County)		(Township)	44827	Keith	43724
(Township)	43123	Jefferson (Fairfield County)	43112	Kelleys Island	43438
Jackson (Guernsey County)		Jefferson (Fayette County)		Kellogg Corners	44410
(Township)	43723	(Township)	43128	Kelloggsville	44030
Jackson (Hancock County)		Jefferson (Franklin County)		Kemp	45806
(Township)	45814	(Township)	43004	Kendall Heights	44646
Jackson (Hardin County)		Jefferson (Greene County)		Kenmore (Part of Akron)	44314
(Township)	45843	(Township)	45335	Kennard	43009

	ZIP
Kennedy Heights (Part of Cincinnati)	45213
Kennonsburg	43773
Keno	45743
Kenridge (Part of Blue Ash)	45242
Kensington	44427
Kensington Park	45305
Kent	44240
Kenton	43326
Kenwood (Hamilton County)	45236
Kenwood (Harrison County)	43901
Kenwood (Lucas County)	43606
Kenwood Heights (Part of Springfield)	45505
Kenwood Knolls	45236
Kenwood Mall	45236
Kenwood Towne Center	45236
Kerr	45643
Kessler	45383
Kettering	45429
Kettlersville	45336
Key	43933
Kidron	44636
Kieferville	45831
Kilbourne	43032
Kile	43064
Kilgore	43988
Killbuck	44637
Killbuck (Township)	44637
Kilvert	45778
Kimball	44847
Kimberly	45764
Kimbolton	43749
Kingman	45177
King Mines	43755
Kings Corners	44904
Kings Creek	43078
Kingsdale Center (Part of Columbus)	43221
Kingsgate	45231
Kingsgate Mall (Part of Mansfield)	44901
Kings Mills	45034
Kingston (Delaware County) (Township)	43074
Kingston (Ross County)	45644
Kingsville	44048
Kingsville (Township)	44048
Kingsville On-the-Lake (Part of North Kingsville)	44068
Kingsway	43420
Kinnickinnick	45601
Kinsman (Township)	44428
Kinsman (Belmont County)	43950
Kinsman (Trumbull County)	44428
Kiousville	43143
Kipling	43750
Kipton	44049
Kirby	43330
Kirkersville	43033
Kirkpatrick	43302
Kirkwood (Belmont County) (Township)	43713
Kirkwood (Shelby County)	45365
Kirkwood Heights	43912
Kirtland	44094
Kirtland Hills	44060
Kitchen	45656
Kitts Hill	45645
Kiwanis Lake	44065
Klondike	44410
Knockemstiff	45601
Knollwood (Part of Beavercreek)	45432
Knollwood Village	43113
Knox (Columbiana County) (Township)	44634
Knox (Guernsey County) (Township)	43725
Knox (Holmes County) (Township)	44638
Knox (Jefferson County) (Township)	43964
Knox (Vinton County) (Township)	45710
Knoxville	43964
Kolmont	43938
Kossuth	45887
Kunkle	43531
Kyger	45620
La Belle View (Part of Steubenville)	43952
Lacarne	43439
La Croft	43920
Lafayette (Allen County)	45854
Lafayette (Coshocton County) (Township)	43845

	ZIP
Lafayette (Madison County)	43140
Lafayette (Medina County)	44256
Lafayette (Medina County) (Township)	44256
Lafferty	43951
Lagonda (Part of Springfield)	45503
Lagrange (Township)	44050
La Grange (Lawrence County)	45638
Lagrange (Lorain County)	44050
Laings	43752
Lake (Ashland County) (Township)	44628
Lake (Logan County) (Township)	43311
Lake (Stark County) (Township)	44720
Lake (Wood County) (Township)	43447
Lake Cable	44718
Lake Darby	43204
Lake Fork	44840
Lakeline	44094
Lake Lorelei	45118
Lake Lucerne	44022
Lake Milton	44429
Lakemore	44250
Lake of the Woods	43021
Lake O'Springs	44718
Lake Seneca	43543
Lakeside (Butler County)	45042
Lakeside (Fairfield County)	43046
Lakeside (Licking County)	43008
Lakeside (Ottawa County)	43440
Lakeside-Marblehead (Part of Marblehead)	43440
Lake Slagle	44720
Lake Sylvan	45369
Lake View (Knox County)	43019
Lakeview (Logan County)	43331
Lakeview Heights	45690
Lakeville (Ashtabula County)	44030
Lakeville (Holmes County)	44638
Lake Waynoka	45171
Lakewood	44107
Lakota Hills	45069
Lamira	43718
Lancaster	43130
Landeck	45833
Landen	45040
Langsville	45741
Lanier (Township)	45381
Lansing	43934
LaPorte	44035
Lapperel	45660
La Rue	43332
Latcha	43447
Latham	45646
Latimer	44428
Lattasburg	44287
Lattaville	45628
Latty	45855
Latty (Township)	45849
Laura	45337
Laurel (Clermont County)	45157
Laurel (Hocking County) (Township)	43149
Laurel Creek	44212
Laurel Ridge	44721
Laurelville	43135
Lawco Lake	45659
Lawndale (Part of Massillon)	44646
Lawrence (Lawrence County)	45659
Lawrence (Lawrence County) (Township)	45645
Lawrence (Stark County) (Township)	44614
Lawrence (Tuscarawas County) (Township)	44612
Lawrence (Washington County) (Township)	45750
Lawrenceville	45502
Lawshe	45660
Layhigh	45013
Layland	44637
Layman	45724
Leaper	45631
Leavittsburg	44430
Leavittsville	44614
Lebanon (Meigs County) (Township)	45770
Lebanon (Monroe County)	45745
Lebanon (Warren County)	45036
Lebanon Correctional Institution	45036

	ZIP
Lecta	45678
Lee (Athens County) (Township)	45710
Lee (Carroll County) (Township)	44615
Lee (Cuyahoga County)	44120
Lee (Monroe County) (Township)	43946
Leesburg (Highland County)	45135
Leesburg (Union County) (Township)	43040
Lees Creek	45138
Leesville (Carroll County)	44639
Leesville (Crawford County)	44827
Leetonia	44431
Lehmkuhl Landing	45865
Leipsic	45856
Leipsic Junction (Part of Leipsic)	45856
Leistville	43113
Lemert	44882
Lemon (Township)	45050
Lemoyne	43441
Lena	45317
Lenox	44047
Lenox (Township)	44047
Leo	45640
Leon	44003
Leonardsburg	43015
Lerado	45176
Leroy (Township)	44077
Le Sourdsville	45042
Lester	44256
Letart (Township)	45771
Letart Falls	45771
Levanna	45167
Lewis (Township)	45121
Lewis Addition	43952
Lewisburg	45338
Lewis Center	43035
Lewistown	43333
Lewisville	43754
Lexington (Township)	44601
Lexington (Richland County)	44904
Lexington (Stark County)	44601
Liberty (Adams County) (Township)	45693
Liberty (Butler County) (Township)	45011
Liberty (Clinton County) (Township)	45177
Liberty (Crawford County) (Township)	44881
Liberty (Darke County) (Township)	45352
Liberty (Delaware County) (Township)	43065
Liberty (Fairfield County) (Township)	43105
Liberty (Guernsey County) (Township)	43725
Liberty (Hancock County) (Township)	45840
Liberty (Hardin County) (Township)	45810
Liberty (Henry County) (Township)	43532
Liberty (Highland County) (Township)	45133
Liberty (Jackson County) (Township)	45640
Liberty (Knox County) (Township)	43050
Liberty (Licking County) (Township)	43031
Liberty (Logan County) (Township)	43357
Liberty (Mercer County) (Township)	45882
Liberty (Montgomery County)	45418
Liberty (Putnam County) (Township)	45856
Liberty (Ross County) (Township)	45647
Liberty (Seneca County) (Township)	44841
Liberty (Trumbull County) (Township)	44420
Liberty (Union County) (Township)	43040
Liberty (Van Wert County) (Township)	45891
Liberty (Washington County) (Township)	45745
Liberty (Wood County) (Township)	43462

	ZIP		ZIP		ZIP
Liberty Center	43532	London (Richland County)	44875	Macedonia	44056
Liberty Plaza	44505	London Correctional		McGill	45880
Lick (Township)	45640	Institution	43140	McGonigle	45013
Licking (Licking County)		Londonderry	43973	Mc Gough	43050
(Township)	43076	Londonderry (Township)	43973	McGuffey	45859
Licking (Muskingum		Londonderry	45647	McGuffey Heights (Part of	
County) (Township)	43830	Long	45331	Youngstown)	44505
Licking View	43701	Long Beach	43449	McIntyre	43910
Liebs Island	43046	Long Bottom	45743	Mack	45211
Lightsville	45362	Long Lake	44638	McKay	44842
Lilly Chapel	43140	Long Run	43917	McKean (Township)	43055
Lima	45801-07	Longs Crossing	44431	McKinley Heights	44446
For specific Lima Zip Codes call		Longstreth	45764	Mack North	45211
(419) 224-5801		Longview Heights (Part of		Macksburg	45746
Lima (Township)	43073	Athens)	45701	Mack South	45211
Limaville	44640	Longvue (Part of Marietta)	45750	Mackstown	43081
Lime City	43551	Loomis	43718	McLean (Township)	45845
Limecrest	45502	Lorain	44052-55	McLuney	43731
Limerick	45601	For specific Lorain Zip Codes call		McMorran	43311
Limestone	43432	(216) 244-4221		Macon	45697
Limestone City	45506	Loramie (Township)	45363	McZena	44638
Lincoln (Morrow County)		Lordstown	44481	Madeira	45243
(Township)	43321	Lore City	43755	Madison (Butler County)	
Lincoln (Richland County)	44905	Lostcreek (Township)	45312	(Township)	45042
Lincoln Heights (Hamilton		Lost Creek Addition	45804	Madison (Clark County)	
County)	45215	Lottridge	45723	(Township)	45368
Lincoln Heights (Jefferson		Louden (Adams County)	45660	Madison (Columbiana	
County)	43952	Louden (Tuscarawas		County) (Township)	43968
Lincoln Heights (Richland		County)	44622	Madison (Fairfield County)	
County)	44903	Loudon (Carroll County)		(Township)	43130
Lincoln Knolls Plaza (Part of		(Township)	44615	Madison (Fayette County)	
Youngstown)	44505	Loudon (Seneca County)		(Township)	43160
Lincoln Village	43228	(Township)	44830	Madison (Franklin County)	
Lindair Estates	45502	Loudonville	44842	(Township)	43125
Lindale	45102	Louisville (Adams County)	45660	Madison (Guernsey County)	
Lindentree	44656	Louisville (Stark County)	44641	(Township)	43773
Lindenwald (Part of		Loveland	45140	Madison (Hancock County)	
Hamilton)	45015	Loveland Park	45140	(Township)	45814
Lindsey	43442	Lovell	43351	Madison (Highland County)	
Lindsley-Gay	44003	Lowell	45744	(Township)	45123
Linndale	44111	Lowellville	44436	Madison (Jackson County)	
Linneman	45804	Lowellville Junction (Part of		(Township)	45656
Linnville (Lawrence County)	45696	Lowellville)	44436	Madison (Lake County)	44057
Linnville (Licking County)	43076	Lower Salem	45745	Madison (Lake County)	
Linton (Township)	43836	Loyal Oak (Part of Norton)	44203	(Township)	44057
Linwood (Part of Cincinnati)	45226	Lucas	44843	Madison (Licking County)	
Linworth	43085	Lucasburg	43723	(Township)	43055
Lippincotts	43078	Lucasville	45648	Madison (Montgomery	
Lisbon (Clark County)	45368	Lucerne	43019	County) (Township)	45426
Lisbon (Columbiana		Luckey	43443	Madison (Muskingum	
County)	44432	Ludington	43730	County) (Township)	43821
Lisman	45659	Ludlow (Township)	45734	Madison (Perry County)	
Litchfield	44253	Ludlow Falls	45339	(Township)	43760
Litchfield (Township)	44253	Lugbill Addition (Part of		Madison (Pickaway County)	
Lithopolis	43136	Archbold)	43502	(Township)	43103
Little Farms	43228	Lumberton	45177	Madison (Richland County)	
Little Hocking	45742	Luray	43025	(Township)	44903
Little Sandusky	43323	Lush Addition	43302	Madison (Sandusky County)	
Little Walnut	43113	Lykens	44818	(Township)	43435
Little Washington	44903	Lykens (Township)	44818	Madison (Scioto County)	
Little York	45414	Lyme (Township)	44811	(Township)	45653
Liverpool (Columbiana		Lynchburg (Columbiana		Madison (Vinton County)	
County) (Township)	43920	County)	44427	(Township)	45698
Liverpool (Medina County)		Lynchburg (Highland		Madison (Williams County)	
(Township)	44280	County)	45142	(Township)	43554
Livingston (Part of		Lyndhurst	44124	Madisonburg	44691
Columbus)	43227	Lyndhurst-Mayfield Heights		Madison Correctional	
Lloydsville	43950	(Part of Mayfield Heights)	44124	Institution	43140
Lock	43011	Lyndon	45681	Madison Hill	44691
Lockbourne	43137	Lynn (Township)	43326	Madison Lake Area	43140
Lockington	45356	Lynns Corners	44406	Madison Mills	43143
Lockland	45215	Lynx	45650	Madison-on-the-Lake	44057
Lock Two	45869	Lyons	43533	Madisonville (Part of	
Lockville	43112	Lyra	45694	Cincinnati)	45227
Lockwood	44450	Lytle	45068	Mad River (Champaign	
Lockwood Corners	44319	McArthur (Logan County)		County) (Township)	43083
Locust Corner	45245	(Township)	43324	Mad River (Clark County)	
Locust Grove (Adams		McArthur (Vinton County)	45651	(Township)	45324
County)	45660	McCance	44627	Mad River (Montgomery	
Locust Grove (Butler		Mc Cappin Mill	45133	County) (Township)	45424
County)	45042	McCartyville	45302	Magnetic Springs	43036
Locust Grove (Mahoning		McClainville	43906	Magnolia	44643
County)	44460	McClimansville	43143	Mahoning	44231
Locust Lake	45102	McClintocksburg	44444	Maineville	45039
Locust Point	43449	McClure	43534	Mainsville	43764
Locust Ridge	45176	McComb	45858	Malaga	43757
Lodi (Athens County)		McConnelsville	43756	Malaga (Township)	43757
(Township)	45735	McCracken Corners	44460	Malinta	43535
Lodi (Medina County)	44254	McCuneville	43782	Mallet Creek	44256
Logan (Auglaize County)		McCutchenville	44844	Malta	43758
(Township)	45887	McDermott	45652	Malta (Township)	43758
Logan (Hocking County)	43138	McDonald (Hardin County)		Malvern	44644
Logan Elm Village	43113	(Township)	43326	Manchester (Adams	
Logansville	43318	McDonald (Trumbull		County)	45144
Logtown	44432	County)	44437	Manchester (Adams	
Lombardsville	45652	McDonaldsville	44720	County) (Township)	45144
London (Madison County)	43140	Macedon	45828		

	ZIP
Manchester (Morgan County) (Township)	43756
Manchester (Summit County)	44216
Mandale	45827
Manhattan (Part of Steubenville)	43952
Mannhassett Village (Part of Mason)	45040
Mansfield	44901-07
For specific Mansfield Zip Codes call (419) 755-4621	
Mantua	44255
Mantua (Township)	44255
Mantua Center	44255
Mantua Corners	44255
Maple Corner	45385
Maple Grove (Geauga County)	44231
Maple Grove (Ross County)	45601
Maple Grove (Seneca County)	44883
Maple Heights (Cuyahoga County)	44137
Maple Heights (Noble County)	43724
Maple Lake	43944
Maple Park	45040
Maple Ridge	44601
Mapleshade (Part of Gallipolis)	45631
Mapleton	44730
Maple Valley (Part of Akron)	44320
Maplewood	45340
Marathon	45145
Marble Cliff	43212
Marble Furnace	45660
Marblehead	43440
Marchand	44720
Marcy	43110
Marengo	43334
Margaretta (Township)	44824
Maria Stein	45860
Mariemont	45227
Marietta	45750
Marietta (Township)	45750
Marion	43301-02
For specific Marion Zip Codes call (614) 389-4621	
Marion (Allen County) (Township)	45833
Marion (Clinton County) (Township)	45107
Marion (Fayette County) (Township)	43145
Marion (Hancock County) (Township)	45840
Marion (Hardin County) (Township)	45812
Marion (Henry County) (Township)	43524
Marion (Hocking County) (Township)	43138
Marion (Marion County) (Township)	43302
Marion (Mercer County) (Township)	45883
Marion (Morgan County) (Township)	43728
Marion (Noble County) (Township)	43788
Marion (Pike County) (Township)	45613
Marion Correctional Institution	43302
Marion East	43302
Mark (Township)	43556
Mark Center	43536
Marlain Acres	45231
Marlboro (Stark County) (Township)	44601
Marlboro (Delaware County) (Township)	43015
Marlboro	44601
Marne	43055
Marquis	44406
Marr	43789
Marseilles	43351
Marseilles (Township)	43351
Marshall	45133
Marshall (Township)	45133
Marshallville	44645
Martel	43335
Martin	43445
Martinsburg	43037
Martins Ferry	43935
Martinsville	45146

	ZIP
Mary Ann (Township)	43055
Marygrove	43558
Marysville	43040
Mason (Lawrence County) (Township)	45696
Mason (Warren County)	45040
Mason Heights (Part of Mason)	45040
Massie (Township)	45032
Massieville	45601
Massillon	44646-48
For specific Massillon Zip Codes call (216) 837-8323	
Massillon State Hospital	44646
Masury	44438
Matville	43146
Maud	45069
Maumee	43537
Maustown	45011
Maximo	44650
Maxville	43748
Mayfield (Butler County)	45044
Mayfield (Cuyahoga County)	44143
Mayfield Heights	44124
Mayflower Village (Part of Massillon)	44647
May Hill	45679
Maynard	43937
Maysville (Allen County)	45810
Maysville (Wayne County)	44606
Mead (Township)	43947
Meade	45644
Meadowbrook	43701
Meadowbrook Lake (Part of Stow)	44224
Meadow Lawn (Part of Middletown)	45044
Mecca	44410
Mecca (Township)	44410
Mechanic (Township)	43804
Mechanicsburg (Champaign County)	43044
Mechanicsburg (Crawford County)	44887
Mechanicsburg (Monroe County)	43793
Mechanicsburg (Wayne County)	44691
Mechanicstown	44651
Mechanicsville	44041
Medina	44256-58
For specific Medina Zip Codes call (216) 722-6511	
Medway	45341
Meeker	43302
Meigs (Adams County) (Township)	45660
Meigs (Morgan County)	43756
Meigs (Muskingum County) (Township)	43727
Meigsville (Township)	43756
Melbern	43506
Mellett Mall (Part of Canton)	44708
Melmore	44845
Melrose	45861
Melvin	45177
Memphis	45135
Mendon	45862
Mentor	44060-61
For specific Mentor Zip Codes call (216) 255-9724	
Mentor Headlands (Part of Mentor)	44060
Mentor-on-the-Lake	44060
Mercer	45862
Mercerville	45631
Mermill	43451
Mesopotamia	44439
Mesopotamia (Township)	44439
Metamora	43540
Metham	43844
Methodist Theological School of Ohio	43015
Metzger	45601
Mexico	44882
Meyers Lake	44730
Miami (Clermont County) (Township)	45147
Miami (Greene County) (Township)	45387
Miami (Hamilton County)	45041
Miami (Hamilton County) (Township)	45002
Miami (Logan County) (Township)	43343
Miami (Montgomery County) (Township)	45342

	ZIP
Miami Heights	45002
Miamisburg	45342-43
For specific Miamisburg Zip Codes call (513) 866-4551	
Miami Shores (Part of Moraine)	45439
Miamitown	45041
Miami Township (Part of Centerville)	45475
Miami University (Part of Oxford)	45056
Miami Valley Center Mall (Part of Piqua)	45356
Miami Villa (Part of Huber Heights)	45424
Miamiville	45147
Michael Manor	45371
Mid City (Part of Dayton)	45402
Middle Bass	43446
Middleboro	45152
Middlebourne	43773
Middlebranch	44652
Middleburg (Jefferson County)	43903
Middleburg (Logan County)	43336
Middleburg (Noble County)	43724
Middleburg Heights	44130
Middlebury (Knox County) (Township)	43019
Middlebury (Van Wert County)	45832
Middlefield	44062
Middlefield (Township)	44062
Middle Point	45863
Middleport	45760
Middleton (Columbiana County)	44408
Middleton (Columbiana County) (Township)	44455
Middleton (Jackson County)	45692
Middleton (Wood County) (Township)	43525
Middleton Corner	45385
Middletown (Butler and Warren County)	45042-44
For specific Middletown Zip Codes call (513) 422-6316	
Middletown (Champaign County)	43009
Middletown (Crawford County)	44833
Midland	45148
Midpark (Part of Parma Heights)	44130
Midtown (Part of Zanesville)	43701
Midvale	44653
Midway	43950
Midway Mall (Part of Elyria)	44035
Mifflin	44805
Mifflin (Ashland County) (Township)	44805
Mifflin (Franklin County) (Township)	43230
Mifflin (Pike County) (Township)	45646
Mifflin (Richland County) (Township)	44843
Mifflin (Wyandot County) (Township)	43351
Milan	44846
Milan (Township)	44846
Milford (Butler County) (Township)	45004
Milford (Clermont County)	45150
Milford (Defiance County) (Township)	43526
Milford (Knox County) (Township)	43011
Milford Center	43045
Mill (Township)	44683
Millbrook	44691
Millbury	43447
Mill Creek (Coshocton County) (Township)	44654
Millcreek (Union County) (Township)	43040
Mill Creek (Williams County) (Township)	43501
Milledgeville	43142
Miller (Knox County) (Township)	43050
Miller (Lawrence County)	45623
Miller City	45864
Millers	45383
Millersburg	44654
Millersport	43046
Miller Station	43976

	ZIP		ZIP		ZIP
Nelsonville	45764	New Petersburg	45123	Northeast (Part of	
Neptune	45822	New Philadelphia	44663	Columbus)	43231
Nettle Lake	43543	New Pittsburg	44691	North Eaton	44044
Nevada	44849	New Pittsburgh	44865	North Fairfield	44855
Neville	45156	New Plymouth	45654	North Feesburg	45130
New Albany (Franklin		New Plymouth Heights	45629	Northfield	44067
County)	43054	Newport (Township)	45768	Northfield Center	
New Albany (Mahoning		Newport (Madison County)	43140	(Township)	44067
County)	44460	Newport (Shelby County)	45845	Northfield Center	44067
New Alexander	44625	Newport (Tuscarawas		North Findlay	45840
New Alexandria	43938	County)	44683	North Fork Village	45601
New Antioch	45177	Newport (Washington		Northgate	45251
Newark	43055-58	County)	45768	North Georgetown	44665
For specific Newark Zip Codes		New Princeton	43844	North Greenfield	43358
call (614) 345-4021		New Reading	43783	North Hampton	45349
Newark Air Force Station	43057	New Richland	43310	North Hill (Part of Akron)	44310
New Athens	43981	New Richmond	45157	North Hills Estates	45224
New Baltimore (Hamilton		New Riegel	44853	North Houston	45333
County)	45030	New Rochester	43450	North Industry	44707
New Baltimore (Stark		New Rome	43228	North Jackson	44451
County)	44601	New Rumley	43984	North Kenova (Part of South	
New Bavaria	43548	New Salem	43148	Point)	45680
New Bedford	43804	New Salisbury	43930	North Kingsville	44068
Newberry (Township)	45318	New Somerset	43964	Northland (Part of	
New Bloomington	43341	New Springfield	44443	Columbus)	43229
New Boston	45662	New Stark	45897	Northland Mall (Part of	
New Bremen	45869	New Straitsville	43766	Columbus)	43229
New Buffalo	44406	New Strasburg	43102	North Lawrence	44666
Newburg (Part of Cleveland)	44105	Newton (Licking County)		North Lewisburg	43060
Newburgh Heights	44105	(Township)	43055	North Liberty	44822
New Burlington	45231	Newton (Miami County)		North Lima	44452
Newbury	44065	(Township)	45339	North Madison (Lake	
Newbury (Township)	44065	Newton (Muskingum		County)	44057
New California	43064	County) (Township)	43735	North Monroeville	44847
New Carlisle	45344	Newton (Pike County)		Northmoor	45315
Newcastle (Township)	43843	(Township)	45661	North Moreland (Part of	
New Castle	45638	Newton (Trumbull County)		Portsmouth)	45662
Newcastle (Coshocton		(Township)	44444	North Mount Vernon	43050
County)	43843	Newton Falls	44444	North Olmsted	44070
New Castle (Belmont		Newtonsville	45158	North Perry	44081
County)	43716	Newtown (Hamilton County)	45244	North Randall	44128
New Cleveland	45875	Newtown (Jefferson		North Richmond	44003
Newcomerstown	43832	County)	43917	Northridge (Clark County)	45502
New Concord	43762	Newtowne Mall (Part of		Northridge (Montgomery	
New Cumberland	44656	New Philadelphia)	44663	County)	45414
New Dover	43040	New Vienna	45159	North Ridgeville	44039
Newell	43941	Newville	44864	North Robinson	44856
Newell Run	45768	New Washington	44854	North Royalton	44133
New England	45778	New Waterford	44445	North Sagamore Heights	45236
Newfain	45660	New Weston	45348	North Salem	43749
New Floodwood	45764	New Westville	47374	North Side (Part of	
New Franklin	44657	New Winchester	44820	Youngstown)	44504
New Garden	44423	Ney	43549	North Star	45350
New Germany (Part of		Nicholsville	45106	North Towne Square Mall	
Beavercreek)	45431	Nile (Township)	45630	(Part of Toledo)	43612
New Guilford	43843	Niles	44446	North Uniontown	45133
New Hagerstown	44695	Nimishillen (Township)	44641	Northup	45658
New Hampshire	45870	Nimisila	44216	Northview	45322
New Harmony	45154	Nipgen	45612	Northwest (Franklin County)	43220
New Harrisburg	44615	Noble (Auglaize County)		Northwest (Williams County)	
New Harrison	45331	(Township)	45885	(Township)	43518
New Haven (Township)	44850	Noble (Cuyahoga County)	44132	Northwest Plaza (Part of	
New Haven (Hamilton		Noble (Defiance County)		Dayton)	45405
County)	45030	(Township)	43512	Northwood (Logan County)	43310
New Haven (Huron County)	44850	Noble (Noble County)		Northwood (Wood County)	43619
New Holland	43145	(Township)	43724	North Woodbury	44813
Newhope (Brown County)	45121	Normandy Heights	45015	North Zanesville	43701
New Hope (Preble County)	45320	Norris	45383	Norton (Delaware County)	43356
New Jasper (Township)	45385	North (Township)	43988	Norton (Summit County)	44203
New Jasper	45385	North Akron (Part of Akron)	44310	Norwalk	44857
New Jerusalem	43311	Northampton (Township)	44221	Norwalk (Township)	44857
New Knoxville	45871	North Auburn	44887	Norwich (Franklin County)	
New Lebanon	45345	North Baltimore	45872	(Township)	43026
New Lexington (Perry		North Bend	45052	Norwich (Huron County)	
County)	43764	North Benton (Mahoning		(Township)	44890
New Lexington (Preble		County)	44449	Norwich (Muskingum	
County)	45381	North Benton (Portage		County)	43767
New Liberty	44413	County)	44449	Norwood (Hamilton County)	45212
New London	44851	North Berne	43130	Norwood (Washington	
New London (Township)	44851	North Bloomfield (Morrow		County)	45750
New Lyme (Township)	44085	County) (Township)	44833	Norwood Heights (Part of	
New Lyme	44085	North Bloomfield (Trumbull		Cincinnati)	45212
New Madison	45346	County)	44450	Nottingham (Cuyahoga	
Newman (Stark County)	44646	North Brewster (Part of		County)	44110
New Market	45133	Brewster)	44613	Nottingham (Harrison	
New Market (Township)	45133	North Bristol	44402	County) (Township)	43907
Newmarket Station (Part of		Northbrook	45231	Nova	44859
Canton)	44702	North Canton	44720	Novelty	44072
New Marshfield	45766	North Clippinger (Part of		Oakdale (Athens County)	45732
New Martinsburg	45123	The Village of Indian Hill)	45243	Oakdale (Montgomery	
New Matamoras	45767	North College Hill	45239	County)	45429
New Miami	45011	North Condit	43074	Oakdale (Stark County)	44646
New Middletown	44442	North Creek	45831	Oakfield (Perry County)	43731
New Moorefield	45502	North Dayton (Darke		Oakfield (Trumbull County)	44450
New Moscow	43812	County)	45390	Oak Grove (Clark County)	45502
New Palestine	45157	North Dayton (Montgomery		Oak Grove (Washington	
New Paris	45347	County)	45404	County)	45750

	ZIP
Oak Harbor	43449
Oak Hill	45656
Oakland (Butler County)	45050
Oakland (Clinton County)	45177
Oakland (Fairfield County)	43102
Oakland Park	43224
Oakley (Part of Cincinnati)	45209
Oakmont	43920
Oak Park	43907
Oak Run (Township)	43143
Oak Shade	43567
Oakview	45805
Oakwood (Cuyahoga County)	44146
Oakwood (Montgomery County)	45419
Oakwood (Paulding County)	45873
Oberlin	44074
Oberlin Beach	44839
Obetz	43207
Oceola	44860
Oco	43950
O'Connor Landing	43310
Octa	43160
Ogden	45177
Ogontz	44814
Ohio (Clermont County) (Township)	45157
Ohio (Gallia County) (Township)	45623
Ohio (Monroe County) (Township)	43931
Ohio City	45874
Ohio Furnace	45638
Ohio Reformatory for Women	43040
Ohio Soldiers and Sailors Home	44870
Ohio State Reformatory	44901
Ohio State University Lima Branch	45804
Okeana	45053
Okolona	43550
Old Fort	44861
Old Gore	43138
Old Mill Creek	44212
Old Plymouth Heights	45629
Old Straitsville	43766
Oldtown	45385
Old Washington	43768
Old West End (Part of Toledo)	43610
Olena	44857
Olentangy	44820
Olive (Meigs County) (Township)	45743
Olive (Noble County) (Township)	43724
Olive Branch	45103
Olive Green (Delaware County)	43074
Olive Green (Noble County)	43724
Oliver (Township)	45693
Olivesburg	44805
Olivett	43713
Olmsted (Township)	44138
Olmsted Falls	44138
Olszeski	43917
Omega	45690
Oneida (Butler County)	45042
Oneida (Carroll County)	44644
Ontario	44862
Opperman	43732
Oran	45365
Orange (Ashland County) (Township)	44805
Orange (Carroll County) (Township)	44639
Orange (Coshocton County)	43832
Orange (Cuyahoga County)	44022
Orange (Delaware County) (Township)	43021
Orange (Hancock County) (Township)	45817
Orange (Meigs County) (Township)	45723
Orange (Shelby County) (Township)	45365
Orangeville	44453
Orbiston	45732
Orchard Beach	44089
Orchard Island	43331
Orchard Park Heights	44904
Oregon	43616
	43618

For specific Oregon Zip Codes call (419) 693-5033

	ZIP
Oregonia	45054
Oreville	43766
Orient	43146
Orient Correctional Institution	43146
Orland	45654
Orrville	44667
Orwell (Township)	44076
Orwell	44076
Osage	43964
Osgood	45351
Osnaburg (Township)	44730
Ostrander	43061
Otsego	43762
Ottawa	45875
Ottawa (Township)	45875
Ottawa Hills	43606
Otterbein	45036
Ottokee	43567
Ottoville	45876
Otway	45657
Outville	43062
Overlook	45431
Overlook Court	43906
Overlook Hills	43952
Overlook Homes	45431
Overlook-Page Manor	45431
Overpeck	45055
Over The Rhine (Part of Cincinnati)	45210
Overton	44691
Owens Hill	43701
Owensville	45160
Oxford	45056
Oxford (Butler County) (Township)	45056
Oxford (Coshocton County) (Township)	43845
Oxford (Delaware County) (Township)	43003
Oxford (Erie County) (Township)	44870
Oxford (Guernsey County) (Township)	43773
Oxford (Tuscarawas County) (Township)	43832
Ozark	43716
Padanaram	44003
Padua	45846
Page Manor	45431
Pagetown	43334
Pageville	45710
Painesville	44077
Painesville (Township)	44077
Painesville on the Lake	44077
Painesville Shopping Center (Part of Painesville)	44077
Paint (Fayette County) (Township)	43106
Paint (Highland County) (Township)	45612
Paint (Holmes County) (Township)	44690
Paint (Madison County) (Township)	43140
Paint (Ross County) (Township)	45612
Paint (Wayne County) (Township)	44659
Painters Creek	45304
Paintersville	45335
Paint Valley	44654
Palermo	44615
Palestine	45352
Palmer (Putnam County)	45831
Palmer (Washington County) (Township)	43787
Palmyra (Township)	44412
Palmyra (Knox County)	43019
Palmyra (Portage County)	44412
Palos	45732
Pancoastburg	43160
Pandora	45877
Pansy	45107
Paradise	44406
Paradise Hill	44805
Paris (Portage County) (Township)	44266
Paris (Stark County) (Township)	44669
Paris (Union County) (Township)	43040
Paris (Portage County)	44266
Paris (Stark County)	44669
Parkdale (Hamilton County)	45240
Parkdale (Jefferson County)	43952

	ZIP
Parkertown	44824
Park Layne (Clark County)	45344
Park Layne (Montgomery County)	45431
Parkman	44080
Parkman (Township)	44080
Park Place (Part of Wyoming)	45215
Park Ridge Acres	45506
Parkview (Part of Fairview Park)	44126
Parkview Heights	45224
Parlett	43907
Parma	44129
Parma Heights	44130
Parmatown Mall (Part of Parma)	44129
Parral	44622
Parrott	43160
Pasadena (Part of Kettering)	45429
Pasco	45365
Pataskala	43062
Patmos	44460
Patriot	45658
Patterson (Darke County) (Township)	45388
Patterson (Hardin County)	45843
Pattersonville	44657
Pattin Addition (Part of Marietta)	45750
Pattonville	45640
Paulding	45879
Paulding (Township)	45879
Paul Laurence Dunbar (Part of Dayton)	45417
Pavonia	44903
Pawnee	44254
Paxton (Township)	45612
Payne	45880
Peacock Acres	45502
Pearlbrook (Part of Cleveland)	44109
Pease (Township)	43935
Pebble (Township)	45690
Pedro	45659
Peebles	45660
Pee Pee (Township)	45690
Pekin (Carroll County)	44657
Pekin (Jefferson County)	43952
Pekin (Warren County)	45036
Pemberton	45353
Pemberville	43450
Penfield	44052
Penfield (Township)	44090
Peniel	45658
Peninsula	44264
Penn (Highland County) (Township)	45135
Penn (Morgan County) (Township)	43787
Pennsville	43787
Penn View	44003
Peoli	43832
Peoria (Butler County)	45056
Peoria (Union County)	43067
Pepper Pike	44124
Perintown	45150
Perkins (Township)	44870
Perry (Allen County) (Township)	45806
Perry (Ashland County) (Township)	44866
Perry (Brown County) (Township)	45118
Perry (Carroll County) (Township)	43988
Perry (Columbiana County) (Township)	44460
Perry (Coshocton County) (Township)	43843
Perry (Fayette County) (Township)	45135
Perry (Franklin County) (Township)	43017
Perry (Gallia County) (Township)	45658
Perry (Hocking County) (Township)	43135
Perry (Lake County)	44081
Perry (Lake County) (Township)	44081
Perry (Lawrence County) (Township)	45638
Perry (Licking County) (Township)	43055
Perry (Logan County) (Township)	43319

	ZIP
Perry (Monroe County) (Township)	43793
Perry (Montgomery County) (Township)	45309
Perry (Morrow County) (Township)	44904
Perry (Muskingum County) (Township)	43701
Perry (Pickaway County) (Township)	43145
Perry (Pike County) (Township)	45616
Perry (Putnam County) (Township)	45837
Perry (Richland County) (Township)	44813
Perry (Shelby County) (Township)	45353
Perry (Stark County) (Township)	44708
Perry (Tuscarawas County) (Township)	44699
Perry (Wood County) (Township)	44817
Perry Addition	45648
Perry Heights	44646
Perrysburg	43551-52
For specific Perrysburg Zip Codes call (419) 874-4440	
Perrysburg Heights	43551
Perrysville (Ashland County)	44864
Perrysville (Carroll County)	43988
Perryton	43822
Peru (Huron County)	44857
Peru (Huron County) (Township)	44847
Peru (Morrow County) (Township)	43334
Petersburg (Carroll County)	44615
Petersburg (Jackson County)	45640
Petersburg (Mahoning County)	44454
Petrea	45640
Petroleum	44438
Pettisville	43553
Pfeiffer Station	43326
Phalanx	44470
Pharisburg	43040
Phillippstown (Part of Columbus)	43201
Phillipsburg	45354
Philo	43771
Philothea	45828
Phoneton	45371
Pickaway (Township)	43113
Pickaway Correctional Institution	43146
Pickerington	43147
Pickrelltown	43357
Piedmont	43983
Pierce (Township)	45245
Pierpont	44082
Pierpont (Township)	44082
Pigeon Creek	44321
Pigeon Run	44646
Pike (Brown County) (Township)	45176
Pike (Clark County) (Township)	45502
Pike (Coshocton County) (Township)	43822
Pike (Fulton County) (Township)	43515
Pike (Knox County) (Township)	44822
Pike (Madison County) (Township)	43029
Pike (Perry County) (Township)	43764
Pike (Stark County) (Township)	44626
Piketon	45661
Pikeville	45331
Pine Grove	45638
Pinehurst	45750
Pine Valley (Part of Dillonvale)	43917
Piney Fork	43941
Pink	45630
Pinkerman	45682
Pioneer	43554
Piqua	45356
Piqua East Mall (Part of Piqua)	45356
Pisgah	45069
Pitchin	45502

	ZIP
Pitsburg	45358
Pitt (Township)	43323
Pittlime (Part of Norton)	44203
Pittsburgh Junction	43986
Pittsfield	44090
Pittsfield (Township)	44090
Placid Meadows	45238
Plain (Franklin County) (Township)	43081
Plain (Stark County) (Township)	44708
Plain (Wayne County) (Township)	44691
Plain (Wood County) (Township)	43402
Plain City	43064
Plainfield	43836
Plain View	43793
Plankton	44882
Planktown	44878
Plantation Acres	45224
Plants	45771
Plantsville	43728
Plattsburg	45368
Plattsville	45365
Playhouse Square (Part of Cleveland)	44115
Pleasant (Brown County) (Township)	45121
Pleasant (Clark County) (Township)	43010
Pleasant (Fairfield County) (Township)	43130
Pleasant (Franklin County) (Township)	43123
Pleasant (Hancock County) (Township)	45858
Pleasant (Hardin County) (Township)	43326
Pleasant (Henry County) (Township)	43527
Pleasant (Knox County) (Township)	43050
Pleasant (Logan County) (Township)	43318
Pleasant (Madison County) (Township)	43143
Pleasant (Marion County) (Township)	43302
Pleasant (Perry County) (Township)	43731
Pleasant (Putnam County) (Township)	45830
Pleasant (Seneca County) (Township)	44861
Pleasant (Van Wert County) (Township)	45891
Pleasant Bend	43548
Pleasant City	43772
Pleasant Corners	43123
Pleasant Grove (Belmont County)	43901
Pleasant Grove (Muskingum County)	43701
Pleasant Heights (Columbiana County)	43920
Pleasant Heights (Jefferson County)	43952
Pleasant Hill (Athens County)	45701
Pleasant Hill (Jefferson County)	43952
Pleasant Hill (Miami County)	45359
Pleasant Hills	45231
Pleasant Home	44287
Pleasant Lea	43130
Pleasant Plain	45162
Pleasant Ridge (Part of Cincinnati)	45213
Pleasant Run	45231
Pleasant Run Farms	45240
Pleasant Valley (Coshocton County)	43812
Pleasant Valley (Pike County)	45661
Pleasant Valley (Ross County)	45601
Pleasant Valley (Vinton County)	45601
Pleasant View (Fayette County)	43128
Pleasant View (Stark County)	44705
Pleasantville	43148
Plumwood	43140
Plymouth (Richland County) (Township)	44865

	ZIP
Plymouth (Ashtabula County) (Township)	44004
Plymouth (Ashtabula County)	44004
Plymouth (Richland County)	44865
Plymouth Center	44004
Poast Town	45042
Poetown	45130
Point (Part of Columbus)	43223
Point Isabel	45153
Point Place (Part of Toledo)	43611
Point Pleasant	45153
Point Rock	45710
Poland	44514
Poland (Township)	44514
Poland Center	44436
Polaris (Part of Columbus)	43240
Polk (Ashland County)	44866
Polk (Crawford County) (Township)	44833
Pomeroy	45769
Pond Run	45684
Poplargrove	45660
Portage (Wood County) (Township)	43451
Portage (Hancock County) (Township)	45872
Portage (Ottawa County) (Township)	43452
Portage	43451
Portage Lakes	44319
Port Clinton	43452
Porter (Delaware County) (Township)	43074
Porter (Gallia County)	45614
Porter (Scioto County) (Township)	45694
Porterfield	45714
Portersville	43730
Port Homer	43964
Port Jefferson	45360
Portland	45770
Portsmouth	45662-63
For specific Portsmouth Zip Codes call (614) 353-2070	
Port Union	45015
Port Washington	43837
Port William	45164
Possum Woods	45506
Post Town	45042
Post Town Heights	45042
Potsdam	45361
Pottery Additon	43952
Powell	43065
Powellsville	45629
Powhatan Point	43942
Prairie (Franklin County) (Township)	43119
Prairie (Holmes County) (Township)	44633
Prairie Meadows	43812
Pratts Fork	45776
Prattsville	45651
Prentiss	45856
Preston Addition	45648
Price Hill (Part of Cincinnati)	45205
Pricetown (Highland County)	45133
Pricetown (Trumbull County)	44429
Pride	45601
Princeton	45015
Proctor	44266
Proctorville	45669
Prospect	43342
Prospect (Township)	43342
Prout	44870
Providence (Township)	43504
Provident	43950
Provincial Point	45244
Public Square (Part of Cleveland)	44114
Pulaski	43506
Pulaski (Township)	43506
Pulaskiville	43338
Pulse	45118
Pultney (Township)	43906
Puritas Park (Part of Cleveland)	44135
Purity	43071
Pusheta (Township)	45895
Put-in-Bay	43456
Put-in-Bay (Township)	43456
Putnam Place (Part of Marietta)	45750
Pymatuning Shores	44003
Pyrmont	45309
Pyro	45656

	ZIP
Quaker City	43773
Qualey	45724
Queen Acres	45013
Quincy	43343
Raccoon (Township)	45685
Racine	45771
Radcliff	45670
Radford Road	45701
Radio Heights	43920
Radnor	43066
Radnor (Township)	43066
Ragersville	44681
Rainsboro	45165
Ra-Mar Estates	45502
Ramsey	43917
Ranchwood	44870
Randall Park (Part of North Randall)	44128
Randolph (Portage County) (Township)	44265
Randolph (Montgomery County) (Township)	45322
Randolph	44265
Range	43143
Range (Township)	43143
Ransom	45381
Rarden	45671
Rarden (Township)	45671
Rathbone (Delaware County)	43015
Rathbone (Washington County)	45750
Rathbone Heights (Part of Marietta)	45750
Ravenna	44266
Ravenna (Township)	44266
Ravenna Army Ammunition Plant	44266
Rawson	45881
Ray	45672
Rayland	43943
Raymond	43067
Rays Corners	44047
Reading (Columbiana County)	44634
Reading (Hamilton County)	45215
Reading (Perry County) (Township)	43783
Recovery (Township)	45846
Red Bank (Part of Fairfax)	45227
Redbird	44057
Redbush	45742
Red Coach Farm (Part of Centerville)	45429
Redfield	43764
Red Fox	44240
Redhaw	44866
Red Lion	45005
Redoak	45167
Red River	45308
Redtown	45732
Reed (Township)	44807
Reedsburg	44691
Reedsmills	43910
Reedsville	45772
Reedtown	44807
Reedurban	44710
Reese Station	43207
Reesville	45166
Reform	43055
Rehoboth	43764
Reily	45056
Reily (Township)	45056
Reinersville	43756
Reminderville	44202
Remington	45140
Remsen Corners	44256
Rendville	43730
Reno	45773
Reno Beach	43412
Rensselaer Park	45216
Republic	44867
Resaca	43140
Residence Park (Part of Dayton)	45417
Revenge	43130
Reynoldsburg	43068
Reynolds Corner (Part of Toledo)	43615
	43617
	43635
For specific Reynolds Corner Zip Codes call (419) 841-1375	
Rialto	45069
Rice (Putnam County)	45831
Rice (Sandusky County) (Township)	43420

	ZIP
Riceland	44667
Richfield (Summit County) (Township)	44286
Richfield (Henry County) (Township)	43516
Richfield (Lucas County) (Township)	43504
Richfield	44286
Richfield Center	43504
Richfield Heights (Part of Richfield)	44286
Rich Hill (Knox County)	43011
Rich Hill (Muskingum County) (Township)	43727
Richland (Allen County) (Township)	45817
Richland (Belmont County) (Township)	43950
Richland (Clinton County) (Township)	45169
Richland (Darke County) (Township)	45380
Richland (Defiance County) (Township)	43512
Richland (Fairfield County) (Township)	43150
Richland (Guernsey County) (Township)	43780
Richland (Holmes County) (Township)	44628
Richland (Logan County) (Township)	43310
Richland (Marion County) (Township)	43302
Richland (Montgomery County)	45431
Richland (Vinton County) (Township)	45651
Richland (Wyandot County) (Township)	43359
Richland Mall (Part of Ontario)	44906
Richmond (Ashtabula County) (Township)	44032
Richmond (Huron County) (Township)	44890
Richmond (Jefferson County)	43944
Richmond Center	44003
Richmond Dale	45673
Richmond Heights	44143
Richmond Mall (Part of Richmond Heights)	44143
Richville	44706
Richwood	43344
Rickard Acres	45005
Rickenbacker Air Force Base	43217
Ridge (Van Wert County) (Township)	45891
Ridge (Wyandot County) (Township)	43316
Ridgefield (Township)	44847
Ridgeland	45640
Ridgeton	44820
Ridgeville (Henry County) (Township)	43555
Ridgeville (Warren County)	45036
Ridgeville Corners	43555
Ridgeway	43345
Ridgewood (Allen County)	43701
Ridgewood (Muskingum County)	43821
Ridgewood Heights	45427
Rigrish	45662
Riley (Putnam County) (Township)	45877
Riley (Sandusky County) (Township)	43420
Rimer	45830
Rinard Mills	45734
Ringgold (Morgan County)	43758
Ringgold (Pickaway County)	43113
Rio Grande	45674
Ripley (Brown County)	45167
Ripley (Holmes County) (Township)	44676
Ripley (Huron County) (Township)	44837
Risingsun	43457
Rittman	44270
River Corners	44275
Riverdale	45661
Riveredge (Township)	44135
Riveredge	44135
Riverlea	43085

	ZIP
Riverside (Montgomery County)	45424
Riverside (Shelby County)	45365
Riverside Park	44683
River Styx	44256
Riverview (Belmont County)	43906
Riverview (Washington County)	45750
Rix Mills	43762
Roachester	45152
Roads	45640
Roaming Rock Shores	44085
Roaming Shores	44085
Roanoke	44683
Robertsville	44670
Robins	43723
Robtown	43103
Robyville	43901
Rochester	44090
Rochester (Township)	44090
Rochester Place (Part of Northwood)	43618
Rockbridge	43149
Rock Camp (Columbiana County)	44432
Rock Camp (Lawrence County)	45675
Rock Creek	44084
Rockdale	45015
Rockford	45882
Rockhill	43977
Rockland (Part of Belpre)	45714
Rock Mills	43160
Rockport	45830
Rock Way	45504
Rockwood (Erie County)	44824
Rockwood (Lawrence County)	45619
Rocky Fall Estates	45133
Rockyhill	45640
Rocky Point	45502
Rocky Ridge	43458
Rocky River	44116
Rodney	45631
Rogers	44455
Rokeby Lock	43756
Rolandus	45771
Rollersville	43431
Rolling Acres Mall (Part of Akron)	44322
Rolling Mill Park	45044
Rome	44085
Rome (Township)	45669
Rome	44878
Rome (Township)	44085
Rome (Athens County) (Township)	45723
Rome (Lawrence County)	45669
Rome Station	44085
Romohr Acres	45244
Rootstown (Township)	44272
Rootstown	44272
Rose (Township)	44643
Rosedale	43029
Rose Farm	43731
Rose Heights (Part of Steubenville)	43952
Rose Hill	45348
Roseland	44906
Roselawn (Part of Cincinnati)	45237
Roselms	45849
Rosemont	44451
Rosemount	45662
Roseville	43777
Rosewood	43070
Roslyn (Part of Kettering)	45429
Ross	45061
Ross (Butler County) (Township)	45061
Ross (Greene County) (Township)	43153
Ross (Jefferson County) (Township)	43944
Rossburg	45362
Rossford	43460
Rossmoyne	45236
Rossville (Part of Hamilton)	45013
Roswell	44663
Round Bottom	43915
Roundhead	43346
Roundhead (Township)	43346
Rousculp	45806
Rowsburg	44866
Roxabell	45628
Roxanna	45068

	ZIP
Roxbury	43787
Royalton (Fairfield County)	43130
Royalton (Fulton County)	
(Township)	43533
Royersville	45638
Rubyville	45662
Rudolph	43462
Ruggles	44837
Ruggles (Township)	44851
Ruggles Beach	44839
Rumley (Harrison County)	
(Township)	43986
Rumley (Shelby County)	45302
Rural	45120
Ruraldale	43720
Rush (Champaign County)	
(Township)	43084
Rush (Scioto County)	
(Township)	45652
Rush (Tuscarawas County)	
(Township)	44683
Rush Creek (Fairfield	
County) (Township)	43107
Rushcreek (Logan County)	
(Township)	43347
Rushmore	45844
Rush Run	43943
Rushsylvania	43347
Rushtown	45652
Rushville	43150
Russell (Geauga County)	
(Township)	44072
Russell (Highland County)	45133
Russell Center	44072
Russell Heights	43968
Russells	43701
Russells Point	43348
Russellville	45168
Russia (Lorain County)	
(Township)	44074
Russia (Shelby County)	45363
Rustic Hills	44256
Rutland	45775
Rutland (Township)	45775
Rye Beach (Part of Huron)	44839
Sabina	45169
Sagamore Hills	44067
Sagamore Hills (Township)	44067
Sahara Sands	44646
St. Albans (Township)	43062
St. Anthony	45846
St. Bernard	45217
St. Charles	45013
St. Clair (Butler County)	
(Township)	45011
St. Clair (Columbiana	
County) (Township)	43920
St. Clairsville	43950
St. Henry	45883
St. Joe	43906
St. Johns	45884
St. Joseph (Mercer County)	45846
St. Joseph (Portage	
County)	44201
St. Joseph (Williams	
County) (Township)	43517
St. Louisville	43071
St. Martin	45118
St. Marys	45885
St. Marys (Township)	45885
St. Paris	43072
St. Pauls	43103
St. Peters	45846
St. Rosa	45886
St. Sebastian	45826
St. Stephens	44807
St. Wendelin	45883
Salem (Auglaize County)	
(Township)	45887
Salem (Champaign County)	
(Township)	43078
Salem (Columbiana County)	44460
Salem (Columbiana County)	
(Township)	44431
Salem (Highland County)	
(Township)	45133
Salem (Jefferson County)	
(Township)	43944
Salem (Meigs County)	
(Township)	45741
Salem (Monroe County)	
(Township)	43915
Salem (Muskingum County)	
(Township)	43802
Salem (Ottawa County)	
(Township)	43449

	ZIP
Salem (Shelby County)	
(Township)	45365
Salem (Tuscarawas County)	
(Township)	43832
Salem (Warren County)	
(Township)	45152
Salem (Washington County)	
(Township)	45745
Salem (Wyandot County)	
(Township)	43351
Salem Center	45741
Salem Heights	44460
Salesville	43778
Saline (Township)	43932
Salineville	43945
Salisbury (Township)	45769
Saltair	45106
Salt Creek (Hocking	
County) (Township)	43135
Salt Creek (Holmes County)	
(Township)	44660
Salt Creek (Muskingum	
County) (Township)	43727
Salt Creek (Pickaway	
County) (Township)	43113
Salt Creek (Wayne County)	
(Township)	44627
Saltillo	44777
Salt Lick (Township)	43782
Salt Rock (Township)	43337
Salt Run	43943
Samantha	45135
Sand Beach	43449
Sand Hill (Erie County)	44870
Sand Hill (Scioto County)	45694
Sand Hill (Washington	
County)	45773
Sand Ridge	45761
Sandrun	45764
Sandusky	44870-71
For specific Sandusky Zip Codes call (419) 626-5525	
Sandusky (Crawford	
County) (Township)	44887
Sandusky (Richland County)	
(Township)	44827
Sandusky (Sandusky	
County) (Township)	43420
Sandusky South	44870
Sandy (Stark County)	
(Township)	44688
Sandy (Tuscarawas County)	
(Township)	44656
Sandy Beach	45885
Sandy Springs	45684
Sandyville	44671
San Margherita	43204
Santa Fe	45895
Santoy	43730
Sarahsville	43779
Sardinia	45171
Sardis	43946
Savannah	44874
Saville Estates	45431
Savona	45331
Sawyerwood	44312
Saybrook	44004
Saybrook (Township)	44004
Saybrook-on-the-Lake	44004
Sayler Park (Part of	
Cincinnati)	45233
Sayre	43731
Scenic Hills	43162
Schauers Acres	45341
Schley	45768
Schoenbrunn	44663
Schooleys	45601
Schrader	45601
Schumm	45898
Scio	43988
Scioto (Delaware County)	
(Township)	43061
Scioto (Jackson County)	
(Township)	45640
Scioto (Pickaway County)	
(Township)	43103
Scioto (Pike County)	
(Township)	45687
Scioto (Ross County)	
(Township)	45601
Sciotodale	45662
Scioto Furnace	45677
Sciotoville (Part of	
Portsmouth)	45662
Scipio (Butler County)	45053
Scipio (Meigs County)	
(Township)	45710

	ZIP
Scipio (Seneca County)	
(Township)	44867
Scotch Ridge	43450
Scott (Adams County)	
(Township)	45679
Scott (Brown County)	
(Township)	45121
Scott (Marion County)	
(Township)	43302
Scott (Sandusky County)	
(Township)	43435
Scott (Van Wert County)	45886
Scottown	45678
Scotts Crossing	45833
Scotty's Beauty Beach	45822
Scroggsfield	44615
Scrub Ridge	45616
Seal (Pike County)	
(Township)	45661
Seal (Wyandot County)	44849
Seaman	45679
Seasons Four	45140
Sebring	44672
Secedar Corners	44425
Sedalia	43151
Sedamsville (Part of	
Cincinnati)	45238
Seilcrest Acres	45140
Sellers Point	43046
Selma	45368
Seneca (Monroe County)	
(Township)	43754
Seneca (Noble County)	
(Township)	43779
Seneca (Seneca County)	
(Township)	44853
Senecaville	43780
Senior	45152
Sentinel	44032
Seven Hills (Cuyahoga	
County)	44131
Seven Hills (Hamilton	
County)	45231
Seven Mile	45062
Seventeen	44629
Severance Center (Part of	
Cleveland Heights)	44118
Seville	44273
Seward	43533
Sewellsville	43713
Shade	45776
Shademore	45244
Shadeville	43137
Shady Bend	43832
Shady Glen	43964
Shady Grove	45324
Shadyside (Belmont	
County)	43947
Shadyside (Columbiana	
County)	43920
Shaker Crossing (Part of	
Kettering)	45429
Shaker Heights	44120
Shalersville (Township)	44266
Shalersville	44255
Shandon	45063
Shane	43944
Shanesville (Part of	
Sugarcreek)	44681
Shannon	43821
Sharon (Franklin County)	
(Township)	43085
Sharon (Medina County)	
(Township)	44274
Sharon (Noble County)	43724
Sharon (Noble County)	
(Township)	43724
Sharon (Richland County)	
(Township)	44875
Sharon Center	44274
Sharon Hills	43085
Sharon Park (Allen County)	45805
Sharon Park (Butler County)	45013
Sharonville	45241
	45262
For specific Sharonville Zip Codes call (513) 563-6850	
Sharon West	44438
Sharpeye	45331
Sharpsburg	45777
Shartz Road	45005
Shauck	43349
Shawnee (Allen County)	
(Township)	45805
Shawnee (Perry County)	43782
Shawnee Hills (Delaware	
County)	43065

	ZIP
Stokes (Logan County) (Township)	43331
Stokes (Madison County) (Township)	43153
Stone	43720
Stone Creek	43840
Stonelick (Township)	45103
Stonelick	45103
Stony Lake	44615
Stony Prairie	43420
Stony Ridge	43463
Stonyrill	45005
Storms	45612
Stout	45684
Stoutsville	43154
Stovertown	43701
Stow	44224
Strasburg	44680
Stratford	43015
Stratton	43961
Streetsboro	44241
Stringtown (Athens County)	45701
Stringtown (Brown County)	45167
Stringtown (Clermont County)	45120
Stringtown (Muskingum County)	43701
Stringtown (Perry County)	43731
Strongs Ridge	44811
Strongsville	44136
Struthers	44471
Stryker	43557
Stuart Manor	43952
Suffield (Township)	44260
Suffield	44260
Sugar Bush Knolls	44240
Sugar Creek (Allen County) (Township)	45807
Sugar Creek (Athens County)	45701
Sugar Creek (Greene County) (Township)	45305
Sugar Creek (Putnam County) (Township)	45830
Sugar Creek (Stark County) (Township)	44662
Sugar Creek (Wayne County) (Township)	44618
Sugarcreek (Tuscarawas County)	44681
Sugarcreek (Tuscarawas County) (Township)	44681
Sugar Grove (Crawford County)	44820
Sugar Grove (Fairfield County)	43155
Sugar Grove (Jefferson County)	43964
Sugar Grove (Miami County)	45318
Sugar Grove (Scioto County)	45663
Sugar Grove Hill	45506
Sugar Ridge	43402
Sugar Tree Ridge	45133
Sugar Valley	45320
Sullivan	44880
Sullivan (Township)	44880
Sulphurgrove (Part of Huber Heights)	45424
Sulphur Springs (Crawford County)	44881
Sulphur Springs (Perry County)	43782
Summerfield	43788
Summerford	43140
Summerside	45244
Summerside Estates	45244
Summersville	43067
Summit (Hamilton County)	45238
Summit (Township)	43754
Summit (Ross County)	45601
Summit (Trumbull County)	44420
Summithill (Ross County)	45601
Summit Mall (Part of Fairlawn)	44333
Summit Station	43073
Summitville	43962
Sumner	45720
Sunbury (Delaware County)	43074
Sunbury (Montgomery County)	45327
Sundale	43767
Sunfish (Township)	45661
Sunny Acres	43952
Sunnyland	45502
Sunny Meade	43725

	ZIP
Sunnyside Beach (Part of Vermilion)	44089
Sunsbury (Township)	43716
Sunset Beach	44429
Sunset Heights	43912
Sunset Point	44077
Sunshine	45684
Sunshine Park	43952
Sun Valley Estates	45505
Superior (Township)	43543
Surrey Hill	44484
Sutton (Township)	45771
Swan (Township)	45622
Swan Creek (Township)	43558
Swanders	45369
Swanktown	45309
Swanton (Fulton County)	43558
Swanton (Lucas County) (Township)	43558
Swickards Additions	43952
Swifton Commons (Part of Cincinnati)	45237
Switzerland (Township)	43942
Sybene	45680
Sycamore (Hamilton County) (Township)	45242
Sycamore (Wyandot County) (Township)	44882
Sycamore	44882
Sycamore Valley	43789
Sychar Road	43050
Sylvania (Township)	43560
Sylvania	43560
Symmes (Butler County)	45014
Symmes (Hamilton County) (Township)	45242
Symmes (Lawrence County) (Township)	45688
Syracuse	45779
Taborville	44022
Tacoma	43713
Taft	45236
Tallmadge	44278
Tama	45822
Tarlton	43156
Tate (Township)	45106
Tatmans	43730
Tawawa	43365
Taylor (Franklin County)	43230
Taylor (Union County) (Township)	43344
Taylor Creek (Township)	43326
Taylorsburg	45315
Taylors Creek	45239
Taylorsville	45133
Taylortown (Jefferson County)	43964
Taylortown (Richland County)	44875
Tedrow	43567
Teegarden	44432
Temperanceville	43713
Ten Hills	45805
Tennyson	45661
Terrace Park	45174
Terre Haute	43078
Terry Acres	45324
Texas (Crawford County) (Township)	44882
Texas (Henry County)	43532
Thackery	43078
Thatcher	43113
The Avenue	44438
The Bend	43512
The Eastern	43908
Thelma City	44601
The Plains	45780
The Village of Indian Hill	45243
Thompson (Delaware County) (Township)	43066
Thompson (Geauga County) (Township)	44086
Thompson	44086
Thompson (Seneca County) (Township)	44828
Thorn (Township)	43076
Thornville	43076
Thorny Acres	45042
Three Locks	45601
Thrifton	45123
Thurman	45685
Thurston	43157
Tiffany Acres	45502
Tiffin (Adams County) (Township)	45693
Tiffin (Defiance County) (Township)	43512

	ZIP
Tiffin (Seneca County)	44883
Tiltonsville	43963
Timberlake	44094
Timberview	43040
Tinny	43435
Tipp City	45371
Tippecanoe	44699
Tipton	45851
Tiro	44887
Tiverton (Township)	43006
Tiverton	43006
Toboso	43055
Tod (Township)	44882
Todds	43728
Toledo	43460
	43601-15
For specific Toledo Zip Codes call (419) 245-6811	
Toledo Dock (Part of Oregon)	43618
Toledo Great Eastern Shopping Center (Part of Northwood)	43616
Toledo Miracle Mile Shopping Center (Part of Toledo)	43613
Tom Corwin	45692
Tomlison Addition	45648
Tontogany	43565
Torch	45781
Toronto	43964
Town and Country Estates	45429
Town and Country Shopping Center (Part of Whitehall)	43213
Townsend (Huron County) (Township)	44826
Townsend (Sandusky County) (Township)	43464
Townview	45427
Townwood	44856
Tradersville	43044
Trail	44624
Trail Run	43946
Tranquility	45679
Traschel	43302
Trebein (Part of Beavercreek)	45434
Tremont City	45372
Trenton (Butler County)	45067
Trenton (Delaware County) (Township)	43021
Triadelphia	43758
Tri-County Mall (Part of Springdale)	45246
Trimble	45782
Trimble (Township)	45782
Trinway	43842
Tri-Village (Part of Columbus)	43212
Trotwood	45426
Trowbridge	43432
Troy (Ashland County) (Township)	44859
Troy (Athens County) (Township)	45723
Troy (Delaware County) (Township)	43015
Troy (Geauga County) (Township)	44021
Troy (Miami County)	45373
Troy (Morrow County) (Township)	44901
Troy (Richland County) (Township)	44904
Troy (Wood County) (Township)	43443
Truetown	45761
Trumbull	44041
Trumbull (Township)	44041
Truro (Township)	43068
Truro	43068
Tuckaho	44003
Tucson	45601
Tully (Marion County) (Township)	43314
Tully (Van Wert County) (Township)	45832
Tunnel	45750
Tunnel Hill	43844
Tuppers Plains	45783
Turnpike Interchange	44444
Turpin Hills	45244
Turtle Creek (Shelby County) (Township)	45365
Turtle Creek (Warren County) (Township)	45036

	ZIP
Tuscalum (Part of Cincinnati)	45226
Tuscarawas (Coshocton County) (Township)	43812
Tuscarawas (Stark County) (Township)	44646
Tuscarawas (Tuscarawas County)	44682
Twain	44212
Twenty Mile Stand	45140
Twightwee	45140
Twin (Darke County) (Township)	45304
Twin (Preble County) (Township)	45381
Twin (Ross County) (Township)	45617
Twin Lakes (Allen County)	45804
Twin Lakes (Portage County)	44240
Twinsburg	44087
Twinsburg (Township)	44087
Twinsburg Heights	44087
Twin Valley	45662
Two Hundred Ten Row	45701
Tymochtee (Township)	44882
Tymochtee	43351
Tyndall	43812
Uhrichsville	44683
Union (Athens County)	45766
Union (Auglaize County) (Township)	45895
Union (Belmont County) (Township)	43759
Union (Brown County) (Township)	45167
Union (Butler County) (Township)	45069
Union (Carroll County) (Township)	44615
Union (Champaign County) (Township)	43009
Union (Clermont County) (Township)	45245
Union (Clinton County) (Township)	45177
Union (Fayette County) (Township)	43160
Union (Hancock County) (Township)	45881
Union (Highland County) (Township)	45133
Union (Knox County) (Township)	43014
Union (Lawrence County) (Township)	45619
Union (Licking County) (Township)	43025
Union (Logan County) (Township)	43311
Union (Madison County) (Township)	43140
Union (Mercer County) (Township)	45862
Union (Miami County) (Township)	45383
Union (Montgomery County)	45322
Union (Morgan County) (Township)	43758
Union (Muskingum County) (Township)	43762
Union (Pike County) (Township)	45648
Union (Putnam County) (Township)	45844
Union (Ross County) (Township)	45628
Union (Scioto County) (Township)	45652
Union (Tuscarawas County) (Township)	44621
Union (Union County) (Township)	43045
Union (Van Wert County) (Township)	45891
Union (Warren County) (Township)	45036
Union City	45390
Union Furnace	43158
Union Landing Siding	45638
Union Plains	45154
Unionport	43966
Union Station	43025
Uniontown (Belmont County)	43950
Uniontown (Stark County)	44685
Unionvale	43907

	ZIP
Unionville (Ashtabula County)	44088
Unionville (Morgan County)	43756
Unionville (Washington County)	45750
Unionville Center	43077
Uniopolis	45888
Unity (Township)	44413
Unity (Adams County)	45693
Unity (Columbiana County)	44413
University (Part of Columbus)	43210
University Center (Part of Cleveland)	44106
University Heights (Allen County)	45804
University Heights (Cuyahoga County)	44118
University View	43212
Upland Heights	43943
Upper (Township)	45645
Upper Arlington (Butler County)	45042
Upper Arlington (Franklin County)	43221
Upper Five Mile	45154
Upper Fox Hollow	45502
Upper Lowell	45744
Upper Sandusky	43351
Urbana	43078
Urbana (Township)	43078
Urbancrest	43123
Utica (Licking County)	43080
Utica (Warren County)	45036
Utopia	45121
Valley (Columbiana County)	44460
Valley (Guernsey County) (Township)	43772
Valley (Scioto County) (Township)	45648
Valley City	44280
Valley City Station	44280
Valley Crossing (Part of Columbus)	43207
Valleydale (Part of Cincinnati)	45216
Valley Forge	44212
Valley Glen	43938
Valley Hi	43360
Valley View (Cuyahoga County)	44131
Valleyview (Franklin County)	43204
Valley View (Jefferson County)	43910
Valley View (Scioto County)	45662
Valley View Estates	44403
Valley View Heights	45244
Valley View Village	43701
Valleywood (Part of Beavercreek)	45430
Vanatta	43055
Van Buren (Darke County) (Township)	45304
Van Buren (Hancock County)	45889
Van Buren (Hancock County) (Township)	45897
Vanburen (Licking County)	43055
Van Buren (Putnam County) (Township)	45856
Van Buren (Shelby County) (Township)	45336
Vandalia	45377
Vanlue	45890
Van Wert	45891
Vaughan (Part of Evendale)	45241
Vaughnsville	45893
Vega	45685
Venedocia	45894
Venice (Erie County)	44870
Venice (Seneca County) (Township)	44807
Venice Heights	44484
Vera Cruz	45118
Vermilion (Township)	44089
Vermilion-on-the-Lake (Part of Vermilion)	44089
Vermillion (Township)	44805
Vernon (Trumbull County) (Township)	44428
Vernon (Clinton County) (Township)	45113
Vernon (Crawford County) (Township)	44827
Vernon (Lawrence County)	45659
Vernon (Richland County)	44875

	ZIP
Vernon (Scioto County) (Township)	45694
Vernon (Trumbull County)	44428
Vernon Heights (Part of Marion)	43302
Verona	45378
Versailles	45380
Vesuvius	45659
Veterans Administration (military housing)	45428
Veterans Administration Medical Center	45601
Veto	45714
Vickery	43464
Vicksville	45732
Vienna	44473
Vienna (Township)	44473
Vienna Center	44473
Vigo	45601
Viking Village	45244
Villa	45503
Villa Nova	45885
Vincent (Lorain County)	44035
Vincent (Washington County)	45784
Vinton	45686
Vinton (Township)	45670
Violet (Township)	43147
Virginia (Township)	43811
Vo-Ash Lake	44615
Volunteer Bay	44089
Vore Ridge	45780
Wabash (Darke County) (Township)	45380
Wabash (Mercer County)	45822
Wacker Heights	43130
Waco	44707
Wade	45767
Wadsworth	44281
Wadsworth (Township)	44281
Waggoner Place	43551
Wagram	43062
Wahlsburg	45121
Wainwright (Jackson County)	45692
Wainwright (Tuscarawas County)	44663
Waite Hill	44094
Wakatomika	43821
Wakefield (Darke County)	45331
Wakefield (Pike County)	45687
Wakeman	44889
Wakeman (Township)	44889
Walbridge	43465
Waldo	43356
Waldo (Township)	43356
Walhonding (Coshocton County)	43843
Walhonding (Guernsey County)	43772
Wallace Heights	43964
Walnut (Fairfield County) (Township)	43046
Walnut (Gallia County) (Township)	45658
Walnut (Pickaway County) (Township)	43103
Walnut Creek	44687
Walnut Creek (Township)	44687
Walnut Grove	43358
Walnut Hills (Hamilton County)	45206
Walnut Hills (Jackson County)	45640
Walnut Hills (Stark County)	44646
Walnutrun	43140
Walton Hills	44146
Wamsley	45657
Wapakoneta	45895
Ward (Township)	43144
Wardwood Acres	45239
Warner	45745
Warnock	43967
Warren	44481-85
For specific Warren Zip Codes call (216) 392-1571	
Warren (Belmont County) (Township)	43713
Warren (Jefferson County) (Township)	43943
Warren (Trumbull County) (Township)	44430
Warren (Tuscarawas County) (Township)	44656
Warren (Washington County) (Township)	45750

	ZIP
Warren Correctional	
Institution	45036
Warrensburg	43061
Warrensville (Township)	44122
Warrensville Heights	44122
Warrenton	43943
Warsaw	43844
Warwick (Summit County)	44216
Warwick (Tuscarawas	
County) (Township)	44663
Washington (Auglaize	
County) (Township)	45871
Washington (Belmont	
County) (Township)	43716
Washington (Brown County)	
(Township)	45171
Washington (Carroll County)	
(Township)	44615
Washington (Clermont	
County) (Township)	45153
Washington (Clinton	
County) (Township)	45114
Washington (Columbiana	
County) (Township)	43945
Washington (Coshocton	
County) (Township)	43842
Washington (Darke County)	
(Township)	47390
Washington (Defiance	
County) (Township)	43549
Washington (Franklin	
County) (Township)	43017
Washington (Guernsey	
County) (Township)	43749
Washington (Hancock	
County) (Township)	45830
Washington (Hardin County)	
(Township)	45835
Washington (Harrison	
County) (Township)	44699
Washington (Henry County)	
(Township)	43532
Washington (Highland	
County) (Township)	45133
Washington (Hocking	
County) (Township)	43138
Washington (Holmes	
County) (Township)	44638
Washington (Jackson	
County) (Township)	45692
Washington (Lawrence	
County) (Township)	45656
Washington (Licking	
County) (Township)	43080
Washington (Logan County)	
(Township)	43348
Washington (Lucas County)	
(Township)	43612
Washington (Mercer	
County) (Township)	45828
Washington (Miami County)	
(Township)	45356
Washington (Monroe	
County) (Township)	45734
Washington (Montgomery	
County) (Township)	45459
Washington (Morrow	
County) (Township)	43338
Washington (Muskingum	
County) (Township)	43701
Washington (Paulding	
County) (Township)	45859
Washington (Pickaway	
County) (Township)	43113
Washington (Preble County)	
(Township)	45320
Washington (Richland	
County) (Township)	44906
Washington (Sandusky	
County) (Township)	43442
Washington (Scioto County)	
(Township)	45663
Washington (Shelby	
County) (Township)	45365
Washington (Stark County)	
(Township)	44601
Washington (Tuscarawas	
County) (Township)	43832
Washington (Union County)	
(Township)	43344
Washington (Van Wert	
County) (Township)	45833
Washington (Warren	
County) (Township)	45054
Washington (Wood County)	
(Township)	43565
Washington Court House	43160

	ZIP
Washingtonville	44490
Waterford (Township)	45786
Waterford (Knox County)	43019
Waterford (Washington	
County)	45786
Waterloo (Township)	45766
Waterloo (Fairfield County)	43110
Waterloo (Lawrence	
County)	45688
Watertown	45787
Watertown (Township)	45787
Waterville	43566
Waterville (Township)	43566
Watkins	43040
Wattsville	44615
Wauseon	43567
Waverly	45690
Waverly Gables	45690
Way	45734
Wayland	44285
Wayne (Ashtabula County)	
(Township)	44093
Wayne (Adams County)	
(Township)	45618
Wayne (Ashtabula County)	44093
Wayne (Auglaize County)	
(Township)	45896
Wayne (Belmont County)	
(Township)	43747
Wayne (Butler County)	
(Township)	45042
Wayne (Champaign County)	
(Township)	43009
Wayne (Clermont County)	
(Township)	45122
Wayne (Clinton County)	
(Township)	45138
Wayne (Columbiana	
County) (Township)	44432
Wayne (Darke County)	
(Township)	45380
Wayne (Fayette County)	
(Township)	45123
Wayne (Jefferson County)	
(Township)	43910
Wayne (Knox County)	
(Township)	43019
Wayne (Monroe County)	
(Township)	45734
Wayne (Muskingum County)	
(Township)	43701
Wayne (Noble County)	
(Township)	43773
Wayne (Pickaway County)	
(Township)	43113
Wayne (Tuscarawas	
County) (Township)	44624
Wayne (Warren County)	
(Township)	45068
Wayne (Wayne County)	
(Township)	44691
Wayne (Wood County)	43466
Wayne Lakes	45331
Waynesburg (Crawford	
County)	44887
Waynesburg (Stark County)	44688
Waynesfield	45896
Waynesville	45068
Weathersfield (Township)	44420
Weaver Station	45331
Webb Heights	43947
Webb Summit	43138
Webster (Darke County)	45309
Webster (Wood County)	
(Township)	43450
Wegee	43947
Welcome	44637
Weller (Township)	44903
Wellington	44090
Wellington (Township)	44090
Wellington Park	45231
Wellman	45068
Wells (Township)	43913
Wellston	45692
Wellsville	43968
Welshfield	44021
Welshtown	45769
Wengerlawn	45309
Wernert (Part of Toledo)	43613
Wesley (Township)	45713
Wesleyan Woods (Part of	
Delaware)	43015
West (Township)	44625
West Akron (Part of Akron)	44307
West Alexandria	45381
West Andover	44003
West Bass Lake	44024

	ZIP
West Bedford	43844
West Bellaire (Part of	
Bellaire)	43906
West Berlin	43015
Westboro	45148
West Brookfield (Part of	
Massillon)	44646
West Carlisle (Coshocton	
County)	43822
West Carlisle (Lorain	
County)	44035
West Carrollton City	45449
West Charleston	45371
West Chesapeake	45619
West Chester (Butler	
County)	45069
	45071
For specific West Chester Zip	
Codes call (513) 777-6262	
West Chester (Tuscarawas	
County)	44699
West Clarksfield	44889
West Covington	45318
West Elkton	45070
West End (Part of	
Ashtabula)	44004
West Enon Estates	45323
Westerly Park	45805
Western Hills	45238
Western Hills Plaza (Part of	
Cincinnati)	45211
Western Reserve Estates	44236
Westerville	43081-82
	43086
For specific Westerville Zip Codes	
call (614) 882-2243	
West Fairport (Part of	
Grand River)	44045
West Farmington	44491
Westfield (Morrow County)	
(Township)	43003
Westfield (Columbiana	
County)	43920
Westfield (Medina County)	
(Township)	44251
Westfield (Morrow County)	43003
Westfield Center	44251
West Florence	45320
Westgate Mall (Part of	
Fairview Park)	44126
Westgate Village (Part of	
Toledo)	43606
West Hill	44403
Westhope	43516
West Independence	44802
West Jefferson (Madison	
County)	43162
West Jefferson (Williams	
County)	43543
West Lafayette	43845
Westlake	44145
West Lakeville (Part of	
Conneaut)	44030
West Lancaster	43128
Westland (Township)	43725
West Lebanon	44618
West Leipsic	45856
West Liberty (Crawford	
County)	44887
West Liberty (Logan	
County)	43357
West Liberty (Morrow	
County)	43334
West Lodi	44811
West Logan	43138
West Manchester	45382
West Mansfield	43358
West Marietta (Part of	
Marietta)	45750
West Marysville (Part of	
Marysville)	43040
West Mecca	44410
West Middletown	45042
West Millgrove	43467
West Milton	45383
Westminster	45850
Westmoor	44833
West Newton	45850
Weston	43569
Weston (Township)	43569
West Park (Cuyahoga	
County)	44111
West Park (Hancock	
County)	45840
West Park (Jefferson	
County)	43952
West Park (Stark County)	44646

	ZIP		ZIP		ZIP
West Point (Columbiana County)	44492	Williamsfield	44093	Woodville (Sandusky County)	43469
West Point (Morrow County)	44833	Williamsfield (Township)	44093	Woodville Gardens	43616
West Portsmouth	45663	Williamsport (Columbiana County)	44432	Woodville Mall (Part of Northwood)	43619
West Richfield (Part of Richfield)	44286	Williamsport (Morrow County)	43338	Woodworth	44512
West Rushville	43163	Williamsport (Pickaway County)	43164	Woodworth Corners	44473
West Salem	44287	Williamstown	45897	Wooster	44691
West Side (Part of Youngstown)	44509	Williston	43468	Wooster (Township)	44691
West Sonora	45338	Willoughby	44094-95	Wooster Heights	44903
West Toledo (Part of Toledo)	43612	For specific Willoughby Zip Codes call (216) 942-9420		Worstville	45880
West Union	45693	Willoughby Hills	44092	Worthington (Franklin County)	43085
West Unity	43570	Willow (Part of Cleveland)	44127	Worthington (Richland County) (Township)	44822
Westview	44028	Willow (Part of Cuyahoga Heights)	44125	Wren	45899
Westville (Champaign County)	43083	Willow Brook Heights	44721	Wright Brothers (Part of Oakwood)	45409
Westville (Columbiana County)	44609	Willowcrest	44452	Wright-Patterson Air Force Base	45433
Westville Lake	44609	Willowdale Lake	44720	Wrightsville (Adams County)	45144
West Warren (Part of Warren)	44485	Willowdell	45380	Wrightsville (Franklin County)	43123
West Wheeling	43906	Willow Grove	43906	Wrightview (Part of Fairborn)	45324
West Williamsfield	44093	Willowick	44094	Wyandot	44849
Westwood (Hamilton County)	45211	Willow Lakes	43701	Wyoming	45215
Westwood (Jefferson County)	43952	Willowville	45103	Wyoming Meadows	45231
Westwood (Wayne County)	44691	Willow Wood	45696	Xavier (Part of Cincinnati)	45207
Westwood Estates (Part of Steubenville)	43952	Wills (Township)	43755	Xenia	45385
West Woodville	45107	Wills Creek	43811	Xenia (Township)	45385
West Worthington	43234-35	Willshire	45898	Yale (Ottawa County)	43468
For specific West Worthington Zip Codes call (614) 793-8789		Willshire (Township)	45898	Yale (Portage County)	44411
		Wilmington	45177	Yankeeburg	45768
Wetzel	45863	Wilmot	44689	Yankee Hills	44403
Weymouth	44256	Wilshire	45122	Yankee Lake	44403
Wharton	43359	Wilshire Heights	45005	Yankeetown	45130
Wheat Ridge	45693	Wilson (Clinton County) (Township)	45169	Yatesville	43106
Wheelersburg	45694	Wilson (Monroe County)	43716	Yellowbud	45601
Wheeling (Belmont County) (Township)	43927	Wiltondale	45224	Yellow Creek (Columbiana County) (Township)	43968
Wheeling (Guernsey County) (Township)	43749	Winameg	43515	Yellow Creek (Jefferson County)	43968
Whetstone (Township)	44820	Winchester	45697	Yellow Springs	45387
Whigville	43788	Winchester (Township)	45697	Yellowtown	43731
Whipple	45788	Winchester	45640	Yelverton	43326
Whisler	45644	Windfall Heights	44256	Yoder	45806
White Cottage	43791	Windham	44288	York (Athens County) (Township)	45764
White Eyes (Township)	43824	Windham (Township)	44288	York (Belmont County) (Township)	43942
White Hall (Athens County)	45701	Windor Park (Part of Xenia)	45385	York (Darke County) (Township)	45380
Whitehall (Franklin County)	43213	Windsor (Ashtabula County)	44099	York (Fulton County) (Township)	43515
Whitehouse	43571	Windsor (Ashtabula County) (Township)	44099	York (Jefferson County)	43901
White Oak (Brown County)	45154	Windsor (Lawrence County) (Township)	45678	York (Medina County) (Township)	44256
Whiteoak (Fayette County)	43143	Windsor (Morgan County) (Township)	43787	York (Morgan County) (Township)	43731
White Oak (Hamilton County)	45239	Windsor (Richland County)	44903	York (Sandusky County) (Township)	44811
White Oak (Highland County) (Township)	45133	Windsor (Warren County)	45162	York (Tuscarawas County) (Township)	44663
White Oak East	45239	Windsor Mills	44099	York (Union County) (Township)	43067
White Oak Meadows	45239	Windy Acres	45502	York (Van Wert County) (Township)	45874
White Oaks (Part of Steubenville)	43952	Winesburg	44690	York Center	43067
White Oak Valley	45121	Winfield	44622	Yorkshire	45388
White Oak West	45239	Wingett Run	45789	Yorkshire Estates	43302
White Pond	44321	Wingston	43462	Yorkville	43971
White's Landing	43464	Winona	44493	Young Hickory	43732
White Sulphur	43061	Winterdale (Part of Wintersville)	43952	Youngs	45657
Whitetree (Part of Cincinnati)	45236	Winterhaven	45305	Youngs Corners	44256
Whitewater	45002	Winterset	43755	Youngstown	44501-15
Whitewater (Township)	45002	Wintersville	43952	For specific Youngstown Zip Codes call (216) 744-6805	
Whitfield	45342	Wintondale	45231		
Wick	44093	Winton Junction	45232	Youngsville	45679
Wickliffe (Lake County)	44092	Winton Place (Part of Cincinnati)	45216	Zahns Corners	45690
Wickliffe (Mahoning County)	44515	Winton Terrace (Part of Cincinnati)	45232	Zaleski	45698
Widowville	44805	Wisterman	45831	Zane (Township)	43336
Wiggonsville	45106	Withamsville	45245	Zane Addition	45601
Wightmans Grove	43420	Wolf	43832	Zanesfield	43360
Wilberforce	45384	Wolfhurst	43912	Zanesville	43701-02
Wildare	44410	Wolf Run	43970	For specific Zanesville Zip Codes call (614) 455-2802	
Wildbrook Acres	45231	Woodbourne	45459		
Wildwood (Part of Middletown)	45042	Woodbourne-Hyde Park	45429	Zenz City	45846
Wilgus	45696	Woodhaven	45005	Zimmer Estates	45431
Wilkesville	45695	Woodington	45331	Zimmerman (Part of Beavercreek)	45434
Wilkesville (Township)	45695	Woodlawn (Hamilton County)	45215	Ziontown	43076
Wilkins Corners	43055	Woodlawn (Miami County)	45373	Zoar (Tuscarawas County)	44697
Wilkshire Hills	44612	Woodlawn Village	45373	Zoar (Warren County)	45152
Willard	44890	Woodmere	44122	Zoarville	44656
Willetsville	45133	Woodridge Plaza (Part of Fairfield)	45014	Zone	43521
Williamsburg	45176	Woods	45056		
Williamsburg (Township)	45176	Woodsdale	45067		
Williams Center	43506	Woodsfield	43793		
Williams Corner	45103	Woodside	43406		
Williamsdale	45011	Woodstock	43084		
		Woodville (Township)	43469		
		Woodville (Clermont County)	45122		

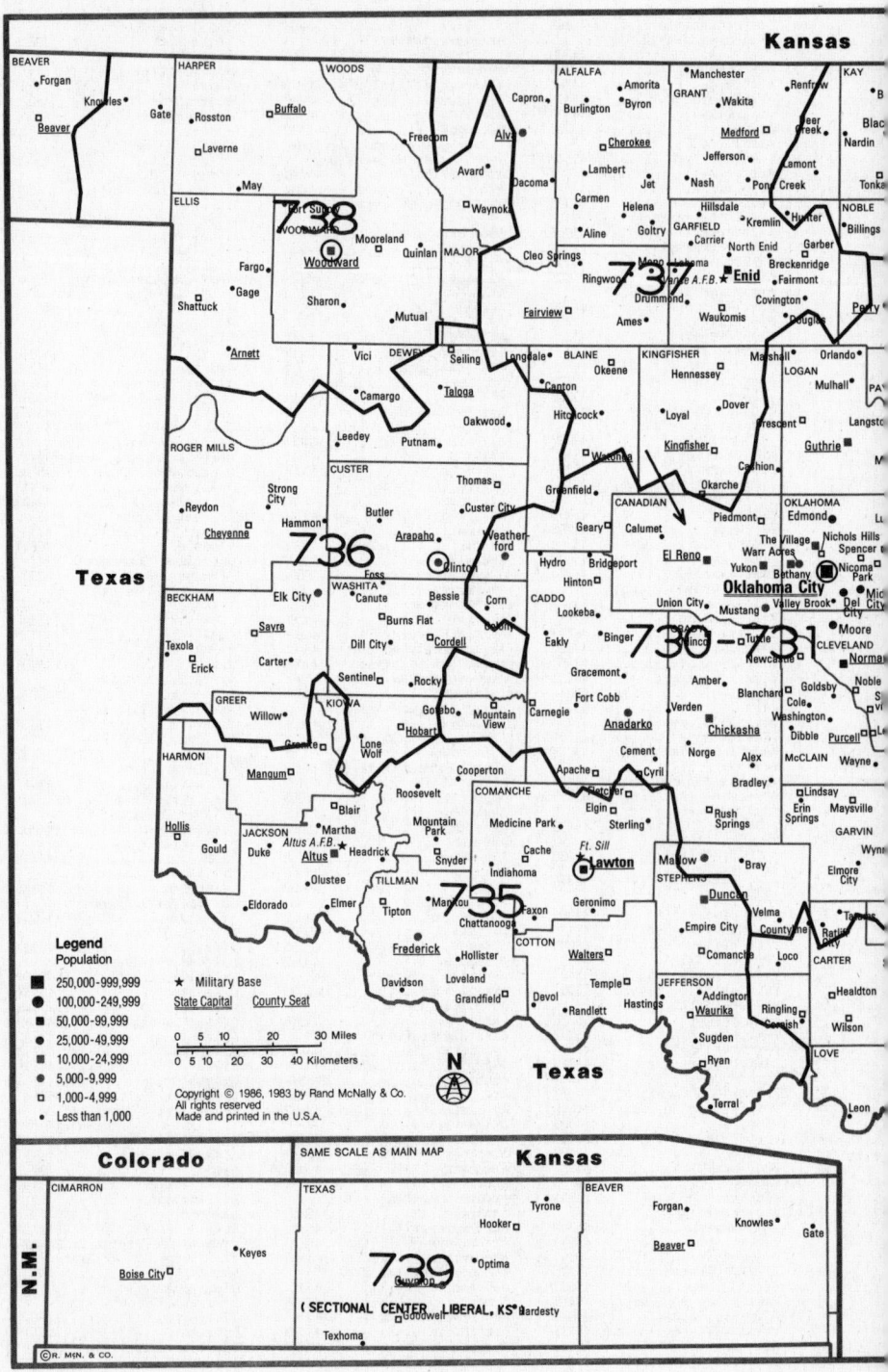

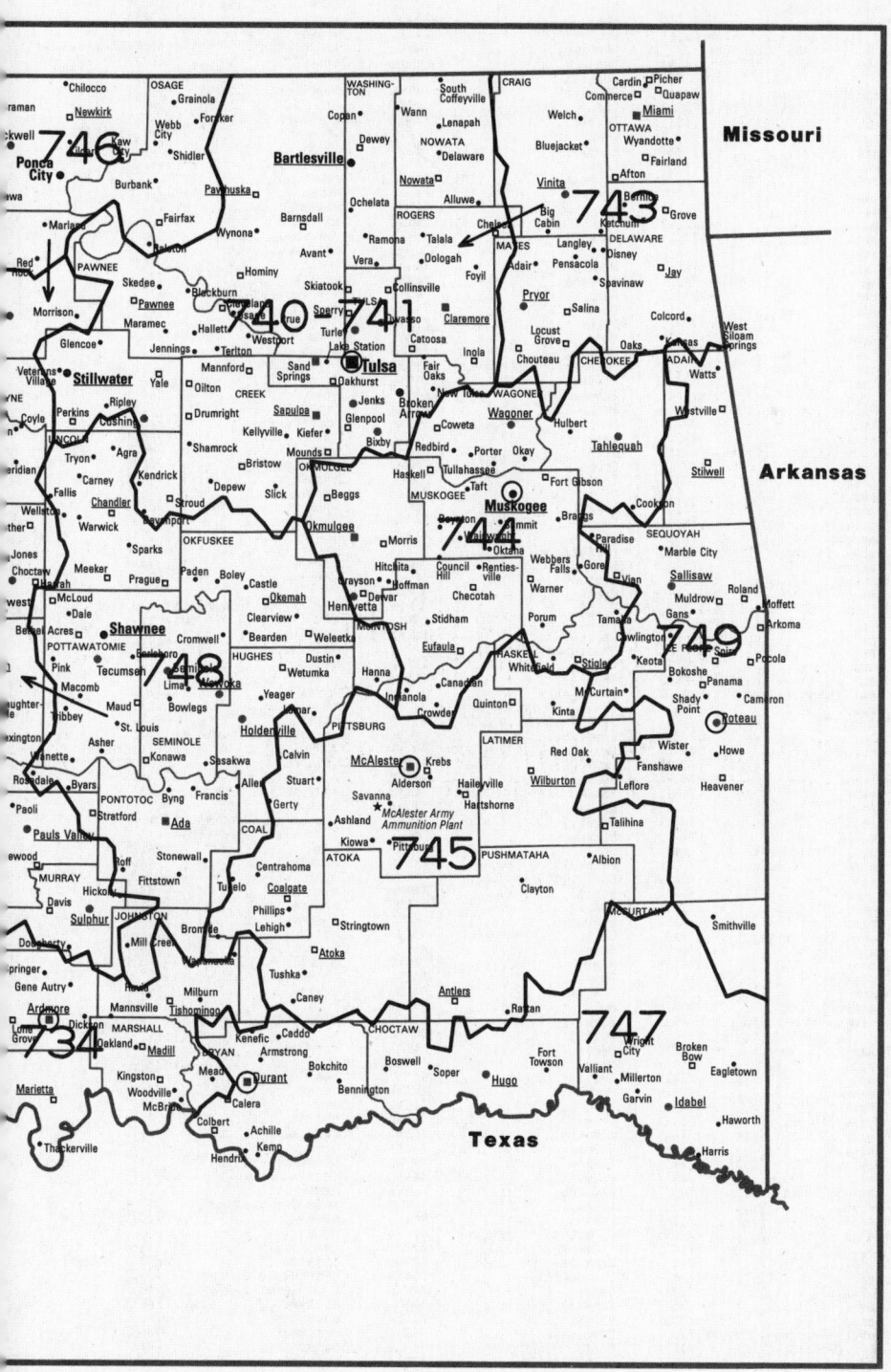

Name	ZIP	Name	ZIP	Name	ZIP
Achille	74720	Binger	73009	Carnegie	73015
Acme	73082	Bison	73720	Carney	74832
Ada	74820-21	Bixby	74008	Carpenter	73644
For specific Ada Zip Codes call (405) 332-6118		Blackburn	74058	Carriage Hills (Part of Lawton)	73501
Adair	74330	Blackgum	74962	Carrier	73727
Adams	73901	Blackwell	74631	Carson	74850
Adamson	74547	Blair	73526	Carter (Beckham County)	73627
Addington	73520	Blanchard	73010	Carter (Cherokee County)	74451
Afton	74331	Blanco	74528	Cartersville	74941
Agawam	73067	Blocker	74529	Cartwright	74731
Agra	74824	Blue	74701	Cashion	73016
Ahloso	74820	Bluejacket	74333	Castle	74833
Ahpeatone	73572	Bluff	74759	Catale	74332
Akins	74955	Boatman	74361	Catoosa	74015
Albany	74721	Boehler	74727	Cedar Crest	74352
Albert	73001	Boggy Depot	74525	Cedar Ridge (Part of Cleveland)	74020
Albion	74521	Bois D'Arc	74601	Cedar Valley	73044
Alderson	74522	Boise City	73933	Cement	73017
Aledo	73654	Bokchito	74726	Center	74820
Alex	73002	Bokhoma	74740	Center City (Part of Oklahoma City)	73102
Alfalfa	73015	Bokoshe	74930	Centerview	74801
Aline	73716	Boley	74829	Centrahoma	74534
Allen	74825	Bond	74426	Centralia	74301
Allison	74730	Boone	73006	Central Mall (Part of Lawton)	73501
Alluwe	74048	Boss	74745	Ceres	74651
Alma	73533	Boswell	74727	Cerrogordo	74740
Altus	73521-23	Boulevard (Part of Norman)	73069	Cestos	73859
For specific Altus Zip Codes call (405) 482-3339		Bowden	74107	Chandler	74834
Alva	73717	Bowlegs	74830	Chase	74401
Amber	73004	Bowlin Spring	74016	Chattanooga	73528
Ames	73718	Bowring	74009	Checotah	74426
Amorita	73719	Box	74962	Chelsea	74016
Anadarko	73005	Boynton	74422	Cherokee	73728
Antioch	73035	Braden	74959	Cherry Tree	74960
Antlers	74523	Bradley	73011	Chester	73838
Apache	73006	Brady	73098	Chewey	74964
Apperson	74633	Braggs	74423	Cheyenne	73628
Apple	74760	Braman	74632	Chickasha	73018, 73023
Arapaho	73620	Bray	73012	For specific Chickasha Zip Codes call (405) 224-1633	
Arcadia	73007	Breckenridge	73701		
Ardmore	73401-03	Brent	74955	Childers	74027
For specific Ardmore Zip Codes call (405) 223-8383		Briartown	74455	Chilli	74578
Arkoma	74901	Bridgeport	73047	Chilocco	74647
Arlington	74864	Briggs	74464	Chitwood	73067
Armstrong	74729	Brinkman	73673	Choctaw	73020
Arnett (Ellis County)	73832	Bristow	74010	Chouteau	74337
Arnett (Harmon County)	73550	Britton (Part of Oklahoma City)	73114	Christie	74965
Arpelar	74548	Brock	73401	Cimarron (Part of Oklahoma City)	73111
Artillery Village	73503	Broken Arrow	74011-14	Cimarron City	73028
Asher	74826	For specific Broken Arrow Zip Codes call (918) 258-6626		Cisco	74745
Ashland	74570	Broken Bow	74728	Citra	74825
Atoka	74525	Bromide	74530	Claremore	74017-18
Atwood	74827	Brooken	74462	For specific Claremore Zip Codes call (918) 341-0614	
Avant	74001	Brooksville	74873		
Avard	73717	Brown	74701	Clarita	74535
Avery	74023	Broxton	73006	Clarksville	74454
Bache	74526	Brush Hill	74426	Clayton	74536
Bacone (Part of Muskogee)		Brushy	74955	Clayton Lake	74536
Bailey	73055	Bryant	74880	Clear Lake	73849
Baker	73950	Buffalo (Harper County)	73834	Clearview	74835
Baldhill	74447	Buffalo (McCurtain County)	74963	Clebit	74728
Balko	73931	Bunch	74931	Clemscot	73437
Ballard	74964	Burbank	74633	Cleora	74331
Banner (Part of El Reno)	73036	Burlington	73722	Cleo Springs	73729
Banty	74723	Burmah	73659	Cleveland	74020
Barber	74471	Burneyville	73430	Clinton	73601
Barnsdall	74002	Burns Flat	73624	Clothier (Part of Oklahoma City)	73160
Baron	74965	Burwell	74754	Cloud Chief	73632
Bartlesville	74003-06	Bushyhead	74016	Cloudy	74562
For specific Bartlesville Zip Codes call (918) 336-0947		Butler	73625	Clyde	73759
Battiest	74722	Butner	74884	Coalgate	74538
Baugh	74020	Byars	74831	Coalton	74437
Baum	73401	Byng	74820	Cobb	74701
Beachton	71945	Byron	73723	Cogar	73059
Bearden	74859	Cache	73527	Colbert	74733
Beaver	73932	Caddo	74729	Colcord	74338
Bee	74748	Cairo	74538	Cole	73010
Beggs	74421	Calera	74730	Coleman	73432
Beland	74401	Calhoun	74956	College (Part of Stillwater)	74074
Bell	74960	Calida	74020	Collinsville	74021
Bellemont	74864	Calumet	73014	Colony	73021
Belvin	74563	Calvin	74531	Comanche	73529
Belzoni	74523	Camargo	73835	Commerce	74339
Bengal	74966	Cambria	74578	Concho (Part of El Reno)	73022
Bennington	74723	Cameron	74932	Conner Correctional Center	74035
Bentley	74525	Cameron University (Part of Lawton)	73505	Connerville	74836
Berlin	73662	Camp Houston	73842	Conser	74937
Bernice	74331	Canadian	74425	Cookietown	73562
Bessie	73622	Caney	74533	Cookson	74427
Bethany	73008	Caney Ridge	74471	Cooperton	73564
Bethel (Comanche County)	73501	Canton	73724	Copan	74022
Bethel (McCurtain County)	74724	Canute	73626	Corbett	73051
Bethel Acres	74801	Capitol Hill (Part of Oklahoma City)	73109	Cordell	73632
Big Cabin	74332	Capron	73725	Corinne	74735
Big Cedar	74939	Cardin	74335		
Big Spring	74883	Carleton	73772		
Billings	74630	Carmen	73726		

	ZIP		ZIP		ZIP
Corn	73024	Edmond	73013	Gaar Corner	74820
Cornish	73456		73034	Gage	73843
Corum	73529		73083	Gans	74936
Cottonwood	74538	For specific Edmond Zip Codes		Garber	73738
Council Hill	74428	call (405) 341-1502		Garden Grove	74801
Countyline	73025	Edna	74010	Garland	74462
Courtney	73456	Eighty Ninth Street (Part of		Garvin	74736
Covington	73730	Oklahoma City)	73159	Gate	73844
Cowden	73632	Eldon	74464	Gay	74743
Coweta	74429	Eldorado	73537	Geary	73040
Cowlington	74941	Elgin	73538	Gene Autry	73436
Cox City	73082	Elk City	73644	Georgetown	74434
Coyle	73027		73648	Geronimo	73543
Cravens	74563	For specific Elk City Zip Codes		Gerty	74531
Crawford	73638	call (405) 225-0294		Gibson	74467
Creosote	74743	Elmer	73539	Gideon	74464
Crescent	73028	Elmore City	73035	Gilcrease (Part of Tulsa)	74127
Criner	73080	Elmwood	73932	Gilmore	74953
Cromwell	74837	El Reno	73036	Glencoe	74032
Crossroads Mall (Part of		Emerson Center	73572	Glendale	74940
Oklahoma City)	73149	Emet	73450	Glenpool	74033
Crowder	74430	Empire City	73533	Glover	74728
Crystal	74555	Empy	74020	Golden	74737
Crystal Lakes	73718	Enid	73701-06	Goldsby	73093
Cumberland	73446	For specific Enid Zip Codes call		Goltry	73739
Curchece	74020	(405) 237-4331		Goodland	74743
Curt's Shopping Center		Enos	73439	Goodwater	74740
(Part of Muskogee)	74401	Enterprise	74561	Goodwell	73939
Cushing	74023	Enville	73448	Gore	74435
Custer City	73639	Erick	73645	Gotebo	73041
Cyril	73029	Erin Springs	73052	Gould	73544
Dacoma	73731	Ethel	74523	Gowen	74545
Daisy	74540	Etowah	73068	Gracemont	73042
Dale	74838	Etta	74471	Grady	73569
Damon	74578	Eucha	74342	Graham	73437
Darwin	74523	Euchee Creek (Part of Sand		Grainola	74652
Davenport	74026	Springs)	74063	Grandfield	73546
Davidson	73530	Eufaula	74432	Grand Lake Towne	74301
Davis	73030	Eva	73939	Granite	73547
Dawson (Part of Tulsa)	74115	Ewing (Part of Clinton)	73601	Grant	74738
Deer Creek	74636	Fairfax	74637	Gray Horse	74637
Degnan	74578	Fairland	74343	Grayson	74437
Delaware	74027	Fairmont	73736	Greasy	74931
Del City	73115	Fair Oaks	74015	Greenfield	73043
Delhi	73662	Fairview	73737	Green Pastures (Part of	
Dempsey	73628	Falconhead	73430	Oklahoma City)	73084
Dennis	74301	Falfa	74571	Green Valley Estates	74962
Depew	74028	Fallis	74881	Greenville	73448
Depot	74501	Fame	74432	Greenwood	74523
Devol	73531	Fanshawe	74935	Griggs	73949
Dewar	74431	Fargo	73840	Grimes	73628
Dewey	74029	Farley (Part of Oklahoma		Grove	74344
Dibble	73031	City)	73107	Guthrie	73044
Dickson	73401	Farmers Hill	74736	Guymon	73942
Dighton	74437	Farris	74542	Haileyville	74546
Dillard	73463	Faxon	73540	Hall Addition (Part of Sand	
Dill City	73641	Fay	73646	Springs)	74063
Disney	74340	Featherston	74561	Hallett	74034
Dixon	74884	Federal Correctional		Hall Park	73069
Donaldson (Part of Tulsa)	74104	Institution	73036	Hammon	73650
Dotyville	74354	Felker	74764	Hanna	74845
Dougherty	73032	Felt	73937	Hanson	74955
Douglas	73733	Fillmore	73432	Happyland	74820
Dover	73734	Finley	74543	Harden City	74871
Dow	74501	First National Bank (Part of		Hardesty	73944
Doyle	73039	Oklahoma City)	73102	Harmon	73832
Drake	73086	Fisher (Part of Sand		Harrah	73045
Driftwood	73728	Springs)	74063	Harris	74740
Drumb	74578	Fittstown	74842	Harrison	74955
Drummond	73735	Fitzhugh	74843	Hartshorne	74547
Drumright	74030	Fletcher	73541	Haskell	74436
Duke	73532	Floris	73938	Hastings	73548
Dunbar	73448	Folsom	73432	Haw Creek	74939
Duncan	73533-34	Fontana Shopping Center		Hawley	73761
	73575	(Part of Tulsa)	74145	Haworth	74740
For specific Duncan Zip Codes		Foraker	74652	Hayward	73730
call (405) 255-7226		Forest Hill	74937	Haywood	74548
Dunjee Park (Part of		Forest Park	73121	Headrick	73549
Oklahoma City)	73084	Forgan	73938	Healdton	73438
Durant	74701-02	Forney	74743	Heavener	74937
For specific Durant Zip Codes call		Forrester	74937	Helena	73741
(405) 924-6464		Fort Cobb	73038	Hendrix	74741
Durham	73642	Fort Coffee	74959	Hennepin	73046
Durwood (Part of Dickson)	73401	Fort Gibson	74434	Hennessey	73742
Dustin	74839	Fort Reno (Part of El Reno)	73036	Henryetta	74437
Eagle City	73658	Fort Sill	73503	Heritage Hills	73507
Eagletown	74734	Fort Supply	73841	Heritage Park Mall (Part of	
Eakly	73033	Fort Towson	74735	Midwest City)	73110
Earl	73447	Foss	73647	Hess	73539
Earlsboro	74840	Foster	73039	Hester	73554
Eastborough	74014	Four Corners	74437	Hewitt (Part of Wilson)	73463
Eastern Oklahoma A&M		Fox	73435	Hext	73645
College	74578	Foyil	74031	Hickory	74865
Eastern State Hospital	74301	Francis	74844	Hicks Addition (Part of	
East Jessie	74871	Frederick	73542	Spencer)	73084
Eastland Mall (Part of Tulsa)	74114	Freedom	73842	Hill	74932
Eastside (Custer County)	73096	French Market (Part of		Hillsdale	73743
East Side (Washington		Oklahoma City)	73116	Hillsdale Free Will Baptist	
County)	74006	Friendship	73521	College	73160
Eddy	74643	Frisco	74871	Hill Top	74570
Edgewater Park	73006	Frogville	74743	Hinton	73047

	ZIP
Hissom Memorial Center ...	74063
Hitchcock	73744
Hitchita	74438
Hobart	73651
Hockerville	74363
Hodgen	74939
Hodge Podge (Part of Tulsa)	74105
Hoffman	74437
Holdenville	74848
Holley Creek	74728
Hollis	73550
Hollister	73551
Homer	74820
Homestead	73763
Hominy	74035
Honobia	74549
Hontubby	74937
Hooker	73945
Hoot Owl	74365
Hopeton	73746
Hough	73942
Howard C. McLeod Correctional Center	74542
Howe	74940
Hoyt	74440
Hugo	74743
Hulbert	74441
Hulen	73572
Humphreys	73521
Hunter	74640
Hyde Park (Part of Muskogee)	74401
Hydro	73048
Idabel	74745
Independence	74937
Indiahoma	73552
Indian Meadows	74464
Indianola	74442
Ingalls	74074
Ingersoll	73728
Inola	74036
Iona	73086
Iron Stob Corner	74736
Irving	73565
Isabella	73747
Jackson	74723
Jacktown	74855
Jamestown	74080
Jay	74346
Jefferson	73759
Jenks	74037
Jennings	74038
Jesse	74871
Jet	73749
Jimtown	73430
Joburn	74556
Joe Harp Correctional Center	73051
John H. Lilley Correctional Center	74829
Johnson	74801
Jollyville	73030
Jones	73049
Joy	73098
Juby's	74020
Jumbo	74557
Kansas	74347
Karen Park (Part of Midwest City)	73110
Katie	73035
Kaw City	74641
Keefeton	74401
Keetonville	74017
Kellond	74523
Kellyville (Creek County)	74039
Kellyville (Ottawa County)	74370
Kemp	74747
Kendrick	74079
Kenefic	74748
Kensington Center (Part of Tulsa)	74103
Kent	74759
Kenton	73946
Kenwood	74365
Keota	74941
Ketchum	74349
Keyes	73947
Kiamichi	74574
Kiefer	74041
Kildare	74601
Kingfisher	73750
Kingston	73439
Kinta	74552
Kiowa	74553
Knowles	73847
Konawa	74849
Kosoma	74557
Krebs	74554
Kremlin	73753
Kulli	74745

	ZIP
Kusa	74437
Lacey	73742
Lahoma	73754
Lake Aluma	73121
Lake Creek	73547
Lake Hiwasse	73007
Lake Humphreys	73055
Lakeside Village	73538
Lake Station (Part of Sand Springs)	74127
Lake Valley	73041
Lake West	74727
Lamar	74850
Lambert	73728
La Mesa (Part of Enid)	73701
Lamont	74643
Lane	74555
Langley	74350
Langston	73050
Lark	73439
Last Chance	74859
Latta	74820
Laverne	73848
Lawrence Creek	74044
Lawton	73501-07
For specific Lawton Zip Codes call (405) 353-1500	
Leach	74364
Leader	74825
Leander	74020
Lebanon	73440
Leedey	73654
Leflore	74942
Lehigh	74556
Leisure Square (Part of Tulsa)	74112
Lenapah	74042
Lenna	74432
Lenora	73667
Leon	73441
Leonard	74043
Lequire	74943
Leroy	74020
Lewisville	74552
Lexington	73051
Lexington Assessment and Recption Center	73051
Liberty (Bryan County)	74741
Liberty (Sequoyah County)	74948
Liberty (Tulsa County)	74101
Lighthouse (Part of Tulsa)	74136
Lima	74884
Limestone (Latimer County)	74578
Limestone (Rogers County)	74017
Lincolnville	74363
Lindsay	73052
Little	74668
Little Chief	74637
Little City	73446
Little Ponderosa	67901
Loco	73442
Locust Grove	74352
Logan	73849
Lona	74552
Lone Grove	73443
Lone Oak	74948
Lone Wolf	73655
Long	74948
Longdale	73755
Longtown	74561
Lookeba	73053
Lotsee	74063
Loveland	73553
Lovell	73028
Loving	74937
Loyal	73756
Lucien	73757
Lugert	73655
Lula	74825
Luther	73054
Lutie	74578
Lynn Addition	74056
Lyons	74960
McAlester	74501-02
For specific McAlester Zip Codes call (918) 423-4048	
McAlester Army Ammunition Plant	74501
MacArthur Park (Part of Lawton)	73507
McBride	73439
McCord	74637
McCurtain	74944
McKey	74962
Mack H. Alford Correctional Center	74569
McKiddyville	73051
McKnight	73550
McLain	74401
McLoud	74851
McMillan	73446

	ZIP
Macomb	74852
McWillie	73716
Madill	73446
Maguire (Part of Slaughterville)	73068
Manard	74434
Manchester	73758
Mangum	73554
Manitou	73555
Mannford	74044
Mannsville	73447
Maple	74948
Maramec	74045
Marble City	74945
Marietta	73448
Marland	74644
Marlow	73055
Marshall	73056
Martha	73556
Martin	74401
Mason	74859
Matoy	74729
Maud	74854
Maxwell	74820
May	73851
Mayfield	73656
May Ridge (Part of Oklahoma City)	73119
Maysville	73057
Mazie	74353
Mead	73449
Medford	73759
Medicine Park	73557
Meeker	74855
Meers	73558
Mehan	74074
Mellette	74432
Melvin	74441
Meno	73760
Meridian (Logan County)	73058
Meridian (Stephens County)	73529
Merritt	73644
Messer	74743
Miami	74354-55
For specific Miami Zip Codes call (918) 542-8235	
Micawber	74882
Middleberg	73010
Midlothian	74834
Midway	74538
Midwest City	73110
Milburn	73450
Milfay	74046
Mill Creek	74856
Miller	74557
Millerton	74750
Milo	73401
Milton	74944
Minco	73059
Moffett	74946
Monroe	74947
Montclair Addition (Part of Heavener)	74937
Moodys	74444
Moon	74740
Moore	73160
Mooreland	73852
Moorewood	73650
Morris	74445
Morrison	73061
Mound Grove	74764
Mounds	74047
Mountain Park	73559
Mountain View	73062
Mount Herman	74728
Mount Zion	74736
Moyers	74557
Mudsand	74759
Muldrow	74948
Mule Barn (Part of Cleveland)	74101
Mulhall	73063
Murphy	74352
Muse	74949
Muskogee	74401-03
For specific Muskogee Zip Codes call (918) 682-7832	
Mustang	73064
Mutual	73853
Nani-Chito	74957
Narcissa	74354
Nardin	74646
Nash	73761
Nashoba	74558
Natura	74421
Navina	73044
Nebo	73086
Needmore	73068
Neff	74953
Nelagony	74056

ZIP		ZIP		ZIP

Newalla (Part of Oklahoma
  City) 74857
Newcastle 73065
Newkirk 74647
New Liberty 73662
New Lima 74884
New Oberlin 74727
Newport 73401
New Tulsa 74429
Nichols Hills 73116
Nicoma Park 73066
Nicut 74948
Nida 74748
Ninnekah 73067
Noble 73068
Nobletown 74884
Non 74531
Norge 73018
Norman 73069-72
  For specific Norman Zip Codes
  call (405) 321-2484
Norris 74563
Northeast (Part of Tulsa) ... 74115
North Enid 73701
North McAlester (Part of
  McAlester) 74501
North Miami 74358
Northside (Part of Tulsa) ... 74106
Northwest (Part of
  Oklahoma City) 73106
Nowata 74048
Nuyaka 74447
Oak Grove (Murray County) 73032
Oak Grove (Pawnee
  County) 74020
Oak Grove (Payne County) 74030
Oak Hill 74728
Oakhurst 74050
Oakland 73446
Oakman 74820
Oak Park (Part of
  Bartlesville) 74003
Oaks 74359
Oakwood 73658
Oberlin 74727
Ochelata 74051
Octavia 74957
Oglesby 74061
Oil Center 74820
Oil City 73463
Oilton 74052
Okarche 73762
Okay 74446
Okeene 73763
Okemah 74859
Okesa 74003
Okfuskee 74859

Oklahoma City 73101-89
  For specific Oklahoma City Zip
  Codes call (405) 278-6122

COLLEGES & UNIVERSITIES

Oklahoma Christian College 73136
Oklahoma City University 73106
University of Oklahoma
  Health Sciences Center 73190

FINANCIAL INSTITUTIONS

Central Bank of Oklahoma
  City 73106
Bank of Oklahoma, National
  Association 73124
Boatman's First National
  Bank of Oklahoma 73102
The First National Bank of
  Midwest City 73110
First Western Federal
  Savings & Loan
  Association 73125
Founders Bank & Trust
  Company 73120
Friendly Bank of Oklahoma
  City 73159
Guaranty Bank & Trust Co. 73127
Liberty Bank and Trust
  Company of Oklahoma
  City, N.A. 73102
Local Federal Savings &
  Loan Association 73116
Midfirst Bank 73118
The Oklahoma Bank 73108

HOSPITALS

Baptist Medical Center of
  Oklahoma 73112
HCA Health of Oklahoma
  Inc.-D.B.A. Presbyterian
  Hospital 73104
Mercy Health Center 73120
South Community Hospital 73109

St. Anthony Hospital 73101
Veterans Affairs Medical
  Center 73104

HOTELS/MOTELS

Embassy Suites 73118
Hilton Inn Northwest 73112
Hilton Inn West 73108
Waterford Hotel 73118

MILITARY INSTALLATIONS

Oklahoma Air National
  Guard, FB6562, Will
  Rogers Airport 73179
Oklahoma City Air Force
  Material Command,
  Tinker Air Force Base ... 73145
United States Property and
  Fiscal Office for
  Oklahoma 73111

Oklahoma State Penitentiary 74501
Okmulgee 74447
Oktaha 74450
Oleta 74735
Olive 74030
Olney 74538
Olustee 73560
Omega 73764
Oneta 74012
Oologah 74053
Optima 73945
Ord 74738
Orienta 73737
Orlando 73073
Orr 73456
Osage 74054
Osage Hills Estates (Part of
  Sand Springs) 74063
Osage Indian Reservation 74056
Oscar 73561
Ouachita Correctional
  Center 74939
Overbrook 73453
Owasso 74055
Paden 74860
Page 74939
Panama 74951
Panola 74559
Paoli 73074
Paradise Hill 74955
Paradise View 74337
Park Hill 74451
Parkland 74824
Park Lane (Part of Lawton) 73501
Patterson 74578
Pauls Valley 73075
Pawhuska 74056
Pawnee 74058
Paw Paw 74948
Payne 73052
Payson 74855
Pearson 74826
Pearsonia 74056
Peckham 74647
Peggs 74452
Penn Square Mall (Part of
  Oklahoma City) 73118
Penn 89th (Part of
  Oklahoma City) 73159
Pensacola 74301
Peoria 74363
Perkins 74059
Pernell 73076
Perry 73077
Pershing 74002
Peterman Ridge 74020
Petersburg 73456
Petros 74937
Pettit 74451
Pettit Bay 74451
Pharoah 74862
Phillips 74538
Picher 74360
Pickens 74752
Pickett 74820
Piedmont 73078
Pierce 74426
Piney 74960
Pink 74873
Pin Oaks Acres 74337
Pittsburg 74560
Platter 74753
Pleasant Hill 74740
Plunkettville 74963
Pocasset 73079
Pocola 74902
Pollard 74740
Ponca City 74601-04
  For specific Ponca City Zip Codes
  call (405) 762-2485

Pond Creek 73766
Pontotoc 74863
Pooleville 73458
Porter 74454
Porter Hill 73538
Porum 74455
Poteau 74953
Powell 73439
Prague 74864
Prattville (Part of Sand
  Springs) 74063
Preston 74456
Proctor 74457
Prue 74060
Pruitt City 73081
Pryor 74361-62
  For specific Pryor Zip Codes call
  (918) 825-0912
Pumpkin Center (Comanche
  County) 73501
Pumpkin Center (Okmulgee
  County) 74445
Purcell 73080
Purdy 73052
Putnam 73659
Pyramid Corners 74333
Quail Creek (Part of
  Oklahoma City) 73120
Quail Springs Mall (Part of
  Oklahoma City) 73134
Qualls 74451
Quapaw 74363
Quay 74085
Quinlan 73852
Quinton 74561
Rabornville 74020
Raiford 74432
Ralston 74650
Ramona 74061
Ranchwood Manor (Part of
  Oklahoma City) 73160
Randlett 73562
Ratliff City 73081
Rattan 74562
Ravia 73455
Reagan 73460
Reck 73463
Redbird 74458
Red Hill 74941
Red Horse (Part of Midwest
  City) 73110
Redland 74948
Red Oak 74563
Red Rock 74651
Reed 73554
Regal (Part of Lawton) 73501
Reichert 74937
Remus 74801
Renfrow 73759
Rentiesville 74459
Retrop 73627
Reydon 73660
Rhea 73654
Richards Spur 73538
Richland 73099
Richville 74501
Rigsby 74020
Ringling 73456
Ringold 74754
Ringwood 73768
Ripley 74062
Roberta 74701
Rock Island 74932
Rocky 73661
Rocky Mountain 74960
Rocky Point 74467
Roff 74865
Roland 74954
Roll 73628
Roosevelt 73564
Rose 74364
Rosedale 74831
Rosston 73855
Rossville 74881
Rubottom 73463
Rufe 74755
Rush Springs 73082
Russell 73554
Russellville 74561
Russett 73447
Ryan 73565
Sacred Heart 74849
Sageeyah 74017
St. Louis 74866
Salem 74437
Salina 74365
Sallisaw 74955
Salt Fork 74640
Sams Point 74501
Sandbluff 74759
Sand Point 73449

	ZIP		ZIP		ZIP
Sand Springs	74063	Stigler	74462	Union (Tulsa County)	74012
Sansbois	74552	Stillwater	74074-76	Union City	73090
Sapulpa	74066-67	For specific Stillwater Zip Codes		Union Valley	74871
For specific Sapulpa Zip Codes		call (405) 377-3867		University (Garfield County)	73701
call (918) 224-0733		Stilwell	74960	University (Pottawatomie	
Sardis	74536	Stockyards (Part of		County)	74801
Sasakwa	74867	Oklahoma City)	73108	University of Science	
Savanna	74565	Stonebluff	74436	and Arts (Part of	
Sawyer	74756	Stonewall	74871	Chickasha)	73018
Sayre	73662	Stony Point (Adair County)	74960	Uptown Shopping Center	
Schulter	74460	Stony Point (Le Flore		(Part of Midwest City)	73110
Scipio	74501	County)	74959	Utica	74726
Scraper	74464	Story	73057	Utica Square (Part of Tulsa)	74152
Scullin	73086	Straight	73942	Valley Brook	73149
Scullyville	74959	Strang	74367	Valley Park	74017
Seiling	73663	Stratford	74872	Valliant	74764
Selman	73834	Stringtown	74569	Vamoosa	74849
Seminole	74818	Strong City	73628	Vance Air Force Base	73701
	74868	Stroud	74079	Vanoss	74820
For specific Seminole Zip Codes		Stuart	74570	Velma	73091
call (405) 382-0152		Sugden	73573	Vera	74082
Sentinel	73664	Sullivan Village (Part of		Verden	73092
Sequoyah	74017	Lawton)	73501	Verdigris	74017
Seward	73044	Sulphur	73086	Vernon	74845
Shady Grove (Pawnee		Summerfield	74966	Vian	74962
County)	74112	Summit	74401	Vici	73859
Shady Grove (Sequoyah		Sumner	73077	Victory	73560
County)	74954	Sungate (Part of Lawton)	73501	Village	73120
Shady Point	74956	Sunkist	74727	Vinco	74059
Shamrock	74068	Sunray	73529	Vinita	74301
Sharon	73857	Sweetwater	73666	Vinson	73571
Shartel (Part of Oklahoma		Swink	74761	Virgil	74756
City)	73118	Tabler	73018	Vista	74849
Sha-To-She	74020	Tablerville	74734	Vivian	74432
Shattuck	73858	Taft	74463	Wade	74723
Shawnee	74801-02	Tahlequah	74436-65	Wagoner	74467
For specific Shawnee Zip Codes		For specific Tahlequah Zip Codes			74477
call (405) 273-2204		call (918) 456-2381		For specific Wagoner Zip Codes	
Shay	73439	Tahona	74932	call (918) 485-2569	
Shepherd Mall (Part of		Tailholt	74471	Wainwright	74468
Oklahoma City)	73107	Talala	74080	Wakita	73771
Sheridan (Comanche		Talihina	74571	Wallville	73052
County)	73505	Tallant	74002	Walters	73572
Sheridan (Tulsa County)	74135	Taloga	73667	Wanette	74878
Sherwood	74728	Tamaha	74462	Wann	74083
Shidler	74652	Tangier	73801	Wapanucka	73461
Shinewell	74740	Tatums	73087	Wardville	74576
Short	72955	Taylor	73562	Warner	74469
Shults	74745	Tecumseh	74873	Warr Acres	73132
Sickles	73053	Temple	73568	Warren	73526
Silo	74701	Teresita	74364	Warwick	74834
Silver City	74038	Terlton	74081	Washington	73093
Skedee	74058	Terral	73569	Washita	73094
Skiatook	74070	Texanna	74426	Waterloo	73034
Slapout	73848	Texhoma	73949	Watonga	73772
Slaughterville	73051	Texola	73668	Watova	74048
Slick	74071	Thackerville	73459	Watson	74963
Smith Village	73115	Thirty-Fourth Street (Part of		Watts	74964
Smithville	74957	Woodward)	73801	Wauhillau	74960
Snow	74567	Thirty Ninth Street (Part of		Waukomis	73773
Snyder	73566	Oklahoma City)	73112	Waurika	73573
Sobol	74735	Thomas	73669	Wayne	73095
Sooner Fashion Mall (Part of		Ti	74528	Waynoka	73860
Norman)	73072	Tiawah	74017	Weatherford	73096
Soper	74759	Timber Brook	74014	Webb	73835
Southard	73770	Timberlane	74020	Webb City	74652
South Coffeyville	74072	Tiner	74728	Webbers Falls	74470
South East (Oklahoma		Tipton	73570	Welch	74369
County)	73109	Tishomingo	73460	Weleetka	74880
Southeast (Tulsa County)	74145	Titanic	74960	Welling	74471
Southroads Mall (Part of		Tom	74740	Wellston	74881
Tulsa)	74135	Tonkawa	74653	Welty	74882
Southside (Part of Tulsa)	74136	Topsy	74366	Wes	74020
Southwest (Part of		Tribbey	74852	West Nichols Hills (Part of	
Oklahoma City)	73119	Trousdale	74878	Oklahoma City)	73116
Sparks	74869	Troy	74856	West Park (Part of	
Spaulding	74848	Trusty Unit	74501	Oklahoma City)	73123
Spavinaw	74366	Tryon	74875	Westport	74020
Speer	74743	Tucker	74959	Westside (Part of Oklahoma	
Spelter City	74437	Tullahassee	74466	City)	73127
Spencer	73084	Tulsa	74101-72	West Siloam Springs	72761
Spencerville	74760	For specific Tulsa Zip Codes call		West Tulsa (Part of Tulsa)	74107
Sperry	74073	(918) 599-6965		Westville	74965
Spiro	74959	Tulsa Promenade (Part of		Wetumka	74883
Sportsmen Acres	74361	Tulsa)	74135	Wewoka	74884
Springer	73458	Tupelo	74572	Wheatland (Part of	
Springlake Park (Part of		Turley	74156	Oklahoma City)	73097
Oklahoma City)	73111	Turner	73430	Wheeless	73933
Stafford	73601	Turpin	73950	Whippoorwill	74009
Stanley	74536	Tushka	74525	White Bead	73075
Stapp	74939	Tuskahoma	74574	White Eagle	74601
Star	74941	Tuskegee	74010	Whitefield	74472
State Capitol (Part of		Tussy	73088	White Oak (Cherokee	
Oklahoma City)	73105	Tuttle	73089	County)	74451
Stealy	73080	Tuxedo (Part of Bartlesville)	74003	White Oak (Craig County)	74301
Stecker	73006	Twin Hills	74447	Whitesboro	74577
Steedman	74825	Twin Oaks	74368	Whittier (Part of Tulsa)	74150
Steel Junction	74728	Tyler	73446	Wichita Mountains Estates	73501
Steen (Part of Enid)	73701	Tyrone	73951	Wilburton	74578
Sterling	73567	Unger	74727	Wildcat Point	74451
Stidham	74461	Union (Cleveland County)	73070	Wild Horse	74035

	ZIP
Williams	74932
William S. Key Correctional Center	73841
Willis	73439
Willow	73673
Wilson (Carter County)	73463
Wilson (Okmulgee County)	74437
Winchester	74421
Winganon	74016
Wister	74966
Wolco	74002
Wolf	74854
Woodford	73458
Woodland Hills Mall (Part of Tulsa)	74133
Woodland View (Part of Tulsa)	74145

	ZIP
Woodlawn Park	73008
Woods	73020
Woodville	73439
Woodward	73801-02
For specific Woodward Zip Codes call (405) 256-7138	
Woody Chapel	73095
Wright City	74766
Wyandotte	74370
Wybark	74401
Wye	74852
Wynnewood	73098
Wynona	74084
Yale	74085
Yanush	74574

	ZIP
Yarnaby	74741
Yeager	74848
Yewed	73728
Yost Lake	74032
Yuba	74721
Yukon	73085
	73099
For specific Yukon Zip Codes call (405) 354-3211	
Zafra	71945
Zena	74346
Zincville	66713
Zion	74960
Zoe	74939

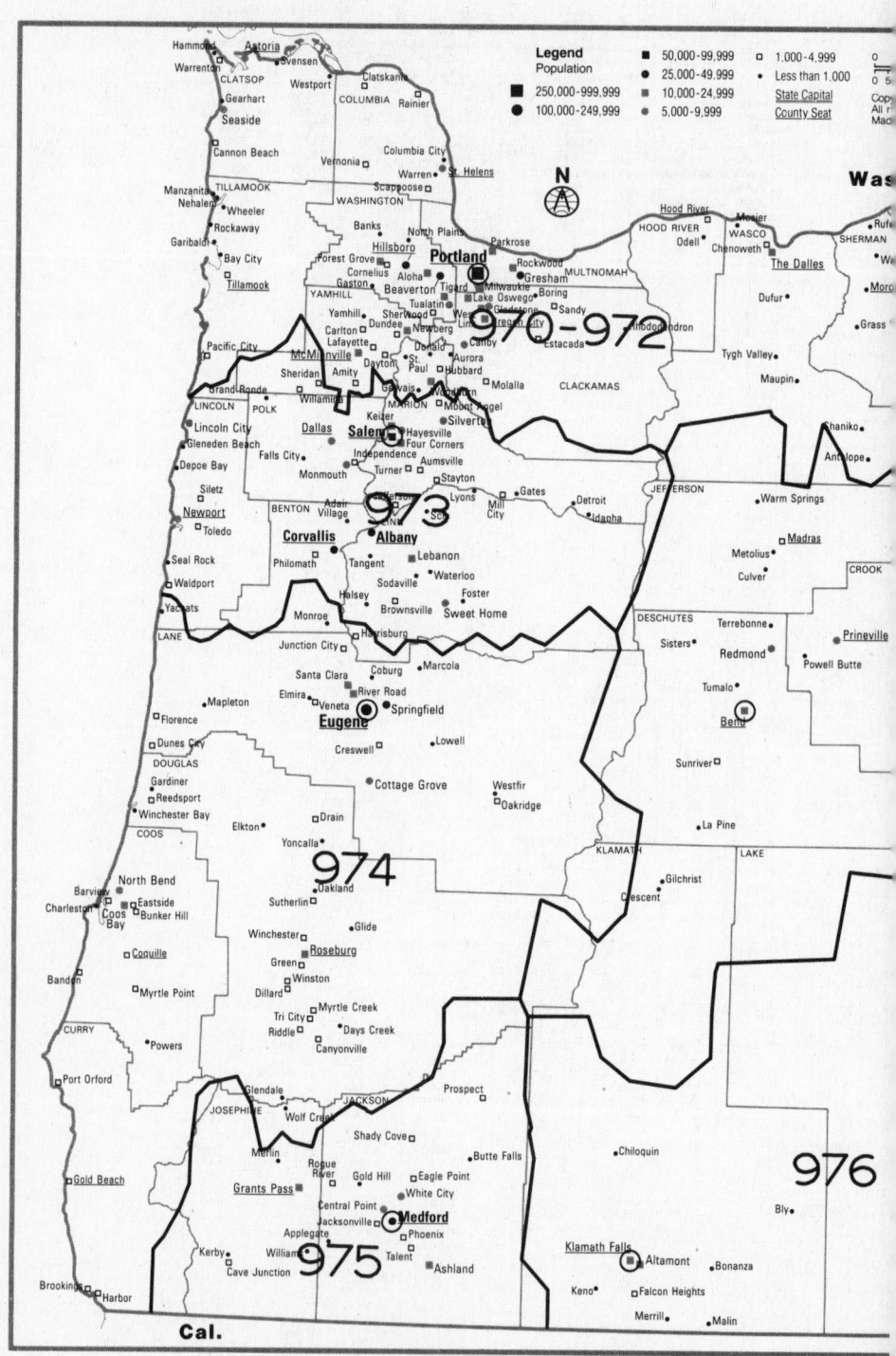

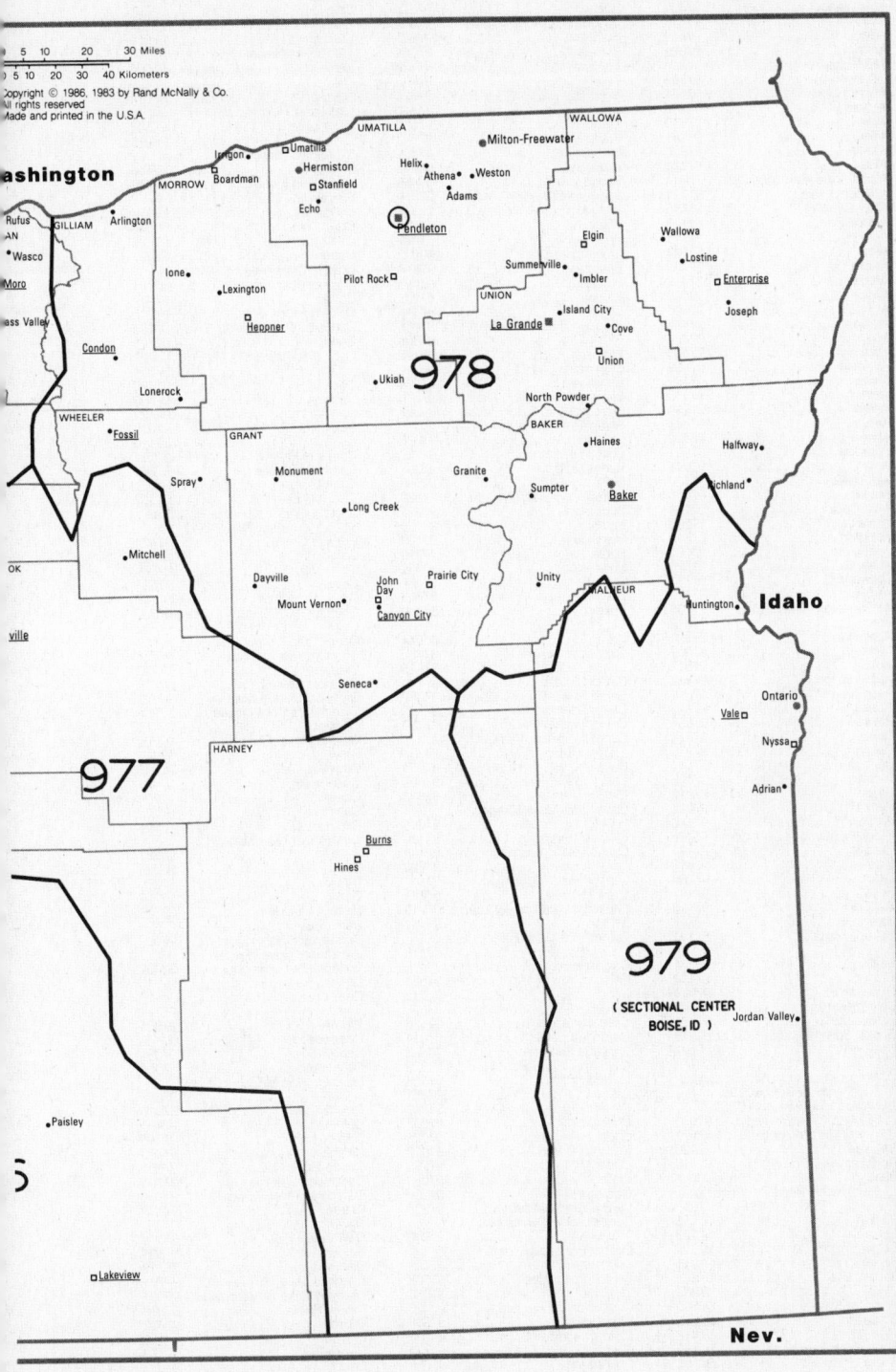

0 5 10   20   30 Miles
0 5 10   20   30   40 Kilometers

ashington

Washington

UMATILLA

WALLOWA

MORROW

GILLIAM

Arlington

Rufus

Wasco

Moro

ass Valley

Condon

WHEELER

Fossil

Spray

Mitchell

ville

OK

Irrigon

Umatilla

Boardman

Hermiston

Stanfield

Echo

Ione

Lexington

Heppner

Lonerock

Milton-Freewater

Helix

Athena   Weston

Adams

Pendleton

Pilot Rock

Summerville

Imbler

UNION

La Grande

Island City

Cove

Union

Elgin

Wallowa

Lostine

Enterprise

Joseph

978

Ukiah

North Powder

BAKER

Haines

Halfway

GRANT

Monument

Granite

Sumpter

Baker

Richland

Long Creek

Dayville

John
Day

Prairie City

Unity

Mount Vernon

Canyon City

MALHEUR

Huntington

Idaho

Seneca

Ontario

Vale

Nyssa

HARNEY

Adrian

977

Burns

Hines

979

(SECTIONAL CENTER
BOISE, ID)

Jordan Valley

Paisley

5

Lakeview

Nev.

	ZIP
Acorn Park (Part of Eugene)	97402
Ada	97493
Adair Village	97330
Adams	97810
Adel	97620
Adrian	97901
Agate Beach (Part of Newport)	97365
Agency Lake	97624
Agness	97406
Aims	97019
Airlie	97361
Ajax	97823
Albany	97321
Albany Yard (Part of Albany)	97321
Alder Creek	97055
Aldrich Point	97103
Alfalfa	97701
Alicel	97824
Alkali Lake	97758
Allegany	97407
Allston	97048
Aloha	97006
Alpine	97456
Alsea	97324
Altamont	97603
Alvadore	97409
Amity	97101
Anchor	97410
Andrews	97720
Anlauf	97428
Annex	83672
Antelope	97001
Apiary	97048
Applegate	97530
Arago	97458
Arch Cape	97102
Arleta	97206
Arlington	97812
Arock	97902
Ashland	97520
Ashwood	97711
Astoria	97103
Astoria Coast Guard Base	97103
Athena	97813
Aumsville	97325
Aurora	97002
Austin	97817
Austin Junction	97817
Avon (Part of Rainier)	97048
Azalea	97410
Bakeoven	97037
Baker City	97814
Ballston	97378
Bandon	97411
Banks	97106
Barlow	97013
Barton	97022
Barview (Coos County)	97420
Barview (Tillamook County)	97136
Basque	89421
Bates	97817
Battin	97266
Bay City	97107
Bay Park	97420
Bayshore	97394
Bayside Garden	97131
Bayview	97394
Beatty	97621
Beaver	97108
Beavercreek	97004
Beaver Homes	97048
Beaver Marsh	97731
Beaver Springs	97048
Beaverton	97005-07
	97075-76
For specific Beaverton Zip Codes call (503) 646-3196	
Beaverton Mall (Part of Beaverton)	97005
Belleview (Part of Ashland)	97520
Bellevue	97128
Bellfountain	97456
Bend	97701-09
For specific Bend Zip Codes call (503) 388-1971	
Berlin	97355
Bethany	97123
Bethel Heights	97304
Beulah	97911
Beverly Beach	97365
Biggs	97065
Bingham Springs	97810
Birkenfeld	97016
Blachly	97412
Black Butte Ranch	97759
Blaine	97108
Blalock	97812
Blodgett	97326
Blooming	97113

	ZIP
Blue River	97413
Bly	97622
Boardman	97818
Bolton (Part of West Linn)	97068
Bonanza	97623
Bonneville	97014
Bonny Slope	97229
Boring	97009
Boyd	97021
Boyer	97347
Bradwood	97016
Breitenbush	97342
Brickerville	97453
Bridal Veil	97010
Bridge	97458
Bridgeport (Baker County)	97819
Bridgeport (Polk County)	97338
Brighton	97136
Brightwood	97011
Broadacres	97002
Broadbent	97414
Brockway	97496
Brogan	97903
Brookings	97415
Brooklyn (Part of Portland)	97266
Brooks	97305
Brothers	97712
Brownlee	97840
Brownsboro	97524
Brownsmead	97016
Brownsville	97327
Bryant (Part of Lake Oswego)	97035
Buchanan	97720
Buena Vista	97351
Bullrun	97055
Bunker Hill	97420
Burlington	97231
Burns	97720
Burnside	97103
Burns Junction	97910
Burnt Woods	97326
Butte Falls	97522
Butteville	97002
Buxton	97109
Cages	97739
Cairo	97914
Calapooya	97386
Camas Valley	97416
Camp Clatsop	97146
Camp Polk	97759
Camp Sherman	97730
Camp Twelve	97391
Campus Station (Part of Corvallis)	97331
Canaan	97054
Canary	97493
Canby	97013
Canemah (Part of Oregon City)	97045
Cannon Beach	97110
Cannon Beach Junction	97138
Canyon City	97820
Canyonville	97417
Cape Meares	97141
Capitol Hill (Part of Portland)	97219
Carlton	97111
Carnation (Part of Forest Grove)	97116
Carpenterville	97415
Carson	97834
Carus	97045
Carver	97015
Cascade Gorge	97536
Cascade Locks	97014
Cascade Summit	97425
Cascadia	97329
Cave Junction	97523
Cayuse	97821
Cecil	97843
Cedar Dale	97038
Cedar Hills	97225
Cedarhurst Park	97023
Cedar Mill	97229
Celilo	97058
Centennial	97236
Central (Part of Portland)	97204
Central Point (Clackamas County)	97045
Central Point (Jackson County)	97502
Central Point West	97502
Chapman	97056
Charleston	97420
Charlestown	97838
Chemawa Indian School	97303
Chemult	97731
Chenoweth	97058
Cherry Grove	97119
Cherry Heights	97058
Cherryville	97055

	ZIP
Cheshire	97419
Chiloquin	97624
Chitwood	97391
Christmas Valley	97641
Clackamas	97015
Clackamas Heights	97045
Clarkes	97004
Clarno	97830
Clatskanie	97016
Clatskanie Heights	97016
Clear Lake	97303
Clifton	97016
Cloverdale (Deschutes County)	97756
Cloverdale (Lane County)	97426
Cloverdale (Tillamook County)	97112
Clow Corner	97338
Coaledo	97420
Coburg	97401
College Crest (Part of Eugene)	97401
Colton	97017
Columbia City	97018
Concord	97222
Condon	97823
Cook (Part of Lake Oswego)	97034
Coos Bay	97420
Cooston	97459
Coquille	97423
Corbett	97019
Cornelius	97113
Cornelius Pass	97231
Coronado Shores	97388
Corvallis	97330-33
	97339
For specific Corvallis Zip Codes call (503) 758-1412	
Cottage Grove	97424
Cottrell	97009
Courtrock	97864
Cove	97824
Cove Orchard	97148
Crabtree	97335
Crane	97732
Crater Lake	97604
Crawfordsville	97336
Crescent	97733
Crescent Lake	97425
Crescent Lake Junction	97425
Creston (Part of Portland)	97206
Creswell	97426
Crooked River Ranch	97760
Crow	97401
Crowfoot	97355
Culp Creek	97427
Culver	97734
Currinsville	97023
Curtin	97428
Cutler City (Part of Lincoln City)	97367
Dairy	97625
Dale	97880
Daley	97702
Dallas	97338
Damascus	97009
Damascus Heights	97009
Dammasch State Hospital	97070
Danebo (Part of Eugene)	97402
Danner	97910
Days Creek	97429
Dayton	97114
Dayville	97825
Deadwood	97430
Dee	97031
Deer Island	97054
De Lake (Part of Lincoln City)	97367
Delena	97016
Dellwood	97420
Delmoor	97146
Denmark	97450
Depoe Bay	97341
Deschutes Junction	97701
Deschutes River Woods	97701
Detroit	97342
Dever	97321
Dew Valley	97411
Dexter	97431
Diamond	97722
Diamond Lake	97731
Diamond Lake Junction	97731
Dickey Prairie	97038
Dillard	97432
Dilley	97116
Dixonville	97470
Dodge	97023
Dodson	97014
Dolph Corner	97338
Donald	97020

	ZIP
Dora	97458
Dorena	97434
Dover	97055
Downing	97016
Downtown (Part of Bend)	97701
Drain	97435
Draperville	97321
Drew	97484
Drewsey	97904
Dufur	97021
Dukes Valley	97031
Dundee	97115
Dunes City	97439
Durham	97223
Durkee	97905
Eagle Creek	97022
Eagle Point	97524
East Gardiner	97467
East Gresham (Part of Gresham)	97030
East Lake	97739
East Parkrose	97230
East Portland (Part of Portland)	97214
Eastside (Part of Coos Bay)	97420
Eastwood (Part of Roseburg)	97470
Echo	97826
Echo Dell	97045
Eckman Lake	97394
Eddyville	97343
Elgarose	97470
Elgin	97827
Elk City	97391
Elkhead	97499
Elkhorn	97358
Elk Lake	97701
Elkton	97436
Ellendale	97338
Ellingson Mill	97884
Elliott Prairie	97071
Elmira	97437
Elsie	97138
Elwood	97017
Emerald Heights (Part of Astoria)	97103
Empire (Part of Coos Bay)	97420
Endersby	97058
Englewood	97420
Enterprise	97828
Errol Heights	97266
Estacada	97023
Eugene	97401-05
	97440
For specific Eugene Zip Codes call (503) 341-3611	
Fairfield	97026
Fair Oaks (Clackamas County)	97222
Fairoaks (Douglas County)	97479
Fairview (Coos County)	97423
Fairview (Multnomah County)	97024
Fairview (Tillamook County)	97141
Falcon Heights	97601
Fall Creek	97438
Falls City	97344
Fargo	97002
Faubion	97049
Fayetteville	97377
Fern Corner	97338
Fern Hill (Clatsop County)	97103
Fern Hill (Columbia County)	97048
Ferns	97338
Fields (Harney County)	97710
Fields (Lane County)	97463
Finn Rock	97488
Fir Grove	97401
Fir Villa	97338
Firwood	97055
Fishers Corner	97045
Fishers Mill	97045
Fish Lake Resort	97524
Five Corners	97630
Flora	97828
Floras Lake	97450
Florence	97439
Forest Grove	97116
Forest Park (Part of Portland)	97210
Forfar	97366
Fort Hill	97396
Fort Klamath	97626
Fort Rock	97735
Fort Stevens (Part of Hammond)	97121
Fortune Branch	97442
Fossil	97830
Foster	97345
Four Corners (Jackson County)	97502

	ZIP
Four Corners (Marion County)	97301
Fox	97831
Franklin	97448
Freewater (Part of Milton-Freewater)	97862
Frenchglen	97736
Friend	97021
Fruitdale	97526
Fruitvale	97365
Gales Creek	97117
Galice	97532
Garden Home	97223
Garden Home-Whitford	97223
Gardiner	97441
Gardiner Ridge	97415
Garfield	97023
Garibaldi	97118
Gaston	97119
Gates	97346
Gateway	97741
Gateway Mall (Part of Springfield)	97477
Gaylord	97458
Gazley	97457
Gearhart	97138
George	97023
Gervais	97026
Gibbon	97810
Gilbert	97266
Gilchrist	97737
Gillespie Corners	97405
Gilliams	97338
Gladstone	97027
Glasgow	97459
Glenada	97439
Glenbrook	97456
Glendale	97442
Gleneden Beach	97388
Glengary	97470
Glenmorrie (Part of Lake Oswego)	97034
Glenwood (Clatsop County)	97146
Glenwood (Lane County)	97401
Glenwood (Washington County)	97116
Glide	97443
Globe	97490
Goble	97048
Gold Beach	97444
Gold Hill	97525
Gooseberry	97843
Goshen	97401
Government Camp	97028
Grand Ronde	97347
Grand Ronde Agency	97347
Granite	97877
Grants Pass	97526-27
For specific Grants Pass Zip Codes call (503) 479-7526	
Grass Valley	97029
Green	97470
Green Acres	97420
Greenberry	97333
Greenhorn	97877
Greenleaf	97430
Greenville (Linn County)	97386
Greenville (Washington County)	97116
Greenway (Part of Tigard)	97223
Gresham	97030
	97080
For specific Gresham Zip Codes call (503) 665-3114	
Haines	97833
Halfway	97834
Halsey	97348
Hammond	97121
Hampton	97712
Happy Valley	97236
Harbeck-Fruitdale	97526
Harbor	97415
Hardman	97836
Harlan	97343
Harney	97720
Harper	97906
Harriman	97601
Harrisburg	97446
Hauser	97459
Hayesville	97303
Hazelwood	97230
Hebo	97122
Heceta Beach	97439
Heceta Junction	97439
Helix	97785
Helvetia	97123
Hemlock (Part of Westfir)	97492
Henley	97603
Henrice	97045
Heppner	97836
Hereford	97837

	ZIP
Hermiston	97838
Highland	97004
Hildebrand	97623
Hilgard	97850
Hillsboro	97123-24
For specific Hillsboro Zip Codes call (503) 294-2308	
Hines	97738
Hobsonville	97107
Holladay Park (Part of Portland)	97212
Holland	97523
Holley	97386
Hollywood (Part of Salem)	97303
Homestead (Baker County)	97840
Homestead (Deschutes County)	97702
Hood River	97031
Horton	97412
Hoskins	97326
Hot Lake	97850
Hubbard	97032
Hugo	97526
Hunter Creek	97444
Huntington	97907
Idanha	97350
Idaville	97141
Idleyld Park	97447
Illahe	97406
Illinois Valley	97523
Imbler	97841
Imnaha	97842
Independence	97351
Indian Ford	97759
Indian Village	97720
Inglis	97016
Interlachen	97060
Ione	97843
Ironside	97908
Irrigon	97844
Irving	97401
Island City	97850
Ivy Station	97103
Jacksonville	97530
Jamieson	97909
Jantzen Beach Center (Part of Portland)	97217
Jasper	97438
Jeffers Garden	97103
Jefferson	97352
Jennings Lodge	97222
Jewell	97138
Jimtown	97834
John Day	97845
Johnson City	97222
Jonesboro	97911
Jordan	97374
Jordan Valley	97910
Joseph	97846
Junction City	97448
Juntura	97911
Kahneeta Hot Springs	97761
Kamela	97801
Kansas City	97116
Keating	97814
Keizer	97303
Kellogg	97462
Kelso	97009
Kendall	97206
Keno	97627
Kent	97033
Kenton (Part of Portland)	97217
Kerby	97531
Kernville	97367
Kimberly	97848
King City	97224
Kingman Kolony	97913
Kingsley Field	97603
Kingston	97383
Kings Valley	97361
Kinton	97005
Kinzua	97830
Kiwanda Beach	97149
Klamath Falls	97601-03
For specific Klamath Falls Zip Codes call (503) 884-9226	
Knappa	97103
Knoll Heights	97702
Lacomb	97355
Ladd Hill	97070
Lafayette	97127
La Grande	97850
Lakecreek	97524
Lake Grove (Part of Lake Oswego)	97035
Lake of the Woods	97601
Lake Oswego	97034-35
For specific Lake Oswego Zip Codes call (503) 294-2308	
Lakeside	97449
Lakeview	97630

	ZIP
Lancaster	97448
Lancaster Mall (Part of Salem)	97301
Langell Valley	97623
Langlois	97450
Langrell	97834
La Pine	97739
Larwood	97374
Latham	97424
Latourell Falls	97014
Laurel	97123
Laurel Grove	97411
Laurelwood	97119
Lawen	97740
Leaburg	97489
Lebanon	97355
Lee's Camp	97141
Leland	97497
Lents (Part of Portland)	97266
Leona	97435
Lewisburg	97330
Lexington	97839
Libby	97420
Liberal	97038
Liberty	97386
Lime	97907
Lincoln	97520
Lincoln Beach	97341
Lincoln City	97367
Lindbergh	97048
Little Albany	97390
Little Sweden	97346
Lloyd Center (Part of Portland)	97232
Locoda	97016
Logsden	97357
London	97424
Lone Elder	97013
Lonerock	97823
Long Creek	97856
Lookingglass (Douglas County)	97470
Looking Glass (Union County)	97827
Lorane	97451
Lorella	97623
Lostine	97857
Lowell	97452
Lower Logan	97045
Lynch (Part of Portland)	97236
Lyons	97358
McCoy	97371
Mc Dermitt	97910
McEwen	97877
McKee Bridge	97530
Mc Kenzie Bridge	97413
McKinley	97458
Macksburg	97013
McMinnville	97128
McNary (Part of Umatilla)	97882
McNulty	97051
Madras	97741
Malin	97632
Mall 205 (Part of Portland)	97216
Manhattan Beach (Part of Rockaway)	97136
Manning	97125
Manzanita	97130
Mapleton	97453
Marcola	97454
Marion	97359
Marion Forks	97350
Marlene Village	97005
Marquam	97362
Marshland	97016
Martin Manor	97225
Marylhurst	97036
Mason Additions (Part of Prineville)	97754
Maupin	97037
Mayger	97016
May Park	97850
Mayville	97830
Maywood Park	97220
Meacham	97859
Meadowbrook	97038
Meadow View	97448
Meda	97112
Medford	97501-04
For specific Medford Zip Codes call (503) 776-1326	
Medford Center (Part of Medford)	97504
Medford Mall (Part of Medford)	97504
Medical Springs	97814
Mehama	97384
Melrose	97470
Melville	97103
Menlo Park (Part of Portland)	97230

	ZIP
Merlin	97532
Merrill	97633
Metolius	97741
Metzger	97223
Midland	97634
Midway (Multnomah County)	97233
Midway (Washington County)	97123
Mikkalo	97812
Miles Crossing	97103
Mill City	97360
Millersburg	97321
Millican	97701
Millington	97420
Millwood	97486
Milo	97429
Milton (Part of Milton-Freewater)	97862
Milton-Freewater	97862
Milwaukie	97222
Minam	97827
Mission	97801
Mist	97016
Mitchell	97750
Modeville	97351
Modoc Point	97624
Mohawk	97477
Mohawk Junction (Part of Springfield)	97477
Mohler	97131
Molalla	97038
Monitor	97071
Monmouth	97361
Monroe	97456
Monument	97864
Moody	97391
Morgan	97843
Moro	97039
Mosier	97040
Mountaindale	97113
Mount Angel	97362
Mount Hebron	97801
Mount Hood	97041
Mount Hood-Parkdale	97041
Mount Hood Village	97049
Mount Pleasant (Part of Oregon City)	97045
Mount Vernon	97865
Mulino	97042
Mulloy	97140
Multnomah (Part of Portland)	97219
Murphy	97533
Myrick	97810
Myrtle Creek	97457
Myrtle Point	97458
Narrows (Harney County)	97721
Narrows (Linn County)	97386
Nashville	97326
Natal	97064
Neahkahnie	97131
Nedonna	97136
Needy	97013
Nehalem	97131
Nelscott (Part of Lincoln City)	97367
Neotsu	97364
Nesika Beach	97444
Neskowin	97149
Netarts	97143
Newberg	97132
New Bridge	97870
New Era	97013
New Hope	97527
New Idanha	97350
New Pine Creek	97635
Newport	97365
Newton Creek	97470
Nimrod	97488
Ninety One	97013
Nonpareil	97479
North Albany	97321
North Bend	97459
North Bend Coast Guard Air Station	97459
North Fork	97467
North Howell	97381
North Plains	97133
North Powder	97867
North Roseburg (Part of Roseburg)	97470
North Santiam	97325
North Springfield	97477
North Umpqua Village	97447
Norway	97460
Norwood	97062
Noti	97461
Nottingham	97702
Nyssa	97913
Nyssa Heights	97913

	ZIP
Oak Grove (Clackamas County)	97267
Oak Grove (Hood River County)	97031
Oak Hills	97225
Oakland	97462
Oakridge	97463
Oak Springs	97037
Oakville	97377
Oakway Mall (Part of Eugene)	97401
Oatfield	97222
O'Brien	97534
Oceanlake (Part of Lincoln City)	97367
Oceanside	97134
Odell	97044
Odessa	97601
Oklahoma Hill	97016
Old Colton	97017
Old Town	97462
Olene	97601
Olex	97812
Olney	97103
Ontario	97914
Ophir	97464
Ordnance	97838
Oregon City	97045
Orenco	97123
Oretech (Part of Klamath Falls)	97601
Oretown	97112
Orient	97030
Orleans	97321
Otis	97368
Otter Rock	97369
Outlook	97045
Owyhee	97913
Oxbow	97840
Pacific City	97135
Page (Part of Albany)	97321
Paisley	97636
Palestine	97321
Paradise Park	97023
Parkdale	97041
Parker	97351
Parkersburg	97411
Park Place	97045
Parkrose	97230
Patterson Junction	97844
Paulina	97751
Pedee	97361
Peel	97443
Pendair Heights (Part of Pendleton)	97801
Pendleton	97801
Pendleton Junction (Part of Pendleton)	97801
Peoria	97377
Perry	97850
Perrydale	97101
Philomath	97370
Phoenix	97535
Piedmont (Part of Portland)	97211
Pigeon Point	97420
Pike	97148
Pilot Rock	97868
Pine	97834
Pine Grove (Hood River County)	97031
Pine Grove (Wasco County)	97037
Pine Ridge	97624
Pioneer (Part of Portland)	97204
Pistol River	97444
Pittsburg	97064
Plainview (Deschutes County)	97701
Plainview (Linn County)	97377
Pleasant Hill	97455
Pleasant Valley (Baker County)	97814
Pleasant Valley (Josephine County)	97532
Pleasant Valley (Tillamook County)	97141
Plush	97637
Pocahontas	97814
Polk Station	97338
Pondosa	97814
Pony Village (Part of North Bend)	97459
Porter Creek	97481
Portland	97201-99
For specific Portland Zip Codes call (503) 294-2308	
Port Orford	97465
Post	97752
Powell Butte	97753
Powellhurst	97236
Powellhurst-Centennial	97236
Powers	97466

	ZIP
Prairie City	97869
Pratum	97301
Prescott	97048
Princeton	97721
Prineville	97754
Prineville Southeast (Part of Prineville)	97754
Pringle Park Plaza (Part of Salem)	97301
Progress	97005
Prospect	97536
Prosper	97411
Quinaby	97303
Quincy	97016
Quines Creek	97442
Rainbow	97413
Rainier	97048
Raleigh Hills	97225
Ramsey	97701
Ramsey Hall	97021
Randolph	97411
Redland	97045
Redmond	97756
Redwood	97526
Reedsport	97467
Remote	97458
Reston	97470
Rhododendron	97049
Rice Hill	97462
Richardson	97490
Richland	97870
Richmond	97874
Rickreall	97371
Riddle	97469
Rieth	97801
Riley	97758
Ritter	97872
Riverdale (Part of Portland)	97219
Rivergrove	97035
River Road	97404
Riverside (Linn County)	97321
Riverside (Malheur County)	97917
Riverside (Umatilla County)	97801
Riverton	97423
Riverview (Columbia County)	97064
Riverview (Lane County)	97448
Roans Estate	97739
Roaring Springs Ranch	97736
Robinwood (Part of West Linn)	97068
Rockaway	97136
Rock Creek (Baker County)	97833
Rock Creek (Gilliam County)	97812
Rockcreek (Washington County)	97225
Rockford	97031
Rockie Four Corners	97375
Rock Point	97525
Rockville	97910
Rockwood	97233
Rocky Point	97601
Rogue River	97537
Rogue Valley Mall (Part of Medford)	97501
Rome	97910
Roseburg	97470
Roseburg North	97470
Rose City Park (Part of Portland)	97213
Rose Lodge	97372
Rosemont	97068
Rowena	97058
Roy	97106
Ruch	97530
Rufus	97050
Ruggs	97836
Rural Dell	97032
Russellville	97216
Rye Valley	97907
Saginaw	97424
St. Benedict	97373
St. Helens	97051
St. Johns (Part of Portland)	97203
St. Louis	97026
St. Paul	97137
Salem	97301-09
For specific Salem Zip Codes call (503) 370-4700	
Salmon Harbor	97467
Salt Creek	97338
Sams Valley	97525
Sand Lake	97112
Sandy	97055
San Marine	97498
Santa Clara	97404
Santiam Terrace	97355
Saunders Lake	97459
Scappoose	97056
Scholls	97123
Scio	97374

	ZIP
Scofield	97109
Scottsburg	97473
Scotts Mills	97375
Seal Rock	97376
Seaside	97138
Seekseequa	97761
Seghers	97119
Sellwood (Part of Portland)	97202
Sellwood Moreland (Part of Portland)	97202
Selma	97538
Seneca	97873
Shadowood	97068
Shady Cove	97539
Shady Dell	97038
Shaniko	97057
Shasta Plaza (Part of Klamath Falls)	97603
Shaw	97325
Shedd	97377
Shelburn	97374
Sheridan	97378
Sherwood	97140
Shorewood	97459
Siletz	97380
Siltcoos	97493
Silver Lake	97638
Silverton	97381
Silvies	97720
Simnasho	97761
Sisters	97759
Sitkum	97458
Six Corners (Part of Sherwood)	97140
Sixes	97476
Skelley	97499
Smithfield	97338
Sodaville	97355
Southbeach	97366
Southgate (Part of Portland)	97266
South Junction	97037
South Lebanon	97355
South Scappoose	97056
Southside (Part of Eugene)	97405
Spicer	97355
Sprague River	97639
Spray	97874
Springbrook	97132
Springdale	97060
Springfield	97477-78
	97482
For specific Springfield Zip Codes call (503) 747-3383	
Springwater	97023
Stafford	97068
Staleys Junction	97109
Stanfield	97875
Starkey	97850
Starvout	97410
Stayton	97383
Steamboat	97447
Stewart Lennox Addition	97601
Stimson Mill	97119
Sublimity	97385
Summer Lake	97640
Summer Lake Hot Springs	97636
Summerville	97876
Summit	97326
Sumner	97420
Sumpter	97877
Sunnycrest	97132
Sunnydale	97435
Sunnyside (Clackamas County)	97015
Sunnyside (Umatilla County)	97862
Sunny Valley	97497
Sunriver	97707
Sunset (Part of West Linn)	97068
Sunset Beach	97146
Sunset Hills (Part of Seaside)	97138
Suntex Valley	97758
Suplee	97751
Surf Pines	97146
Surprise Valley	97457
Sutherlin	97479
Suver	97361
Suver Junction	97361
Svensen	97103
Swedetown	97016
Sweet Home	97386
Swisshome	97480
Sylvan (Part of Portland)	97221
Table Rock	97501
Taft (Part of Lincoln City)	97367
Takilma	97523
Talbot	97352
Talent	97540
Tallman	97355
Tangent	97389
Taylorville	97016

	ZIP
Telocaset	97883
Tenmile	97481
Terrebonne	97760
Thatcher	97116
The Dalles	97058
Thornhollow	97810
Three Lynx	97023
Three Rivers	97701
Thurston (Part of Springfield)	97482
Tide	97480
Tidewater	97390
Tiernan	97453
Tierra Del Mar	97112
Tigard	97223
Tillamook	97141
Tiller	97484
Tillican	97701
Timber	97144
Timber Grove	97004
Timberline Lodge	97028
Toketee Falls	97447
Toledo	97391
Tollgate	97886
Tolovana Park	97145
Tongue Point Village	97103
Top	97864
Tophill	97109
Town Center (Part of Portland)	97229
Trail	97541
Trask	97141
Treharne	97064
Trent	97431
Triangle Lake	97412
Tri-City	97457
Trout Creek (Harney County)	97710
Trout Creek (Hood River County)	97041
Troutdale	97060
Troy	97828
Tualatin	97062
Tumalo	97701
Turner	97392
Twelve Mile	97030
Twickenham	97750
Twin Rocks	97136
Twomile	97411
Tygh Valley	97063
Ukiah	97880
Umapine	97862
Umatilla	97882
Umatilla Indian Reservation	97801
Umpqua	97486
Union	97883
Union Creek	97536
Union Gap	97462
Union Mills	97042
Union Point	97327
Unionvale	97114
Unity (Baker County)	97884
Unity (Lane County)	97438
University (Lane County)	97403
University (Multnomah County)	97201
Upper Highland	97004
Upper Hood River Valley	97044
Upper Soda	97345
Vale	97918
Valley Falls	97630
Valley Junction	97396
Valley River Center (Part of Eugene)	97401
Valley View	97321
Valsetz	97380
Van	97904
Vaughn	97487
Veneta	97487
Verboort	97116
Vermont Hills	97219
Vernonia	97064
Vida	97488
Viola	97023
Vista (Part of Salem)	97302
Waconda	97026
Wagontire	97738
Wagon Trail Ranch	97739
Wakonda Beach	97394
Walden	97424
Waldport	97394
Walker	97426
Wallowa	97885
Wallowa Lake Resort	97846
Walterville	97489
Walton	97490
Wamic	97063
Wapato	97119
Wapinitia	97037
Warm Springs	97761

	ZIP
Warm Springs Indian Reservation	97761
Warren	97053
Warrendale	97014
Warrenton	97146
Wasco	97065
Washington Park Zoo Railway (Part of Portland)	97221
Waterloo	97355
Watseco	97136
Weatherby	97905
Wecoma Beach (Part of Lincoln City)	97367
Wedderburn	97491
Welches	97067
Wemme	97067
Western Evangelical Seminary	97045
Westfall	97920
Westfir	97492
West Haven-Sylvan	97225
West Lake (Clatsop County)	97146
Westlake (Lane County)	97493
West Linn	97068
Weston	97886
Westport	97016
West Salem (Part of Salem)	97304
West Scio	97374
West Side (Lake County)	97630
West Side (Lane County)	97402

	ZIP
West Slope	97225
West Stayton	97325
West St. Helens (Part of St. Helens)	97051
West Union	97123
Wetmore	97830
Weyerhaeuser Townsite	97601
Wheeler	97147
Wheeler Heights (Part of Wheeler)	97147
Whiskey Hill	97032
White City	97503
Whiteson	97101
Wilbur	97494
Wilderville	97543
Wildwood	97049
Wilhoit	97038
Willakenzie (Part of Eugene)	97401
Willamette (Part of West Linn)	97068
Willamette City (Part of Oakridge)	97463
Willamina	97396
Willbridge (Part of Portland)	97231
Williams	97544
Willowcreek	97918
Willowdale	97741
Willsburg Junction (Part of Milwaukie)	97222
Wilson Beach	97141

	ZIP
Wilsonville	97070
Wimer	97537
Winchester	97495
Winchester Bay	97467
Windmaster Corner	97031
Winema Beach	97112
Wingville	97814
Winston	97496
Winterville	97411
Witch Hazel	97123
Wocus	97601
Wolf Creek	97497
Women's Release Unit	97301
Wonder	97543
Woodburn	97071
Woods	97112
Woodson	97016
Wood Village	97060
Worden	97601
Wren	97326
Wyeth	97014
Yachats	97498
Yamhill	97148
Yankton	97051
Yaquina	97365
Yoder	97032
Yoncalla	97499
Yonna	97623
Zigzag	97049

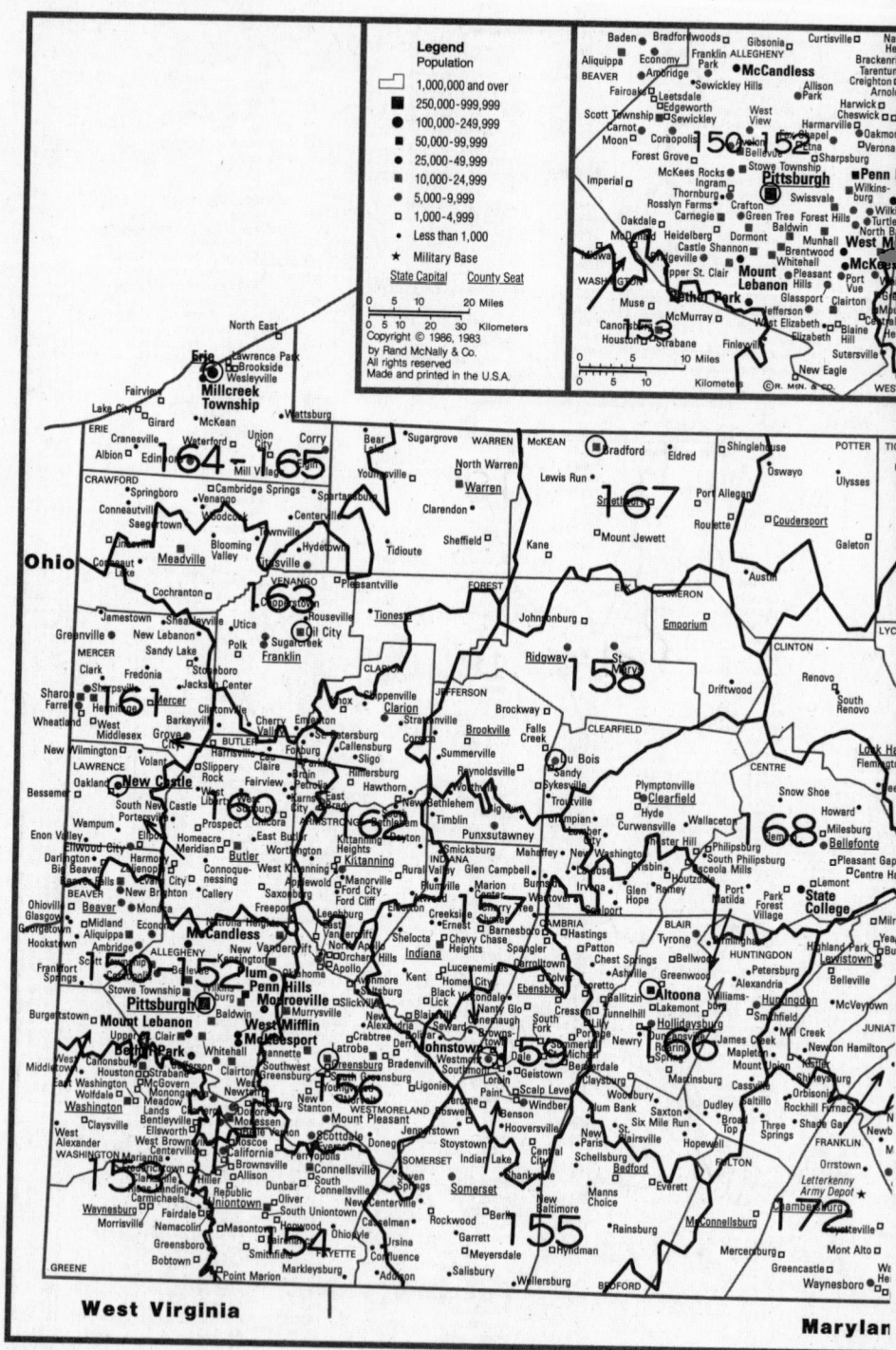

Legend

Population

☐ 1,000,000 and over

■ 250,000-999,999

● 100,000-249,999

● 50,000-99,999

● 25,000-49,999

■ 10,000-24,999

□ 5,000-9,999

□ 1,000-4,999

★ Less than 1,000

★ Military Base

State Capital   County Seat

0 5 10   20 Miles

0 5 10   20   30 Kilometers

Ohio

West Virginia

Maryland

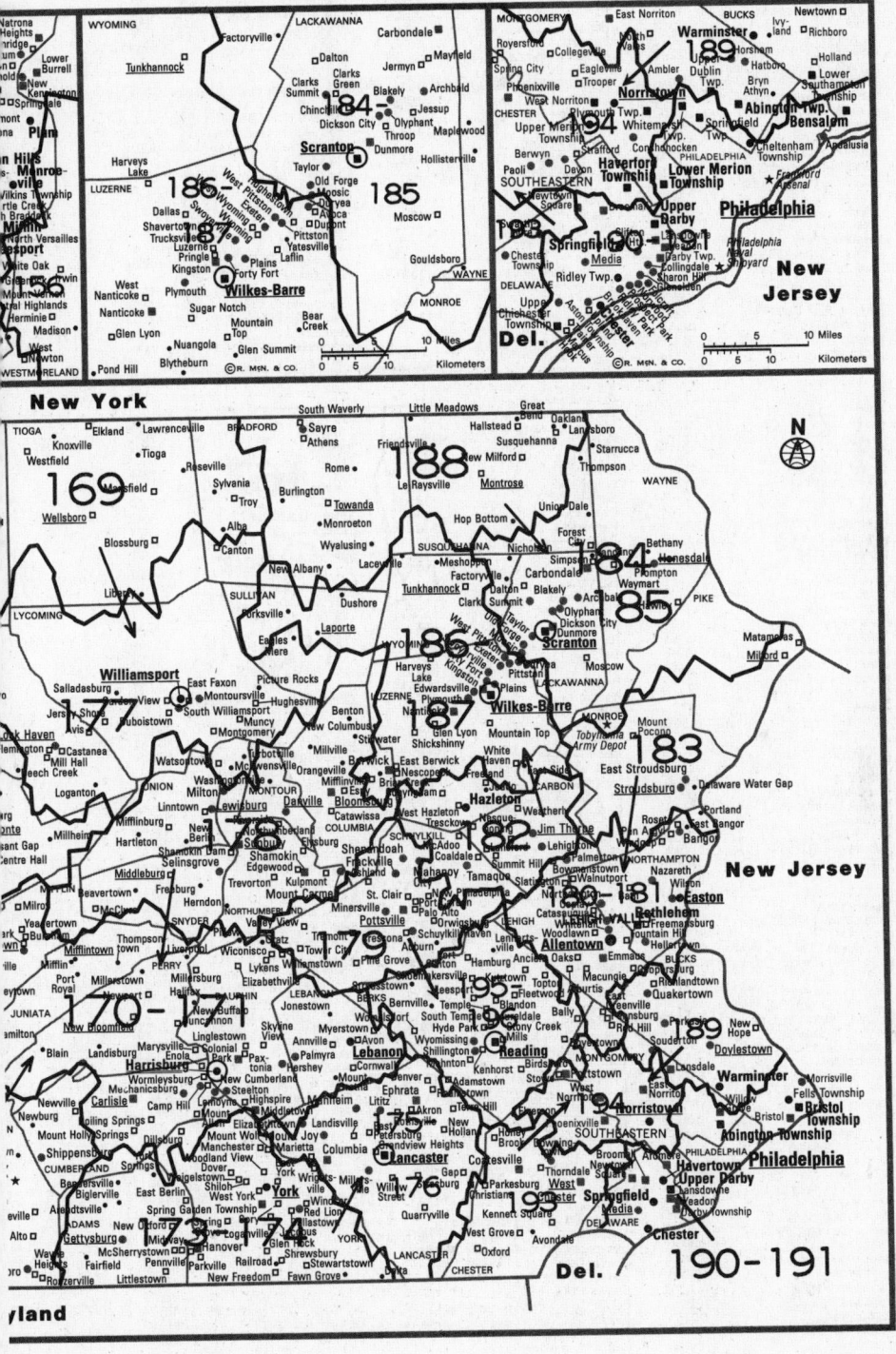

	ZIP
Aspinwall	15215
Aston	19014
Aston (Township)	19014
Asylum (Township)	18848
Atco	12764
Atglen	19310
Athens (Bradford County)	18810
Athens (Bradford County) (Township)	18810
Athens (Crawford County) (Township)	16360
Athol	19519
Atkinsons Mills	17051
Atlantic (Clearfield County)	16651
Atlantic (Crawford County)	16111
Atlantic (Westmoreland County)	15671
Atlas	17851
Atlasburg	15004
Atwood	16249
Auburn (Schuylkill County)	17922
Auburn (Susquehanna County) (Township)	18630
Auburn Center	18623
Auburn Four Corners	18630
Audenried	18201
Audubon	19407
Aughwick	17066
Augustaville	17801
Aultman	15713
Austin	16720
Austinburg	16928
Austinville	16914
Avalon	15202
Avella	15312
Avella Heights	15312
Avella Highlands	15312
Avis	17721
Avoca	18641
Avondale	19311
Avondale Knolls	19086
Avon Heights	17042
Avonia	16423
Avonmore	15618
Axemann	16823
Ayr (Township)	17212
Bachmanville	17033
Baden	15005
Baederwood	19046
Bagdad	15656
Baggaley	15650
Baidland	15063
Bailey	17074
Baileys Corner	16926
Baileyville	16865
Bainbridge	17502
Bair	17405
Bairdford	15006
Bairdstown	15717
Bakers Crossroads	16668
Bakers Summit	16614
Baker Station	19390
Bakerstown (station)	15044
Bakerstown	15007
Bakersville	15501
Bala	19004
Bala-Cynwyd	19004
Bala-Cynwyd Shopping Center	19004
Bald Eagle (Blair County)	16686
Bald Eagle (Clinton County) (Township)	17751
Bald Hill (Clearfield County)	16850
Bald Hill (Greene County)	15327
Baldwin (Allegheny County)	15234
Baldwin (Township)	15234
Baldwin (Delaware County)	19013
Balliettsville	18037
Balls Eddy	18461
Balls Mills	17728
Balltown	16347
Bally	19503
Balsinger	15484
Banbury Crossing	17036
Bando	15501
Banetown	15301
Baney Settlement	16830
Bangor	18013
Banian Junction	16661
Banks (Carbon County) (Township)	18254
Banks (Indiana County) (Township)	15742
Banksville (Part of Pittsburgh)	15216
Banner Ridge	15757
Bannerville	17841
Banning	15428
Baptist Bible College and School of Theology	18411
Barbours	17701

	ZIP
Bard	15534
Baresville	17331
Bareville	17540
Barkeyville	16038
Barlow	17325
Barnards	16222
Barnes (Cambria County)	15737
Barnes (Jefferson County)	15825
Barnes (Warren County)	16347
Barnesboro	15714
Barneston	19344
Barnesville	18214
Barnett (Forest County) (Township)	15828
Barnett (Jefferson County) (Township)	15860
Barneytown	17052
Barnitz	17013
Barnsley	19363
Barr (Township)	15760
Barree	16611
Barree (Township)	16669
Barren Hill	19444
Barret Plan	15001
Barrett (Clearfield County)	16830
Barrett (Monroe County) (Township)	18342
Barronvale	15557
Barr Slope	15734
Barrville	17084
Barry (Township)	17921
Barry Heights (Part of Norristown)	19401
Bart	17503
Bart (Township)	17562
Barto	19504
Bartonsville	18321
Bartville	17509
Basket	19547
Bassards Corners	16038
Bastress (Township)	17701
Bath	18014
Bath Addition	19007
Bath Manor	19007
Bauerstown	15209
Baumgardner	17584
Baumstown	19508
Bausman	17504
Bavington	15019
Baxter	15829
Beachdale	15530
Beach Haven	18601
Beach Lake	18405
Beachly	15424
Beadling	15241
Beale (Township)	17082
Beallsville	15313
Beans Cove	15535
Bear Creek	18602
Bear Creek (Township)	18602
Bear Creek Lake	18229
Bear Gap	17824
Bear Lake	16402
Bear Rocks	15610
Beartown (Franklin County)	17268
Beartown (Lancaster County)	17555
Bear Valley	17872
Beatty	15650
Beatty Hills	19008
Beaufort Farms	17110
Beaumont	18618
Beaver (Beaver County)	15009
Beaver (Clarion County) (Township)	16232
Beaver (Columbia County) (Township)	17815
Beaver (Crawford County) (Township)	16406
Beaver (Jefferson County) (Township)	15864
Beaver (Snyder County) (Township)	17813
Beaver Acres	15136
Beaver Brook	18201
Beaver Center	16435
Beaverdale (Cambria County)	15921
Beaverdale (Northumberland County)	17851
Beaverdale-Lloydell	15921
Beaver Dam	16407
Beaver Falls	15010
Beaver Lake	17758
Beaver Meadows	18216
Beaver Springs	17812
Beavertown (Blair County)	16662
Beavertown (Huntingdon County)	16685
Beavertown (Snyder County)	17813

	ZIP
Beavertown (York County)	17019
Beaver Valley	16640
Beccaria	16616
Beccaria (Township)	16627
Bechtelsville	19505
Beckersville	19540
Becks	17901
Becks Run (Part of Pittsburgh)	15201
Bedford	15522
Bedford (Township)	15522
Bedminster	18910
Bedminster (Township)	18910
Beech Creek	16822
Beech Creek (Township)	16822
Beecherstown	17307
Beech Flats	17724
Beech Glen	17758
Beech Grove	15822
Beechmont	15071
Beechton	15824
Beechview (Part of Pittsburgh)	15216
Beechwood	15834
Beechwood Park	19014
Beechwoods	15840
Beersville	18067
Beesons	15445
Beham	15376
Bela	16049
Belair	17601
Belair Park	17601
Belardiey	19007
Belden	15522
Belfast (Fulton County) (Township)	17238
Belfast (Northampton County)	18064
Belfast Junction	18042
Belfry	19401
Belknap	16222
Bell (Clearfield County) (Township)	16627
Bell (Jefferson County) (Township)	15767
Bell (Westmoreland County) (Township)	15650
Bell Acres	15143
Bella Vista	17754
Belle Bridge (Part of Lincoln)	15037
Bellefield (Part of Pittsburgh)	15213
Bellefonte	16823
Bellegrove	17003
Bellemont	17562
Belle Valley	16509
Belle Vernon (Fayette County)	15012
Belle Vernon (Washington County)	15012
Belleville	17004
Bellevue	15202
Bell Mountain (Part of Dickson City)	18508
Bell Point	15613
Bellrun	16748
Bells Camp	16727
Bells Landing	15757
Bells Mills	15767
Belltown	17841
Bellview	15301
Bellwood	16617
Belmar	16323
Belmont	15904
Belmont Corner	18453
Belmont Hills	19020
Belmont Homes	15904
Belmont Terrace	19406
Belsano	15922
Belsena Mills	16661
Belton	16117
Beltzhoover (Part of Pittsburgh)	15210
Ben Avon (Allegheny County)	15202
Ben Avon (Indiana County)	15701
Ben Avon Heights	15202
Bencetown	15734
Bendersville	17306
Bendertown	17859
Benedicks	17315
Benezett	15821
Benezette (Township)	15821
Benfer	17812
Benjamin (Part of Perkasie)	18944
Benner (Township)	16823
Bensalem	19020-21
For specific Bensalem Zip Codes call (215) 639-5050	
Benscreek (Cambria and Somerset County)	15905

	ZIP
Buffalo (Butler County) (Township)	16055
Buffalo (Perry County) (Township)	17045
Buffalo (Union County) (Township)	17837
Buffalo (Washington County)	15301
Buffalo (Washington County) (Township)	15323
Buffalo Cross Roads	17837
Buffalo Mills	15534
Buffalo Springs	17042
Buffalo Valley	16262
Buffington (Fayette County)	15468
Buffington (Indiana County) (Township)	15961
Buhl (Part of Sharon)	16146
Buhls	16033
Bulger	15019
Bullion	16374
Bullis Mill	16731
Bullskin (Township)	15666
Bully Hill	16323
Bunches	17070
Bungalow Park	18104
Bunker Hill (Cumberland County)	17055
Bunker Hill (Lebanon County)	17042
Bunker Hill (Schuylkill County)	17901
Bunkertown	17049
Bunola	15020
Burbank	16749
Burd Coleman Village (Part of Cornwall)	17016
Burgettstown	15021
Burholme (Part of Philadelphia)	19111
Burlington	18814
Burlington (Township)	18848
Burnham	17009
Burning Well	16735
Burnside (Centre County) (Township)	16845
Burnside (Clearfield County)	15721
Burnside (Clearfield County) (Township)	16692
Burnside (Northumberland County)	17872
Burnstown	16117
Burnt Cabins	17215
Burnwood	18465
Burrell (Armstrong County) (Township)	16226
Burrell (Indiana County) (Township)	15716
Burrous	16922
Burson Plan	15322
Bursonville	18077
Burtville	16743
Bush Addition	16823
Bushkill (Northampton County) (Township)	18064
Bushkill (Pike County)	18324
Bushkill Center	18064
Bush Patch (Part of Old Forge)	18518
Bustleton (Part of Philadelphia)	19115
Bute	15489
Butler	16001-03
For specific Butler Zip Codes call (412) 287-1706	
Butler (Adams County) (Township)	17307
Butler (Butler County) (Township)	16045
Butler (Luzerne County) (Township)	18222
Butler (Schuylkill County) (Township)	17921
Butler Junction	16229
Buttermilk Falls	15658
Buttonwood (Luzerne County)	18702
Buttonwood (Lycoming County)	17771
Buttonwood Glen	18901
Buttonwood Manor	18901
Butztown	18017
Buyerstown	17535
Buzzingtown	15642
Byberry (Part of Philadelphia)	19116
Bycot	18928
Byers	19480
Byersdale	15005
Byrnedale	15827
Byrnesville	17927

	ZIP
Byromtown	16239
Bywood	19082
Bywood Heights	19082
Cabbage Hill	15106
Cabot	16023
Cacoossing	19608
Cadis	18837
Cadogan (Township)	16212
Cadogan	16212
Caernarvon (Berks County) (Township)	19543
Caernarvon (Lancaster County) (Township)	17555
Cains	17527
Cairnbrook	15924
Caldwell	17745
Caledonia	15868
Caledonia Park	17222
California (Bucks County)	18951
California (Washington County)	15419
Calkins	18443
Callapoose	18444
Caliensburg	16213
Callery	16024
Callimont	15552
Caln	19320
Caln (Township)	19320
Calumet	15621
Calumet-Norvelt	15621
Calvert	17771
Calvert Hills (Part of Altoona)	16601
Calvin	16622
Camargo	17566
Cambra	18611
Cambria (Township)	15931
Cambridge (Chester County)	19344
Cambridge (Crawford County) (Township)	16403
Cambridge Springs	16403
Camden Hill (Part of West Mifflin)	15122
Cameron	15834
Cammal	17723
Camp Akiba	18352
Campbelltown (Lebanon County)	17010
Campbelltown (McKean County)	16735
Camp Bnai Brith	18461
Camp Curtin (Part of Harrisburg)	17110
Camp Grove	17830
Camp Hill (Allegheny County)	15106
Camp Hill (Cumberland County)	17001
	17011
For specific Camp Hill Zip Codes call (717) 737-1461	
Camp Hill Shopping Mall (Part of Camp Hill)	17011
Camp Indian Run	19344
Camp Jo-Ann	15668
Camp Mystic	16403
Camp Perry	16114
Camp Starlight	18461
Camptown	18815
Camp Westmont	18449
Canaan	18472
Canaan (Township)	18472
Canadensis	18325
Canadohta Lake	16438
Canal (Township)	16314
Canan Station	16601
Candlebrook	19406
Candor	15019
Cannelton	16115
Canoe (Township)	15772
Canoe Camp	16933
Canoe Creek	16648
Canoe Ridge	15772
Canonsburg	15317
Canton (Bradford County) (Township)	17724
Canton (Bradford County)	17724
Canton (Washington County) (Township)	15301
Capital City Plaza	17011
Caprivi	17013
Carbon (Huntingdon County) (Township)	16678
Carbon (Mercer County)	16154
Carbon (Westmoreland County)	15601
Carbon Center	16001
Carbondale	18407
Carbondale (Township)	18407
Cardale	15420

	ZIP
Cardiff	15943
Cardington	19082
Carlisle	17013
Carlisle Barracks	17013
Carlisle Springs	17013
Carlson	16735
Carlton	16311
Carlton Heights	17252
Carmichaels	15320
Carnegie	15106
Carnot	15108
Carnot-Moon	15108
Carnwath	16861
Carol Acres	17036
Carpenter Corner	16153
Carpenter Town (Lackawanna County)	18414
Carpentertown (Westmoreland County)	15666
Carriage Hill	19067
Carrick (Part of Pittsburgh)	15210
Carrier (Part of Summerville)	15864
Carroll (Clinton County)	17747
Carroll (Perry County) (Township)	17090
Carroll (Washington County) (Township)	15063
Carroll (York County) (Township)	17019
Carroll Park (Columbia County)	17815
Carroll Park (Montgomery County)	19151
Carrolltown	15722
Carroll Valley	17320
Carson (Part of Pittsburgh)	15203
Carsontown	17776
Carson Valley	16635
Carsonville	17032
Carter Camp	16922
Cartwright	15823
Carver Court	19320
Carversville	18913
Carverton	18644
Casanova	16860
Cascade (Township)	17771
Cashtown (Adams County)	17310
Cashtown (Franklin County)	17201
Cass (Huntingdon County) (Township)	16623
Cass (Schuylkill County) (Township)	17901
Cassandra	15925
Casselman	15557
Cassville	16623
Castanea	17726
Castanea (Township)	17726
Castanea (census designated place)	17726
Caste Village (Part of Whitehall)	15236
Castle Garden	15832
Castle Rock	19073
Castle Shannon	15234
Castle Valley	18914
Castlewood	16101
Castor (Part of Philadelphia)	19149
Cataract	16871
Catasauqua	18032
Catawissa	17820
Catawissa (Township)	17820
Caterbury Manor	15061
Catharine (Township)	16693
Cavettsville	15085
Ceasetown	18612
Cecil	15321
Cecil (Township)	15057
Cecil-Bishop	15057
Cedarbrook	19095
Cedarbrook Hills	19095
Cedarbrook Mall	19095
Cedar Cliff Manor	17011
Cedar Creek	15012
Cedar Heights	19428
Cedar Hollow	19355
Cedarhurst	15243
Cedar Knoll	19320
Cedar Lane	17519
Cedar Ledge	17724
Cedar Ridge (Adams County)	17350
Cedar Ridge (Beaver County)	15061
Cedar Run	17727
Cedars	19423
Cedar Springs	17751
Cedarville	19464
Celia	16123
Cementon	18052
Centennial (Adams County)	17331
Centennial (Centre County)	16870

	ZIP
Cleveland (Township)	17820
Cleversburg	17257
Cliff Mine	15108
Clifford (Township)	18413
Clifford (Snyder County)	17870
Clifford (Susquehanna County)	18413
Clifton (Dauphin County)	17057
Clifton (Lackawanna County) (Township)	18424
Clifton (Lackawanna County)	18424
Clifton Heights	19018
Climax (Armstrong County)	16216
Climax (Clarion County)	16216
Climax (Indiana County)	15944
Clinton (Allegheny County)	15026
Clinton (Armstrong County)	16229
Clinton (Butler County) (Township)	16001
Clinton (Fayette County)	15469
Clinton (Lycoming County) (Township)	17752
Clinton (Venango County) (Township)	16373
Clinton (Wayne County) (Township)	18472
Clinton (Wyoming County) (Township)	18419
Clintondale	17751
Clintonville	16372
Cloe	15767
Clonmell	19390
Clover (Township)	15829
Cloverdale Park	18915
Clover Hill	15423
Clover Run	15757
Clune	15727
Cly	17370
Clyde	15944
Clyde No. 3	15322
Clymer (Indiana County)	15728
Clymer (Tioga County) (Township)	16943
Coal (Township)	17872
Coal Bluff	15332
Coal Brook	15425
Coal Cabin Beach	17314
Coal Castle	17901
Coal Center	15423
Coal City	16374
Coaldale (Dauphin County)	17048
Coaldale (Schuylkill County)	18218
Coal Glen	15824
Coal Hill	16301
Coal Hollow	15846
Coal Junction	15531
Coalmont	16678
Coalport (Carbon County)	18229
Coalport (Clearfield County)	16627
Coal Run (Clearfield County)	16666
Coal Run (Somerset County)	15552
Coal Run (Northumberland County)	17866
Coaltown (Butler County)	16057
Coaltown (Lawrence County)	16101
Coatesville	19320
Cobalt Ridge	19058
Cobblerville	17218
Cobbs Corners	16434
Cobham	16351
Coburn (Blair County)	16601
Coburn (Centre County)	16832
Cocalico	17517
Cochran Acres	15001
Cochrans Mills	16226
Cochranton	16314
Cochranville	19330
Cocolamus	17014
Codorus	17311
Codorus (Township)	17327
Coffeetown (Lebanon County)	17078
Coffeetown (Lehigh County)	18069
Coffeetown (Northampton County)	18042
Cogan House (Township)	17771
Cogan Station	17728
Cokeburg	15324
Cokeburg Junction	15331
Cold Point	19462
Cold Run	19508
Cold Spring (Franklin County)	17222
Cold Spring (Huntingdon County)	16652
Cold Spring (Lebanon County) (Township)	17028

	ZIP
Cold Spring (York County)	17360
Cold Spring Park	19464
Cold Springs Crossing	19426
Colebrook (Clinton County) (Township)	17734
Colebrook (Lebanon County)	17015
Colebrookdale	19512
Colebrookdale (Township)	19512
Colegrove	16749
Coleman	15541
Colemanville	17565
Colerain (Bedford County) (Township)	15522
Colerain (Huntingdon County)	16683
Colerain (Lancaster County) (Township)	17536
Coles	17948
Colesburg	16915
Coles Creek	17814
Colesville	18015
Coleville (Centre County)	16823
Coleville (McKean County)	16749
Colfax	16652
College (Beaver County)	15010
College (Centre County) (Township)	16801
College (Northampton County)	18042
College A (Part of East Stroudsburg)	18301
College Heights	19605
College Hill (Part of Beaver Falls)	15010
College Manor	18612
College Misericordia	18612
College Park (Montgomery County)	19031
College Park (Union County)	17837
College View Heights	18016
Collegeville	19426
Colley (Township)	18614
Collier (Allegheny County) (Township)	15106
Collier (Fayette County)	15401
Collingdale	19023
Collins	17566
Collinsburg	15089
Collinsville	17302
Collinswood Acres	15017
Collomsville	17701
Colmar	18915
Colona (Part of Monaca)	15061
Colonial Crest	17111
Colonial Hills (Berks County)	19608
Colonial Hills (Mifflin County)	17044
Colonial Manor	17603
Colonial Park (Dauphin County)	17109
Colonial Park (Delaware County)	19064
Colonial Park (Lancaster County)	17540
Colonial Park (Northumberland County)	17847
Colonial Village	19087
Colony Park	19608
Columbia (Bradford County) (Township)	16914
Columbia (Lancaster County)	17512
Columbia Cross Roads	16914
Columbus	16405
Columbus (Township)	16405
Colver	15927
Colwyn	19023
Comly	17772
Commerce (Part of Philadelphia)	19108
Commodore	15729
Compass	17527
Conashaugh Lake	18337
Concord (Butler County) (Township)	16025
Concord (Delaware County) (Township)	19331
Concord (Erie County) (Township)	16407
Concord (Franklin County)	17217
Concord (Westmoreland County)	15012
Concord Park	19047
Concordville	19331
Conemaugh (Cambria County) (Township)	15902
Conemaugh (Indiana County) (Township)	15725
Conemaugh (Somerset County) (Township)	15905

	ZIP
Conestoga (Township)	17516
Conestoga (Chester County)	19520
Conestoga (Lancaster County)	17516
Conestoga Farms	19317
Conestoga Woods	17602
Coneville	16748
Conewago (Adams County) (Township)	17331
Conewago (Dauphin County) (Township)	17022
Conewago (York County) (Township)	17404
Conewago Heights	17345
Conewango (Township)	16365
Confluence	15424
Congo	19504
Congruity	15601
Conifer	15864
Connaughton	19428
Conneaut (Crawford County) (Township)	16424
Conneaut (Erie County) (Township)	16401
Conneaut Lake	16316
Conneaut Lake Park	16316
Conneaut Lakeshore	16316
Conneautville	16406
Connellsville	15425
Connellsville (Township)	15425
Connersville	17851
Connerton	17935
Connoquenessing	16027
Connoquenessing (Township)	16053
Conoy (Township)	17502
Conrad	16720
Conshohocken	19428
Continental (Part of Philadelphia)	19106
Conway	15027
Conyngham (Columbia County) (Township)	17851
Conyngham (Luzerne County)	18219
Conyngham (Luzerne County) (Township)	18655
Cook (Township)	15687
Cooke (Township)	17241
Cookport	15729
Cooksburg	16217
Cookseytown	18707
Cooks Mills	15545
Cooks Run	17778
Coolbaugh (Township)	18466
Coolbaughs	18324
Coolspring (Fayette County)	15445
Coolspring (Jefferson County)	15730
Coolspring (Mercer County) (Township)	16137
Cool Valley (Washington County)	15317
Cool Valley (Westmoreland County)	15601
Coon Hunter	17842
Coontown	16735
Cooper (Clearfield County) (Township)	16839
Cooper (Montour County) (Township)	17821
Coopersburg	18036
Cooper Settlement	16834
Cooperstown (Butler County)	16059
Cooperstown (Venango County)	16317
Cooperstown (Westmoreland County)	15650
Coopersville	17509
Copella	18014
Copesville	19380
Coplay	18037
Coral	15731
Coraopolis	15108
Coraopolis Heights	15108
Corinne	19380
Cork Lane	18640
Corliss (Part of Pittsburgh)	15204
Corner Ketch	19335
Corner Store	19460
Corning	18092
Cornish	15451
Cornog	19343
Cornplanter (Township)	16301
Cornpropst	16652
Cornwall	17016
Cornwall Center (Part of Cornwall)	17016

Name	ZIP
Cornwells Heights-Eddington	19020
Corrine	19380
Corry	16407
Corsica	15829
Cortez (Jefferson County)	15767
Cortez (Lackawanna County)	18436
Corwins Corners	16701
Corydon (Township)	16701
Coryville	16731
Costello	16720
Cosytown	17225
Coterell Lake	18470
Cottage	16669
Cottage Grove	16105
Cottage Hill	16242
Cottageville	18901
Cotton Town	16625
Couchtown	17047
Coudersport	16915
Coulters	15028
Council Crest	18201
Country Club Estates (Armstrong County)	16201
Country Club Estates (Lancaster County)	17601
Country Club Estates (Montgomery County)	19444
Country Club Heights	17601
Country Gardens	17540
Country Hills	15642
Countryside	17011
County Line	18966
County Line Park	18914
Coupon	16629
Court at King of Prussia, The	19406
Courtdale	18704
Courtney	15029
Cove	17020
Covedale	16693
Cove Gap	17236
Coventryville	19464
Coverdale (Part of Bethel Park)	15102
Coveville	18325
Covington (Tioga County) (Township)	16917
Covington (Clearfield County) (Township)	16836
Covington (Lackawanna County) (Township)	18424
Covington	16917
Covode	15767
Cowan	17844
Cowanesque	16918
Cowansburg	15642
Cowanshannock (Township)	16222
Cowans Village	17224
Cowansville	16218
Cowden	15057
Coxeville	18216
Coy	15748
Coy Junction	15748
Coyleville	16034
Crabapple	15380
Crabtree	15624
Crabtree Hollow	19053
Crackersport	18104
Crafton	15205
Craig	18414
Craigheads	17013
Craigs	17948
Craigs Meadow	18301
Craigsville	16262
Craley	17312
Cramer	15954
Cranberry (Venango County) (Township)	16319
Cranberry (Butler County) (Township)	16046
Cranberry (Luzerne County)	18201
Cranberry (Venango County)	16319
Cranberry Estates	16046
Cranberry Ridge	18201
Cranesville	16410
Crates	16240
Crawford (Township)	17740
Crawfordtown	15733
Creamery	19430
Creekside	15732
Creighton	15030
Crenshaw	15824
Crescent (Township)	15046
Crescentdale (Part of Wampum)	16157
Crescent Heights	15427
Crescent Lake (Monroe County)	18332
Crescent Lake (Pike County)	18337
Cresco	18326
Creslo	15951
Cresmont	17931
Cresmont Farms	19335
Cress	17268
Cresson	16630
Cresson (Township)	16630
Cressona	17929
Crestmont (Clinton County)	17745
Crestmont (Montgomery County)	19090
Crestmont Village	15001
Crestview	19040
Crestwood	18444
Creswell	17516
Crete	15701
Criders Corners	16046
Crimson Maple	18837
Croft	16830
Cromby	19460
Cromwell (Township)	17260
Crooked Creek	16652
Crookham	15332
Crosby	16724
Cross Creek	15021
Cross Creek (Township)	15312
Cross Fork	17729
Crossgrove	17841
Crossingville	16412
Cross Keys (Adams County)	17350
Cross Keys (Blair County)	16635
Cross Keys (Bucks County)	18901
Cross Keys (Juniata County)	17021
Crossroads (Northampton County)	18014
Cross Roads (York County)	17322
Crosswicks	19046
Crown	16220
Croydon	19021
Croydon Acres	19021
Croydon Crest	19021
Croydon Heights	19021
Croydon Manor	19021
Croydon Park	19021
Croyle (Township)	15955
Crozer Park Gardens (Part of Chester)	19013
Crucible	15325
Crum Creek Manor	19013
Crum Lynne	19022
Crum Lynne (Part of Ridley Park)	19078
Crystal	15439
Crystal Lake	18407
Crystal Spring	15536
Crystal View	15084
Cuba Mills	17059
Cuddy	15031
Cuddy Hill	15031
Culbertson	17201
Culmerville	15084
Culp	16601
Culpepper Woods	19444
Cumberland (Adams County) (Township)	17325
Cumberland (Greene County) (Township)	15320
Cumberland Park	17011
Cumberland Valley (Township)	15522
Cumberland Village	15320
Cumbola	17930
Cummings (Township)	17776
Cummingstown	17013
Cummingswood Park	15610
Cumru (Township)	19540
Cupola	19344
Curllsville	16221
Curren Terrace (Part of Norristown)	19401
Curry Run	15757
Curryville	16631
Curtin	16841
Curtin (Township)	16841
Curtis Hills	19095
Curtis Park (Centre County)	16866
Curtis Park (Delaware County)	19079
Curtisville	15032
Curwensville	16833
Cush Creek	15712
Cussewago (Township)	16433
Custards	16314
Custer City	16725
Custis Woods	19038
Cutler Summit	16923
Cyclone	16726
Cymbria Mine	15714
Cynwyd Estates	19004
Cynwyd Hills	19004
Cypher	16650
Daggett	16936
Dagus	15846
Daguscahonda	15853
Dagus Mines	15831
Daisytown (Cambria County)	15902
Daisytown (Washington County)	15427
Dale (Cambria County)	15902
Dale (Clearfield County)	16881
Dale Summit	16801
Daleville (Chester County)	19330
Daleville (Lackawanna County)	18424
Dalevue	16801
Daley	15924
Dallas	18612
Dallas (Township)	18612
Dallas City	16701
Dallastown	17313
Dalmatia	17017
Dalton	18414
Damascus	18415
Damascus (Township)	18415
Danboro	18916
Danielsville	18038
Dannersville	18067
Danville	17821
Danville State Hospital	17821
Darby	19023
Darby (Township)	19036
Darby Township (census designated place)	19036
Darlington (Beaver County)	16115
Darlington (Township)	16115
Darlington (Delaware County)	19063
Darlington (Westmoreland County)	15658
Darlington Corners	19380
Darragh	15625
Darthmouth Farms	17036
Dartmouth Hills	19406
Dauberville	19517
Daugherty (Township)	15066
Dauphin	17018
Davidsburg	17315
Davidson (Township)	17758
Davidson Heights	15001
Davidsville	15928
Davis Grove	19044
Davistown (Fayette County)	15446
Davistown (Greene County)	15349
Dawson	15428
Dawson Manor	19040
Dawson Ridge	15009
Dawson Run	16370
Day	16258
Daylesford	19312
Dayton (Armstrong County)	16222
Dayton (Dauphin County)	17098
Deal	15552
Dean	16636
Dean (Township)	16636
Deanville	16242
Dearth	15401
Decatur (Clearfield County) (Township)	16666
Decatur (Mifflin County) (Township)	17841
Deckard	16314
Deckers Point	15759
Deckertown	18446
Deemers Cross Roads	15851
Deemston	15333
Deep Dale East	19058
Deep Dale West	19058
Deep Run	18944
Deep Valley	15352
Deer Creek (Township)	16145
Deercroft	19444
Deerfield (Tioga County) (Township)	16928
Deerfield (Warren County) (Township)	16351
Deer Lake (Fayette County)	15421
Deer Lake (Schuylkill County)	17961
Deer Mt. Lake (mail Swiftwater)	18370
Deer Mt. Lake (mail Scotrun)	18355
Deer Park	18938
Defiance	16633
Degolia	16701
Deiblers Station	17821
Delabole	18072

	ZIP
Faunce	16863
Fawn (Allegheny County) (Township)	15084
Fawn (York County) (Township)	17321
Fawn Grove	17321
Faxon	17701
Fayette (Juniata County) (Township)	17049
Fayette (Lawrence County)	16156
Fayette City	15438
Fayetteville	17222
Fayfield	17402
Fay Terrace	16125
Fearnot	17968
Feasterville	19047
Feasterville Gardens	19047
Feasterville Heights	19047
Feasterville-Trevose	19047
Federal	15071
Federal Correctional Institution	16701
Federal Penitentiary	17837
Federal Prison Camp	17810
Federal Reserve (Part of Pittsburgh)	15230
Federal Square (Part of Harrisburg)	17108
Fell (Township)	18421
Fellsburg	15012
Fellwick	19034
Felton	17322
Feltonville	19013
Fenelton	16034
Ferguson (Centre County) (Township)	16801
Ferguson (Clearfield County) (Township)	16833
Ferguson (Fayette County)	15431
Fergusonville	19007
Fermanagh (Township)	17059
Fern	16319
Fern Brook	18612
Ferndale (Bucks County)	18921
Ferndale (Cambria County)	15905
Ferndale (Northumberland County)	17872
Ferndale (Schuylkill County)	17985
Fern Glen	18241
Fern Hill	19380
Fernridge	18610
Fern Village	19040
Fernville	17815
Fernway	16063
Fernwood (Clearfield County)	16680
Fernwood (Delaware County)	19050
Fernwood-Yeadon	19050
Ferrelton	15563
Fertigs	16364
Fertility	17602
Fetterville	17555
Fiddle Lake	18465
Fiddlers Green	15946
Fidelity (Part of Philadelphia)	19109
Fieldmore Springs	16354
Fife Shire Acres	15317
Fifficktown	15956
Fiketown	15459
Filbert	15435
Fillmore	16823
Finch Hill	18407
Findlay (Township)	15026
Findley (Township)	16137
Finland	18073
Finleyville (Bedford County)	16679
Finleyville (Washington County)	15332
Fireside Terrace (Part of York)	17404
Fisher	16225
Fisherdale	17824
Fisher Heights (Butler County)	16001
Fisher Heights (Washington County)	15063
Fishers Corner	19013
Fishers Ferry	17801
Fishertown (Bedford County)	15539
Fishertown (Cambria County)	15956
Fisherville	17032
Fishing Creek (Township)	17859
Fiske	16639
Fitch Corner	18615
Fitz Henry	15479
Five Corners	16404
Five Forks	17268
Five Points	15001

	ZIP
Five Points (Part of Ohioville)	15059
Five Points (Berks County)	19606
Five Points (Butler County)	16057
Five Points (Chester County)	19348
Five Points (Clearfield County)	15753
Five Points (Erie County)	16509
Five Points (Indiana County)	15732
Five Points (Luzerne County)	18249
Five Points (Mercer County)	16133
Five Points (rural) (Mercer County)	16150
Five Points (Northumberland County)	17772
Five Points (Venango County)	16342
Five Points (Westmoreland County)	15601
Fivepointville	17517
Flat Rock (Centre County)	16870
Flat Rock (Fayette County)	15459
Flatwoods	15486
Fleetville	18420
Fleetwing Estates	19057
Fleetwood	19522
Fleming	16835
Flemington	17745
Flicksville	18050
Flinton	16640
Flintville	17042
Floradale	17307
Floreffe (Part of Jefferson)	15025
Florence	15021
Florida Park	19073
Florin (Part of Mount Joy)	17552
Flourtown	19031
Flourtown Gardens	19031
Flying Hills	19607
FM Corners (Part of Hermitage)	16148
Fogelsville	18051
Folcroft	19032
Foleys Siding (Part of Castle Shannon)	15234
Folsom	19033
Folstown	18707
Fombell	16123
Font	19335
Fontana	17042
Footedale	15468
Foot of Ten	16635
Forbes Road	15633
Force	15841
Ford City	16226
Ford Cliff	16228
Fordham	15767
Ford View	16226
Fordville	17364
Fordyce	15370
Forest	16879
Forest Castle (Part of Exeter)	18643
Forest City	18421
Forest Grove (Allegheny County)	15108
Forest Grove (Bucks County)	18922
Foresthill (Union County)	17844
Forest Hill (York County)	17356
Forest Hills (Allegheny County)	15221
Forest Hills (Lancaster County)	17540
Forest Hills Manor	19006
Forest Inn	18235
Forest Lake	18801
Forest Lake (Township)	18801
Forest Park (Bucks County)	18914
Forest Park (Luzerne County)	18702
Forestville (Butler County)	16035
Forestville (Schuylkill County)	17901
Forge	16686
Forks (Columbia County)	17859
Forks (Northampton County) (Township)	18042
Forks (Sullivan County) (Township)	18614
Forkston	18629
Forkston (Township)	18629
Forksville	18616
Forsythia Gate	19053
Fort Allen Plan	15601
Fortenia	18431
Fort Fetter	16648
Fort Hill (Somerset County)	15540

	ZIP
Fort Hill (Westmoreland County)	15687
Fort Hunter	17110
Fort Indiantown Gap	17003
Fort Littleton	17223
Fort Loudon	17224
Fortney	17339
Fort Roberston	17047
Fortuna	18915
Fort Washington	19034
Forty Fort	18704
Forward (Allegheny County) (Township)	15063
Forward (Butler County) (Township)	16033
Fossilville	15534
Foster (Indiana County)	15681
Foster (Luzerne County) (Township)	18224
Foster (McKean County) (Township)	16701
Foster (Schuylkill County) (Township)	17901
Foster Brook	16701
Fostoria	16617
Foundryville	18603
Fountain	17938
Fountain Dale	17320
Fountain Hill	18015
Fountain House Corners	16433
Fountain Springs	17921
Fountainville	18923
Fourth Avenue (Part of Pittsburgh)	15222
Foustown	17404
Foustwell	15953
Fowler Heights	15701
Fowlersville	18603
Fox (Elk County) (Township)	15846
Fox (Sullivan County) (Township)	17724
Foxburg (Cambria County)	15773
Foxburg (Clarion County)	16036
Foxburg (Jefferson County)	15767
Fox Chapel	15238
Fox Chase (Lancaster County)	17601
Fox Chase (Philadelphia County)	19111
Fox Chase Manor	19117
Foxcroft (Delaware County)	19008
Foxcroft (Montgomery County)	19046
Foxdale (Part of New Stanton)	15672
Fox Hill (Franklin County)	17268
Fox Hill (Luzerne County)	18702
Fox Run	16046
Foxton Lake	18847
Foxtown	15697
Foxtown Hill	18360
Frackville	17931
Frailey (Township)	17981
Francis	16417
Francis Mine	15021
Franconia	18924
Franconia (Township)	18924
Frank	15018
Frankford (Part of Philadelphia)	19124
Frankfort Springs	15050
Franklin (Adams County) (Township)	17307
Franklin (Beaver County) (Township)	16123
Franklin (Bradford County) (Township)	18848
Franklin (Butler County) (Township)	16052
Franklin (Cambria County)	15909
Franklin (Carbon County) (Township)	18235
Franklin (Chester County) (Township)	19350
Franklin (Columbia County) (Township)	17820
Franklin (Erie County) (Township)	16412
Franklin (Fayette County) (Township)	15486
Franklin (Greene County) (Township)	15370
Franklin (Huntingdon County) (Township)	16865
Franklin (Luzerne County) (Township)	18640
Franklin (Lycoming County) (Township)	17742
Franklin (Snyder County) (Township)	17861

	ZIP
Franklin (Susquehanna County) (Township)	18801
Franklin (Venango County)	16323
Franklin (York County) (Township)	17019
Franklin Acres	16046
Franklin Center (Delaware County)	19063
Franklin Center (Erie County)	16412
Franklindale	18832
Franklin Farms	15301
Franklin Forks	18801
Franklin Hill	18822
Franklin Park	15143
Franklintown	17323
Franklinville	16683
Frankstown	16648
Frankstown (Township)	16648
Frazer (Allegheny County) (Township)	15084
Frazer (Chester County)	19355
Frederick	19435
Fredericksburg (Armstrong County)	16041
Fredericksburg (Ski Gap) (Blair County)	16625
Fredericksburg (Clovercreek) (Blair County)	16662
Fredericksburg (Crawford County)	16335
Fredericksburg (Lebanon County)	17026
Fredericksville	19539
Fredericktown	15333
Fredericktown Hill	15333
Fredonia	16124
Freeburg	17827
Freedom (Adams County) (Township)	17307
Freedom (Beaver County)	15042
Freedom (Blair County) (Township)	16637
Freehold (Township)	16402
Freeland	18224
Freemansburg	18017
Freemansburg Heights	18017
Freemansville	19607
Freeport (Armstrong County)	16229
Freeport (Erie County)	16428
Freeport (Greene County) (Township)	15352
Freeport Junction (Part of Freeport)	16229
French Creek (Mercer County) (Township)	16311
Frenchcreek (Venango County) (Township)	16323
Frenchs Corners	16210
Frenchtown	16327
Frenchville	16836
Freysville	17356
Fricks	18927
Fricks Lock	19464
Friedens (Lehigh County)	18080
Friedens (Somerset County)	15541
Friedensburg	17933
Friedensville	18017
Friendship Heights	15467
Friendship Village	19320
Friendsville	18818
Friesville	16625
Frisbie	17961
Frisco	16117
Fritztown	19608
Frogtown (Armstrong County)	16028
Frogtown (Clarion County)	16224
Frogtown (Huntingdon County)	16877
Frogtown (York County)	17070
Froman	15332
Frostburg	15740
Frosts	16239
Frugality	16639
Fruitville (Lancaster County)	17601
Fruitville (Montgomery County)	19473
Frutcheys	18301
Fryburg	16326
Frystown	17067
Fuhrmans Mill	17331
Fulmor Heights	19040
Fulton (Township)	17563
Fulton Run	15701
Furlong	18925
Furnace Hill (Fayette County)	15431

	ZIP
Furnace Hill (Mercer County)	16159
Furnace Run	16210
Furniss	17563
Gabby Heights	15301
Gabelsville	19512
Gahagen	15926
Gaibleton	15747
Gaines	16921
Gaines (Township)	16921
Galeton	16922
Galilee	18415
Gallagher (Township)	17745
Gallagherville	19335
Gallatin	15063
Gallery at Market East, The (Part of Philadelphia)	19107
Gallitzin	16641
Gallitzin (Township)	16641
Galloway (Part of Sugarcreek)	16323
Gamble (Township)	17771
Ganister	16693
Gans	15439
Gap	17527
Gapsville	15533
Garards Fort	15334
Gardeau	16720
Garden City (Allegheny County)	15146
Garden City (Delaware County)	19013
Gardendale	19061
Garden Heights (Part of Altoona)	16602
Garden Hills	17603
Garden View (Lycoming County)	17701
Gardenview (Mifflin County)	17084
Gardenville	18926
Gardner	16101
Gardners	17324
Garfield	19506
Garland	16416
Garman	15714
Garrett	15542
Garrett Hill	19010
Garretts Run	16201
Garrison	15352
Gascola	15235
Gaskill (Township)	15715
Gastonville	15336
Gastown	15774
Gatchellville	17352
Gates	15410
Gatesburg	16877
Gateway Center (Part of Pittsburgh)	15222
Gateway Shopping Center (Part of Edwardsville)	18704
Gauff Hill	18017
Gayly	15146
Gaysport (Part of Hollidaysburg)	16648
Gay Street (Part of West Chester)	19380
Gearhartville	16866
Geeseytown	16648
Geiger	15501
Geigertown	19523
Geistown	15904
Gelatt	18825
General Warren Village	19355
Genesee	16923
Genesee (Township)	16923
Geneva	16316
Geneva Hill	15010
Georges (Township)	15401
George School (Part of Newtown)	18940
Georgetown (Adams County)	17340
Georgetown (Armstrong County)	15656
Georgetown (Beaver County)	15043
Georgetown (Luzerne County)	18702
Georgetown (Northampton County)	18064
Georgeville	15759
German (Township)	15458
German Corners	18053
Germania	16922
Germans	18235
Germansville	18053
Germantown (Adams County)	17340
Germantown (Franklin County)	17222

	ZIP
Germantown (Philadelphia County)	19144
Germantown (Pike County)	18428
Germany (Township)	17340
Geryville	18073
Getty Heights	15701
Gettysburg	17325
Ghenne Heights	15063
Ghennes Heights	15063
Ghent	18850
Giant Oaks	15317
Gibbon Glade	15440
Gibbs Hill	16735
Gibraltar	19508
Gibson (Township)	18842
Gibson	15314
Gibson (Cameron County) (Township)	15832
Gibson (Susquehanna County)	18820
Gibsonia	15044
Gibsonton	15012
Gifford	16732
Gilbert	18331
Gilberton	17934
Gilbertsville	19525
Gilfoyle	16239
Gillespie	15438
Gillett	16925
Gillingham	16836
Gilmore (Fayette County)	15401
Gilmore (Township)	15352
Gilmore (McKean County)	16727
Gilmore (Washington County)	15057
Gilmore Acres	15235
Gilpin (Township)	15656
Ginger Hill	15063
Ginter	16651
Ginther	18252
Gipsy	15741
Girard (Clearfield County) (Township)	16836
Girard (Erie County)	16417
Girard (Erie County) (Township)	16417
Girard Avenue (Part of Philadelphia)	19122
Girardville	17935
Girty	15686
Gitts Run	17331
Gladden	15057
Gladden Heights	15057
Glade (Somerset County)	15530
Glade (Warren County) (Township)	16365
Glade (Warren County)	16365
Glade City	15552
Glades	17402
Gladhill	17320
Gladstone (Part of Lansdowne)	19050
Gladwyne	19035
Glanford (Part of Pittsburgh)	15230
Glasgow (Beaver County)	15059
Glasgow (Cambria County)	16644
Glasgow (Montgomery County)	19464
Glass City	16866
Glasser	15061
Glassmere	15030
Glassport	15045
Glassworks	15338
Glatfelter	17360
Gleason	17724
Gleasonton	17760
Glen Acres	19380
Glen Ashton Farms	19020
Glenburn	18414
Glenburn (Township)	18414
Glen Campbell	15742
Glen Carbon	17901
Glencoe	15538
Glendale (Allegheny County)	15106
Glendale (Luzerne County)	18641
Glendale Gardens (Part of Glenolden)	19036
Glendale Manor	18701
Glendon (Northampton County)	18042
Glendon (Schuylkill County)	17948
Glen Dower	17901
Glen Eden	16033
Glenfield	15143
Glen Forney	17268
Glen Gormely	15071
Glenhall	19380
Glen Hazel	15870
Glen Hope	16645

Name	ZIP
Glenhurst (Part of Bryn Athyn)	19009
Gleniron	17845
Glenloch	19380
Glen Lyon	18617
Glen Mawr	17737
Glen Mills	19342
Glenmoore (Chester County)	19343
Glen Moore (Lancaster County)	17601
Glenolden	19036
Glen Richey	16863
Glen Riddle	19037
Glen Riddle-Lima	19037
Glen Rock	17327
Glen Rose	19320
Glen Roy	19362
Glenruadh	16505
Glen Savage	15538
Glenshaw	15116
Glenside	19038
Glenside Gardens	19038
Glenside Heights	19038
Glen Summit	18707
Glenville	17329
Glenwall Village	15001
Glenwillard	15046
Glenwood (Allegheny County)	15230
Glenwood (Dauphin County)	17109
Glenwood (Erie County)	16501
Glenwood (Mifflin County)	17044
Glenwood (Susquehanna County)	18446
Glenwood Junction (Part of Pittsburgh)	15230
Glenworth	17901
Glosser View	17701
Glyde	15301
Glyndon	16434
Gnatstown	17331
Goat Hill	15301
Godfrey	15656
Goff	16020
Goheenville	16259
Gold	16923
Golden Hill	18623
Golden Key Lake	18337
Goldenridge	19057
Golden Rod Farms	16830
Good	17268
Goodhope	17055
Good Hope Farms	17055
Good Intent	15323
Goodmans Corners	16364
Goods Corner	15906
Good Spring	17981
Goodtown	15530
Goodville	17528
Goodyear	17324
Goosetown	19320
Gordon	17936
Gordonville	17529
Goshen	16830
Goshen (Township)	16873
Goshenville	19380
Gosser Hill	15656
Gouglersville	19608
Gouldsboro	18424
Gourley	15061
Gowen	18241
Gowen City	17828
Grace Park	19081
Graceton	15748
Graceville	15537
Gracey	17228
Gradwohl Terrace	18017
Gradyville	19039
Grafton (Indiana County)	15716
Graham	16866
Graham (Township)	16858
Grampian	16838
Grampian Hills (Part of Williamsport)	17701
Grand Valley	16420
Grandview (Armstrong County)	16201
Grandview (Butler County)	16045
Grandview (Elk County)	15857
Grandview (Indiana County)	15701
Grandview (Washington County)	15063
Grandview Heights	17601
Grandview Park (Elk County)	15857
Grand View Park (Montgomery County)	19426
Grange	15767
Grange Corners	16433
Grange Hall Center	16433

Name	ZIP
Grangeville	17331
Granite	17325
Grant (Elk County)	15821
Grant (Indiana County) (Township)	15759
Grant City	16051
Grantham	17027
Grantley	17403
Grant Street (Part of Pittsburgh)	15219
Grantville	17028
Granville (Mifflin County) (Township)	17044
Granville (Part of California)	15423
Granville (Bradford County) (Township)	16926
Granville	17029
Granville Center	16926
Granville Summit	16926
Grapeville	15634
Grassflat	16839
Grassmere	17814
Grassy (Part of Olyphant)	18447
Graterford	19426
Gratz	17030
Gratztown	15089
Gravity	18436
Gray (Clearfield County)	16881
Gray (Township)	15337
Gray (Somerset County)	15544
Graydon	17322
Grays Landing	15461
Gray Station	15717
Graysville (Greene County)	15337
Graysville (Huntingdon County)	16865
Grazier	15953
Grazierville	16686
Greason	17013
Great Bend	18821
Great Bend (Township)	18822
Greater Pittsburgh International Airport 911th TAC	15231
Greater Point Marion	15474
Greble	17067
Greece City	16025
Greeley	18425
Green (Forest County) (Township)	16353
Green (Indiana County) (Township)	15724
Greenawalds	18104
Greenbank	17557
Greenbrae	16201
Greenbrier (Centre County)	16875
Greenbrier (Dauphin County)	17036
Greenbrier (Delaware County)	19073
Greenbrier (Northumberland County)	17867
Greenbrook	19007
Greenburr	17747
Greencastle	17225
Green Circle	18451
Greencrest Park	16125
Greendale	16735
Greendown Acres	16635
Greene (Beaver County) (Township)	15050
Greene (Clinton County) (Township)	17747
Greene (Erie County) (Township)	16509
Greene (Franklin County) (Township)	17254
Greene (Greene County) (Township)	15320
Greene (Lancaster County)	17518
Greene (Mercer County) (Township)	16125
Greene (Pike County) (Township)	18426
Greene Junction (Part of South Connellsville)	15425
Greenfield (Allegheny County)	15217
Greenfield (Blair County) (Township)	16625
Greenfield (Cambria County)	16613
Greenfield (Erie County) (Township)	16428
Greenfield (Lackawanna County) (Township)	18407
Greenfield (Mercer County)	16137
Greenfields (Berks County)	19605
Green Fields (Dauphin County)	17098
Green Hill	19380

Name	ZIP
Green Hills (Delaware County)	19079
Green Hills (Washington County)	15301
Green Lane	18054
Green Lane Farms	17011
Greenlawn Park	19007
Greenmount	17325
Green Oaks	16301
Greenock	15047
Green Park	17031
Green Point	17038
Green Ridge (Delaware County)	19014
Green Ridge (Lackawanna County)	18509
Green Ridge (Luzerne County)	18201
Greenridge (Westmoreland County)	15642
Greenridge Farms	19006
Greensboro	15338
Greensburg	15601
Greens Landing	18810
Greenspring	17241
Green Springs	17331
Greentown	18426
Green Tree (Allegheny County)	15220
Green Tree (Chester County)	19355
Green Valley (Allegheny County)	15137
Green Valley (Jefferson County)	15825
Green Village	17201
Greenville (Clearfield County)	16839
Greenville (Mercer County)	16125
Greenville (Township)	15552
Greenville East	16125
Greenwald	15670
Greenwich (Berks County) (Township)	19530
Greenwich (Cambria County)	15714
Greenwood (Clearfield County) (Township)	15757
Greenwood (Columbia County)	17846
Greenwood (Columbia County) (Township)	17859
Greenwood (Blair County)	16601
Greenwood (Crawford County) (Township)	16316
Greenwood (Juniata County) (Township)	17094
Greenwood (Perry County) (Township)	17062
Greenwood Hills (Dauphin County)	17109
Green Wood Hills (Franklin County)	17222
Greenwood Village	16001
Gregg (Allegheny County)	15071
Gregg (Centre County) (Township)	16875
Gregg (Union County) (Township)	17810
Gregory (Part of Larksville)	18704
Grenoble	18974
Gresham	16354
Greshville	19512
Gretna	15301
Grey Nuns	19067
Grier City	18214
Griesemersville	19512
Griffiths	16735
Grill	19607
Grimesville	17701
Grimms Crossroads	17356
Grimville	19530
Grindstone	15442
Grindstone-Rowes Run	15442
Gringo	15001
Grisemore	15728
Groffdale	17557
Grovania	17821
Grove (Cameron County) (Township)	15861
Grove (Chester County)	19380
Grove Chapel	15701
Grove City	16127
Grover	17735
Groveton	15108
Grugan (Township)	17745
Gruvertown	18013
Guenot Settlement	16836
Guernsey	17307
Guffey (McKean County)	16740

	ZIP		ZIP		ZIP
Guffey (Westmoreland County)	15642	Hanover (Beaver County) (Township)	15026	Haverford (Montgomery County)	19041
Guilford	17201	Hanover (Lehigh County)		Havertown	19083
Guilford (Township)	17201	(Township)	18103	Hawkeye	15612
Guilford Hills	17201	Hanover (Luzerne County)		Hawk Run	16840
Guilford Springs	17201	(Township)	18702	Hawksville	17566
Guitonville	16239	Hanover (Luzerne County)	18634	Hawley	18428
Guldens	17325	Hanover (Northampton		Hawleywood	18428
Gulich (Township)	16671	County)	18017	Hawstone	17044
Gulph	19406	Hanover (Northampton		Hawthorn	16230
Gulph Mills	19428	County) (Township)	18017	Haycock (Township)	18951
Gump	15370	Hanover (Washington		Haydentown	15478
Gum Tree	19320	County) (Township)	15021	Hayesville	19363
Guth	18104	Hanover (York County)	17331	Hayfield (Township)	16433
Guthriesville	19335	Hanoverdale	17036	Haymaker	16731
Guthsville	18069	Hanover Green	18702	Haynie	16254
Guys Mills	16327	Hanover Heights	19464	Hays (Allegheny County)	15230
Gwynedd	19436	Hanover Hills	17036	Hays (Fayette County)	15401
Gwynedd Square	19446	Hanover Junction	17360	Hays Creek	18661
Gwynedd Valley	19437	Hansotte Plan	16226	Hays Grove	17241
Haafsville	18031	Happy Valley (Part of		Hays Mills	15552
Habrenfield Hills	18612	Exeter)	18643	Haysville (Allegheny County)	15143
Hackelbernie (Part of Jim		Harbor	16101	Haysville (Butler County)	16041
Thorpe)	18229	Harborcreek	16421	Hayti	19320
Hackett	15367	Harborcreek (Township)	16421	Hazel Hurst	16733
Haddenville	15401	Harding	18615	Hazel Kirk	15063
Haddock	18201	Hardy Hill	15431	Hazelwood (Part of	
Hadley	16130	Harford	18823	Pittsburgh)	15207
Haffey	15147	Harford (Township)	18823	Hazen	15825
Hagersville	18944	Harford Heights	15642	Hazle (Township)	18201
Hahnstown	17522	Harlan	15829	Hazlebrook	18201
Hahntown	15642	Harlansburg	16101	Hazleton	18201
Haines (Township)	16820	Harleigh	18225	Hazle Village (Part of	
Haines Acres	17402	Harlem	18062	Hazleton)	18201
Haleeka	17728	Harleysville	19438	Hazzard (Part of	
Halfmoon (Township)	16877	Harmar (Township)	15024	Monongahela)	15063
Halford Hills	19401	Harmar Heights	15024	Heacock Meadows	19067
Halfville	17543	Harmarville	15238	Headlee Heights	15334
Halfway	17042	Harmonsburg	16422	Heart Lake	18801
Halfway House	19464	Harmonville	19428	Heath (Township)	15860
Halifax	17032	Harmony (Beaver County)		Heatherwold	19086
Halifax (Township)	17032	(Township)	15003	Heathville	15864
Hall (Allegheny County)	15146	Harmony (Butler County)	16037	Hebe	17830
Hall (Beaver County)	15061	Harmony (Clearfield County)	16692	Heberlig	17241
Hallowell	19044	Harmony (Forest County)		Hebron (Lebanon County)	17042
Halls	17756	(Township)	16370	Hebron (Potter County)	
Hallstead	18822	Harmony (Jefferson County)	15767	(Township)	16915
Hallston	16057	Harmony (Susquehanna		Hebron Center	16915
Hallton	15860	County) (Township)	18847	Heckscherville	17901
Hallwood	18621	Harmony Grove	17315	Hecktown	18017
Halsey	16735	Harmony Hill	19335	Hecla	17960
Hamburg	19526	Harmony Township	15003	Hector (Township)	16948
Hametown	17327	Harmonyville	19464	Hegarty Crossroads	16671
Hamilton (Adams County)		Harnedsville	15424	Hegins	17938
(Township)	17316	Harpers	18088	Hegins (Township)	17938
Hamilton (Franklin County)		Harper Tavern	17003	Heidelberg (Allegheny	
(Township)	17201	Harper Village	15001	County)	15106
Hamilton (Jefferson County)	15744	Harris (Township)	16827	Heidelberg (Berks County)	
Hamilton (McKean County)		Harris Acres	16801	(Township)	19567
(Township)	16333	Harrisburg	17101-30	Heidelberg (Lebanon	
Hamilton (Monroe County)		For specific Harrisburg Zip Codes		County) (Township)	17088
(Township)	18354	call (717) 257-2150		Heidelberg (Lehigh County)	
Hamilton (Northumberland		Harrison (Allegheny County)		(Township)	18053
County)	17801	(Township)	15065	Heidelberg (York County)	
Hamilton (Tioga County)		Harrison (Bedford County)		(Township)	17362
(Township)	16912	(Township)	15550	Heidlersburg	17372
Hamiltonban (Township)	17325	Harrison (Potter County)		Heights Plaza	15065
Hamilton Heights	17201	(Township)	16927	Heilmandale	17042
Hamilton Mall (Part of		Harrison City	15636	Heilwood	15745
Allentown)	18101	Harrison Valley	16927	Heise Run	16901
Hamilton Park	17603	Harrisonville	17228	Heistersburg	15433
Hamlin (Lebanon County)	17026	Harristown	17562	Helen Furnace	16214
Hamlin (McKean County)		Harrisville	16038	Helen Mills	15823
(Township)	16733	Harrity	18235	Helfenstein	17939
Hamlin (Wayne County)	18427	Harrow	18942	Helixville	15559
Hammersley Fork	17764	Harshaville	15026	Hellam	17406
Hammett	16510	Hartleton	17829	Hellam (Township)	17368
Hammond	16946	Hartley (Township)	17835	Hellertown	18055
Hammondville	15666	Hartranft	19401	Helvetia	15848
Hamorton	19348	Hartsfield	16930	Hemlock (Columbia County)	
Hampden (Berks County)	19604	Hartstown	16131	(Township)	17815
Hampden (Cumberland		Hartsville	18974	Hemlock (Warren County)	16365
County) (Township)	17055	Harvey Plan	15042	Hemlock Grove (Pike	
Hampden Heights (Part of		Harveys Lake	18618	County)	18426
Reading)	19604	Harveyville	18655	Hemlock Grove (Sullivan	
Hampshire Heights	15601	Harwick	15049	County)	17758
Hampton (Adams County)	17350	Harwood	18201	Hempfield (Mercer County)	
Hampton (Allegheny		Harwood Park	19082	(Township)	16125
County) (Township)	15101	Hasentab's	16635	Hempfield (Westmoreland	
Hampton Station	16301	Hasson Heights	16301	County) (Township)	15601
Hampton Township	15101	Hastings	16646	Hempfield Manor	15601
Hancock	19539	Hatboro	19040	Henderson (Clearfield	
Haneyville	17745	Hatfield (Fayette County)	15401	County)	16651
Hankey Farms	15071	Hatfield (Montgomery		Henderson (Huntingdon	
Hanlin	15021	County)	19440	County) (Township)	16652
Hannah	16870	Hatfield (Township)	19440	Henderson (Jefferson	
Hannahstown	16023	Hauto (Part of		County) (Township)	15767
Hannastown	15635	Nesquehoning)	18240	Henderson (Mercer County)	16153
Hannaville	16314	Haverford (Delaware		Henderson Park	19406
Hann Hill (Part of		County) (Township)	19083	Hendersonville (Butler	
Hermitage)	16159			County)	16046

	ZIP		ZIP		ZIP
Hughes Park	19406	Indian Lake (Somerset		Jacksonville (Lehigh	
Hughestown	18640	County)	15926	County)	18066
Hughesville	17737	Indianland	18088	Jacksonville (Northampton	
Hughs	18621	Indian Mountain Lake	18210	County)	18014
Hulltown	15428	Indianola	15051	Jacksonwald	19606
Hulmeville	19047	Indian Orchard	18431	Jacksville	16057
Hulton (Part of Oakmont)	15139	Indian Pines	15205	Jacktown	15642
Humbolt	18201	Indian Springs Estates	15701	Jacktown Acres	15642
Hummelstown	17036	Industry	15052	Jacobs Creek	15448
Hummels Wharf	17831	Inez	16915	Jacobs Mills	17331
Humphreys	15601	Ingleby	16882	Jacobus	17407
Humphreyville	19320	Inglenook	17032	Jalappa	19526
Hungerford (Part of		Inglesmith	17211	James City	16734
Shrewsbury)	17361	Ingomar	15127	James Creek	16657
Hungry Hollow	15656	Ingram	15205	Jamestown (Cambria	
Hunker	15639	Inkerman	18640	County)	15946
Hunlock (Township)	18621	Intercourse	17534	Jamestown (Carbon	
Hunlock Creek	18621	Iola	17846	County)	18235
Hunlock Gardens	18621	Iona	17042	Jamestown (Mercer County)	16134
Hunter	17872	Irishtown (Adams County)	17350	Jamesville	18014
Hunter Hill	19462	Irishtown (Clearfield County)	16838	Jamison (Bucks County)	18929
Hunters Run	17324	Irishtown (Fayette County)	15431	Jamison (Fayette County)	15401
Hunterstown	17325	Irishtown (McKean County)	16738	Jamison (Forest County)	16370
Huntersville	17756	Irishtown (Mercer County)	16137	Jamison City	17814
Huntingdon	16652	Iron Bridge	15666	Japan	18224
Huntingdon Furnace	16686	Iron Springs	17320	Jarrettown	19025
Huntingdon Heights	15642	Ironton	18037	Jay (Township)	15827
Huntingdon Manor	17540	Ironville (Blair County)	16686	Jeanesville	18201
Huntingdon Meadows	19006	Ironville (Lancaster County)	17512	Jeannette	15644
Huntingdon Valley	19006	Irvin (Part of West Mifflin)	15122	Jeddo	18224
Hunting Park (Part of		Irvine	16329	Jednota	17057
Philadelphia)	19140	Irving	17963	Jefferis Crossing	15401
Huntington (Adams County)		Irvona	16656	Jefferson (Township)	15021
(Township)	17372	Irwin (Venango County)		Jefferson	15687
Huntington (Luzerne		(Township)	16038	Jefferson (Allegheny	
County) (Township)	18655	Irwin (Westmoreland		County)	15025
Huntington Mills	18622	County)	15642	Jefferson (Berks County)	
Huntley	15832	Isabella	15447	(Township)	19506
Huntsdale	17013	Iselin	15681	Jefferson (Butler County)	
Huntsville	18612	Iselin Heights	15801	(Township)	16001
Husband	15501	Island Lake	18462	Jefferson (Dauphin County)	
Huston (Blair County)		Island Park	17801	(Township)	17032
(Township)	16693	Ithan	19085	Jefferson (Fayette County)	
Huston (Centre County)		Itley	16412	(Township)	15473
(Township)	16844	Iva	17562	Jefferson (Greene County)	15344
Huston (Clearfield County)		Ivarea	16410	Jefferson (Greene County)	
(Township)	15849	Ivyland	18974	(Township)	15344
Huston Run	15332	Ivy Mills (Part of Chester		Jefferson (Lackawanna	
Hustontown	17229	Heights)	19342	County) (Township)	18436
Hutchins	16740	Ivy Ridge (Part of		Jefferson (Mercer County)	
Hutchinson (Fayette		Philadelphia)	19101	(Township)	16150
County)	15401	Ivywood	18451	Jefferson (Schuylkill County)	17922
Hutchinson (Westmoreland		Jacks Creek	17044	Jefferson (Somerset	
County)	15640	Jacks Mountain	17320	County) (Township)	15501
Hyde	16843	Jackson (Butler County)		Jefferson (Washington	
Hyde Park (Berks County)	19605	(Township)	16063	County)	15312
Hyde Park (Westmoreland		Jackson (Cambria County)		Jefferson Center	16001
County)	15641	(Township)	15909	Jeffersonville	19408
Hydetown	16328	Jackson (Columbia County)		Jenkins (Township)	18640
Hyde Villa	19605	(Township)	17814	Jenkintown	19046
Hyndman	15545	Jackson (Dauphin County)		Jenkintown Manor	19117
Hynemansville	18066	(Township)	17032	Jenks (Township)	16239
Hyner	17738	Jackson (Greene County)		Jenner (Township)	15531
Icedale	19344	(Township)	15341	Jenners	15546
Icksburg	17037	Jackson (Huntingdon		Jenners Crossroads	15531
Idaho	15774	County) (Township)	16669	Jennerstown	15547
Idamar	15734	Jackson (Lebanon County)		Jennersville	19390
Idaville	17337	(Township)	17042	Jenningsville	18629
Idetown (Part of Harveys		Jackson (Luzerne County)		Jericho	15861
Lake)	18612	(Township)	18708	Jericho Mills	17059
Idlewood (Part of Crafton)	15205	Jackson (Lycoming County)		Jermyn	18433
Imler	16655	(Township)	17765	Jerome	15937
Imlertown	15522	Jackson (Mercer County)		Jerome Junction (Part of	
Immaculata	19345	(Township)	16133	Benson)	15935
Imperial	15126	Jackson (Monroe County)		Jersey Mills	17739
Imperial-Enlow	15126	(Township)	18352	Jersey Shore	17740
Independence	15001	Jackson (Northumberland		Jerseytown	17815
Independence (Beaver		County) (Township)	17830	Jessup (Lackawanna	
County) (Township)	15026	Jackson (Perry County)		County)	18434
Independence (Snyder		(Township)	17006	Jessup (Susquehanna	
County)	17864	Jackson (Snyder County)		County) (Township)	18801
Independence (Washington		(Township)	17889	Jessup-Peckville (Part of	
County) (Township)	15312	Jackson (Susquehanna		Jessup)	18434
Independence (Washington		County)	18825	Jewtown	15745
County)	15312	Jackson (Susquehanna		Jim Thorpe	18229
Indiana (Allegheny County)		County) (Township)	18825	Jimtown	15501
(Township)	15051	Jackson (Tioga County)		Joanna	19543
Indiana (Indiana County)	15701	(Township)	16936	Joanna Heights	19543
Indian Creek (Bucks		Jackson (Venango County)		Jobs Corners	16936
County)	19057	(Township)	16317	Joffre	15053
Indian Creek (Cumberland		Jackson (York County)		Johnsonburg (Elk County)	15845
County)	17055	(Township)	17362	Johnsonburg (Indiana	
Indian Crossing	16731	Jackson Center	16133	County)	15772
Indian Head (Erie County)	16441	Jackson Corner	16652	Johnsons Corner	19317
Indian Head (Fayette		Jackson Crossing	16365	Johnstown (Cambria	
County)	15446	Jackson Hall	17201	County)	15901-15
Indian Hills	16201	Jackson Knolls	16101	For specific Johnstown Zip Codes	
Indian King	19380	Jackson Summit	16936	call (814) 533-4935	
Indian Lake (Luzerne		Jacksonville (Centre		Johnstown (Union County)	17844
County)	18661	County)	16841	Johnsville	18974

	ZIP		ZIP		ZIP
Kushequa	16735	Landreth Manor	19007	Lawton	18828
Kutztown (Berks County)	19530	Landstreet	15935	Layfield	19525
Kutztown (Lebanon County)	17067	Lane (Part of Freeport)	16229	Layton	15473
Kylers Corners	15846	Lanesboro	18827	Leacock	17540
Kylertown	16847	Lanes Mills	15824	Leacock (Township)	17572
Kyleville	17302	Langdon	17763	Leacock-Leola-Bareville	17540
La Anna	18326	Langdondale	16650	Leaders Heights	17403
La Belle	15450	Langeloth	15054	Leaf Park	17603
Laboratory	15301	Langhorne	19047	Leak Run (Part of	
Labott	17364		19053	Monroeville)	15146
Lacey Park	18974	For specific Langhorne Zip Codes		Leaman Place	17562
Laceyville	18623	call (215) 757-6777		Leamersville	16635
Lack (Township)	17021	Langhorne Gables	19047	Learn Settlement	15729
Lackawannock (Township)	16137	Langhorne Gardens	19047	Leasuresville	16055
Lackawaxen	18435	Langhorne Manor	19047	Leather Corner Post	18069
Lackawaxen (Township)	18425	Langhorne Terrace	19047	Leatherwood	16242
Lacock	15301	Lansdale	19446	Lebanon (Lebanon County)	17042
Laddsburg	18833	Lansdowne	19050	Lebanon (Wayne County)	
Lafayette	16738	Lansdowne Park Gardens		(Township)	18431
Lafayette (Township)	16738	(Part of Collingdale)	19023	Lebanon Plaza	17042
Lafayette Hill	19444	Lanse	16849	Lebanon South	17042
Lafayette Park	19444	Lansford	18232	Lebo	17040
Lafferty Hill (Part of		Lantz Corners	16740	Le Boeuf (Township)	16441
Baldwin)	15227	Lapidea Hills	19013	Le Boeuf Gardens	16441
Laflin	18702	La Plume	18440	Leck Kill	17836
La Gonda	15301	La Plume (Township)	18440	Leckrone	15454
Lahaska	18931	Laporte	18626	Lecontes Mills	16850
Laings Garden	19007	Laporte (Township)	17758	Lederach	19450
Lairds Crossing	16262	Larabee	16731	Ledgedale	18463
Lairdsville	17742	Lardintown	16055	Lee	18617
La Jose	15753	Large (Part of Jefferson)	15025	Leechburg	15656
Lake (Luzerne County)		Larimer (Somerset County)		Leech Hill	16943
(Township)	18621	(Township)	15552	Leedom Estates	19078
Lake (Mercer County)		Larimer (Westmoreland		Leedom Gardens	19078
(Township)	16153	County)	15647	Lee Mine	18634
Lake (Wayne County)		Larke	16693	Lee Park	18702
(Township)	18436	Larksville	18704	Leeper	16233
Lake Ariel	18436	Larrys Creek	17740	Leesburg	16156
Lake Carey	18657	Larryville	17740	Leesburg Station	16156
Lake City	16423	Larue	17327	Lees Cross Roads	17257
Lake Como	18437	Lashley	17267	Leesport	19533
Lake Donegal	15610	Lathrop (Township)	18446	Leet (Township)	15003
Lake Harmony	18624	Latimore	17372	Leetonia	17727
Lake Heritage	17325	Latimore (Township)	17372	Leetsdale	15056
Lake Idlewild	18470	Latrobe	15650	Lehigh (Carbon County)	
Lake Jo-Ann	15367	Latrobe Shopping Center	15650	(Township)	18255
Lakeland	18436	Lattimer Mines	18234	Lehigh (Lackawanna	
Lake Lynn	15451	Laughlin Corner	15043	County)	18424
Lake Meade	17316	Laughlin Junction (Part of		Lehigh (Lackawanna	
Lake Monroe	18335	Pittsburgh)	15207	County) (Township)	18424
Lakemont	16602	Laughlintown	15655	Lehigh (Northampton	
Lakemont Terrace (Part of		Laurel (Cumberland County)	17324	County) (Township)	18088
Altoona)	16602	Laurel (York County)	17322	Lehigh (Wayne County)	
Lake Naomi	18350	Laurel Bend	19007	(Township)	18424
Lake Pleasant	16438	Laureldale	19605	Lehigh Furnace	18080
Lake Quinn	18472	Laurel Falls	15552	Lehigh Gap (Carbon	
Lake Sheridan	18446	Laurel Gardens	15229	County)	18071
Lakeside (Bucks County)	19053	Laurel Hill (Fayette County)	15431	Lehigh Gap (Lehigh County)	18080
Lakeside (Susquehanna		Laurel Hill (Washington		Lehighton	18235
County)	18834	County)	15057	Lehigh University (Part of	
Lake Stonycreek	15541	Laurel Lake (Luzerne		Bethlehem)	18015
Laketon Heights	15235	County)	18707	Lehigh Valley General Mail	
Lakeview	18847	Laurel Lake (Susquehanna		Facility	18001-02
Lakeview Heights	17111	County)	18812	For specific Lehigh Valley General	
Lakeville	18438	Laurel Mountain	15655	Mail Facility Zip Codes call (215)	
Lake Waynewood	18436	Laurel Park	17845	882-3256	
Lake Wesauking	18848	Laurel Ridge	15009	Lehigh Valley Mall	18052
Lake Winola	18625	Laurel Run	18702	Lehman (Luzerne County)	18627
Lakewood (Erie County)	16505	Laurelton	17835	Lehman (Luzerne County)	
Lakewood (Wayne County)	18439	Laurelville (Fayette County)	15666	(Township)	18612
Lake Wynonah	17972	Laurelville (Lancaster		Lehman (Pike County)	
Lamar	16848	County)	17557	(Township)	18324
Lamar (Township)	17750	Laurys Station	18059	Lehman (York County)	17362
Lamartine	16375	Lausanne (Township)	18255	Leibeyville	17960
Lamberton	15458	Lavansville	15501	Leidy (Township)	17764
Lambertsville	15563	Lavelle	17943	Leinbachs	19605
Lambs Creek	16933	Laverock	19118	Leisenring	15455
Lamonts Corners (Part of		Lawn	17041	Leith	15401
Hermitage)	16150	Lawnherst	18042	Leithsville	18055
La Mott	19012	Lawnton	17111	Lemasters	17231
Lampeter	17537	Lawrence (Clearfield		Lemon (Township)	18657
Lanark	18034	County) (Township)	16830	Lemon	18657
Lancaster	17601-05	Lawrence (Tioga County)		Lemont	16851
For specific Lancaster Zip Codes		(Township)	16946	Lemont Furnace	15456
call (717) 665-4199		Lawrence (Washington		Lemoyne	17043
Lancaster (Butler County)		County)	15055	Lenape	19380
(Township)	16037	Lawrence Park (Delaware		Lenape Heights	16226
Lancaster (Lancaster		County)	19008	Lenape Park	16226
County) (Township)	17603	Lawrence Park (Erie		Lenhartsville	19534
Lancaster Avenue (Part of		County) (Township)	16511	Lenker Manor	17111
Philadelphia)	19104	Lawrence Park (Erie		Lenkerville	17061
Lancaster Bible College	17601	County)	16511	Lenni	19052
Lancaster Junction	17545	Lawrenceville (Allegheny		Lenni Heights	19037
Landenberg	19350	County)	15201	Lennox Park (Part of	
Lander	16345	Lawrenceville (Lackawanna		Trainer)	19015
Landingville	17942	County)	18642	Lenover	19365
Landisburg	17040	Lawrenceville (Tioga		Lenox (Township)	18446
Landis Farms	17601	County)	16929	Lenoxville	18446
Landis Store	19512	Lawsonham	16248	Lenwood Heights	17236
Landis Valley	17604	Lawson Heights	15650	Leola	17540
Landisville	17538	Lawsville Center	18801	Leolyn	17765

	ZIP		ZIP		ZIP
Leona	16914	Lincoln Heights (Berks		Locust Grove	17402
Leopard	19312	County)	19508	Locust Grove Gardens	17402
Leopard Lakes	19312	Lincoln Heights		Locust Lakes Village	18347
Le Raysville	18829	(Westmoreland County)	15644	Locust Point	17055
Le Roy	17743	Lincoln Hill	15301	Locust Ridge	15116
Leroy (Township)	17724	Lincoln Park (Allegheny		Locust Run	17094
Lester	19113	County)	15235	Locust Summit	17840
Letort	17582	Lincoln Park (Berks County)	19609	Locust Valley (Lehigh	
Letterkenny (Township)	17244	Lincoln Park (Delaware		County)	18036
Letterkenny Army Depot	17201	County)	19079	Locust Valley (Schuylkill	
Level Corner	17744	Lincoln Place (Part of		County)	18214
Level Green	15085	Pittsburgh)	15122	Lofty	18201
Levittown	19054-59	Lincoln Terrace	18042	Logan (Blair County)	
For specific Levittown Zip Codes		Lincoln University	19352	(Township)	16602
call (215) 949-3131		Lincolnville	16404	Logan (Clinton County)	
Levittown Center	19054	Lincolnway	17404	(Township)	17747
Levittown Discount World		Linconia	19047	Logan (Huntingdon County)	
(Part of Tullytown)	19055	Lindaville	18824	(Township)	16611
Levittown-Tullytown	19007	Linden (Lycoming County)	17744	Logan (Indiana County)	15742
Lewis (Lycoming County)		Linden (Washington		Logan (Philadelphia County)	19141
(Township)	17771	County)	15317	Logan Mills	17747
Lewis (Northumberland		Linden Hall	16828	Logans Ferry (Part of Plum)	15068
County) (Township)	17772	Lindenhurst	19067	Logans Ferry Heights (Part	
Lewis (Union County)		Linds Crossing	16648	of Plum)	15068
(Township)	17880	Lindsey (Part of		Logan Square (Part of	
Lewisberry	17339	Punxsutawney)	15767	Norristown)	19401
Lewisburg	17837	Line Lexington	18932	Loganton	17747
Lewis Crossing	15458	Line Mountain	17941	Loganville	17342
Lewis Run	16738	Linesville	16424	Log Pile	15301
Lewistown (Mifflin County)	17044	Linfield	19468	London	16127
Lewistown (Schuylkill		Linglestown	17112	London Britain (Township)	19350
County)	18252	Linn	15442	Londonderry (Bedford	
Lewistown Junction	17044	Linntown	17837	County) (Township)	15545
Lewisville (Chester County)	19351	Linville Circle (Part of		Londonderry (Chester	
Lewisville (Indiana County)	15725	Lancaster)	17602	County) (Township)	19330
Lexington	17543	Linwood	19061	Londonderry (Dauphin	
Liberty (Adams County)		Linwood Park	19061	County) (Township)	17057
(Township)	17320	Linwood Terrace	19061	London Grove	19348
Liberty (Allegheny County)	15133	Lionville	19353	London Grove (Township)	19390
Liberty (Bedford County)		Lionville-Marchwood	19353	Lonely Acres	15722
(Township)	16678	Lippincott	15370	Lone Pine	15301
Liberty (Centre County)		Lisbon	16373	Lonewood	15145
(Township)	16826	Lisburn	17055	Long Acre Park (Part of	
Liberty (McKean County)		Listie	15549	Yeadon)	19050
(Township)	16749	Listonburg	15424	Long Branch	15423
Liberty (Mercer County)		Litchfield	18810	Long Bridge	15658
(Township)	16127	Litchfield (Township)	18810	Longbrook	17758
Liberty (Montour County)		Lithia Springs	17857	Longfellow	17044
(Township)	17821	Lithia Valley (Part of		Longlevel	17368
Liberty (Susquehanna		Factoryville)	18419	Long Pond	18334
County) (Township)	18801	Lititz	17543	Long Run	18235
Liberty (Tioga County)	16930	Little Beaver (Township)	16141	Longs Crossroad	16661
Liberty (Tioga County)		Little Britain (Township)	19363	Longsdale	19539
(Township)	16930	Little Chicago	15320	Longsdorf	17241
Liberty Corners	18848	Little Cooley	16404	Longstown	17402
Liberty Square	17518	Little Corners	16335	Longswamp	19539
Library	15129	Little Gap	18058	Longswamp (Township)	19539
Lickdale	17038	Little Hickory	16353	Longview (Part of Bethel	
Licking (Township)	16049	Little Hope	16428	Park)	15102
Licking Creek (Township)	17228	Little Italy	18956	Longwood	19348
Lickingville	16332	Little Kansas	17051	Lookout	18417
Lightner	17404	Little Mahanoy (Township)	17823	Loomis Park	18702
Light Street	17839	Little Marsh	16950	Loop Station	16648
Ligonier	15658	Little Meadows	18830	Lopez	18628
Ligonier (Township)	15658	Littlestown	17340	Lorain	15902
Lilly	15938	Little Summit	15431	Lorane	19606
Lillyville	16123	Little Washington (Chester		Lorberry	17963
Lima	19037	County)	19335	Lords Valley	18428
Limehill	18853	Little Washington		Lorenton	16938
Limekiln	19535	(Cumberland County)	17241	Loretto	15940
Limeport	18060	Live Easy	15320	Loretto Road	15931
Limerick	19468	Liverpool	17045	Loshs Run	17020
Limerick (Township)	19468	Liverpool (Township)	17045	Lost Creek	17946
Lime Ridge	17815	Livonia	16872	Lottsville	16402
Lime Rock	17543	Llandrilla	19004	Loux Corner	18927
Limestone (Clarion County)	16234	Llanfair	15930	Lovedale	15037
Limestone (Clarion County)		Llangelan Hills	19073	Lovejoy	15729
(Township)	16234	Llewellyn	17944	Lovell	16407
Limestone (Lycoming		Llewelyn Corners	18602	Lovelton	18629
County) (Township)	17740	Lloydell	15921	Lovely	15521
Limestone (Montour		Lloydesville	15650	Lover	15022
County) (Township)	17821	Llyswen (Part of Altoona)	16602	Lowber (Fayette County)	15438
Limestone (Union County)		Loag	19520	Lowber (Westmoreland	
(Township)	17844	Lobachsville	19547	County)	15660
Limestone (Warren County)		Lochiel	17837	Lowe Lake	18470
(Township)	16365	Lochvale	15742	Lower Allen	17011
Limestoneville	17847	Locke Mills	17063	Lower Allen (Township)	17011
Lime Valley	17584	Lock Haven	17745	Lower Alsace (Township)	19606
Limeville	17527	Lock No. 4 (Part of		Lower Askam	18706
Lincoln (Allegheny County)	15037	Charleroi)	15022	Lower Augusta (Township)	17801
Lincoln (Bedford County)		Lockport (Clinton County)	17745	Lower Brownville	17976
(Township)	15521	Lockport (Mifflin County)	17044	Lower Burrell	15068
Lincoln (Huntingdon		Lockport (Westmoreland		Lower Chanceford	
County) (Township)	16638	County)	15923	(Township)	17302
Lincoln (Lancaster County)	17522	Locksley	19342	Lower Chichester	
Lincoln (Somerset County)		Lockview	15022	(Township)	19061
(Township)	15501	Locust (Columbia County)		Lower Frankford (Township)	17013
Lincoln Acres	15642	(Township)	17820	Lower Frederick (Township)	19492
Lincoln Beach	15068	Locust (Indiana County)	15771	Lower Gwynedd (Township)	19437
Lincoln Colliery	17963	Locustdale	17945	Lower Heidelberg	
Lincoln Falls	18616	Locust Gap	17840	(Township)	19604

	ZIP		ZIP		ZIP
Lower Longswamp	19539	Lyon Valley	18066	Magill Heights	15024
Lower Macungie (Township)	18062	Mable	17921	Magnolia Gardens	19007
Lower Mahanoy (Township)	17017	Mable Hill	15327	Magnolia Hill	19007
Lower Makefield (Township)	19067	McAdoo	18237	Mahaffey	15757
Lower Merion (Township)	19003	McAdoo Heights	18237	Mahanoy (Township)	17776
Lower Mifflin (Township)	17241	McAlevys Fort	16652	Mahanoy City	17948
Lower Milford (Township)	18036	McAlisters Crossroads	15086	Mahanoy Plane (Part of	
Lower Moreland (Township)	19006	McAlisterville	17049	Gilberton)	17949
Lower Mount Bethel		MacArthur (Part of		Mahoning (Armstrong	
(Township)	18063	Aliquippa)	15001	County)	16259
Lower Nazareth (Township)	18017	McCalmont (Township)	15711	Mahoning (Armstrong	
Lower Orchard	19058	McCandless (Township)	15237	County) (Township)	16242
Lower Oxford (Township)	19363	McCandless Township		Mahoning (Carbon County)	
Lower Paxton	17109	(census designated		(Township)	18235
Lower Paxton (Township)	17109	place)	15237	Mahoning (Lawrence	
Lower Peanut	15480	McCartney	16661	County) (Township)	16132
Lower Pottsgrove		McCauley	16651	Mahoning (Montour County)	
(Township)	19464	McChesneytown	15650	(Township)	17821
Lower Providence		McChesneytown-		Mahoning Manor	17847
(Township)	19401	Loyalhanna	15620	Mahoningtown (Part of New	
Lower Sagon	17877	McClarran	15650	Castle)	16102
Lower Salford (Township)	19438	Mc Cleary	15050	Maiden Creek	19510
Lower Saucon (Township)	18015	McClellan	17032	Maidencreek (Township)	19605
Lower Southampton		McClellandtown	15458	Main (Township)	17815
(Township)	19047	McClellan Heights	17403	Mainesburg	16932
Lower Swatara (Township)	17057	McClintock	16301	Mainland	19451
Lower Towamensing		McClure (Fayette County)	15666	Mainsville	17257
(Township)	18071	McClure (Snyder County)	17841	Mainville	17815
Lower Turkeyfoot		McConnellsburg	17233	Maitland	17044
(Township)	15424	McConnells Mill	15301	Maizeville (Part of Gilberton)	17934
Lower Tyrone (Township)	15428	McConnellstown	16660	Majeriks Corners	16441
Lower Windsor (Township)	17368	McCormick (mail		Malden Place (Part of	
Lower Yoder (Township)	15906	Smicksburg)	16256	Centerville)	15417
Lowhill (Lehigh County)		McCormick (mail Marion		Mall (Part of Monroeville)	15146
(Township)	18069	Center)	15759	Malta	17017
Low Hill (Washington		McCoysville	17058	Malvern	19355
County)	15429	McCullocks Mills	17035	Mammoth	15664
Lowville	16442	McCullough	15636	Mamont	15632
Loyalhanna	15661	McDonald	15057	Manada Gap	17112
Loyalhanna (Township)	15681	Macdonaldton	15530	Manatawny	19547
Loyalhanna Woodlands		Macedonia (Bradford		Manayunk (Part of	
No. 1	15670	County)	18848	Philadelphia)	19127
Loyalsock (Township)	17701	Macedonia (Juniata County)	17059	Manchester (Allegheny	
Loyalsockville	17754	McElhattan	17748	County)	15233
Loyalton	17048	McEwensville	17749	Manchester (Wayne	
Loyalville	18612	McGareys	15825	County) (Township)	18417
Loysburg	16659	McGees Mills	15757	Manchester (York County)	17345
Loysville	17047	McGillstown	17003	Manchester (York County)	
Lucernemines	15754	McGovern	15342	(Township)	17402
Lucesco	15656	McGrann	16236	Mandata	17830
Lucinda	16235	McGregor	16222	Manheim (Lancaster	
Luciusboro	15748	McHenry (Township)	17723	County)	17545
Lucknow	17110	McIlhaney	18322	Manheim (Lancaster	
Lucky	17322	McIntyre (Indiana County)	15756	County) (Township)	17601
Lucon	19473	McIntyre (Lycoming County)		Manheim (York County)	
Lucy Crossing (Part of		(Township)	17763	(Township)	17329
Glendon)	18042	McKean	16426	Manifold	15301
Lucy Furnace	17066	McKean (Township)	16426	Manito	15650
Ludlow	16333	McKean Corners	16351	Mann (Township)	17211
Ludwigs Corner	19343	McKeansburg	17960	Mannitto Haven	15670
Luke Fidler	17872	McKee	16637	Manns Choice	15550
Lumber (Township)	15834	McKee Half Falls	17864	Mannsville	17074
Lumber City (Clearfield		McKeesport	15130-35	Manoa	19083
County)	16833	For specific McKeesport Zip		Manor (Armstrong County)	
Lumber City (Mifflin County)	17084	Codes call (412) 672-9721		(Township)	16226
Lumberville	18933	McKees Rocks	15136	Manor (Township)	17603
Lumstead	16201	Mackeyville	17750	Manor (Westmoreland	
Lundys Lane	16401	McKinley	19117	County)	15665
Lungerville	17774	McKinley Hill (Part of Point		Manor Hill	16652
Lurgan	17232	Marion)	15474	Manor Hills (Part of Yeadon)	19050
Lurgan (Township)	17240	McKinney	17232	Manor Park Terrace	16226
Luthersburg	15848	McKnight	15237	Manor Ridge	17603
Luthers Mills	18848	McKnightstown	17343	Manor Shopping Center	17603
Lutztown	17013	McKnight Village	15237	Manorville	16238
Lutzville	15537	McLane	16426	Manown	15063
Luxor	15662	McMichaels	18360	Mansfield	16933
Luzerne (Fayette County)	15433	McMurray	15317	Mantzville	18252
Luzerne (Township)	15417	McNett (Township)	17765	Manver	15765
Luzerne (Luzerne County)	18709	McPherron	15753	Maple Beach	19007
Lycippus	15650	McSherrystown	17344	Mapledale	16323
Lycoming (Township)	17728	Macungie	18062	Maple Glen (Montgomery	
Lykens	17048	McVeytown	17051	County)	19002
Lykens (Township)	17048	McVille	16229	Maple Glen (Washington	
Lyleville	16627	McWilliams	16242	County)	15417
Lynch	16347	Maddensville	17229	Maple Grove (Berks	
Lynchville	15857	Madera	16661	County)	18011
Lyndell	19354	Madge	16735	Maple Grove (Chester	
Lyndon	17602	Madison (Armstrong		County)	19363
Lyndora	16045	County) (Township)	16259	Maple Grove (Clarion	
Lynn (Lehigh County)		Madison (Clarion County)		County)	16248
(Township)	19529	(Township)	16248	Maple Grove (Fayette	
Lynn (Susquehanna		Madison (Columbia County)		County)	15622
County)	18844	(Township)	17846	Maple Grove Park	19540
Lynnewood	19150	Madison (Lackawanna		Maple Hill (Lycoming	
Lynnewood Gardens	19012	County) (Township)	18444	County)	17752
Lynnport	18066	Madison (Westmoreland		Maple Hill (Montgomery	
Lynnville	18066	County)	15663	County)	19422
Lynnwood (Fayette County)	15012	Madisonburg	16852	Maple Hill (Schuylkill	
Lynnwood (Luzerne County)	18702	Madisonville	18444	County)	17976
Lynnwood-Pricedale	15012	Madley	15534	Maple Hills	17319
Lyon Station	19536	Magee	16351	Maple Hollow	16635

	ZIP
Militia Hill	19034
Millardsville	17067
Millbach	17073
Millbank	15658
Millbourne	19082
Millbrook (Centre County)	16801
Millbrook (Mercer County)	16133
Mill Brook (Pike County)	18426
Millburn	16137
Mill City	18414
Millcreek (Clarion County) (Township)	16225
Millcreek (Erie County) (Township)	16506
Millcreek (Erie County)	16505
Mill Creek (Huntingdon County)	17060
Millcreek (Lebanon County) (Township)	17073
Mill Creek (Lycoming County) (Township)	17756
Mill Creek (Mercer County) (Township)	16145
Mill Creek (Schuylkill County)	17901
Mill Creek Falls	19007
Millcreek Mall	16509
Milledgeville	16311
Miller (Huntingdon County) (Township)	16652
Miller (Perry County) (Township)	17094
Miller Heights	18017
Miller Manor	18067
Miller Plan	15042
Miller Run	15936
Millers	16403
Millersburg	17061
Miller Shaft	15946
Millerstown (Allegheny County)	15084
Millerstown (Blair County)	16662
Millerstown (Clarion County)	16334
Millerstown (Perry County)	17062
Millersville	17551
Millerton	16936
Millertown	15446
Mill Grove	17820
Mill Hall	17751
Millheim	16854
Milligantown	15069
Milmont	17845
Millport (Lancaster County)	17540
Millport (Potter County)	16748
Millrift	18340
Mill Run (Blair County)	16601
Mill Run (Fayette County)	15464
Mills	16937
Millsboro	15348
Millstone (Township)	15860
Milltown (Bradford County)	18840
Milltown (Chester County)	19380
Millvale	15209
Millview	18616
Mill Village	16427
Millville	17846
Millway	17543
Millwood	15627
Millwood Manor	15068
Milmont Park	19033
Milnesville	18239
Milnor	17225
Milroy	17063
Milton (Armstrong County)	16222
Milton (Northumberland County)	17847
Milton Grove	17552
Milwaukee	18411
Mina	16915
Mineral (Township)	16342
Mineral Point	15942
Mineral Springs	16855
Miners Mills (Part of Wilkes-Barre)	18705
Miners Village (Part of Cornwall)	17016
Minersville	17954
Minesite (Part of Allentown)	18103
Mingoville	16856
Minisink Hills	18341
Minister	16347
Minnequa	17724
Miola	16214
Miquon	19452
Miquon Hills	19452
Mission Hill	17601
Mitchell Park (Part of Hatboro)	19040
Mix Run	15832
Mocanaqua	18655
Moc-A-Tek Lake	18436

	ZIP
Mocking Bird Hill	15642
Modena	19358
Moffit	15327
Mogees	19401
Mohns Hill	19608
Mohnton	19540
Mohrsville	19541
Molino	17961
Mollenauer (Part of Bethel Park)	15102
Molltown	19522
Monaca	15061
Monaghan (Township)	17404
Monarch	15431
Monessen	15062
Mongul	17257
Moninger	15342
Moniteau	16061
Monocacy Station	19542
Monongahela (Greene County) (Township)	15338
Monongahela (Washington County)	15063
Monongahela Junction (Part of Duquesne)	15110
Monroe (Bedford County) (Township)	15537
Monroe (Bradford County) (Township)	18848
Monroe (Clarion County)	16232
Monroe (Clarion County) (Township)	16255
Monroe (Cumberland County) (Township)	17055
Monroe (Juniata County) (Township)	17086
Monroe (Snyder County) (Township)	17831
Monroe (Wyoming County) (Township)	18657
Monroe Heights (Part of Monroeville)	15146
Monroeton	18832
Monroeville	15146
Monroeville Mall (Part of Monroeville)	15146
Mont Alto	17237
Montandon	17850
Mont Clare	19453
Montdale	18447
Montello	19608
Monterey (Berks County)	19530
Monterey (Franklin County)	17214
Monterey (Lancaster County)	17540
Montgomery (Franklin County) (Township)	17236
Montgomery (Indiana County) (Township)	15712
Montgomery (Lycoming County)	17752
Montgomery (Montgomery County) (Township)	18936
Montgomerys Ferry	17074
Montgomery Square	18936
Montgomeryville	18936
Montour (Allegheny County)	15244
Montour (Columbia County) (Township)	17815
Montour Junction (Part of Coraopolis)	15108
Montoursville	17754
Montrose (Berks County)	19607
Montrose (Susquehanna County)	18801
Montrose Hill	15238
Montsera	17013
Monument	16822
Moon	15108
Moon (Township)	15108
Moon Crest	15108
Moon Run	15136
Moore (Township)	18014
Mooredale	17013
Mooresburg	17821
Moores Corners	16057
Moorestown	18014
Moorheadville	16428
Moosic	18507
Moosic Lake	18416
Morado (Part of Beaver Falls)	15010
Morann	16663
Moravia	16157
Moravian (Part of Bethlehem)	18018
Mordansville	17815
Morea	17948
Moreland (Township)	17756
Moreland Farms	19040
Moreland Manor	19040

	ZIP
Morewood	19040
Morgan (Allegheny County)	15064
Morgan (rural) (Fayette County)	15456
Morgan (Fayette County)	15425
Morgan (Township)	15346
Morgan Hill	15031
Morgans Hill	18042
Morgantown	19543
Morningside (Part of Pittsburgh)	15206
Morrell	15431
Morris (Tioga County) (Township)	16938
Morris (Washington County) (Township)	15329
Morris (Clearfield County) (Township)	16821
Morris (Greene County) (Township)	15364
Morris (Huntingdon County) (Township)	16611
Morris (Tioga County)	16938
Morris Cross Roads	15451
Morrisdale	16858
Morris Run	16939
Morrisville (Bucks County)	19067
Morrisville (Greene County)	15370
Morrows Corner	16210
Morstein	19380
Morton	19070
Mortonville	19320
Morwood	18969
Morysville	19512
Moscow	18444
Moselem	19526
Moselem Springs	19522
Mosgrove	16259
Moshannon	16859
Mosherville	16925
Mosiertown	16433
Mosserville	18066
Moss Plan	15074
Mostoller	15563
Mottarns Mill	15771
Moudy Hill	15946
Moulstown	17331
Mount Aetna	19544
Mountaindale (Cambria County)	16639
Mountain Dale (Dauphin County)	17110
Mountain Grove	17815
Mountainhome	18342
Mountain Lake	18848
Mountain Top (Lancaster County)	17555
Mountain Top (Luzerne County)	18707
Mountain Valley Lake	17921
Mount Airy (Clarion County)	16255
Mount Airy (Lancaster County)	17578
Mount Airy (Philadelphia County)	19119
Mount Airy Terrace	18708
Mount Allen	17055
Mount Alton	16738
Mount Bethel	18343
Mount Braddock	15465
Mount Carbon	17901
Mount Carmel	17851
Mount Carmel (Township)	17851
Mount Chestnut	16001
Mount Chestnut Springs	16001
Mount Cobb	18436
Mount Eagle	16841
Mount Etna	16693
Mount Gretna	17064
Mount Gretna Heights	17064
Mount Holly Springs	17065
Mount Hope	17320
Mount Independence	15456
Mount Jackson	16101
Mount Jewett	16740
Mount Joy (Adams County) (Township)	17340
Mount Joy (Clearfield County)	16830
Mount Joy (Lancaster County)	17552
Mount Joy (Lancaster County) (Township)	17022
Mount Joy (Westmoreland County)	15666
Mount Laffee	17901
Mount Laurel	18201
Mount Lebanon (Township)	15228
Mount Lebanon	15228
Mount Misery	17350
Mount Morris	15349

	ZIP
Mount Nebo (Allegheny County)	15143
Mount Nebo (Lancaster County)	17565
Mount Oliver	15210
Mount Patrick	17045
Mount Penn	19606
Mount Pleasant (Adams County)	17331
Mount Pleasant (Adams County) (Township)	17325
Mount Pleasant (Berks County)	19506
Mount Pleasant (Columbia County) (Township)	17815
Mount Pleasant (Delaware County)	19087
Mount Pleasant (Juniata County)	17059
Mount Pleasant (Lebanon County)	17042
Mount Pleasant (Mifflin County)	17063
Mount Pleasant (Northampton County)	18013
Mount Pleasant (Northumberland County)	17801
Mount Pleasant (Perry County)	17006
Mount Pleasant (Schuylkill County)	17901
Mount Pleasant (Tioga County)	16938
Mount Pleasant (Washington County) (Township)	15340
Mount Pleasant (Wayne County) (Township)	18472
Mount Pleasant (Westmoreland County)	15666
Mount Pleasant (Westmoreland County) (Township)	15664
Mount Pleasant (York County)	17019
Mount Pleasant Mills	17853
Mount Pocono	18344
Mountrock (Cumberland County)	17013
Mount Rock (Franklin County)	17257
Mount Rock (Mifflin County)	17044
Mount Royal	17315
Mount Sterling	15461
Mount Tabor	17324
Mount Troy	15212
Mount Union (Franklin County)	17222
Mount Union (Huntingdon County)	17066
Mount Vernon (Allegheny County)	15135
Mount Vernon (Chester County)	19363
Mount Vernon (Lancaster County)	17527
Mount Vernon (Westmoreland County)	15601
Mountville	17554
Mount Washington (Allegheny County)	15211
Mount Washington (Beaver County)	15010
Mount Wilson	17042
Mount Wolf	17347
Mount Zion (Hampden twp.) (Cumberland County)	17013
Mount Zion (South Middleton twp.) (Cumberland County)	17055
Mount Zion (Lebanon County)	17042
Mount Zion (Luzerne County)	18643
Mount Zion (Monroe County)	18301
Mount Zion (York County)	17402
Moween	15681
Mowersville	17257
Mowry	17921
Moyer	15425
Moylan	19065
Mozart	18925
Mt Pocahontas	18210
Muddycreek (Township)	16051
Muddy Creek Forks	17302
Muhlenberg (Berks County) (Township)	19560
Muhlenberg (Luzerne County)	18621
Muhlenberg Park	19605

	ZIP
Muir	17957
Mullertown	17331
Mumbauersville	18073
Mummasburg	17325
Muncy	17756
Muncy (Township)	17756
Muncy Creek (Township)	17756
Muncy Valley	17758
Munderf	15825
Mundys Corner	15909
Munhall	15120
Munson	16860
Munster	15940
Munster (Township)	15938
Murdock	15501
Murdocksville	15026
Murphy Siding	15425
Murraysville (Part of Murrysville)	15668
Murrell	17522
Murrinsville	16020
Murry Hill	15317
Murrysville	15668
Muse	15350
Mustard	15037
Mutual	15601
Myersburg	18854
Myerstown (Cumberland County)	17324
Myerstown (Lebanon County)	17067
Mylo Park	15931
Myobeach	18630
Myoma	16046
Myrtle	14721
Mystic Park	16404
Naces Corner	18927
Naceville	18960
Nadine	15147
Naginey	17063
Nagles Crossroad	16668
Nan Lynn Gardens	18974
Nansen	16735
Nanticoke	18634
Nantmeal Village	19343
Nanty Glo	15943
Naomi	15438
Napier (Township)	15559
Napierville	17522
Narberth	19072
Narbrook Park (Part of Narberth)	19072
Narrows Creek	15801
Narrows Shopping Center (Part of Edwardsville)	18704
Narrowsville	18972
Narvon	17555
Nashua	16101
Nashville (Indiana County)	15771
Nashville (York County)	17362
Nassau Village	19078
Natalie	17851
National Hill	15031
Natrona	15065
Natrona Heights	15065
Nauvoo	16938
Naval Air Development Center	18974
Nazareth	18064
Nealmont	16686
Neason Hill	16335
Neath	18829
Nebo	15622
Nectarine	16038
Ned	15352
Needful	16881
Needmore	17238
Neelyton	17239
Neffs	18065
Neffs Mills	16669
Neffsville	17601
Neiffer	19473
Neiltown	16341
Neiman	17327
Nellie	15486
Nelson	16940
Nelson (Township)	16940
Nemacolin	15351
Nemanie	18451
Nescopeck	18635
Nescopeck (Township)	18635
Neshaminy	18976
Neshaminy Falls	19047
Neshaminy Hills	19047
Neshaminy Valley	19020
Neshaminy Woods	19047
Neshannock	16105
Neshannock (Township)	16105
Neshannock Falls	16156
Nesquehoning	18240

	ZIP
Nether Providence (Township)	19086
Nether Providence Township (census designated place)	19013
Neville (Township)	15225
Neville Island	15225
New Albany	18833
New Alexandria	15670
New Athens	16248
New Baltimore (Somerset County)	15553
New Baltimore (York County)	17331
New Beaver	16141
New Bedford	16140
New Berlin	17855
New Berlinville	19545
Newberry (Lycoming County)	17701
Newberry (York County) (Township)	17370
Newberrytown	17319
New Bethlehem	16242
New Bloomfield	17068
Newboro	15468
New Boston	17948
New Bridgeville	17356
New Brighton	15066
New Britain	18901
New Britain (Township)	18914
New Buena Vista	15550
New Buffalo	17069
Newburg (Blair County)	16601
Newburg (Cumberland County)	17240
Newburg (Northampton County)	18017
Newburg Homes	18042
New Castle	16101-08
For specific New Castle Zip Codes call (412) 656-7200	
New Castle (Township)	17970
New Castle Northwest	16105
New Centerville	15557
Newchester	17350
New Columbia	17856
New Columbus (Carbon County)	18240
New Columbus (Luzerne County)	17878
Newcomer	15401
New Cumberland	17070
New Cumberland Army Depot	17105
New Danville	17603
New Derry	15671
New Eagle	15067
Newell	15466
New England	18252
New Enterprise	16664
New Era	18833
Newfield (Allegheny County)	15147
Newfield (Potter County)	16948
New Florence	15944
Newfoundland	18445
New Franklin	17201
New Freedom	17349
New Freeport	15352
New Galena	18914
New Galilee	16141
New Garden	19374
New Garden (Township)	19350
New Geneva	15467
New Germantown	17071
New Germany	15946
New Grass Manor	18612
New Grenada	16674
New Hamburg	16124
New Hanover	19525
New Hanover (Township)	19525
New Hanover Square	19435
Newhard	18080
New Holland	17557
New Homestead (Part of Pittsburgh)	15120
New Hope	18938
New Ireland	16438
New Jerusalem	19522
New Kensington	15068
New Kingstown	17072
Newkirk	18252
New Lebanon	16145
New Lexington	15557
Newlin (Chester County) (Township)	19380
Newlin (Columbia County)	17820
New London (Chester County)	19360
New London (Township)	19360

	ZIP		ZIP		ZIP
New London (Warren County)	16351	Normalville	15469	North Shenango (Township)	16424
Newlonsburg (Part of Murrysville)	15668	Norman	15825	North Springfield	16430
		Norristown	19401-04	North Strabane (Township)	15317
New Mahoning	18235	For specific Norristown Zip Codes call (215) 275-9780		North Towanda	18848
Newmanstown	17073			North Towanda (Township)	18848
Newmansville	16353	Norrisville	16406	Northumberland	17857
New Market	17070	North Abington (Township)	18414	North Union (Fayette County) (Township)	15401
New Milford	18834	Northampton (Bucks County) (Township)	18954	North Union (Schuylkill County) (Township)	18241
New Milford (Township)	18834	Northampton (Northampton County)	18067	North Vandergrift	15690
New Millport	16861	Northampton (Somerset County) (Township)	15538	North Vandergrift-Pleasant View	15690
New Mines	17923	Northampton Hills	18966	North Versailles (Township)	15137
New Oxford	17350	North Annville (Township)	17038	North Versailles	15137
New Paris	15554	North Apollo	15673	Northview Heights (Part of Economy)	15005
New Park	17352	North Aronimink	19082	Northview Homes (Part of Economy)	15005
New Philadelphia	17959	North Bangor	18013	Northvue	16001
Newport (Lawrence County)	16157	North Barnesboro (Part of Barnesboro)	15714	North Wales	19454
Newport (Luzerne County) (Township)	18634	North Beaver (Township)	16102	North Warren	16365
Newport (Perry County)	17074	North Belle Vernon	15012	North Washington (Butler County)	16048
Newportville	19056	North Bend	17760	North Washington (Westmoreland County)	15613
Newportville Terrace	19020	North Bessemer	15235	Northway Mall	15237
New Providence	17560	North Bethlehem (Township)	15360	North Waynesburg	17268
New Richmond	16327	North Bingham	16923	North Weissport	18235
New Ringgold	17960	North Braddock	15104	Northwest Harborcreek	16510
Newry	16665	North Branch (Township)	18629	North Whitehall (Township)	18037
New Salem	15468	Northbrook	19380	Northwood	16686
New Salem-Buffington	15468	Northbrook Hills	17601	North Woodbury (Township)	16662
New Schaefferstown	19506	North Buffalo (Township)	16201	Northwood Heights	18042
New Sewickley (Township)	15074	North Butler	16001	North York	17404
New Sheffield	15001	North Catasauqua	18032	Norvelt	15674
Newside	18080	North Centre (Township)	18603	Norwegian (Township)	17951
New Smithville	19530	North Charleroi	15022	Norwich (Township)	16724
New Stanton	15672	North Codorus (Township)	17362	Norwin Heights	15642
New Street	17901	North Cornwall (Township)	17042	Norwood (Allegheny County)	15136
New Texas	17563	North Cornwall	17016	Norwood (Delaware County)	19074
Newton (Township)	18411	North Coventry (Township)	19464	Nossville	17213
Newtonburg	15757	North East	16428	Nottingham (Bucks County)	19020
Newton Hamilton	17075	North East (Township)	16428	Nottingham (Township)	15332
Newton Lake	18407	Northeast Madison (Township)	17047	Nottingham (Chester County)	19362
Newtown (Bucks County)	18940	North Edinburg	16116	Nowrytown	15681
Newtown (Bucks County) (Township)	18940	North End (Part of Wilkes-Barre)	18705	Noxen	18636
New Town (Centre County)	16666	Northern Lights Shopping Center (Part of Economy)	15005	Noxen (Township)	18636
Newtown (Clearfield County)	16878	North Essington	19029	Noyes (Township)	17764
Newtown (Delaware County) (Township)	19073	North Fayette (Township)	15071	Nuangola	18637
Newtown (Lancaster County)	17512	North Fork	16950	Nuangola Station	18707
Newtown (Lehigh County)	18031	North Franklin (Township)	15301	Number Five Mine	16137
Newtown (Luzerne County)	18706	North Fredericktown	15333	Number Thirty Seven	15963
Newtown Grant	18940	North Freedom	16240	Numidia	17858
Newtown Square	19073	North Hamilton (Part of Doylestown)	18901	Nu Mine	16244
New Tripoli	18066	North Hanover Mall (Part of Hanover)	17331	Nuremberg	18241
New Vernon	16145	North Heidelberg (Township)	19506	Nutts Corners	16127
New Vernon (Township)	16145	North Hills (Montgomery County)	19038	Nyesville	17201
Newville (Bucks County)	18914	North Hills (Northumberland County)	17847	Oakbottom	17566
Newville (Cumberland County)	17241	North Hopewell (Township)	17322	Oakdale (Allegheny County)	15071
Newville (Lancaster County)	17023	North Huntingdon (Township)	15642	Oakdale (Luzerne County)	18224
New Virginia (Part of Hermitage)	16146	North Irwin	15642	Oakdale Manor	19067
New Washington	15757	North Jackson	18847	Oakeola	19036
New Wilmington	16142	North Larchmont	19073	Oakford	19047
Niagara	18453	North Lebanon (Township)	17042	Oak Forest	15370
Niantic	19504	North Liberty	16127	Oak Grove (Clearfield County)	16858
Nicetown (Part of Philadelphia)	19140	North Londonderry (Township)	17078	Oak Grove (Schuylkill County)	17963
Nichola	16262	North Mahoning (Township)	15771	Oakgrove (Westmoreland County)	15658
Nicholson (Fayette County) (Township)	15461	North Mall Factory Outlet Center (Part of York)	17404	Oak Hall	16827
Nicholson (Wyoming County)	18446	North Manheim (Township)	17901	Oak Hill (North Versailles twp.) (Allegheny County)	15137
Nicholson (Wyoming County) (Township)	18446	North McKees Rocks	15136	Oak Hill (Wilkins twp.) (Allegheny County)	15145
Nickel Mines	17562	North Mehoopany	18629	Oak Hill (Clearfield County)	16845
Nickleville	16373	North Middleton (Township)	17013	Oak Hills	16001
Nicklin	16323	Northmoreland (Township)	18612	Oakland (Allegheny County)	15213
Nicktown	15762	North Mountain	17758	Oakland (Butler County) (Township)	16061
Nilan	15474	North Newton (Township)	17241	Oakland (Cambria County)	15904
Niles	16323	North Oakland	16025	Oakland (Lawrence County)	16101
Niles Valley	16935	North Orwell	18837	Oakland (Mercer County)	16137
Ninepoints	17509	North Philadelphia (Part of Philadelphia)	19132	Oakland (Susquehanna County)	18847
Nine Row	15927	North Philipsburg	16866	Oakland (Susquehanna County) (Township)	18847
Nineveh (Clarion County)	16232	North Pine Grove	16260	Oakland (Venango County) (Township)	16317
Nineveh (Greene County)	15353	North Point (Bedford County)	16679	Oakland Beach	16316
Nippenose (Township)	17720	Northpoint (Indiana County)	15763	Oakland Hills I	18016
Nisbet	17759	North Radcliffe	19007	Oakland Mills	17076
Nittany	16841	North Rochester	15074	Oakland Park	18101
Niverton	15558	North Rome	18854	Oak Lane (Part of Philadelphia)	19126
Nixon	16001	North Scottdale	15683	Oaklane Manor	19012
Noble	19046	North Scranton (Part of Scranton)	18508	Oakleigh	17111
Noble Hill	15215	North Sewickley	15010	Oaklyn	17801
Noblestown	15071	North Sewickley (Township)	15010		
Nockamixon (Township)	18930				
Noll Acres	17055				
Nolo	15765				
Nook	17058				
Nordmont	17758				
Normal Square	18235				

	ZIP
Oakmont (Allegheny County)	15139
Oakmont (Cambria County)	15904
Oakmont Villa	17036
Oak Park (mobile home park) (Montgomery County)	19446
Oak Park (Montgomery County)	19440
Oak Park (Northumberland County)	17857
Oak Ridge (Armstrong County)	16245
Oak Ridge (Clearfield County)	16661
Oakryn	17563
Oaks	19456
Oak Shade	17566
Oaktree Hollow	19007
Oakview	19026
Oakview Park	19026
Oakville (Cumberland County)	17257
Oakville (Westmoreland County)	15650
Oakwood	16101
Oakwood Park (Part of Laflin)	18702
Obelisk	19492
Oberlin	17113
Oberlin Gardens	17113
Observatory (Part of Pittsburgh)	15214
Odenthal	15946
Odenwelder (Part of West Easton)	18042
Odin	16915
Ogden	19061
Ogdensburg	17765
Ogle (Butler County)	16046
Ogle (Somerset County) (Township)	15963
Ogletown	15963
Ogontz	19012
Ogontz Campus	19001
O'Hara (Township)	15238
Ohio (Township)	15237
Ohiopyle	15470
Ohioview (Part of Industry)	15052
Ohioville	15059
Ohl	15864
Oil City (Cambria County)	15925
Oil City (Venango County)	16301
Oil Creek (Crawford County) (Township)	16354
Oil Creek (Venango County)	16301
Oilcreek (Venango County) (Township)	16341
Oklahoma (Clearfield County)	15801
Oklahoma (Westmoreland County)	15613
Okome	17739
Olanta	16863
Old Bethany	15688
Old Boston	18640
Old Clarendon (Part of Clarendon)	16313
Old Concord	15329
Old Crabtree	15650
Old Enon	16120
Old Forge	18518
Oldframe	15478
Old Junction (Part of Somerset)	15501
Old Line	17545
Old Lycoming (Township)	17701
Old Meadow	15683
Old Orchard (Monroe County)	18370
Old Orchard (Northampton County)	18042
Old Port	17082
Old Stanton (Part of New Stanton)	15672
Old Zionsville	18068
Oleopolis	16301
Oley	19547
Oley (Township)	19547
Oley Furnace	19547
Oliphant Furnace	15401
Oliveburg	15764
Oliver (Fayette County)	15472
Oliver (Jefferson County) (Township)	15825
Oliver (Mifflin County) (Township)	17044
Oliver (Perry County) (Township)	17074
Oliver No. 2	15401
Oliver No. 3	15401

	ZIP
Olivers Mills (Part of Laurel Run)	18702
Olivet	15618
Olney (Part of Philadelphia)	19120
Olwen Heights	18444
Olyphant	18447
Oneida (Butler County)	16001
Oneida (Huntingdon County) (Township)	16652
Oneida (Schuylkill County)	18242
Onnalinda	15955
Ono	17077
Ontario	15330
Ontelaunee (Township)	19605
Opp	17756
Oppermans Corner	19425
Option (Part of Baldwin)	15236
Orange (Columbia County) (Township)	17859
Orange (Luzerne County)	18612
Orangeville	17859
Orbisonia	17243
Orchard Beach	16428
Orchard Crossing	16686
Orchard Hill (Part of Mount Pleasant)	15666
Orchard Hills	15613
Orefield	18069
Oregon (Lancaster County)	17540
Oregon (Wayne County) (Township)	18431
Oregon Hill	16938
Ore Hill	16673
Oreland	19075
Oreland Gardens	19075
Oreminea	16693
Ore Valley	17403
Orient	15420
Oriental	17045
Oriole	17740
Ormrod	18037
Ormsby	16726
Orners Corner	16601
Orrstown	17244
Orrtanna	17353
Orrville	15144
Orson	18449
Orvilla	19440
Orviston	16864
Orwell	18837
Orwell (Township)	18837
Orwigsburg	17961
Orwin	17980
Osborne	15143
Osceola	16942
Osceola (Township)	16942
Osceola Mills	16666
Osgood	16125
Oshanter	16830
Ostend	15757
Osterburg	16667
Osterhout	18657
Oswayo	16915
Oswayo (Township)	16748
Ottawa	17821
Otter Creek (Township)	16125
Otto (Township)	16745
Ottsville	18942
Ott Town	15537
Outcrop	15478
Outlet	18612
Outwood	17963
Oval	17740
Overbrook (Allegheny County)	15210
Overbrook (Philadelphia County)	19151
Overbrook Hills	19151
Overfield (Township)	18414
Overholt Acres	15642
Overleigh	19004
Overlook	17601
Overlook Heights	16801
Overlook Springs	18049
Overton	18833
Overton (Township)	18833
Overview	17053
Owensdale	15425
Oxbow Meadows	18914
Oxford (Adams County) (Township)	17350
Oxford (Chester County)	19363
Oxford Valley	19030
Oyster Point	17602
Packer Point	18255
Packerton	18235
Paddytown	15551
Pageville	16401
Paint (Clarion County) (Township)	16254
Paint (Somerset County)	15963

	ZIP
Paint (Somerset County) (Township)	15963
Paintersville (Mifflin County)	17044
Paintersville (Westmoreland County)	15672
Paintertown	15642
Paisley	15320
Paletown	18944
Palm	18070
Palmdale	17033
Palmer (Township)	18042
Palmer Heights	18042
Palmer Park	18042
Palmerton	18071
Palmerton East (Part of Palmerton)	18071
Palmertown	15716
Palmyra (Lebanon County)	17078
Palmyra (Pike County) (Township)	18451
Palmyra (Wayne County) (Township)	18428
Palo Alto (Bedford County)	15545
Palo Alto (Schuylkill County)	17901
Palomino Farms	18976
Pancoast	15851
Panic	15851
Panorama Village	16801
Pansy	15864
Pansy Hill	17042
Panther	18445
Paoli	19301
Paper Mills (Part of Bryn Athyn)	19009
Paradise (Lancaster County)	17562
Paradise (Lancaster County) (Township)	17562
Paradise (Monroe County) (Township)	18326
Paradise (Schuylkill County)	17963
Paradise (York County) (Township)	17301
Paradise Falls	18326
Paradise Valley	18326
Pardee	18866
Pardeesville	18201
Pardoe	16137
Pardus	15851
Paris	15021
Park (Part of Vandergrift)	15690
Parkchester	19380
Park Crest	18214
Parker (Armstrong County)	16049
Parker (Butler County) (Township)	16001
Parker Ford	19457
Parkersville	19380
Parkesburg	19365
Park Forest Village	16801
Park Gate	16117
Park Heights	17331
Parkhill	15945
Park Hills (Centre County)	16801
Park Hills (York County)	17331
Parkland	19047
Park Manor	19607
Park Meadows	15642
Park Place	17948
Parks (Township)	15690
Parkside	19015
Parkside Courts	18104
Parkside Manor (Part of Parkside)	19015
Parkstown	16101
Parktown Estates	19067
Parkview	15215
Parkview Gardens	18052
Park View Heights (Part of Bellefonte)	16823
Parkville	17331
Parkway Center (Part of Green Tree)	15220
Parkway Center Mall (Part of Pittsburgh)	15220
Park Way Manor	18104
Parkwood	15774
Parnassus (Part of New Kensington)	15068
Parryville	18244
Parsonville (Butler County)	16050
Parsonville (Clearfield County)	16651
Parvin	17751
Paschall (Part of Philadelphia)	19142
Passer	18036
Patchel Run (Part of Sugarcreek)	16323
Patchinville	15724
Patterson (Township)	15010
Patterson Grove	18655

	ZIP
Patterson Heights	15010
Patterson Hill (Part of Lincoln)	15037
Pattersons Mill	15312
Patterson Township	15010
Pattersonville	17967
Patton (Cambria County)	16668
Patton (Township)	16801
Patton (Washington County)	15301
Pattonville	16226
Paulton	15613
Paupack (Pike County)	18451
Paupack (Wayne County) (Township)	18428
Paupack Gardens	18451
Pavia	16655
Paxinos	17860
Paxtang	17111
Paxtang Manor	17111
Paxton	17017
Paxtonia	17111
Paxtonville	17861
Peacedale	19363
Peach Bottom (Lancaster County)	17563
Peach Bottom (York County) (Township)	17314
Peach Bottom Village	17563
Peach Glen	17306
Pealertown	17859
Peanut (Lawrence County)	16116
Peanut (Westmoreland County)	15627
Pearl	16342
Pebble Hill	18901
Pecan	16342
Pechin	15431
Pecks Pond	18328
Peckville (Part of Blakely)	18452
Pemberton	16683
Pen Argyl	18072
Penarth	19004
Penbrook	17103
Penbryn	17765
Pendle Hill	19086
Penfield	15849
Penllyn	19422
Pen Mar	17268
Penn (Berks County) (Township)	19506
Penn (Butler County) (Township)	16001
Penn (Centre County) (Township)	16832
Penn (Chester County) (Township)	19390
Penn (Clearfield County) (Township)	16838
Penn (Cumberland County) (Township)	17257
Penn (Huntingdon County) (Township)	16647
Penn (Lancaster County) (Township)	17545
Penn (Lycoming County) (Township)	17737
Penn (Perry County) (Township)	17020
Penn (Snyder County) (Township)	17870
Penn (Westmoreland County)	15675
Penn (Westmoreland County) (Township)	15636
Penn (York County) (Township)	17331
Penn Allen	18064
Pennbrook (Part of Lansdale)	19446
Penn Center (Part of Philadelphia)	19102
Penncraft	15433
Penndel	19047
Pennersville	17268
Penn Estates	18320
Pennfield	19007
Penn Five	16666
Penn Forest (Township)	18210
Penn Glyn (Part of Irwin)	15642
Pennhall	16875
Penn Heights (Part of Hanover)	17331
Penn Hill	17563
Penn Hill Homes	19022
Penn Hills (Township)	15235
Penn Hills	15235
Penn Hills Shopping Center	15235
Pennhurst Center	19475
Penn Lake Park	18661
Pennline	16424
Penn Pines	19018

	ZIP
Penn Pitt	15338
Penn Rose Park	17601
Penn Run	15765
Pennsburg	18073
Pennsbury (Township)	19317
Pennsbury Heights	19067
Pennsbury Village	15205
Penns Creek	17862
Pennsdale	17756
Pennside (Berks County)	19606
Pennside (Erie County)	16401
Penns Park	18943
Penn Square Village	19401
Pennsville (Fayette County)	15425
Pennsville (Northampton County)	18067
Penns Woods	15642
Pennsylvania Furnace	16865
Penn Taft (Part of West Mifflin)	15222
Pennvale	17701
Penn Valley	19072
Penn Valley Terrace	19047
Penn Village (Part of Pottstown)	19464
Pennville	17331
Pennwyn	19607
Penn Wynne	19151
Penobscot	18707
Penowa	15312
Penryn	17564
Pequea	17565
Pequea (Township)	17584
Percy	15456
Perdix	17020
Perkasie	18944
Perkiomen (Township)	19426
Perkiomen Heights	18073
Perkiomen Junction	19460
Perkiomen Village	19426
Perkiomenville	18074
Perrine Corners	16153
Perry (Armstrong County) (Township)	16041
Perry (Berks County) (Township)	19526
Perry (Clarion County) (Township)	16049
Perry (Fayette County) (Township)	15482
Perry (Greene County) (Township)	15349
Perry (Jefferson County) (Township)	15767
Perry (Lawrence County) (Township)	16117
Perry (Mercer County) (Township)	16130
Perry (Snyder County) (Township)	17853
Perrymont	15237
Perryopolis	15473
Perry Square (Part of Erie)	16507
Perrysville	15237
Perryville (Clarion County)	16049
Perryville (Lycoming County)	17728
Perryville (Westmoreland County)	15618
Perulack	17021
Peters (Franklin County) (Township)	17236
Peters (Washington County) (Township)	15317
Petersburg	16669
Peters Corner	18934
Peters Creek (Part of Clairton)	15025
Petersville	18067
Petrolia	16050
Pettis	16335
Pheasant Hill	17601
Pheasant Ridge	18901
Philadelphia	**19101-60**

For specific Philadelphia Zip Codes call (215) 895-9000

COLLEGES & UNIVERSITIES

	ZIP
Chestnut Hill College	19118
Drexel University	19104
Hahnemann University-The School of Health Sciences and Humanities	19102
Holy Family College	19114
LaSalle University	19141
The University of the Arts	19102
Philadelphia College of Pharmacy and Science	19104
Philadelphia College of Textiles and Science	19144

	ZIP
St. Joseph's University	19131
Temple University	19122
University of Pennsylvania	19104

FINANCIAL INSTITUTIONS

	ZIP
Beneficial Savings Bank	19107
Brown Brothers Harriman & Co	19102
Cheltenham Bank	19111
Fidelity Federal Savings & Loan Association	19135
Fox Chase Federal Savings & Loan Association	19111
Frankford Trust Company	19124
Prime Savings Bank	19111
Roxborough-Manayunk Federal Savings & Loan Association	19128
Third Federal Savings & Loan Association of Philadelphia	19124

HOSPITALS

	ZIP
Albert Einstein Medical Center	19141
Children's Hospital of Philadelphia	19104
Episcopal Hospital	19125
Frankford Hospital of the City of Philadelphia	19114
Friedman Hospital of the Home for the Jewish Aged	19141
Germantown Hospital and Medical Center	19144
Graduate Hospital	19146
Hahnemann University Hospital	19102
Hospital of Philadelphia College of Osteopathic Medicine	19131
Hospital of the Medical College of Pennsylvania	19129
Hospital of the University of Pennsylvania	19104
Methodist Hospital	19148
Nazareth Hospital	19152
Pennsylvania Hospital	19107
Presbyterian Medical Center of Philadelphia	19104
Temple University Hospital	19140
Thomas Jefferson University Hospital	19107
Veterans Affairs Medical Center	19104

HOTELS/MOTELS

	ZIP
The Barclay Hotel	19103
Four Seasons Hotel Philadelphia	19103
Guest Quarters Suite Hotel	19153
Holiday Inn-Independence Mall	19106
The Latham	19103
Philadelphia Airport Marriott	19153
The Warwick	19103
Wyndham Franklin Plaza Hotel	19103

MILITARY INSTALLATIONS

	ZIP
Defense Industrial Supply Center	19111
Defense Personnel Support Center	19101
Fort Mifflin Distribution Center, U.S. Army Corps. of Engineers	19153
Naval Publications and Forms Center	19120
Naval Regional Medical Clinic	19145
Naval Station, Philadelphia	19112
Philadelphia Naval Shipyard	19112

	ZIP
Philatelic (Part of State College)	16801
Philipsburg (Centre County)	16866
Philipsburg (Washington County)	15419
Phillips (Fayette County)	15401
Phillips (Tioga County)	16918
Phillipston	16248
Phillipsville (Chester County)	19320
Phillipsville (Erie County)	16442
Philmont	19006
Philmont Manor	19006
Philmont Park	19006
Phoenix Park	17901
Phoenixville	19460
Piatt (Township)	17740

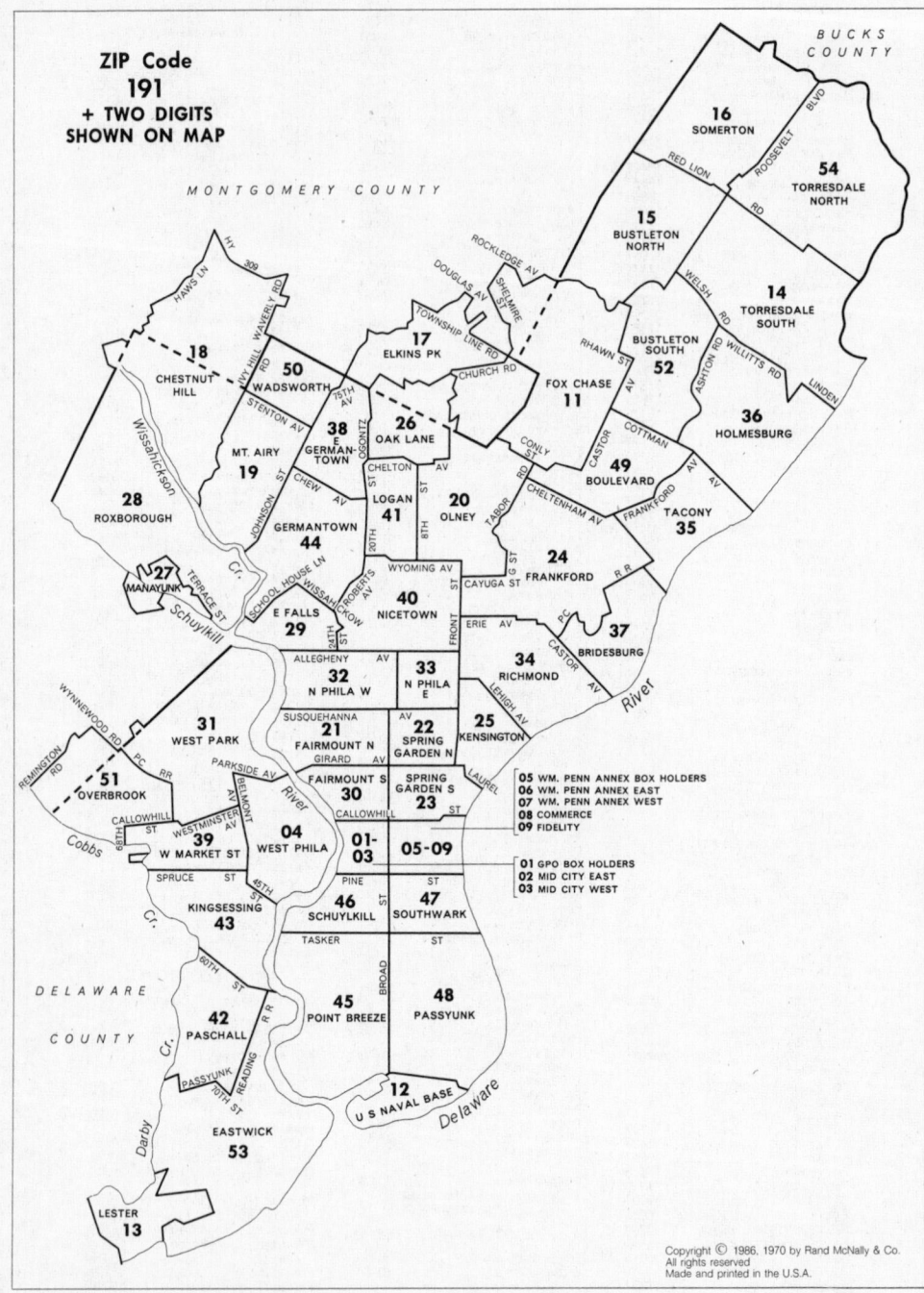

ZIP Code
191
+ TWO DIGITS
SHOWN ON MAP

BUCKS COUNTY

MONTGOMERY COUNTY

16 SOMERTON

54 TORRESDALE NORTH

15 BUSTLETON NORTH

14 TORRESDALE SOUTH

18 CHESTNUT HILL

17 ELKINS PK

52 BUSTLETON SOUTH

36 HOLMESBURG

50 WADSWORTH

26 OAK LANE

11 FOX CHASE

49 BOULEVARD

38 E GERMANTOWN

19 MT AIRY

35 TACONY

28 ROXBOROUGH

41 LOGAN

20 OLNEY

24 FRANKFORD

44 GERMANTOWN

27 MANAYUNK

40 NICETOWN

37 BRIDESBURG

29 E FALLS

34 RICHMOND

32 N PHILA W

33 N PHILA E

31 WEST PARK

21 FAIRMOUNT N

22 SPRING GARDEN N

25 KENSINGTON

51 OVERBROOK

30 FAIRMOUNT S

23 SPRING GARDEN S

39 W MARKET ST

04 WEST PHILA

01-03

05-09

05 WM. PENN ANNEX BOX HOLDERS
06 WM. PENN ANNEX EAST
07 WM. PENN ANNEX WEST
08 COMMERCE
09 FIDELITY

01 GPO BOX HOLDERS
02 MID CITY EAST
03 MID CITY WEST

43 KINGSESSING

46 SCHUYLKILL

47 SOUTHWARK

42 PASCHALL

45 POINT BREEZE

48 PASSYUNK

DELAWARE COUNTY

12 U S NAVAL BASE

Delaware

53 EASTWICK

13 LESTER

	ZIP
Picture Rocks	17762
Pierce (Allegheny County)	15025
Pierce (Armstrong County)	16240
Pierceville	17327
Pigeon	16239
Pike (Berks County) (Township)	19547
Pike (Bradford County) (Township)	18829
Pike (Clearfield County) (Township)	16833
Pike (Potter County) (Township)	16922
Pikeland	19425
Pikes Peak	15765
Piketown	17112
Pikeville	19547
Pilgrim Gardens	19026
Pilgrimham	16232
Pillow	17080
Pine (Allegheny County) (Township)	15090
Pine (Armstrong County) (Township)	16259
Pine (Clearfield County) (Township)	15849
Pine (Clinton County)	17748
Pine (Columbia County) (Township)	17846
Pine (Crawford County) (Township)	16424
Pine (Indiana County) (Township)	15745
Pine (Lycoming County) (Township)	16938
Pine (Mercer County) (Township)	16127
Pine Bank	15352
Pine Beach	18428
Pinebrook	17011
Pine Creek (Clinton County) (Township)	17721
Pinecreek (Jefferson County) (Township)	15825
Pinecrest	19047
Pinecroft	16601
Pinedale (Part of Deer Lake)	17961
Pine Flats	15728
Pine Forge	19548
Pine Glen (Centre County)	16845
Pine Glen (Mifflin County)	17044
Pine Grove (Perry County)	17047
Pine Grove (Schuylkill County)	17963
Pine Grove (Schuylkill County) (Township)	17963
Pine Grove (Susquehanna County)	18446
Pinegrove (Venango County) (Township)	16301
Pine Grove (Warren County) (Township)	16345
Pine Grove Furnace	17324
Pine Grove Mills	16868
Pine Hill (Armstrong County)	16201
Pine Hill (Schuylkill County)	17901
Pine Hill (Somerset County)	15530
Pine Ridge	19063
Pine Run (Bucks County)	18901
Pine Run (Lycoming County)	17744
Pine Summit	17846
Pine Swamp	19520
Pinetown	17339
Pinetree (Part of Scottdale)	15683
Pine Valley	16405
Pine Valley Estates	18901
Pine View	18707
Pineville (Bucks County)	18946
Pineville (Warren County)	16420
Pinewood	19054
Piney	16214
Piney (Township)	16255
Piney Fork	15129
Pinola	17257
Pipersville	18947
Pitcairn	15140
Pitman	17964
Pitt Gas	15322
Pittock	15136
Pitts	16901
Pittsburgh	15122-23
	15201-90

For specific Pittsburgh Zip Codes
call (412) 359-7860

COLLEGES & UNIVERSITIES

	ZIP
Carlow College	15213
Carnegie Mellon University	15213
Duquesne University	15282
La Roche College	15237
Point Park College	15222
University of Pittsburgh	15260

FINANCIAL INSTITUTIONS

	ZIP
Allegheny Valley Bank of Pittsburgh	15201
Bell Federal Savings & Loan Association of Bellevue	15222
Dollar Bank, A Federal Savings Bank	15222
First Home Savings Association	15219
First South Savings Association	15203
Great American Federal Savings & Loan Association	15236
Intega National Bank/Pittsburgh	15278
Landmark Savings Association	15222
North Side Deposit Bank	15212
Pittsburgh Home Savings Association	15222
Pittsburgh National Bank	15222
West View Savings Bank	15237

HOSPITALS

	ZIP
Allegheny General Hospital	15212
Magee-Womens Hospital	15213
Mercy Hospital of Pittsburgh	15219
Montefiore University Hospital	15213
North Hills Passavant Hospital	15237
Presbyterian-University Hospital	15213
Shadyside Hospital	15232
St. Clair Memorial Hospital	15243
St. Francis Medical Center	15201
St. Margaret Memorial Hospital	15215
Veterans Affairs Medical Center	15240
Western Pennsylvania Hospital	15224

HOTELS/MOTELS

	ZIP
Holiday Inn Pittsburg Airport	15231
Best Western Parkway Center Inn	15220
Days Inn-Pittsburgh	15216
Harley of Pittsburgh	15235
Hyatt Pittsburgh at Chatham Center	15219
Pittsburgh Green Tree Marriott	15205
Sheraton Hotel at Station Square	15219

MILITARY INSTALLATIONS

	ZIP
911th Airlift Group, Greater Pittsburgh International Airport, (AFRES)	15231
Hays Army Ammunition Plant	15207
Pennsylvania Air National Guard, FB6381, Greater Pittsburgh International Airport	15231
United States Army Engineer District, Pittsburgh	15222
Charles E. Kelley Support Facility, Maintenance Division, Neville Island	15225
Pittsburgh Plate Plan	16226
Pittsburgh Valley	17516
Pittsfield	16340
Pittsfield (Township)	16340
Pittston	18640-44

For specific Pittston Zip Codes
call (717) 654-3313

	ZIP
Pittston Junction (Part of Wilkes-Barre)	18705
Pittsville	16374
Plainfield (Cumberland County)	17081
Plainfield (Northampton County) (Township)	18064
Plain Grove (Township)	16156
Plains	18705
Plains (Township)	18705
Plainsville	18705
Plainview	17325
Planebrook	19355
Plank	16938
Platea	16417
Plateau Heights	16335
Plattsville	16646
Plaza (Part of Butler)	16001
Plaza Heights (Part of Hanover)	17331
Pleasant (Township)	16365
Pleasant Corners	18235
Pleasant Gap	16823
Pleasant Grove (Lancaster County)	17563
Pleasant Grove (Washington County)	15323
Pleasant Hall	17246
Pleasant Hill (Cambria County)	15738
Pleasant Hill (Cooper twp.) (Clearfield County)	16839
Pleasant Hill (Decatur twp.) (Clearfield County)	16866
Pleasant Hill (Delaware County)	19063
Pleasant Hill (Fayette County)	15425
Pleasant Hill (Indiana County)	15701
Pleasant Hill (Lawrence County)	16123
Pleasant Hill (Lebanon County)	17042
Pleasant Hill (York County)	17331
Pleasant Hills (Allegheny County)	15236
Pleasant Hills (Dauphin County)	17112
Pleasant Mount	18453
Pleasant Union	15552
Pleasant Unity	15676
Pleasant Valley (Blair County)	16602
Pleasant Valley (Bucks County)	18951
Pleasant Valley (Lancaster County)	17604
Pleasant Valley (Potter County) (Township)	16743
Pleasant Valley (Schuylkill County)	17963
Pleasant Valley (Westmoreland County)	15642
Pleasant Valley Estates	18058
Pleasant View (Armstrong County)	15690
Pleasantview (Beaver County)	15010
Pleasant View (Centre County)	16823
Pleasant View (Franklin County)	17201
Pleasantview (Juniata County)	17082
Pleasant View (York County)	17356
Pleasant Village (Part of Altoona)	16602
Pleasantville	16341
Pleasureville	17402
Pleasureville Heights	17402
Plowville	19540
Plum (Township)	16354
Plum (Allegheny County)	15239
Plum (Venango County)	16354
Plumbridge	19056
Plumb Sock	15329
Plum Creek (Allegheny County)	15239
Plumcreek (Armstrong County) (Township)	15774
Plumer	16301
Plummer	15458
Plum Run	17238
Plumsock	19073
Plumstead (Township)	18923
Plumsteadville	18949
Plumville	16246
Plunketts Creek (Township)	17701
Plymouth (Luzerne County)	18651
Plymouth (Luzerne County) (Township)	18651
Plymouth (Montgomery County) (Township)	19401
Plymouth Junction (Part of Larksville)	18651
Plymouth Meeting	19462
Plymouth Meeting Mall	19462
Plymouth Valley	19401
Plymptonville	16830
Pocahontas	15552
Pocono (Township)	18372
Pocono Country Place	18466
Pocono Farms	18466
Pocono Farms East	18466
Pocono Heights	18301

	ZIP		ZIP		ZIP
Pocono Lake	18347	Potts Grove		Quicks Bend	18846
Pocono Lake Preserve	18348	(Northumberland County)	17865	Quicktown	18444
Pocono Manor	18349	Pottstown	19464-65	Quiggleville	17728
Pocono Mt. Lake Forest	18328	For specific Pottstown Zip Codes		Quincy	17247
Pocono Park	18360	call (215) 323-2100		Quincy (Township)	17247
Pocono Pines	18350	Pottstown Landing	19464	Quincy Hollow	19057
Pocono Summit	18346	Pottsville	17901	Raccoon (Township)	15001
Pocono Summit Estates	18346	P&OV Junction	15136	Racine	15010
Pocopson	19366	Powder Mill Village	15687	Radebaugh	15601
Pocopson (Township)	19366	Powder Valley	18092	Radnor (Township)	19087
Poets Village	15701	Powell	18832	Radnor Township (census	
Pogue	17264	Powells Valley	17032	designated place)	19087
Point (Bedford County)	15559	Powelton	16677	Rahns	19426
Point (Northumberland		Powys	17728	Railroad	17355
County) (Township)	17857	Poyntelle	18454	Raineytown	15428
Point Breeze (Part of		Prentisvale	16731	Rainsburg	15522
Pittsburgh)	15208	Prescott	17042	Ralpho (Township)	17872
Point Breeze (Part of		Prescottville	15851	Ralphton	15563
Philadelphia)	19145	President	16353	Ralston	17763
Point Marion	15474	President (Township)	16301	Ramblewood	16865
Point Phillip	18014	Presidential Heights		Ramey	16671
Point Pleasant	18950	(Allegheny County)	15237	Ramona	17067
Point Ridge Farms	17011	Presidential Heights		Ramsay Terrace (Part of	
Point View	16693	(Franklin County)	17201	Mount Pleasant)	15666
Pokeytown	15563	Presque Isle	16505	Ramsaytown	15825
Poland	15327	Presston	15136	Ramsey	17740
Polk (Jefferson County)		Presto	15142	Ranavilla	17011
(Township)	15825	Preston (Luzerne County)	18706	Rand (Part of Baldwin)	15227
Polk (Monroe County)		Preston (Wayne County)		Randolph (Township)	16327
(Township)	18333	(Township)	18455	Rankin	15104
Polk (Venango County)	16342	Preston Hill	17935	Ranshaw	17866
Polktown	17268	Preston Park	18455	Ransom	18653
Polk Valley	18055	Pretoria	15935	Ransom (Township)	18411
Pomeroy	19367	Price (Township)	18301	Rapho (Township)	17545
Pomeroy Heights	19320	Priceburg (Part of Dickson		Rasler Run	15425
Pond Bank	17201	City)	18519	Rasleytown	18072
Pond Creek	18661	Pricedale	15072	Rasselas	15870
Pond Eddy	12770	Pricetown	19522	Rathbun	15834
Ponderosa	18451	Priceville	18417	Rathmel	15851
Pond Hill	18660	Primos	19018	Rattigan	16025
Pont	16401	Primos-Secane	19018	Raubsville	18042
Poplar Grove (Fayette		Primrose (Schuylkill County)	17901	Rauchtown	17740
County)	15425	Primrose (Washington		Rauschs	17960
Poplar Grove (Lancaster		County)	15057	Raven Creek	17814
County)	17543	Princeton	16101	Raven Run	17946
Porkey	16347	Pringle	18704	Ravine	17966
Portage (Cambria County)	15946	Pritchards Corner	16150	Rawlinsville	17532
Portage (Potter County)		Prittstown	15666	Rayburn (Township)	16201
(Township)	16720	Proctor	17701	Raymilton	16342
Portage (Cambria County)		Progress	17109	Raymond	16923
(Township)	15946	Prompton	18456	Rayne (Township)	15747
Portage (Cameron County)		Prospect	16052	Raytown	15742
(Township)	15834	Prospect Gardens	17602	Rea	15356
Portage Creek	16743	Prospect Heights	18017	Reade (Township)	16619
Port Allegany	16743	Prospect Park (Cameron		Reading	19601-12
Port Barnett	15825	County)	15834	For specific Reading Zip Codes	
Port Blanchard	18640	Prospect Park (Delaware		call (215) 921-7050	
Port Carbon	17965	County)	19076	Reading (Township)	17350
Port Clinton	19549	Prospectville	19002	Reading Mines	15563
Porter (Jefferson County)		Prosperity	15329	Reagantown	15679
(Township)	16222	Providence (Township)	17560	Reamstown	17567
Porter (Lycoming County)		Providence Downe	19063	Reamstown Heights	17567
(Township)	17740	Providence Square	19426	Rebel Hill	19406
Porter (Pike County)		Providence Village	19086	Rebersburg	16872
(Township)	18301	Provins Works	15461	Rebuck	17867
Porter (Schuylkill County)		Pughtown	19464	Rector	15677
(Township)	17980	Puite	17110	Redbank (Armstrong	
Porter (Clarion County)		Pulaski (Lawrence County)		County) (Township)	16240
(Township)	16242	(Township)	16143	Redbank (Clarion County)	
Porter (Clinton County)		Pulaski (Beaver County)		(Township)	16224
(Township)	17751	(Township)	15066	Red Bank (Union County)	17844
Porter (Huntingdon County)		Pulaski	16143	Redbird	15946
(Township)	16611	Punxsutawney	15767	Red Bridge (Franklin	
Porter (Jefferson County)	15767	Purcell	15535	County)	17201
Porters Sideling	17354	Purchase Line	15729	Red Bridge (McKean	
Portersville	16051	Puritan (Cambria County)	15946	County)	16735
Port Griffith	18640	Puritan (Fayette County)	15458	Redclyffe	16239
Port Indian	19401	Putnam (Township)	16917	Red Cross	17823
Port Jenkins	18661	Putneyville	16242	Redds Mill	15022
Port Kennedy	19406	Puttstown	16678	Red Gate Farms	18901
Portland	18351	Puzzletown	16635	Red Hill (Blair County)	16601
Portland Mills	15853	Pymatuning (Township)	16125	Red Hill (Montgomery	
Port Matilda	16870	Pyrra	16226	County)	18076
Port Providence	19453	Quakake	18245	Redington	18055
Port Royal	17082	Quaker Hills (Part of		Red Lion (Berks County)	18062
Port Trevorton	17864	Millersville)	17551	Red Lion (Chester County)	19348
Port Vue	15133	Quaker Lake	18812	Red Lion (York County)	17356
Possum Hollow (Part of		Quakertown	18951	Red Mill	15840
New Beaver)	16157	Quaker Valley	17307	Red Oak	18436
Potetown	16673	Quarryville	17566	Red Rock (Luzerne County)	17814
Potosi	17327	Quecreek	15555	Red Rock (McKean County)	16727
Potter (Beaver County)		Queen (Bedford County)	16670	Red Rose Gate	19056
(Township)	15061	Queen (Forest County)	16321	Redrun	17517
Potter (Centre County)		Queen City	17820	Redstone	15438
(Township)	16875	Queensgate Shopping		Redstone (Township)	15442
Potter Brook	16950	Center (Part of York)	17404	Redstone Junction	15472
Pottersdale	16871	Queens Grant	19067	Reduction	15479
Potters Mills	16875	Queens Run	17745	Reed (Dauphin County)	
Potterville	18837	Queenstown	16041	(Township)	17032
Pottsgrove (Montgomery		Quemahoning (Township)	15563	Reed (Northumberland	
County)	19464	Quentin	17083	County)	17860

	ZIP		ZIP		ZIP
Rose Point	16101	Rutherford Park	17036	Salona	17767
Roses	16239	Ruthford	15955	Saltillo	17253
Roseto	18013	Ruthfred Acres (Part of		Saltlick (Township)	15446
Rose Valley (Delaware		Bethel Park)	15102	Saltsburg	15681
County)	19063	Rutland (Township)	16933	Salunga	17538
Rose Valley (Montgomery		Rutledge	19070	Salunga-Landisville	17538
County)	19002	Rutledgedale	18469	Saluvia	17228
Rose Valley Acres	19063	Ryan (Township)	18214	Sample Heights	15116
Roseville (Jefferson County)	15825	Ryans Corner	18940	Sample Run (Part of	
Roseville (Tioga County)	16933	Rydal	19046	Clymer)	15728
Rosewood Gardens	18974	Ryde	17051	Sampson	15063
Roslyn (Chester County)	19380	Rye (Township)	17053	Sanatoga	19464
Roslyn (Montgomery		Ryerson Station	15380	Sanatoga Park	19464
County)	19001	Ryot	15521	Sanbourn	16651
Ross (Allegheny County)		Rywal Park	19020	Sandbeach	17033
(Township)	15237	Sabinsville	16943	Sand Hill (Lebanon County)	17042
Ross (Luzerne County)		Sabula	15801	Sandhill (Monroe County)	18354
(Township)	18656	Saco (Bradford County)	18848	Sand Hill (Westmoreland	
Ross (Monroe County)		Saco (Lackawanna County)	18436	County)	15666
(Township)	18353	Sacramento	17968	Sand Patch	15552
Ross Common	18353	Saddle Brook	18101	Sand Springs	18222
Rossford	16226	Saddlebrook Village I and II	19565	Sandts Eddy	18042
Rossiter	15772	Sadlers Corner	16301	Sandy	15801
Rosslyn Farms	15106	Sadsbury (Chester County)		Sandy (Township)	15801
Rossmere	17601	(Township)	19369	Sandy Bank	19063
Rossmoyne	17011	Sadsbury (Crawford		Sandy Creek (Allegheny	
Ross Siding	17723	County) (Township)	16316	County)	15147
Rosston	16226	Sadsbury (Lancaster		Sandy Creek (Mercer	
Ross Township	15237	County) (Township)	17509	County) (Township)	16125
Rossville	17358	Sadsburyville	19369	Sandycreek (Venango	
Rostraver	15012	Saegersville	18053	County) (Township)	16323
Rostraver (Township)	15012	Saegertown	16433	Sandy Hill	19401
Rote	17751	Safe Harbor	17516	Sandy Hollow	16248
Rothsville	17543	Sagamore (Armstrong		Sandy Lake	16145
Rough and Ready	17941	County)	16250	Sandy Lake (Township)	16153
Roulette	16746	Sagamore (Fayette County)	15446	Sandy Plains	15322
Roulette (Township)	16746	Sagamore Hills	18101	Sandy Ridge	16677
Round Top (Adams County)	17325	Saginaw	17347	Sandy Ridge Acres	18901
Round Top (Bedford		Sagon	17872	Sandy Run (Bucks County)	19067
County)	16679	St. Augustine	16636	Sandy Run (Greene County)	15338
Roundtown	17404	St. Benedict	15773	Sandy Run (Luzerne	
Rouseville	16344	St. Boniface	16675	County)	18224
Rouzerville	17250	St. Charles	16242	Sandy Shore	18428
Rowes Run	15442	St. Clair (Schuylkill County)	17970	Sandy Valley	15851
Rowland	18457	St. Clair (Westmoreland		Sandyville	18324
Rowland Park	19012	County)	15601	Sanford	16340
Rowles	15757	St. Clair (Westmoreland		Sankertown	16630
Roxborough (Part of		County) (Township)	15954	Sarah Furnace	16248
Philadelphia)	19128	St. Clairsville	16667	Sardis (Part of Murrysville)	15668
Roxbury (Cumberland		St. Davids	19087	Sartwell	16731
County)	17055	St. George	16374	Sarver	16055
Roxbury (Franklin County)	17251	St. Johns	18247	Sarversville	16055
Roxbury (Somerset County)	15530	St. Joseph	18818	Sassamansville	19472
Royal (Fayette County)	15422	St. Lawrence (Berks		Satterfield	18614
Royal (Susquehanna		County)	19606	Satterfield Junction	18614
County)	18446	St. Lawrence (Cambria		Saucon Acres	18034
Royalton	17057	County)	16668	Saulsburg	16652
Royer	16693	St. Leonard	18940	Saville	17074
Royersford	19468	St. Marys	15857	Saville (Township)	17037
Roystone	16347	St. Michael	15951	Sawtown	16301
Roytown	15501	St. Michael-Sidman	15951	Saxonburg	16056
Rozel Park	18966	St. Nicholas	17948	Saxton	16678
Ruble	15478	St. Paul	15552	Saybrook	16347
Ruchsville	18037	St. Peters	19470	Saylorsburg	18353
Rudytown	17070	St. Petersburg	16054	Sayre	18840
Ruffcreek	15329	St. Thomas	17252	Scalp Level	15963
Ruffs Dale	15679	St. Thomas (Township)	17201	Scammells Corner	19067
Ruggles	18636	St. Vincent College	15650	Scandia	16345
Rummel	15963	St. Vincent Shaft	15650	Scenery Hill	15360
Rummerfield	18853	Salco	15530	Schaefferstown	17088
Rundell	16406	Salem (Clarion County)		Schellsburg	15559
Running Brooke	15701	(Township)	16232	Schenley	15682
Runville	16823	Salem (Clearfield County)	15801	Scherersville	18104
Rupert	17815	Salem (Franklin County)	17201	Schlusser	17013
Ruppsville	18106	Salem (Luzerne County)		Schnecksville	18078
Rural Ridge	15075	(Township)	18603	Schoeneck (Lancaster	
Rural Valley	16249	Salem (Mercer County)	16125	County)	17578
Ruscombmanor (Township)	19522	Salem (Mercer County)		Schoeneck (Northampton	
Rush (Susquehanna		(Township)	16130	County)	18064
County) (Township)	18801	Salem (Snyder County)	17870	Schoentown (Part of Port	
Rush (Centre County)		Salem (Wayne County)		Carbon)	17965
(Township)	16866	(Township)	18444	Schofer	19530
Rush (Dauphin County)		Salem (Westmoreland		Schollard	16137
(Township)	17980	County) (Township)	15601	School Lane	17603
Rush (Northumberland		Salem Harbor	19020	School Lane Hills	17604
County) (Township)	17821	Salemville	16664	School Valley Farms	17520
Rush (Schuylkill County)		Salford	18957	Schubert	19507
(Township)	18252	Salford (Township)	18969	Schultzville	19504
Rush	18801	Salford Heights	19438	Schulzville	18411
Rushland	18956	Salfordville	18958	Schuster Heights	16229
Rushtown	17821	Salida (Part of Baldwin)	15227	Schuyler	17772
Rushville	18839	Salina	15680	Schuylkill (Chester County)	
Russell	16345	Salisbury (Lancaster		(Township)	19460
Russell Hill	18657	County) (Township)	17535	Schuylkill (Philadelphia	
Russellton	15076	Salisbury (Lehigh County)		County)	19146
Russellville (Chester		(Township)	18103	Schuylkill (Schuylkill County)	
County)	19363	Salisbury (Somerset County)	15558	(Township)	17952
Russellville (Huntingdon		Salisbury Heights	17527	Schuylkill Haven	17972
County)	16657	Salix	15952	Schuylkill Hills	19401
Rutan	15341	Salix-Beauty Line Park	15952	Schwenksville	19473
Rutherford	17111	Salladasburg	17740	Sciota	18354

	ZIP		ZIP		ZIP
Sconnelltown	19380	Shaners Crossroads	15656	Ships Parts Control Center,	
Scotch Hill	16233	Shanesville	19512	USN	17055
Scotch Hollow	16666	Shankles (Part of Du Bois)	15801	Shiremanstown	17011
Scotia (Part of Jefferson)	15025	Shanksville	15560	Shire Oaks	15322
Scotland	17254	Shanktown	15777	Shirks Corner	19473
Scotrun	18355	Shannondale	16240	Shirley (Township)	17066
Scott (Allegheny County)		Shannon Heights	15235	Shirleysburg	17260
(Township)	15106	Shanor Heights	16001	Shoaf	15478
Scott (Columbia County)		Shanor-Northvue	16001	Shocks Mills	17547
(Township)	17815	Sharon (Mercer County)	16146	Shoemaker	15946
Scott (Lackawanna County)		Sharon (Potter County)		Shoemakers (Monroe	
(Township)	18447	(Township)	16748	County)	18301
Scott (Lawrence County)		Sharon Center	16748	Shoemakers (Schuylkill	
(Township)	16101	Sharon Hill	19079	County)	17948
Scott (Wayne County)		Sharon North (Part of		Shoemakersville	19555
(Township)	18462	Hermitage)	16146	Shoenberger	16686
Scott Center	18462	Sharon Park (Part of Sharon		Shoenersville	18103
Scottdale	15683	Hill)	19079	Shohola	18458
Scott Haven	15083	Sharpsburg (Allegheny		Shohola (Township)	18458
Scottsville	15001	County)	15215	Shope Gardens	17057
Scott Township	15106	Sharpsburg (Huntingdon		Shorbes Hill	17331
Scranton	18501-19	County)	17060	Shortsville	16935
For specific Scranton Zip Codes		Sharps Hill	15215	Shraders	17084
call (717) 969-5100		Sharpsville	16150	Shrewsbury (Lycoming	
Scrubgrass (Township)	16373	Sharrertown	15427	County) (Township)	17737
Scullton	15557	Shartlesville	19554	Shrewsbury (Sullivan	
Scyoc	17021	Shavertown (Delaware		County) (Township)	17758
Seamentown	15729	County)	19061	Shrewsbury (York County)	17361
Seanor	15953	Shavertown (Luzerne		Shrewsbury (York County)	
Searights	15401	County)	18708	(Township)	17327
Sebring	16930	Shawanese (Part of Harveys		Shumans	17815
Secane	19018	Lake)	18654	Shunk	17768
Secane Highlands	19018	Shaw Mine	15057	Shy Beaver	16657
Seek (Part of Coaldale)	18218	Shawmut	15823	Sickles Corner	16601
Seelyville	18431	Shawnee on Delaware	18356	Siddonsburg	17019
Seemsville	18067	Shawtown	15642	Sidman	15955
Seger	15627	Shawville	16873	Siegfried (Part of	
Seidersville	18015	Shay	16226	Northampton)	18067
Seipstown	18031	Sheakleyville	16151	Sigel	15860
Seisholtzville	18062	Shearersburg	15656	Siglerville	17063
Seitzland	17327	Sheatown	18634	Sigmund	18092
Seitzville	17360	Sheffield	16347	Silkworth	18621
Selea	17264	Sheffield (Township)	16347	Silvara	18623
Selinsgrove	17870	Sheffield Heights	15001	Silver Creek	17959
Sellersville	18960	Sheffield Terrace	15001	Silverdale	18962
Seltzer	17974	Sheffield Village	19401	Silver Ford Heights	17066
Seminole	16253	Shehawken	18462	Silver Lake (Township)	18812
Seneca	16346	Shellsville	17028	Silver Lake (Wayne County)	18469
Seneca Valley	15642	Shelly	18951	Silver Lake (York County)	17339
Sereno	17846	Shellytown	16693	Silver Lake (Bucks County)	18940
Sergeant	16735	Shelocta	15774	Silver Lake (Susquehanna	
Sergeant (Township)	16740	Sheltontown	16403	County)	18812
Seven Fields	16046	Shelvey	15846	Silver Spring (Cumberland	
Seven Hills	18837	Shenandoah	17976	County) (Township)	17055
Seven Pines	17082	Shenandoah Heights	17976	Silver Spring (Lancaster	
Sevenpoints	17801	Shenango (Lawrence		County)	17575
Seven Springs	15622	County) (Township)	16101	Silverville	16055
Seven Stars (Adams		Shenango (Mercer County)	16125	Simmonstown	17527
County)	17325	Shenango (Mercer County)		Simpson	18407
Seven Stars (Juniata		(Township)	16159	Singersville	17018
County)	17062	Shenango Valley Mall (Part		Sinking Spring	19608
Seven Valleys	17360	of Hermitage)	16146	Sinking Valley	16601
Seward	15954	Shenkel	19464	Sinnamahoning	15861
Sewickley (Allegheny		Shenks Ferry	17309	Sinsheim	17362
County)	15143	Shepherd Hills	18101	Sipesville	15561
Sewickley (Westmoreland		Shepherdstown	17055	Sitka	15431
County) (Township)	15637	Sheppton	18248	Six Mile Run	16679
Sewickley Heights	15143	Sheridan (Lebanon County)	17073	Six Points	16049
Sewickley Hills	15143	Sheridan (Schuylkill County)	17980	Sixty-Ninth Street Center	19082
Seybertown	16028	Sherman	18847	Sizerville	15834
Seyfert	19508	Shermans Dale	17090	Skelp	16601
Shade (Township)	15924	Shermansville	16316	Skidmore	16101
Shade Gap	17255	Sherrett	16218	Ski Haven Lake Estates	18326
Shadeland	16435	Sherwood Acres	15061	Skinners Eddy	18623
Shades Glen	18661	Sheshequin	18850	Skippack	19474
Shade Valley	17213	Sheshequin (Township)	18848	Skippack (Township)	19474
Shadle	17853	Shetters Grove	17405	Skyline Heights	17402
Shado-wood Village	15701	Shickshinny	18655	Skyline View	17112
Shady Acres	17834	Shields (Part of Edgeworth)	15143	Skytop	18357
Shady Grove	17256	Shieldsburg	15670	Sky View	18426
Shady Plain	15613	Shillington	19607	Slabtown (Clearfield County)	15724
Shadyside (Part of		Shiloh (Clearfield County)	16881	Slabtown (Franklin County)	17268
Pittsburgh)	15232	Shiloh (York County)	17404	Slackwater	17551
Shaffer	15801	Shiloh East	17405	Slatedale	18079
Shaffers Corner	15401	Shimerville	18049	Slatefield	18038
Shaffersville	16652	Shimpstown	17236	Slateford	18343
Shaft (Schuylkill County)	17976	Shindle	17841	Slateford Junction	18343
Shaft (Somerset County)	15530	Shinglehouse	16748	Slate Hill	17314
Shafton	15642	Shingletown	16801	Slate Lick	16229
Shaler (Township)	15116	Shintown	17764	Slate Run	17769
Shalercrest	15223	Shipmans Eddy	16365	Slate Valley	18038
Shaler Township (census		Shippen (Cameron County)		Slateville	19529
designated place)	15116	(Township)	15834	Slatington	18080
Shamokin	17872	Shippen (Tioga County)		Slickport	16646
Shamokin (Township)	17860	(Township)	16901	Slickville	15684
Shamokin Dam	17876	Shippensburg	17257	Sligo	16255
Shamrock (Fayette County)	15401	Shippensburg (Township)	17257	Slippery Rock (Butler	
Shamrock (Somerset		Shippensburg State College	17257	County)	16057
County)	15557	Shippenville	16254	Slippery Rock (Butler	
Shamrock Station	19539	Shippingport	15077	County) (Township)	16057
Shaner	15642				

	ZIP
Slippery Rock (Lawrence County) (Township)	16101
Slippery Rock Park	16057
Slocum (Township)	18660
Slocum Corners	18660
Slovan	15078
Slovene National Benefit Society	16120
Smallwood (Part of California)	15423
Smethport	16749
Smicksburg	16256
Smiley	15401
Smith (Blair County)	16665
Smith (Indiana County)	15717
Smith (Township)	15078
Smith Bridge	15380
Smithdale	15089
Smithfield (Bradford County) (Township)	18831
Smithfield (Fayette County)	15478
Smithfield (Huntingdon County) (Township)	16652
Smithfield (Huntingdon County)	16652
Smithfield (Monroe County) (Township)	18335
Smithfield Center	16652
Smith Gardens	17345
Smithland	16242
Smithmill	16680
Smithport	15742
Smiths	17362
Smiths Corner	18950
Smiths Corners	16374
Smiths Ferry (Part of Ohioville)	15059
Smithton	15479
Smithtown (Bucks County)	18947
Smithtown (Jefferson County)	15840
Smithville	17560
Smock	15480
Smokeless	15944
Smokerun	16681
Smoketown (Bucks County)	18951
Smoketown (Franklin County)	17222
Smoketown (Lancaster County)	17576
Smullton	16854
Smyerstown	15772
Smyrna	17509
Snake Spring (Township) ..	15522
Snedekerville	16914
Snively Corners	16232
Snowball Gate.............	19056
Snowden	15129
Snowdenville	19475
Snow Shoe	16874
Snow Shoe (Township)	16829
Snyder (Blair County) (Township)	16686
Snyder (Jefferson County) (Township)	15824
Snyder Corner	17356
Snyders	17960
Snydersburg	16257
Snydersville	18360
Snydertown (Centre County)	16841
Snydertown (Fayette County)	15425
Snydertown (Northumberland County)	17877
Snydertown (Westmoreland County)	15620
Snyderville	16222
Social Island	17201
Soho (Part of Pittsburgh)..	15219
Soldier	15851
Solebury	18963
Solebury (Township)	18963
Somerset (Somerset County)	15501
Somerset (Somerset County) (Township)	15501
Somerset (Washington County) (Township)	15330
Somers Lane	16929
Somerton (Part of Philadelphia)	19116
Somerville	16028
Sonestown	17770
Sonman	15946
Soradoville	17841
Soudersburg	17577
Souderton	18964
Soukesburg	15956
South Abington (Township)	18410

	ZIP
South Altoona (Part of Altoona)	16602
Southampton (Bedford County) (Township)	17211
Southampton (Bucks County)	18966
Southampton (Cumberland County) (Township)	17257
Southampton (Franklin County) (Township)	17244
Southampton (Somerset County) (Township)	15552
South Annville (Township)	17042
South Auburn	18630
South Beaver (Township)	16115
South Bend	15686
South Bend (Township) ...	15774
South Bethlehem	16242
South Bradford	16701
South Buffalo (Township)	16229
South Burgettstown (Part of Burgettstown)	15021
South Canaan	18459
South Canaan (Township)	18472
South Carnegie	15106
South Centre (Township)...	17815
South Clarksville	15322
South Clearfield (Part of Clearfield)	16830
South Coatesville	19320
South Connellsville	15425
South Coventry (Township)	19464
South Creek (Township) ...	16925
Southdale	18655
South Duquesne (Part of Duquesne)	15110
Southeastern	19397-99
For specific Southeastern Zip Codes call (215) 964-6448	
Southeastern Facility	19399
South Easton (Part of Easton)	18042
South Eaton	18657
South Enola	17025
South Erie (Part of Erie)...	16508
Southerwood	15610
South Fayette (Township)	15064
South Fork	15956
South Franklin (Township)	15301
South Gibson	18842
South Greensburg	15601
South Hanover (Township)	17033
South Heidelberg (Township)	19565
South Heights	15081
South Hermitage	17555
South Hills (Allegheny County)	15216
South Hills (Mifflin County)	17044
South Hills Village	15241
South Huntingdon (Township)	15089
South Lakemont	16602
Southland 4 Seasons Centre (Part of Pleasant Hills)	15236
South Lebanon (Township)	17042
South Londonderry (Township)	17010
South Mahoning (Township)	15747
South Manheim (Township)	17972
South Meadville	16335
South Media	19063
South Middleton (Township)	17007
Southmont	15905
South Montrose	18843
South Mountain	17261
South Mountain Restoration Center	17261
South New Castle	16101
South Newton (Township)	17266
South Oil City (Part of Oil City)	16301
South Park (Township)	15129
South Philipsburg	16866
South Pottstown	19464
South Pymatuning (Township)	16150
South Renovo	17764
South Rockwood	15557
South Shenango (Township)	16134
South Side (Allegheny County)	15203
South Side (Butler County)	16045
South Side (Lackawanna County)	18505
Southside (Northampton County)	18015
South Sterling	18460
South Strabane (Township)	15301
South Tamaqua	18252

	ZIP
South Temple	19560
South Towanda	18848
South Union (Township) ...	15401
South Uniontown	15401
South Versailles (Township)	15028
Southview	15361
Southwark (Part of Philadelphia)	19147
South Waverly..............	14892
Southwest (Warren County) (Township)	16354
Southwest (Westmoreland County)	15685
Southwest Greensburg	15601
Southwest Madison (Township)	17047
South Whitehall (Township)	18104
South Williamsport	17701
South Woodbury (Township)	16664
Southwood Hills	17403
Spaces Corners	16201
Spangenberg Lake	18436
Spangler	15775
Spangsville	19512
Sparta (Crawford County) (Township)	16434
Sparta (Washington County)	15329
Spartansburg	16434
Spears Grove	17021
Speedwell	17543
Speers	15012
Spike Island	16666
Spillway Lake	15473
Spindley City	16641
Spinnerstown	18968
Spinners Point	18464
Split Rock	18624
Sporting Hill (Cumberland County)	17055
Sporting Hill (Lancaster County)	17545
Sportsburg	15767
Spraggs..................	15362
Sprankle Mills	15767
Spring (Berks County) (Township)	19609
Spring (Snyder County) (Township)	17812
Spring (Centre County) (Township)	16823
Spring (Crawford County) (Township)	16406
Spring (Perry County) (Township)	17040
Spring Bank	16872
Springboro	16435
Spring Brook (Township)...	18444
Spring Church	15686
Spring City	19475
Spring Creek (Elk County) (Township)	15853
Spring Creek (Lehigh County)	18011
Spring Creek (Warren County) (Township)	16436
Spring Creek (Warren County)	16436
Springdale	15144
Springdale (Township)	15049
Springdell	19320
Springettsbury (Township)	17402
Springetts Manor-Yorklyn	17402
Springfield (Bradford County)	16914
Springfield (Bradford County) (Township)	18831
Springfield (Bucks County) (Township)	18951
Springfield (Cumberland County)	17241
Springfield (Delaware County) (Township)	19064
Springfield (Delaware County)	19064
Springfield (Erie County) (Township)	16443
Springfield (Fayette County) (Township)	15464
Springfield (Huntingdon County) (Township)	17243
Springfield (Mercer County) (Township)	16137
Springfield (Montgomery County) (Township)	19118
Springfield (York County) (Township)	17327
Springfield Falls	16137
Springfield Mall	19064
Spring Garden (Bucks County)	18940

	ZIP		ZIP		ZIP
Spring Garden (Lancaster County)	17535	Starners Station	17324	Stony Point (Franklin County)	17262
Spring Garden (Philadelphia County)	19122	Starr (Forest County)	16353	Stony Point (Greene County)	15344
Spring Garden (Schuylkill County)	17972	Starr (Warren County)	16420	Stony Run	19557
Spring Garden (Union County)	17810	Starrucca	18462	Stormstown	16870
Spring Garden (Westmoreland County)	15666	Starview	17347	Stormville	18360
Spring Garden (York County) (Township)	17403	Starview Heights	17402	Stottsville	19367
Spring Garden (York County)	17403	State College	16801-05	Stouchsburg	19567
Spring Glen	17978	For specific State College Zip Codes call (814) 238-2435		Stoufferstown	17201
Spring Grove	17362	State Correctional Institution at Dallas (Luzerne County)	18612	Stoughstown	17257
Springhaven Estates	19086	State Correctional Institution (Lycoming County)	17756	Stover	16686
Springhill (Bradford County)	18853	State Correctional Institution (Montgomery County)	19426	Stoverdale	17036
Springhill (Fayette County) (Township)	15478	State Correction Institution	17011	Stoverstown	17362
Springhill (Greene County) (Township)	15352	State Hill (Berks County)	19608	Stowe (Allegheny County) (Township)	15136
Spring Hill (Cambria County)	15946	State Hill (Chester County)	17527	Stowe (Montgomery County)	19464
Spring Hill (Delaware County)	19018	State Line (Bedford County)	15545	Stowell	18623
Springhope	15559	State Line (Erie County)	16428	Stowe Township (census designated place)	15136
Spring House	19477	State Line (Franklin County)	17263	Stoystown	15563
Springhouse Farms	18104	Steamburg	16424	Straban (Township)	17325
Spring Meadow	15554	Steel City	18015	Strabane	15363
Spring Meadows	19565	Steelstown	17003	Strafford	19087
Spring Mill	19428	Steelton	17113	Strangford	15717
Spring Mills	16875	Steelville	19370	Strasburg	17579
Springmont	19609	Steene	18472	Strasburg (Township)	17602
Spring Mount (Huntingdon County)	16877	Steffins Hill	15010	Strattanville	16258
Spring Mount (Montgomery County)	19478	Steinbachs Corner	18847	Strausstown	19559
Spring Run	17262	Steinsburg	18951	Strawberry Ridge	17821
Springs	15562	Steinsville	19529	Strawbridge	17758
Springtown (Bucks County)	18081	Stemlersville	18235	Straw Pump	15642
Springtown (Franklin County)	17221	Sterling (Township)	18445	Strickhousers	17360
Springtown (Luzerne County)	18707	Sterling (Clearfield County)	16651	Stricklerstown	17073
Springtown (Northumberland County)	17777	Sterling (Wayne County)	18463	Strinestown	17345
Springvale	17356	Sterling Run	15832	Stringtown (Armstrong County)	16226
Spring Valley (Berks County)	19560	Sterlingworth	18104	Stringtown (Greene County)	15320
Spring Valley (Bucks County)	18901	Sterrettania	16415	Strobleton	16353
Spring Valley (Clearfield County)	16878	Stetlersville	18069	Strodes Mills	17044
Spring Valley (Northampton County)	18015	Steuben (Township)	16404	Stronach	16833
Spring Valley Estates	17201	Stevens (Bradford County) (Township)	18854	Strong	17851
Spring Valley Farms	18901	Stevens (Lancaster County)	17578	Strongstown	15957
Springville (Township)	18844	Stevens Point	18847	Stroud (Township)	18360
Springville (Venango County)	16342	Stevenstown	17019	Stroudsburg	18360
Springville (Cumberland County)	17007	Stevensville	18845	Stroudsburg West	18360
Springville (Lancaster County)	17535	Stewardson (Township)	17729	Strum	15478
Springville (Susquehanna County)	18844	Stewart (Township)	15470	Studa	15312
Sproul	16682	Stewart Run	16341	Stull	18636
Spruce Creek	16683	Stewartstown	17363	Stump Creek	15863
Spruce Creek (Township)	16683	Stewartsville	15642	Stumptown	16666
Spruce Hill	17082	Stickney	16701	Sturgeon	15082
Spruce Hill (Township)	17082	Sticks	17329	Sturgeon-Noblestown	15071
Sprucetown	15474	Stiefler Corner	16670	Sturgis (Part of Archbald)	18447
Spry	17403	Stier	18013	Suburban Village	19380
Squab Hollow	15846	Stifflertown	15724	Sudan	15063
Square Corner	17325	Stiles	18052	Suedburg	17963
Squirrel Hill (Part of Pittsburgh)	15217	Stiles Hill	16943	Sugarcreek (Armstrong County) (Township)	16218
Stack Town	15502	Still Creek	18252	Sugarcreek (Venango County)	16323
Stafore Estates	18017	Stilleys Siding (Part of Jefferson)	15025	Sugar Grove (Greene County)	15380
Stahlstown	15687	Stillwater	17878	Sugar Grove (Mercer County) (Township)	16125
Stairville	18660	Stillwater Lake Estates	18346	Sugargrove (Warren County)	16350
Stalker	12741	Stiltz	17327	Sugar Grove (Warren County) (Township)	16350
Stambaugh	15456	Stines Corner	18066	Sugar Hill	15824
Standard	15666	Stobo	15061	Sugarloaf (Luzerne County) (Township)	18251
Standard Shaft	15666	Stockdale	15483	Sugarloaf (Columbia County) (Township)	17814
Standing Stone	18854	Stockertown	18083	Sugarloaf	18249
Standing Stone (Township)	18853	Stockton	18201	Sugar Notch	18706
Stanhope	17963	Stockton Number Eight	18201	Sugar Run	18846
Stanley	15801	Stockton Number Seven	18201	Sugartown	19355
Stanton (Jefferson County)	15825	Stockton Number Six	18201	Sullivan (Township)	16932
Stanton (Luzerne County)	15825	Stoddartsville	18610	Summerdale	17093
Stanton Heights (Allegheny County)	15201	Stokesdale	16901	Summerhill (Cambria County)	15958
Stanton Heights (Westmoreland County)	15672	Stoneboro	16153	Summerhill (Crawford County) (Township)	16406
Stanwood Gardens	19020	Stone Church	18343	Summerhill (Cambria County) (Township)	15921
Star Brick	16365	Stone Glen	17018	Summer Hill (Columbia County)	18603
Starford	15777	Stoneham	16313	Summerson	15821
Star Junction	15482	Stone Hill	17516	Summerville (Jefferson County)	15864
Starkville	18657	Stone House	16258	Summerville (Susquehanna County)	18822
Starlight	18461	Stonehurst	19006	Summit (Butler County) (Township)	16001
		Stonerstown	16678	Summit (Cambria County)	16630
		Stonersville	19508	Summit (Crawford County) (Township)	16424
		Stonetown	19508		
		Stonevilla	15601		
		Stoneybreak	17267		
		Stonington	17801		
		Stonybrook	17402		
		Stonybrook Heights	17402		
		Stonybrook-Wilshire	17402		
		Stonycreek (Cambria County) (Township)	15906		
		Stonycreek (Somerset County) (Township)	15541		
		Stony Creek Mills	19606		
		Stonyfork	16901		
		Stony Point (Bucks County)	18930		
		Stony Point (Crawford County)	16316		

Place	ZIP	Place	ZIP	Place	ZIP
Valley (Chester County) (Township)	19320	Vienna	15376	Ward (Tioga County) (Township)	17724
Valley (Montour County) (Township)	17821	Viennese Woods	15209	Warfordsburg	17267
Valley Falls	19006	Viewmont Mall (Part of Dickson City)	18519	Warminster (Township)	18974
Valley Forge	19481-85	Village	15241	Warminster	18974
For specific Valley Forge Zip Codes call (215) 783-0232		Village Green	19013	Warminster Heights	18974
Valley Forge Christian College	19460	Village Green-Green Ridge	19013	Warner	15022
Valley Forge Estates	19087	Village of Cross Creek	17402	Warren (Bradford County) (Township)	18851
Valley Forge Homes	19406	Village of Olde Hickory	17601	Warren (Franklin County) (Township)	17236
Valley Forge Manor	19460	Village of the Four Seasons	18470	Warren (Warren County)	16365
Valley Furnace	17959	Village of Westover	17055	Warren Center	18851
Valley Green (Delaware County)	19026	Village Shires	18966	Warrendale	15086
Valley Green (York County)	17319	Villa Green	17403	Warren South	16365
Valley Green Estates	17319	Villa Maria	16155	Warren State Hospital	16365
Valley Green Heights	17319	Villanova	19085	Warrensville	17701
Valley Green West	17319	Vinco	15909	Warrington	18976
Valley-Hi	15533	Vinemont	17569	Warrington (Bucks County) (Township)	18976
Valley Stream	18707	Vintage	17562	Warrington (York County) (Township)	17019
Valley View (Cambria County)	15906	Vintondale	15961	Warrior Ridge	16669
Valley View (Centre County)	16823	Violet Hill	17403	Warrior Run	18706
Valley View (Chester County)	19344	Violet Wood	19057	Warriors Mark	16877
Valley View (Lancaster County)	17545	Vira	17044	Warriors Mark (Township)	16686
Valley View (Schuylkill County)	17983	Virginia Farms	15717	Warsaw (Jefferson County) (Township)	15851
Valley View (York County)	17403	Virginia Hills West	15126	Warsaw (Lackawanna County)	18512
Valley View Farms	19006	Virginia Mills	17320	Warsaw (Luzerne County)	18702
Valley View Heights	16226	Virginville	19564	Warwick (Chester County) (Township)	19520
Van	16319	Voganville	17522	Warwick (Lancaster County) (Township)	17543
Van Buren	15329	Vogleyville	16001	Warwick (Bucks County) (Township)	18929
Vance	15301	Volant	16156	Warwick	19470
Vances Mills	15401	Vosburg	18657	Washington (Armstrong County) (Township)	16218
Vanceville	15330	Vowinckel	16260	Washington (Berks County) (Township)	19512
Vanderbilt	15486	Vulcan	18214	Washington (Butler County) (Township)	16061
Vandergrift	15690	Wabash (Part of Pittsburgh)	15220	Washington (Cambria County) (Township)	15938
Vandergrift Heights (Part of Vandergrift)	15690	Wadesville	17901	Washington (Clarion County) (Township)	16326
Vandling	18421	Wadsworth (Part of Philadelphia)	19150	Washington (Dauphin County) (Township)	17048
Vandyke	17082	Wagner	17841	Washington (Erie County) (Township)	16412
Vankirk	15301	Wagnersville	18042	Washington (Fayette County) (Township)	15012
Van Meter	15479	Wagontown	19376	Washington (Franklin County) (Township)	17268
Van Ormer	16639	Wahlville	16033	Washington (Greene County) (Township)	15370
Vanport (Township)	15009	Wahnetah (Part of Jim Thorpe)	18229	Washington (Indiana County) (Township)	15732
Van Voorhis	15366	Wakena	15681	Washington (Jefferson County) (Township)	15840
Van Wert	17059	Walbert	18104	Washington (Lawrence County) (Township)	16156
Varden	18436	Walcksville	18235	Washington (Lehigh County) (Township)	18080
Vaux Town (Part of New Britain)	18901	Walden Woods	15126	Washington (Lycoming County) (Township)	17810
Vawter	18810	Walkchalk	16201	Washington (Northampton County) (Township)	18010
Venango (Butler County) (Township)	16049	Walker (Centre County) (Township)	16841	Washington (Northumberland County) (Township)	17867
Venango (Crawford County)	16440	Walker (Huntingdon County) (Township)	16660	Washington (Schuylkill County) (Township)	17963
Venango (Crawford County) (Township)	16440	Walker (Juniata County) (Township)	17059	Washington (Snyder County) (Township)	17842
Venango (Erie County) (Township)	16442	Walker (Schuylkill County) (Township)	18252	Washington (Washington County)	15301
Venetia	15367	Walkers Mill	15106	Washington (Westmoreland County) (Township)	15613
Venice	15057	Walkertown	15427	Washington (Wyoming County) (Township)	18657
Venturetown	16365	Wall	15148	Washington (York County) (Township)	17316
Venus	16364	Wallace (Township)	19343	Washington Boro	17582
Vera Cruz	18049	Wallace Junction (Part of Girard)	16417	Washington Crossing	18977
Verdilla	17870	Wallaceton	16876	Washington Heights (Part of Lemoyne)	17043
Vere Cruz	17569	Wallaceville	16354	Washington Hill (Part of Pottstown)	19464
Vermilion Hill	19054	Wallenpaupack Lake Estates	18436	Washington Square Gardens	19401
Vernfield	19438	Waller	17814	Washingtonville	17884
Vernon (Crawford County) (Township)	16335	Wallingford	19086	Wassergass	18055
Vernon (Wyoming County)	18657	Wallingford Hills	19086	Waterfall	16689
Vernondale	16509	Wallis Run	17771	Waterford (Erie County)	16441
Vernon Park (Part of Philadelphia)	19144	Walls Corners	18414	Waterford (Erie County) (Township)	16411
Verona	15147	Wallsville	18414	Waterford (Westmoreland County)	15658
Versailles	15132	Walltown	16838		
Vestaburg	15368	Walmo	16101		
Vesta Heights	15333	Walnut	17082		
Vesta No 6 (Part of Centerville)	15429	Walnut Bend	16301		
Veterans Administration Hospital (Blair County)	16602	Walnut Bottom	17266		
Veterans Administration Hospital (Butler County)	16001	Walnut Gardens	18052		
Veterans Administration Medical Center (Lebanon County)	17042	Walnut Grove	17074		
Veterans Hospital (Allegheny County)	15240	Walnut Hill (Fayette County)	15401		
Veterans Hospital (Chester County)	19320	Walnut Hill (Greene County)	15327		
Veterans Hospital (Luzerne County)	18702	Walnut Hill (Montgomery County)	19001		
Vicksburg (Blair County)	16648	Walnutport	18088		
Vicksburg (Union County)	17883	Walnuttown	19522		
Victory (Township)	16342	Walsall	15904		
Victory Heights	16323	Walston	15781		
Victory Hills	15063	Walston Junction (Part of Punxsutawney)	15767		
		Walters	18042		
		Waltersburg	15488		
		Waltonville	17036		
		Waltz	15679		
		Waltz Landing	18428		
		Waltzvale	16671		
		Wampum	16157		
		Wanamakers	19529		
		Wanamie	18634		
		Wandin	15729		
		Wanneta	16401		
		Wapwallopen	18660		
		Ward (Delaware County)	19331		

	ZIP		ZIP		ZIP
Waterford (York County) ...	17402	Welty	15666	Westfield Terrace	17070
Waterloo	17021	Wendel	15691	West Finley	15377
Waterloo Mills	19333	Wendover	15601	West Finley (Township) ...	15377
Waterman	15748	Wenks	17304	Westford	16134
Waterside	16695	Wentlings Corners	16232	West Franklin (Armstrong	
Waterson	16258	Werleys Corner	18066	County) (Township)	16262
Water Street	16611	Wernersville	19565	West Franklin (Bradford	
Waterton	18655	Wernersville Heights	19565	County)	18832
Waterville	17776	Wernersville State Hospital	19565	West Freedom	16049
Waterworks, The (Part of		Wertz	16693	Westgate Hills	18017
Pittsburgh)	15212	Wertzville	17055	West Goshen (Township)	19380
Watkins	15722	Wescosville	18106	West Goshen	19380
Watrous	16921	Wesley	16038	West Goshen Hills	19380
Watson (Lycoming County)		Wesley Chapel	15909	West Goshen Park	19380
(Township)	17740	Wesleyville	16510	West Grove	19390
Watson (Warren County)		Wessex Hills	15108	West Hamburg	19526
(Township)	16351	West (Township)	16669	West Hanover (Township)	17112
Watson Farm	16239	West Abington (Township)	18419	West Hazleton	18201
Watson Run	16316	West Acres	17837	West Hemlock (Township)	17821
Watsontown	17777	West Alexander	15376	West Hempfield (Township)	17601
Watters	16033	West Aliquippa (Part of		West Hickory	16370
Wattersonville	16218	Aliquippa)	15001	West Hill	17013
Watts (Township)	17020	West Ambler	19002	West Hills	16201
Wattsburg	16442	West Annville	17003	West Hills Estates	17701
Waverly	18471	West Apollo (Part of		West Hoffman	15101
Wawa (Part of Chester		Oklahoma)	15613	West Homestead	15120
Heights)	19017	West Auburn	18623	Westinghouse Village	19029
Wawaset	19380	Westaway	19444	West Jeannette (Part of	
Wayland Corners	16335	West Bangor (Northampton		Jeannette)	15644
Waymart	18472	County)	18072	West Jonestown	17038
Wayne (Armstrong County)		West Bangor (York County)	17314	West Keating (Township)	16871
(Township)	16222	West Beaver (Township) ...	17841	West Kittanning	16201
Wayne (Clinton County)		West Belt Junction (Part of		West Lampeter (Township)	17537
(Township)	17748	Pittsburgh)	15230	West Lancaster	17603
Wayne (Crawford County)		West Bend	15433	Westland	15378
(Township)	16314	West Berwick (Part of		West Lawn (Berks County)	19609
Wayne (Dauphin County)		Berwick)	18603	West Lawn (Union County)	17837
(Township)	17032	West Bethlehem (Township)	15345	West Lebanon (Indiana	
Wayne (Delaware County)	19087	West Bingham	16923	County)	15783
Wayne (Erie County)		West Bolivar	15923	West Lebanon (Township)	17042
(Township)	16407	West Bradford (Township)	19335	West Lebanon (Lebanon	
Wayne (Greene County)		West Branch (Cambria		County)	17042
(Township)	15362	County)	15714	West Leechburg	15656
Wayne (Lawrence County)		West Branch (Potter		West Leisenring	15489
(Township)	16117	County) (Township)	16922	West Lenox	18826
Wayne (Mifflin County)		West Brandywine		West Leroy	17724
(Township)	17051	(Township)	19320	West Liberty (Butler County)	16057
Wayne (Schuylkill County)		West Bridgewater	15009	West Liberty (Clearfield	
(Township)	17933	West Bristol	19007	County)	15801
Waynecastle	17225	West Brownsville	15417	West Library (Part of Bethel	
Wayne Heights	17268	West Brunswick (Township)	17961	Park)	15102
Waynesboro	17268	West Buffalo (Township) ...	17844	Westline	16740
Waynesburg	15370	West Burlington	16947	West Mahanoy (Township)	17976
Waynesburg Lakes	15329	West Burlington (Township)	16914	West Mahoning (Township)	16256
Waynesville	17032	Westbury	15071	West Manayunk	19151
Weatherly	18255	West Caln (Township)	19376	West Manchester	
Weaverland	17519	West Cameron	17872	(Township)	17404
Weaversville	18067	West Cameron (Township)	17872	West Manchester Mall (Part	
Weavertown (Berks County)	19518	West Carroll (Township) ...	15737	of York)	17345
Weavertown (Lancaster		West Catasauqua	18052	West Manheim (Township)	17331
County)	17505	West Chester	19380-83	West Market (Part of	
Weavertown (Lebanon		For specific West Chester Zip		Philadelphia)	19139
County)	17042	Codes call (215) 696-4808		West Marlborough	
Weavertown (Washington		West Chillisquaque		(Township)	19348
County)	15317	(Township)	17850	West Mayfield	15010
Weber City	15834	West Clifford	18470	West Mead (Township)	16335
Webster	15087	West Cocalico (Township)	17578	West Meyersdale (Part of	
Webster Mills	17233	Westcolang	18428	Meyersdale)	15552
Weedville	15868	West Conshohocken	19428	West Middlesex	16159
Wegley	15642	West Cornwall (Township)	17042	West Middletown	15379
Wehnwood (Part of Altoona)	16601	West Creek	15834	West Mifflin	15122-23
Weidasville	18078	West Creek Hills	17011	For specific West Mifflin Zip	
Weidmanville	17522	West Cressona (Part of		Codes call (412) 466-5120	
Weigelstown	17315	Cressona)	17929	West Milton	17886
Weigh Scales	17872	West Damascus	18469	Westminster (Erie County)	16506
Weikert	17885	West Decatur	16878	Westminster (Luzerne	
Weilersville	18011	West Deer (Township)	15076	County)	18702
Weinel's Crossroads	15656	West Derry	15627	Westminster Manor	15241
Weir Lake	18058	West Donegal (Township)	17022	West Monocacy	19518
Weisel	18944	West Earl (Township)	17508	Westmont (Cambria	
Weisenberg (Township) ...	18066	West Easton	18042	County)	15905
Weishample	17938	West Eldred	16731	Westmont (Lebanon	
Weissport	18235	West Elizabeth	15088	County)	17042
Weissport East	18235	West Ellwood Junction (Part		West Monterey	16049
Weldbank	16313	of Koppel)	16136	Westmont Plan	16201
Weldon	19006	West End (Dauphin County)	17102	Westmoreland City	15692
Wellersburg	15564	West End (Washington		West Moshannon	16651
Wellington Estates	18901	County)	15301	West Myerstown	17067
Welliversville	17815	West Enola	17025	West Nanticoke	18634
Wellmans Corners	18834	West Export (Part of Export)	15632	West Nantmeal (Township)	19520
Wells (Bradford County)		West Fairfield	15944	West New Kensington	15030
(Township)	16925	West Fairview	17025	West Newton	15089
Wells (Fulton County)		Westfall (Township)	18336	West Nicholson	18446
(Township)	16691	West Fallowfield (Chester		West Norriton (Township)	19401
Wellsboro	16901	County) (Township)	19330	West Norriton	19401
Wellsboro Junction	16901	West Fallowfield (Crawford		West Nottingham	
Wellscreek	15541	County) (Township)	16131	(Township)	19362
Wells Tannery	16691	West Falls	18615	Weston	18256
Wellsville	17365	West Fayetteville	17222	Weston Place	17976
Welsh Hill	18470	Westfield	16950	Westover (Bucks County)	19067
Welsh Run	17225	Westfield (Township)	16950		

	ZIP
Westover (Clearfield County)	16692
West Overton	15683
Westover Woods	19401
West Park (Allegheny County)	15136
West Park (Philadelphia County)	19131
West Pen Argyl	18072
West Penn (Township)	17960
West Pennsboro (Township)	17241
West Perry (Township)	17086
West Pike	16922
West Pikeland (Township)	19425
West Pike Run (Township)	15427
West Pittsburg	16160
West Pittston	18643
West Point (Cambria County)	15942
West Point (Montgomery County)	19486
West Point (Westmoreland County)	15601
Westport	17778
West Pottsgrove	19464
West Pottsgrove (Township)	19464
West Providence (Township)	15537
West Reading	19611
West Renovo	17764
West Ridge	17603
West Rockhill (Township)	18960
West Sadsbury (Township)	19365
West Salem (Township)	16125
West Salisbury	15565
West Scranton (Part of Scranton)	18504
West Shenango (Township)	16134
West Side (Part of West Newton)	15089
West Spring Creek	16407
West Springfield	16443
West St. Clair (Township)	15521
West Sunbury	16061
West Tarentum (Part of Tarentum)	15084
West Taylor (Township)	15906
West Telford (Part of Telford)	18969
Westtown	19395
Westtown (Township)	19395
Westtown Acres	19380
West Union	15364
West Valley	16201
West Vandergrift (Part of Vandergrift)	15690
West View (Allegheny County)	15229
Westview (Beaver County)	15009
Westville	15824
West Vincent (Township)	19425
West Warren	13812
West Wayne	19087
West Waynesburg	15370
West Wheatfield (Township)	15944
West Whiteland (Township)	19341
West William Penn	17976
West Willow	17583
West Wilmerding	15137
West Winfield	16023
Westwood (Cambria County)	15905
Westwood (Chester County)	19320
Westwood Park	19083
West Wyoming	18644
West Wyomissing	19609
West York	17404
West Zollarsville	15345
Wetherills Corner	19460
Wetmore	16735
Wetmore (Township)	16735
Wetona	16914
Wexford	15090
Weyant	16655
Wharton (Potter County) (Township)	16720
Wharton (Fayette County) (Township)	15437
Wharton	16720
Wheatfield (Township)	17020
Wheatland	16161
Wheatland Hills	17604
Wheat Sheaf	19067
Wheeler	15425
Wheelerville	17768
Whig Hill	16353
Whipkeys-Dam	15551
Whiskerville	16040
Whitaker	15120
White (Beaver County) (Township)	15010

	ZIP
White (Cambria County) (Township)	15906
White (Fayette County)	15490
White (Indiana County)	15681
White (Indiana County) (Township)	15701
White Bear	19508
White Cottage	15341
White Deer	17887
White Deer (Township)	17887
Whitehall (Township)	18052
Whitehall (Adams County)	17340
Whitehall (Allegheny County)	15227
Whitehall (Lehigh County)	18052
White Hall (Dauphin County)	17110
White Hall (Montour County)	17821
Whitehall Mall	18052
Whitehall Park	19401
White Haven	18661
White Hill	17011
White Horse (Chester County)	19073
White Horse (Lancaster County)	17527
White House	15478
Whiteland Crest	19341
Whiteland Farms	19355
Whiteley (Township)	15370
Whitemarsh (Township)	19428
Whitemarsh Downs	19075
Whitemarsh Estates	19444
Whitemarsh Greens	19444
Whitemarsh Hills	19444
Whitemarsh Valley Farms	19444
White Mills	18473
White Oak (Allegheny County)	15131
White Oak (Lancaster County)	17545
White Oak (Westmoreland County)	15068
White Oak Manor	18042
White Oaks	18701
White Pine	17771
Whitesburg	16201
Whites Corner	16927
Whites Crossing	18407
Whites Ferry	18657
Whiteside	16651
Whitesprings	17844
White Squaw Mission	17353
Whitestown	16052
Whites Valley	18453
White Valley (Part of Murrysville)	15632
Whitewood	19057
Whitfield	19609
Whitford Hills	19341
Whitney	15693
Whitney Lake	18428
Whitneyville	16901
Whitpain (Township)	19422
Whitsett	15473
Wick	16057
Wickerham Manor	15063
Wickerham Manor-Fisher	15063
Wickerton	19390
Wickham Village	15001
Wickhaven	15492
Wiconisco	17097
Wiconisco (Township)	17097
Widener College (Part of Chester)	19013
Widnoon	16261
Wiegletown	16101
Wiester (Part of Murrysville)	15632
Wiggans	17948
Wigwam	16731
Wila	17074
Wilawana	18840
Wilbur	15563
Wilburton	17888
Wilco Hill	15087
Wilcox	15870
Wild Acres Country Club	18328
Wildcat	16248
Wilden Acres	18042
Wildwood	15091
Wildwood Terrace	18701
Wiley	17363
Wiley Heights	15320
Wilgus	15742
Wilkes-Barre	18701-73
For specific Wilkes-Barre Zip Codes call (717) 829-5468	
Wilkes-Barre (Township)	18702
Wilkes-Barre Township (census designated place)	18702
Wilkes Manor	18977

	ZIP
Wilkins (Township)	15145
Wilkinsburg	15221
Wilkins Township (census designated place)	15145
Willet	15732
William Penn Annex (Part of Philadelphia)	19107
William Penn Manor	18017
Williams (Dauphin County) (Township)	17098
Williams (Northampton County) (Township)	18042
Williamsburg (Blair County)	16693
Williamsburg (Clarion County)	16214
Williams Grove	17055
Williamson	17270
Williamsport	17701-03
For specific Williamsport Zip Codes call (717) 322-2732	
Williamstown	17098
Willistown (Township)	19355
Willock (Part of Baldwin)	15236
Willopenn	18966
Willowbrook	19061
Willowburn	19085
Willowdale	19348
Willow Grove (Lawrence County)	16101
Willow Grove (Montgomery County)	19090
Willow Grove Naval Air Station	19090
Willow Grove Park	19090
Willow Hill	17271
Willow Lake	17901
Will-O-Wood	19007
Willow Springs (Columbia County)	17815
Willow Springs (Westmoreland County)	15642
Willow Street	17584
Willow View Heights	17584
Wills Creek	15545
Wilmer	19460
Wilmerding	15148
Wilmington (Lawrence County) (Township)	16105
Wilmington (Mercer County) (Township)	16142
Wilmore	15962
Wilmore Heights	15958
Wilmot (Township)	18846
Wilpen	15658
Wilshire Hills (Lancaster County)	17603
Wilshire Hills (York County)	17402
Wilson (Allegheny County)	15025
Wilson (Berks County)	19608
Wilson (Northampton County)	18042
Wilson Creek	15557
Wilson Heights	18426
Wilsons Corners	19460
Wimmers	18436
Winburne	16879
Windber	15963
Winder Village	19007
Windfall	17724
Windgap	18091
Windham (Bradford County) (Township)	18837
Windham (Wyoming County) (Township)	18623
Windham Center	18837
Winding Brook Manor	18062
Winding Hill	17055
Winding Hill Heights	17055
Windom	17603
Wind Ridge	15380
Windsor (Berks County) (Township)	19526
Windsor (York County)	17366
Windsor (York County) (Township)	17356
Windsor Castle	19526
Windsor Farms	17110
Windsor Park (Cumberland County)	17055
Windsor Park (York County)	17403
Windward Heights	16001
Winfield (Butler County) (Township)	16023
Winfield (Union County)	17889
Wingate	16880
Wingerton	17268
Winslow	15767
Winslow (Township)	15851
Winstead	15474
Winterburne	15849
Winterdale	18461

	ZIP		ZIP		ZIP
Winterstown	17356	Woodward (Clearfield		Wysox (Township)	18854
Wintersville	17087	County) (Township)	16651	Yardley	19067
Wiscasset	18344	Woodward (Clinton County)		Yardley Farms	19067
Wishaw	15851	(Township)	17745	Yardley Hunt	19067
Wismer	18947	Woodward (Lycoming		Yarnell	16823
Wissahickon Village	19444	County) (Township)	17744	Yatesboro	16263
Wissinoming (Part of		Woodward Acres	15601	Yatesville (Luzerne County)	18640
Philadelphia)	19135	Woodycrest	16801	Yatesville (Schuylkill County)	17976
Witinski Villa	18706	Woolrich	17779	Yeadon	19050
Witmer	17585	Wopsononock	16636	Yeagertown	17099
Wittmer	15116	Worcester	19490	Yellow Creek	16650
Wolf (Township)	17737	Worcester (Township)	19490	Yellow Hammer	16322
Wolf Creek (Township)	16127	Worden Place (Part of		Yellow House	19518
Wolfdale	15301	Harveys Lake)	18618	Yellowwood	19007
Wolf Run	16749	Worleytown	17225	Yerkes	19426
Wolfsburg	15522	Worman	19518	Yocumtown	17319
Wolfs Corner	16353	Wormleysburg	17043	Yoe	17313
Wolfs Crossroads	17801	Worth (Butler County)		York	17315
Wolftown (Part of North		(Township)	16057	York	17401-07
Braddock)	15104	Worth (Centre County)		For specific York Zip Codes call
Womelsdorf	19567	(Township)	16870	(717) 848-2381
Wood	16694	Worth (Mercer County)		York (Township)	17403
Wood (Township)	16674	(Township)	16133	Yorkana	17402
Woodale	18301	Worthington	16262	York County (Shopping
Woodbine	17302	Worthville	15784	Center)	17402
Woodbourne	19047	Woxall	18979	York Haven	17370
Woodbridgetown	15478	Wright (Township)	18707	Yorklyn	17402
Woodbury (Bedford County)	16695	Wrights	16743	York New Salem	17371
Woodbury (Bedford County)		Wrights Corners	16749	York Road (Bucks County)	18974
(Township)	16695	Wrightsdale	17563	York Road (York County)	17331
Woodbury (Blair County)		Wrightstown	18940	York Run	15401
(Township)	16693	Wrightstown (Township)	18980	Yorkshire	17402
Woodchoppertown	19512	Wrightsville (Warren County)	16340	York Springs	17372
Woodcock	16433	Wrightsville (York County)	17368	Yostville	18444
Woodcock (Township)	16433	Wurtemburg	16117	Young (Indiana County)
Woodcock Grange	16433	Wurtemburg Heights	16117	(Township)	15725
Woodcrest	19380	Wyalusing	18853	Young (Jefferson County)
Wooddale	15425	Wyalusing (Township)	18853	(Township)	15767
Woodglen	15442	Wyano	15695	Youngdale	17748
Woodhaven Estates	15001	Wyattville (Part of		Youngsburg	19320
Woodhill	18940	Sugarcreek)	16323	Youngstown (Luzerne
Woodland (Clearfield		Wycombe	18980	County)	18221
County)	16881	Wydnor	18015	Youngstown (Westmoreland
Woodland (Mifflin County)	17084	Wyebrooke	19344	County)	15696
Woodland Heights		Wylandville	15330	Youngsville (Northampton
(Venango County)	16301	Wylie	15037	County)	18038
Woodland Park	17701	Wylie (Part of Pittsburgh)	15219	Youngsville (Warren County)	16371
Woodland View	17402	Wylie (Part of Clairton)	15025	Youngwood	15697
Woodlawn (Lancaster		Wyncote	19095	Yukon	15698
County)	17603	Wyncote Hills	19095	Zebleys Corner	19061
Woodlawn (Lehigh County)	18104	Wyncroft	19063	Zehners	17960
Woodlawn (Westmoreland		Wyndham Hills	17403	Zelienople	16063
County)	15644	Wyndmoor	19118	Zerbe (Northumberland
Woodlawn Park	15001	Wyndmoor Valley	19075	County) (Township)	17881
Woodlyn	19094	Wynn	15401	Zerbe (Schuylkill County)	17981
Woodlyn Manor	19094	Wynnewood (Bucks		Zieglerville	19492
Woodlyn Park	19094	County)	19067	Zimmerman	15501
Woodrow	15340	Wynnewood (Montgomery		Zion (Centre County)	16823
Woodruff	15341	County)	19096	Zion (Luzerne County)	18643
Woodside (Bucks County)	19067	Wynnewood Shopping		Zion Grove	17985
Woodside (Fayette County)	15478	Center	19096	Zionhill	18981
Woodside (Luzerne County)	18224	Wyoming	18644	Zions View	17404
Woodside-Drifton	18221	Wyoming Camp Ground	18643	Zionsville	18092
Woods of Sandy Ridge	18901	Wyoming Valley Mall	18702	Zollarsville	15345
Woodstown	15935	Wyomissing	19610	Zooks Corner	17602
Woodvale Heights	15901	Wyomissing Hills	19609	Zooks Dam	17059
Woodville	15106	Wyomissing Junction (Part		Zora	17320
Woodville State Hospital	15106	of Wyomissing)	19610	Zucksville	18042
Woodward (Centre County)	16882	Wysox	18854	Zullinger	17272

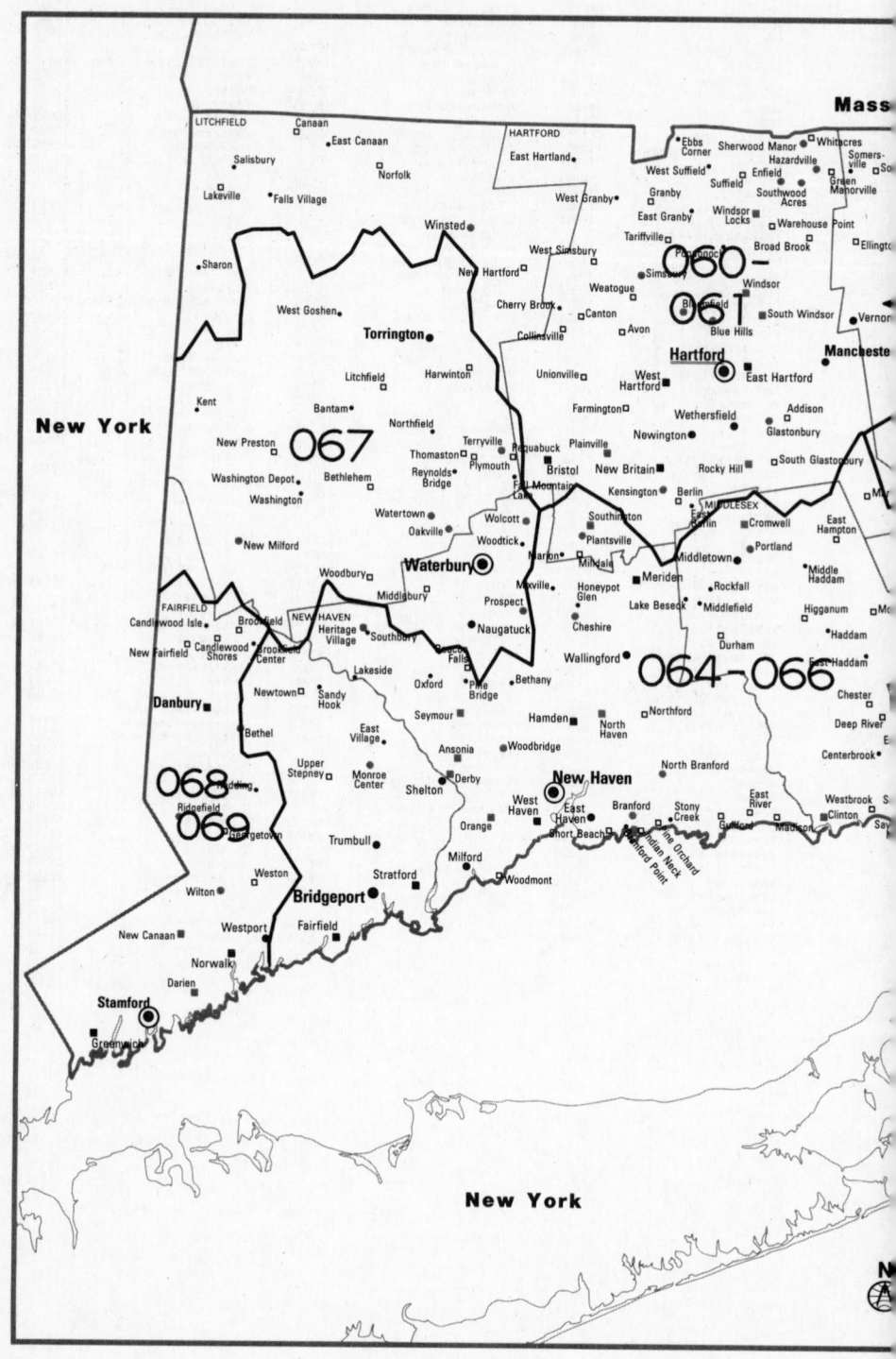

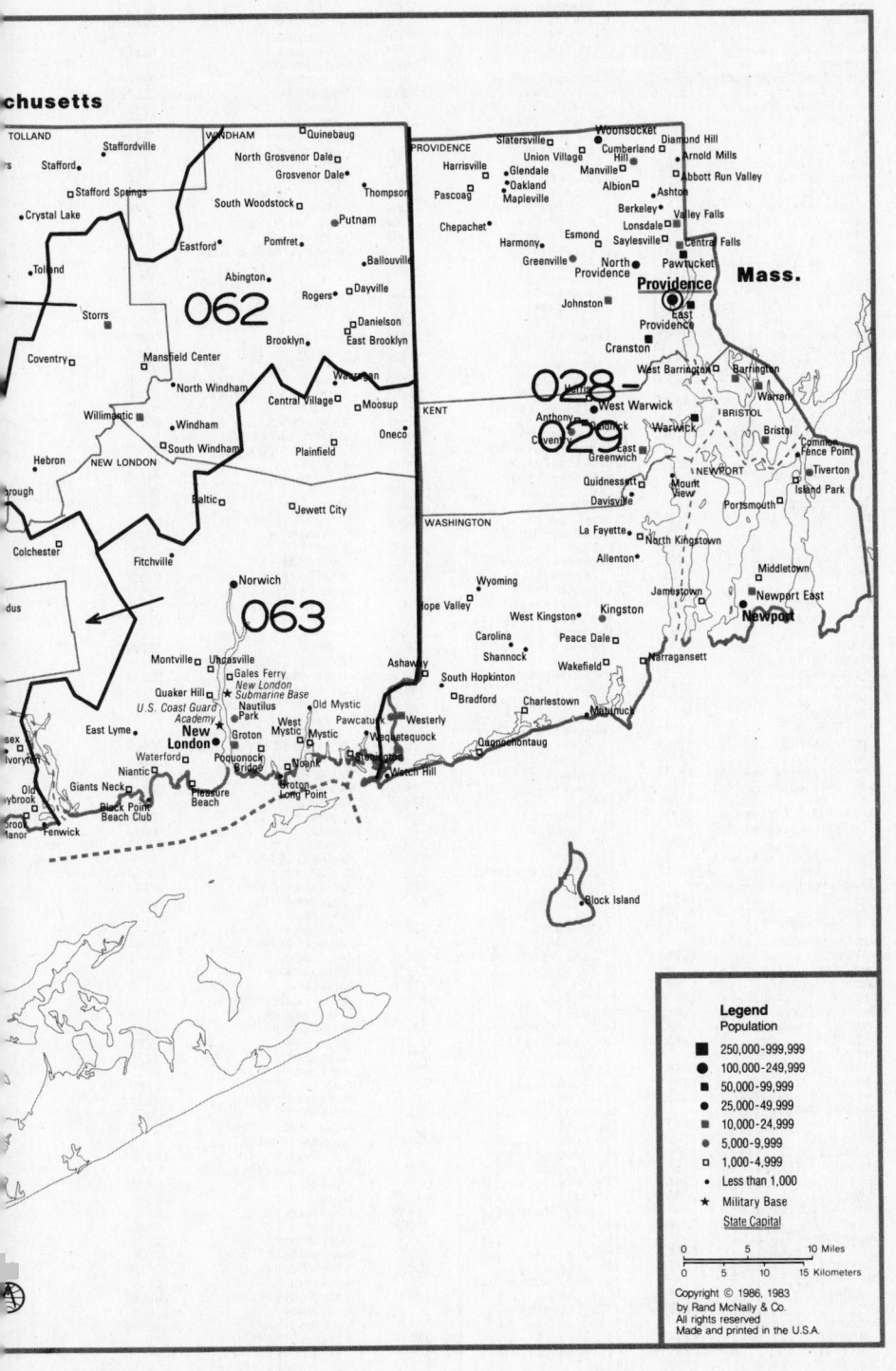

chusetts

TOLLAND

Staffordville

Stafford

Stafford Springs

Crystal Lake

Tolland

Storrs

Coventry

Hebron

rough

Colchester

dus

sex

Ivoryton

Old
aybrook

brook
Manor   Fenwick

WINDHAM   Quinebaug

North Grosvenor Dale

Grosvenor Dale

Thompson

South Woodstock

Eastford   Pomfret

Abington

Rogers   Dayville

Brooklyn   East Brooklyn

Danielson

Mansfield Center

North Windham   Wauregan

Central Village   Moosup

Willimantic   Windham   Oneco

South Windham   Plainfield

NEW LONDON

Baltic

Jewett City

Fitchville

Norwich

062

063

Montville   Uncasville

Quaker Hill   Gales Ferry
         New London
         Submarine Base
U.S. Coast Guard   Nautilus
Academy   Park   Old Mystic

East Lyme   West   Pawcatuck
         Mystic Mystic
New   Groton
London
Waterford   Poquonock
         Bridge   Noank
Niantic

Giants Neck

Black Point
Beach Club

Putnam

Ballouville

PROVIDENCE

Slatersville   Woonsocket   Diamond Hill

Harrisville   Union Village   Cumberland   Arnold Mills
         Glendale   Hill
Pascoag   Mapleville   Oakland   Manville   Abbott Run Valley
                  Albion   Ashton
Chepachet   Berkeley   Valley Falls
                  Lonsdale
Harmony   Esmond   Saylesville   Central Falls

Greenville   North   Pawtucket
         Providence
         Johnston   **Providence**
                  East
                  Providence

Cranston

KENT

West Barrington   Barrington

Hope   West Warwick   Warren

Anthony   Redrick   Warwick   BRISTOL   Bristol
Coventry   Common
East   Fence Point
Greenwich   Mount
                  View   Tiverton
Quidnessett   NEWPORT   Island Park
Davisville   Portsmouth

WASHINGTON

La Fayette   North Kingstown

Allenton   Middletown

Wyoming   Jamestown   Newport East

Hope Valley   Kingston   **Newport**

West Kingston

Carolina

Shannock   Peace Dale

Ashaway   Wakefield

South Hopkinton   Narragansett

Bradford   Charlestown

Westerly   Quonochontaug   Manunuck

Watch Hill

Mass.

028—029

Block Island

	ZIP
Abbott Run Valley	02864
Adamsville	02801
Albion	02802
Allendale	02911
Allenton	02852
Alton	02894
Annawomscutt	02806
Annex (Part of Providence)	02903
Anthony	02816
Apple Blossom (Part of Cranston)	02920
Arcadia	02832
Arctic	02893
Arkwright	02816
Arlington (Part of Cranston)	02920
Arnold Mills	02864
Arnold's Neck (Part of Warwick)	02886
Ashaway	02804
Ashton	02864
Auburn (Part of Cranston)	02910
Austin	02822
Avondale	02891
Barberville	02832
Barrington	02806
Barrington (Town)	02806
Bayridge (Part of Warwick)	02818
Bayside (Part of Warwick)	02889
Bay Spring	02806
Bay View (Part of East Providence)	02914
Beach Terrace	02809
Bellefonte (Part of Cranston)	02920
Belleville	02852
Berkeley	02864
Beverage Hill (Part of Pawtucket)	02860
Bishops Heights	02857
Black Plain	02822
Block Island	02807
Bonnet Shores	02882
Boon Lake	02822
Bowdish Lake	02814
Bradford	02808
Branch Village	02895
Brenton Village (Part of Newport)	02840
Bridgeport	02878
Bridgetown	02874
Briggs Beach	02837
Bristol (Town)	02809
Bristol	02809
Bristol Colony	02872
Bristol Ferry	02871
Bristol Highlands	02809
Bristol Narrows	02809
Broadway (Part of Newport)	02840
Brookfield (Part of Cranston)	02920
Brown (Part of Providence)	02912
Brush Neck Cove (Part of Warwick)	02886
Bryant College of Business Administration	02917
Bullocks Point (Part of East Providence)	02914
Burdickville	02808
Burrillville (Town)	02830
Buttonwoods (Part of Warwick)	02886
Canonchet	02832
Carnegie Heights	02865
Carolina	02812
Carpenters Beach	02879
Cedar Grove Estates	02822
Cedar Point	02835
Cedar Tree Point (Part of Warwick)	02886
Centerdale	02911
Centerville (Kent County)	02893
Centerville (Washington County)	02832
Central Falls	02863
Charlestown	02813
Charlestown (Town)	02813
Charlestown Beach	02813
Chepachet	02814
Chepiwanoxet (Part of Warwick)	02886
Cherry Valley	02814
Cherry Valley Beach	02814
Chopmist	02857
Clarke's Village	02835
Clayville	02815
Clyde	02893
Coasters Harbor (Part of Newport)	02840
Coggeshall	02885
Coles (Part of Warwick)	02889
Columbia Heights	02875
Common Fence Point	02871

	ZIP
Commons	02837
Comstock Gardens (Part of Cranston)	02910
Conanicut Park	02835
Conimicut (Part of Warwick)	02889
Corey's Lane	02871
Coventry	02816
Coventry (Town)	02816
Coventry Center	02816
Cowesett (Part of Warwick)	02886
Cranston	02910
Crescent Park (Part of East Providence)	02914
Crompton	02893
Cross Mills	02813
Cumberland	02864
Cumberland (Town)	02864
Cumberland Hill	02864
Curtis Corners	02883
Darlington (Part of Pawtucket)	02861
Davisville (P.O.)	02854
Davisville	02852
Diamond Hill	02864
Dunns Corners	02891
Durfee Hill	02814
Eagleville	02878
East Greenwich (Town)	02818
East Greenwich	02818
East Matunuck	02879
East Natick (Part of Warwick)	02893
East Providence	02914
East Providence Wharf (Part of East Providence)	02914
East Side (Part of Providence)	02906
East Warren	02885
Echo Lake	02814
Eden Park (Part of Cranston)	02920
Edgewood (Part of Cranston)	02905
Elmwood (Part of Providence)	02907
Enos (Part of Cranston)	02920
Escoheag	02821
Esmond	02917
Exeter	02822
Exeter (Town)	02822
Fairbanks Corner	02827
Finast (Part of East Providence)	02914
Fiskeville (Part of Cranston)	02823
Fogland Point	02878
Forestdale	02824
Fort Adams (Part of Newport)	02840
Foster	02825
Foster (Town)	02825
Fox Point (Part of Providence)	02906
Frenchtown	02818
Friar (Part of Providence)	02918
Fruit Hill	02911
Galilee	02882
Garden City (Part of Cranston)	02920
Garden City Shopping Center (Part of Cranston)	02920
Gazzaville	02839
Geneva	02911
Georgiaville	02917
Glendale	02826
Glocester (Town)	02814
Goat Island (Part of Newport)	02840
Goulds	02883
Graniteville	02911
Grants Mills	02838
Greene	02827
Green Hill	02879
Greenville	02828
Greenwood (Part of Warwick)	02886
Greystone	02911
Hamilton	02852
Hampden Meadows	02806
Harmony	02829
Harris	02816
Harrisville	02830
Haversham	02891
Highland Beach (Part of Warwick)	02889
Hill's Grove (Part of Warwick)	02886
Hog Island	02809
Homestead	02872
Hope	02831
Hope Valley	02832
Hopkins Hollow	02827

	ZIP
Hopkinton	02833
Hopkinton (Town)	02833
Howard (Part of Cranston)	02920
Hoxsie (Part of Warwick)	02889
Hughesdale	02919
Indian Lake Shores	02879
India Point (Part of Providence)	02903
Island Park	02871
Jackson	02823
Jamestown (Town)	02835
Jamestown	02835
Jamestown Center	02835
Jamestown Shores	02835
Jerusalem	02879
Johnston (Town)	02919
Johnston	02919
Kent Corner (Part of East Providence)	02914
Kent Heights (Part of East Providence)	02914
Kenyon	02836
Kingston	02881
Knightsville (Part of Cranston)	02920
La Fayette	02852
Lake Bel Air	02895
Lake Mishnock	02817
Lakewood (Part of Warwick)	02888
Langworthy Corner	02891
Laurel Hill	02859
Laurel Park	02885
Leonard Corner (Part of East Providence)	02914
Liberty	02877
Limerock	02865
Lincoln	02865
Lincoln (Town)	02860
Lincoln Park (Part of Warwick)	02888
Lippit	02893
Lippitt Estate	02864
Little Compton	02837
Little Compton (Town)	02837
Lockwood Corner (Part of Warwick)	02889
Longmeadow (Part of Warwick)	02889
Lonsdale (Lincoln Town) (Providence County)	02864
Lonsdale (Cumberland Town) (Providence County)	02865
Lymansville	02911
Manton (Part of Providence)	02909
Manville	02838
Maple Root Village	02816
Mapleville	02839
Marieville	02904
Matunuck	02879
Mellville	02840
Melville	02840
Meshanticut (Part of Cranston)	02920
Middletown (Town)	02840
Middletown	02840
Misquamicut	02891
Mohegan	02830
Mohegan Bluffs	02807
Mooresfield	02874
Moosup Valley	02827
Moscow	02832
Mount Pleasant (Part of Providence)	02908
Mount Vernon	02825
Mount View	02852
Nannaquaket	02878
Narragansett	02882
Narragansett (Town)	02882
Narragansett Heights	02878
Nasonville	02830
Natick (Part of Warwick)	02893
Nausauket (Part of Warwick)	02886
Naval Construction Battalion Center	02854
Nayatt	02806
New Harbor	02807
Newport	02840
Newport East	02840
New Shoreham (Town)	02807
Nichols Corner	02818
Nooseneck	02816
North (Part of Providence)	02908
North Foster	02825
North Kingstown	02852-54
For specific North Kingstown Zip Codes call (401) 294-4641	
North Providence (Town)	02911
North Providence	02911
North Quidnessett	02852

	ZIP		ZIP		ZIP
North Scituate	02857	River Point	02893	Touisset Highlands	02885
North Smithfield (Town)	02876	Riverside (Part of East		Tuckertown	02879
Norwood (Part of Warwick)	02888	Providence)	02915	Tunipus	02837
Oakland	02830	River Vue (Part of Warwick)	02889	Union Village	02895
Oakland Beach (Part of		Rockville	02873	Usquepaug	02892
Warwick)	02886	Rocky Point (Part of		Valley Falls	02864
Oak Lawn (Part of		Warwick)	02889	Vaughn Hollow	02827
Cranston)	02920	Rumford (Part of East		Wakefield	02879-83
Old Harbor	02807	Providence)	02916	For specific Wakefield Zip Codes	
Olney Arnold Estates (Part		Rumstick Point	02806	call (401) 783-2691	
of Cranston)	02920	Sakonnet	02837	Wakefield-Peacedale	02883
Olneyville (Part of		Sandy Point (Kent County)	02818	Walnut Hill (Part of	
Providence)	02909	Sandy Point (Washington		Woonsocket)	02895
Palace Garden (Part of		County)	02807	Warren (Town)	02885
Warwick)	02888	Saunderstown	02874	Warren	02885
Parcel Post Annex	02891	Saundersville	02857	Warren Point	02837
Pascoag	02859	Saylesville	02865	Warwick	02886-89
Pawtucket	02860-63	Scituate (Town)	02857	For specific Warwick Zip Codes	
For specific Pawtucket Zip Codes		Shady Harbor	02891	call (401) 737-6200	
call (401) 722-1073		Shannock	02875	Warwick Mall (Part of	
Peace Dale	02883	Shawomet (Part of		Warwick)	02886
Perryville	02879	Warwick)	02889	Warwick Neck (Part of	
Pettaquamscutt Lake		Shelter Harbor	02891	Warwick)	02889
Shores	02874	Shores Acres	02852	Washington Park (Part of	
Phenix	02893	Silver Lake (Part of		Cranston)	02905
Phillipsdale (Part of East		Providence)	02909	Watch Hill	02891
Providence)	02914	Simmonsville	02919	Watchmocket Square (Part	
Pilgrim (Part of Warwick)	02888	Slatersville	02876	of East Providence)	02914
Pine Hill	02822	Slocum	02877	Waterford	01504
Pleasant View (Part of		Smithfield (Town)	02917	Waterman Four Corners	02857
Pawtucket)	02860	Smith Hill (Part of		Weekapaug	02891
Plum Beach	02874	Providence)	02908	West Barrington	02806
Plum Point	02874	Sockannosset (Part of		Westcott (Part of Warwick)	02893
Poccasett Heights	02871	Cranston)	02920	Westcott Beach	02814
Point Judith	02882	South Foster	02825	Westerly	02891
Pontiac (Part of Warwick)	02886	South Hopkinton	02813	Westerly (Town)	02891
Popasquash Point	02809	South Kingstown (Town)	02879	West Glocester	06260
Portsmouth	02871	South Providence (Part of		West Greenville	02828
Portsmouth (Town)	02871	Providence)	02905	West Greenwich (Town)	02817
Potowomut (Part of		South Warren	02885	West Greenwich Center	02827
Warwick)	02818	Spragueville	02828	West Kingston	02892
Potter Hill	02891	Spring Green (Part of		West Warwick	02893
Primrose	02895	Warwick)	02888	West Warwick (Town)	02893
Print Works (Part of		Spring Grove	02814	Weybosset Hill (Part of	
Cranston)	02920	Spring Lake Beach	02826	Providence)	02903
Providence	02901-09	Squantum (Part of East		Whipple	02830
	02940	Providence)	02914	White Rock	02891
For specific Providence Zip Codes		Stillwater	02917	Wickford Junction	02852
call (401) 276-6850		Summit	02827	Wildes Corner (Part of	
Prudence Island	02872	Tarkiln	02830	Warwick)	02886
Prudence Park	02872	The Anchorage	02840	Wood Estates	02816
Quidnessett	02852	The Hummocks	02871	Wood River Junction	02894
Quidnick	02816	Thornton	02919	Woodville (Providence	
Quinnville	02865	Tiverton	02878	County)	02911
Quonochontaug	02813	Tiverton (Town)	02878	Woodville (Washington	
Rhode Island Mall (Part of		Tiverton Four Corners	02878	County)	02832
Warwick)	02886	Tockwotten (Part of		Woonsocket	02895
Rice City	02827	Providence)	02903	Wyoming	02898
Rice Plat	02857	Tonomy Hill (Part of		Yorktown Manor	02852
Richmond (Town)	02812	Newport)	02840		

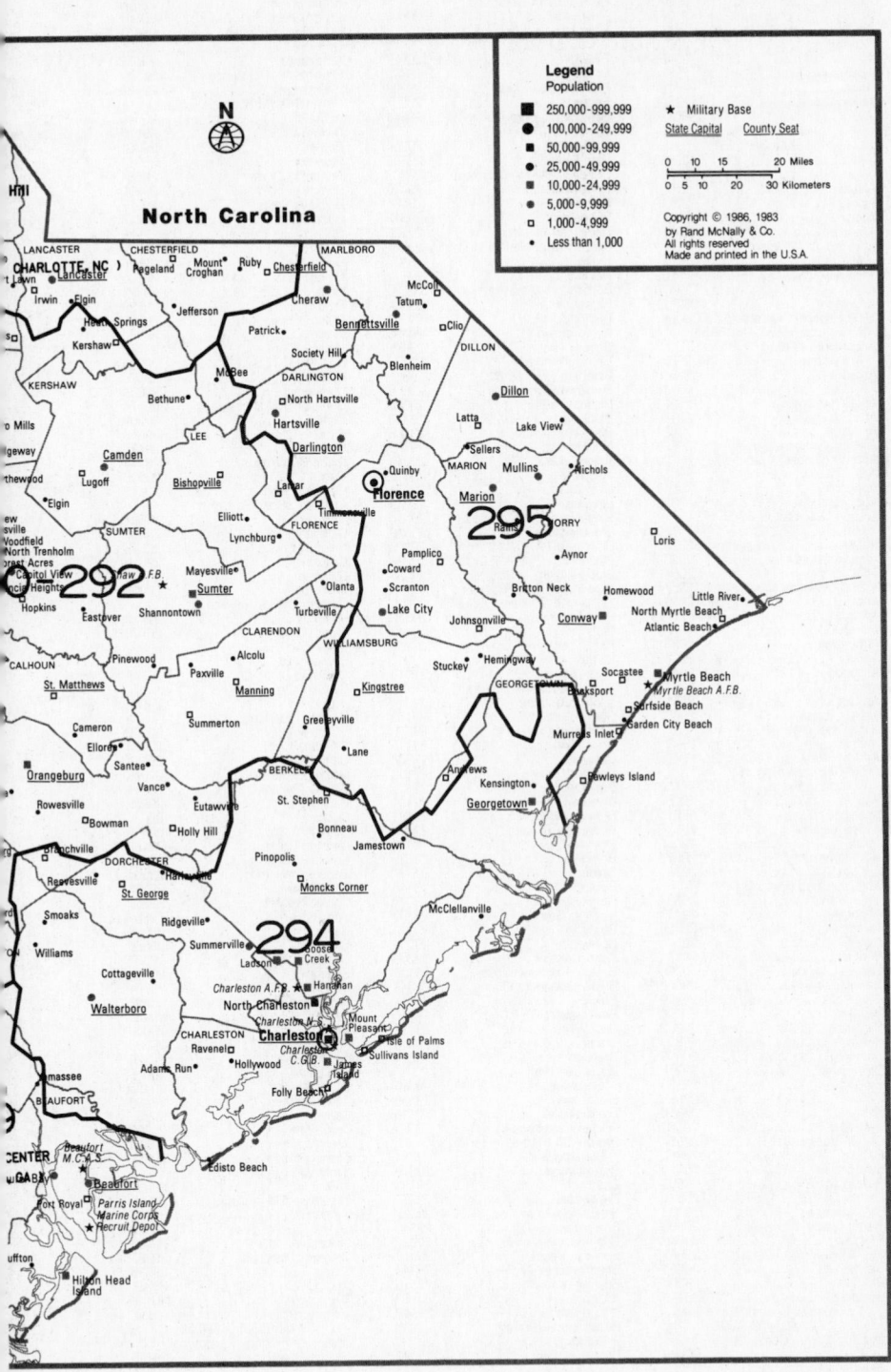

North Carolina

N

Legend
Population
■ 250,000-999,999
● 100,000-249,999
■ 50,000-99,999
■ 25,000-49,999
■ 10,000-24,999
● 5,000-9,999
□ 1,000-4,999
• Less than 1,000

★ Military Base
State Capital   County Seat

0   10   15   20 Miles
0 5 10   20   30 Kilometers

	ZIP		ZIP		ZIP
Abbeville	29620	Belle Meade (Greenville		Brook Forest	29605
Abney	29067	County)	29603	Brook Green Park	29501
Academy Acres	29488	Belle Meade (Lexington		Brookhaven Estates	29801
Adamsburg	29379	County)	29172	Brooklyn	29720
Adams Run	29426	Bellinger	29927	Brooksville	29582
Adamsville	29570	Bells	29475	Brownsville (Dorchester	
Adger	29180	Belmont	29203	County)	29483
Adrian	29526	Belton	29627	Brownsville (Marlboro	
Aiken	29801-04	Belvedere (Aiken County)	29841	County)	29516
For specific Aiken Zip Codes call		Belvedere (Richland		Brownway	29526
(803) 648-2351		County)	29204	Bruner	29061
Aiken Estates	29803	Ben Avon	29302	Brunson	29911
Aiken West	29801	Bendale (Part of Columbia)	29203	Brunsons Crossroads	29554
Alcolu	29001	Beneventum	29440	Bryans Crossroads	29590
Alcot	29010	Bennett	29405	Buckeye Forest	29377
Allen	29511	Bennettsville	29512	Buck Hall	29429
Allendale	29810	Bent Tree	29678	Buckingham Landing	29928
Allendale Correctional		Berea (Greenville County)	29611	Bucksport	29526
Institute	29827	Berlin	29137	Bucksville	29526
Allsbrook	29569	Bethany	29710	Buffalo (McCormick County)	29835
Alvin	29479	Bethera	29430	Buffalo (Union County)	29321
Anderson	29621-25	Bethesda	29584	Buford	29720
For specific Anderson Zip Codes		Bethune	29009	Buford Crossroads	29720
call (803) 226-1595		Beufordtown	29453	Bufords Bridge	29843
Anderson Mall (Part of		Beverly Hills	29445	Bullock Creek	29742
Anderson)	29621	Beverly Woods	29301	Bunker Hill	29536
Andrews	29510	Bingham	29565	Burgess	29576
Angelus	29718	Birdtown Crossroads	29550	Burnettown	29834
Angle Siding	29902	Bishopville	29010	Burnt Church Crossroads	29474
Anne Village	29440	Blackjack	29180	Burton	29902
Ansel	29651	Blacks	29166	Bynum	29556
Antioch (Kershaw County)	29020	Blacksburg	29702	Byrd	29477
Antioch (Lancaster County)	29720	Blackstock	29014	Byrds Crossroads	28114
Antreville	29655	Blackville	29817	Cades	29518
Appleton	29810	Blair	29015	Caesars Head	28718
Appleton Mills	29625	Blakedale	29649	Caldwell Street (Part of	
Aragon Mills (Part of Rock		Blenheim	29516	Rock Hill)	29731
Hill)	29730	Bloomingvale	29510	Calhoun (Part of Clemson)	29631
Arcadia	29320	Bloomville	29102	Calhoun Falls	29628
Arcadia Lakes	29206	Blossom	29583	Callison	29819
Arial	29640	Blue Heaven	29638	Camden	29020
Ariel Crossroads	29574	Blue Ridge Community Pre-		Cameron	29030
Arkwright	29301	Release Center	29609	Campbell Work Release	
Arlington	29651	Blue Town	29512	Center	29210
Armenia	29706	Bluff	29142	Camp Creek	29720
Arthurtown	29201	Bluff Estates	29209	Camp Croft	29302
Asbury	29340	Bluffton	29910	Campobello	29322
Ashepoo	29446	Blythewood	29016	Campton	29349
Ashland	29010	Bob Jones University (Part		Canaan (Orangeburg	
Ashleigh	29817	of Greenville)	29614	County)	29038
Ashley Forest	29407	Bob Marina	29163	Canaan (Spartanburg	
Ashley Hall (Part of		Boiling Springs	29316	County)	29302
Charleston)	29401	Bolentown	29115	Canadys	29433
Ashley Heights	29405	Bon Aire	29902	Cane Savannah	29154
Ashley Junction (Part of		Bon Air Terrace	29150	Canterbury	29673
North Charleston)	29406	Bonham	29379	Capitol (Part of Columbia)	29211
Ashton	29082	Bonneau	29431	Capitol View	29209
Ashwood	29010	Bonneau Beach	29431	Carlisle	29031
Aspen Heights	29646	Bonniview Estates	29803	Carmel	29058
Atkins	29080	Boones Creek	29676	Carolina Circle	29488
Atlantic Beach	29582	Bordeaux	29835	Caromi Village	29456
Auburn	29550	Borden	29017	Carters Crossroads	29554
Augusta Road (Part of		Boulder Bluff	29445	Cartersville	29161
Greenville)	29604	Bounty Land	29678	Carver Heights	29204
Avondale	29407	Bowling Green	29703	Carvers Bay	29554
Awendaw	29429	Bowman	29018	Cash	29520
Aynor	29511	Bowyer	29059	Cashville	29388
Badham	29471	Boyden Arbor	29206	Cassatt	29032
Baileys Landing	29936	Boykin (Kershaw County)	29128	Catarrah	29718
Baker Crossroads	29569	Boykin (Marlboro County)	28343	Catawba	29704
Bald Rock	29379	Bradley	29819	Cateechee	29667
Baldwin	29706	Bradleyville	29841	Catholic Hill	29488
Ballentine	29002	Branchville	29432	Cave	29810
Balltown	29801	Brand	29360	Cayce	29033
Bamberg	29003	Brandon	29611	Cedar Grove	29526
Barkersville	29916	Branwood (Part of		Cedar Hill	29835
Barksdale	29360	Greenville)	29610	Cedar Springs	29455
Barnes	29655	Brasstown	29658	Cedar Terrace	29209
Barnwell	29812	Brattonsville	29726	Celriver	29732
Barrineau	29560	Brazen Crossroads	29583	Cementon	29059
Bartell Crossroads	29554	Breeze Hill (Part of		Centenary	29519
Barton	29827	Burnettown)	29834	Center Crossroads	29554
Bascomville	29729	Breezewood	29819	Centerville (Anderson	
Batesburg	29006	Brentwood	29405	County)	29621
Bath	29816	Brewerton	29692	Centerville (Dillon County)	29565
Baton Rouge	29706	Briarcliffe Acres	29572	Central	29630
Baxter Forks	29569	Briarcreek	29340	Central Pacolet	29372
Bayboro	29569	Brighton	29922	Challedon	29210
Bay Shores	29665	Brighton Beach	29910	Chaparral Ranches	29461
Bay Springs	29584	Brightsville	28343	Chapin	29036
Bay View	29204	Bristow	29516	Chappells	29037
Beaufort	29901-05	Britton	29153	Charleston	29401-25
For specific Beaufort Zip Codes		Brittons Neck	29546	For specific Charleston Zip Codes	
call (803) 524-4746		Broad Street (Part of		call (803) 745-4350	
Beaufort Marine Corps Air		Sumter)	29150	Charleston Heights (Part of	
Station	29904	Broadway Lake	29621	North Charleston)	29405
Beckhamville	29055	Brock	29691		29415
Beech Island	29842	Brock Circle	29654	For specific Charleston Heights	
Bel-Clear Heights	29841	Brockington	29556	Zip Codes call (803) 745-4359	
Beldoc	29836	Brogdon	29150	Charles Towne Square (Part	
Belle Isle Gardens	29440	Brookdale	29115	of North Charleston)	29406

	ZIP
Chartwell	29210
Cheddar	29627
Cheraw	29520
Cherokee	29302
Cherokee Falls	29702
Cherokee Forest	29687
Cherokee Gardens	29678
Cherry Grove Beach (Part of North Myrtle Beach)	29582
Cherry Hill Estates	29902
Cherryvale	29154
Chesnee	29323
Chester	29706
Chesterfield	29709
Chestnut Hills	29605
Chickasaw Point	29693
Chicora Place (Part of North Charleston)	29405
Choppee	29440
Citadel (Part of Charleston)	29409
Citadel Mall (Part of Charleston)	29407
City View	29611
Claremont	29150
Clarks Hill	29821
Claussen	29505
Clayton	29015
Clearmont	29693
Clear Pond	29003
Clearspring	29681
Clearwater	29822
Cleburne	29440
Clemson	29631-34
For specific Clemson Zip Codes call (803) 654-2531	
Clemson University	29631
Cleora	29824
Cleveland	29635
Clifton	29324
Clinton	29325
Clio	29525
Clover	29710
Clubhouse Crossroads (Dorchester County)	29472
Club House Crossroads (Lexington County)	29054
Clyde	29101
Coastal (Part of North Myrtle Beach)	29582
Coastal Work Release Center	29405
Cochrantown	29526
Cokesbury	29653
Cold Point	29360
Coldstream	29210
College Acres	29803
Colliers	29838
Colonial Heights	29902
Colonial Village	29715
Columbia	29201-92
For specific Columbia Zip Codes call (803) 733-4646	
Columbia Bible College	29203
Columbia Mall	29204
Coneross	29693
Conestee	29636
Congaree	29044
Connecticut Park	29341
Converse	29329
Conway	29526-27
For specific Conway Zip Codes call (803) 248-6313	
Cooks Crossroads	29644
Cool Branch	29031
Cooley Springs	29323
Cool Spring	29511
Coosaw	29940
Coosawhatchie	29912
Cope	29038
Cordesville	29434
Cordova	29039
Cornwell	29014
Coronaca	29649
Cottageville	29435
Couchtown	29801
Country Club Estates	29730
Country Homes	29646
Courtenay	29678
Coward	29530
Cowpens	29330
Crafts-Farrow	29203
Crane Forest	29203
Crescent	29388
Crescent Beach (Part of North Myrtle Beach)	29582
Creston	29030
Crestview	29501
Crocketts Crossroads	29720
Crocketville	29913
Crooks Crossroads	29554

	ZIP
Crosland Park (Part of Aiken)	29801
Cross	29436
Cross Anchor	29331
Cross Anchor Correctional Institution	29335
Crosscreek Mall (Part of Greenwood)	29646
Cross Hill	29332
Cross Keys	29379
Crosswell	29640
Cummings	29944
Cusaac Crossroads	29541
Cypress Crossroads	29069
Cypress Fork	29001
Dacusville	29640
Daisy	29569
Dale	29914
Dalewood	29653
Dalzell	29040
Danwood	29541
Darlington	29532
Daufuskie Island	29915
Davis Crossroads	29148
Davis Station	29041
Deans	29684
De Bordieu Colony	29440
Deer Park	29405
DeKalb	29175
Delemar Crossroads	29470
Delmar	29070
Delphos	29726
Delta	29178
Denmark	29042
Denny Terrace	29203
Dentsville	29204
Denver	29625
Deweys Hill (Part of North Charleston)	29406
Dillon	29536
Dinkins	29128
Dinkins Mill	29128
Dixiana	29172
Dixie	29720
Dog Bluff	29511
Donalds	29638
Dongola	29526
Dorange	29471
Dorchester	29437
Dorchester Estates	29485
Dorchester Terrace	29405
Douglass	29014
Dovesville	29540
Drake	29516
Drawdy	29488
Drayton (Charleston County)	29407
Drayton (Spartanburg County)	29333
Draytonville	29340
Drexel Lake Hills	29206
Dry Branch	29803
Dubose	29150
Du Bose Crossroads	29153
Du Bose Park	29020
Dudley	29728
Due West	29639
Duford	29581
Dunbar (Georgetown County)	29440
Dunbar (Marlboro County)	29525
Duncan	29334
Dunean	29601
Dunes	29577
Dupont	29407
Dusty Bend (Part of Camden)	29020
Dutch Fork	29210
Dutchman	29374
Dutchman Correctional Institution	29335
Dutch Square	29210
Dutch Village	29063
Dyson	29666
Eadytown	29468
Earle Homes	29624
Earles	29510
Earles Grove	29678
Earlwood Park	29532
Early Branch	29916
Easley	29640-42
For specific Easley Zip Codes call (803) 859-9411	
East Bay (Part of Charleston)	29403
East Gaffney	29340
East Gantt	29609
East Greer	29651
East Hartsville	29550
Eastmont	29209
Eastover	29044
East Side Acres	29488

	ZIP
East Sumter	29150
East View	29669
Eau Claire (Part of Columbia)	29203
Ebenezer (Florence County)	29501
Ebenezer (York County)	29732
Eden	29645
Edenwood	29033
Edgefield	29824
Edgemoor	29712
Edgewood (Part of Columbia)	29204
Edisto	29038
Edisto Beach	29438
Edisto Island	29438
Edmund	29073
Effingham	29541
Ehrhardt	29081
Elgin (Kershaw County)	29045
Elgin (Lancaster County)	29720
Elko	29826
Elliott	29046
Elloree	29047
Elmwood Park	29803
Emanuelville	29536
Emerald Place	29646
Emerald Valley	29210
Emory	29138
Enchanted Hills	29678
Enoree	29335
Epworth	29666
Equinox Mill	29625
Estill	29918
Eureka	29847
Eureka Mill	29706
Eutaw Springs	29048
Eutawville	29048
Evans Crossroad	29720
Evergreen	29541
Evergreen Hills	29625
Fairfax	29827
Fairfield (Part of Hilton Head Island)	29928
Fairfield Terrace	29203
Fair Forest (Greenwood County)	29646
Fairforest (Spartanburg County)	29336
Fairmont	29301
Fair Play	29643
Fairview (Greenville County)	29651
Fairview (Oconee County)	29678
Fairview Crossroads	29070
Farrel Crossroads	29432
Farrow Terrace	29203
Fechtig	29916
Federal (Florence County)	29503
Federal (Greenville County)	29603
Felderville	29047
Fenwick Hills	29455
Ferndale (Charleston County)	29406
Ferndale (Spartanburg County)	29301
Filbert	29710
Fingerville	29338
Finklea	29569
Finland	29042
Fisher Hill	29520
Five Forks (Anderson County)	29621
Five Forks (Greenville County)	29681
Five Forks (Pickens County)	29657
Five Points (Oconee County)	29693
Five Points (Richland County)	29205
Flamingo Acres	29512
Flat Rock	29624
Flat Shoals	29691
Fletcher	29570
Florence	29501-06
For specific Florence Zip Codes call (803) 662-9501	
Florence Mall (Part of Florence)	29501
Floyd Dale	29542
Floyds Crossroads	29581
Folly Beach	29439
Folly Field (Part of Hilton Head Island)	29928
Forest	29437
Forest Acres (Oconee County)	29691
Forest Acres (Richland County)	29206
Forest Beach (Part of Hilton Head Island)	29928
Forestbrook	29577

ZIP   ZIP   ZIP

	ZIP		ZIP		ZIP
Knox	29706	Lydia	29079	Morningside	29607
Ladson	29456	Lydia Mills	29325	Morris Acres	29455
La France	29656	Lykesland	29061	Moselle	29929
Lake City	29560	Lyman	29365	Mountain Brook	29209
Lake Forest (Greenville		Lynchburg	29080	Mountain Lakes	29706
County)	29606	Lyndhurst	29812	Mountain Rest	29664
Lake Forest (Pickens		Lynwood	29816	Mountain View	29323
County)	29640	McAlister Square (Part of		Mount Carmel	29840
Lake Forest Estates	29841	Greenville)	29607	Mount Croghan	29727
Lake Lanier	29356	Mac Arthurs Junction	29638	Mount Gallagher	29692
Lakemont	29635	McBee	29101	Mount Holly	29445
Lake Murray Shores	29070	McBeth	29431	Mount Olive	29581
Lake Shores	29649	McClellanville	29458	Mount Pleasant	29464-65
Lakeview (Chester County)	29714	McColl	29570	For specific Mount Pleasant Zip
Lake View (Dillon County)	29563	McConnells	29726	Codes call (803) 884-8221
Lakewood	29732	McCormick	29835	Mount View	29687
Lakewood Manor	29301	McCormick Correctional		Mountville	29370
Lake Wylie	29710	Institution	29835	Mt. Calvary	29536
Lamar	29069	McCormick Crossroads	29536	Mulberry	29150
Lambertown	29510	McCutchen Crossroads	29010	Mullins	29574
Lambs (Part of North		McDonald	29440	Murphy Estates	29841
Charleston)	29405	MacDougall Youth		Murrells Inlet	29576
Lancaster	29720-21	Correction Center	29472	Myrtle Beach	29572
For specific Lancaster Zip Codes		Macedonia	29330		29575
call (803) 283-4969		McKellar Farms	29646		29577-78
Lancaster Mill	29720	McKenzie Crossroads	29114	For specific Myrtle Beach Zip
Lando	29724	McPhersonville	29916	Codes call (803) 626-9533
Landrum	29356	Maddens	29360	Myrtle Beach Air Force
Landsford	29704	Madison (Aiken County)	29829	Base	29579
Lane	29564	Madison (Oconee County)	29693	Myrtle Island	29910
Lanford	29335	Magnolia Park	29853	Myrtle Square (Part of
Langley	29834	Mallory	29565	Myrtle Beach)	29577
Larkin	29377	Manning	29102	Naval Hospital	29902
Lathem (Part of Easley)	29640	Manning Crossroads	29536	Naval Weapons	29445
Latimer	29628	Manville	29010	Naval Weapons Station	29408
Latta	29565	Maple Crossroads	29526	Neeses	29107
Laurel Bay	29902	Maplewood	29340	Nesmith	29580
Laurens	29360	Marietta	29661	Nevitt Forest	29621
Leawood	29601	Marine Corps Air Station	29904	Newberry	29108
Lebanon (Anderson County)	29621	Marion	29571	New Cut	29720
Lebanon (Fairfield County)	29180	Marlboro	29512	New Easley Highway (Part
Leeds	29031	Mars Bluff	29506	of Greenville)	29611
Leesburg (Part of Columbia)	29209	Martin	29836	New Ellenton	29809
Leesville	29070	Maryville (Charleston		New Holland Crossroads	29006
Legareville	29455	County)	29407	New Hope	29530
Lena	29918	Maryville (Georgetown		Newport	29730
Leo	29560	County)	29440	New Prospect	29349
Lesslie	29730	Masons Crossroads	29621	New Road	29945
Lester	29512	Mathews (Part of		Newry	29665
Level Land	29655	Greenwood)	29646	Newtonville	29512
Lewis	29706	Mathews Heights	29646	New Town	29536
Lewis Crossroads	29532	Mauldin	29662	New Zion	29111
Lexington	29071-73	Mayesville	29104	Neyles	29488
For specific Lexington Zip Codes		Mayfair	29687	Nichols	29581
call (803) 359-9355		Mayfair Mill (Part of Pickens)	29671	Nicholson Village	29801
Liberty	29657	Mayo	29368	Nimmons	29685
Liberty Hill (Charleston		Mayo Mills	29368	Nine Times	29685
County)	29406	Mayson	29138	Ninety Six	29666
Liberty Hill (Kershaw		Meadowlake	29203	Nixons Crossroads	29566
County)	29074	Mechanicsville	29532	Nixonville	29526
Liberty Hill (McCormick		Meggett	29449	Nixville	29944
County)	29835	Melrose	29803	Norris	29667
Lieber Correctional		Merchant	29138	North	29112
Institution	29472	Middendorf	29550	North Aiken (Part of Aiken)	29801
Limehouse	29927	Midland Park	29405	North Anderson (Part of
Limestone	29115	Midland Valley	29829	Anderson)	29623
Lincoln Shire	29203	Midway (Bamberg County)	29003	North Augusta	29841
Lincolnville	29483	Midway (Kershaw County)	29032	Northbridge (Part of
Lions Beach	29461	Midway (Lancaster County)	29720	Charleston)	29407
Litchfield Beach	29585	Midway Crossroads	29554	North Bridge Terrace (Part
Little Africa	29323	Midway Village	29577	of Charleston)	29405
Little Camden	29201	Miley	29933	North Charleston	29406
Little Chicago	29322	Mill Creek	29163		29418-20
Little Eastatoe	29685	Millers Crossroads	29838	For specific North Charleston Zip
Little Mountain	29075	Millett	29836	Codes call (803) 569-2610
Little River	29566	Mill Village (Part of		North Conway (Part of
Little Rock	29567	Bennettsville)	29512	Conway)	29526
Little Texas	29690	Millwood (Sumter County)	29150	North Forest Beach (Part of
Livingston	29076	Millwood (Williamsburg		Hilton Head Island)	29928
Lobeco	29931	County)	29556	Northgate (Cherokee
Lockhart	29364	Millwood Gardens	29150	County)	29341
Lockhart Junction	29353	Milton	29325	Northgate (Florence County)	29501
Lodge	29082	Mink Point Plantation	29902	North Greenwood	29649
Lone Star	29077	Minturn	29573	North Hartsville	29550
Long Bay Estates	29572	Mitchellville	29936	Northlake	29621
Long Branch	29853	Mitford	29055	North Litchfield Beach	29585
Longcreek (Oconee		Modoc	29838	North Mullins (Part of
County)	29658	Monaghan	29611	Mullins)	29574
Long Creek (Pickens		Monarch Mill	29379	North Myrtle Beach	29582
County)	29640	Moncks Corner	29461		29597-98
Long Leaf	29488	Monetta	29105	For specific North Myrtle Beach
Long Point	29569	Monroe Crossroads	29512	Zip Codes call (803) 249-1023
Longs	29568	Montague	29601	North Pacolet	29322
Longtown	29130	Mont Clare	29532	North Santee	29458
Loris	29569	Monticello	29106	Northside Correctional
Lowenstein Mills	29621	Montmorenci	29839	Center	29303
Lowndesville	29659	Montrose	29520	North Summerville (Part of
Lowrys	29706	Moore	29369	Summerville)	29483
Lucknow	29010	Moores Crossroads	29518	North Trenholm	29206
Lugoff	29078	Moreland	29407	North Winyah Heights (Part
Luray	29932	Morgan	29927	of Georgetown)	29440

	ZIP
Northwood Estates	29405
Northwoods Mall (Part of Charleston)	29405
Norway	29113
Oakdale (Cherokee County)	29330
Oakdale (York County)	29730
Oak Dale (Clarendon County)	29111
Oakdale (Florence County)	29501
Oak Grove (Dillon County)	29565
Oak Grove (Lexington County)	29073
Oak Hill	29801
Oakland (Beaufort County)	29902
Oakland (Sumter County)	29150
Oakland Crossroads	29547
Oakland Mill (Part of Newberry)	29108
Oakley	29461
Oak Ridge	29058
Oaks Crossroads	29142
Oakvale	29673
Oakway	29693
Oakwood	29801
Oatland	29440
Oats	29069
Ocean Drive Beach (Part of North Myrtle Beach)	29582
Ocean Forest (Part of Myrtle Beach)	29577
Oceanview	29412
Oconee Estates	29678
Oconee Station	29691
Ogden	29730
Olanta	29114
Olar	29843
Old House	29936
Old Madison	29693
Olympia..................	29201
Ora	29360
Orangeburg	29115-17
For specific Orangeburg Zip Codes call (803) 536-1720	
Orchard Park (Part of Greenville)	29615
Orr Mill	29621
Orrville	29621
Orum	29583
Osborn	29426
Osceola	29744
Oswego	29150
Otranto	29405
Outland	29554
Owings	29645
Oyster Point.............	29412
Pacolet	29372
Pacolet Mills	29373
Pacolet Park (Part of Pacolet Mills)...........	29373
Padgetts	29481
Pageland.................	29728
Palmer Work Release Center	29501
Palmetto	29532
Palmetto Estates	29902
Palmetto Fort.............	29464
Pamplico	29583
Panola (Clarendon County)	29125
Panola (Greenwood County)	29646
Paramount Park	29605
Paris	29609
Parker	29611
Parkers Ferry	29426
Parkersville	29585
Park Place	29609
Parksville	29844
Parler	29142
Parr	29065
Parris Island	29905
Parris Island Marine Corps Recruit Depot	29905
Parrot Point	29412
Patrick	29584
Pauline	29374
Pawleys Island	29585
Paxville	29102
Peach Valley	29303
Peak	29122
Pecan Terrace	29605
Pecan Way Terrace (Part of Orangeburg)	29115
Pee Dee	29571
Pelham	29651
Pelion...................	29123
Pelzer..................	29669
Pendleton	29670
Peniel Crossroads	29161
Pepperhill (Part of North Charleston)	29418
Percival Crossroads	29693
Perry....................	29124

	ZIP
Perry Correctional Institution	29669
Philip....................	29464
Phoenix	29646
Pickens	29671
Pickett Post	29691
Piedmont	29673
Piercetown	29697
Pierpont	29407
Pimlico..................	29461
Pine Grove (Darlington County)...............	29532
Pine Grove (Hampton County)...............	29924
Pinehaven (Part of Charleston)	29405
Pinehurst (Dorchester County)...............	29483
Pinehurst (Greenwood County)...............	29646
Pine Island	29577
Pineland (Charleston County)...............	29429
Pineland (Jasper County)	29934
Pineridge (Darlington County)...............	29101
Pineridge (Lexington County)...............	29172
Pine Valley	29210
Pineville................	29468
Pinewood (Spartanburg County)...............	29303
Pinewood (Sumter County)	29125
Pinopolis	29469
Pisgah	29128
Plantation Pines	29180
Plantersville	29440
Playcards	29569
Plaza (Part of Sumter)	29150
Pleasantburg (Part of Greenville)	29606
Pleasant Grove	29671
Pleasant Hill (Georgetown County)..............	29554
Pleasant Hill (Lancaster County)..............	29058
Pleasant Lane	29824
Pleasant Valley	29605
Pleasant View	29569
Plum Branch	29845
Pocotaligo	29945
Poe	29609
Polaris Missile Facility Atlantic	29408
Polk Village	29902
Pomaria	29126
Pontiac	29045
Poovey Farm	29720
Poplar Springs	29369
Port Royal...............	29935
Port Royal Plantation (Part of Hilton Head Island)	29928
Poston..................	29555
Powdersville.............	29673
Pregnall	29437
Primus	29720
Princeton................	29654
Pritchardville	29910
Promised Land	29819
Prospect Crossroads	29560
Prosperity	29127
Providence	29059
Pumpkintown.............	29671
Puncheon Creek	29510
Purysburg Landing	29927
Quail Hollow	29169
Quinby	29506
Quinby Estates (Part of Quinby)...............	29506
Quinby Forest (Part of Quinby)...............	29501
Rabon Crossroads	29511
Rains	29589
Rantowles...............	29449
Ravenel	29470
Ravenwood (Part of Forest Acres)	29206
Red Bank	29073
Red Bank Landing	29048
Red Bluff Crossroads	29569
Red Hill (Horry County)	29526
Red Hill (rural) (Horry County)..............	29544
Red Hill (Lee County)	29020
Red Top	29455
Reevesville	29471
Rehobeth	29544
Reid Park	29520
Reidville................	29375
Rembert	29128
Remount (Part of North Charleston)	29406

	ZIP
Renfrew..................	29690
Renno	29325
Retreat	29693
Return	29678
Reynold.................	29817
Rhems	29440
Ribault Park (Part of Beaufort)	29902
Richburg	29729
Rich Hill Crossroads	29058
Richland	29675
Richland Mall (Part of Forest Acres)	29206
Richland Springs	29138
Richmond Hills	29609
Richtex	29180
Ridgecrest	29801
Ridgeland	29912
	29936
For specific Ridgeland Zip Codes call (803) 726-5528	
Ridge Spring	29129
Ridgeville	29472
Ridgeway	29130
Ridgewood (Charleston County)	29456
Ridgewood (Oconee County)...............	29678
Ridgewood (Richland County)...............	29203
Rimini	29131
Ringle Heights	29440
Rion	29132
Ritter...................	29488
Riverdale................	29536
River Falls	29661
Riverland	29412
Riverland Terrace	29412
Rivermont	29210
Rivers General Mail Facility (Part of North Charleston)	29411
Riverside (Abbeville County)	29692
Riverside (Anderson County)	29624
Riverside (Greenville County)	29611
Riverside (Lancaster County)	29720
Riverside Park	29210
Riverview	29715
Robat	29379
Robbins.................	29831
Robbins Circle	29706
Robertville..............	29922
Robinson	29101
Rock Bluff	29556
Rockbridge..............	29206
Rock Hill (York County)	29730-34
For specific Rock Hill Zip Codes call (803) 327-4187	
Rock Hill (Fairfield County)	29065
Rockton.................	29180
Rockville	29487
Rocky Bottom	29685
Roddy	29704
Rodman	29706
Roebuck	29376
Rogers Fallout	29544
Rosehill Park	29340
Roseida	29902
Rosinville	29477
Round O	29474
Rowell	29704
Rowesville	29133
Ruby	29741
Ruffin	29475
Russellville..............	29476
St. Andrews (Charleston County)..................	29407
	29417
For specific St. Andrews Zip Codes call (803) 766-4031	
St. Andrews (Richland County)..............	29210
St. Charles	29104
St. George	29477
St. Helena Island	29920
St. Julian	29048
St. Matthews	29135
St. Paul	29148
St. Paul Forks	29526
St. Stephen	29479
Salak	29646
Salem (Florence County)...	29583
Salem (Oconee County) ...	29676
Salem Crossroads	29015
Salley	29137
Salters	29590
Saluca	29646
Saluda	29138

ZIP | ZIP | ZIP

Saluda Gardens (Part of West Columbia) 29169
Saluda Terrace (Part of West Columbia) 29169
Samaria 29006
Sampit 29440
Sanders Corner 29062
Sandridge (Berkeley County) 29059
Sand Ridge (Horry County) 29526
Sandwood 29206
Sandy Flat 29687
Sandy Ridge 29666
Sandy Springs.............. 29677
Sans Souci 29609
Sans Souci Heights 29609
Santee 29142
Santee Circle 29461
Santuc 29379
Sardinia 29143
Sardis 29161
Satchel Ford Terrace 29206
Savannah Bluff 29526
Sawyerdale 29112
Saxon 29301
Saylors Crossroads 29627
Scanlonville 29464
Schofield 29843
Schultz Hill (Part of North Augusta) 29841
Scotia 29939
Scottsville 29104
Scranton 29591
Seabrook 29940
Seabrook Island 29455
Sea Pines (Part of Hilton Head Island) 29928
Seaside 29412
Secessionville 29412
Sedalia 29379
Seiglers Crossroads 29801
Seigling 29810
Seivern 29164
Sellers 29592
Selma 29536
Seneca 29678-79
For specific Seneca Zip Codes call (803) 882-8422
Seneca Landing 29678
Seven Mile (Part of North Charleston) 29405
Seven Oaks (Lexington County) 29210
Shady Rest (Part of Bennettsville)............. 29512
Shalimar 29341
Shannon Hill 29010
Shannontown 29150
Sharon 29742
Shaw Air Force Base 29152
Shaw Heights 29152
Sheldon 29941
Shell 29526
Shell Point 29902
Shepard 29032
Sheppard Park 29483
Sherwood Acres........... 29301
Shiloh (Oconee County) ... 29678
Shiloh (Sumter County) 29080
Shiloh Estates 29678
Shipyard Plantation (Part of Hilton Head Island) 29928
Shirley 29922
Shoals Junction 29638
Shulerville 29479
Silver 29102
Silver Bluff Estates........ 29803
Silverstreet 29145
Simpson 29130
Simpsonville 29681
Singing Pines 29678
Singleton 29135
Six Mile 29682
Six Points 29801
Skyview Terrace........... 29210
Slansville 29483
Slater 29683
Slater-Marietta 29661
Slighs 29127
Smallwood (Fairfield County) 29130
Smallwood (Laurens County)................... 29325
Smith 29730
Smithboro 29574
Smith Mills 29554
Smoaks 29481
Smyrna 29743
Snelling 29812
Sniders Crossroads........ 29475
Snowden 29464

Socastee................... 29577
Society Hill 29593
South Anderson (Part of Anderson) 29624
South Congaree 29172
Southern Meadows 29678
Southern Shops 29303
South Forest Estates 29605
South Greenwood (Part of Greenwood) 29646
South Hartsville 29550
South Hills 29379
South Lynchburg 29080
South Mullins (Part of Mullins) 29574
South Park (Part of Florence) 29505
Southpark Shopping Center (Part of Florence) 29505
Southside.................. 29505
South Sumter 29150
South Windermere (Part of Charleston) 29407
Soviet Union 29693
Spartanburg 29301-18
For specific Spartanburg Zip Codes call (803) 585-0301
Spaulding Heights 29501
Spiderweb 29841
Spring Branch 29571
Springdale (Lancaster County) 29720
Springdale (Lexington County) 29170
Springfield (Orangeburg County) 29146
Springfield (Spartanburg County) 29349
Spring Hill (Lee County)... 29128
Spring Hill (Richland County) 29117
Springmaid Beach 29577
Spring Mills 29067
Springtown 29481
Spring Valley 29646
Springwood 29204
Stallsville 29485
Stark Terrace.............. 29203
Starmount 29172
Starr 29684
Startex 29377
Stateburg 29150
State College (Part of Orangeburg) 29115
State Farm 29128
Steedman 29070
Stiefeltown 29851
Stokes 29488
Stokes Bridge 29010
Stomp Springs 29325
Stoneboro 29558
Stoney Hill 29127
Stono 29412
Stover 29014
Stratford Hall 29803
Stratton Capers 29405
Strawberry 29461
Stuart Point 29940
Stuckey 29554
Sullivans Island 29482
Summer Hill (Part of North Augusta) 29841
Summerland (Part of Batesburg)............... 29006
Summerton................. 29148
Summerville 29483-85
For specific Summerville Zip Codes call (803) 873-3571
Summit 29070
Sumter 29150-51
.... 29153-54
For specific Sumter Zip Codes call (803) 773-9312
Sunnyside (Part of Greer) 29651
Sunset 29685
Surfside Beach 29575
.... 29587
For specific Surfside Beach Zip Codes call (803) 238-2523
Suttons 29510
Swansea 29160
Sweden 29042
Sweetwater (Aiken County) 29841
Sweetwater (Barnwell County)................... 29812
Switzer 29369
Switzerland................ 29936
Sycamore 29846
Syracuse 29532
Talatha.................... 29803
Tall Pines 29536

Tamassee.................. 29686
Tanglewood (Beaufort County).................. 29902
Tanglewood (Greenville County).................. 29611
Tanglewood (Oconee County).................. 29678
Tanglewood (Orangeburg County).................. 29115
Tarboro 29943
Tatum 29594
Taxahaw 29067
Taylors 29687
Tega Cay 29715
Temperance Hill 29571
Ten Mile (Part of Charleston) 29406
Ten Mile (Charleston County).................. 29464
Terrells Crossroads 29518
Texas 29477
The Farms (Part of Hanahan) 29410
The Groves (Part of Mount Pleasant) 29464
The Meadows 29678
Thor 29123
Three Trees 29412
Tibwin 29458
Tifton 29532
Tigerville 29688
Tillman 29943
Timberlake 29678
Timmonsville 29161
Tirzah 29745
Toddville 29526
Tokeena Crossroads 29678
Toney Creek 29627
Townville 29689
Toxaway (Part of Anderson) 29621
Tradesville 29720
Tranquil Acres............. 29456
Travelers Rest 29690
Trenton 29847
Triangle (Part of Belton).... 29627
Trio 29595
Troy 29848
Tuckertown 29031
Tugtown 29059
Turbeville 29162
Twin Lake Hill 29209
Tyler 29536
Ulmer 29849
Una (Darlington County) ... 29069
Una (Spartanburg County) 29378
Union 29379
Union Bleachery 29609
Union Crossroads 29111
Unity 28173
University (Part of Columbia) 29208
University of South Carolina at Coastal Carolina 29526
Utica 29678
Valencia Heights 29205
Valley Falls 29303
Vance 29163
Van Wyck.................. 29744
Varnville 29944
Vaucluse 29850
Verdery 29819
Victor Mills (Part of Greer) 29651
Village Creek 29678
Virginia Acres 29803
Voorhees College 29042
Waddell Gardens (Part of Beaufort)................. 29902
Wade Hampton 29607
Wadmalaw Island 29487
Wadsworth 29301
Wagener 29164
Walden Correctional Institute 29210
Walhalla................... 29691
Wallace 29596
Walnut Grove 29374
Walterboro 29488
Wampee 29568
Wando 29492
Wando Woods 29405
Ward 29166
Ware Place 29669
Ware Shoals 29692
Warren Crossroads 29470
Warrenville 29851
Warsaw 29510
Wateree 29044
Waterford Estates 29440
Waterloo 29384
Watkins Store 29803

	ZIP
Watson Village (Part of Anderson)	29624
Watts Mills	29360
Waverly Mills	29585
Waylyn	29405
Wedgefield	29168
Welcome (Anderson County)	29621
Welcome (Greenville County)	29611
Wellford	29385
Wellington Mill	29624
Wesleyan	29630
West Andrews (Part of Andrews)	29510
West Columbia	29169-72
For specific West Columbia Zip Codes call (803) 796-0455	
West Gantt	29605
Westgate Mall (Part of Spartanburg)	29301
West Marion	29571
Westminster	29693
Westover Acres (Part of West Columbia)	29169
West Pelzer	29669
West Springs	29353
West Union	29696
Westview	29301
Westville (Greenville County)	29611
Westville (Kershaw County)	29175
Whetstone	29664
Whipper Barony (Part of North Charleston)	29405
White Bluff Crossroads	29067

	ZIP
White Hall (Colleton County)	29446
Whitehall (Greenwood County)	29646
Whitehall (Lexington County)	29210
White Oak	29176
White Plains (Anderson County)	29697
White Plains (Chesterfield County)	29718
White Pond	29853
White Rock	29177
White Stone	29386
Whitesville	29461
Whitetown	29845
Whitmire	29178
Whitney	29303
Wilder	29431
Wilkinson Heights	29115
Wilkinsville	29340
Wilksburg	29706
Williams	29493
Williams Estate	29720
Williamston	29697
Willington	29835
Williston	29853
Willowbrook	29445
Wilson	29102
Wilson Creek	29646
Wilsons Cross Roads	29532
Windsor	29856
Windsor Estates	29204
Windsor Forest	29501
Windsor Lake Park	29206
Windsor Park	29520
Windsor Plantation	29440

	ZIP
Windwood	29461
Windy Hill	29506
Windy Hill Beach (Part of North Myrtle Beach)	29582
Winnsboro	29180
Winnsboro Mills	29180
Winona	29506
Winthrop College (Part of York)	29730
Wisacky	29010
Wolfton	29112
Women's Correctional Center	29210
Woodburn Hills	29301
Woodfield	29206
Woodfields	29605
Woodford	29112
Woodland Hills	29210
Woodrow	29040
Woodruff	29388
Woodside	29610
Woodville	29669
Woodward	29014
Workman	29111
Yarn Mill	29520
Yauhannah	29440
Yeamans Hall (Part of Hanahan)	29410
Yemassee	29945
Yenome	29814
Yonges Island	29449
York	29745
Yorkshire	29209
Yoruba Village	29941
Youngs	29388
Zion	29574

	ZIP
Aberdeen	57401-02
For specific Aberdeen Zip Codes	
call (605) 226-2555	
Academy	57369
Agar	57520
Agency Village	57262
Akaska	57420
Albee	57259
Alcester	57001
Alexandria	57311
Allen	57714
Alpena	57312
Altamont	57226
Ames	57362
Amherst	57421
Andover	57422
Antelope	57555
Ardmore	57715
Arlington	57212
Arlington Beach	57212
Armour	57313
Arpan	57762
Artas	57437
Artesian	57314
Ashton	57424
Astoria	57213
Athol	57424
Aurora	57002
Aurora Center	57375
Avon	57315
Badger	57214
Baltic	57003
Bancroft	57316
Barnard	57426
Batesland	57716
Bath	57427
Bear Butte	57785
Bear Creek	57636
Belle Fourche	57717
Belvidere	57521
Bemis	57238
Beresford	57004
Bethlehem	57708
Big Bend	57702
Big Springs	57001
Big Stone City	57216
Bijou Hills	57370
Bison	57620
Black Hawk	57718
Blacktail	57754
Blumengard Colony	57438
Blunt	57522
Bonesteel	57317
Bon Homme Colony	57063
Bonilla	57348
Bowdle	57428
Box Elder	57719
Bradley	57217
Brandon	57005
Brandt	57218
Brentford	57429
Bridger	57748
Bridgewater	57319
Bristol	57219
Britton	57430
Broadland	57350
Brookings	57006
Brownsville	57754
Bruce	57220
Bryant	57221
Buffalo	57720
Buffalo Gap	57722
Buffalo Ridge	57115
Buffalo Trading Post	57018
Bullhead	57621
Burbank	57010
Burke	57523
Bushnell	57276
Butler	57219
Cactus Flat	57567
Camp Crook	57724
Canistota	57012
Canova	57321
Canton	57013
Capa	57552
Caputa	57725
Carpenter	57526
Carter	57322
Carthage	57323
Castle Rock	57760
Castlewood	57223
Cavour	57324
Cedar Butte	57527
Cedar Grove Colony	57369
Center	57058
Center Point	57070
Centerville	57014
Central City	57754
Chamberlain	57325
Chancellor	57015
Chautauqua	57042

	ZIP
Chelsea	57465
Cherry Creek	57622
Chester	57016
Cheyenne Crossing	57754
Cheyenne River Indian	
Reservation	57625
Claire City	57224
Claremont	57432
Clark	57225
Clark Colony	57258
Clayton	57332
Clearfield	57580
Clear Lake	57226
Colman	57017
Colome	57528
Colonial Pine Hills	57701
Colton	57018
Columbia	57433
Conde	57434
Corn Creek	57560
Corona	57227
Corsica	57328
Corson	57005
Cottonwood	57775
Crandall	57434
Crazy Horse	57730
Creighton	57729
Cresbard	57435
Crocker	57229
Crooks	57020
Crow Creek Indian	
Reservation	57339
Crow Lake	57382
Custer	57730
Dallas	57529
Dante	57329
Davis	57021
Deadwood	57732
De Grey	57501
Dell Rapids	57022
Delmont	57330
Dempster	57234
Denby	57716
De Smet	57231
Dimock	57331
Dixon	57533
Doland	57436
Dolton	57319
Downtown (Part of	
Aberdeen)	57401
Draper	57531
Dupree	57623
Eagle Butte	57625
East Sioux Falls	57101
Eden	57232
Edgemont	57735
Egan	57024
Elk Point	57025
Elkton	57026
Ellis	57101
Ellsworth Air Force Base	57706
Elmore	57754
Elm Springs	57736
Elm Springs Colony	57334
Emery	57332
Empire	57788
Empire Mall, The (Part of	
Sioux Falls)	57101
Enning	57737
Epiphany	57321
Erwin	57233
Esmond	57353
Estelline	57234
Ethan	57334
Eureka	57437
Fairburn	57738
Fairfax	57335
Fairpoint	57787
Fairview	57027
Faith	57626
Farmer	57311
Farmingdale	57725
Faulkton	57438
Fedora	57337
Ferney	57439
Firesteel	57628
Flandreau	57028
Flandreau Indian	
Reservation	57028
Fleetwood (Part of Brandon)	57005
Florence	57235
Forestburg	57314
Fort Pierre	57532
Fort Thompson	57339
Frankfort	57440
Franklin	57042
Frederick	57441
Freeman	57029
Froehlich Addition	57104
Fruitdale	57742
Fulton	57340

	ZIP
Galena	57732
Gannvalley	57341
Garden City	57236
Garretson	57030
Gary	57237
Gayville	57031
Geddes	57342
Gettysburg	57442
Glad Valley	57629
Glencross	57630
Glendale Colony	57440
Glenham	57631
Goodwin	57238
Graceville Colony	57076
Greenfield	57010
Green Grass	57625
Greenwood	57380
Gregory	57533
Grenville	57239
Groton	57445
Grover	57201
Hamill	57534
Hammer	57255
Hanna	57754
Harrington	57551
Harrisburg	57032
Harrison	57344
Harrold	57536
Hartford	57033
Hartford Beach	57227
Hayes	57537
Hayti	57241
Hayward Addition	57106
Hazel	57242
Hecla	57446
Henry	57243
Hereford	57785
Hermosa	57744
Herreid	57632
Herrick	57538
Hetland	57244
Hiawatha Beach	57279
Hidden Timber	69201
Highmore	57345
Hill City	57745
Hillhead	57270
Hillside	57328
Hillside Colony	57436
Hillview	57437
Hisega	57701
Hisle	57577
Hitchcock	57348
Holabird	57540
Holmquist	57274
Hooker	57070
Hoover	57760
Hosmer	57448
Hot Springs	57747
Houghton	57449
Hoven	57450
Howard	57349
Howes	57748
Hub City	57069
Hudson	57034
Huffton	57432
Humboldt	57035
Hurley	57036
Huron	57350
Huron Colony	57350
Ideal	57541
Igloo	57735
Imlay	57780
Interior	57750
Iona	57542
Ipswich	57451
Irene	57037
Iron Lightning	57623
Iroquois	57353
Isabel	57633
James	57445
Java	57452
Jefferson	57038
Johnson Siding	57701
Joubert	57344
Junction City	57010
Junius	57042
Kadoka	57543
Kaylor	57354
Keldron	57634
Kenel	57642
Kennebec	57544
Keyapaha	57545
Keystone	57751
Kidder	57430
Kimball	57355
Kingsburg	57062
Kones Corner	57223
Kranzburg	57245
Kyle	57752
La Bolt	57246
Ladner	57720

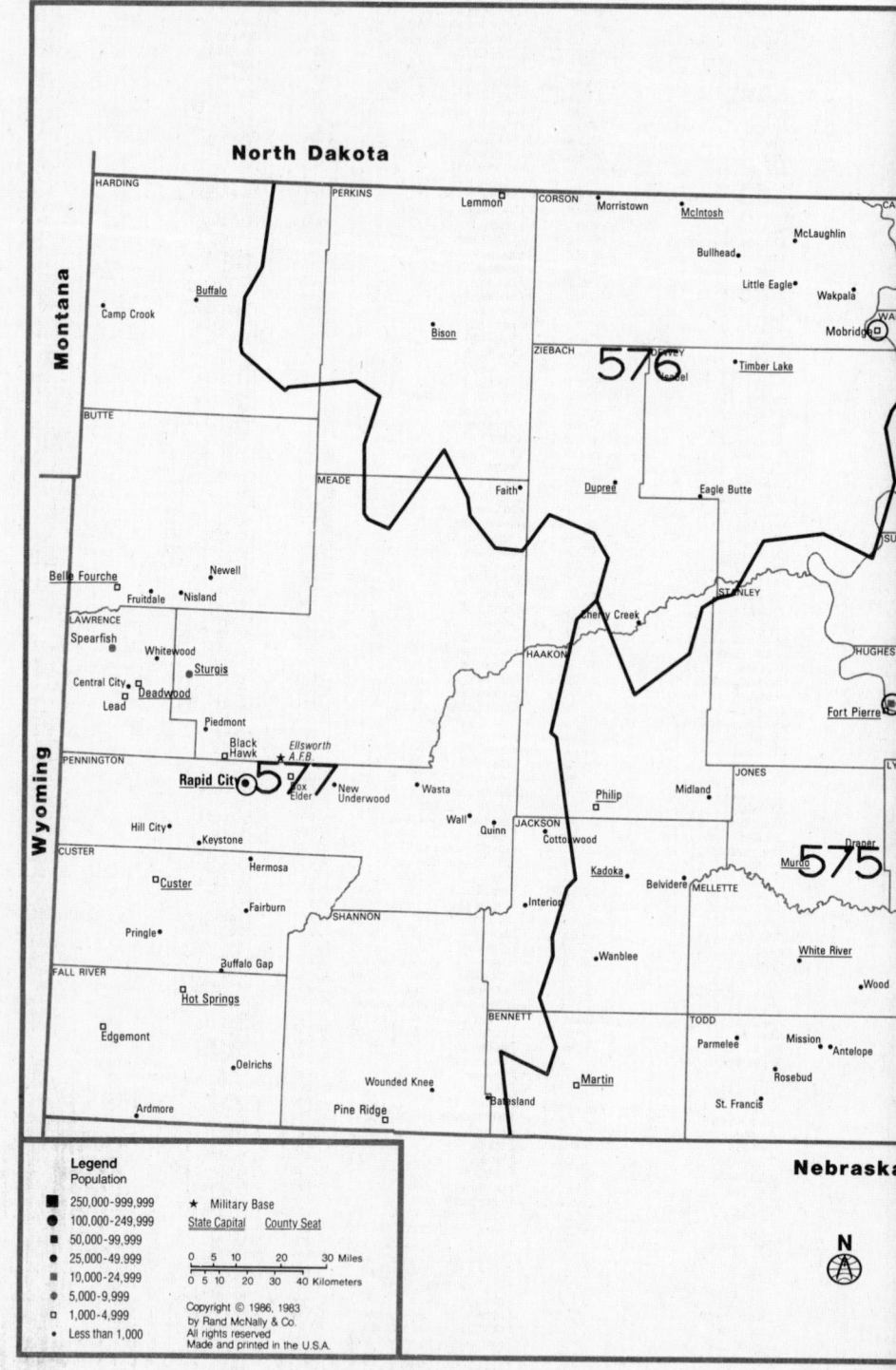

North Dakota

Montana

Wyoming

HARDING
PERKINS
Lemmon
CORSON
Morristown
McIntosh
McLaughlin
Bullhead
Little Eagle
Wakpala
Buffalo
Camp Crook
Bison
Mobridge
ZIEBACH
DEWEY
576
Isabel
Timber Lake
BUTTE
MEADE
Faith
Dupree
Eagle Butte
Belle Fourche
Newell
Fruitdale
Nisland
Cherry Creek
STANLEY
LAWRENCE
Spearfish
HAAKON
HUGHES
Whitewood
Sturgis
Central City
Deadwood
Lead
Piedmont
Fort Pierre
Black Hawk
Ellsworth A.F.B.
PENNINGTON
Rapid City
577
Box Elder
New Underwood
Wasta
Philip
Midland
JONES
Hill City
Keystone
Wall
Quinn
JACKSON
Cottonwood
Draper
CUSTER
Hermosa
Murdo
575
Custer
Kadoka
Belvidere
MELLETTE
Fairburn
SHANNON
Interior
Pringle
White River
Buffalo Gap
Wanblee
Wood
FALL RIVER
Hot Springs
BENNETT
TODD
Edgemont
Parmelee
Mission
Antelope
Oelrichs
Rosebud
Wounded Knee
Martin
St. Francis
Ardmore
Pine Ridge
Batesland

Nebraska

Legend
Population

- 250,000-999,999   ★ Military Base
- 100,000-249,999   <u>State Capital</u>   <u>County Seat</u>
- 50,000-99,999
- 25,000-49,999   0 5 10   20   30 Miles
- 10,000-24,999   0 5 10   20   30   40 Kilometers
- 5,000-9,999
- 1,000-4,999   Copyright © 1986, 1983
- Less than 1,000   by Rand McNally & Co.
                    All rights reserved
                    Made and printed in the U.S.A.

N

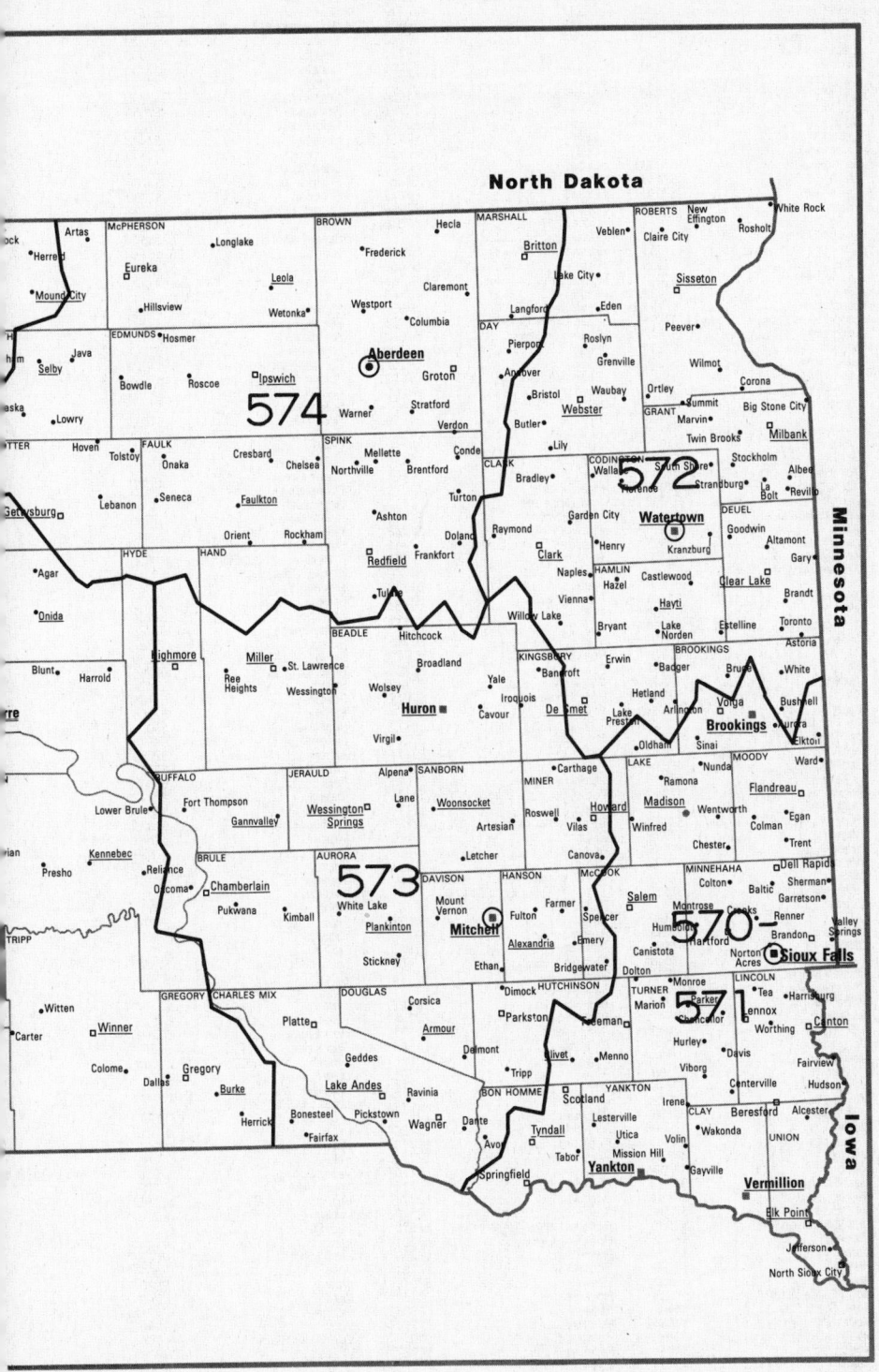

Name	ZIP	Name	ZIP	Name	ZIP
Lake Andes	57356	Ogala Lakota College	57752	St. Charles	57571
Lake Campbell	57006	Oglala	57764	St. Francis	57572
Lake City	57247	Okaton	57562	St. Lawrence	57373
Lake Norden	57248	Okreek	57563	St. Onge	57779
Lake Preston	57249	Ola	57325	Salem	57058
Lane	57358	Oldham	57051	Sanator	57730
Langford	57454	Olivet	57052	Savoy	57754
Lantry	57636	Olsonville	69201	Scenic	57780
La Plant	57652	Onaka	57466	Scotland	57059
Lead	57754	Onida	57564	Selby	57472
Lebanon	57455	Opal	57765	Seneca	57473
Lemmon	57638	Oral	57766	Shadehill	57653
Lennox	57039	Ordway	57433	Shady Beach	57227
Leola	57456	Orient	57467	Sharps Corner	57752
Lesterville	57040	Orland	57042	Sherman	57060
Letcher	57359	Ortley	57256	Silver City	57701
Lily	57274	Osceola	57316	Sinai	57061
Linden Beach	57227	Owanka	57767	Sioux Falls	57055-57
Littleburg	57555	Parade	57647		57101-07
Little Eagle	57639	Parker	57053		57116-18
Lodgepole	57640	Parkston	57366	For specific Sioux Falls Zip Codes	
Lone Tree	57024	Parmelee	57566	call (605) 332-8360	
Longlake	57457	Patricia	57551	Sisseton	57262
Long Lake Colony	57481	Pearl Creek Colony	57353	Sisseton Indian Reservation	57262
Longvalley	57547	Pearsons Corner	57070	Smiths Park	57075
Loomis	57301	Pedro	57729	Smithwick	57782
Lower Brule	57548	Peever	57257	So Dak Park	57279
Lower Brule Indian		Peninsula Park	57075	Soldier Creek	57555
Reservation	57548	Perkins	57062	Sorum	57620
Lowry	57472	Philip	57567	South Shore	57263
Lucas	57523	Pickerel	57239	Spearfish	57783
Ludlow	57755	Pickstown	57367	Spencer	57374
Lyons	57041	Piedmont	57769	Spink	57025
McCook Lake	57038	Pierpont	57468	Spink Colony	57440
McIntosh	57641	Pierre	57501	Spring Creek	57572
McLaughlin	57642	Pine Ridge	57770	Spring Creek Colony	58439
Madison	57042	Pine Ridge Indian		Springfield	57062
Madsen Beach	57279	Reservation	57770	Spring Valley	57036
Mahto	57643	Plainview	57748	Spring Valley Colony	57382
Manchester	57353	Plainview Colony	57741	Standing Rock Indian	
Manderson	57756	Plankinton	57368	Reservation (SD part)	58538
Manderson-White Horse		Plano	57340	Stanley Corner	57319
Creek	57756	Platte	57369	Stephan	57346
Mansfield	57460	Platte Colony	57369	Stickney	57375
Marcus	57757	Pluma	57732	Stockholm	57264
Marcy Colony	57366	Pollock	57648	Stone Bridge	57223
Marion	57043	Polo	57467	Stoneville	57787
Marlow	57270	Porcupine	57772	Storla	57359
Martin	57551	Potato Creek	57750	Strandburg	57265
Marty	57361	Prairie City	57649	Stratford	57474
Marvin	57251	Prairie Village	57042	Sturgis	57785
Maurine	57626	Presho	57568	Summit	57266
Maxwell Colony	57059	Pringle	57773	Sunnyview	57006
Mayfield	57037	Promise	57601	Swett	57551
Meadow	57644	Provo	57774	Tabor	57063
Meckling	57044	Pukwana	57370	Tacoma Park	57433
Mellette	57461	Pumpkin Center	57035	Tea	57064
Menno	57045	Putney	57445	Thomas	57241
Midland	57552	Quinn	57775	Thunder Butte	57623
Midway	57037	Quinn Table	57790	Thunder Hawk	57638
Milbank	57252	Ralph	57650	Tilford	57769
Milesville	57553	Ramona	57054	Timber Lake	57656
Millboro	57580	Rapid City	57701-02	Tolstoy	57475
Miller	57362	For specific Rapid City Zip Codes		Toronto	57268
Miller Dale Colony	57362	call (605) 394-8600		Trail City	57657
Milltown	57366	Rapid Valley	57701	Trent	57065
Mina	57462	Ravinia	57357	Tripp	57376
Miranda	57438	Raymond	57258	Trojan	57754
Mission	57555	Red Elm	57623	Troy	57265
Mission Hill	57046	Redfield	57469	Tschetter Colony	57052
Mission Ridge	57532	Redig	57776	Tulare	57476
Mitchell	57301	Redowl	57777	Turkey Ridge	57036
Mobridge	57601	Red Scaffold	57626	Turton	57477
Monroe	57047	Red Shirt	57744	Tuthill	57574
Montrose	57048	Ree Heights	57371	Twin Brooks	57269
Morningside	57350	Reliance	57569	Two Strike	57570
Morristown	57645	Renner	57055	Tyndall	57066
Mosher	57580	Reva	57651	Union Center	57787
Mound City	57646	Revillo	57259	Unityville	57058
Mount Vernon	57363	Richland	57025	University (Part of	
Mud Butte	57758	Ridgeview	57652	Brookings)	57007
Murdo	57559	Riverside Colony	57350	Usta	57626
Mystic	57745	Rochford	57778	Utica	57067
Naples	57271	Rockerville	57701	Vale	57788
Nemo	57759	Rockham	57470	Valley Springs	57068
New Effington	57255	Rockport	57311	Valley View	57072
Newell	57760	Roscoe	57471	Vayland	57381
New Holland	57364	Rosebud	57570	Veblen	57270
New Underwood	57761	Rosebud Indian Reservation	57570	Vedin Corner	57037
Nisland	57762	Rosedale Colony	57301	Verdon	57434
Nora	57001	Rosholt	57260	Vermillion	57069
Norbeck	57438	Roslyn	57261	Vetal	57551
Norris	57560	Roswell	57349	Viborg	57070
North Eagle Butte	57625	Roubaix	57754	Victor	57260
North Sioux City	57049	Rowena	57056	Vienna	57271
North Spearfish	57783	Rumford	57774	Vilas	57349
Northville	57465	Rumpus Ridge	57012	Villa Trailer Court	57706
Norton Acres	57104	Running Water	57062	Virgil	57379
Nunda	57050	Rushmore Mall (Part of		Vivian	57576
Oacoma	57365	Rapid City)	57701	Volga	57071
Oelrichs	57763	Rutland	57057	Volin	57072

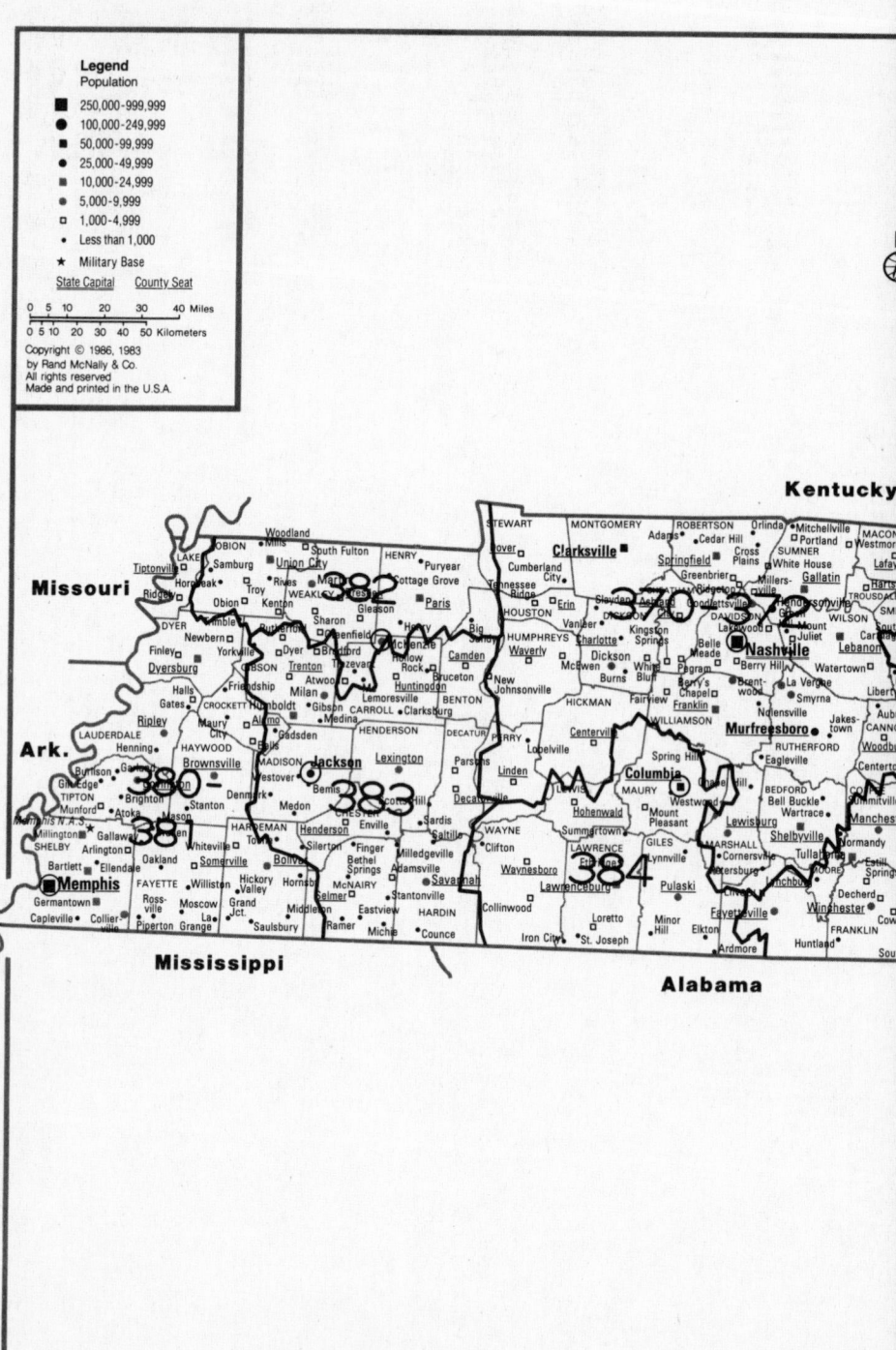

Legend
Population

■ 250,000-999,999

● 100,000-249,999

■ 50,000-99,999

● 25,000-49,999

● 10,000-24,999

● 5,000-9,999

□ 1,000-4,999

. Less than 1,000

★ Military Base

State Capital   County Seat

0 5 10   20   30   40 Miles

0 5 10 20 30 40 50 Kilometers

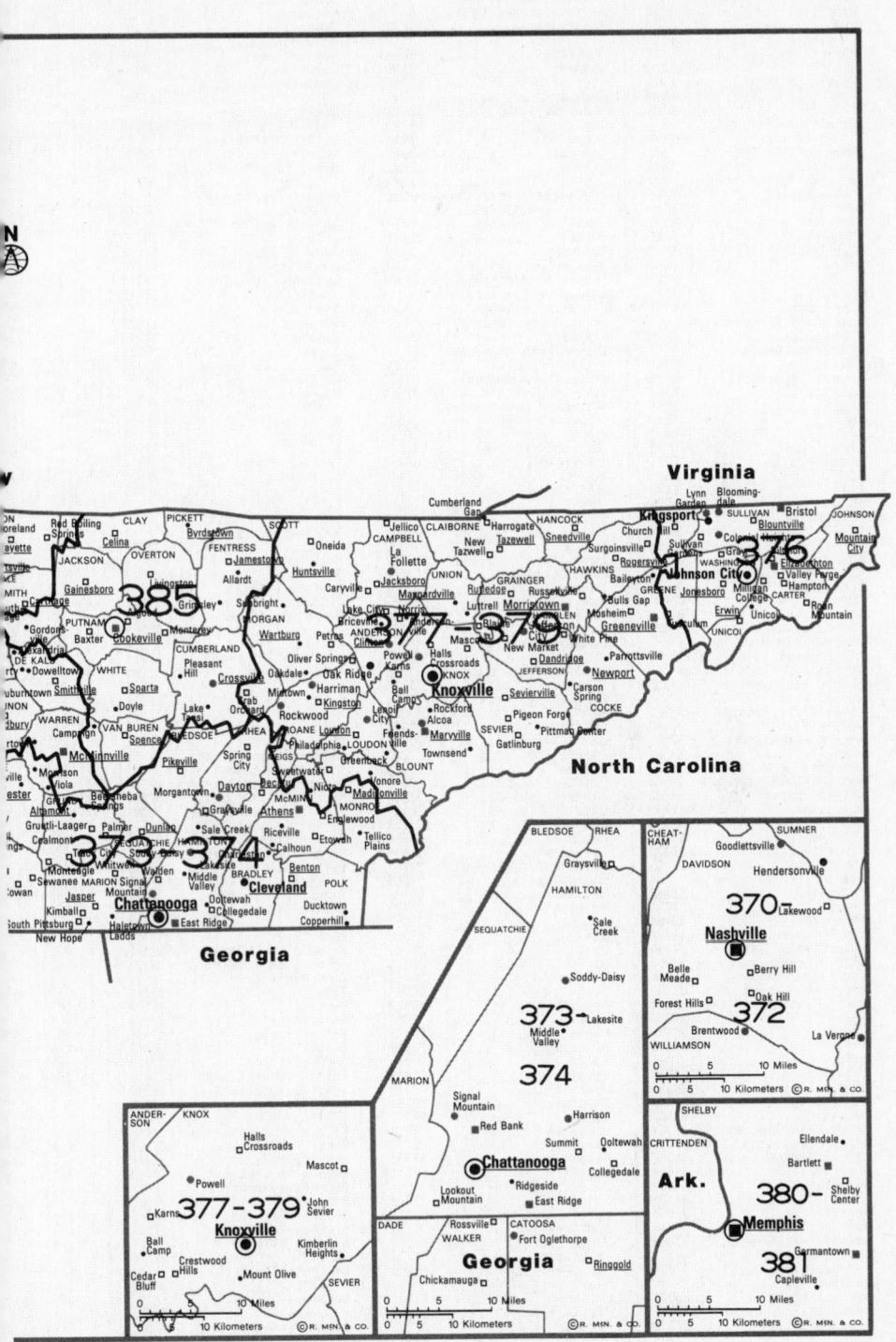

	ZIP
Acklen (Part of Nashville)	37212
Acton	38357
Adair	38301
Adams	37010
Adams Crossroads	37055
Adamsville	38310
Aetna	37033
Afton	37616
Airport	37110
Airport Estates (Part of Nashville)	37217
Airport Mail Facility (Part of Nashville)	37217
Airport Mail Facility (Part of Memphis)	38130
Air View	37301
Akard Addition	37620
Alamo	38001
Alanthus Hill	37879
Albany	37743
Albright	37066
Alcoa	37701
Alder Branch	37862
Alder Springs (Campbell County)	37766
Alder Springs (Union County)	37807
Alexander Springs	38456
Alexandria	37012
Algood	38501
Allardt	38504
Allens	38012
Allens Chapel	37166
Allensville	37862
Allisona	37046
Allons	38541
Alloway	37337
Allred	38542
Almaville	37014
Almira	38011
Almy	37755
Alpha	37814
Alpha Heights	37814
Alpine	38543
Altamont	37301
Alto	37324
Alton Park (Part of Chattanooga)	37409
Altonville	37857
Alumwell	37857
Alynwick	37804
Amherst (Part of Knoxville)	37931
Amity Heights	37620
Amqui (Part of Nashville)	37115
Anark	38344
Anderson (Franklin County)	37376
Anderson (Overton County)	38574
Anderson Heights	37617
Andersonville	37705
Anes	37091
Angeltown	37022
Anglea	37022
Anglers Cove	37763
Annadale (Part of Cleveland)	37312
Annadel	37770
Anthony Hill	38460
Antioch (Davidson County)	37013
Antioch (DeKalb County)	37166
Antioch (Jackson County)	38562
Antioch (Loudon County)	37771
Antioch (Polk County)	37307
Antioch (Tipton County)	38058
Apison	37302
Appleton	38457
Arcadia	37660
Archer	37091
Archville	37369
Arcott	38551
Ardmore	38449
Arkland	38487
Arlington (Houston County)	37061
Arlington (Knox County)	37917
Arlington (Shelby County)	38002
Armathwaite	38504
Armona	37804
Armour	38401
Arms Mill	37807
Arno	37046
Arnold Air Force Base	37389
Arnold Engineering Development Center	37389
Arnolds Chapel	38544
Arp	38063
Arrington	37014
Arrowhead	37920
Arthur	37707
Asbury (Coffee County)	37355
Asbury (Haywood County)	38069
Asbury (Knox County)	37914
Asbury (Lauderdale County)	38063

	ZIP
Asbury (Pickett County)	38577
Asbury (Stewart County)	37175
Asbury Estates	37801
Ashburn	37172
Ash Hill	37046
Ashland	38485
Ashland City	37015
Ashport	38063
Ashwood	38401
Asia	37398
Aspen Hill	38478
Athendale	38401
Athens	37303
Athens	37371
For specific Athens Zip Codes call (615) 745-5100	
Atkins	37079
Atoka	38004
Atwood	38220
Auburntown	37016
Aulon (Part of Memphis)	38101
Austin Peay State University (Part of Clarksville)	37040
Austin Springs (Washington County)	37601
Austin Springs (Weakley County)	38226
Avoca (Part of Bristol)	37620
Avondale (Grainger County)	37861
Avondale (Sumner County)	37075
Avondale Springs	37861
Ayers	38030
Bacchus	37879
Bacon Gap	37763
Bagdad	37145
Baggettsville	37172
Bailey	38017
Baileyton	37743
Bailey Town	37821
Bain	38320
Bairds Mills	37087
Baker Crossroads	38555
Bakers (Part of Nashville)	37072
Bakers Crossroads	38583
Bakersworks	37029
Bakerton	37150
Bakertown (Davidson County)	37013
Bakertown (Moore County)	37352
Bakerville	37185
Bakewell	37304
Bald Point	37881
Ball Camp	37921
Ballplay (Monroe County)	37385
Ball Play (Polk County)	37362
Balltown	37331
Baltimore	37843
Baneberry	37890
Bangham	38501
Banner	37738
Banner Hill	37650
Banner Springs	38556
Baptist (Part of Nashville)	37203
Baptist Ridge	38568
Barefoot	37186
Barfield	37129
Bargerton	38351
Barkertown	37365
Barnardsville	37763
Barnes	38573
Barnesville	38483
Barr	38040
Barren Plain	37172
Barretville	38053
Barthelia	37031
Bartlebaugh	37416
Bartlett	38134
Barton Springs	37814
Bates Hill	37110
Bath Springs	38311
Batley	37716
Battlewood Estates	37064
Baugh	38449
Baugh Spring	37353
Baxter	38544
Bazel Town (Part of Harriman)	37748
Beacon	38363
Beamswitch	38230
Beans Creek	37345
Bean Station	37708
Bear Creek	37892
Beardstown (Part of Lobelville)	37097
Bear Spring	37058
Beartown	37660
Bearwallow	37015
Beasley	37034
Beauty Hill	38315
Beaver	38011
Beaverdam Springs	37147

	ZIP
Beaver Ridge	37921
Beckwith	37122
Bedford	37160
Beech Bluff	38313
Beech Bottom	37083
Beech Fork	37714
Beech Grove (Anderson County)	37769
Beechgrove (Coffee County)	37018
Beech Grove (Grainger County)	37881
Beech Grove (Hawkins County)	37711
Beech Grove (Trousdale County)	37074
Beech Grove (Weakley County)	38230
Beech Hill (Franklin County)	37398
Beech Hill (Giles County)	38478
Beech Hill (Macon County)	37074
Beechnut	37617
Beech Springs	37764
Beechwood	37020
Beersheba Springs	37305
Bel Air	38261
Bel Aire (Coffee County)	37388
Bel Aire (Rutherford County)	37130
Bel-Aire Heights (Part of Winchester)	37398
Belfast	37019
Belinda City	37122
Belk	37166
Bella Mara Estates	37854
Bell Buckle	37020
Bell Campground	37849
Belle Aire (Knox County)	37922
Belle Aire (White County)	38583
Belle Brook Estate (Part of Bristol)	37620
Belle Eagle	38012
Belle Founte	37312
Belle Meade (Blount County)	37801
Belle Meade (Davidson County)	37205
Belleville	37334
Bellevue (Part of Nashville)	37221
Bellevue Estates	37331
Bell Mill	37363
Bells	38006
Bellsburg	37036
Bell Town (Cheatham County)	37082
Belltown (Monroe County)	37385
Belltown (Polk County)	37317
Bellview (Bledsoe County)	37367
Bellview (Lincoln County)	37334
Bellwood	37087
Belmont (Anderson County)	37705
Belmont (Coffee County)	37355
Belmont (Jefferson County)	37725
Belmont West	37919
Belvidere	37306
Bemis (Part of Jackson)	38314
Bending Chestnut	37064
Benton	37307
Benton Springs	37307
Berclair (Part of Memphis)	38117
Berea (Giles County)	38478
Berea (Warren County)	38581
Berlin	37091
Berry Hill	37204
Berrys Chapel	37064
Bertha	37765
Bessie	38079
Bethany	37110
Bethel (Anderson County)	37716
Bethel (Benton County)	38320
Bethel (Blount County)	37882
Bethel (Carroll County)	38344
Bethel (Cheatham County)	37015
Bethel (DeKalb County)	37166
Bethel (Giles County)	38477
Bethel (Haywood County)	38012
Bethel (Maury County)	38482
Bethel (Perry County)	37096
Bethel Springs	38315
Bethesda (Greene County)	37641
Bethesda (Williamson County)	37046
Bethlehem (Bedford County)	37160
Bethlehem (Campbell County)	37766
Bethlehem (Hardin County)	38310
Bethlehem (Henry County)	38222
Bethlehem (Monroe County)	37354
Bethlehem (Williamson County)	37064
Bethpage	37022

	ZIP		ZIP		ZIP
Betsy Willis	37342	Bolton	38002	Brooks (Part of Hohenwald)	38462
Beulah (Greene County)	37810	Boma	38544	Brotherton	38501
Beulah (Union County)	37807	Bon Air (Sumner County)	37022	Browder (Loudon County)	37771
Beverly	37918	Bon Air (White County)	38583	Browder (Marion County)	37347
Bible Hill	38363	Bon Aqua	37025	Brown Cross Roads	38469
Bidwell	37144	Bon Aqua Junction	37098	Brown Ellis	37748
Big Boy Junction	38030	Bon De Croft	38583	Brownington	37398
Bigbyville	38401	Bone Cave	38581	Browns	37083
Big Creek (Hancock		Bonicord	38024	Browns Shop	37144
County)	37869	Bonnertown	38457	Brownsville	38012
Big Creek (Hawkins County)	37857	Bonny Kate	37920	Browntown	38578
Big Creek (Monroe County)	37354	Bonsack	38554	Brownwood Acres	37064
Big Ivy	38372	Bonwood (Part of Jackson)	38301	Broylesville	37681
Big Lick	38555	Boom	38573	Bruceton	38317
Big Mountain	37840	Boone	37601	Bruceville	38024
Big Piney	37774	Boones Creek	37615	Bruner Grove	37713
Big Ridge Park	37807	Booneville	37334	Brunswick	38014
Big Rock	37023	Boonshill	38459	Brush Creek (Sequatchie	
Big Sandy	38221	Boothspoint	38030	County)	37327
Big Sinks	37866	Bordeaux (Part of Nashville)	37218	Brush Creek (Smith County)	38547
Big Spring (Blount County)	37737	Borden Mills (Part of		Brush Creek (Williamson	
Big Spring (Carter County)	37643	Kingsport)	37660	County)	37062
Big Spring (Meigs County)	37322	Boston	37064	Brushy Mountain State	
Big Springs (Hancock		Bowen	37861	Penitentiary	37845
County)	37731	Bowling	38555	Bryan Hill (Part of Dayton)	37321
Big Springs (Overton		Bowman	38555	Bryant Station	37091
County)	38570	Bowmantown	37690	Bryson	38453
Big Springs (Rutherford		Boxwood Hills	37922	Bryson Mountain	40965
County)	37037	Boyd	37722	Brysonville	37190
Big Spring Union	37752	Boyd Mill Estates (Part of		Buchanan	38222
Biltmore	37643	Franklin)	37064	Buckeye	37847
Binfield	37804	Boyds Creek	37862	Buck Lodge	37148
Bingham	37064	Brace	38483	Buckner	37166
Binghamton (Part of		Brackentown	37148	Bucksnort	37140
Memphis)	38112	Bradburn Hill	37743	Bucktown (Hardin County)	38372
Birchwood	37308	Bradbury	37763	Bucktown (Loudon County)	37771
Bird Crossroad	37862	Braden (Fayette County)	38010	Buena Vista	38318
Bird Song	38320	Braden (Union County)	37870	Buffalo (Humphreys County)	37078
Bishop	38024	Bradford	38316	Buffalo (Scott County)	37756
Bivens	38472	Bradleytown	38030	Buffalo Springs	37861
Black Center	38320	Bradshaw	38459	Buffalo Valley	38548
Black Creek	37852	Bradyville	37026	Bufords	38472
Black Fox (Bradley County)	37311	Braemar	37658	Bugscuffle	37183
Black Fox (Grainger		Braid Cove	37087	Buladeen	37643
County)	37888	Brainerd (Part of		Bullards Gap	38562
Black Jack	37355	Chattanooga)	37411	Bull Creek	37756
Blackman	37129	Brakebill	37354	Bullet Creek	37369
Black Oak	37841	Bransford	37022	Bull Run (Anderson County)	37849
Blackwell	37861	Bratcher's	37110	Bull Run (Davidson County)	37015
Blaine	37709	Brattontown	37083	Bulls Gap	37711
Blair	37748	Braxton	37190	Bumpass Cove	37650
Blair Gap	37660	Bray	37881	Bumpus Mills	37028
Blair Lane	37087	Brayton	37338	Buncombe	37617
Blakeville	37144	Braytown	37710	Bungalow Town	37804
Blanche	38488	Brazil	38382	Bunker Hill	38478
Blanche Chapel	38449	Breckinredge South	37064	Buntontown	37640
Blaney Forest (Part of East		Brentlawn (Part of		Burbank	37687
Ridge)	37412	Springfield)	37172	Burchfield Heights	37830
Blanton Chapel	37355	Brentwood (Hamblen		Burem	37857
Bledsoe (Lincoln County)	37144	County)	37814	Burgen	37026
Bledsoe (Sumner County)	37022	Brentwood (Williamson		Burke	37367
Block City (Part of Mount		County)	37024	Burlington (Part of Knoxville)	37914
Carmel)	37642		37027	Burlington Heights (Part of	
Blockhouse	37801	For specific Brentwood Zip Codes		Cleveland)	37312
Blondy (Part of Hohenwald)	38462	call (615) 373-1661		Burlison	38015
Bloomingdale	37660	Brentwood Mall (Part of		Burns	37029
Bloomington	38549	Brentwood)	37027	Burnt Church	38372
Bloomington Heights	37660	Brewer Addition (Part of		Burristown	38562
Bloomington Springs	38545	Athens)	37303	Burrville	37872
Blount Hills	37804	Brewstertown	37852	Burt	37190
Blountville	37617	Briar Thicket	37713	Burton (Part of Rogersville)	37857
Blowing Cave Mill	37862	Briarwood	37040	Burwood	37179
Blowing Springs	37716	Briceville	37710	Busby (Part of Loretto)	38469
Bluebank	38079	Brick Church	38478	Busselltown	37771
Blue Creek	38472	Brick Mill	37742	Butler	37640
Bluefields (Part of Nashville)	37214	Bride	38019	Butlers Landing	38551
Blue Goose	38351	Bridgeport	37821	Bybee (Cocke County)	37713
Bluegrass	37722	Bridwell Heights	37617	Bybee (Warren County)	37110
Blue Hill	37110	Bright Hope	37743	Byrdstown	38549
Blue Ridge (Part of Bristol)	37620	Brighton (Lincoln County)	37335	Cabin Row	37171
Blue Spring	37643	Brighton (Tipton County)	38011	Cabo	38332
Blue Springs (DeKalb		Brims Corner	38001	Cades	38358
County)	37166	Bristol	37620-25	Cades Cove	37882
Blue Springs (Hamilton		For specific Bristol Zip Codes call		Cadet (Part of Franklin)	37064
County)	37341	(615) 968-2355		Cagle	37327
Bluff City	37618	Britton Ford	38256	Cain Mill	37860
Bluff Creek	38547	Brittontown	37616	Cainsville	37085
Bluff Springs	37110	Brittsville	37336	Cairo (Crockett County)	38001
Bluhmtown	37166	Broad Acres	37849	Cairo (Sumner County)	37066
Blunts Landing	37096	Broadmoor	38024	Cairo Bend	37087
Blythe Ferry	37321	Broad Street (Part of		Calderwood	37801
Board Valley	38583	Cookeville)	38501	Calfkiller	38574
Boatland	38556	Broadview (Crockett		Calhoun	37309
Bodenham	38478	County)	38034	Calico	37322
Boggs	37861	Broadview (Franklin County)	37398	Calistia	37049
Bogota	38007	Broadway	38351	Callins	38230
Bohannon Addition (Part of		Brockdell	37367	Calls	37330
Athens)	37303	Brockland Acres	37814	Camargo	37334
Boiling Springs	38544	Brock's	38230	Cambria	37325
Bold Spring	37101	Brookhaven (Part of		Cambridge	38581
Bolivar	38008	Crossville)	38555	Camden	38320

	ZIP
Camelot (Cumberland County)	38555
Camelot (Hawkins County)	37857
Camilla Homes	38004
Campaign	38550
Camp Austin	37829
Campbell Army Airfield	42223
Campbell Junction	38555
Campbells	38451
Campbellsville	38478
Camp Creek	37743
Camp Ground	38237
Camp Marymount	37062
Camp Monterey Lake	38574
Camp Nakanawa	38555
Camp Relax	37166
Camps	37869
Camp Ta-Pa-Win-Go	37694
Camp Woodlee	37110
Canadaville	38028
Cane Ridge (Part of Nashville)	37013
Caney Branch	37743
Caney Creek	37891
Caney Ford	37748
Caney Spring	37091
Caney Valley	37879
Cantrell	38485
Capitol Hill (Franklin County)	37330
Capitol Hill (Scott County)	37756
Capleville	38118
Caravelle Estates	37122
Cardiff	37854
Carlisle	37058
Carlock	37331
Carnegie (Part of Johnson City)	37601
Carpenter Campground	37804
Carroll	37087
Carroll Reece (Part of Johnson City)	37601
Carrs Branch	37825
Carson Spring	37821
Carter	37643
Carters Creek	38401
Carthage	37030
Carthage Junction (Part of Gordonsville)	38567
Cartwright (Sequatchie County)	37397
Cartwright (Smith County)	37145
Caryville	37714
Cash Point	38449
Cassville	38583
Castalian Springs	37031
Castle Heights	37821
Cat Corner	38240
Cates	38079
Cates Trailor	37764
Catlettsburg	37862
Cato	37057
Catons Grove	37722
Catoosa	37770
Cave	38559
Cave Spring	37879
Cavvia	38341
Cedar Bluff (Sevier County)	37862
Cedarbluff (Trousdale County)	37087
Cedar Bluff Two	37722
Cedar Chapel	38075
Cedar Creek	37743
Cedar Creek Landing	37096
Cedarcrest	37857
Cedarfork (Claiborne County)	37879
Cedar Fork (Loudon County)	37846
Cedar Grove (Bedford County)	37034
Cedar Grove (Carroll County)	38321
Cedar Grove (Carter County)	37601
Cedar Grove (Henderson County)	38371
Cedar Grove (Humphreys County)	37078
Cedar Grove (Pickett County)	38577
Cedar Grove (Roane County)	37763
Cedar Grove (Rutherford County)	37060
Cedar Grove (Sullivan County)	37660
Cedar Grove (rural) (Sullivan County)	37618
Cedar Grove (Wilson County)	37087
Cedar Hill (Putnam County)	38544

	ZIP
Cedar Hill (Robertson County)	37032
Cedar Springs	37303
Cedar Valley (Part of Bristol)	37620
Celina	38551
Center (Crockett County)	38337
Center (Lawrence County)	38464
Center (Monroe County)	37385
Center Grove (Franklin County)	37388
Center Grove (Jackson County)	38562
Center Hill (Cannon County)	37190
Center Hill (Warren County)	37110
Center Point (Chester County)	38332
Center Point (Giles County)	38478
Center Point (Hardeman County)	38042
Center Point (Lawrence County)	38468
Center Point (Sequatchie County)	37327
Center Point (Stewart County)	37058
Center Point (White County)	38587
Center Star	38454
Centersville	37742
Centertown	37110
Centerville (Hickman County)	37033
Centerville (Wilson County)	37087
Central (Carter County)	37601
Central (Gibson County)	38382
Central (Lauderdale County)	38063
Central (Obion County)	38253
Central Heights	37617
Central Point	37861
Central State Psychiactric Hospital (Part of Nashville)	37217
Central View	38587
Cerro Gordo	38372
Chable	30708
Chalklevel (Benton County)	38320
Chalk Level (Hawkins County)	37857
Champ	37359
Chanceytown	37391
Chandler	37777
Chantay Acres (Part of Columbia)	38401
Chanute	38577
Chapel Hill (Marshall County)	37034
Chapel Hill (Maury County)	38474
Chapman Grove	37763
Chapmans	38478
Chapmansboro	37035
Charity	37334
Charles Creek Estates	37110
Charleston (Bradley County)	37310
Charleston (Tipton County)	38069
Charleys Branch	37710
Charlotte	37036
Charlotte Park (Part of Nashville)	37209
Charlton Green (Part of Franklin)	37064
Chaska	37766
Chattanooga	37401-22
For specific Chattanooga Zip Codes call (615) 499-8256	
Cherokee	38380
Cherokee Harshaw	37743
Cherokee Heights	37801
Cherokee Hills (Roane County)	37763
Cherokee Hills (Sevier County)	37865
Cherokee Hills (Part of Sevierville)	37862
Cherry	38041
Cherry Acres (Part of Gruetli-Laager)	37339
Cherrybrook	37912
Cherry Chapel	38372
Cherry Grove	37333
Cherry Hill	38582
Cherry Valley	37184
Chesney	37848
Chester Estates (Part of Fairview)	37062
Chesterfield	38351
Chestnut Bluff	38040
Chestnut Glade	38237
Chestnut Grove (Jefferson County)	37725
Chestnut Grove (Perry County)	37096

	ZIP
Chestnut Grove (Stewart County)	37058
Chestnut Grove (Sumner County)	37148
Chestnut Grove (Union County)	37807
Chestnut Hill (Cumberland County)	38555
Chestnut Hill (Jefferson County)	37725
Chestnut Hill (Sumner County)	37148
Chestnut Mound	38552
Chestnut Orchard	37172
Chestnut Ridge (Greene County)	37641
Chestnutridge (Lincoln County)	37144
Chestoa	37650
Chestua	37354
Chestuee	37312
Chewalla	38393
Chic	38030
Chickamauga (Part of Chattanooga)	37421
Chickasaw Heights (Part of Paris)	38242
Childers Hill	38326
Chilhowee View	37801
China Grove	38233
Chinquapin Grove	37618
Chinubee	38486
Chipman	37022
Chittum	37879
Choptack	37857
Chota	37801
Chotham	38382
Choto	37922
Choto Hills	37777
Christiana	37037
Christian Bend	37642
Christianburg	37874
Christie Hill	37801
Christmasville (Carroll County)	38201
Christmasville (Haywood County)	38012
Chuckey	37641
Church Hill	37642
	37645
For specific Church Hill Zip Codes call (615) 357-5981	
Churchton	38059
Citico Beach	37885
Clacks Gap	37748
Clairfield	37715
Clark Addition	37804
Clarkrange	38553
Clarksburg	38324
Clarksville	37040-43
For specific Clarksville Zip Codes call (615) 647-3392	
Clarksville Base	42223
Clarktown	38583
Claxton (Anderson County)	37849
Claxton (McMinn County)	37303
Claybrook	38301
Clay Hill	37892
Claylick	37187
Clayton	38260
Clearbranch	37650
Clear Creek Mill	37332
Clearmont	37110
Clear Springs (Greene County)	37681
Clear Springs (Knox County)	37806
Clear Springs (McMinn County)	37309
Clearwater	37303
Clements Lake Estates (Part of Fairview)	37062
Clementsville	37150
Cleveland	37311-12
	37320
	37323
	37364
For specific Cleveland Zip Codes call (615) 472-6597	
Clevenger	37821
Cliff Springs	38574
Clifftops	37356
Clifton (Clifton City)	38425
Clifton	38485
Clifty	38583
Clinton	37716
Clopton	38011
Cloud Creek	37857
Clouds	37879
Clouse Hill	37387

	ZIP
Clovercroft	37064
Cloverdale (Obion County)	38240
Cloverdale (Shelby County)	38053
Cloverdale (White County)	38583
Clover Hill (Blount County)	37804
Cloverhill (Davidson County)	37214
Cloverport	38381
Club Springs	38560
Coal Chute	37643
Coalfield	37719
Coal Hill (Morgan County)	37748
Coal Hill (Scott County)	37872
Coaling	37051
Coalmont	37313
Cobbs	38006
Coble	37033
Coffee Landing	38310
Coffee Ridge	37650
Cog Hill	37325
Cokercreek	37314
Cold Spring (Bledsoe County)	37367
Cold Spring (Johnson County)	37683
Cold Springs (Blount County)	37886
Cold Springs (Hawkins County)	37873
Coldwater	37334
Colesburg	37055
Coles Ferry	37087
Coles Store	38544
Coletown	37317
College (Bledsoe County)	37327
College (Blount County)	37801
Collegedale	37315
College Grove	37046
College Grove Estates	37854
College Hill (Part of Dayton)	37321
College Park	37601
College Park Estates	37801
Colliers Corner	37760
Collierville	38017
Collins (Grundy County)	37365
Collins (Hawkins County)	37857
Collinwood	38450
Colonial Acres	38225
Colonial Circle	37865
Colonial Heights	37663
Colonial Village (Part of Knoxville)	37920
Columbia	38401-02

For specific Columbia Zip Codes call (615) 388-6161

	ZIP
Columbia Hill	38574
Columbus Hill	38562
Comfort	37380
Commerce	37184
Community Acres	37180
Como	38223
Compton	37130
Conasauga	37316
Concord (Carroll County)	38344
Concord (Gibson County)	38382
Concord (Humphreys County)	37185
Concord (Knox County)	37922
Concord (Rhea County)	37332
Concord (Rutherford County)	37153
Concord-Farragut	37922
Conklin	37659
Conner Heights (Part of Pigeon Forge)	37863
Conyersville	38251
Cookeville	38501-03

For specific Cookeville Zip Codes call (615) 526-7141

	ZIP
Cool Springs	38259
Cooper	38556
Coopers	38317
Coopertown	37172
Copperhill	37317
Corbin Hill	37840
Cordell	37756
Corder Cross Roads	37348
Cordova	38018
Corinth (Knox County)	37918
Corinth (Sumner County)	37148
Cornersville	37047
Coro Lake	38109
Corona	72338
Corryton	37721
Cortner	37360
Cosby	37722
Coster (Part of Knoxville)	37917
Cottage Grove	38224
Cottage Home	37095
Cottonport	37322
Cottontown	37048
Cottonwood Estates	37064

	ZIP
Cottonwood Grove	38080
Cotula	37766
Couchville (Part of Nashville)	37214
Coulterville	37373
Counce	38326
Country Club	38008
Country Haven Estates	37179
Country Roads	37064
Countrywood Estates	37064
Countyline (Moore County)	37352
County Line (Sevier County)	37865
Courtland	37172
Cove Creek (Campbell County)	37714
Cove Creek (Carter County)	37687
Cove Creek Cascades	37862
Cove Lake Estates	37714
Covington	38019
Cowan	37318
Cowanstown	37640
Cowards	37921
Cowenville	38567
Coxville	38343
Cozyette	38380
Crab Orchard	37723
Crabtree	37687
Crackers Neck	37683
Craggie Hope	37082
Craigfield	37025
Crandull	37688
Cranmore Cove	37321
Cravenstown	37589
Crawfish Valley	38464
Crawford	38554
Creekwood (Bedford County)	37160
Creekwood (Wilson County)	37122
Crenshaw	37920
Crescent	37129
Creson (Part of Fayetteville)	37334
Creston	38555
Crestwood	37763
Crestwood Hills	37918
Crewstown	38464
Crieve Hall (Part of Nashville)	37211
Crippen Gap	37918
Crisp Spring	37357
Crockett	38253
Crockett Mills	38021
Cronanville	38079
Cross	37617
Cross Anchor	37743
Cross Bridges	38474
Cross Keys	37046
Crossland	42049
Cross Lanes	37186
Cross Plains	37049
Cross Road	37841
Crossroads (Benton County)	38320
Cross Roads (Cannon County)	37190
Crossroads (Crockett County)	38006
Cross Roads (DeKalb County)	37059
Cross Roads (Dyer County)	38034
Cross Roads (Fentress County)	38556
Crossroads (Hardin County)	38372
Cross Roads (mail Ethridge) (Lawrence County)	38456
Crossroads (mail Leoma) (Lawrence County)	38468
Cross Roads (Macon County)	37186
Crossroads (Shelby County)	38017
Cross Roads (Stewart County)	37178
Crossroads (Wayne County)	38450
Crosstown (Shelby County)	38104
Crosstown (Tipton County)	38004
Crossville	38555
	38557

For specific Crossville Zip Codes call (615) 484-6521

	ZIP
Crosswinds	37122
Crowley Store	38230
Crown Point Estates	37122
Crucifer	38345
Crump	38327
Crunk	37073
Crystal	38261
Crystal Springs	37348
Cuba (Hawkins County)	37811
Cuba (Shelby County)	38053
Cuba Landing	37185
Cub Creek	38562
Culleoka	38451

	ZIP
Culpepper	37149
Cumberland City	37050
Cumberland Estates (Part of Knoxville)	37921
Cumberland Furnace	37051
Cumberland Gap	37724
Cumberland Heights (Grundy County)	37313
Cumberland Heights (Montgomery County)	37040
Cumberland Springs	37321
Cumberland View	37757
Cumberland View Estates	37769
Cummings	38583
Cummingsville	38585
Cunningham	37052
Cupp Mill	37825
Curlee	37190
Curve	38063
Cusick	37865
Cuzick	37771
Cypress	38001
Cypress Creek	38222
Cypress Inn	38452
Daisy (Part of Soddy-Daisy)	37379
Dale Hollow	38551
Dalewood (Part of Nashville)	37207
Dallas Gardens	37379
Dallas Hills	37379
Dalton Heights (Part of Morristown)	37814
Dancyville	38069
Dandridge	37725
Dante	37921
Darden	38328
Darks Mill	38401
Daugherty Estates	37062
Daus	37327
Davenport	37110
Davidson	38589
Davidson Chapel	38382
Davis Chapel (Campbell County)	37766
Davis Chapel (Carroll County)	38344
Davis Springs	37692
Daylight	37110
Daysville	37854
Dayton	37321
Dayton Spur	38555
Deanburg	38366
Deans	37033
DeArmond	37748
Deason	37020
De Busk	37743
Decatur	37322
Decaturville	38329
Decherd	37324
Deep Springs	37725
Deerfield (Lawrence County)	38464
Deerfield (Williamson County)	37064
Deerfield Acres	37620
Deer Lodge	37726
Deermont	37829
Defeated	37030
Defense Depot (Part of Memphis)	38114
Delano	37325
Delina	37047
Dellrose	38453
Dellwood	37804
Del Rio	37727
Demory	37766
Denmark	38391
Dennis Cove	37658
Denton	37722
Dentville	37325
Denver (Cannon County)	37149
Denver (Humphreys County)	37054
De Priest Bend (Part of Lobelville)	37097
De Rossett	38583
Detroit	38015
Devonia	37710
Diana	37047
Dibrell	37110
Dickel	37388
Dickey Bluff Peninsula	37381
Dickson	37055-56

For specific Dickson Zip Codes call (615) 446-2556

	ZIP
Dickson Town	38455
Difficult	37145
Dill	37367
Dilley	37730
Dillton	37130
Disco	37737
Dismal	37095

	ZIP		ZIP		ZIP
Disney	37769	East Brainerd	37421	Emory Heights (Part of	
Dixie	38261	Eastbrook (Part of Estill		Harriman)	37748
Dixie Lee Junction (Part of		Springs)	37330	Englewood (McMinn	
Farragut)	37771	East Chattanooga (Part of		County)	37329
Dixon Springs	37057	Chattanooga)	37406	Englewood (Obion County)	38261
Dixonville	38053	East Cleveland	37311	English Mountain Resort	37862
Doaks Crossroads	37087	East Cyruston	37334	Enigma	38548
Dockery	37310	East Due West (Part of		Eno	37055
Dodson (Roane County)	37748	Nashville)	37115	Enon	37150
Dodson (White County)	38583	Easter Seal	37087	Ensor	38544
Dodson Estates (Part of		East Etowah	37331	Enterprise (Hawkins County)	37857
Nashville)	37076	East Fork	37862	Enterprise (Maury County)	38474
Dodsons	38472	Eastgate Mall (Part of		Enville	38332
Doeville	37640	Chattanooga)	37411	Epperson	37385
Dog Hill	38050	Eastgate Shopping Center		Erasmus	38555
Dogtown (Carter County)	37643	(Part of Memphis)	38117	Erie	37846
Dog Town (Grundy County)	37313	East Jamestown	38556	Erin	37061
Dogtown (Polk County)	37391	East Junction (Part of		Erlanger (Part of	
Dogwood	37763	Memphis)	38101	Chattanooga)	37403
Dogwood Heights	37879	East Lake (Part of		Ernestville	37650
Dollar	38313	Chattanooga)	37407	Erwin	37650
Donelson (Part of Nashville)	37214	Eastland	38583	Essary Springs	38061
Donnels Chapel	37149	East Memphis (Part of		Estes Kefauver (Part of	
Donoho	37030	Memphis)	38111	Johnson City)	37601
Doran Addition	37660	East Miller's Cove	37886	Estill Springs	37330
Dorton	38555	East Ridge	37412	Ethridge	38456
Dossett	37716	Eastside (Cannon County)	37190	Etowah	37331
Dotson	37888	East Side (Carter County)	37643	Etter	38549
Dotson Branch	38501	East Side (Dickson County)	37029	Euchee	37880
Dotson's Camp Ground	37888	Eastside (Sullivan County)	37664	Eulia	37186
Dotsontown	37681	Eastside (Warren County)	38581	Eureka (Bradley County)	37323
Dotsonville	37191	East Springbrook (Part of		Eureka (Hardin County)	38372
Doty Chapel	37616	Alcoa)	37701	Eureka (Roane County)	37854
Double Bridges	38040	East Sweetwater	37874	Eurekaton	38075
Double Springs (McMinn		East Union	38301	Eva	38333
County)	37303	Eastview (Greene County)	37743	Evansville	38024
Double Springs (Putnam		Eastview (McNairy County)	38367	Evensville	37332
County)	38544	East View (Meigs County)	37336	Evergreen	37687
Douglas	37064	Eastwood (Part of La		Evins Mill	37166
Douglas Estates	37725	Vergne)	37086	Ewingville (Part of Franklin)	37064
Dover (Hamblen County)	37814	Eaton	38331	Excell	37040
Dover (Stewart County)	37058	Eaton Crossroad	37771	Factory	38485
Dowelltown	37059	Eaton Forest	37771	Fair Acres (Hickman	
Dowler Heights	37377	Ebenezer	37347	County)	37025
Downtown (Part of		Echo Hills	37743	Fair Acres (Sullivan County)	37660
Maryville)	37801	Eddie Hill	37087	Fairfield (Bedford County)	37183
Downtown (Part of		Edenwold (Part of Nashville)	37115	Fairfield (Hamblen County)	37814
Cleveland)	37311	Edgefield (Part of Bristol)	37620	Fairfield (Hickman County)	37033
Downtown (Part of		Edgemont (Cocke County)	37821	Fairfield (Sumner County)	37186
Chattanooga)	37402	Edgemont (Sullivan County)	37620	Fairfield Glade	38555
Doyle	38559	Edgemoor	37716	Fair Garden	37862
Drapers Crossroads	37083	Edgewater (Rhea County)	37321	Fairgrounds (Part of	
Dresden	38225	Edgewater (Wilson County)	37122	Shelbyville)	37160
Driftwood (Part of Bristol)	37620	Edgewood (Dyer County)	38059	Fairlane Estates (Part of	
Dripping Springs	37398	Edgewood (Sullivan County)	37660	Shelbyville)	37160
Drop	38583	Edgewood Acres	37804	Fairmont (Part of Bristol)	37620
Drummonds	38023	Edgewood Heights	37849	Fairmount	37377
Drycreek	37659	Edison	38343	Fairview (Blount County)	37801
Dry Hill (Johnson County)	37640	Edith	38063	Fairview (Bradley County)	37312
Dry Hill (Lauderdale County)	38040	Edwards Point	37377	Fairview (Carroll County)	38201
Dry Hollow (Part of		Edwina	37821	Fairview (Carter County)	37658
Kingsport)	37660	Egam	37334	Fairview (Clay County)	38541
Duck Creek	37869	Egypt (Part of Memphis)	38128	Fairview (Coffee County)	37360
Duck River	38454	Eidson	37731	Fairview (Fentress County)	38556
Ducktown (Polk County)	37326	Elba	38066	Fairview (Gibson County)	38233
Ducktown (Washington		Elbethel	37160	Fairview (mail Mohawk)	
County)	37681	Elbridge	38240	(Greene County)	37810
Dudney Hill	38562	Elgin	37732	Fairview (mail Afton)	
Due West (Part of Nashville)	37115	Elizabeth	38034	(Greene County)	37616
Duff	37766	Elizabethton	37643-44	Fairview (Lawrence County)	38469
Dukedom	38226	For specific Elizabethton Zip		Fair View (Lincoln County)	37334
Dulaney	37743	Codes call (615) 543-5801		Fairview (Macon County)	37186
Dull	37036	Elkhead	37366	Fairview (Madison County)	38343
Dumplin	37820	Elkhorn	38242	Fairview (McMinn County)	37303
Dunbar	38311	Elk Mills	37640	Fairview (Meigs County)	37322
Duncantown	37330	Elk Mill Village (Part of		Fairview (Pickett County)	38549
Dunlap	37327	Fayetteville)	37334	Fairview (Putnam County)	38501
Duplex	37064	Elkmont	37738	Fairview (Roane County)	37763
Du Pont	37865	Elkmont Springs	38449	Fairview (Scott County)	37756
Durhamville	38063	Elkton	38455	Fairview (Stewart County)	37058
Dutch	37888	Elk Valley	37847	Fairview (Warren County)	37110
Dutch Valley	37716	Ellejoy	37865	Fairview (Washington	
Dyer	38330	Ellendale	38029	County)	37659
Dyersburg	38024-25	Ellington Park	37064	Fairview (Wayne County)	38463
For specific Dyersburg Zip Codes		Ellis Mills	37050	Fairview (White County)	38583
call (901) 285-5491		Ellisville	38004	Fairview (Williamson	
Dykes Crossroads	38555	Elm Grove	38015	County)	37062
Dyllis	37748	Elm Springs	37888	Fairview Heights (Jefferson	
Dyson Grove	37640	Elmwood	38560	County)	37725
Eads	38028	Elora	37328	Fairview Heights (Williamson	
Eagan	37730	Elverton	37748	County)	37062
Eagle Creek	38341	Elza	37830	Fairyland	38555
Eagle Furnace	37854	Embreeville	37650	Faix	38549
Eagle Hill	38242	Emerald Acres	37814	Falcon	38375
Eagleton Village (census		Emerts Cove	37862	Fall Branch	37656
designated place)	37801	Emery Mill	37367	Fall Creek	37160
Eagleton Village	37804	Emmanuel School of		Falling Water	37343
Eagleville	37060	Religion	37601	Fallriver	38468
Earleyville	37110	Emmett	37620	Falls Mill	37306
East (Part of Nashville)	37206	Emory Gap (Part of		Fanchers Mills	38583
East Acres	38053	Harriman)	37748	Fancy Meadows	37871

	ZIP
Farmers Exchange	38462
Farmers Valley	37096
Farmington (Marshall County)	37091
Farmington (Williamson County)	37064
Farner	37333
Farragut	37922
Farris Chapel	37398
Farrport (Part of Alcoa)	37701
Faulkner Springs	37110
Faxon	38221
Fayette Corners	38075
Fayetteville	37334
Federal Correctional Institution	38116
Federal Reserve (Part of Nashville)	37203
Fellowship	37122
Fennel Store	37709
Fernvale	37064
Fernwood	37814
Few Chapel	37101
Fielden Store	37820
Fincastle	37766
Findlay (Part of Sparta)	38583
Finger	38334
Finley	38030
Fisherville	38017
Fishery	37650
Fish Springs	37640
Fisk University (Part of Nashville)	37203
Five Points (Lawrence County)	38457
Five Points (Madison County)	38366
Five Points (Rhea County)	37321
Flag Branch	37743
Flag Pond	37657
Flat Branch Junction	37387
Flat Creek (Bedford County)	37160
Flat Creek (Overton County)	38570
Flat Gap (Hancock County)	37881
Flatgap (Jefferson County)	37760
Flat Hollow	37870
Flat Rock (Morgan County)	37726
Flat Rock (Smith County)	37087
Flattop	37379
Flatwood (Tipton County)	38015
Flatwood (Warren County)	37110
Flatwoods (Lawrence County)	38456
Flatwoods (Perry County)	37096
Flewellyn	37172
Flintville	37335
Flippin	38063
Floraton	37149
Florence	37129
Flourville	37659
Flowertown	37360
Fly	38482
Flynns Lick	38562
Foothills Mall (Part of Maryville)	37804
Forbus	38577
Ford	37771
Ford Chapel	37825
Fordtown (Campbell County)	37766
Fordtown (Sullivan County)	37663
Forest Chapel	37186
Forest Grove (Davidson County)	37080
Forest Grove (Meigs County)	37322
Forest Hill (Blount County)	37801
Forest Hill (Shelby County)	38139
Forest Hills (Bedford County)	37160
Forest Hills (Davidson County)	37215
Forest Hills (Knox County)	37919
Forest Hills (Sullivan County)	37620
Forest Home	37064
Forest Home Farms	37064
Forest Mills	37355
Forge Ridge	37752
Forked Deer	38037
Fork Mountain	37710
Fork of Pike	37095
Fork Ridge	40965
Forrest Park (Part of Tullahoma)	37388
Forsythe (Part of Memphis)	38101
Fort Campbell	42223
Fort Campbell South	42223
Fort Donelson Shores	37058
Fort Henry Mall (Part of Kingsport)	37664

	ZIP
Fort Loudon Estates	37771
Fort Pillow Prison and State Farm	38041
Fort Robinson (Part of Kingsport)	37660
Fosterville	37063
Foundry Hill	38251
Fountain City (Part of Knoxville)	37918
Fountain Head	37148
Fountain Heights	38401
Fourmile Board Hill	38485
Four Points	37820
Fowler-Grove	37713
Fowlers	38320
Fowlkes	38033
Fox Bluff	37015
Foxbranch	37765
Foxfire	38555
Frankewing	38459
Frankfort	37770
Franklin	37064-65
	37068
For specific Franklin Zip Codes call (615) 794-2784	
Franklin East	37064
Fraterville	37769
Frayser (Part of Memphis)	38127
Fredonia (Coffee County)	37355
Fredonia (Montgomery County)	37040
Free Communion	38573
Free Hills	38551
Freeland	38222
Free State	38562
Freewill	38562
Fremont	38261
French Broad	37727
Frettin	38052
Friendship (Bledsoe County)	37381
Friendship (Crockett County)	38034
Friendship (Hamilton County)	37341
Friendship (Hawkins County)	37881
Friendship (Sullivan County)	37620
Friends Station	37820
Friendsville	37737
Frisco	37642
Frog Jump (Crockett County)	38040
Frog Jump (Gibson County)	38382
Frog Level	37731
Front Street (Part of Memphis)	38103
Frost Bottom	37840
Fruitland	38343
Fruitvale	38336
Fruit Valley	37153
Fulton	38041
Gabtown	37656
Gadsden	38337
Gainesboro	38562
Gainsville	38049
Gaitherville	38464
Galaxy Heights (Part of Chattanooga)	37343
Galbraith Springs	37811
Galen	37083
Gallatin	37066
Gallaway	38036
Gandy	38464
Gann	38358
Gapcreek	37643
Gardner	38237
Garland	38019
Garretts	38329
Gassaway	37095
Gates	38037
Gath	37110
Gatlinburg	37738
Gattistown	37359
Gause	37035
Gay	37110
Gentry	38544
Georgetown (Gibson County)	38382
Georgetown (Hamilton County)	37336
Georgetown (McMinn County)	37370
George W. Lee (Part of Memphis)	38126
Georgia Crossing	37398
Germantown (Davidson County)	37189
Germantown (Shelby County)	38138
Gerren Heights	37367
Gibbs (Part of Union City)	38261

	ZIP
Gibbs Crossroads	37145
Gibson	38338
Gibson Hall	37879
Gibsontown (Part of Kingsport)	37660
Gibson Wells	38343
Gift	38019
Gilchrist	38310
Gildfield	38002
Gilfield	37686
Gillises Mills	38372
Gilmore	38301
Gilt Edge	38015
Gin House Lake	38058
Gladdice	38562
Glade Creek	38583
Glades (Morgan County)	37726
Glades (Sevier County)	37738
Gladeville	37071
Glass	38240
Gleason	38229
Glen	37342
Glen Alice	37854
Glencliff (Part of Nashville)	37211
Glendale (Hamilton County)	37405
Glendale (Lawrence County)	38469
Glendale (Loudon County)	37742
Glendale (Maury County)	38401
Glendale Estates	38478
Glen Del Acres	37860
Glenhaven (Part of Fairview)	37062
Glen Mary	37852
Glenmore Estates	37853
Glen Oaks	37122
Glenobey	38556
Glenview (Part of Nashville)	37217
Glenwood	37185
Glenwylde	37051
Glimp	38041
Glover	37172
Glover Hill	37347
Glynnwood Lake	38028
Gnat Hill	37355
Goat City	38355
Godwin	38401
Goffton	38501
Goin	37825
Golddust	38063
Goldpoint	37343
Goodbars	38581
Goodfield	37322
Good Hope (Campbell County)	37762
Good Hope (Dyer County)	38059
Goodlettsville	37070
	37072
For specific Goodlettsville Zip Codes call (615) 859-2766	
Good Luck	38369
Goodspring	38460
Good Springs	37331
Goose Horn	38588
Gooseneck (Anderson County)	37705
Gooseneck (Blount County)	37737
Gordon (Part of Pulaski)	38478
Gordonsburg	38462
Gordonsville	38563
Gorman	37101
Goshen	37642
Gossburg	37018
Graball (Gibson County)	38358
Graball (Marshall County)	37047
Graball (Sumner County)	37148
Graham	37137
Grammer Estates	37062
Grand Junction	38039
Grand Valley	38067
Grandview (Greene County)	37641
Grandview (Knox County)	37920
Grandview (Rhea County)	37337
Grandview Estates	37764
Grandview Terrace	37620
Granite	37716
Grannys Branch	38221
Grant	38563
Grantsboro	37766
Granville	38564
Grasshopper	37308
Grassland	37064
Grassy Cove	38555
Grassy Creek	37317
Grassy Fork	37753
Grassy Valley	37743
Gratio	38240
Gravel Hill (McNairy County)	38339
Gravel Hill (Washington County)	37681
Gravelly Hill (Part of Jefferson City)	37760

	ZIP
Graveltown	37145
Graveston	37721
Gray	37615
Gray Acres	37620
Graysville	37338
Graytown	37033
Graywinds	37122
Green Ack	37840
Green Acres (Giles County)	38478
Green Acres (Knox County)	37921
Green Acres (Roane County)	37763
Green Acres (Sullivan County)	37660
Greenback	37742
Greenbriar	37185
Greenbriar Village (Part of Crossville)	38555
Greenbrier (Cheatham County)	37015
Green Brier (Pickett County)	38549
Greenbrier (Robertson County)	37073
Greenbrier (Williamson County)	37064
Greenbrier Lake	37087
Greeneville	37743-44
For specific Greeneville Zip Codes call (615) 638-2221	
Greenfield	38230
Greenfield Bend	38487
Greenfields (Part of Kingsport)	37660
Green Grove	37074
Green Harbor	37138
Greenhaw	37324
Green Hill (Jefferson County)	37725
Green Hill (Warren County)	37110
Green Hill (Wilson County)	37138
Green Hills (Part of Nashville)	37215
Greenland	37642
Green Meadow (Blount County)	37701
Green Meadow (Bradley County)	37311
Green Meadows	38556
Green Pond	38554
Greens	37110
Greens Mill	37343
Greentown	37387
Greenvale	37184
Green Valley (Knox County)	37919
Green Valley (Williamson County)	37064
Green Valley (Macon County)	37083
Green Village (Part of Church Hill)	37642
Greenwood (Macon County)	37150
Greenwood (Rutherford County)	37046
Greenwood (Wilson County)	37087
Greystone	37743
Griffith	37367
Griffith Creek	37397
Grimsley	38565
Grinders	37033
Gronanville	38079
Gruetl (Part of Gruetli-Laager)	37339
Gruetli-Laager	37339
Gudger	37354
Guild	37340
Gulf Park	37919
Gum	37130
Gum Creek	37324
Gum Flat	38006
Gum Spring	37821
Gum Springs (Lawrence County)	38468
Gum Springs (Macon County)	37145
Guntown	37857
Guys	38339
Habersham	37766
Hackberry	37142
Hales Crossroads	37814
Hales Point	38040
Halesville	37095
Haletown-Ladds	37340
Haley	37183
Half Acre	37166
Halls (Knox County)	37918
Halls (Lauderdale County)	38040
Halls Creek	37185
Halls Crossroads	37918
Hallshare Estates	38320
Halls Hill	37118
Halls Mills	37160

	ZIP
Hall Town (Sumner County)	37148
Halltown (Trousdale County)	37074
Hallview Meadows (Part of Fairview)	37062
Hamburg	38376
Hamilville (Part of Chattanooga)	37343
Hamilton Mill	38453
Hamilton Place (Part of Chattanooga)	37421
Hamlin Town	37715
Hammon Chapel	37683
Hampshire	38461
Hampton	37658
Hamptons Crossroads	38583
Hampton Station	37040
Handleyton	37148
Hanging Limb	38554
Happy Hill	38478
Happy Top	37337
Happy Valley	37878
Harbin	37854
Harbison	37721
Harbor Town	38221
Harbour Island	37138
Harbuck	37391
Hardin Estates	37771
Hardy	38501
Harmon	37688
Harmony (Franklin County)	37398
Harmony (Jackson County)	38562
Harmony (Washington County)	37659
Harmony Grove	37727
Harmony Hills	37660
Harms	37334
Harpeth	37064
Harpeth Estates	37064
Harpeth Hills	37064
Harpeth Meadows (Part of Franklin)	37064
Harpeth Valley	37187
Harpeth Valley Park (Part of Nashville)	37221
Harrill Hills (Part of Knoxville)	37918
Harriman	37748
Harriman Junction (Part of Harriman)	37748
Harris	38261
Harrisburg	37862
Harrison	37341
Harrison Hills	37771
Harrogate	37752
Harrogate-Shawnee	37752
Harrtown	37617
Hartford	37753
Hartmantown	37659
Hartsville	37074
Haskins Chapel	37091
Hatchertown	37862
Hatchie	38392
Havley Springs (Part of Morristown)	37814
Havron Chapel	37347
Hawkinsville	38034
Hawthorne	37160
Haydenburg	38588
Hayes	38583
Hayes Fork	37058
Haynes	38077
Haynesfield (Part of Bristol)	37620
Hays	38057
Haysboro (Part of Nashville)	37216
Haysville	37083
Head of Barren	37825
Heard	38573
Heatherwood Hill	37064
Heatoncreek	37687
Hebbertsburg	37723
Hebron	38052
Heiskell	37754
Helena	38556
Helenwood	37755
Heloise	38030
Helton	37012
Helton Springs	37861
Heltonville	37708
Hemlock Hills	37650
Henard Mill	37857
Henardtown	37857
Henderson	38340
Hendersonville	37075
	37077
For specific Hendersonville Zip Codes call (615) 824-8789	
Hendon	37338
Hendron	37920
Henley (Part of Decherd)	37324
Henning	38041
Henrietta	37015

	ZIP
Henry	38231
Henrys Crossroads	37764
Henry Street (Part of Morristown)	37814
Henryville	38483
Hensley Chapel	38583
Herbert Domain	37367
Heritage Estates	38555
Heritage Hills	37801
Hermitage (Part of Nashville)	37076
Hermitage Hills (Part of Nashville)	37076
Hermitage Springs	37150
Hermon	37616
Hiawassee	37357
Hickerson	37388
Hickey	38582
Hickman	38567
Hickory Bend (Part of Nashville)	37214
Hickory Flat	38321
Hickory Flats	38310
Hickory Grove (Gibson County)	38382
Hickory Grove (Sumner County)	37031
Hickory Grove (Warren County)	37110
Hickory Hill (Part of Lynchburg)	37352
Hickory Hill (Shelby County)	38125
	38141
For specific Hickory Hill Zip Codes call (615) 759-7818	
Hickory Hill Estates (Part of Tullahoma)	37388
Hickory Hills	37064
Hickory Hollow Mall (Part of Nashville)	37211
Hickory Point	37040
Hickory Star Landing	37807
Hickory Tree	37618
Hickory Valley (Hardeman County)	38042
Hickory Valley (Union County)	37807
Hickory Withe	38043
Hicks Chapel	37397
Hicksville (Part of Jackson)	38301
Hico	38344
Hico Station	38344
Hide-A-Way Hills	38555
Highcliff	37762
Highgate	37064
Highland (DeKalb County)	37166
Highland (Jackson County)	38562
Highland (Overton County)	38570
Highland (Wayne County)	38450
Highland Academy	37148
Highland Acres	37804
Highland Forest (Part of Rockwood)	37854
Highland Heights (Davidson County)	37207
Highland Heights (Giles County)	38478
Highland Heights (Shelby County)	38122
Highland Junction	38589
Highland Manor	37341
Highland Park (Campbell County)	37766
Highland Park (Hamilton County)	37404
Highland Park (Loudon County)	37771
Highland Park (Sullivan County)	37660
Highland Springs	37709
Highlandview	37920
High Point (Campbell County)	37714
High Point (Scott County)	37841
Hilham	38568
Hillcrest (Cumberland County)	38555
Hillcrest (Hamblen County)	37814
Hillcrest (Sullivan County)	37618
Hillcrest (Part of Kingsport)	37660
Hilldale (Part of Clarksville)	37043
Hill Estates (Part of Franklin)	37064
Hilliard	38344
Hillsboro	37342
Hillsboro Acres	37064
Hillsdale	37057
Hillside	38237
Hills View	37370
Hilltop (Bedford County)	37160
Hilltop (Montgomery County)	37040

	ZIP		ZIP		ZIP
Hilltop (Rutherford County)	37167	Hubbard	37801	Jarrell	38201
Hill Top (Washington		Hubertville	37172	Jasper	37347
County)	37601	Hudson	38464	Jaybird (Cocke County)	37821
Hill Town	38482	Hugarth	38556	Jaybird (Hamblen County)	37814
Hillvale	37716	Hughes Loop	38358	Jeannette	38363
Hillville	38075	Hughett	37852	Jearoldstown	37641
Hillwood (Part of Nashville)	37205	Hughey	37334	Jefferson	37166
Himesville	37160	Hulan Hollow (Part of Erwin)	37650	Jefferson City	37760
Hindscreek	37716	Humboldt	38343	Jefferson Estates	37877
Hinds Creek Valley	37807	Humphrey	37865	Jefferson Springs	37167
Hinkle	37871	Hunter	37643	Jellico	37762
Hinkledale	38201	Hunter Hills	37379	Jena	37742
Hitchcox	37367	Hunters Point	37087	Jenkins Hill (Part of	
Hiwassee College	37354	Hunters Ridge	37064	Sevierville)	37862
Hiwassee Hills	37354	Huntersville	38301	Jenkinsville	38024
Hixon	37301	Hunting Creek Farms	37064	Jere Baxter (Part of	
Hixson (Part of		Huntingdon	38344	Nashville)	37216
Chattanooga)	37343	Huntland	37345	Jernigan Town	37188
Hobbs Hill	37387	Huntsville (Loudon County)	37771	Jersey (Part of	
Hodges	37820	Huntsville (Scott County)	37756	Chattanooga)	37416
Hoggtown	37030	Hurdlow (Part of Lynchburg)	37306	Jessie	37110
Hohenwald	38462	Hurley	38357	Jewell	38225
Holiday City (Part of		Hurley Acres	37814	Jewett	37337
Memphis)	38118	Huron	38345	Jimtown	37821
Holiday Hills (Cumberland		Hurricane (Houston County)	37175	Joelton (Part of Nashville)	37080
County)	38555	Hurricane (Jackson County)	38562	John Sevier	37914
Holiday Hills (Roane		Hurricane (Wilson County)	37087	Johnson Bible College	37920
County)	37763	Hurricane Hill	38063	Johnson City	37601-15
Holiday Shores	37028	Hurricane Mills	37078	For specific Johnson City Zip	
Holladay (Benton County)	38341	Hustburg	37134	Codes call (615) 461-8251	
Holladay (Putnam County)	38501	Hutsell (Part of Athens)	37303	Johnsons	37048
Holland Mill	37616	Hygeia Springs	37073	Johnsons Chapel	38583
Hollow Rock	38342	Hyndsver	38237	Johnsons Grove	38006
Hollow Springs	37026	Iconium	37190	Johntown	37074
Holly Grove (Haywood		Idaho	38468	Jones	38006
County)	38006	Idaville	38004	Jonesborough	37659
Holly Grove (Marshall		Ideal Valley	37381	Jones Chapel	38549
County)	37091	Idlewild (Gibson County)	38346	Jones Cove	37862
Holly Grove (Tipton County)	38011	Idlewild (McMinn County)	37303	Jones Mill	38224
Holly Leaf	38258	Idlewood (Part of Franklin)	37064	Jones Valley	38482
Holly Springs	38570	Ilemar	37122	Jonesville (Fentress County)	38553
Hollywood (Maury County)	38451	Imperial Estates	37921	Jonesville (Roane County)	37840
Hollywood (Shelby County)	38108	Independence (Hancock		Joppa (Grainger County)	37861
Hollywood Hills	37066	County)	37731	Joppa (White County)	38587
Holston Army Ammunition		Independence (Overton		Jordonia (Part of Nashville)	37218
Plant	37662	County)	38573	Jug Town	37130
Holston Heights (Part of		Independence Estates	37087	Juno	38351
Kingsport)	37660	India	38242	Kagley	37801
Holston Hills (Knox County)	37914	Indian Bluff	37710	Kansas (Jefferson County)	37760
Holston Hills (Sullivan		Indian Cave	37709	Kansas (Sumner County)	37066
County)	37620	Indian Creek	37757	Karns	37921
Holston Institute	37617	Indian Hills	37087	Kaywood (Part of	
Holston Valley	37620	Indian Mound (DeKalb		Tullahoma)	37388
Holts Corner	37034	County)	38583	Kedron (Giles County)	38477
Holttown	37821	Indian Mound (Stewart		Kedron (Maury County)	37174
Holy Hill	37683	County)	37079	Keefe	38080
Homestead	38555	Indian Ridge (Grainger		Keeling	38069
Honeycutt	37857	County)	37709	Keenburg	37643
Hood Lake (Part of		Indian Ridge (Washington		Keese (Part of Decherd)	37324
Lawrenceburg)	38464	County)	37601	Keith Springs	37398
Hoodoo	37018	Indian Springs	37617	Kellertown	37183
Hookers Bend	38361	Ingleside Hill (Part of		Kelley Town (Part of Oliver	
Hoop	37879	Athens)	37303	Springs)	37840
Hoovers Gap	37037	Inglewood (Part of		Kelso	37348
Hopewell (Bradley County)	37312	Nashville)	37216	Keltonburg	37166
Hopewell (Carroll County)	38348	Inskip (Part of Knoxville)	37912	Kemmer Hill (Part of Spring	
Hopewell (Claiborne		Interstate Park	37032	City)	37381
County)	37879	Irish Cut	37821	Kempville	37030
Hopewell (Davidson County)	37138	Iron City	38463	Kendricks Creek	37663
Hopewell (Gibson County)	38389	Ironsburg	37385	Kennedy Creek	37016
Hopewell (Tipton County)	38011	Irving College	37110	Kenneytown	37743
Hopewell Springs	37354	Irwinton Shores	37880	Kenton	38233
Hopper Bluff	37861	Isabella	37346	Kepler	37857
Hopson	37687	Isham	37892	Kerrville	38053
Hornbeak	38232	Island Home (Part of		Kettle Mills	38461
Horner	37096	Knoxville)	37920	Key	38583
Hornertown	37147	Island Park	37618	Keystone (Part of Johnson	
Hornsby	38044	Isoline	38555	City)	37601
Horn Springs	37087	Isom	38461	Killians Chapel (Part of	
Horse Creek (Greene		Ivy	37369	Altamont)	37301
County)	37641	Ivy Bluff	37110	Kilsyth	37766
Horse Creek (Sullivan		Ivydell	37766	Kimball	37347
County)	37660	Ivy Point (Part of Nashville)	37072	Kimberlin Heights	37920
Horse Shoe	37643	Ivyton	38543	Kimberly Acres	37122
Horseshoe Bend	38560	Jacksboro	37757	Kimbrough Crossroad	37890
Horsleys	37074	Jacks Creek	38347	Kimery	38230
Housley Addition (Part of		Jackson	38301-08	Kimmins	38462
Athens)	37303		38314	Kimsey	37391
Houston	38471	For specific Jackson Zip Codes		Kin Cove	37087
Houston Valley	37743	call (901) 422-5369		Kinderhook	38482
Howard (Monroe County)	37885	Jackson Heights (Part of		King	37715
Howard (Sevier County)	37865	Murfreesboro)	37129	Kingfield	37064
Howard Springs	38570	Jackson Ridge	37060	Kingsport	37660-65
Howard Hill (Part of		Jacksons Chapel	37036	For specific Kingsport Zip Codes	
Kingsport)	37660	Jackson Square (Part of		call (615) 245-5111	
Howard Quarter	37879	Oak Ridge)	37830	King Springs (Part of	
Howard Springs	38555	Jacobs Hill	37087	Johnson City)	37601
Howell (Lincoln County)	37334	Jakestown	37130	Kings Ridge (Part of	
Howell (White County)	38583	Jamestown (Fentress		Chattanooga)	37343
Howell Hill	37334	County)	38556	Kingston	37763
Howley	38321	Jamestown (Tipton County)	38015	Kingston Heights	37763

	ZIP		ZIP		ZIP
Kingston Hills	37919	Langford Farms	37138	Lincoya Hills (Part of	
Kingston Mill	37160	Lanier	37801	Nashville)	37214
Kingston Springs	37082	Lantana	38555	Linden	37096
Kingston Woods	37919	Lapata	38059	Lindsay Mill	37769
Kinzel Springs	37882	Lascassas	37085	Link	37037
Kirk	38017	Lassiter Corner	38232	Linsdale	37325
Kirkland (Lincoln County)	38488	Latham	38225	Linton (Part of Nashville)	37216
Kirkland (Williamson		Laurel (Anderson County)	37716	Linwood	37087
County)	37046	Laurel (Sevier County)	37862	Lisbon	38052
Kite	37857	Laurel Bloomery	37680	Little Barren (Claiborne	
Kittrell	37149	Laurel Bluff	37763	County)	37825
Kleburne	37174	Laurel Brook	37321	Little Barren (Union County)	37825
Kline	37398	Laurelburg	38581	Littlebrook (Part of	
Klondike	37857	Laurel Cove	38585	Rockford)	37853
Knapp	37769	Laurel Grove	37710	Littlecrab	38556
Knob Creek (Lauderdale		La Vergne	37086	Little Creek	37752
County)	38063	Lavinia	38348	Little Doe	37640
Knob Creek (Sevier County)	37865	Law	38351	Little Emory	37748
Knoxville	37901-98	Law Chapel	37801	Little Hope (Rutherford	
For specific Knoxville Zip Codes		Lawnville	37763	County)	37129
call (615) 558-4528		Lawrenceburg	38464	Little Hope (Wayne County)	38485
Knoxville College (Part of		Lawson Crossroad	37882	Littlelot	38454
Knoxville)	37921	Lawton	38375	Little Milligan	37640
Kodak	37764	Leach	38344	Little River	37804
Kodak Estates	37764	Leadvale (Cocke County)	37821	Little White Oak	37766
KoKo	38069	Leadvale (Jefferson County)	37890	Litton	37367
Kontika	37087	Leana	37129	Litz Manor (Part of	
Kyles Ford	37765	Leapwood	38310	Kingsport)	37660
Laager (Part of Gruetli-		Lea Springs	37709	Liverwort	37040
Laager)	37339	Leatherwood	38485	Livingston	38570
Laconia	38045	Lebanon	37087-88	Lobelville	37097
Lacy	38052	For specific Lebanon Zip Codes		Locke	38053
Lafayette	37083	call (615) 444-2672		Lockertsville	37015
La Follette	37766	Ledgemere	37160	Lockmiller Addition (Part of	
La Grange	38046	Lee	37367	Athens)	37303
Laguardo	37087	Lee College (Part of		Locust Grove	38059
Lake City	37769	Cleveland)	37311	Locust Mount	37659
Lake Colonial Estates	37014	Leeland	37064	Locust Springs	37616
Lake Crest	37663	Leemans Corner	37087	Lodge	37380
Lake Drive	38079	Leesburg	37659	Lodi	38486
Lake Farm Estates	37167	Lee Valley	37869	Logans Lake	38334
Lake Forest (Grainger		Leeville	37087	Lois (Part of Lynchburg)	37359
County)	37861	Leewood (Part of Memphis)	38101	Lomax Crossroads	38462
Lake Forest (Hamilton		Leftwich	38401	Lone Mountain (Claiborne	
County)	37343	Legate	37079	County)	37773
Lake Forest (Knox County)	37920	Leighs Chapel	38019	Lone Mountain (Scott	
Lakeharbor	37763	Leighton	38391	County)	37852
Lake Harbor Estates	37416	Leinart	37716	Lone Oak	37377
Lake Haven	37087	Leipers Fork	37064	Lone Oaks (Part of Atoka)	38004
Lake Hills (Part of		Lenoir City	37771	Lone Star	37660
Tullahoma)	37388	Lenow	38018	Long Branch (Hamilton	
Lakeland	38002	Lenox	38047	County)	37343
Lakemont	37777	Leoma	38468	Long Branch (Lawrence	
Lakemont Cabin Area	37811	Leonard	37620	County)	38464
Lakemont Heights (Part of		Leoni	37190	Long Creek	37843
Rockwood)	37854	Lewisburg	37091	Long Hollow (Part of La	
Lakemoor	37920	Lewis Chapel	37327	Follette)	37766
Lakemoore (Part of		Lexie	37306	Long Island	37660
Morristown)	37814	Lexie Crossroads	37306	Long Rock	38344
Lake Placid	38340	Lexington	38351	Longs Mills	37303
Lake Road (Part of		Liberty (Benton County)	38320	Longtown	38049
Fairview)	37062	Liberty (Decatur County)	38374	Longview	37020
Lakeshore Estates	37416	Liberty (DeKalb County)	37095	Longwood	37064
Lake Side (Hamilton		Liberty (Franklin County)	37398	Lonsdale (Part of Knoxville)	37921
County)	37343	Liberty (Giles County)	38477	Lookout Mountain	37350
Lakeside (Monroe County)	37885	Liberty (Jackson County)	38564	Lookout Valley (Part of	
Lakeside Estates (Part of		Liberty (Johnson County)	37683	Chattanooga)	37419
Estill Springs)	37330	Liberty (Lincoln County)	37334	Loon Bay	37028
Lakeside Heights	37890	Liberty (Morgan County)	37887	Loonewood	38585
Lakesite	37379	Liberty (mail Gallatin		Loretto	38469
Lake Tansi Village	38555	(Sumner County)	37066	Lorraine	37381
Lake Tullahoma Estates		Liberty (mail Bethpage)		Lost Creek	38583
(Part of Tullahoma)	37388	(Sumner County)	37022	Lost Mountain	37743
Lakeview (Blount County)	37777	Liberty (Washington		Loudon	37774
Lakeview (Claiborne		County)	37641	Louise	37051
County)	37825	Liberty (Weakley County)	38229	Louisville	37777
Lakeview (Hamblen County)	37814	Liberty Grove	38469	Love Joy	38574
Lakeview (McMinn County)	37303	Liberty Hill (Grainger		Lovelace	37641
Lakeview (Roane County)	37763	County)	37888	Love Lady	38549
Lakeview (Robertson		Liberty Hill (Greene County)	37641	Loveland (Part of Knoxville)	37924
County)	37172	Liberty Hill (McMinn County)	37329	Lovell Heights	37922
Lakeview Commercial Park		Liberty Hill (Williamson		Love Station	37650
(Part of Franklin)	37064	County)	37025	Lovetown	38474
Lakeview Estates	37777	Liberty Hill (Wilson County)	37012	Lower Mill	37343
Lake View Heights (Part of		Lick Creek (Benton County)	38221	Lower Mockeson	38468
Harriman)	37748	Lick Creek (Decatur		Lowland	37778
Lakeview Manor	38256	County)	38363	Lowryville	38372
Lakeview Park (Part of		Lickskillet	37807	Luckett	38063
Dandridge)	37725	Lickton (Part of Nashville)	37189	Lucky	37110
Lakewood	37138	Lightfoot	38063	Lucy	38053
Lakewood Village	37381	Lilamay	37015	Luna	37019
Lamar (Part of Memphis)	38114	Lillydale	37650	Lunns Store	37034
Lambert	38068	Lily Grove	37825	Lupton City (Part of	
Lamont	37172	Limbs	38255	Chattanooga)	37351
Lamontville	37309	Limestone	37681	Luray	38352
Lancaster	38569	Limestone Cove	37692	Lusk	37327
Lancaster Hill	38567	Linary	38555	Luskville	37309
Lancelot Acres	38478	Lincoln	37334	Luther	37869
Lancing	37770	Lincoln Park (Part of		Luttrell (Loudon County)	37846
Lane	38240	Knoxville)	37917	Luttrell (Union County)	37779
Laneview	38382			Lutts	38471

	ZIP
Lyles	37098
Lynchburg	37352
Lynn Garden	37665
Lynnville	38472
Lyons View (Part of Knoxville)	37919
McAllister Hill	37346
McAllisters Crossroads	37171
McAnna	38260
McBurg	38459
McCains	38401
McClamerys Stand (Part of Collinwood)	38450
McCloud	37857
McClures Bend	37030
McCoinsville	38562
McConnell	38237
McCullough	38024
McDonald	37353
McDonald Hill	37857
Macedonia (Carroll County)	38201
Macedonia (McMinn County)	37329
Macedonia (Obion County)	38233
Macedonia (White County)	38583
McElroy	38559
Mace's Hill	37057
McEwen	37101
McGeetown	37317
McIllwain	38341
McKenzie	38201
	38257

For specific McKenzie Zip Codes call (901) 352-7977

	ZIP
McKinley	37601
McKinnon	37175
McKnight	38482
McLemoresville	38235
McLin's Corner	38034
McMahan	37862
McMillan	37914
McMinnville	37110
McNairy	38315
Macon	38048
McPheeter Bend	37642
Maddox	38372
Madge	38002
Madie	38080
Madison	37115-16

For specific Madison Zip Codes call (615) 868-1883

	ZIP
Madison College (Part of Nashville)	37115
Madison Hall	38301
Madison Square (Part of Nashville)	37115
Madisonville	37354
Maggart	38560
Magnolia	37175
Magnolia Place (Part of Franklin)	37064
Major	37087
Malesus (Part of Jackson)	38301
Mall (Part of Cookeville)	38501
Mall, The (Part of Johnson City)	37601
Mall of Memphis, The (Part of Memphis)	38118
Mallory (Part of Memphis)	38109
Mallorys (Part of Franklin)	37064
Maloney Heights	37920
Maloneyville	37918
Manchester	37355
Mankinville	37130
Manlyville	38256
Mansfield	38236
Mansfield Gap	37877
Mansford	37398
Manson	38556
Maple Grove (Clay County)	38541
Maple Grove (Macon County)	37083
Maple Grove (Meigs County)	37880
Maple Hill	37620
Maplehurst	37618
Maplewood (Part of Nashville)	37216
Marble City (Part of Knoxville)	37919
Marbledale	37914
Marble Hall	37857
Marble Hill (Blount County)	37737
Marble Hill (Moore County)	37398
Marble Plains	37398
Marbleton	37692
Marguerite	37814
Marion (Claiborne County)	37715
Marion (Montgomery County)	37051

	ZIP
Market Square Mall (Part of Knoxville)	37902
Markham	38079
Marlborough	38317
Marlow	37716
Marlyn Hills (Part of Bristol)	37620
Marrowbone	37015
Mars Hill	38464
Martel Estates	37771
Martha	37087
Martha Washington	38553
Martin	38237
Martin Creek	38544
Martin Springs	37380
Marvin	37818
Marys Grove	38488
Maryville	37801-04

For specific Maryville Zip Codes call (615) 983-7801

	ZIP
Mascot	37806
Mason	38049
Mason Grove	38343
Masonhall	38233
Masseyville	38315
Maupin Row (Part of Johnson City)	37601
Maury City	38050
Maxey	38059
Maxwell	37306
Maxwell Chapel	38568
May Acres	37877
Mayhome	37184
Mayland	38555
Maynardville	37807
Mayview Heights	37849
Meacham	38024
Meades Quarry (Part of Knoxville)	37920
Meadorville	37083
Meadow	37742
Meadowbrook (Blount County)	37804
Meadowbrook (Greene County)	37616
Meadow Brook (Warren County)	37110
Meadow Green Acres	37064
Meadow Mead (Part of Paris)	38242
Meadow View (Hamilton County)	37336
Meadowview (Lawrence County)	38464
Meadowview Gardens (Part of Harriman)	37748
Meadowwood Acres (Part of Fairview)	37062
Mechanicsville	37190
Medford	37769
Medina	38355
Medon	38356
Melrose (Blount County)	37886
Melrose (Davidson County)	37204
Melville Hill (Part of Soddy-Daisy)	37379
Melvine	37367
Melwood	38315
Memorial	37150

	ZIP
Memphis	38101-87

For specific Memphis Zip Codes call (901) 775-3872

COLLEGES & UNIVERSITIES

	ZIP
Christian Brothers College	38104
Memphis State University	38152
Rhodes College	38112
University of Tennessee-Memphis	38163

FINANCIAL INSTITUTIONS

	ZIP
Bank of Bartlett	38134
Boatmen's Bank of Tennessee	38103
The Community Bank of Germantown	38119
First American National Bank	38103
First Tennessee Bank National Association	38103
Leader Federal Bank for Savings	38103
National Bank of Commerce	38150
Nationsbank	38112
Union Planters National Bank	38103
United American Bank of Memphis	38119

HOSPITALS

	ZIP
Baptist Memorial Hospital	38146
Methodist Hospital-Central	38104
Regional Medical Center at Memphis	38103
St. Francis Hospital	38119
St. Joseph Hospital	38105
Veterans Affairs Medical Center	38104

HOTELS/MOTELS

	ZIP
Holiday Inn International Airport	38116
Holiday Inn Overton Square	38104
Ramada	38115
Ramada Hotel Convention Center	38103

MILITARY INSTALLATIONS

	ZIP
Defense Distribution Depot, Memphis	38114
Tennessee Air National Guard, FB6422, Memphis International Airport	38118
United States Army Engineer District, Memphis	38103
Memphis State University (Part of Memphis)	38111
Mendenhall (Part of Memphis)	38117
Mengelwood	38047
Mentor	37777
Mercer	38392
Meredith Cave	37766
Merry Oaks (Part of Nashville)	37214
Michie	38357
Middlebrook Heights (Part of Knoxville)	37919
Middleburg (Hardeman County)	38008
Middleburg (Henderson County)	38374
Middle City	38024
Middle Creek	37862
Middle Fork	38352
Middle Settlement	37777
Middleton	38052
Middle Valley	37343
Middle Valley Estates	37343
Midfields	37665
Midland	37020
Midland Shopping Center (Part of Alcoa)	37701
Midtown	37748
Midtown Heights	37748
Midway (Cannon County)	37026
Midway (Cocke County)	37727
Midway (Cumberland County)	38555
Midway (DeKalb County)	37166
Midway (Dyer County)	38030
Midway (Franklin County)	37375
Midway (Greene County)	37818
Midway (Johnson County)	37640
Midway (Knox County)	37871
Midway (Obion County)	38261
Midway (Roane County)	37763
Midway (Warren County)	37110
Midway (Washington County)	37601
Mifflin	38352
Milan	38358
Milan Army Ammunition Plant	38358
Milburnton	37681
Miles Crossroads	37150
Mile Straight (Part of Soddy-Daisy)	37379
Milky Way	38478
Mill Brook	37681
Mill Creek (Anderson County)	37705
Mill Creek (Hickman County)	37098
Mill Creek (Morgan County)	37872
Mill Creek (Putnam County)	38501
Milldale	37172
Milledgeville	38359
Miller's Store	38225
Millersville	37072
Millertown	37914
Milican	37862
Milligan College	37682
Millington	38053
Millsfield	38024
Mill Spring	37820
Milltown (Humphreys County)	37101
Milltown (Jackson County)	38588
Milltown (Macon County)	37150

	ZIP
Milltown (Marshall County)	37091
Millview	37064
Milo	37381
Milton	37118
Mimms (Part of Nashville)	37211
Mimosa	37334
Mimosa Estates	37777
Mimosa Heights	37777
Mineral Park	37353
Mineral Springs	38574
Mink	38485
Minnick	38240
Minor Hill	38473
Mint	37801
Miser Station	37777
Miston	38056
Mitchell	37148
Mitchellville	37119
Mixie	38342
Moccasin	38485
Mohawk	37810
Mohawk Crossroad	37711
Molino	37334
Mon	37087
Mona	37129
Monoville	37030
Monroe	38573
Monsanto	38402
Montague (Davidson County)	37216
Montague (Rhea County)	37321
Monteagle	37356
Monterey	38574
Montezuma	38340
Montgomery Junction	37756
Monticello (Williamson County)	37064
Monticello (Wilson County)	37122
Montpier Farms	37064
Montvale	37801
Moodyville	38549
Mooneyham	38585
Moons	38256
Moon Shadows	37341
Mooreland Heights (Part of Knoxville)	37920
Mooresburg	37811
Mooresburg Springs	37811
Moores Chapel	38358
Moores College	38581
Mooresville	37091
Mooretown	37190
Mooring	38080
Morgan Springs	37321
Morganton	37742
Morgantown	37321
Morganville	37397
Morley	37766
Morny (Part of Nashville)	37080
Morris Chapel (Benton County)	38320
Morris Chapel (Hardin County)	38361
Morrison	37357
Morrison City	37660
Morrison Creek	38562
Morristown	37813-16
For specific Morristown Zip Codes call (615) 586-1291	
Moscow	38057
Mosheim	37818
Moss	38575
Mossy Grove	37748
Mountain City	37683
Mountain Dale	37650
Mountain Home (Part of Johnson City)	37684
Mountain View (Part of Dayton)	37321
Mountain View Acres (Part of Winchester)	37398
Mount Airy	37327
Mount Ararat	37095
Mount Carmel (Decatur County)	38329
Mount Carmel (Greene County)	37711
Mount Carmel (Hawkins County)	37642
Mount Carmel (Tipton County)	38019
Mount Carmel (Washington County)	37641
Mount Crest	37367
Mount Cumberland	37329
Mount Denson	37172
Mount Gilead (Henderson County)	38321
Mount Gilead (White County)	38583

	ZIP
Mount Harmony (McMinn County)	37826
Mount Harmony (Monroe County)	37385
Mount Helen	38504
Mount Herman (Bedford County)	37160
Mount Herman (Weakley County)	38230
Mount Hope	38485
Mount Horeb	37760
Mount Joy	38474
Mount Juliet	37122
Mount Lebanon	38464
Mount Leo	37110
Mount Moriah	38320
Mount Nebo	38463
Mount Olive (Grundy County)	37110
Mount Olive (Knox County)	37920
Mount Olive (Marion County)	37397
Mount Olive (Rutherford County)	37130
Mount Pelia	38237
Mount Pisgah	38587
Mount Pleasant (Greene County)	37743
Mount Pleasant (Henry County)	38222
Mount Pleasant (Maury County)	38474
Mount Pleasant (Putnam County)	38501
Mount Pleasant (Scott County)	37852
Mount Tabor	37804
Mount Tucker Addition	37617
Mount Union (Jackson County)	38564
Mount Union (Pickett County)	38549
Mount Vernon (Monroe County)	37358
Mount Vernon (Rutherford County)	37153
Mount Vernon (Sumner County)	37022
Mount View (Davidson County)	37211
Mount View (Grundy County)	37356
Mount View (Scott County)	37852
Mount Vinson	38379
Mount Zion (Cheatham County)	37015
Mount Zion (Monroe County)	37885
Mount Zion (Montgomery County)	37051
Mount Zion (Obion County)	38232
Mount Zion (Warren County)	37110
Mourberry	38583
Mowbray	37379
Mud Creek (McNairy County)	38310
Mud Creek (Warren County)	38581
Muddy Pond	38574
Mudsink	37064
Mulberry	37359
Mulberry Gap	37869
Mulberry Hill	37058
Mulloy	37048
Munford	38058
Murfreesboro	37129-33
For specific Murfreesboro Zip Codes call (615) 893-2201	
Murray-Lake Hills (Part of Chattanooga)	37416
Murray Store	37826
Myers (Part of Winchester)	37398
Nameless	38545
Nance	38001
Nance Ferry	37709
Nances Grove	37820
Nankipoo	38040
Napier	38462
Narrow Valley	37861
Nash	38544
Nashville	37201-49
For specific Nashville Zip Codes call (615) 885-1005	

COLLEGES & UNIVERSITIES

	ZIP
Belmont College	37212
David Lipscomb College	37204
Tennessee State University	37209
Vanderbilt University	37212

	ZIP
FINANCIAL INSTITUTIONS	
Dominion Bank of Middle Tennessee	37219
Fidelity Federal Bank, F.S.B.	37219
First American National Bank of Nashville	37237
Metropolitan Federal Savings & Loan Association, F.A.	37219
Security Federal Savings & Loan Association	37204
Nationsbank	37219
Third National Bank in Nashville	37219

	ZIP
HOSPITALS	
Baptist Hospital	37236
Centennial Medical Center	37203
Nashville Metropolitan Bordeaux Hospital	37218
St. Thomas Hospital	37205
Vanderbilt University Hospital and Clinic	37232
Veterans Affairs Medical Center	37203

	ZIP
HOTELS/MOTELS	
Doubletree Hotel	37219
Holiday Inn-Briley Parkway	37210
Holiday Inn Crowne Plaza	37219
Regal Maxwell House	37228
Marriott Nashville	37210
Sheraton Music City	37214
Loews Vanderbilt Plaza Hotel	37203

	ZIP
MILITARY INSTALLATIONS	
Tennessee Air National Guard, FB6421, Nashville International Airport	37217
United States Army Engineer District, Nashville	37202
United States Property and Fiscal Office for Tennessee	37204

	ZIP
Natco (Part of Columbia)	38401
National Cemetery (Part of Memphis)	38122
Natural Bridge	37843
Nauvoo	38024
Neapolis	38401
Neboville	38059
Needmore (Hamblen County)	37891
Needmore (Marshall County)	37091
Needmore (Maury County)	38474
Needmore (Montgomery County)	37079
Needmore (Wilson County)	37138
Neely	38391
Neely Crossroads	38551
Nelsontown (Part of Kingsport)	37660
Nemo	37887
Nenny	37891
Neptune	37015
Netherland	38501
Neubert	37920
Neva	37683
Newbern	38059
New Bethel	37331
New Canton	37642
New Castle	38075
Newcomb	37762
New Corinth	37861
New Deal	37048
New Dellrose	38453
New Due West (Part of Nashville)	37115
Newell Station	37865
New Era	38555
New Harmony (Bledsoe County)	37367
New Harmony (Macon County)	37074
New Haven (Lawrence County)	38464
New Haven (Scott County)	37841
New Herman	37160
New Hope (Cheatham County)	37080
New Hope (Hancock County)	37869
New Hope (Hardin County)	38310
New Hope (Hawkins County)	37857

	ZIP		ZIP		ZIP
New Hope (Houston County)	37175	Oak Dale (Overton County)	38573	Old Hickory Mall (Part of Jackson)	38301
New Hope (Humphreys County)	37101	Oakdale (White County)	38583	Old Kingsport (Part of Kingsport)	37660
New Hope (Marion County)	37380	Oakfield	38362	Old Laguardo	37122
New Hope (McNairy County)	38339	Oak Grove (Campbell County)	37769	Old Lawton	38375
New Hope (Roane County)	37854	Oak Grove (Carter County)	37643	Old Salem	37345
New Hope (Williamson County)	37062	Oak Grove (Claiborne County)	37752	Old Springville	38256
New Hope (Wilson County)	37087	Oak Grove (Clay County)	38575	Old Sweetwater	37874
New Hope (Jackson County)	38568	Oak Grove (Dickson County)	37055	Old Washington	37321
New Hope (Lincoln County)	37334	Oak Grove (Franklin County)	37324	Old Winesap	38555
New Johnsonville	37134	Oak Grove (Giles County)	38460	Old Zion	38583
New Line	37814	Oak Grove (Hardin County)	38372	Olivehill	38475
New Loyston	37705	Oak Grove (Henry County)	38222	Oliver Springs	37840
Newmansville	37616	Oak Grove (Jefferson County)	37725	Olivet	38372
New Market	37820	Oak Grove (Lewis County)	38462	One Hundred Oaks Regional Mall (Part of Nashville)	37204
New Markham	38079	Oak Grove (Madison County)	38301	Oneida	37841
New Middleton	38563	Oak Grove (Marion County)	37397	Only	37140
New Midway	37763	Oak Grove (Monroe County)	37354	Ooltewah	37363
Newport	37821	Oak Grove (mail Livingston) (Overton County)	38570	Opossum	38063
New Prospect	38464	Oak Grove (mail Hilham) (Overton County)	38568	Opossum Creek Pines	37379
New Providence (Loudon County)	37771	Oakgrove (Pickett County)	38573	Oral	37771
New Providence (Montgomery County)	37042	Oak Grove (Polk County)	37307	Orchard View	37840
New River	37755	Oak Grove (Sumner County)	37022	Orebank	37664
New Salem (Hamilton County)	37379	Oak Grove (Tipton County)	38019	Ore Spring	38225
New Salem (Jackson County)	38562	Oak Grove (Union County)	37866	Orlinda	37141
New Salem (Scott County)	37841	Oak Grove (Warren County)	37357	Orme	37380
New Tazewell	37825	Oak Grove (Washington County)	37615	Orysa	38063
Newton	38555	Oak Grove (Weakley County)	38237	Osage	38242
New Town (Marshall County)	37047	Oak Grove Heights	37921	Osemont Chapel	37190
New Town (Maury County)	37174	Oakhaven (Part of Memphis)	38116	Ostella	37091
Newtown (Polk County)	37317	Oak Hill (Carter County)	37658	Oswego	37762
New Union	37355	Oak Hill (Cocke County)	37843	Otes	37857
New Victory	37659	Oak Hill (Cumberland County)	38555	Otter Creek	38555
New Zion (Carroll County)	38344	Oak Hill (Davidson County)	37220	Ottway	37743
New Zion (Macon County)	37186	Oak Hill (Overton County)	38580	Overall	37130
Nickletown	37347	Oak Hill (Pickett County)	38549	Overlook	37804
Nicks Creek	37756	Oak Hill (Sullivan County)	37620	Ovilla	38464
Nine Mile	37367	Oak Hill (Washington County)	37659	Ovoca	37388
Ninth Model	37382	Oakhurst (Part of Maryville)	37801	Owens	37172
Niota	37826	Oakland (Fayette County)	38060	Owl City	38079
Nixon	38372	Oakland (Grainger County)	37861	Owlhollow	37398
Noah	37355	Oakland (Henry County)	38242	Owl Hoot	38080
Nolensville	37135	Oakland (Jefferson County)	37760	Ozone	37842
Nonaburg	37329	Oakland (Knox County)	37918	Pactolus	37663
Nonaville	37122	Oakland (Robertson County)	37172	Pailo	37327
Nonconnah (Part of Memphis)	38116	Oakland (Warren County)	37110	Paint Rock (Loudon County)	37846
Norene	37136	Oakland (Washington County)	37690	Paint Rock (Roane County)	37846
Norma	37756	Oaklawn	37166	Palestine (Henderson County)	38351
Normandy	37360	Oakleigh Estates	37620	Palestine (Robertson County)	37172
Norris	37828	Oakley	38541	Pall Mall	38577
North (Davidson County)	37208	Oaklyn	38555	Palmer	37365
North (Shelby County)	38107	Oak Park (Part of Tullahoma)	37388	Palmersville	38241
North Chattanooga (Part of Chattanooga)	37405	Oakplain	37015	Palmyra	37142
Northcott	37660	Oak Plains	37040	Pandora	37640
Northcutts Cove (Grundy County)	37110	Oak Ridge	37830-31	Paperville (Part of Bristol)	37620
Northcutt's Cove (Warren County)	37110	For specific Oak Ridge Zip Codes call (615) 483-3507		Paradise Acres	37122
Northeast (Part of Nashville)	37207	Oak Tree	37062	Paragon Mills (Part of Nashville)	37211
Northern Hills (Part of Chattanooga)	37343	Oak View	37886	Paris	38242
Northgate Shopping Center (Part of Memphis)	38107	Oakville (Part of Memphis)	38118	Parkburg	38366
North Glen Estates (Part of Chattanooga)	37343	Oakwood (Knox County)	37917	Park City (Knox County)	37914
North Hills (Part of Knoxville)	37917	Oakwood (Montgomery County)	37191	Park City (Lincoln County)	37334
North Johnson City (Part of Johnson City)	37601	Oakwood Estates	37064	Parker	38577
North Knoxville (Part of Knoxville)	37917	Obion	38240	Parker's Cross Roads	38388
Northpoint	37874	Ocana	37075	Parkey	37869
North Riverside	38462	Ocoee	37361	Park Grove	38464
Northside (Part of Jackson)	38301	O'Connors	38583	Park Settlement	37862
North Springs	38588	Odd Fellows Hall	38478	Park Shore	37343
Norwood (Anderson County)	37840	Odens Bend	37066	Parkshore Estates	37343
Norwood (Knox County)	37912	Officers Chapel	38501	Parksville	37307
Notchy Creek	37354	Offutt	37716	Parkview	37854
Nough	37727	Ogden	37321	Parkway Village (Part of Memphis)	38118
Nubia	37186	Okalona	38570	Parrottsville	37843
Nucarbon	38468	Okolona (Carter County)	37601	Parsons	38363
Number One (Part of Gallatin)	37066	Okolona (Hawkins County)	37642	Paschall	37064
Nunnelly	37137	Old Antioch	38562	Pasquo (Part of Nashville)	37221
Nutbush	38012	Old Chihowee	37865	Pate Hill	37818
Oak City	37865	Olde Mill	37343	Patterson	37153
Oakdale (Hawkins County)	37873	Oldfort	37362	Patterson Crossroads	37752
Oakdale (Macon County)	37186	Old Glory	37804	Patty	37325
Oakdale (Morgan County)	37829	Old Hickory (Part of Nashville)	37138	Paulette	37807
				Paw Paw Ridge	38030
				Payne Cove	37366
				Paynes Store	37022
				Peabody	37766
				Peak	37716
				Peakland	37322
				Peanut	37843
				Pea Ridge (DeKalb County)	37095
				Pea Ridge (Lawrence County)	38464
				Pearl City	37334
				Peavine	38555
				Pebble Hill	38357
				Peckerwood Point	38004

	ZIP		ZIP		ZIP
Rebel Acres (Part of Pulaski)	38478	Roberts	38582	Royer Estates (Part of Murfreesboro)	37130
Rebel Meadows (Part of Franklin)	37064	Robertson Fork	38472	Rucker	37130
Red Ash	37714	Robinson Crossroads	37921	Rudderville	37064
Red Bank	37415	Rockbridge	37022	Rudolph	38012
Red Boiling Springs	37150	Rock City (Smith County)	37030	Rugby	37733
Red Hill (Bradley County)	37323	Rock City (Sullivan County)	37664	Rugby Hills (Part of Memphis)	38127
Red Hill (Claiborne County)	37752	Rock Creek (Pickett County)	38556	Rural Hill (Davidson County)	37217
Red Hill (Coffee County)	37355	Rock Creek (Unicoi County)	37650	Rural Hill (Wilson County)	37071
Red Hill (Fentress County)	38556	Rockdale	38474	Rural Vale	37385
Red Hill (Lawrence County)	38464	Rockford	37853	Russel Fork	37766
Red Hill (Marion County)	37397	Rock Haven	37708	Russell Crossroad	37743
Red Hill (Pickett County)	38549	Rock Hill (Hancock County)	37765	Russell Hill	37145
Red Hill (Weakley County)	38225	Rock Hill (Henderson County)	38351	Russellville	37860
Red House	37709	Rock Hill (Sullivan County)	37694	Rusty (Part of Fairview)	37062
Red Row	38474	Rock House	37075	Rutherford	38369
Redwing Farms	37064	Rock Island	38581	Rutherford Estates	38401
Reeds Lake	38004	Rockland (Part of Hendersonville)	37075	Ruthton	37620
Reed Spring	37846	Rock Ledge Estates	37363	Ruthville	38237
Reeds Store	37046	Rock Springs (Dickson County)	37036	Rutledge	37861
Reedtown	37821	Rock Springs (Dyer County)	38024	Rutledge Falls	37355
Reel Cove	37397	Rock Springs (Henderson County)	38388	Rutledge Hill	37342
Reesetown	37391	Rock Springs (Rutherford County)	37167	Ryall Springs	37421
Rehoboth	38024			Sadie	37643
Reliance	37369	Rock Springs (Sullivan County)	37663	Sadlers	37010
Reubensville	37148	Rock Station	38581	Safford	38328
Reverie	72395	Rockvale	37153	Safley	37110
Revilo	38468	Rockville	37874	Sagewood Estates	38401
Rheatown	37641	Rockwood	37854	Sailors Rest	37050
Rialto	38019	Rockwood Hill	37743	St. Andrews	37372
Rice Bend	37657	Rocky Branch	37886	St. Bethlehem	37155
Riceville	37370	Rocky Creek	37031	St. Clair (Hawkins County)	37711
Rich	38472	Rocky Fork (Rutherford County)	37167	Saint Clair (Rhea County)	37381
Rich Acres (Part of Johnson City)	37601	Rocky Fork (Unicoi County)	37657	St. James	37743
Richard City	37380	Rocky Grove	37722	St. Joseph	38481
Richardson	38023	Rocky Hill (Part of Knoxville)	37919	St. Paul	38023
Richland (Davidson County)	37209	Rocky Mound	37186	Saint Peters	38012
Richland (Grainger County)	37709	Rocky Point (Hamblen County)	37860	Sainville	37355
Richmond	37144	Rocky Point (Putnam County)	38501	Sale Creek	37373
Richview Acres	37865			Salem (Cocke County)	37843
Richwood	38024	Rocky Ridge	38573	Salem (Lewis County)	37033
Rickman	38580	Rocky Spring (Monroe County)	37354	Salem (Montgomery County)	37040
Riddleton	37151	Rocky Spring (Sullivan County)	37686	Salem (Tipton County)	38004
Ridenour	37705	Rocky Valley	37820	Salem (Weakley County)	38255
Ridge	37879	Roddy	37381	Saltillo	38370
Ridgedale (Knox County)	37931	Roe Junction	37814	Samburg	38254
Ridgedale (Sullivan County)	37620	Roellen	38024	Sampson	37367
Ridgefield (Part of Kingsport)	37660	Rogana	37022	Sanders	37387
Ridge Lake North (Part of Chattanooga)	37343	Rogers Creek	37303	Sand Hill	38229
Ridgely	38080	Rogers Spring	38052	Sandlick	37825
Ridgeside	37411	Rogersville	37857	Sand Ridge	38351
Ridgetop (Lewis County)	38461	Rolling Acres (Jefferson County)	37877	Sand Springs	38574
Ridgetop (Robertson County)	37152	Rolling Acres (Williamson County)	37062	Sand Switch	37375
Ridgeview	37814			Sandy	38589
Ridgeville (Part of Lynchburg)	37352	Rolling Hills (Hickman County)	37025	Sandy Hook	38474
Ridgewood	37714	Rolling Hills (Marshall County)	37091	Sandy Lane	37385
Ridley	38401	Rolling Hills (Unicoi County)	37650	Sandy Point	38320
Riggs	37046	Rolling Hills (Warren County)	37110	Sandy Ridge	37725
Riggs Crossroads	37046	Rolling Meadows (Part of Franklin)	37064	Sandy Spring	37032
Right	38361	Rome	37030	Sanford	37370
Rim Rock Mesa	38583	Romeo	37711	Sanford Hill (Part of Henderson)	38340
Rinda	38230	Rose Creek	38375	Sango	37040
Rinnie	38555	Rosedale	37710	Santa Fe	38482
Riovista (Part of Elizabethton)	37643	Rose Hill (Madison County)	38301	Saratoga Springs	37367
Ripley	38063	Rose Hill (Union County)	37807	Sardis	38371
Ritchie	37879	Rosemark	38053	Saulsbury	38067
Ritta	37918	Rose Valley	37079	Saundersville (Part of Hendersonville)	37075
Riva Lake Camp	37398	Roseville	37183	Savannah	38372
Riverdale	37914	Roslin	38556	Sawdust	38401
Rivergate Mall (Part of Nashville)	37072	Ross Camp Ground	37642	Sawyers Mill	38320
River Hill	37650	Rosser	38344	Scandlyn	37840
River Oaks	37341	Rossview	37040	Scarboro (Part of Oak Ridge)	37830
River Rest	37064	Rossville	38066	Scattersville	37148
Riversburg	38478	Rotherwood	37642	Scenic Point Estates	37777
Riverside (Claiborne County)	37879	Round Pond	37040	Scoot Mill	37810
Riverside (Coffee County)	37355	Round Rock	37714	Scottsboro (Part of Nashville)	37218
Riverside (Davidson County)	37218	Round Top	37012	Scotts Hill	38374
Riverside (Decatur County)	38363	Routon	38231	Screamer	38474
Riverside (Shelby County)	38113	Rover	37060	Seeber Flats	37710
Riverside (Sullivan County)	37618	Rowland	38581	Selmer	38375
Riverton	38556	Royal	37160	Sentinel Heights (Part of Dayton)	37363
Riverview (Claiborne County)	37752	Royal Blue	37847	Sequatchie	37374
Riverview (Sullivan County)	37660	Royal Oak (Part of Manchester)	37355	Sequoia Grove (Part of Cleveland)	37312
Riverview (Unicoi County)	37650			Sequoia Hills	37743
Riverview Estates	37033	Royal Oaks (Williamson County)	37068	Sequoyah Estates (Part of Madisonville)	37354
Rives	38253	Royal Oaks (Wilson County)	37122	Sequoyah Hills	37343
Roan Mountain	37687			Sequoyah Village (Part of Madisonville)	37354
Roaring Springs	37616			Serles	38008
Roarks Cove	37324			Settlers Point	37064
Robbins (Pickett County)	38549			Seven Islands	37920
Robbins (Scott County)	37852			Seven Oaks	37922

	ZIP
Valley Brook (Wilson County)	37122
Valley Creek	37715
Valley Forge	37643
Valley Hills (Part of Bristol)	37620
Valley View Heights	37716
Van Buren	38042
Vandever	38555
Van Dyke	38242
Van Hill	37857
Vanleer	37181
Vannatta	37160
Vanntown	37335
Vardy	37869
Vasper	37714
Vaughn's Gap (Part of Nashville)	37205
Vaughns Grove	38382
Verdun	37841
Vernon	37137
Vernon Heights	37664
Verona	37091
Verona Hills	37122
Versailles	37153
Vesta	37087
Vestal (Part of Knoxville)	37920
Veterans Administration (Part of Murfreesboro)	37129
Veto	38477
Viar	38024
Victoria	37397
Victory	37766
Vildo	38075
Villa Gardens (Part of Knoxville)	37918
Village Green (Part of Farragut)	37922
Vine	37087
Vinegar Hill	37620
Vine Ridge	38554
Vinson	37110
Viola	37394
Virtue (Part of Farragut)	37922
Vise	38329
Volunteer Heights (Part of Crossville)	38555
Vonore	37885
Vose (Part of Alcoa)	37701
Waco	38472
Walden	37377
Walden Creek	37862
Waldens Ridge (Bledsoe County)	37381
Waldens Ridge (Rhea County)	37321
Wales	38478
Walkertown (Greene County)	37616
Walkertown (Hardin County)	38372
Walland	37886
Walling	38587
Walnut Acres	37064
Walnut Grove (Gibson County)	38233
Walnut Grove (Hardin County)	38372
Walnut Grove (Lauderdale County)	38063
Walnut Grove (Meigs County)	37322
Walnut Grove (Sevier County)	37862
Walnut Grove (Sullivan County)	37618
Walnut Grove (Sumner County)	37048
Walnut Grove (Tipton County)	38015
Walnut Grove (Trousdale County)	37074
Walnut Hill (Crockett County)	38006
Walnut Hill (Roane County)	37748
Walnut Hill (Sullivan County)	37620
Walnut Log	38261
Walnut Shade	37150
Walter Crossroad	37743
Walterhill	37129
Wa-Ni Village	37861
Ware Branch	37341
Warren	38068
Warrens Bluff	38351
Warrensburg	37818
Wartburg	37887
Wartrace	37183
Warwicktown	37807
Washburn	37888
Washington	37321
Washington College	37681
Washington Heights (Part of Chattanooga)	37406

	ZIP
Watauga	37694
Watauga Flats	37601
Watauga Point (Part of Elizabethton)	37643
Waterstown	37886
Watertown	37184
Water Valley	38487
Waterville	37323
Watkins (DeKalb County)	37166
Watkins (Tipton County)	38019
Watt Heights (Part of Calhoun)	37309
Watts Bar Dam	37395
Watts Bar Estates	37381
Waverly	37185
Wayland Springs	38463
Waynesboro	38485
Wayside	37110
Weakly Creek	38464
Wear Valley	37862
Weaver	37620
Webber City	38456
Webbs Chapel	37166
Webbtown	37083
Webster	37854
Wedgewood Hills	37922
Welch Crossroad	37866
Welchland	38585
Welch's Camp	37714
Well Spring	37870
Wells Station (Part of Memphis)	38122
Wellsville	37801
Wellwood	38006
Wesleyanna	37303
West (Davidson County)	37209
West (Gibson County)	38358
West Cyruston	37334
Westel	37854
West Emory	37922
Western Heights	37857
Western Institute (Part of Bolivar)	38074
Westfield Estates (Part of Franklin)	37064
West Forest (Part of Knoxville)	37919
West Fork	38543
West Greene (Part of Greeneville)	37743
West Harpeth	37064
Westhaven Village (Part of Knoxville)	37921
West Hills (Jefferson County)	37820
West Hills (Knox County)	37919
West Hills (Monroe County)	37354
West Hills (Roane County)	37748
West Junction (Part of Memphis)	38101
West Knoxville (Part of Knoxville)	37919
West Maryville (Part of Maryville)	37801
West Meade (Part of Nashville)	37205
West Miller Cove	37886
Westmoreland	37186
Westmoreland Heights (Part of Knoxville)	37919
West Nashville (Part of Nashville)	37209
West Oneida (Part of Oneida)	37841
Westover	38301
Westpoint	38486
Westport	38387
West Robbins	37852
West Shiloh	38379
Westside Heights (Part of Tullahoma)	37388
West Springbrook (Part of Alcoa)	37701
West Town Mall (Part of Knoxville)	37919
West Union	38225
West View (Knox County)	37921
Westview (Weakley County)	38237
West View Acres	37087
West View Park	37660
Westwood	38401
Westwood Gardens (Part of Jackson)	38301
Westwood Hills	37801
Westwood Homes	37355
Wetmore	37325
Wheel	37160
Wheelerton	38453
Whispering Hills	38261
Whispering Pine	37601
Whitaker	37160

	ZIP
White (Shelby County)	38117
	38119-20
For specific White Zip Codes call (615) 672-3281	
White (Warren County)	37110
White Bluff (Dickson County)	37187
White Bluff (Trousdale County)	37074
White City	37387
White Fern	38313
Whitehaven (Part of Memphis)	38116
Whitehaven Plaza (Part of Memphis)	38116
Whitehead Hills	37687
White Hill (Robertson County)	37072
White Hill (Van Buren County)	38581
White Horn	37711
White House	37188
White Oak (Campbell County)	37766
White Oak (Morgan County)	37829
Whiteoak Crossing	38425
White Oak Flat	37036
White Oaks (Part of Manchester)	37355
White Pine	37890
White Rock	37687
Whitesand	37743
Whitesburg	37891
White Schoolhouse Corners	37840
Whites Creek (Davidson County)	37189
White's Creek (Rhea County)	37381
Whiteside	37396
Whiteville	38075
Whitleyville	38588
Whitlock	38242
Whitthorne	38348
Whittle Springs (Part of Knoxville)	37917
Whitway	38358
Whitwell	37397
Widow Town	37862
Wilder	38589
Wilder Chapel	37324
Wildersville	38388
Wild Plum	38555
Wildwood	37801
Wildwood Lake	37311
Wilhite	38501
Wilkinsville	38004
Willard	37074
Willette	37150
Williams (Lauderdale County)	38063
Williams (Macon County)	37083
Williamsburg	37331
Williams Creek	37841
Williams Crossroads	38544
Williamsport	38487
Williams Springs	37888
Willis	37765
Willis Spring	37362
Williston	38076
Willow Grove (Bedford County)	37360
Willow Grove (Clay County)	38541
Willow Grove (Haywood County)	38012
Wilmore Estates	37890
Wilson Station	37329
Wilsonville	37821
Winchester	37398
Winchester Springs	37398
Windle	38570
Windletown	38554
Windrock	37840
Windrow	37153
Windy City	38343
Windy Hill (Part of Bristol)	37620
Winesap	38555
Winfield	37892
Wingo	38258
Winklers	37150
Winner	37643
Winona	37756
Winton Town	37355
Wirmingham	38573
Withamtown	37022
Witt	37814
Wixtown	37186
Wolf Creek (Cocke County)	37727
Wolf Creek (DeKalb County)	38582
Wolf Creek (Rhea County)	37381
Wolf Hill	37022

	ZIP		ZIP		ZIP
Wolf River	38577	Woodlawn (Washington		Yankeetown	38583
Womack (Sumner County)	37066	County)	37659	Yell	37091
Womack (Warren County)	37110	Woodlawn (Wayne County)	38450	Yellow Store	37873
Woodbine (Part of		Woodmont (Part of		Yett Addition	37862
Nashville)	37211	Nashville)	37215	Yettland (Part of Sevierville)	37862
Woodbury	37190	Woodrow	37617	Yorkely	38472
Woodcliff	38574	Woods Ferry	37066	Yorktown (Part of Franklin)	37064
Wooddale	37914	Woodstock	38053	Yorkville	38389
Wooded Acres (Part of		Woods Valley	37051	Young Bend	37166
Knoxville)	37921	Woodville	38063	Youngs	38301
Woodland (Davidson		Woody	38555	Youngville	37172
County)	37206	Wooldridge	37762	Y Section	37601
Woodland (Haywood		Wrigley	37098	Yukon	38488
County)	38012	Wyatts Chapel	37058	Yuma	38390
Woodland Acres	37919	Wyatt Village	37708	Yum Yum	38068
Woodland Mills	38271	Wyly	38320	Zack	38320
Woodlawn (Cumberland		Wynn	37766	Zion Grove	37862
County)	38555	Wynnburg	38077	Zion Hill (Part of	
Woodlawn (Montgomery		Yager	37110	Surgoinsville)	37857
County)	37191				

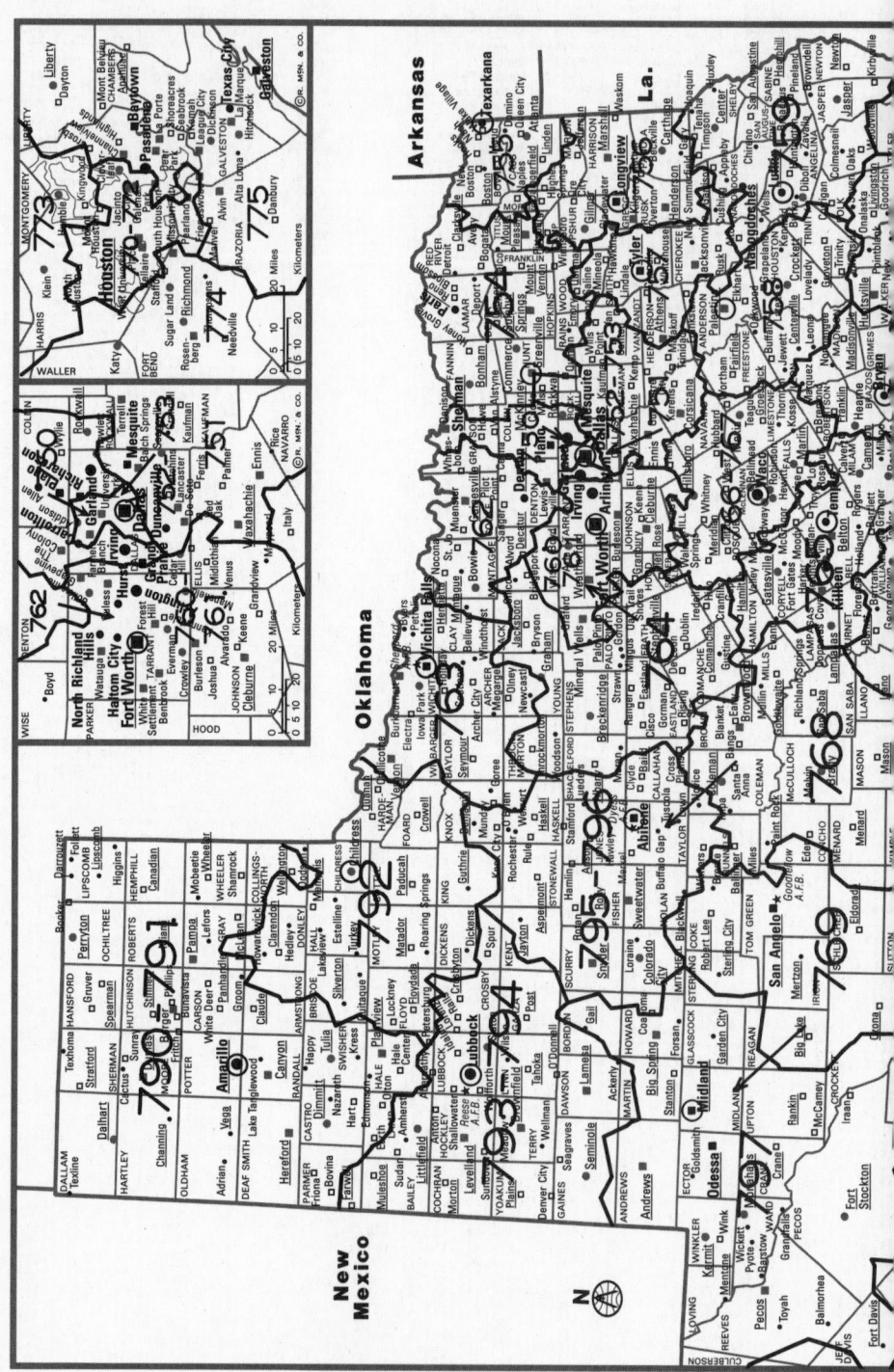

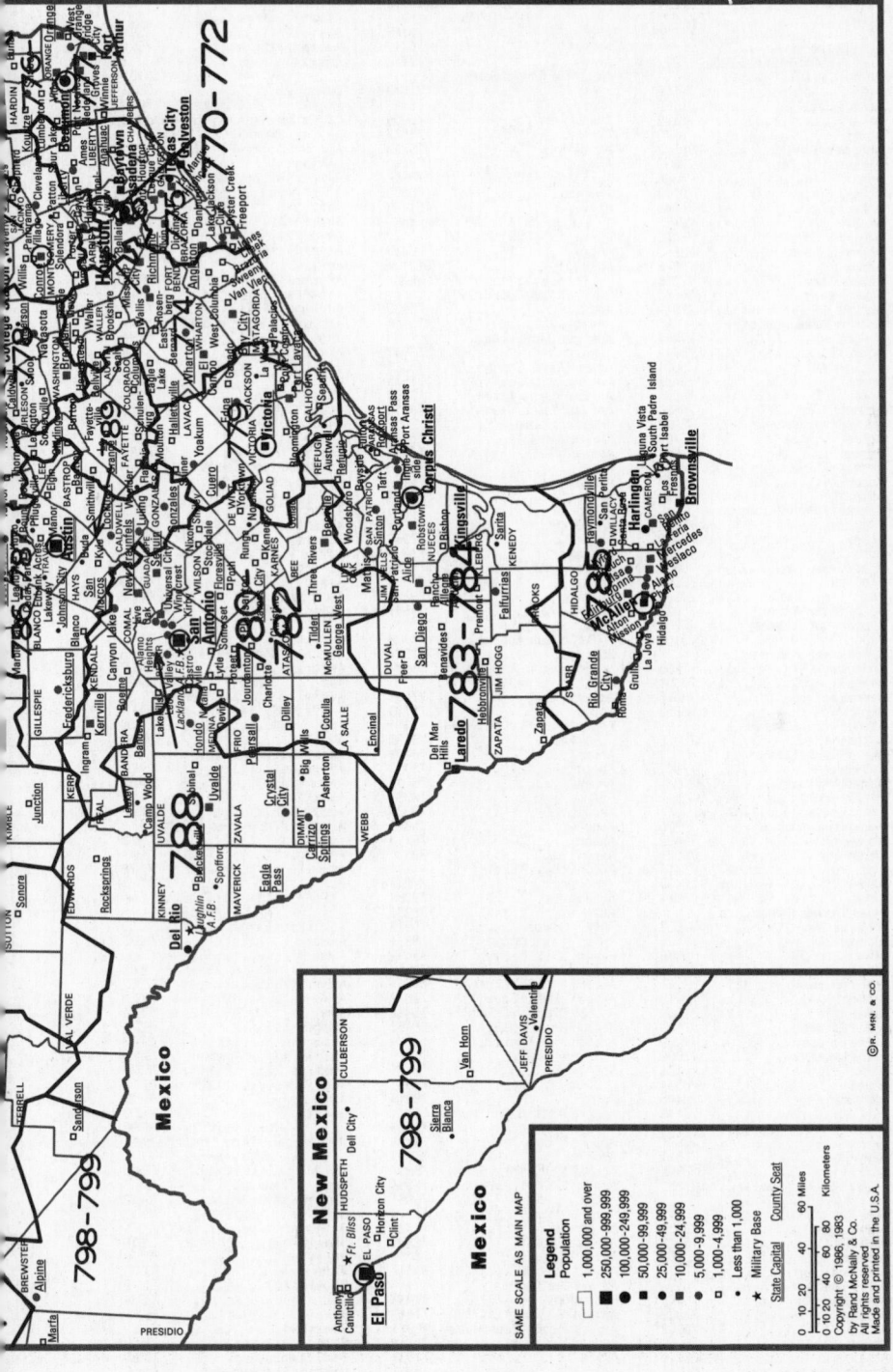

	ZIP		ZIP		ZIP
A (Part of San Antonio)	78207	Almont	75559	Argyle	76226
Abbott	76621	Aloe	77901	Argyle Plaza (Part of	
Aberfoyle	75496	Alpine	79830-31	Houston)	77035
Abernathy	79311	For specific Alpine Zip Codes call		Ariola	77625
Abilene	79601-08	(915) 837-2524		Arizona	77367
	79697-99	Alsa	75169	Arlam	75946
For specific Abilene Zip Codes		Alsdorf	75119	Arledge Ridge	75418
call (915) 673-6485		Altair	77412	Arlington	76003-07
Abilene Christian College		Alta Loma (Part of Santa			76010-19
(Part of Abilene)	79699	Fe)	77510		76094
Ables Springs	75160	Alto	75925		76096
Abner	75142	Altaga	75069	For specific Arlington Zip Codes	
Abram	78572	Alton	78572	call (817) 274-3385	
Abram-Perezville	78572	Alto Springs	76653	Arlington Downs (Part of	
Acala	79839	Alum	78160	Arlington)	76010
Ace	77326	Alum Creek	78957	Arlington Heights (Part of	
Ackerly	79713	Alvarado	76009	Fort Worth)	76147
Acton	76048	Alvin	77511-12	Armstrong	78338
Acuff	79401	For specific Alvin Zip Codes call		Arneckeville	77954
Acworth	75426	(713) 331-4747		Arnett (Coryell County)	76528
Adams Gardens	78550	Alvord	76225	Arnett (Hockley County)	79336
Adams Hill	78245	Amarillo	79101-59	Arp	75750
Adams Oaks	77365	For specific Amarillo Zip Codes		Arrowhead Lake	77378
Adamsville	76550	call (806) 379-2140		Arrowhead Shores	76048
Addicks	77079	Ambia	75460	Arrowhead Village	78130
Addicks Barker (Part of		Ambrose	75414	Arroyo (Part of Harlingen)	78550
Houston)	77218	American Technological		Arroyo City	78586
Addielou	75412	University	76540	Arsenal (Part of San	
Addison	75001	Ames (Coryell County)	76528	Antonio)	78283
Addran	75482	Ames (Liberty County)	77575	Art	76820
Adell	76086	Amherst (Lamar County)	75460	Artesian Forest	77304
Ad Hall	76520	Amherst (Lamb County)	79312	Artesia Wells	78001
Adina	78947	Amigoland Mall (Part of		Arthur City	75411
Adkins	78101	Brownsville)	78520	Arvana	79331
Admiral	79504	Ammansville	78945	Asa	76707
Adrian	79001	Amy	75432	Ash (Henderson County)	75751
Adsul	75956	Anadarko	75667	Ash (Houston County)	75835
Afton	79220	Anahuac	77514	Ashby	77465
Aggieland (Part of College		Anchor	77515	Asherton	78827
Station)	77844	Anchorage	78065	Ashland	75640
Agnes	76082	Ander	77963	Ashmore	79342
Agua Dulce	78330	Anderson	77830	Ashtola	79226
Agua Nueva	78361	Anderson Mill	78750	Ashworth	75142
Aguilares	78369	Andice	78628	Asia	75939
Aiken (Floyd County)	79221	Andrews	79714	Aspermont	79502
Aiken (Shelby County)	75935	Andrewsville	75683	Astrodome (Part of	
Airlawn (Part of Dallas)	75235	Angelo State University		Houston)	77025
Airport City	78108	(Part of San Angelo)	76909	Astro Hills	78130
Airport Mail Facility (Part of		Angleton	77515-16	Atascocita (Part of Humble)	77346
Houston)	77205	For specific Angleton Zip Codes		Atascosa	78002
Airville	76501	call (409) 849-7500		Ater	76528
Alamo	78516	Angleton South	77515	Athens	75751
Alamo Alto	79853	Angus	75110	Atlanta	75551
Alamo Beach (Bandera		Angus Valley (Part of		Atlas	75460
County)	78063	Austin)	78758	Atoy	75785
Alamo Beach (Calhoun		Anna	75409	Atreco (Part of Port Arthur)	77640
County)	77979	Annarose	78022	Attoyac	75961
Alamo Heights	78208-09	Annetta	76008	Atwell	76437
For specific Alamo Heights Zip		Annetta North	76087	Aubrey	76227
Codes call (512) 826-0461		Annetta South	76086	Auburn	76050
Alamo Ranchettos	79735	Anneville	76023	Audobon Park (Part of	
Alanreed	79002	Annona	75550	Houston)	77338
Alazan	75961	Anson	79501	Augusta	75844
Alba	75410	Anson Jones (Part of		Aurora	76078
Albany	76430	Houston)	77009	Austin	78701-69
Albert	78671	Antelope	76389	For specific Austin Zip Codes call	
Albert Thomas (Part of		Anthony	88021	(512) 929-1255	
Nassau Bay)	77058	Anthony Harbor	75929	Austin Lake Estates	78759
Albion	75426	Antioch (Cass County)	75551	Austonio	75835
Alco	75949	Antioch (Delta County)	75432	Austwell	77950
Alderbranch	75801	Antioch (Henderson County)	75758	Authon	76086
Aldine (census designated		Antioch (Houston County)	75851	Autumn Woods	77362
place)	77018	Antioch (Jasper County)	77612	Avalon	76623
Aldine	77039	Antioch (Madison County)	75852	Avery	75554
Aldine Estates	77039	Antioch (Rusk County)	75652	Avinger	75630
Aldine Gardens	77039	Antioch (mail Timpson		Avoca	79503
Aldine Meadows	77039	(Shelby County)	75975	Avonbell (Part of Amarillo)	79106
Aledo	76008	Antioch (mail Center)		Avondale	76179
Aleman	76531	(Shelby County)	75935	Avon Park	76708
Alexander	76446	Anton	79313	Axtell	76624
Aley	75143	Apache Addition (Part of		Azle	76020
Alfred	78332	Seguin)	78155		76098
Algerita	76877	Apache Shores	78734	For specific Azle Zip Codes call	
Algoa	77511	Apolonia	77830	(817) 444-4612	
Alice	78332-33	Apparel Mart (Part of Dallas)	75207	Bacliff	77518
For specific Alice Zip Codes call		Appelt Hill	77964	Bagby	75446
(512) 664-5541		Appleby	75961	Bagwell	75412
Alief (Part of Houston)	77411	Apple Springs	75926	Bailey	75413
Allamore	79855	Aquilla	76622	Baileyboro	79371
Allen	75002	Aransas Pass	78336	Bailey's Prairie	77515
Allenfarm	77868	Arbala	75482	Baileyville	76570
Allenhurst	77414	Arbor	75847	Bainer	79339
Allens Chapel	75492	Arbor Oaks (Part of		Bainville	78119
Allens Point	75446	Houston)	77088	Baird	79504
Alleyton	78935	Arcadia (Galveston County)	77517	Baker	76086
Allison	79003	Arcadia (Shelby County)	75935	Bakersfield	79752
Allmon	79250	Archer City	76351	Balch	79358
Alma	75119	Arcola	77583	Balch Springs	75180
Almeda (Part of Houston)	77045	Arden	76901	Balcones (Part of Austin)	78759
Almeda Mall (Part of		Argenta	78368	Balcones Heights	78201
Houston)	77034	Argo	75558	Balcones Village	78750

ZIP		ZIP		ZIP

Bald Hill 75901
Bald Prairie 77856
Baldwin 75661
Ballinger 76821
Balmorhea 79718
Balsora 76426
Bammel 77040
Bammel Timbers 77040
Banana Junction 76708
Bancroft (Part of Pinehurst) 77630
Bandera 78003
Bandera Falls 78063
Bangs 76823
Banquete 78339
Barbarosa 78130
Barclay 76656
Bardin Road (Part of
  Arlington) 76018
  76096
  For specific Bardin Road Zip
  Codes call (817) 472-8290
Bardwell 75101
Barker 77413
Barksdale 78828
Barnes 75960
Barnhart 76930
Barnum 75939
Barrett 77532
Barrington Oaks (Part of
  Austin) 78759
Barry 75102
Barstow 79719
Bartlett 76511
Bartley Woods 75492
Barton Creek Square (Part
  of Austin) 78746
Bartons Chapel 76458
Bartonville 76226
Barwise 79235
Bascom 75705
Basin 79834
Basin Springs 76264
Bassett 75574
Bassett Center (Part of El
  Paso) 79925
Bastrop 78602
Bastrop Bayou 77515
Bastrop Beach 77515
Bateman 78662
Batesville (Red River
  County) 75426
Batesville (Zavala County) 78829
Batson 77519
Battle 76664
Baxter 75751
Bay City 77404
  77414
  For specific Bay City Zip Codes
  call (409) 245-2051
Bay Harbor 77554
Baylor University (Part of
  Waco) 76706
Bay Oaks 77571
Bayou Bend (Part of
  Houston) 77088
Bayou Chantilly (Part of
  Dickinson) 77539
Bayou Vista 77563
Bay Plaza (Part of Baytown) 77520
Bayport (Part of Houston) 77058
Bayside 78340
Bayside Terrace 77571
Baytown 77520-22
  For specific Baytown Zip Codes
  call (713) 420-2508
Bayview (Cameron County) 78566
Bay View (Galveston
  County) 77518
Bayview Estates 76945
Bayway (Part of Baytown) 77520
Baywood (Part of Seabrook) 77586
Bazette 75144
Beach 77301
Beach City 77520
Beacon Hill (Part of San
  Antonio) 78201
Beadle 77414
Bear Grass 75846
Beasley 77417
Beattie 76442
Beaukiss 78621
Beaumont 77701-26
  For specific Beaumont Zip Codes
  call (409) 842-7200
Beaumont Place 77028
Beauxart Gardens 77705
Beaver Dam 75559
Bebe 78603
Becker 75142
Beckville 75631
Becton 79343

Bedford 76021-22
  76095
  For specific Bedford Zip Codes
  call (214) 647-2996
Bedias 77831
Bee Cave 78746
Beech Grove 75951
Beechnut (Part of Houston) 77072
Beechwood 75948
Bee House 76525
Beeville 78102-04
  For specific Beeville Zip Codes
  call (512) 358-3727
Belcherville 76255
Belfalls 76579
Belgrade 75928
Belk 75411
Bellaire 77401-02
  For specific Bellaire Zip Codes call
  (713) 668-0521
Bellaire Addition 75704
Bellaire West (Part of
  Houston) 77072
Bell Branch 76651
Bellevue 76228
Bellmead 76705
Bells 75414
Bellview 75410
Bellville 77418
Belmar (Part of Amarillo) 79106
Belmena 76520
Belmont 78604
Belott 75835
Belton 76513
Ben Arnold 76517
Benavides 78341
Ben Bolt 78342
Benbrook 76126
Benchley 77801
Bend 76824
Bending Bough 77373
Ben Franklin 75415
Ben Hur 76664
Benjamin 79505
Bennett 76066
Bennett Estates 77302
Benoit 76882
Bent Tree (Part of Dallas) 75287
Bentwood (Part of San
  Angelo) 76904
Bentwood Acres 75076
Ben Wheeler 75754
Berclair 78107
Berea (Houston County) ... 75835
Berea (Marion County) 75657
Bergheim 78004
Bergstrom Air Force Base 78743
Berlin 77833
Bernardo 78933
Berry Street (Part of Fort
  Worth) 76109
Berryville 75763
Bertram 78605
Bessmay 77612
Best 76932
Bethany 71007
Bethel (Anderson County) 75861
Bethel (Ellis County) 75165
Bethel (Henderson County) 75751
Bethlehem (Bowie County) 75559
Bethlehem (Collin County) 75442
Bethlehem (Upshur County) 75644
Beto Unit 75861
Beto 2 Unit 75801
Bettie 75644
Beulah 75941
Beverly 76711
Beverly Hills (Part of Dallas) 75211
Bevil Oaks 77706
Bevilport 75951
Beyersville 78615
Biardstown 75462
Big Bend National Park ... 79834
Bigfoot 78005
Biggs Army Air Base 79908
Big Lake 76932
Big Oaks 75630
Big Sandy 75755
Big Spring 79720-21
  For specific Big Spring Zip Codes
  call (915) 263-7391
Big Square 79027
Big Thiket 77369
Big Town Shopping Center
  (Part of Mesquite) 75149
Big Valley Ranchettes 76522
Big Wells 78830
Billington 76624
Billpark (Part of Houston) 77012
Biloxi 75928
Birch 77879

Birdville (Part of Haltom
  City) 76117
Birnam Woods 77379
Birome 76625
Birthright 75482
Biry 78016
Bisbee 76063
Bishop 78343
Bivins 75555
Black 79035
Blackfoot 75853
Black Hills 75110
Black Jack (Cherokee
  County) 75789
Black Jack (Robertson
  County) 77859
Blackland 75189
Blackoak 75431
Blackwell 79506
Blakeney 75412
Blanchard 77351
Blanco 78606
Blanconia 78102
Blandlake 75972
Blanket 76432
Bleakwood 75956
Bledsoe 79314
Bleiblerville 78931
Blessing 77419
Blevins 76524
Blewett 78801
Blodgett 75686
Bloomburg 75556
Bloomdale 75069
Bloomfield 76258
Blooming Grove 76626
Bloomington 77951
Blossom 75416
Blue 78947
Bluegrove 76352
Blue Haven Estates 75169
Blue Lake Estates 78654
Blue Mound 76131
Blue Ridge (Collin County) 75424
Blue Ridge (Falls County) 76661
Blueroan 77434
Bluetown 78592
Blue Water Key 75758
Bluff Dale 76433
Bluff Springs (Parker
  County) 76020
Bluff Springs (Travis
  County) 78744
Bluffton 78607
Blum 76627
Blumenthal 78624
Bluntzer 78380
Board 76442
Bob Harris (Part of
  Pasadena) 77506
Bob Lyons (Part of
  Galveston) 77554
Bobo 75974
Bobville 77333
Boca Chica (Part of
  Brownsville) 78520
Boerne 78006
Bogata 75417
Bois D'Arc 75801
Boling 77420
Boling-Iago 77420
Bolivar 76266
Bolton 75686
Bomarton 76380
Bon Ami 75956
Bonanza (Hill County) 76692
Bonanza (Hopkins County) 75420
Bonham 75418
Bonita 76255
Bonnerville 75840
Bonney 77583
Bonnie View 78393
Bono 76031
Bon Wier 75928
Booker 79005
Boonsville 76426
Booth 77469
Boquillas 79834
Borden 78962
Borderland 79932
Bordersville (Part of
  Houston) 77338
Borger 79007-08
  For specific Borger Zip Codes call
  (806) 273-3761
Bosqueville 76708
Boston (Part of New
  Boston) 75570
Boswell 77340
Bovina 79009
Bowie 76230

	ZIP		ZIP		ZIP
Bowser	76872	Brushy	77845	Campbell	75422
Box Church	76642	Brushy Bend Park	78681	Campbellton	78008
Boxelder	75550	Brushy Creek (Anderson		Camp Dallas	75034
Boxwood	75683	County)	75801	Camp Maxey	75473
Boyce	75165	Brushy Creek (Williamson		Campo Alto	78516
Boyd (Fannin County)	75418	County)	78681	Camp Ruby	77351
Boyd (Wise County)	76023	Brushy Creek North	78681	Camp San Saba	76825
Boys Ranch	79010	Bryan	77801-06	Camp Springs	79526
Boz	75165	For specific Bryan Zip Codes call		Camp Stanley	78206
Brachfield	75681	(409) 779-1988		Camp Strake	77301
Bracken	78266	Bryans Mill	75568	Camp Swift	78602
Brackettville	78832	Bryson	76427	Campti	75935
Brad	76475	Buchanan Dam	78609	Camp Valley	78140
Bradfield	75566	Buchanan Lake Village	78672	Camp Verde	78010
Bradford	75853	Buchel	77954	Camp Wood	78833
Bradshaw	79567	Buck Creek	75949	Cana	75169
Brady (McCulloch County)	76825	Buckeye	77414	Canada Verde	78114
Brady (Shelby County)	75935	Buckholts	76518	Canadian	79014
Branch	75407	Buckhorn (Austin County)	77418	Canal City	77617
Branchville	76520	Buckhorn (Newton County)	75928	Candelaria	79843
Brandon	76628	Buckingham	75080	Candlelight Oaks (Part of	
Bransford (Part of		Buckner	76462	Houston)	77088
Colleyville)	76034	Buda	78610	Caney	77414
Brashear	75420	Buena Vista (Bexar County)	78112	Caney City	75148
Brazoria	77422			Caney Creek Estates	77357
Brazos	76472	For specific Buena Vista Zip		Cannon	75495
Brazos Mall (Part of Lake		Codes call (512) 650-1630		Canton	75103
Jackson)	77566	Buena Vista (Burnet		Canutillo	79835
Brazos Point	76652	County)	78611	Canyon (Lubbock County)	79408
Breckenridge	76424	Buena Vista (Shelby		Canyon (Randall County)	79015
Bremond	76629	County)	75975	Canyon City	78130
Brenham	77833-34	Buffalo	75831	Canyon Creek (Part of	
For specific Brenham Zip Codes		Buffalo Gap (Taylor County)	79508	Richardson)	75080
call (409) 836-2652		Buffalo Gap (Travis County)	78734	Canyon Creek Estates	78130
Brentwood Manor	77901	Buffalo Springs	76228	Canyon Lake	78130
Breslau	77964	Buford	79512	Canyon Lake Acres	78130
Briar	76020	Bugbee Heights	79078	Canyon Lake Estates	78130
Briarcliff	78669	Bug Tussle	75449	Canyon Lake Forest	78130
Briaroaks	76028	Bula	79320	Canyon Lake Hills	78130
Briary	76570	Bullard	75757	Canyon Lake Island	78130
Brice	79226	Bullock	76470	Canyon Lake Mobile Home	
Bridge Chapel	75455	Bulverde	78163	Estates	78130
Bridge City	77611	Buna	77612	Canyon Lake Shores	78130
Bridgeport	76426	Bunavista (Part of Borger)	79007	Canyon Lake Village	78130
Brierwood Bay	75763	Buncomb	75633	Canyon Lake Village West	78130
Briggs	78608	Bunger	76450	Canyon Springs Resort	78130
Bright Star (Rains County)	75410	Bunker Hill	75486	Canyon Valley	79356
Bright Star (Van Zandt		Bunker Hill Village	77024	Canyon View Acres	78163
County)	75169	Bunyan	76446	Capital Plaza (Part of	
Briscoe	79011	Burkburnett	76354	Austin)	78723
Bristol	75119	Burke	75941	Capitol (Part of Austin)	78701
Britton	76063	Burkett	76828	Caplen	77617
Broaddus	75929	Burkeville	75932	Capps Corner	76265
Broadway (Crosby County)	79243	Burleigh	77418	Cap Rock	79357
Broadway (Lamar County)	75460	Burleson	76028	Caprock Shopping Center	
Broadway Junction	75460		76097	(Part of Lubbock)	79404
Broadway Square (Part of		For specific Burleson Zip Codes		Caps	79606
Tyler)	75701	call (817) 295-8158		Caradan	76844
Brock	76086	Burlington	76519	Carancahua	77465
Brock Junction	76086	Burnell	78119	Carbon	76435
Brogado	79718	Burnet	78611	Carbondale	75567
Bronco	79355	Burns (Bowie County)	75561	Cardinal (Part of Athens)	75751
Bronson	75930	Burns (Cooke County)	76258	Carey	79222
Bronte	76933	Burr	77488	Carey Estates (Part of	
Brookeland	75931	Burris Crossing	79853	Seabrook)	77586
Brookesmith	76827	Burrow	75189	Carlisle	75862
Brook Forest	77357	Burton	77835	Carlos	77830
Brook Glen Addition (Part of		Busby	79543	Carl Range (Part of Irving)	75062
La Porte)	77571	Bushland	79012	Carlsbad	76934
Brookhollow (Part of Dallas)	75247	Bushwhacker Peninsula	75147	Carl's Corner	76645
Brookshier	76933	Bustamante	78361	Carlton	76436
Brookshire	77423	Busterville	79358	Carmine	78932
Brookside Village	77581	Butler (Bastrop County)	78621	Carmona	75939
Brookston	75421	Butler (Freestone County)	75855	Caro	75961
Broom City	75839	Byers	76357	Carolina Cove	77367
Broome	76951	Bynum	76631	Carpenter	78101
Brown College	77880	Byrd	75119	Carpenters Bluff	75020
Browndell	75931	Byrds	76801	Carricitos	78586
Brownfield	79316	Cabot Kingsmill	79065	Carrizo Springs	78834
Browning	75705	Cactus	79013	Carroll	75771
Brownsboro (Caldwell		Caddo	76429	Carroll Springs	75853
County)	78644	Caddo Mills	75135	Carrollton	75006-08
Brownsboro (Henderson		Cadiz	78102		75010-11
County)	75756	Cain City	78624	For specific Carrollton Zip Codes	
Brownsville	78520-26	Calaveras	78114	call (214) 418-7858	
For specific Brownsville Zip Codes		Caldwell	77836	Carrolton Park Two (Part of	
call (512) 546-2411		Caledonia	75946	Dallas)	75006
Brownwood	76801-04	Calf Creek	76825	Carson	75488
For specific Brownwood Zip		Call	75933	Carta Valley	78840
Codes call (915) 646-0656		Calliham	78007	Carterville	75563
Brownwood (Part of		Callisburg	76240	Carthage	75633
Orange)	77630	Call Junction	75933	Cartwright (Kaufman	
Broyles	75801	Calvary	75773	County)	75142
Bruceville (Part of Bruceville-		Calvert	77837	Cartwright (Wood County)	75494
Eddy)	76630	Camden	75934	Casa Piedra	79843
Bruceville-Eddy	76630	Camelot	78239	Casa View (Part of Dallas)	75228
Brumley	75686	Cameron	76520	Cash	75402
Brundage	78834	Cameron Park	78521	Cason	75636
Bruni	78344	Camey	75034	Cass	75556
Brunswick	75925	Camilla	77331	Cassie	78611
Brushie Prairie	76641	Camp Air	76856	Castell	76831

	ZIP		ZIP		ZIP
Castle Hills	78213	Chaparral Hills	78840	Clemville	77414
Castlewood	77039	Chaparral Park	78652	Cleveland	77327-28
Castolon	79834	Chapman	75652	For specific Cleveland Zip Codes	
Castroville	78009	Chapman Ranch	78347	call (713) 592-3951	
Catarina	78836	Chappel	76877	Clever Creek	75935
Cat Spring	78933	Chappell Hill	77426	Cliffside	79106
Causeway Beach	75143	Charco	77963	Clifton (Bosque County)	76634
Cave Creek	78624	Charleston	75432	Clifton (Van Zandt County)	75169
Cave Springs	75670	Charlie	76306	Climax	75407
Caviness	75460	Charlotte	78011	Cline	78801
Cawthon	77868	Chase Field Naval Air		Clint	79836
Cayote	76689	Station	78103	Clinton (DeWitt County)	77954
Cayuga	75832	Chat	76645	Clinton (Hunt County)	75135
Cedar Branch (Henderson		Chateau Woods	77301	Clodine	77469
County)	75147	Chatfield	75105	Close City	79356
Cedar Branch (Houston		Cheapside	77954	Cloverleaf	77015
County)	75844	Cheek	77705	Club Lake Estates	75708
Cedar Creek (Anderson		Cherokee	76832	Clute	77531
County)	75839	Cherry Mound	75020	Clyde	79510
Cedar Creek (Bastrop		Cherry Spring	78624	Coady	77520
County)	78612	Chester	75936	Coahoma	79511
Cedar Elm (Part of San		Chesterville	77435	Coal Mine (Part of Lytle)	78052
Antonio)	78249	Chico	76431	Cobb Creek	75852
Cedar Grove (Cass County)	75560	Chicota	75425	Cobb Switch	75160
Cedar Grove (Coryell		Chief	75142	Cochran	77418
County)	76522	Chihuahua	78572	Cockrell Hill	75211
Cedar Grove (El Paso		Childress	79201	Coffee City	75763
County)	79915	Chillicothe	79225	Coffeeville	75683
Cedar Grove (Harris		Chilton	76632	Coffield Unit	75861
County)	77532	Chimney Corners (Part of		Coit	76653
Cedar Hill (Dallas County)	75104	Austin)	78731	Coke	75431
Cedar Hill (Floyd County)	79241	China	77613	Coldhill	75708
Cedar Hills	78621	China Grove (Bexar County)	78223	Coldspring	77331
Cedar Lake	77414	China Grove (Scurry		Coleman	76834
Cedar Lane	77415	County)	79526	Coleman Cove	75929
Cedar Mills Resort	76245	China Spring	76633	Colfax	75103
Cedar Park	78613	Chinati	79843	College Country Estates	75020
Cedar Point	77520	Chireno	75937	College Hill	75559
Cedar Shores Estates	76671	Chita	75862	College Mound	75160
Cedar Springs (Falls		Choate	78119	Collegeport	77428
County)	76570	Chocolate Bayou	77511	College Station	77840-45
Cedar Springs (Upshur		Choice	75935	For specific College Station Zip	
County)	75683	Chriesman	77838	Codes call (409) 693-4152	
Cedar Valley	78736	Christine	78012	Colleyville	76034
Cedarview	75104	Christoval	76935	Collin Creek Mall (Part of	
Cee Vee	79223	C H Rouse Estates	77365	Plano)	75075
Cego	76524	Church Hill (Cherokee		Collinsville	76233
Cele	78653	County)	75766	Colmesneil	75938
Celeste	75423	Church Hill (Rusk County)	75652	Cologne	77901
Celina	75009	Churchill Bridge	77422	Colonial (Part of Waco)	76707
Center (Limestone County)	76642	Cibolo	78108	Colorado City	79512
Center (Shelby County)	75935	Cielo Vista (Part of El Paso)	79925	Colquitt	75160
Center City	76844	Cielo Vista Mall (Part of El		Colton	78744
Center Grove	75455	Paso)	79925	Columbus	78934
Center Line	77879	Cienegas Terrace	78840	Comal	78130
Center Point (Camp		Circle	79064	Comanche	76442
County)	75686	Circle Back	79371	Comanche Cove	76048
Center Point (Ellis County)	76651	Circle D-KC Estates	78602	Comanche Harbor	76048
Center Point (Kerr County)	78010	Circleville (Travis County)	78736	Comanche Village	76544
Center Point (Panola		Circleville (Williamson		Combes	78535
County)	75691	County)	76574	Combine	75159
Center Point (mail		Cisco	76437	Comfort	78013
Weatherford) (Parker		Cistern	78941	Commerce	75428
County)	76087	Citrus City	78572	Como	75431
Center Point (mail Azle)		Citrus Grove	77465	Comstock	78837
(Parker County)	76020	Civic Center (Part of		Comyn	76444
Center Point (Titus County)	75455	Houston)	77208	Concan	78838
Center Point (Upshur		Clairemont	79549	Concepcion	78349
County)	75755	Clairette	76457	Concho	76866
Centerview	75833	Clardy	75468	Concord (Cherokee County)	75789
Centerville (Leon County)	75833	Clarendon	79226	Concord (Leon County)	77850
Centerville (Trinity County)	75845	Clareville	78102	Concord (Morris County)	75571
Central (Angelina County)	75969	Clark	77327	Concord (Rusk County)	75681
Central (Tarrant County)	76102	Clarks	77979	Concrete	77954
Central Gardens	77627	Clarksville	75426	Cone	79321
Central Heights (Jefferson		Clarksville City	75647	Conlen	79022
County)	77627	Clarkwood (Part of Corpus		Connor	77864
Central Heights		Christi)	78406	Conroe	77301-05
(Nacogdoches County)	75961	Claude	79019		77384-85
Central High	75925	Clauene	79336	For specific Conroe Zip Codes	
Centralia	75834	Clawson	75901	call (409) 756-8908	
Central Mall (Bowie County)	75501	Clay	77839	Constitution Village (Part of	
Central Mall (Jefferson		Claydesta Station (Part of		Sherman)	75495
County)	77640	Midland)	79710	Content	79519
Central Park (Bexar County)	78216	Clayton (Jefferson County)	77627	Converse	78109
Central Park (Harris County)	77011	Clayton (Panola County)	75637	Conway	79068
Central Unit	77478	Claytonville (Fisher County)	79556	Cooks Point	77836
Cestohowa	78113	Claytonville (Swisher		Cookville	75558
Chaffee Village	76544	County)	79052	Cool	76086
Chalk	79248	Clear Creek	76544	Cool Crest	78245
Chalk Bluff	76705	Clear Lake City (Part of		Coolidge	76635
Chalk Mountain	76401	Houston)	77062	Cooper	75432
Chalybeate	75494	Clear Lake Shores	77565	Cooper Creek	76201
Chambersville	75069	Clear Spring	78130	Copano Village	78382
Chambliss	75409	Clearview	78602	Copeland	75701
Champion Forest	77303	Cleburne	76031-33	Copeville	75121
Chances Store	77839	For specific Cleburne Zip Codes		Coppell	75019
Chandler	75758	call (817) 645-3991		Copperas Cove	76522
Channelview	77530	Clegg	78022	Copper Canyon	76226
Channelwood	77530	Clemens Unit	77422	Corbet	75110
Channing	79018	Clemons	77423	Cordele	77957

	ZIP
Corine	75766
Corinth (Denton County)	76205
Corinth (Eastland County)	76437
Corinth (Jones County)	79553
Corinth (Leon County)	75831
Corinth (Van Zandt County)	75140
Corley	75567
Cornersville	75494
Cornett	75568
Cornudas	79847
Coronado	79912-13
For specific Coronado Zip Codes call (915) 584-3362	
Corpus Christi	78401-82
For specific Corpus Christi Zip Codes call (512) 886-2200	
Corral City	76226
Corrigan	75939
Corsicana	75110
Corsicana Junction (Part of Corsicana)	75110
Coryell	76689
Cost	78614
Cotton Center (Fannin County)	75418
Cotton Center (Hale County)	79021
Cottondale	76073
Cotton Flat	79701
Cotton Gin	75860
Cotton Mill Spur (Part of Denison)	75020
Cottonwood (Brazos County)	77803
Cottonwood (Callahan County)	79504
Cottonwood (Falls County)	76655
Cottonwood (Kaufman County)	75158
Cottonwood (Lamar County)	75486
Cottonwood (Madison County)	77864
Cottonwood (McLennan County)	76691
Cottonwood Shores	78654
Cotulla	78014
Coughran	78064
Council Creek Village	78611
Country Campus	77340
Country Club Lake Estates	76904
Country Club Terrace (Potter County)	79106
Country Club Terrace (Victoria County)	77901
Country Colony	77372
Country Place Acres	77355
Countryside Plaza (Part of San Antonio)	78216
Country Squire Estates	77630
County Line (Camp County)	75686
County Line (Hale County)	79363
Coupland	78615
Courtney	77868
Cove (Chambers County)	77520
Cove (Orange County)	77630
Cove Spring	75766
Covington	76636
Covington Woods (Part of Sugar Land)	77478
Cox	75644
Coyanosa	79730
Coy City	78118
Cozy Corner	78945
Crabb	77469
Crabbs Prairie	77340
Craft	75766
Crafton	76431
Craig	75652
Crandall	75114
Crane	79731
Cranfills Gap	76637
Crawford	76638
Creagleville	75140
Crecy	75845
Creechville	75119
Creedmoor	78747
Creekwood Acres	77375
Creekwood Addition	77372
Crenneland	77650
Crescent	77488
Crescent Heights	75751
Cresson	76035
Cresthaven (Part of San Antonio)	78213
Crestwood (Ector County)	79762
Crestwood (Marion County)	75630
Crestwood Farms	77356
Crews	79567
Crimcrest (Part of Henderson)	75652

	ZIP
Cripple Creek Farms (mail Magnolia)	77355
Cripple Creek Farms (mail Pinehurst)	77362
Cripple Creek Farms West	77362
Cripple Creek North	77355
Crisp	75119
Crockett	75835
Crosby	77532
Crosbyton	79322
Cross (Grimes County)	77861
Cross (McMullen County)	78026
Cross Cut	76801
Crossing (Part of De Soto)	75115
Cross Mountain	78255-56
For specific Cross Mountain Zip Codes call (512) 641-7828	
Cross Plains	76443
Crossroads (Bexar County)	78201
Crossroads (Camp County)	75686
Cross Roads (Cass County)	75656
Crossroads (Midway) (Cass County)	77962
Cross Roads (Delta County)	75432
Cross Roads (Denton County)	76227
Crossroads (Harrison County)	75670
Cross Roads (Henderson County)	75148
Cross Roads (Milam County)	76520
Cross Roads (Rusk County)	75662
Cross Roads (Van Zandt County)	75140
Croton	79232
Crow	75765
Crowell	79227
Crowley	76036
Cruz Calle	78349
Cryer Creek	76626
Crystal Beach	77650
Crystal City	78839
Crystal Creek Forest	77301
Crystal Lake	75801
Crystal Lakes Estates	77351
Cuadrilla	79836
Cuero	77954
Cullen Mall (Part of Corpus Christi)	78412
Culleoka	75407
Cumby	75433
Cundiff	76458
Cuney	75759
Cunningham	75434
Curtis	75951
Curvitas	78595
Cushing	75760
Cusseta	75566
Cut	75835
Cut and Shoot	77302
Cuthand	75417
Cuthbert	79512
Cyclone	76519
Cypress (Franklin County)	75494
Cypress (Harris County)	77429
	77433
For specific Cypress Zip Codes call (713) 373-0279	
Cypress Bend	77040
Cypress Cove	78130
Cypress Creek	78028
Cypress Creek Estates	77429
Cypress Mill	78654
Dabney	78801
Da Costa	77901
Dacus	77356
Daingerfield	75638
Daisetta	77533
Dalby Springs	75559
Dale	78616
Dalhart	79022
Dallardsville	77332
Dallas	75201-99
	75301-98
For specific Dallas Zip Codes call (214) 647-2996	

COLLEGES & UNIVERSITIES

	ZIP
Dallas Baptist University	75211
Southern Methodist University	75275
University of Texas Southwestern Medical Center	75235

FINANCIAL INSTITUTIONS

	ZIP
Bank One	75201
Comerica Bank	75201

	ZIP
Cullen/Frost Bank of Dallas, N.A.	75201
First City, Texas-Dallas	75201
First Interstate Bank of Texas, N.A.	75202
Guaranty Savings Bank, F.S.B.	75225
Hibernia National Bank in Dallas	75201
Inwood National Bank	75209
North Dallas Bank & Trust Company	75230
NorthPark National Bank	75225
Team Bank	75235
Texas Commerce Bank, N.A.	75201
United National Bank	75201
Bank United of Texas, F.S.B.	75248

HOSPITALS

	ZIP
Baylor University Medical Center	75246
Dallas County Hospital District-Parkland Memorial Hospital	75235
Humana Hospital-Medical City Dallas	75230
Methodist Medical Center	75208
Presbyterian Hospital of Dallas	75231
RHD Memorial Medical Center	75234
St. Paul Medical Center	75235
Veterans Affairs Medical Center	75216

HOTELS/MOTELS

	ZIP
The Adolphus Hotel	75202
Dallas Marriott Quorom	75240
Doubletree Hotel at Campbell Center	75206
Fairmont Hotel	75201
Holiday Inn Brookhollow	75247
Hyatt Regency Dallas at Reunion	75207
Lexington Hotel Suites	75237
Loews Anatole Hotel	75207
Plaza of the Americas Hotel	75201
Preston Suites Hotel	75240
Sheraton Mockingbird	75243
Sheraton Park Central Hotel & Towers	75251
Stouffer Dallas Hotel	75207
The Summit Hotel	75234

MILITARY INSTALLATIONS

	ZIP
Naval Air Station, Dallas	75211
Texas Air National Guard, FB6431, Hensley Field	75211
United States Army Engineer Division, Southwestern	75242
Dallas-Fort Worth Airport (Part of Coppell)	75261
Dalrock	75088
Dalton	75568
Dalworthington Gardens	76010
Dalys	75844
Dam B	75979
Damon	77430
Danbury	77534
Danciger	77431
Danevang	77432
Daniel Unit	79549
Danville (Collin County)	75069
Danville (Gregg County)	75662
Daphne	75455
Darco	75670
Darrouzett	79024
Daugherty	75440
Davenport	75412
Davilla	76523
Davis Prairie	76687
Davisville (Angelina County)	75901
Davisville (Leon County)	75833
Dawn	79025
Dawson	76639
Dayton	77535
Dayton Lakes	77535
Deadwood	75633
Dean (Clay County)	76303
Dean (Hockley County)	79363
Deanville	77852
De Berry	75639
Decatur	76234
Decker (Nolan County)	79506
Decker (Travis County)	78653
Decker Prairie	77355
De Cordova Bend Estates	76049

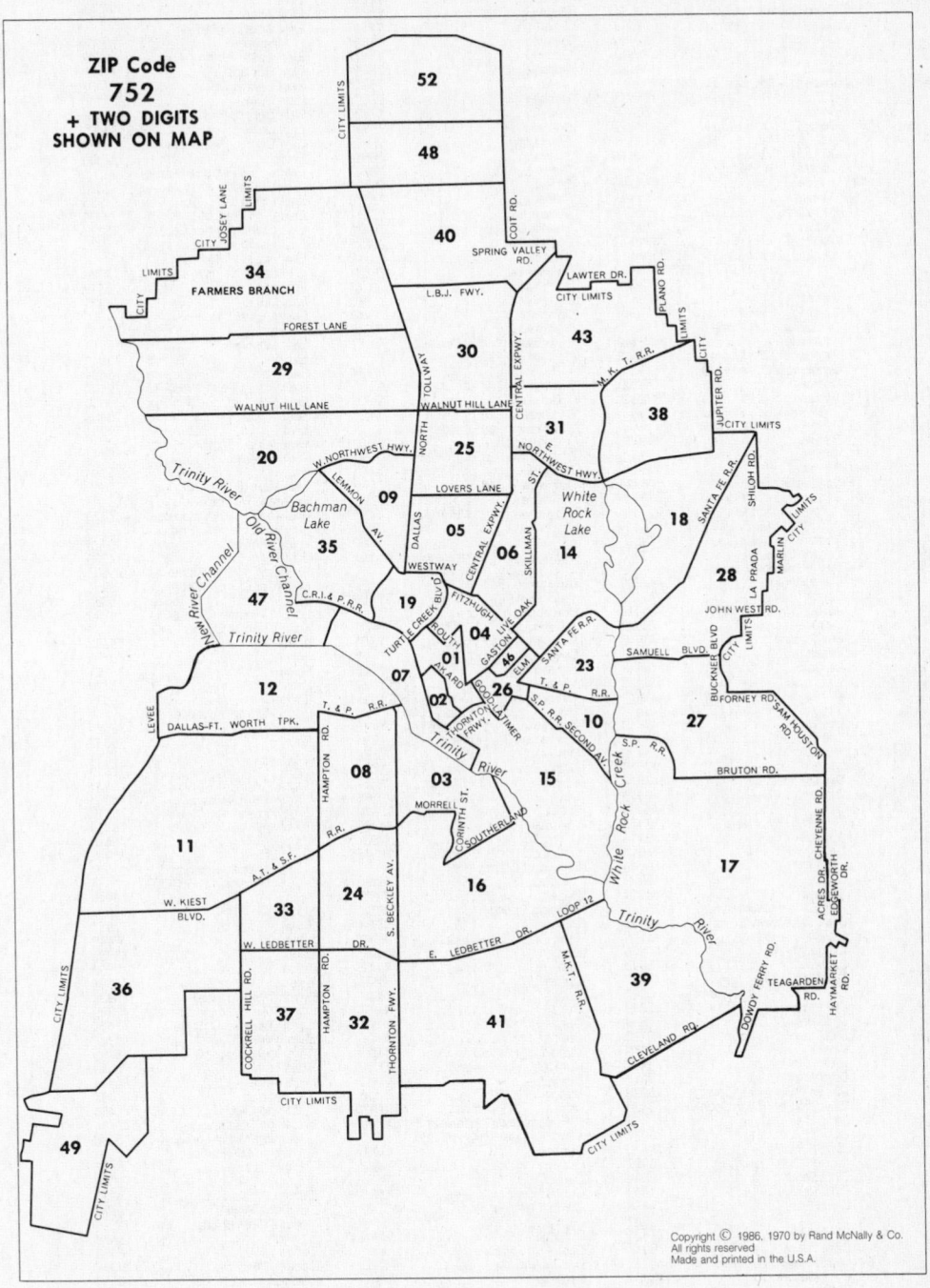

ZIP Code
752
+ TWO DIGITS
SHOWN ON MAP

52

48

40

34
FARMERS BRANCH

30

43

29

38

20

31

25

09

Bachman
Lake

05

35

18

47

19

04

28

12

07

46

01

23

02

26

10

27

03

15

11

08

17

24

16

33

37

32

41

39

36

49

	ZIP
Deep Water Point Estates	75121
Deer Creek	76365
Deer Haven	78654
Deer Park	77536
Deerwood East	77445
De Kalb	75559
Delba	75452
Delbert L. Atkinson (Part of Pasadena)	77505
De Leon	76444
Delhi	78953
Delia	76635
Dell City	79837
Del Mar Hills (Part of Laredo)	78041
Delmita	78536
Del Monte	77627
Delray	75633
Del Rio	78840-42

For specific Del Rio Zip Codes call (512) 775-3571

	ZIP
Delrose	75644
Del Valle	78617
Demi-John Island	77541
Democrat (Comanche County)	76442
Democrat (Mills County)	76442
De Moss (Part of Houston)	77074
Denhawken	78160
Denison	75020-21

For specific Denison Zip Codes call (903) 465-1464

	ZIP
Denning	75972
Dennis	76439
Denny	76653
Denson Springs	75844
Denton (Denton County)	76201-07

For specific Denton Zip Codes call (817) 387-8555

	ZIP
Denton (Callahan County)	79510
Denver City	79323
Denver Harbor (Part of Houston)	77020
Deport	75435
Derby	78017
Dermott	79549
Desdemona	76445
Desert	75424
De Soto	75115
	75123

For specific De Soto Zip Codes call (214) 223-6500

	ZIP
Dessau	78753
Detmold	76577
Detroit	75436
Devers	77538
Devils Pocket	77612
Devine	78016
Dew	75860
Dewalt	77478
Dewees	78114
Deweyville	77614
Dewville	78140
Dexter	76240
D'Hanis	78850
Dial (Fannin County)	75446
Dial (Hutchinson County)	79007
Dialville	75785
Diamondhead	77356
Diana	75640
Diboll	75941
Dicey	76086
Dickens	79229
Dickinson	77539
Dido	76179
Dies	75979
Dike	75437
Dilley	78017
Dilworth (Gonzales County)	78629
Dilworth (Red River County)	75426
Dime Box	77853
Dimmitt	79027
Dimple	75426
Dinero	78022
Ding Dong	76542
Dinsmore	77488
Direct	75486
Dirgin	75691
Divide	75420
Divot	78017
Dixie (Grayson County)	76273
Dixie (Jasper County)	75951
Dixon	75402
Doans	76384
Dobbin	77333
Dobrowolski	78026
Dodd	79347
Dodd City	75438
Dodge	77334
Dodson	79230
Dogwood	75979

	ZIP
Dogwood Acres (Part of Houston)	77022
Dogwood City	75762
Dolen	77327
Dominion	78257
Domino	75572
Donall Estates	78611
Donie	75838
Donna	78537
Don Tol	77420
Doole	76836
Dorchester	75459
Doss	78618
Dot	76524
Dothan	76437
Dotson	75669
Double Bayou	77514
Double Diamond Estates	79036
Double Oak	76226
Doucette	75942
Dougherty	79231
Douglass	75943
Douglassville	75560
Downing	76442
Downsville	76706
Downtown (Part of Amarillo)	79105
Downtown (Part of Beaumont)	77704
Downtown (Part of Brownsville)	78522
Downtown (Part of Bryan)	77801
Downtown (Part of Corpus Christi)	78401
Downtown (Part of Dallas)	75201
Downtown (Part of El Paso)	79901
Downtown (Part of Freeport)	77541
Downtown (Part of Irving)	75015
	75017
	75060

For specific Downtown Zip Codes call (214) 254-4197

	ZIP
Downtown (Part of Longview)	75606
Downtown (Part of Lubbock)	79401
Downtown (Part of McAllen)	78501
Downtown (Part of San Antonio)	78205
	78291-99

For specific Downtown Zip Codes call (512) 227-3399

	ZIP
Downtown (Part of Tyler)	75710
Downtown (Part of Waco)	76701
Doyle	76642
Dozier	79079
Drasco	79567
Draw	79373
Dreka	75973
Dresden	75102
Dreyer	77984
Driftwood (Hays County)	78619
Driftwood (Henderson County)	75143
Driners	75937
Dripping Springs	78620
Driscoll	78351
Drop	76247
Dryden	78851
Dubina	78956
Dublin	76446
Dudley	79601
Duffau	76457
Dugas Addition	77611
Dugger	78155
Dumas	79029
Dumont	79232
Dunbar	75440
Duncanville	75116
	75137-38

For specific Duncanville Zip Codes call (214) 298-3603

	ZIP
Dundee	76366
Dunlap	79248
Dunlay	78861
Dunn	79516
Dunnan (Part of Houston)	77022
Duplex	75447
Durango	76656
Duster	76444
Dye Mound	76265
Dyersdale	77016
Eagle Lake	77434
Eagle Mountain	76135
Eagle Mountain Acres	76020
Eagle Pass	78852-53

For specific Eagle Pass Zip Codes call (512) 773-3210

	ZIP
Earles Camp	79521
Earles Chapel	75764
Early	76801

	ZIP
Earlywine	77833
Earth	79031
East Afton	79220
East Amarillo (Part of Amarillo)	79104
East Austin (Part of Austin)	78702
East Bernard	77435
East Caney	75482
East Center	75140
East Columbia	77486
East Delta	75450
East Donna (Part of Donna)	78537
Easterly	77856
Eastex Oaks Village (Part of Houston)	77338
Eastgate	77535
East Glen (Part of El Paso)	79936
East Grand (Part of Dallas)	75223
East Hamilton	75973
East Houston (Part of Houston)	77028
Eastland	76448
East Liberty	75935
East Mayfield (Part of Hemphill)	75948
East Mountain	75644
Easton	75641
East Point	75494
East Ridge (Part of Amarillo)	79107
East Side	75639
East Tawakoni	75453
East Tempe	77351
East Texas (Part of Commerce)	75428
Eastvale	75056
East View (Part of Kilgore)	75662
Eastview Terrace	78101
Eastwood (Part of Houston)	77023
Eastwood Heights (Part of El Paso)	79925
Eaton	77856
Ebenezer (Camp County)	75686
Ebenezer (Jasper County)	75951
Ebony	76864
Echo (Coleman County)	76834
Echo (Orange County)	77630
Echo Hills	75763
Eckert	78675
Ecleto	78111
Ector	75439
Edcouch	78538
Eddy (Part of Bruceville-Eddy)	76524
Eden	76837
Edgar	77954
Edge	77803
Edgecliff	76134
Edgewater Estates	78368
Edgewood	75117
Edgeworth	76569
Edhube	75418
Edinburg	78539-40

For specific Edinburg Zip Codes call (512) 383-3866

	ZIP
Edith	76945
Edmonson	79032
Edna	77957
Edna Hill	76446
Edom	75756
Edroy	78352
Egan	76031
Egypt (Leon County)	75833
Egypt (Montgomery County)	77355
Egypt (Wharton County)	77436
Elam (Part of Dallas)	75217
Elam Springs	75755
Elbert	76359
El Calmino	75948
El Campo	77437
El Campo Club	77465
El Campo South	77437
El Centro (Part of Laredo)	78040
El Centro Mall (Part of Pharr)	78577
El Cenzio	78043
Eldorado	76936
Eldorado Center	76639
Eldridge (Part of Sugar Land)	77478
Electra	76360
Electric City	79007
Elevation	76556
El Gato	78516
Elgin	78621
Eliasville	76438
El Indio	78860
El Jardin (Part of Brownsville)	78520
El Jardin Del Mar (Part of Pasadena)	77586
Elk	76624

	ZIP		ZIP		ZIP
Elkhart	75839	Ethel	76233	Files Valley	76055
El Lago	77586	Etoile	75944	Fincastle	75763
Ellinger	78938	Etter	79029	Fink	75076
Ellington Air Force Base		Eubank Acres	78753	Finney (Hale County)	79072
(Part of Houston)	77209	Eula	79510	Finney (King County)	79248
Elliott (Robertson County)	77859	Eulalie	75975	First Colony	77479
Elliott (Wilbarger County)	76364	Euless	76039-40	Fischer	78623
Ellis (Part of Levelland)	79338	For specific Euless Zip Codes call		Fisk	76834
Ellis Unit	77340	(817) 283-6636		Fitze	75946
Elmaton	77440	Eulogy	76652	Fitzhugh	78703
Elmdale	79601	Eureka	75110	Five Points (El Paso	
Elmendorf	78112	Eustace	75124	County)	79903
Elm Flat	75144	Evadale	77615		79923
Elm Grove (Cherokee		Evant	76525	For specific Five Points Zip Codes	
County)	75785	Evergreen (Grimes County)	77861	call (915) 566-9371	
Elm Grove (Fayette County)	78959	Evergreen (San Jacinto		Five Points (Ellis County)	75165
Elm Grove (San Saba		County)	77327	Flagg	79027
County)	76872	Evergreen Park	77662	Flamingo Bay (Part of	
Elm Grove (Wharton		Everitt	77327	Seabrook)	77586
County)	77434	Everman	76140	Flanagan	75691
Elm Mott	76640	Ewell	75644	Flat	76526
Elmo	75118	Exchange Park (Part of		Flat Fork	75974
Elmont	75495	Dallas)	75245	Flatonia	78941
Elm Ridge (Grayson		Eylau	75501	Flat Prairie	77835
County)	75020	Ezzell	77964	Flats	75472
Elm Ridge (Milam County)	76520	Fabens	79838	Flatwood	75754
Elmtown	75801	Fairbanks (Part of Houston)	77040	Fleetwood Oaks	77079
Elmwood (Anderson		Fairchilds	77469	Fletcher	77656
County)	75801	Fairfield	75840	Flint	75762
Elmwood (Guadalupe		Fairgreen	77039	Flint Creek	76450
County)	78155	Fairland	78654	Flo	75831
Eloise	76680	Fairlie	75428	Flomot	79234
El Oso	78119	Fairmount	75948	Flora	75437
El Paso (El Paso County)	79821	Fairoaks	75838	Florence	76527
	79901-99	Fair Oaks Ranch	78006	Florence Hill (Part of Grand	
For specific El Paso Zip Codes		Fair Park (Part of Dallas)	75210	Prairie)	75052
call (915) 775-7542		Fair Play	75631	Floresville	78114
El Paso (Fisher County)	79543	Fairview (Bailey County)	79371	Florey	79714
El Pinon Estates	75929	Fairview (Bosque County)	76689	Florine (Part of San Antonio)	78209
El Rancho	79766	Fairview (Brazos County)	77803	Flour Bluff (Part of Corpus	
El Rancho Estates	76008	Fairview (Cass County)	75563	Christi)	78418
El Refugio	78582	Fairview (Collin County)	75002	Flower Hill	78934
Elroy	78617	Fairview (Gaines County)	79360	Flower Mound	75028
Elsa	78543	Fairview (Harris County)	77006	Floy	78941
El Sauz	78582	Fairview (Howard County)	79720	Floyd	75401
El Toro	77957	Fairview (Rusk County)	75784	Floydada	79235
Elwood (Fannin County)	75447	Fairview (Wilson County)	78114	Fluvanna	79517
Elwood (Madison County)	75852	Fairview (Wise County)	76078	Flynn	77855
Ely	75439	Fairy	76457	Fodice	75851
Elysian Fields	75642	Faker	75686	Follett	79034
Emberson	75486	Falcon	78564	Folley	79255
Emblem	75482	Falcon Heights	78545	Fondren (Part of Webster)	77598
Emerald Valley	78250	Falcon Mesa	78076	Fords Corner	75972
Emhouse	75110	Falcon Village	78545	Fordtran	77995
Emmett	76641	Falfurrias	78355	Forest	75925
Emory	75440	Fallon	76667	Forestburg	76239
Encantada	78586	Falls City	78113	Forest Chapel	75411
Encantada-Ranchito El		Fambrough	76424	Forest Glade	76667
Calaboz	78520	Familiner	79346	Forest Grove (Collin	
Enchanted Oaks (Harris		Fannett	77705	County)	75069
County)	77373	Fannin	77960	Forest Grove (Henderson	
Enchanted Oaks		Fargo	76384	County)	75758
(Henderson County)	75147	Farmer	76460	Forest Heights	77630
Enchanted River Estates	78003	Farmers Branch	75234	Forest Hill (Lamar County)	75446
Encinal	78019	Farmers Valley	76384	Forest Hill (Potter County)	79107
Encino	78353	Farmersville	75442	Forest Hill (Tarrant County)	76119
Energy	76452	Farmington	75058	Forest Hill (Wood County)	75783
Engle	78956	Farnsworth	79033	Forest Hill Estates	76528
English	75426	Farr Addition	79756	Forest Hills (Part of Tyler)	75702
Enloe	75441	Farrar	75838	Forest North Estates	78729
Ennis	75119-20	Farrsville	75977	Forest Spring	77351
For specific Ennis Zip Codes call		Farwell	79325	Forney	75126
(214) 875-3894		Fashing	78008	Forreston	76041
Enoch	75644	Fate	75132	Forsan	79733
Enochs	79324	Faught	75462	Fort Bliss (census	
Ensign	75119	Faulkner	75416	designated place)	79906
Enterprise (Cherokee		Fawil	75928		79916
County)	75766	Fayburg	75424	For specific Fort Bliss (census	
Enterprise (Van Zandt		Fayetteville	78940	designated place) Zip Codes call	
County)	75169	Faysville	78539	(915) 562-4036	
Eola	76937	Federal Correctional		Fort Bliss	79916
Eolian	76424	Institution (Bastrop		Fort Clark Springs	78832
Era	76238	County)	78602	Fort Davis	79734
Erath	76708	Federal Correctional		Fort Gates	76528
Erin	75951	Institution (Bowie County)	75501	Fort Hancock	79839
Erwin	77830	Federal Correctional		Fort Hood	76544
Escobares	78582	Institution (Dallas County)	75159	Fort McKavett	76841
Escobas	78361	Federal Correctional		Fort Ringgold	78582
Eskota	79561	Institution (Tarrant		Fort Spunky	76031
Esmond Estates (Part of		County)	76119	Fort Stockton	79735
Odessa)	79762	Federal Prison Camp	79720		
Esperanza	79839	Fedor	78947	**Fort Worth**	76101-85
Esquire Estates	75147	Fellowship	75961	For specific Fort Worth Zip Codes	
Esselle	78008	Fentress	78622	call (817) 625-3628	
Estacado	79343	Ferris	75125		
Estacado Estates (Part of		Fetzer	77363	*COLLEGES & UNIVERSITIES*	
Amarillo)	79109	Fiddlers Green	75034		
Estelline	79233	Field Creek	76869	Southwestern Baptist	
Estes	78382	Fieldton	79326	Theological Seminary	76122
Estes Addition	76071	Fife	76825	Texas Christian University	76129
				Texas Wesleyan College	76105

	ZIP
FINANCIAL INSTITUTIONS	
American Bank of Haltom City	76117
Bank One, Texas, N.A.	76102
Bank of Commerce	76102
Central Bank & Trust	76104
Comerica Bank-Texas	76107
First Interstate Bank of Texas, N.A.	76102
Overton Bank & Trust, N.A.	76109
Southwest Bank	76133
Summit National Bank	76102
Team Bank	76102
Texas Commerce Bank, National Association	76102
HOSPITALS	
All Saints Episcopal Hospital of Fort Worth	76104
Harris Methodist-Fort Worth	76104
HCA Medical Plaza Hospital	76104
Saint Joseph Hospital	76104
Tarrant County Hospital District	76104
HOTELS/MOTELS	
Residence Inn	76107
The Worthington	76102
MILITARY INSTALLATIONS	
Carswell Air Force Base	76127
United States Army Engineer District, Fort Worth	76102
United States Property and Fiscal Office for Fort Worth	76108
Fort Worth Town Center (Part of Fort Worth)	76115
Forum 303 Mall (Part of Arlington)	76010
Foster (Fort Bend County)	77469
Foster (Terry County)	79316
Foster Hills	75951
Foster Place (Part of Houston)	77021
Foster Store	77836
Fouke	75765
Fountain View	77032
Four Corners (Brazoria County)	77422
Four Corners (Fort Bend County)	77469
Four Corners (Montgomery County)	77301
Four Way	79018
Fowlerton	78021
Fox	76086
Fox Landing	75938
Fox Run	77373
Foxwood	77362
Frame Switch	76574
Francis (Part of West Orange)	77630
Francitas	77961
Frankell	76470
Franklin	77856
Frankston	75763
Fred	77616
Fredericksburg	78624
Fredonia (Gregg County)	75662
Fredonia (Mason County)	76842
Fredonia Hill (Part of Nacogdoches)	75961
Freedom (Lubbock County)	79412
Freedom (Rains County)	75440
Freeneytown	75667
Freeport	77541
Freer	78357
Freestone	75838
Freeway Oaks Estates	77365
Freiheit	78130
Frelsburg	78950
French Creek Village (Part of San Antonio)	78240
Frenstat	77836
Fresenius	77656
Fresno	77545
Freyburg	78956
Friday	75845
Friendship (Jasper County)	75966
Friendship (Lamb County)	79371
Friendship (Leon County)	75846
Friendship (Smith County)	75647
Friendship (Upshur County)	75644
Friendship (Van Zandt County)	75140
Friendswood	77546
Friona	79035

	ZIP
Frisco	75034
Fritch	79036
Frog	75160
Frognot	75424
Frontier Lakes	77378
Fronton	78582
Frosa	76678
Frost	76641
Fruitland	76230
Fruitvale	75127
Frydek	77474
Frys Gap	75766
Fulbright	75436
Fuller Springs	75901
Fulshear	77441
Fulton	78358
Fulton Beach (Part of Fulton)	78358
Funston	79501
Furney Richardson	75860
Gail	79738
Gainesville	76240-41
For specific Gainesville Zip Codes call (817) 665-5811	
Galena Park	77547
Galilee	77340
Gallatin	75764
Gallaway	71049
Galle	78638
Galleria (Part of Dallas)	75240
Galleria, The (Part of Houston)	77056
Galveston	77550-54
For specific Galveston Zip Codes call (409) 763-1819	
Galvez Mall (Part of Galveston)	77551
Ganado	77962
Garceno	78582
Garciasville	78547
Garden Acres (Part of Fort Worth)	76028
Garden City (Glasscock County)	79739
Garden City (Harris County)	77018
Gardendale (Ector County)	79758
Gardendale (La Salle County)	78014
Garden Oaks (Part of Houston)	77206
Garden Ridge	78266
Garden Valley	75771
Garden Villas	77901
Garfield (DeWitt County)	78164
Garfield (Travis County)	78617
Garland (Dallas County)	75040-48
For specific Garland Zip Codes call (214) 272-5541	
Garland (Bowie County)	75559
Garland (Red River County)	75550
Garner	76086
Garrett	75119
Garretts Bluff	75411
Garrison	75946
Garth	77520
Garvin	76023
Garwood	77442
Gary	75643
Gasoline	79255
Gastonia	75114
Gatesville	76528
Gatesville Unit	76528
Gateway Shopping City (Part of Beaumont)	77701
Gatewood	77039
Gause	77857
Gay Hill (Fayette County)	78945
Gay Hill (Washington County)	77833
Geneva	75947
Geneva Estates	78736
Genoa (Part of Houston)	77034
George	77871
Georges Creek	76031
Georgetown	78626-28
For specific Georgetown Zip Codes call (512) 863-2325	
George West	78022
George W. Singer (Part of Lubbock)	79424
Georgia	75486
Gerald	76640
Geronimo	78115
Geronimo Forest	78254
Geronimo Village	78253
Gethsemane	75657
Gholson	76705
Gibtown	76486
Giddings	78942
Gilchrist	77617
Gill	75670

	ZIP
Gillett	78116
Gilliland	79260
Gilmer	75644
Gilpin	79370
Ginger	75410
Girard	79518
Girvin	79740
Givens	75462
Gladewater (Gregg County)	75647
Gladewater (Titus County)	75455
Glass	76690
Glaze City	77984
Glazier	79014
Glen Cove (Coleman County)	76834
Glen Cove (Galveston County)	77565
Glencrest (Part of Fort Worth)	76119
Glendale	75862
Glenfawn	75760
Glen Flora	77443
Glenn Heights	75115
Glen Rose	76043
Glenwood (Potter County)	79103
Glenwood (Upshur County)	75644
Glidden	78943
Globe	75486
Glory	75462
Gober	75443
Godley	76044
Gold	78624
Golden	75444
Golden Beach	78643
Golden Oaks	78628
Golden Triangle Mall (Part of Denton)	76206
Goldfinch	78005
Goldsboro	79519
Goldsmith	79741
Goldthwaite	76844
Goliad	77963
Golinda	76655
Gomez	79316
Gonzales	78629
Goober Hill	75973
Goodfellow Air Force Base	76908
Good Hope	77964
Goodland	79371
Goodlett	79252
Goodlow	75144
Goodlow Park	75144
Goodnight (Armstrong County)	79226
Goodnight (Navarro County)	75144
Goodrich	77335
Good Springs	75667
Goodville	76632
Gordon (Lynn County)	79356
Gordon (Palo Pinto County)	76453
Gordonville	76245
Goree	76363
Goree Unit	77340
Gorman	76454
Goshen	77340
Gough	75448
Gould	75766
Gouldbusk	76845
Graceton	75644
Graford	76449
Graham (Garza County)	79356
Graham (Jasper County)	75951
Graham (Young County)	76450
Granada Estates	78737
Granbury	76048-49
For specific Granbury Zip Codes call (817) 573-5515	
Grand Bluff	75631
Grandfalls	79742
Grand Prairie	75050-54
For specific Grand Prairie Zip Codes call (214) 264-5751	
Grand Saline	75140
Grandview (Dawson County)	79351
Grand View (El Paso County)	79930
Grandview (Gray County)	79039
Grandview (Johnson County)	76050
Grange Hall	75670
Granger	76530
Grangerland	77302
Granite Shoals	78654
Granjeno	78572
Granview Beach	78611
Granville W. Elder (Part of Houston)	77013
Grape Creek	76901
Grapeland	75844
Grapetown	78624

ZIP		ZIP		ZIP	
Grapevine	76051	Gustine	76455	Havana	78572
	76092	Guthrie	79236	Hawkins	75765
	76099	Guy	77444	Hawkinsville	77414
For specific Grapevine Zip Codes call (817) 488-9012		Guys Store	75833	Hawley	79525
		Hacienda Heights (Part of El		Hawthorne	77358
Grassland	79356	Paso)	79915	Hayden	75169
Graves (Part of Midland)	79708	Hackberry (Bexar County)	78210	Haynesville	76360
Gray	75657	Hackberry (Cottle County)	79248	Hays	78666
Grayback	76360	Hackberry (Denton County)	75068	Hazy Hollow	77355
Grayburg	77659	Hackberry (Garza County)	79356	Headlea Estates (Part of	
Grays Chapel	75801	Hackberry (Lavaca County)	78956	Odessa)	79762
Grays Prairie	75158	Hagansport	75487	Headsville	76653
Graytown	78114	Hagerman	75090	Heald	79057
Great Northwest	78250	Hagerville	75847	Hearne	77859
Great Oaks	78681	Hail	75492	Heath	75087
Great Southwest (Part of		Hainesville	75773	Hebbronville	78361
Fort Worth)	76005	Halbert	75973	Hebco (Part of San Antonio)	78218
Green	78119	Hale Center	79041	Hebron	75056
Green Acres	77058	Halesboro	75417	Heckville	79329
Green Hill	75455	Halfway	79072	Hedley	79237
Green Lake	77979	Hall (Marion County)	75657	Hedwig Village	77024
Green Pastures	78640	Hall (San Saba County)	76871	Heidelberg	78570
Greenridge (Part of		Hallettsville	77964	Heidenheimer	76533
Houston)	77022	Halloway Heights	77047	Heights (Galveston County)	77590
Greens Bayou (Part of		Halls Bluff	75835	Heights (Harris County)	77008
Houston)	77015	Hallsburg	76705	Helena	78118
Greens Camp	79521	Halls Store	71007	Helmic	75845
Greens Creek	76446	Hallsville	75650	Helotes	78023
Greenspoint Mall (Part of		Halsell	76365	Hemphill	75948
Houston)	77018	Haltom City	76117	Hempstead	77445
Green Valley	76227	Hamby	79601	Henderson	75652-53
Greenview	75420	Hamilton	76531	For specific Henderson Zip Codes call (903) 657-1481	
Greenview Hills (Part of		Hamlin	79520		
Irving)	75062	Hamon	78629	Henderson Chapel	76866
Greenview Manor	77032	Hampton	75936	Henderson Heights	79763
Greenville	75401-04	Hamshire	77622	Henkhaus	77984
For specific Greenville Zip Codes call (903) 455-5363		Hancock Oak Hills	78130	Henly	78620
		Hancock Shopping Center		Henning	75946
Greenville Avenue (Part of		(Part of Austin)	78751	Henrietta	76365
Dallas)	75206	Handley (Part of Fort Worth)	76124	Henrys Chapel	75789
Greenvine	77835	Hankamer	77560	Hereford	79045
Greenway	78223	Hannibal	76401	Heritage Northwest	78245
Greenway Plaza (Part of		Hanover	76520	Heritage Oaks	77365
Houston)	77046	Hansford	79081	Hermleigh	79526
Greenwood (Hopkins		Happy	79042	Herring (Part of San Angelo)	76901
County)	75478	Happy Hill	76009	Herty (Part of Lufkin)	75901
Greenwood (Midland		Happy Union	79072	Hewitt	76643
County)	79701	Happy Valley	79566	Hext	76848
Greenwood (Parker County)	76086	Harbin	76446	Hickey	75667
Greenwood (Wise County)	76246	Harbor Grove (Part of		Hickory Creek (Denton	
Greenwood Acres (Llano		Hickory Creek)	75065	County)	75065
County)	78609	Harborlight	75948	Hickory Creek (Hunt	
Greenwood Acres (Orange		Hardin	77561	County)	75423
County)	77626	Hardin-Simmons (Part of		Hickory Hill	75686
Greenwood Forest	78028	Abilene)	79698	Hickory Hills	77356
Greenwood Village	77093	Hardy	76265	Hickory Hollow	75929
Greggton (Part of		Hare	76574	Hickston	78959
Longview)	75604	Hargill	78549	Hico	76457
Gregory	78359	Harker Heights	76543	Hidalgo	78557
Gresham	75703	Harkeyville	76877	Hidden Echo	77336
Grey Forest	78023	Harlandale (Part of San		Hidden Forest (Part of San	
Gribble (Part of Farmers		Antonio)	78214	Antonio)	78232
Branch)	75234	Harlem	77469	Hidden Hill	75065
Grice	75644	Harleton	75651	Hidden Hills Harbor	75147
Griffin	75789	Harlingen	78550-52	Hidden Valley (Part of	
Griffing (Part of Port Arthur)	77640	For specific Harlingen Zip Codes call (512) 423-1464		Houston)	77088
Griffing Park (Part of Port				Hide-A-Way Lake	75771
Arthur)	77640	Harmon	75446	Higginbotham	79360
Griffith (Cochran County)	79346	Harmony (Anderson		Higgins	79046
Griffith (Ellis County)	76084	County)	75801	Highbank	76680
Grigsby	75935	Harmony (Parker County)	76086	High Hill	78956
Grit (Mason County)	76856	Harmony (Rusk County)	75684	High Island	77623
Grit (Rains County)	75410	Harmony Grove	77340	Highland (Erath County)	76446
Groceville	77301	Harmony Hill	75691	Highland (Johnson County)	76031
Groesbeck	76642	Harper	78631	Highland Acres (Grayson	
Groom	79039	Harriet	76901	County)	75076
Grosvenor	76801	Harrisburg (Harris County)	77012	Highland Acres (Harris	
Groves	77619	Harrisburg (Jasper County)	75951	County)	77018
Groveton	75845	Harrison	76682	Highland Acres (Hunt	
Grow	79248	Harrold	76364	County)	75453
Gruenau	78164	Hart	79043	Highland Addition (Harris	
Gruene	78130	Hartburg	77630	County)	77018
Grulla	78548	Hart Camp	79339	Highland Addition (Parker	
Gruver	79040	Hartley	79044	County)	76082
Guadalupe	77901	Harts Bluff	75455	Highland Bayou	77563
Guadalupe Heights	78028	Hart Spur (Part of Hurst)	76053	Highland Creek Lakes	78736
Guajillo	78332	Hartzo	75657	Highland Estates (Part of	
Guerra	78360	Harvard	75686	Victoria)	77901
Gulf Camp	79756	Harvest Acres (Montgomery		Highland Haven	78654
Gulfgate Shopping Center		County)	77372	Highland Hills (Bexar	
(Part of Houston)	77087	Harvest Acres (Tom Green		County)	78223
Gulfway (Part of Corpus		County)	76905	Highland Hills (Dallas	
Christi)	78412	Harvest Heights	77088	County)	75241
Gum Springs (Cass County)	75560	Harvey	77845	Highland Mall (Part of	
Gum Springs (Harrison		Harwood	78632	Austin)	78757
County)	75601	Haskell	79521	Highland Park	75205
Gun Barrel City	75147	Haslam	75954	Highland Range Estates	76901
Gunsight	76437	Haslet	76052	Highlands	77562
Gunter (Grayson County)	75058	Hasse	76456	Highland Village	75067
Gunter (Wood County)	75410	Hatchel	79567	Highland Waters	78003
Gussettville	78022	Hatchetville	75437	Highpoint	77093

	ZIP
Highsaw	75763
Hi Ho	77630
Hiland Shores	75076
Hill and Dale Acres	77372
Hill City	76476
Hill Country Village	78232
Hillcrest	77511
Hillebrandt	77705
Hillister	77624
Hillje	77455
Hills	78659
Hillsboro	76645
Hillside Estates	75763
Hillside Gardens	77039
Hilltop (Coryell County)	76528
Hilltop (Gillespie County)	78624
Hilltop (Grayson County)	75020
Hilltop Acres	78253
Hilltop Lakes	77871
Hilshire Village	77055
Hinckley	75460
Hindes	78026
Hines	76384
Hinkles Ferry	77422
Hiram	75160
Hitchcock	77563
Hitchland	73942
Hoard	75773
Hobbs	79526
Hobson	78117
Hochheim	77967
Hockley	77447
Hodges	79525
Hodgson	75559
Hoen	76691
Hogan Acres	76028
Hogansville	75410
Hogg	77836
Holiday Beach	78382
Holiday Estates	75169
Holiday Harbor	75630
Holiday Hills	75453
Holiday Hills Estates	76424
Holiday Lake Estates	77335
Holiday Lakes	77515
Holiday Oaks	77372
Holland (Bell County)	76534
Holland (Hardin County)	77625
Holland Quarters	75633
Holliday	76366
Hollis	77864
Holly	75851
Holly Grove	77351
Holly Springs (Camp County)	75686
Holly Springs (Jasper County)	75951
Holly Springs (Nacogdoches County)	75946
Holly Springs (Van Zandt County)	75754
Holly Terrace	77365
Hollywood Addition	77627
Hollywood Heights	77627
Hollywood Park	78232
Holman	78962
Holt	76872
Homer (Angelina County)	75901
Homer (Jasper County)	75951
Homestead Meadows	79927
Homewood	75951
Hondo	78861
Honea	77356
Honey Grove (Cass County)	75551
Honey Grove (Fannin County)	75446
Honey Island	77625
Hood	76240
Hooks	75561
Hoover	79065
Hoovers Valley	78611
Hope	77995
Hopewell (Franklin County)	75457
Hopewell (Houston County)	75835
Hopewell (Leon County)	75833
Horizon City	79927
Horn Hill	76642
Horseshoe Bay	78654
Horseshoe Bay South	78654
Horseshoe Bay West	78654
Horseshoe Falls	78130
Hortense	77351
Horton (Delta County)	75428
Horton (Jasper County)	75951
Horton (Panola County)	75639
Hostyn	78945
Hot Wells	79851
Houmont Park	77044
Houseman Addition	77662
Houston	77001-99

	ZIP
	77101-99
	77201-93
	77315

For specific Houston Zip Codes call (713) 227-1474

COLLEGES & UNIVERSITIES

	ZIP
Houston Baptist University	77074
Rice University	77251
South Texas College of Law	77002
Texas Southern University	77004
University of Houston-Clear Lake	77058
University of Houston-Downtown	77002
University of Houston-Houston Texas	77204
University of St. Thomas	77006
University of Texas Health Science Center at Houston	77225

FINANCIAL INSTITUTIONS

	ZIP
American Bank	77002
Bank One, Texas, N.A.	77002
BancTEXAS Houston, N.A.	77063
Bank of Houston	77002
Charter National Bank-Houston	77008
Cullen Center Bank & Trust	77002
Enterprise Bank-Houston	77023
First City,Texas	77002
First Gibraltar Bank, F.S.B	77060
Guardian Savings & Loan Association	77057
Harrisburg Bank	77012
Lockwood National Bank of Houston	77020
Med Center Bank and Trust	77030
Merchants Bank Houston	77008
NationsBank	77002
Northwest Bank	77092
Post Oak Bank	77056
River Oaks Bank & Trust Company	77019
South Main Bank	77002
Team Bank	77056
Texas Commerce Bank, National Association	77002
United Savings Association of Texas, F.S.B.	77027
University State Bank	77005

HOSPITALS

	ZIP
AMI Park Plaza Hospital	77004
AMI Twelve Oaks Hospital	77027
Harris County Hospital District	77030
Hermann Hospital	77030
Houston Northwest Medical Center	77090
Memorial City Medical Center	77024
Memorial Hospital System	77074
Methodist Hospital	77030
HCA Spring Branch Medical Center	77055
St. Joseph Hospital	77002
St. Luke's Episcopal Hospital	77030
Texas Children's Hospital	77030
University of Texas M.D. Anderson Cancer Center	77030
Veterans Affairs Medical Center	77030

HOTELS/MOTELS

	ZIP
Adam's Mark Houston	77042
Embassy Suites Hotel	77074
Four Seasons Hotel, Houston	77010
Holiday Inn Crowne Plaza-Galleria	77027
Holiday Inn-Houston Intercontinental	77032
Houston Airport Marriott	77032
Hyatt Regency Houston	77002
J.W. Marriott Hotel	77056
Quality Inn-Intercontinental Airport	77205
The Ritz Carlton,Houston	77027
Residence Inn Astrodome	77030
Sheraton Crown Hotel & Conference Center	77032
The Westchase Hilton & Towers	77042
The Westin Galleria	77056
The Westin Oaks	77056

MILITARY INSTALLATIONS

	ZIP
Coast Guard Air Station, Houston	77034
Texas Air National Guard, FB6433, Ellington Field	77034
Lyndon B. Johnson Space Center	77058

	ZIP
Howard	75165
Howardwick	79226
Howe	75459
Howland	75460
Hoxie	76574
Hoyt (Part of Alba)	75410
Hoyte	76520
Hub	79035
Hubbard	76648
Huckabay	76401
Hudson	75901
Hudson Oaks	76086
Huffines	75555
Huffman	77336
Hufsmith	77337
Hughes Springs	75656
Hughey	75662
Hulen Mall (Part of Fort Worth)	76133
Hulen Park (Part of Texas City)	77590
Hull	77564
Humble	77325
	77338-39
	77345-47
	77396

For specific Humble Zip Codes call (713) 446-3152

	ZIP
Humble Camp	78377
Humble Heights (Part of Houston)	77338
Hungerford	77448
Hunt	78024
Hunter	78130
Hunters Creek Village	77024
Hunters Retreat	77355
Huntington	75949
Huntsville	77340-42

For specific Huntsville Zip Codes call (409) 295-7741

	ZIP
Hurlwood	79407
Hurnville	76365
Huron	76692
Hurst	76053-54

For specific Hurst Zip Codes call (817) 284-3464

	ZIP
Hurstown	75973
Hurst Springs	76634
Hutchins	75141
Hutto	78634
Huxley	75973
Huxley Bay	75973
Hye	78635
Hylton	79506
Iago	77420
Ida	75491
Idalou	79329
Idyle Hour Acres	78728
Ike	75165
Illinois Bend	76265
Impact	79603
Imperial	79743
Imperial Valley (Part of Houston)	77022
Inadale	79545
Independence	77833
India	75125
Indian Creek	76801
Indian Gap	76531
Indian Harbor Estates	76048
Indian Hill	75977
Indian Hills	78006
Indian Lake (Cameron County)	78586
Indian Lake (Newton County)	77630
Indian Lodge	76652
Indian Oaks (Henderson County)	75163
Indian Oaks (Waller County)	77466
Indianola	77979
Indian Rock	75644
Indian Shores	77532
Indian Springs	77351
Indian Trails (Part of Victoria)	77901
Indian Village	77351
Indian Waters	78003
Indian Woods	77355
Industrial (Part of Dallas)	75207
Industry	78944
Inez	77968

	ZIP		ZIP		ZIP
Ingleside	78362	Jonah	78626	Kilowatt (Part of Orange)	77630
Ingleside on the Bay	78362	Jones	75140	Kimball	76652
Ingram	78025	Jonesboro	76538	Kimbro	78653
Ingram Park Mall (Part of		Jones Creek (Brazoria		Kinard Estates	77630
San Antonio)	78238	County)	77541	King (Coryell County)	76528
Inks Lake Village	78609	Jones Creek (Wharton		King (Red River County)	75550
Inwood (Part of Dallas)	75209	County)	77437	King City (Part of	
Inwood Forest (Part of		Jones Prairie	76520	Cleveland)	77327
Houston)	77088	Jonestown	78645	King Ranch	78363
Inwood Place	77016	Jonesville	75659	Kingsbury	78638
Inwood Village (Part of		Joplin	76458	Kings Cove	78611
Dallas)	75206	Joppa	78605	Kingsland	78639
Iola	77861	Jordan (Part of Amarillo)	79159	Kingsland Estates	78639
Iowa Colony	77583	Josephine	75164	Kingsley (Part of Garland)	75041
Iowa Park	76367	Joshua	76058	Kings Mill	79065
Ira	79527	Josserand	75845	Kings Point	78073
Iraan	79744	Jot 'Em Down	75469	Kingston	75401
Irby	79521	Jourdanton	78026	Kings Village	78727
Iredell	76649	Joy (Clay County)	76365	Kingsville	78363-64
Ireland	76538	Joy (Smith County)	75647	For specific Kingsville Zip Codes	
Irene	76650	Jozye	77864	call (512) 592-2801	
Ironton	75766	Juanita Craft (Part of Dallas)	75315	Kingsville Naval Station	78363
Irving	75014-17	Jubilee Springs	76502	Kingswood	75104
	75038-39	Jud	79544	Kingtown	75961
	75060-63	Judson	75660	Kingwood	77339
For specific Irving Zip Codes call		Juliff	77583	Kinkler	77964
(214) 986-6557		Julius Melcher (Part of		Kiomatia	75436
Irving Mall (Part of Irving)	75062	Houston)	77027	Kirby	78219
Irvington (Part of Houston)	77022	Jumbo	75669	Kirbyville	75956
Island (Galveston County)	77550	Junction	76849	Kirkland	79201
Island (Madison County)	75852	Juno	76943	Kirkpatrick Addition	75704
Italy	76651	Jupiter Pharmacy (Part of		Kirtley	78957
Itasca	76055	Richardson)	75080	Kirvin	75848
Ivan	76424	Justiceburg	79330	Kittrell	75862
Ivanhoe	75447	Justin	76247	Kleberg (Part of Dallas)	75253
Iveys Crossing	79853	Kadane Corner	76360		75336
Ivy	76854	Kalgary	79370	For specific Kleberg Zip Codes	
Izoro	76522	Kamay	76369	call (214) 286-5460	
Jacinto City	77029	Karney	77979	Klein	77379
Jacksboro	76458	Kanawha	75436	Klondike (Dawson County)	79331
Jackson (Marion County)	75657	Karen	77355	Klondike (Delta County)	75448
Jackson (Shelby County)	75954	Karnack	75661	Klump	77833
Jackson (Van Zandt		Karnes City	78118	Knapp	79527
County)	75103	Katemcy	76825	Knickerbocker	76939
Jacksonville	75766	Katy	77449-50	Knippa	78870
Jacobia	75401		77491-94	Knob Hill	75034
Jamaica Beach	77554	For specific Katy Zip Codes call		Knollwood	75090
James	75935	(713) 578-0942		Knott	79748
James Moody (Part of		Kaufman	75142	Knox City	79529
Victoria)	77901	Kayare (Part of Harlingen)	78550	Koerth	77964
Jamestown (Newton		Keechi	75831	Kohrville	77040
County)	75966	Keenan	77356	Kokomo	76454
Jamestown (Smith County)	75140	Keene	76059	Komensky	77775
Jaques Spur (Part of		Keeter	76023	Kona Kai	77650
Denison)	75020	Keith	77861	Kopernik Shores	78520
Jardin	75428	Keller	76244	Kopperl	76652
Jarrell	76537		76248	Kosciusko	78160
Jarvis Christian College	75765	For specific Keller Zip Codes call		Kosse	76653
Jasper	75951	(817) 431-1311		Kountze	77625
Jasper Heights (Part of		Kellerville	79057	Kovar	78941
Marshall)	75670	Kelly	75409	Kress	79052
Jayton	79528	Kellyville	75657	Kreutzberg	78006
Jean	76374	Kelsey	75644	Krugerville	76227
Jeddo	78953	Kelton	79096	Krum	76249
Jefferson	75657	Keltys (Part of Lufkin)	75901	Kubala Store	78164
Jefferson City Shopping		Kemah	77565	Kurten	77862
Center (Part of Port		Kemp	75143	Kuykendahl Village (Part of	
Arthur)	77640	Kempner	76539	Houston)	77068
Jefferson Heights (Part of		Kendalia	78027	Kyle	78640
San Angelo)	76901	Kendleton	77451	Kyote	78005
Jenkins	75638	Kenedy	78119	Labatt	78114
Jennings	75462	Kenefick	77535	La Blanca	78558
Jensen Drive (Part of		Kennard	75847	La Casita	78582
Houston)	77026	Kennedale	76060	La Casita-Garciasville	78547
Jensens Point	77465	Kenney	77452	Laceola	77864
Jericho	79226	Kensing	75450	Lackland Air Force Base	78236
Jermyn	76459	Kent	79855	Lackland Heights	78227
Jerrys Quarters	77833	Kentuckytown	75491	Lackland Terrace (Part of	
Jersey Village	77040	Kenwood Place	77339	San Antonio)	78227
Jerusalem	77422	Kerens	75144	La Coste	78039
Jester Unit	77469	Kermit	79745	La Cuchilla (Part of Mission)	78572
Jewett	75846	Kerrick	79051	Lacy	75845
J. Frank Dobie (Part of San		Kerrville	78028-29	Lacy-Lakeview	76705
Antonio)	78220	For specific Kerrville Zip Codes		Ladonia	75449
Jiba	75142	call (512) 257-5040		LaFayette	75686
Joaquin	75954	Kessler Park (Part of Dallas)	75208	La Feria	78559
Joe Pool (Part of Dallas)	75224	Kevin	77327	Lagarto	78022
John Foster (Part of		Key	79331	La Gloria	78591
Pasadena)	77502	Key Ranch Estates	75163	Lago	78586
Johnson	79316	Keystone Park (Part of		Lago Vista	78645
Johnson City	78636	Dallas)	75240	La Grange	78945
Johnsons Station (Part of		Kickapoo	75763	Laguna Heights	78578
Arlington)	76015	Kildare	75562	Laguna Park	76634
Johnstown	75169	Kildare Junction	75555	Laguna Tres Estates	76049
Johnsville	76401	Kilgore	75662-63	Laguna Vista	78578
Johntown	75417	For specific Kilgore Zip Codes call		Laguna Vista Estates	75751
Joiner	78945	(903) 984-2313		La Hacienda Estates	78759
Joinerville	75658	Killeen	76540-47	La Homa	78572
Joliet	78648	For specific Killeen Zip Codes call		Laird Hill	75666
Jolly	76303	(817) 634-0281		Lajitas	79852
Jollyville	78729	Killeen Mall (Part of Killeen)	76543	La Joya	78560

	ZIP
La Junta	76020
Lake Air Center (Part of Waco)	76710
Lake Barbara (Part of Clute)	77531
Lake Bonanza	77356
Lake Bridgeport	76426
Lake Brownwood	76801
Lake Chateau Woods	77302
Lake Cherokee	75652
Lake City	78387
Lake Conroe Forrest	77301
Lake Conroe West	77301
Lake Corsicana (Part of Corsicana)	75110
Lake Creek	75450
Lake Creek Estates	77355
Lake Dallas	75065
Lake Gardens	76901
Lake Halbert (Part of Corsicana)	75110
Lakehills	78063
Lake Jackson	77566
Lake Jackson Farms	77566
Lake Kiowa	76240
Lakeland	77302
Lakeland Heights (Part of Grand Prairie)	75050
Lakeland Park	78759
Lake Livingston	77376
Lake Meredith Estates	79036
Lake Pauline	79252
Lake Placid	78155
Lakeport	75603
Lake Ransom Canyon Village	79366
Lake Rolling Wood	77301
Lake Shadows	77532
Lake Shore	76801
Lakeshore Estates	75630
Lakeshore Estates West	75630
Lake Shore Gardens	78368
Lakeside (Galveston County)	77565
Lakeside (San Patricio County)	78368
Lakeside (Tarrant County)	76108
Lakeside Acres	78006
Lakeside Beach	78669
Lakeside City	76308
Lakeside Heights	78639
Lakeside Park	77530
Lakeside Village	76671
Lake Splendora	77372
Lake Tanglewood	79118
Lake Tejas	77371
Lake Thomas	79527
Laketon	79065
Lake Victor	76550
Lakeview (Cherokee County)	75766
Lakeview (Floyd County)	79235
Lakeview (Hall County)	79239
Lakeview (Jefferson County)	77640
Lakeview (Lynn County)	79345
Lakeview (McLennan County)	76705
Lakeview (Orange County)	77662
Lakeview (Swisher County)	79088
Lakeview (Tarrant County)	76135
Lakeview (Tom Green County)	76903
Lakeview Estates (Johnson County)	76031
Lakeview Estates (Orange County)	77662
Lakeview Estates (Van Zandt County)	75169
Lakeview Hills	78645
Lake View Park	78130
Lakeway	78734
Lake Whitney Estates	76692
Lake Wildwood	77302
Lakewood (Dallas County)	75214
Lakewood (Harris County)	77520
Lakewood (Orange County)	77662
Lakewood (San Augustine County)	75929
Lakewood Estates	77304
Lakewood Forest	78639
Lakewood Harbor	76634
Lakewood Heights (Part of Houston)	77336
Lakewood Hills (Comal County)	78130
Lakewood Hills (Hood County)	76049
Lakewood Village	76205
Lake Worth	76135
Lamar	78382

	ZIP
Lamar Park (Part of Corpus Christi)	78411
La Marque	77568
Lamar University (Part of Beaumont)	77710
Lamasco	75488
Lamesa	79331
Lamkin	76455
Lampasas	76550
Lamplight Village	78758
Lanark	75572
Lancaster (Dallas County)	75134
	75146
For specific Lancaster Zip Codes call (214) 227-2551	
Lancaster (El Paso County)	79907
Landa Park Highlands (Part of New Braunfels)	78130
Lane	75423
Lane City	77453
Lanely	75831
Laneport	76574
Lane Prairie	76058
Laneville	75667
Langtry	78871
Lanham	76538
Lanier	75563
Lannius	75438
Lantana	78586
La Paloma	78586
La Plaza (Part of McAllen)	78503
La Porte	77571-72
For specific La Porte Zip Codes call (713) 471-0284	
La Pryor	78872
La Puerta	78582
Laredo	78040-44
For specific Laredo Zip Codes call (512) 723-2043	
La Reforma	78536
Lariat	79325
Larue	75770
La Salle (Calhoun County)	77979
La Salle (Jackson County)	77969
Lasara	78561
Las Colinas (Part of Irving)	75014
	75016
For specific Las Colinas Zip Codes call (214) 556-1229	
Las Milpas	78577
Las Rusias	78586
Lassater	75630
Las Yescas	78586
Latch	75644
Latexo	75849
La Tina	78586
Latium	77835
Latonia	77422
La Tuna	79821
Laughlin Air Force Base	78843
Laureles	78586
Laurel Heights (Part of San Antonio)	78212
Lavada	75487
La Vernia	78121
La Villa	78562
Lavon	75166
Lavon Beach Estates	75442
La Ward	77970
Lawn	79530
Lawrence	75160
Lawrence Park (Part of Amarillo)	79109
Lawrence Springs	75140
Lawson	75149
Lazare	79252
Lazbuddie	79053
Leaday	76888
League City	77573-74
For specific League City Zip Codes call (713) 554-6281	
Leagueville	75778
Leakey	78873
Leander	78641
Leary	75501
Leasure Acres	76528
Lebanon	75034
Ledbetter	78946
Ledbetter Hills (Part of Dallas)	75211
Leedale	76569
Leesburg	75451
Leesville	78122
Lefors	79054
Leggett	77350
Legion (Part of Kerrville)	78028
Lehman	79346
Leigh	75661
Lela	79079
Lelia Lake	79240
Leming	78050

	ZIP
Lena	78963
Lenorah	79749
Lenz	78118
Leo (Cooke County)	76234
Leo (Lee County)	78947
Leona	75850
Leonard	75452
Leon Junction	76552
Leon Springs	78229
Leon Valley	78238
	78240
	78250-51
	78268
For specific Leon Valley Zip Codes call (512) 680-5074	
Leroy	76654
Lesley	79239
Letney Park	75951
Le Tourneau (Part of Longview)	75601
Levelland	79336-38
For specific Levelland Zip Codes call (806) 894-3250	
Leveretts Chapel	75684
Levi	76655
Levita	76528
Lewis Addition	77465
Lewisville	75028-29
	75056-57
	75067
For specific Lewisville Zip Codes call (214) 221-2755	
Lexington	78947
Lexington Woods	77373
Liberty (Hamilton County)	76531
Liberty (Liberty County)	77575
Liberty (Lubbock County)	79401
Liberty (Newton County)	75966
Liberty (Rusk County)	75652
Liberty City	75647
Liberty Grove	75098
Liberty Hill (Houston County)	75844
Liberty Hill (Milam County)	76567
Liberty Hill (Titus County)	75455
Liberty Hill (Williamson County)	78642
Liggett (Part of Irving)	75060
Lilac	76577
Lilbert	75760
Lillian	76061
Lily Grove	75961
Lily Island	75934
Lincoln	78948
Lincoln Park	76227
Lindale	75771
Linden	75563
Lindenau	77954
Lindenwood	77630
Lindsay	76250
Lindsay Addition	79772
Lingleville	76461
Link Five (Part of La Porte)	77571
Linkwood Addition	76008
Linn	78563
Linn Flat	75961
Linwood	75925
Lipan	76462
Lipscomb	79056
Lisbon (Part of Dallas)	75216
Lissie	77454
Littig	78621
Little Boy	77662
Little Elm	75068
Littlefield	79339
Little Flock	77879
Little Hope	75494
Little Mexico	79735
Little New York	78629
Little Ridge	75121
Little River	76554
Little Rock	77625
Lively	75143
Live Oak (Bexar County)	78233
Liveoak (Palo Pinto County)	76472
Live Oak Ranchettes	78641
Liverpool	77577
Livingston	77351
Llano	78643
Lobo	79855
Locker	76871
Lockett	76384
Lockettville	79358
Lockhart	78644
Lockhill (Part of San Antonio)	78230
	78278
For specific Lockhill Zip Codes call (512) 493-2174	
Lockney	79241
Locust	75076

	ZIP
Locust Grove	79014
Lodi	75564
Loeb	77656
Loebau	78948
Logan (Marion County)	75657
Logan (Panola County)	71049
Logan Heights (Part of El Paso)	79904
Log Cabin	75148
Log Cabin Estates	75148
Lohn	76852
Loire	78064
Lois	76272
Lolaville	75034
Lolita	77971
Lollipop	75763
Loma	77876
Loma Alta (McMullen County)	78072
Loma Alta (Val Verde County)	78840
Loma Terrace (Part of El Paso)	79907
Loma Vista	78829
Lomax (Harris County)	77571
Lomax (Howard County)	79720
Lometa	76853
London	76854
Lone Camp	76484
Lone Cedar	76626
Lone Elm	75165
Lone Grove	78643
Lone Mountain	75644
Lone Oak (Bexar County)	78101
Lone Oak (Colorado County)	78940
Lone Oak (Erath County)	76446
Lone Oak (Hunt County)	75453
Lone Pine	75801
Lone Star (Floyd County)	79241
Lone Star (Kaufman County)	75142
Lone Star (Morris County)	75668
Lone Star (Titus County)	75558
Long Branch	75669
Longfellow	79848
Longford Place	77630
Long Hollow	77865
Long Lake (Anderson County)	75801
Long Lake (Montgomery County)	77355
Long Mott	77972
Long Point (Harris County)	77055
Long Point (Harrison County)	75661
Long Point (Washington County)	77835
Longview	75601-15

For specific Longview Zip Codes call (903) 753-7644

	ZIP
Longview Heights	75601
Longview Mall (Part of Longview)	75601
Longworth	79543
Lonoke Place	77093
Looneyville	75760
Loop	79342
Lopeno	78564
Lopezville	78589
Loraine	79532
Lorena	76655
Lorenzo	79343
Los Angeles	78014
Los Barreras	78582
Los Campos	78840
Los Ebanos	78565
Los Fresnos	78566
Los Indios	78567
Los Jardines (Part of San Antonio)	78237
Losoya	78221
Los Ricos Pobres	78013
Los Saenz (Part of Roma)	78584
Lost Creek	78746
Lost Lakes	77357
Los Velas	78582
Los Ybanez	79331
Lott	76656
Louise	77455
Love Chapel	75656
Lovelace	76645
Lovelady	75851
Lovell Lake	77706
Loving	76460
Lowake	76855
Lowry Crossing	75069
Loyola Beach	78379
Lozano	78568

	ZIP
Lubbock	79401-99

For specific Lubbock Zip Codes call (806) 763-6408

	ZIP
Lucas	75002
Luckenbach	78624
Lucky Ridge	76023
Lueders	79533
Luella	75090
Lufkin	75901-15

For specific Lufkin Zip Codes call (409) 634-7749

	ZIP
Luling	78648
Lull	78539
Lumberton	77711
Lums Chapel	79339
Lund	78621
Luther	79720
Lutie	79079
Lydia	75554
Lyford	78569
Lynchburg	77520
Lyncrest	77086
Lyndon B. Johnson Space Center	77058
Lynn Grove	77868
Lyons	77863
Lytle	78052
Lytton Springs	78616
Mabank	75147
Mabelle	76380
Mabry	75426
McAdoo	79243
McAllen	78501-04

For specific McAllen Zip Codes call (512) 686-1771

	ZIP
McBeth	77515
McCamey	79752
McCaulley	79534
McClanahan	76661
McCook	78539
McCoy (Atascosa County)	78053
McCoy (Floyd County)	79235
McCoy (Panola County)	75643
McCreless Mall (Part of San Antonio)	78223
McDade	78650
McDade Estates	77304
Macdona	78054
Macedonia (Austin County)	77474
Macedonia (Bowie County)	75501
Macedonia (Brazoria County)	77422
Macedonia (Liberty County)	77327
McElroy	75968
McFaddin	77973
McGalin	77612
McGee Landing	75948
McGregor	76657
McKenzie	75630
McKibben	79081
McKinney	75069-70

For specific McKinney Zip Codes call (214) 542-5031

	ZIP
McKnight	75652
McLean	79057
McLendon (Part of McLendon-Chisholm)	75087
McLendon-Chisholm	75087
McLeod	75565
McMahan	78616
McMillin	76877
McMurray (Part of Abilene)	79697
McNair	77520
McNair Village	76544
McNary	79839
McNeil (Caldwell County)	78640
McNeil (Travis County)	78651
Macon	75457
McQueeney	78123
Mc Rea Lake	77302
Macune	75972
Macy	77882
Madero	78572
Madisonville	77864
Madras	75426
Magasco	75968
Magic (Part of San Antonio)	78229 / 78280

For specific Magic Zip Codes call (512) 616-0777

	ZIP
Magnet	77488
Magnolia	77355
Magnolia Beach	77979
Magnolia Bend	77302
Magnolia Gardens	77044
Magnolia Hills	77355
Magnolia Springs	75957
Magpetco (Part of Port Neches)	77651
Mahl	75961
Mahomet	78605

	ZIP
Mahoney	75482
Main Place (Part of Dallas)	75202
Majors	75457
Malakoff	75148
Mallard	76251
Mall Del Norte (Part of Laredo)	78040
Mall of Abilene (Part of Abilene)	79606
Malone	76660
Malta	75570
Mambrino	76048
Manchaca	78652
Manchester	75412
Manda	78653
Manheim	78659
Mankin	75163
Mankins	76366
Manor	78653
Manor East Shopping Center (Part of Bryan)	77801
Mansfield	76063
Manvel	77578
Maple (Bailey County)	79344
Maple (Red River County)	75417
Maple Crest Acres (Part of Vidor)	77662
Maple Springs	75455
Mapleton	75835
Marathon	79842
Marble Falls	78654
March Trailer Court	75169
Marfa	79843
Margaret	79227
Marie	76933
Marietta	75566
Marilee	75058
Marion	78124
Markham	77456
Markley	76460
Marlin	76661
Marquez	77865
Marshall	75670-71

For specific Marshall Zip Codes call (903) 938-4086

	ZIP
Marshall Creek	76262
Marshall Ford	78732
Marshall Meadows (Part of San Antonio)	78240
Marshall Springs	75455
Mart	76664
Martindale	78655
Martinez	78219
Martin Luther King (Part of Houston)	77033
Martins Mills	75754
Martin Springs	75482
Martinsville	75958
Marvin	75462
Mary Hardin-Baylor (Part of Belton)	76513
Maryneal	79535
Marysville	76252
Mason	76856
Mason Lake Estates	77327
Massey Lake	75861
Masterson	79058
Matador	79244
Matagorda	77457
Mathews	77434
Mathis	78368
Matinburg	75686
Maud	75567
Mauriceville	77626
Maverick	76865
Maxdale	76542
Maxey	75421
Maxwell	78656
May	76857
Maydelle	75772
Mayfair (Part of Houston)	77022
Mayfield (Hale County)	79041
Mayfield (Hill County)	76055
Mayflower (Newton County)	75977
Mayflower (Rusk County)	75691
Mayhill	76205
Maynard	77358
Maypearl	76064
Maysfield	76555
Meador Grove	76557
Meadow	79345
Meadowcreek (Part of San Angelo)	76904
Meadowood Acres	78252
Meadows	77477
Mecca	77871
Medicine Mound	79252
Medill	75460
Medina	78055
Medio (Part of Houston)	77022
Meek Estates	75163

	ZIP
New Boston	75570
New Braunfels	78130-33

For specific New Braunfels Zip Codes call (512) 625-7736

	ZIP
New Bremen	78950
Newburg	76442
Newby	75846
New Caney	77357
New Caney Heights	77357
Newcastle	76372
New Chapel Hill	75701
New Clarkson	76570
New Colony	75563
New Corn Hill	76537
New Deal	79350
New Fountain	78861
Newgulf	77462
New Harmony (Shelby County)	75973
New Harmony (Smith County)	75704
Newharp	76239
New Hebron	75685
New Home	79383
New Hope (Cherokee County)	75766
New Hope (Collin County)	75069
New Hope (Dallas County)	75149
New Hope (Henderson County)	75756
New Hope (Jones County)	79553
New Hope (Rusk County)	75662
New Hope (San Jacinto County)	77327
New Hope (Smith County)	75703
New Hope (Wood County)	75773
New Katy	78653
Newlin	79245
New London	75682
New Lynn	79381
New Mine	75686
New Moore	79351
Newport (Clay County)	76254
Newport (Harris County)	77532
New Prospect (Rusk County)	75652
New Prospect (Shelby County)	75652
New River Lake Estates	77327
New Salem (Falls County)	76570
New Salem (Palo Pinto County)	76472
New Salem (Rusk County)	75652
Newsome	75451
New Summerfield	75780
New Sweden (McCulloch County)	76825
New Sweden (Travis County)	78653
New Taiton	77437
Newton	75966
New Ulm	78950
New Waverly	77358
New Wehdem	77833
New Willard	77351
New York	75770
Neylandville	75401
Nickel	78629
Nickelberry	75566
Nickel Creek	88220
Niederwald	78640
Nigton	75926
Nimitz (Part of San Antonio)	78216
	78279

For specific Nimitz Zip Codes call (512) 341-5351

	ZIP
Nimrod	76437
Nineveh	75833
Nix	76550
Nixon	78140
Noack	76574
Nobility	75424
Noble	75470
Nockenut	78160
Nocona	76255
Nogalus	75845
Nolan	79537
Nolanville	76559
Nolte	78155
Nome	77629
Nona	77625
Noodle	79536
Noonday	75762
Nopal	78164
Nordheim	78141
Norias	78338
Norman Crossing	76574
Normandy	78877
Normangee	77871
Normanna	78142
Norse	76634

	ZIP
North Amarillo (Part of Amarillo)	79117
Northampton	77379
North Austin (Part of Austin)	78751
Northaven (Part of Dallas)	75229
North Beach (Part of Corpus Christi)	78402
North Bonami	75956
North Broadway (Part of San Antonio)	78217
North Caney	75482
North Cedar	75926
North Cleveland	77327
Northcliff	78108
North Concho Lake Estates	76901
Northcrest	76705
Northcrest Estates (Part of Victoria)	77901
Northcross Mall (Part of Austin)	78757
Northeast (Part of Austin)	78752
North East Mall (Part of Hurst)	76053
Northeast Station (Part of Odessa)	79764
Northern Hills	75020
Northfield	79201
Northgate (El Paso County)	79914
	79924

For specific Northgate Zip Codes call (915) 755-5821

	ZIP
Northgate (Victoria County)	77901
North Groesbeck	79252
North Heights (Part of Amarillo)	79107
North Hills Mall (Part of North Richland Hills)	76118
North Houston	77086
North Houston General Mail Facility (Part of Houston)	77315
North Houston Heights	77039
North Lake (Dallas County)	75238
Northlake (Denton County)	76247
Northlake Estates	78628
North Line Oaks	77301
Northline Shopping Center (Part of Houston)	77022
Northline Terrace	77093
North Oaks	78753
North Orange Heights	77630
Northpark (Part of Dallas)	75225
Northpark Malll (Part of El Paso)	79924
North Port Arthur (Part of Port Arthur)	77642
North Richland Hills	76118
Northrup	78942
North Rusk (Part of Rusk)	75785
North San Antonio Hills	78253
North San Pedro	78380
North Shepherd (Part of Houston)	77088
Northside Village (Part of Houston)	77015
North Springs	77373
North Star Mall (Part of San Antonio)	78216
Northtown Mall (Part of Dallas)	75234
Northwest (Part of Austin)	78757
Northwest Hills	78024
Northwest Mall (Part of Houston)	77292
Northwest Park	77086
Northwest Plaza (Part of Dallas)	75238
Northwood	78758
Northwood Hills Village (Part of Dallas)	75240
North Zulch	77872
Norton	76865
Norwood	75972
Notrees	79759
Nottingham Forest	77630
Nottingham Woods	75835
Novice (Coleman County)	79538
Novice (Lamar County)	75462
Novohrad	77975
Noxville	78631
Nugent	79601
Nursery	77976
Oakalla	76542
Oak Canyon	77302
Oak Creek Addition (Part of Grapevine)	76051
Oak Crest Estates	78628
Oak Dale (Erath County)	76401
Oakdale (Hopkins County)	75482
Oak Flat (Angelina County)	75949
Oak Flat (Nacogdoches County)	75760

	ZIP
Oak Flat (Rusk County)	75681
Oak Forest (Harris County)	77018
Oak Forest (Travis County)	78759
Oak Grove (Bowie County)	75554
Oak Grove (Wood County)	75783
Oak Grove (Camp County)	75686
Oak Grove (Ellis County)	75119
Oak Grove (Kaufman County)	75142
Oak Grove (Tarrant County)	76028
Oak Hill (Jasper County)	75951
Oak Hill (Johnson County)	76031
Oak Hill (Rusk County)	75652
Oakhill (Travis County)	78735
Oak Hills Acres	77362
Oakhill Station (Part of Austin)	78749
Oakhurst	77359
Oak Island	77514
Oak Lake	76705
Oakland (Cherokee County)	75785
Oakland (Colorado County)	78951
Oakland (Rusk County)	75652
Oakland (Van Zandt County)	75103
Oak Lawn (Part of Dallas)	75219
Oaklawn Village (Part of Texarkana)	75501
Oak Leaf	75154
Oak Point	75034
Oak Ridge (Cooke County)	76240
Oak Ridge (Kaufman County)	75160
Oak Ridge (Llano County)	78654
Oak Ridge (Nacogdoches County)	75961
Oak Ridge (Parker County)	76086
Oak Ridge North	77302
Oaks (Bee County)	78119
Oaks (Tarrant County)	76114
Oaks North	78260
Oak Terrace	77365
Oak Trail Shores	76048
Oak Valley	75110
Oakview	77611
Oak Village North	78266
Oakville	78060
Oakwilde	77093
Oakwood	75855
Oakwood Village and Westwood Plaza (Part of Abilene)	79603
Oatmeal	78605
O'Brien	79539
Oceanshore	77650
Ocee	76638
Odell	79247
Odell Addition (Part of Grapevine)	76051
Odem	78370
Odessa	79760-69

For specific Odessa Zip Codes call (915) 332-6436

	ZIP
Odom	75147
Odonnell	79351
Oenaville	76501
O'Farrell	75551
Oglesby	76561
Oilla	77630
Oilton	78371
Oklahoma	77355
Oklahoma Flat	79339
Oklahoma Lane	79325
Oklaunion	76373
Okra	76435
Ola	75142
Old Boston	75570
Old Bowling	77865
Old Brazoria (Part of Brazoria)	77422
Old Dime Box	77853
Olden	76466
Oldenburg	78945
Old Ferry	78669
Old Glory	79540
Old Ivy	75847
Old Kinkler	77964
Old Larissa	75757
Old London	75682
Old Mill (Part of Leon Valley)	78238
Old Mobeetie (Part of Mobeetie)	79061
Old Moulton	77975
Old Ocean	77463
Old River Lake	77327
Old River Terrace	77530
Old River-Winfree	77520
Olds	75951
Old Sabinetown	75948

	ZIP		ZIP		ZIP
Old Salem	75933	Pantego	76094	Peerless	75482
Old Union (Bowie County)	75574	Papalote	78387	Peggy	78062
Old Union (Limestone		Paradise	76073	Pelham	76648
County)	76687	Paradise Bay	75143	Pelican Bay	76020
Old Union (Titus County)	75455	Paradise Hills	75929	Pendleton	76564
Old Waverly	77358	Paris	75460-62	Pendleton Harbor	75948
Oletha	76687	For specific Paris Zip Codes call		Penelope	76676
Olfen	76875	(903) 784-3381		Peniel (Part of Greenville)	75401
Olin	76457	Park	78945	Penitas	78576
Olive	77625	Park Cities (Part of		Pennington	75856
Olivia	77979	University Park)	75205	Penwell	79776
Olmito	78575	Parkdale (Part of Dallas)	75227	Peoria	76645
Olmos (Bee County)	78389	Parkdale Mall (Part of		Pep	79353
Olmos (Starr County)	78582	Beaumont)	77706	Percilla	75844
Olmos Park	78212	Parkdale Plaza (Part of		Perezville	78572
Olney	76374	Corpus Christi)	78411	Perico	79087
Olton	79064	Parker (Collin County)	75002	Permian Mall (Part of	
Omaha	75571	Parker (Johnson County)	76050	Odessa)	79762
Omen	75789	Parker Point	75980	Pernitas Point	78022
Onalaska	77360	Parker Square (Part of		Perrin	76486
One Seventy Seven Lake		Wichita Falls)	76308	Perrin Field	75020
Estates	77356	Park Forest (Part of Dallas)	75240	Perrin Heights	75020
Onion Creek	78747	Park Glen (Part of Houston)	77072	Perry	76677
Opdyke	79336	Park Place (Part of		Perry Landing (Part of	
Opdyke West	79336	Houston)	77017	Jones Creek)	77541
Opelika	75778	Park Row (Part of Katy)	77449	Perryton	79070
Oplin	79510	Parks at Arlington, The (Part		Perryville	75494
O'Quinn	78945	of Arlington)	76015	Pershing (Part of Austin)	78702
Ora	75949	Park Springs	76270	Pershing Park	76544
Oran	76449	Parkview (Part of Fort		Personville	76642
Orange	77630-32	Stockton)	79735	Pert	75801
For specific Orange Zip Codes call (409) 883-9351		Parkview Estates	78155	Peters	77474
		Parkwood	77612	Petersburg	79250
Orangedale	78102	Parkwood Estates	77032	Peterson	77627
Orangefield	77639	Parnell	79201	Peters Prairie	75426
Orange Grove (Harris		Parvin	75009	Petersville	77995
County)	77039	Pasadena	77501-08	Petrolia	76377
Orange Grove (Jim Wells		For specific Pasadena Zip Codes call (713) 475-5140		Petronila	78380
County)	78372			Pettway	76629
Orangeville	75491	Pasadena Town Square		Pettibone	76520
Orchard	77464	(Part of Pasadena)	77506	Pettit	79336
Ore City	75683	Patilo	76642	Pettus	78146
Orient	76901	Patman	75656	Petty (Lamar County)	75470
Orla	79770	Patrich	75652	Petty (Lynn County)	79373
Orme (Part of Arlington)	76010	Patricia	79331	Petty's Chapel	75110
Osage	76528	Patrick (Dallas County)	75125	Pflugerville	78660
Oscar	76501	Patrick (McLennan County)	76708	Phalba	75147
Osceola	76055	Patroon	75973	Pharr	78577
Ottine	78658	Pattison	77466	Phelan	78602
Otto	76675	Patton	76689	Phelps	77340
Ovalo	79541	Pattonfield	75644	Phillips	79007
Overland Plaza (Part of		Patton Park	76544	Phillipsburg	77426
Arlington)	76003	Patton Village	77372	Pickens	75751
Overton	75684	Pattonville	75468	Pickett	75110
Ovilla	75154	Pauline	75124	Pickton	75471
Owens (Brown County)	76801	Pauls Store	75973	Pidcoke	76528
Owens (Crosby County)	79357	Pawelekville	78113	Piedmont (Grimes County)	77830
Owensville	77856	Pawnee	78145	Piedmont (Upshur County)	75644
Owentown	75708	Paxton	75954	Pierce	77467
Oyster Creek	77541	Paynes Corner	79360	Pierces Chapel	75766
Ozona	76943	Payne Springs	75124	Piggly Wiggly (Part of	
Pacio	75450	Payton Colony	78606	Bryan)	77801
Pack Unit	77868	Peach Creek	77488	Pike	75424
Padgett	76374	Peach Creek Estates	77372	Pilgrim Ridge	77367
Padre-Staples Mall (Part of		Peach Tree (Brazos County)	77801	Pilgrims Rest	75410
Corpus Christi)	78411	Peachtree (Jasper County)	75951	Pilot Grove	75491
Paducah	79248	Peacock	79542	Pilot Knob	78744
Pagoda	75862	Peadenville	76067	Pilot Point	76258
Paige	78659	Pearl	76528	Pine	75686
Paint Rock	76866	Pearland	77581	Pine Acres	77357
Pakan	79079		77584	Pine Branch	75417
Palacios	77465		77588	Pine Crest	77301
Palava	79556	For specific Pearland Zip Codes call (713) 485-2814		Pine Forest (Hopkins	
Palestine (Anderson				County)	75471
County)	75801-02	Pearl City	77995	Pine Forest (Orange	
For specific Palestine Zip Codes call (903) 729-2435		Pear Ridge (Part of Port		County)	77662
		Arthur)	77640	Pine Grove (Cherokee	
Palestine (Polk County)	75936	Pearsall	78061	County)	75766
Palito Blanco	78332	Pearsons Chapel	75851	Pine Grove (Newton	
Palmer	75152	Pear Valley	76867	County)	75966
Palmetto (Part of Oakhurst)	77359	Peaster	76485	Pine Grove (Orange	
Palm Harbor	78382	Pebble Beach	75121	County)	77630
Palmhurst	78572	Pebble Hills (Part of El		Pine Hill (Cherokee County)	75766
Palm Park	78223	Paso)	79925	Pinehill (Rusk County)	75652
Palm Valley	78550		79937	Pinehurst (Montgomery	
Palmview	78572	For specific Pebble Hills Zip Codes call (915) 598-2295		County)	77362
Palo Alto	78343			Pinehurst (Orange County)	77630
Paloduro	79226	Pecan (Part of Del Rio)	78840	Pine Island	77445
Palo Pinto	76484	Pecan Acres (Orange		Pine Lake	77356
Paluxy	76467	County)	77662	Pineland	75968
Pampa	79065-66	Pecan Acres (Wise County)	76071	Pine Mills	75773
For specific Pampa Zip Codes call (806) 665-5713		Pecan Gap	75469	Pine Park	75948
		Pecangrove (Coryell		Pine Prairie	77340
Pancake	76528	County)	76528	Pine Ridge	77625
Pandale	76943	Pecan Grove (Fort Bend		Pine Springs (Culberson	
Pandora	78143	County)	77469	County)	88220
Panhandle	79068	Pecan Hill	75154	Pine Springs (Smith County)	75702
Panna Maria	78144	Pecan Lake Area	77835	Pine Trail Shores	75762
Panola	75685	Pecan Plantation	76048	Pine Valley	75941
Panorama Estates	75169	Pecos	79772	Pineview	75494
Panorama Village	77301	Peeltown	75158		

	ZIP
Rattan	75432
Ravenna	75476
Rayburn	77327
Rayburn Hideaway	75937
Rayford	77373
Rayland	76384
Raymondville	78580
Ray Point	78071
Raywood	77582
Reagan	76680
Reagan Wells	78801
Reagor Springs	75165
Realitos	78376
Reata Trails	78628
Redbank	75561
Red Bird Mall (Part of Dallas)	75237
Red Bluff	79770
Red Branch	75855
Redford	79846
Red Gate	78539
Red Hill (Cass County)	75560
Red Hill (Lamar County)	75473
Red Lake	75855
Redland (Angelina County)	75901
Redland (Leon County)	75833
Redland (Van Zandt County)	75754
Redlawn	75925
Redlick	75501
Redmond Terrace (Part of College Station)	77840
Red Oak (Ellis County)	75154
Red Oak (Kaufman County)	75142
Red Ranger	76569
Red River Army Depot	75501
Red Rock	78662
Red Springs (Baylor County)	76380
Red Springs (Bowie County)	75501
Red Springs (Smith County)	75701
Red Top	76450
Redtown (Anderson County)	75839
Red Town (Angelina County)	75901
Redwater	75573
Redwood	78666
Reedville	78656
Reese	75766
Reese Air Force Base	79489
Refugio	78377
Regency	76864
Rehburg	77835
Rehobeth	75633
Reilly Springs	75482
Rek Hill	78940
Reklaw	75784
Relampago	78570
Reliance	77801
Remolino	78582
Rendon	76028
Reno (Lamar County)	75462
Reno (Parker County)	76020
Retreat (Grimes County)	77868
Retreat (Hill County)	76627
Retreat (Navarro County)	75110
Retrieve Unit	77515
Retta	76028
Rhea	79035
Rhea Mills	75069
Rhineland	76371
Rhome	76078
Rhonesboro	75494
Ricardo	78363
Rice (Navarro County)	75155
Rice (Smith County)	75701
Rices Crossing	76574
Richards	77873
Richardson	75080-85

For specific Richardson Zip Codes call (214) 235-8353

	ZIP
Richardson Square (Part of Richardson)	75081
Richland (Dallas County)	75243
Richland (Navarro County)	76681
Richland (Rains County)	75472
Richland Hills	76118
Richland Mall (Part of Waco)	76710
Richland Park (Part of Fort Worth)	76118
Richland Plaza (Part of North Richland Hills)	76118
Richland Springs	76871
Richmond	77406
	77469

For specific Richmond Zip Codes call (713) 342-2021

	ZIP
Richwood	77531
Riderville	75633
Ridge (Mills County)	76864
Ridge (Robertson County)	77856
Ridgecrest (Part of Amarillo)	79109
Ridgecrest Addition	77630
Ridgeheights	79701
Ridgemere (Part of Amarillo)	79107
Ridgeway	75482
Ridglea (Part of Fort Worth)	76116
Ridgmar Mall (Part of Fort Worth)	76116
Ridings	75476
Riesel	76682
Rimwick Forrest	77355
Rincon	78582
Ringgold	76261
Rio Farms	78538
Rio Frio	78879
Rio Grande City	78582
Rio Hondo	78583
Rio Llano Ranch	78643
Riomedina	78066
Rio Pecos	79740
Rios	78349
Rio Vista	76093
Rising Star	76471
Rita	77857
River Bend (Newton County)	75932
River Bend (Sabine County)	75948
River Bend Estates	78003
River Brook	77302
Riverby	75488
Rivercenter (Part of San Antonio)	78205
Riverdrive Mall (Part of Laredo)	78040
River Hill	75633
Riverland	76365
River Oak Lake Estates	78758
River Oaks (Harris County)	77019
River Oaks (Tarrant County)	76114
River Oaks Ranch	78063
River Plantation	77302
River Ridge	75951
Riverside (Tarrant County)	76111
Riverside (Walker County)	77367
Riverside Crest (Part of Houston)	77338
River Woods Estates	77050
Riviera	78379
Riviera Beach	78379
Roach	75551
Roach Town	75758
Roane	75110
Roanoke	76262
Roans Prairie	77875
Roaring Springs	79256
Robbins	75846
Robert Lee	76945
Robertson	79343
Robinson	76706
Robinson Plaza (Part of Robinson)	76706
Robstown	78380
Roby	79543
Rochelle	76872
Rochester	79544
Rock Creek	76708
Rockdale	76567
Rockett	75165
Rockford	75462
Rock Harbor	76048
Rockhill (Collin County)	75069
Rock Hill (Jasper County)	75951
Rock Hill (Wood County)	75783
Rockhouse	78950
Rock Island (Colorado County)	77470
Rock Island (Polk County)	75939
Rockland	75970
Rockne	78602
Rockport	78382
Rock Prairie	77801
Rocksprings	78880
Rockwall	75087
Rockwood	76873
Rocky Branch	75638
Rocky Creek Park	77835
Rocky Hill	76661
Rocky Mound	75686
Rocky Point	75440
Rocky Springs (Angelina County)	75949
Rocky Springs (Tyler County)	75970
Roddy	75147
Rodney	76639
Roganville	75956
Rogers	76569
Rogers Hill	76691
Rolling Hills (Hunt County)	75453
Rolling Hills (Potter County)	79108
Rolling Hills (Waller County)	77445
Rolling Hills Shores	76086
Rolling Meadows	75603
Rolling Oaks	75169
Rolling Oaks Mall (Part of San Antonio)	78247
Rollingwood	78746
Roma	78584
Roman Forest	77357
Roman Hills	77356
Romayor	77368
Romero	79022
Romney	76471
Roosevelt (Kimble County)	76874
Roosevelt (Lubbock County)	79401
Ropesville	79358
Rosalie	75417
Rosanky	78953
Roscoe	79545
Rosebud	76570
Rose City	77662
Rosedale	76661
Rose Hill (Harris County)	77375
Rose Hill (San Jacinto County)	77331
Rose Hill (Wood County)	75773
Rose Hill Acres	77656
Rosenberg	77471
Rosenthal	76655
Rosevine	75930
Rosewood	75644
Rosharon	77583
Rosita (Duval County)	78384
Rosita (Starr County)	78582
Ross	76684
Rosser	75157
Rosston	76263
Rossville	78065
Rotan	79546
Round Mountain	78663
Round Prairie	75144
Round Rock	78664
	78680-81

For specific Round Rock Zip Codes call (512) 255-3516

	ZIP
Round Timber	76380
Round Top	78954
Roundup	79313
Rowden	79504
Rowena	76875
Rowlett	75088
Roxton	75477
Royal Forest	77303
Royal Lane (Part of Dallas)	75230
Royal Oaks (Henderson County)	75143
Royal Oaks (Llano County)	78639
Royal Oaks (Orange County)	77626
Royalty	79779
Royalwood	77028
Roy Miller (Part of Corpus Christi)	78465
Roy Royall (Part of Houston)	77093
Royse City	75189
Royston	79543
Rucker	76444
Rugby	75435
Ruidosa	79843
Rule	79547
Rumley	76539
Run	78537
Runaway Bay	76426
Runge	78151
Rural Shade	75144
Rushwood	77067
Rusk	75785
Rutersville	78945
Ruth Springs	75163
Ryanville	78377
Rye	77369
Sabanna	76437
Sabathany	76086
Sabinal	78881
Sabine	77640
Sabine Pass	77655
Sabine Sands	75928
Sabinetown	75948
Sachse	75040
Sacul	75788
Saddle and Surrey	77356
Sadler	76264
Sagerton	79548
Saginaw	76179
St. Claire Cove	77650
St. Elmo	75859
St. Francis	79107
St. Francis Village	76036

	ZIP
St. Hedwig	78152
St. Jo	76265
Saint John	78956
Saint John Colony	78616
St. Lawrence	79739
St. Louis (Part of Tyler)	75702
St. Paul (Brazoria County)	77422
St. Paul (Collin County)	75098
St. Paul (Falls County)	76661
St. Paul (San Patricio County)	78387
Salado	76571
Salem (Bastrop County)	78953
Salem (Milam County)	76520
Salem (Smith County)	75789
Salesville	76067
Salineno	78585
Salmon	75839
Salona	76230
Salt Flat	79847
Salt Gap	76836
Saltillo	75478
Sam Houston (Part of Houston)	77002
Sam Houston College (Part of Huntsville)	77341
Samnorwood	79077
Sam Rayburn	75951
Sanaloma Estates	78628
San Angelo	76901-09

For specific San Angelo Zip Codes call (915) 655-5681

San Antonio 78201-99

For specific San Antonio Zip Codes call (512) 657-8302

COLLEGES & UNIVERSITIES

	ZIP
Incarnate Word College	78209
Our Lady of the Lake University of San Antonio	78207
St. Mary's University	78228
Trinity University	78212
University of Texas Health Science Center at San Antonio	78284
University of Texas at San Antonio	78285

FINANCIAL INSTITUTIONS

	ZIP
Bank One, N.A.	78205
The Bank of San Antonio	78205
Broadway National Bank	78209
First City, Texas-San Antonio, N.A.	78216
First Federal Savings Bank	78209
Frost National Bank of San Antonio	78205
Groos Bank, National Association	78216
International Bank of Commerce	78209
Jefferson State Bank	78201
Kelly Field National Bank	78238
Nationsbank of Texas, N.A.	78205
Sunbelt Federal Savings, F.S.B.	78217
Texas Commerce Bank-San Antonio, N.A.	78209
U.S.A.A. Federal Savings Bank	78288
Westside Bank	78207

HOSPITALS

	ZIP
Audie L. Murphy Memorial Veterans Hospital	78284
Baptist Medical Center	78205
Bexar County Hospital District	78229
Humana Hospital-San Antonio	78229
Santa Rosa Health Care Corporation	78207
Southwest Texas Methodist Hospital	78229

HOTELS/MOTELS

	ZIP
Embassy Suites Northwest	78230
The Hilton Palacio del Rio	78205
Holiday Inn Riverwalk North	78204
Marriott Riverwalk	78205
Ramada Inn Airport	78209
Hotel St. Anthony	78205

MILITARY INSTALLATIONS

	ZIP
Brooks Air Force Base	78235
Camp Bullis	78234
Camp Stanley Storage Activity	78269
Fort Sam Houston	78234
Kelly Air Force Base	78241

	ZIP
Lackland Air Force Base	78236
Texas Air National Guard, FB6432, Kelly Air Force Base	78241
San Augustine	75972
San Benito	78586
San Carlos	78539
Sanco	76945
Sanctuary	76020
Sanderson	79848
Sand Flat (Rains County)	75440
Sandflat (Smith County)	75706
Sand Flat (Van Zandt County)	75140
Sand Hill (Floyd County)	79235
Sand Hill (Upshur County)	75644
Sandia	78383
San Diego	78384
Sandjack	75928
Sand Lake	75119
Sandoval	76574
Sand Ridge (Houston County)	75835
Sand Ridge (Wharton County)	77434
Sand Springs (Howard County)	79720
Sand Springs (Wood County)	75773
Sandusky	76273
Sandy	78665
Sandy Acres	79703
Sandy Corner	77437
Sandy Creek	76556
Sandy Fork	76632
Sandy Harbor	78654
Sandy Hill	77833
Sandy Point	77583
Sandy Ridge	77351
San Elizario	79849
San Felipe	77473
Sanford	79078
Sanford Estates	79036
San Gabriel	76577
San Gabriel Heights	78628
Sanger	76266
San Geromino	78023
San Isidro	78588
San Jacinto (Part of Amarillo)	79106
San Jose	78332
San Juan (Hidalgo County)	78589
San Juan (Nueces County)	78406
San Leanna	78748
San Leon	77539
San Marcos	78666-67

For specific San Marcos Zip Codes call (512) 392-3451

	ZIP
San Patricio	78368
San Pedro	78520
San Perlita	78590
San Saba	76877
Sansom Park	76114
Santa Anna	76878
Santa Catarina	78582
Santa Cruz	78582
Santa Elena	78591
Santa Fe	77510
	77517

For specific Santa Fe Zip Codes call (409) 925-2934

	ZIP
Santa Maria	78592
Santa Monica	78580
Santa Rita (Part of San Angelo)	76901
Santa Rosa	78593
Santo	76472
San Ygnacio	78067
Saragosa	79780
Saratoga	77585
Sarco	77963
Sardis (Cass County)	75656
Sardis (Ellis County)	76065
Sargent	77414
Sarita	78385
Sash	75446
Saspamco	78112
Satin	76685
Satsuma	77040
Sattler	78130
Sauney Stand	77426
Savage	79357
Savoy	75479
Sayers	78602
Sayersville	78653
Scenic Heights	78130
Scenic Hills	78108
Scenic Oaks	78023
Scenic Terrace	78130
Schattel	78005

	ZIP
Schertz	78154
Schicke Point	77465
Schoolerville	76531
School Land	78140
Schroeder	77963
Schulenburg	78956
Schumansville	78130
Schwab City	77351
Schwertner	76573
Scissors	78537
Scotland	76379
Scotsdale (Ector County)	79762
Scotsdale (El Paso County)	79925
Scott	75169
Scottsville	75688
Scranton	76437
Scrappin Valley	75977
Scroggins	75480
Scurry	75158
Seabrook	77586
Sea Crest Park	77520
Seadrift	77983
Seagoville	75159
Seagraves	79359
Sea Isle	77554
Seale	76687
Sealy	77474
Seaton	76501
Seawillow	78644
Sebastian	78594
Sebastopol	75862
Seco Mines	78852
Security	77327
Sedalia	75495
Segno	77351
Segovia	76849
Seguin	78155-56

For specific Seguin Zip Codes call (512) 379-2594

	ZIP
Sejita	78376
Selden	76401
Selfs	75446
Selma	78209
Selman City	75689
Seminary Hill (Part of Fort Worth)	76115
Seminole	79360
Senate	76458
Senior	78073
Sequoia Estates	77032
Serbin	78942
Serenada	78628
Serna (Part of San Antonio)	78218
	78266

For specific Serna Zip Codes call (512) 655-0151

	ZIP
Seth Ward	79072
Seven Oaks	77350
Seven Pines	75601
Seven Points	75143
Seven Sisters	78357
Sexton	75972
Sexton City	75684
Seymore	75482
Seymour	76380
Shadow Glen	77530
Shadow Lake Estates	77365
Shadowland	75435
Shadowland Retreat	77365
Shady Acres (Brazoria County)	77422
Shady Acres (Burnet County)	78654
Shady Brook Acres	77355
Shady Grove (Angelina County)	75941
Shady Grove (Cherokee County)	75785
Shady Grove (Dallas County)	75050
Shady Grove (Kerr County)	78028
Shady Grove (Marion County)	75657
Shady Grove (Nacogdoches County)	75961
Shady Grove (Navarro County)	76679
Shady Grove (Panola County)	75669
Shady Grove (Rains County)	75440
Shady Grove (Smith County)	75706
Shady Grove (Upshur County)	75755
Shady Hollow	78739
Shady Oaks (Henderson County)	75751
Shady Oaks (Tarrant County)	76053

	ZIP
Steep Hollow	77801
Stellar	78949
Stephen F. Austin University (Part of Nacogdoches)	75962
Stephenville	76401
Sterley	79241
Sterling City	76951
Sterlings Island	77367
Sterrett	75165
Stewards Mill	75840
Stewart	75691
Stewart Heights (Part of Baytown)	77520
Stieren	78632
Stilson	77535
Stinnett	79083
Stith	79536
Stockard	75751
Stockdale	78160
Stockman	75975
Stock Yards (Part of Fort Worth)	76106
Stoneburg	76230
Stoneham	77868
Stonewall	78671
Stonewall Mall (Part of Corpus Christi)	78410
Stony	76259
Stout	75494
Stowell	77661
Stranger	76653
Stratford	79084
Stratton	77954
Stratton Ridge	77531
Strawn	76475
Streetman	75859
Strickland	75968
String Prairie	78953
Structure	78621
Stuart Place	78550
Study Butte	79852
Stumptown	75931
Sturdivant	76067
Sturgeon	76273
Styx	75143
Sublett (Part of Arlington)	76063
Sublime	77986
Sudan	79371
Suffolk	75644
Sugar Land	77478-79
	77487
For specific Sugar Land Zip Codes call (713) 494-2042	
Sugar Valley	77480
Sullivan City	78595
Sulphur Bluff	75481
Sulphur Springs (Angelina County)	75980
Sulphur Springs (Hopkins County)	75482-83
For specific Sulphur Springs Zip Codes call (903) 885-5215	
Sulphur Springs (Rusk County)	75760
Summerall	75147
Summerfield (Castro County)	79085
Summerfield (Upshur County)	75644
Summer Hill	75751
Summit Heights	79930-31
For specific Summit Heights Zip Codes call (915) 565-6589	
Sumner	75486
Sun (Part of Denison)	75020
Sundown	79372
Sunnyside (Castro County)	79027
Sunny Side (Waller County)	77445
Sunnyslope (Part of Texarkana)	75501
Sunnyvale	75149
Sunray	79086
Sunrise (El Paso County)	79904
Sunrise (Falls County)	76661
Sunrise Acres (Part of El Paso)	79904
Sunrise Beach	78643
Sunrise Mall (Cameron County)	78521
Sunrise Mall (Nueces County)	78412
Sunset (Lubbock County)	79416
Sunset (Montague County)	76270
Sunset Mall (Part of San Angelo)	76904
Sunset Marketown (Part of Amarillo)	79102
Sunset Ridge	77301
Sunset Valley	78745
Sunshine Hill	76360
Sun Valley (El Paso County)	79924

	ZIP
Sun Valley (Lamar County)	75462
Surf Oaks (Part of Seabrook)	77586
Surfside Beach	77541
Sutherland Springs	78161
Swamp City	75647
Swan	75706
Swan Lagoon (Part of Nassau Bay)	77058
Swanson Hill	75801
Sweeny	77480
Sweeny Switch	78368
Sweet Home (Guadalupe County)	78155
Sweet Home (Lavaca County)	77987
Sweetwater (Comanche County)	76442
Sweetwater (Nolan County)	79556
Swenson	79502
Swift	75961
Swiss Alp	78956
Swiss Village	78611
Sycamore	75932
Sylvan	75462
Sylvan Beach (Part of La Porte)	77571
Sylvester	79560
Tabor	77801
Tacoma	75633
Tadmor	75847
Taft	78390
Taft Southwest	78390
Tahoka	79373
Talco	75487
Tall Pines	75630
Talpa	76882
Talty	75160
Tamega	78605
Tamina	77302
Tandy Center (Part of Fort Worth)	76102
Tanglewood	78947
Tanglewood Forest	78748
Tanglewood Island	76424
Tanglewood Manor	77357
Tankersly	76901
Tarkington Acres	77327
Tarkington Prairie	77327
Tarleton (Part of Stephenville)	76402
Tarpley	78883
Tarrant (Part of Fort Worth)	76039
Tarzan	79783
Tatum	75691
Tavener	77435
Taylor	76574
Taylor Lake Village	77586
Taylorsville	78662
Taylor Town	75462
Taylorville	75452
Teague	75860
Teaselville	75757
Tecula	75766
Tehuacana	76686
Telegraph	76883
Telephone	75488
Telferner	77988
Telico	75119
Tell	79259
Temple	76501-05
For specific Temple Zip Codes call (817) 773-0792	
Temple Mall (Part of Temple)	76502
Temple Springs	75951
Tenaha	75974
Tennessee	75975
Tennessee Colony	75861
Tennyson	76953
Terlingua	79852
Terrell	75160
Terrell Hills	78209
Terrell Station	79781
Terrell Wells (Part of San Antonio)	78221
Terrys Chapel	76570
Terryville	77995
Texarkana	75501-07
For specific Texarkana Zip Codes call (903) 838-9537	
Texas Christian University (Part of Fort Worth)	76129
Texas City	77590-92
For specific Texas City Zip Codes call (409) 948-2591	
Texas City Junction (Part of Texas City)	77590
Texas City Junction (Part of Hitchcock)	77563

	ZIP
Texas Lutheran (Part of Seguin)	78155
Texas Womans University (Part of Denton)	76204
Texhoma	73949
Texline	79087
Texon	76932
Thalia	79227
Thayer	78570
The Bluffs (Part of San Angelo)	76901
The Colony	75056
Thedford	75771
The Grove	76576
The Heights (Part of Alvin)	77511
The Homestead	78736
The Knobbs	78650
Thelma (Bexar County)	78221
Thelma (Limestone County)	76642
The Meadows (Part of Meadows)	77477
The Oaks	78130
Theon	76537
Thermo	75482
The Shores (Part of Amarillo)	79110
The Woodlands	77380
The Y	75551
Thicket	77374
Thomas	75644
Thomas Manor (Part of El Paso)	79915
Thomaston	77989
Thompson	77040
Thompson Heights	75020
Thompsons	77481
Thompsonville	78959
Thornberry	76306
Thorndale	76577
Thornton	76687
Thorntonville	79756
Thorp Spring	76048
Thousand Oaks (Part of San Antonio)	78232
	78247
	78258-61
	78270
For specific Thousand Oaks Zip Codes call (512) 494-9671	
Thrall	76578
Three Leagues	79331
Three Points	78660
Three Rivers	78071
Three Way	76401
Thrifty	76801
Throckmorton	76483
Thurber	76463
Tidwell	75401
Tidwell Prairie	76629
Tierra Linda Ranch	78028
Tigertown	75446
Tiki Island	77554
Tilden	78072
Tilmon	78616
Timber Cove (Part of Taylor Lake Village)	77586
Timberlake	77429
Timberlake Acres	77365
Timber Lakes Estates	77380
Timber Ridge (Bexar County)	78251
Timber Ridge (Montgomery County)	77380
Timothy	75105
Timpson	75975
Tin Top	76086
Tioga	76271
Tira	75482
Tivoli	77990
Tivydale	78624
Tobe Hahn (Part of Beaumont)	77706
Toco	75421
Tod (Part of Seabrook)	77586
Todd City	75801
Todd Mission	77363
Togo	78957
Tokio	79376
Tolar	76476
Tolbert	76384
Toledo Village (Newton County)	75932
Toledo Village (Sabine County)	75948
Tolosa	75143
Tomball	77375
	77377
For specific Tomball Zip Codes call (713) 255-3027	
Tom Bean	75489
Tonkowon Country	78628

	ZIP		ZIP		ZIP
Tool	75143		75372	Vidor	77662
Topsey	76522	For specific University Zip Codes			77670
Tornillo	79853	call (214) 739-3331		For specific Vidor Zip Codes call	
Tours	76691	University (Part of Austin)	78712	(409) 769-4247	
Tow	78672	University of Dallas (Part of		Vienna	77964
Town and Country Center		Irving)	75061	View	79606
(Part of Houston)	77024	University of Texas at El		Viewpoint	75460
Town Bluff	75979	Paso (Part of El Paso)	79902	Vigo Park	79088
Town East Mall (Part of		University Park (Bexar		Vilas	76534
Mesquite)	75149	County)	78228	Villa Cavazos	78520
Town Oaks (Part of		University Park (Dallas		Village (Part of Highland	
Marshall)	75670	County)	75205	Park)	75205
Town Plaza (Part of		University Park (Wichita		Village Mills	77663
Victoria)	77901	County)	76308	Village Shores	78130
Town West	77478	University Place (Part of		Village Station (Part of	
Toyah	79785	Nacogdoches)	75961	Midland)	79704
Toyahvale	79786	Upper Meyersville	78164	Villa Nueva	78520
Tracy	76567	Upshaw	75943	Villareales	78582
Tradewinds	75143	Upton	78957	Vincent	79511
Trammells	77045	Urbana	77371	Vineyard	76458
Travis	76656	Utility (Part of San Antonio)	78219	Vinton	79821
Travis Peak	78654	Utley	78602	Violet	78380
Trawick	75961	Utopia	78884	Virginia Point	77554
Trent	79561	Uvalde	78801-02	Vista del Sol (Part of El	
Trenton	75490	For specific Uvalde Zip Codes call		Paso)	79935
Trevat	75845	(512) 278-3911		Vistula	75851
Tri Cities	75751	Valdasta	75424	Voca	76887
Trickham	76878	Valentine	79854	Volente	78641
Tri-Lake Estates	77356	Valera	76884	Von Ormy	78073
Trimmier Friendship	76542	Valle de Oro	79010	Voss	76888
Trinidad	75163	Valle Vista Mall (Part of		Votaw	77376
Trinity	75862	Harlingen)	78550	Voth (Part of Beaumont)	77709
Trinity Park	75098	Valleycreek	75452	Vsetin	77964
Trophy Club	76262	Valley Hi (Part of San		Waco	76701-16
Tropical Acres	77901	Antonio)	78227	For specific Waco Zip Codes call	
Troup	75789	Valley Lodge (Part of		(817) 757-6585	
Trout Creek	75933	Simonton)	77476	Wade	78372
Troy	76579	Valley Mills	76689	Wadsworth	77483
Truby	79525	Valley Spring	76885	Waelder	78959
Truce	76230	Valley View (Comal County)	78130	Wainwright (Part of San	
Trumbull	75125	Valley View (Cooke County)	76272	Antonio)	78208
Truscott	79260	Valley View (McLennan		Wainwright Heights	76544
Tucker	75801	County)	76701	Waka	79093
Tuleta	78162	Valley View (Mitchell		Wake	79243
Tulia	79088	County)	79512	Wakefield	75939
Tulip	75447	Valley View (Runnels		Wake Village	75501
Tulsita	78119	County)	76821	Walburg	78673
Tundra	75103	Valley View (Upshur		Waldeck	78946
Tunis	77836	County)	75644	Walden	77356
Tupelo	75155	Valley View (Wichita		Walden Place	77093
Turkey	79261	County)	76367	Walden Woods (Part of	
Turkey Creek (Part of		Valley View Center (Part of		Houston)	77012
Copperas Cove)	76522	Dallas)	75244	Waldrip	76852
Turlington	75840	Valley Wells	78830	Walhalla	78954
Turnersville	76528	Val Verde	76518	Walkers Mill	75650
Turnertown	75689	Val Verde Park Estates	78840	Walker Village	76544
Turney	75766	Van	75790	Wall	76957
Turtle Bayou	77514	Van Alstyne	75495	Wallace	75103
Tuscola	79562	Vance	78828	Wallace Chapel	75686
Tuttle Addition	77488	Vancourt	76955	Waller	77484
Tuxedo	79553	Vandalia	75426	Wallis	77485
Twine Cedar Retreat	75948	Vanderbilt	77991	Wallisville	77597
Twin Shores	77378	Vanderpool	78885	Walnut Bend	76273
Twin Valley Terrace	78073	Vandyke	76442	Walnut Creek	77355
Twitty	79090	Vanetia	77865	Walnut Forest	78753
Tye	79563	Van Horn	79855	Walnut Grove (Collin	
Tyler	75701-13	Van Vleck	77482	County)	75069
For specific Tyler Zip Codes call		Varisco	77801	Walnut Grove (Smith	
(903) 595-8621		Vasco	75450	County)	75703
Tynan	78391	Vashti	76228	Walnut Hill (Part of Dallas)	75220
Type	78621	Vattmannville	78379	Walnut Hills	77303
Uhland	78640	Vaughan	76645	Walnut Springs (Bosque	
Umbarger	79091	Vealmoor	79720	County)	76690
Uncertain	75661	Veal Station	76082	Walnut Springs	
Union (Brazos County)	77801	Vedas Camp	79521	(Montgomery County)	77355
Union (Franklin County)	75478	Vega	79092	Walston Springs	75801
Union (Lubbock County)	79364	Venable Village	76544	Walton (Cass County)	71082
Union (Scurry County)	79549	Ventura	77355	Walton (Van Zandt County)	75751
Union (Terry County)	79316	Venus	76084	Wamba	75503
Union (Wilson County)	78140	Vera	76383	Waneta	75844
Union Academy	75801	Verbena	79356	Waples	76048
Union Bluff	76645	Verdi	78064	Warda	78960
Union Bower (Part of Irving)	75060	Verhalen	79772	Ward Prairie	75840
Union Center	76471	Verhelle	77954	Wards Creek	75574
Union Grove (Bell County)	76513	Veribest	76886	Waring	78074
Union Grove (Cherokee		Vernon	76384-85	Warren	77664
County)	75766	For specific Vernon Zip Codes call		Warren City	75647
Union Grove (Upshur		(817) 552-9391		Warrenton	78961
County)	75647	Verona	75424	Warsaw	75142
Union High	76639	Veterans Administration		Washburn	79019
Union Hill (Bosque County)	76652	(Part of Waco)	76711	Washington	77880
Union Hill (Henderson		Viboras	78361	Waskom	75692
County)	75756	Vick	76937	Wastella	79545
Union Hill (Upshur County)	75644	Vickery (Part of Dallas)	75231	Watauga	76148
Union Springs	75961	Victoria (Victoria County)	77901-05	Water Front Park	78130
Union Valley	75189	For specific Victoria Zip Codes		Waterloo (Grayson County)	75020
Unity	75486	call (512) 575-2363		Waterloo (Williamson	
Universal City	78148	Victoria (Limestone County)	76664	County)	76574
University (Part of Dallas)	75205-06	Victory City	75561	Waterman	75935
		Victory Gardens	77630	Waters Bluff	75792
		Vidauri	78377	Water Valley	76958

	ZIP
Waterwood (San Jacinto County)	77359
Waterwood (Walker County)	77340
Watkins	75103
Watson	76550
Watsonville	76063
Watt	76664
Waxahachie	75165
Wayside	79094
Wealthy	77871
Weatherford	76086-87
For specific Weatherford Zip Codes call (817) 594-3072	
Weaver	75478
Webberville	78653
Webbville	76828
Webster (Harris County)	77598
Webster (Wood County)	75494
Weches	75844
Wedgewood (Part of Fort Worth)	76163
Weedhaven	77979
Weeping Mary	75925
Weesatche	77993
Weimar	78962
Weinert	76388
Weir	78674
Weirville	75482
Welch	79377
Welch Store	75973
Welcome	78944
Weldon	75851
Welfare	78006
Wellborn	77881
Wellington	79095
Wellman	79378
Wells (Cherokee County)	75976
Wells (Lynn County)	79351
Wells Branch	78728
	78753
For specific Wells Branch Zip Codes call (915) 622-4566	
Wellswood	75929
Wentworth	75103
Weser	77963
Weslaco	78596
Weslayan (Part of Houston)	77005
Wesley	77833
Wesley Grove	77831
West	76691
West Austin (Part of Austin)	78703
West Baytown (Part of Baytown)	77520
West Bluff	77630
Westbrook	79565
West Camp	79325
Westchase (Part of Houston)	77042
Westchester (Part of Grand Prairie)	75054
Westcliff	76513
West Cliff Park (Part of Amarillo)	79124
West Columbia	77486
West Delta	75448
Western Hills (Part of Copperas Cove)	76522
Western Plaza Mall (Part of Amarillo)	79101
Westfield (Harris County)	77090
Westfield (Wharton County)	77437
Westfield Estates	77093
West Galveston (Part of Jamaica Beach)	77551
Westgate (Harris County)	77429
Westgate (Tom Green County)	76901
Westgate Mall (Part of Amarillo)	79121
Westgate Mall (Part of Austin)	78704
Westgate Towne Centre (Part of Abilene)	79605
Westhaven	78130
Westheimer (Part of Houston)	77042
Westhill Addition	77437
Westhoff	77994
West Lake (Jasper County)	75951
Westlake (Tarrant County)	76248
Westlake (Travis County)	78746
West Lake Hills	78746
Westlakes (Part of San Antonio)	78245
Westlakes Mercado (Part of San Antonio)	78227
Westlawn	77630
Westminster	75485
West Mountain	75647
West Odessa	79764

	ZIP
	79769
For specific West Odessa Zip Codes call (915) 381-6707	
Weston	75097
West Orange	77630
Westover	76380
Westover Hills	76107
West Payne	77437
Westphalia	76656
West Point (Fayette County)	78963
West Point (Lynn County)	79373
West Sinton	78370
West Tawakoni	75474
West Texas State University (Part of Canyon)	79016
West University Place	77005
West Vernon (Part of Vernon)	76384
Westview (Part of Waco)	76710
Westville	75862
West Waco (Part of Waco)	76710
Westway	79835
Westwood	75951
Westwood Mall (Part of Houston)	77036
Westworth Village	76114
Wetmore (Part of San Antonio)	78247
Wetsel	75069
Wexford Park	77662
Whaley	75570
Wharton	77488
Whatley	75657
Wheatland	76116
Wheeler	79096
Wheeler Springs	75835
Wheelock	77882
Whispering Oaks (Bexar County)	78230
Whispering Oaks (Rains County)	75453
Whispering Pines (Montgomery County)	77302
Whispering Pines (Walker County)	77358
Whispering Winds	78264
Whisperwood (Part of Lubbock)	79416
White City (San Augustine County)	75929
White City (Wilbarger County)	76384
White Deer	79097
Whiteface	79379
Whiteflat	79234
White Hall (Bell County)	76557
White Hall (Coryell County)	76528
White Hall (Grimes County)	77868
Whitehall (Kaufman County)	75147
Whitehouse	75791
Whiteland	76858
White Mound	75090
White Oak (Gregg County)	75693
White Oak (Montgomery County)	77365
White Oak (Morris County)	75571
White Oak (Titus County)	75455
White Oak Valley Estates	77301
White Rock (Dallas County)	75218
White Rock (Grayson County)	75491
White Rock (Hunt County)	75423
White Rock (Red River County)	75426
White Rock (Robertson County)	76629
White Rock (San Augustine County)	75972
Whitesboro	76273
White Settlement	76108
Whitestar	79234
White Stone (Part of Cedar Park)	78641
Whitetail	78628
Whiteway	76538
Whitewright	75491
Whitharral	79380
Whitman	77833
Whitney	76692
Whitsett	78075
Whitt	76490
Whitton	75103
Whon	76889
Wichita Falls	76301-11
For specific Wichita Falls Zip Codes call (817) 766-4188	
Wichita Valley Farms	76301
Wickett	79788
Wiedeville	77833
Wieland	75402
Wiergate	75977

	ZIP
Wiggins	76691
Wigginsville	77301
Wilcox	77879
Wildcat (Part of Plano)	75023
Wilderville	76570
Wild Horse	79855
Wild Hurst	75925
Wildorado	79098
Wild Peach Village	77422
Wildwood (Hardin County)	77663
Wildwood (Walker County)	77367
Wilford Hall U.S.A.F. Hospital (Part of San Antonio)	78236
Wilkins	75755
Wilkinson	75455
Willacy County Housing Authority	78580
Willamar	78580
William Beaumont Army Medical Center	79920
William Penn	77833
William Rice (Part of Houston)	77005
Williams	76471
Williamsburg (Lamar County)	75460
Williamsburg (Lavaca County)	77964
William Spear Addition	75704
Willis	77378
Willow City	78675
Willow Grove (McLennan County)	76712
Willow Grove (Shelby County)	75954
Willow Park	76086
Willow Place (Part of Houston)	77070
Willow Point	76426
Willow Springs (Fayette County)	78940
Willow Springs (Rains County)	75440
Wills Point	75169
Wilmer	75172
Wilmeth	79567
Wilson (Falls County)	76519
Wilson (Lynn County)	79381
Wilson Lake	77351
Wimberley	78676
Winchell	76827
Winchester	78964
Windcrest	78239
Windcrest Mall (Part of San Antonio)	78221
Windemere (Burnet County)	78669
Windemere (Travis County)	78660
Windom	75492
Windsor Park Mall (Part of San Antonio)	78218
Windthorst	76389
Winedale	77835
Winfield	75493
Winfree (Chambers County)	77535
Winfree (Orange County)	77630
Wingate	79566
Wink	79789
Winkler	75859
Winnie	77665
Winningkoff (Part of Lucas)	75069
Winnsboro	75494
Winona	75792
Winter Haven	78839
Winter Hill	75943
Winters	79567
Winwood Mall (Part of Odessa)	79762
Witting	77975
Wixon Valley	77803
Wizard Wells	76458
Woden	75978
Wolfe City	75496
Wolfforth	79382
Womack	76634
Woodbine	76240
Woodbranch	77357
Woodbury	76645
Wood-Canyon Waters	75147
Woodcreek	78676
Woodcreek North	78676
Woodcrest	77301
Woodhaven Estates	77304
Wood Hollow	77365
Woodlake (Bexar County)	78244
Woodlake (Grayson County)	75020
Woodlake (Trinity County)	75865
Woodland (Bell County)	76513
Woodland (Red River County)	75436
Woodland Estates	75948

	ZIP
Woodland Hills (Henderson County)	75143
Woodland Hills (Hill County)	76692
Woodland Lakes	77355
Woodland Shores	75630
Woodlawn (Angelina County)	75901
Woodlawn (Harrison County)	75694
Woodlawn Lakes	77355
Woodley	75670
Woodloch	77301
Woodridge Park	78264
Woodrow (Fort Bend County)	77430
Woodrow (Lubbock County)	79401
Woods	75974
Woodsboro	78393
Woods of Shavano (Part of San Antonio)	78249
Woodson	76491
Wood Springs	75701
Woodville	75979
Woodway (McLennan County)	76710

	ZIP
Woodway (Victoria County)	77901
Woody Acres	77365
Woosley	75472
World Trade Center (Part of Dallas)	75207
Wortham	76693
Worthing	77964
Wright City	75684
Wrightsboro	78677
Wyldwood	78612
Wylie (Collin County)	75098
Wylie (Franklin County)	75494
Wylie (Taylor County)	79606
Wynne Unit	77340
Wynnewood Village (Part of Dallas)	75224
Wynnrock Estates	78737
Yancey	78886
Yantis	75497
Yarboro	77868
Yarbrough Plaza (Part of El Paso)	79912
Yard	75861

	ZIP
Yarrelton	76518
Yaupon Cove	77351
Yellowpine	75948
Yoakum	77995
Yorktown	78164
Young	75840
Youngsport	76542
Yowell	75428
Ysleta (Part of El Paso)	79907
	79917

For specific Ysleta Zip Codes call (915) 859-7033

	ZIP
Zabcikville	76501
Zapata	78076
Zavalla	75980
Zephyr	76890
Zionsville	77833
Zippville	78155
Zorn	78666
Zuehl	78124
Zunkerville	78119
Zybach	79011

	ZIP
Abraham	84635
Adamsville	84713
Alpine	84003
Alta	84092
Altamont	84001
Alton	84710
Altonah	84002
Amalga	84335
American Fork	84003-04
For specific American Fork Zip Codes call (801) 756-3241	
Aneth	84510
Angle	84712
Annabella	84711
Antimony	84712
Arcadia	84012
Arsenal (Part of Sunset)	84015
Aspen Acres	84055
Atwood (Part of Murray)	84107
Aurora	84620
Austin	84754
Avon	84328
Axtell	84621
Ballard	84066
Bauer	84071
Bear River City	84301
Beaver	84713
Beaverdam	84306
Belmont Heights	84070
Benjamin	84660
Ben Lomond (Part of Ogden)	84404
Bennion	84118
	84123
For specific Bennion Zip Codes call (801) 974-2200	
Benson	84335
Beryl	84714
Beryl Junction	84714
Bicknell	84715
Big Water	84741
Bingham Canyon	84006
Birdseye	84629
Blanding	84511
	84533
For specific Blanding Zip Codes call (801) 678-2627	
Bloomington	84770
Bluebell	84007
Bluff	84512
Bluffdale	84065
Bonanza	84078
Boneta	84051
Bonnie (Part of Orem)	84057
Bothwell	84337
Boulder	84716
Bountiful	84010-11
For specific Bountiful Zip Codes call (801) 295-5589	
Bowery Haven	84701
Brendel	84540
Brian Head	84719
Bridgeland	84012
Brigham City	84302
Brighton	84121
Brooklyn	84754
Bryce	84764
Bryce Canyon	84717
Burbank	84751
Burmester	84029
Burrville	84701
Bushnell (Part of Brigham City)	84302
Cache Junction	84304
Cache Valley Mall (Part of Logan)	84321
Caineville	84775
Callao	84034
Call Fort	84302
Cannonville	84718
Carbonville	84501
Castle Dale	84513
Castleton	84532
Castle Valley	84532
Cedar City	84720-21
For specific Cedar City Zip Codes call (801) 586-6701	
Cedar Hills	84062
Cedar Valley	84013
Cedarview	84066
Center Creek	84032
Centerfield	84622
Centerville	84014
Central (Sevier County)	84754
Central (Washington County)	84722
Charleston	84032
Chester	84623
Circleville	84723
Cisco	84515
Clarkston	84305

	ZIP
Clawson	84516
Clear Creek (Box Elder County)	83342
Clear Creek (Carbon County)	84526
Clearfield	84015-16
For specific Clearfield Zip Codes call (801) 773-0205	
Cleveland	84518
Clinton	84015
Clover	84069
Clyde (Part of Orem)	84057
Coalville	84017
College Ward	84321
Collinston	84306
Columbia	84520
Columbia Junction (Part of East Carbon)	84520
Copperton	84006
Corinne	84307
Cornish	84308
Cottonwood	84121
Cottonwood Heights	84121
Cottonwood Mall	84112
Cottonwood West	84117
	84121
For specific Cottonwood West Zip Codes call (801) 974-2200	
Cove	84320
Crescent	84070
Croydon	84018
Cushing (Part of Midvale)	84047
Daniel	84032
Defas Park	84031
Delta	84624
Deseret	84624
Devils Slide	84050
Deweyville	84309
Downtown (Part of Salt Lake City)	84101
Draper	84020
Dry Fork	84078
Duchesne	84021
Dugway (Tooele County)	84022
Dugway Proving Ground	84022
Dutch John	84023
East Bay (Part of Provo)	84605
East Carbon	84520
Eastland Township	84535
East Layton (Part of Layton)	84041
East Midvale	84047
East Millcreek	84117
East Portal	84102
Eastwood Hills	84106
Echo	84024
Eden	84310
Elberta	84626
Elgin	84525
Elk Ridge	84660
Elmo	84521
Elsinore	84724
Elwood	84337
Emery	84522
Emory	84024
Enoch	84720
Enterprise (Morgan County)	84050
Enterprise (Washington County)	84725
Ephraim	84627
Erda	84074
Escalante	84726
Esk Dale	84728
Etna	84313
Eureka	84628
Fairfield	84013
Fairgrounds (Part of Salt Lake City)	84116
Fairview	84629
Farmington	84025
Farr West	84404
Fashion Place (Part of Murray)	84107
Faust	84080
Fayette	84630
Ferron	84523
Fielding	84311
Fillmore	84631
Fish Lake	84701
Flowell	84631
Foothill (Part of Salt Lake City)	84108
Fort Duchesne	84026
Fountain Green	84632
Francis	84036
Freedom	84646
Freeport Center (Part of Clearfield)	84016
Fremont	84747
Fruita	84775
Fruit Heights	84037
Fruitland	84027

	ZIP
Gandy	84728
Garden City	84028
Garland	84312
Garrison	84728
Genola	84655
Glendale	84729
Glenwood	84730
Gorder (Part of Ogden)	84403
Goshen	84633
Goshute Indian Reservation	84034
Gouldings Trading Post	86033
Grand Vu	84515
Granger (Part of West Valley City)	84119
Granite	84092
Grantsville	84029
Greendale	84023
Green Lake	84023
Green River	84525
Greenville	84731
Greenwich	84732
Grouse Creek	84313
Grover	84773
Gunlock	84733
Gunnison	84634
Gusher	84030
Hailstone	84032
Halchita	84531
Hamilton Fort	84720
Hanksville	84734
Hanna	84031
Hardy (Part of Lindon)	84062
Harrisburg Junction	84770
Harrisville	84404
Hatch	84735
Hatton	84637
Hayden	84053
Heber City	84032
Helper	84526
Henefer	84033
Henrieville	84736
Herriman	84065
Hiawatha	84527
Hidden Lake	84055
Highland	84003
Highlands	84050
Hildale	84784
Hill Air Force Base	84056
Hinckley	84635
Holden	84636
Holiday Park	84055
Holladay	84117
Holladay-Cottonwood	84117
	84121
For specific Holladay-Cottonwood Zip Codes call (801) 974-2200	
Honeyville	84314
Hooper	84315
Hoovers	84750
Howell	84316
Hoytsville	84017
Hunter (Part of West Valley City)	84120
Huntington	84528
Huntsville	84317
Hurricane	84737
Hyde Park	84318
Hyrum	84319
Ibapah	84034
Indianola	84629
Ioka	84066
Ivins	84738
Jensen	84035
Jerusalem	84646
Joseph	84739
Junction	84740
Kamas	84036
Kanab	84741
Kanarraville	84742
Kanesville	84315
Kanosh	84637
Kaysville	84037
Kearns	84118
Keetley	84032
Kelton	84336
Kenilworth	84529
Kimball Junction	84060
Kingston	84743
Koosharem	84744
Lake Point	84074
Lake Shore	84660
Lakeside Resort	84701
Laketown	84038
Lakeview	84601
Lapoint	84039
Lark	84065
La Sal	84530
La Sal Junction	84530
La Verkin	84745
Lawrence	84528

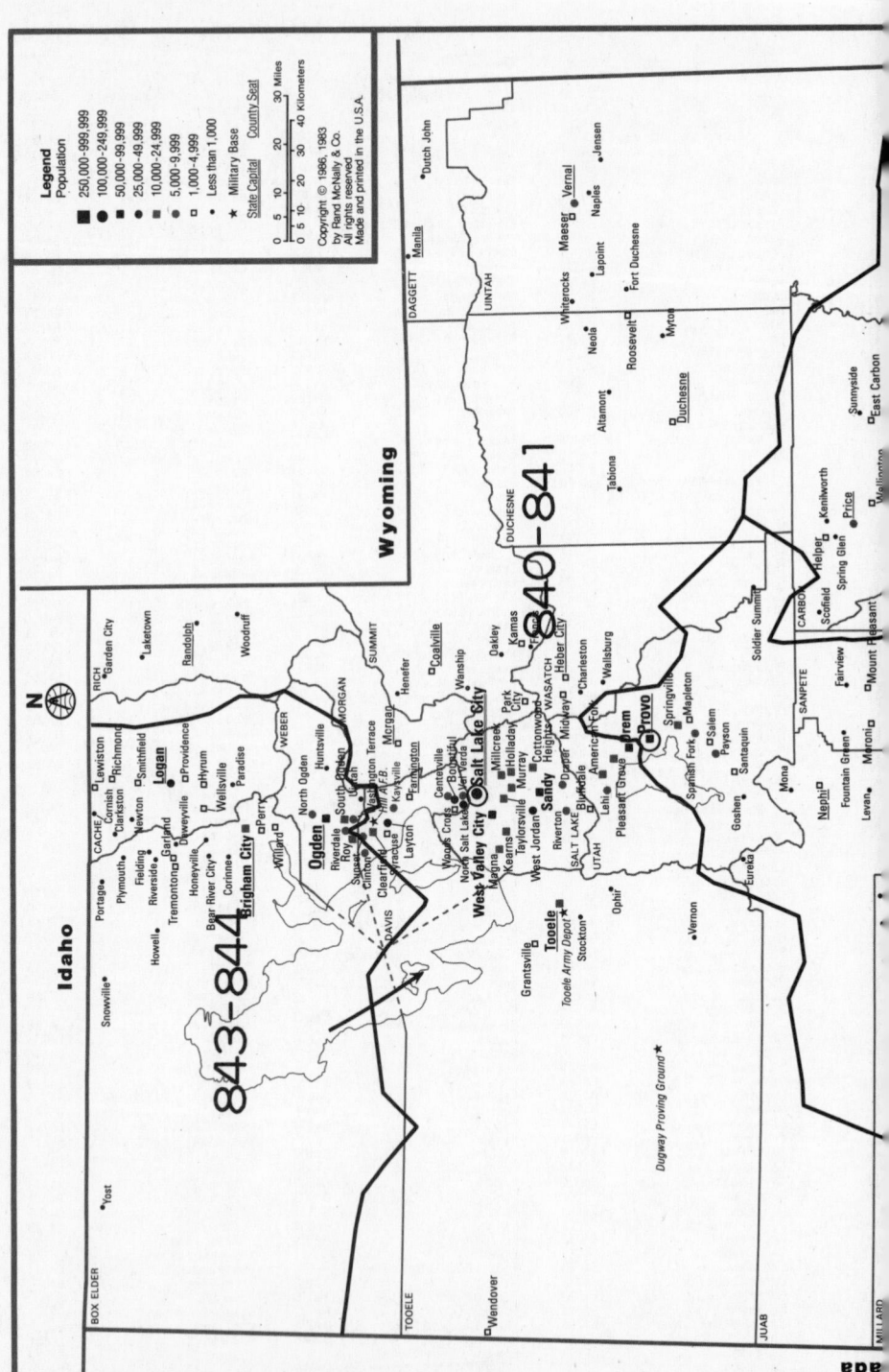

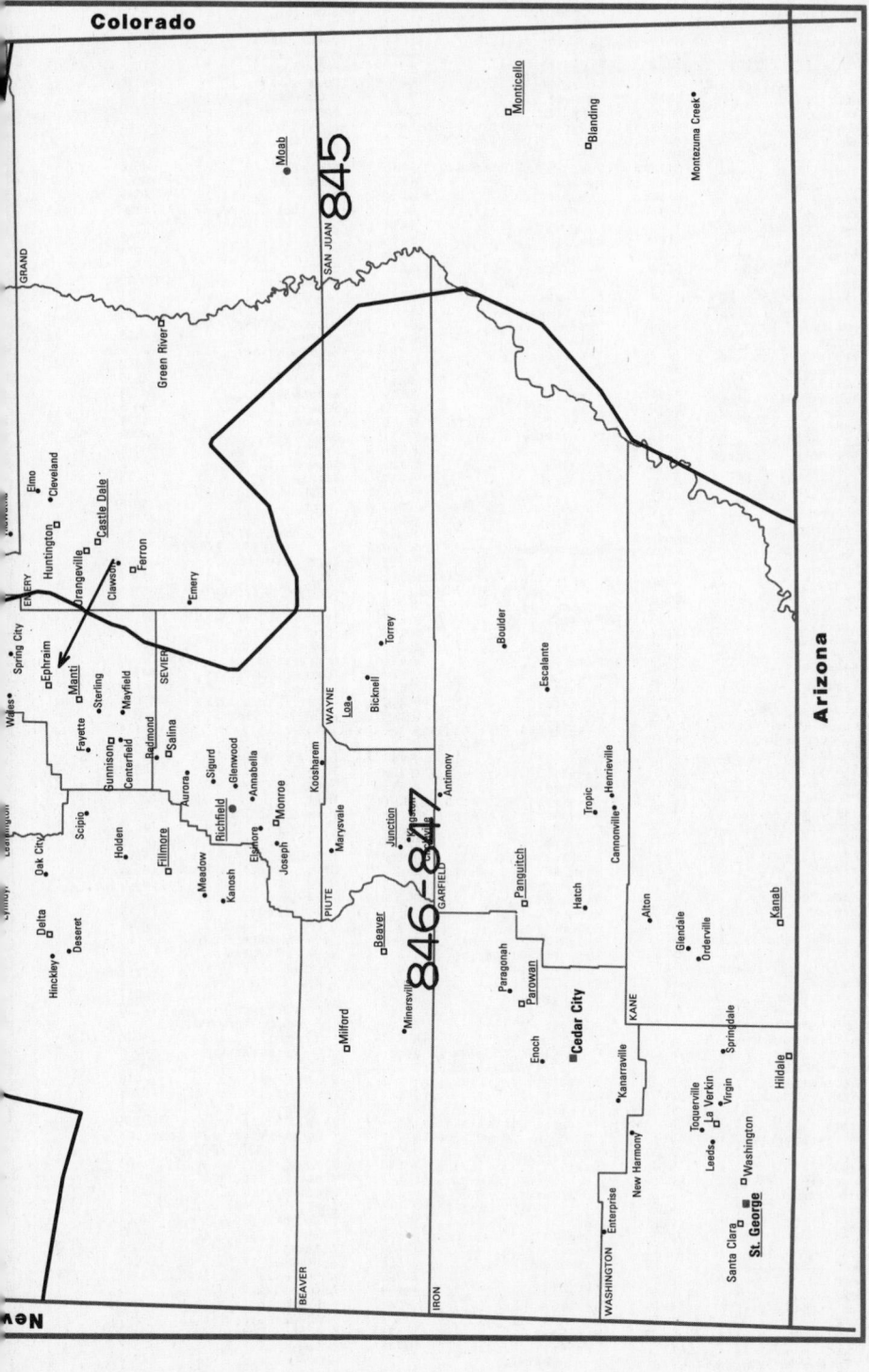

Colorado

Arizona

845

846-847

GRAND

SAN JUAN

Monticello

Blanding

Montezuma Creek

Moab

Green River

Elmo
Cleveland
Castle Dale
Ferron

Emery

EMERY

Huntington
Orangeville
Clawson

Spring City
Ephraim
Manti
Sterling
Mayfield

Wales

SEVIER

WAYNE

Loa
Bicknell
Torrey

Boulder

Escalante

Fayette
Gunnison
Centerfield
Redmond
Salina
Glenwood
Sigurd
Annabella
Aurora
Richfield
Elsinore
Monroe
Joseph
Koosharem

Scipio

Leamington

Oak City

Holden

Fillmore

Meadow
Kanosh

Delta
Deseert
Hinckley

Sigurd

PIUTE

Marysvale

Junction

Antimony

Tropic
Henrieville
Cannonville

Panguitch

Hatch

GARFIELD

Beaver

Minersville

Milford

BEAVER

IRON

Paragonah
Parowan

Cedar City

Enoch

Kanarraville

Alton

Glendale
Orderville

Kanab

KANE

Springdale

Hildale

New Harmony

Toquerville
Leeds
La Verkin
Virgin
Washington

Enterprise

WASHINGTON

Santa Clara
St. George

New

Syracuse

	ZIP
Layton	84040-41
For specific Layton Zip Codes call (801) 544-1203	
Layton Hills Mall (Part of Layton)	84041
Leamington	84638
Leeds	84770-71
For specific Leeds Zip Codes call (801) 673-3312	
Leeton	84066
Lehi	84043
Leland	84660
Levan	84639
Lewiston	84320
Liberty	84310
Lincoln	84074
Lindon	84042
Little Bonanza	84008
Little Cottonwood Creek Valley	84121
Littleton	84050
Loa	84747
Logan	84321-23
For specific Logan Zip Codes call (801) 752-7246	
Long Valley Junction	84758
Lund	84720
Lyman	84749
Lynn	83346
Lynndyl	84640
Madsen (Part of Honeyville)	84314
Maeser	84078
Magna	84044
Mammoth	84601
Manderfield	84713
Manila	84046
Manti	84642
Mantua	84302
Mapleton	84663
Marion	84036
Marriott	84404
Martin	84526
Marysvale	84750
Mayfield	84643
Meadow	84644
Meadowville	84038
Mendon	84325
Mexican Hat	84531
Middleton	84770
Midvale	84047
Midway	84049
Milburn	84629
Milford	84751
Millcreek (Grand County)	84515
Millcreek (Salt Lake County)	84109
Mills	84639
Millville	84326
Milton	84050
Minersville	84752
Moab	84532
Modena	84753
Molen	84523
Mona	84645
Monarch	84066
Monroe	84754
Montezuma Creek	84534
Monticello	84535
Monti Verdi	84050
Monument Valley	84536
Moore	84523
Morgan	84050
Moroni	84646
Mountain Green	84050
Mountain Home	84051
Mount Carmel	84755
Mount Carmel Junction	84755
Mount Emmons	84001
Mount Olympus	84117
Mount Pleasant	84647
Murray	84107
Myton	84052
Naples	84078
Navajo Indian Reservation	86515
Neola	84053
Nephi	84648
Newcastle	84756
New Harmony	84757
Newton	84327
Nibley	84321
North Creek	84713
North Logan	84321
North Ogden	84404
North Salt Lake	84054
Oak City	84649
Oak Creek	84629
Oakley	84055
Oasis	84650
Ogden	84401-14
For specific Ogden Zip Codes call (801) 627-4437	

	ZIP
Ogden ALC Hardness Test Center	84401
Ogden City Mall (Part of Ogden)	84401
Oljato	86033
Olmstead	84604
Ophir	84071
Oquirrh	84084
Orangeville	84537
Orderville	84758
Orem	84057-59
For specific Orem Zip Codes call (801) 225-2071	
Ouray	84063
Pallas (Part of Murray)	84107
Palmyra	84660
Panguitch	84759
Paradise	84328
Paragonah	84760
Park City	84060
	84068
For specific Park City Zip Codes call (801) 649-9191	
Park Terrace	84106
Park Valley	84329
Parowan	84761
Partoun	84083
Payson	84651
Penrose	84337
Peoa	84061
Perry	84302
Peruvian Park	84093
Peterson	84050
Pickelville (Part of Garden City)	84028
Pine Mountain	84055
Pine Valley	84781
Pintura	84720
Pioneer (Part of Salt Lake City)	84147
Plain City	84404
Pleasant Grove	84042
	84062
For specific Pleasant Grove Zip Codes call (801) 785-3231	
Pleasant View	84404
Plymouth	84330
Polls	84050
Portage	84331
Portersville	84050
Price	84501
Promontory	84307
Providence	84332
Provo	84601-06
For specific Provo Zip Codes call (801) 374-2000	
Randlett	84063
Randolph	84064
Redmond	84652
Red Wash	84078
Redwood	84119
Richfield	84701
Richmond	84333
Richville	84050
Riverdale	84405
River Heights	84321
Riverside	84334
Riverton	84065
Rockville	84763
Roosevelt	84066
Roper (Part of South Salt Lake)	84115
Rosette	84329
Round Valley	84038
Roy	84067
Rush Valley	84069
St. George	84770-71
For specific St. George Zip Codes call (801) 673-3312	
Salem	84653
Salina	84654
Salt Lake City	84101-99
For specific Salt Lake City Zip Codes call (801) 974-2200	
Samak	84036
Sandy	84070
	84090-94
For specific Sandy Zip Codes call (801) 255-3442	
Santa Clara	84765
Santaquin	84655
Scipio	84656
Scofield	84526
Sevier	84766
Sherwood Park	84093
Shivwits	84765
Sigurd	84657
Silver Fork	84121
Silver Reef	84746
Skull Valley Indian Reservation	84029

	ZIP
Slaterville	84404
Smithfield	84335
Snowbird	84092
Snowville	84336
Snyderville	84060
Soldier Summit	84601
South Jordan	84065
South Ogden	84403
South Salt Lake	84115
South Weber	84405
Spanish Fork	84660
Spring City	84662
Springdale	84767
Springdell	84604
Spring Glen	84526
Spring Lake	84651
Springville	84663-64
For specific Springville Zip Codes call (801) 489-4561	
Standrod	83342
Stansbury Park	84074
Starr	84645
Sterling	84665
Stockton	84071
Stoddard	84050
Sugar House (Part of Salt Lake City)	84106
Sugarville	84624
Summit	84772
Summit Point	84535
Sunnyside	84539
Sunset	84015
Sutherland	84624
Swan Creek	84028
Syracuse	84075
Tabiona	84072
Talmage	84073
Taylor	84401
Taylorsville	84118-19
	84123
For specific Taylorsville Zip Codes call (801) 974-2200	
Taylorsville-Bennion	84118-19
	84123
For specific Taylorsville-Bennion Zip Codes call (801) 974-2200	
Teasdale	84773
Terra	84022
Thatcher	84337
Thompson	84540
Thompsonville	84750
Ticaboo	84533
Tooele	84074
Tooele Army Depot	84074
Toquerville	84774
Torrey	84775
Town (Part of Ogden)	84401
Tremonton	84337
Trenton	84338
Tridell	84076
Trolley Square (Part of Salt Lake City)	84102
Tropic	84776
Trout Creek	84083
Ucolo	84535
Uintah	84405
Uintah and Ouray Indian Reservation	84026
Union	84047
University (Part of Provo)	84602
University Mall (Part of Orem)	84057
Upalco	84007
Upton	84017
Utah State Prison	84020
Utah State University (Part of Logan)	84322
Utida (Part of Cornish)	84308
Uvada	84753
Val Verda	84010
Venice	84701
Vermillion	84657
Vernal	84078-79
For specific Vernal Zip Codes call (801) 789-2393	
Vernon	84080
Veyo	84782
Vineyard	84057
Virgin	84779
Vivian Park	84604
Wales	84667
Wallsburg	84082
Wanship	84017
Warren	84404
Washakie Indian Reservation	83203
Washington	84780
Washington Terrace	84403
Wellington	84542
Wellsville	84339
Wendover	84083

	ZIP		ZIP		ZIP
West Bountiful	84087	West Weber	84401	Woodland Hills	84653
West Jordan	84084	Wheelon	84306	Woodruff	84086
	84088	White City	84070	Woods Cross	84087
For specific West Jordan Zip		Whiterocks	84085	Yost	83342
Codes call (801) 255-4022		Wildwood	84604	ZCMI Center (Part of Salt	
West Point	84015	Willard	84340	Lake City)	84111
West Valley City	84120	Wilson	84401	Zion National Park	84767
West Warren	84404	Woodland	84036		

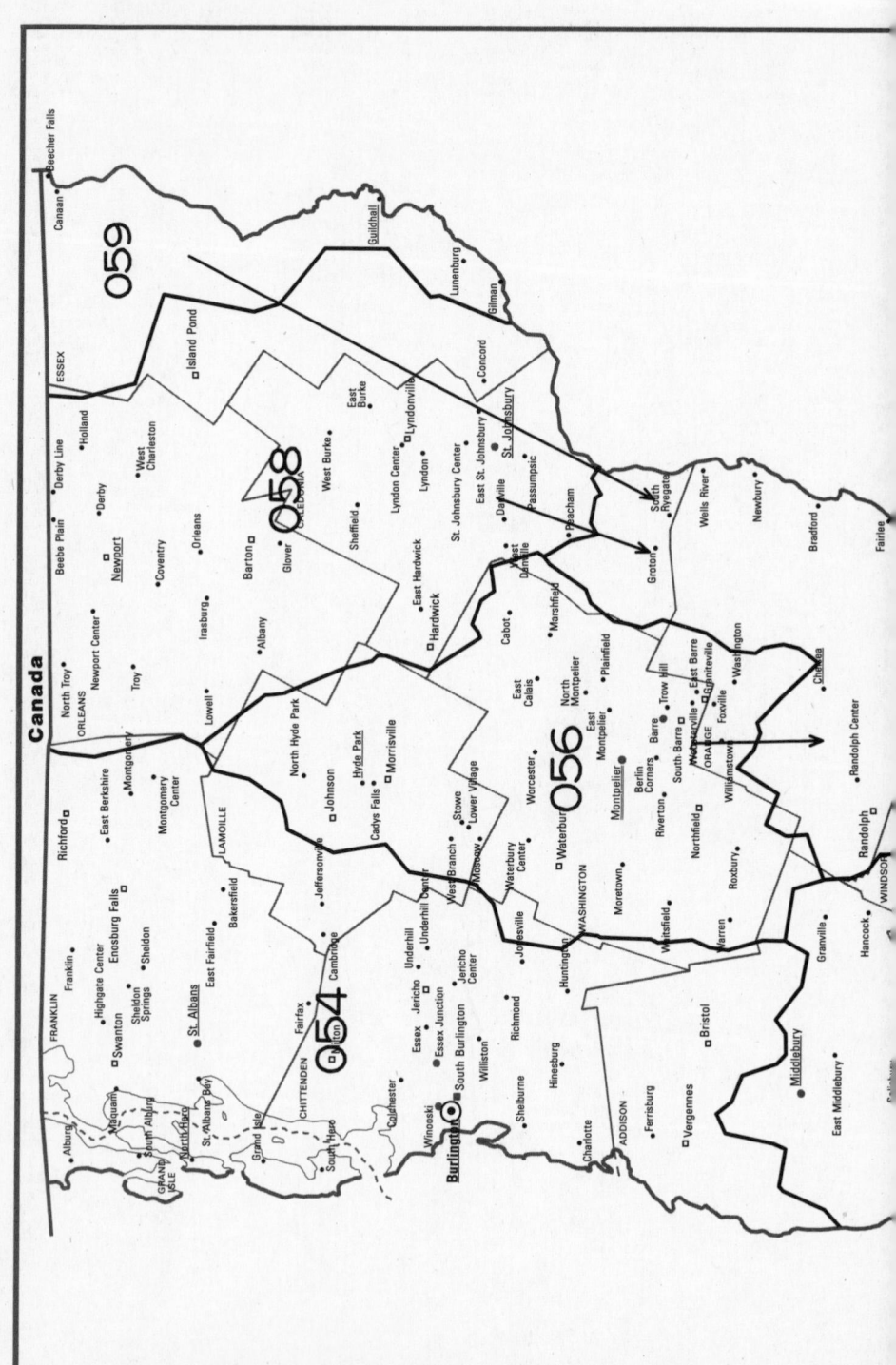

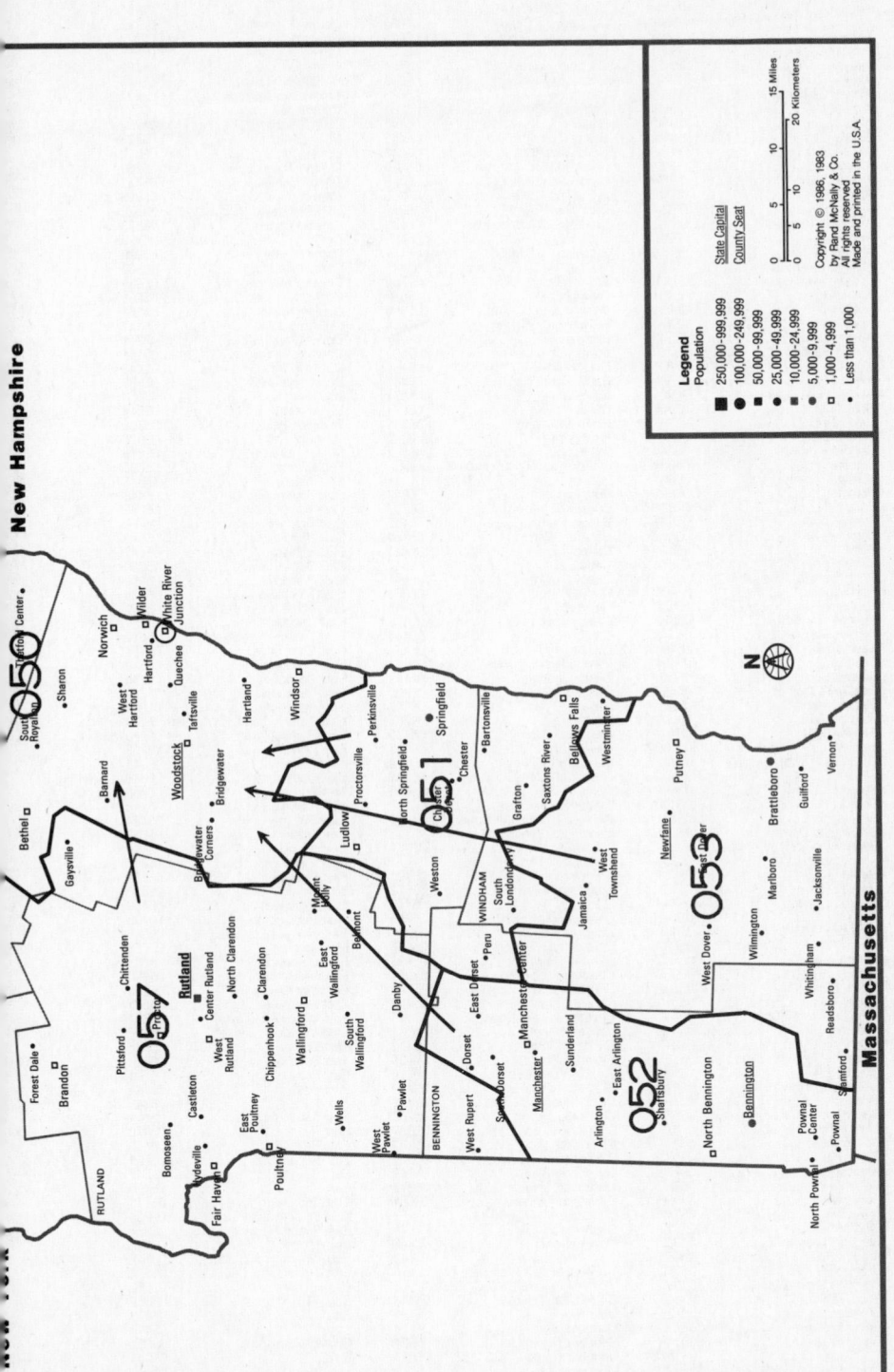

	ZIP		ZIP		ZIP
Abnaki	05474	Bridgewater (Town)	05034	Cornwall	05753
Adamant	05640	Bridgewater Center	05035	Cornwall (Town)	05753
Addison	05491	Bridgewater Corners	05035	Coventry	05825
Addison (Town)	05491	Bridport	05734	Coventry (Town)	05825
Albany	05820	Bridport (Town)	05734	Craftsbury	05826
Albany (Town)	05820	Brighton (Town)	05846	Craftsbury (Town)	05826
Albany Center	05845	Brimstone Corner	05083	Craftsbury Common	05827
Alburg	05440	Brimstone Corners	05761	Cream Hill	05734
Alburg (Town)	05440	Bristol	05443	Crystal Beach	05732
Alburg Center	05440	Bristol (Town)	05443	Cuttingsville	05738
Alburg Springs	05440	Brockways Mills	05143	Danby	05739
Alfrecha	05759	Brookfield	05036	Danby (Town)	05739
Alpine Village	05674	Brookfield (Town)	05036	Danby Corners	05739
Ames Hill	05344	Brookfield Center	05036	Danville	05828
Amsden	05151	Brookline (Town)	05345	Danville (Town)	05828
Andover (Town)	05143	Brookside (Chittenden		Danville Center	05828
Arlington	05250	County)	05494	Derby	05829
Arlington (Town)	05250	Brookside (Windham		Derby (Town)	05829
Arlington (census		County)	05341	Derby Line	05830
designated place)	05250	Brooksville	05753	Deweys Mills	05059
Arnold Bay	05491	Brownington	05860	Dorset	05251
Ascutney	05030	Brownington (Town)	05860	Dorset (Town)	05251
Athens	05143	Brownington Center	05860	Dover	05341
Athens (Town)	05143	Brownsville	05037	Dover (Town)	05341
Avalon Beach	05750	Brunswick (Town)	03590	Downers	05151
Averill	05901	Buck Hollow	05454	Downingville	05443
Averill (Town)	05901	Buels Gore (Town)	05487	Dows Crossing	05836
Averys Gore (Town)	05903	Burke	05871	Dowsville	05660
Bailey's Mills	05062	Burke (Town)	05871	Dummerston	05346
Bakersfield	05441	Burke Mountain	05832	Dummerston (Town)	05346
Bakersfield (Town)	05441	Burlington	05401-02	Duxbury	05676
Baltimore (Town)	05144		05405-06	Duxbury (Town)	05676
Barnard	05031	For specific Burlington Zip Codes		Eagle Point	05855
Barnard (Town)	05031	call (802) 863-6033		East Albany	05845
Barnet	05821	Burnham Hill	05843	East Alburg	05440
Barnet (Town)	05821	Burnham Hollow	05757	East Arlington	05252
Barnet Center	05821	Butlers Corners	05452	East Barnard	05068
Barnumtown	05472	Butternut Bend	05761	East Barre	05649
Barre	05641	Button Bay	05491	East Berkshire	05447
Barre (Town)	05678	Cabot	05647	East Bethel	05032
Barre Transfer (Part of		Cabot (Town)	05647	East Braintree	05060
Montpelier)	05602	Cadys Falls	05661	East Brookfield	05036
Barton	05822	Calais	05648	East Burke	05832
Barton (Town)	05822	Calais (Town)	05648	East Cabot	05647
Bartonsville	05143	Cambridge	05444	East Calais	05650
Basin Harbor	05491	Cambridge (Town)	05444	East Cambridge	05464
Bayside	05404	Cambridge Junction	05464	East Charleston	05833
Beanville	05060	Cambridgeport	05141	East Charlotte	05445
Beaulieu's Corner	05459	Canaan	05903	East Clarendon	05759
Beebe Plain	05823	Canaan (Town)	05903	East Concord	05906
Beecher Falls	05902	Castleton	05735	East Corinth	05040
Bellows Falls	05101	Castleton (Town)	05735	East Craftsbury	05826
Belmont	05730	Cavendish	05142	East Dorset	05253
Belvidere (Town)	05492	Cavendish (Town)	05142	East Dover	05341
Belvidere Center	05492	Cavendish Center	05142	East Dummerston	05346
Belvidere Corners	05492	Cedar Beach	05445	East Enosburg	05450
Belvidere Junction	05492	Center Rutland	05736	East Fairfield	05448
Bennington	05201	Centerville (Lamoille County)	05655	East Fletcher	05464
Bennington (Town)	05201	Centerville (Windsor		East Franklin	05457
Bennington College (Part of		County)	05001	East Granville	05669
North Bennington)	05201	Champlain (Part of South		East Hardwick	05836
Benson	05731	Burlington)	05401	East Haven	05837
Benson (Town)	05731	Charleston (Town)	05872	East Haven (Town)	05837
Benson Landing	05743	Charlotte	05445	East Highgate	05459
Berkshire	05447	Charlotte (Town)	05445	East Hubbardton	05735
Berkshire (Town)	05450	Checkerberry	05468	East Jamaica	05343
Berlin (Town)	05602	Chelsea	05038	East Johnson	05656
Berlin Corners	05602	Chelsea (Town)	05038	East Lyndon	05851
Bethel	05032	Chelsea West Hill	05041	East Middlebury	05740
Bethel (Town)	05032	Chester	05143	East Monkton	05443
Bethel Gilead	05060	Chester (Town)	05143	East Montpelier	05651
Binghamville	05444	Chester-Chester Depot	05143	East Montpelier (Town)	05651
Birdland	05474	Chester Depot	05144	East Montpelier Center	05602
Bliss Pond	05640	Chimney Corner	05446	East Orange	05086
Blissville	05764	Chimney Point	05491	East Peacham	05862
Bloomfield	03590	Chipman Lake	05739	East Pittsford	05701
Bloomfield (Town)	03590	Chipmans Point	05760	East Poultney	05741
Blossoms Corners	05775	Chippenhook	05777	East Putney	05346
Bolton	05676	Chiselville	05250	East Randolph	05041
Bolton (Town)	05676	Chittenden	05737	East Richford	05476
Bolton Valley	05477	Chittenden (Town)	05737	East Roxbury	05663
Boltonville	05081	Clarendon	05759	East Rupert	05761
Bomoseen	05732	Clarendon (Town)	05759	East Ryegate	05042
Bondville	05340	Clarendon Springs	05777	East Sheldon	05450
Bordoville	05450	Cleveland Corner	05661	East Shoreham	05770
Bowlsville	05742	Cloverdale	05489	East St. Johnsbury	05838
Bradford	05033	Colbyville	05676	East Sutton Ridge	05867
Bradford (Town)	05033	Colchester	05446	East Thetford	05043
Bragg	05055		05449	East Wallingford	05742
Braintree	05060	For specific Colchester Zip Codes		East Warren	05674
Braintree (Town)	05060	call (802) 655-1376		Eden	05652
Braintree Hill	05060	Colchester (Town)	05446	Eden (Town)	05652
Brandon	05733	Cold River	05738	Eden Mills	05653
Brandon (Town)	05733	Concord	05824	Egypt	05448
Brattleboro	05301-04	Concord (Town)	05824	Elmore (Town)	05657
	05351	Concord Corner	05824	Ely	05044
For specific Brattleboro Zip Codes		Copperfield	05079	Enosburg (Town)	05450
call (802) 254-4110		Corinth	05039	Enosburg Center	05450
Brattleboro Center	05301	Corinth (Town)	05039	Enosburg Falls	05450
Bread Loaf	05753	Corinth Center	05039	Essex	05451
Bridgewater	05034	Corinth Corners	05039	Essex (Town)	05451

	ZIP
Essex Junction	05451-53
For specific Essex Junction Zip	
Codes call (802) 878-3085	
Ethan Allen Shopping	
Center (Part of	
Burlington)	05404
Evansville	05860
Fairfax	05454
Fairfax (Town)	05454
Fairfax Falls	05454
Fairfield	05455
Fairfield (Town)	05455
Fairfield Station	05455
Fair Haven (Town)	05743
Fair Haven	05743
Fairlee	05045
Fairlee (Town)	05045
Fays Corner	05477
Fayston (Town)	05660
Ferdinand (Town)	05905
Fernville	05733
Ferrisburg	05456
Ferrisburg (Town)	05456
Fieldsville	05089
Fletcher	05444
Fletcher (Town)	05744
Florence	05488
Fonda	05745
Forest Dale	05654
Foxville	05457
Franklin	05457
Franklin (Town)	05457
Freedleyville	05253
Gallup Mills	05858
Garfield	05661
Gassetts	05144
Gaysville	05746
Georgia	05454
Georgia (Town)	05478
Georgia Center	05478
Georgia Plains	05468
Gilman	05904
Glastenbury (Town)	05262
Glover	05839
Glover (Town)	05839
Goodrich Four Corners	05055
Goose City	05341
Goose Green	05039
Gordon Landing	05458
Goshen	05733
Goshen (Town)	05733
Goulds Mills	05156
Grafton	05146
Grafton (Town)	05146
Grahamville	05149
Granby	05840
Granby (Town)	05840
Grand Isle	05458
Grand Isle (Town)	05458
Graniteville	05654
Graniteville-East Barre	05654
Granville (Town)	05747
Granville	05747
Green Acres	05477
Green Bay	05046
Greenbush	05151
Green River	05301
Greensboro	05841
Greensboro (Town)	05841
Greensboro Bend	05842
Greens Corners	05478
Groton	05046
Groton (Town)	05046
Guildhall	05905
Guildhall (Town)	05905
Guilford	05301
Guilford (Town)	05301
Guilford Center	05301
Halifax	05358
Halifax (Town)	05358
Halls Lake	05081
Hammondsville	05062
Hancock	05748
Hancock (Town)	05748
Hanksville	05487
Hardscrabble	05156
Hardwick	05843
Hardwick (Town)	05843
Hardwick Center	05843
Hardwick Steet	05836
Harmonyville	05353
Harrisville	05301
Hartford	05047
Hartford (Town)	05047
Hartland	05048
Hartland (Town)	05048
Hartland Four Corners	05049
Harvey	05828
Healdville	05758
Heartwellville	05350
Hectorville	05471

	ZIP
Hewitts Corners	05053
Highgate (Town)	05459
Highgate Center	05459
Highgate Falls	05459
Highgate Springs	05460
Hinesburg	05461
Hinesburg (Town)	05461
Hinesburg	05301
Holden	05763
Holland	05830
Holland (Town)	05830
Hortonia	05760
Hortonville	05758
Houghtonville	05146
Hubbard Corner	05478
Hubbardton	05732
Hubbardton (Town)	05732
Huntington	05462
Huntington (Town)	05462
Huntington Center	05462
Huntville	05454
Hutchins	05471
Hyde Park	05655
Hyde Park (Town)	05655
Hydeville	05750
Indian Point (Part of	
Newport)	05855
Inwood	05821
Ira	05777
Ira (Town)	05777
Irasburg	05845
Irasburg (Town)	05845
Irasville	05673
Island Pond	05846
Isle La Motte	05463
Isle La Motte (Town)	05463
Jacksonville	05342
Jamaica	05343
Jamaica (Town)	05343
Jay	05859
Jay (Town)	05859
Jay Peak	05859
Jeffersonville	05464
Jenneville	05089
Jericho	05465
Jericho (Town)	05465
Jericho Center	05465
Jerusalem	05443
Joes Pond	05873
Johnson	05656
Johnson (Town)	05656
Jonesville	05466
Kansas	05252
Keeler Bay	05486
Kendall	05043
Kendricks Corner	05150
Killington	05751
Kimball	05822
Kirby (Town)	05824
Kirby Corner	05495
Lake Dunmore	05769
Lake Elmore	05657
Lake Fairlee	05044
Lake Hortonia	05743
Lake Morey	05045
Lake Park	05855
Lake Raponda	05363
Lake Rescue	05149
Lake St. Catherine	05764
Lakewood	05488
Landgrove	05148
Landgrove (Town)	05148
Lapham Bay	05734
Larrabees Point	05770
Leicester	05733
Leicester (Town)	05733
Leicester Junction	05778
Lemington	03576
Lemington (Town)	03576
Lewis (Town)	05905
Lewiston	05055
Lilliesville	05032
Lincoln	05443
Lincoln (Town)	05443
Lindsay Beach	05855
Londonderry	05148
Londonderry (Town)	05148
Long Point	05473
Lowell	05847
Lowell (Town)	05847
Lower Branch	05600
Lower Cabot	05658
Lower Granville	05747
Lower Plain	05033
Lower Village	05672
Lower Waterford	05848
Lower Websterville	05641
Ludlow	05149
Ludlow (Town)	05149
Lunenburg	05906
Lunenburg (Town)	05906

	ZIP
Lyman	05001
Lympus	05032
Lyndon	05849
Lyndon (Town)	05849
Lyndon Center	05850
Lyndon State College	05851
Lyndonville	05851
McIndoe Falls	05050
Mackville	05843
Mad River Glen	05673
Maidstone (Town)	05905
Maidstone Lake	03590
Mallets Bay	05404
Manchester (Town)	05254
Manchester	05254
Manchester (station)	05255
Manchester Center	05255
Maple Dell	05156
Maquam	05488
Marlboro	05344
Marlboro (Town)	05344
Marshfield	05658
Marshfield (Town)	05658
Mary Meyer	05353
Mechanicsville	05477
Medburyville	05363
Melville	05478
Mendon	05701
Mendon (Town)	05701
Merrill Corner	05845
Middlebury	05753
Middlebury (Town)	05753
Middlesex	05602
Middlesex (Town)	05602
Middlesex Center	05602
Middletown	05143
Middletown Springs	05757
Middletown Springs (Town)	05757
Mile Point	05491
Miles Pond	05858
Millbrook	05053
Mill Village (Orange County)	05079
Mill Village (Orleans County)	05827
Milton	05468
Milton (Town)	05468
Miltonboro	05468
Monkton	05469
Monkton (Town)	05469
Monkton Ridge	05473
Montgomery	05470
Montgomery (Town)	05470
Montgomery Center	05471
Montpelier	05601-02
For specific Montpelier Zip Codes	
call (802) 828-4404	
Moretown	05660
Moretown (Town)	05660
Moretown Common	05660
Morgan	05853
Morgan (Town)	05853
Morgan Center	05853
Morristown	05661
Morristown (Town)	05661
Morrisville	05661
Moscow	05662
Mosquitoville	05042
Mount Holly	05758
Mount Holly (Town)	05758
Mount Snow	05356
Mount Tabor	05739
Mount Tabor (Town)	05739
Nashville	05465
Neshobe Beach	05732
Newark	05871
Newark (Town)	05871
Newark Hollow	05871
New Boston (Norwich	
Town) (Windsor County)	05772
New Boston (Stockbridge	
Town) (Windsor County)	05055
Newbury	05051
Newbury (Town)	05051
Newbury Center	05081
Newfane	05345
Newfane (Town)	05345
New Haven (Town)	05472
New Haven	05472
New Haven Mills	05443
Newport	05855
Newport (Town)	05857
Newport Center	05857
North Bennington	05257
North Brattleboro	05304
North Burlington (Part of	
Burlington)	05401
North Calais	05650
North Cambridge	05464
North Chester	05144
North Clarendon	05759
North Concord	05858
North Danville	05819

	ZIP
North Derby	05855
North Dorset	05253
North Duxbury	05676
North Fairfax	05454
North Fayston	05660
North Ferrisburg	05473
Northfield	05663
Northfield (Town)	05663
Northfield Center	05663
Northfield Falls	05664
North Hartland	05052
North Hero	05474
North Hero (Town)	05474
North Hyde Park	05665
North Montpelier	05666
North Orwell	05760
North Pomfret	05053
North Pownal	05260
North Randolph	05041
North Royalton	05068
North Rupert	05761
North Sheldon	05485
North Sherburne	05751
North Shrewsbury	05738
North Springfield	05150
North Thetford	05054
North Troy	05859
North Tunbridge	05077
North Vernon	05354
North Westminster	05101
North Windham	05148
North Wolcott	05680
Norton	05907
Norton (Town)	05907
Norwich	05055
Norwich (Town)	05055
Norwich University (Part of Northfield)	05663
Oakland	05478
Oil City	05072
Old Bennington	05201
Old Church	05600
Orange	05641
Orange (Town)	05641
Orchard Lane	05156
Orleans	05860
Orwell	05760
Orwell (Town)	05760
Panton	05491
Panton (Town)	05491
Paper Mill Village	05257
Passumpsic	05861
Pawlet	05761
Pawlet (Town)	05761
Peacham	05862
Peacham (Town)	05862
Pearl	05458
Peaseville	05143
Pedden Acres	05156
Pekin	05667
Perkinsville	05151
Peru	05152
Peru (Town)	05152
Peth	05060
Pierces Corner	05759
Pikes Falls	05343
Pittsfield	05762
Pittsfield (Town)	05762
Pittsford	05763
Pittsford (Town)	05763
Plainfield	05667
Plainfield (Town)	05667
Pleasant Valley	05444
Plymouth	05056
Plymouth (Town)	05056
Plymouth Kingdom	05149
Plymouth Union	05056
Pomfret	05053
Pomfret (Town)	05053
Post Mills	05058
Potash Bay	05491
Potash Point	05491
Pottersville	05680
Poultney	05764
Poultney (Town)	05764
Pownal	05261
Pownal (Town)	05261
Pownal Center	05261
Prindle Corner	05445
Proctor (Town)	05765
Proctor	05765
Proctorsville	05153
Prosper	05091
Putnamville	05602
Putney	05346
Putney (Town)	05346
Quechee	05059
Queen City Park (Part of South Burlington)	05401
Ralston Corner	05824
Randolph	05060

	ZIP
Randolph (Town)	05060
Randolph Center	05061
Rawsonville	05155
Reading	05062
Reading (Town)	05062
Reading Center	05062
Readsboro	05350
Readsboro (Town)	05350
Readsboro Falls	05350
Red Village	05851
Reedville	05143
Rhode Island Corner	05477
Rices Mills	05075
Richford	05476
Richford (Town)	05476
Richmond	05477
Richmond (Town)	05477
Ricker Mills	05046
Ripton	05766
Ripton (Town)	05766
Riverton	05663
Robinson	05767
Rochester	05767
Rochester (Town)	05767
Rockingham	05101
Rockingham (Town)	05101
Rockville	05443
Rocky Dale	05443
Round Pond	05069
Roxbury	05669
Roxbury (Town)	05669
Roxbury Flat	05669
Royalton	05068
Royalton (Town)	05068
Rupert	05768
Rupert (Town)	05768
Russellville	05738
Russtown	05001
Rutland	05701-02
For specific Rutland Zip Codes call (802) 773-0222	
Ryegate	05042
Ryegate (Town)	05042
St. Albans	05478
St. Albans (Town)	05481
St. Albans Bay	05481
St. Albans Hill	05478
St. Albans Shopping Center (Part of St. Albans)	05478
St. George (Town)	05495
St. Johnsbury	05819
St. Johnsbury (Town)	05819
St. Johnsbury Center	05863
Saint Michael's College	05404
St. Rocks	05478
Salisbury (Town)	05769
Salisbury	05769
Samsonville	05450
Sanderson Corner	05454
Sandgate	05250
Sandgate (Town)	05250
Saxtons River	05154
Scottsville	05739
Searsburg	05363
Searsburg (Town)	05363
Seymour Lake	05853
Shadow Lake	05839
Shady Rill	05602
Shaftsbury	05262
Shaftsbury (Town)	05262
Shaftsbury Center	05262
Sharon	05065
Sharon (Town)	05065
Shawville	05457
Sheddsville	05089
Sheffield	05866
Sheffield (Town)	05866
Sheffield Square	05866
Shelburne	05482
Shelburne (Town)	05482
Shelburne Falls	05482
Shelburne Road Section (Part of South Burlington)	05401
Sheldon	05483
Sheldon (Town)	05483
Sheldon Junction	05483
Sheldon Springs	05485
Sherburne (Town)	05751
Shoreham	05770
Shoreham (Town)	05770
Shoreham Center	05770
Shrewsbury	05738
Shrewsbury (Town)	05738
Simonsville	05143
Simpsonville	05353
Smithville	05149
Smugglers Notch	05464
Sodom	05257
Somerset (Town)	05345
South Albany	05875
South Alburg	05440

	ZIP
South Barre	05670
South Burlington	05403
South Cabot	05658
South Cambridge	05464
South Corinth	05039
South Danville	05828
South Dorset	05251
South Duxbury	05660
South End	05739
Southern Vermont College	05201
South Hero	05486
South Hero (Town)	05486
South Lincoln	05443
South Londonderry	05155
South Lunenburg	05906
South Newbury	05051
South Newfane	05351
South Northfield	05663
South Peacham	05821
South Pomfret	05067
South Poultney	05764
South Randolph	05041
South Reading	05153
South Richford	05476
South Royalton	05068
South Ryegate	05069
South Starksboro	05487
South Strafford	05070
South Tunbridge	05068
South Vershire	05079
South Walden	05843
South Wallingford	05773
South Wardsboro	05355
South Washington	05675
South Wheelock	05851
South Windham	05359
South Woodbury	05681
South Woodstock	05071
Spoonerville	05144
Springfield	05156
Springfield (Town)	05156
Stamford	05352
Stamford (Town)	05352
Stannard	05842
Stannard (Town)	05842
Starksboro	05487
Starksboro (Town)	05487
Stevens Mills	05476
Stevensville	05489
Stockbridge	05772
Stockbridge (Town)	05772
Stowe	05672
Stowe (Town)	05672
Strafford	05072
Strafford (Town)	05072
Stratton (Town)	05360
Stratton Mountain	05155
Sudbury	05733
Sudbury (Town)	05733
Sugarbush Valley	05674
Summer Point	05491
Summit	05758
Sunderland	05250
Sunderland (Town)	05250
Sutton	05867
Sutton (Town)	05867
Swanton	05488
Swanton (Town)	05488
Tafts Corner	05495
Taftsville	05073
Talcville	05767
Tarbellville	05742
The Bluffs (Part of Newport)	05855
The Island	05161
Thetford	05074
Thetford (Town)	05074
Thetford Center	05075
Thompsonburg	05148
Thompson's Point	05445
Tinmouth	05773
Tinmouth (Town)	05773
Topsham	05076
Topsham (Town)	05076
Topsham Four Corners	05040
Townshend	05353
Townshend (Town)	05353
Trow Hill	05641
Troy	05868
Troy (Town)	05868
Tunbridge	05077
Tunbridge (Town)	05077
Tyson	05149
Una Bella	05201
Underhill	05489
Underhill (Town)	05489
Underhill Center	05490
Union Village	05043
University Mall (Part of South Burlington)	05401
University of Vermont (Part of Burlington)	05405

	ZIP		ZIP		ZIP
Upper Graniteville	05654	West Brattleboro	05301	West Swanton	05488
Vergennes	05491	West Bridgewater	05035	West Topsham	05086
Vernon	05354	West Bridport	05734	West Townshend	05359
Vernon (Town)	05354	West Brookfield	05060	West Wardsboro	05360
Vershire	05079	West Burke	05871	West Waterford	05819
Vershire (Town)	05079	West Castleton	05743	West Windsor (Town)	05037
Vershire Center	05079	West Charleston	05872	West Woodstock	05091
Vershire Heights	05079	West Corinth	05039	Weybridge	05753
Victory (Town)	05858	West Cornwall	05753	Weybridge (Town)	05753
Waitsfield	05673	West Danville	05873	Weybridge Hill	05753
Waitsfield (Town)	05673	West Dover	05356	Wheelock	05851
Waitsfield Common	05673	West Dummerston	05357	Wheelock (Town)	05851
Waits River	05086	West Enosburg	05450	White River Junction	05001
Walden	05873	West Fairlee	05083	Whitesville	05142
Walden (Town)	05873	West Fairlee (Town)	05083	Whiting	05778
Walden Heights	05873	West Fairlee Center	05044	Whiting (Town)	05778
Wallace Pond	05903	Westfield	05874	Whitingham	05361
Wallingford	05773	Westfield (Town)	05874	Whitingham (Town)	05361
Wallingford (Town)	05773	Westford	05494	Wilder	05088
Waltham (Town)	05491	Westford (Town)	05494	Williamstown	05679
Wardsboro	05355	West Georgia	05478	Williamstown (Town)	05679
Wardsboro (Town)	05355	West Glover	05875	Williamsville	05362
Wardsboro Center	05355	West Groton	05046	Williston (Town)	05495
Warners Grant (Town)	05903	West Halifax	05358	Williston	05495
Warren	05674	West Hartford	05084	Williston Road Section (Part	
Warren (Town)	05674	West Haven	05743	of South Burlington)	05401
Warrens Gore (Town)	05903	West Haven (Town)	05743	Wilmington	05363
Washington	05675	West Hill	05450	Wilmington (Town)	05363
Washington (Town)	05675	West Lincoln	05443	Windham	05359
Washington Heights	05657	West Milton	05468	Windham (Town)	05359
Waterbury	05676	Westminster	05158	Windsor (Town)	05089
Waterbury (Town)	05676	Westminster (Town)	05158	Windsor	05089
Waterbury Center	05677	Westminster Station (Part of		Winhall (Town)	05340
Waterford (Town)	05848	Westminster)	05159	Winooski	05404
Waterville	05492	Westminster West	05346	Winooski Park	05404
Waterville (Town)	05492	Westmore	05860	Wolcott	05680
Weathersfield (Town)	05151	Westmore (Town)	05860	Wolcott (Town)	05680
Weathersfield Bow	05156	West Newbury	05085	Woodbury	05681
Weathersfield Center	05151	West Norwich	05055	Woodbury (Town)	05681
Websterville	05678	Weston	05161	Woodford	05201
Wells	05774	Weston (Town)	05161	Woodford (Town)	05201
Wells (Town)	05774	Weston Priory	05161	Woodford Hollow	05201
Wells River	05081	West Pawlet	05775	Woodstock	05091
West Addison	05491	West Rupert	05776	Woodstock (Town)	05091
West Arlington	05250	West Rutland (Town)	05777	Worcester	05682
West Barnet	05821	West Rutland	05777	Worcester (Town)	05682
West Berkshire	05450	West Salisbury	05769	Wrightsville (Part of	
West Bolton	05465	West Springfield	05156	Montpelier)	05602
West Branch	05672				

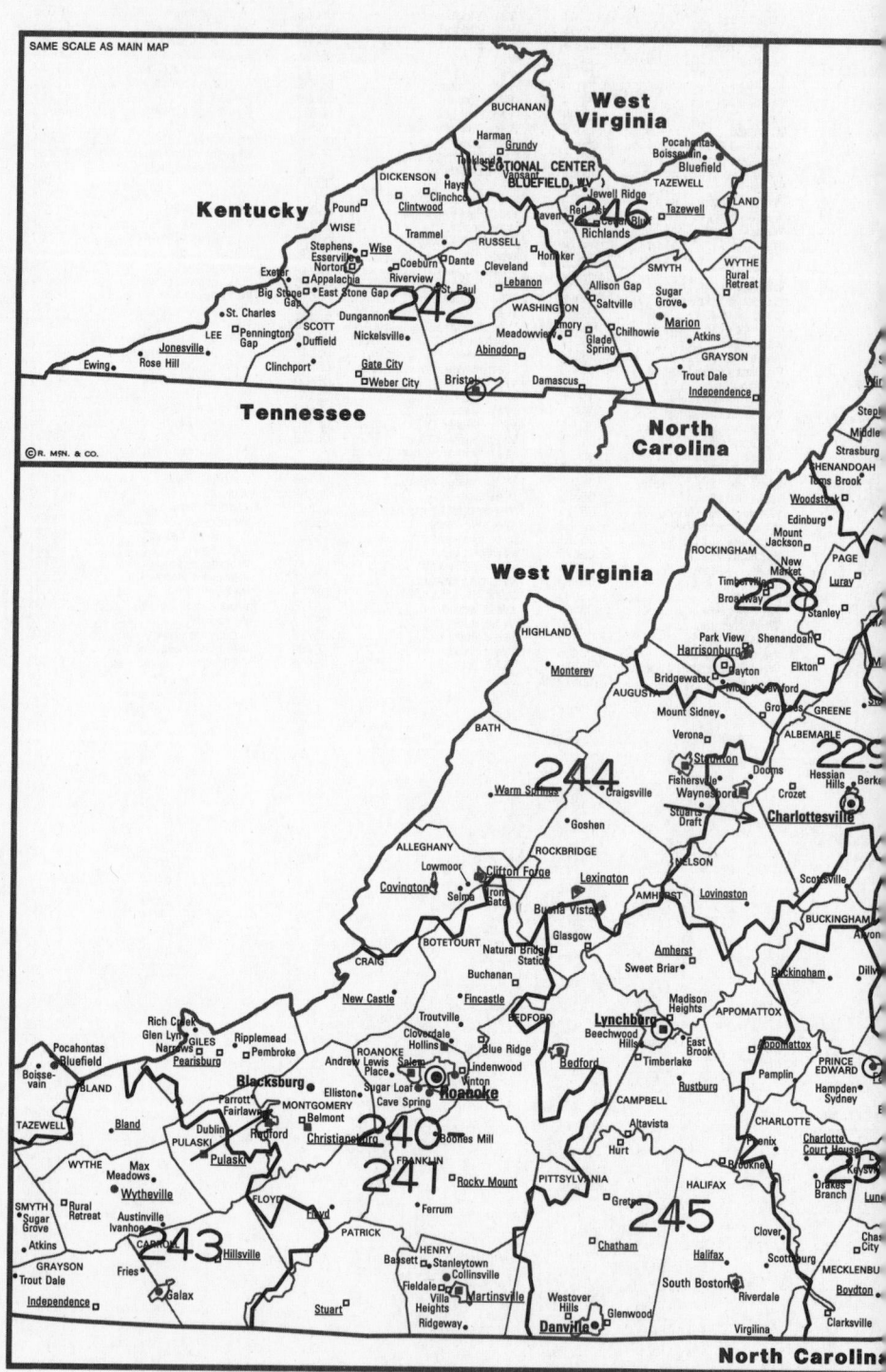

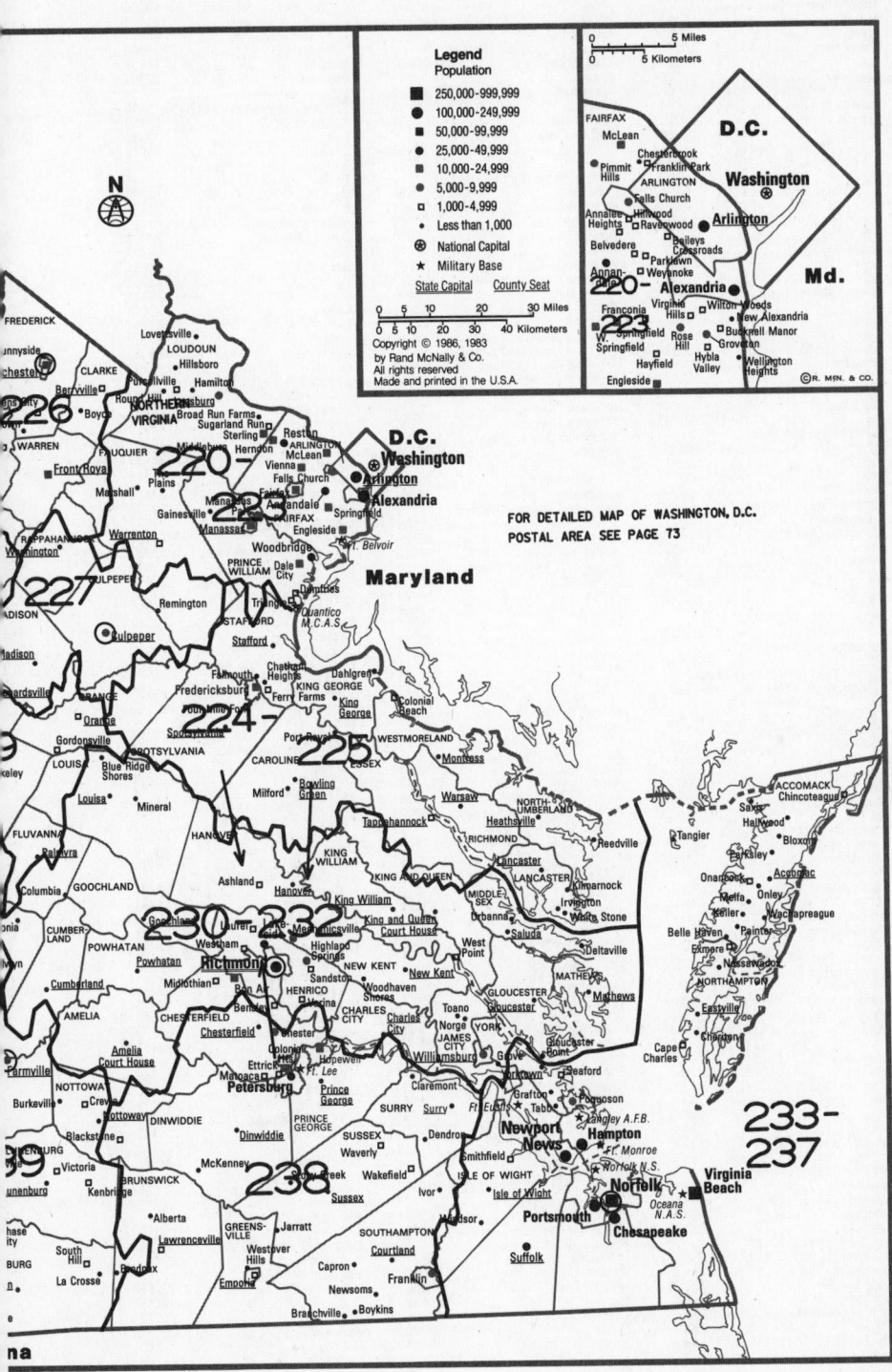

Legend
Population
- ■ 250,000-999,999
- ● 100,000-249,999
- ■ 50,000-99,999
- ■ 25,000-49,999
- ■ 10,000-24,999
- ● 5,000-9,999
- □ 1,000-4,999
- • Less than 1,000
- ⊗ National Capital
- ★ Military Base

State Capital   County Seat

0   5   10   20   30 Miles
0 5 10 20   30   40 Kilometers

0   5 Miles
0   5 Kilometers

FOR DETAILED MAP OF WASHINGTON, D.C.
POSTAL AREA SEE PAGE 73

Maryland

233-237

	ZIP		ZIP		ZIP
Aarons Creek	24598	Annex	24401	Balcony Falls (Part of	
Abbey Oaks	22180	Ante	23847	Glasgow)	24555
Abbott	24127	Antioch	24590	Ballards Crossroads	23315
Abilene	23923	Appalachia	24216	Ballentine Place (Part of	
Abingdon	24210	Apple Blossom Mall (Part of		Norfolk)	23509
Accomac	23301	Winchester)	22601	Balls Hills	22101
Accotink	22060	Apple Grove	23117	Ballston	22203
Accotink Heights	22003	Appomattox	24522	Ballston Common	22203
Achilles	23001	Aqua	24435	Ballsville	23139
Achsah	22727	Aquia Harbor	22554	Baltimore Corner	23850
Acorn	22469	Aragona Village (Part of		Balty	22546
Acredale (Part of Virginia		Virginia Beach)	23455	Banco	22711
Beach)	23464	Ararat	24053	Bandy	24602
	23467	Arbor Estates (Part of		Bane	24134
For specific Acredale Zip Codes		Suffolk)	23434	Banner	24230
call (804) 424-7237		Arborhill	24401	Banners Corner	24224
Acree Acres	23692	Arcadia	24066	Barbours Creek	24127
Ada	22115	Arch Mills	24066	Barboursville	22923
Addison Heights	22202	Arcola	22010	Barcroft	22204
Aden	22123	Arcturus	22308	Barfoot	24151
Adial	22938	Ardmore (Part of Fairfax)	22030	Barham	23881
Adkins Store	23140	Argyle Heights	22405	Barharnsville	23011
Adner	23149	Ark	23003	Barley	23847
Adria	24630	Arlington	22201-19	Barnesville	23964
Adsit	23856	For specific Arlington Zip Codes		Barnett	24266
Advance Mills	22968	call (703) 525-4838		Barnetts	23030
Adwolf	24354	Arlington (Part of Hopewell)	23860	Barracks	22901
Afton	22920	Arlington Forest	22203	Barracks Road (Part of	
Agricola	24574	Arlington Hall	22212	Charlottesville)	22903
Aiken Summit	24054	Arlington Heights	22204	Barren Ridge	24401
Aily	24237	Arlington Village	22204	Barren Springs	24313
Air Mail Facility (Part of		Arlingwood	22207	Barrett Acres (Part of	
Norfolk)	23519	Armel	22602	Suffolk)	23434
Airmont	22141	Armistead Forest (Part of		Bartlett	23314
Ajax	24161	Portsmouth)	23703	Bartlick	24256
Alanthus	22714	Armstrong	24460	Bartons Crossroad	24378
Alanton (Part of Virginia		Armstrong Gardens (Part of		Bartonville	22602
Beach)	23450	Hampton)	23669	Barytes (Part of Bristol)	24201
Albemarle (Part of Norfolk)	23503	Aroda	22709	Basham	24138
Alberene	22959	Arrington	22922	Basic (Part of Waynesboro)	22980
Alberta	23821	Arrowhead (Part of Virginia		Baskerville	23915
Albin	22603	Beach)	23462	Baskerville Correctional Unit	23915
Alcoma	23921	Arthur	24162	Bassett	24055
Aldie	22001	Artillery Ridge	22408	Bassett Forks	24055
Alexander Corner (Part of		Artrip	24225	Bastian	24314
Portsmouth)	23707	Arvonia	23004	Basye	22810
Alexandria (Independent		Asberrys	24377	Batesville	22924
City)	22301-32	Ashburn	22011	Bath Alum	24460
For specific Alexandria		Ashby	23040	Battersea (Part of	
(Independent City) Zip Codes call		Ashland	23005	Petersburg)	23803
(703) 549-4201		Ashton Heights	22201	Battery	22560
Alfonso	22421	Ashville	22115	Battery Park (Henrico	
Algonquin Park (Part of		Ashwood	24445	County)	23228
Norfolk)	23505	Aspen	23959	Battery Park (Isle of Wight	
Alhambra	22951	Aspenwall	24528	County)	23304
Alice Heights	23234	Assawoman	23302	Battle Beach	23851
Alleghany	24426	Atkins	24311	Battle Creek	23851
Alleghany Spring	24162	Atlantic (Accomack County)	23303	Battlefield Green	22407
Allen	24226	Atlantic (Part of Virginia		Battlefield Park (Part of	
Allencrest	22207	Beach)	23458	Petersburg)	23805
Allens Creek	24553	Atlantic Park (Part of		Bavon	23013
Allenslevel	23936	Virginia Beach)	23451	Bayberry Estates	22485
Allentown	23301	Atlee	23111	Bay Colony (Part of Virginia	
Allison Gap	24370	Atoka	22115	Beach)	23451
Allisonia	24347	Attoway	24354	Bayford	23354
Allmondsville	23061	Auburn	22019	Bay Island (Part of Virginia	
Allwood	24521	Augusta Correctional Center	24430	Beach)	23451
Alma	22851	Augusta Springs	24411	Bay Lake Beach (Part of	
Almagro (Part of Danville)	24541	Aurora Hills	22202	Virginia Beach)	23455
Almira (Part of Pound)	24279	Austinville	24312	Baylake Pines (Part of	
Alonzaville	22644	Avalon	22473	Virginia Beach)	23455
Alpha	23936	Avalon Terrace (Part of		Baynesville	22520
Alpine	22003	Virginia Beach)	23462	Bayport	23079
Alps	22514	Averett	24580	Bayside (Accomack	
Alsop	22553	Avon	22920	County)	23417
Altavista	24517	Avondale	23111	Bayside (Part of Virginia	
Alto	24483	Avon Forest	22039	Beach)	23455
Alton	24520	Axtel	24562	Bay View	23310
Alum Ridge	24091	Axton	24054	Bayville Park (Part of	
Alvarado	24210	Aylett	23009	Virginia Beach)	23455
Amburg	23043	Aylor	22727	Baywood	24333
Amelia Court House	23002	Azalea Acres (Part of		Beach	23832
Amherst (Amherst County)	24521	Norfolk)	23518	Beach Grove	22967
Amherst (Fairfax County)	22015	Azalea Court	23227	Beaconsdale (Part of	
Amissville	22002	Azalea Gardens (Part of		Newport News)	23607
Ammon	23822	Hampton)	23669	Bealeton	22712
Amonate	24601	Bachelors Hall	24541	Beamantown (Part of Big	
Ampthill	23234	Backbay (Part of Virginia		Stone Gap)	24219
Ampthill Heights (Part of		Beach)	23457	Beamon (Part of Suffolk)	23434
Richmond)	23234	Bacons Castle	23883	Bear Wallow	24622
Amsterdam	24175	Bacons Fork	23950	Beaufont Hills (Part of	
Andersonville	23911	Bacova	24412	Richmond)	23225
Andover	24215	Bacova Junction	24445	Beaumont	23014
Andrew Lewis Place	24153	Baden	24228	Beaverdam	23015
Angola	23901	Bagby	22514	Beaverlett	23016
Ankum	23868	Bagleys Mills	23970	Beazley	22560
Annalee Heights	22042	Bailey	24605	Beckham	24538
Annandale	22003	Baileys Crossroads	22041	Bedford (Independent City)	24523
Annandale Acres	22003	Bailey's Crossroads (census		Bee	24217
Annandale Gardens	22003	designated place)	22041	Beech Fork	23974
Annandale Terrace	22003			Beech Springs	24263

	ZIP
Brooklyn	24594
Brookneal	24528
Brook Vale	22503
Brookville (Part of Alexandria)	22304
Brookwood (Part of Virginia Beach)	23452
Brookwood Manor	23141
Brosville	24541
Brown Field (Part of Quantico)	22134
Brown Grove	23005
Brownsburg	24415
Browns Corner	23141
Browns Cove	22932
Browns Store	22473
Brown Town (Amherst County)	24521
Browntown (Warren County)	22610
Broyhill Crest	22003
Broyhill Forest	22207
Broyhill Park	22042
Brucetown	22622
Bruington	23023
Brumley Gap	24210
Bruno	24258
Brunswick	23868
Brush Tavern	24502
Bryan Park	23228
Bryan Parkway	23228
Bryant	22967
Bryants Corner	23847
Bryn Mawr	22101
Buchanan	24066
Buckhall	22110
Buckingham (Part of Arlington)	22203
Buckingham (Buckingham County)	23921
Buckingham (Chesterfield County)	23112
Buckingham Circle	22901
Buckland	22065
Bucknell Heights	22307
Bucknell Manor	22307
Buckner	23024
Buckroe Beach (Part of Hampton)	23664
Buckton	22657
Buena	22733
Buena Vista (Independent City)	24416
Buffalo Forge	24555
Buffalo Gap	24479
Buffalo Hill	24521
Buffalo Hills	22044
Buffalo Junction	24529
Buffalo Ridge	24171
Buffalo Springs	24529
Bufford Cross Roads	23847
Bull Run	22110
Bull Run Mountain Estates	22069
Bumpass	23024
Bundy	24265
Bunker Hill	24523
Burdette	23851
Burgess	22432
Burgundy Village	22303
Burke	22009
	22015
For specific Burke Zip Codes call (703) 978-9113	
Burke Heights	22015
Burke Hills	22015
Burkes Garden	24608
Burkes Shop	22580
Burketown	24486
Burkeville	23922
Burks Garden (Part of Tazewell)	24651
Burnam Woods	23168
Burnleys	22923
Burnside Farms	23111
Burnsville	24487
Burnt Chimney	24184
Burnt Store	23950
Burnt Tree	22960
Burr Hill	22433
Burrowsville	23842
Burson Place	24201
Burton (Part of Virginia Beach)	23455
Burtons Shop	24651
Bush Hill	22310
Bush Hill Woods	22310
Bush Mill	24271
Busthead	24609
Bustleburg	22450
Butterworth	23840
Butts Corner	22039
Butylo	22504

	ZIP
Bybee	22963
Byllesby	24350
Bynum Store	23924
Byrdton	22482
Cabin Point	23881
Cadet (Part of Big Stone Gap)	24219
Cady	23069
Caira	23040
Caledonia	23038
Callaghan	24426
Callands	24530
Callao	22435
Callaville	23856
Callaway	24067
Callison	24445
Calno	23069
Calvary	22664
Calverton	22016
Cambria (Part of Christiansburg)	24073
Cambridge	23235
Camden Heights (Part of Norfolk)	23502
Camellia Shores (Part of Norfolk)	23518
Camelot	22003
Cameron Station (Part of Alexandria)	22304
Cameron Valley (Part of Alexandria)	22314
Camp	24375
Camp Barrett	22134
Campbell	22947
Camp Creek	24091
Campostella Heights (Part of Norfolk)	23523
Camps Mill (Part of Suffolk)	23434
Camptown	24528
Cana	24317
Candlewax	24260
Cannady	24656
Canova	22110
Canterburg	22655
Canterbury	23229
Canterbury Hills	22901
Canterbury Woods	22003
Canton	24221
Capahosic	23061
Cape Charles	23310
Cape Henry (Part of Virginia Beach)	23454
Cape Henry Shores (Part of Virginia Beach)	23451
Cape Story by the Sea (Part of Virginia Beach)	23451
Capeville	23313
Capitol (Part of Richmond)	23219
Capon Road	22657
Capron	23829
Captain's Cove	23356
Carbo	24225
Cardinal	23025
Cardinal Forest	22152
Cardova	22701
Cardwell	23039
Cardwell Town	24370
Caret	22436
Carfax	24230
Carloover	24445
Carolanne Farms (Part of Virginia Beach)	23462
Caroline Correctional Unit	23069
Caroline Pines	22546
Carriage Hill (Fairfax County)	22181
Carriage Hill (Part of Virginia Beach)	23452
Carrie	24225
Carrollton	23314
Carrsbrook	22901
Carrsville	23315
Carsley	23890
Carson	23830
Carsonville	24348
Carters Mills	24053
Cartersville	23027
Carterton	24266
Carver Court (Part of Hampton)	23669
Carver Gardens	23185
Carysbrook	23055
Casanova	22017
Cascade	24069
Cash	23061
Cash Corner	22942
Cashville	23417
Caskie	24553
Castle Craig	24550
Castle Heights	23917
Castleton	22716

	ZIP
Castlewood	24224
Catalpa	22701
Catawba (Halifax County)	24577
Catawba (Roanoke County)	24070
Catharpin	22018
Catherton (Part of Manassas)	22110
Catlett	22019
Cats Bridge	23420
Cauthornville	23029
Cavalcade	22003
Cavalier Park (Part of Virginia Beach)	23451
Cave Mountain	24579
Cave Spring	24018
Cavetown	22835
Caylor	24248
Cedar Bluff (Tazewell County)	24609
Cedar Bluff (Washington County)	24236
Cedar Branch (Part of Saltville)	24370
Cedar Forest	24569
Cedar Fork	22546
Cedar Green	24401
Cedar Grove (Halifax County)	24520
Cedar Grove (Mecklenburg County)	23970
Cedar Grove (Northampton County)	23310
Cedar Grove Acres (Part of Chesapeake)	23320
Cedarhill	24565
Cedar Lawn	23231
Cedar Level (Part of Hopewell)	23860
Cedar Point	23063
Cedar Springs	24368
Cedarville (Warren County)	22630
Cedarville (Washington County)	24361
Cedon	22580
Celt	22973
Centenary	24590
Center Cross	22437
Center Star	23841
Centerville (Accomack County)	23412
Centerville (Augusta County)	22812
Centerville (Bedford County)	24523
Centerville (Goochland County)	23103
Centerville (Halifax County)	24592
Centerville (James City County)	23188
Centerville (Louisa County)	23117
Central (Part of Arlington)	22203
Central (Part of Richmond)	23219
Central Facility	22079
Central Garage	23086
Central Gardens	23223
Central Hill	23487
Centralia	23831
Centralia Gardens	23234
Central Martinsville (Part of Martinsville)	24112
Central Plains	22963
Central Point	22514
Central State Hospital	23803
Centre Heights	22020
Centreville	22020
Centreville Farms	22020
Ceres	24318
Chadswyck (Part of Chesapeake)	23321
Chalet Woods	22020
Chalk Level	24557
Chamberlain Village	22134
Chamberlayne	23227
Chamberlayne Farms	23227
Chamberlayne Heights	23227
Chamberlayne North	23227
Chamblissburg	24179
Champlain	22438
Chance	22439
Chancellor	22407
Chancellors Green	22407
Chancellorsville	22553
Chaneys	24565
Chantilly	22021-22
For specific Chantilly Zip Codes call (703) 968-7272	
Chantilly Estates	22021
Chapel	24124
Chapel Acres	22153
Chapel Hill (Part of Alexandria)	22302

ZIP

	ZIP
Chapel Park (Part of Newport News)	23606
Chapel Square	22003
Charity	24185
Charlemont	24526
Charles City	23030
Charlie Hope	23923
Charlotte Court House	23923
Charlottesville (Independent City)	22901-08
For specific Charlottesville (Independent City) Zip Codes call (804) 286-2282	
Chase City	23924
Chatham	24531
Chatham Heights	22405
Chatham Hill	24370
Chatmoss	24112
Chatmoss-Laurel Park	24112
Cheapside	23310
Check	24072
Cheriton	23316
Cherokee Heights (Part of Norfolk)	23518
Cherry Acres (Part of Hampton)	23669
Cherrydale	22207
Cherry Hill (Charles City County)	23030
Cherry Hill (Dinwiddie County)	23872
Cherry Hill (Prince William County)	22026
Chesapeake (Independent City)	23320-28
For specific Chesapeake (Independent City) Zip Codes call (804) 547-2144	
Chesapeake (Northampton County)	23310
Chesapeake Beach (Northumberland County)	22539
Chesapeake Beach (Part of Virginia Beach)	23455
Chesapeake Heights (Part of Hampton)	23664
Chesapeake Manor (Part of Norfolk)	23513
Chesconessex	23417
Chesdin Manor	23885
Chesopeian Colony (Part of Virginia Beach)	23452
Chesswood	23234
Chester	23831
Chesterbrook	22101
Chesterbrook Gardens	22101
Chesterbrook Woods	22101
Chester Estates (Part of Bristol)	24201
Chesterfield	23832
Chesterfield Heights (Part of Norfolk)	23504
Chester Gap	22623
Chestnut Hill (Fairfax County)	22003
Chestnut Hill (King George County)	22485
Chestnut Knob	24112
Chestnut Level	24527
Chestnut Yard	24381
Chevalle	22110
Chewings Corner	22534
Chickahominy Haven	23089
Chickahominy Shores	23089
Childress	24073
Childry	24577
Chilesburg	22546
Chilhowie	24319
Chiltons	22520
Chimney Run	24484
Chincoteague	23336
Chinquapin Village (Part of Alexandria)	22302
Chisford	22520
Christchurch	23031
Christensons Corner	23188
Christians	24479
Christiansburg	24068
	24073
For specific Christiansburg Zip Codes call (703) 382-3912	
Christie	24598
Chuckatuck (Part of Suffolk)	23432
Chula	23002
Church Hill (Part of Richmond)	23223
Churchill	22043
Churchland (Part of Portsmouth)	23703
Church Road	23833
Church View	23032

	ZIP
Churchville	24421
Cifax	24556
Circlewoods	22031
Cismont	22947
Civic Center (Part of Richmond)	23240
Clam	23308
Clancie	23156
Claraville	22473
Claremont (Part of Arlington)	22206
Claremont (Surry County)	23899
Clarendon	22201
Claresville	23847
Clarkes Gap	22075
Clarksville (Mecklenburg County)	23927
Clarksville (Washington County)	24340
Clarkton	24577
Clary	22657
Claudville	24076
Clay Bank	23061
Claypool Hill	24609
Clays Mill	24589
Clayville	23139
Clear Brook (Frederick County)	22624
Clearbrook (Roanoke County)	24014
Clearfield	22151
Clearfork	24314
Clearview Manor	22101
Clearwater Park	24426
Clell	24631
Clermont Woods	22310
Cleveland	24225
Cliffield	24637
Clifford	24533
Cliffview	24333
Clifton (Fairfax County)	22024
Clifton (Orange County)	22733
Cliftondale	24422
Clifton Forge (Independent City)	24422
Climax	24531
Clinchburg	24321
Clinchco	24226
Clinchport	24244
Clintwood	24228
Clito	24330
Clover (Part of Alexandria)	22314
Clover (Halifax County)	24534
Cloverdale (Botetourt County)	24077
Cloverdale (Fluvanna County)	23022
Clover Hill	22821
Club Court	23227
Cluster Springs	24535
Coalcreek	24333
Coaldan	24641
Coal Kiln	23420
Coal Mine	22657
Coan Stage	22473
Cobbdale (Part of Fairfax)	22030
Cobbs Creek	23035
Cobham	22929
Cobham Park	22572
Cobham Wharf	23883
Cochran	23821
Cody	24577
Coeburn	24230
Coffee	24551
Cohasset	23055
Cohoke	23181
Coke	23072
Colchester	22079
Cold Harbor Farms	23111
Coldwater	23108
Coleman Falls	24536
Coleman Place (Part of Norfolk)	23502
Coles Creek	24151
Coles Point	22442
Coliseum Mall (Part of Hampton)	23666
Colleen	22922
College (Part of Fredericksburg)	22401
	22404
For specific College Zip Codes call (703) 373-4871	
College Park (Part of Alexandria)	22314
College Park (Part of Staunton)	24401
College Park (Part of Suffolk)	23703
Colley	24220
Collierstown	24450

	ZIP
Collingwood	22308
Collins Crossing	22580
Collinsville	24078
Collinwood	24266
Cologne	23037
Colonial Beach	22443
Colonial Forest	23111
Colonial Heights (Independent City)	23834
Colonial Heights (Part of Hampton)	23664
Colonial Heights (Part of Norfolk)	23518
Colonial Heights (Washington County)	24201
Colonial Place (Part of Norfolk)	23508
Colonial Village	22201
Colonial Williamsburg (Part of Williamsburg)	23185
Colosse	23315
Colthurst	22901
Coltons Mill	24523
Columbia	23038
Columbia Forest	22204
Columbia Furnace	22824
Columbia Heights	22204
Columbia Park (Part of Hopewell)	23860
Columbia Pines	22003
Colvin Run	22066
Comans Well	23897
Comers Rock	24326
Comet	23430
Commodore Park (Part of Norfolk)	23503
Commonwealth	22901
Commonwealth Acres	23875
Community	22306
Comorn	22405
Compton	22650
Conaway	24603
Concord (Brunswick County)	23876
Concord (Campbell County)	24538
Concord Heights	22401
Conde	22115
Confederate Heights	23222
Conicville	22842
Conners Grove	24380
Conners Valley	24324
Contra	22437
Cookstown	22553
Cool Spring	22308
Coolwell	24521
Cooper	23092
Cootes Store	22815
Copper Hill	24079
Copper Valley	24141
Corbin	22446
Corinth	23866
Corn Valley	24260
Cornwall	24416
Coronado (Part of Norfolk)	23513
Cottage Heights (Part of Norfolk)	23504
Cottage Park (Part of Norfolk)	23503
Cottage Road Park (Part of Norfolk)	23505
Coulson	24381
Coulwood	24260
Council	24260
Countis Corner	24201
Country Club Hills (Part of Arlington)	22207
Country Club Hills (Part of Fairfax)	22030
Country Club Manor	22207
Country Club View	22032
Country Creek	22181
Countryside	22170
Counts	24237
County Line Cross Roads	23923
Court House	22216
Courtland	23837
Courtland Park	22041
Courtney	23060
Cove Colony	22503
Cove Creek (Bland County)	24314
Cove Creek (Tazewell County)	24651
Covesville	22931
Covingston Corner	23047
Covington (Independent City)	24426
Cox's Chapel	24363
Crab Orchard	24230
Crackers Neck (Scott County)	24271

	ZIP		ZIP		ZIP
Crackers Neck (Wise County)	24219	Darlington Heights	23935	Douglas Park (Part of Portsmouth)	23701
Craddockville	23341	Darnell Town	24265	Douglass Park	22204
Cradock (Part of Portsmouth)	23702	Darvills	23824	Doveville	22032
Craigs Mills	24201	Darwin	24228	Dowden Terrace	22311
Craig Springs	24127	Daugherty	23301	Downings	22460
Craigsville	24430	Davenport	22439	Downtown (Part of Charlottesville)	22902
Crandon	24315	Davis	24472	Downtown (Part of Leesburg)	22075
Cranes Nest	24230	Davis Corner (Part of Virginia Beach)	23462	Downtown (Part of Lynchburg)	24505
Craney Island Estates	23111	Davis Wharf	23345	Downtown (Part of Manassas)	22110
Creeds (Part of Virginia Beach)	23457	Dawley Corner (Part of Virginia Beach)	23457	Downtown (Part of Blacksburg)	24063
Crescent Hill (Part of Hopewell)	23860	Dawn	23047	Downtown (Part of Roanoke)	24001
Crescent Hills	22207	Dayton	22821	Doylesville	22932
Cresthill	22639	Deans (Part of Suffolk)	23435	Drakes Branch	23937
Crestview (Henrico County)	23226	Deatonville	23083	Dranesville	22070
Crestview (Prince Edward County)	23901	De Bree (Part of Norfolk)	23517	Draper	24324
Crestwood Manor	22003	De Busk Mill	24340	Drewryville	23844
Crewe	23930	Deel	24656	Drill	24260
Criders	22820	Deep Bottom	23075	Driver (Part of Suffolk)	23435
Criglersville	22727	Deep Creek (Accomack County)	23417	Drouin Hill	23075
Crimora	24431	Deep Creek (Part of Chesapeake)	23323	Drum Bay	24469
Cripple Creek	24322	Deep Creek (Part of Newport News)	23606	Dry Branch	24132
Crittenden (Part of Suffolk)	23433	Deep Hole	23336	Dryburg	24589
Critz	24082	Deerborne (Part of Richmond)	23234	Dryden	24243
Croaker	23188	Deerfield	24432	Dry Fork (Pittsylvania County)	24549
Croatan Beach (Part of Virginia Beach)	23451	Deerfield Correctional Center	23829	Dry Fork (Wise County)	24230
Crockett	24323	Deerfield Estates	23832	Drytown	24630
Crockett Springs	24162	Deer Park (Part of Manassas)	22110	Duane	23009
Crofton	24179	Deer Park Groove (Part of Newport News)	23607	Dublin	24084
Cromwell (Part of Norfolk)	23509	Deerrock	22938	Dudley	24558
Crooked Oak	24343	Defense General Supply Center	23234	Duffield	24244
Crossbrook	24215	De Jarnett	22514	Dugspur	24325
Crosses Corner	23069	Delaplane	22025	Dugwell	24151
Cross Junction	22625	Delaware	23851	Duke Gardens (Part of Alexandria)	22304
Crosskeys	22841	Delmar	24236	Dumbarton	23228
Crossroads (Albemarle County)	22959	Del Ray (Part of Alexandria)	22301	Dumfries	22026
Crossroads (Halifax County)	24577	Delta (Part of Alexandria)	22304	Dunavant	22401
Crossroads Mall (Part of Roanoke)	24012	Deltaville	23043	Dunbar	24216
Crosswinds	22153	Delton	24324	Dunbar Gardens (Part of Hampton)	23666
Crouch	22437	Denaro	23002	Dunbrooke	22560
Crows	24426	Denbigh (Part of Newport News)	23602	Duncan Gap	24293
Crozet	22932	Denby Park (Part of Norfolk)	23505	Duncans Mills	22435
Crozier	23039	Dendron	23839	Duncanville	24210
Crymes Store	23974	Denmark	24450	Dundalow (Part of Suffolk)	23434
Crystal Hill	24539	Denniston	24520	Dundas	23938
Crystal Spring Knolls	22207	Dentons Corner	23921	Dunford Town	24602
Cuckoo	23117	Derby	24216	Dungadin Heights	22630
Cullen	23934	Desha	22560	Dungannon	24245
Culmore	22041	Detrick	22652	Dunlop (Part of Colonial Heights)	23834
Culpeper	22701	Devon Manor (Part of Norfolk)	23503	Dunn Loring	22027
Cumberland	23040	Devonshire Gardens	22042	Dunn Loring Woods	22180
Cummings Heights	24210	Dewey	24279	Dunnsville	22454
Cumnor	23085	DeWitt	23840	Durrett Town	22920
Cunningham	22963	Dewitt Hospital	22060	Dutton	23050
Curdsville	23936	Diamond Springs (Part of Virginia Beach)	23455	Duty	24217
Currioman Landing	22520	Diascund	23089	Dwale	24228
Currituck Farms	23150	Dickensdale	23230	Dwina	24230
Cuscowilla	23917	Dickensonville	24224	Dye	24649
Customhouse (Part of Norfolk)	23514	Diggs	23045	Dyers Store	24112
Cypress Chapel (Part of Suffolk)	23434	Diggs Park (Part of Norfolk)	23523	Dyke	22935
Cypress Manor	23851	Dillard's Landing	23140	Eads	22202
Cypress Point (James City County)	23089	Dillwyn	23936	Eagle Rock	24085
Cypress Point (Surry County)	23899	Dinwiddie	23841	Earlhurst	24426
Dabney Estates	23885	Dinwiddie Gardens	23803	Earls	23002
Dabneys	23042	Disputanta	23842	Earlysville	22936
Dahlgren	22448	Ditchley	22482	East Aberdeen Gardens (Part of Hampton)	23666
Dahlia	27866	Dixie (Fluvanna County)	23055	East Brook	24501
Dalbys	23310	Dixie (Mathews County)	23050	East End (Part of Richmond)	23223
Dale City	22193	Dixie Hill	22030	Eastern Park (Part of Virginia Beach)	23452
Dalecrest (Part of Alexandria)	22304	Dockery	23970	Eastern State Hospital	23185
Dale Enterprise	22801	Doe Hill	24433	East Falls Church	22205
Daleville	24083	Dogtown	23063	Eastham	22901
Damascus	24236	Dogue	22451	East Hampton (Part of Hampton)	23669
Dam Neck (Part of Virginia Beach)	23461	Dogue Creek Village	22060	East Highland Park	23222
Dam Neck Corner (Part of Virginia Beach)	23454	Dogwood Hill (Part of Staunton)	24401	East Hilton (Part of Newport News)	23607
Danbury Forest	22151	Dogwood Knoll	23111	East Lexington	24450
Dandy	23692	Dolphin	23843	Eastmoreland	23231
Daniel	22960	Donna Lee Gardens	22046	East Norton (Part of Norton)	24273
Daniel Boone	24251	Dooms	22980	East Norview (Part of Norfolk)	23513
Danieltown	23821	Doran	24612	East Ocean View (Part of Norfolk)	23503
Danripple	24592	Dorchester (Part of Richmond)	23234	Easton Place (Part of Norfolk)	23502
Dante	24237	Dorchester (Wise County)	24273	Eastover (Part of Suffolk)	23434
Danville (Independent City)	24540-43	Dorchester Junction	24273	Eastover Gardens	23231
For specific Danville (Independent City) Zip Codes call (804) 792-3766		Dorset Woods	23075		
		Doswell	23047		
Dare	23692	Dot	24277		
		Double Tollgate	22663		

	ZIP		ZIP		ZIP
East Point (Accomack County)	23417	Eureka Park (Part of Virginia Beach)	23452	Fauquier Springs	22186
East Point (Rockingham County)	22827	Eustaces Corner	22728	Favonia	24382
		Euwanee Park (Part of Norfolk)	23503	Fawcett Gap	22602
East Radford (Part of Radford)	24141	Everets (Part of Suffolk)	23434	Fayette Park	23222
East Stone Gap	24246	Evergreen	23399	Featherstone	22191
East Suffolk Gardens (Part of Suffolk)	23434	Evergreen Hills	24201	Featherstone Shores	22191
Eastville	23347	Evergreen Shores	23696	Federal Correctional Institution	23803
Eastville Station (Part of Eastville)	23347	Evington	24550	Federal Reserve (Part of Richmond)	23219
Ebenezer	24565	Ewell	23185		
Ebony	23845	Ewing	24248	Fentress (Part of Chesapeake)	23322
Eclipse (Part of Suffolk)	23433	Exeter	24216	Fentress (Part of Virginia Beach)	23451
Edge	24554	Exmore	23350		
Edgehill (King George County)	22485	Faber	22938	Fenwick Park	22042
		Fagg	24073	Fergusonville	23930
Edgehill (Southampton County)	23851	Fairchester (Part of Fairfax)	22030	Ferncliff	23084
Edgehill Park	23803	Fair City Mall (Part of Fairfax)	22031	Ferndale Gardens	23803
Edgemont (Part of Covington)	24426	Fairfax (Independent City)	22021-22	Ferndale Park	23803
			22030-39	Ferrum	24088
Edgemont Park	24210	For specific Fairfax (Independent City) Zip Codes call (703) 273-5571		Ferry Farms	22405
Edgerton	23868			Fieldale	24089
Edgewater (Part of Norfolk)	23508			Fife	23054
Edgewood (Part of Petersburg)	23805	Fairfax Acres	22030	Figsboro	24112
Edinburg	22824	Fairfax Circle (Part of Fairfax)	22031	File	22427
Ednam Forest	22901	Fairfax Forest	22031	Fincastle	24090
Edom	22834	Fairfax Station	22039	Finchley	23927
Edsall Park	22151	Fairfax Villa	22030	Fine Creek Mills	23139
Edwards Shop	22718	Fairfax Woods (Part of Fairfax)	22030	Finneywood	23924
Edwardsville	22456	Fairfield (Essex County)	22454	First Colony	23185
Effinger	24450	Fairfield (Rockbridge County)	24435	First Street (Part of Radford)	24141
Eggleston	24086	Fairhaven	22303	Fishers Hill	22626
Eheart	22923	Fair Hill	22031	Fishersville	22939
Elam	23960	Fairland	22312	Five Forks (Amherst County)	24521
Elberon	23846	Fairlawn (Part of Covington)	24426	Five Forks (Bedford County)	24523
Elephant Fork (Part of Suffolk)	23434	Fairlawn (Part of Pulaski County)	24141	Five Forks (Carroll County)	24343
Elevon	22438	Fairlawn Estates (Part of Norfolk)	23502	Five Forks (Dinwiddie County)	23833
Elizabeth Park (Part of Norfolk)	23502	Fairlawn Heights	23075	Five Forks (Halifax County)	24592
Elizabeth River Shores (Part of Virginia Beach)	23464	Fairlee	22031	Five Forks (Part of Hopewell)	23860
Elizabeth River Terrace (Part of Virginia Beach)	23464	Fair Meadows (Part of Virginia Beach)	23462	Five Forks (James City County)	23185
Elk Creek	24326	Fair Meadows Estates (Part of Virginia Beach)	23462	Five Forks (Madison County)	22960
Elk Garden	24266	Fairmont Manor (Part of Norfolk)	23509	Five Forks (Nelson County)	24553
Elk Hill	23063	Fairmount Park (Part of Norfolk)	23509	Five Forks (Prince Edward County)	23958
Elko	23150	Fair Oaks (Part of Fairfax)	22032	Five Lakes	23141
Elkrun	22728	Fair Oaks (Henrico County)	23075	Five Mile Fork	22407
Elkton	22827	Fair Port	22539	Five Oaks	24630
Elkwood	22718	Fairview (Fairfax County)	22306	Flactem Manor	23805
Ellett	24073	Fairview (Part of Fairfax)	22031	Flagpond	24221
Elliston	24087	Fairview (Mecklenburg County)	23924	Flat Gap	24279
Elliston-Lafayette	24087	Fairview (Montgomery County)	24149	Flat Iron	22520
Ellisville	23093	Fairview (Northampton County)	23310	Flatridge	24378
Ellsworth (Part of Norfolk)	23505	Fairview (Page County)	22635	Flat Rock (Powhatan County)	23139
Elma	22971	Fairview (Scott County)	24244	Flatrock (Russell County)	24260
Elmhurst (Part of Norfolk)	23513	Fairview Beach	22405	Flat Run	22508
Elmo	24592	Fairview Heights (Part of Clifton Forge)	24422	Flat Spur	24237
Elmont	23005	Fairview Heights (Part of Lexington)	24450	Flat Top	24230
Elmwood Estates	22101	Fairwood	24378	Flatwood	24312
El-Nido	22101	Fairwood Acres	22039	Flatwoods	24090
Elon	24572	Falconbridge	23234	Fleeburg	22849
Elsom	23181	Falconerville	24521	Fleenors	24201
Eltham	23181	Falling Creek	23234	Fleenortown	24263
Elysian Woods	22192	Falling Spring	24445	Fleet (Part of Norfolk)	23511
Emmerton	22572	Falls Church (Independent City)	22040-46	Fleet Branch Post Office (Part of Norfolk)	23511
Emory	24327	For specific Falls Church (Independent City) Zip Codes call (703) 532-8822		Fleeton	22539
Emory-Meadow View	24327			Flemington	22228
Emporia (Independent City)	23847			Fletcher	22973
Endicott	24088	Falls Hill	22043	Fletcherville	22186
Enfield	23106	Falls Mills	24613	Flint Hill (Bedford County)	24121
Engleside	22309	Fallville	24326	Flint Hill (Rappahannock County)	22627
English Hills	23228	Falmouth	22405	Flood	24458
Enonville	23936	Fancy Gap	24328	Floris	22071
Eppes Fork	27584	Fancy Hill	24521	Floyd	24091
Erica	22520	Farmers	22580	Foneswood	22461
Esmont	22937	Farmers Fork (Essex County)	22509	Fontaine	24148
Esnon	23924	Farmers Fork (Richmond County)	22572	Ford	23850
Esserville	24273	Farmers Store	24360	Fordham (Part of Hampton)	23663
Estabrook (Part of Norfolk)	23509	Farmingdale (Part of Hopewell)	23860	Forest	24551
Estabrook Park (Part of Norfolk)	23513	Farmington (Albemarle County)	22903	Forest Acres	23805
Estaline	24430	Farmington (Henrico County)	23229	Forest Hill (Part of Richmond)	23225
Estes	22716	Farmville	23901	Forest Hills (Part of Virginia Beach)	23450
Ethel	22572	Farnham	22460	Forest Lake Hills	23111
Ethridge Estates	23805			Forest Park (Part of Hampton)	23666
Etlan	22719			Forest Park (Part of Norfolk)	23518
Ettrick	23803			Forestville (Fairfax County)	22066
Euclid (Part of Virginia Beach)	23462			Forestville (Shenandoah County)	22847
Euclid Place (Part of Virginia Beach)	23462			Fork Ridge	24639
Euclid Terrace (Part of Virginia Beach)	23462			Forks of Buffalo	24521
Eureka	23947			Forks Of Water	24413

	ZIP
Forksville	23950
Fork Union	23055
Formosa	23962
Fort Belvoir	22060
Fort Blackmore	24250
Fort Chiswell	24360
Fort Defiance	24437
Fortener Addition	24354
Fort Hill (Henrico County)	23226
Fort Hill (Part of Lynchburg)	24502
Fort Hunt	22306
Fort Lee (Henrico County)	23075
Fort Lee (Prince George County)	23801
Fort Lewis Terrace (Part of Salem)	24153
Fort Mitchell	23941
Fort Myer	22211
Fort Myer Heights	22209
Fort Pickett	23824
Fort Valley	22652
Foster	23056
Fosters Falls	24360
Four Corners	22182
Four Mile Fork	22408
Fourway (Part of Tazewell)	24630
Fox	24348
Foxhall (Part of Norfolk)	23502
Fox Hill (Part of Hampton)	23664
Fox Mill Estates	22070
Foxwells	22578
Fractionville	24210
Fraleytown	24244
Franconia	22310
Franconia Commons	22310
Franklin (Independent City)	23851
Franklin Farms	23805
Franklin Forest	22101
Franklin Heights	24151
Franklin Junction (Part of Suffolk)	23438
Franklin Park	22101
Franks Mill	24401
Franktown	23354
Frederick Hall	23117
Frederick Heights	22602
Fredericksburg (Independent City)	22401-08

For specific Fredericksburg (Independent City) Zip Codes call (703) 373-6543

	ZIP
Fredericksburg (Rockbridge County)	24473
Freeman	23856
Freemont	24343
Freeport	23061
Freeshade Corner	23071
Free Union	22940
Fremac (Part of Virginia Beach)	23451
Friendship	24340
Fries	24330
Fringer	24066
Frogtown	22012
Front Royal	22630
	22651

For specific Front Royal Zip Codes call (703) 635-4540

	ZIP
Frytown	22186
Fuqua Farms	23234
Fulks Run	22830
Fulton (Part of Richmond)	23231
Furnace	22827
Furnace Hill	24354
Furnace Mountain	22075
Gainesboro	22603
Gaines Mill Estates	23111
Gainesville	22065
Gala	24085
Galax (Independent City)	24333
Gallops Corner (Part of Virginia Beach)	23464
Galts Mill	24572
Gammons Store	23042
Garden City (Part of Arlington)	22207
Garden City (Part of Hampton)	23661
Garden Wood Park (Part of Virginia Beach)	23455
Gardner	24260
Gardners Crossroads	23117
Garfield Estates	22191
Gargatha	23421
Garland Heights	23234
Garrisonville	22463
Garrisonville Estates	22554
Garysville	23860
Gasburg	23857
Gate City	24251
Gatewood	22534

	ZIP
Gatewood Park (Part of Virginia Beach)	23454
Gaylord	22611
Gaynor Heights	24112
Gayton	23075
Geer	22973
Genito	23139
Genoa	22830
George Mason University	22030
Georges Fork	24228
Georges Mill	22080
Georges Tavern	23063
Georgetown	22842
Georgetown South (Part of Manassas)	22110
Georgetown Village	22191
George Washington (Part of Alexandria)	22305
George Washington Village	22060
Georgian Hamlet	22110
Gether	22514
Getz	22842
Ghent (Part of Norfolk)	23517
Gholsonville	23893
Gibson Station	24248
Gidsville	24521
Gilbert Gardens	23231
Gilmore Mills	24579
Ginter Park (Part of Richmond)	23227
Gladehill	24092
Gladesboro	24343
Glade Spring	24340
Gladstone	24553
Gladys	24554
Glamorgan	24293
Glasgow	24555
Glass	23072
Glebe Point	22432
Gleedsville	22075
Glen Alden	22030
Glen Allen	23058
	23060

For specific Glen Allen Zip Codes call (703) 270-2846

	ZIP
Glenbrook Hills	23075
Glencarlyn	22204
Glendale (Part of Newport News)	23607
Glendale Acres	23030
Glen Echo	23223
Glenford	24210
Glen Forest	22041
Glenita	24244
Glen Lyn	24093
Glenmore	24562
Glenns	23149
Glen Oaks	22015
Glenrochie	24210
Glen Rock (Part of Norfolk)	23502
Glen Roy Estates	23061
Glenshellah (Part of Portsmouth)	23707
Glenvar	24153
Glen Wilton	24438
Glenwood (Part of Danville)	24541
Glenwood Farms	23223
Glenwood Park (Part of Norfolk)	23505
Gloucester	23061
Gloucester Banks	23062
Gloucester Courthouse	23061
Gloucester Point	23062
Goblintown	24171
Goddin Hill	23005
Gogginsville	24151
Goldbond	24094
Golddale	22568
Gold Hill	23123
Goldvein	22720
Gonyon	22473
Goochland	23063
Goodall	23192
Goode	24556
Goods Mills	24471
Goodview	24095
Goodwins Ferry	24128
Goose Pimple Junction	24201
Gordonsville	22942
Gore	22637
Goshen	24439
Goshen Cross Road	23015
Gossan Mines	24333
Gouldin	23192
Gowrie Park (Part of Norfolk)	23509
Grady	24530
Grafton	23692
Grafton Village	22405
Grahams Forge	24360

	ZIP
Granby Shores (Part of Norfolk)	23503
Grandin Road (Part of Roanoke)	24015
Grand View (Part of Hampton)	23664
Grangeville	23410
Granite Hills (Part of Richmond)	23225
Granite Springs	22553
Grant	24378
Grant's Field	23803
Granville	23030
Grapefield	24314
Grassland	22733
Grass Ridge	22101
Grassy Creek (Henry County)	24112
Grassy Creek (Russell County)	24224
Gratton	24651
Gravel Hill (Part of Richmond)	23225
Graves Mill	22721
Graves Store	24104
Gray	23897
Graysontown	24141
Gray's Pointe	22033
Graysville	23301
Great Bridge (Part of Chesapeake)	23320
	23328

For specific Great Bridge Zip Codes call (804) 482-1193

	ZIP
Great Falls	22066
Great Neck Manor (Part of Virginia Beach)	23450
Green Acres (Part of Fairfax)	22030
Greenbackville	23356
Green Bay	23942
Greenbriar (Chesterfield County)	23831
Greenbrier (Fairfax County)	22033
Greenbrier Mall (Part of Chesapeake)	23320
Greenbush	23357
Green Cove	24236
Greendale (Henrico County)	23228
Greendale (Washington County)	24210
Greendale Manor	23230
Greenes Corner	23024
Greenfield (Nelson County)	22920
Greenfield (Pittsylvania County)	24557
Greenfield (Washington County)	24361
Greenfield Farms (Part of Portsmouth)	23703
Greenlee	24579
Greenmount	22801
Green Oaks (Part of Newport News)	23601
Green Pond	24531
Greens Folly Apartments	24592
Green Spring	22603
Green Springs (Louisa County)	22942
Green Springs (Washington County)	24210
Green Valley (Part of Bristol)	24201
Greenville (Augusta County)	24440
Greenville (Fauquier County)	22123
Greenville Correctional Unit	24440
Greenway Downs	22042
Greenway Hills (Part of Fairfax)	22030
Greenwich (Prince William County)	22123
Greenwich (Part of Virginia Beach)	23462
Greenwood (Albemarle County)	22943
Greenwood (Henrico County)	23060
Greenwood (Part of Norfolk)	23513
Greenwood (Rockingham County)	22827
Greenwood Farms (Part of Hampton)	23666
Gregory Corner	23968
Gressitt	23137
Gretna	24557
Griffinsburg	22701
Griffith	24422
Grimes	22624
Grimsleyville	24639
Grimstead	23064
Grindall Creek	23234
Grit	24563

	ZIP		ZIP		ZIP
Grizzard	23879	Hassen Heights (Part of		Hill Top (Part of Martinsville)	24112
Groseclose	24368	Bristol)	24201	Hilltop (Part of Suffolk)	23451
Grotons	23399	Hatchers	23139	Hilltop Manor (Part of	
Groton Town	23359	Hat Creek	24528	Virginia Beach)	23454
Grottoes	24441	Hatton	24590	Hilltop-Oceana (Part of	
Grove	23185	Haven Heights (Part of		Virginia Beach)	23454
Grove Hill	22849	Virginia Beach)	23462	Hilltown	24330
Grove Park (Part of		Hawkinstown	22842	Hillwood	22042
Portsmouth)	23707	Hawthorne (Part of Norton)	24273	Hiltons	24258
Groveton (census		Hayes	23072	Hilton Village (Part of	
designated place)	22303	Hayfield (Fairfax County)	22310	Newport News)	23601
Groveton	22306	Hayfield (Frederick County)	22638	Hinesville	24549
Groveton Gardens	22303	Haymarket	22069	Hinnom	22520
Groveton Heights	22306	Haynesville	22472	Hinton	22831
Grundy	24614	Haynesville Correctional Unit	22472	Hitesburg	24598
Guilford (Accomack County)	23308	Haysi	24256	Hiwassee	24347
Guilford (Fairfax County)	22310	Hayters Gap	24210	Hixburg	23958
Guilford Heights	23899	Haywood	22722	Hoadly	22191
Guinea	22580	Hazel	24237	Hobson (Part of Suffolk)	23436
Guinea Mills	23040	Hazel Heights (Part of		Hockley	23137
Gum Spring	23065	Bristol)	24201	Hockman (Part of Bluefield)	24605
Gum Tree	23005	Head Waters	24442	Hodges	24554
Gunn Hall Manor (Part of		Healing Springs	24445	Hodges Manor (Part of	
Virginia Beach)	23454	Health Science (Part of		Portsmouth)	23701
Gunston Heights	22079	Richmond)	23219	Hodgesville	24151
Gunston Manor	22079	Healys	23071	Hoges Chapel	24136
Gunton Park	24360	Heards	22920	Holcomb Rock	24503
Gwathmey	23005	Heathsville	22473	Holdcroft	23030
Gwynn	23066	Hebron (Augusta County)	24401	Holiday Hills (Part of	
Hacksneck	23358	Hebron (Carroll County)	24333	Richmond)	23235
Haddonfield	24279	Hebron (Dinwiddie County)	23894	Holiday Point Estates (Part	
Hadensville	23067	Hechler Village	23223	of Suffolk)	23434
Hagans	24263	Heights (Part of Petersburg)	23803	Holland (Part of Suffolk)	23437
Hague	22469	Helmet	23148	Hollindale	22306
Hale Creek	24634	Hematite	24426	Hollin Hall	22308
Halemhurst (Part of Fairfax)	22032	Hendricks Store	24121	Hollin Hills	22307
Hales Bottom	24605	Henry	24102	Hollins	24019
Halfway	22171	Henry Clay Heights	23111	Hollins College	24020
Halifax	24558	Henry Fork	24151	Holly Brook	24315
Halifax Correctional Unit	24558	Henrytown (Part of Saltville)	24370	Holly Forest	22039
Hall Addition	24354	Hepners	22842	Holly Forks	23011
Hallieford	23068	Herald	24230	Holly Grove	23024
Hallowing Point Estates	22079	Heritage Court	23228	Holly Hills	23139
Hallsboro	23113	Heritage Square	22003	Hollymead	22901
Halls Hill	22207	Heritage Village	22003	Holly Park	22032
Hallwood (Accomack		Herman	23967	Holly Point	23430
County)	23359	Hermitage	22980	Hollywood (Part of Suffolk)	23434
Hallwood (Part of Hampton)	23664	Hermitage Farms	23228	Holman	22853
Hamburg (Page County)	22835	Hermitage Park	23228	Holmes Run Acres	22042
Hamburg (Shenandoah		Hermosa	24577	Holmes Run Heights	22003
County)	22824	Herndon	22070-71	Holmes Run Park	22042
Hamilton	22068		22090-94	Holston	24210
Hamiltontown	24273	**For specific Herndon Zip Codes**		Holston Mill	24354
Hamlin	24224	**call (703) 437-3740**		Holts Crossing	24554
Hampden Sydney	23943	Hessian Hills	22901	Home Creek	24614
Hampton (Independent City)	23651-70	Hewlett	22546	Homeville	23890
For specific Hampton		Hickory Flat	24333	Homewood	22015
(Independent City) Zip Codes call		Hickory Ground (Part of		Honaker	24260
(804) 826-7586		Chesapeake)	23322	Honey Branch	24283
Hampton Institute (Part of		Hickory Grove Acres	22069	Honeyville	22851
Hampton)	23668	Hickory Haven	23103	Hood	22723
Hampton Terrace (Part of		Hickory Hill	22901	Hopeton	23421
Hampton)	23669	Hickory Junction	24260	Hopewell (Independent City)	23860
Hanckel	24361	Hicks Island	23089	Hopewell (Pittsylvania	
Handsom	23859	Hicksville	24314	County)	24549
Hanging Rock	24153	Hiddenbrook	22070	Hopkins	23421
Hanover	23069	Hideaway Park	22031	Horizon Hills (Part of Bristol)	24201
Hanover Heights	24266	Hidenwood (Part of		Horners	22520
Hansonville	24266	Newport News)	23606	Hornsbyville	23692
Happy Creek	22630	High Knob	22630	Horntown	23395
Harbors of Newport	22191	Highland	24084	Horse Gap (Part of Pound)	24279
Harborton	23389	Highland Gardens	23222	Horse Head	22473
Harbor View	22079	Highland Homes	22405	Horse Pasture	24112
Hardings	22482	Highland Park (Part of		Horsepen	24619
Hardware	24590	Arlington)	22205	Horsey	23396
Hardwood	24245	Highland Park (Part of		Hotchkiss	24460
Hardy	24101	Hopewell)	23860	Hot Springs	24445
Hardyville	23070	Highland Park (Part of		Howardsville (Albemarle	
Hare Valley	23350	Portsmouth)	23707	County)	24562
Harless	24073	Highland Park (Prince		Howardsville (Loudoun	
Harman (Buchanan County)	24618	William County)	22110	County)	22012
Harman (Tazewell County)	24602	Highland Park (Part of		Howellsville	22630
Harman Junction	24614	Richmond)	23222	Howertons	22454
Harmony (Halifax County)	24520	Highlands	22201	Howland	22473
Harmony (Shenandoah		Highland Springs	23075	Hubbard Springs	24263
County)	22824	High Meadows	24201	Huckleberry Hills	23805
Harpersville (Part of		High Point (Part of		Huddle	24382
Newport News)	23607	Hopewell)	23860	Huddleston	24104
Harrell Siding (Part of		Hightown (Highland County)	24444	Hudgins	23076
Suffolk)	23434	Hightown (Rockingham		Hudson Crossroads	22842
Harris Grove	23692	County)	22834	Hudson Terrace (Part of	
Harrisonburg (Independent		Highview Park	22207	Newport News)	23607
City)	22801	Hilander Park	24201	Huffman	24128
Harriston	24441	Hill	24251	Huffville	24138
Harrisville	22660	Hillbrook	22003	Hughes Store	23030
Harrowgate	23831	Hillcrest	23040	Hull Street (Part of	
Harryhogan	22435	Hillcrest Estates	22110	Richmond)	23224
Hartfield	23071	Hillsboro	22132	Hume	22639
Harts Shop	23117	Hillsdale (Part of Suffolk)	23434	Hunterdale	23851
Hartwood	22471	Hillsman Corner	24502	Hunter Estates	22079
Harvey	24219	Hillsville	24343		

	ZIP		ZIP		ZIP
Hunters Valley	22181	Jennings	23930	King George	22485
Huntersville (Part of Norfolk)	23504	Jennings Gap	24421	Kingsbury Manor	22980
Huntsville (Part of Suffolk)	23435	Jennings Mission	24251	Kings Corner	23089
Huntingcreek Hills	23234	Jennings Store	24244	Kings Crossroads	23964
Huntington (Fairfax County)	22303	Jericho (Carroll County)	24381	Kingsdale	23851
Huntington (Henrico		Jericho (Part of Suffolk)	23434	Kings Fork (Part of Suffolk)	23434
County)	23229	Jerome	22824	Kings Grant (Part of Virginia	
Huntington Heights (Part of		Jersey	22481	Beach)	23452
Newport News)	23607	Jessup Farms	23234	Kings Hill	23231
Huntly	22640	Jester Gardens (Part of		Kingsland	23234
Hunton	23060	Chesapeake)	23320	Kings Park	22151
Hunts Village	22032	Jetersville	23083	Kings Park West	22032
Hupp	22853	Jewell Hollow	22835	Kings Point	23185
Hurley	24620	Jewell Ridge	24622	Kings Store	24091
Hurricane	24293	Jewell Valley	24622	Kingston	24550
Hurt	24563	Johnsontown	23405	Kingston Chase	22070
Huske	23882	Joliff (Part of Chesapeake)	23321	Kingstown	24019
Hustle	22476	Jolivue	24401	Kingsville	23901
Hyacinth	22477	Jollett	22827	Kingswood	23185
Hybla Valley	22306	Jones	22553	Kingswood Court	23111
Hybla Valley Farms	22306	Jonesboro	23824	Kingtown (Part of Bristol)	24201
Hyco	24592	Jones Corner	22427	King William	23086
Hylas	23146	Jones Creek (Part of		Kino	22560
Hylton Park	23235	Martinsville)	24112	Kinsale	22488
Iberis	22503	Jonesville	24263	Kiptopeke	23310
Ida	22835	Jordan Mines	24449	Kire	24094
Idlewilde (Part of Covington)	24426	Josephine	24273	Kirkside	22306
Idylwood	22043	Joyce Heights (Part of		Klotz	24150
Igo	22405	Fairfax)	22030	Knightly	24437
Imboden	24216	Joyner	23829	Knob Hill (Part of Virginia	
Independence	24348	Justisville	23421	Beach)	23464
Independent Hill	22110	Ka	24245	Koehler	24112
Index	22485	Karo	22630	Konnarock	24236
Indian Field	22572	Kathmoor	22310	Laburnum Manor	23222
Indian Gap	24656	Keats	27553	Lacey Forest	22205
Indian Neck	23148	Kecoughtan (Part of		Lacey Spring	22833
Indian River (Part of		Hampton)	23667	Lackey	23694
Chesapeake)	23325	Keeling	24566	La Crosse	23950
Indian River Estates (Part of		Keene	22946	Ladd	22980
Virginia Beach)	23462	Keene Mill Manor	22152	Ladysmith	22501
Indian Rock	24066	Keen Mountain	24624	Lafayette	24087
Indian Run Park	22312	Keezletown	22832	Lafayette Boulevard (Part of	
Indian Springs (Chesterfield		Keith	23009	Norfolk)	23509
County)	23234	Keller	23401	Lafayette Park (Part of	
Indian Springs (Fairfax		Kells Corner	23924	Norfolk)	23509
County)	22312	Kelsa	24620	Lahore	22502
Indian Valley	24105	Kemmerer Gem No. 2	24282	Lake	22511
Indika	23487	Kemp's Place	23231	Lake Barcroft (cesus	
Ingham	22849	Kempsville (Part of Virginia		designated place)	22041
Ingleside (Part of Norfolk)	23502	Beach)	23462	Lake Barcroft	22044
Ingram	24597	Kempsville Colony (Part of		Lake Caroline	22546
Inlet	22701	Virginia Beach)	23464	Lake Crystal Farms	23235
Inman	24216	Kempsville Gardens (Part of		Lake Jackson	22110
Ino	22437	Virginia Beach)	23462	Lake Monticello	22963
Interior	24094	Kempsville Heights (Part of		Lake Of The Woods	22508
Intervale	24426	Virginia Beach)	23462	Lake Ridge	22192
Ira	24620	Kenbridge	23944	Lakeside (Henrico County)	23228
Irisburg	24054	Kendall Acres	23234	Lakeside (Part of Newport	
Irondale	24219	Kendall Grove	23347	News)	23606
Iron Gate (Alleghany		Kenilworth (Part of Norfolk)	23503	Lakeside (Part of Salem)	24153
County)	24448	Kennard	22572	Lakeside Heights	23692
Irongate (Prince William		Kennelworth (Part of		Lakeside Hills	23228
County)	22110	Petersburg)	23803	Lakeside Village	23038
Ironto	24087	Kent	24382	Lakeview Acres	23901
Irving	24174	Kent Gardens	22101	Lakeville Estates (Part of	
Irvington	22480	Kent Park (Part of Norfolk)	23509	Virginia Beach)	23464
Irwin	23063	Kents Store	23084	Lakewood (Fairfax County)	22041
Isaac	23851	Kentuck	24586	Lakewood (James City	
Island Creek	24343	Kenwood (Hanover County)	23005	County)	23185
Island Farm	22560	Kenwood (Part of Hopewell)	23860	Lakewood (Part of Norfolk)	23509
Island Ford	22827	Keokee	24265	Lakewood (Pittsylvania	
Isle of Wight	23397	Kerfoot	22025	County)	24541
Isom	24228	Kermit	24251	Lamberts Point (Part of	
Ivakota	22024	Kerns	24250	Norfolk)	23508
Ivanhoe	24350	Kernstown (Part of		Lambsburg	24351
Ivondale	22572	Winchester)	22602	Lanahan	24088
Ivor	23866	Kerrs Creek	24450	Lancaster	22503
Ivy	22945	Keswick	22947	Landmark Center (Part of	
Jacksons Ferry	24312	Keysville	23947	Alexandria)	22304
Jamaica	23079	Key West	22901	Landmark Plaza (Part of	
James River Estates	23238	Kibler	24053	Alexandria)	22312
James Store	23080	Kidds Fork	22514	Landmark Square (Part of	
Jamesville	23398	Kidd's Store	24590	Manassas)	22110
Janaf Shopping Center		Kidville	22939	Land of Promise (Part of	
(Part of Norfolk)	23502	Kiels Gardens	22030	Virginia Beach)	23457
Janey	24631	Kiger Hill	24450	Land O'Pines	23832
Jarratt	23867	Kilby (Part of Suffolk)	23434	Landtown (Part of Virginia	
Jasper	24244	Kilby Shores (Part of		Beach)	23456
Java	24565	Suffolk)	23434	Lanes Corner (Hanover	
Jefferson (Fairfax County)	22042	Kildare Annex	23230	County)	23005
Jefferson (Powhatan		Kilmarnock	22482	Lanes Corner (Spotsylvania	
County)	23139	Kilmarnock Wharf	22482	County)	22553
Jefferson Manor	22303	Kimages	22030	Lanesville	23086
Jefferson Mews (Part of		Kimballton	24150	Laneview	22504
Herndon)	22070	Kimberly Hills	23901	Lanexa	23089
Jefferson Park	23860	Kimberling	24315	Langhorne Acres	22031
Jeffersonton	22724	Kimberly Acres	23234	Langley	22101
Jefferson Village	22042	Kinderhook	22973	Langley Forest	22101
Jeffress	23927	Kindrick	24382	Langley Research Center	
Jenkins Bridge	23399	King and Queen Court		(Part of Hampton)	23665
Jenkins Neck	23072	House	23085		

	ZIP
Langley View (Part of Hampton)	23669
Lankford Corner	22473
Lantz Mills	22824
Lara	22503
Larchmont (Part of Arlington)	22201
Larchmont (Part of Norfolk)	23508
Larkspur (Part of Virginia Beach)	23462
Larrys Store	24598
Larwood Acres	24201
Lassiter Courts (Part of Newport News)	23607
Laswell	24360
Latanes	22443
Laurel (Henrico County)	23060
Laurel (Russell County)	24260
Laurel Branch	24091
Laureldale	24236
Laurel Dell	23228
Laurel Fork	24352
Laurel Grove	24594
Laurel Grove Estates	23111
Laurel Hill (Augusta County)	24482
Laurel Hill (Shenandoah County)	22641
Laurel Manor (Part of Virginia Beach)	23451
Laurel Mills	22716
Laurel Oak	23234
Laurel Park (Henrico County)	23228
Laurel Park (Henry County)	24112
Lawndale Farms	23231
Lawrenceville	23868
Lawrenceville Hills	23868
Lawson	23430
Lawson Forest (Part of Virginia Beach)	23455
Lawson's Store (Mecklenburg County)	23924
Lawsons Store (Russell County)	24224
Lawyers	24501
Laymantown	24064
LC Page (Part of Norfolk)	23518
Leaksville	22835
Leatherwood	24112
Lebanon	24266
Lebanon Church	22641
Leck	24230
Leda	24577
Lee	23039
Lee Acres	23875
Lee Boulevard Heights	22044
Leedstown	22443
Lee Forest	22030
Lee Hall (Part of Newport News)	23603
Lee Heights	22207
Lee-Hi Village	22030
Leemaster	24656
Lee Meadows	22032
Lee Mont	23403
Lee Park	23150
Leesburg	22075
Leesville	24571
Lee Town	24614
Leewood	22151
Lenah	22001
Lennig	24577
Lenox (Part of Norfolk)	23503
Lenox (Part of Virginia Beach)	23451
Leon	22725
Lerty	22520
Lester Manor	23086
Level Run	24563
Lewinsville	22101
Lewinsville Heights	22101
Lewisetta	22505
Lewis Gardens	23150
Lewis Park	22030
Lewiston	23005
Lewisville	22611
Lexington (Independent City)	24450
Liberia Woods (Part of Manassas)	22110
Liberty (Halifax County)	24577
Liberty (Tazewell County)	24651
Lick Fork	24230
Lick Run	24085
Lick Skillet	24370
Lightfoot	23090
Lignum	22726
Lilian	22539
Lilly	22821
Lime Hill	24201
Limeton	22610

	ZIP
Lincoln	22078
Lincolnia	22312
Lincolnia Heights	22312
Lincolnia Park	22312
Lincoln Park (Fairfax County)	22030
Lincoln Park (Part of Norfolk)	23513
Lindell	24210
Linden	22642
Lindenwood	24179
Lindsay	22942
Linkhorn (Part of Virginia Beach)	23454
Linkhorn Estates (Part of Virginia Beach)	23454
Linkhorn Shores (Part of Virginia Beach)	23451
Linlier (Part of Virginia Beach)	23451
Linville	22834
Lipps	24273
Lithia	24066
Little Haven (Part of Virginia Beach)	23452
Little Plymouth	23091
Little River Hills (Part of Fairfax)	22031
Little River Pines	22031
Little River Shopping Center	22003
Little Rocky Run	22024
Littleton	23890
Little Vienna Estates	22181
Litwalton	22503
Litz	24340
Lively	22507
Lloyd Place (Part of Suffolk)	23434
Loch Laird (Part of Buena Vista)	24416
Loch Lomond	22110
	22111
For specific Loch Lomond Zip Codes call (703) 368-2145	
Lockhart Flats	24228
Locust Creek	23024
Locust Dale	22948
Locust Grove	22508
Locust Hill (Middlesex County)	23092
Locust Hill (Wythe County)	24360
Locust Mound	23410
Locustville	23404
Lodge	22435
Lodi	24340
Lodore	23002
Lofton	24472
Logan	22553
Loisdale Estates	22150
Lombardy Grove	23970
London Bridge (Part of Virginia Beach)	23454
London Towne	22020
Lone Fountain	24421
Lone Gum	24104
Longbottom (Part of Grundy)	24614
Long Branch	24237
Long Dale (Alleghany County)	24422
Longdale (Henrico County)	23060
Longdale Furnace	24422
Long Island	24569
Long Point (Part of Portsmouth)	23703
Longshop	24060
Long Spur	24084
Longview	23430
Looney's Creek	24614
Loretto	22509
Lorfax Heights	22079
Lorne	22546
Lorraine	23075
Lorton	22079
	22199
For specific Lorton Zip Codes call (703) 339-6128	
Lost Corner	22663
Lost Forest	23234
Lottsburg	22511
Loudoun Heights	25425
Louisa	23093
Love	22952
Loves Mill	24319
Loves Shop	24558
Lovettsville	22080
Lovingston	22949
Lower Brandon	23881
Lower Elk Creek	24326
Lower Exeter	24216
Lowery Hills	24201
Lowesville	22951

	ZIP
Lowmoor	24457
Lowry	24570
Loxley Place (Part of Portsmouth)	23702
Luck	24565
Lucketts	22075
Lumberton	23890
Lummis (Part of Suffolk)	23434
Lunenburg	23952
Luray	22835
Lurich	24124
Lusters Gate	24060
Luttrellville	22435
Lydia	22973
Lyells	22572
Lyman Park	22134
Lynchburg (Independent City)	24501-06
For specific Lynchburg (Independent City) Zip Codes call (804) 528-8900	
Lynch Station	24571
Lyndhurst	22952
Lynhaven (Part of Alexandria)	22305
Lynn Grove	23222
Lynnhaven (Part of Hampton)	23666
Lynnhaven (Part of Virginia Beach)	23450
Lynnhaven Acres (Part of Virginia Beach)	23452
Lynnhaven Colony (Part of Virginia Beach)	23451
Lynnhaven Mall (Part of Virginia Beach)	23452
Lynn Shores (Part of Virginia Beach)	23452
Lynn Spring	24649
Lynnwood (Rockingham County)	24471
Lynnwood (Part of Virginia Beach)	23452
Lynwood	22191
Lyon Park	22201
Lyon Village	22201
Mabe	24244
McAdam	24301
Macanie	22842
McCall Gap	24340
McChesney Heights (Part of Bristol)	24201
McClung	24460
McClure	24269
McConnell	24251
McCoy	24111
McCrady	24370
McDonalds Mill	24060
McDonald's Small Farms	23060
McDowell	24458
Macedonia	23308
Maces Springs	24258
McGaheysville	22840
McHenry	22553
Machipongo	23405
McKendree	24558
McKenney	23872
McKinley	24459
McLean	22101-06
	22043
	22067
For specific McLean Zip Codes call (703) 790-9100	
McLean Estates	22101
McLean Hamlet	22102
McLean Manor	22101
McMullen	22973
McNeals Corner	22503
Macon	23101
Madison	22727
Madison College (Part of Harrisonburg)	22801
Madison Heights	24572
Madison Manor	22205
Madison Mills	22953
Madison Run	22942
Madisonville	23958
Madrid	22980
Madrillon Farms	22182
Maggie	24127
Magnolia (Part of Suffolk)	23434
Magnolia Gardens (Part of Suffolk)	23434
Maidens	23102
Major	24526
Makemie Park	23442
Malbrook	22044
Malcolm	24201
Malibu (Part of Virginia Beach)	23452
Mallow	24426

	ZIP		ZIP		ZIP
Malmaison	24527	Meadowbrook (Part of		Mobjack	23118
Manakin	23103	Norfolk)	23505	Modern (Part of Hampton)	23666
Manakin Farms	23103	Meadowbrook Forest (Part		Modest Town	23412
Manakin Sabot	23103	of Norfolk)	23518	Moffats Creek	24459
Manassas (Independent		Meadowcrest (Part of		Mogarts Beach	23430
City)	22110-11	Bristol)	24201	Mollusk	22517
For specific Manassas		Meadowood	23227	Monaskon	22503
(Independent City) Zip Codes call		Meadows of Dan	24120	Moneta	24121
(703) 368-2145		Meadows of Newgate	22020	Moneys Corner	22070
Manassas Park		Meadow View (Chesterfield		Monroe	24574
(Independent City)	22111	County)	23234	Monroe Gardens (Part of	
Manbur	23150	Meadowview (Washington		Hampton)	23669
Manchester Mills	23875	County)	24361	Monroe Hall	22443
Maness	24282	Meadville	24558	Montague	22504
Mangohick	23104	Mears	23409	Montclair	22026
Mannboro	23105	Mears Station	23409	Montebello	24464
Manquin	23106	Mearsville	23409	Monterey	24465
Manry	23888	Mechanicsburg	24315	Montevideo	22840
Mantua	22031	Mechanicsville (Hanover		Montezuma	22821
Mantua Hills	22031	County)	23111	Montezuma Gardens	23223
Manville	24251	Mechanicsville (Rockingham		Montford	22960
Maple Grove (Rockbridge		County)	22853	Montgomery	24023
County)	24450	Mechums River	22901	Monticello Park (Part of	
Maple Grove (Spotsylvania		Mecklenburg Correctional		Alexandria)	22305
County)	22407	Center	23917	Monticello Village (Part of	
Maple Grove		Media Park	23231	Norfolk)	23509
(Westmoreland County)	22443	Meetze	22186	Monticello Woods	22150
Maplewood	23002	Meherrin	23954	Montpelier (Charles City	
Mappsburg	23420	Melfa	23410	County)	23030
Mappsville	23407	Melrose (Campbell County)	24554	Montpelier (Hanover	
Marble Valley	24432	Melrose (Part of Roanoke)	24017	County)	23192
Marcem (Part of Gate City)	24251	Melrose Gardens	22172	Montpelier Station	22957
Marengo	23950	Melton	22942	Montrose	23231
Margo	22553	Memorial Heights	22306	Montrose Heights (Part of	
Marion	24354	Mendota	24270	Richmond)	23231
Marion Hill	23231	Mentow	24104	Montrose Terrace	23231
Marionville	23408	Meredithville	23873	Montross	22520
Markham (Fauquier County)	22643	Meridian Park	22046	Montvale	24122
Markham (Pittsylvania		Merrifield	22031	Montvue	22901
County)	24557	Merrimac	24060	Monument Heights	23226
Mark Haven Beach	22454	Merrimack Park (Part of		Moon	23119
Marksville	22851	Norfolk)	23503	Mooreland	23075
Marlan Forest	22307	Merrimac Shores (Part of		Mooreland Farms	23229
Marlbank	23692	Hampton)	23669	Moores Corner	22554
Marlboro	23224	Merry Point	22513	Moorings	23839
Marlbrook	24483	Messongo	23399	Moran	23966
Marrowbone Heights	24148	Metomkin	23421	Morattico	22523
Marshall	22115	Mew	24224	Morefield	24283
Marshall Heights	23072	Michaux	23139	Morningside Hills	24210
Marsh Run	22712	Midcity Shopping Center		Morning Star	22835
Marstella Estates	22186	(Part of Portsmouth)	23707	Morrisdale	23831
Martha Gap	24256	Middlebrook	24459	Morrison (Part of Newport	
Martin Siding	23405	Middleburg	22117	News)	23601
Martins Store	22920	Middleridge	22032	Morrisonville	22080
Martinsville (Independent		Middleton	23228	Morrisville	22712
City)	24112-15	Middleton Gardens (Part of		Morven	23002
For specific Martinsville		Salem)	24153	Mosby	22042
(Independent City) Zip Codes call		Middletown (Frederick		Mosby Woods (Part of	
(703) 632-4745		County)	22645	Fairfax)	22030
Marumsco Acres	22191	Middletown (Northampton		Moscow	22843
Marumsco Hills	22191	County)	23413	Moseley	23120
Marumsco Plaza	22191	Middletowne Farms	23185	Moss Run	24426
Marumsco Village	22191	Midland	22728	Mossy Creek	22812
Marumsco Woods	22191	Midlothian	23112-13	Motley	24563
Marvin	24639	For specific Midlothian Zip Codes		Motleys Mill	24531
Marye	22553	call (804) 794-5177		Motorun	23163
Marysville	24554	Midway (Halifax County)	24598	Mountain Falls	22602
Maryus	23107	Midway (Mecklenburg		Mountain Gap	22075
Mascot	23108	County)	23915	Mountain Grove	24484
Mason Cove	24153	Midway (Tazewell County)	24609	Mountain Hill	24586
Mason Creek (Part of		Mike	24538	Mountain Lake	24136
Salem)	24153	Mila	22473	Mountain Valley	24112
Masonville	22003	Milan (Part of Norfolk)	23508	Mountain View (Giles	
Massanetta Springs	22801	Miles	23025	County)	24134
Massanutten	22840	Milford	22514	Mountain View (King	
Massaponax	22407	Military Circle (Part of		George County)	22406
Massies Mill	22954	Norfolk)	23502	Mountain View (Pulaski	
Mathews	23109	Millboro	24460	County)	24084
Matoaca	23803	Millboro Spring	24460	Mountain View (Rockbridge	
Mattaponi	23110	Mill Creek Park	22003	County)	24416
Maurertown	22644	Millenbeck	22503	Mountain View (Washington	
Maury Place (Part of		Miller Park (Part of		County)	24210
Newport News)	23601	Lynchburg)	24501	Mount Airy	24557
Mavisdale	24627	Millers Tavern	23115	Mount Alto	22937
Max Creek	24347	Mill Gap	24465	Mount Carmel (Halifax	
Maxie	24628	Mill Garden	22553	County)	24520
Maximum Security Facility	22079	Milltown	22080	Mount Carmel (Smyth	
Max Meadows	24360	Millwood	22646	County)	24354
Maxwell	24651	Milteer Acres (Part of		Mountcastle	23140
Mayberry	24120	Suffolk)	23434	Mount Clifton	22842
Maybrook	24136	Mineral	23117	Mount Clinton	22801
Mayfair Place	23223	Mine Run	22568	Mount Crawford	22841
Mayfield	23230	Minimum Security Facility	22079	Mountfair	22932
Mayfield Farms	23111	Minnieville	22193	Mount Garland	23117
Mayflower	24521	Minor	22560	Mount Hermon	24541
Mayo (Halifax County)	24598	Mint Spring	24463	Mount Heron	24631
Mayo (Henry County)	24165	Miona	23415	Mount Holly	22524
Maytown (Part of Coeburn)	24230	Miskimon	22473	Mount Jackson	22842
Meade	22560	Mission Home	22940	Mount Landing	22560
Meadowbrook (Chesterfield		Mitchells	22729	Mount Laurel	24534
County)	23234	Mitchelltown	24445	Mount Meridian	24441

	ZIP
Mount Nebo	23235
Mount Olive	22660
Mount Pisgah	24467
Mount Pleasant	24521
Mount Pleasant Estates	22405
Mount Sidney	24467
Mount Solon	22843
Mount Vernon	22121
Mount Vernon Forest	22309
Mount Vernon Park	22309
Mount Vernon Square	22306
Mount Vernon Terrace	22309
Mount Vernon Valley	22309
Mount Vernon Woods	22309
Mountville	22117
Mount Vinco	23921
Mount Williams	22602
Mount Zephyr	22309
Mount Zion	24554
Mouth of Laurel	24609
Mouth of Wilson	24363
Mt. Ararat	23927
Mt. Cross	24540
Mt. View	24354
Mud Fork	24630
Mulch	22460
Munden (Part of Virginia Beach)	23457
Mundy Point	22435
Munson Hill	22041
Murat	24450
Murpheyville	24368
Murphy	24656
Murrayfield	24319
Museville	24531
Mustoe	24468
Mutton Hunk	23421
Myndus	22949
Myrtle (Part of Suffolk)	23434
Nace	24175
Naffs	24065
Nahor	22963
Nain	22603
Namozine Store	23833
Nancy Wrights Corner	22580
Nandua	23420
Nansemond (Part of Suffolk)	23434
Nansemond Shores (Part of Suffolk)	23434
Naola	24574
Narrows	24124
Naruna	24576
Nash Ford	24225
Nasons	22733
Nassawadox	23413
Nathalie	24577
National Airport	20001
National Heights	23231
Natural Bridge	24578
Natural Bridge Station	24579
Natural Well	24445
Naval Base (Part of Norfolk)	23511
Naval Weapons Laboratory	22448
Naval Weapons Station	23691
Navy Annex	20370
Naxera	23122
Naylors Beach	22572
Nealy Ridge	24226
Nebo	24318
Needmore (Smyth County)	24319
Needmore (Wise County)	24273
Neenah	22520
Neersville	22132
Negro Foot	23192
Nellysford	22958
Nelson	24580
Nelson Estates	23231
Nelsonia	23414
Nelson Park	23185
Nesting	23079
Nethers	22740
Nettleridge	24171
New Alexandria	22307
New Baltimore	22186
Newbern	24126
Newberry	22170
New Birchett Estates	23875
New Bohemia	23842
New Canton	23123
New Castle	24127
New Church	23415
Newcomb Hall (Part of Charlottesville)	22904
New Design (Part of Danville)	24541
New Ellett	24060
New Glasgow	24521
New Gosport (Part of Portsmouth)	23702
New Hampden	24413

	ZIP
New Hope (Augusta County)	24469
New Hope (Charles City County)	23030
Newington	22122
Newington Station	22153
Newington Woods	22153
New Kent	23124
Newland	22572
New London	24551
New Market	22844
Newmarket North (Part of Hampton)	23605
Newmarket South (Part of Newport News)	23605
New Point	23125
Newport (Giles County)	24128
Newport (Page County)	22849
Newport News (Independent City)	23601-12
For specific Newport News (Independent City) Zip Codes call (804) 247-5241	
New Post	22408
New River	24129
News Ferry	24592
Newsoms	23874
Newstead Farm	23875
New Store	23901
Newton Park (Part of Norfolk)	23523
Newtown (King and Queen County)	23126
Newtown (Lancaster County)	22503
Newtown (Rockbridge County)	24450
Newtown (Rockingham County)	22827
Newville (Prince George County)	23842
Newville (Sussex County)	23890
Niceleytown	24422
Nickelsville	24271
Niday	24124
Nimrod Hall	24460
Ninde	22526
Nineveh	22630
Nokesville	22123
Nomini Grove	22572
Nora	24272
Norfolk (Independent City)	23501-29
	23612
For specific Norfolk (Independent City) Zip Codes call (804) 629-2198	

COLLEGES & UNIVERSITIES

Norfolk State University	23504

FINANCIAL INSTITUTIONS

New Atlantic Bank, N.A.	23510
Dominion Bank, National Association	23510
First Virginia Bank of Tidewater	23510
Life Savings Bank	23510

HOSPITALS

DePaul Medical Center	23505
Lake Taylor Hospital	23502
Sentara Leigh Hospital	23502
Sentara Norfolk General Hospital	23507

HOTELS/MOTELS

Best Western Center Inn	23502
Hotel Norfolk	23510
Holiday Inn-Ocean View	23503
Norfolk Airport Hilton	23502
Quality Inn-Lake Wright	23502
Ramada Inn-Airport	23502

MILITARY INSTALLATIONS

Armed Forces Staff College	23511
Naval Air Station, Norfolk	23511
Naval Amphibious Base, Little Creek	23521
Naval Material Transportation Office, Norfolk, Air Terminal	23512
Naval Supply Center, Norfolk, Material Operations Department, Ocean Terminal	23512
Naval Supply Center, Norfolk, Material Operations Department	23512

	ZIP
Navy Material Transportation Office, Norfolk	23511
United States Army Engineer District, Norfolk	23510
Norge	23127
Norland	24228
Norman	22701
North (Part of Arlington)	22207
North (Mathews County)	23128
North Bristol (Part of Bristol)	24201
North Fairlington	22206
Northfields	22901
North Fork	22132
North Gap	24366
North Garden	22959
North Halifax	24577
North Holston	24370
North Jericho (Part of Suffolk)	23434
North Linkhorn Park (Part of Virginia Beach)	23451
North Post	22060
North Rolleston (Part of Norfolk)	23502
North Run Hills	23228
Northside (Part of Richmond)	23222
North Springfield	22151
North Stanton	24577
North Tazewell (Part of Tazewell)	24630
North View	23970
North Virginia Beach (Part of Virginia Beach)	23451
North Weems	22576
North Wellville	23824
Northwest (Part of Chesapeake)	23322
North Woodley	22042
Norton (Independent City)	24273
Nortonsville	22935
Norvello	23917
Norview (Part of Norfolk)	23513
Norwood (Bedford County)	24551
Norwood (Nelson County)	24581
Nottingham (Part of Richmond)	23235
Nottingham (Scott County)	24251
Nottoway	23955
Nottoway Correctional Center	23922
Novelty	24137
Novum	22735
Nurney (Part of Suffolk)	23434
Nurneysville (Part of Suffolk)	23434
Nutbush	23942
Nuttall	23061
Nuttsville	22528
Oakcrest (Part of Alexandria)	22302
Oakcrest (Part of Arlington)	22202
Oakdale	24450
Oakdale Farms (Part of Norfolk)	23505
Oak Forest	23040
Oak Grove (Carroll County)	24381
Oak Grove (Loudoun County)	22170
Oak Grove (Spotsylvania County)	22407
Oak Grove (Washington County)	24201
Oak Grove (Westmoreland County)	22443
Oak Hall	23416
Oak Hill (Augusta County)	22980
Oak Hill (Page County)	22650
Oak Hill (Grayson County)	24363
Oak Hill (Henrico County)	23223
Oak Hill Estates	23005
Oakhurst (Part of Petersburg)	23805
Oakland (Part of Suffolk)	23432
Oakland Park	23350
Oakleaf Terrace (Part of Norfolk)	23523
Oak Level (Halifax County)	24558
Oaklevel (Henry County)	24055
Oakley	22437
Oakpark	22730
Oak Ridge (Fairfax County)	22180
Oakridge (Part of Suffolk)	23434
Oakridge Estates (Prince William County)	22110
Oakridge Estates (Part of Suffolk)	23434
Oakton	22124
Oak Valley Estates	22181
Oakville	24522
Oakwood (Part of Arlington)	22213

	ZIP		ZIP		ZIP
Oakwood (Buchanan County)	24631	Pamlico (Part of Norfolk)	23503	Piedmont	24441
Oakwood (Fairfax County)	22310	Pamplin	23958	Pierces Corner	22503
Oakwood (Part of Norfolk)	23513	Panoramic Hills	22003	Pierces Shop	22960
Oakwood Forest	24426	Pardee	24216	Pigeon Hill	22611
Oatlands	22075	Paris	22130	Pilgrims Knob	24634
Occoquan	22125	Park (Part of Waynesboro)	22980	Pilot	24138
Occoquan Facility	22079	Parker	22508	Pimmit	22043
Occupacia	22476	Parkers Shores	22577	Pimmit Hills	22043
Oceana (Part of Virginia Beach)	23454	Parkfairfax (Part of Alexandria)	22302	Pine	24324
Ocean Park (Part of Virginia Beach)	23455	Parkglen	22204	Pineaire (Part of Suffolk)	23434
Ocean View (Part of Norfolk)	23503	Parklawn	22312	Pine Chapel Village (Part of Hampton)	23666
Oconita	24263	Park Lee Place	23234	Pinecrest	22312
Ocran	22578	Park Place (Part of Norfolk)	23508	Pinecrest Heights	22003
Oilville	23129	Parksley	23421	Pinedale	23229
Old Courthouse	22182	Parkview (Part of Newport News)	23605	Pine Grove (Clarke County)	22012
Old Creek Estates	22032	Park View (Part of Portsmouth)	23707	Pine Grove (Page County)	22851
Old Dominion	22969	Parkview (Rockingham County)	22801	Pine Grove (Washington County)	24270
Old Dominion Gardens	22101	Parkview Hills	22101	Pine Grove Court (Part of Hampton)	23669
Olde Forge	22032	Parkwood	22408	Pine Grove Terrace (Part of Hampton)	23669
Oldewood	22043	Parnassus	24421	Pine Hill	23111
Oldfield (Part of Virginia Beach)	23451	Parrott	24132	Pinehurst (Part of Portsmouth)	23703
Old Glade Spring	24340	Parsonage	24224	Pine Ridge (mail Annandale)	22003
Old Hampton (Part of Hampton)	23669	Partlow	22534	Pine Ridge (mail Fairfax)	22031
Oldhams	22529	Passapatanzy	22405	Pinero	23061
Old Somerset	22972	Passing	22427	Pine Springs	22042
Old Tavern	22171	Pastoria	23421	Pine Tree	23027
Oldtown	24333	Patna	24487	Pinetta	23061
Old Well	23959	Patrician Manor (Part of Hampton)	23666	Pineville	22840
Olinger	24219	Patrick Henry Correctional Unit	24148	Pinewood Lake	22309
Olive (Part of Portsmouth)	23701	Patrick Henry Heights	23111	Pinewood Lawns	22309
Omaha	24228	Patrick Henry Mall (Part of Newport News)	23607	Pinewood Park (Part of Manassas Park)	22110
Omega	24592	Patrick Springs	24133	Pinewood South	22309
Onancock	23417	Patterson (Buchanan County)	24631	Piney Grove	24589
Onemo	23130	Patterson (Wythe County)	24343	Piney River	22964
Onley	23418	Pattonsville	24244	Pinners Point (Part of Portsmouth)	23707
Ontario	23937	Pauls Cross Roads	22560	Pipers Gap	24333
Opal	22186	Paynes Store	22553	Pisgah	24651
Opequon	22602	Paytes	22553	Pitmans Corner	22576
Ophelia	22530	Peach Bottom	24333	Pittmantown (Part of Suffolk)	23438
Oranda	22657	Peaks	23069	Pittsville	24139
Orange	22960	Peapatch	24622	Pizarro	24091
Orange Hunt	22153	Pearisburg (Giles County)	24134	Plain View	23137
Orapax Farms	23141	Pearly	24614	Plantersville	23937
Orbit	23487	Peary	23138	Plasterco	24370
Orchard Hill	23234	Pedlar Mills	24574	Plaza, The (Part of Lynchburg)	24501
Orchid	23117	Pedro	22559	Pleasant Gap	24549
Orchid Lake	23065	Pemberton	23063	Pleasant Grove (Henry County)	24112
Ordinary	23131	Pembroke	24136	Pleasant Grove (Lunenburg County)	23947
Oregon Acres (Part of Portsmouth)	23707	Pembroke Mall (Part of Virginia Beach)	23450	Pleasant Grove (Mecklenburg County)	23970
Oreton	24219	Pembroke Manor (Part of Virginia Beach)	23455	Pleasant Grove Estates	23920
Oriskany	24130	Pender	22033	Pleasant Heights	24370
Orkney Springs	22845	Penderbrook	22033	Pleasant Hill (Part of Harrisonburg)	22801
Orlando (Part of Suffolk)	23434	Pendleton	23117	Pleasant Hill (Part of Suffolk)	23434
Orlean	22128	Penhook	24137	Pleasant Ridge (Fairfax County)	22003
Orleans Village	22312	Penn Acres	23235	Pleasant Ridge (Part of Virginia Beach)	23451
Oronoco	24483	Penn Daw	22303	Pleasant Shade	23847
Osaka	24216	Penn Daw Terrace	22307	Pleasant Valley (Buckingham County)	23936
Osbornes Chapel	24221	Pennington Gap	24277	Pleasant Valley (Fairfax County)	22021
Osborns Gap	24228	Penn Laird	22846	Pleasant Valley (Rockingham County)	22848
Osceola	24210	Penn Lee	22282	Pleasantview	24574
Osso	22405	Penns Store	24165	Plum Creek	24340
Othma	23153	Pennsytown (Part of Norfolk)	23513	Plum Point	23181
Otter Lake	24523	Penola	22546	Plum Tree	23024
Otter River	24571	Pentagon	20301	Plymouth	23974
Otterville	24523	Penvir	24124	Poages Mill	24018
Ottobine	22821	Peola Mills	22740	Pocahontas (Part of Petersburg)	23803
Ottoman	22503	Pepper	24141	Pocahontas (Tazewell County)	24635
Overall	22610	Perrin	23072	Pocahontas Correctional Unit	23832
Overbrook (Part of Norfolk)	23513	Perrowville	24551	Pocket	24282
Overlee Knolls	22205	Perryville (Part of Saltville)	24370	Poetown (Part of Grundy)	24614
Owens	22485	Perth	24577	Poff	24091
Owens Brooke (Part of Manassas)	22110	Petersburg (Independent City)	23803-06	Pohick Estates	22079
Owenton	23148	For specific Petersburg (Independent City) Zip Codes call (804) 732-4631		Point Breeze	22454
Oxford (Part of Richmond)	23235			Point Eastern	22546
Oyster	23419			Point Pleasant	24315
Oyster Point (Part of Newport News)	23606	Peterson Chapel	24244	Pons	23866
Ozeana	22454	Petunia	24382	Poole Siding	23833
Paces	24592	Peytonsburg	24565	Pope	23829
Paeonian Springs	22129	Phenix	23959	Poplar Camp	24360
Page	24631	Philadelphia (Part of Suffolk)	23434	Poplar Cove	23417
Page Hollow	24370	Philbeck Crossroads	23968		
Paige	22580	Phillip	24201		
Paineville	23083	Phillis	23917		
Paint Bank	24131	Philomont	22131		
Painter	23420	Philpott	24055		
Paint Lick	24637	Phoebus (Part of Hampton)	23663		
Palls	23086	Piankatank Shores	23071		
Palmer	22578	Pickaway	24597		
Palmer Crossroads	27563	Pico	24066		
Palmer Springs	23917				
Palmyra (Fluvanna County)	22963				
Palmyra (Part of Suffolk)	23434				

	ZIP		ZIP		ZIP
Roland Park (Part of Norfolk)	23509	Sandy Level	24161	Shenandoah (Page County)	22849
Rolling Brook	22192	Sandy Point	22579	Shenandoah Farms	22630
Rolling Hills	22309	Sandy River	24054	Shenandoah Place	23226
Rolling Meadows	23875	Sanford	23426	Shenandoah Retreat	22012
Rolling Valley	22152	Sangerville	22812	Shenandoah Shores	22630
Rollins Fork	22544	Sanville	24055	Shepherds Hill	24265
Rondo	24531	Sarah	23130	Shepherds Store	23038
Roosevelt Gardens (Part of Norfolk)	23513	Saratoga	22153	Sheppards	23901
		Saratoga Place (Part of Suffolk)	23434	Sherando	22952
Roseann	24614	Saumsville	22644	Sherwill	24538
Rose Bower	24522	Saunders (Part of Richmond)	23220	Sherwood Forest	24401
Rosedale	24280			Sherwood Hall	22306
Rose Hill (Fairfax County)	22310	Savage Crossing (Part of Suffolk)	23434	Sheva	24531
Rose Hill (Lee County)	24281	Savageville	23417	Shields	23306
Rose Hill Farms	22310	Savedge	23881	Shiloh (King George County)	22549
Roseland	22967	Saxe	23967		
Rosemont (Part of Alexandria)	22301	Saxis	23427	Shiloh (Southampton County)	23827
Rosemont (Fairfax County)	22101	Sayersville	24602	Shiny Rock	23927
Rosemont (Part of Suffolk)	23434	Scarborough Neck	23306	Shipman	22971
Rosemont (Part of Virginia Beach)	23452	Scenic Park (Part of Bristol)	24201	Shirley	23030
Roseville	22554	Schley	23154	Shirley Duke (Part of Alexandria)	22304
Roslyn Hills	23229	Schoolfield (Part of Danville)	24541	Shirley Gate Park	22030
Rosslyn	22209	Schuyler	22969	Shirlington	22206
	22219	Scotland	23883	Shockoe	24531
For specific Rosslyn Zip Codes call (703) 575-4336		Scott Addition	24210	Shores	22963
		Scottie Farms	23075	Short Lane	23061
Roth	24631	Scottsburg	24589	Short Pump	23060
Rough Creek	23959	Scotts Crossroads	23924	Shorts Creek	24312
Round Bottom	24124	Scotts Fork	23002	Shortt Gap	24647
Round Hill	22141	Scottsville	24590	Shoulders Hill (Part of Suffolk)	23435
Round Top	24293	Scottswood	23851	Shrevewood	22043
Roundtree	22042	Scrabble	22749	Shumansville	22514
Rowe	24646	Scruggs	24121	Shumate	24124
Roxbury (Charles City County)	23140	Seaboard	24641	Siddon	24580
Roxbury (Henrico County)	23229	Seaford	23696	Sigma (Part of Virginia Beach)	23456
Royal City (Part of Grundy)	24614	Seaford Shores	23696	Signpine	23061
Royal Court	22003	Sealston	22547	Sign Post	23395
Ruark	23043	Seapines (Part of Virginia Beach)	23451	Siler	22603
Rubermont	23974	Searcy	23831	Silva	23415
Ruby	22545	Seatack (Part of Virginia Beach)	23451	Silver Beach	23398
Ruckersville	22968	Seaview	23429	Silver Springs	22310
Rudee Inlet (Part of Virginia Beach)	23451	Seawright Spring	24467	Silverwood (Part of Chesapeake)	23320
Rue	23421	Sebrell	23837	Simeon	22901
Ruff	23016	Sedalia	24526	Simmonsville	24127
Rugby	24363	Sedgefield (Part of Newport News)	23607	Simons Corner	22572
Rural Retreat	24368	Sedgefield Manor	23228	Simonsdale (Part of Portsmouth)	23701
Rushmere	23430	Sedley	23878	Simonson	22460
Rushmere Shores	23430	Selden	23061	Simpkins	23310
Russell	24260	Selma	24474	Simpsons	24072
Russell Creek	24283	Seminary	24219	Sinai	24592
Rustburg	24588	Seminary Valley (Part of Alexandria)	22304	Sinclair Farms (Part of Hampton)	23669
Rustburg Correctional Unit	24588	Senora	22503	Singers Glen	22850
Rustic	23030	Seven Corners	22044	Sinking Creek	24127
Rutherford	22032	Seven Corners Shopping Center	22044	Sinnickson	23395
Ruther Glen	22546	Seven Fountains	22652	Sissons Corner	22473
Ruthland	23228	Seven Mile Ford	24373	Sixmile Post	24151
Ruthville	23147	Seven Pines	23150	Skeetrock	24228
Ryan	22011	Seven Pines Villa	23150	Skeggs	24646
Rye Cove	24244	Severn	23155	Skinquarter	23120
Sabot	23103	Severn Manor	23072	Skippers	23879
Sadler Heights (Part of Suffolk)	23434	Shacklefords	23156	Skipwith	23968
Sago	24137	Shacklefords Fork	23156	Skipwith Farms (Henrico County)	23229
St. Brides (Part of Chesapeake)	23322	Shadow	23163	Skipwith Farms (Part of Williamsburg)	23185
St. Charles	24282	Shadow Valley (Part of Bristol)	24201	Skyland	22835
St. Clair	24605	Shadwell	22947	Skyland Estates	22642
St. Clair Bottom	24319	Shady Grove (Greene County)	22940	Skymont (Part of Staunton)	24401
St. Davids Church	22652			Slabtown	24251
St. Elmo (Part of Alexandria)	22305	Shady Grove (Halifax County)	24598	Slate	24614
St. Joy	23921			Slate Mills	22740
St. Just	22567	Shady Grove (Washington County)	24210	Sleepy Hole (Part of Suffolk)	23435
St. Luke	22664	Shady Oak	22066	Sleepy Hollow	22042
St. Paul	24283	Shadyside	23405	Sleepy Hollow Estates (Fairfax County)	22044
St. Stephens	22019	Shanghai	23110		
St. Stephens Church	23148	Shannondale	24630	Sleepy Hollow Estates (Henrico County)	23229
Salem (Culpeper County)	22701	Shannon Hills	24148	Sleepy Hollow Manor	22044
Salem (Independent City)	24153	Shannon Park	22577	Sleepy Hollow Run	22003
Salem Woods	23234	Sharps	22548	Sleepy Hollow Woods	22003
Salisbury	23113	Shawnee Land	22602	Sliders	23936
Salona Village	22101	Shawsville	24162	Sloantown	24244
Saltpetre	24085	Shawver Mill	24651	Smithfield	23430
Saltville	24370	Shea Terrace (Part of Portsmouth)	23707	Smiths Cross Roads	23970
Saluda	23149			Smoky Ordinary	23868
Salvia	23148	Sheep Town	24312	Snake Creek	24343
Samos	23180	Sheffield Court	23235	Snapp	24340
Sanburne Park	23150	Sheffield Terrace	24148	Snell	22553
Sand Bridge (Part of Virginia Beach)	23456	Shelby	22727	Snowden (Amherst County)	24526
Sandidges	24521	Shelfar	23117	Snowden (Fairfax County)	22308
Sands	23874	Shelors Mill	24091	Snowflake	24251
Sandston	23150	Shelton (Part of Virginia Beach)	23455	Snow Hill	23156
Sandy Bottom (Part of Suffolk)	23432			Snowville	24347
Sandy Fork	23927	Shenandoah (Part of Hopewell)	23860	Soles	23050
Sandy Hook	23153				

	ZIP
Solomons Store	23060
Solsburg	22827
Somers	22503
Somerset	22972
Somerton (Part of Suffolk)	23438
Somerville	22739
Sonans	24531
Sorocco (Part of Suffolk)	23434
Soudan	23927
South	22204
Southampton (Part of Hampton)	23669
Southampton Correctional Center	23829
South Anna	23117
South Boston (Independent City)	24592
South Chesconessex	23417
South Clinchfield	24225
Southern Estates	23805
Southern Pine	23803
South Fairlington	22206
South Garden	22959
South Hill	23970
South Jackson	22842
South Martinsville (Part of Martinsville)	24112
South Norfolk (Part of Chesapeake)	23324
South Plains (Part of Petersburg)	23805
Southport	22191
Southridge	22101
South Roanoke (Part of Roanoke)	24014
Southside (Part of Richmond)	23224
South Suffolk (Part of Suffolk)	23434
South Woodley	22042
Spainville	23824
Sparkling Springs	22834
Sparta	22552
Speedwell	24374
Speegleville (Part of Hampton)	23666
Spencer	24165
Sperryville	22740
Spitler	22835
Spivey Store	24251
Splash Dam	24256
Spotsylvania	22553
Spotsylvania Courthouse	22553
Spottswood	24475
Spout Spring	24593
Springbrook Forest	22003
Spring City	22225
Springcreek	22812
Springdale (Part of Bristol)	24201
Springdale (Henrico County)	23222
Springfield (census designated place)	22150-53
For specific Springfield (census designated place) Zip Codes call (703) 451-1533	
Springfield (Fairfax County)	22150
Springfield (Page County)	22835
Springfield (Rockbridge County)	24066
Springfield Estates	22150
Springfield Forest	22150
Springfield Mall Regional Shopping Center	22150
Springfield Plaza	22150
Spring Garden (Part of Bristol)	24201
Spring Garden (Pittsylvania County)	24527
Spring Grove	23881
Springhaven Estates	22102
Spring Hill	24401
Spring Meadows	23111
Spring Mills	24538
Springvale	22066
Spring Valley (Grayson County)	24330
Spring Valley (Stafford County)	22405
Springville	24630
Springwood	24066
Sprouses Corner	23936
Stacy	24614
Stafford	22554-55
For specific Stafford Zip Codes call (703) 659-4775	
Stafford Correctional Unit	22554
Staffordshire	23235
Staffordsville	24167
Stage Junction	23038
Staleys Cross Roads	24368
Stanardsville	22973

	ZIP
Stanley	22851
Stanleytown (Henry County)	24168
Stanleytown (Scott County)	22435
Stapleton	24572
Starkey	24018
Starnes	24250
Star Tannery	22654
Statesville	23874
Station Hills	22039
Staunton (Independent City)	24401
Staunton Park (Part of Staunton)	24401
Steeleburg	24609
Steeles Tavern	24476
Steinman	24226
Stella	24133
Stemphleytown	22821
Stephens	24293
Stephens City	22655
Stephenson	22656
Sterling	22170
Sterling Point (Part of Portsmouth)	23703
Stevensburg	22741
Stevens Creek	24330
Stevensville	23161
Stewart (Part of Richmond)	23221
Stewartsburg	24416
Stewartsville	24179
Stickleyville	24244
Stingray Point	23043
Stith	24534
St Louis	22131
Stockton	24054
Stoddert	23901
Stokesland (Part of Danville)	24541
Stokesville	22843
Stone Bridge	22663
Stone Creek	24277
Stonega	24285
Stone Mountain	24523
Stones Mill	24382
Stone Springs (Part of Harrisonburg)	22801
Stonewall	24538
Stonewall Acres	22110
Stonewall Manor	22180
Stoneybrook	22553
Stony	24245
Stony Battery	24354
Stony Creek	23882
Stony Man	22835
Stony Point	22901
Stony Point Mills	23040
Stony Ridge	24630
Stormont	23149
Story	23837
Stott	23898
Stovall	24577
Stover	24421
Straightstone	24569
Strasburg	22657
Strasburg Junction	22657
Stratford (Fairfax County)	22308
Stratford (Westmoreland County)	22558
Stratford Hills (Part of Arlington)	22207
Stratford Hills (Part of Richmond)	23225
Stratford Landing	22308
Stratford-on-the-Potomac	22308
Stratford Village	23222
Strathmeade Springs	22003
Strathmore	23022
Stringtown	22611
Stroupes Store	24382
Stuart	24171
Stuarts Draft	24477
Stubbs	22553
Studley	23162
Stukeley Hall Farms	23227
Stumptown (Loudoun County)	22075
Stumptown (Northampton County)	23347
Suburban Apartments	23230
Sudley	22110
Sudley Manor	22110
Suffolk (Independent City)	23432-39
For specific Suffolk (Independent City) Zip Codes call (804) 539-5191	
Sugar Grove	24375
Sugar Hill	24528
Sugarland Run	22170
Sugar Loaf	24018
Suiter	24314
Sulgrave Manor	22309
Sumerduck	22742
Summerdeon	24479

	ZIP
Summit (Smyth County)	24375
Summit (Spotsylvania County)	22408
Sun	24224
Sunbeam	23851
Sunnybank	22539
Sunnybrook	22182
Sunnybrook Estates	22110
Sunnyside (Cumberland County)	23040
Sunnyside (Frederick County)	22603
Sunny View	22309
Sunset Heights	22331
Sunset Hills	22090
Sunset Manor	22312
Sunset Village (Part of Salem)	24153
Supply	22559
Surrey Square	22032
Surry	23883
Susan	23163
Sussex	23884
Sussex Hilton (Part of Newport News)	23605
Sutherland (Dinwiddie County)	23885
Sutherland (Wise County)	24273
Sutherland Manor	23885
Sutherlin	24594
Sutton Place	22031
Sutton Woods	22180
Swansea Manor (Part of Newport News)	23601
Swansonville	24549
Sweet Briar	24595
Sweet Briar Park	23075
Sweet Chalybeate	24426
Sweet Hall	23181
Swift Creek (Part of Colonial Heights)	23834
Swift Run	22827
Switch Back	24445
Swoope	24479
Swords Creek	24649
Sycamore	24557
Sydnorsville	24151
Sylvania Heights	22408
Sylvatus	24343
Syria	22743
Syringa	23169
Tabb	23693
Tabscott	23038
Tacoma	24230
Taft	22578
Talbot Park (Part of Norfolk)	23505
Tall Oaks	22003
Tallysville	23124
Tamworth	23027
Tangier	23440
Tannersville	24377
Tappahannock	22560
Tara	22205
Taro	23934
Tarpon	24228
Tasley	23441
Tatum	22567
Tauxemont	22308
Taylors Store	24184
Taylorstown	22075
Taylors Valley	24236
Taylorsville	23047
Tazewell	24651
Tazewell Correctional Unit	24651
Teas	24375
Temperanceville	23442
Temple Hall Estates	23168
Temple Hill	24224
Templeman	22520
Tenso	24226
Tenth Legion	22815
Terrys Fork	24138
Tetotum	22485
Thaxton	24174
The English Hills	22039
The Hollow	24053
The Knolls	22191
Thelma	22942
The Manors	22192
Theological Seminary (Part of Alexandria)	22304
The Plains	22171
The Ridge	23917
Thessalia	24134
The Timbers	22152
The Villas	22191
Thomas Bridge	24354
Thomas Corner (Part of Norfolk)	23502
Thomasson Park	22134
Thomas Terrace	24501

	ZIP
Thomastown	24445
Thompson Valley	24651
Thornburg	22565
Thornhill	22960
Thoroughfare	22014
Thoroughgood (Part of Virginia Beach)	23455
Three Forks	24588
Threemile Corner	23117
Three Springs	24201
Three Square (Goochland County)	23063
Three Square (Louisa County)	23024
Threeway	22469
Tibbstown	22942
Tibitha	22539
Ticktown	23301
Tidemill	23072
Tidewater	22572
Tidwells	22520
Tight Squeeze	24531
Tignor	22514
Timberlake	24502
Timberly Heights (Part of Petersburg)	23803
Timber Ridge	24450
Timberville	22853
Timothy Park	22309
Tiny	24220
Tiptop	24630
Tito	24244
Tivis	24256
Toano	23168
Tobaccoville	23139
Todds Tavern	22553
Toga	23936
Tola	23959
Toms Bottom	24256
Toms Brook	22660
Toms Creek	24230
Tookland	24614
Topnot	22657
Topping	23169
Toshes	24139
Totaro	23856
Tower Mall (Part of Portsmouth)	23703
Town and Country Estates	22180
Townsend	23443
Trade Center (Part of Alexandria)	22304
Trammel	24289
Trapp	22176
Treemont	23234
Treherneville	23307
Tremont Gardens	22042
Trenholm	23139
Trents Mill	23040
Trevilians	23170
Triangle	22172
Trigg	22134
Trinity	24175
Triplet	23868
Trout Dale	24378
Troutville	24175
Trower	23480
Troy	22974
Trueblue	22701
Truxillo	23002
Tuckahoe	23229
Tuckahoe Park	23229
Tuckahoe Village	23229
Tucker Hill	22488
Tuggle	23901
Tunstall	23124
Turbeville	24596
Turnbull	22186
Turners Crossroads	23879
Turner Store	23873
Turnpike (Part of Fairfax)	22031
Tuscarora	22454
Twin Pines (Part of Portsmouth)	23703
Twin Poplars	22938
Twin Springs	24271
Twymans Mill	22727
Tye River	22922
Tyler Gardens (Part of Falls Church)	22046
Tyler Park	22042
Tylerton	22405
Tyro	22976
Tysons Corner (census designated place)	22102
Tysons Corner (Shopping Center)	22103
Tysons Corner	22102
Tysons Green	22182
Union (Bedford County)	24174
Union (Floyd County)	24380

	ZIP
Union Hall	24176
Union Level	23970
Unionville	22567
Unison	22141
United States Marine Reservation	22134
Unity	23898
University (Part of Charlottesville)	22903
University Heights (Albemarle County)	22901
University Heights (Henrico County)	23229
University of Richmond (Part of Richmond)	23173
Uno	22738
Upper Brandon	23881
Upperville	22176
Upright	22454
Upshaw	23009
Urbanna	23175
Vails Mill	24236
Vale	22124
Valentine Hills	23228
Valentines	23887
Valley Brook	22042
Valley Creek	24271
Valley Mall (Part of Harrisonburg)	22801
Valley Mills	24479
Valley Ridge	24426
Valley View	22306
Valley View Mall (Part of Roanoke)	24012
Valleywood	22191
Van Buren Furnace	22644
Vanderpool	24465
Vandola	24541
Vandyke (Buchanan County)	24639
Van Dyke (Tazewell County)	24609
Vannoy Acres	22030
Vannoy Park	22024
Vansant	24656
Varina	23231
Varina Grove	23075
Vaucluse	22655
Vaughn	22835
Vawter Corner	23093
Velma	23108
Venia	24260
Vera	24522
Verbena	22827
Verdi	22435
Vernon Hill	24597
Verona	24482
Vertain Park	22032
Vesta	24177
Vests Store	23139
Vesuvius	24483
Vicey	24256
Vicker	24073
Vicker Heights	24073
Vicksville	23878
Victoria	23974
Vienna	22180-83
For specific Vienna Zip Codes call (703) 938-2125	
Viers	24256
Viewtown	22746
Village	22570
Villa Heights	24112
Villamay	22307
Villamont	24178
Villboro	22580
Vint Hill Farms	22186
Vint Hill Farms Station	22186
Vinton	24179
Virgilina	24598
Virginia Beach (Independent City)	23450-67
For specific Virginia Beach (Independent City) Zip Codes call (804) 340-6227	
Virginia City	24283
Virginia Forest (Part of Falls Church)	22046
Virginia Gardens (Part of Norfolk)	23505
Virginia Heights (Part of Arlington)	22204
Virginia Heights (Henrico County)	23231
Virginia Highlands	22202
Virginia Hills (Part of Bristol)	24201
Virginia Hills (Fairfax County)	22310
Virginia State University (Part of Petersburg)	23803
Virginia Union University (Part of Richmond)	23220

	ZIP
Vir-Mar Beach	22473
Volens	24577
Volney	24379
Vulcan	22567
Wabun	24153
Wachapreague	23480
Wadesville	22611
Wake	23176
Wakefield (Part of Alexandria)	22304
Wakefield (Sussex County)	23888
Wakefield Chapel	22003
Wakefield Forest	22003
Wake Forest	24060
Wakenva	24237
Waldrop	22942
Walhaven	22310
Walkers	23089
Walker Store	23924
Walkers Well	24531
Walkerton	23177
Wallace	24201
Wallaces Store	23937
Wallops Flight Center	23337
Wallops Island	23337
Walnut Grove	24270
Walnut Hill (Part of Petersburg)	23805
Walters	23315
Walters Woods	22044
Walton	24141
Walton Furnace	24360
Walton Park	23112
Waltons Store	24104
Wan	23061
Ward	24620
Wardell	24609
Wards Corner (Part of Norfolk)	23505
Wards Mill	24333
Wardtown	23482
Ware Neck	23178
Wares Crossroads	23117
Wares Wharf	22454
Warfield	23889
Warminster	24599
Warm Springs	24484
Warner	23179
Warren	24590
Warrenton	22186
Warren Woods (Part of Fairfax)	22030
Warsaw	22572
Warwick (Part of Newport News)	23601
Warwick on the James (Part of Newport News)	23601
Warwick Village (Part of Alexandria)	22305
Washington	22747
Washington Corner	22580
Washington Gardens (Part of Hampton)	23669
Washington National Airport	22201
Washington Park	23847
Watauga	24210
Waterford	22190
Waterlick	22657
Waterloo	22663
Water View (Middlesex County)	23180
Waterview (Part of Portsmouth)	23707
Watson	22075
Wattsville	23483
Waugh	24526
Waverly	23890
Waverly Hills	22207
Waverly Village	22407
Waxpool	22010
Wayland	23235
Waynesboro (Independent City)	22980
Waynewood	22308
Wayside	23030
Weal	24531
Webbtown	22611
Weber City (Fluvanna County)	23022
Weber City (Scott County)	24290
Wedgewood	23229
Weedonville	22485
Weems	22576
Weirwood	23484
Welchs	22580
Welcome	22485
Wellford	22572
Wellington (Fairfax County)	22308
Wellington (Prince William County)	22110
Wellington Heights	22308

	ZIP		ZIP		ZIP
West Arlington	22213	White Oaks	22307	Withams	23488
West Augusta	24485	White Oak Swamp	23150	Wittens Mills	24630
West Bottom	23022	White Plains	23893	Wolfglade	24333
Westbourne	23230	White Post	22663	Wolford	24658
Westbriar	23075	White Shop	23086	Wolftown	22748
Westchester (Chesterfield		White Stone	22578	Wolf Trap (Fairfax County)	22182
County)	23235	Whitesville	23421	Wolf Trap (Halifax County)	24592
Westchester (Fairfax		Whitethorne	24060	Womacks	23923
County)	22031	Whitetop	24292	Wood	24250
Westdale	23229	Whiteville	23040	Woodberry Forest	22989
West Dante	24272	Whitewood	24657	Woodberry Hills (Part of	
West End Manor	23229	Whitley	23487	Danville)	24541
Western (Part of		Whitlock	22942	Woodbridge	22191-94
Petersburg)	23803	Whitmell	24549	For specific Woodbridge Zip	
West Falls Church (Part of		Whittle	24531	Codes call (703) 494-6427	
Falls Church)	22046	Wickford	22310	Woodbrook	22901
Westfield (Part of Bristol)	24201	Wicomico	23184	Woodford	22580
West Fork	24069	Wicomico Church	23579	Woodhaven Shores	23141
West Fredericksburg (Part		Wide Water	22554	Woodland Hills	24210
of Fredericksburg)	22401	Widewater Beach	22554	Woodlawn (Carroll County)	24381
West Galax (Part of Galax)	24333	Wightman	23924	Woodlawn (Part of	
West Gate	22110	Wilburdale	22003	Hopewell)	23860
West Gate of Lomond	22110	Wilda	24477	Woodlawn Manor	22309
West Ghent (Part of		Wilde Acres	22602	Woodlawn Mansion	22060
Norfolk)	23507	Wilderness	22553	Woodlawn Park	22309
Westgrove	22307	Wilderness Corner	22553	Woodlawn Terrace (Fairfax	
Westham	23229	Wildwood (Fluvanna		County)	22309
Westhampton (Fairfax		County)	22963	Woodlawn Terrace (Henrico	
County)	22043	Wildwood (Henrico County)	23227	County)	23150
Westhampton (Part of		Wildwood Farms	23842	Woodlawn Village	22060
Richmond)	23226	Wilkinsons Store	23833	Woodlee (Part of Staunton)	24401
Westhaven (Part of		Wilkinson Terrace	23234	Woodley Hills	22309
Portsmouth)	23707	Willard Park (Part of Norfolk)	23509	Woodley Hills (mobile home	
West Hope	23882	Williamsburg (Independent		park)	22306
Westland	22578	City)	23185-88	Woodman Terrace	23228
West Langley	22101	For specific Williamsburg		Woodmont (Part of	
Westlawn	22042	(Independent City) Zip Codes call		Arlington)	22207
West Leigh	22901	(804) 229-4668		Woodmont (Chesterfield	
West Lexington (Part of		Williamsburg Manor	22308	County)	23235
Covington)	24450	Williams Mill	24251	Woodridge	24590
Westmoreland (Albemarle		Williamson Road (Part of		Woodrow Wilson	22939
County)	22901	Roanoke)	24012	Woodrum (Part of Staunton)	24401
Westmoreland		Williamsville	24487	Woods Cross Roads	23190
(Westmoreland County)	22577	Willis	24380	Woodside Estates	22102
Westmoreland Heights	22043	Willisville	22176	Woods Mill	22938
Westmoreland Park	22046	Willis Wharf	23486	Woodson	22951
West Norfolk (Part of		Willoughby Terrace (Part of		Woods Store	24091
Portsmouth)	23703	Norfolk)	23503	Woodstock	22664
Westover (Part of Arlington)	22205	Willow	24521	Woodville	22749
Westover (Charles City		Willowbrook	23024	Woodway	24277
County)	23030	Willow Hill	23881	Woolwine	24185
Westover (Pittsylvania		Willow Lakes (Part of		Worlds	24530
County)	24541	Chesapeake)	23320	Worsham	23901
Westover Hills (Augusta		Willow Lawn	23230	Worshams	23139
County)	22980	Willow Run	22003	Wren	23959
Westover Hills (Part of		Willow Spring	24266	Wright (Part of Norfolk)	23505
Danville)	24541	Willow Woods	22003	Wrights Shop	24572
Westover Hills (Greensville		Wills Corner	23430	Wrightsville	22427
County)	23847	Willston	22044	Wurno	24301
Westover Hills (Part of		Wilmington	22963	Wylliesburg	23976
Richmond)	23225	Wilroy (Part of Suffolk)	23434	Wyndale	24210
West Petersburg	23803	Wilsons	23894	Wythe (Part of Hampton)	23661
West Piney	24382	Wilson Springs	24473	Wytheville	24382
West Point	23181	Wilton Woods	22310	Yacht Haven Estates	22309
West Raven	24639	Winchester (Independent		Yale	23897
West Springfield	22152	City)	22601-04	Yancey Mills	22932
Wests Store	24577	For specific Winchester		Yanceyville	23093
Westview (Augusta County)	24479	(Independent City) Zip Codes call		Yards	24659
West View (Goochland		(703) 662-2553		Yellow Branch	24550
County)	23063	Windmill Point	22578	Yellow Springs	24361
Westview Hills	22152	Windsor	23487	Yellow Sulphur Springs	24073
West Warm Springs	24484	Windsordale	23229	Yellow Tavern	23060
Westwood	23226	Windsor Estates	22310	York Manor	23075
Westwood Estates	24210	Windsor Farms (Part of		Yorkshire	22110
Westwood Forest	22182	Richmond)	23221	Yorkshire Acres	22110
Westwood Park	22046	Windsor Park	22310	Yorkshire Park	22110
Westwood Place	24426	Windsor Place	23075	York Terrace	23185
Weyanoke	22312	Windsor Shades	23140	Yorktown	23690-93
Weyers Cave	24486	Windy Hill Estates	23111	For specific Yorktown Zip Codes	
Whaley (Part of Suffolk)	23438	Winesap	24572	call (804) 898-3098	
Whaleyville (Part of Suffolk)	23438	Winfall	24554	Yorktown Naval Weapons	
Wheatfield	22641	Wingina	24599	Station	23691
Wheatland	22132	Winona (Part of Norfolk)	23509	Yost	24460
Wheeler	24248	Winslow Hills	22310	Youngers Store	24558
Whitacre	22625	Winston	22701	Yuma	24251
White City	23847	Wintergreen	22958	Zacata	22581
White Gate	24134	Winterham	23002	Zack	24459
White Hall (Albemarle		Winterpock	23832	Zanoni	23191
County)	22987	Wirtz	24184	Zenda	22801
Whitehall (Frederick County)	22603	Wise	24293	Zepp	22644
White Head Hall	23828	Wisharts Point	23303	Zion	22942
White Hill	24477	Wistar Farms	23228	Zion Crossroads	22942
White House	24580	Witch Duck (Part of Suffolk)	23462	Ziontown	23075
White Marsh	23183		23466	Zuni	23898
White Mill	24210	For specific Witch Duck Zip			
White Oak (Halifax County)	24558	Codes call (804) 497-1033			
White Oak (Stafford County)	22405				

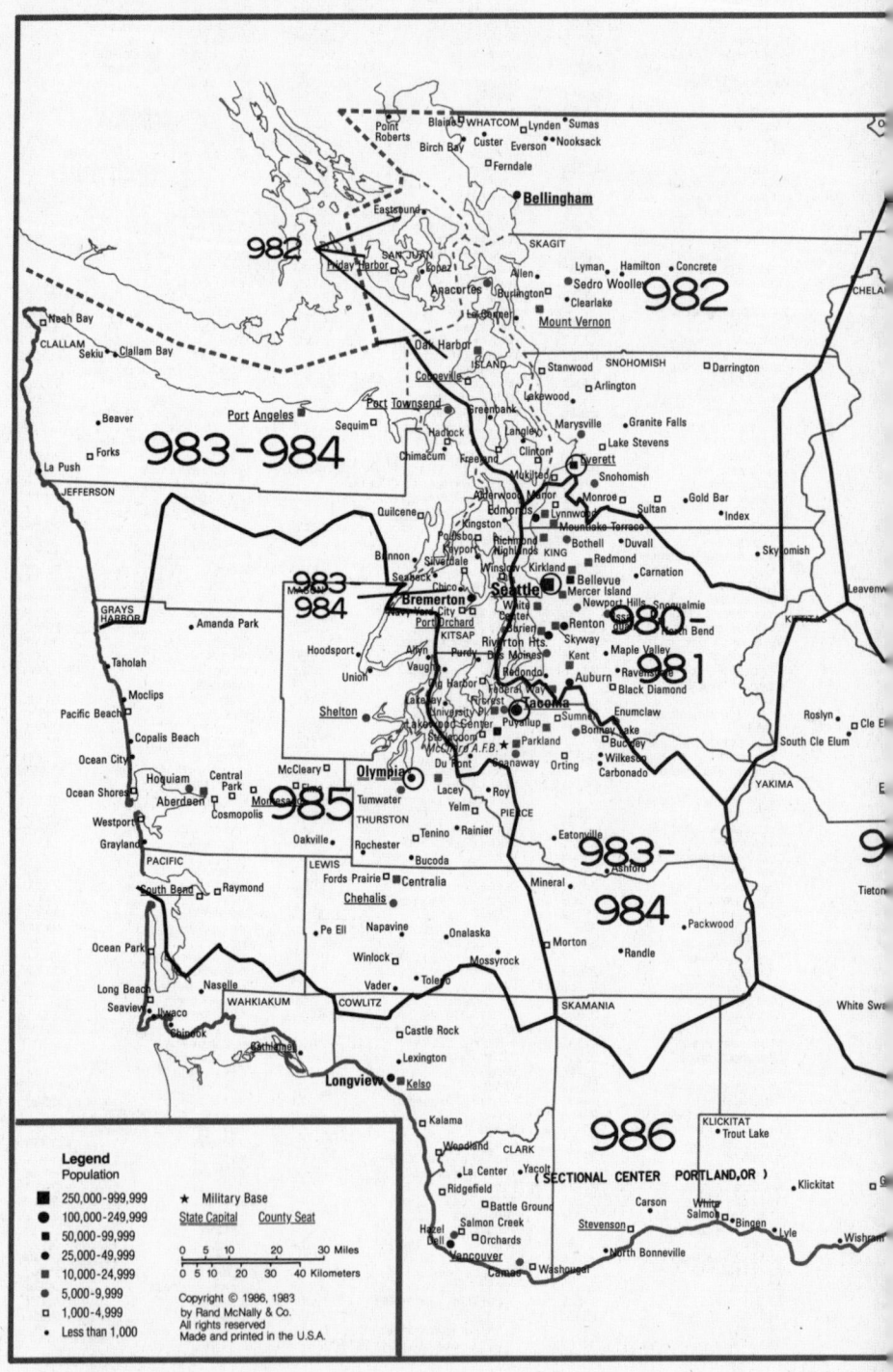

982

982

SAN JUAN

983-984

983
984

980-
981

985

983-
984

986

SECTIONAL CENTER PORTLAND,OR)

Legend
Population
■ 250,000-999,999
● 100,000-249,999
● 50,000-99,999
● 25,000-49,999
● 10,000-24,999
□ 5,000-9,999
□ 1,000-4,999
• Less than 1,000

★ Military Base
State Capital   County Seat

0 5 10   20   30 Miles
0 5 10 20 30 40 Kilometers

Copyright © 1986, 1983
by Rand McNally & Co.
All rights reserved
Made and printed in the U.S.A.

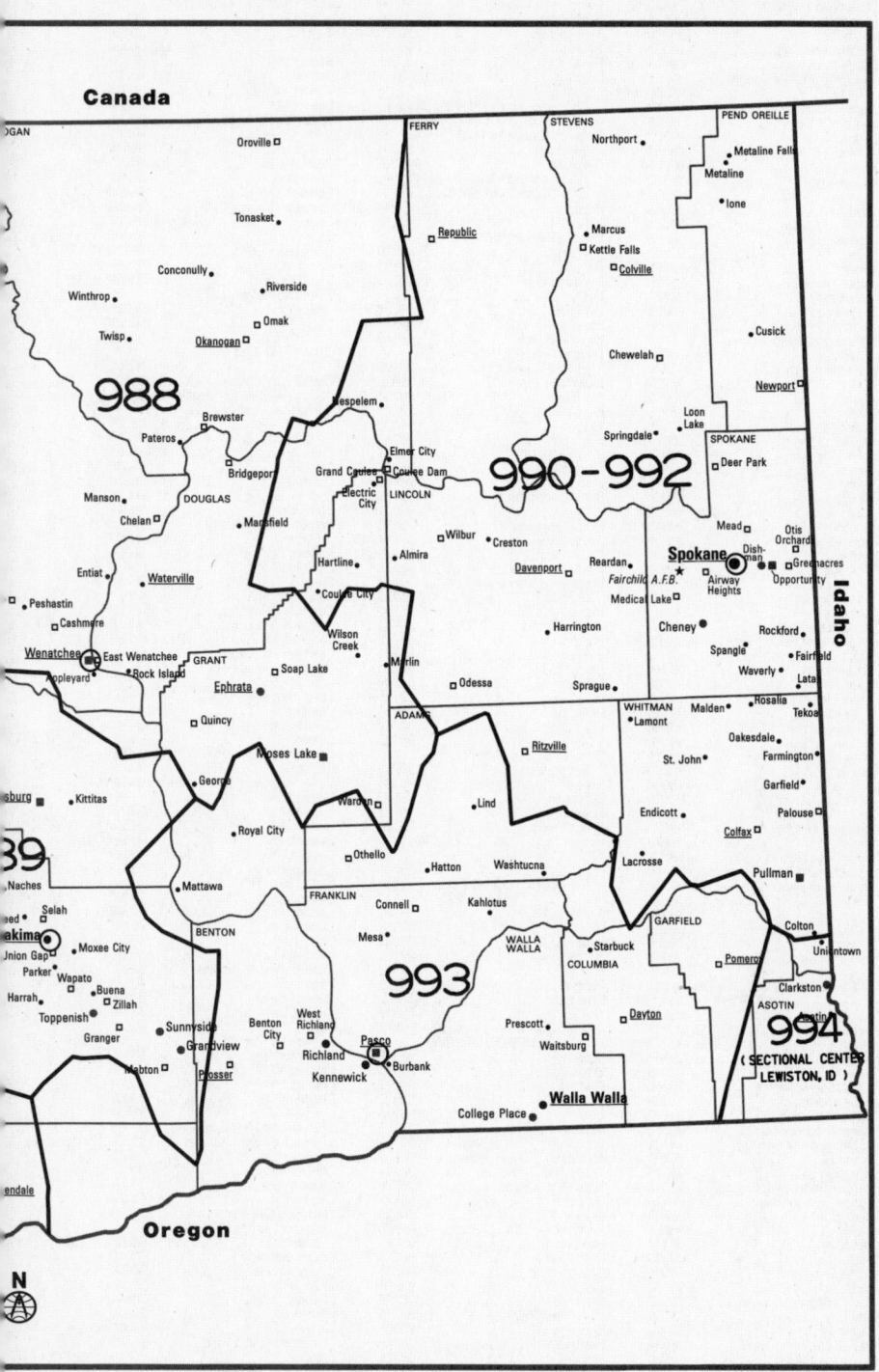

	ZIP
Aberdeen	98520
Aberdeen Gardens	98520
Academy	99031
Acme	98220
Adamsview Park	98951
Addy	99101
Adelaide (Part of Federal Way)	98003
Adelma Beach	98368
Admiral's Cove	98239
Adna	98522
Adrian	98851
Aeneas	98855
Agate Point	98110
Agnew	98362
Ahtanum	98903
Airway Heights	99001
Ajlune	98564
Albion	99102
Alder	98328
Alder Terrace	98926
Alderton	98371
Alderwood	98225
Alderwood Manor	98036
Alderwood Manor-Bothell North	98021
Alexander Beach	98221
Alger	98233
Algona	98001
Allen	98232
Allentown	98178
Allyn	98524
Allyn-Grapeview	98524
Almira	99103
Aloha	98571
Alpental	98068
Alpha	98570
Altoona	98643
Amanda Park	98526
Amber	99004
Amboy	98601
American Lake	98493
Anacortes	98221
Anatone	99401
Anderson Island	98303
Angle Lake (Part of SeaTac)	98188
Annapolis (Part of Port Orchard)	98366
Appleton	98602
Arbor Heights (Part of Seattle)	98146
Arcadia	98584
Arden	99114
Ardenvoir	98811
Argyle	98250
Ariel	98603
Arletta	98335
Arlington	98223
Arlington Heights	98223
Armar	98270
Arrowhead (King County)	98011
Arrowhead (Pierce County)	98498
Arrowhead Beach	98292
Artic	98537
Artondale	98335
Ashford	98304
Asotin	99402
Auburn	98001-02
	98071
For specific Auburn Zip Codes call (206) 833-0540	
Ault Field	98277
Avery	98617
Avon	98273
Ayer	99348
Azwell	98846
Baby Island Heights	98260
Baileysburg	99328
Bainbridge Island	98110
Baker Heights	98273
Ballard (Part of Seattle)	98107
B and G	98201
Bangor	98315
Bangor Submarine Base	98315
Bangor Trident Base	98315
Barberton	98665
Baring	98224
Barstow	99141
Basin City	99343
Battle Ground	98604
Battle Point	98110
Bay Center	98527
Bay City	98520
Bayne	98022
Bay Shore	98584
Bay View (Island County)	98260
Bayview (Skagit County)	98273
Bazinet Eddition	98532
Beachcombers Hidden Beach	98253
Beachcrest	98501

	ZIP
Beacon Hill	98632
Beaux Arts Village	98004
Beaver	98305
Beaver Valley	98365
Beckett Point	98368
Belfair	98528
Bellevue	98004-09
	98015
For specific Bellevue Zip Codes call (206) 454-2489	
Bellevue Square (Part of Bellevue)	98004
Bellingham	98225-27
For specific Bellingham Zip Codes call (206) 676-8303	
Belmont	99104
Belvidere	99116
Bench Drive (Part of Aberdeen)	98520
Benge	99105
Benson Hill	98055
Benton City	99320
Bethel	98366
Beverly	99321
Beverly Beach	98249
Beverly Park (Part of Everett)	98203
Bickleton	99322
Big Bend	98251
Big Lake	98273
Bingen	98605
Birch Bay	98230
Birchfield	98901
Birdsview	98237
Bissell	99137
Bitter Lake (Part of Seattle)	98133
Biz Point	98221
Black Diamond	98010
Black Lake	99114
Black River	98178
Black River (Part of Renton)	98055
Black River Junction (Part of Renton)	98055
Blaine	98230
Blakely Island	98222
Blanchard	98232
Blewett	98826
Blockhouse	98620
Blue Creek	99109
Blue Lake	99115
Blueslide	99180
Blyn	98382
Boise	98022
Bonneville Spur (Part of Bellingham)	98225
Bonney Lake	98390
Bordeaux	98556
Bossburg	99126
Boston Harbor	98506
Bothell	98011-12
	98021
	98041
For specific Bothell Zip Codes call (206) 486-3243	
Boulevard Park	98188
Bow	98232
Bowman Beach	98381
Boyds	99107
Brady	98563
Breidablick	98370
Bremerton	98310-12
	98337
For specific Bremerton Zip Codes call (206) 373-1456	
Brewster	98812
Briarwood	98031
Bridgeport	98813
Brief	98822
Brier	98036
Brinnon	98320
Broadmoor (Part of Seattle)	98112
Broadway (Part of Seattle)	98102
Brookdale	98444
Brooklane Village	98926
Brooklyn	98537
Browns Point	98422
Brownstown	98920
Brownsville	98310
Bruceport	98586
Brush Prairie	98606
Bryant	98223
Bryn Mawr	98178
Bryn Mawr-Skyway	98178
Buckeye	99005
Buckhorn	98245
Buckley	98321
Bucoda	98530
Buena	98921
Buena Vista	98292
Bunker	98532
Burbank	99323

	ZIP
Burbank Heights	99301
Burien (census designated place)	98062
Burien	98166
Burley	98322
Burlington	98233
Burnett	98321
Burton	98013
Bush Point	98249
Butler Acres	98626
Butler Cove	98501
BZ Corner	98672
Cabin Creek	98925
Camaloch	98292
Camano City	98292
Camano Country Club	98292
Camas	98607
Camelot	98002
Campbell's Glen	98236
Camp Murray	98498
Camp Union	98312
Campus (Part of Bellingham)	98225
Canal Tract	98320
Cape George	98368
Capital Mall (Part of Olympia)	98502
Capitol City Country Club	98501
Capitol Hill (Part of Seattle)	98102
Cap Sante (Part of Anacortes)	98221
Carbonado	98323
Care Free Loop	98331
Carlisle	98536
Carlsborg	98324
Carlton	98814
Carnation	98014
Carrier Annex (Part of Everett)	98204
Carrolls	98609
Carson	98610
Carson River Valley	98610
Carylon Beach	98501
Cascade-Fairwood	98055
Cascade Mall	98055
Cascade Park East	98684
Cascade Park West	98684
Cascade Terrace	98371
Cascade Valley	98837
Cascade Vista	98058
Cashmere	98815
Castle Rock	98611
Cathan	98270
Cathcart	98290
Cathlamet	98612
Cavelero Beach	98292
Cedar Creek Corrections Center	98556
Cedardale	98273
Cedar Falls	98045
Cedar Grove	98038
Cedarhome	98292
Cedar Mountain	98055
Cedarview	98390
Cedarville	98568
Cedonia	99137
Center	98376
Centerville	98613
Central (Part of Yakima)	98901
Centralia	98531
Central Park	98520
Central Valley	98370
Ceres	98532
Charleston (Part of Bremerton)	98312
Charleston Beach	98310
Charter Oak	98604
Chattaroy	99003
Chehalis	98532
Chehalis Indian Reservation	98568
Chehalis Village	98568
Chelan	98816
Chelan Falls	98817
Chelatchie	98601
Cheney	99004
Cherokee Bay Park	98038
Cherry Crest (Part of Bellevue)	98004
Cherry Gardens	98019
Cherry Grove	98604
Cherry Point	98230
Chesaw	98844
Chewelah	99109
Chico	98312
Chimacum	98325
Chinook	98614
Christopher (Part of Auburn)	98002
Chuckanut Village (Part of Bellingham)	98225
Chumstick	98826
Churchlake	98390

	ZIP		ZIP		ZIP
Cicero	98223	Dallesport	98617	East Union (Part of Seattle)	98122
Cinebar	98533	Danville	99121	Eastview Hills	98204
Cispus	98377	Darlington (Part of Everett)	98203	East Wenatchee	98802
City Center (Part of		Darrington	98241	East Wenatchee Bench	98801
Bellingham)	98225	Dash Point	98402	Eatonville	98328
Clallam Bay	98326	Davenport	99122	Echo	99114
Claquato	98532	Day Creek	98284	Echo Lake	98133
Claremont (Part of Everett)	98201	Day Island	98466	Eden	98643
Clarkston	99403	Dayton (Columbia County)	99328	Edgecomb	98223
Clarkston Heights	99403	Dayton (Mason County)	98584	Edgemoor (Part of	
Clarkston Heights-Vineland	99403	Decatur	98221	Bellingham)	98225
Clay City	98328	Deep Creek	99022	Edgewater (Part of Everett)	98203
Clayton	99110	Deep River	98638	Edgewood	98372
Clearbrook	98247	Deer Harbor	98243	Edgewood-North Hill	98371
Clear Lake (Pierce County)	98328	Deer Island	98390	Edison	98232
Clearlake (Skagit County)	98235	Deer Lake	98148	Edmonds	98020
Clear Lake (Spokane		Deer Park	99006		98026
County)	99022	Delano	99133	For specific Edmonds Zip Codes	
Clearview	98290	Delano Beach	98349	call (206) 774-6667	
Clearwater	98331	Delphi	98501	Edwall	99008
Cle Elum	98922	Delphi Country Club	98501	Eglon	98346
Cleveland	99356	Del Ridge	98501	Elbe	98330
Cliffdell	98937	Deming	98244	Elberton	99130
Cline (Part of Springdale)	99173	Denison	99006	Eldon	98555
Clinton	98236	Denny Creek	98045	Eldorado Hills	98310
Clipper	98244	Denny Park	98011	Electric City	99123
Cloverland	99402	Desert Aire	99344	Elk	99009
Clover Park	98499	Des Moines	98188	Elk Plain	98387
Clyde Hill	98004	Devereaux Lake	98528	Ellensburg	98926
Coal Creek	98632	Dewey	98221	Ellisford	98855
Coalfield	98059	Dexter by the Sea	98590	Ellisport	98070
Cohasset Beach	98595	Diablo	98283	Ellsworth	98664
Colbert	99005	Diamond	99111	Ellsworth North	98664
Colby	98366	Diamond Lake	99156	Ellsworth South	98664
Colchester	98366	Dieringer	98390	Elma	98541
Coles Corner	98826	Dines Point	98253	Elmer City	99124
Colfax	99111	Disautel	98841	Eltopia	99330
College (Part of Pullman)	99163	Discovery Bay	98368	Endicott	99125
College Place	99324	Dishman	99213	Enterprise	99129
Colton	99113	Dixie	99329	Entiat	98822
Columbia (Part of Seattle)	98118	Dockton	98070	Enumclaw	98022
Columbia Beach	98236	Dodge	99347	Ephrata	98823
Columbia Heights	98632	Doe Bay	98279	Erlands Point	98312
Columbia Shopping Center		Dollar's Corner	98604	Erlands Point-Kitsap Lake	98312
(Part of Kennewick)	99336	Donald	98951	Espanola	99022
Columbia Valley Gardens	98632	Doty	98539	Esperance	98043
Colville	99114	Douglas	98858	Ethel	98542
Colville Indian Agency	99155	Downing	98812	Etna	98674
Colville Indian Reservation	99155	Downtown (Part of		Eufaula Heights	98632
Conconully	98819	Vancouver)	98660	Eureka (Walla Walla County)	99348
Concora (Part of Tukwila)	98188	Downtown (Part of Tacoma)	98402	Eureka (Whatcom County)	98225
Concrete	98237	Draper Spring	98619	Evaline	98596
Conifer View (Part of		Driftwood Acres	98940	Evans	99126
Bothell)	98011	Driftwood Point	98390	Everett	98201-08
Connell	99326	Driftwood Shores	98292	For specific Everett Zip Codes call	
Conway	98238	Dryad	98532	(206) 355-9505	
Cook	98605	Dryden	98821	Everett Mall (Part of Everett)	98204
Cooper Point	98501	Duluth	98642	Evergreen	98684
Copalis Beach	98535	Dumas Bay-Twin Lakes		Evergreen Estates	98501
Copalis Crossing	98536	(Part of Federal Way)	98023	Evergreen Shores	98501
Cornwall (Part of		Dungeness	98382	Everson	98247
Bellingham)	98225	Du Pont	98327	Ewan	99127
Cosmopolis	98537	Dusty	99143	Factoria	98006
Cottage Lake	98072	Duvall	98019	Fairchild Air Force Base	99011
Cottage Lake Bridle Trail	98033	Duwamish	98188	Fairfield	99012
Cottonwood Beach	98230	Eagledale	98110	Fair Harbor	98546
Cougar	98616	Eaglemount	98368	Fairhaven (Part of	
Coulee City	99115	Earlington (Part of Renton)	98055	Bellingham)	98225
Coulee Dam	99116	Earlmount (Part of		Fairmont	98204
Country Homes	99218	Redmond)	98052	Fairview (Kitsap County)	98310
Countryside Beach	98501	East Aberdeen (Part of		Fairview (Yakima County)	98901
Coupeville	98239	Aberdeen)	98520	Fairview-Sumach	98903
Covington	98042	East Coulee Dam (Part of		Fairwood (King County)	98058
Covington-Sawyer-		Coulee Dam)	99116	Fairwood (Spokane County)	99218
Wilderness	98042	East Everett	98205	Fall City	98024
Cowiche	98923	East Farms	99025	Fargher Lake	98675
Cozy Nook	99109	Eastgate (King County)	98007	Farmington	99128
Creosote	98110	Eastgate (Walla Walla			99128
Crescent Bar	98848	County)	99362	For specific Farmington Zip Codes	
Creston	99117	East Heights	99133	call (509) 287-2631	
Crocker	98360	East Hill-Meridian	98031	Fawn Lake	98584
Crockett Lake Estates	98239		98042	Federal (Part of Seattle)	98104
Cromwell	98335	For specific East Hill-Meridian Zip		Federal Way	98003
Crossroads (Part of		Codes call (206) 852-3950			98023
Bellevue)	98008	East Hoquiam (Part of			98063
Crown Hill (Part of Seattle)	98117	Hoquiam)	98550	For specific Federal Way Zip	
Crystal Mountain	98022	East Kittitas	98926	Codes call (206) 927-8100	
Crystal Spring	98110	Eastmont	98205	Felida	98685
Crystal Springs	98466	East Olympia	98540	Felton Stone Lodge	99026
Crystal Village	98022	Easton	98925	Ferndale	98248
Cumberland	98022	East Port Orchard	98366	Fern Hill (Part of Tacoma)	98412
Cunningham	99327	East Quilcene	98376	Fern Prairie	98607
Curlew	99118	East Raymond	98577	Fernwood	98366
Curtis	98538	East Renton Highlands	98024	Fife	98424
Cushman Dam	98548	East Seattle (Part of Mercer		Fife Heights	98424
Cusick	99119	Island)	98040	Finley	99337
Custer (Pierce County)	98413	East Selah	98901	Fircrest	98466
Custer (Whatcom County)	98240	Eastsound	98245	Fircrest Eddition	98532
Dabob	98376	East Spokane	99212	Firdale	98577
Daisy	99167	East Stanwood (Part of		Firgrove	98204
Dalkena	99156	Stanwood)	98292	Fir Tree	98540

	ZIP		ZIP		ZIP
Moxee	98936	Odessa	99159	Pocahontas Bay	99009
Muckleshoot Indian		Offutt Lake	98589	Point Roberts	98281
Reservation	98002	Okanogan	98840	Point White	98110
Mukilteo	98275	Olalla	98359	Pomeroy	99347
Munson Point	98584	Olalla Valley	98359	Pomona	98901
Murdock	98617	Oldport	98501	Pomona Heights	98903
Murphy's Corner	98012	Old Tacoma (Part of		Ponder	98499
Mushroom Corner	98501	Tacoma)	98466	Ponderosa Estates	98390
Naches	98929	Old Willapa	98577	Pontius Park	98021
	98937	Olga	98279	Portage	98013
For specific Naches Zip Codes		Olympia	98501-07	Portage Point	98262
call (509) 653-2467		For specific Olympia Zip Codes		Port Angeles	98362
Nahcotta	98637	call (206) 357-2286		Port Angeles East	98362
Nahwatzel Lake	98584	Olympic Corrections Center	98331	Port Blakely	98110
Napavine	98565	Olympic View	98383	Port Discovery	98368
Naselle	98638	Olympus Ocean Estates	98571	Porter	98541
National	98304	Omak	98841	Port Gamble	98364
Naval Supply Center Puget		Onalaska	98570	Port Gamble Indian	
Sound	98314	Oneida	98643	Reservation	98346
Naval Torpedo Station	98345	Onion Creek	99114	Port Hadlock	98339
Navy Yard City	98310	Opportunity	99206	Port Ludlow	98365
Neah Bay	98357	Orcas	98280	Port Madison	98110
Neilton	98566	Orchard Avenue	99211	Port Madison Indian	
Nemah	98586	Orchard Prairie	99207	Reservation	98310
Nespelem	99155	Orchards	98662	Port Orchard	98366
Nespelem Community	99155	Orchards North	98662	Port Stanley	98261
Newaukum	98002	Orchards South	98662	Port Townsend	98368
Newcastle	98055	Orient	99160	Possession	98236
Newhalem	98283	Orillia (Part of Kent)	98032	Possession Shores	98236
New London	98550	Orin	99114	Potlatch	98584
Newman Lake	99025	Orondo	98843	Poulsbo	98370
Newport (King County)	98004	Oroville	98844	Poverty Bay (Part of Federal	
Newport (Pend Oreille		Orting	98360	Way)	98003
County)	99156	Osceola	98022	Prairie	98284
Newport Hills (census		Oso	98223	Prairie Center (Part of	
designated place)	98002	Ostrander	98626	Coupeville)	98239
Newport Hills	98006	Othello	99327	Prairie Ridge	98390
Newport Shores (Part of		Otis Orchards	99027	Prescott	99348
Bellevue)	98004	Otis Orchards-East Farms	99025	Preston	98050
Newton	98550	Outlook	98938	Priest Point	98271
Nighthawk	98827	Oyhut	98550	Proctor (Part of Tacoma)	98407
Nile	98937	Oysterville	98641	Proebstel	98662
Nine Mile Falls	99026	Ozette	98326	Prosser	99350
Nisqually Indian Community	98503	Pacific	98047	Prune Hill	98607
Nisqually Indian Reservation	98597	Pacific Beach	98571	Puget Island	98612
Nisson	98550	Packwood	98361	Puget Sound Naval Base	98314
Nooksack	98276	Paine Field-Lake Stickney	98204	Puget Sound Naval	
Nordland	98358	Painted Hills	99206	Shipyard	98314
Norma Beach	98292	Palisades	98845	Pullman	99163-65
Norman	98292	Palmer	98051	For specific Pullman Zip Codes	
Normandy Park	98166	Palouse	99161	call (509) 334-3212	
North Beach	98245	Panhandle Lake	98584	Purdy	98332
North Bend	98045	Paradise Estates	98304	Purdy Treatment Center for	
North Bonneville	98639	Paradise Inn	98398	Women	98332
North City	98155	Park	98284	Puyallup	98371-74
North City-Ridgecrest	98155	Parker	98939	For specific Puyallup Zip Codes	
North Cove	98547	Parkland	98444	call (206) 845-2334	
North Fort Lewis	98434	Park Orchard	98031	Queen Anne (Part of	
Northgate (Part of Seattle)	98125	Park Rapids	99114	Seattle)	98109
Northgate Shopping Center		Parkwater	99211	Queensborough	98021
(Part of Seattle)	98125	Parkway Plaza (Part of		Queets	98331
North Hill	98166	Tukwila)	98188	Quendall (Part of Renton)	98055
North Lake	98002	Parkwood	98366	Quilcene	98376
North Lynnwood	98036	Pasadena Park	99206	Quillayute Indian	
North Marysville (census		Pasco	99301-02	Reservation	98350
designated place)	98201	For specific Pasco Zip Codes call		Quinault	98575
North Marysville	98270	(509) 547-8481		Quinault Indian Reservation	98587
North Omak	98841	Pataha City	99347	Quincy	98848
Northport	99157	Pateros	98846	Rainer Valley (Part of	
North Prosser	99350	Paterson	99345	Seattle)	98118
North Puyallup	98372	Peach Acres	98465	Rainier	98576
Northrup (Part of Bellevue)	98008	Pearcot	98801	Rainier Beach (Part of	
North Town (Part of		Pearson	98370	Seattle)	98102
Spokane)	99207	Pe Ell	98572	Rainier Terrace	98371
Northtown Mall (Part of		Pend Orielle Village	99153	Ralston	99169
Spokane)	99207	Penn Cove Park	98277	Rambler Park	98908
Northwood	98264	Peone	99021	Randle	98377
Northwoods	98616	Perrinville (Part of Edmonds)	98020	Raugust	98837
North Yelm	98597	Peshastin	98847	Ravensdale	98051
Norwood Village (Part of		Picnic Point	98335	Raymond	98577
Bellevue)	98004	Pillar Rock	98643	Reardan	99029
Noth Creek-Canyon Park	98012	Pinebrook (Part of		Redmond	98052-53
	98021	Vancouver)	98660		98073
For specific Noth Creek-Canyon		Pine City	99170	For specific Redmond Zip Codes	
Park Zip Codes call (206) 486-		Pinecliff	98937	call (206) 885-1296	
3243		Pinecroft	99214	Redondo	98054
Novelty	98019	Pine Glen	98925	Rees Corner	98290
Nugents Corner	98247	Pinehurst (Part of Everett)	98203	Reintree	98072
Oakbrook	98497	Pine Lake	98027	Renton	98055-59
Oakesdale	99158	Ping	99347	For specific Renton Zip Codes call	
Oak Harbor	98277	Pioneer	98642	(206) 255-8920	
Oakland (Part of Tacoma)	98409	Pioneer Square (Part of		Renton Village (Part of	
Oak Park (Part of Camas)	98607	Seattle)	98104	Renton)	98055
Oakville	98568	Pipe Lake	98038	Republic	99166
O'Brien (Part of Kent)	98032	Plain	98826	Retsil	98378
Obstruction Pass	98279	Plaza	99170	Rhodesia Beach	98527
Ocean City	98569	Pleasant Harbor	98320	Rhododendron Park	98390
Ocean Grove	98571	Pleasant Hill	98626	Rice	99167
Ocean Park	98640	Pleasant Prairie	99207	Richland	99352
Ocean Shores	98569	Pleasant Valley	98665	Richmond Beach	98160
Ocosta	98520	Plymouth	99346		

	ZIP		ZIP		ZIP
Richmond Beach-Innis Arden	98160	Seatons Grove	99116	Shine	98365
Richmond Highlands	98133	**Seattle**	98101-99	Shoalwater Indian Reservation	98590
Ridgecrest	98155	For specific Seattle Zip Codes call (206) 285-1650		Shore Acres	98335
Ridgefield	98642			Shorewood	98106
Ridgetop	98383	*COLLEGES & UNIVERSITIES*		Shorewood Beach	98333
Riiho Park	98640			Shrine Beach	98816
Rimrock	98937	Griffin College	98121	Shuwah	98331
Ritzville	99169	Seattle University	98122	Sierra Division	98239
Riverbend	98821	University of Washington	98195	Sifton	98662
Rivercrest	98204			Sightly	98649
Riverside (Okanogan County)	98849	*FINANCIAL INSTITUTIONS*		Silcott	99403
		American Marine Bank	98110	Silvana	98287
Riverside (Spokane County)	99201	First Interstate Bank of Washington, N.A.	98104	Silvana Terraces	98292
Riverton Heights	98188	Key Bank of Washington	98104	Silver Beach (Part of Bellingham)	98225
Riverview Hills	99005	Metropolitan Federal Savings & Loan Association of Seattle	98101	Silver Brook	98377
Robe	98252			Silver Creek	98585
Robinswood (Part of Bellevue)	98008	Olympic Savings Bank	98101	Silverdale	98383
Roche Harbor	98250	Seattle-First National Bank	98104	Silverlake (Cowlitz County)	98645
Rochester	98579	Security Pacific Bank Washington, N.A.	98168	Silver Lake (Snohomish County)	98208
Rockford	99030	U.S. Bank of Washington, National Association	98101	Silver Lake (Spokane County)	99022
Rock Island	98850	Washington Federal Savings & Loan Association	98101	Silver Lake-Firecrest	98201
Rockport	98283	Washington Mutual Savings Bank	98101	Similk Beach	98221
Rocky Butte	98812			Sisco Heights	98223
Rocky Point (Cowlitz County)	98626	*HOSPITALS*		Skagit City	98273
Rocky Point (Island County)	98292	Group Health Cooperative Central Hospital	98112	Skagit Country Club	98233
Rocky Point (Kitsap County)	98310	Harborview Medical Center	98105	Skamania	98648
Rocky Woods	98387	Providence Medical Center	98122	Skamokawa	98647
Rodena Beach	98239	Swedish Hospital Medical Center	98104	Skokomish Indian Reservation	98584
Rollingbay	98061	University of Washington Medical Center	98195	Skykomish	98288
Rolling Hills	98277	Veterans Affairs Medical Center	98108	Skyway	98178
Ronald	98940	Virginia Mason Medical Center	98101	Sleepy Hollow	98647
Roosevelt (Klickitat County)	99356			Smithville	98635
Roosevelt (Snohomish County)	98290	*HOTELS/MOTELS*		Smokey Point	98223
Roosevelt Beach	98571	Edgewater Inn	98121	Smyrna	99357
Rosalia	99170	Holiday Inn Crowne Plaza	98101	Snee Oosh	98257
Rosario	98245	Sea-Tac Marriott	98188	Snohomish	98290-91
Rosario Beach	98221	Ramada Inn-Downtown Seattle	98121	For specific Snohomish Zip Codes call (206) 568-4313	
Rosburg	98643	Red Lion Hotel-SeaTac	98188	Snoqualmie	98065
Rosedale	98335	Seattle Airport Hilton	98188	Snoqualmie Pass	98068
Rose Hill (Part of Kirkland)	98033	The Seattle Hilton	98101	Soap Lake	98851
Rose Valley	98626	Seattle Sheraton Hotel & Towers	98101	South Aberdeen (Part of Aberdeen)	98520
Rosewood	99208	The Sorrento Hotel	98104	South Bay	98501
Roslyn	98941	The Westin Hotel	98101	South Beach (Kitsap County)	98110
Roy	98580			South Beach (Whatcom County)	98281
Royal Camp	99344	*MILITARY INSTALLATIONS*		South Bellingham (Part of Bellingham)	98225
Royal City	99357	Air Force Water Port Logistics Office	98134	South Bend	98586
Ruby	99119	Coast Guard Support Center, Seattle	98134	South Broadway	98902
Ruff	98832	Fort Lawton	98433	Southcenter (Part of Tukwila)	98188
Ruston	98407	(MTMC) Pacific Northwest Outport	98134	South Cle Elum	98943
Ryderwood	98581	Naval Station, Puget Sound	98115	South Colby	98384
Sahalee	98052-53	Supervisor of Shipbuilding, Conversion and Repair, Seattle	98115	South Elma	98541
For specific Sahalee Zip Codes call (206) 885-1296		United States Engineer District, Seattle	98124	Southgate (Pierce County)	98499
St. Andrews	99115	13th Coast Guard District, Seattle	98134	Southgate (Thurston County)	98501
St. John	99171			South Hill	98373
St. Urbans	98596	Seattle Heights (Part of Edmonds)	98036	South Montesano	98563
Salkum	98582	Seaview	98644	South Park (Part of Seattle)	98108
Salmon Beach (Part of Tacoma)	98424	Sedro Woolley	98284	South Park Village	98366
Salmon Creek	98665	Sekiu	98381	South Point	98365
	98685-86	Selah	98942	South Prairie	98385
For specific Salmon Creek Zip Codes call (206) 695-4462		Selleck	98051	South Seattle (Part of Seattle)	98102
Saltwater	98188	Sequim	98382	Southshore Mall (Part of Aberdeen)	98520
Samish Island	98232	Sequoia	99026	Southside (Part of Everett)	98208
Samish Lake	98226	Seven Mile	99026	South Snohomish	98290
San de Fuca	98239	Shadle Center (Part of Spokane)	99205	South Sound (Part of Lacey)	98503
Sandy Hook	98236	Shadle Garland (Part of Spokane)	99205	South Tacoma (Part of Tacoma)	98409
Sandy Hook Park	98370	Shaker Church	98271	South Union	98501
Sandy Point	98260	Shana Park	98501	South Wenatchee	98801
Santiago Beach	98587	Shangri-La Shores	98239	Southworth	98386
Sappho	98305	Shaw Island	98286	Spanaway	98387
Sara	98642	Shawnee	99111	Spangle	99031
Saratoga Beach	98260	Shelter Bay	98257	Special Offender Center	98272
Saratoga Heights	98260	Shelton	98584	Spokane	99201-28
Saratoga Shores	98292	Sheridan Beach	98155	For specific Spokane Zip Codes call (509) 459-0222	
Satsop	98583	Sheridan Park (Part of Bremerton)	98310	Spokane Indian Reservation	99129
Satus	98948	Sherwood Forest (Part of Bellevue)	98008	Sprague	99017
Sauk River Estates	98283				99032
Sawyer	98951			For specific Sprague Zip Codes call (206) 257-2269	
Scandia	98370			Spring Creek	98940
Scatchet Head	98236			Springdale	99173
Schawana	99321			Spring Glen	98024
Schneiders Prairie	98502			Squaxin Island Indian Reservation	98584
Schwarder	98908			Stabler	98610
Scopa (Part of Renton)	98055				
Scott Lake	98501				
Sea Acres	98279				
Seabeck	98380				
Seabold	98110				
Sea First (Part of Seattle)	98104				
Seahurst	98062				
Seal Rock	98320				
Seamount Estates	98320				
SeaTac	98188				
Seatac Mall (Part of Federal Way)	98003				

	ZIP		ZIP		ZIP
Wickersham	98220	Wishram	98673	Yakima	98901-09
Wilbur	99185	Wishram Heights	98673	For specific Yakima Zip Codes	
Wilburton (Part of Bellevue)	98004	Withrow	98858	call (509) 575-5827	
Wildcat Lake	98310	Wollochet	98335	Yakima Indian Reservation	98948
Wilderness	98501	Woodinville	98072	Yakima Mall (Part of	
Wiley	98908	Woodland	98674	Yakima)	98901
Wilkeson	98396	Woodland Beach	98292	Yale	98603
Willada	99171	Woodland Creek	98501	Yardley	99202
Willapa	98577	Woodland Park	98603	Yarrow Point	98004
Willard	98605	Woodlawn (Part of		Yelm	98597
Willow Grove	98632	Hoquiam)	98550	Yeomalt	98110
Wilson Creek	98860	Woodmont Beach	98032	Yesler Terrace (Part of	
Winchester	98848	Woodsmuir	98501	Seattle)	98104
Winlock	98596	Woodway	98020	Yokeko Point	98221
Winona	99125	Wycoff (Part of Bremerton)	98312	Yoman Ferry	98303
Winthrop	98862	Wye Lake	98366	Zenith	98188
Winton	98826	Yacht Haven	98250	Zillah	98953
Wishkah	98520	Yacolt	98675		

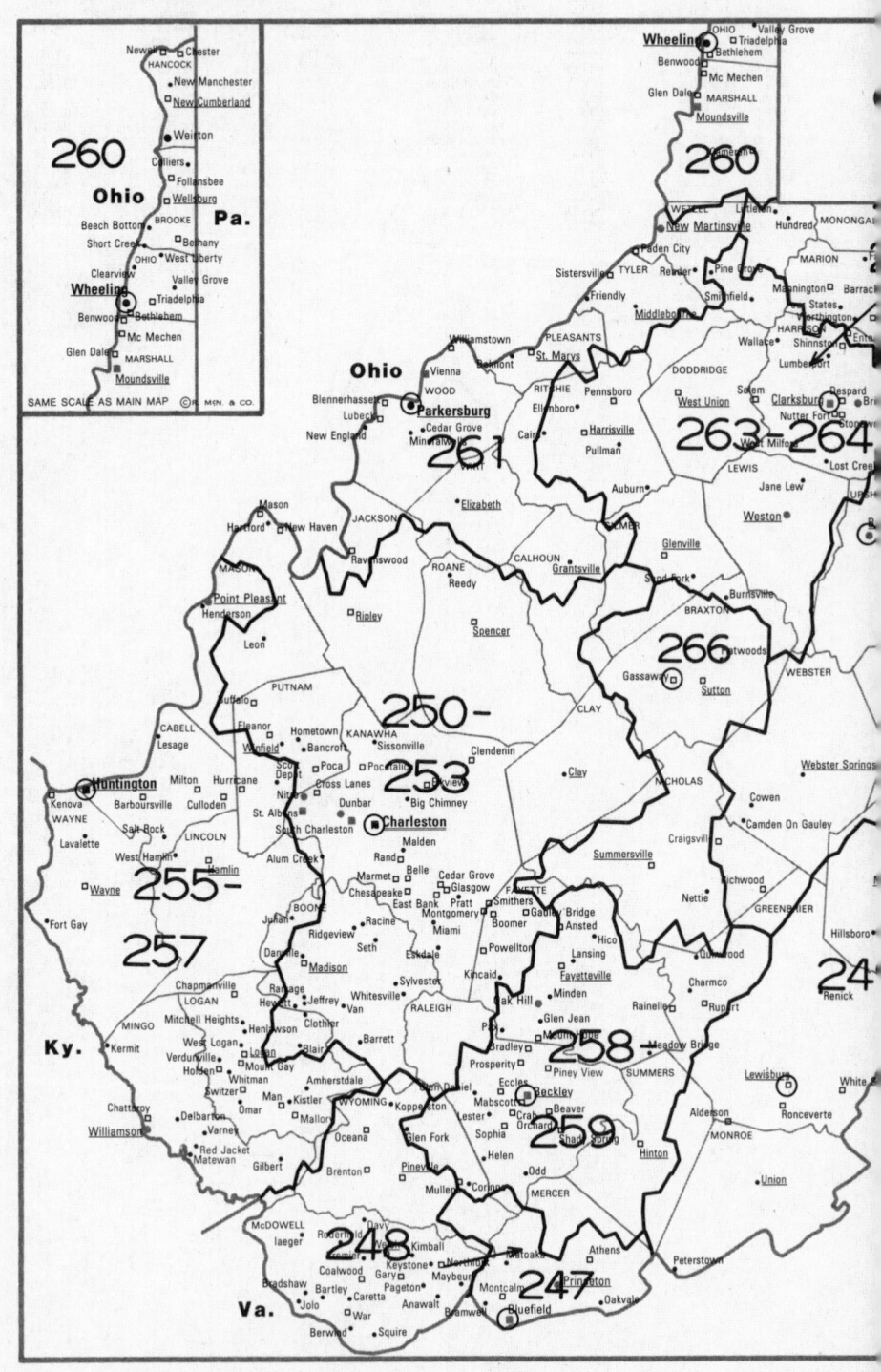

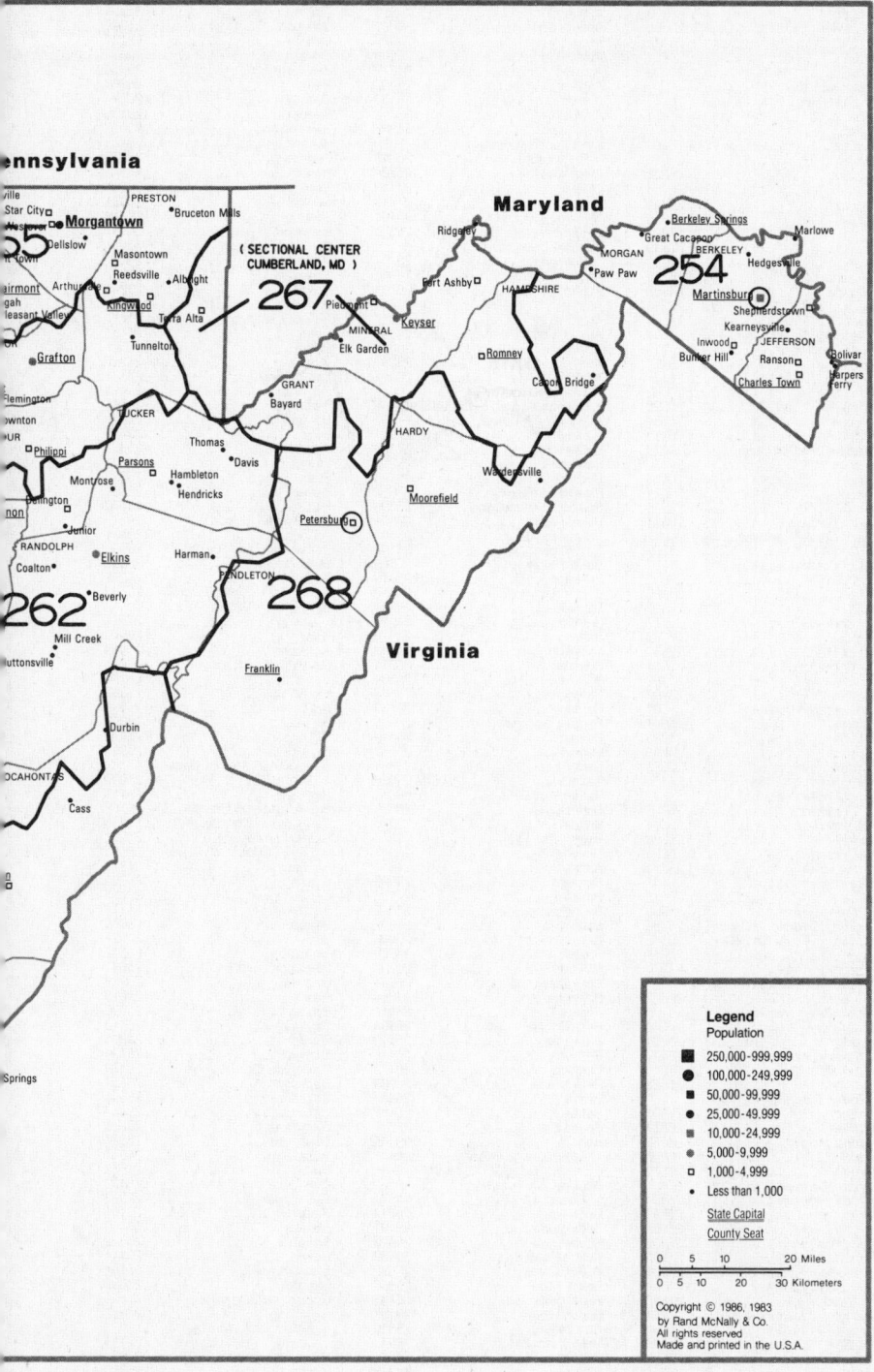

Maryland

Pennsylvania

ville
Star City
Westover
•Morgantown
Dellslow
•Bruceton Mills
PRESTON
Masontown
Reedsville
Albright

(SECTIONAL CENTER
CUMBERLAND, MD)

267

Ridgeley
MORGAN
•Paw Paw

•Berkeley Springs
Great Cacapon
BERKELEY
Hedgesville
Marlowe

254

Martinsburg
Shepherdstown
Kearneysville
JEFFERSON
Inwood
Bunker Hill
Ranson
Charles Town
Bolivar
Harpers
Ferry

airmont
gah
leasant Valley
Arthur
Kingwood
Terra Alta
Piedmont
MINERAL
Elk Garden
Keyser

Grafton
Tunnelton

Port Ashby
HAMPSHIRE
Romney
Capon Bridge

Flemington
ownton
UR
Philippi
Montrose
lington
GRANT
Bayard

TUCKER
Thomas
Parsons
Hambleton
Hendricks
Davis

HARDY

Wardensville
Moorefield

non
Junior
RANDOLPH
Coalton
•Elkins
Harman

Petersburg

262
•Beverly
Mill Creek
luttonsville

PENDLETON

268

Virginia

Franklin

•Durbin

OCAHONTAS
•Cass

Springs

	ZIP		ZIP		ZIP
Aarrons Fork	25071	Arthurdale	26520	Bellepoint (Part of Hinton)	25951
Abbott	26201	Artie	25008	Belleville	26133
Abney	25847	Arvilla	26135	Bellmeade	25550
Abraham	25918	Asbury	24916	Bellview (Part of Fairmont)	26554
Accoville	25606	Asbury Church	26801	Bellwood	25962
Acme	25122	Asco	24828	Belmont	26134
Ada	24701	Ashford	25009	Belva	26656
Adaline	26033	Ashland	24810	Belvedere Heights	25414
Adamston (Part of		Ashley	26456	Bemis	26268
Clarksburg)	26301	Ashton	25503	Benbush	26292
Adamsville	26431	Aspinall	26412	Bendale	26452
Adlai	26170	Astor	26347	Ben Lomond	25515
Adolph	26280	Astor Junction (Part of		Bennett	26423
Adrian	26210	Flemington)	26347	Benson	26378
Advent	25231	Atenville	25524	Benson Park	25302
Afton	26764	Athens	24712	Bens Run	26135
Aggregate	26241	Atwell	24813	Benton Ferry	26554
Airport Road	25813	Atwood	26167	Bentree	25018
Ajax	25676	Auburn	26325	Benwood	26031
Albright	26519	Augusta (Hampshire		Benwood Junction (Part of	
Alderson	24910	County)	26704	Benwood)	26031
Alexander	26218	Augusta (Mercer County)	24740	Berea	26327
Algoma	24868	Aurora	26705	Bergoo	26298
Alice	26342	Austen	26410	Berkeley	25401
Alkol	25501	Auto	24917	Berkeley Springs	25411
Allendale	26003	Auville (Part of Iaeger)	24844	Berlin	26452
Allen Junction	25810	Auviltown	26290	Bernie	25521
Allensville	25427	Avis (Part of Hinton)	25951	Berryburg	26347
Allister	26167	Avon	26411	Berry Siding	26621
Alloy	25002	Avondale (Doddridge		Berryville	25411
Alma	26320	County)	26456	Bertha Hill	26541
Alpena	26254	Avondale (McDowell		Berwind	24815
Alpha	26408	County)	24811	Beryl	26726
Alpheus (Part of Gary)	24836	Bablin	26376	Besoco	25857
Alpoca	24710	Backus	25976	Bessemer	25401
Alta	26656	Baden	25123	Bethany	26032
Altizer	25234	Baisden (Logan County)	25652	Bethel Place	26181
Alton	26210	Baisden (Mingo County)	25608	Bethesada	25570
Alum Bridge	26321	Baker	26801	Bethlehem (Harrison	
Alum Creek (Kanawha		Baker Heights	25401	County)	26431
County)	25003	Baker Park	25177	Bethlehem (Ohio County)	26003
Alum Creek (Lincoln		Baker Ridge	26505	Betty Zane	26003
County)	25003	Bakerton	25410	Beverly	26253
Alvon	24986	Bald Knob	25010	Beverly Hills (Cabell County)	25705
Alvy	26322	Baldwin	26351	Beverly Hills (Marion	
Amandaville	25177	Ballard	24918	County)	26554
Amboy	26705	Ballengee	24919	Bias	25670
Ambrosia	25550	Balls Gap	25541	Bickmore	25019
Ameagle	25004	Bancroft	25011	Big Battle	26426
Amelia	25160	Bandytown	25204	Bigbend	26136
Amherstdale	25607	Barboursville	25504	Big Chimney	25302
Amherstdale-Robinette	25607	Bardane	25430	Big Creek	25505
Amigo	25811	Bargers Springs	24935	Big Four	24853
Amma	25005	Barker	26419	Big Isaac	26426
Anawalt	24808	Barksdale	25951	Big Moses	26320
Andersonville	26033	Barn	25841	Big Mountain (Part of Cedar	
Andrew	25154	Barnabus	25638	Grove)	25039
Angel Terrace (Part of		Barnet Run	26610	Big Otter	25113
Charleston)	25303	Barrackville	26559	Big Run (Marion County)	26582
Angerona	25241	Barrett	25013	Big Run (Marshall County)	26033
Anjean	25984	Barrs	25276	Big Run (Webster County)	26217
Anmoore	26323	Barry Mine	26347	Big Run (Wetzel County)	26561
Annamoriah	26141	Bartley	24813	Big Sandy	24816
Annamoriah Flats	26141	Bartow	24920	Bigson	25206
Ansted	25812	Basin	24726	Big Springs	26137
Anthony	24938	Basnettsville	26570	Big Sycamore	25111
Antioch (Doddridge County)	26456	Basore	26812	Billings	25270
Antioch (Mineral County)	26743	Bass	26836	Bim	25021
Aplin	25244	Baxter	26560	Bingamon	26591
Apple Farm	25274	Bayard	26707	Bingamon Junction	26591
Apple Grove (Mason		Bear Creek	26624	Bingham	25958
County)	25502	Beard Heights	24954	Birch River	26610
Apple Grove (McDowell		Beards Fork	25014	Birchton	25209
County)	24844	Bear Mountain Mine	26334	Birds Creek	26410
Aracoma	25601	Bearsville	26149	Bishop	24604
Arborland Acres	25177	Beason	26415	Bismarck	26739
Arbovale	24915	Beatrice	26178	Blackberry City	25678
Arbuckle	25123	Beatysville	26133	Black Betsy	25159
Arbutus Park (Part of		Beaver	25813	Black Bottom	25601
Clarksburg)	26301	Bebee	26155	Black Eagle	25882
Archer	26377	Becco	25607	Blackhawk	25306
Archer Heights	26035	Beckley	25801-02	Blacksville	26521
Arcola	26206	For specific Beckley Zip Codes		Black Wolf	24871
Ardel	25570	call (304) 252-4202		Blaine	21538
Arden (Barbour County)	26405	Beckley Junction (Part of		Blair (Jefferson County)	25432
Arden (Berkeley County)	25401	Mabscott)	25871	Blair (Logan County)	25022
Argonne	25649	Beckwith	25814	Blairton	25401
Argyle	25654	Bedington	25401	Blakeley	25160
Arkansas	26801	Beebe	25625	Blandville	26328
Arlee	25106	Beech Bottom	26030	Blaser	26444
Arlington (Harrison County)	26301	Beech Creek	25682	Blennerhassett	26101
Arlington (McDowell		Beech Glen	26656	Blocton	25685
County)	24810	Beechgrove	26415	Bloomery (Hampshire	
Arlington (Upshur County)	26234	Beech Hill	25187	County)	26817
Arnett	25007	Beechwood	25810	Bloomery (Jefferson	
Arnette	26619	Beelick Knob	25976	County)	25414
Arnettsville	26505	Beeson	24714	Bloomingrose	25024
Arnold Hill	26241	Belgrove	25248	Blount	25025
Arnoldsburg	25234	Belington	26250	Blue	26149
Arroyo	26047	Bellburn	25958	Blue Creek	25026
Arthur	26816	Belle	25015	Bluefield	24701

	ZIP		ZIP		ZIP
Blue Jay	25816	Bula	26521	Chapman Addition	26070
Blue Ridge Acres	25425	Bulger	26501	Chapmanville	25508
Blue Rock	26280	Bull	25669	Charleston	25301-75
Bluestone	24701	Bull Run	26547	For specific Charleston Zip Codes	
Blue Sulphur Springs	24910	Bulltown	26631	call (304) 357-4116	
Blueville (Part of Grafton)	26354	Bunker Hill (Berkeley		Charleston Ordnance	
Bluewell	24701	County)	25413	Center (Part of South	
Blundon	25071	Bunker Hill (Kanawha		Charleston)	25303
Board	25253	County)	25309	Charleston Town Center	
Boaz	26187	Bunners Ridge	26554	(Part of Charleston)	25375
Bob White	25028	Burchfield	26562	Charles Town	25414
Boggs	26299	Burlington	26710	Charlton Heights (Part of	
Bolair	26288	Burning Springs (Kanawha		Gauley Bridge)	25040
Bolivar	25425	County)	25015	Charmco	25958
Bolt	25817	Burning Springs (Wirt		Chatham Hill	26571
Bomont	25030	County)	26141	Chattaroy	25667
Bona Vista (Part of		Burnsville	26335	Chauncey	25612
Charleston)	25311	Burnsville Junction (Part of		Cheat Lake	26505
Bonnie	26619	Burnsville)	26335	Cheat Neck	26505
Bonnivale	26150	Burnt Factory	25411	Chelyan	25035
Booher	26320	Burnt House	26178	Cherokee	25122
Boomer	25031	Burnwell	25034	Cherry Falls	26288
Boonesborough (Part of		Burton	26562	Cherry Grove	26804
Gauley Bridge)	25057	Butchersville	26452	Cherry Run	25427
Booth	26522	Cabell	25871	Chesapeake (Kanawha	
Boothsville	26554	Cabin Creek	25035	County)	25315
Borderland	25665	Cabins	26855	Chesapeake (Marion	
Boreman	26101	Cabot	25163	County)	26554
Borgman	26444	Cabot Station	26147	Chester	26034
Bottom Creek	24853	Cairo	26337	Chesterville	26150
Boulder	26201	Caldwell	24925	Chestnut Heights	26070
Bowan Ridge	25701	Calis	26033	Chestnut Hill (Part of	
Bowden	26254	Callaway	25880	Weirton)	26062
Bowlby	26541	Calvert (Part of St. Albans)	25177	Chestnut Ridge	26505
Bowles	25523	Calvin	26660	Chiefton	26301
Boyd	26234	Cambria	26386	Childs	26162
Boyer	24915	Camden	26338	Chimney Corner	25085
Bozoo	24923	Camden On Gauley	26208	Chloe	25235
Bradley (Boone County)	25051	Cameron	26033	Christian	25611
Bradley (Raleigh County)	25818	Camp	26320	Churchville	26338
Bradshaw	24817	Campbelltown	24954	Cicerone	25243
Braeholm	25607	Camp Creek	25820	Cinco	25306
Bragg	25918	Campus	24827	Cinderella	25661
Bramwell	24715	Canaan	26234	Circleville	26804
Branchland	25506	Canaan Heights	26260	Cirtsville	25801
Brandonville	26523	Canaan Valley	26260	Cisco	26161
Brandywine	26802	Canebrake	24819	Claremont	25936
Braxton	26619	Cane Fork	25075	Clarence	25244
Bream	25071	Canfield (Braxton County)	26601	Clarksburg	26301-02
Breeden	25666	Canfield (Randolph County)	26241	For specific Clarksburg Zip Codes	
Brenton	24818	Cannelton	25036	call (304) 623-4796	
Bretz (Preston County)	26524	Canton	26456	Clay	25043
Bretz (Tucker County)	26287	Cantwell	26362	Claypool (Logan County)	25617
Brewsterdale	24619	Canvas	26662	Claypool (Summers County)	25976
Briarwood Estates	26101	Canyon	26505	Claysville	26743
Brick Church	25514	Capehart	25123	Clayton	24910
Bridgeport	26330	Capels	24820	Clear Creek	25044
Bridgeport Hill (Part of		Capitol (Part of Charleston)	25311	Clear Fork	24822
Bridgeport)	26330	Capon Bridge	26711	Clearview	26003
Bridgeway	26149	Capon Springs	26823	Clem	26623
Brink	26582	Carbon	25122	Clemtown	26405
Bristol	26332	Carbondale	25036	Clendenin	25045
Broaddus (Part of Philippi)	26416	Caretta	24821	Cleveland	26215
Broadmoor	26181	Carl	26676	Clifftop	25831
Broad Oaks (Part of		Carlisle	25917	Clifton	25237
Clarksburg)	26301	Carl Lee Ray	26181	Clifton Mills	26525
Brohard	26138	Carlos	24844	Clinton (Boone County)	25013
Brookhaven (Kanawha		Carolina	26563	Clinton (Ohio County)	26059
County)	25143	Carolina Heights	25177	Clintonville	24928
Brookhaven (Monongalia		Carpendale	26753	Clio	25046
County)	26505	Carrollton	26238	Clothier	25047
Brooklyn	25840	Carswell	24853	Clouston	26033
Brooklyn Junction (Part of		Carter	26218	Clover	25276
New Martinsville)	26155	Cascade	26547	Cloverdale	24963
Brooks	25957	Cashmere	24918	Clover Lick	24927
Brookside	26705	Cass	24927	Clyde (Kanawha County)	25302
Brounland	25314	Cassity	26278	Clyde (Wetzel County)	26186
Brown	26448	Cassville (Monongalia		Coal Branch Heights (Part	
Brownlow	26354	County)	26527	of Charleston)	25301
Brownsburg	24954	Catawba	26554	Coalburg	25035
Browns Mills	26505	Cave	26807	Coal City	25823
Brownsville (Fayette County)	25085	Cazy	25028	Coaldale	24724
Brownsville (Lewis County)	26452	Cedar Grove (Kanawha		Coal Fork	25147
Brownton	26334	County)	25039	Coal Fork (census	
Brownwood	25864	Cedar Grove (Wood		designated place)	25306
Bruceton Mills	26525	County)	26101	Coal Mountain	24823
Bruno	25611	Cedarville	26611	Coalton	26257
Brush Fork	24701	Center Hill	26143	Coal Valley	25047
Brushy		Center Point	26339	Coalwood	24824
run	26866	Centerville	25555	Coburn	26562
Brydon	26435	Central	26101	Coco	25071
Bryson	25865	Centralia	26612	Cofoco	25147
Bubbling Spring	26865	Central Station	26456	Coketon	26292
Buck	25951	Century	26214	Colcord	25048
Buckeye	24924	Century No. 2	26238	Cold Stream	26711
Buckhannon	26201	Ceredo	25507	Coldwater	26411
Bud	24716	Ceres	24701	Colebank	26405
Buena Vista	25320	Cham	25654	Coleman	25517
Buffalo	25033	Chapel	26624	Colfax	26566
Buffalo Creek	25530	Chapman (Braxton County)	26412	Colliers	26035
Buff Lick	25039	Chapman (Webster County)	26288	Collinsdale	25034

Name	ZIP	Name	ZIP	Name	ZIP
Columbia	25118	Dameron	25849	Eagle	25136
Combs Addition	25617	Danese	25831	Earling	25632
Comfort	25049	Daniels	25832	Earnshaw	26585
Conaway	26149	Dans Run	26763	East Bank	25067
Concord	26410	Danville	25053	East Beckley (Part of Beckley)	25801
Confidence	25168	Darkesville	25428	East Dailey	26253
Congo	26050	Dartmont	25009	East Gulf	25915
Conings	26443	Dartmoor	26250	East Huntington (Part of Huntington)	25702
Cool Ridge	25825	Davenport	26175	East Kermit	25674
Cooper (Part of Bramwell)	24715	Davin	25617	East Lynn	25512
Coopertown	25148	Davis (Logan County)	25625	East Nitro (Part of Nitro)	25143
Copen	26615	Davis (Tucker County)	26260	East Oak Hill	25901
Copley	26452	Davis Creek	25003	Easton	26505
Cora	25614	Davisville	26142	East Pea Ridge	25705
Cordova	24966	Davy	24828	East Salem	26426
Core	26529	Dawes	25054	East Side (Kanawha County)	25301
Corinne	25826	Dawmont	26344	Eastside (Marion County)	26554
Corinth	26713	Dawson	24910	East View	26301
Corley (Barbour County)	26250	Daybrook	26570	East Vivian	24891
Corley (Braxton County)	26621	Daysville	26201	East Williamson (Part of Williamson)	25661
Corliss	25962	Deansville	26201	Eaton	26180
Cornstalk	24901	Deanville	26452	Eccles	25836
Cornwallis	26337	Decota	25122	Echo	25570
Cortland	26260	Deep Valley (Marion County)	26582	Eckman	24829
Corton	25045	Deep Valley (Tyler County)	26360	Eden (Ohio County)	26003
Costa	25051	Deep Water	25057	Eden (Upshur County)	26234
Cottageville	25239	Deer Creek	24927	Edgarton	25672
Cottle	26207	Deer Run	26807	Edgemont (Part of Fairmont)	26554
Cotton	25046	Deer Walk	26180	Edgewood (Harrison County)	26301
Cottontown	26562	Dehue	26654	Edgewood (Kanawha County)	25302
Country Club Acres (Part of South Charleston)	25309	Delbarton	25670	Edgewood (Ohio County)	26003
Countsville	25243	Dellslow	26531	Edgewood Acres (Part of Charleston)	25302
Courtright	26330	Delong	26170	Edison	24701
Cove (Part of Weirton)	26062	Delray	26714	Edmond	25837
Cove Creek	25534	Dempsey	25840	Edna	26505
Cove Gap	25534	Denver (Marshall County)	26033	Edray	24954
Covel	24719	Denver (Preston County)	26444	Edwight	25189
Cowen	26206	Denver Heights	26033	Effie	25514
Cox Landing	25537	Derryhale	25846	Egeria (Mercer County)	25841
Coxs Mills	26342	Despard	26301	Egeria (Raleigh County)	25902
Coxtown (Part of Weston)	26452	Dessie	26623	Eggleton	25523
Crab Orchard	25827	Devon	25682	Eglon	26716
Crag	25962	Dewitt	25901	Elana	25266
Craigmoor	26408	Diamond (Kanawha County)	25015	Elbert (Part of Gary)	24830
Craigsville	26205	Diamond (Logan County)	25625	Eldora	26554
Cranberry	25828	Diana	26217	Eleanor	25070
Craneco	25630	Dickinson	25015	Elgood	24740
Cranesville	26764	Dickson	25535	Elizabeth	26143
Crany	24870	Dille	26617	Elk	26271
Crawford	26343	Dingess	25671	Elk City	26416
Crawley	24931	Dingy	26623	Elk Forest	25311
Creamery	24910	Dink	25113	Elk Garden	26717
Crede	25302	Dixie	25059	Elkhorn	24831
Cremo	26141	Doane	25511	Elkhurst	25164
Crescent	25136	Dobra	25183	Elkins	26241
Cressmont	25043	Dock	25177	Elkridge (Fayette County)	25161
Creston	26141	Dog Patch	25636	Elkridge (McDowell County)	24868
Crichton	25961	Dog Run	25043	Elk Run Junction	25209
Crickmer	25831	Dola	26386	Elkview	25071
Crooked Creek	25639	Donaldson	26206	Elkwater	26273
Crosby	25125	Doortown	26288	Ella	26055
Cross Lanes	25312-13	Dorcas	26847	Ellamore	26267
For specific Cross Lanes Zip Codes call (304) 776-3201		Dorothy	25060	Ellenboro	26346
Crossroads	26589	Dothan	25833	Elliber Spring	26852
Crow	25813	Dott	24736	Ellison	25969
Crown (Logan County)	25606	Douglas (Calhoun County)	25235	Elm Grove	26003
Crown (Monongalia County)	26505	Douglas (Tucker County)	26292	Elmira	26618
Crown Hill	25052	Downtown (Part of Huntington)	25701	Elm Terrace (Part of Wheeling)	26003
Crow Summit	26164	Downtown (Part of Wheeling)	26003	Elmwood (Mason County)	25123
Crum	25669	Drennen	26667	Elmwood (Wayne County)	25570
Crumpler	24825	Drews Creek	25140	Elmwood Heights	26187
Crystal	24747	Droop	24946	Eloise	25511
Crystal Lake	26456	Drybranch	25061	Elton	25965
Crystal Springs (Randolph County)	26241	Dry Creek	25062	Emma	25124
Crystal Springs (Wood County)	26181	Dryfork	26263	Emmart	26447
Cubana	26237	Dry Hill	25801	Emmett	25620
Cucumber	24826	Duck	25063	Emmons	25009
Culloden	25510	Dudeon	25248	Emoryville	26717
Cumberland Heights	24701	Dudley Gap	25541	Endicott	26581
Cunard	25840	Duffields	25442	Engle	25425
Curtin	26288	Duffy	26376	English	24832
Curtisville	26582	Duhring	24747	Ennis	24887
Cusicks Crossing	26562	Dukes	25252	Enoch	25043
Custer Addition	26301	Dunbar	25064	Enon	26651
Cutlips	26619	Duncan	25252	Enterprise (Harrison County)	26568
Cuzzart	26530	Dundon	25043	Enterprise (Wirt County)	26160
Cyclone	24827	Dunloup	25880	Entry Mountain	26807
Cyrus	25530	Dunlow	25511	Epperly	25823
Czar	26224	Dunmore	24934	Erbacon	26203
Dabney	25654	Dunns	25841	Erie	26301
Dahmer	26807	Duo	25984	Erwin	26705
Dailey	26259	Dupont Circle	26181	Eskdale	25075
Daisy	25505	Dupont City	25015		
Dakota	26554	Durbin	26264		
Dale	26377	Durgon	26836		
Dallas	26036	Dutchman	26148		
Dallison	26180	Dutch Ridge	25045		
		Dyer	26206		

	ZIP		ZIP		ZIP
Esty	24966	Forks of Hurricane	25514	Glasgow	25086
Etam	26425	Fort Ashby	26719	Glen	25088
Ethel	25076	Fort Branch	25076	Glen Alum	25651
Eunice	25209	Fort Gay	25514	Glencoe	25119
Eureka	26144	Fort Grand	26533	Glen Dale	26038
Evans	25241	Fort Hill (Part of Charleston)	25303	Glendale Heights	26038
Evansdale (Part of		Fort Martin	26541	Glen Daniel	25844
Morgantown)	26505	Fort Neal (Part of		Glendon	26623
Evansville	26440	Parkersburg)	26103	Glen Easton	26039
Evenwood	26254	Fort Run	26836	Glen Elk (Part of	
Everettville	26533	Fort Seybert	26806	Clarksburg)	26301
Evergreen	26218	Fort Spring	24936	Glen Falls	26301
Evergreen Hills	25239	Foster	25081	Glen Ferris	25090
Everson	26554	Fosterville	25181	Glen Fork	25845
Excelsior (McDowell		Four Mile	26419	Glengary	25421
County)	24892	Four States	26572	Glenhayes	25519
Excelsior (Upshur County)	26201	Frame	25071	Glen Jean	25846
Exchange	26619	Frametown	26623	Glenmore	26241
Extra	25033	Francis (Harrison County)	26554	Glen Morgan	25847
Factory	25411	Francis (Raleigh County)	25915	Glenray	24910
Fairdale	25839	Frank	24920	Glen Rogers	25848
Fairfax Estates (Part of		Frankford	24938	Glen View	25827
Charleston)	25314	Franklin (Brooke County)	26070	Glenville	26351
Fairlea	24902	Franklin (Pendleton County)	26807	Glen White	25849
Fairmont	26554-55	Franklintown	25441	Glenwood (Mason County)	25520
For specific Fairmont Zip Codes		Fraziers Bottom	25082	Glenwood (Ohio County)	26003
call (304) 366-1610		Freed	26138	Glenwood Park	24701
Fairmor (Part of Westover)	26505	Freeman (Part of Bramwell)	24724	Glover Gap	26585
Fairplain	25271	Freemansburg	26452	Gluck	24844
Fairview (Jackson County)	25252	Freeport (Preston County)	26764	Godby	25508
Fairview (Marion County)	26570	Freeport (Wirt County)	26180	Godfrey	24735
Fairview (Marshall County)	26055	Freeze Fork	25076	Goffs	26362
Fairview (Mason County)	25253	French Creek	26218	Goldtown	25248
Fairview (Mingo County)	25661	Frenchton	26219	Goodhope	26378
Fairview (Wood County)	26181	Frew	26149	Goodman	25667
Fallen Timber	26437	Friars Hill	24939	Goodwill	24747
Falling Rock	25079	Friendly	26146	Gordon	25093
Falling Waters	25419	Friendly View	25062	Gore	26301
Falls	26833	Frogtown	25625	Gormania	26720
Falls Mill	26620	Frost	24954	Gormley	26267
Falls Mills	26146	Frozen Camp	25252	Goshen	26234
Fallsview	25002	Fry	25524	Gould	26218
Fanco	25606	Fulton (Part of Wheeling)	26003	Grace	25270
Fanny	24834	Gaines	26234	Grafton	26354
Fanrock	24834	Gallagher	25083	Graham	25253
Far	26167	Gallipolis Ferry	25515	Graham Heights	26554
Farley	25979	Galloway	26349	Grand Central Mall (Part of	
Farmington	26571	Galloway Junction	26349	Vienna)	26105
Farnum	26369	Galmish	26167	Grandview	25813
Faulkner	26241	Gandeeville	25243	Grangeville	26582
Fayetteville	25840	Gap Mills	24941	Grantsville	26147
Federal (Part of Bluefield)	24701	Gap of the Ridge	24701	Grant Town	26574
Federal Correctional Institute		Gardner	24740	Granville	26534
(Monroe County)	24910	Garland	24811	Grape Island	26170
Federal Correctional		Garretts Bend	25564	Grapevine	24844
Institution (Summers		Garrison	25209	Grassy Meadows	24943
County)	24910	Garten	25840	Grave Creek	26041
Federal Mine (Part of Grant		Garwood	24726	Graydon	25938
Town)	26574	Gary	24836	Graysville	26055
Federal Ridge	26170	Gassaway	26624	Great Cacapon	25422
Fellowsville	26410	Gaston	26452	Green Bank	24944
Fenwick	26202	Gaston Junction (Part of		Green Bottom	25537
Ferguson	25511	Fairmont)	26554	Greenbrier	24810
Ferrellsburg	25524	Gates	24983	Green Castle	26180
Fetterman (Part of Grafton)	26354	Gatewood	25840	Greendale	26656
Filbert (Part of Gary)	24830	Gauley Bridge	25085	Green Hill	26155
Finch	26170	Gauley Mill	26208	Greenland (Grant County)	26833
Finley	25003	Gawthrop	26201	Greenland (Wood County)	26181
Fireco	25856	Gay	25244	Green Spring	26722
Fisher	26818	Gaymont	25938	Greenstown	25901
Fitzpatrick	25801	Gem	26335	Green Sulphur Springs	25966
Five Block	25022	Genoa	25517	Green Valley (Mercer	
Five Forks (Calhoun		Georges Run	26456	County)	24701
County)	26145	Georgetown (Lewis County)	26372	Green Valley (Nicholas	
Five Forks (Preston County)	26525	Georgetown (Marshall		County)	25981
Five Forks (Ritchie County)	26362	County)	26033	Greenview	25053
Fivemile (Kanawha County)	25306	Georgetown (Monongalia		Greenville	24945
Fivemile (Mason County)	25106	County)	26505	Greenwood (Boone County)	25010
Flat Rock	25123	Gerrardstown	25420	Greenwood (Doddridge	
Flats	25140	Ghent	25843	County)	26360
Flat Top	25841	Giatto	24736	Greer (Mason County)	25550
Flat Top Lake	25843	Gilbert	25621	Greer (Monongalia County)	26505
Flatwoods (Braxton County)	26621	Gilbert Creek	25608	Greggsville (Part of	
Flatwoods (Jackson		Gilboa	26671	Wheeling)	26003
County)	26164	Giles	25054	Grey Eagle	25674
Flemington	26347	Gilkerson	25512	Griffithsville	25521
Flinderation	26332	Gill	25557	Grimms Landing	25095
Flint	26456	Gilliam	24897	Grippe	25314
Flipping	24747	Gillman Bottom	25617	Grove	26411
Floe	25235	Gilman	26241	Groves	25063
Flower	26611	Gilmer	26350	Grubbs Corner	25401
Flowing Acres	25414	Gip	26618	Guardian	26217
Fola	25019	Given	25245	Gum Spring	26505
Follansbee	26037	Glace	24942	Gunville	25123
Folsom	26348	Glade Farms	26525	Guthrie	25312
Forest Hill	24935	Glade Springs	25832	Guyandotte (Part of	
Forest Hills (Kanawha		Gladesville	26374	Huntington)	25702
County)	25314	Glade View	26206	Guyan Estates	25504
Forest Hills (Ohio County)	26003	Gladwin	26241	Guyan Terrace	25601
Forks of Cacapon	25434	Glady	26268	Gypsy	26361
Forks of Coal	25003	Glady Creek	26554	Hacker Valley	26222

	ZIP		ZIP		ZIP
Hagans	26529	Hillcrest (Part of Fairmont)	26554	Intermont	26851
Hager	25563	Hilldale	25951	Inwood	25428
Hales Gap	24701	Hillsboro	24946	Ireland	26376
Hall	26201	Hillsdale	24976	Irona	26537
Hallburg	25063	Hilltop	25855	Iroquis	25928
Halleck	26505	Hillview (Cabell County)	25702	Isaban	24846
Halltown	25423	Hillview (Marion County)	26554	Isom	25121
Halo	26206	Hillview Terrace	26041	Israel	26444
Hambleton	26269	Hilton Village	25962	Itmann	24847
Hamlin	25523	Hinch	25682	Iuka	26149
Hammond	26566	Hines	25967	Ivy	26201
Hampden	25623	Hinkleville	26201	Ivydale	25113
Hampton	26201	Hinton	25951	Jacksonburg	26377
Hampton Heights (Part of		Hiorra	26410	Jackson Flats	24873
Charleston)	25314	Hite	26588	Jacksons Mills	26452
Hancock	25411	Hitop	25160	Jacobs Fork	24884
Handley	25102	Hix	25951	Jacox	24946
Hanna	26180	Hodgesville	26201	Jamestown	25446
Hannahsville	26290	Hogsett	25515	Jamison Mine No. Nine	26571
Hanover	24839	Hokes Mill	24970	Jane Lew	26378
Hansford	25103	Holbrook	26456	Janie	25209
Hany	25511	Holcomb	26261	Jarrolds Valley (Part of	
Harding	26250	Holden	25625	Whitesville)	25209
Hardy	24740	Holly	25122	Jarvisville	26332
Harewood Mine	25031	Holly Grove	25103	Jawood	25811
Harlin	26456	Hollywood	24983	Jayenn	26554
Harman	26270	Homeland	26378	Jeffrey	25114
Harmco (Part of Mullens)	25882	Hometown	25109	Jenkinjones	24848
Harmony	25246	Homewood	26452	Jenks	25563
Harmony Grove	26505	Hominy Falls	26679	Jenningston	26254
Harper (Pendleton County)	26807	Hoodsville	26588	Jenny Gap	25865
Harper (Raleigh County)	25851	Hoo Hoo	25865	Jere	26546
Harper Heights	25801	Hookersville	26651	Jerrys Run	26133
Harpers Ferry	25425	Hooverson Heights	26037	Jesse	24849
Harpertown	26241	Hoover Town	26218	Jimtown (Harrison County)	26386
Harris Ferry	26181	Hopemont	26764	Jimtown (Morgan County)	25411
Harrison (Clay County)	25105	Hopeville	26855	Job	26270
Harrison (Mineral County)	26717	Hopewell (Barbour County)	26416	Jockeycamp Run	26456
Harrisville	26362	Hopewell (Fayette County)	25938	Jodie	26674
Harters Hill	26591	Hopewell (Marion County)	26554	Joetown	26582
Hartford	25247	Hopewell (Preston County)	26525	Johnnycake	24844
Hartland	25043	Hopkins Fork	25181	Johnsontown (Berkeley	
Hartmansville	26717	Horner	26372	County)	25427
Harts	25524	Horsepen	24619	Johnsontown (Jefferson	
Harvey	25901	Horse Shoe Run	26769	County)	25430
Harveytown (Part of		Horton	26296	Johnstown	26385
Huntington)	25704	Hosterman	26264	Joker	26141
Hastings	26377	Hotchkiss	25920	Jolo	24850
Hatcher (Mercer County)	24740	Hoult	26554	Jonben	25856
Hatcher (Wyoming County)	24870	Howells Mill	25545	Jones Springs	25427
Hatfield Bottom (Part of		Howesville	26444	Jordan	26554
Matewan)	25678	Hoy	26704	Jordan Run	26833
Havaco	24841	Hubball	25506	Josephine	25857
Haywood	26366	Hubbardstown	25555	Josephs Mills	26320
Haywood Junction	26431	Hudson	26519	Joy	26456
Hazelgreen	26367	Huff Junction	25634	Judson	24910
Hazelton	26535	Hughart	24928	Judy Gap	26814
Hazelwood	26241	Hughes	26404	Julia	24966
Hazy	25189	Hugheston	25110	Julian	25529
Headsville	26710	Hugo	25168	Jumping Branch	25969
Heaters	26627	Hull	24844	Junction	26824
Heatherfield	25443	Humphrey	26133	Junior	26275
Heavener Grove	26201	Hundred	26575	Justice	24851
Hebron	26346	Hunt	26635	Justice Addition	25601
Hedgesville	25427	Hunter's Ridge (Part of		Kabletown	25414
Hedgeview	25637	Charleston)	25314	Kalamazoo	26416
Heizer	25159	Huntersville	24954	Kanawha	26142
Helen	25853	Hunting Ground	26804	Kanawha City (Part of	
Helens Run	26591	Huntington	25701-79	Charleston)	25304
Helvetia	26224	For specific Huntington Zip Codes		Kanawha Drive	26351
Hemlock	26224	call (304) 526-9600		Kanawha Estates (Part of	
Hemphill (Part of Welch)	24842	Huntington Mall (Part of		Charleston)	25304
Henderson	25106	Barboursville)	25504	Kanawha Falls	25115
Hendricks	26271	Hur	26151	Kanawha Head	26228
Henlawson	25624	Hurricane	25526	Kanawha Station	26142
Henning	24938	Hurst	26321	Kansooth	26033
Henrietta	26147	Hutchinson	26591	Kasson	26405
Hensley	24843	Huttonsville	26273	Katy	26554
Hensley Heights	25635	Huttonsville Correctional		Katy Lick	26301
Hepzibah (Harrison County)	26369	Center	26273	Kayford	25122
Hepzibah (Taylor County)	26330	Iaeger	24844	Kearneysville	25430
Hereford	25252	Idamay	26576	Kedron	26201
Herndon	24726	Ikes Fork	24845	Keeler Glade	26525
Herndon Heights	24726	Independence (Clay		Keenan	24983
Hernshaw	25107	County)	25125	Kegley	24731
Herold	26601	Independence (Jackson		Keister	24901
Herring	26547	County)	25275	Keith	25148
Hettie	26376	Independence (Preston		Kelly	25022
Hetzel	25076	County)	26374	Kelly Hill	25045
Hewett	25108	Indian (Part of St. Albans)	25177	Kellysville	24732
Hiawatha	24729	Indian Meadows	25545	Kenna	25248
Hickman Run	26554	Indian Mills	24935	Kenova	25530
Hickory Chapel	25550	Indore	25111	Kent	26055
Hico	25854	Industrial	26375	Kentuck	25249
Highland	26346	Industrial (Part of		Kera Landing	25262
Highland Lake Terrace	26181	Clarksburg)	26301	Kerens	26276
Highland Park	26241	Industry	26152	Kermit	25674
Highlawns (Part of		Ingleside	24740	Keslers Cross Lanes	26675
Rivesville)	26588	Ingram Branch	25119	Kessler	25984
High View	26808	Inkerman	26801	Kettle	25243
Hildebrand	26505	Institute	25112	Key	26814

	ZIP		ZIP		ZIP
Organ Cave	24970	Pine Creek	25625	Quinnimont	25910
Orgas	25148	Pine Grove (Kanawha		Quinwood	25981
Orient Hill	25958	County)	25143	Rachel	26587
Orlando	26412	Pine Grove (Marion County)	26554	Racine	25165
Orleans Road	25422	Pine Grove (Wetzel County)	26419	Racy	26161
Orma	25268	Pineknob	25140	Rada	26852
Orr	26764	Pineville	24874	Radnor	25517
Ortin Heights	25143	Piney	26167	Ragland	25690
Orville	25654	Piney View	25906	Rainelle	25962
Osage	26543	Pinoak	24733	Raines Corner	24951
Osborne	25045	Pipestem	25979	Raintown	24946
Osbornes Mills	25045	Pisgah	26525	Raleigh	25911
Oscar	24966	Pleasant Creek	26416	Ramage	25166
O'Toole	24808	Pleasant Dale	26704	Ramp	25985
Otsego	25882	Pleasant Hill	26147	Ramsey	25912
Ottawa	25149	Pleasant Home	26133	Rand	25306
Otto	25276	Pleasant Valley (Hancock		Randall	26543
Ovapa	25150	County)	26062	Ranger	25557
Overfield	26416	Pleasant Valley (Marion		Ranson	25438
Owings	26431	County)	26554	Raven	26651
Oxford	26456	Pleasant Valley (Marshall		Ravencliff	25913
Packs Branch	25880	County)	26033	Raven Rock	26170
Packsville	25209	Pleasant Valley (Monongalia		Raven Rocks	26763
Pad	25286	County)	26505	Ravenswood	26164
Paden City	26159	Pleasant Valley (Ohio		Rawl	25691
Page	25152	County)	26003	Rayburn	25550
Pageton	24871	Pleasant View (Jackson		Raymond City	25159
Paint Creek Junction (Part		County)	26164	Raysal	24879
of Pratt)	25162	Pleasant View (Lincoln		Reader	26167
Palace Valley	26224	County)	25506	Ream (Part of Gary)	24836
Palermo	25546	Pleasant View (Marion		Reamer	25045
Palestine (Greenbrier		County)	26588	Red Creek	26289
County)	24910	Pleasure Valley	26283	Redhill	26101
Palestine (Wirt County)	26160	Pliny	25158	Red House	25168
Pansy	26847	Plum Orchard	25271	Red Jacket	25692
Panther	24872	Pluto	25951	Red Run	26271
Paradise	25124	Plymouth	25011	Red Spring	25976
Parchment Valley	25271	Poca	25159	Redstar	25914
Parcoal	26288	Pocatalico	25320	Red Sulphur Springs	24918
Pardee	25630	Poe	26683	Red Warrior Junction	25122
Park Addition	26070	Point Lick Junction	25306	Reedson	25442
Parkersburg	26101-02	Point Mills (Part of Valley		Reedsville	26547
For specific Parkersburg Zip		Grove)	26059	Reedy	25270
Codes call (304) 485-7770		Point Pleasant	25550	Reedyville	25276
Parkview (Ohio County)	26003	Points	25437	Reeses Mill	26726
Parkview (Taylor County)	26354	Polard	26149	Reger	26201
Par Metta Crest	26184	Polemic	26601	Renick	24966
Parsley Bottom	25676	Polk Gap	25870	Renicks Valley	24966
Parsons	26287	Pondco	25208	Rensford	25306
Patterson Creek	26753	Pond Creek	26133	Replete	26222
Paw Paw	25434	Pond Gap	25160	Reston	25130
Pax	25904	Pond Junction (Part of		Reynoldsville	26422
Paynesville	24873	Madison)	25130	Rhodell	25915
Peach Creek	25639	Pool	26684	Richard	26505
Peanut	26582	Port Amherst	25306	Richardson	25234
Pear	25918	Porters Falls	26162	Richland	24901
Pea Ridge	25705	Porterwood	26283	Richwood	26261
Pecks Mill	25547	Porto Rico	26411	Rider	26385
Pecks Run	26201	Posey	25180	Ridersville	25411
Peeltree	26238	Potomac	15376	Ridgedale	26505
Peewee	25252	Potomac Manor	21538	Ridge Farms	26588
Pemberton	25905	Potomac Park	25419	Ridgeley	26753
Pence Springs	24962	Powell	26554	Ridgeview (Boone County)	25169
Peniel	25270	Powell Creek	25130	Ridgeview (Logan County)	25637
Pennsboro	26415	Powellton	25161	Ridgeville	26710
Pentress	26544	Powhatan	24877	Ridgeway	25440
Peora	26431	Pratt	25162	Riffle	26601
Pepper	26330	Premier	24878	Rift	24892
Perkins	26634	Prenter	25163	Rig	26836
Perry	26851	Price	25540	Riley	25927
Persinger	26651	Price Hill (Boone County)	25130	Rinehart	26448
Petersburg	26847	Price Hill (Raleigh County)	25818	Ringold	26505
Peterson	26423	Price Hill Junction (Part of		Rio	26755
Peterstown	24963	Mount Hope)	25880	Ripley	25271
Petroleum	26161	Pricetown (Lewis County)	26452	Ripley Landing	25262
Pettit Heights	26070	Pricetown (Wetzel County)	26437	Ripling Waters	25248
Pettry	24712	Prichard	25555	Rippon	25441
Pettry Bottom	25189	Priestly	25003	Rita	25632
Pettus	25209	Prince	25907	Riverbend	25177
Pettyville	26101	Princeton	24740	Riverlake Estates	25177
Peytona	25154	Princewick	25908	Riverlawn (Part of St.	
Pharoah	25555	Procious	25164	Albans)	25177
Pheasant Run	26276	Proctor	26055	Riverside (Kanawha County)	25086
Phico	25508	Propstburg	26802	Riverside (Monongalia	
Philippi	26416	Prospect Valley	26431	County)	26505
Platt	25015	Prosperity	25909	Riverton	26814
Pickaway	24976	Prudence	25901	Rivesville	26588
Pickens	26230	Pruntytown	26354	Rivesville Junction (Part of	
Pickle Street	26321	Pullman	26421	Rivesville)	26588
Pickshin	25857	Pumpkintown	26257	Roach	25504
Pie	25670	Purgitsville	26852	Roanoke	26423
Piedmont	26750	Puritan	25670	Roberts	26456
Pierce	26292	Pursglove	26546	Robertsburg	25172
Pierpont (Monongalia		Pursley	26175	Robey	26386
County)	26505	Quaker	25511	Robinette	25607
Pierpont (Wyoming County)	25870	Quarrier	25122	Robson	25173
Pigeon	25164	Queens	26237	Rock	24747
Pike	26346	Queen Shoals	25045	Rock Camp	24951
Pikeside	25401	Quick	25045	Rock Castle	25272
Pinch	25156	Quiet Dell	26408	Rock Cave	26234
Pine Bluff	26431	Quinland	25205	Rock Creek	25174

	ZIP
Rockford	26385
Rock Forge	26505
Rock Gap	25411
Rock Lake	26554
Rock Lake Village (Part of South Charleston)	25309
Rock Lick (Fayette County)	25879
Rocklick (Marshall County)	26033
Rock Oak	26801
Rockport	26169
Rockridge	24873
Rock Run	26456
Rocksdale	25234
Rockton	26623
Rock View	24880
Rockville	25540
Rocky Fork	25312
Rodemer	26764
Roderfield	24881
Rohr	26547
Rolfe	24897
Rollins Branch	24870
Romance	25248
Romines Mills	26385
Romney	26757
Romont	25812
Ronceverte	24970
Ronda	25182
Roneys Point	26059
Rosebud	26386
Roseby Rock	26041
Rosedale (Fayette County)	25901
Rosedale (Gilmer County)	26636
Rosedale (Monongalia County)	26541
Rosemont	26424
Roseville Addition	25177
Rossmore	25643
Rough Run	26866
Round Bottom	26575
Round Knob	25033
Rowlesburg	26425
Roxalana (Kanawha County)	25064
Roxalana (Roane County)	25259
Ruddle	26807
Rumble	25009
Runa	26679
Rupert	25984
Rush Creek	25276
Rush Run	25274
Rusk	26161
Russelldale	26710
Russellville	26680
Russellville Road	25981
Russett	26147
Ruth	25314
Ruthbelle	26519
Rutherford	26362
Rutledge	25311
Ryanville	26330
Rymer	26582
Sabine	25916
Sabraton (Part of Morgantown)	26505
Sago	26201
St. Albans	25177
St. Clara	26321
St. Cloud	26575
St. George	26290
St. Joe (Part of Albright)	26519
St. Joseph	26055
St. Marys	26170
Salem	26426
Salt Hill	25271
Saltlick Bridge	26627
Saltpetre	25514
Salt Rock	25559
Salt Sulphur Springs	24983
Saltwell	26330
Sam Black Church	24928
Sanderson	25045
Sand Fork	26430
Sand Hill	26003
Sandlick	24701
Sand Lick Junction	26435
Sand Ridge	25274
Sand Run	26201
Sandstone	25985
Sandy Huff	24844
Sandy Summit	25252
Sandyville	25275
Sanford	26554
Sanger	25901
Sanoma	26160
Sarah Ann	25644
Sardis	26301
Sarton	24973
Sassafras	25287
Sattes (Part of Nitro)	25143
Saulsbury	26150
Saulsville	25876

	ZIP
Saunders	25630
Saxman	26202
Saxon	25180
Scarbro	25917
Scarlet	25670
Scary	25177
Scherr	26726
Schrader	25071
Schultz	26170
Scott Depot	25560
Scrabble	25443
Seaman	25252
Secondcreek	24974
Security Hills	25414
Sedalia	26426
Seebert	24946
Selbyville	26236
Seminole	26361
Seneca Rocks	26884
Seng Creek	25209
Servia	25063
Seth	25181
Seven Pines	26582
Shadow Lawn (Part of Charleston)	25311
Shady Brook (Part of Weston)	26452
Shady Spring	25918
Shafer	26290
Shamrock	25614
Shanghai	25427
Shanks	26761
Shannondale	25425
Sharon	25182
Sharon Heights	25621
Sharples	25183
Shawvers Crossing	24931
Shegon	25649
Shenandoah Junction	25442
Shepherdstown	25443
Sheridan	25506
Sherman	26173
Sherrard	26003
Sherwood	26456
Shiloh (Raleigh County)	25844
Shiloh (Tyler County)	26146
Shinnston	26431
Shirley	26434
Shively	25508
Shoals	25562
Shock	26638
Short Creek	26058
Short Creek Valley	26003
Short Gap	26726
Short Line Junction (Part of Clarksburg)	26301
Shrewsbury	25015
Shriver	26546
Sias	25563
Sidneyville	25271
Sigman	25168
Silver Grove	25425
Silver Hill	26155
Silver Lake	26769
Silverton	26164
Simoda	26814
Simon	24882
Simpson	26435
Sinclair	26405
Sinks Grove	24976
Sir Johns Run	25411
Sissonville	25320
Sistersville	26175
Six	24824
Six Mile	25053
Skeetersville	25442
Skelton	25919
Skygusty	24883
Slab Fork	25920
Slabtown	25621
Slagle	25654
Slanesville	25444
Slate	26143
Slatyfork	26291
Sleepy Creek	25411
Smithburg	26436
Smith Crossroads	25411
Smithers	25186
Smithfield (Jefferson County)	25430
Smithfield (Wetzel County)	26437
Smithtown	26505
Smithville (Marion County)	26588
Smithville (Ritchie County)	26178
Smoke Hole	26866
Smoot	24977
Snider	26537
Snowden	25573
Snow Flake	24936
Snow Hill	25311
Snowshoe	26209

	ZIP
Sod	25564
Sodom	25183
Somerville	26181
Sophia	25921
South Charleston	25303
South Fork Junction	24883
South Hills (Kanawha County)	25314
South Hills (Monongalia County)	26505
South Madison (Part of Madison)	25130
South Malden	25306
South Park (Kanawha County)	25304
South Park (Lewis County)	26378
South Parkersburg (Part of Parkersburg)	26101
South Ruffner (Part of Charleston)	25304
Southside	25187
South Side Junction (Part of Thurmond)	25936
South Worthington	26591
Spangler	25160
Spanishburg	25922
Spaulding	25666
Spears	25540
Speed	25276
Speedway	24712
Spelter	26438
Spencer	25276
Spencer Hospital	25276
Spice	24946
Sprague	25926
Sprattsville	25621
Spread	25043
Sprigg	25693
Spring Creek	24966
Spring Dale (Fayette County)	25986
Springdale (Ohio County)	26003
Springfield	26763
Spring Gap	25444
Spring Hill (Harrison County)	26301
Spring Hill (Kanawha County)	25309
Springton	24736
Spring Valley	25701
Spurlockville	25565
Squire	24884
Stanaford	25927
Standard	25083
Star City	26505
Staten	25274
Statler Run	26570
Statts Mills	25279
Stealey (Part of Clarksburg)	26301
Steeles	24844
Steelton (Part of New Martinsville)	26155
Steep Gut Hollow	25687
Stephenson	25928
Steptown	25674
Stevenboro	26444
Stewart	26101
Stewart Chapel	26301
Stewartstown	26505
Stickney	25189
Stillman	26234
Stinson	25235
Stirrat	25645
Stohrs Cross Roads	25411
Stollings	25646
Stone Branch	25508
Stonecoal	25674
Stoneville	24834
Stonewall (Part of Charleston)	25302
Stonewood	26301
Stony Bottom	24927
Stony River	26739
Stotesbury	25921
Stotlers Crossroads	25411
Stouts Mills	26439
Stover	25844
Stowe	25607
Strange Creek	26639
Streby	26833
Streeter	25969
Stringtown (Barbour County)	26250
Stringtown (Marion County)	26582
Stringtown (Randolph County)	26263
Stringtown (Roane County)	25276
Strouds	26208
Stumptown	25280
Sturgisson	26411
Sugar Camp	26411
Sugar Grove	26815
Sugar Tree	25521

	ZIP		ZIP		ZIP
Wheeling Island (Part of Wheeling)	26003	Williams Mountain	25163	Woodcliff Acres	26181
Whipple	25917	Williamson	25661	Woodland	26055
Whirlwind	25524	Williamsport	26710	Woodland Heights (Part of Charleston)	25314
Whitby	25823	Williamstown	26187	Woodland Park (Part of Parkersburg)	26101
Whitehall	26554	Willis Branch	25880	Woodrow	24954
White Oak (Raleigh County)	25989	Willow Bend	24983	Woodruff	26033
Whiteoak (Ritchie County)	26421	Willow Island	26134	Woodville	25572
White Oak Springs	26764	Willowton	24740	Woodward Woods (Part of Charleston)	25312
White Pine	26147	Wilmore	24844	Worth	24897
White Rock	26554	Wilsie	26641	Worthington	26591
Whites Addition	25637	Wilson	26707	Wriston	25840
Whites Creek	25555	Wilsonburg	26461	Wyatt	26463
White Sulphur Springs	24986	Wilsondale	25699	Wyco	25943
Whitesville	25209	Wilsontown	26234	Wylo	25611
Whitman	25652	Winding Gulf	25823	Wymer	26254
Whitman Junction	25652	Windom	24859	Wyoma	25515
Whitmer	26296	Windsor Heights	26075	Wyoming	24898
Whittaker	25083	Windy	26143	Yards	24659
Wick	26185	Winebrenners Crossroad	25401	Yates Crossing	25545
Wickham	25871	Winfield (Marion County)	26554	Yawkey	25573
Widemouth	24736	Winfield (Putnam County)	25213	Yellow Creek	26136
Widen	25211	Wingrove	25917	Yellow Spring	26865
Wikel	24945	Winifrede	25214	Yolyn	25654
Wilbur (Logan County)	25632	Winifrede Junction (Part of Chesapeake)	25315	Youngs Bottom	25071
Wilbur (Tyler County)	26320	Winona	25942	Yukon	24899
Wilcoe (Part of Gary)	24895	Wiseburg	25275	Zela	26651
Wildcat	26376	Witcher	25015	Zenith	24951
Wilding	26164	Wolfcreek	24993	Zevely	26537
Wiley Ford	26767	Wolfe	24751	Zigler	26807
Wileyville	26186	Wolf Pen	24896	Zinnia	26426
Wilkinson	25653	Wolf Run	26033	Zion	26218
Willard	26431	Wolf Summit	26462		
William	26292	Wood	25123		
Williamsburg	24991				

	ZIP		ZIP		ZIP
Abbotsford	54405	Appleton	54911-15	Barnum	54631
Abells Corners	53121	For specific Appleton Zip Codes		Barre (Town)	54601
Abrams	54101	call (414) 734-7141		Barre Mills	54601
Abrams (Town)	54101	Applewood	53711	Barron	54812
Ackerville	53086	Arbor Vitae	54568	Barron (Town)	54812
Ackley (Town)	54409	Arbor Vitae (Town)	54568	Barronett (Barron County)	54813
Ada	53020	Arcade Acres	54971	Barronett (Washburn	
Adams (Adams County)	53910	Arcadia	54612	County) (Town)	54871
Adams (Adams County)		Arcadia (Town)	54612	Barron Junction (Part of	
(Town)	53934	Arena	53503	Barron)	54812
Adams (Green County)		Arena (Town)	53503	Bartelme (Town)	54416
(Town)	53504	Argonne	54511	Barton (Town)	53095
Adams (Jackson County)		Argonne (Town)	54511	Barton	53095
(Town)	54615	Argyle	53504	Basco	53508
Adams (Walworth County)	53120	Argyle (Town)	53504	Bashaw (Burnett County)	54871
Adams Beach	54929	Arkansaw	54721	Bashaw (Washburn County)	
Addison	53002	Arkdale	54613	(Town)	54871
Addison (Town)	53002	Arland	54004	Bass Bay (Part of Muskego)	53150
Adell	53001	Arland (Town)	54004	Bassett	53101
Adrian (Town)	54648	Arlington	53911	Bass Lake (Sawyer County)	
Advance	54111	Arlington (Town)	53555	(Town)	54843
Afton	53501	Armenia (Town)	54646	Bass Lake (Washburn	
Agenda (Town)	54514	Armstrong (Fond du Lac		County) (Town)	54875
Ahnapee (Town)	54201	County)	53079	Basswood	53573
Ainsworth (Town)	54462	Armstrong (Oconto County)		Batavia	53001
Air Mail Facility (Part of		(Town)	54149	Bateman	54729
Milwaukee)	53237	Armstrong Creek	54103	Bay City	54723
Akan (Town)	54655	Armstrong Creek (Town)	54103	Bayfield	54814
Alaska	54216	Arnott	54481	Bayfield (Town)	54814
Alban (Town)	54473	Arpin	54410	Bay Park Square (Part of	
Albany (Green County)	53502	Arpin (Town)	54410	Ashwaubenon)	54304
Albany (Green County)		Artesia Beach	53049	Bay Settlement (Part of	
(Town)	53502	Arthur (Chippewa County)		Green Bay)	54301
Albany (Pepin County)		(Town)	54727	Bay Shore Shopping Center	
(Town)	54755	Arthur (Grant County)	53818	(Part of Glendale)	53217
Albertville	54730	Ashford	53010	Bayside	53217
Albion	53534	Ashford (Town)	53010	Bayview (Bayfield County)	
Albion (Town)	53534	Ashippun	53003	(Town)	54891
Albion (Jackson County)		Ashippun (Town)	53003	Bay View (Milwaukee	
(Town)	54615	Ashland	54806	County)	53207
Albion (Trempealeau		Ashland (Town)	54846	Beachs Corners	54627
County) (Town)	54738	Ash Ridge	54664	Bear Bluff (Town)	54666
Alden (Town)	54017	Ashton	53562	Bear Creek (Outagamie	
Alderley	53066	Ashton Corners	53562	County)	54922
Algoma (Kewaunee County)	54201	Ashwaubenon	54304	Bear Creek (Sauk County)	
Algoma (Winnebago		Askeaton	54126	(Town)	53577
County) (Town)	54901	Astico	53925	Bear Creek (Waupaca	
Allen	54770	Athelstane	54104	County) (Town)	54922
Allens Grove	53114	Athelstane (Town)	54104	Bear Lake (Barron County)	
Allenton	53002	Athens	54411	(Town)	54868
Allenville	54904	Atlanta (Town)	54819	Bear Lake (Rusk County)	54728
Allouez (Town)	54301	Atlas	54853	Bear Valley	53937
Allouez	54301	Attica	53502	Beaver (Marinette County)	
Alma (Buffalo County)	54610	Atwater	53922	(Town)	54114
Alma (Buffalo County)		Atwood	54460	Beaver (Polk County)	
(Town)	54610	Auburn (Chippewa County)		(Town)	54889
Alma (Jackson County)		(Town)	54757	Beaver (Clark County)	
(Town)	54611	Auburn (Fond du Lac		(Town)	54446
Alma Center	54611	County) (Town)	53040	Beaver	54114
Almena	54805	Auburndale	54412	Beaver Brook (Town)	54871
Almena (Town)	54826	Auburndale (Town)	54412	Beaver Dam	53916
Almon (Town)	54416	Auburn Lake	53010	Beaver Dam (Town)	53916
Almond	54909	Augusta	54722	Beaver Edge	53916
Almond (Town)	54909	Aurora	49801	Beecher (Town)	54156
Alpha	54840	Aurora (Town)	49801	Beecher	54156
Alto	53919	Aurora (Taylor County)		Beecher Lake	54156
Alto (Town)	53919	(Town)	54433	Beechwood	53001
Altoona	54720	Aurora (Waushara County)		Beetown	53802
Alvin	54542	(Town)	54923	Beetown (Town)	53802
Alvin (Town)	54542	Auroraville	54923	Beldenville	54003
Amberg	54102	Avalanche	54665	Belgium	53004
Amberg (Town)	54102	Avalon	53505	Belgium (Town)	53004
Amery	54001	Avoca	53506	Bell (Town)	54827
Amherst	54406	Avon (Town)	53520	Bell Center	54631
Amherst (Town)	54977	Avon (Lafayette County)	53530	Belle Plaine	54166
Amherst Junction	54407	Avon (Rock County)	53520	Belle Plaine (Town)	54166
Amnicon (Town)	54874	Aztalan (Town)	53038	Belleville	53508
Amnicon Falls	54874	Babcock	54413	Bellevue	54311
Anacker	53901	Badger Army Ammunition		Bellevue (Town)	54311
Anderson (Burnett County)		Plant	53913	Bell Heights (Part of	
(Town)	54840	Bad River Indian		Appleton)	54911
Anderson (Iron County)		Reservation	54806	Bellinger	54771
(Town)	54565	Bagley (Grant County)	53801	Bellwood	54820
Angelica	54162	Bagley (Oconto County)		Belmont (Lafayette County)	53510
Angelica (Town)	54162	(Town)	54161	Belmont (Lafayette County)	
Angelo	54656	Baileys Harbor	54202	(Town)	53818
Angelo (Town)	54656	Baileys Harbor (Town)	54202	Belmont (Portage County)	
Angus	54817	Bakerville	54449	(Town)	54909
Aniwa	54408	Baldwin	54002	Beloit	53511-12
Aniwa (Town)	54414	Baldwin (Town)	54028	For specific Beloit Zip Codes call	
Annaton	53825	Balsam Lake	54810	(608) 365-7755	
Anson	54729	Balsam Lake (Town)	54024	Beloit Mall (Part of Beloit)	53511
Anson (Town)	54748	Bancroft	54921	Belvidere (Town)	54610
Anston	54301	Bangor	54614	Benderville	54301
Anthony	54755	Bangor (Town)	54653	Benet Lake	53102
Antigo	54409	Baraboo	53913	Bennett	54873
Antigo (Town)	54409	Baraboo (Town)	53951	Bennett (Town)	54873
Applecreek	54911	Barksdale	54806	Benoit	54816
Apple River (Town)	54810	Barksdale (Town)	54806	Benton	53803
		Barnes (Town)	54873	Benton (Town)	53803
		Barneveld	53507		

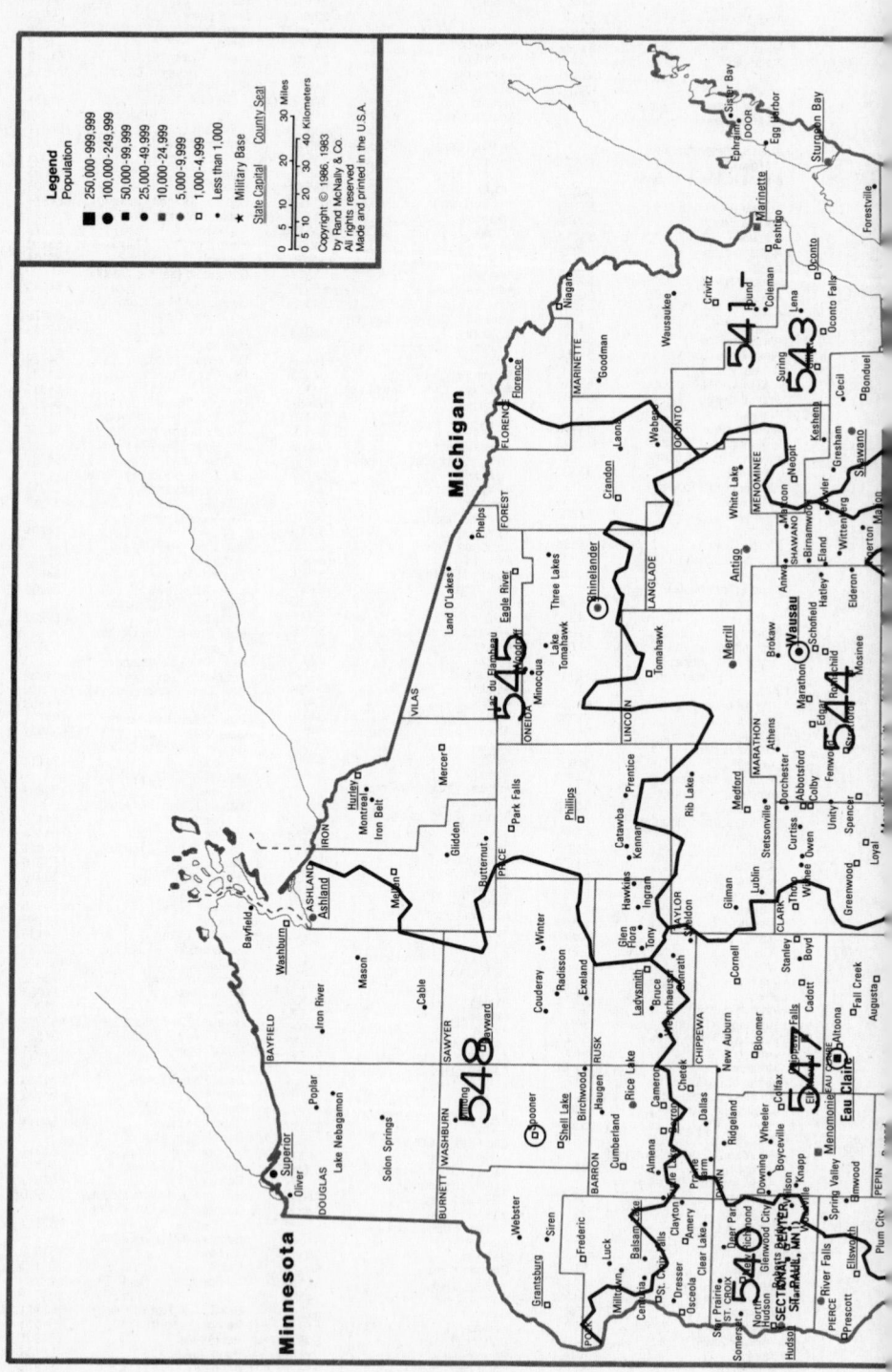

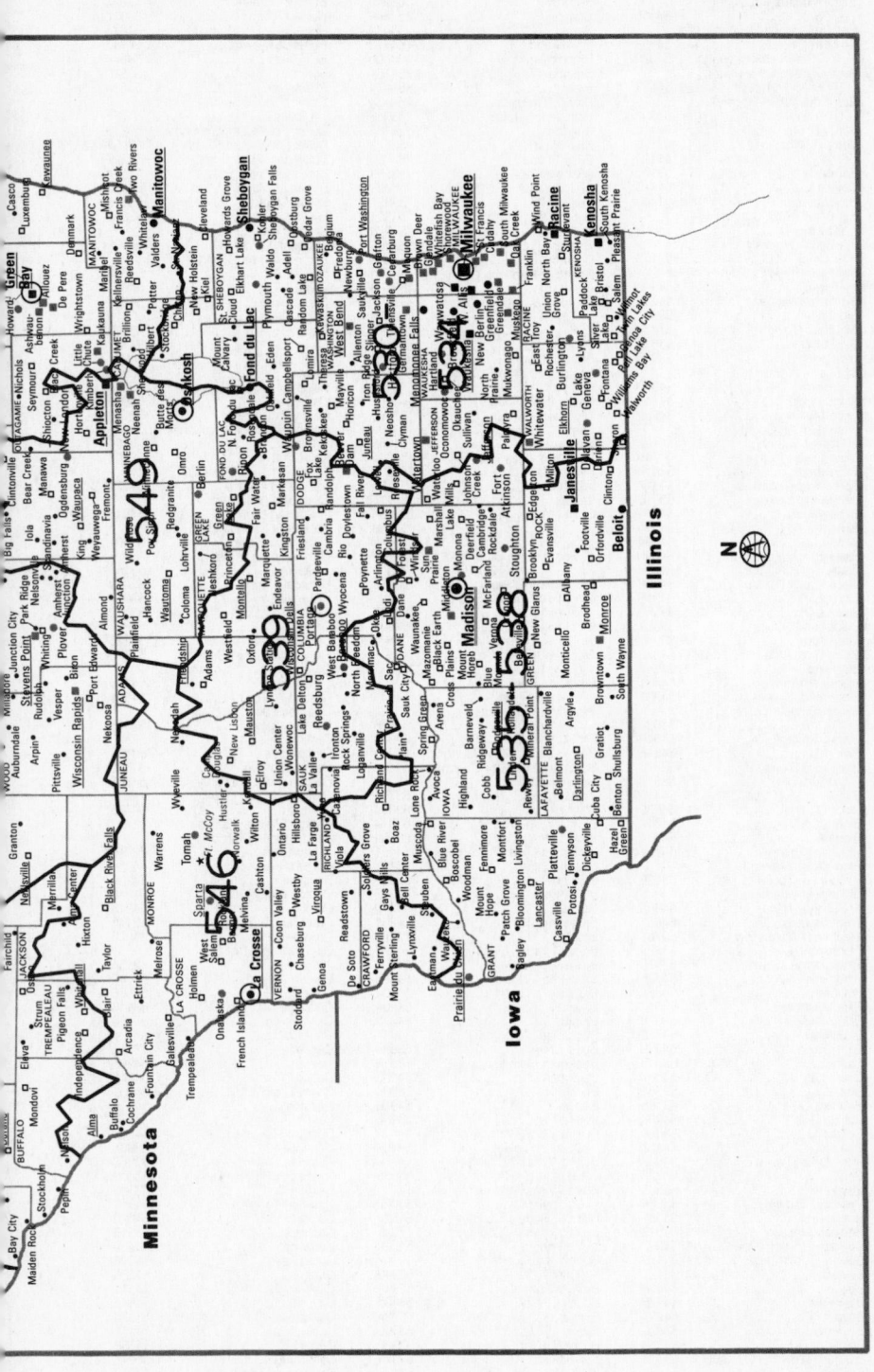

	ZIP
Bergen (Marathon County) (Town)	54455
Bergen (Vernon County) (Town)	54658
Berlin (Green Lake County)	54923
Berlin (Green Lake County) (Town)	54923
Berlin (Marathon County) (Town)	54401
Bern (Town)	54411
Berry (Town)	53528
Bethel	54410
Bethesda	53186
Bevent	54440
Bevent (Town)	54440
Big Bend (Rusk County) (Town)	54819
Big Bend (Waukesha County)	53103
Big Falls (Rusk County) (Town)	54848
Big Falls (Waupaca County)	54926
Big Flats	53934
Big Flats (Town)	54613
Big Patch	53818
Big Spring	53965
Billings Park (Part of Superior)	54880
Binghamton	54106
Birch (Ashland County)	54559
Birch (Lincoln County) (Town)	54442
Birch Creek (Town)	54745
Birchwood	54817
Birchwood (Town)	54817
Birchwood Lake	53010
Birnamwood	54414
Birnamwood (Town)	54414
Biron	54494
Black Brook (Town)	54005
Black Creek	54106
Black Creek (Town)	54106
Black Earth	53515
Black Earth (Town)	53560
Black Hawk	53588
Black River	53081
Black River Falls	54615
Blackwell	54541
Blackwell (Town)	54541
Black Wolf (Town)	54901
Blaine (Burnett County) (Town)	54830
Blaine (Portage County)	54909
Blair	54616
Blanchard (Town)	53516
Blanchardville	53516
Blenker	54415
Bloom (Town)	54639
Bloom City	54617
Bloomer	54724
Bloomer (Town)	54724
Bloomfield (Walworth County) (Town)	53128
Bloomfield (Waushara County) (Town)	54965
Bloomingdale	54667
Blooming Grove (Town)	53701
Bloomington	53804
Bloomington (Town)	53810
Bloomville	54435
Blueberry	54854
Blue Mounds	53517
Blue Mounds (Town)	53572
Blue River	53518
Bluff Siding	54629
Bluffview	53913
Boardman	54017
Boaz	53581
Bohners Lake	53105
Bolt	54208
Boltonville	53040
Bonduel	54107
Bone Lake (Town)	54837
Borth	54923
Boscobel	53805
Boscobel (Town)	53805
Bosstown	53581
Boulder Junction	54512
Boulder Junction (Town)	54512
Bovina (Town)	54170
Bowers	53121
Bowler	54416
Boyceville	54725
Boyd	54726
Boydtown	53826
Brackett	54742
Bradford (Town)	53505
Bradley	54487
Bradley (Town)	54487
Bradley (Part of Milwaukee)	53223
Branch	54203
Brandon	53919
Branstad	54840
Brant	53014
Brantwood	54513
Braund Addition	54660
Brazeau (Town)	54161
Breed	54174
Breed (Town)	54174
Briarcrest Estates	53545
Briarton	54162
Briarwood	53575
Brice Prairie	54650
Brickson Park	53558
Bridge Creek (Town)	54722
Bridgeport	53821
Bridgeport (Town)	53821
Briggsville	53920
Brigham (Town)	53507
Brighton	53139
Brighton (Kenosha County) (Town)	53139
Brighton (Marathon County) (Town)	54488
Brill	54818
Brillion	54110
Brillion (Town)	54110
Bristol (Kenosha County) (Town)	53104
Bristol (Dane County) (Town)	53590
Bristol	53104
Bristow	54665
Brockway (Town)	54615
Brodhead	53520
Brodtville	53801
Brokaw	54417
Brookfield	53005
	53008
	53045
For specific Brookfield Zip Codes call (414) 782-5070	
Brookfield (Town)	53186
Brookfield Square (Part of Brookfield)	53005
Brookhaven	54494
Brooklyn (Green County)	53521
Brooklyn (Green County) (Town)	53521
Brooklyn (Green Lake County) (Town)	54941
Brooklyn (Washburn County) (Town)	54888
Brooks	53921
Brookside (Adams County)	53910
Brookside (Oconto County)	54101
Brookwood (Part of Madison)	53711
Brothertown	53014
Brothertown (Town)	53014
Brown Deer	53209
Browning (Town)	54451
Browns Lake	53105
Brownsville	53006
Browntown	53522
Bruce	54819
Bruemmerville	54201
Brule	54820
Brule (Town)	54820
Brunswick (Town)	54701
Brushville	54965
Brussels	54204
Brussels (Town)	54204
Bryant	54418
Buchanan (Town)	54911
Buck Creek	53581
Buckhorn Corner	53916
Buckman	54208
Budd	54665
Budsin	54960
Buena Park	53185
Buena Vista (Portage County) (Town)	54467
Buena Vista (Richland County) (Town)	53556
Buena Vista (Waukesha County)	53072
Buffalo (Buffalo County)	54622
Buffalo (Buffalo County) (Town)	54629
Buffalo (Marquette County) (Town)	53949
Buffalo Estates	53949
Bundy	54435
Bunker Hill	53924
Burke (Town)	53590
Burke	53590
Burkhardt	54016
Burlington	53105
Burlington (Town)	53105
Burnett	53922
Burnett (Town)	53922
Burnett Corners	53922
Burns (Town)	54614
Burns	54614
Burnside (Town)	54747
Burr Oak	54644
Burton	53820
Busseyville	53534
Butler (Clark County) (Town)	54771
Butler (Milwaukee County)	53213
Butler (Waukesha County)	53007
Butte des Morts	54927
Butternut	54514
Butternut Island	53039
Byrds Creek	53518
Byron	53009
Byron (Fond du Lac County) (Town)	53009
Byron (Monroe County) (Town)	54618
Cable	54821
Cable (Town)	54821
Caddy Vista	53108
Cadiz (Town)	53522
Cadott	54727
Cady (Town)	54027
Cainville	53536
Calamine	53565
Calamus (Town)	53916
Caldwell	53149
Caledonia (Racine County) (Town)	53108
Caledonia	53108
Caledonia (Trempealeau County) (Town)	54630
Caledonia (Waupaca County) (Town)	54940
Caledonia (Columbia County) (Town)	53901
Calhoun (Part of New Berlin)	53151
Calumet (Town)	53049
Calumetville	53049
Calvary	53057
Cambria	53923
Cambridge	53523
Cameron (Barron County)	54822
Cameron (Wood County) (Town)	54449
Campbell (Town)	54601
Campbellsport	53010
Camp Douglas	54618
Campia	54868
Camp Lake	53109
Camp Leonard	53558
Canton (Barron County)	54868
Canton (Buffalo County) (Town)	54736
Capitol (Part of Madison)	53701
Capitol Court (Part of Milwaukee)	53216
Carey (Town)	54534
Carlsville	54235
Carlton (Town)	54216
Carnot	54213
Carol Beach Estates	53143
Caroline	54928
Carrollville (Part of Oak Creek)	53154
Carson (Town)	54443
Carter	54566
Carthage College	53140
Cary (Town)	54466
Caryville	54701
Cascade	53011
Casco	54205
Casco (Town)	54216
Casey (Town)	54801
Cashton	54619
Cassel (Town)	54426
Cassian (Town)	54529
Cassville	53806
Cassville (Town)	53806
Castle Rock (Town)	53809
Castle Rock	53569
Caswell (Town)	54511
Cataract	54620
Catawba	54515
Catawba (Town)	54459
Cato (Town)	54206
Cato	54206
Cavour	54511
Cayuga	54546
Cazenovia	53924
Cecil	54111
Cedar	54559
Cedarburg	53012
Cedarburg (Town)	53012
Cedar Creek	53095
Cedar Falls	54751
Cedar Grove	53013

	ZIP
Dodge (Town)	54625
Dodge Correctional Institution	53963
Dodges Corners	53149
Dodgeville	53533
Dodgeville (Town)	53533
Doering	54435
Donald	54433
Dorchester	54425
Doty (Town)	54149
Dotyville	53057
Douglas (Town)	53930
Dousman	53118
Dover (Buffalo County) (Town)	54755
Dover (Racine County) (Town)	53182
Dovre (Town)	54757
Downing	54734
Downing Junction (Part of Downing)	54734
Downsville	54735
Downtown (Part of Oshkosh)	54901
Doyle (Town)	54868
Doylestown	53928
Drammen (Town)	54739
Draper (Town)	54896
Draper	54896
Dresser	54009
Drummond (Town)	54832
Drummond	54832
Drywood	54727
Duck Creek (Part of Howard)	54301
Dudley	54435
Dunbar	54119
Dunbar (Town)	54156
Dunbarton	53586
Dundas	54130
Dundee	53010
Dunkirk (Town)	53589
Dunkirk	53589
Dunn (Dane County) (Town)	53558
Dunn (Dunn County) (Town)	54751
Duplainville	53186
Dupont (Town)	54950
Durand	54736
Durand (Town)	54736
Durham (Part of Muskego)	53130
Durham Hill (Part of Franklin)	53132
Duvall	54217
Dyckesville	54217
Eagle (Richland County) (Town)	53573
Eagle (Waukesha County)	53119
Eagle (Waukesha County) (Town)	53119
Eagle Corners	53573
Eagle Lake	53139
Eagle Lake Manor	53139
Eagle Point (Town)	54729
Eagle River	54521
Eagleton	54724
Eagleville	53149
Earl	54875
East Bristol	53925
East Delavan	53115
East Ellsworth (Part of Ellsworth)	54010
East End (Part of Superior)	54880
East Farmington	54020
East Friesland	53956
East Krok	54216
Eastman	54626
Eastman (Town)	53826
Easton	53910
Easton (Adams County) (Town)	53910
Easton (Marathon County) (Town)	54471
East Side (Part of Madison)	53704
East Towne Mall (Part of Madison)	53704
East Troy	53120
East Troy (Town)	53120
East Waupun	53963
Eastwood	54494
Eaton (Brown County) (Town)	54217
Eaton (Clark County) (Town)	54437
Eaton (Manitowoc County) (Town)	53042
Eau Claire	54701-03
For specific Eau Claire Zip Codes call (715) 836-6470	
Eau Galle (Dunn County) (Town)	54737
Eau Galle	54737

	ZIP
Eau Galle (St. Croix County) (Town)	54028
Eau Pleine (Marathon County) (Town)	54484
Eau Pleine (Portage County) (Town)	54443
Eden (Fond du Lac County)	53019
Eden (Fond du Lac County) (Town)	53010
Eden (Iowa County) (Town)	53526
Edgar	54426
Edgerton	53534
Edgewater	54834
Edgewater (Town)	54834
Edgewood	53072
Edithton Beach	53143
Edmund	53535
Edson	54726
Edson (Town)	54726
Edwards	53015
Edwards Park (Part of McFarland)	53558
Egg Harbor	54209
Egg Harbor (Town)	54209
Eidsvold	54768
Eileen (Town)	54806
Eisenstein (Town)	54552
Eland	54427
Elba (Town)	53925
Elcho	54428
Elcho (Town)	54428
Elderon	54429
Elderon (Town)	54440
Eldorado	54932
Eldorado (Town)	54932
Eleva	54738
Elk (Town)	54555
Elk Creek	54747
Elk Grove (Town)	53807
Elk Grove	53807
Elkhart Lake	53020
Elkhorn	53121
Elk Mound	54739
Elk Mound (Town)	54739
Ella	54721
Ellenboro (Town)	53813
Ellington (Town)	54944
Ellis	54481
Ellison Bay	54210
Ellisville	54217
Ellsworth	54011
Ellsworth (Town)	54003
Elm Grove	53122
Elmhurst	54409
Elm Island	53185
Elmore	53010
Elm Tree Corners (Part of Howard)	54301
Elmwood	54740
Elmwood Park	54405
Elmwood Plaza (Part of Racine)	53403
El Paso	54003
El Paso (Town)	54003
Elroy	53929
Elton	54430
Embarrass	54933
Emerald	54012
Emerald (Town)	54012
Emerald Grove	53545
Emery (Town)	54513
Emmet (Dodge County) (Town)	53094
Emmet (Marathon County) (Town)	54426
Empire (Town)	54935
Enchanted Valley Estates	53562
Endeavor	53930
Enterprise	54463
Enterprise (Town)	54463
Ephraim	54211
Erdman	53083
Erin (St. Croix County)	54017
Erin (Washington County) (Town)	53027
Erin Prairie (Town)	54002
Esadore Lake	54451
Esdaile	54723
Esofea	54667
Estella (Town)	54732
Ettrick	54627
Ettrick (Town)	54627
Eureka (Polk County) (Town)	54024
Eureka (Winnebago County)	54934
Eureka Center	54024
Euren	54205
Evansville	53536
Evergreen (Langlade County) (Town)	54491

	ZIP
Evergreen (Marathon County) (Town)	54455
Evergreen (Washburn County) (Town)	54801
Excelsior (Richland County)	53518
Excelsior (Sauk County) (Town)	53961
Exeland	54835
Exeter (Town)	53508
Exile	54761
Fahey Heights	53575
Fairbanks (Town)	54486
Fairburn	54923
Fairchild	54741
Fairchild (Town)	54741
Fairfield (Rock County)	53114
Fairfield (Sauk County) (Town)	53913
Fairplay	53811
Fairview (Crawford County)	54628
Fairview (Milwaukee County)	53219
Fairview Beach	54901
Fair Water	53931
Fall City	54739
Fall Creek	54742
Fall River	53932
Falun	54840
Fargo	54665
Farmersville	53050
Farmhill	54740
Farmington	53094
Farmington (Jefferson County) (Town)	53094
Farmington (La Crosse County) (Town)	54644
Farmington (Polk County) (Town)	54017
Farmington (Washington County) (Town)	53040
Farmington (Waupaca County) (Town)	54981
Fayette	53530
Fayette (Town)	53530
Federal Correctional Institution	53952
Fence	54120
Fence (Town)	54120
Fennimore	53809
Fennimore (Town)	53809
Fenwood	54426
Fern (Town)	54121
Ferron Park	54801
Ferryville	54628
Fifield	54524
Fifield (Town)	54524
Fillmore	53021
Finley	54646
Finley (Town)	54646
Fish Creek	54212
Fisk	54904
Fitchburg	53713
Five Corners (Outagamie County)	54911
Five Corners (Ozaukee County)	53012
Five Points	53518
Flambeau (Price County) (Town)	54555
Flambeau (Rusk County)...	54745
Flambeau (Rusk County) (Town)	54848
Flintville	54301
Florence	54121
Florence (Town)	54121
Folsom	54655
Fond du Lac	54935-37
For specific Fond du Lac Zip Codes call (414) 921-9300	
Fontana	53125
Fontenoy	54208
Footville	53537
Ford (Town)	54433
Forest (St. Croix County) (Town)	54012
Forest (Vernon County) (Town)	54639
Forest (Fond du Lac County) (Town)	54935
Forest (Richland County) (Town)	54664
Forest	54012
Forest Junction	54123
Forest Mall (Part of Fond du Lac)	54935
Forestville	54213
Forestville (Town)	54213
Fort Atkinson	53538
Fort McCoy	54656
Fort Winnebago (Town)	53901
Forward	53572

	ZIP		ZIP		ZIP
Foster (Clark County)		Germania (Shawano		Greenleaf	54126
(Town)	54493	County) (Town)	54486	Greenridge Park	53558
Foster (Eau Claire County)	54758	Germantown (Juneau		Greenstreet	54227
Fountain (Town)	53929	County) (Town)	53948	Green Valley (Shawano	
Fountain City	54629	Germantown (Washington		County) (Town)	54127
Fountain Prairie (Town)	53932	County)	53022	Green Valley (Marathon	
Four Corners (Burnett		Germantown (Washington		County) (Town)	54455
County)	54837	County) (Town)	53076	Green Valley	54127
Four Corners (Douglas		Gibbsville	53070	Greenville	54942
County)	54880	Gibraltar (Town)	54212	Greenville (Town)	54942
Foxboro	54836	Gibson (Town)	54228	Greenwood (Clark County)	54437
Fox Creek	54810	Gilbert	54487	Greenwood (Taylor County)	
Fox Lake	53933	Gile (Part of Montreal)	54525	(Town)	54451
Fox Lake (Town)	53933	Gillett	54124	Greenwood (Vernon	
Fox Lake Correctional		Gillett (Town)	54124	County) (Town)	54634
Institution	53933	Gillingham	53581	Gregorville	54201
Fox Point	53217	Gills Rock	54210	Grellton	53094
Fox River	53105	Gilman (Pierce County)		Gresham	54128
Fox River Mall (Part of		(Town)	54767	Grimms	54230
Appleton)	54911	Gilman (Taylor County)	54433	Grover (Marinette County)	
Francis Creek	54214	Gilmanton	54743	(Town)	54157
Frankfort (Marathon County)		Gilmanton (Town)	54743	Grover (Taylor County)	
(Town)	54426	Gingles (Town)	54806	(Town)	54451
Frankfort (Pepin County)		Glasgow	54627	Grow (Town)	54563
(Town)	54721	Gleason	54435	Guenther (Town)	54455
Franklin (Jackson County)	54659	Glenbeulah	53023	Gull Lake (Town)	54875
Franklin (Jackson County)		Glencoe (Town)	54629	Gurney	54528
(Town)	54659	Glendale (Town)	54638	Gurney (Town)	54528
Franklin (Kewaunee County)		Glendale (Milwaukee		Hackett (Town)	54555
(Town)	54216	County)	53209	Hager City	54014
Franklin (Manitowoc		Glendale (Monroe County)	54638	Halder	54455
County) (Town)	54230	Glen Flora	54526	Hale	54758
Franklin (Milwaukee County)	53132	Glen Haven	53810	Hale (Town)	54758
Franklin (Sauk County)		Glen Haven (Town)	53810	Hales Corners	53130
(Town)	53943	Glenmore (Town)	54208	Hallie	54729
Franklin (Sheboygan		Glenwood (Town)	54012	Hallie (Town)	54729
County)	53073	Glenwood City	54013	Halsey (Town)	54411
Franklin (Vernon County)		Glidden	54527	Hamburg	54411
(Town)	54665	Globe	54456	Hamburg (Marathon	
Franksville	53126	Goetz (Town)	54727	County) (Town)	54411
Franzen (Town)	54499	Goodman	54125	Hamburg (Vernon County)	
Frazer	54162	Goodman (Town)	54125	(Town)	54621
Frederic	54837	Goodnow	54529	Hamilton (Town)	54669
Fred John (Part of		Goodrich (Town)	54451	Hammel (Town)	54451
Milwaukee)	53225	Goodrich	54411	Hammond	54015
Fredonia	53021	Gooseville	53075	Hammond (Town)	54002
Fredonia (Town)	53075	Gordon (Town)	54838	Hampden (Town)	53960
Freedom (Outagamie		Gordon (Ashland County)		Hamples Corners	54911
County) (Town)	54131	(Town)	54527	Hampton (Part of	
Freedom (Sauk County)		Gordon (Douglas County)	54838	Milwaukee)	53218
(Town)	53951	Gotham	53540	Hancock	54943
Freedom (Forest County)		Grafton	53024	Hancock (Town)	54943
(Town)	54566	Grafton (Town)	53024	Haney (Town)	54631
Freedom	54131	Grand Avenue, The (Part of		Hannibal	54439
Freeman (Town)	54628	Milwaukee)	53203	Hanover	53542
Freistadt (Part of Mequon)	53097	Grand Chute (Town)	54911	Hansen (Town)	54489
Fremont (Clark County)		Grand Marsh	53936	Hansonville	54822
(Town)	54420	Grand Rapids (Town)	54494	Happy Corners	53807
Fremont (Waupaca County)	54940	Grand View	54839	Harbor (Part of Milwaukee)	53204
Fremont (Waupaca County)		Grand View (Town)	54839	Harding (Town)	54452
(Town)	54940	Granite Heights	54401	Harmony (Marinette County)	54143
French Island	54601	Grant (Clark County) (Town)	54436	Harmony (Price County)	
Frenchville	54627	Grant (Dunn County)		(Town)	54515
Friendship (Adams County)	53934	(Town)	54730	Harmony (Rock County)	
Friendship (Fond du Lac		Grant (Monroe County)		(Town)	53545
County) (Town)	54937	(Town)	54666	Harmony (Vernon County)	
Friesland	53935	Grant (Portage County)		(Town)	54665
Frog Creek (Town)	54859	(Town)	54494	Harmony Grove	53555
Fulton	53534	Grant (Rusk County) (Town)	54848	Harris (Town)	53949
Fulton (Town)	53534	Grant (Shawano County)		Harrison (Lincoln County)	
Fussville (Part of		(Town)	54950	(Town)	54435
Menomonee Falls)	53051	Granton	54436	Harrison (Marathon County)	
Gale (Town)	54630	Grantsburg	54840	(Town)	54409
Galesville	54630	Grantsburg (Town)	54840	Harrison (Waupaca County)	
Galloway	54432	Gratiot	53541	(Town)	54945
Garden Valley (Town)	54611	Gratiot (Town)	53541	Harrison (Calumet County)	
Garden Village	53511	Gravesville	53014	(Town)	54911
Gardner (Town)	54204	Green Acres	53121	Harrison (Grant County)	
Garfield (Jackson County)		Green Bay	54301-24	(Town)	53818
(Town)	54758	For specific Green Bay Zip Codes		Harrison	54435
Garfield (Polk County)		call (414) 498-3993		Harrisville	53949
(Town)	54001	Green Bay (Town)	54229	Harshaw	54529
Garfield (Portage County)	54407	Green Bay Plaza (Part of		Hartford	53027
Garnet	53049	Green Bay)	54303	Hartford (Town)	53027
Gays Mills	54631	Greenbush	53026	Hartland (Pierce County)	
Genesee	53149	Greenbush (Town)	53026	(Town)	54011
Genesee (Town)	53149	Greendale	53129	Hartland (Shawano County)	
Genesee Depot	53127	Greenfield (La Crosse		(Town)	54107
Geneva (Town)	53121	County) (Town)	54623	Hartland (Waukesha	
Genevista	53147	Greenfield (Milwaukee		County)	53029
Genoa	54632	County)	53220	Harvey Estates	53589
Genoa (Town)	54624	Greenfield (Monroe County)		Hatchville	54751
Genoa City	53128	(Town)	54660	Hatfield	54754
Georgetown (Grant County)	53807	Greenfield (Sauk County)		Hatley	54440
Georgetown (Polk County)		(Town)	53913	Hauer	54876
(Town)	54853	Greenfield Park (Part of		Haugen	54841
Georgetown (Price County)		Fitchburg)	53711	Haven	53083
(Town)	54537	Green Grove (Town)	54460	Hawkins	54530
Germania (Iron County)	54550	Green Lake	54941	Hawkins (Town)	54530
Germania (Marquette		Green Lake (Town)	54941	Hawthorne	54842
County)	54960	Green Lake Terrace	54941	Hawthorne (Town)	54842

	ZIP
Knowles	53048
Knowlton	54455
Knowlton (Town)	54455
Knox (Town)	54513
Kodan	54201
Kohler	53044
Kohlsville	53095
Kolberg	54213
Komensky (Town)	54754
Koshkonong (Jefferson County) (Town)	53538
Koshkonong (Rock County)	53538
Kossuth (Town)	54220
Krakow	54137
Kroghville	53594
Krok	54216
Kronenwetter (Town)	54455
Kunesh	54162
Lac Courte Oreilles Indian Reservation	54876
Lac du Flambeau	54538
Lac du Flambeau (Town)	54538
Lac du Flambeau Indian Reservation	54538
Lac La Belle	53066
La Crosse	54601-03
For specific La Crosse Zip Codes call (608) 782-6034	
La Crosse Mall (Part of La Crosse)	54601
Ladoga	53963
Ladysmith	54848
La Farge	54639
Lafayette (Chippewa County) (Town)	54729
Lafayette (Monroe County) (Town)	54656
Lafayette (Walworth County) (Town)	53121
La Follette (Town)	54872
La Grange (Walworth County) (Town)	53190
La Grange (Monroe County) (Town)	54660
La Grange	53190
Lake (Marinette County) (Town)	54159
Lake (Price County) (Town)	54552
Lake Beulah	53120
Lake Camelot	54475
Lake Church	53004
Lake Como Beach	53147
Lake Delton	53940
Lake Eau Claire	54722
Lake Emily	54407
Lakefield	53024
Lake Five	53017
Lake Geneva	53147
Lake George (Kenosha County)	53104
Lake George (Oneida County)	54501
Lake Hallie	54729
Lake Holcombe (Town)	54745
Lake Ivanhoe	53147
Lake Keesus	53029
Lakeland (Town)	54813
Lakeland College	53081
Lake Lorraine	53115
Lake Mills	53551
Lake Mills (Town)	53551
Lake Nebagamon	54849
Lake Ripley	53523
Lake Shangrila	60002
Lake Sherwood	54457
Lakeside (Town)	54874
Lake Tomahawk (Town)	54539
Lake Tomahawk	54539
Laketown (Town)	54006
Lake Wazeecha	54494
Lake Windsor	53598
Lake Wisconsin	53555
Lake Wissota	54729
Lakewood	54138
Lakewood (Town)	54138
Lamartine	53065
Lamartine (Town)	53065
Lamont	53530
Lamont (Town)	53530
Lampson	54888
Lanark (Town)	54981
Lancaster	53813
Land O'Lakes	54540
Land O'Lakes (Town)	54540
Landstad	54107
Langes Corners	54208
Langlade	54491
Langlade (Town)	54465
Lannon	53046
Laona	54541
Laona (Town)	54541

	ZIP
La Pointe	54850
La Pointe (Town)	54850
La Prairie (Town)	53545
Lark	54126
Larrabee (Manitowoc County)	54241
Larrabee (Waupaca County) (Town)	54929
Larsen	54947
LaRue	53951
Lasleys Point	54986
Lauderdale	53121
La Valle	53941
La Valle (Town)	53941
LaVerne Dilweg (Part of Green Bay)	54303
Lawrence (Brown County) (Town)	54115
Lawrence (Marquette County)	53964
Lawrence (Rusk County) (Town)	54526
Lawton	54003
Layton Park (Part of Milwaukee)	53215
Leadmine	53807
Lebanon	53047
Lebanon (Dodge County) (Town)	53047
Lebanon (Waupaca County) (Town)	54961
Ledges	53532
Leeds	53571
Leeds (Town)	53571
Leeds Center	53911
Leeman	54170
Leipsig	53916
Leland	53951
Lemington	54835
Lemonweir (Town)	53948
Lena	54139
Lena (Town)	54139
Lenroot (Town)	54843
Leola (Town)	54921
Leon	54656
Leon (Monroe County) (Town)	54646
Leon (Waushara County) (Town)	54965
Leonards Point	54904
Leopolis	54948
LeRoy	53048
LeRoy (Town)	53048
Leslie	53510
Lessor (Town)	54107
Levis (Town)	54456
Lewis	54851
Lewiston	53965
Lewiston (Town)	53965
Leyden	53545
Liberty (Grant County) (Town)	53825
Liberty (Manitowoc County) (Town)	54245
Liberty (Outagamie County) (Town)	54170
Liberty (Vernon County) (Town)	54664
Liberty Grove (Town)	54202
Liberty Pole	54665
Liddell	54729
Lilly Lake	53105
Lily	54445
Lima (Grant County) (Town)	53818
Lima (Pepin County) (Town)	54736
Lima (Rock County) (Town)	53190
Lima (Sheboygan County) (Town)	53085
Lima Center	53190
Limeridge	53942
Lincoln (Adams County) (Town)	53964
Lincoln (Bayfield County) (Town)	54856
Lincoln (Buffalo County) (Town)	54610
Lincoln (Burnett County) (Town)	54893
Lincoln (Eau Claire County) (Town)	54722
Lincoln (Forest County) (Town)	54520
Lincoln (Kewaunee County) (Town)	54205
Lincoln (Monroe County) (Town)	54666
Lincoln (Polk County) (Town)	54001
Lincoln (Trempealeau County) (Town)	54773

	ZIP
Lincoln (Vilas County) (Town)	54521
Lincoln (Wood County) (Town)	54449
Lincoln	54205
Lind (Town)	54983
Lind Center	54981
Linden	53553
Linden (Town)	53565
Lindina (Town)	53948
Lindsey	54449
Linn (Town)	60034
Linton	53147
Linwood (Town)	54481
Lisbon (Juneau County) (Town)	53950
Lisbon (Waukesha County) (Town)	53089
Little Black	54451
Little Black (Town)	54451
Little Chicago	54448
Little Chute	54140
Little Falls (Monroe County) (Town)	54656
Little Falls (Polk County)	54001
Little Grant (Town)	53813
Little Hope	54981
Little Kohler	53021
Little Prairie	53119
Little Rapids	54115
Little Rice (Town)	54564
Little River (Town)	54153
Little Rose	54484
Little Round Lake	54843
Little Sturgeon	54235
Little Suamico	54141
Little Suamico (Town)	54141
Little Wolf (Town)	54949
Livingston	53554
Loddes Mill	53583
Lodi	53555
Lodi (Town)	53555
Loganville	53943
Lohrville	54970
Lombard	54771
Lomira	53048
Lomira (Town)	53006
London	53523
London Square Mall (Part of Eau Claire)	54701
Lone Rock (Juneau County)	54618
Lone Rock (Richland County)	53556
Long Lake	54542
Long Lake (Town)	54542
Long Lake (Fond du Lac County)	53011
Long Lake (Washburn County) (Town)	54817
Longwood	54498
Longwood (Town)	54498
Lookout	54755
Loomis	54159
Lorain (Town)	54837
Loretta	54896
Lost Lake	53956
Louisburg	53807
Louis Corners	53042
Lowell	53557
Lowell (Town)	53579
Lower Nemahbin Lake	53066
Lowville (Town)	53955
Loyal	54446
Loyal (Town)	54446
Loyd	53924
Lublin	54447
Lucas (Town)	54751
Luck	54853
Luck (Town)	54837
Ludington	54742
Ludington (Town)	54742
Lugerville	54555
Lund	54769
Lunds	54166
Luxemburg	54217
Luxemburg (Town)	54217
Lykens	54810
Lymantown	54552
Lyndhurst	54128
Lyndon (Juneau County) (Town)	53944
Lyndon (Sheboygan County) (Town)	53073
Lyndon Station	53944
Lynn	54436
Lynn (Town)	54436
Lynne (Town)	54564
Lynxville	54640
Lyons	53148
Lyons (Town)	53148
McAllister	54177

	ZIP
McCartney	53806
McFarland	53558
Mackford (Town)	53946
McKinley (Polk County) (Town)	54829
McKinley	54829
McKinley (Taylor County) (Town)	54766
Mackville	54911
McMillan (Town)	54449
McNaughton	54543
Madge (Town)	54870
Madison	53701-44
For specific Madison Zip Codes call (608) 246-1249	
Madsen	54220
Magenta (Part of Eau Claire)	54701
Magnolia	53534
Magnolia (Town)	53536
Maiden Rock	54750
Maiden Rock (Town)	54750
Maine (Marathon County) (Town)	54401
Maine (Outagamie County) (Town)	54170
Mallwood	53534
Malone	53049
Manawa	54949
Manchester	53945
Manchester (Green Lake County) (Town)	53945
Manchester (Jackson County) (Town)	54615
Manitowish	54547
Manitowish Waters (Town)	54545
Manitowish Waters	54545
Manitowoc	54220-21
For specific Manitowoc Zip Codes call (414) 682-6166	
Manitowoc Rapids (Town)	54220
Manitowoc Rapids (Part of Manitowoc)	54220
Maple	54854
Maple (Town)	54854
Maple Bluff	53704
Maple Creek (Town)	54961
Maple Grove (Barron County) (Town)	54744
Maple Grove (Manitowoc County)	54230
Maple Grove (Manitowoc County) (Town)	54110
Maple Grove (Shawano County) (Town)	54162
Maple Heights	53014
Maple Hills	53125
Maplehurst (Town)	54498
Maple Plain (Town)	54829
Mapleton	53066
Maple Valley (Town)	54174
Maplewood	54226
Marathon	54448
Marathon (Town)	54448
Marblehead	53019
Marcellon (Town)	53901
March Rapids	54484
Marengo	54855
Marengo (Town)	54855
Maribel	54227
Marietta (Town)	53805
Marinette	54143
Marion (Grant County) (Town)	53805
Marion (Juneau County) (Town)	53948
Marion (Waupaca County)	54950
Marion (Waushara County) (Town)	54960
Markesan	53946
Marquette	53947
Marquette (Town)	53946
Marshall (Dane County)	53559
Marshall (Richland County) (Town)	53581
Marshall (Rusk County) (Town)	54731
Marshfield (Fond du Lac County) (Town)	53057
Marshfield (Wood County)	54449
Marshfield (Wood County) (Town)	54449
Marshland	54629
Martell	54767
Martell (Town)	54767
Martinsville	53528
Martintown	61089
Marxville	53560
Mary Lake	53597
Marytown	53061
Mason	54856

	ZIP
Mason (Town)	54856
Mather	54641
Matteson (Town)	54929
Mattoon	54450
Mauston	53948
Maxville	54736
Maxville (Town)	54736
May Corner	54157
Mayfair Mall (Part of Wauwatosa)	53226
Mayfield	53037
Mayville (Clark County) (Town)	54425
Mayville (Dodge County)	53050
Mazomanie	53560
Mazomanie (Town)	53560
Mead (Town)	54437
Meadowbrook (Town)	54835
Mecan (Town)	53949
Medary (Town)	54650
Medford	54451
Medford (Town)	54451
Medina (Dane County) (Town)	53559
Medina (Outagamie County)	54951
Meeker (Part of Germantown)	53022
Meeme (Town)	53063
Meeme	53063
Meenon (Town)	54893
Meggers	53061
Mellen	54546
Melnik	54247
Melrose	54642
Melrose (Town)	54642
Melrose Park	54901
Melvina	54619
Memorial Mall (Part of Sheboygan)	53081
Menasha	54952
Menasha (Town)	54952
Menchalville	54206
Menekaunee (Part of Marinette)	54143
Menominee (Town)	54150
Menomonee Falls	53051-52
For specific Menomonee Falls Zip Codes call (414) 251-2260	
Menomonie	54751
Menomonie (Town)	54751
Menomonie Junction (Part of Menomonie)	54751
Mentor (Town)	54746
Mequon	53097
Mercer	54547
Mercer (Town)	54547
Meridean	54755
Merrill	54452
Merrill (Town)	54452
Merrillan	54754
Merrimac	53561
Merrimac (Town)	53561
Merton	53056
Merton (Town)	53029
Meteor (Town)	54835
Metomen (Town)	54971
Metz	54940
Mid-City (Part of Milwaukee)	53208
Middle Inlet	54114
Middle Inlet (Town)	54114
Middle Ridge	54614
Middleton	53562
Middleton (Town)	53562
Middleton Junction	53562
Midway (Brown County)	54301
Midway (La Crosse County)	54650
Mifflin	53580
Mifflin (Town)	53580
Mikana	54857
Mikesville	54901
Milan	54453
Milford	53551
Milford (Town)	53551
Milladore	54454
Milladore (Town)	54412
Millard	53121
Mill Center	54301
Millersville (Part of Howards Grove-Millersville)	53083
Millhome	53042
Millston	54643
Millston (Town)	54643
Millstone Heights	53532
Milltown	54858
Milltown (Town)	54858
Millville	53827
Millville (Town)	53827
Milton (Buffalo County) (Town)	54629
Milton (Rock County)	53563

	ZIP
Milton (Rock County) (Town)	53563
Milton Junction (Part of Milton)	53563
Milwaukee	53201-35
For specific Milwaukee Zip Codes call (414) 291-2444	

COLLEGES & UNIVERSITIES

	ZIP
Alverno College	53215
Cardinal Stritch College	53217
Marquette University	53233
Milwaukee School of Engineering	53201
Mount Mary College	53222
University of Wisconsin-Milwaukee	53201

FINANCIAL INSTITUTIONS

	ZIP
Associated Commerce Bank	53203
Badger Bank, F.S.B.	53211
Bank One, Milwaukee, N.A.	53201
Continental Savings Bank	53202
First Bank, N.A.	53259
First Bank Southeast, N.A.	53202
First Wisconsin National Bank of Milwaukee	53202
First Wisconsin Trust Company	53202
Guaranty Bank, S.S.B.	53223
Federated Bank	53226
KK Federal Bank	53207
Lincoln Savings Bank, S.A.	53215
M&I Marshall & Ilsley Bank	53202
M&I Wauwatosa State Bank	53213
Mutual Savings Bank of Wisconsin, S.A.	53223
St. Francis Bank, F.S.B.	53207
Security Bank, S.S.B.	53203
Valley Bank	53226
Wauwatosa Savings & Loan Association	53213
West Allis Savings Bank, S.A.	53214

HOSPITALS

	ZIP
Columbia Hospital	53211
Milwaukee County Medical Complex	53226
St. Francis Hospital	53215
St. Joseph's Hospital	53210
St. Luke's Medical Center	53215
St. Mary's Hospital	53211
St. Michael Hospital	53209
Sinai Samaritan Medical Center	55233
Veterans Affairs Medical Center	53295

HOTELS/MOTELS

	ZIP
The Astor Hotel	53202
Best Western Midway Motor Lodge	53226
Grand Milwaukee Hotel	53207
Holiday Inn-South Airport	53221
Howard Johnson Lodge	53226
Hyatt Regency Milwaukee	53203
The Marc Plaza Hotel	53203
The Pfister Hotel	53202

MILITARY INSTALLATIONS

	ZIP
Coast Guard Group, Milwaukee	53207
440th Support Group, General Mitchell International Airport (AFRES)	53207
Wisconsin Air National Guard, FB6491, General Mitchell International Airport	53207
84th Division(Training)	53218

	ZIP
Mindoro	54644
Mineral Point	53565
Mineral Point (Town)	53565
Minnesota Junction	53032
Minocqua	54548
Minocqua (Town)	54548
Minong	54859
Minong (Town)	54859
Mishicot	54228
Mishicot (Town)	54228
Mitchell (Town)	53093
Modena	54755
Modena (Town)	54755
Moeville	54011
Mole Lake	54520

	ZIP
Mole Lake Indian Reservation	54520
Molitor (Town)	54451
Monches	53029
Mondovi	54755
Mondovi (Town)	54755
Monico (Town)	54501
Monico	54501
Monona	53716
Monroe (Adams County) (Town)	54613
Monroe (Green County)	53566
Monroe (Green County) (Town)	53566
Monroe Center	54613
Montana	54747
Montana (Town)	54747
Montello	53949
Montello (Town)	53949
Monterey	53066
Montfort	53569
Monticello (Green County)	53570
Monticello (Lafayette County) (Town)	54810
Montpelier (Town)	54217
Montreal	54550
Montrose (Town)	53508
Moon	54455
Moose Junction	54830
Moquah	54806
Morgan (Town)	54154
Morgan (Oconto County)	54154
Morgan (Shawano County)	54128
Morris (Town)	54486
Morrison	54126
Morrison (Town)	54126
Morrisonville	53571
Morris Park	53558
Morse	54527
Morse (Town)	54546
Moscow (Town)	53507
Mosel (Town)	53015
Mosinee	54455
Mosinee (Town)	54455
Mosling	54124
Moundville (Town)	53930
Mountain	54149
Mount Calvary	53057
Mount Hope	53816
Mount Hope (Town)	53816
Mount Horeb	53572
Mount Ida	53809
Mount Ida (Town)	53809
Mount Morris	54982
Mount Morris (Town)	54982
Mount Pleasant (Green County) (Town)	53502
Mount Pleasant (Racine County) (Town)	53401
Mount Sterling	54645
Mount Tabor	54638
Mount Vernon	53572
Mount Zion	53805
Mukwa (Town)	54961
Mukwonago	53149
Mukwonago (Town)	53149
Murphy Corner	54130
Murry (Town)	54819
Muscoda	53573
Muscoda (Town)	53573
Muskego	53150
Myra	53095
Nabob	53095
Namakagon (Town)	54821
Namur	54204
Naples (Town)	54755
Nasbro	53006
Nasewaupee (Town)	54235
Nashotah	53058
Nashville (Town)	54520
Nasonville	54449
Navarino	54107
Navarino (Town)	54107
Necedah	54646
Necedah (Town)	54646
Neda	53035
Neenah	54956-57
For specific Neenah Zip Codes call (414) 725-4818	
Neillsville	54456
Nekimi (Town)	54901
Nekoosa	54457
Nelma	49935
Nelson	54756
Nelson (Town)	54756
Nelsonville	54458
Nenno	53002
Neopit	54150
Neosho	53059
Nepeuskun (Town)	54971
Neshkoro	54960

	ZIP
Neshkoro (Town)	54960
Neuern	54217
Neva (Town)	54424
Neva Corners	54424
Newald	54511
New Amsterdam	54636
Newark	53511
Newark (Town)	53511
New Auburn	54757
New Berlin	53151
Newbold (Town)	54501
Newburg	53060
Newburg Corners	54614
New Centerville	54002
New Chester (Town)	53936
New Denmark (Town)	54208
New Diggings	61075
New Diggings (Town)	61075
New Fane	53040
New Franken	54229
New Glarus	53574
New Glarus (Town)	53574
New Haven (Adams County) (Town)	53920
New Haven (Dunn County) (Town)	54005
New Holstein	53061
New Holstein (Town)	53061
New Hope (Town)	54407
New Lisbon	53950
New London	54961
New Lyme (Town)	54656
New Miner	54646
New Munster	53152
New Odanah	54861
Newport (Town)	53965
New Post	54828
New Prospect	53010
New Richmond	54017
New Rome	54457
Newry	54619
Newton (Manitowoc County)	53063
Newton (Manitowoc County) (Town)	53063
Newton (Marquette County) (Town)	53964
Newton (Vernon County)	54665
Newtonburg	54220
Newville	53534
Niagara	54151
Niagara (Town)	49870
Nichols	54152
Nippersink Manor	53128
Nokomis (Town)	54487
Nora	53531
Norman	54216
Norrie	54414
Norrie (Town)	54414
Norske	54945
North Andover	53810
North Bay (Door County)	54202
North Bay (Racine County)	53402
North Bend	54642
North Bend (Town)	54642
North Branch	54611
North Bristol	53590
North Cape	53126
Northeim	53063
Northfield	54635
Northfield (Town)	54635
North Fond du Lac	54937
North Freedom	53951
North Hudson	54016
North Lake (Walworth County)	53121
North Lake (Waukesha County)	53064
North Lancaster (Town)	53813
Northland	54945
Northland Mall (Part of Milwaukee)	53209
North Leeds	53911
North Lowell	53039
North Menomonie (Part of Menomonie)	54751
North Park	53402
Northport (Door County)	54210
Northport (Waupaca County)	54961
North Prairie	53153
Northridge (Part of Milwaukee)	53223
North Shore (Part of Glendale)	53217
North Tomah	54660
Northway Mall (Part of Marshfield)	54449
Northwoods Beach	54843
North York	54846
Norton	54730
Norwalk	54648

	ZIP
Norway (Town)	53182
Norway Grove	53532
Norwegian Bay	54940
Norwood (Town)	54409
Nutterville	54401
Nye	54020
Oak Center	53065
Oak Creek	53154
Oakdale	54649
Oakdale (Town)	54649
Oakfield	53065
Oakfield (Town)	53065
Oak Grove (Dodge County) (Town)	53039
Oak Grove (Pierce County) (Town)	54021
Oak Grove (Barron County) (Town)	54868
Oak Grove	53039
Oak Hill	53156
Oakhill Correctional Institution	53575
Oakland (Jefferson County) (Town)	53538
Oakland (Jefferson County)	53538
Oakland (Burnett County) (Town)	54893
Oakland (Douglas County) (Town)	54874
Oakley	53550
Oakridge	53179
Oak Shores	53125
Oakwood (Part of Oak Creek)	53154
Oakwood Mall (Part of Eau Claire)	54703
Oasis (Town)	54966
Oconomowoc	53066
Oconomowoc (Town)	53069
Oconomowoc Lake	53066
Oconto	54153
Oconto (Town)	54139
Oconto Falls	54154
Oconto Falls (Town)	54154
Odanah	54861
Ogdensburg	54962
Ogema	54459
Ogema (Town)	54459
Oil City	54648
Ojibwa	54862
Ojibwa (Town)	54862
Okauchee	53069
Okauchee Lake	53058
Okee	53555
Old Albertville	54730
Old Ashippun	53003
Old Lebanon	53094
Oliver	54880
Olivet	54767
Oma (Town)	54534
Omro	54963
Omro (Town)	54901
Onalaska	54650
Onalaska (Town)	54650
Oneida	54155
Oneida (Town)	54155
Oneida Indian Reservation	54155
Ono	54750
Ontario	54651
Oostburg	53070
Orange (Town)	54618
Orange Mill	54618
Oregon	53575
Oregon (Town)	53575
Orfordville	53576
Orienta (Town)	54865
Orihula	54940
Orion	53573
Orion (Town)	53573
Osborn (Town)	54165
Osceola (Fond du Lac County) (Town)	53010
Osceola (Polk County)	54020
Osceola (Polk County) (Town)	54020
Oshkosh	54901-04
For specific Oshkosh Zip Codes call (414) 236-0200	
Osman	53063
Osseo	54758
Ostrander	54961
Otsego	53925
Otsego (Town)	53925
Ottawa (Town)	53118
Otter Creek (Dunn County) (Town)	54772
Otter Creek (Eau Claire County) (Town)	54722
Oulu (Town)	54847
Ourtown	53085
Owen	54460

	ZIP		ZIP		ZIP
Oxbo	54552	Plainville	53965	Preston (Adams County)	
Oxford	53952	Plat	53017	(Town)	53934
Oxford (Town)	53952	Platteville	53818	Preston (Grant County)	53809
Pacific (Town)	53954	Platteville (Town)	53818	Preston (Trempealeau	
Packwaukee (Town)	53953	Plaza 8 (Part of Sheboygan)	53081	County) (Town)	54616
Packwaukee	53953	Pleasant Prairie	53158	Price (Jackson County)	54741
Paddock Lake	53168	Pleasant Ridge	53533	Price (Langlade County)	
Padus	54566	Pleasant Springs (Town)	53589	(Town)	54418
Palmyra	53156	Pleasant Valley (Eau Claire		Primrose (Town)	53593
Palmyra (Town)	53156	County) (Town)	54701	Princeton	54968
Paoli	53508	Pleasant Valley (St. Croix		Princeton (Town)	54968
Pardeeville	53954	County) (Town)	54015	Prospect (Part of New	
Parfreyville	54981	Pleasant Valley (Vernon		Berlin)	53151
Paris (Grant County) (Town)	53807	County)	54658	Pukwana Beach	53049
Paris (Kenosha County)		Pleasant View	54615	Pulaski (Brown County)	54162
(Town)	53182	Pleasantville	54758	Pulaski (Iowa County)	
Paris	53182	Plover (Marathon County)		(Town)	53506
Park Falls	54552	(Town)	54414	Pulcifer	54164
Parkland (Town)	54874	Plover (Portage County)	54467	Purdy	54665
Parklawn (Part of		Plover (Portage County)		Quarry	54230
Milwaukee)	53216	(Town)	54467	Quincy (Town)	53910
Park Plaza (Part of		Plugtown	53805	Quincy Details	53934
Oshkosh)	54902	Plum City	54761	Quinney	53014
Park Ridge	54481	Plum Lake (Town)	54560	Racine	53401-08
Parrish	54435	Plymouth (Juneau County)		For specific Racine Zip Codes call	
Parrish (Town)	54435	(Town)	53929	(414) 632-1661	
Patch Grove	53817	Plymouth (Rock County)		Radisson	54867
Patch Grove (Town)	53821	(Town)	53545	Radisson (Town)	54867
Patzau	54836	Plymouth (Sheboygan		Randall (Burnett County)	54840
Pearson	54462	County)	53073	Randall (Kenosha County)	
Peck (Town)	54424	Plymouth (Sheboygan		(Town)	60071
Pecks Station	53121	County) (Town)	53073	Randolph (Columbia	
Peebles	54935	Point Loomis Shopping		County) (Town)	53923
Peeksville (Town)	54527	Center (Part of		Randolph (Dodge County)	53956
Pelican (Town)	54501	Milwaukee)	53221	Random Lake	53075
Pelican Lake	54463	Poland	54301	Range	54001
Pella	54950	Polar	54418	Rankin	54201
Pella (Town)	54950	Polar (Town)	54418	Rantoul (Town)	53014
Pell Lake	53157	Polifka Corners	54247	Rattman Heights	53701
Pembine	54156	Polk (Town)	53076	Ravenoaks	53575
Pembine (Town)	54156	Polley	54433	Rawson (Part of Oak Creek)	53172
Pence	54550	Polonia	54423	Raymond	53126
Pence (Town)	54550	Poniatowski	54426	Raymond (Town)	53126
Peninsula Center	54202	Poplar	54864	Readfield	54969
Pensaukee	54153	Popple Lake	54729	Readstown	54652
Pensaukee (Town)	54153	Popple River	54542	Red Banks	54940
Pepin	54759	Popple River (Town)	54542	Red Cedar (Town)	54751
Pepin (Town)	54759	Porcupine	54721	Red Cliff	54814
Peplin	54455	Portage	53901	Red Cliff Indian Reservation	54806
Perkinstown	54451	Port Andrew	53518	Redgranite	54970
Perry (Town)	53572	Port Edwards	54469	Red Mound	54624
Pershing (Town)	54433	Port Edwards (Town)	54457	Red River (Kewaunee	
Peru (Dunn County) (Town)	54764	Porter (Town)	53545	County) (Town)	54205
Peru (Portage County)	54407	Porterfield	54159	Red River (Shawano	
Peshtigo	54157	Porterfield (Town)	54159	County)	54166
Peshtigo (Town)	54143	Portland (Dodge County)	53594	Red Springs (Town)	54128
Petersburg	54631	Portland (Dodge County)		Redville	54498
Petty Acres	53589	(Town)	53594	Reedsburg	53959
Pewaukee	53072	Portland (Monroe County)	54619	Reedsburg (Town)	53959
Pewaukee (Town)	53072	Portland (Monroe County)		Reedsville	54230
Phantom Lake	53149	(Town)	54619	Reeseville	53579
Pheasant Branch (Part of		Port Plaza Mall (Part of		Reeve	54004
Middleton)	53562	Green Bay)	54301	Regency Mall (Part of	
Phelps	54554	Port Washington	53074	Racine)	53406
Phelps (Town)	54554	Port Washington (Town)	53074	Reid (Town)	54440
Phillips	54555	Port Wing	54865	Reighmoor	54963
Phipps	54843	Port Wing (Town)	54865	Remington (Town)	54413
Phlox	54464	Poskin	54866	Reseburg (Town)	54437
Piacenza	54986	Post Lake	54428	Reserve	54876
Pickerel	54465	Postville	53516	Retreat	54624
Pickett	54964	Potawatomi Indian		Rewey	53580
Piehl (Town)	54501	Reservation	54520	Rhine	53020
Pierce (Town)	54216	Potosi	53820	Rhine (Town)	53020
Pigeon (Town)	54773	Potosi (Town)	53820	Rhinelander	54501
Pigeon Falls	54760	Potter	54160	Rib Falls	54426
Pike Lake	54440	Potter Lake	53120	Rib Falls (Town)	54426
Pilsen (Bayfield County)		Potts Corners	54639	Rib Lake	54470
(Town)	54806	Pound	54161	Rib Lake (Town)	54470
Pilsen (Kewaunee County)	54217	Pound (Town)	54139	Rib Mountain (Town)	54401
Pine Bluff	53528	Powell	54547	Rib Mountain	54401
Pine Creek	54625	Powers Lake	53159	Rice Lake	54868
Pine Grove (Brown County)	54301	Poygan (Town)	54963	Rice Lake (Town)	54868
Pine Grove (Portage		Poynette	53955	Richardson	54004
County) (Town)	54921	Poy Sippi	54967	Richfield (Washington	
Pine Lake (Iron County)	54534	Poysippi (Town)	54967	County) (Town)	53076
Pine Lake (Oneida County)		Praag	54610	Richfield (Wood County)	
(Town)	54501	Prairie Corners	53807	(Town)	54449
Pine River (Lincoln County)		Prairie du Chien	53821	Richfield (Adams County)	
(Town)	54452	Prairie du Chien (Town)	53821	(Town)	53934
Pine River (Waushara		Prairie du Sac	53578	Richfield	53076
County)	54965	Prairie du Sac (Town)	53583	Richford	54930
Pine Tree Mall (Part of		Prairie Farm	54762	Richford (Town)	54930
Marinette)	54143	Prairie Farm (Town)	54762	Richland (Richland County)	
Pine Valley (Town)	54456	Prairie Lake (Town)	54728	(Town)	53581
Pipe	53049	Pray	54466	Richland (Rusk County)	
Pipersville	53094	Preble (Part of Green Bay)	54302	(Town)	54526
Pittsford (Town)	54301	Prentice	54556	Richland Center	53581
Pittsville	54466	Prentice (Town)	54556	Richmond (Walworth	
Plain	53577	Prescott	54021	County) (Town)	53115
Plainfield	54966	Presque Isle	54557	Richmond (Shawano	
Plainfield (Town)	54966	Presque Isle (Town)	54557	County) (Town)	54166

Name	ZIP
Richmond (St. Croix County) (Town)	54017
Richmond	53115
Richwood (Dodge County)	53094
Richwood (Richland County) (Town)	53518
Ridgeland	54763
Ridgeville (Town)	54648
Ridgeway	53582
Ridgeway (Town)	53582
Rief's Mills	54247
Rietbrock (Town)	54411
Rileys	53593
Rileys Point	54235
Ringle	54471
Ringle (Town)	54471
Rio	53960
Rio Creek	54231
Riplinger	54479
Ripon	54971
Ripon (Town)	54971
Rising Sun	54628
River Falls	54022
River Falls (Town)	54022
River Hills	53209
	53217
For specific River Hills Zip Codes call (414) 962-8644	
Rivermoor	54963
Riverside	53541
Riverview (Town)	54149
Riverwood	54613
River Wood Estates	53589
Roberts	54023
Robinson	53147
Rochester	53167
Rochester (Town)	53105
Rock (Rock County) (Town)	53545
Rock (Wood County) (Town)	54466
Rockbridge	53581
Rockbridge (Town)	53581
Rock Creek (Town)	54764
Rockdale	53523
Rock Elm	54740
Rock Elm (Town)	54740
Rock Falls (Dunn County)	54764
Rock Falls (Lincoln County) (Town)	54442
Rockfield	53077
Rock Lake	53179
Rockland (Brown County) (Town)	54115
Rockland (La Crosse County)	54653
Rockland (Manitowoc County) (Town)	54207
Rock Springs	53961
Rockton	54639
Rockville (Grant County)	53820
Rockville (Manitowoc County)	53042
Rockwood	54220
Rocky Run	54481
Rodell	54722
Rogersville	54974
Rolling (Town)	54409
Rolling Acres	53589
Rolling Ground	54655
Rolling Prairie	53039
Rolling View	53589
Romance	54632
Rome (Adams County) (Town)	54457
Rome (Jefferson County)	53178
Roosevelt (Burnett County) (Town)	54813
Roosevelt (Oneida County)	54501
Roosevelt (Taylor County) (Town)	54447
Root River (Part of Milwaukee)	53227
Rose (Town)	54984
Rosecrans	54227
Rose Lawn	54165
Rosemere (Part of Manitowoc)	54220
Rosendale	54974
Rosendale (Town)	54964
Rosholt	54473
Rosiere	54205
Ross (Forest County) (Town)	54511
Ross (Vernon County)	54665
Ross D. Sills	53125
Rostok	54216
Rothschild	54474
Round Lake (Town)	54843
Rowleys Bay	54210
Roxbury	53583
Roxbury (Town)	53583

Name	ZIP
Royalton	54975
Royalton (Town)	54975
Rozellville	54484
Rubicon (Town)	53078
Rubicon	53078
Ruby (Town)	54745
Rudolph	54475
Rudolph (Town)	54475
Rural	54981
Rushford (Town)	54963
Rush Lake	54971
Rush River (Town)	54002
Rusk (Burnett County) (Town)	54801
Rusk (Dunn County)	54751
Rusk (Rusk County) (Town)	54728
Russell (Bayfield County) (Town)	54814
Russell (Lincoln County) (Town)	54435
Russell (Sheboygan County) (Town)	53079
Russell (Trempealeau County) (Town)	54747
Rutland (Town)	53589
Sabin	53581
Sacred Heart School of Theology	53130
St. Anna	53061
St. Anthony	53002
St. Cloud	53079
St. Croix Falls	54024
St. Croix Falls (Town)	54824
St. Croix Indian Reservation	54830
St. Francis	53207
Saint George	53085
St. Germain	54558
St. Germain (Town)	54558
St. John	54129
St. Joseph (Fond du Lac County)	53079
St. Joseph (La Crosse County)	54601
St. Joseph (Town)	54016
St. Kilian	53010
St. Lawrence (Washington County)	53027
St. Lawrence (Waupaca County) (Town)	54962
St. Marie (Town)	54968
St. Martins (Part of Franklin)	53132
St. Marys	54619
St. Michaels	53040
St. Nazianz	54232
St. Peter	53049
St. Wendel (Part of Cleveland)	53015
Salem	53168
Salem (Kenosha County) (Town)	53168
Salem (Pierce County) (Town)	54750
Salem Oaks	53168
Salvatorian Center (Part of New Holstein)	53062
Sampson (Chippewa County) (Town)	54757
Sampson (Oconto County)	54171
Sanborn	54806
Sanborn (Town)	54861
Sand Bay (Bayfield County)	54814
Sand Bay (Door County)	54235
Sand Creek	54765
Sand Creek (Town)	54765
Sand Lake (Burnett County) (Town)	54893
Sandlake (Polk County)	54009
Sand Lake (Sawyer County) (Town)	54876
Sand Prairie	53518
Sandusky	53937
Saratoga (Town)	54494
Sarona	54870
Sarona (Town)	54870
Sauk City	53583
Saukville	53080
Saukville (Town)	53074
Saxeville	54976
Saxeville (Town)	54976
Saxon	54559
Saxon (Town)	54559
Saylesville (Dodge County)	53078
Saylesville (Waukesha County)	53186
Sayner	54560
Scandinavia	54977
Scandinavia (Town)	54977
Scarboro	54217
Schleswig (Town)	53042
Schley (Town)	54452
Schnappsville	54411

Name	ZIP
Schoepke (Town)	54463
Schofield	54476
School Hill	53042
Schraven Circle	54937
Scott (Brown County) (Town)	54229
Scott (Burnett County) (Town)	54893
Scott (Columbia County) (Town)	53923
Scott (Crawford County) (Town)	53518
Scott (Lincoln County) (Town)	54452
Scott (Monroe County) (Town)	54666
Scott (Sheboygan County) (Town)	53001
Sechlerville	54635
Seeleys	54843
Seif (Town)	54456
Seneca	54654
Seneca (Crawford County) (Town)	54654
Seneca (Green Lake County) (Town)	54923
Seneca (Shawano County) (Town)	54978
Seneca (Wood County) (Town)	54494
Sevastopol (Town)	54235
Seven Mile Creek (Town)	53944
Sextonville	53584
Seymour (Eau Claire County) (Town)	54701
Seymour (Eau Claire County)	54703
Seymour (Lafayette County) (Town)	53586
Seymour (Outagamie County)	54165
Seymour (Outagamie County) (Town)	54165
Shamrock	54615
Shanagolden	54527
Shanagolden (Town)	54527
Shantytown	54473
Sharon (Portage County) (Town)	54473
Sharon (Walworth County)	53585
Sharon (Walworth County) (Town)	53585
Shawano	54166
Shawano North Beach	54166
Sheboygan	53081-83
For specific Sheboygan Zip Codes call (414) 458-3741	
Sheboygan Falls	53085
Sheboygan Falls (Town)	53085
Sheil	53575
Shelby (Town)	54601
Sheldon (Monroe County)	54651
Sheldon (Rusk County)	54766
Shell Lake	54871
Shennington	54618
Shepley	54499
Sheridan (Dunn County) (Town)	54751
Sheridan (Waupaca County)	54981
Sherman (Clark County) (Town)	54479
Sherman (Dunn County) (Town)	54751
Sherman (Iron County) (Town)	54552
Sherman (Sheboygan County) (Town)	53075
Sherman Center	53075
Sherry	54454
Sherry (Town)	54454
Sherwood (Calumet County)	54169
Sherwood (Clark County) (Town)	54466
Shields (Dodge County) (Town)	53094
Shields (Marquette County) (Town)	53949
Shiocton	54170
Shirley	54115
Shopiere	53511
Shoreview	53179
Shorewood	53211
Shorewood Hills	53705
Shortville	54456
Shoto	54241
Shullsburg	53586
Shullsburg (Town)	53586
Sidney	54456
Sigel (Chippewa County) (Town)	54727

	ZIP		ZIP		ZIP
Sigel (Wood County) (Town)	54494	Spring Prairie	53121	Summit Corners	53066
Silica	53049	Spring Prairie (Town)	53121	Summit Lake	54485
Silver Cliff (Town)	54104	Springstead	54552	Sumner (Barron County)	
Silver Creek	53075	Springvale (Columbia		(Town)	54868
Silver Lake (Kenosha		County) (Town)	53960	Sumner	54822
County)	53170	Springvale (Fond du Lac		Sumner (Jefferson County)	
Silver Lake (Walworth		County) (Town)	54974	(Town)	53538
County)	53121	Spring Valley (Manitowoc		Sumner (Trempealeau	
Silver Lake (Waushara		County)	53063	County) (Town)	54758
County)	54982	Spring Valley (Pierce		Sumpter (Town)	53951
Sinsinawa	53824	County)	54767	Sunburst	53701
Sioux	54891	Spring Valley (Rock County)		Sunnyslope (Part of New	
Sioux Creek (Town)	54728	(Town)	53576	Berlin)	53151
Siren	54872	Springville (Adams County)		Sun Prairie	53590
Siren (Town)	54872	(Town)	53965	Sun Prairie (Town)	53559
Sister Bay	54234	Springville (Vernon County)	54665	Sunset	54401
Skanawan (Town)	54442	Springwater (Town)	54984	Sunset Beach	53916
Slab City	54107	Spruce	54139	Superior	54880
Slabtown	53549	Spruce (Town)	54139	Superior (Town)	54880
Slades Corner	53105	Stanbery	54875	Superior (Village)	54880
Slinger	53086	Standart	53533	Suring	54174
Slovan	54205	Stanfold (Town)	54812	Sussex	53089
Smelser (Town)	53807	Stangelville	54208	Swiss (Town)	54830
Sobieski	54171	Stanley (Barron County)		Sylvan	54664
Sobieski Corners	54141	(Town)	54822	Sylvan (Town)	54664
Soldiers Grove	54655	Stanley (Chippewa County)	54768	Sylvania	53177
Solon Springs	54873	Stanton (Dunn County)		Sylvester (Town)	53550
Solon Springs (Town)	54873	(Town)	54725	Symco	54949
Somers	53171	Stanton (St. Croix County)		Tabor	53404
Somers (Town)	53171	(Town)	54017	Taegesville	54401
Somerset	54025	Stark (Town)	54639	Taft (Town)	54771
Somerset (Town)	55082	Starks	54501	Tainter (Town)	54730
Somo (Town)	54564	Starlake	54561	Tainter Lake	54730
Soperton	54566	Star Prairie	54026	Tamarack	54612
South Beaver Dam	53916	Star Prairie (Town)	54025	Tarrant	54736
South Byron	53006	Star Valley	54655	Taus	54206
South Chase	54162	Starview Heights	53545	Taycheedah	54935
South Chippewa (Part of		State Line	53140	Taycheedah (Town)	54935
Chippewa Falls)	54729	State Street (Part of Racine)	53404	Taycheedah Correctional	
South Fork (Town)	54530	Steffenrud Addition	54656	Institution	54935
Southgate Mall (Part of		Stella (Town)	54501	Taylor	54659
Milwaukee)	53215	Stephenson (Town)	54114	Teegarden	54751
South Itasca (Part of		Stephenson Island (Part of		Tell	54610
Superior)	54880	Marinette)	54143	Tennyson	53820
South Janesville (Part of		Stephensville	54944	Terrace Park	53532
Janesville)	53545	Sterling (Polk County)		Tess Corners (Part of	
South Kenosha	53143	(Town)	54006	Muskego)	53130
South Lancaster (Town)	53813	Sterling (Vernon County)		Teutonia (Part of	
South Luxemburg (Part of		(Town)	54624	Milwaukee)	53206
Luxemburg)	54217	Stetsonville	54480	Texas (Town)	54401
South Milwaukee	53172	Stettin (Town)	54401	Theresa	53091
South Necedah (Part of		Steuben	54657	Theresa (Town)	53050
Necedah)	54646	Stevens Point	54481	Thiensville	53092
South Randolph	53956	Stevenstown	54636		53097
South Range	54874	Stiles	54139	For specific Thiensville Zip Codes	
Southridge (Part of		Stiles (Town)	54139	call (414) 242-1720	
Greendale)	53129	Stiles Junction	54139	Thiry Daems	54217
South Side (Part of		Stinnett (Town)	54875	Thompson	53027
Madison)	53715	Stitzer	53825	Thompsonville	53126
South Wayne	53587	Stockbridge	53088	Thornapple (Town)	54819
Sparta	54656	Stockbridge (Town)	53014	Thornton	54166
Sparta (Town)	54656	Stockbridge-Munsee Indian		Thorp	54771
Spaulding	54466	Reservation	54416	Thorp (Town)	54768
Spencer	54479	Stockholm	54769	Three Lakes	54562
Spencer (Town)	54479	Stockholm (Town)	54769	Three Lakes (Town)	54562
Spider Lake (Town)	54843	Stockton (Town)	54481	Tibbets	53121
Spirit	54513	Stockton	54481	Tichigan Lake	53185
Spirit (Town)	54513	Stoddard	54658	Tiffany (Dunn County)	
Spirit Falls	54564	Stonebank	53066	(Town)	54725
Split Rock	54486	Stone Lake	54876	Tiffany (Rock County)	53511
Spokeville	54479	Stone Lake (Town)	54876	Tigerton	54486
Spooner	54801	Stoughton	53589	Tilden	54729
Spooner (Town)	54801	Strader	54722	Tilden (Town)	54729
Sprague	54646	Stratford	54484	Tilleda	54978
Spread Eagle	54121	Strickland (Town)	54895	Tipler	49935
Spring Bluff	54930	Strongs Prairie (Town)	54613	Tipler (Town)	49935
Springbrook (Washburn		Strum	54770	Tisch Mills	54240
County) (Town)	54875	Stubbs (Town)	54819	Token Creek	53532
Spring Brook (Dunn County)		Sturgeon Bay	54235	Tomah	54660
(Town)	54751	Sturgeon Bay (Town)	54235	Tomah (Town)	54660
Springbrook	54875	Sturtevant	53177	Tomahawk	54487
Springdale (Town)	53593	Suamico	54173	Tomahawk (Town)	54487
Springfield (Dane County)		Suamico (Town)	54173	Tonet	54217
(Town)	53528	Sugar Bush (Brown County)	54217	Tony	54563
Springfield (Jackson		Sugar Bush (Outagamie		Towerville	54655
County) (Town)	54659	County)	54961	Townsend	54175
Springfield (Marquette		Sugar Camp	54501	Townsend (Town)	54175
County) (Town)	53964	Sugar Camp (Town)	54501	Trade Lake	54837
Springfield (St. Croix		Sugar Creek (Town)	53121	Trade Lake (Town)	54837
County) (Town)	54013	Sugar Grove	54655	Trade River	54840
Springfield (Walworth		Sugar Island	53094	Trego	54888
County)	53176	Sullivan	53178	Trego (Town)	54888
Springfield Corners	53529	Sullivan (Town)	53549	Trempealeau	54661
Spring Green	53588	Summit (Douglas County)		Trempealeau (Town)	54661
Spring Green (Town)	53588	(Town)	54836	Trenton (Dodge County)	
Spring Grove (Town)	53550	Summit (Juneau County)		(Town)	53916
Spring Hill Edition	53589	(Town)	53948	Trenton (Pierce County)	
Spring Lake (Pierce County)		Summit (Langlade County)		(Town)	54014
(Town)	54767	(Town)	54435	Trenton (Washington	
Spring Lake (Waushara		Summit (Waukesha County)		County) (Town)	53095
County)	54960	(Town)	53058	Trevor	53179

	ZIP		ZIP		ZIP
Tri City (Part of Oak Creek)	53154	Vignes	54235	Wauzeka	53826
Trimbelle	54011	Vilas (Dane County)	53527	Wauzeka (Town)	53826
Trimbelle (Town)	54011	Vilas (Langlade County)		Waverly	54740
Tripoli	54564	(Town)	54424	Wayne (Town)	53010
Tripp (Town)	54847	Villard (Part of Milwaukee)	53209	Wayne (Lafayette County)	
Troy (Walworth County)		Vineyard	53575	(Town)	53587
(Town)	53120	Vinland (Town)	54901	Wayne (Washington	
Troy (Sauk County) (Town)	53583	Viola	54664	County)	53010
Troy (St. Croix County)		Viroqua	54665	Wayside	54126
(Town)	54022	Viroqua (Town)	54665	Webb Lake	54830
Troy	53121	Voltz Lake	53179	Webb Lake (Town)	54830
Troy Center	53120	Wabeno	54566	Webster (Burnett County)	54893
True (Town)	54526	Wabeno (Town)	54566	Webster (Vernon County)	
Truesdell	53143	Wagner (Town)	54177	(Town)	54639
Truman	53530	Waino	54820	Weirgor	54835
Trusler Circle	53575	Waldo	53093	Weirgor (Town)	54835
Tuckaway (Part of		Waldwick	53565	Wellington (Town)	54651
Milwaukee)	53221	Waldwick (Town)	53565	Wells (Town)	54656
Tuleta Hills	53946	Wales	53183	Wentworth	54874
Tunnel City	54662	Walhain	54217	Werley	53809
Turtle (Town)	53511	Walsh	54159	Wescott (Town)	54166
Turtle Lake (Barron County)	54889	Walworth	53184	West Allis	53214
Turtle Lake (Barron County)		Walworth (Town)	53184	West Baraboo	53913
(Town)	54004	Wandawega	53121	West Bend	53095
Turtle Lake (Walworth		Wanderoos	54001	West Bend (Town)	53095
County)	53115	Warner (Town)	54437	West Bloomfield	54983
Tustin	54940	Warren (St. Croix County)		Westboro	54490
Twelfth Street Junction (Part		(Town)	54023	Westboro (Town)	54490
of Superior)	54880	Warren (Waushara County)		Westby	54667
Twelve Corners	54106	(Town)	54923	West De Pere (Part of De	
Twenty-Eighth Street		Warrens	54666	Pere)	54115
Junction (Part of		Warrentown	54750	Western (Part of Milwaukee)	53210
Superior)	54880	Wascott (Town)	54890	Westfield (Marquette	
Twin Bluffs	53581	Wascott	54890	County)	53964
Twin Grove	53550	Washburn (Bayfield County)	54891	Westfield (Marquette	
Twin Lakes	53181	Washburn (Bayfield County)		County) (Town)	53964
Two Creeks	54241	(Town)	54891	Westfield (Sauk County)	
Two Creeks (Town)	54241	Washburn (Clark County)		(Town)	53943
Two Rivers	54241	(Town)	54456	Westford (Dodge County)	
Two Rivers (Town)	54241	Washington (Door County)		(Town)	53916
Ubet	54009	(Town)	54246	Westford (Richland County)	
Underhill	54176	Washington (Eau Claire		(Town)	53924
Underhill (Town)	54176	County) (Town)	54742	West Jacksonport	54209
Union (Rock County)	53536	Washington (Green County)		West Kewaunee (Town)	54216
Union (Burnett County)		(Town)	53570	West Lima	54639
(Town)	54830	Washington (La Crosse		Westlyn	54494
Union (Door County) (Town)	54204	County) (Town)	54619	West Marshland (Town)	54840
Union (Eau Claire County)		Washington (Rusk County)		West Milwaukee	53214
(Town)	54701	(Town)	54819	Weston (Clark County)	
Union (Grant County)	53818	Washington (Sauk County)		(Town)	54456
Union (Pierce County)		(Town)	53937	Weston (Dunn County)	54751
(Town)	54750	Washington (Shawano		Weston (Dunn County)	
Union (Rock County)		County) (Town)	54107	(Town)	54751
(Town)	53536	Washington (Vilas County)		Weston (Marathon County)	54476
Union (Vernon County)		(Town)	54521	Weston (Marathon County)	
(Town)	54634	Washington Island	54246	(Town)	54476
Union (Waupaca County)		Waterford	53185	West Plainfield	54966
(Town)	54949	Waterford (Town)	53185	West Point (Town)	53555
Union Center	53962	Waterford North	53185	Westport (Dane County)	
Union Church	53126	Waterford Woods	53185	(Town)	53597
Union Grove	53182	Waterloo (Grant County)		Westport (Richland County)	53518
Unity (Clark County) (Town)	54488	(Town)	53820	West Prairie	54665
Unity (Marathon County)	54488	Waterloo (Jefferson County)	53594	West Racine (Part of	
Unity (Trempealeau County)		Waterloo (Jefferson County)		Racine)	53405
(Town)	54770	(Town)	53551	West Rosendale	54974
University (Part of Madison)	53715	Watertown	53094	West Salem	54669
Upham (Town)	54485	Watertown (Town)	53094	West Sweden (Town)	54837
Upper Third Street (Part of		Waterville (Pepin County)		West Towne Mall (Part of	
Milwaukee)	53212	(Town)	54721	Madison)	53719
Upson	54565	Waterville (Waukesha		Weyauwega	54983
Uptown (Part of Racine)	53403	County)	53066	Weyauwega (Town)	54983
Urne	54736	Watterstown (Town)	53805	Weyerhaeuser	54895
Utica (Crawford County)		Waubeek (Town)	54736	Wheatland	53105
(Town)	54655	Waubeesee	53185	Wheatland (Vernon County)	
Utica (Dane County)	53523	Waubeka	53021	(Town)	54624
Utica (Waukesha County)	53066	Waubesa Heights	53558	Wheatland (Kenosha	
Utica (Winnebago County)		Waucousta	53010	County) (Town)	53105
(Town)	54964	Waukau	54980	Wheaton (Town)	54739
Valders	54245	Waukechon (Town)	54166	Wheeler	54772
Valley	54639	Waukesha	53186-88	Whitcomb	54486
Valley Junction	54660		53146	White Creek	53965
Valley View Mall (Part of La		For specific Waukesha Zip Codes		Whitefish Bay (Door	
Crosse)	54601	call (414) 542-5377		County)	54235
Valmy	54235	Waumandee	54622	Whitefish Bay (Milwaukee	
Valton	53968	Waumandee (Town)	54622	County)	53217
Van Buskirk	54534	Waunakee	53597	Whitehall	54773
Vance Creek (Town)	54868	Waupaca	54981	White Lake	54491
Vandenbroek (Town)	54130	Waupaca (Town)	54981	Whitelaw	54247
Vandyne	54979	Waupun (Dodge County)	53963	White Oak Springs (Town)	53586
Vaudreuil	54615	Waupun (Fond du Lac		White River (Town)	54855
Veedum	54466	County) (Town)	53963	Whitestown (Town)	54639
Vermont (Town)	53515	Wausau	54401-02	Whitewater	53190
Vernon (Town)	53103	For specific Wausau Zip Codes		Whitewater (Town)	53190
Verona	53593	call (715) 842-0731		Whiting	54481
Verona (Town)	53593	Wausau Center (Part of		Whittlesey	54451
Vesper	54489	Wausau)	54401	Wien (Town)	54426
Veterans Administration		Wausaukee	54177	Wild Rose	54984
Hospital (Part of		Wausaukee (Town)	54177	Wildwood	54028
Shorewood Hills)	53705	Wautoma	54982	Wilkinson (Town)	54895
Victory	54624	Wautoma (Town)	54982	Willard (Clark County)	54493
Vienna (Town)	53532	Wauwatosa	53213		

	ZIP		ZIP		ZIP
Willard (Rusk County)		Winnebago Indian		Woodman	53827
(Town)	54731	Reservation	53965	Woodman (Town)	53827
Williams Bay	53191	Winnebago Mission	54615	Woodmohr (Town)	54724
Williamstown (Town)	53032	Winneboujou	54820	Wood River (Town)	54840
Willow (Town)	53924	Winneconne	54986	Woodruff	54568
Willow Springs (Lafayette		Winneconne (Town)	54927	Woodruff (Town)	54568
County) (Town)	53565	Winter	54896	Woodstock	53581
Willow Springs (Waukesha		Winter (Town)	54896	Woodville (Calumet County)	
County)	53051	Wiota	53587	(Town)	54129
Wilmore Heights	54971	Wiota (Town)	53587	Woodville (St. Croix County)	54028
Wilmot	53192	Wiscona (Part of Glendale)	53209	Woodworth	53194
Wilson (Dunn County)		Wisconsin Correctional		Worcester (Town)	54555
(Town)	54733	Center System	53575	Worden (Town)	54771
Wilson (Eau Claire County)		Wisconsin Dells	53965	Wrightstown	54180
(Town)	54726	Wisconsin Rapids	54494-95	Wrightstown (Town)	54115
Wilson (Eau Claire County)	54726	For specific Wisconsin Rapids Zip		Wuertsburg	54411
Wilson (Lincoln County)		Codes call (715) 423-2130		Wyalusing	53801
(Town)	54487	Withee	54498	Wyalusing (Town)	53801
Wilson (Rusk County)		Withee (Town)	54771	Wyeville	54671
(Town)	54817	Wittenberg	54499	Wyocena	53969
Wilson (Sheboygan County)		Wittenberg (Town)	54499	Wyocena (Town)	53960
(Town)	53081	Witwen	53583	Wyoming (Iowa County)	
Wilson (St. Croix County)	54027	Wolfcreek	54024	(Town)	53588
Wilton	54670	Wolf Lake	53079	Wyoming (Waupaca	
Wilton (Town)	54670	Wolf River (Langlade		County) (Town)	54945
Winchester (Vilas County)	54545	County) (Town)	54491	Yahara Heights	53597
Winchester (Vilas County)		Wolf River (Winnebago		Yellow Lake	54830
(Town)	54545	County) (Town)	54940	York (Clark County) (Town)	54436
Winchester (Winnebago		Wonewoc	53968	York (Dane County) (Town)	53925
County)	54947	Wonewoc (Town)	53929	York (Green County) (Town)	53516
Winchester (Winnebago		Wood (Milwaukee County)	53295	York (Jackson County)	54758
County) (Town)	54947	Wood (Wood County)		York Center	53559
Wind Lake	53185	(Town)	54466	Yorkville	53182
Wind Point	53402	Woodboro	54501	Yorkville (Town)	53182
Windsor	53598	Woodboro (Town)	54501	Young America	53095
Windsor (Town)	53598	Wooddale	54817	Yuba	54639
Windsor Hills	53532	Woodford	53599	Zachow	54182
Windsor Prairie	53532	Woodhull	54932	Zander	54208
Winfield (Town)	53959	Woodland (Dodge County)	53099	Zenda	53195
Wingville (Town)	53569	Woodland (Sauk County)		Zittau	54940
Winnebago	54985	(Town)	53968		
Winnebago Heights	53049				

	ZIP
Adkins Valley	82801
Afton	83110
Airport (Part of Cheyenne)	82001
Aladdin	82710
Albany	82070
Albin	82050
Alcova	82620
Allendale	82601
Almy	82930
Alpine	83128
Alpine Junction (Part of Alpine)	83128
Alta	83422
Alva	82711
Antelope Valley-Crestview	82716
Arapahoe	82510
Arminto	82630
Arrow Head Lodge	82836
Arvada	82831
Atlantic City	82520
Auburn	83111
Baggs	82321
Bairoil	82322
Banner	82832
Barnum	82639
Bar Nunn	82601
Basin	82410
Bear Lodge	82836
Beckton	82801
Bedford	83112
Beulah	82712
Big Horn	82833
Big Piney	83113
Bill	82631
Bondurant	82922
Bonneville	82649
Bosler	82051
Bosler Junction	82051
Boulder	82923
Boxelder	82637
Bronx	83115
Brundage Place	82801
Buffalo	82834
Buford	82052
Burlington	82411
Burns	82053
Burntfork	82938
Burris	82512
Byron	82412
Calpet	83123
Canyon	82190
Carlile	82713
Carpenter	82054
Carter	82937
Casper	82601-09
	82630
	82646
For specific Casper Zip Codes call (307) 266-4000	
Centennial	82055
Chatham	82401
Cheyenne	82001-09
For specific Cheyenne Zip Codes call (307) 772-6583	
Chugwater	82210
Clareton	82701
Clark	59008
Clay	82723
Clearmont	82835
Cody	83114
Cokeville	83114
Colony	57717
Colter Bay	83001
Cora	82925
Cowley	82420
Creston	82301
Creston Junction	82301
Crowheart	82512
Daniel	83115
Dayton	82836
Deaver	82421
Devils Tower	82714
Diamondville	83116
Dixon	82323
Douglas	82633
Downer	82801
Dubois	82513
Dwyer	82201
Eastridge Mall (Part of Casper)	82601
East Thermopolis	82443
Eden	82926
Edgerton	82635
Egbert	82053
Elk Mountain	82324
Elmo (Part of Hanna)	82327
Emblem	82422
Encampment	82325
Esterbrook	82633
Ethete	82520
Etna	83118

	ZIP
Evanston	82930-31
For specific Evanston Zip Codes call (307) 789-2912	
Evansville	82636
Fairview	83119
Farson	82932
Fishing Bridge	82190
Fontenelle	83101
Fort Bridger	82933
Fort Laramie	82212
Fort Steele	82301
Fort Washakie	82514
Four Corners	82715
Fox Farm-College	82007
Foxpark	82070
Francis E. Warren Air Force Base	82001
Frannie	82423
Freedom	83120
Frontier	83121
Frontier Mall (Part of Cheyenne)	82001
Garland	82435
Garrett	82058
Gas Camp 1	82643
Gillette	82716-17
For specific Gillette Zip Codes call (307) 682-3727	
Glendo	82213
Glenrock	82637
Granger	82934
Granite Canon	82059
Grant Village	82190
Grass Creek	82443
Green River	82935
Greybull	82426
Grover	83122
Guernsey	82214
Halfway	83113
Hamilton Dome	82427
Hanna	82327
Happy Jack Ranchettes	82007
Harriman	82059
Hartville	82215
Hawk Springs	82217
Hiland	82638
Hillsdale	82060
Hilltop (Part of Casper)	82609
Hoback Junction	83001
Horse Creek	82061
Hudson	82515
Hulett	82720
Huntley	82218
Hyattville	82428
Iron Mountain	82001
Jackson	83001-02
For specific Jackson Zip Codes call (307) 733-3650	
Jackson Lake Lodge	83013
James Town	82935
Jay Em	82219
Jeffrey City	82310
Jelm	82063
Jenny Lake	83012
Kaycee	82639
Kearny	82832
Keeline	82220
Kelly	83011
Kemmerer	83101
Keystone	82070
Kinnear	82516
Kirby	82430
La Barge	83123
Lagrange	82221
Lake	82190
Lake Creek Resort	82070
Lamont	82301
Lance Creek	82222
Lander	82520
Laramie	82070-71
For specific Laramie Zip Codes call (307) 742-2109	
Leiter	82837
Leo	82327
Linch	82640
Lingle	82223
Little America	82929
Lonetree	82936
Lost Cabin	82642
Lost Springs	82224
Lovell	82431
Lucerne	82443
Lucky MacCamp	82501
Lusk	82225
Lyman	82937
Lysite	82642
McFadden	82080
McKinley	82633
McKinnon	82938
Manderson	82432
Mantua	82435

	ZIP
Manville	82227
Marbleton	83113
Mayoworth	82639
Medicine Bow	82329
Meeteetse	82433
Meriden	82081
Merna	83115
Midvale	82501
Midwest	82643
Midwest Heights	82601
Milford	82520
Mills	82644
Moneta	82601
Moorcroft	82721
Moose	83012
Moran	83013
Morton	82501
Mountain Home	82070
Mountain View (Natrona County)	82604
Mountain View (Uinta County)	82936
	82939
For specific Mountain View Zip Codes call (307) 782-3718	
Muddy Gap	82301
Museum (Part of Cheyenne)	82001
Natrona	82646
Newcastle	82701
New Haven	82720
Node	82228
North Rock Springs	82901
Number One (Part of Cheyenne)	82001
O'Donnell Spur	82435
Old Faithful	82190
Opal	83124
Orchard Valley	82007
Orin	82633
Orpha	82633
Osage	82723
Oshoto	82724
Osmond	83110
Otto	82434
Pahaska	82414
Paradise Valley (Part of Casper)	82601
Parkerton	82637
Parkman	82838
Pavillion	82523
Piedmont	82933
Pine Bluffs	82082
Pinedale	82941
Pine Haven	82721
Point of Rocks	82942
Powder River	82648
Powell	82435
Prospector Village	82717
Rafter J Ranch	83001
Ralston	82440
Ranchester	82839
Ranchettes	82009
Rawhide Village	82717
Rawlins	82301
Recluse	82725
Red Buttes Village	82604
Red Desert	82336
Red Lane	82443
Reliance	82943
Reno (Part of Wright)	82732
Reno Junction (Part of Wright)	82732
Riovista	82935
Riverside	82325
Riverton	82501
Riverview	57735
Robertson	82944
Rock River	82058
	82083
For specific Rock River Zip Codes call (307) 378-2248	
Rock Springs	82901-02
For specific Rock Springs Zip Codes call (307) 362-9792	
Rockypoint	82724
Rolling Hills	82637
Rozet	82727
Ryan Park	82331
Saddlestring	82840
Sand Draw	82501
Saratoga	82331
Savery	82332
Seminoe Dam	82334
Shawnee	82229
Shell	82441
Sheridan	82801
Sheridan Gardens	82801
Shirley Basin	82615
Shoshoni	82649
Sinclair	82334
Slater	82201

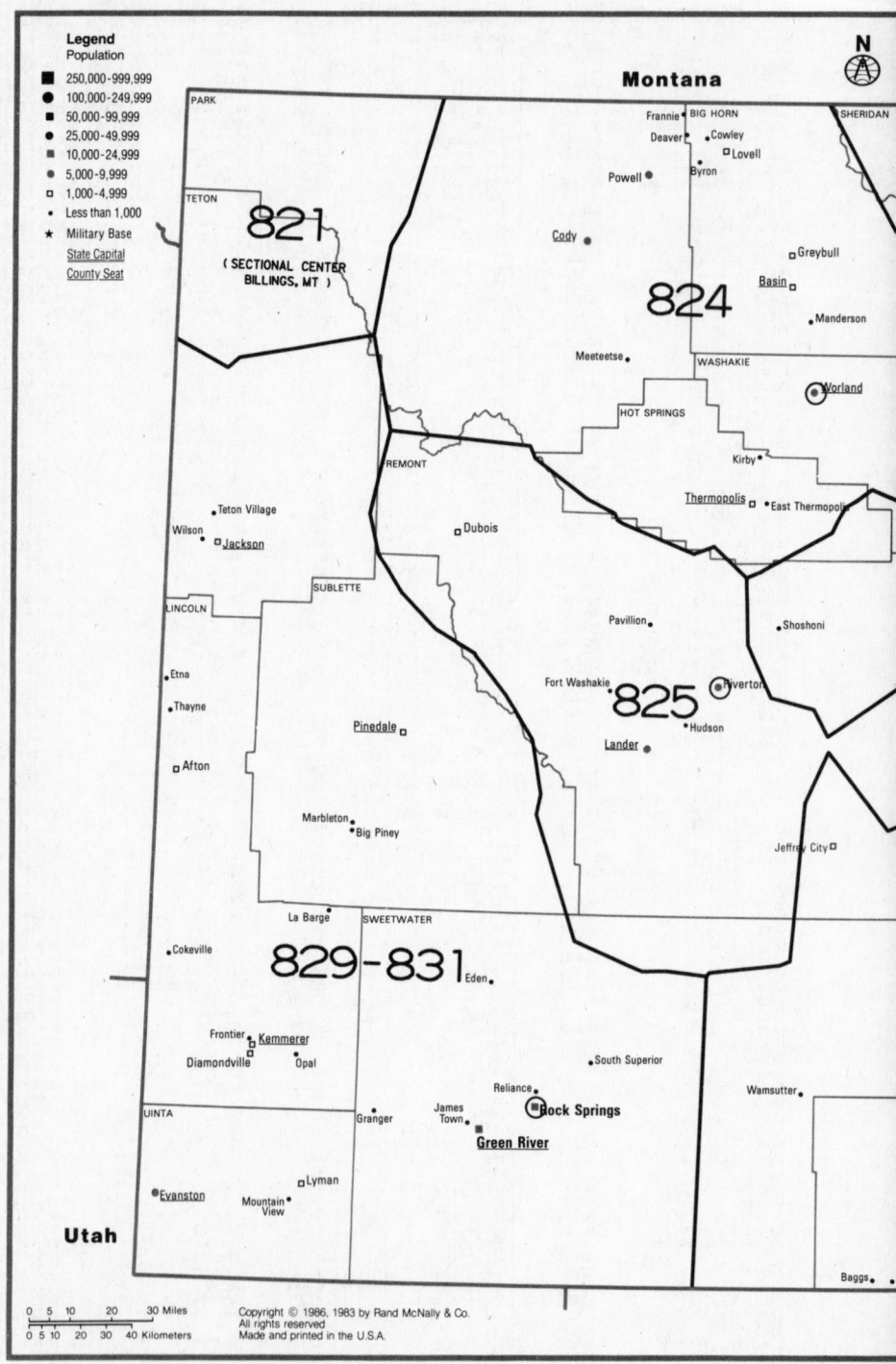

Legend
Population
- 250,000-999,999
- 100,000-249,999
- 50,000-99,999
- 25,000-49,999
- 10,000-24,999
- 5,000-9,999
- 1,000-4,999
- Less than 1,000
- ★ Military Base
- State Capital
- County Seat

N

Montana

PARK

821

(SECTIONAL CENTER
BILLINGS, MT)

TETON

Frannie   BIG HORN   SHERIDAN
Deaver   Cowley
Powell   Lovell
          Byron

Cody

824

Greybull
Basin
Manderson

Meeteetse   WASHAKIE

HOT SPRINGS   Worland

FREMONT   Kirby

Teton Village   Thermopolis   East Thermopolis
Wilson
Jackson   Dubois

SUBLETTE

LINCOLN   Pavillion   Shoshoni

Etna

Thayne   Fort Washakie   **825**   Riverton
                              Hudson
Pinedale   Lander

Afton

Marbleton
Big Piney   Jeffrey City

La Barge   SWEETWATER

Cokeville   **829-831** Eden

                South Superior

Frontier Kemmerer   Reliance   Wamsutter
Diamondville Opal   Rock Springs

UINTA   Granger   James   Green River
                    Town

Lyman
Evanston   Mountain
            View

Utah   Baggs

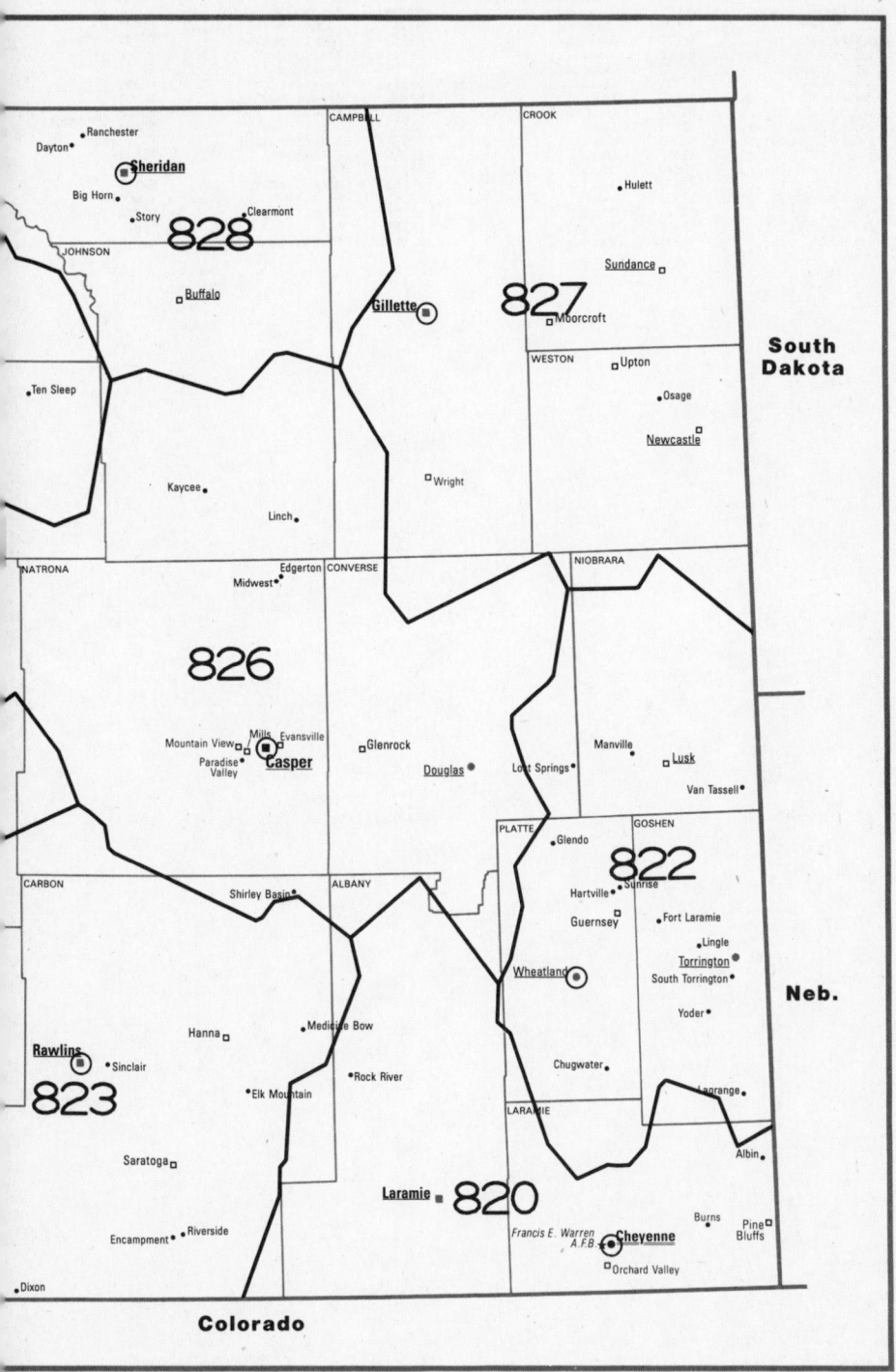

CAMPBELL

CROOK

Ranchester
Dayton
Sheridan

Hulett

Big Horn
Story   Clearmont

828

JOHNSON

Buffalo

Sundance

827

Gillette

Moorcroft

WESTON
Upton

**South
Dakota**

Ten Sleep

Osage

Kaycee

Newcastle

Wright

Linch

NATRONA   CONVERSE
Edgerton
Midwest

NIOBRARA

826

Mountain View   Mills   Evansville
Paradise   **Casper**
Valley

Glenrock

Manville

Lusk

Douglas   Lost Springs

Van Tassell

PLATTE   GOSHEN

CARBON   ALBANY

Shirley Basin

Glendo

822

Hartville   Sunrise

Guernsey   Fort Laramie

Lingle
Torrington
South Torrington

Neb.

Hanna   Medicine Bow

Wheatland

Yoder

Rawlins
Sinclair

823

Elk Mountain   Rock River

Chugwater

Lagrange

LARAMIE

Saratoga

Albin

Laramie   **820**

Encampment   Riverside

Burns   Pine
Bluffs

Francis E. Warren   **Cheyenne**
A.F.B.

Dixon

Orchard Valley

Colorado

	ZIP		ZIP		ZIP
Sleepy Hollow	82716	Thayne	83127	Wapiti Valley	82450
Smoot	83126	Thermopolis	82443	Warren AFB	82005
South Greeley	82007	Three Forks	82301	Western Hills (Part of	
South Jackson	83001	Tie Siding	82084	Cheyenne)	82001
South Laramie	82070	Torrington	82240	West Lance Creek	82222
South Pass City	82520	Tower Junction	82190	West Laramie	82070
South Torrington	82240	Turnerville	83112	Weston	82731
Spotted Horse	82831	Ucross	82835	West Thumb	82190
Story	82842	Ulm	82835	Wheatland	82201
Sundance	82729	University (Part of Laramie)	82071	Willwood	82435
Sunrise (Natrona County)	82604	Upton	82730	Wilson	83014
Sunrise (Platte County)	82215	Urie	82937	Wind River Indian	
Sunshine	82433	Uva	82201	Reservation	82514
Superior	82945	Valley	82414	Wolf	82844
Sussex	82639	Van Tassell	82242	Woods Landing	82063
Sweetwater Station	82520	Veteran	82243	Worland	82401
Taylor	82643	Walcott	82335	Wright	82732
Ten Sleep	82442	Warnsutter	82336	Wyarno	82845
Teton Village	83025	Wapiti	82450	Wyodak	82716

NOTES

NOTES

NOTES

NOTES

NOTES

NOTES

NOTES

NOTES

NOTES

NOTES

NOTES

NOTES

NOTES

NOTES